www.wadsworth.com

wadsworth.com is the World Wide Web site for Wadsworth Publishing Company and is your direct source to dozens of online resources.

At *wadsworth.com* you can find out about supplements, demonstration software, and student resources. You can also send e-mail to many of our authors and preview new publications and exciting new technologies.

wadsworth.com
Changing the way the world learns®

CONTEMPORARY ISSUES IN BIOETHICS

FIFTH EDITION

Edited by

Tom L. Beauchamp & LeRoy Walters

Kennedy Institute of Ethics and Department of Philosophy

Georgetown University

Wadsworth Publishing Company

I(T)P® An International Thomson Publishing Company

Belmont, CA • Albany, NY • Boston • Cincinnati • Detroit • Johannesburg • London • Madrid
Melbourne • Mexico City • New York • Pacific Grove, CA • Scottsdale, AZ • Singapore • Tokyo • Toronto

Philosophy Editor: Peter Adams
Assistant Editor: Kerri Abdinoor
Senior Editorial Assistant: Mindy Newfarmer
Marketing Manager: Dave Garrison
Print Buyer: Karen Hunt
Permissions Editor: Susan Walters

Production: Matrix Productions Inc.
Copy Editor: Cheryl Smith
Cover Design: Carole Lawson
Compositor: ColorType
Printer: R. R. Donnelley & Sons, Harrisonburg

Printed in the United States of America
  2 3 4 5 6 7 8 9 10

For more information, contact Wadsworth Publishing Company, 10 Davis Drive, Belmont, CA
94002, or electronically at http://www.wadsworth.com

International Thomson Publishing Europe
Berkshire House
168-173 High Holborn
London, WC1V 7AA, United Kingdom

International Thomson Editores
Seneca, 53
Colonia Polanco
11560 México D. F. México

Nelson ITP, Australia
102 Dodds Street
South Melbourne
Victoria 3205 Australia

International Thomson Publishing Asia
60 Albert Street #15-01
Albert Complex
Singapore 189969

Nelson Canada
1120 Birchmount Road
Scarborough, Ontario
Canada M1K 5G4

International Thomson Publishing Japan
Hirakawa-cho Kyowa Building, 3F
2-2-1 Hirakawa-cho, Chiyoda-ku
Tokyo 102, Japan

International Thomson Publishing Southern Africa
Building 18, Constantia Square
138 Sixteenth Road, P.O. Box 2459
Halfway House, 1685 South Africa

Library of Congress Cataloging-in-Publication Data

Contemporary issues in bioethics / [edited by] Tom L. Beauchamp &
   LeRoy Walters. — 5th ed.
        p.   cm.
   Includes bibliographical references.
   ISBN 0-534-50476-0
      1. Medical ethics.   2. Bioethics.   I. Beauchamp, Tom L.
   II. Walters, LeRoy.
   R724.C67   1999
   174′ .2 — dc21   98-48339

 This book is printed on acid-free, recycled paper.

CONTENTS

CHAPTER 3: THE MANAGEMENT OF MEDICAL INFORMATION   117

PART III The Beginning and End of Life

CHAPTER 4: ABORTION AND MATERNAL-FETAL

RELATIONS   189

CHAPTER 5: EUTHANASIA AND ASSISTED SUICIDE   271

PART IV   Access to Health Care

CHAPTER 6:   JUSTICE IN THE DISTRIBUTION OF HEALTH CARE   355

PART V   Biomedical Research and Technology

CHAPTER 7:   RESEARCH INVOLVING HUMAN AND ANIMAL SUBJECTS   427

CHAPTER 8: EUGENICS AND HUMAN GENETICS   511

PREFACE

This fifth edition of *Contemporary Issues in Bioethics* differs significantly from the fourth and earlier editions. It attempts to reflect current changes in the bioethics field and assumes a more global perspective. For example, it incorporates new materials on ethical dilemmas arising in Africa, Asia, and Europe, as well as in Canada and the United States. Seventy-five of the 124 selections in this edition are new, when compared with the selections in the fourth edition. This edition also includes a new chapter on research ethics, involving human and animal subjects, and combines the two death-and-dying chapters of the fourth edition into a single chapter.

In each chapter we have tried to give students and faculty members a sense of the cutting-edge of contemporary ethical discussion and debate. For example, the chapter on the right to die includes excerpts from the precedent-setting Supreme Court decisions on physician-assisted suicide from 1997. Chapter 6, on access to health care, discusses managed care for the first time in the editions of this anthology. The research chapter includes several striking historical examples of the abuse of human subjects — in the Tuskegee syphilis study, in Nazi Germany, in the recently-revealed radiation experiments in the United States, and in China under Japanese occupation. Chapter 9, on reproduction, considers cloning. In the final chapter on AIDS, questions of newborn screening and research in third-world contexts both receive substantial attention.

This book has again been a collaborative effort from start to finish. Tom Beauchamp has assumed primary responsibility for Chapters 1 and 3–6. LeRoy Walters took the lead on Chapters 2 and 7–10. However, we have shared a common goal — to identify and reprint a spectrum of views on each of our topics — views advanced by some of the most articulate and widely respected spokespersons in the field of bioethics. In this effort we have both been ably assisted by Padma Shah, our research assistant, who was tireless in locating and evaluating candidate documents from an almost-overwhelming flood of literature. In addition, Tom Beauchamp received valuable assistance from Sanyin Siang in the accumulation of materials for four chapters. Padma and Sanyin also provided sage advice that helped us make our selections more pertinent and the introductions more readable for students. Sue Walters and Barbara Bost helped with proofreading, and seven students also collaborated in the preparation of page proofs: April Carnahan, Michael Hammer, Erika Ann Jeschke, Philip LeVine, Sarah Moesker, Julia Jacoby, and Rhett Millsaps.

We have again been fortunate to be assisted by the finest library and information-retrieval colleagues in the world. In particular, we acknowledge the exceptional work of Doris Goldstein, Director of Library and Information Services, and her colleagues, Frances Abramson, Laura Bishop, Nichelle Cherry, Martina Darragh, Lucinda Huttlinger, Joy Kahn, Pat McCarrick, Patricia Martin, Hannelore Ninomiya, Anita Nolen, Cecily Orr, Clementine Pellegrino, Susan Poland, Kathleen Reynolds, and Jamey Trainer. We also thank all of our faculty colleagues at the Kennedy Institute and the Philosophy Department for their constant intellectual stimulation.

Moheba Hanif has accompanied us in the work on this edition from the beginning of the project, and it is she alone who was responsible for securing permission to reprint the selections that we include in this edition, as well as for final preparation of several features of the manuscript.

At Wadsworth Publishing Company, we are grateful for the expert advice of Peter Adams, the Philosophy Editor. At Matrix Productions, Merrill Peterson has efficiently overseen the copyediting process and the conversion of our text into pages. At ColorType, multiple type-setters with whom we have not communicated directly have carefully keyed thousand of characters. We are grateful to the reviewers of the previous edition: Donald Becker, University of Texas, Austin; Candace C. Gauthier, University of North Carolina, Wilmington; Richard T. Hull, SUNY, Buffalo; Douglas C. Long, University of North Carolina, Chapel Hill; Lynn Lumbrezer, University of Toledo; and Lynn Pasquerella, University of Rhode Island. And we also wish to thank the reviewers of this edition: Donald Becker, University of Texas, Austin; Peter Horn, Capital University; Terrence McConnell, University of North Carolina, Greensboro; and Lynn Pasquerella, University of Rhode Island.

Finally, we want to acknowledge the patience and support of our spouses, Ruth and Sue, and of our children, Karine and Zack, and David and Robert, throughout the always-arduous process of reading, selecting, editing, introducing, and proofreading.

We hope that this book will stimulate discussion in academic settings and contribute to the development of more enlightened public policies on these important biomedical topics.

November 1998
Tom L. Beauchamp, LeRoy Walters
Kennedy Institute of Ethics
and Department of Philosophy
Georgetown University

1.
Ethical Theory and Bioethics

The moral problems discussed in this book have emerged from professional practice in the fields of clinical medicine, biomedical research, nursing, public health, and the social and behavioral sciences. The goal of this first chapter is to provide a basis in ethical theory and bioethics sufficient for reading and criticizing the selections in the later chapters.

FUNDAMENTAL PROBLEMS

THE STUDY OF MORALITY

Some Basic Definitions. The field of ethics includes the study of social morality as well as philosophical reflection on its norms and practices. The terms "ethical theory" and "moral philosophy" refer exclusively to philosophical reflection on morality. The term "morality," by contrast, refers to traditions of belief about right and wrong human conduct. Morality is a social institution with a history and a code of learnable rules. Like political constitutions and languages, morality exists before we are instructed in its relevant rules, and thus it has a trans-individual status as a body of guidelines for action.

Individuals do not create their morality by making their own rules, and morality cannot be purely a personal policy or code. The core parts of morality exist before their acceptance by individuals. We learn about these moral responsibilities and moral ideals as we grow up. We also gradually learn to distinguish the general morality that holds for all persons (sometimes called the common morality) from rules that bind only members of special groups, such as physicians. We learn moral rules alongside other important social rules, which is one reason it later becomes difficult to distinguish the two. For example, we are constantly reminded in our early years that we must observe social rules of etiquette such as saying "Please" when we want something and "Thank you" when we receive it, as well as more specific rules such as "A judge is addressed as 'judge.'" We are also taught rules of prudence, including "Don't touch a hot stove," together with rules of housekeeping, dressing, and the like.

But the whole of these rules does not amount to morality. Morality enters the picture when certain actions ought or ought not to be performed because of the considerable impact these actions can be expected to have on the interests of other people. We first learn maxims such as "It is better to give than to receive" and "Respect the rights of others." These are elementary instructions in morality; they express what society expects of us and of everyone in terms of taking the interests of other people into account. We thus learn about moral instructions and expectations, and gradually we come to understand morality as a set of normative standards about doing good, avoiding harm, respecting others, keeping promises, and acting fairly. We also absorb standards of character and moral excellence.

Following this analysis, the terms "ethical" and "moral" are to be understood in this introduction as identical in meaning, and "ethics" will be used as a general term referring to *both* morality and ethical theory. The terms "moral philosophy," "ethical theory," and "philosophical ethics" will be reserved for philosophical theories about the moral life.

Four Approaches to the Study of Ethics.   Morality can be studied and developed in a variety of ways. In particular, four ways of either studying moral beliefs or doing moral philosophy appear prominently in the literature of ethics. Two of these approaches describe and analyze morality without taking moral positions, and these approaches are therefore called "nonnormative." Two other approaches do involve taking moral positions, and are therefore "normative." These four approaches can be grouped as follows:

A. *Nonnormative approaches*
   1. Descriptive ethics
   2. Metaethics
B. *Normative approaches*
   3. General normative ethics
   4. Practical normative ethics

It would be a mistake to regard these categories as expressing rigid, sharply differentiated approaches. They are often undertaken at the same time, and they overlap in goal and content. Nonetheless, when understood as broad polar contrasts exemplifying models of inquiry, these distinctions are important.

First among the two nonnormative fields of inquiry into morality is descriptive ethics, or the factual description and explanation of moral behavior and beliefs. Anthropologists, sociologists, and historians who study moral behavior employ this approach when they explore how moral attitudes, codes, and beliefs differ from person to person and from society to society. Their works often dwell in detail on matters such as professional codes and practices, codes of honor, and rules governing permissible killing in a society. Although philosophers do not typically engage in descriptive ethics in their work, some have combined descriptive ethics with philosophical ethics — for example, by analyzing the ethical practices of American Indian tribes or researching Nazi experimentation during World War II.

The second nonnormative field, metaethics, involves analysis of the meanings of central terms in ethics, such as "right," "obligation," "good," "virtue," and "responsibility." The proper analysis of the term "morality" and the distinction between the moral and the nonmoral are typical metaethical problems. Crucial terms in bioethics, including "physician-assisted suicide," "informed consent," and "universal access" to health care, can be and should be given careful conceptual attention, and they are so treated in various chapters in this volume. (Descriptive ethics and metaethics may not be the only forms of nonnormative inquiry. In recent years there has been an active discussion of the biological bases of moral behavior and of the ways in which humans do and do not differ from animals.)

General normative ethics attempts to formulate and defend basic principles and virtues governing the moral life. Ideally, any ethical theory will provide a system of moral principles or virtues and reasons for adopting them, and will defend claims about the range of their applicability. In the course of this chapter the most prominent of these theories will be examined, as will various principles of respect for autonomy, justice, and beneficence that have played a major role in some of these theories.

General normative theories are sometimes used to justify positions on particular moral problems such as abortion, euthanasia, the distribution of health care, and research involving human subjects. Usually, however, no direct move can be made from theory or principles to particular judgments, and theory and principles therefore typically only *facilitate* the development of policies, action-guides, or judgments. In general, the attempt to delineate practical action guides is referred to as "practical ethics" (B.4 above).

Substantially the same general ethical theories and principles apply to problems across different professional fields and in areas beyond professional ethics as well. One might appeal to principles of justice, for example, in order to illuminate and resolve issues of taxation, health care distribution, criminal punishment, and affirmative action in hiring. Similarly, principles of veracity (truthfulness) are invoked to discuss secrecy and deception in international politics, misleading advertisements in business ethics, balanced reporting in journalistic ethics, and the disclosure of the nature and extent of an illness to a patient in medical ethics.

MORAL DILEMMAS AND DISAGREEMENTS

In the teaching of ethics, moral problems are often examined through cases, particularly law cases, clinical cases, and public policy cases. These cases, which appear in virtually every chapter in this book, vividly display dilemmas and disagreements that require students to identify and grapple with real moral problems.

Moral Dilemmas. In a case presented in Chapter 3, two judges became entangled in apparent moral disagreement when confronted with a murder trial. A woman named Tarasoff had been killed by a man who previously had confided to a therapist his intention to kill her as soon as she returned home from a summer vacation. Owing to obligations of confidentiality between patient and physician, a psychologist and a consulting psychiatrist did not report the threat to the woman or to her family, though they did make one unsuccessful attempt to commit the man to a mental hospital.

One judge held that the therapist could not escape liability: "When a therapist determines, or pursuant to the standards of his profession should determine, that his patient presents a serious danger of violence to another, he incurs an obligation to use reasonable care to protect the intended victim against such danger." Notification of police and direct warning to the family were mentioned as possible instances of due care. The judge argued that, although medical confidentiality must generally be observed by physicians, it was overridden in this particular case by an obligation to the possible victim and to the "public interest in safety from violent assault."

In the minority opinion, a second judge stated his firm disagreement. He argues that a patient's rights are violated when rules of confidentiality are not observed, that psychiatric treatment would be frustrated by nonobservance, and that patients would subsequently lose confidence in psychiatrists and would fail to provide full disclosures. He also suggested that violent assaults would actually increase because mentally ill persons would be discouraged from seeking psychiatric aid.[1]

The Tarasoff case is an instance of a moral dilemma, because strong moral reasons support the rival conclusions of the two judges. The most difficult and recalcitrant moral controversies that we encounter in this volume generally have at least some dilemmatic features. They may even involve what Guido Calabresi has called "tragic choices." Everyone who has been faced with a difficult decision — such as whether to have an abortion, to have a pet "put to sleep," or to commit a member of one's family to a mental institution — knows through deep anguish what is meant by a personal dilemma.

Dilemmas occur whenever good reasons for mutually exclusive alternatives can be cited; if any one set of reasons is acted upon, events will result that are desirable in some respects but undesirable in others. Here an agent morally ought to do one thing and also morally ought to do another thing, but the agent is precluded by circumstances from doing both. Although the moral reasons behind each alternative are good reasons, neither set of reasons clearly outweighs the other. Parties on both sides of dilemmatic disagreements thus can *correctly* present moral reasons in support of their competing conclusions. The reasons behind each alternative are good and weighty, and neither set of reasons is obviously the best set. Most moral dilemmas therefore present a need to balance rival claims in untidy circumstances.

One possible response to the problem of public moral dilemmas and disputes is that we do not have and are not likely ever to have a single theory or method for resolving public disagreements. In any pluralistic culture there may be many sources of moral value and consequently a pluralism of moral points of view on many issues: bluffing in business deals, providing national health insurance to all citizens, involuntarily committing the mentally disturbed, civil disobedience in pursuit of justice, and so on. If this response is correct, we can understand why there seem to be intractable moral dilemmas and controversies both inside and outside professional philosophy. However, there also are ways to alleviate at least some dilemmas and disagreements, as we shall now see.

The Resolution of Moral Disagreements. No single set of considerations is an entirely reliable method for resolving disagreement and controversy, but several methods for dealing constructively with moral disagreements have been employed in the past. Each deserves recognition as a method of constructively contending with disagreement.

1. *Obtaining Objective Information.* First, many moral disagreements can be at least facilitated by obtaining factual information concerning points of moral controversy. It has often been assumed that moral disputes are produced solely by differences over moral principles or their interpretation and application, rather than by a lack of information. However, disputes over what morally ought or ought not to be done often have nonmoral elements as central ingredients. For example, debates about the justice of government allocation of health dollars to preventive and educational strategies (see Chapter 6) have often bogged down over factual issues of whether these strategies actually function to prevent illness and promote health.

In some cases new information facilitates negotiation and compromise. New information about the alleged dangers involved in certain kinds of scientific research, for instance, have turned public controversies regarding the risks of science and the rights of scientific researchers in unanticipated directions. In several controversies over research with a high level of uncertainty, it has been feared that the research might create an irreversible and dangerous situation (for example, by releasing an organism of pathogenic capability that known antibodies would be unable to combat and that could produce widespread contagion).

Controversies about sweetening agents for drinks, toxic substances in the workplace, pesticides in agriculture, radiation therapies, and vaccine dissemination, among others, have been laced with issues of both values and facts. Current controversies over whether there should be compulsory screening for AIDS sometimes turn chiefly on factual claims about how much can be learned by screening, how many persons are threatened, whether health education campaigns can successfully teach safe sex practices, and the like.

The arguments used by disagreeing parties in these cases sometimes turn on a dispute about liberty or justice and therefore sometimes are primarily normative, but they may also rest on purely factual disagreements. New information may have only a limited bearing on the resolution of some of these controversies, whereas in others it may have a direct and almost overpowering influence. The problem is that rarely, if ever, is all the information obtained that would be sufficient to settle factual disagreements.

2. *Providing Definitional Clarity.* Second, controversies have been calmed by reaching conceptual or definitional agreement over the language used by disputing parties. Controversies over the morality of euthanasia, for example, are often needlessly entangled because disputing parties use different senses of the term and have invested heavily in their particular definitions. For example, it may be that one party equates euthanasia with mercy killing and another party equates it with voluntarily elected natural death. Some even hold that euthanasia is by definition *nonvoluntary* mercy killing. Any resulting moral controversy over "euthanasia" is ensnared in terminological problems (see Chapters 6 and 7), rendering it doubtful that the parties are even discussing the same problem. Fortunately, conceptual analysis does often facilitate discussion of issues, and many essays in this volume dwell at some length on conceptual analysis.

3. *Adopting a Code.* Third, resolution of moral problems can be facilitated if disputing parties can come to agreement on a common set of moral guidelines. If this method requires a complete shift from one starkly different moral point of view to another, disputes will virtually never be eased. Differences that divide persons at the level of their most cherished principles are deep divisions, and conversions are infrequent. Various forms of discussion and negotiation can, however, lead to the adoption of a new or changed moral framework that can serve as a common basis for discussion.

For example, a national commission appointed to study ethical issues in research involving human subjects unanimously adopted a common framework of moral principles. These principles provided a general background for deliberation about particular problems. Commissioners utilized three moral principles: respect for persons, beneficence, and justice. The principles were then used, along with other considerations, to justify a position on a wide range of moral problems that confronted the commission.[2] This common framework of principles facilitated discussion of controversies and opened up avenues of agreement that might otherwise not have been spotted.

Virtually every professional association in medicine and nursing has a code of ethics, and the reason for the existence of these codes is to give guidance in a circumstance of uncertainty or dispute. Their rules apply to all persons in the relevant professional roles in medicine, nursing, and research and often help resolve charges of unprofessional or unethical conduct. These codes are very general and cannot be expected to cover every possible case, but agreed-upon general principles do provide an important starting point.

4. *Using Examples and Counterexamples.* Fourth, resolution of moral controversies can be aided by a constructive method of example and opposed counterexample. Cases or examples favorable to one point of view are brought forward, and counterexamples to these cases are thrown up against the examples and claims of the first. This form of debate occurred when the commission mentioned in the preceding section considered the level of risk that can justifiably be permitted in scientific research involving children as subjects, where no therapeutic benefit is offered to the child. On the basis of principles of acceptable risk used in their own previous deliberations, commissioners were at first inclined to accept the view that only low risk or "minimal risk" procedures could be justified in the case of children (where "minimal risk" refers analogically to the level of risk present in standard medical examinations of patients). Examples from the history of medicine were cited that revealed how certain significant diagnostic, therapeutic, and preventive advances in medicine would have been unlikely, or at least slowed, unless procedures that posed a higher level of risk had been employed. Counterexamples of overzealous researchers who placed children

at too much risk were then thrown up against these examples, and the debate continued in this way for several months.

Eventually a majority of commissioners abandoned their original view that nontherapeutic research involving more than minimal risk was unjustified. The majority accepted the position that a higher level of risk can be justified by the benefits provided to other children, as when a group of terminally ill children becomes the subject of research in the hope that something will be learned about their disease that can be applied to other children. Once a consensus on this particular issue crystallized, resolution was achieved on the primary moral controversy about the involvement of children as research subjects (although two commissioners never agreed).

5. *Analyzing Arguments.* Fifth and finally, one of the most important methods of philosophical inquiry is the exposing of inadequacies, gaps, fallacies, and unexpected consequences of an argument. If an argument rests on accepting two incoherent points of view, then pointing out the incoherence will require a change in the argument. There are many subtle ways of attacking an argument. For example, in Chapter 4 there are discussions of the nature of "persons," and these discussions are carried into Chapter 5, dealing with problems of the right to die and euthanasia. Some writers on these topics have not appreciated that their arguments about persons were so broad that they carried important but unnoticed implications for both infants and animals. Their arguments implicitly provided reasons they had not noticed for denying rights to infants (rights that adults have), or for granting (or denying) the same rights to fetuses that infants have, and in some cases for granting (or denying) the same rights to animals that infants have.

It may, of course, be correct to hold that infants have fewer rights than adults, or that fetuses and animals should be granted the same rights as infants. The point is that if a moral argument leads to conclusions that a proponent is not prepared to defend and did not previously anticipate, the argument will have to be changed, and this process may reduce the distance between the parties who were initially in disagreement. This style of argument may be supplemented by one or more of the other four ways of reducing moral disagreement. Much of the work published in journals takes the form of attacking arguments, using counterexamples, and proposing alternative principles.

To accept this ideal of criticism is not to assume that conflicts can always be eliminated. The moral life will always be plagued by forms of conflict and incoherence. Our pragmatic goal should be a method that helps in a circumstance of disagreement, not a method that will always eradicate problems. We need not claim that moral disagreements can always be resolved, or even that every rational person must accept the same method for approaching problems. However, if something is to be done to alleviate disagreement, a resolution is more likely to occur if the methods outlined in this section are used.

THE PROBLEM OF RELATIVISM

The fact of moral disagreement raises questions about whether there can be correct or objective moral judgments and whether an inescapable relativism underlies moral thinking.

Cultural Relativism. Relativists often appeal to anthropological data indicating that moral rightness and wrongness vary from place to place and that there are no absolute or universal moral standards that could apply to all persons at all times. They maintain that rightness is contingent on cultural beliefs and that the concepts of rightness and wrongness are meaningless apart from the specific contexts in which they arise. The claim is that patterns of culture can only be understood as unique wholes and that moral beliefs about normal behavior are closely connected to a set of social expectations in a culture.

Although cultural practices and individual beliefs vary, it does not follow that people *fundamentally* disagree about ultimate moral standards. Two cultures may agree about an ultimate principle of morality yet disagree about how to apply the principle in a particular situation or practice. The two cultures may even agree on all the basic principles of morality, yet disagree about how to live by these principles in particular circumstances.

For example, if personal payments for special services are common in one culture and punishable as bribery in another, then it is undeniable that these customs are different, but it does not follow that the moral principles underlying the customs are relative. One culture may exhibit a belief that practices of grease payments produce a social good by eliminating government interference and by lowering the salaries paid to functionaries, while the people of another culture may believe that the overall social good is best promoted by eliminating all special favors. Both justifications rest on an appraisal of the overall social good, but the people of the two cultures apply this principle in disparate and apparently competing ways.

This possibility suggests that a basic or fundamental conflict between cultural values can only occur if apparent cultural disagreements about proper principles or rules occur at the level of ultimate moral principles. Otherwise, the apparent disagreements can be understood in terms of, and perhaps be arbitrated by, appeal to deeper shared values. If a moral conflict were truly fundamental, then the conflict could not be removed even if there were perfect agreement about the facts of a case, about the concepts involved, and about background beliefs.

We need, then, to distinguish *relativism of judgments* from *relativism of standards*: Different judgments may rely upon the same general standards for their justification. Relativism of judgment is so pervasive in human social life that it would be foolish to deny it. When people differ about whether one policy for keeping hospital information confidential is more acceptable than another, they differ in their judgments, but they need not have different moral standards of confidentiality. They may hold the same moral standard on protecting confidentiality, but differ over how to implement that standard.

Showing the falsity of a relativism of standards is more than we can hope to achieve here, but we can show how difficult it would be to show that it is true. Suppose, for the sake of argument, that disagreement exists at the deepest level of moral belief; that is, suppose that two cultures disagree on basic or fundamental norms. It does not follow even from a relativity of *standards* that there is no ultimate norm or set of norms in which everyone *ought* to believe. Consider an analogy to religious disagreement: From the fact that people have incompatible religious or atheistic beliefs, it does not follow that there is no single correct set of religious or atheistic propositions. Nothing more than skepticism is justified by the facts about religion that are adduced by anthropology; and, similarly, nothing more than this skepticism would be justified if fundamental conflicts of social belief were discovered in ethics.

Normative Relativism.   Consider now a second type of relativism. Some relativists interpret "What is right at one place or time may be wrong at another" to mean that *it is right* in one context to act in a way that *it is wrong* to act in another. This thesis is normative, because it makes a value judgment; it delineates *which standards or norms correctly determine right and wrong behavior.* One form of this normative relativism asserts that one ought to do what one's society determines to be right (a group or social form of normative relativism), and a second form holds that one ought to do what one personally believes is right (an individual form of normative relativism).

This normative position has sometimes crudely been translated as "Anything is right or wrong whenever some individual or some group judges that it is right or wrong." However, less crude formulations of the position can be given, and more or less plausible examples can be adduced. One can hold the view, for example, that in order to be right something must be conscientiously and not merely customarily believed. Alternatively, it might be formulated as the view that whatever is believed to be right is right if it is part of a well-formed traditional moral code of rules in a society — for example, a medical code of ethics developed by a professional society.

The evident inconsistency of this form of relativism with many of our most cherished moral beliefs is one major reason to be doubtful of it. No general theory of normative relativism is likely to convince us that a belief is acceptable merely because others believe it in a certain way, although that is exactly the commitment of this theory. At least some moral views seem relatively more enlightened, no matter how great the variability of beliefs. The idea that practices such as slavery cannot be evaluated across cultures by some common standard seems morally unacceptable, not morally enlightened. It is one thing to suggest that such beliefs might be *excused,* still another to suggest that they are *right.*

We can evaluate this second form of relativism by focusing on (1) the objectivity of morals within cultures and (2) the stultifying consequences of serious commitment to moral relativism. (The first focus provides an argument against *individual* relativism and the second provides an argument against a *cultural* source of relativism.)

We noted previously that morality is concerned with practices of right and wrong transmitted within cultures from one generation to another. The terms of social life are set by these practices, whose rules are pervasively acknowledged and shared in that culture. Within the culture, then, a significant measure of moral agreement (objectivity) exists, and morality cannot be modified through a person's individual preferences.

For example, a hospital corporation cannot develop its professional ethics in any way it wishes. No hospital chain can draw up a code that brushes aside the need for confidentiality of patient information or that permits surgeons to proceed without adequate consents from patients; and a physician cannot make up his or her individual "code" of medical ethics. If codes deviate significantly from standard or accepted rules, they will rightly be rejected as subjective and mistaken.

Room for invention or alteration in morality is therefore restricted by the broader understanding of social morality. Beliefs cannot become *moral* standards simply because an individual so labels them. Because individual (normative) relativism claims that moral standards can be invented or labeled, the theory seems *factually* mistaken. This critique of *individual* relativism does not count against *cultural* relativism, however, because a cultural relativist could easily accept this critique. Our discussion needs to shift, then, to a second argument, which is directed at cultural forms of normative relativism.

The problem is this: In circumstances of disagreement, moral reflection is needed to resolve moral issues whether or not people accept different norms. When two parties argue about a serious, divisive, and contested moral issue — for example, conflicts of interest — most of us think that some fair and justified compromise may be reached despite the differences of belief causing the dispute. People seldom infer from the mere fact of a conflict between beliefs that there is no way to judge one view as correct or as better argued or fairer-minded than the other. The more implausible the position advanced by one party, the more convinced others become that some views are mistaken or require supplementation.

People seldom conclude, then, that there is not a better and worse ethical perspective or a more reasonable form of negotiation. If cultural normative relativists deny the acceptability of these beliefs, they seem to give up too early on the possibility that moral agreement may be achieved.

Morality in the Narrow and Broad Senses. Another way to think about relativism is through the idea that the morality shared by all morally serious persons in all societies is not *a morality*; it is simply morality. It is universal because it contains ethical precepts found wherever morality is found. In recent years, the favored category to express this perspective has been human rights,[3] but parts of morality are also found in standards of obligation and virtue. These norms constituting a shared morality can be called "morality in the narrow sense," because the morality we share in common is only a small slice of the entire moral life. Morality in the broad sense includes divergent moral norms and positions that spring from different cultural, philosophical, and religious roots.

Many people are curious about and even skeptical of the idea of a common morality. They think that virtually nothing is shared across cultures and different moral traditions, but this skepticism may involve a confusion over the broad and narrow senses of "morality." While the broad sense allows for ample diversity and disagreement, the narrow sense captures what we all already know and appreciate about morality. The following are examples of universal precepts that all morally serious persons share in common: Tell the truth; Respect the privacy of others; Protect confidential information; Obtain consent before invading another person's body; Do not kill; Do not cause pain; Do not steal or otherwise deprive of goods; and Prevent harm from occurring to others.

It is no objection to these rules to note that in some circumstances they can be validly overridden by other norms with which they conflict. All norms can be validly overridden in some circumstances in which they compete with other moral claims. For example, we might not tell the truth in order to prevent someone from killing another person; and in order to protect the rights of one person, a person might have to disclose confidential information about another person. Principles, duties, and rights are not unbending standards, but they also do not, from a moral point of view, appear to be relative.

MORAL JUSTIFICATION

Typically we have no difficulty in deciding whether to act morally. We make moral judgments through a mix of appeals to rules, paradigm cases, role models, and the like. These moral beacons work well as long as we are not asked to deliberate about or justify our judgments. However, when we experience moral doubt or uncertainty, we are led to moral deliberation, and often from there to a need to justify our beliefs. As we deliberate, we usually consider which among the possible courses of action is morally justified, i.e., which has the strongest moral reasons behind it. The reasons we finally accept express the conditions under which we believe some course of action is morally justified.

The objective of justification is to establish one's case by presenting a sufficient set of reasons for belief and action. Not all reasons, however, are good reasons, and even good reasons are not always sufficient for justification. There is, then, a need to distinguish a reason's *relevance* to a moral judgment from its final *adequacy* for that judgment; and also to distinguish an *attempted* justification from a *successful* justification. For example, a good reason for involuntarily committing certain mentally ill persons to institutions is that they present a clear and present danger to other persons. By contrast, a reason for commitment that is sometimes offered as a good reason, but which many people consider a bad reason (because it involves a deprivation of liberty), is that some mentally ill persons present a clear and present danger to themselves, or require treatment for a serious mental disorder.

If someone holds that involuntary commitment on grounds of danger to self is a good reason and is solely sufficient to justify commitment, that person should be able to give some account of why this reason is good and sufficient. That is, the person should be able to give further justifying reasons for the belief that the reason offered is good and sufficient. The person might refer, for example, to the dire consequences for the mentally ill that will occur if no one intervenes. The person might also invoke certain principles about the moral importance of caring for the needs of the mentally ill. In short, the person is expected to give a set of reasons that amounts to an argued defense of his or her perspective. These appeals are usually either to a coherent group of moral principles or to consequences of actions, and they form the substantive basis of justification.

Although the justification of moral *judgments* is often the issue, philosophers are no less concerned with the justification of ethical *theories.* Which theory, we can now ask, is the best theory? Or do all theories fail tests for plausibility and coherence?

TYPES OF ETHICAL THEORY

If there is to be a meaningful ethics in the cultures of medicine and research, practitioners in these fields must be able to implement standards that are more than loose abstractions. We need a way to make moral theory of direct relevance to professional practice and public policy. Bringing theory directly to bear on issues of practice, professional responsibility, and public policy are largely the subjects of later chapters in this book. At present we are concerned primarily with the nature of the theories that either underlie our practices and policies or that could be used to revise practice and policy.

Some persons interested in ethics do not see the need for abstract theory or for any revisions of prevailing practices that might flow from a theory. They find present moral conventions and rules comfortable and adequate. However, other persons are concerned about relating ethical theory to practice, and they take the competing view that traditional or operative standards are often incomplete, poorly understood, and inconsistent—as well as suffering from the lack of a uniform theory that would make the body of rules coherent and relevant. Those who take this viewpoint are inclined to revise present practices and policies, and they often look to some system of ethical theory to provide a basis for revisions.

To deal with these issues, the reader should be prepared not only to understand ethical theory but also to make some assessment of its value for bioethics. Our objective in this section is not to show how ethical theory can resolve problems in health care, but to present several types of ethical theory. These theories should be situated under the category that we earlier called general normative ethics. We will concentrate on utilitarianism, Kantianism, character ethics, the ethics of care, and casuistry. Some knowledge of these theories is indispensable for reflective study in biomedical ethics, because a sizable part of the field's literature draws on methods and conclusions found in these theories. In almost every chapter in this volume at least one author relies upon some version of one of these theories.

UTILITARIAN THEORIES

Utilitarianism is rooted in the thesis that an action or practice is right (when compared to any alternative action or practice) if it leads to the greatest possible balance of good consequences or to the least possible balance of bad consequences in the world as a whole. Utilitarians hold that there is one and only one basic principle of ethics: the principle of utility. This principle asserts that we ought always to produce the maximal balance of positive

casuistry / —specious argument

value over disvalue (or the least possible disvalue, if only undesirable results can be achieved). The classical origins of this theory are found in the writings of Jeremy Bentham (1748–1832) and John Stuart Mill (1806–1873).

Utilitarians invite us to consider the larger objective or function of morality as a social institution, where "morality" is understood to include our shared rules of justice and other principles of the moral life. The point of the institution of morality, they insist, is to promote human welfare by minimizing harms and maximizing benefits: There would be no point in having moral codes unless they served this purpose. Utilitarians thus see moral rules as the means to the fulfillment of individual needs as well as to the achievement of broad social goals.

Mill's Utilitarianism. In several types of ethical theory, classic works of enduring influence form the basis for development of the theory. The most influential exposition of utilitarianism is John Stuart Mill's book *Utilitarianism* (1863). In this work Mill refers to the principle of utility as the Greatest Happiness Principle: "Actions are right in proportion as they tend to promote happiness, wrong as they tend to produce the reverse of happiness, i.e., pleasure or absence of pain." Mill's view seems to be that the purpose of morality is to tap natural human sympathies so as to benefit others while at the same time controlling unsympathetic attitudes that cause harm to others. The principle of utility is conceived as the best means to these basic human goals.

For Mill and other utilitarians, moral theory is grounded in a theory of the general goals of life, which they conceive as the pursuit of pleasure and the avoidance of pain. The production of pleasure and pain assumes moral and not merely personal significance when the consequences of our actions affect the pleasurable or painful states of others. Moral rules and moral and legal institutions, as they see it, must be grounded in a general theory of value, and morally good actions are alone determined by these final values.

Essential Features of Utilitarianism. Several essential features of utilitarianism may be extracted from the reasoning of Mill and other utilitarians. In particular, four conditions must be satisfied in order to qualify as a utilitarian theory.

1. *The Principle of Utility: Maximize the Good.* First, actors are obliged to maximize the good: We ought always to produce the greatest possible balance of value over disvalue (or the least possible balance of disvalue, if only bad results can be achieved). But what is the good or the valuable? This question takes us to the second condition.

2. *A Theory of Value: The Standard of Goodness.* The goodness or badness of consequences is to be measured by items that count as the primary goods or utilities. Many utilitarians agree that ultimately we ought to look to the production of *agent-neutral* or intrinsic values, those that do not vary from person to person. That is, what is good in itself, not merely what is good as a means to something else, ought to be produced. Bentham and Mill are hedonists; they believe that only pleasure or happiness (which are synonymous terms in this context) can be intrinsically good. Pluralistic utilitarian philosophers, by contrast, believe that no single goal or state constitutes the good and that many values besides happiness possess intrinsic worth—for example, the values of friendship, knowledge, love, personal achievement, culture, freedom, and liberties can all qualify.

Both the hedonistic and the pluralistic approaches have nonetheless seemed to some recent philosophers relatively problematic for purposes of objectively aggregating widely different interests in order to determine where maximal value, and therefore right action, lies. Many utilitarians interpret the good as that which is *subjectively* desired or wanted. The satisfaction of desires or wants is seen as the goal of our moral actions. To maximize an individual's utility is to maximize what he or she has chosen or would choose from the available alternatives.

3. *Consequentialism.* All utilitarian theories decide which actions are right and which wrong by the consequences of the actions. Consequentialism is the position that actions are morally right or wrong according to their consequences, rather than by virtue of any intrinsic moral features they may have, such as truthfulness or fidelity. Here the utilitarian need not demand that all future consequences or even all avoidable consequences be anticipated. A utilitarian demands only that we take account of what can reasonably be expected to produce the greatest balance of good or least balance of harm. In judging the *agent* of the action, we should assess whether the agent conscientiously attempts to produce the best utilitarian outcome.

4. *Impartiality (Universalism).* Finally, in a utilitarian theory the consequences affecting all parties must receive equal and impartial consideration. Utilitarianism thus stands in sharp contrast to egoism, which proposes maximizing consequences for oneself rather than for all parties affected by an action. In seeking a blinded impartiality, utilitarianism aligns good and mature moral judgment with moral distance from the choices to be made.

Act and Rule Utilitarianism. Utilitarian moral philosophers are conventionally divided into several types, and it is best to think of "utilitarianism" as a label designating a family of theories that use a consequentialist principle. A significant dispute has arisen among utilitarians over whether the principle of utility is to be applied to *particular acts* in particular circumstances or to *rules of conduct* that determine which acts are right and wrong. For the rule utilitarian, actions are justified by appeal to rules such as "Don't deceive" and "Don't break promises." These rules, in turn, are justified by appeal to the principle of utility. An act utilitarian simply justifies actions directly by appeal to the principle of utility. Act utilitarianism is thus characterized as a "direct" or "extreme" theory because the act utilitarian directly asks, "What good and evil consequences will result directly from this action in this circumstance?" — not "What good and evil consequences will result generally from this sort of action?"

Consider the following case, which occurred in the state of Kansas and which anticipates some issues about euthanasia encountered in Chapter 5. An elderly woman lay ill and dying. Her suffering came to be too much for her and her faithful husband of fifty-four years to endure, so she requested he kill her. Stricken with grief and unable to bring himself to perform the act, the husband hired another man to kill his wife. An act utilitarian might reason that *in this case* hiring another to kill the woman was justified, although *in general* we would not permit persons to perform such actions. After all, only this woman and her husband were directly affected, and relief of her pain was the main issue. It would be unfortunate, the act utilitarian might reason, if our "rules" against killing failed to allow for selective killings in extenuating circumstances, because it is extremely difficult to generalize from case to case. The jury, as it turned out, convicted the husband of murder, and he was sentenced to twenty-five years in prison. An act utilitarian might maintain that a *rigid* application of rules inevitably leads to injustices and that rule utilitarianism cannot escape this problem of undue rigidity of rules.

Many philosophers object vigorously to act utilitarianism, charging its exponents with basing morality on mere expediency. On act-utilitarian grounds, they say, it is desirable for a physician to kill babies with many kinds of birth defects if the death of the child would relieve the family and society of a burden and inconvenience and would lead to the greatest good for the greatest number. Many opponents of act utilitarianism have thus argued that strict rules, which cannot be set aside for the sake of convenience, must be maintained. Many of these apparently desirable rules can be justified by the principle of utility, so utilitarianism need not be abandoned if act utilitarianism is judged unworthy.

Rule utilitarians hold that rules have a central position in morality and cannot be compromised in particular situations. Compromise threatens the rules themselves. The rules' effectiveness is judged by determining whether the observance of a given rule would maximize social utility better than would any substitute rule (or having no rule). Utilitarian rules are, in theory, firm and protective of all classes of individuals, just as human rights firmly protect all individuals regardless of social convenience and momentary need.

Nonetheless, we can ask whether rule-utilitarian theories offer anything more than act utilitarianism. Dilemmas often arise that involve conflicts among moral rules—for example, rules of confidentiality conflict with rules protecting individual welfare, as in the Tarasoff case. If there are no rules to resolve these conflicts, perhaps the rule utilitarian cannot be distinguished from the act utilitarian.

KANTIAN THEORIES

We have seen that utilitarianism conceives the moral life in terms of intrinsic value and the means to produce this value. A second type of theory departs significantly from this approach. Often called *deontological* (i.e., a theory that some features of actions other than or in addition to consequences make actions obligatory), this type is now increasingly called *Kantian*, because of its origins in the theory of Immanuel Kant (1724–1804).

Duty from Rules of Reason. Kant believed that an act is morally praiseworthy only if done neither for self-interested reasons nor as the result of a natural disposition, but rather from *duty.* That is, the person's motive for acting must be a recognition of the act as resting on duty. It is not good enough, in Kant's view, that one merely performs the morally correct action, because one could perform one's duty for self-interested reasons having nothing to do with morality. For example, if an employer discloses a health hazard to an employee only because he or she fears a lawsuit, and not because of a belief in the importance of truth telling, then this employer acts rightly but deserves no moral credit for the action.

Kant tries to establish the ultimate basis for the validity of moral rules in pure reason, not in intuition, conscience, or utility. He thinks all considerations of utility and self-interest secondary, because the moral worth of an agent's action depends exclusively on the moral acceptability of the rule on the basis of which the person is acting. An action has moral worth only when performed by an agent who possesses a good will, and a person has a good will only if moral duty based on a universally valid rule is the sole motive for the action. Morality, then, provides a rational framework of principles and rules that constrain and guide everyone, without regard to their personal goals and interests.

Kant's supreme principle, also called "the moral law," is expressed in several ways in his writings. In what appears to be his favored formulation, the principle is stated as follows: "I ought never to act except in such a way that I can also will that my maxim should become a universal law." This Kantian principle has often been compared to the golden rule, but Kant calls it the "categorical imperative." He gives several examples of moral maxims required by this fundamental principle: "Help others in distress"; "Do not commit suicide"; and "Work to develop your abilities." The categorical imperative is categorical, he argues, because it admits of no exceptions and is absolutely binding. It is imperative because it gives instruction about how one must act.

Kant clarifies this basic moral law—the condition of morality, in his view—by drawing a distinction between a categorical imperative and a hypothetical imperative. A hypothetical imperative takes the form "If I want to achieve such and such a valued end, then I must do so and so." These prescriptions—so reminiscent of utilitarian thinking—tell us what we must do, provided that we already have certain desires, interests, or goals. An example is "If you want to regain your health, then you must take this medication," or "If you want to improve infant mortality rates, then you must improve your hospital facilities." These imperatives are not commanded for their own sake. They are commanded as means to an end that has already been willed or accepted. Hypothetical imperatives are not moral imperatives in Kant's philosophy because moral imperatives tell us what must be done independently of our goals or desires.

Kant emphasizes the notion of "rule as universal law." Rules that determine duty are made correct by their universality, that is, the fact that they apply to everyone. This criterion of universality offers some worthwhile lessons for bioethics. Some of the clearest cases of immoral behavior involve a person trying to make a unique exception of himself or herself purely for personal reasons. This conduct could not be made universal, or the rules presupposed by the idea of "being an exception" would be destroyed. If carried out consistently by others, this conduct would violate the rules presupposed by the system of morality, thereby rendering the system inconsistent—that is, having inconsistent rules of operation.

Kant's view is that wrongful practices, including invasion of privacy, theft, and manipulative suppression of information are "contradictory"; that is, they are not consistent with the very duties they presuppose. In cases of lying, for example, the universalization of rules that allow lying would entitle everyone to lie to you, just as you would be entitled to lie to them. Such rules are inconsistent with the practice of truth telling that they presuppose. Similarly, fraud in research is inconsistent with the practice of publishing the truth. How could one cheat in research if there were no criteria that assumed honesty? All such practices are inconsistent with a rule or practice that they presuppose.

The Requirement to Never Treat Persons as Means. Kant states his categorical imperative in another and distinctly different formulation. This form may be more widely quoted and endorsed in contemporary ethics than the first form, and certainly it is more frequently invoked in bioethics. This formulation stipulates that "One must act to treat every person as an end and never as a means only."[4] Thus, one must treat persons as having their own autonomously established goals.

It has commonly been said that Kant is arguing categorically that we can never treat another as a means to our ends. This interpretation, however, misrepresents his views. He argues only that we must not treat another *exclusively* as a means to our own ends. When adult human research subjects are asked to volunteer, for example, they are treated as a means to a researcher's ends. However, they are not exclusively used for others' purposes, because they do not become mere servants or objects. Their consent justifies using them as means to the end of research.

Kant's imperative demands only that persons in such situations be treated with the respect and moral dignity to which all persons are always entitled, including the times when they are used as means to the ends of others. To treat persons merely as means, strictly speaking, is to disregard their personhood by exploiting or otherwise using them without regard to their own thoughts, interests, and needs. It involves a failure to acknowledge that every person has a worth and dignity equal to that of every other person and that this worth and dignity cannot be compromised for utilitarian or any other reasons.

CONTEMPORARY CHALLENGES TO
THE TRADITIONAL THEORIES

Thus far we have treated only two types of theory: utilitarianism and Kantianism. These theories combine a variety of moral considerations into a surprisingly systematized framework, centered around a single major principle. Much is attractive in these theories, and they have been the dominant models in ethical theory throughout much of the twentieth century. From this perspective, one must choose between them, as if there were no available alternative. However, much recent philosophical writing has focused on weaknesses in these theories and on ways in which the two theories actually affirm a similar conception of the moral life oriented around universal principles and rules.

Critics of utilitarian and Kantian models believe that the contrast between the two types of theory has been overestimated and that they do not merit the attention they have received and the lofty position they have occupied. Three accounts popular in bioethics as replacements for, or perhaps supplements to, utilitarian and Kantian theories are (1) virtue theory (which is character-based), (2) the ethics of care (which is relationship-based), and (3) casuistry (which is case-based). These are the topics of the next three sections.

VIRTUE ETHICS

In discussing utilitarian and Kantian theories, we have looked chiefly at obligations and rights. Beyond obligations and rights, we often reflect on the agents who perform actions, have motives, and follow principles. Here we commonly make judgments about good and evil character in persons.

Virtue ethics descends from the classical Greek tradition represented by Plato and Aristotle. Here the cultivation of virtuous traits of character is viewed as morality's primary function. Aristotle held that virtue is neither a feeling nor an innate capacity, but rather a disposition bred from an innate capacity properly trained and exercised. People acquire virtues much as they do skills such as carpentry, playing an instrument, or cooking. They become just by performing just actions and become temperate by performing temperate actions. Virtuous character, says Aristotle, is cultivated and made a part of the individual, much like a language or tradition.

However, an ethics of virtue is more than habitual training. One must also have a correct *motivational structure*. A conscientious person, for example, not only has a disposition to act conscientiously, but a morally appropriate desire to be conscientious. The person characteristically has a moral concern and reservation about acting in a way that would not be conscientious.

Imagine a Kantian who always performs his or her obligation because it is an obligation, but intensely dislikes having to allow the interests of others to be of importance. Such a person does not cherish, feel congenial toward, or think fondly of others, and respects them only because obligation requires it. This person can, on a theory of moral obligation such as Kant's (or Mill's), perform a morally right action, have an ingrained disposition to perform that action, and act with obligation as the foremost motive. It is possible (1) to be disposed to do what is right, (2) to intend to do it, and (3) to do it, while also (4) yearning to be able to avoid doing it. If the motive is improper, a vital moral ingredient is missing; and if a person *characteristically* lacks this motivational structure, a necessary condition of virtuous character is absent.

Consider a physician who meets his moral obligations because they are his obligations and yet has underlying motives that raise questions of character. This physician detests his job and hates having to spend time with every patient who comes through the door. He cares not about being of service to people or creating a better environment in the office. All he wants to do is make money, avoid malpractice suits, and meet his obligations. Although this man never acts immorally from the perspective of duty, something in his character is deeply defective morally. The admirable compassion and dedication guiding the lives of many health professionals is absent in this person, who merely engages in rule-following behavior.

Virtue ethics may seem only of intellectual interest, but it has practical value in that a morally good person with right desires or motives is more likely to understand what should be done, to perform required acts, and to form moral ideals than is a morally bad or indifferent person. A trusted person has an ingrained motivation and desire to do what is right and to care about whether it is done. Whenever the feelings, concerns, and attitudes of others are the morally relevant matters, rules and principles are not as likely as human warmth and sensitivity to lead a person to notice what should be done. From this perspective, virtue ethics is at least as fundamental in the moral life as principles of basic obligation.

A proponent of character ethics need not claim that analysis of the virtues subverts or discredits ethical principles and rules. It is enough to argue that ethical theory is more complete if the virtues are included and that moral motives deserve to be at center stage in a way some leading traditional theories have inadequately appreciated.

THE ETHICS OF CARE

Related to virtue ethics in some respects is a relatively new body of moral reflection often called the "ethics of care." This theory develops some of the themes in virtue ethics about the centrality of character, but the ethics of care focuses on a set of character traits that people all deeply value in close personal relationships: sympathy, compassion, fidelity, love, friendship, and the like. Noticeably absent are universal moral rules and impartial utilitarian calculations such as those espoused by Kant and Mill.

To understand this approach, consider the traditional theories' criterion of impartiality in moral judgment. This criterion of distanced fairness and treating similar cases similarly makes eminently good sense for courts, but does it make good sense of intimate moral relationships? The care perspective views this criterion as cutting away too much of morality in order to get to a standpoint of detached fairness. Lost in the traditional *detachment* of impartiality is *attachment*—that which we care about most and which is closest to us. In seeking blindness, we may be made blind and indifferent to the special needs of others. So, although impartiality is a moral virtue in some contexts, it may be a moral vice in others. The care perspective is especially important for roles such as parent, friend, physician, and nurse, where contextual response, attentiveness to subtle clues, and discernment are likely to be more important morally than impartial treatment.

Being cautious about abstract principles of obligation—the instruments of impartiality—is also characteristic of the ethics of care. Defenders of the ethics of care find principles often to be irrelevant, vacuous, or ineffectual in the moral life. A defender of principles could say that principles of care, compassion, and kindness structure our understanding of when it is appropriate to respond in caring, compassionate, and kind ways, but there is something hollow about this claim. It seems to best capture our moral experience to say that we rely on our emotions, our capacity for sympathy, our sense of friendship, and our knowledge of how caring people behave.

Exponents of the ethics of care have also criticized the autonomous, unified, rational beings that typify both the Kantian and the utilitarian conception of the moral self. They argue that moral decisions often require a sensitivity to the situation, as well as an awareness of the beliefs, feelings, attitudes, and concerns of each of the individuals involved and of the relationships of those individuals to one another.

Additional reasons exist for thinking that a morality centered on care and concern cannot be squeezed into a morality of rules. For example, it seems very difficult to express the responsibilities of a health care professional adequately through principles and rules. We can generalize about how caring physicians and nurses respond in encounters with patients, but these generalizations do not amount to principles, nor will such generalizations be subtle enough to give sound guidance for the next patient. Each situation calls for a different set of responses, and behavior that in one context is caring seems to intrude on privacy or be offensive in another context.

A morality centered on care and concern can potentially serve health care ethics in a constructive and balanced fashion, because it is close to the processes of reason and feeling exhibited in clinical contexts. Disclosures, discussions, and decision making in health care typically become a family affair, with support from a health care team. The ethics of care fits this context of relationships, whereas rights theory, for example, seems poorly equipped for it. The ethics of care frames responsibilities in terms of meeting the health as well as other human needs of patients and their families, role commitments, concerns about causing harm, protecting positive family relationships, and the like.

CASUISTRY

A third alternative to classical theories has been labeled "casuistry." It focuses on decision-making using particular cases, where the judgments reached rely on judgments reached in prior cases. Casuists are skeptical of the power of principles and theory to resolve problems in specific cases. They think that many forms of moral thinking and judgment do not involve appeals to general guidelines, but rather to narratives, paradigm cases, and precedents established by previous cases.[5]

Consider the way a physician thinks in making a judgment and then a recommendation to a patient. Many individual factors, including the patient's medical history, the physician's successes with other similar patients, paradigms of expected outcomes, and the like will play a role in formulating a judgment and recommendation to this patient, which may be very different from the recommendation made to the next patient with the same malady. The casuist views moral judgments and recommendations similarly. One can make successful moral judgments of agents, actions, and policies, casuists say, only when one has an intimate understanding of particular situations and an appreciation of treating similar cases similarly.

An analogy to case law is helpful in understanding the casuist's point. In case law, the normative judgment of courts of law become authoritative, and it is reasonable to hold that these judgments are primary for later judges who assess other cases — even though the particular features of each new case will be different. Matters are similar in ethics, say casuists. Normative judgments about certain cases emerge through case comparisons. A case under current consideration is placed in the context of a set of cases that shows a family resemblance, and the similarities and differences are assessed. The relative weight of competing values is presumably determined by the comparisons to analogous cases. Moral guidance is provided by an accumulated mass of influential cases, which represent a consensus in society and in institutions reached by reflection on cases. That consensus then becomes authoritative and is extended to new cases.[6]

Cases like the *Tarasoff* case have been enormously influential in bioethics. Writers have used it as a form of authority for decisions in new cases. Features of their analyses have then been discussed throughout the literature of biomedical ethics, and they become integral to the way we think and draw conclusions in the field. However, for a case to work well, it must be believed that decisions can be reached in new cases by a process of comparing similar cases. Too many unique features in a case make it difficult to use the case for purposes of generalization to other cases.

At first sight, casuistry seems strongly opposed to the frameworks of principles in traditional moral theory. However, closer inspection of casuistry shows that its primary concern (like the ethics of care) is with an excessive reliance in recent philosophy on impartial, universal action-guides. Two casuists, Albert Jonsen and Stephen Toulmin, write that "*good* casuistry . . . applies general principles to particular cases with discernment." As a history of similar cases and similar judgments mounts, we become more confident in our general judgments. A "locus of moral certitude" arises in the judgments, and the stable elements crystallize into tentative principles. As confidence in these generalizations increases, they are accepted less tentatively and moral knowledge develops.[7]

Today's casuists have resourcefully reminded us of the importance of analogical reasoning, paradigm cases, and practical judgment. Bioethics, like ethical theory, has sometimes unduly minimized this avenue to moral knowledge. Casuists also have rightly pointed out that generalizations are often best learned, accommodated, and implemented by using cases, case discussion, and case methods. These insights can be utilized by connecting them to an appropriate set of concepts, principles, and theories that control the judgments we make about cases.

ETHICAL PRINCIPLES

The common morality, we saw earlier, contains numerous moral precepts that express how a similar range of cases should be treated. These precepts have been expressed as principles that are basic in biomedical ethics. These principles are generally accepted in classical ethical theories and seem to be presupposed in traditional medical codes, which have relied heavily upon the implications of the general principle "Do no harm" as well as other general principles.

Ideally, a set of general principles will serve as an analytical framework of basic principles that expresses the general values underlying rules in the common morality and guidelines in professional ethics. Three general moral principles have proved to be serviceable as a framework of principles for bioethics: respect for autonomy, beneficence, and justice. These three principles should not be construed as jointly forming a complete moral system or theory, but they can provide the beginnings of a framework through which we can begin to reason about problems in bioethics. Each is treated in a separate section below.

One caution is in order about the nature and use of such principles. Moral thinking and judgment must take account of many considerations besides ethical principles and rules, and principles do not contain sufficient content to determine judgments in a great many cases. Often the most prudent course is to search for more information about cases and policies, rather than to try to decide prematurely on the basis of either principles or some general theoretical commitments. More information sometimes will resolve problems and in other cases will help fix the principles that are most important in the circumstances.

Principles provide a starting point for moral judgment and policy evaluation, but, as we saw in the previous section and will see below in the section on public policy, more content is needed than that supplied by principles alone. They are tested and reliable starting points, but they rarely are sufficient for moral thinking.[8]

RESPECT FOR AUTONOMY

One principle at the center of modern bioethics is respect for autonomy. It is rooted in the liberal moral and political tradition of the importance of individual freedom and choice. In moral philosophy personal autonomy refers to personal self-governance: personal rule of the self by adequate understanding while remaining free from controlling interferences by others and from personal limitations that prevent choice. "Autonomy" thus means freedom from external constraint and the presence of critical mental capacities such as understanding, intending, and voluntary decision-making capacity.[9]

To respect an autonomous agent is to recognize with due appreciation that person's capacities and perspective, including his or her right to hold certain views, to make certain choices, and to take certain actions based on personal values and beliefs. The moral demand that we respect the autonomy of persons can be expressed as a principle of respect for autonomy: Autonomy of action should not be subjected to control by others. The principle provides the basis for the right to make decisions, which in turn takes the form of specific autonomy-related rights.

For example, in the debate over whether autonomous, informed patients have the right to refuse self-regarding, life-sustaining medical interventions, the principle of respect for autonomy suggests a morally appropriate response. But the principle covers even simple exchanges in the medical world, such as listening carefully to patients' questions, answering the questions in the detail that respectfulness would demand, and not treating patients in a patronizing fashion.

Respect for autonomy has historically been connected to the idea that persons possess an intrinsic value independent of special circumstances that confer value. As expressed in Kantian ethics, autonomous persons are ends in themselves, determining their own destiny, and are not to be treated merely as means to the ends of others. Thus, the burden of moral justification rests on those who would restrict or prevent a person's exercise of autonomy.

To respect the autonomy of self-determining agents is to recognize them as *entitled* to determine their own destiny, with due regard to their considered evaluations and view of the world. They must be accorded the moral right to have their own opinions and to act upon them (as long as those actions produce no moral violation). Thus, in evaluating the self-regarding actions of others, we are obligated to respect them as persons with the same right to their judgments as we possess to our own, and they in turn are obligated to treat us in the same way.

Medical and nursing codes have begun in recent years to include rules that are explicitly based on this principle. For example, the first principle of the American Nurses' Association *Code* reads as follows:

The fundamental principle of nursing practice is respect for the inherent dignity and worth of every client. Nurses are morally obligated to respect human existence and the individuality of all persons who are the recipients of nursing actions. . . . Truth telling and the process of reaching informed choice underlie the exercise of self-determination, which is basic to respect for persons. Clients should be as fully involved as possible in the planning and implementation of their own health care.[10]

The controversial problems with the noble-sounding principle of respect for autonomy, as with all moral principles, arise when we must interpret its significance for particular contexts and determine precise limits on its application and how to handle situations when it conflicts with such other moral principles as beneficence and justice. Among the best known problems of conflict are found in cases of overriding refusals of treatment by patients, as in Jehovah's Witnesses' refusals of blood transfusions.

Many controversies involve questions about the conditions under which a person's right to autonomous expression demands actions by others and also questions about the restrictions society may rightfully place on choices by patients or subjects when these choices conflict with other values. If an individual's choices endanger the public health, potentially harm another party, or involve a scarce resource for which a patient cannot pay, it may be justifiable to restrict exercises of autonomy. If restriction is in order, the justification will rest on some competing moral principle such as beneficence or justice. This issue of both specifying and balancing the demands made by conflicting moral principles can now be seen to apply to each of these principles.

BENEFICENCE

The welfare of patients is the goal of health care. This welfare objective is medicine's context and justification: Clinical therapies are aimed at the promotion of health by cure or prevention of disease. This value has long been treated as a foundational value — and sometimes as *the* foundational value — in medical and nursing ethics. Among the most quoted principles in the history of codes of medical ethics is the maxim *primum non nocere:* "Above all, do no harm." Although the origins of this abstract principle are obscure and its implications often unclear, it has appeared in many medical writings and codes, and it was present in nursing codes as early as Florence Nightingale's *Pledge for Nurses.* Many current medical and nursing codes assert that the health professional's "primary commitment" is to protect the patient from harm and to promote the patient's welfare.

Other duties in medicine, nursing, public health, and research are expressed in terms of a *more positive* obligation to come to the assistance of those in need of treatment or in danger of injury. In the International Code of Nursing Ethics, for example, it is said that "[T]he nurse shares with other citizens the responsibility for initiating and supporting actions to meet the health and social needs of the public."[11] Various sections of the Principles of Medical Ethics of the American Medical Association express a virtually identical point of view.

The range of duties requiring abstention from harm and positive assistance may be conveniently clustered under the single heading of "beneficence." This term has a broad set of meanings, including the doing of good and the active promotion of good, kindness, and charity. But in the present context the principle of beneficence has a narrower meaning: It requires us to abstain from injuring others and to help others further their important and legitimate interests, largely by preventing or removing possible harms. Presumably such acts are required when they can be performed with minimal risk to the actors; one is not under an obligation of beneficence in all circumstances of risk.

According to William Frankena, the principle of beneficence can be expressed as including the following four elements: (1) One ought not to inflict evil or harm (a principle of nonmaleficence). (2) One ought to prevent evil or harm. (3) One ought to remove evil or harm. (4) One ought to do or promote good.[12] Frankena suggests that the fourth element may not be an obligation at all (being an act of benevolence that is over and above obligation) and contends that these elements appear in a hierarchical arrangement so that the first takes precedence over the second, the second over the third, and the third over the fourth.

There are philosophical reasons for separating passive nonmaleficence (as expressed in 1) and active beneficence (as expressed in 2–4). Ordinary moral thinking often suggests that certain duties not to injure others are more compelling than duties to benefit them. For example, we do not consider it justifiable to kill a dying patient in order to use the patient's organs to save two others. Similarly, the obligation not to injure a patient by abandonment seems to many stronger than the obligation to prevent injury to a patient who has been abandoned by another (under the assumption that both are moral duties).

Despite the attractiveness of this hierarchical ordering rule, it is not firmly sanctioned by either morality or ethical theory. The obligation expressed in (1) may not *always* outweigh those expressed in (2)–(4). For example, the harm inflicted in (1) may be negligible or trivial, whereas the harm to be prevented in (2) may be substantial: Saving a person's life by a blood transfusion clearly justifies the inflicted harm of venipuncture on the blood donor. One of the motivations for separating nonmaleficence from beneficence is that they themselves conflict when one must *either* avoid harm *or* bring aid. In such cases, one needs a decision procedure for choosing one alternative rather than another. But if the weights of the two principles can vary, as they can, there can be no mechanical decision rule asserting that one obligation must always outweigh the other.

One of the most vexing problems in ethical theory is the extent to which the principle of beneficence generates *general moral duties* that are incumbent on everyone — not because of a professional role but because morality itself makes a general demand of beneficence. Any analysis of beneficence, in the broad sense delineated above, would potentially demand severe sacrifice and extreme generosity in the moral life, for example, giving a kidney for transplantation or donating bone marrow. As a result, some philosophers have argued that this form of beneficent action is virtuous and a moral *ideal,* but not an obligation. We are not *required* by the general canons of morality to promote the good of persons, even if we are in a position to do so and the action is morally *justified.*

Several proposals have been offered in moral philosophy to resolve this problem by showing that beneficence *is* a principle of obligation, but these theoretical ventures are extraneous to our concerns here. The scope or range of acts required by the obligation of beneficence is an undecided issue, and perhaps an undecidable one. Fortunately, we do not need a resolution in the present context. That we are morally obligated on *some* occasions to assist others — at least in professional roles such as nursing, medicine, and research — is hardly a matter of moral controversy. Beneficent acts are demanded by the roles involved in fiduciary relationships between health care professionals and patients, lawyers and clients, researchers and subjects (at least in therapeutic research), bankers and customers, and so on.

We can treat the basic roles and concepts that give substance to the principle of beneficence in medicine as follows: The positive benefits the physician and nurse are obligated to seek all involve the alleviation of disease and injury, if there is a reasonable hope of cure. The harms to be prevented, removed, or minimized are the pain, suffering, and disability of injury and disease. In addition, the physician and nurse are enjoined from *doing* harm if interventions inflict unnecessary pain and suffering on patients.

Those engaged in both medical practice and research know that risks of harm presented by interventions must be weighed against possible benefits for patients, subjects, and the public. The physician who professes to "do no harm" is not pledging never to cause harm, but rather to strive to create a positive balance of goods over inflicted harms. This is recognized in the Nuremberg Code, which enjoins: "The degree of risk to be taken should never exceed that determined by the humanitarian importance of the problem to be solved by the experiment."

JUSTICE

Every civilized society is a cooperative venture structured by moral, legal, and cultural principles that define the terms of social cooperation. Beneficence and respect for autonomy are principles in this fabric of social order, but *justice* has been the subject of more treatises on the terms of social cooperation than any other principle. A person has been treated justly if treated according to what is fair, due, or owed. For example, if equal political rights are due all citizens, then justice is done when those rights are accorded.

The term *distributive justice* refers to fair, equitable, and appropriate distribution in society determined by justified norms of distribution that structure part of the terms of social cooperation. Usually this term refers to the distribution of primary social goods, such as economic goods and fundamental political rights. But burdens are also within its scope. Paying for forms of national health insurance is a distributed burden; medicare checks and grants to do research are distributed benefits.[13]

Recent literature on distributive justice has tended to focus on considerations of fair economic distribution, especially unjust distributions in the form of inequalities of income between different classes of persons and unfair tax burdens on certain classes. But many problems of distributive justice exist besides issues about income and wealth, including the issues raised in prominent contemporary debates over health care distribution, as discussed in Chapter 6.

There is no single principle of justice. Somewhat like principles under the heading of beneficence, there are several *principles* of justice, each requiring specification in particular contexts. But common to almost all theories of justice is a minimal, beginning principle: Like cases should be treated alike, or, to use the language of equality, equals ought to be treated equally and unequals unequally. This elementary principle is referred to as the formal principle of justice, or sometimes as the formal principle of equality — formal because it states no particular respects in which people ought to be treated. It merely asserts that whatever respects are under consideration, if persons are equal in those respects, they should be treated alike. Thus, the formal principle of justice does not tell us how to determine equality or proportion in these matters, and it therefore lacks substance as a specific guide to conduct. Equality must here be understood as "equality in the relevant respects." Many controversies about justice arise over what should be considered the relevant characteristics for equal treatment. Principles that specify these relevant characteristics are often said to be *material* because they identify relevant properties for distribution.

The following is a sample list of major candidates for the position of valid material principles of distributive justice (though longer lists have been proposed): (1) To each person an equal share. (2) To each person according to individual need. (3) To each person according to acquisition in a free market. (4) To each person according to individual effort. (5) To each person according to societal contribution. (6) To each person according to merit. There is no obvious barrier to acceptance of more than one of these principles, and some theories of justice accept all six as valid. Most societies use several principles in the belief that different rules are appropriate to different situations.

Because the formal and material principles leave space for differences in the interpretation of how justice applies to particular situations, philosophers have developed diverse *theories* of justice that provide material principles, specify the principles, and defend the choice of principles. These theories attempt to be more specific than the formal principle by elaborating how people are to be compared and what it means to give people their due. Egalitarian theories of justice emphasize equal access to primary goods; libertarian theories emphasize rights to social and economic liberty; and utilitarian theories emphasize a mixed use of such criteria so that public and private utility are maximized.

The utilitarian theory follows the main lines of the explanation of utilitarianism above, and thus economic justice is viewed as one among a number of problems concerning how to maximize value. The ideal economic distribution, utilitarians argue, is any arrangement that would have this maximizing effect.

Egalitarianism holds that distributions of burdens and benefits in a society are just to the extent they are equal, and deviations from equality in distribution are unjust. Most egalitarian accounts of justice are guardedly formulated, so that only *some* basic equalities among individuals take priority over their differences. In recent years an egalitarian theory discussed above in the section on Kantian theories has enjoyed wide currency: John Rawls's *A Theory of Justice*. This book has as its central contention that we should distribute all economic goods and services equally except in those cases in which an unequal distribution would actually work to everyone's advantage, or at least would benefit the worst off in society.

Sharply opposed to egalitarianism is the libertarian theory of justice. What makes libertarian theories *libertarian* is the priority afforded to distinctive processes, procedures, or mechanisms for ensuring that liberty rights are recognized in economic practice—typically the rules and procedures governing social liberty and economic acquisition and exchange in free market systems. Because free choice is the pivotal goal, libertarians place a premium on the principle of respect for autonomy. In some libertarian systems, this principle is the sole basic moral principle, and there thus are no other principles of justice. We will see in Chapter 6 that many philosophers believe that this approach is fundamentally wrong because economic value is generated through an essentially communal process that our health policies must reflect if justice is to be done.

Libertarian theorists, however, explicitly reject the conclusion that egalitarian patterns of distribution represent a normative ideal. People may be equal in a host of morally significant respects (for example, entitled to equal treatment under the law and equally valued as ends in themselves), but the libertarian contends that it would be a basic violation of *justice* to regard people as deserving of equal economic returns. In particular, people are seen as having a fundamental right to own and dispense with the products of their labor as they choose, even if the exercise of this right leads to large inequalities of wealth in society. Equality and utility principles, from this libertarian perspective, sacrifice basic liberty rights to the larger public interest by coercively extracting financial resources through taxation.

These three theories of justice all capture some of our intuitive convictions about justice, and each exhibits strengths as a theory of justice. Perhaps, then, there are several equally valid, or at least equally defensible, theories of justice and just taxation. This problem will be studied further in Chapter 6.

The Prima Facie Nature of Principles. W. D. Ross, a prominent twentieth-century British philosopher, developed a theory intended to assist us in resolving problems of a conflict between principles. Ross's views are based on an account of what he calls prima facie duties, which he contrasts with actual duties. A prima facie duty is a duty that is always to be acted upon unless it conflicts on a particular occasion with an equal or stronger duty. A prima facie duty, then, is always right and binding, all other things being equal; it is conditional on not being overridden or outweighed by competing moral demands. One's *actual* duty, by contrast, is determined by an examination of the respective weights of competing prima facie duties.

Ross argues that several valid principles, all of which can conflict, express moral duties (that is, obligations). These principles do not, Ross argues, derive from either the principle of utility or Kant's categorical imperative. For example, our promises create duties of fidelity, wrongful actions create duties of reparation, and the generous gifts of our friends create duties of gratitude. Ross defends several additional duties, such as duties of self-improvement, nonmaleficence, beneficence, and justice. Unlike Kant's system and the utilitarian system, Ross's list of duties is not based on any overarching principle. He defends it simply as a reflection of our ordinary moral conventions and beliefs.

The idea that moral principles are absolute values that cannot be overridden has had a long but troubled history. Both utilitarians and Kantians have defended their basic rule (the principle of utility and the categorical imperative) as absolute, but this claim to absoluteness has been widely challenged. For Ross's reasons, among others, many moral philosophers have with increasing frequency come to regard principles, duties, and rights not as unbending standards but rather as strong prima facie moral demands that may be validly overridden in circumstances of competition with other moral claims.

Although no philosopher or professional code has successfully presented a system of moral rules that is free of conflicts and exceptions, this fact is no cause for either skepticism or alarm. Prima facie duties reflect the complexity of the moral life, in which a hierarchy of rules and principles is impossible. The problem of how to weight different moral principles remains unresolved, as does the best set of moral principles to form the framework of biomedical ethics. Nonetheless, the general categories of prima facie principles discussed above have proven serviceable as a basic starting point and source for reflection on cases and problems. The main difficulty with these principles is that in most difficult contexts they must be specified.

The Specification of Principles. Practical moral problems often cannot, as we noted earlier, be resolved by appeal to highly general principles. Practical problems typically require that we make our general norms suitably specific.[14] To be practical, moral principles must be made specific for a context and must make room for considerations of feasibility and institutional policies. Even specific norms are often too indeterminate and need further specification.

A simple example of specification of commitments to obtain consent is found in the following provision in the "Ethical Guidelines for the Practice of Forensic Psychiatry" of the American Academy of Psychiatry and the Law: "The informed consent of the subject of a forensic evaluation is obtained when possible. Where consent is not required, notice is given to the evaluee of the nature of the evaluation. If the evaluee is not competent to give consent, substituted consent is obtained in accordance with the laws of the jurisdiction."[15]

A progressive specification of general principles is central to bioethics, especially in the formulation of institutional and public policy. However, we cannot reasonably expect that strategies of specification will always eliminate competing proposals for the resolution of contingent conflicts. In problematic cases, several specifications will emerge that are well-defended. Nonetheless, specification, together with a moral justification that defends one's chosen specification, is essential in bioethics. Indeed, perhaps nothing is more central to the method of bioethics.

LAW AND POLICY

Moral principles are often already embedded in public morality, public policies, and institutional practices, but if these values are already in place, how can moral reflection on philosophical theory assist us in the complicated task of forming and criticizing institutional policies, public policies, and laws?

ETHICS AND PUBLIC AFFAIRS

Institutional and public policies are almost always motivated by and incorporate moral considerations. Policies such as those that fund health care for the indigent and those that protect subjects of biomedical research are examples. Moral analysis is part of good policy formation, not merely a method for evaluating already formed policy. A "policy," in the relevant sense, is comprised of a set of normative, enforceable guidelines that govern a particular area of conduct and that have been accepted by an official body, such as an institutional board of trustees, an agency of government, or a legislature. The policies of corporations, hospitals, trade groups, and professional societies are private rather than public, but the discussion below is directed at all forms of policy.

Many articles in this volume are concerned with the use of ethical theory for the formulation of public affairs. Joel Feinberg has made a suggestive comment about one way in which the problems raised in these essays might be viewed from an ideal vantage point:

> It is convenient to think of these problems as questions for some hypothetical and abstract political body. An answer to the question of when liberty should be limited or how wealth ideally should be distributed, for example, could be used to guide not only moralists, but also legislators and judges toward reasonable decisions in particular cases where interests, rules, or the liberties of different parties appear to conflict. . . . We must think of an ideal legislator as somewhat abstracted from the full legislative context, in that he is free to appeal directly to the public interest unencumbered by the need to please voters, to make "deals" with colleagues, or any other merely "political" considerations. . . . The principles of the ideal legislator . . . are still of the first practical importance, since they provide a target for our aspirations and a standard for judging our successes and failures.[16]

However, policy formation and criticism usually involve complex interactions between moral values and cultural and political values. A policy will be shaped by empirical data and information in relevant fields such as medicine, economics, law, and the like. By taking into consideration factors such as efficiency and clientele acceptance, we interpret principles so that they provide a practical strategy for real-world problems that incorporate the demands of political procedures, legal constraints, uncertainty about risk, and the like.[17] For example, in this book we will consider policies pertaining to physician-assisted suicide, public allocations for health care, regulation of risk in the workplace, protection of animal and human subjects of research, legislative definitions of death, liability for failures of disclosure and confidentiality, policies to control developments in genetics, the control of epidemics, and a host of other moral problems of institutional and public policy.

A specific example of ethics at work in the formulation of policy is found in the work of the previously mentioned National Commission for the Protection of Human Subjects of Biomedical and Behavioral Research, which was established by a federal law. Its mandate was to develop ethical guidelines for the conduct of research involving human subjects and to make recommendations to the Department of Health and Human Services (DHHS). To discharge its duties, the commission studied the nature and extent of various forms of research, its purposes, the ethical issues surrounding the research, present federal regulations, and the views of representatives of professional societies and federal agencies. The commission engaged in extensive deliberations on these subjects in public, a process in which moral reasoning played as central a role as the information and methods supplied from other fields.

Subsequent government regulations regarding research issued by the relevant agency (DHHS) were developed on the basis of work provided by the commission. These public laws show the imprint of the commission in virtually every clause. The regulations cannot be regarded as exclusively ethical in orientation, but much distinctive ethical material is found in the commission documents, and ethical analysis provided the framework for its deliberations and recommendations. The commission also issued one exclusively philosophical volume, which sets forth the moral framework that underlies the various policy recommendations it made. It is among the best examples of the use of moral frameworks for actual (not merely theoretical or programmatic) policy development and of a philosophical publication issued through a government-sponsored body.

Several U.S. federal branches, agencies, and courts regularly use ethical premises in the development of their health policies, rules, or decisions. These include the Centers for Disease Control (CDC), the National Institutes of Health (NIH), the Agency for Health Care Policy and Research (AHCPR), and the U.S. Supreme Court. Ethical analysis also often plays a prominent role in policy formation in bioethics. Examples include the widely examined work of the Oregon legislature on rationing in health care, the New York Task Force on Life and the Law, and the New Jersey Bioethics Commission. Their reports and legislative actions raise vital questions explored at various points in this book about the proper relation between government and professional groups in formulating standards of practice.

MORALITY AND LAW

The "morality" of many actions that have a public impact is commonly gauged by whether the law prohibits that form of conduct. Law is the public's agent for translating morality into explicit social guidelines and practices and for determining punishments for offenses. Both case law (judge-made law expressed in court decisions) and statutory law (federal and state statutes and their accompanying administrative regulations) set standards for science, medicine, and health care, and these sources have deeply influenced bioethics.

In these forms law has placed many issues before the public. Case law, in particular, has established influential precedents that provide material for reflection on both legal and moral questions. Prominent examples include judicial decisions about informed consent and terminating life-sustaining treatment. The line of court decisions since the Karen Ann Quinlan case in the mid-1970s, for example, constitutes an important body of material for moral reflection. Most of the chapters in this book contain selections from case law, and selections in the chapters frequently mention actual or proposed statutory law.

Moral evaluation is, nonetheless, very different from *legal* evaluation. Issues of legal liability, costs of the system, practicability within the litigation process, and questions of compensation demand that legal requirements be different from moral requirements. The law is not the repository of our moral standards and values, even when the law is directly concerned with moral problems. A law-abiding person is not necessarily morally sensitive or virtuous, and from the fact that something is legally acceptable, it does not follow that it is morally acceptable.

The judgment that an act is morally acceptable also does not imply that the law should permit it. For example, the moral position that various forms of euthanasia are morally justified is consistent with the thesis that the government should legally prohibit these acts, on grounds that it would not be possible to control potential abuses.

Bioethics in the United States is currently involved in a complex and mutually stimulating relationship with law. The law often appeals to moral duties and rights, places sanctions on violators, and in general strengthens the social importance of moral beliefs. Morality and law share concerns over matters of basic social importance and often acknowledge the same principles, obligations, and criteria of evidence. Nevertheless, the law rightly backs away from attempting to legislate against everything that is morally wrong.

LEGAL AND MORAL RIGHTS

Much of the modern ethical discussion that we encounter throughout this volume turns on ideas about rights, and many public policy issues concern rights or attempts to secure rights. Our political tradition itself has developed from a conception of human rights. However, until the seventeenth and eighteenth centuries, problems of social and political philosophy were rarely discussed in terms of rights. New political views were introduced at this point in history, including the notion of universal natural (or human) rights. Rights quickly came to be understood as powerful assertions of claims that demand respect and status.

Substantial differences exist between moral and legal rights, because legal systems do not formally require reference to moral systems for their understanding or grounding, nor do moral systems formally require reference to legal systems. One may have a legal right to do something patently immoral, or have a moral right without any corresponding legal guarantee. Legal rights are derived from political constitutions, legislative enactments, case law, and the executive orders of the highest state official. Moral rights, by contrast, exist independently of and form a basis for criticizing or justifying legal rights.

Philosophers have often drawn a distinction between positive and negative rights. A right to well-being — generally the right to receive goods and services — is a positive right, and a right to liberty — generally a right not to be interfered with — is a negative right. The right to liberty is a negative right because no one has to do anything to honor it. Presumably all that must be done to honor negative rights is to leave people alone. The same is not true with respect to positive rights. To honor those rights someone has to provide something. For example, if a person has a human right to well-being and is starving, then someone has an obligation to provide that person with food. This important distinction between positive and negative rights is analyzed in Chapter 6 under the subject of the right to health care.

Because general negative rights are rights of noninterference, their direct connection to individual self-determination is apparent. Because general positive rights require that all members of the community yield some of their resources to advance the welfare of others by providing social goods and services, there is a natural connection in theories that emphasize positive rights to a sense of "the commons" that limits the scope of individualism. The broader the scope of positive rights in a theory, the more likely that theory is to emphasize a scheme of social justice that confers positive rights to redistributions of resources.

Accordingly, a moral system composed of a powerful set of general negative obligations and rights is antithetical to a moral system composed of a powerful set of general positive obligations and rights, just as a strong individualism is opposed to a strong communitarianism. Many of the conflicts that we encounter throughout this book spring from these basic differences over the existence and scope of negative and positive rights and obligations, especially regarding the number, types, and weight of positive rights and obligations.

LAW, AUTHORITY, AND AUTONOMY

As important as autonomy rights are, no autonomy right is strong enough to entail a right to unrestricted exercises of autonomy. Acceptable liberty must be distinguished from unacceptable, but how are we to do so?

Liberty-Limiting Principles. Various principles have been advanced in the attempt to establish valid grounds for the limitation of autonomy. The following four "liberty-limiting principles" have all been defended.

1. *The Harm Principle:* A person's liberty is justifiably restricted to prevent harm to others caused by that person.
2. *The Principle of Paternalism:* A person's liberty is justifiably restricted to prevent harm to self caused by that person.
3. *The Principle of Legal Moralism:* A person's liberty is justifiably restricted to prevent that person's immoral behavior.
4. *The Offense Principle:* A person's liberty is justifiably restricted to prevent offense to others caused by that person.

Each of these four principles represents an attempt to balance liberty and other values. The harm principle is universally accepted as a valid liberty-limiting principle, but the other three principles are highly controversial. Only one of these controversial principles is pertinent to the controversies that arise in this volume: paternalism. Here the central problem is whether this form of justification for a restriction of liberty may ever validly be invoked, and, if so, how the principle is to be formulated.

Paternalism. The word "paternalism" refers to treating individuals in the way that a parent treats his or her child. Paternalism is the intentional limitation of the autonomy of one person by another, where the person who limits autonomy appeals exclusively to grounds of benefit for the person whose autonomy is limited. The essence of paternalism is an overriding of a person's autonomy on grounds of providing them with a benefit — in medicine, a medical benefit.

Examples in medicine include involuntary commitment to institutions for treatment, intervention to stop "rational" suicides, resuscitating patients who have asked not to be resuscitated, withholding medical information that patients have requested, compulsory care, denial of an innovative therapy to patients who wish to try it, and some government efforts to promote health. Other health-related examples include laws requiring motorcyclists to wear helmets and motorists to wear seat belts and the regulations of governmental agencies such as the Food and Drug Administration that prevent people from purchasing possibly harmful or inefficacious drugs and chemicals. In all cases the motivation is the beneficent promotion of individuals' health and welfare.

Paternalism has been under attack in recent years, especially by defenders of the autonomy rights of patients. The latter hold that physicians and government officials intervene too often and assume too much paternalistic control over patients' choices. Philosophers and lawyers have generally supported the view that the autonomy of patients is the decisive factor in the patient-physician relationship and that interventions can be valid only when patients are in some measure unable to make voluntary choices or to perform autonomous actions. The point is that patients can be so ill that their judgments or voluntary abilities are significantly affected, or they are incapable of grasping important information about their case, and thus in no position to reach carefully reasoned decisions about their medical treatment or their purchase of drugs. Beyond this form of intervention, many have argued, paternalism is not warranted.

However, paternalism also has defenders, even under some conditions in which autonomous choice is overridden. Any careful proponent of a principle of paternalism will specify precisely which goods and needs deserve paternalistic protection and the conditions under which intervention is warranted. Some writers have argued that one is justified in interfering with a person's autonomy only if the interference protects the person against his or her own actions where those actions are extremely and unreasonably risky (for example, refusing a life-saving therapy in nonterminal situations) or are potentially dangerous and irreversible in effect (as some drugs are). According to this position, paternalism is justified if and only if the harms prevented from occurring to the person are greater than the harms or indignities (if any) caused by interference with his or her liberty and if it can be universally justified, under relevantly similar circumstances, always to treat persons in this way.

This moderate formulation of paternalism still leaves many critics resolutely opposed to all possible uses of this principle. Their arguments against paternalism turn on some defense of the importance of the principle of respect for autonomy. We will many times encounter such appeals in this volume, especially as applied to rightful state intervention in order to benefit patients or subjects without their authorization.

T.L.B.

NOTES

1. *Tarasoff v. Regents of the University of California,* California Supreme Court (17 California Reports, 3d Series, 425. Decided July 1, 1976). Reprinted in Chapter 3.

2. These principles and their analysis by the National Commission for the Protection of Human Subjects of Biomedical and Behavioral Research have been published as *The Belmont Report: Ethical Principles and Guidelines for the Protection of Human Subjects of Research* (Washington, D.C.: U.S. Government Printing Office, DHEW Publication, 1978).

3. See, for example, Ronald Dworkin, *Taking Rights Seriously* (Cambridge, MA: Harvard University Press, 1977); Judith Jarvis Thomson, *The Realm of Rights* (Cambridge, MA: Harvard University Press, 1990); Ruth Macklin, "Universality of the Nuremberg Code," in *The Nazi Doctors and the Nuremberg Code,* ed. George J. Annas and Michael Grodin (New York: Oxford University Press, 1992), pp. 240–57.

4. Immanuel Kant, *Foundations of the Metaphysics of Morals,* trans. Lewis White Beck (Indianapolis, IN: Bobbs-Merrill Company, 1959), p. 47.

5. Albert R. Jonsen, "Casuistry as Methodology in Clinical Ethics," *Theoretical Medicine* 12 (December 1991); Jonsen and S. Toulmin, *Abuse of Casuistry* (Berkeley: University of California Press, 1988); Jonsen, "Casuistry: An Alternative or Complement to Principles?" *Kennedy Institute of Ethics Journal* 5 (1995): 237–51.

6. John D. Arras, "Principles and Particularity: The Role of Cases in Bioethics," *Indiana Law Journal* 69 (Fall 1994): 983–1014 (with two replies); and "Getting Down to Cases: The Revival of Casuistry in Bioethics," *Journal of Medicine and Philosophy* 16 (1991): 29–51.

7. Jonsen and Toulmin, *Abuse of Casuistry,* pp. 16–19, 66–67; Jonsen, "Casuistry and Clinical Ethics," pp. 67, 71.

8. Some reservations about principles have been expressed. See *Principles of Health Care Ethics,* ed. Raanan Gillon and Ann Lloyd (London: John Wylie & Sons, 1994); Stephen Toulmin, "The Tyranny of Principles," *Hastings Center Report* 11 (1981); K. Danner Clouser and Bernard Gert, "A Critique of Principlism," *The Journal of Medicine and Philosophy* 15 (April 1990): 219–36; K. Danner Clouser, "Common Morality as an Alternative to Principlism," *Kennedy Institute of Ethics Journal* 5 (1995): 219–36.

9. For autonomy-based theory, see Robert Nozick, *Anarchy, State, and Utopia* (New York: Basic Books, 1974); H. Tristram Engelhardt, Jr., *The Foundations of Bioethics,* 2d ed. (New York: Oxford University Press, 1996); Joel Feinberg, *The Moral Limits of the Criminal Law* (New York: Oxford University Press, 1984–87); Jay Katz, *The Silent World of Doctor and Patient* (New York: The Free Press: 1984).

10. American Nurses' Association, *Code for Nurses with Interpretive Statements* (Kansas City, MO: ANA, 1985), pp. 2–3.

11. 1953 and 1973 International Codes of Nursing Ethics of the International Council of Nurses.

12. William Frankena, *Ethics,* 2d ed. (Englewood Cliffs, NJ: Prentice-Hall, 1973), p. 47.

13. For accounts of justice that have influenced contemporary bioethics, see John Rawls, *A Theory of Justice* (Cambridge: Harvard University Press, 1971); Norman Daniels, *Just Health Care* (New York: Cambridge University Press, 1985); Allen Buchanan, "Health-Care Delivery and Resource Allocation," in *Medical Ethics,* ed. Robert Veatch, 2d ed. (Boston: Jones and Bartlett Publishers, 1997); Daniel Callahan, *Setting Limits: Medical Goals in an Aging Society* (New York: Simon & Schuster, 1987).

14. Henry S. Richardson, "Specifying Norms as a Way to Resolve Concrete Ethical Problems," *Philosophy and Public Affairs* 19 (Fall 1990): 279–310.

15. As revised October 1991, p. 2.
16. Joel Feinberg, *Social Philosophy* (Englewood Cliffs, NJ: Prentice-Hall, 1973), pp. 2–3.
17. Dennis Thompson, "Philosophy and Policy," *Philosophy and Public Affairs* 14 (Spring 1985), 205–18.

SUGGESTED READINGS

MORALITY AND MORAL PHILOSOPHY

Beauchamp, Tom L. *Philosophical Ethics.* 2d ed. New York: McGraw-Hill, 1991.
Holmes, Robert L. *Basic Moral Philosophy.* Belmont, CA: Wadsworth Publishing Co., 1993.
MacIntyre, Alasdair. *A Short History of Ethics.* New York: Macmillan, 1966.
Regan, Tom, ed. *Matters of Life and Death.* 3rd ed. New York: Random House, 1992.
Singer, Peter. *Practical Ethics.* 2d ed. New York: Cambridge University Press, 1993.
Sinnot-Armstrong, Walter. *Moral Dilemmas.* Oxford: Basil Blackwell, 1988.
Sumner, L. W., and Boyle, J. *Philosophical Perspectives on Bioethics.* Toronto: University of Toronto Press, 1996.

RELATIVISM AND DISAGREEMENT

Brandt, Richard B. "Ethical Relativism." In Edwards, Paul, ed. *Encyclopedia of Philosophy.* New York: Macmillan, 1967, Vol. 3, 75–78.
Buchanan, Allen. "Judging the Past," *Hastings Center Report* 26 (May–June 1996), 25–30.
Gert, Bernard; Culver, Charles; and Clouser, K. Danner. *Bioethics: A Return to Fundamentals.* New York: Oxford University Press, 1997.
Krausz, Michael, and Meiland, Jack W., eds. *Relativism: Cognitive and Moral.* Notre Dame, IN: University of Notre Dame Press, 1982.
Krausz, Michael, ed. *Relativism: Interpretation and Confrontation.* Notre Dame, IN: University of Notre Dame Press, 1989.
Rachels, James. "Can Ethics Provide Answers?" *Hastings Center Report* 10 (June 1980), 32–40.
Stocker, Michael. *Plural and Conflicting Values.* Oxford: Clarendon Press, 1990.

JUSTIFICATION

Brandt, R. B. *Morality, Utilitarianism, and Rights.* Cambridge: Cambridge University Press, 1992.
Gert, Bernard. *Morality: A New Justification of the Moral Rules.* New York: Oxford University Press, 1988.
Griffiths, A. Phillips, "Ultimate Moral Principles: Their Justification." In Edwards, Paul, ed. *Encyclopedia of Philosophy.* New York: Macmillan, 1967. Vol. 8, 177–182.
The Monist 71 (July 1988). Special issue on "Justification."
Pennock, J. Roland, and Chapman, John W., eds. *NOMOS XXVIII: Justification.* New York: New York University Press, 1986.

UTILITARIANISM

Bentham, Jeremy. *An Introduction to the Principles of Morals and Legislation.* Oxford: Clarendon Press, 1970.
Frey, R. G., ed. *Utility and Rights,* Minneapolis, MN: University of Minnesota Press, 1984.
Gorovitz, Samuel, ed. *Mill: Utilitarianism, with Critical Essays.* New York: Bobbs-Merrill, 1971.
Griffin, James. *Well-Being: Its Meaning, Measurement and Moral Importance.* Oxford: Clarendon Press, 1986.
Kagan, Shelly. *The Limits of Morality.* Oxford: Clarendon Press, 1989.
Mill, John Stuart. *Collected Works of John Stuart Mill.* Toronto: University of Toronto Press, 1969– .
Scheffler, Samuel, ed. *Consequentialism and Its Critics.* Oxford: Oxford University Press, 1988.

KANTIAN AND DEONTOLOGICAL THEORIES

Donagan, Alan. *The Theory of Morality.* Chicago: University of Chicago Press, 1977.
Guyer, Paul, ed. *The Cambridge Companion to Kant.* Cambridge: Cambridge University Press, 1992.
Kant, Immanuel. *Ethical Philosophy.* In Ellington, J., ed. Indianapolis: Hackett, 1983.
Rawls, John. "The Priority of Right and Ideas of the Good." *Philosophy & Public Affairs* 17 (1988).
Rawls, John. *A Theory of Justice.* Cambridge, MA: Harvard University Press, 1971.

Rawls, John. "Themes in Kant's Moral Philosophy." In Förster, Eckart, ed. *Kant's Transcendental Deductions.* Stanford: Stanford University Press, 1989.

Ross, William D. *The Right and the Good.* Oxford: Oxford University Press, 1930.

ETHICS OF CARE

Blustein, Jeffrey. *Care and Commitment: Taking the Personal Point of View.* New York: Oxford University Press, 1991.

Carse, Alisa. "The Voice of Care: Implications for Bioethical Education." *Journal of Medicine and Philosophy* 16 (1991), 5–28.

Gilligan, Carol. *In a Different Voice.* Cambridge, MA: Harvard University Press, 1982.

Holmes, Helen Bequaert, and Purdy, Laura M., eds. *Feminist Perspectives in Medical Ethics.* Bloomington, IN: Indiana University Press, 1992.

Journal of Clinical Ethics 3 (1992). Special issue: See Hilde L. Nelson, "Against Caring," Nel Noddings, "In Defense of Caring," and Toni M. Vezeau, "Caring: From Philosophical Concerns to Practice."

Noddings, Nel. *Caring: A Feminine Approach to Ethics and Moral Education.* Berkeley: University of California Press, 1984.

Sherwin, Susan. *No Longer Patient: Feminist Ethics and Health Care.* Philadelphia: Temple University Press, 1992.

Wolf, Susan, ed. *Feminism & Bioethics.* New York: Oxford, 1996.

VIRTUE ETHICS

Aristotle, *Nicomachean Ethics.* Irwin, Terence, trans. Indianapolis: Hackett Publishing Co., 1985.

Crisp, Roger, and Slote, Michael, eds. *Virtue Ethics.* Oxford: Oxford University Press, 1997.

Flanagan, Owen, and Rorty, Amélie Oksenberg, eds. *Identity, Character, and Morality.* Cambridge, MA: MIT Press, 1990.

French, Peter A.; Uehling, Theodore E. Jr.; and Wettstein, Howard K. *Midwest Studies in Philosophy Volume XIII—Ethical Theory: Character and Virtue.* Notre Dame, IN: University of Notre Dame Press, 1988.

Hume, David. *A Treatise of Human Nature.* Oxford: Clarendon Press, 1978.

MacIntyre, Alasdair. *After Virtue.* 2d ed. Notre Dame, IN: University of Notre Dame Press, 1984.

Nussbaum, Martha. *Love's Knowledge.* Oxford: Oxford University Press, 1990.

Sherman, Nancy. *The Fabric of Character: Aristotle's Theory of Virtue.* Oxford: Clarendon Press, 1989.

CASUISTRY

Arras, John. "Getting Down to Cases: The Revival of Casuistry in Bioethics." *Journal of Medicine and Philosophy* 16 (1991).

Arras, John. "Principles and Particularity: The Role of Cases in Bioethics." *Indiana Law Journal* 69 (1994), 983–1014.

Brody, Baruch. *Life and Death Decision Making.* New York: Oxford University Press, 1988.

Jonsen, Albert. "Casuistry as Methodology in Clinical Ethics." *Theoretical Medicine* 12 (1991).

Jonsen, Albert, and Toulmin, Stephen. *The Abuse of Casuistry: A History of Moral Reasoning.* Berkeley: University of California Press, 1988.

Toulmin, Stephen. "The Tyranny of Principles." *Hastings Center Report* 11 (December 1981), 31–39.

MORAL PRINCIPLES

Beauchamp, Tom L., and Childress, James F. *Principles of Biomedical Ethics.* 4th ed. New York: Oxford University Press, 1994. Chaps. 3–6.

Clouser, K. Danner, and Gert, Bernard. "A Critique of Principlism." *The Journal of Medicine and Philosophy* 15 (1990).

DeGrazia, David. "Moving Forward in Bioethical Theory: Theories, Cases, and Specified Principlism." *Journal of Medicine and Philosophy* 17 (1992), 511–39.

Engelhardt, H. Tristram, Jr. *The Foundations of Bioethics.* 2d ed. New York: Oxford University Press, 1996.

Gillon, Raanan, and Lloyd, Ann, eds. *Principles of Health Care Ethics.* London: John Wylie & Sons, 1994.

Kennedy Institute of Ethics Journal 5 (1995): Special Issue on Principlism.

National Commission for the Protection of Human Subjects of Biomedical and Behavioral Research. *The Belmont Report.* Washington, D.C.: DHEW Publication No. OS 78-0012, 1978.

Pellegrino, Edmund, and Thomasma, David. *For the Patient's Good: The Restoration of Beneficence in Health Care*. New York: Oxford University Press, 1988.

Richardson, Henry. "Specifying Norms as a Way to Resolve Concrete Ethical Problems." *Philosophy & Public Affairs* 19 (1990), 279–310.

Veatch, Robert M. *A Theory of Medical Ethics*. New York: Basic Books, 1981.

ETHICS AND PUBLIC POLICY

Areen, Judith, et al. *Law, Science, and Medicine*. Mineola, NY: Foundation Press, 1984. Supplementary volume, 1987.

Brock, Dan W. "Truth or Consequences: The Role of Philosophers in Policy-Making." *Ethics* 97 (1987), 786–91.

Thompson, Dennis. "Philosophy and Policy." *Philosophy & Public Affairs* 14 (1985), 205–18.

Weisbard, Alan J. "The Role of Philosophers in the Public Policy Process." *Ethics* 97 (1987), 776–85.

MORALITY AND LAW

Dworkin, Ronald. *Taking Rights Seriously*. Cambridge, MA: Harvard University Press, 1977.

Feinberg, Joel. *The Moral Limits of the Criminal Law*. 4 vols. New York: Oxford University Press, 1984–1987.

Lyons, David. *Ethics and the Rule of Law*. Cambridge: Cambridge University Press, 1984.

Meyer, Michael J., and Parent, W. A., eds. *The Constitution of Rights*. Ithaca, NY: Cornell University Press, 1992.

Winston, Morton E., ed. *The Philosophy of Human Rights*. Belmont, CA: Wadsworth Publishing Co., 1989.

LIBERTY, AUTHORITY, AND PATERNALISM

Beauchamp, Tom L., and McCullough, Laurence B. *Medical Ethics*. Englewood Cliffs, NJ: Prentice-Hall, 1984. Chap. 4.

Childress, James. *Who Should Decide?: Paternalism in Health Care*. New York: Oxford University Press, 1982.

Feinberg, Joel. *The Moral Limits of the Criminal Law*. New York: Oxford University Press, 1984–1987. Especially Vol. 3, *Harm to Self*.

Kleinig, John. *Paternalism*. Totowa, NJ: Rowman and Allenheld, 1983.

Sartorius, Rolf, ed. *Paternalism*. Minneapolis: University of Minnesota Press, 1983.

VanDeVeer, Donald. *Paternalistic Intervention: The Moral Bounds on Benevolence*. Princeton, NJ: Princeton University Press, 1986.

BIBLIOGRAPHIES AND ENCYCLOPEDIAS
WITH BIBLIOGRAPHIES

Bioethicsline: Computer Retrieval Service.

Encyclopedia of Bioethics, ed. Reich, Warren. 2d ed. New York: Macmillan, 1995.

Encyclopedia of Ethics, ed. Becker, Lawrence, and Becker, Charlotte, New York: Garland Publishing Inc., 1992.

Lineback, Richard H., ed. *Philosopher's Index*. Vols. 1– . Bowling Green, OH: Philosophy Documentation Center, Bowling Green State University. Issued quarterly.

Part II

PATIENT-PROFESSIONAL RELATIONSHIPS

2.
Rights and Responsibilities

INTRODUCTION

That medicine and nursing are applied sciences none would deny. But these practices also involve the common human transactions of contracts and services. Interesting responsibilities and rights emerge from this human side of medical and nursing research and practice. Professional obligations have long been recognized in codes of ethics, but only recently has much systematic thought been given to the moral and legal rights of patients. In this chapter, both traditional conceptions of, and emerging problems in, the relationships between health professionals and patients are explored.

PROFESSIONAL CODES AND STATEMENTS

The first four selections in this chapter are samples of codes and statements that have been developed by health professionals in both ancient and modern times. The Hippocratic Oath took the form of a series of religious vows. More recent codes, including that of the American Nurses Association (ANA), generally contain secular statements of moral rules. The central affirmation of such codes is that, in treating the (frequently vulnerable) patient, the health professional will not exploit his or her position of relatively controlling power and influence.

The statement entitled "Fundamental Elements of the Patient-Physician Relationship," written by the Council on Ethical and Judicial Affairs of the American Medical Association (AMA), represents a departure from earlier AMA codes and a synthesis of several diverse themes. Unlike the "Principles of Medical Ethics" (1980), which had enumerated the moral obligations of physicians, the "Fundamental Elements" focus primarily on patients' rights. In fact, one hears in the "Elements" reminiscences of a much earlier document, the 1972 "Statement on a Patients's Bill of Rights" by the American Hospital Association. The rights asserted on behalf of patients by the "Elements" are relatively robust and include the important welfare right to "adequate health care" (see Point 6). The "Fundamental Elements" also portray the physician as an advocate for patients, a role introduced for nurses by the 1976 ANA "Code for Nurses" and still present in the 1985 revision (see Section 3.1 of the nurses' code). A new theme presented by the "Fundamental Elements" is the shared responsibility of patients for their own health care and therefore, presumably, for their own health. The 1994 revision of the 1990 "Elements" adds a final sentence: "Physicians should advocate for patients in dealing with third parties when appropriate." This cryptic statement may reflect the concern of many physicians that their desire to do or recommend what is best for their patients is increasingly constrained by the requirements of health insurance companies and managed care organizations.

The ANA code deftly blends several ethical traditions. The initial emphasis on the fundamental principle of "respect for the inherent dignity and worth" of every client is reminiscent of Kantian ethics. At the same time, however, the well-being and rights of clients are cited as considerations to be taken into account by nurses. While the primary focus of the ANA code is on the rights and welfare of the individual client, the theme of interdependence is also introduced in a way that justifies at least the temporary "overriding" of individual autonomy rights for the sake of the common good. Other notable emphases in the nurses' code are the nurse's duty to function as whistle-blower (sections 3.1 and 3.2), to participate in groups that review the quality and appropriateness of health care (including ethics committees), and to be politically active in efforts to achieve "a just distribution of health care and nursing resources" (section 11.2).

The final professional code reprinted in this chapter is a more personal and contextual statement by eight well-known U.S. physicians. The authors express concern that financial motives — both on the part of physicians and third parties — are undermining the traditional patient-physician relationship. They urge a return to the patient-centered beneficence and the professional virtues that are so prominently featured in the Hippocratic Oath and the Hippocratic tradition. In their view, any other policy will undermine the trust that patients have had, and should have, in their physicians.

Two questions arise concerning the status of these codes and statements: (1) What is their relation to law? and (2) What is their relation to general ethical principles? The first three codes and statements, though quasi-legal in form, are self-legislative documents developed by particular professions. As such, they have only the force that the profession chooses to attribute to them. In most professions, including medicine and nursing, professional self-discipline and self-policing has usually been less than vigorous. In contrast, the patient-physician covenant avoids legal and quasi-legal categories and instead makes an explicit ethical appeal to members of the medical profession. By implication the authors of the covenant suggest that, at least in some cases, moral obligations may trump legal considerations. For example, if a managed care organization contractually prohibits participating physicians from talking with patients about alternative treatments that are not covered by the organization, a conscientious physician may conclude that he or she is morally obligated to defy a contractual obligation.

Two possible relationships between professional codes or statements and general ethical principles can be envisioned. The codes and statements may constitute autonomous, self-contained systems of ethics that are unrelated to external validating principles. On the other hand, the codes and statements may be viewed as specific applications of universal ethical principles. According to the latter conception, the codes or statements consist primarily of moral rules or rights that implicitly appeal to general ethical principles, and perhaps even to particular ethical theories. On this view, the same canons of logical coherence and consistency that are applied to any other system of moral rights or rules can also be employed in the critical evaluation of the professional codes and statements. (See the discussion of morality and law in Chapter 1.)

THE VIRTUES AND OBLIGATIONS OF PROFESSIONALS

This section of Chapter 2 elaborates several of the themes introduced by the professional codes and statements but discusses complementary emphases, as well. Central to most professional documents has been an emphasis on the moral obligations of each professional or the moral rights of each patient in their one-on-one relationship. But are there other approaches to ethics that focus less on moral rights and obligations? And what of the obligations of each professional (and each patient, for that matter) to third parties?

In his essay in this chapter Edmund Pellegrino distinguishes among three standards by which professional behavior can be judged. The first standard is the least stringent: It asks, "Has the professional violated any legal rules or administrative regulations in his or her treatment of the patient?" The second standard is the one employed in most essays in this chapter — and indeed in this book. This standard evaluates professional performance on the basis of its conformity with widely accepted ethical principles and moral rules, such as the principle of respect for the autonomy of persons. The third and most stringent standard is one that requires professionals not only to fulfill their moral obligations but to be virtuous as well. In what ways does virtue go beyond mere conformity with moral rules? First, a virtuous person performs morally right actions for the right reasons, as an expression of his or her genuine concern for the welfare of others. Second, in some cases a virtuous person will behave in a self-sacrificial way, going beyond the obligations that are imposed, for example, by the usual requirements of justice. Pellegrino is under no illusion that all health professionals are necessarily virtuous persons. However, he recommends the cultivation of character as an important adjunct to the clarification of moral concepts and the development of coherent theories of rights and obligations. (See Chapter 1 for a general discussion of virtue ethics.)

A second alternative approach to professional ethics focuses on care, or caring, rather than on virtue in general. Nancy Jecker and Donnie Self attempt to clarify the notion of care and to show how care has been, and ought to be, associated with the nursing and medical professions. Drawing on the research of Carol Gilligan and others, Jecker and Self note that caring has often been construed as a virtue that is especially characteristic of nurses. However, Jecker and Self also raise the question whether caring might also be a moral obligation of both nurses and physicians. If caring is regarded as a moral obligation, one might raise a further question: How is such a moral obligation related to the general principles of bioethics discussed in Chapter 1, and particularly to the principles of beneficence and nonmaleficence?

At first glance, it might seem that the primary moral obligation of health professionals is always to promote the welfare (or respect the autonomy) of their patients. However, even at a purely descriptive level, we know that physicians and nurses must make decisions about how to allocate time among the multiple patients for whom they almost always bear responsibility. Further, both patients and health professionals live in a world of economic constraints. There is no easy way for either patients or professionals to avoid taking these constraints and conflicting obligations into account in their decision making.

In his essay, "The Ideal Advocate and Limited Resources," Normal Daniels develops and refines the notion of patient advocacy that was introduced by the last three selections in the preceding section. According to Daniels, the traditional depiction of the physician as patient advocate has included five important elements, of which the last two have become increasingly controversial. The first problematic element is that a physician's clinical decisions must be "free from consideration of the physician's interests"; the second is that his or her decisions must be "uninfluenced by judgments about the patient's worth." Daniels argues that a just health care system that would be compatible with these constraints can and should be constructed in the United States. Within such a system, a physician acting as gatekeeper could continue to fulfill the role of Ideal Advocate for his or her patients.

PATIENTS' RIGHTS AND RESPONSIBILITIES

The original version of the "Statement on a Patients' Bill of Rights" was affirmed by the American Hospital Association's (AHA's) Board of Directors in November of 1972. The document surprised many observers of health care in the United States because it seemed more like a product of the consumer movement or the American Civil Liberties Union than like a policy statement by the organization representing the nation's hospitals. In fact, commentators on the genesis of the 1972 statement have noted that the National Welfare Rights Association—a group representing the interests of poor people—played a major role in suggesting the topics to be included in the document.[1] In this edition we reprint a revision of the 1972 statement that was adopted by the AHA's Board of Directors in October 1992. There is a less confrontational tone in the revised document. In fact, the preamble to the 1992 "Patient's Bill of Rights" accents the importance of collaboration between patients and health care providers. Several of the specific rights asserted in the 1972 statement have been expressed somewhat less forcefully in the 1992 bill of rights. For example, the patient's right to "complete current information concerning his diagnosis, treatment, and prognosis in terms the patient can reasonably be expected to understand" (1972) has become the patient's right to "relevant, current, and understandable information concerning diagnosis, treatment, and prognosis" (1992). Also new to the 1992 revision is a concluding section on the responsibilities of patients.

The "Consumer Bill of Rights and Responsibilities" (1997) continues in the tradition of the AHA document yet introduces important nuances. The "Consumer Bill" was produced by a combined public- and private-sector presidential commission[2] in the hope that many of its provisions would be enacted into federal law or regulation. The commission was chaired by the secretaries of the federal Department of Labor and the Department of Health and Human Services. Several provisions of the 1997 document seem to be aimed at perceived abuses of patients by hospitals or managed care organizations. For example, the "prudent layperson" standard is adopted by the presidential commission as the appropriate guide for determining whether the use of emergency health services is reasonable—and therefore reimbursable. A new positive (or welfare) right is asserted on behalf of patients, namely, the right to "a choice of health care providers." The "Consumer Bill" also opposes discrimination against consumers on the basis of "race, ethnicity, national origin, religion, sex, age, mental or physical disability, sexual orientation, genetic information, or source of payment" (see Point 5). What actions would in fact constitute discrimination depends on the precise interpretation of important phrases such as "consumers eligible for coverage under the terms and conditions of a health plan or program." Like the AHA "Patient's Bill of Rights," the "Consumer Bill" concludes with an enumeration of patient responsibilities, several of which were clearly borrowed from the earlier document.

With the Council of Europe's "Convention for Protection of Human Rights and Dignity of the Human Being" (1997), the reader clearly enters a thought-world quite far removed from the one presupposed in the two preceding documents. The "Convention" is a legal document; in fact, it is a legally binding international treaty among the signatory nations.[3] The intellectual tradition in which this document is rooted is the United Nations' (UN's) Universal Declaration of Human Rights (December 1948), as well as in a long series of later UN and European human rights documents. There is a solemn quality to the provisions of this convention, as if its authors are not only creating human rights, but also discovering rights that are somehow written into the nature of things. In other words, the convention is intellectually akin to the writings of John Locke on natural rights and to the Declaration of Independence adopted in 1776 by thirteen British colonies in North America.

The central theme of the European convention is announced in Article 2: "The interests and welfare of the human being shall prevail over the sole interest of society or science." Given this focus on the primacy of the individual human being and his or her rights and interests, the "free and informed consent" of the individual to health-related interventions understandably assumes a major role in the convention (see Articles 5–9). Unlike the two U.S. bills of rights, the European convention clearly announces a human right to "equitable access to health care," with the proviso that the parties to the convention will need to "[take] into account health needs and available resources" (Article 3). Thus, the human rights asserted in the convention encompass both negative (liberty) rights and positive (welfare) rights. Several specific conclusions of the convention are quite controversial, including Article 13, which seems to rule out germ-line genetic intervention even if the goal is to prevent disease, and Article 14, which limits the preselection of a future child's gender to cases in which a sex-linked disease is being avoided. In Article 18 the signatories agree to provide "adequate protection" to human embryos in vitro. Article 21 prohibits the buying and selling of human organs and tissues and can be interpreted to forbid the sale or purchase of human sperm or eggs, as well. The serious purpose of the European convention is reemphasized in Articles 23 to 25, where legal remedies and sanctions for violations of the convention are discussed.

The three documents reprinted in this section reflect three different stages of normative discussion and public policy making. The patients' rights enunciated by the American Hospital Association and the President's Advisory Commission on Consumer Protection and Quality in the Health Care Industry are moral rights. The presidential commission clearly intended that at least some of these moral rights would be translated into federal law or regulation; a lack of consensus has precluded any action by the United States Congress that would make these rights legally enforceable in the private health care sector. In contrast, the Council of Europe has recognized several comprehensive health-related human rights and has adopted policies on several biomedical procedures and transactions in a convention that is legally binding for Council members. (For a general discussion of legal and moral rights and ethics and public affairs, see Chapter 1.)

PROFESSIONALS AND SPECIFIC PATIENT POPULATIONS

The final section of Chapter 2 focuses on the moral obligations of health professionals toward five groups of patients: African-Americans, women, the elderly, the "socially undesirable," and the seriously mentally ill. In her essay entitled "Under the Shadow of Tuskegee," Vanessa Northington Gamble argues that the mistrust that African-Americans sometimes feel toward members of the health professions is rooted in a long history of discrimination, exploitation, and abuse. During the nineteenth century both black slaves and free black people were subjected to painful and inhumane research procedures that, in the opinion of critics, would never have been performed on European-Americans. According to Gamble, African-Americans also experienced discrimination in their quest for health care, often being relegated to the inferior wards of hospitals and receiving second-rate services. Even in the twentieth century, African-Americans frequently encounter racial stereotypes in medical literature and in their interactions with health professionals. Gamble concludes that the Tuskegee syphilis study — far from being an aberration — actually typifies the attitudes of many white physicians and exemplifies the mistreatment of black patients that occurs even in the latter part of the twentieth century. (For further discussion of the Tuskegee syphilis study, see Chapter 7.)

The treatment of women by health providers and their level of participation in clinical research are the principal foci of the essay by the AMA's Council on Ethical and Judicial Affairs. The Council notes that women are underrepresented in clinical research and that they are less likely than men to be offered several important diagnostic or therapeutic interventions, for example, kidney dialysis and kidney transplants. On the other hand, according to some studies, women's health complaints are more likely to be attributed to emotional causes than are similar complaints expressed by men. The Council's prescriptions for change include a reexamination of their attitudes toward patients by physicians and increasing participation by women in leadership roles within medicine.

In their essay "The Goals of Medicine in an Aging Society," Christine Cassel and Bernice Neugarten ask whether there is a natural life span that human beings ought not to exceed and question whether people aged 65 and above consume a disproportionate share of health care resources in the United States. Their answer to the first question is no; this answer is based on data showing that increasing numbers of Americans are remaining in relatively good health even as they live longer than people in earlier generations lived. Cassel and Neugarten provide a more nuanced answer to the second question, noting that only a small percentage of Medicare patients (about 17 percent) account for over 60 percent of Medicare payments. In their view, these relatively high payments on a relatively small number of patients are likely to be reduced in the future as patients make their wishes known through advance directives and as medicine achieves a better balance between heroic and humanistic patterns of practice.

Nancy Jecker's essay examines the social class and social status of patients, rather than issues of age, gender, or ethnic heritage. Jecker's opening case study involves a homeless man who is comatose as a result of having ingested antifreeze. In the analysis that follows, the author reminds readers of a historical precedent from the early 1960s — the attempt of a Seattle committee to allocate the scarce resource of kidney dialysis based on the relative social worth of the candidates for dialysis. Critics of the Seattle committee argued that this criterion would surely lead to the exclusion of "creative nonconformists who rub the bourgeoisie the wrong way but who historically have contributed so much to the making of America." Jecker's constructive proposal is that healthcare providers should always act as the advocates for their patients and that, in the absence of society-wide guidelines for allocating scarce resources, local institutions should rely on broad-based advisory committees whose recommendations are likely to represent diverse points of view and to be accepted as legitimate by the surrounding community. (There are obvious points of contact between Jecker's proposal and Norman Daniels' comments on the role of physicians as "ideal advocates" for their patients.)

Professional obligations to the seriously mentally ill are the focus of Paul Chodoff's essay. Chodoff, a psychiatrist, questions whether the emphasis on patients' rights has not been carried too far by civil liberties lawyers and their allies in the health professions. In the context of mental illness, and in cases involving persons of questionable competence to care for themselves, an overly zealous respect for the rights of patients may, in Chodoff's view, lead to unmitigated disaster. Thus, he argues, the temporary loss of freedom through involuntary commitment may sometimes be in the long-term best interest of patients.

In the five essays of this section patient-centered beneficence and justice emerge as the dominant ethical principles. Health care providers are urged to be advocates for the patient's good, not the good of society. Several authors also invoke the notion of justice, interpreted as equality, to critique both past and current abuse or neglect of relatively vulnerable groups. When difficult decisions about fairness in cost containment or resource allocation need to be made, the authors argue, the decisions should be made at the level of local or national policy, not at the bedside. Respect for patient autonomy also plays a role in these essays, especially in Cassel and Neugarten's emphasis on paying close attention to the preferences of aging people about their treatment. At the same time, however, Chodoff argues that long-term patient benefit can sometimes trump short-term respect for autonomy, especially in encounters with patients whose autonomous status is either compromised or uncertain. (For a more detailed discussion of these general ethical principles, see Chapter 1.)

L. W.

NOTES

1. Laurens H. Silver, "The Legal Accountability of Nonprofit Hospitals," in Clark C. Havighurst, ed., *Regulating Health Facilities Construction* (Washington, DC: American Enterprise Institute for Public Policy Research, 1974), pp. 183–200, esp. pp. 190–97; see also George J. Annas, "Patients' Rights: I. Origin and Nature of Patients' Rights," in Warren Thomas Reich, ed., *Encyclopedia of Bioethics,* revised ed. (New York: Simon and Schuster Macmillan, 1995), pp. 1925–27, and David J. Rothman, *Strangers at the Bedside* (New York: Basic Books, 1991), pp. 145–47.

2. For more information about this commission and its work, see The President's Advisory Commission on Consumer Protection and Quality in the Health Care Industry, *Quality First: Better Health Care for All Americans: Final Report to the President of the United States* (Washington, DC: U.S. Government Printing Office, 1998), esp. pp. v–xi.

3. For more detailed discussion of this convention, see Maurice A. M. de Wachter, "The European Convention on Bioethics," *Hastings Center Report* 27 (January/February 1997), 12–23, and F. William Dommel, Jr., and Duane Alexander, "The Convention on Biomedicine and Human Rights of the Council of Europe," *Kennedy Institute of Ethics Journal* 7 (September 1997), 259–76.

Professional Codes and Statements

The Hippocratic Oath (ca. Fourth Century B.C.)

I swear by Apollo Physician and Asclepius and Hygieia and Panaceia and all the gods and goddesses, making them my witnesses, that I will fulfill according to my ability and judgment this oath and this covenant:

To hold him who has taught me this art as equal to my parents and to live my life in partnership with him, and if he is in need of money to give him a share of mine, and to regard his offspring as equal to my brothers in male lineage and to teach them this art — if they desire to learn it — without fee and covenant; to give a

Reprinted with permission of the publisher from "The Hippocratic Oath," in Ludwig Edelstein, *Ancient Medicine,* edited by Oswei Temkin and C. Lillian Temkin (Baltimore: Johns Hopkins University Press, 1967).

share of precepts and oral instruction and all the other learning to my sons and to the sons of him who has instructed me and to pupils who have signed the covenant and have taken an oath according to the medical law, but to no one else.

I will apply dietetic measures for the benefit of the sick according to my ability and judgment; I will keep them from harm and injustice.

I will neither give a deadly drug to anybody if asked for it, nor will I make a suggestion to this effect. Similarly I will not give to a woman an abortive remedy. In purity and holiness I will guard my life and my art.

I will not use the knife, not even on sufferers from stone, but will withdraw in favor of such men as are engaged in this work.

Whatever houses I may visit, I will come for the benefit of the sick, remaining free of all intentional injustice, of all mischief and in particular of sexual relations with both female and male persons, be they free or slaves.

What I may see or hear in the course of the treatment or even outside of the treatment in regard to the life of men, which on no account one must spread abroad, I will keep to myself holding such things shameful to be spoken about.

If I fulfill this oath and do not violate it, may it be granted to me to enjoy life and art, being honored with fame among all men for all time to come; if I transgress it and swear falsely, may the opposite of all this be my lot.

AMERICAN MEDICAL ASSOCIATION, COUNCIL ON ETHICAL AND JUDICIAL AFFAIRS

Fundamental Elements of the Patient-Physician Relationship (1994)

From ancient times, physicians have recognized that the health and well-being of patients depends upon a collaborative effort between physician and patient. Patients share with physicians the responsibility for their own health care. The patient-physician relationship is of greatest benefit to patients when they bring medical problems to the attention of their physicians in a timely fashion, provide information about their medical condition to the best of their ability, and work with their physicians in a mutually respectful alliance. Physicians can best contribute to this alliance by serving as their patients' advocates and by fostering these rights:

1. The patient has the right to receive information from physicians and to discuss the benefits, risks, and costs of appropriate treatment alternatives. Patients should receive guidance from their physicians as to the optimal course of action. Patients are also entitled to obtain copies or summaries of their medical records, to have their questions answered, to be advised of potential conflicts of interest that their physicians might have, and to receive independent professional opinions.

2. The patient has the right to make decisions regarding the health care that is recommended by his or her physician. Accordingly, patients may accept or refuse any recommended medical treatment.

3. The patient has the right to courtesy, respect, dignity, responsiveness, and timely attention to his or her needs.

4. The patient has the right to confidentiality. The physician should not reveal confidential communications or information without the consent of the patient, unless provided for by law or by the need to protect the welfare of the individual or the public interest.

5. The patient has the right to continuity of health care. The physician has an obligation to cooperate in the coordination of medically indicated care with other health care providers treating the patient. The physician may not discontinue treatment of a patient as long as further treatment is medically indicated, without giving the patient

reasonable assistance and sufficient opportunity to make alternative arrangements for care.

6. The patient has a basic right to have available adequate health care. Physicians, along with the rest of society, should continue to work toward this goal. Fulfillment of this right is dependent on society providing resources so that no patient is deprived of necessary care because of an inability to pay for the care. Physicians should continue their traditional assumption of a part of the responsibility for the medical care of those who cannot afford essential health care. Physicians should advocate for patients in dealing with third parties when appropriate.

Originally adopted June 1990. Updated June 1994.

AMERICAN NURSES ASSOCIATION

Code for Nurses (1985)

1

The nurse provides services with respect for human dignity and the uniqueness of the client, unrestricted by considerations of social or economic status, personal attributes, or the nature of health problems.

1.1 RESPECT FOR HUMAN DIGNITY

The fundamental principle of nursing practice is respect for the inherent dignity and worth of every client. Nurses are morally obligated to respect human existence and the individuality of all persons who are the recipients of nursing actions. Nurses therefore must take all reasonable means to protect and preserve human life when there is hope of recovery or reasonable hope of benefit from life-prolonging treatment.

Truth telling and the process of reaching informed choice underlie the exercise of self-determination, which is basic to respect for persons. Clients should be as fully involved as possible in the planning and implementation of their own health care. Clients have the moral right to determine what will be done with their own person; to be given accurate information, and all the information necessary for making informed judgments; to be assisted with weighing the benefits and burdens of options in their treatment; to accept, refuse, or terminate treatment without coercion; and to be given necessary emotional support. Each nurse has an obligation to be knowledgeable about the moral and legal rights of all clients and to protect and support those rights. In situations in which the client lacks the capacity to make a decision, a surrogate decision maker should be designated.

Individuals are interdependent members of the community. Taking into account both individual rights and the interdependence of persons in decision making, the nurse recognizes those situations in which individual rights to autonomy in health care may temporarily be overridden to preserve the life of the human community; for example, when a disaster demands triage or when an individual presents a direct danger to others. The many variables involved make it imperative that each case be considered with full awareness of the need to preserve the rights and responsibilities of clients and the demands of justice. The suspension of individual rights must always be considered a deviation to be tolerated as briefly as possible.

1.2 STATUS AND ATTRIBUTES OF CLIENTS

The need for health care is universal, transcending all national, ethnic, racial, religious, cultural, political, educational, economic, developmental, personality, role, and sexual differences. Nursing care is delivered without prejudicial behavior. Individual value systems and life-styles should be considered in the planning of health care with and for each client. Attributes of clients influence nursing practice to the extent that they represent factors the nurse must understand, consider, and respect in tailoring care to personal needs and in maintaining the individual's self-respect and dignity.

1.3 THE NATURE OF HEALTH PROBLEMS

The nurse's respect for the worth and dignity of the individual human being applies, irrespective of the nature of the health problem. It is reflected in care given the person who is disabled as well as one without disability, the person with long-term illness as well as one with acute illness, the recovering patient as well as one in the last phase of life. This respect extends to all who require the services of the nurse for the promotion of health, the prevention of illness, the restoration of health, the alleviation of suffering, and the provision of supportive care of the dying. The nurse does not act deliberately to terminate the life of any person.

The nurse's concern for human dignity and for the provision of high quality nursing care is not limited by personal attitudes or beliefs. If ethically opposed to interventions in a particular case because of the procedures to be used, the nurse is justified in refusing to participate. Such refusal should be made known in advance and in time for other appropriate arrangements to be made for the client's nursing care. If the nurse becomes involved in such a case and the client's life is in jeopardy, the nurse is obliged to provide for the client's safety, to avoid abandonment, and to withdraw only when assured that alternative sources of nursing care are available to the client.

The measures nurses take to care for the dying client and the client's family emphasize human contact. They enable the client to live with as much physical, emotional, and spiritual comfort as possible, and they maximize the values the client has treasured in life. Nursing care is directed toward the prevention and relief of the suffering commonly associated with the dying process. The nurse may provide interventions to relieve symptoms in the dying client even when the interventions entail substantial risks of hastening death.

1.4 THE SETTING FOR HEALTH CARE

The nurse adheres to the principle of nondiscriminatory, nonprejudicial care in every situation and endeavors to promote its acceptance by others. The setting shall not determine the nurse's readiness to respect clients and to render or obtain needed services.

2

The nurse safeguards the client's right to privacy by judiciously protecting information of a confidential nature.

2.1 THE CLIENT'S RIGHT TO PRIVACY

The right to privacy is an inalienable human right. The client trusts the nurse to hold all information in confidence. This trust could be destroyed and the client's welfare jeopardized by injudicious disclosure of information provided in confidence. The duty of confidentiality, however, is not absolute when innocent parties are in direct jeopardy.

2.2 PROTECTION OF INFORMATION

The rights, well-being, and safety of the individual client should be the determining factors in arriving at any professional judgment concerning the disposition of confidential information received from the client relevant to his or her treatment. The standards of nursing practice and the nursing responsibility to provide high quality health services require that relevant data be shared with members of the health team. Only information pertinent to a client's treatment and welfare is disclosed, and it is disclosed only to those directly concerned with the client's care.

Information documenting the appropriateness, necessity, and quality of care required for the purposes of peer review, third-party payment, and other quality assurance mechanisms must be disclosed only under defined policies, mandates, or protocols. These written guidelines must assure that the rights, well-being, and safety of the client are maintained.

2.3 ACCESS TO RECORDS

If in the course of providing care there is a need for the nurse to have access to the records of persons not under the nurse's care, the persons affected should be notified and, whenever possible, permission should be obtained first. Although records belong to the agency where the data are collected, the individual maintains the right of control over the information in the record. Similarly, professionals may exercise the right of control over information they have generated in the course of health care.

If the nurse wishes to use a client's treatment record for research or nonclinical purposes in which anonymity cannot be guaranteed, the client's consent must be obtained first. Ethically, this ensures the client's right to privacy; legally, it protects the client against unlawful invasion of privacy.

3

The nurse acts to safeguard the client and the public when health care and safety are affected by incompetent, unethical, or illegal practice by any person.

3.1 SAFEGUARDING THE HEALTH AND SAFETY OF THE CLIENT

The nurse's primary commitment is to the health, welfare, and safety of the client. As an advocate for the client, the nurse must be alert to and take appropriate action regarding any instances of incompetent, unethical, or illegal practice by any member of the health care team or the health care system, or any action on the part of others that places the rights or best interests of the client in jeopardy. To function effectively in this role, nurses must be aware of the employing institution's policies and procedures, nursing standards of practice, the Code for Nurses, and laws governing nursing and health care practice with regard to incompetent, unethical, or illegal practice.

3.2 ACTING ON QUESTIONABLE PRACTICE

When the nurse is aware of inappropriate or questionable practice in the provision of health care, concern should be expressed to the person carrying out the questionable practice and attention called to the possible detrimental effect upon the client's welfare. When factors in the health care delivery system threaten the welfare of the client, similar action should be directed to the responsible administrative person. If indicated, the practice should then be reported to the appropriate authority within the institution, agency, or larger system.

There should be an established process for the reporting and handling of incompetent, unethical, or illegal practice within the employment setting so that such reporting can go through official channels without causing fear of reprisal. The nurse should be knowledgeable

about the process and be prepared to use it if necessary. When questions are raised about the practices of individual practitioners or of health care systems, written documentation of the observed practices or behaviors must be available to the appropriate authorities. State nurses' associations should be prepared to provide assistance and support in the development and evaluation of such processes and in reporting procedures.

When incompetent, unethical, or illegal practice on the part of anyone concerned with the client's care is not corrected within the employment setting and continues to jeopardize the client's welfare and safety, the problem should be reported to other appropriate authorities such as practice committees of the pertinent professional organizations or the legally constituted bodies concerned with licensing of specific categories of health workers or professional practitioners. Some situations may warrant the concern and involvement of all such groups. Accurate reporting and documentation undergird all actions.

3.3 REVIEW MECHANISMS

The nurse should participate in the planning, establishment, implementation, and evaluation of review mechanisms that serve to safeguard clients, such as duly constituted peer review processes or committees, and ethics committees. Such ongoing review mechanisms are based on established criteria, have stated purposes, include a process for making recommendations, and facilitate improved delivery of nursing and other health services to clients wherever nursing services are provided.

4

The nurse assumes responsibility and accountability for individual nursing judgments and actions.

• • •

5

The nurse maintains competence in nursing.

• • •

6

The nurse exercises informed judgment and uses individual competency and qualifications as criteria in seeking consultation, accepting responsibilities, and delegating nursing activities.

• • •

7

The nurse participates in activities that contribute to the ongoing development of the profession's body of knowledge.

7.1 THE NATURE AND DEVELOPMENT OF KNOWLEDGE

Every profession must engage in scholarly inquiry to identify, verify, and continually enlarge the body of knowledge that forms the foundation for its practice. A unique body of verified knowledge provides both framework and direction for the profession in all of its activities and for the practitioner in the provision of nursing care. The accrual of scientific and humanistic knowledge promotes the advancement of practice and the well-being of the profession's clients. Ongoing scholarly activity such as research and the development of theory is indispensable to the full discharge of a profession's obligations to society. Each nurse has a role in this area of professional activity, whether as an investigator in furthering knowledge, as a participant in research, or as a user of theoretical and empirical knowledge.

7.2 PROTECTION OF RIGHTS
OF HUMAN PARTICIPANTS IN RESEARCH

Individual rights valued by society and by the nursing profession that have particular application in research include the right of adequately informed consent, the right to freedom from risk of injury, and the right of privacy and preservation of dignity. Inherent in these rights is respect for each individual's rights to exercise self-determination, to choose to participate or not, to have full information, and to terminate participation in research without penalty.

It is the duty of the nurse functioning in any research role to maintain vigilance in protecting the life, health, and privacy of human subjects from both anticipated and unanticipated risks and in assuring informed consent. Subjects' integrity, privacy, and rights must be especially safeguarded if the subjects are unable to protect themselves because of incapacity or because they are in a dependent relationship to the investigator. The investigation should be discontinued if its continuance might be harmful to the subject.

7.3 GENERAL GUIDELINES
FOR PARTICIPATING IN RESEARCH

Before participating in research conducted by others, the nurse has an obligation to (a) obtain information

about the intent and the nature of the research and (b) ascertain that the study proposal is approved by the appropriate bodies, such as institutional review boards.

Research should be conducted and directed by qualified persons. The nurse who participates in research in any capacity should be fully informed about both the nurse's and the client's rights and obligations.

8

The nurse participates in the profession's efforts to implement and improve standards of nursing.

•   •   •

9

The nurse participates in the profession's efforts to establish and maintain conditions of employment conducive to high quality nursing care.

•   •   •

10

The nurse participates in the profession's effort to protect the public from misinformation and misrepresentation and to maintain the integrity of nursing.

•   •   •

11

The nurse collaborates with members of the health professions and other citizens in promoting community and national efforts to meet the health needs of the public.

11.1 COLLABORATION WITH OTHERS
TO MEET HEALTH NEEDS

The availability and accessibility of high quality health services to all people require collaborative planning at the local, state, national, and international levels that respects the interdependence of health professionals and clients in health care systems. Nursing care is an integral part of high quality health care, and nurses have an obligation to promote equitable access to nursing and health care for all people.

11.2 RESPONSIBILITY TO THE PUBLIC

The nursing profession is committed to promoting the welfare and safety of all people. The goals and values of nursing are essential to effective delivery of health services. For the benefit of the individual client and the public at large, nursing's goals and commitments need adequate representation. Nurses should ensure this representation by active participation in decision making in institutional and political arenas to assure a just distribution of health care and nursing resources.

11.3 RELATIONSHIPS WITH OTHER DISCIPLINES

The complexity of health care delivery systems requires a multidisciplinary approach to delivery of services that has the strong support and active participation of all the health professions. Nurses should actively promote the collaborative planning required to ensure the availability and accessibility of high quality health services to all persons whose health needs are unmet.

RALPH CRAWSHAW, ET AL.

Patient-Physician Covenant (1995)

Medicine is, at its center, a moral enterprise grounded in a covenant of trust. This covenant obliges physicians to be competent and to use their competence in the patient's best interests. Physicians, therefore, are both intellectually and morally obliged to act as advocates for the sick wherever their welfare is threatened and for their health at all times.

Today, this covenant of trust is significantly threatened. From within, there is growing legitimation of the physician's materialistic self-interest; from without, for-profit forces press the physician into the role of commercial agent to enhance the profitability of health care organizations. Such distortions of the physician's responsibility degrade the physician-patient relationship that is the central element and structure of clinical care. To capitulate to these alterations of the trust relationship is to significantly alter the physician's role as healer, carer, helper, and advocate for the sick and for the health of all.

By its traditions and very nature, medicine is a special kind of human activity — one that cannot be pursued effectively without the virtues of humility, honesty, intellectual integrity, compassion, and effacement of excessive self-interest. These traits mark physicians as members of a moral community dedicated to something other than its own self-interest.

Our first obligation must be to serve the good of those persons who seek our help and trust us to provide it. Physicians, as physicians, are not, and must never be, commercial entrepreneurs, gateclosers, or agents of fiscal policy that runs counter to our trust. Any defection from [the] primacy of the patient's well-being places the patient at risk by treatment that may compromise quality of or access to medical care.

We believe the medical profession must reaffirm the primacy of its obligation to the patient through national, state, and local professional societies; our academic, research, and hospital organizations; and especially through personal behavior. As advocates for the promotion of health and support of the sick, we are called upon to discuss, defend, and promulgate medical care by every ethical means available. Only by caring and advocating for the patient can the integrity of our profession be affirmed. Thus we honor our covenant of trust with patients.

Ralph Crawshaw, MD
David E. Rogers, MD
Edmund D. Pellegrino, MD
Roger J. Bulger, MD
George D. Lundberg, MD
Lonnie R. Bristow, MD
Christine K. Cassel, MD
Jeremiah A. Barondess, MD

Reprinted by permission of the authors and the publisher from the *Journal of the American Medical Association* 273 (May 17, 1995), 1553. Copyright © 1995, American Medical Association.

EDMUND D. PELLEGRINO

The Virtuous Physician and the Ethics of Medicine

Consider from what noble seed you spring: You were created not to live like beasts, but for pursuit of virtue and of knowledge.

Dante, *Inferno* 26, 118–120

THE VIRTUOUS PERSON,
THE VIRTUOUS PHYSICIAN

Virtue implies a character trait, an internal disposition, habitually to seek moral perfection, to live one's life in accord with the moral law, and to attain a balance between noble intention and just action. Perhaps C. S. Lewis has captured the idea best by likening the virtuous man to the good tennis player: "What you mean by a good player is the man whose eye and muscles and nerves have been so trained by making innumerable good shots that they can now be relied upon. . . . They have a certain tone or quality which is there even when he is not playing. . . . In the same way a man who perseveres in doing just actions gets in the end a certain quality of character. Now it is that quality rather than the particular actions that we mean when we talk of virtue" [1].

On almost any view, the virtuous person is someone we can trust to act habitually in a 'good' way — courageously, honestly, justly, wisely, and temperately. He is committed to *being* a good person and to the pursuit of perfection in his private, professional and communal life. He is someone who will act well even when there is no one to applaud, simply because to act otherwise is a violation of what it is to be a good person. No civilized society could endure without a significant num-

ber of citizens committed to this concept of virtue. Without such persons no system of general ethics could succeed, and no system of professional ethics could transcend the dangers of self-interest. That is why, even while rights, duties, obligations may be emphasized, the concept of virtue has 'hovered' so persistently over every system of ethics.

Is the virtuous physician simply the virtuous person practicing medicine? Are there virtues peculiar to medicine as a practice? Are certain of the individual virtues more applicable to medicine than elsewhere in human activities? Is virtue more important in some branches of medicine than others? How do professional skills differ from virtue? These are pertinent questions propadeutic to the later questions of the place of virtue in professional medical ethics.

I believe these questions are best answered by drawing on the Aristotelian-Thomist notion of virtues and its relationship to the ends and purposes of human life. The virtuous physician on this view is defined in terms of the ends of medicine. To be sure, the physician, before he is anything else, must be a virtuous person. To be a virtuous physician he must also be the kind of person we can confidently expect will be disposed to the right and good intrinsic to the practice he professes. What are those dispositions?

To answer this question requires some exposition of what we mean by the good in medicine, or more specifically the good of the patient — for that is the end the patient and the physician ostensibly seek. Any theory of virtue must be linked with a theory of the good because virtue is a disposition habitually to do the good. Must we therefore know the nature of the good the virtuous man is disposed to do? As with the definition of virtue we are caught here in another perennial

Reprinted from Earl E. Shelp (ed.), *Virtue and Medicine: Exploration in the Character of Medicine* (Philosophy and Medicine Series, No. 17), pp. 243–255. © 1985 by D. Reidel Publishing Company. Reprinted by permission of Kluwer Academic Publishers.

philosophical question — what is the nature of the Good? Is the good whatever we make it to be or does it have validity independent of our desires or interest? Is the good one, or many? Is it reducible to riches, honors, pleasures, glory, happiness, or something else?

I make no pretense to a discussion of a general theory of the good. But any attempt to define the virtuous physician or a virtue-based ethic for medicine must offer some definition of the good of the patient. The patient's good is the end of medicine, that which shapes the particular virtues required for its attainment. That end is central to any notion of the virtues peculiar to medicine as a practice.

I have argued elsewhere that the architectonic principle of medicine is the good of the patient as expressed in a particular right and good healing action [2]. This is the immediate good end of the clinical encounter. Health, healing, caring, coping are all good ends dependent upon the more immediate end of a right and good decision. On this view, the virtuous physician is one so habitually disposed to act in the patient's good, to place that good in ordinary instances above his own, that he can reliably be expected to do so.

But we must face the fact that the 'patient's good' is itself a compound notion. Elsewhere I have examined four components of the patient's good: (1) clinical or biomedical good; (2) the good as perceived by the patient; (3) the good of the patient as a human person; and (4) the Good, or ultimate good. Each of these components of patient good must be served. They must also be placed in some hierarchical order when they conflict within the same person, or between persons involved in clinical decisions [3].

Some would consider patient good, so far as the physician is concerned, as limited to what applied medical knowledge can achieve in *this* patient. On this view the virtues specific to medicine would be objectivity, scientific probity, and conscientiousness with regard to professional skill. One could perform the technical tasks of medicine well, be faithful to the skills of good technical medicine per se, but without being a virtuous person. Would one then be a virtuous physician? One would have to answer affirmatively if technical skill were all there is to medicine.

Some of the more expansionist models of medicine — like . . . that of the World Health Organization (total well-being) — would require compassion, empathy, advocacy, benevolence, and beneficence, i.e., an expanded sense of the affective responses to patient need [4]. Some might argue that what is required,

therefore, is not virtue, but simply greater skill in the social and behavioral sciences applied to particular patients. On this view the physician's habitual dispositions might be incidental to his skills in communication or his empathy. He could achieve the ends of medicine without necessarily being a virtuous person in the generic sense.

It is important at this juncture to distinguish the virtues from technical or professional skills, as MacIntyre and, more clearly, Von Wright do. The latter defines a skill as 'technical goodness' — excellence in some particular activity — while virtues are not tied to any one activity but are necessary for "the good of man" ([5], pp. 139–140). The virtues are not "characterized in terms of their results" ([6], p. 141). On this view, the technical skills of medicine are not virtues and could be practiced by a non-virtuous person. Aristotle held *techne* (technical skills) to be one of the five intellectual virtues but not one of the moral virtues.

The virtues enable the physician to act with regard to things that are good for man, when man is in the specific existential state of illness. They are dispositions always to seek the good intent inherent in healing. Within medicine, the virtues do become in MacIntyre's sense acquired human qualities ". . . the possession and exercise of which tends to enable us to achieve those goods which are internal to practices and the lack of which effectively prevents us from achieving any such goods" ([7], p. 178).

We can come closer to the relationship of virtue to clinical actions if we look to the more immediate ends of medical encounters, to those moments of clinical truth when specific decisions and actions are chosen and carried out. The good the patient seeks is to be healed — to be restored to his prior, or to a better, state of function, to be made 'whole' again. If this is not possible, the patient expects to be helped, to be assisted in coping with the pain, disability or dying that illness may entail. The immediate end of medicine is not simply a technically proficient performance but the use of that performance to attain a good end — the good of the patient — his medical or biomedical good to the extent possible but also his good as he the patient perceives it, his good as a human person who can make his own life plan, and his good as a person with a spiritual destiny if this is his belief [8]. It is the sensitive balancing of these senses of the patient's good which the virtuous physician pursues to perfection.

To achieve the end of medicine thus conceived, to practice medicine virtuously, requires certain dispositions: conscientious attention to technical knowledge and skill to be sure, but also compassion—a capacity to feel something of the patient's experience of illness and his perceptions of what is worthwhile; beneficence and benevolence—doing and wishing to do good for the patient; honesty, fidelity to promises, perhaps at times courage as well—the whole list of virtues spelled out by Aristotle: ". . . justice, courage, temperance, magnificence, magnanimity, liberality, placability, prudence, wisdom" (*Rhetoric*, 1, c, 13666, 1–3). Not every one of these virtues is required in every decision. What we expect of the virtuous physician is that he will exhibit them when they are required and that he will be so habitually disposed to do so that we can depend upon it. He will place the good of the patient above his own and seek that good unless its pursuit imposes an injustice upon him, or his family, or requires a violation of his own conscience.

While the virtues are necessary to attain the good internal to medicine as a practice, they exist independently of medicine. They are necessary for the practice of a good life, no matter in what activities that life may express itself. Certain of the virtues may become duties in the Stoic sense, duties because of the nature of medicine as a practice. Medicine calls forth benevolence, beneficence, truth telling, honesty, fidelity, and justice more than physical courage, for example. Yet even physical courage may be necessary when caring for the wounded on battlefields, in plagues, earthquakes, or other disasters. On a more ordinary scale courage is necessary in treating contagious diseases, violent patients, or battlefield casualties. Doing the right and good thing in medicine calls for a more regular, intensive, and selective practice of the virtues than many other callings.

A person who is a virtuous person can cultivate the technical skills of medicine for reasons other than the good of the patient—his own pride, profit, prestige, power. Such a physician can make technically right decisions and perform skillfully. He could not be depended upon, however, to act against his own self-interest for the good of his patient.

In the virtuous physician, explicit fulfillment of rights and duties is an outward expression of an inner disposition to do the right and the good. He is virtuous not because he has conformed to the letter of the law, or his moral duties, but because that is what a good person does. He starts always with his commitment to be a certain kind of person, and he approaches clinical quandaries, conflicts of values, and his patient's interests as a good person should.

Some branches of medicine would seem to demand a stricter and broader adherence to virtue than others. Generalists, for example, who deal with the more sensitive facets and nuances of a patient's life and humanity must exercise the virtues more diligently than technique-oriented specialists. The narrower the specialty the more easily the patient's good can be safeguarded by rules, regulations, rights and duties; the broader the specialty the more significant are the physician's character traits. No branch of medicine, however, can be practiced without some dedication to some of the virtues [9].

Unfortunately, physicians can compartmentalize their lives. Some practice medicine virtuously, yet are guilty of vice in their private lives. Examples are common of physicians who appear sincerely to seek the good of their patients and neglect obligations to family or friends. Some boast of being 'married' to medicine and use this excuse to justify all sorts of failures in their own human relationships. We could not call such a person virtuous. Nor could we be secure in, or trust, his disposition to act in a right and good way even in medicine. After all, one of the essential virtues is balancing conflicting obligations judiciously.

As Socrates pointed out to Meno, one cannot really be virtuous in part:

Why did not I ask you to tell me the nature of virtue as a whole? And you are very far from telling me this; but declare every action to be virtue which is done with a part of virtue; as though you had told me and I must already know the whole of virtue, and this too when frittered away into little pieces. And therefore my dear Meno, I fear that I must begin again, and repeat the same question: what is virtue? For otherwise, I can only say that every action done with a part of virtue is virtue; what else is the meaning of saying that every action done with justice is virtue? Ought I not to ask the question over again; for can any one who does not know virtue know a part of virtue? (*Meno*, 79)

VIRTUES, RIGHTS AND DUTIES IN MEDICAL ETHICS

Frankena has neatly summarized the distinctions between virtue-based and rights- and duty-based ethics as follows:

In an ED (ethics of duty) then, the basic concept is that a certain kind of external act (or doing) ought to be done in certain circumstances; and that of a certain disposition being a virtue is a dependent one. In an EV (ethics of virtue) the basic concept is that of a disposition or way of being—something one has, or if not, does—as a virtue, as morally good; and that of an action's being virtuous or good or even right, is a dependent one [10].

There are some logical difficulties with a virtue-based ethic. For one thing, there must be some consensus on a definition of virtue. For another there is a circularity in the assertion that virtue is what the good man habitually does, and that at the same time one becomes virtuous by doing good. Virtue and good are defined in terms of each other and the definitions of both may vary among sincere people in actual practice when there is no consensus. A virtue-based ethic is difficult to defend as the sole basis for normative judgments.

But there is a deficiency in rights- and duty-ethics as well. They too must be linked to a theory of the good. In contemporary ethics, theories of good are rarely explicitly linked to theories of the right and good. Von Wright, commendably, is one of the few contemporary authorities who explicitly connects his theory of good with his theory of virtue. . . .

In most professional ethical codes, virtue- and duty-based ethics are intermingled. The Hippocratic Oath, for example, imposes certain duties like protection of confidentiality, avoiding abortion, not harming the patient. But the Hippocratic physician also pledges: ". . . in purity and holiness I will guard my life and my art." This is an exhortation to be a good person and a virtuous physician, in order to serve patients in an ethically responsible way.

Likewise, in one of the most humanistic statements in medical literature, the first century A.D. writer, Scribonius Largus, made *humanitas* (compassion) an essential virtue. It is thus really a role-specific duty. In doing so he was applying the Stoic doctrine of virtue to medicine [11].

The latest version (1980) of the AMA 'Principles of Medical Ethics' similarly intermingles duties, rights, and exhortations to virtue. It speaks of 'standards of behavior', 'essentials of honorable behavior', dealing 'honestly' with patients and colleagues and exposing colleagues 'deficient in character'. The *Declaration of Geneva,* which must meet the challenge of the widest array of value systems, nonetheless calls for practice 'with conscience and dignity' in keeping with 'the honor and noble traditions of the profession'. Though their first allegiance must be to the Communist ethos, even the Soviet physician is urged to preserve 'the high

title of physician', 'to keep and develop the beneficial traditions of medicine' and to 'dedicate' all his 'knowledge and strength to the care of the sick'.

Those who are cynical of any protestation of virtue on the part of physicians will interpret these excerpts as the last remnants of a dying tradition of altruistic benevolence. But at the very least, they attest to the recognition that the good of the patient cannot be fully protected by rights and duties alone. Some degree of supererogation is built into the nature of the relationship of those who are ill and those who profess to help them.

This too may be why many graduating classes, still idealistic about their calling, choose the Prayer of Maimonides (not by Maimonides at all) over the more deontological Oath of Hippocrates. In that 'prayer' the physician asks: ". . . may neither avarice nor miserliness, nor thirst for glory or for a great reputation engage my mind; for the enemies of truth and philanthropy may easily deceive me and make me forgetful of my lofty aim of doing good to thy children." This is an unequivocal call to virtue and it is hard to imagine even the most cynical graduate failing to comprehend its message.

All professional medical codes, then, are built of a three-tiered system of obligations related to the special roles of physicians in society. In the ascending order of ethical sensitivity they are: observance of the laws of the land, then observance of rights and fulfillment of duties, and finally the practice of virtue.

A legally based ethic concentrates on the minimum requirements—the duties imposed by human laws which protect against the grosser aberrations of personal rights. Licensure, the laws of torts and contracts, prohibitions against discrimination, good Samaritan laws, definitions of death, and the protection of human subjects of experimentation are elements of a legalistic ethic.

At the next level is the ethics of rights and duties which spells out obligations beyond what law defines. Here, benevolence and beneficence take on more than their legal meaning. The ideal of service, of responsiveness to the special needs of those who are ill, some degree of compassion, kindliness, promise-keeping, truth-telling, and non-maleficence and specific obligations like confidentiality and autonomy, are included. How these principles are applied, and conflicts among them resolved in the patient's best interests, are subjects of widely varying interpretation. How sensitively these issues are confronted depends more on the physician's character than his capability at ethical discourse or moral casuistry.

Virtue-based ethics goes beyond these first two levels. We expect the virtuous person to do the right and the good even at the expense of personal sacrifice and legitimate self-interest. Virtue ethics expands the notions of benevolence, beneficence, conscientiousness, compassion, and fidelity well beyond what strict duty might require. It makes some degree of supererogation mandatory because it calls for standards of ethical performance that exceed those prevalent in the rest of society [12].

At each of these three levels there are certain dangers from over-zealous or misguided observance. Legalistic ethical systems tend toward a justification for minimalistic ethics, a narrow definition of benevolence or beneficence, and a contract-minded physician-patient relationship. Duty- and rights-based ethics may be distorted by too strict adherence to the letter of ethical principles without the modulations and nuances the spirit of those principles implies. Virtue-based ethics, being the least specific, can more easily lapse into self-righteous paternalism or an unwelcome over-involvement in the personal life of the patient. Misapplication of any moral system even with good intent converts benevolence into maleficence. The virtuous person might be expected to be more sensitive to these aberrations than someone whose ethics is more deontologically or legally flavored.

The more we yearn for ethical sensitivity the less we lean on rights, duties, rules, and principles, and the more we lean on the character traits of the moral agent. Paradoxically, without rules, rights, and duties specifically spelled out, we cannot predict what form a particular person's expression of virtue will take. In a pluralistic society, we need laws, rules, and principles to assure a dependable minimum level of moral conduct. But that minimal level is insufficient in the complex and often unpredictable circumstances of decision-making, where technical and value desiderata intersect so inextricably.

The virtuous physician does not act from unreasoned, uncritical intuitions about what feels good. His dispositions are ordered in accord with that 'right reason' which both Aristotle and Aquinas considered essential to virtue. Medicine is itself ultimately an exercise of practical wisdom—a right way of acting in difficult and uncertain circumstances for a specific end,

i.e., the good of a particular person who is ill. It is when the choice of a right and good action becomes more difficult, when the temptations to self-interest are most insistent, when unexpected nuances of good and evil arise and no one is looking, that the differences between an ethics based in virtue and an ethics based in law and/or duty can most clearly be distinguished.

Virtue-based professional ethics distinguishes itself, therefore, less in the avoidance of overtly immoral practices than in avoidance of those at the margin of moral responsibility. Physicians are confronted, in today's morally relaxed climate, with an increasing number of new practices that pit altruism against self-interest. Most are not illegal, or, strictly speaking, immoral in a rights- or duty-based ethic. But they are not consistent with the higher levels of moral sensitivity that a virtue-ethics demands. These practices usually involve opportunities for profit from the illness of others, narrowing the concept of service for personal convenience, taking a proprietary attitude with respect to medical knowledge, and placing loyalty to the profession above loyalty to patients.

Under the first heading, we might include such things as investment in and ownership of for-profit hospitals, hospital chains, nursing homes, dialysis units, tie-in arrangements with radiological or laboratory services, escalation of fees for repetitive, high-volume procedures, and lax indications for their use, especially when third party payers 'allow' such charges.

The second heading might include the ever decreasing availability and accessibility of physicians, the diffusion of individual patient responsibility in group practice so that the patient never knows whom he will see or who is on call, the itinerant emergency room physician who works two days and skips three with little commitment to hospital or community, and the growing over-indulgence of physicians in vacations, recreation, and 'self-development.'

The third category might include such things as 'selling one's services' for whatever the market will bear, providing what the market demands and not necessarily what the community needs, patenting new procedures or keeping them secret from potential competitor-colleagues, looking at the investment of time, effort, and capital in a medical education as justification for 'making it back', or forgetting that medical knowledge is drawn from the cumulative experience of a multitude of patients, clinicians, and investigators.

Under the last category might be included referrals on the basis of friendship and reciprocity rather than skill, resisting consultations and second opinions as affronts to one's competence, placing the interest of the referring physician above those of the patients, [and] looking the other way in the face of incompetence or even dishonesty in one's professional colleagues.

These and many other practices are defended today by sincere physicians and even encouraged in this era of competition, legalism, and self-indulgence. Some can be rationalized even in a deontological ethic. But it would be impossible to envision the physician committed to the virtues assenting to these practices. A virtue-based ethic simply does not fluctuate with what the dominant social mores will tolerate. It must interpret benevolence, beneficence, and responsibility in a way that reduces self-interest and enhances altruism. It is the only convincing answer the profession can give to the growing perception clearly manifest in the legal commentaries in the FTC [Federal Trade Commission] ruling that medicine is nothing more than business and should be regulated as such.

A virtue-based ethic is inherently elitist, in the best sense, because its adherents demand more of themselves than the prevailing morality. It calls forth that extra measure of dedication that has made the best physicians in every era exemplars of what the human spirit can achieve. No matter to what depths a society may fall, virtuous persons will always be the beacons that light the way back to moral sensitivity; virtuous physicians are the beacons that show the way back to moral credibility for the whole profession.

Albert Jonsen, rightly I believe, diagnoses the central paradox in medicine as the tension between self-interest and altruism [13]. No amount of deft juggling of rights, duties, or principles will suffice to resolve that tension. We are all too good at rationalizing what we want to do so that personal gain can be converted from vice to virtue. Only a character formed by the virtues can feel the nausea of such intellectual hypocrisy.

To be sure, the twin themes of self-interest and altruism have been inextricably joined in the history of medicine. There have always been physicians who reject the virtues or, more often, claim them falsely. But, in addition, there have been physicians, more often than the critics of medicine would allow, who have been truly virtuous both in intent and act. They have been, and remain, the leaven of the profession and the hope of all who are ill. They form the sea-wall that will not be eroded even by the powerful forces of commercialization, bureaucratization, and mechanization inevitable in modern medicine.

We cannot, need not, and indeed must not, wait for a medical analogue of MacIntyre's 'new St. Benedict' to show us the way. There is no new concept of virtue waiting to be discovered that is peculiarly suited to the dilemmas of our own dark age. We must recapture the courage to speak of character, virtue, and perfection in living a good life. We must encourage those who are willing to dedicate themselves to a "higher standard of self effacement" [14].

We need the courage, too, to accept the obvious split in the profession between those who see and feel the altruistic imperatives in medicine, and those who do not. Those who at heart believe that the pursuit of private self-interest serves the public good are very different from those who believe in the restraint of self-interest. We forget that physicians since the beginnings of the profession have subscribed to different values and virtues. We need only recall that the Hippocratic Oath was the Oath of physicians of the Pythagorean school at a time when most Greek physicians followed essentially a craft ethic [15]. A perusal of the Hippocratic Corpus itself, which intersperses ethics and etiquette, will show how differently its treatises deal with fees, the care of incurable patients, and the business aspects of the craft.

The illusion that all physicians share a common devotion to a high-flown set of ethical principles has done damage to medicine by raising expectations some members of the profession could not, or will not, fulfill. Today, we must be more forthright about the differences in value commitment among physicians. Professional codes must be more explicit about the relationships between duties, rights, and virtues. Such explicitness encourages a more honest relationship between physicians and patients and removes the hypocrisy of verbal assent to a general code, to which an individual physician may not really subscribe. Explicitness enables patients to choose among physicians on the basis of their ethical commitments as well as their reputations for technical expertise.

Conceptual clarity will not assure virtuous behavior. Indeed, virtues are usually distorted if they are the subject of too conscious a design. But conceptual clarity will distinguish between motives and provide criteria for judging the moral commitment one can expect from the profession and from its individual members. It can also inspire those whose virtuous inclinations need re-enforcement in the current climate of commercialization of the healing relationship.

To this end the current resurgence of interest in virtue-based ethics is altogether salubrious. Linked to a theory of patient good and a theory of rights and duties, it could provide the needed groundwork for a reconstruction of professional medical ethics as that work matures. Perhaps even more progress can be made if we take Shakespeare's advice in *Hamlet:* "Assume the virtue if you have it not. . . . For use almost can change the stamp of nature."

NOTES

1. Lewis, C.: 1952, *Mere Christianity,* Macmillan Co., New York.

2. Pellegrino, E.: 1983, 'The Healing Relationship: The Architectonics of Clinical Medicine', in E. Shelp (ed.), *The Clinical Encounter,* D. Reidel, Dordrecht, Holland, pp. 153–172.

3. Pellegrino, E.: 1983, 'Moral Choice, The Good of the Patient and the Patient's Good', in J. Moskop and L. Kopelman (eds.), *Moral Choice and Medical Crisis,* D. Reidel, Dordrecht, Holland.

4. Engel, G.: 1980, 'The Clinical Application of the Biopsychosocial Model', *American Journal of Psychiatry* 137: 2, 535–544.

5. Von Wright, G.: 1965, *The Varieties of Goodness,* The Humanities Press, New York.

6. Ibid.

7. MacIntyre, A.: 1981, *After Virtue,* University of Notre Dame Press, Notre Dame, Indiana.

8. Pellegrino, E.: 1979, 'The Anatomy of Clinical Judgments: Some Notes on Right Reason and Right Action', in H. T. Engelhardt, Jr., *et al.* (eds.), *Clinical Judgment: A Critical Appraisal,* D. Reidel, Dordrecht, Holland, pp. 169–194. Pellegrino, E.: 1979, 'Toward a Reconstruction of Medical Morality: The Primacy of the Act of Profession and the Fact of Illness', *Journal of Medicine and Philosophy* 4: 1, 32–56.

9. May, W.: Personal communication, 'Virtues in a Professional Setting', unpublished.

10. Frankena, W.: 1982, 'Beneficence in an Ethics of Virtue', in E. Shelp (ed.), *Beneficence and Health Care,* D. Reidel, Dordrecht, Holland, pp. 63–81.

11. Cicero: 1967, *Moral Obligations,* J. Higginbotham (trans.), University of California Press, Berkeley and Los Angeles. Pellegrino, E.: 1983, '*Scribonius Largus* and the Origins of Medical Humanism', address to the American Osler Society.

12. Reeder, J.: 1982, 'Beneficence, Supererogation, and Role Duty', in E. Shelp (ed.), *Beneficence and Health Care,* D. Reidel, Dordrecht, Holland, pp. 83–108.

13. Jonsen, A.: 1983, 'Watching the Doctor', *New England Journal of Medicine* 308: 25, 1531–1535.

14. Cushing, H.: 1929, *Consecratio Medici, and Other Papers,* Little, Brown and Co., Boston.

15. Edelstein, L.: 1967, 'The Professional Ethics of the Greek Physician', in O. Temkin (ed.), *Ancient Medicine: Selected Papers of Ludwig Edelstein,* Johns Hopkins University Press, Baltimore.

NANCY S. JECKER AND DONNIE J. SELF

Separating Care and Cure: An Analysis of Historical and Contemporary Images of Nursing and Medicine

Care as a central organizing concept is a relative newcomer to moral theory (Blum, 1988; Kittay and Meyers, 1987; Noddings, 1984, 1987, 1989; Pearsall, 1986) and moral development theory (Gilligan, 1982, 1986; Gilligan and Wiggins, 1987; Lyons, 1983). However, its roots in American nursing trace back to nursing's early history. In the late nineteenth century, Florence Nightingale thought medical therapeutics and 'curing' were of less importance to patient outcome and willingly left this realm to the physician. Caring, the arena she considered of greatest importance, she assigned to the nurse (Reverby, 1987a, 1987b).[1]

Although the nurses and physicians entertain a more sophisticated picture of their professions today, the image of caring as the exclusive province of nurses continues to influence public perceptions. Because patients exert influence over professionals' self-perceptions, patients' attitudes have the potential to strengthen and reinforce traditional stereotypes, obstruct efforts to redefine professional relationships and provide political

From *Journal of Medicine and Philosophy* 16 (June 1991), 285–306. © 1991 by Kluwer Academic Publishers. Reprinted by permission of Kluwer Academic Publishers.

fuel for traditional hierarchies. In this way, the idea that 'doctors cure and nurses care' continues to exercise a pervasive influence on health professionals' self-images and inter-professional relationships. In addition to these practical consequences, the care-cure division easily can produce a lack of philosophical clarity regarding the concept of care itself. In particular, dissociating the labor of physicians from the realm of care narrows our understanding of care, while treating nursing work as an exclusive care paradigm encourages one-dimensional thinking about care.

This essay provides a philosophical critique of professional stereotypes in medicine. In the course of this critique, we also offer a detailed analysis of the concept of care in health care. More precisely, our aims are to (1) identify factors that contribute to viewing care as the exclusive province of nurses; (2) fine tune the concept of care by exploring alternative forms of care; and (3) illustrate, through the use of cases, diverse models of caring.

GENDER-BASED EXPLANATIONS OF PROFESSIONAL STEREOTYPES

In a popular text on nursing ethics, Andrew Jameton observes that "Physicians are . . . said to focus on the *cure* function, while nurses focus on the *care* functions" (1984, p. 10). Jameton goes on to explain that nurses are expected to perform such functions as follow hospital procedures, report significant incidents and mishaps to supervisors, and organize work on wards and hospital departments. Presumably, physicians order procedures, make medical decisions and take charge of wards and departments. What are the origins of this apparent division of labor? Why does the perception that nurses, and only nurses, perform care functions remain with us? Since nursing and medicine are largely gender segregated professions, the answers to these questions may lie as much in gender-related tendencies as in the histories of nursing and medicine.

One explanation for this apparent division is suggested by Gilligan and Pollak (1989). They report that the association of danger with intimacy is a more salient feature in the fantasies of men than of women. In their study, men projected more danger into situations of close, personal affiliation than situations of impersonal achievement. For example, male subjects expressed "a fear of being caught in a smothering relationship or humiliated by rejection or deceit" (1989, p. 246). Females, by contrast, perceived more danger

in situations of impersonal achievement than situations of personal affiliation. For instance, females "connected danger with the isolation that they associated with competitive success" (1989, p. 246). If male and female attitudes toward attachment and separation do cluster in the way this study suggests, this indicates one fairly obvious explanation for care and cure stereotypes in the health professions. Female nurses would tend to cultivate skill at caring activities, because these activities involve the intimacy and close personal affiliation that women, as a group, prefer. Curing activities would, on the whole, be shunned by nurses, because such activities involve forms of impersonal achievement that women, as a group, find threatening. The opposite tendency should occur in medicine, a male dominated profession, namely: physicians would be likely to stress scientific and technical achievement, while downplaying patient contact and physician-patient relationships.

Consistent with the above line of reasoning is a second possible explanation. According to this second account, the detached objectivity of scientific fields generally, and medical science in particular, discourages many women from excelling at them. Keller maintains that the goal of post-enlightenment science has been a method of perception that affirms empirical reality, while denying subjectivity (1985). This method of knowing implies a purely mechanical view of persons and objects: "no longer filling the void with living form," scientists in the modern age "learned to fill it with dead form" (Keller, 1985, pp. 69–70). In our culture, such a view of self and world is, according to Keller, pervasively associated with masculinity (1985, p. 71).

If Keller is correct about both the association between science and objectivity and the association between objectivity and masculinity, her analysis sheds light on the alleged cure-care division. Following Keller's analysis, once scientific medicine became the dominant mode of medicine in this country, a method of perception that denied the significance of subjectivity took hold. Such an approach focused attention on patients' physical signs and symptoms, while downplaying the significance of their subjective preferences, feelings and experiences. The masculine image this method portrayed in the culture induced males to practice medicine, but encouraged women to assume healing roles that fit better the culture's idea of femininity.

A third explanation of professional stereotypes in nursing and medicine also appeals to gender stereotypes. This explanation holds that our culture associates ethics and humanism with femininity rather than masculinity. For example, ethics and values frequently are referred to as being learned at mother's knee. Morantz-Sanchez (1985) traces this association between ethics and femininity to the early nineteenth century. She argues that during this time, the popular image of women shifted from the biblical and puritan idea of an innately sexual temptress to the idea of women as naturally passionless, spiritual and moral. When women were no longer seen as the inheritors of Eve's questionable legacy" (Morantz-Sanchez, 1985, p. 22), their prudery confined the social roles they were qualified to fill. In particular, women were judged unqualified to enter the medical profession because, unlike men, they could not restrain their natural sympathies as a physician must. For example, women could not be brought into the dissecting room and undergo other rigors of medical training without destroying their innate moral sensibilities.

Referring to the modern tradition, Jameton makes the point that it is "women [not men who] have carried the humane tradition in modern western cultures: they educate children, soften the blows of the world, nurture others and humanize modern life. Nursing and medicine have reified this stereotype" (1987, p. 67). Jameton also notes the longstanding tradition of ethics in the female dominated profession of nursing, and the comparatively weaker and more recent tradition of ethics in medicine. According to Jameton, since 1900 not a single decade has passed without publication of at least one basic text in nursing ethics. Moreover, in its very first volume (1901), *The American Journal of Nursing* published an article on ethics. In the 1920s and 1930s, the *Journal* carried a regular column of ethics cases. In addition to ethics publications, ethics courses have a long history in nursing: they were included in the first formal training programs for nurses. In medicine, by contrast, the tradition of ethics teaching in a sustained and consistent manner is much more recent. It was not until the 1970s that medicine incorporated a significant formal ethics curriculum into medical school classes, and even then "it resulted in large part from outside pressures" (Jameton, 1987, p. 67). Assuming Morantz-Sanchez's and Jameton's historical analyses are correct, they illuminate another possible source of professional stereotypes. If our culture associates ethical concern and response with femininity, one would expect females in general to gravitate toward roles that call upon these abilities. Men who wished to enter the health care profession would fill other roles.

It should be noted that all of the above explanations take for granted the idea that American nursing and medicine are gender segregated professions. This assumption is historically accurate, since a generation or more ago over ninety percent of medical students and physicians were white men (Relman, 1989), and nursing has long been dominated by women. Yet despite this historical precedence, today more men are becoming nurses and women are much more likely to enter the medical profession. In 1972, for example, 1,694 men graduated from American nursing schools, a fourfold increase over 1963, and in 1981 the number of men graduating from R.N. programs jumped to 3,492 (Rowland, 1984). Since women continue to dominate nursing, it is not surprising that overall they occupy more high-level administrative and supervisory positions than men. Yet, the percentage of male nurses who have reached administrative or supervisory positions is much larger than the percentage of female nurses who have reached administrative or supervisory positions (Rowland, 1984). Thus men who do enter nursing are more likely to be in positions where their presence and influence is felt.

Likewise, in the American medical profession, the percentage of female applicants and matriculants to medical school began to rise abruptly in 1970–1971. The number of applications from men, which had been rising steeply, reached a peak in 1974–1976 and has been falling ever since (Relman, 1989). Although few women serve on medical faculty (Eisenberg, 1989), and women are underrepresented in positions of power in academic institutions and as leaders in medical organizations (Levinson, Tolle, Lewis, 1989), their presence in medicine is growing and their influence in shaping medicine's professional identity is increasing.

For these reasons, the above explanations of professional stereotypes are incomplete as they stand. A more complete account would need to explain recent changes in the gender constitution of each profession, perhaps by appealing to shifts in the culture's gender ideals. For example, new gender ideals for men may lie behind changes currently underway in the medical profession. For example, the Association of American Medical Colleges has substantially revised its Medical College Admission Test (MCAT) to place greater emphasis on 'humanistic' skills in selecting physicians; the American Board of Internal Medicine has requested directors of residency programs to assess compassion, respect for patients and integrity in candidates for board certification; and the American Medical Association recently embarked on a major quality assurance initiative which will include research into attributes of 'interpersonal exchange' (Nelson, 1989). Alternatively, a fuller explanation might uncover ways in which traditional gender attitudes persist, despite greater integration of men in nursing and women in medicine. For example, despite greater numbers of male nurses, the American nursing profession is still overwhelmingly female: ninety-seven percent of the total nurse population is female (American Nurses' Association, 1987). Moreover, the majority (56.3 percent) of men cite employment availability as their reason for entering nursing, while most women (62.1 percent) cite interest in people (Rowland, 1984). This suggests that practical economic considerations, rather than a desire to enter a caring role, are more frequent motives among men. Furthermore, the fact that more men are entering nursing may simply indicate that more men are willing to challenge prevailing stereotypes, rather than indicating that these stereotypes and the expectations associated with them no longer apply. Evidence for this is that males who become nurses are more likely than female nurses to be viewed as gay or asked why they do not become doctors (Rowland, 1984). Male nurses also report greater difficulty than female nurses in telling others of their occupational choice: in one study, only sixty-six percent felt comfortable doing so, as compared with eighty-three percent of women (Rowland, 1984). Finally, although more men are choosing nursing, gender segregation reportedly persists between nursing specialties. Men's highest priorities after graduation are jobs in critical or acute care settings, whereas women prefer pediatric and public health fields (Rowland, 1984). In one study of nursing students, male students preferred, in rank order: emergency nursing, then outpatient, intensive care, medical-surgical, psychiatric, and coronary care nursing, and lastly, anesthesia. By contrast, female students ranked pediatric nursing first, then public health, medical-surgical, obstetrics/maternity, and psychiatric nursing (Rowland, 1984).

HISTORICAL EXPLANATIONS
OF PROFESSIONAL STEREOTYPES

Another kind of explanation for the cure-care division has less to do with hypothesized gender differences and more to do with the unique histories of the nursing and medical professions. First, the history of nursing, and its domestic roots in particular, may shed light on the association of nursing with care. Although historians sometimes ignore these roots and begin the history of nursing with the introduction of formal training programs for nurses in the 1870s, a growing number of revisionist historians reject this approach. For example, Reverby makes the point that American nursing "did not appear *de novo* at the end of the nineteenth century . . . [instead,] nursing throughout the colonial era and most of the nineteenth century took place within the family" (1987a, p. 5). O'Brien also finds the roots of nursing "deep in the domestic world of the family" (1987). And Starr maintains that "care of the sick was part of the domestic economy for which the wife assumed responsibility. She would call on the networks of kin and community for advice and assistance when illness struck" (1982, p. 32).

According to these historians, the history of American nursing begins prior to the 1870s. During this earlier period, mothers, daughters and sisters nursed their families at home, sometimes aided by female neighbors who called themselves 'professed' or 'born' nurses and had previous experience caring for their own families (O'Brien, 1987, p. 13). So long as the locus of nursing remained domestic, its primary task was the nurturing of loved ones through ongoing feeding, clothing, bathing and comforting.

Increasingly, the nurturing tasks in which home-based nurses engaged during the colonial era were set apart from the responsibility of their physician counterparts. First, the medical manuals that domestic nurses consulted drew a sharp line between "what could be accomplished by a loving mother and nurse and what needed the skilled consultation of a physician" (O'Brien, 1987, p. 13). The popular 18th century book, *Domestic Medicine,* assured readers that physicians need be consulted rarely, and that most people underestimate their own abilities and knowledge (Buchanan, 1778). Second, the very fact that nurses lived with their patients and constantly were immersed in the practical activity of caring for them, meant that their job took on a distinctive character. In contrast to nurses, physicians made house calls or were visited by patients in offices. Patients were not primarily relatives, but neighbors and townspeople. The physician's job was to offer expert advice or perform specific medical procedures, while nurses carried out physicians' instructions. Thus, physicians used their presumed expertise to direct the caring process, while nurses who lived with patients carried out the actual tasks of ongoing care.

According to this account, the association of American nursing with care traces back to the time when nurses' chief task was caring for sick offspring in the home. Later in the nineteenth century, when nurses left the domestic front to care for patients in hospitals and during wartime, and when they attended the first professional training schools, these early domestic roots continued to shape nursing's identity. In these new locations, nurses' roles continued to include traditional domestic tasks, such as bed making, feeding and hygiene. Thus, a significant emphasis of early training programs was on practical skills. Later educational reforms which sought to introduce scientific content into the nursing curriculum stirred heated debate, attesting to the continued influence of the domestic tradition on the nursing profession.

While American nursing was linked intimately with caregiving activities, American physicians achieved professional status and identity by fashioning a separate sphere. Given the association between caring and 'women's work', physicians surely had little incentive to identify their own professional function as caring. As Benner and Wrubel note, "caring is devalued because caring is associated with women's work and women's work is devalued and most often unpaid" (1989, p. 368). During the colonial era, physicians had only part time medical practices. They earned a livelihood performing other tasks, such as clergy, teaching and farming (Conrad and Schneider, 1990). Not until the nineteenth century did medicine become a full time vocation, but during this period its dangerous and often unsuccessful therapies undermined its prestige. According to Starr, "while some physicians were seeking to make themselves into an elite profession with a monopoly of practice, much of the public refused to grant them any such privileges" (1982, p. 31). In addition, physicians were fiercely competitive with homeopaths and other medical sects for a share of the medical market. Thus, much of American medicine's early history was characterized by repeated efforts to gain repute and professional standing. The first state licensing laws, which granted to physicians with special training and class sole authority to practice medicine, were repealed during the Jacksonian period (Starr, 1982).

Later in the nineteenth century, with the formation of the American Medical Association, physicians were finally successful in their efforts to professionalize medicine and control medical markets. Medicine was credited with the decline in incidence and mortality of diseases, such as leprosy, malaria, smallpox and cholera, thereby increasing the public's faith in its healing powers. During the latter part of the nineteenth century, the rise of scientific medicine ushered in significant progress and ensured the continued prestige and dominance of the medical profession.

The early history of American medicine suggests a possible explanation for the association of medicine with cure, rather than care. The presence of fierce competition and marginal status during its early years forged a mission for medicine that focused on achieving cultural authority and an elite status for its practitioners. Efforts to gain authority and status required physicians to stand apart from laypersons and develop exclusive modes of language, technique and theory. This put physicians at odds with activities, such as patient empathy and care, that call upon abilities of engagement and identification with others. The scientific paradigm that became the language and practice of medicine further reinforced a separation between physician and patient. This paradigm pictured the human being as a machine, and disease as an objective entity that interfered with the human being's mechanical functioning. Such a perspective implied that the 'ghost in the machine' was superfluous to the healing process.

RETHINKING THE CONCEPT OF CARE

Having considered several possible explanations for the association of nursing with care, and medicine with cure, we need to consider next whether these common stereotypes are justified. To address this question, we now turn to a critical analysis of the concept of care. To begin with, it should be noted that the very idea of separating care from cure assumes that these ideas are distinct and non-overlapping. An alternative view sees caring as part of the very meaning of curing. According to this view, physicians who cure also care. Interestingly, the *Oxford English Dictionary* supports this interpretation of cure. Cure comes from the Latin word "curare" meaning "to care for, take care of". Cure refers to "care, heed, concern; to do one's (busy) care, to give one's care or attention to some piece of work; to apply one's self diligently". This definition renders the idea of a physician who cures without caring unintelligible. A person who heals a wound, or otherwise restores a patient to health, cures only if this outcome is the result of devoted caring.

On this reading, although curing entails applying one's care to some one or thing, caring does not imply curing. Thus, physicians can and often do *care* for patients, while suspending attempts to *cure* them. This occurs, for example, when physicians withdraw medical treatments they judge futile, while continuing palliative measures. Hauerwas notes the practical importance of acknowledging the possibility of caring *without* curing. Physicians who fail to recognize the possibility of caring without curing might attempt futile therapies, based on the false belief that efforts to cure patients are all they have to offer.

The *Oxford English Dictionary* distinguishes two distinct senses of care. First, care means "a burdened state of mind arising from . . . concern about anything . . . mental perturbation", and "serious or grave mental attention, the charging of the mind". In this first sense, to "have a care" or "keep a care" is to be in a subjective state of concern about something. Second, care refers to "oversight with [a] view of protection, preservation, or guidance; hence to have the care of". In this second sense, care implies an activity of looking out for or safeguarding the interests of others.

We shall designate the first sense of care, 'caring about'. Caring about indicates an attitude, feeling, or state of mind directed toward a person or circumstance (Hauerwas, 1978, p. 145). To assert that 'My nurse cares about me' or that 'Everyone ought to care about the environment' refers to care in this first sense. The second sense of care involves the exercise of a skill, with or without a particular attitude or feeling toward the object upon which this skill is exercised. We shall refer to this as 'caring for'. For example, we use care in this sense when we say that 'Nurse Jones is caring for your mother' or 'The mechanic down the street offered to take care of my car'. Caring in both senses is a relational term, referring to an attitude or skill directed to someone or something. One's concern about others may be more or less deep, and one's skill at caring for others may display more or less ability. Thus, we refer to the quality of caring to describe how deeply one feels, or how good or poor one is at caring for another. Whereas caring about can occur at a distance from its object, caring for usually requires direct contact with the one who is cared for. Excellence at caring for particular patients typically requires repeated contacts and skill in ascertaining each patient's particular needs. Thus, an expert caregiver learns "through re-peated experience with patients . . . to perceive the particular rather than the typical, care becomes individualized rather than standardized and planning becomes anticipatory of change rather than simply responsive to change" (Benner and Wrubel, 1989, p. 382).

Applying these definitions of cure and care to the medical setting enables us to say that a health professional who cares *about* a patient makes a cognitive or emotional decision that the welfare of the patient is of great importance. Caring about requires keeping the patient's best interest in the forefront of mind and heart. By contrast, a health professional who cares *for* a patient engages in a deliberate and ongoing activity of responding to the patient's needs. Caring for, executed in an exemplary or excellent way, involves deciphering the patient's particular condition and needs. This calls upon verbal skills of questioning and listening and requires attending to and translating nonverbal cues. Caring for thus requires cultivating a capacity to understand others' subjective experiences. Understood in this light, caring for draws upon and teaches a way of knowing that involves "awareness of the complexities of a particular situation" and "inner . . . resources that have been garnered through experience in living" (Benoliel, 1987). The source of this knowledge tends to be participation in relationships with others and observation of others' actions, rather than verbal debate and conversation or the reading of texts (Benner, 1983). Knowledge in this form is practical and interpersonal (Schultz and Meleis, 1988). In the case of unconscious or mentally compromised patients and infants, caring for especially draws upon a person's skill at interpreting gestures, postures, sounds, grimaces, eye scans and bodily movements (Jecker, 1990a). For instance, through intimate engagement, a daughter who serves as a caretaker for a disoriented elderly parent may be able to decipher what counts as pain and comfort, or boredom and interest to the parent. Evidence is gleaned through partaking in daily rituals, such as bathing and feeding, and interpreting the parent's responses.

Caring *about* does not imply caring for. For example, a ward supervisor may care deeply about her patients, without being engaged in the activity of caring directly for them. Nor does caring *for* entail caring about. For instance, one who skillfully cares for patients may be meticulous in her efforts to interpret patients' needs, without actually caring about patients: she may regard them as just one more puzzle to be solved, excel at caring for its own sake, or simply seek to impress colleagues or a boss.

While it is fairly easy to tell who cares *for* a patient, it can be exceedingly difficult to construe who cares *about* a patient. Some professionals may prefer colleagues and supervisors to think they care about their patients, even if they in fact are preoccupied with other matters. Others may learn to cover up the fact that they do care about patients. For example, the idea of masculinity to which some aspire discourages outward expressions of care and concern for others. It would be difficult to gauge whether males who express masculinity in this way care about their patients. Still others may appear uncaring because they learn deference in conflict. For example, women or nurses who are taught to follow orders blindly may appear not to take a genuine interest in their patients. Historically, nurses were instructed to discharge medical orders in an obedient, unquestioning manner (Jameton, 1987), but this expectation does not necessarily entail the absence of caring about.

EXAMPLES OF CARE

In order to bring the concept of care into sharper focus, it is useful to review cases in which individuals exhibit care in different ways. In the course of this review, we shall consider in more detail the protective qualities associated with different kinds of care and the positive and negative forms these qualities can take.

1. CASE ONE: CARING FOR AND ABOUT A PATIENT

I was taking care of a 40-year-old female who had been hospitalized for 3 months in another hospital and came to our hospital the day before to have her abdominal fistulas [external openings for collecting bodily wastes] corrected. The night before I met her, the bag collecting her drainage fell off three times and was reapplied the same way each time by her former nurse due to the patient's insistence that nothing else works. Her skin was very excoriated in spots and tender. When I removed the leaking bag I noticed that the problem was that she had a large crease between two recessed fistulas. I attempted to reapply it to avoid these. She was resistant to my suggestions, and protested my efforts to replace the bag. So I told her that she should trust me because I've had numerous similar situations with which I've had positive outcomes. I pointed out that if the bag was not replaced to avoid the fistulas it would continue to fall off and her pain and discomfort would only increase. She reconsid-

ered. I told her that I was sure I could get a bag to stay on her for at least 24 hours, if not more. She said she'd love that to happen and told me I could do what I wanted. ([quoted in part from] Benner, 1984, pp. [130–131])

In this first case, a nurse appears to care both for and about a patient. Each effort calls upon a distinct set of responses. Caring *for* manifests itself in the activities of removing the leaking bag, locating the problem in adhering it to the patient's skin and replacing the bag. Caring *about* is shown by the *manner* in which the nurse cares for the patient, a manner which expresses concern and involves efforts to reassure and gain the patient's confidence.

Notice too the nurse's response to her patient's initial resistance. This response exhibits the nurse's ability to persuade a recalcitrant patient that a certain procedure (replacing the bag) is in the patient's best interest and that she can execute this procedure successfully. A different response would have been simply to say, 'you *must* let me do this'. The difference between these two responses reveals alternative forms of parentalism (Taylor, 1985). In the medical setting, parentalism is an attempt to justify performing (or omitting) an action that is contrary to a patient's expressed wishes, yet judged to be in a patient's best interest. Were the nurse in this situation to respond to the refusal of treatment by saying 'that's my final word', she would illustrate a kind of parentalism that justifies medical actions by presuming to abrogate a patient's *rights*. An alternative mode of parentalism invokes a morality of *responsibility*, rather than rights (Taylor, 1985; Ruddick, 1989). Here, one appeals to the patient's self-interest and personal responsibility, rather than invoking one's own authority to override the patient. For example, the nurse in case one displays this latter kind of parentalism by effectively laying out for the patient the consequences that attach to different alternatives: replacing the bag properly ensures that it will adhere; not doing so may result in the bag falling off and so heighten the patient's pain and discomfort. In this way, the patient is led to choose between taking responsibility for safeguarding her own interests, or behaving in a less responsible fashion.

Parentalism that is based on promoting the patient's sense of personal responsibility elicits our powers of practical persuasion, and it is often cultivated by those who care *for* others. This is because those charged with caring for others are more often in the position of having to gain others' cooperation. Those who care about, but not for, may need only to confirm in their *own* mind that a certain course of action is justified.

Both kinds of parentalism can be instantiated in positive and negative ways. For example, parentalism that fosters the patient's sense of responsibility can be a positive force. However, this kind of parentalism can also deteriorate into a manipulative tool, for example, when it is used merely to produce guilt in patients, block the expression of patients' feelings, or manipulate patients to acquiesce to decisions they do not prefer in order to gain petty conveniences for caregivers (Taylor, 1985).

The other form of parentalism, that appeals to the health professional's rights and authority over the patient, can represent both positive and negative approaches as well. Negative expressions include a doctor or nurse who knowingly assumes greater authority than she is morally entitled to claim. Or negative parentalism occurs when the justified exercise of authority is conjoined with callousness, e.g., bullying a patient or giving patients orders in an abrupt or cruel fashion. By contrast, an example of positive parentalism of this sort is overriding the rights of someone that one is close to in order to protect that person's interests. Hardwig, for example, notes that in the context of close personal relationships, parentalistic behavior is often warranted and failing to show parentalism can signal a failure to fulfill special responsibilities (Hardwig, 1984). Elsewhere (Jecker, 1989, 1990b, 1990c), it is argued that the responsibilities of individuals in close relationships are different and often greater than the responsibilities that exist between acquaintances or strangers. If this approach is correct, then whether or not abrogating others' rights is justified in the health care setting depends, in part, upon whether particular health professionals stand in close relationships with their patients. Between virtual strangers, interference with others for their own good is less often desirable and more apt to overstep moral boundaries between persons.

2. CASE TWO: CARING FOR, BUT NOT ABOUT A PATIENT

A demented thirty-year-old man had AIDS for eight months. His final admission to our hospital was prompted by the development of large decubitus ulcers. On the ward his oral intake was minimal, and the attending physician instructed me to administer parenteral nutrition. I didn't like taking care of this patient. I kept thinking that he had brought this fate upon himself by his gay lifestyle. Gays repulsed me, and I was unable to feel any compassion for this fellow. I also found his medical problems disgusting and resented the fact that caring for him exposed me to life threatening risks. The patient had copious diarrhea; the decubiti were oozing fluids; and administering parenteral nutrition was complicated by high, spiking fevers that twice necessitated removal of the central line. ([quoted in part from] Cooke, 1986)

In case two a nurse is involved in caring *for* a patient. Caring for is manifest in the activities of treating the patient's ulcers and administering parenteral nutrition. Although the nurse is engaged in the activity of caregiving, her negative feelings about the patient suggest that she lacks an attitude of caring *about* the patient. Mustering such an attitude would require the nurse to reject or subdue her negative responses to the patient. On the other hand, particular nurses will always dislike particular patients, and subduing negative feelings will not necessarily change or mitigate bad feelings. Attempting and failing to reduce negative feelings may simply compound a nurse's difficulties by festering guilt or lowering self-esteem. Where dislike for patients is likely to persist, it is important to keep separate the ideas of *dislike* and *disrespect*. A nurse who dislikes a particular patient may still express respect toward the patient as a fellow human being, for example, through her ongoing activity of caring *for* the patient. Thus, although the nurse may not care *about* the patient, she can still regard the patient in a positive manner and express this regard in action.

3. CASE THREE: CARING ABOUT, BUT NOT FOR A PATIENT

A twenty-seven-year-old model was admitted to the emergency room after an automobile accident that caused multiple fractures and burns over sixty-five percent of his body. Glass had penetrated both eyes so severely as to leave him blind, although a good chance for survival existed. In the emergency room, the patient was met by friends who candidly told him that his physician expects that his life can be saved. Later when I, the physician, met with the patient to discuss treatment, the patient bluntly told me that he had enjoyed a life in which he had identified with his body and physical pleasure and abilities. He had few intellectual or other interests. On these grounds, he flatly refused treatment and asked me to keep him comfortable. My only concern was to promote this patient's welfare. I had seen many burn patients begin with a negative attitude toward treatment and then undergo a change of heart. Based on these experiences I decided to order aggressive treatment and arranged for a psychiatric consult. ([quoted in part from] Brody and Engelhardt, 1987, pp. 327–328)

The third case is about a physician who cares about a patient, but may not be engaged, in an ongoing way, in caring for the patient. For example, the physician orders burn treatments, but may not be the one who actually will provide these treatments to the patient. Unlike the nurse in case one, the physician in this case does not need to gain the patient's cooperation immediately. Moreover, the physician expresses parentalism by appealing to her authority and presumed superior knowledge to justify overriding the patient's wishes. The justification she gives for this is the silent refrain: "I know better; I've seen many burn patients in this situation change their mind". A different kind of parentalism would involve persuading the patient, as well as herself, of the wisdom of continued treatment. The alternative response intends to justify an action *to the patient* through iteration of the consequences of different choices. By contrast, the physician in case three seeks to justify the action mainly *to herself.* Thus her reasoning is 'silent' and she does not attempt negotiation of a solution agreeable to the patient.

4. CASE FOUR: CARING NEITHER FOR NOR ABOUT A PATIENT

I supervise a ward of terminally ill cancer patients. I deliberately avoid getting emotionally involved with these patients because I realize it would be terribly depressing. Fortunately, most of my responsibilities involve management of nurses, paper work and general organization, so I by and large can steer clear of patients and families. Most of the time, I limit my contact with nursing staff while eschewing patient contact. This enables me to direct my energy toward problems I can solve effectively and prevents me from feeling overwhelmed and powerless about dying patients.[2]

The nurse in this last case does not assume the responsibility of caring *for* patients. Nor does she display an attitude of caring *about* patients on her ward. Instead, she strives to maintain a neutral or indifferent stance. Presumably, such a stance affords her a sense of control in an otherwise emotionally charged environment.

FORMS OF CARE IN HEALTH CARE PROFESSIONS

The foregoing analysis of the concept of care places us in a better position to consider traditional stereotypes with a critical eye. In rethinking the idea that 'doctors cure and nurses care', it is helpful to be aware of four possible models of caring. These models parallel the cases discussed above:

1. Health professionals who care for and about their patients,
2. Health professionals who care for, but not about their patients,
3. Health professionals who care about, but not for their patients,
4. Health professionals who care neither for nor about their patients.

In the first model, health professionals care for and about patients. Since caring for is an ongoing and deliberate activity, a health professional whose patient contact is limited to brief visits or to discrete medical interventions, such as taking vital signs, does not fit the first model. Rather, to care in the sense defined by the first model a health professional must both carry out the tasks required to provide health care to the patient and possess an attitude of being concerned about what happens to the patient.

The difference between the first and second models of caring is that in the second it does not ultimately matter much to the professional what happens to patients. Nonetheless, it would be misleading to say that the second professional 'does not care'. After all, the second kind of health professional cares *all the time:* he or she is an ongoing caregiver, even though she lacks an attitude of caring *about* patients. This lack may impede her ability to care for patients, but (as noted above), it need not.

Similarly, it would be misleading to state that health professionals whose caring exemplifies the third model 'do not care.' Such professionals (who care about but not for their patients) may think about patients with great frequency, pray for their recovery and be deeply moved to witness it. These kinds of professionals do indeed care, but their care is more remote by virtue of being removed from the immediate context of the patient. This does not imply that caring *about* is 'intellectual' or 'cold', but it does represent a more abstract mode of caring.

The grounds for saying that a health professional 'does not care' can only be that the professional cares neither for nor about patients. In the fourth model, health professionals do not care in either sense. An *uncaring* health professional is neither a caregiver nor concerned about the welfare of patients. Multiple factors may contribute to health professionals' lacking an attitude of caring about patients. In the cases discussed in the previous section, the absence of caring is prompted, in part, by feeling superior, being emotionally indifferent, needing control, blaming the patient for the disease and disliking the patient. Caring neither for nor about patients often will be an unacceptable role for health professionals. Yet it also may represent a legitimate coping tool, for example, when one's responsibilities are experienced as overwhelming and the need to distance oneself emotionally is felt forcefully.

It is now time to ask how the above models can serve to deepen our understanding of nurses' and physicians' professional roles. To begin with, it is never correct to hold that nurses who function as caregivers do not care. Caring, in the sense of *caring for*, is an inextricable part of their role. The history of nursing is *essentially* a history of caring in this sense. In the colonial era, home-based nurses always cared in the sense of caring *for* family members. Nursing also has a caring tradition in the sense of caring *about* patients. As noted earlier, the first training programs for nurses sought to cultivate moral virtues, including devotion to the welfare of patients.

Despite the historical tradition of care by nurses, there are, and always have been, nurses who do not care much *about* patients in general, or *about* particular patients they nurse. Moreover, as more and more nurses become engaged in administrative and supervisory roles, they may do less caring *for* patients. On these grounds, it is misleading to accept the traditional stereotype that 'nurses care'. This stereotype obscures the fact that over time nursing has changed in its stratification and fields of specialization. These changes have meant that in some areas nurses have less direct patient contact and are less engaged in caring *for* patients. In addition, the traditional stereotype obscures the fact that there always have been nurses who do not care *about* patients.

Turning to physicians, a similar cautionary note is in order. Although some physicians may be less likely to care for patients, and so less likely to exemplify the first two models of caring, many physicians obviously care profoundly *about* patients. Moreover, physicians are a diverse group. In a [university] hospital, medical students or residents-in-training may seek or be delegated a considerable amount of caring for responsibilities, while attendings or senior staff may assume very little. Likewise, in health maintenance organizations, physician assistants and nurse practitioners may be uti-

lized to perform a majority of caring for activities. By contrast, in private practices, physicians may undertake most of the caring for responsibilities. Such physicians may establish ongoing relationships with each patient over several years, e.g., monitoring medications, performing regular check-ups and treating minor emergencies. However, regardless of whether physicians care directly *for* patients, they usually assume a stance of caring *about* patients. Attempting to *cure* a patient is ordinarily an expression of a physician's caring about the patient. It is unfortunate, as well as confusing, then, to assume that doctors cure, as *opposed* to care. Thus, to the extent that the care-cure distinction informs our present thinking, it wrongly denies to the medical profession a caring role and unfortunately clouds our conception of the complexities of nursing care.

CONCLUSION

In closing, this [essay] has intended to take a careful look at professional stereotypes in nursing and medicine. Doing so required clarifying the concept of care and articulating different models of caring. That the concept of care is multiform and the models of caring many should attune us to the dangers of buying into popular stereotypes. Holding tenaciously to traditional stereotypes can prevent us from seeing the evidence that both medicine and nursing are caring professions and both men and women care for and about their patients.

Appreciating the richness of the concept of care also should infuse new energy into research on care in health care and professional settings. The following are suggested research topics that merit further consideration. (1) How can cure and care be joined and integrated into the curriculum of both nursing and medical schools? (2) Is care a virtue? If so, under what circumstances might it deteriorate into a vice? Is care ever a duty or obligation? (3) Is caring a way of knowing? How do cure and care relate to both scientific and intuitive forms of knowledge? (4) What is the proper balance between cure and care in developing an ethic for specific patient groups, such as the elderly, the terminally ill and the chronically ill? Although answering these questions is a tall order, our analysis shows the importance and promise of further research in this area.

NOTES

1. Throughout this paper, we will use the terms 'care' and 'caring' interchangeably. There may be important shades of meaning

unique to each term, but exploring this is beyond the scope of the present inquiry.

2. Whereas the previous cases are drawn from the medical ethics literature, we could find no cases in the literature to illustrate the fourth model. We believe this is significant if it represents a lack of attention to the ethical problems of health care workers who exemplify this model.

REFERENCES

American Nurses' Association: 1987, *Facts About Nurses,* American Nurses' Association, Kansas City, Missouri.

Benner, P.: 1983, 'Recovering the knowledge embedded in clinical practice', *Image: Journal of Nursing Scholarship* 15, 30–41.

Benner, P.: 1984, *From Novice to Expert: Excellence and Power in Clinical Nursing Practice,* Addison-Wesley Publishing Company, Menlo Park, California.

Benner, P., and Wrubel, J.: 1989, *The Primacy of Caring,* Addison-Wesley Publishing Company, Menlo Park, California.

Benoliel, J.Q.: 1987, 'Response to 'toward holistic inquiry in nursing: A proposal for synthesis of patterns and methods', *Scholarly Inquiry for Nursing Practice: An International Journal* 1, 147–152.

Blum, L.A.: 1988, 'Gilligan and Kohlberg: Implications for moral theory', *Ethics* 98, 472–491.

Brody, B.A., and Engelhardt, H.T.: 1987, *Bioethics: Readings and Cases,* Prentice-Hall, Englewood Cliffs, New Jersey.

Buchanan, W.: 1778, *Domestic Medicine, The Third American Edition,* John Trumbull, Boston.

Conrad, P., and Schneider, J.W.: 1990, 'Professionalization, monopoly, and the structure of medical practice', in P. Conrad and R. Kern (eds.), *The Sociology of Health and Illness: Critical Perspectives, Third Edition,* St. Martin's Press, New York, pp. 141–147.

Cooke, M.: 1986, 'Ethical issues in the care of patients with AIDS', *Quality Review Bulletin,* October, 343–346.

Eisenberg, C.: 1989, 'Medicine is no longer a man's profession', *New England Journal of Medicine* 321, 1542–1544.

Gilligan, C.: 1982, *In a Different Voice: Psychological Theory and Women's Development,* Harvard University Press, Cambridge, Massachusetts.

Gilligan, C.: 1986, 'Remapping the moral domain: New images of the self in relationship', in T.C. Heller, M. Sosna, and D.E. Wellbery (eds.), *Reconstructing Individualism: Autonomy, Individuality, and the Self in Western Thought,* Stanford University Press, Stanford, California, pp. 237–252.

Gilligan, C., and Wiggins, G.: 1987, 'The origins of morality in early childhood', in J. Kagan and S. Lamb (eds.), *The Emergence of Morality in Young Children,* University of Chicago Press, Chicago, pp. 277–305.

Gilligan, C., and Pollak, S.: 1989, 'The vulnerable and invulnerable physician', in C. Gilligan, J.V. Ward, and J.M. Taylor (eds.), *Mapping the Moral Domain,* Harvard University Press, Cambridge, Massachusetts, pp. 245–262.

Hardwig, J.: 1984, 'Should women think in terms of rights?,' *Ethics* 94, 441–455.

Hauerwas, S.: 1978, 'Care', in W.T. Reich (ed.), *The Encyclopedia of Bioethics,* Free Press, New York, Vol. 1, 145–150.

Levinson, W., Tolle, S., and Lewis, C.: 1989, 'Women in academic medicine', *New England Journal of Medicine* 321, 1511–1517.

Jameton, A.: 1984, *Nursing Practice: The Ethical Issues,* Prentice-Hall, Englewood Cliffs, New Jersey.

Jameton, A.: 1987, 'Physicians and nurses: A historical perspective', in B.A. Brody and H.T. Engelhardt, *Bioethics, Readings and Cases,* Prentice-Hall, Englewood Cliffs, New Jersey, pp. 66–73.

Jecker, N.S.: 1989, 'Are filial duties unfounded'? *American Philosophical Quarterly* 26, 73–80.

Jecker, N.S.: 1990a, 'The role of intimate others in medical decision making', *The Gerontologist* 30, 65–71.

Jecker, N.S.: 1990b, 'Conceiving a child to save a child: Reproductive and filial ethics', *The Journal of Clinical Ethics* 1, 99–103.

Jecker, N.S.: 1990c, 'Anencephalic infants and special relationships', *Theoretical Medicine* 11, 333–342.

Keller, E.F.: 1985, *Reflections on Gender and Science,* Yale University Press, New Haven, Connecticut.

Kittay, E.F., and Meyers, D.T. (eds.): 1987, *Women and Moral Theory,* Rowman and Littlefield, Totowa, New Jersey.

Lyons, N.P.: 1983, 'Two perspectives: On self, relationships, and morality', *Harvard Educational Review* 53, 125–145.

MacIntyre, A.: 1987, 'How virtues become vices', in B.A. Brody and H.T. Engelhardt (eds.), *Bioethics: Readings and Cases,* Prentice-Hall, Englewood Cliffs, New Jersey, pp. 100–101.

Morantz-Sanchez, R.M.: 1985, *Sympathy and Science: Women Physicians in American Medicine,* Oxford University Press, New York.

Nelson, A.R.: 1989, 'Humanism and the art of medicine: Our commitment to care', *Journal of the American Medical Association* 262, 1228–1230.

Noddings, N.: 1984, *Caring: A Feminine Approach to Ethics and Moral Education,* University of California Press, Berkeley.

Noddings, N.: 1987, 'Do we really want to produce good people?', *Journal of Moral Education* 16, 177–188.

Noddings, N.: 1989, *Women and Evil,* University of California Press, Berkeley.

O'Brien, P.: 1987, 'All a woman's life can bring: The domestic roots of nursing in Philadelphia, 1830–1885', *Nursing Research* 36, 12–17.

Pearsall, M. (ed.): 1986, *Women and Values,* Wadsworth Publishing Company, Belmont, California.

Relman, A.: 1989, 'The changing demography of the medical profession', *New England Journal of Medicine* 321, 1540–1542.

Reverby, S.: 1987a, 'A caring dilemma: Womanhood and nursing in historical perspective', *Nursing Research* 36, 5–11.

Reverby, S.: 1987b, *Ordered to Care: The Dilemma of American Nursing,* Cambridge University Press, New York.

Rowland, H.S.: 1984, *The Nurse's Almanac, 2nd edition,* Aspen Systems Corporation, Rockville, Maryland.

Ruddick, S.: 1989, *Maternal Thinking,* Beacon Press, Boston.

Schultz, P.R., and Meleis, A.I.: 1988, 'Nursing epistemology: Traditions, insights, questions', *Image: Journal of Nursing Scholarship* 20, 217–221.

Starr, P.: 1982, *The Social Transformation of American Medicine,* Basic Books, New York.

Taylor, S.G.: 1985, 'Rights and responsibilities: Nurse-patient relationships', *Image: Journal of Nursing Scholarship* 17, 9–13.

NORMAN DANIELS

The Ideal Advocate and Limited Resources

1. INTRODUCTION

Recently, a friend of mine confided to me that he is not sure he will be able to continue practicing medicine if current trends in the health care system continue. He complained that various reforms — actual and proposed — in the financing of health care make him feel that he will not be able to remain the unbiased agent or advocate for his patients. He feels he has always been such an advocate and that medical ethics requires him to be one. To represent his patient's best interests, he feels he must be free to make medical decisions aimed at the best treatments and outcome which are *medically possible* for his patient.

Of course, he knows he cannot be a completely autonomous agent. Though this was not part of his early medical training, he has learned that his patient should have the ultimate say in what is done and that he must act with his patient's informed consent. But my friend is now concerned about threats to his autonomy that come not from the patient, but from outside the doctor-patient relationship. He feels he cannot in good conscience comply with hospital pressures to discharge his Medicare patients before he thinks they are ready. He finds repugnant a recent capitation scheme proposed for physicians at his hospital. Under the plan, doctors would be financially rewarded for not ordering certain diagnoses or consultations. He insists these are threats to his "moral character" and to his "psyche" as a physician.

I do not think my friend's complaints are unfamiliar. Similar remarks can be heard in scrub rooms, hospital staff meetings, and letters columns in medical journals. Many physicians believe that the 'old' retrospective fee-for-service schemes facilitated acting as the unfettered agent of the patient, but that cost-containment schemes destroy morally essential features of the doctor-patient relationship by restricting physician autonomy. I want [to] explore some general questions underlying these reactions and beliefs. Specifically, I want to address these questions: What kinds of autonomy have been granted American physicians, and how do these fit with ethical constraints on how a physician may act concerning his patient? Do the pre-cost-containment arrangements many physicians prefer institutionally embody or facilitate the ideal doctor-patient relationship? Can we, or how can we, reconcile the fact of resource limitations with the plausible view that physicians should remain neutral advocates of their patients' best interests? In answering these questions, I shall argue that we can reconcile resource limitations with what I will call the Ideal Advocate model of the doctor-patient relationship, but that doing so requires that our health care institutions be just.

2. PHYSICIAN AUTONOMY AND IDEAL ADVOCACY

It will help to analyze briefly the dimensions of autonomy traditionally claimed by U.S. physicians. We can pick out four main dimensions: (1) Whom to treat, (2) Where to practice, (3) What to specialize in, and (4) How to treat?

Unlike their colleagues in many other countries, U.S. physicians retain the power to decide *whom* they will treat. They may consider facts about the individual patient or his method of reimbursement. Choices about both *where* to practice and *what* to specialize in are of course subject to what might be called 'market'

From *Theoretical Medicine* 8 (February 1987), 69–80. © 1987 by D. Reidel Publishing Company. Reprinted by permission of Kluwer Academic Publishers.

constraints. They are subject to facts about the availability of training positions, practices to enter, indebtedness, and other factors. But few of these market constraints are themselves the results of centralized planning, and so there is an extensive, unregulated space for physicians' choice.

These first three dimensions of autonomy are similar in that they all are responsive to physician interests — some would say physicians' 'rights' — rather than patient interests. Granting these dimensions of autonomy to physicians has a major negative impact, for example, on programs to improve access to health care for underserved groups. Thus, only a minority of physicians will treat Medicaid patients. But I am not chiefly interested here in these three dimensions of autonomy. Rather, it is the fourth dimension, *clinical autonomy,* autonomy in *how* to treat, that is most directly affected by the recent cost-containment measures.

Granting physicians clinical autonomy is justified by reference to the patient's interests, not the physician's. Thus autonomy in treatment decisions is constrained by what might be called an 'ethic of advocacy (or agency)', The autonomy we grant the physician is necessary precisely if he is to act in his patient's best interest, and for this reason it also includes some constraints on the physician. The clinical decisions must be: (A) competent: up to professional standards of care; (B) respectful of patient autonomy; (C) respectful of other patient rights, e.g., confidentiality; (D) free from consideration of the physician's interests; (E) uninfluenced by judgments about the patient's worth.

The first of these constraints, the competency constraint, is enforced by peer review and tort law. The four remaining constraints are special features of the kind of fiduciary relationship that holds between a physician, with his greater knowledge and skill, and the patient, on whose behalf the physician acts as agent or advocate. Much recent clinical medical ethics has focused on patient autonomy and rights [constraints (B) and (C)]. Because they have little to do with the problem of cost-containment, I will not talk about them here. But the "purity" constraints, as I will call constraints (D) and (E), are at the heart of the issue. Constraint (D) requires that the physician not allow consideration of his economic or career interests to influence his treatment of his patient. Constraint (E) is interpreted by some to mean that the physician should

not put a price on his patient's life — should not decide how much it is worth to save or extend a particular patient's life. More narrowly interpreted, constraint (E) bars a physician from considering facts other than medical need or likelihood of treatment success in making clinical decisions for a particular patient. I shall call the Ideal Advocate model the view that physicians should be autonomous in their clinical decision-making and pursuit of their patients' best interests, while abiding by constraints (A)–(E) of the ethic of agency.

An important loose-end remains here. Some people believe that the Ideal Advocate is necessarily also an Unrestricted Ideal Advocate. That is, the physician should be subject to no external constraints on treatments he can pursue for his patient. Our retrospective fee-for-service reimbursement schemes may have contributed to this belief. They give the appearance that no resource constraints affect clinical decision-making: just treat, and then bill. Of course, these arrangements hide the way in which rationing actually takes place, by ability to pay, that is, to buy insurance. But this form of rationing seems to leave the clinician untouched. There seem to be no direct incentives to physicians to consider their own interest or the relative worth of the patient in decisions about how to treat (though the physician can refuse to treat at all, which clearly has something to do with his interests and possibly with his assessment of patient worth). In reality, retrospective fee-for-service schemes contain incentives for physicians to treat too much. But this tendency has been viewed as a lesser evil than incentives to deny beneficial care.

Because pre-cost-containment arrangements seem to embody the virtues of the Unrestricted Ideal Advocate, many physicians may have come to think of them as the form medicine must take if it is to be morally acceptable. Similarly, because current cost-containment measures introduce a concern about resource limitations through incentives which threaten the purity constraints (D) and (E), it is easy for physicians to overgeneralize and to think that any challenge to the Unrestricted Ideal Advocate must undermine the Ideal Advocate. A glance at some history may put this issue in perspective.

3. A HISTORY LESSON

Paul Starr has recently described the rise of the American medical profession from an early period in which the medical profession lacked the cultural authority and power it now enjoys.[1] He shows that physicians did not acquire their cultural power merely because they were "healers" and society has always revered healers. He documents the ways in which physicians resisted "capture" by hospitals and other emerging institutions, because hospitals in the U.S. remained dependent on physicians for referrals. In contrast, in many European countries, physicians were often salaried employees of hospitals from early on. Consequently they too had an interest in undercutting the independence of non-hospital-based physicians. Starr also documents the ways in which physicians and their professional associations and lobbies resisted "capture" by institutions developed to improve access to health care through new financing and insurance schemes. For example, when Medicare and Medicaid were established, physicians retained the power to determine whether they would treat such patients and how many they would treat. They also retained the retrospective, fee-for-service reimbursement scheme that characterized private insurance schemes. If we add to this the control physicians retain over where they locate their practices and what specialties they enter, we arrive at a unique pattern of physician autonomy and power, one that has had a negative effect on access to care for important subgroups in the population.

By exposing the details of the idiosyncratic history that led to this result, Starr shows us that the arrangements we presently have [are] not the result of an "inner logic" or ethical necessity that characterizes the doctor-patient relationship. We should not transform features of the relationships and institutions that result from such a unique historical process into a "nature." We have not stumbled on the *natural form* of the professional-patient relationship. When we see the details of this history, we lose any inclination we might have had to believe that the autonomy and power that has been granted American physicians is based either on the inner necessities of the doctor-patient relationship or on a reasoned social calculation about how to guarantee equitable access to high-quality care at acceptable costs. Rather we see ingenious lobbying by the medical profession, strategic exercises of economic strength, and the effective use of cultural authority. The results have been a series of exasperating political compromises embedded in financing reforms throughout this century. But past political success on this uneven historical battleground is hardly a *justification* of

the institutions which grant and protect the profession's power. Might does not make right, and the peculiarities and vagaries of the historical process undermine claims that it is procedurally fair. Moreover, the very idiosyncrasy of the profession's historical success undercuts claims that "legitimate" expectations would weigh in favor of preserving the status quo.

An important feature of the history Starr documents is the way in which some physicians, we must suppose quite sincerely, made explicitly ethical arguments in favor of the broad institutional powers and authority they sought. Starr cites the code of ethics the AMA adopted in 1934 which claimed it was "unprofessional" for a physician to permit making "a direct profit" from his work: "The making of a profit from medical work is beneath the dignity of professional practice, is unfair competition with the profession at large, is harmful alike to the profession of medicine and the welfare of the people, and is against sound public policy."[2] As Starr points out, it was unprofessional only for someone *other* than a doctor to make a profit from a physician's work. It was acceptable, however, for another doctor to make such a profit! How exquisitely refined this principle of professional ethics is! The first of ten principles for medical service adopted by the AMA in 1934 (current codes are less explicit about converting economic considerations into ethical ones) says that "All features of medical service in any method of medical practice should be under the control of the medical profession." The fifth claimed that the "medical profession alone can determine the adequacy and character" of the institutions involved in medical care, which should be construed as "but expansions of the equipment of the physician."[3] Starr notes that "the doctors took professional authority, patient confidentiality, and free choice to require a specific set of economic relations." For example, "However the cost of medical service may be distributed . . . the immediate cost should be borne by the patient if able to pay at the time the service is rendered."[4] Thus, as Starr concludes, "the AMA insisted that all health insurance plans accept the private physician's monopoly control of the medical market and complete authority over all aspects of medical institutions,"[5] and it did so by deriving these controls from its view of professional ethics.

Of course the fact that physicians later embraced many of the institutional arrangements which they earlier thought unethical does not mean they were morally inconsistent. Rather it suggests that their moral concerns about some features of the doctor-patient relationship had led them to make false claims about ethically acceptable institutional arrangements. Obviously, this is a pattern of which we must be wary. (I am not even considering the more cynical view that all these moral concerns are secondary to economic interests and are appealed to only to disguise bald self-interest; Starr is less generous.)

Let me summarize the argument I have been making in this historical section. First, the kinds of control physicians have in our society over whom they will treat, where they will locate, what they will specialize in, as well as the autonomy they retain within largely retrospective fee-for-service reimbursement schemes — this autonomy and power of physicians is the result of a very particular, even idiosyncratic series of historical events. When we examine the power struggles that yielded physicians these results, we find no evidence that the institutional arrangements were the product of a social consensus in which all parties agreed that the Ideal Advocate model necessitated such full-blown autonomy and powers. Second, at points in that history, some physicians sincerely believed that Ideal Advocacy did require that particular institutional arrangements be established and others opposed. Physicians later embraced institutions which they had earlier thought ethically unacceptable, suggesting that Ideal Advocacy had fewer implications for institutional arrangements than physicians had previously believed. Third, in view of this history, we should be very careful not to assume that important, morally desirable features of medical decision-making can be preserved only if we maintain the institutional arrangements with which we are familiar. These arrangements are not necessarily the historical product of respect for that moral core of the doctor-patient relationship. They have, if Starr is right, a less respectable birthright.

This history lesson brings me to a central claim. The shape of professional relationships, and thus the scope and content of professional ethics, should depend on what kinds of institutions are needed to guarantee the just distribution of the goods provided by those relationships. It is justice that should be primary here, as should other general moral principles, and professional ethics should govern roles circumscribed by just institutions. Professional ethics should not be the tail that

wags the dog. Ludicrous professional codes, such as the 1934 AMA principles, are but an extreme result of reversing priorities in this way.

4. JUSTICE AND IDEAL ADVOCACY

To see how the ethic of agency and the Ideal Advocate model can fit within a just health care system, we must consider what justice requires. As we shall see, justice will require that we abandon the Unrestricted Ideal Advocate in favor of a more modest Ideal Advocate. I have provided elsewhere a detailed account of what a just health care system might look like.[6] Here I shall offer but a brief summary of that argument.

We can begin with the question, Is health care 'special'? Should we distinguish it from other goods, say video recorders, because of its special moral importance? And does that moral importance mean there are social obligations to distribute it in particular ways, ways which might not coincide with the results of market distribution? I believe the answer to all these questions is "yes".

Health care — I mean the term quite broadly — does many important things for people. Some extends lives, some reduces pain and suffering, some merely gives important information about one's condition. I have argued that a central, unifying function of health care is to maintain and restore functional organization, let us say 'functioning', that is typical or normal for our species. This central function of health care derives its moral importance from the following fact: normal functioning has a central effect on the opportunity open to an individual. More specifically, an individual's fair share of the normal opportunity range for his society is impaired when disease or disability impairs normal functioning. I believe this means there are social obligations to provide health care services that protect and restore normal functioning. In short, the principle of justice that should govern the design of health care institutions is a principle that calls for guaranteeing fair equality of opportunity.

This principle of justice has implications for access and resource allocation. It implies that there should be no financial, geographical or discriminatory barriers to a level of care which promotes normal functioning. It also implies that resources [should] be allocated in ways that are effective in promoting normal functioning. That is, we can use the effect on normal opportunity range as a crude way of ranking the moral importance of health care services. This does not mean that any technology which might have a positive impact on normal functioning for some individuals should be introduced: we must weigh new technologies against alternatives to judge the overall impact of introducing them on fair equality of opportunity—this gives a slightly new sense to the term 'opportunity cost'. The point is that social obligations to provide just health care must be met within the conditions of moderate scarcity that we face. This approach is not one which gives individuals a basic right to have all their health care needs met. Rather, there is a social obligation to provide individuals only with those services which are part of the design of a system that on the whole protects equal opportunity.

This view has implications for the autonomy and powers we might grant physicians. Specifically, institutions must give providers incentives that yield equitable access to care. This may mean restricting some of the powers now held by providers to choose whom they are willing to treat, what specialties they will enter, and where they will locate. These restrictions need violate no fundamental liberties of providers, though realistic options open to individual providers might be dramatically different from those enjoyed under current incentives. Similarly, providers will find themselves in a framework that restricts the resources that may be devoted to treating certain conditions in order that a more equitable distribution of resources overall results. There will be some things that providers cannot do for their patients—providers will not be able to be the unrestricted advocates of their patients, but will have to do the best they can for them under the restrictions that exist in the system.[7]

What is crucial to understand about these restrictions on the Ideal Advocate is their underlying justification. Under conditions of moderate resource scarcity, there will be some things we cannot do for certain classes of patients because doing them would mean we would not be able to meet the requirements of justice regarding other classes of patients. Notice that there are two central features underlying these kinds of rationing decisions. First, weighing the opportunity cost of one class of treatments or technologies against another must take place in a *closed* system. When beneficial care is denied it must be because the resources will be better used elsewhere in the system. Second, principles of justice must govern the decisions about priorities within this closed system—and thus define what counts as "better" uses of services. Thus, the just distribution of health care resources implies that we cannot implement the Unrestricted Ideal Advocate model. Rather, we can now state how the Ideal Advocate model must be qualified: physicians should be the advocates of their patients, abiding by the ethic of agency, within the limits imposed by just resource allocation. The physician as Ideal Advocate cannot do things which would be unfair or unjust to other patients. This is the sense in which justice is primary, or provides the framework within which professional ethics can be elaborated.

Stringent—but just—rationing schemes need not threaten the ethic of advocacy. The purity constraint (D), which requires clinical decisions to be free from consideration of the physician's interests, is perfectly compatible with the just rationing of limited health care resources. British physicians, for example, who deny beneficial care that may be available to patients in the United States, do not do so because of any economic incentives that directly reward them for denying care.[8] It is possible to construct institutions in which physicians pursue their patients' best interests and respect fair resource limitations without their incentive for denying care deriving from economic incentives to them.

Similarly, a physician need not violate the constraint (E) that he avoid judgments about a patient's worth. Judgments about the just distribution of health care resources must be social and public ones. For example, the fair equality of opportunity principle I described might require us to forego treatments or technologies which consume resources more effectively used elsewhere to protect opportunity. But this principled social decision does not involve the physician in making any judgments of social worth. The physician acts as a "gatekeeper," but he is abiding by a just social decision, not his own determination that it is not worth the resources to treat a particular class of patients in a particular way. Physicians can still do the best they can for their patients within the limits imposed by justice, which is all that constraints (D) and (E) require.

We can now better see why American cost-containment measures have seemed so threatening to the idea that a physician must be the advocate for his patients. Constraints on physician autonomy embodied within current cost-restraint measures carry with them no such justification grounded in requirements of justice. In the United States, there is no assurance that when a patient is required to forego beneficial treatment, say a needed day in the hospital beyond the DRG [Diagnosis Related

Group] standard, the saving in resources works to the advantage of other patients whom justice requires we treat instead. Rather, services that might well benefit one patient are foregone simply because it is not profitable to treat him compared to another, and the system of incentives has no principle guiding it other than the intention of reducing 'unnecessary' services. Indeed, decisions about the dissemination of new technologies are made without the system being closed at all: opportunity costs are not considered at all, let alone by reference to a principle of justice.

The Ideal Advocate who plays the role of "gatekeeper" in a just system can nevertheless reassure himself that his denials of care are *fair.* It is because this reassurance is most definitely lacking for the U.S. physician under existing cost-containment schemes that we hear the complaints my friend expressed. When he denies beneficial care, the American physician can be rather sure that the savings will not go to more urgently needed care elsewhere in the system. He may know, for example, the savings will be returned to investors for a for-profit hospital or be consumed elsewhere in a hospital budget which has never been examined to see what implicit assumptions about health care priorities govern it. To be compelled to play the role of "gatekeeper" under these circumstances may interfere with Ideal Advocacy in a morally unacceptable way. In the long run it can erode patient confidence that physicians will act as their advocates or agents. My physician friend was right to feel threatened by cost-containment measures with such implications.

5. A PALLIATIVE FOR COST-CONSTRAINTS?

The problem with current cost-containment measures is that they are not part of an overall effort to make the U.S. health care system more just. They compromise the physician, who must deny beneficial care for reasons other than those imposed by justice. The measures fail to preserve important features of the Ideal Advocate model, especially the purity constraints on clinical decisions. These are serious flaws, and only quite basic reforms — drastic reconstructive surgery — could eliminate them. Contrary to what many physicians believe, we would have to undertake more, not less, extensive planning within our health care system, and we would have to do so with a commitment to justice. In the current political climate, no one seems

ready to finance such measures, yet nothing short of them can let us preserve the Ideal Advocate model and face resource scarcity at the same time.

Since I am loathe to suggest a band-aid or palliative when only major interventions will produce real reform, I hesitate to advance the following suggestion. Nevertheless, one feature of the current situation that clearly exacerbates it is that physicians have no public way of resisting pressures to deny beneficial care. They have no way to appeal what they take to be unacceptable pressures in particular cases. Physicians — and other medical personnel — need some hearing board to which they can appeal against hospital policies and third-party restrictions. It is not clear what form such a board should take, but perhaps some expanded role for hospital ethics committees is in order. Instead of merely approving plug-pulling, they might consider the ethical issues involved in decision-making under cost-constraints. This would provide a broader, more public forum in which disputes between physicians and hospital administrators might be aired. It might also provide a setting in which evidence about the effects of the cost-constraints can be gathered — effects on access and quality of care, not just on costs.

Such appeals to ethics committees are costly and may be time-consuming. And it is difficult to imagine many hospitals surrendering authority over policies to such committees. Indeed, only about 10% of all hospitals have such committees at all. In contrast, it is easy to imagine physicians trying to do quiet end-runs around the cost-constraints instead, even if it involves some compromise to integrity. But some way of protecting the physician — and ultimately the patient — against policies which are aimed at profit, not fair allocation, is definitely in order. Such boards might give us a way to monitor the cost-containment process, but they are no substitute for careful research into effects on access to care and quality of care. Unfortunately, the government which was so quick to install DRGs — without full consideration of them — has taken only small steps to measure their real effects. Funding for this research is hard to come by.

I think there is another argument for establishing a mechanism for this type of review. The measures we have so far encountered may be mild compared to what we may encounter next — especially if there is no defined forum for appeal against what we already have. I am particularly concerned that our halfway measures in the direction of cost-containment will be seen as typical failures of "regulation" and that there will be a further push to make the health care market more competitive and entrepreneurial. This would only postpone facing the problem of rationing equitably in the face of resource limitations. Hearing boards might thus offer some preventive effects. In any case, they provide another context in which the physician can attempt to abide by the Ideal Advocate model, and this may slow the erosion of physician commitment to important moral ideals.

Acknowledgment: Research for this paper was funded by grants from the National Endowment for the Humanities Basic Research Program and the Retirement Research Foundation. I am indebted to David Ozar for editorially carving this paper out of a much longer take, "Are Physicians Treating Patients Too Well?" delivered at the Loyola-Strich School of Medicine, Loyola University of Chicago, April, 1985.

NOTES

1. Paul Starr, *Social Transformation of American Medicine* (New York: Basic Books, 1982). Material in this section draws on my review of Starr's book, "Understanding Physician Power," *Philosophy and Public Affairs* 13:4, pp. 347–357.

2. Starr, *Social Transformation*, p. 216.

3. Starr, *Social Transformation*, p. 299.

4. Starr, *Social Transformation*, p. 300.

5. Starr, *Social Transformation*, p. 300.

6. Norman Daniels, *Just Health Care* (New York: Cambridge University Press, 1985).

7. For further discussion of the relationship between provider liberties and the requirements of justice, see my *Just Health Care*, Ch. 6.

8. See my "Why Saying 'No' to Patients in the United States Is So Hard," *New England Journal of Medicine* 314 (May 22, 1986), [1380–1383]; also see Henry Aaron and William Schwartz, *The Painful Prescription* (Washington: Brookings Institution, 1984).

Patients' Rights and Responsibilities

AMERICAN HOSPITAL ASSOCIATION

A Patient's Bill of Rights (1992)

INTRODUCTION

Effective health care requires collaboration between patients and physicians and other health care professionals. Open and honest communication, respect for personal and professional values, and sensitivity to differences are integral to optimal patient care. As the setting for the provision of health services, hospitals must provide a foundation for understanding and respecting the rights and responsibilities of patients, their families, physicians, and other caregivers. Hospitals must ensure a health care ethic that respects the role of patients in decision making about treatment choices and other aspects of their care. Hospitals must be sensitive to cultural, racial, linguistic, religious, age, gender, and other differences as well as the needs of persons with disabilities.

The American Hospital Association presents A Patient's Bill of Rights with the expectation that it will contribute to more effective patient care and be supported by the hospital on behalf of the institution, its medical staff, employees, and patients. The American Hospital Association encourages health care institutions to tailor this bill of rights to their patient community by translating and/or simplifying the language of this bill of rights as may be necessary to ensure that patients and their families understand their rights and responsibilities.

BILL OF RIGHTS

These rights can be exercised on the patient's behalf by a designated surrogate or proxy decision maker if the patient lacks decision-making capacity, is legally incompetent, or is a minor.

1. The patient has the right to considerate and respectful care.
2. The patient has the right to and is encouraged to obtain from physicians and other direct caregivers relevant, current, and understandable information concerning diagnosis, treatment, and prognosis.

    Except in emergencies when the patient lacks decision-making capacity and the need for treatment is urgent, the patient is entitled to the opportunity to discuss and request information related to the specific procedures and/or treatments, the risks involved, the possible length of recuperation, and the medically reasonable alternatives and their accompanying risks and benefits.

    Patients have the right to know the identity of physicians, nurses, and others involved in their care, as well as when those involved are students, residents, or other trainees. The patient also has the right to know the immediate and long-term financial implications of treatment choices, insofar as they are known.
3. The patient has the right to make decisions about the plan of care prior to and during the course of treatment and to refuse a recommended treatment or plan of care to the extent permitted by law and hospital policy and to be informed of the medical consequences of this action. In case of such refusal, the patient is entitled to other appropriate care and services that the hospital provides or transfer to another hospital. The hospital should notify patients of any policy that might affect patient choice within the institution.
4. The patient has the right to have an advance directive (such as a living will, health care proxy, or durable power of attorney for health care) concerning treatment or designating a surrogate decision maker with the expectation that the hospital will honor the intent of that directive to the extent permitted by law and hospital policy.

    Health care institutions must advise patients of their rights under state law and hospital policy to make informed medical choices, ask if the patient has an advance directive, and include that information in patient records. The patient has the right to timely information about hospital policy that may limit its ability to implement fully a legally valid advance directive.
5. The patient has the right to every consideration of privacy. Case discussion, consultation, examination, and treatment should be conducted so as to protect each patient's privacy.
6. The patient has the right to expect that all communications and records pertaining to his/her care will be treated as confidential by the hospital, except in cases such as suspected abuse and public health hazards when reporting is permitted or required by law. The patient has the right to expect that the hospital will emphasize the confidentiality of this information when it releases it to any other parties entitled to review information in these records.
7. The patient has the right to review records pertaining to his/her medical care and to have the information explained or interpreted as necessary, except when restricted by law.
8. The patient has the right to expect that, within its capacity and policies, a hospital will make reasonable response to the request of a patient for appropriate and medically indicated care and services. The hospital must provide evaluation, service, and/or referral as indicated by the urgency of the case. When medically appropriate and legally permissible, or when a patient has so requested, a patient may be transferred to another facility. The institution to which the patient is to be transferred must first have accepted the patient for transfer. The patient must also have the benefit of complete information and explanation concerning the need for, risks, benefits, and alternatives to such a transfer.
9. The patient has the right to ask and be informed of the existence of business relationships among the hospital, educational institutions, other health care providers, or payers that may influence the patient's treatment and care.

10. The patient has the right to consent to or decline to participate in proposed research studies or human experimentation affecting care and treatment or requiring direct patient involvement, and to have those studies fully explained prior to consent. A patient who declines to participate in research or experimentation is entitled to the most effective care that the hospital can otherwise provide.

11. The patient has the right to expect reasonable continuity of care when appropriate and to be informed by physicians and other caregivers of available and realistic patient care options when hospital care is no longer appropriate.

12. The patient has the right to be informed of hospital policies and practices that relate to patient care, treatment, and responsibilities. The patient has the right to be informed of available resources for resolving disputes, grievances, and conflicts, such as ethics committees, patient representatives, or other mechanisms available in the institution. The patient has the right to be informed of the hospital's charges for services and available payment methods.

The collaborative nature of health care requires that patients, or their families/surrogates, participate in their care. The effectiveness of care and patient satisfaction with the course of treatment depend, in part, on the patient fulfilling certain responsibilities. Patients are responsible for providing information about past illnesses, hospitalizations, medications, and other matters related to health status. To participate effectively in decision making, patients must be encouraged to take responsibility for requesting additional information or clarification about their health status or treatment when they do not fully understand information and instructions. Patients are also responsible for ensuring that the health care institution has a copy of their written advance directive if they have one. Patients are responsible for informing their physicians and other caregivers if they anticipate problems in following prescribed treatment.

Patients should also be aware of the hospital's obligation to be reasonably efficient and equitable in providing care to other patients and the community. The hospital's rules and regulations are designed to help the hospital meet this obligation. Patients and their families are responsible for making reasonable accommodations to the needs of the hospital, other patients, medical staff, and hospital employees. Patients are responsible for providing necessary information for insurance claims and for working with the hospital to make payment arrangements, when necessary.

A person's health depends on much more than health care services. Patients are responsible for recognizing the impact of their life-style on their personal health.

CONCLUSION

Hospitals have many functions to perform, including the enhancement of health status, health promotion, and the prevention and treatment of injury and disease; the immediate and ongoing care and rehabilitation of patients; the education of health professionals, patients, and the community; and research. All these activities must be conducted with an overriding concern for the values and dignity of patients.

PRESIDENT'S ADVISORY COMMISSION ON CONSUMER PROTECTION AND QUALITY IN THE HEALTH CARE INDUSTRY

Consumer Bill of Rights and Responsibilities (1997)

1. INFORMATION DISCLOSURE

Consumers have the right to receive accurate, easily understood information, and some consumers require assistance in making informed health care decisions about their health plans, professionals and facilities.

•   •   •

2. CHOICE OF PROVIDERS AND PLANS

Consumers have the right to a choice of health care providers that is sufficient to ensure access to appropriate high-quality health care. . . . [P]ublic and private group purchasers should, wherever feasible, offer consumers a choice of high-quality health insurance plans.

•   •   •

3. ACCESS TO EMERGENCY SERVICES

Consumers have the right to access emergency health care services when and where the need arises. Health plans should provide payment when a consumer presents to an emergency department with acute symptoms of sufficient severity—including severe pain—such that a "prudent layperson" could reasonably expect the absence of medical attention to result in placing that

World Wide Web source: http://www.hcqualitycommission.gov. Also available in The President's Advisory Commission on Consumer Protection and Quality in the Health Care Industry, *Quality First: Better Health Care for All Americans* (Washington, DC: U.S. Government Printing Office, 1998), Appendix A, pp. A–5 to A–12.

consumer's health in serious jeopardy, serious impairment to bodily functions, or serious dysfunction of any bodily organ or part.

•   •   •

4. PARTICIPATION IN TREATMENT DECISIONS

Consumers have the right and responsibility to fully participate in all decisions related to their health care. Consumers who are unable to fully participate in treatment decisions have the right to be represented by parents, guardians, family members, or other conservators.

•   •   •

5. RESPECT AND NONDISCRIMINATION

Consumers have the right to considerate, respectful care from all members of the health care industry at all times and under all circumstances. An environment of mutual respect is essential to maintain a quality health care system.

Consumers must not be discriminated against in the delivery of health care services consistent with the benefits covered in their policy, or as required by law, based on race, ethnicity, national origin, religion, sex, age, mental or physical disability, sexual orientation, genetic information, or source of payment.

Consumers eligible for coverage under the terms and conditions of a health plan or program, or as required by law, must not be discriminated against in marketing and enrollment practices based on race, ethnicity, national origin, religion, sex, age, mental or physical disability, sexual orientation, genetic information, or source of payment.

• • •

6. CONFIDENTIALITY OF HEALTH INFORMATION

Consumers have the right to communicate with health care providers in confidence and to have the confidentiality of their individually identifiable health care information protected. Consumers also have the right to review and copy their own medical records and request amendments to their records.

• • •

7. COMPLAINTS AND APPEALS

Consumers have the right to a fair and efficient process for resolving differences with their health plans, health care providers, and the institutions that serve them, including a rigorous system of internal review and an independent system of external review.

• • •

8. CONSUMER RESPONSIBILITIES

In a health care system that protects consumers' rights, it is reasonable to expect and encourage consumers to assume reasonable responsibilities. Greater individual involvement by consumers in their care increases the likelihood of achieving the best outcomes and helps support a quality improvement, cost-conscious environment. Such responsibilities include:

- Take responsibility for maximizing health habits, such as exercising, not smoking, and eating a healthy diet.

- Work collaboratively with health care providers in developing and carrying out agreed-upon treatment plans.
- Disclose relevant information and clearly communicate wants and needs.
- Use the health plan's internal complaint and appeal processes to address concerns that may arise.
- Avoid knowingly spreading disease.
- Recognize the reality of risks and limits of the science of medical care and the human fallibility of the health care professional.
- Be aware of a health care provider's obligation to be reasonably efficient and equitable in providing care to other patients and the community.
- Become knowledgeable about their health plan coverage and health plan options (when available) including all covered benefits, limitations, and exclusions, rules regarding use of network providers, coverage and referral rules, appropriate processes to secure additional information, and the process to appeal coverage decisions.
- Show respect for other patients and health workers.
- Make a good-faith effort to meet financial obligations.
- Abide by administrative and operational procedures of health plans, health care providers, and government health benefit programs.
- Report wrongdoing and fraud to appropriate resources or legal authorities.

• • •

COUNCIL OF EUROPE

Convention for Protection of Human Rights and Dignity of the Human Being with Regard to the Application of Biology and Biomedicine: Convention on Human Rights and Biomedicine (1997)

PREAMBLE

The Member States of the Council of Europe, the other States and the European Community signatories hereto,

Bearing in mind the Universal Declaration of Human Rights proclaimed by the General Assembly of the United Nations on 10 December 1948;

Bearing in mind the Convention for the Protection of Human Rights and Fundamental Freedoms of 4 November 1950;

Bearing in mind the European Social Charter of 18 October 1961;

Bearing in mind the International Covenant on Civil and Political Rights and the International Covenant on Economic, Social and Cultural Rights of 16 December 1966;

Bearing in mind the Convention for the Protection of Individuals with Regard to Automatic Processing of Personal Data of 28 January 1981;

Bearing also in mind the Convention on the Rights of the Child of 20 November 1989;

Considering that the aim of the Council of Europe is the achievement of a greater unity between its members and that one of the methods by which that aim is to be pursued is the maintenance and further realisation of human rights and fundamental freedoms;

Conscious of the accelerating developments in biology and medicine;

Convinced of the need to respect the human being both as an individual and as a member of the human species and recognising the importance of ensuring the dignity of the human being;

Conscious that the misuse of biology and medicine may lead to acts endangering human dignity;

Affirming that progress in biology and medicine should be used for the benefit of present and future generations;

Stressing the need for international co-operation so that all humanity may enjoy the benefits of biology and medicine;

Recognising the importance of promoting a public debate on the questions posed by the application of biology and medicine and the responses to be given thereto;

Wishing to remind all members of society of their rights and responsibilities;

Taking account of the work of the Parliamentary Assembly in this field, including Recommendation 1160 (1991) on the preparation of a Convention on bioethics;

Resolving to take such measures as are necessary to safeguard human dignity and the fundamental rights and freedoms of the individual with regard to the application of biology and medicine;

Have agreed as follows:

CHAPTER 1   GENERAL PROVISIONS

Article 1. (Purpose and object)

Parties to this Convention shall protect the dignity and identity of all human beings and guarantee everyone, without discrimination, respect for their integrity and other rights and fundamental freedoms with regard to the application of biology and medicine.

From *Kennedy Institute of Ethics Journal* 7(1997), 277–290. The part of the Convention reprinted here appears on pp. 277–285.

Each Party shall take in its internal law the necessary measures to give effect to the provisions of this Convention.

Article 2. (Primacy of the human being)

The interests and welfare of the human being shall prevail over the sole interest of society or science.

Article 3. (Equitable access to health care)

Parties, taking into account health needs and available resources, shall take appropriate measures with a view to providing, within their jurisdiction, equitable access to health care of appropriate quality.

Article 4. (Professional standards)

Any intervention in the health field, including research, must be carried out in accordance with relevant professional obligations and standards.

CHAPTER II   CONSENT

Article 5. (General rule)

An intervention in the health field may only be carried out after the person concerned has given free and informed consent to it.

This person shall beforehand be given appropriate information as to the purpose and nature of the intervention as well as on its consequences and risks.

The person concerned may freely withdraw consent at any time.

Article 6. (Protection of persons not able to consent).

1. Subject to Articles 17 and 20 below, an intervention may only be carried out on a person who does not have the capacity to consent, for his or her direct benefit.

2. Where, according to law, a minor does not have the capacity to consent to an intervention, the intervention may only be carried out with the authorisation of his or her representative or an authority or a person or body provided for by law.

The opinion of the minor shall be taken into consideration as an increasingly determining factor in proportion to his or her age and degree of maturity.

3. Where, according to law, an adult does not have the capacity to consent to an intervention because of a mental disability, a disease or for similar reasons, the intervention may only be carried out with the authori-

sation of his or her representative or an authority or a person or body provided for by law.

The individual concerned shall as far as possible take part in the authorisation procedure.

4. The representative, the authority, the person or the body mentioned in paragraphs 2 and 3 above shall be given, under the same conditions, the information referred to in Article 5.

5. The authorisation referred to in paragraphs 2 and 3 above may be withdrawn at any time in the best interests of the person concerned.

Article 7. (Protection of persons who have mental disorder)

Subject to protective conditions prescribed by law, including supervisory, control and appeal procedures, a person who has a mental disorder of a serious nature may be subjected, without his or her consent, to an intervention aimed at treating his or her mental disorder only where, without such treatment, serious harm is likely to result to his or health.

Article 8. (Emergency situation)

When because of an emergency situation the appropriate consent cannot be obtained, any medically necessary intervention may be carried out immediately for the benefit of the health of the individual concerned.

Article 9. (Previously expressed wishes)

The previously expressed wishes relating to a medical intervention by a patient who is not, at the time of the intervention, in a state to express his or her wishes shall be taken into account.

CHAPTER III   PRIVATE LIFE
AND RIGHT TO INFORMATION

Article 10. (Private life and right to information)

1. Everyone has the right to respect for private life in relation to information about his or her health.

2. Everyone is entitled to know any information collected about his or her health. However, the wishes of individuals not to be so informed shall be observed.

3. In exceptional cases, restrictions may be placed by law on the exercise of the rights contained in paragraph 2 in the interests of the patient.

CHAPTER IV   HUMAN GENOME

Article 11. (Non-discrimination)

Any form of discrimination against a person on grounds of his or her genetic heritage is prohibited.

Article 12. (Predictive genetic tests)

Tests which are predictive of genetic diseases or which serve either to identify the subject as a carrier of a gene responsible for a disease or to detect a genetic predisposition or susceptibility to a disease may be performed only for health purposes or for scientific research linked to health purposes, and subject to appropriate genetic counselling.

Article 13. (Interventions on the human genome)

An intervention seeking to modify the human genome may only be undertaken for preventive, diagnostic or therapeutic purposes and only if its aim is not to introduce any modification in the genome of any descendants.

Article 14. (Non-selection of sex)

The use of techniques of medically assisted procreation shall not be allowed for the purpose of choosing a future child's sex, except where serious hereditary sex-related disease is to be avoided.

CHAPTER V   SCIENTIFIC RESEARCH

Article 15. (General rule)

Scientific research in the field of biology and medicine shall be carried out freely, subject to the provisions of this Convention and the other legal provisions ensuring the protection of the human being.

Article 16. (Protection of persons undergoing research)

Research on a person may only be undertaken if all the following conditions are met:

  i. there is no alternative of comparable effectiveness to research on humans,
  ii. the risks which may be incurred by that person are not disproportionate to the potential benefits of the research,
  iii. the research project has been approved by the competent body after independent examination of its scientific merit, including assessment of the importance of the aim of the research, and multidisciplinary review of its ethical acceptability,
  iv. the persons undergoing research have been informed of their rights and the safeguards prescribed by law for their protection,
  v. the necessary consent as provided for under Article 5 has been given expressly, specifically and is documented. Such consent may be freely withdrawn at any time.

Article 17. (Protection of persons not able to consent to research)

1. Research on a person without the capacity to consent as stipulated in Article 5 may be undertaken only if all the following conditions are met:

  i. the conditions laid down in Article 16, subparagraphs (i) to (iv), are fulfilled;
  ii. the results of the research have the potential to produce real and direct benefit to his or her health;
  iii. research of comparable effectiveness cannot be carried out on individuals capable of giving consent;
  iv. the necessary authorisation provided for under Article 6 has been given specifically and in writing, and
  v. the person concerned does not object.

2. Exceptionally and under the protective conditions prescribed by law, where the research has not the potential to produce results of direct benefit to the health of the person concerned, such research may be authorised subject to the conditions laid down in paragraph 1, sub-paragraphs (i), (iii), (iv) and (v) above, and to the following additional conditions:

  i. the research has the aim of contributing, through significant improvement in the scientific understanding of the individual's condition, disease or disorder, to the ultimate attainment of results capable of conferring benefit to the person concerned or to other persons in the same age category or afflicted with the same disease or disorder or having the same condition.
  ii. the research entails only minimal risk and minimal burden for the individual concerned.

Article 18. (Research on embryos in vitro)

1. Where the law allows research on embryos in vitro, it shall ensure adequate protection of the embryo.

2. The creation of human embryos for research purposes is prohibited.

CHAPTER VI ORGAN AND TISSUE REMOVAL FROM LIVING DONORS FOR TRANSPLANTATION PURPOSES

Article 19. (General rule)

1. Removal of organs or tissue from a living person for transplantation purposes may be carried out solely for the therapeutic benefit of the recipient and where there is no suitable organ or tissue available from a deceased person and no other alternative therapeutic method of comparable effectiveness.

2. The necessary consent as provided for under Article 5 must have been given expressly and specifically either in written form or before an official body.

Article 20. (Protection of persons not able to consent to organ removal)

1. No organ or tissue removal may be carried out on a person who does not have the capacity to consent under Article 5.

2. Exceptionally and under the protective conditions prescribed by law, the removal of regenerative tissue from a person who does not have the capacity to consent may be authorised provided the following conditions are met:

    i. there is no compatible donor available who has the capacity to consent,
    ii. the recipient is a brother or sister of the donor,
    iii. the donation must have the potential to be life-saving for the recipient,
    iv. the authorisation provided for under paragraphs 2 and 3 of Article 6 has been given specifically and in writing in accordance with the law and with the approval of the competent body,
    v. the potential donor concerned does not object.

CHAPTER VII PROHIBITION OF FINANCIAL GAIN AND DISPOSAL OF A PART OF THE HUMAN BODY

Article 21. (Prohibition of financial gain)

The human body and its parts shall not, as such, give rise to financial gain.

Article 22. (Disposal of a removed part of the human body)

When in the course of an intervention any part of a human body is removed, it may be stored and used for a purpose other than that for which it was removed, only if this is done in conformity with appropriate information and consent procedures.

CHAPTER VIII INFRINGEMENTS OF THE PROVISIONS OF THE CONVENTION

Article 23. (Infringement of the rights or principles)

The parties shall provide appropriate judicial protection to prevent or to put a stop to an unlawful infringement of the rights and principles set forth in this Convention at short notice.

Article 24. (Compensation for undue damage)

The person who has suffered undue damage resulting from an intervention is entitled to fair compensation according to the conditions and procedures prescribed by law.

Article 25. (Sanctions)

Parties shall provide for appropriate sanctions to be applied in the event of infringement of the provisions contained in this Convention.

CHAPTER IX RELATION BETWEEN THIS CONVENTION AND OTHER PROVISIONS

Article 26. (Restrictions on the exercise of the rights)

1. No restrictions shall be placed on the exercise of the rights and protective provisions contained in this Convention other than such as are prescribed by law and are necessary in a democratic society in the interest of public safety, for the prevention of crime, for the protection of public health or for the protection of the rights and freedoms of others.

2. The restrictions contemplated in the preceding paragraph may not be placed on Articles 11, 13, 14, 16, 17, 19, 20 and 21.

Article 27. (Wider protection)

None of the provisions of this Convention shall be interpreted as limiting or otherwise affecting the possibility for a Party to grant a wider measure of protection with regard to the application of biology and medicine than is stipulated in this Convention.

CHAPTER X   PUBLIC DEBATE
Article 28. (Public debate)

Parties to this Convention shall see to it that the fundamental questions raised by the developments of biology and medicine are the subject of appropriate public discussion in the light, in particular, of relevant medical, social, economic, ethical and legal implications, and that their possible application is made the subject of appropriate consultation.

. . .

Professionals and Specific Patient Populations

VANESSA NORTHINGTON GAMBLE

Under the Shadow of Tuskegee: African Americans and Health Care

INTRODUCTION

On May 16, 1997, in a White House ceremony, President Bill Clinton apologized for the Tuskegee Syphilis Study, the 40-year government study (1932 to 1972) in which 399 Black men from Macon County, Alabama, were deliberately denied effective treatment for syphilis in order to document the natural history of the disease[1] "The legacy of the study at Tuskegee," the president remarked, "has reached far and deep, in ways that hurt our progress and divide our nation. We cannot be one America when a whole segment of our nation has no trust in America."[2] The president's comments underscore that in the 25 years since its public disclosure, the study has moved from being a singular historical event to a powerful metaphor. It has come to symbolize racism in medicine, misconduct in human research, the arrogance of physicians, and government abuse of Black people.

The continuing shadow cast by the Tuskegee Syphilis Study on efforts to improve the health status of Black Americans provided an impetus for the campaign for a presidential apology.[3] Numerous articles, in both the professional and popular press, have pointed out that the study predisposed many African Americans to distrust medical and public health authorities and has led to critically low Black participation in clinical trials and organ donation.[4]

The specter of Tuskegee has also been raised with respect to HIV/AIDS prevention and treatment programs. Health education researchers Dr. Stephen B. Thomas and Dr. Sandra Crouse Quinn have written extensively on the impact of the Tuskegee Syphilis Study on these programs.[5] They argue that "the legacy of this experiment, with its failure to educate the study participants and treat them adequately, laid the foundation for today's pervasive sense of black distrust of public health authorities."[6] The syphilis study has also been used to explain why many African Americans oppose needle exchange programs. Needle exchange programs provoke the image of the syphilis study and Black fears about genocide. These programs are not viewed as mechanisms to stop the spread of HIV/AIDS but rather as fodder for the drug epidemic that has devastated so many Black neighborhoods.[7] Fears that they will be used as guinea pigs like the men in the syphilis study have also led some African Americans with AIDS to refuse treatment with protease inhibitors.[8]

Reprinted by permission of the publisher from *American Journal of Public Health* 87 (November 1997), 1774–1778. Copyright © 1997, American Public Health Association.

The Tuskegee Syphilis Study is frequently described as the singular reason behind African-American distrust of the institutions of medicine and public health. Such an interpretation neglects a critical historical point: the mistrust predated public revelations about the Tuskegee study. Furthermore, the narrowness of such a representation places emphasis on a single historical event to explain deeply entrenched and complex attitudes within the Black community. An examination of the syphilis study within a broader historical and social context makes plain that several factors have influenced, and continue to influence, African Americans' attitudes toward the biomedical community.

Black Americans' fears about exploitation by the medical profession date back to the antebellum period and the use of slaves and free Black people as subjects for dissection and medical experimentation.[9] Although physicians also used poor Whites as subjects, they used Black people far more often. During an 1835 trip to the United States, French visitor Harriet Martineau found that Black people lacked the power even to protect the graves of their dead. "In Baltimore the bodies of coloured people exclusively are taken for dissection," she remarked, "because the Whites do not like it, and the coloured people cannot resist."[10] Four years later, abolitionist Theodore Dwight Weld echoed Martineau's sentiment. "Public opinion," he wrote, "would tolerate surgical experiments, operations, processes, performed upon them [slaves], which it would execrate if performed upon their master or other whites."[11] Slaves found themselves as subjects of medical experiments because physicians needed bodies and because the state considered them property and denied them the legal right to refuse to participate.

Two antebellum experiments, one carried out in Georgia and the other in Alabama, illustrate the abuse that some slaves encountered at the hands of physicians. In the first, Georgia physician Thomas Hamilton conducted a series of brutal experiments on a slave to test remedies for heatstroke. The subject of these investigations, Fed, had been loaned to Hamilton as repayment for a debt owed by his owner. Hamilton forced Fed to sit naked on a stool placed on a platform in a pit that had been heated to a high temperature. Only the man's head was above the ground. Over a period of 2 to 3 weeks, Hamilton placed Fed in the pit five or six times and gave him various medications to determine which enabled him best to withstand the heat. Each ordeal ended when Fed fainted and had to be revived. But note that Fed was not the only victim

in this experiment; its whole purpose was to make it possible for masters to force slaves to work still longer hours on the hottest of days.[12]

In the second experiment, Dr. J. Marion Sims, the so-called father of modern gynecology, used three Alabama slave women to develop an operation to repair vesicovaginal fistulas. Between 1845 and 1849, the three slave women on whom Sims operated each underwent up to 30 painful operations. The physician himself described the agony associated with some of the experiments[13]: "The first patient I operated on was Lucy. . . . That was before the days of anaesthetics, and the poor girl, on her knees, bore the operation with great heroism and bravery." This operation was not successful, and Sims later attempted to repair the defect by placing a sponge in the bladder. This experiment, too, ended in failure. He noted:

> The whole urethra and the neck of the bladder were in a high state of inflammation, which came from the foreign substance. It has to come away, and there was nothing to do but to pull it away by main force. Lucy's agony was extreme. She was much prostrated, and I thought that she was going to die; but by irrigating the parts of the bladder she recovered with great rapidity.

Sims finally did perfect his technique and ultimately repaired the fistulas. Only after his experimentation with the slave women proved successful did the physician attempt the procedure, with anesthesia, on White women volunteers.

EXPLOITATION AFTER THE CIVIL WAR

It is not known to what extent African Americans continued to be used as unwilling subjects for experimentation and dissection in the years after emancipation. However, an examination of African-American folklore at the turn of the century makes it clear that Black people believed that such practices persisted. Folktales are replete with references to night doctors, also called student doctors and Ku Klux doctors. . . . According to folk belief, these sinister characters would kidnap Black people, usually at night and in urban areas, and take them to hospitals to be killed and used in experiments. . . .

Reports about the medical exploitation of Black people in the name of medicine after the end of the Civil War were not restricted to the realm of folklore.

Until it was exposed in 1882, a grave robbing ring operated in Philadelphia and provided bodies for the city's medical schools by plundering the graves at a Black cemetery. According to historian David C. Humphrey, southern grave robbers regularly sent bodies of southern Blacks to northern medical schools for use as anatomy cadavers.[14]

During the early 20th century, African-American medical leaders protested the abuse of Black people by the White-dominated medical profession and used their concerns about experimentation to press for the establishment of Black-controlled hospitals.[15] Dr. Daniel Hale Williams, the founder of Chicago's Provident Hospital (1891), the nation's first Black-controlled hospital, contended that White physicians, especially in the South, frequently used Black patients as guinea pigs.[16] Dr. Nathan Francis Mossell, the founder of Philadelphia's Frederick Douglass Memorial Hospital (1895), described the "fears and prejudices" of Black people, especially those from the South, as "almost proverbial." He attributed such attitudes to southern medical practices in which Black people, "when forced to accept hospital attention, got only the poorest care, being placed in inferior wards set apart for them, suffering the brunt of all that is experimental in treatment, and all this is the sequence of their race variety and abject helplessness."[17] The founders of Black hospitals claimed that only Black physicians possessed the skills required to treat Black patients optimally and that Black hospitals provided these patients with the best possible care.[18]

Fears about the exploitation of African Americans by White physicians played a role in the establishment of a Black veterans hospital in Tuskegee, Ala. In 1923, 9 years before the initiation of the Tuskegee Syphilis Study, racial tensions had erupted in the town over control of the hospital. The federal government had pledged that the facility, an institution designed exclusively for Black patients, would be run by a Black professional staff. But many Whites in the area, including members of the Ku Klux Klan, did not want a Black-operated federal facility in the heart of Dixie, even though it would serve only Black people.[19]

Black Americans sought control of the veterans hospital, in part because they believed that the ex-soldiers would receive the best possible care from Black physicians and nurses, who would be more caring and sympathetic to the veterans' needs. Some Black newspapers even warned that White southerners wanted command of the hospital as part of a racist plot to kill and sterilize African-American men and to establish an "experiment station" for mediocre White physicians.[20] Black physicians did eventually gain the right to operate the hospital, yet this did not stop the hospital from becoming an experiment station for Black men. The veterans hospital was one of the facilities used by the United States Public Health Service in the syphilis study.

During the 1920s and 1930s, Black physicians pushed for additional measures that would battle medical racism and advance their professional needs. Dr. Charles Garvin, a prominent Cleveland physician and a member of the editorial board of the Black medical publication *The Journal of the National Medical Association,* urged his colleagues to engage in research in order to protect Black patients. He called for more research on diseases such as tuberculosis and pellagra that allegedly affected African Americans disproportionately or idiosyncratically. Garvin insisted that Black physicians investigate these racial diseases because "heretofore in literature, as in medicine, the Negro has been written about, exploited and experimented upon sometimes not to his physical betterment or to the advancement of science, but the advancement of the Nordic investigator." Moreover, he charged that "in the past, men of other races have for the large part interpreted our diseases, often tinctured with inborn prejudices."[21]

FEARS OF GENOCIDE

These historical examples clearly demonstrate that African Americans' distrust of the medical profession has a longer history than the public revelations of the Tuskegee Syphilis Study. There is a collective memory among African Americans about their exploitation by the medical establishment. The Tuskegee Syphilis Study has emerged as the most prominent example of medical racism because it confirms, if not authenticates, long-held and deeply entrenched beliefs with the Black community. To be sure, the Tuskegee Syphilis Study does cast a long shadow. After the study had been exposed, charges surfaced that the experiment was part of a governmental plot to exterminate Black people.[22] Many Black people agreed with the charge that the study represented "nothing less than an official, premeditated policy of genocide."[23] Furthermore, this was not the first or last time that allegations of genocide have been launched against the government and the medical profession. The sickle cell anemia screening programs of the 1970s and birth control programs have also provoked such allegations.[24]

In recent years, links have been made between Tuskegee, AIDS, and genocide. In September 1990, the article "AIDS: Is It Genocide?" appeared in *Essence,* A Black woman's magazine. The author noted: "As an increasing number of African-Americans continue to sicken and die and as no cure for AIDS has been found some of us are beginning to think the unthinkable: Could AIDS be a virus that was manufactured to erase large numbers of us? Are they trying to kill us with this disease?"[25] In other words, some members of the Black community see AIDS as part of a conspiracy to exterminate African Americans.

Beliefs about the connection between AIDS and the purposeful destruction of African Americans should not be cavalierly dismissed as bizarre and paranoid. They are held by a significant number of Black people. For example, a 1990 survey conducted by the Southern Christian Leadership Conference found that 35% of the 1056 Black church members who responded believed that AIDS was a form of genocide.[26] A *New York Times*/WCBS TV News poll conducted the same year found that 10% of Black Americans thought that the AIDS virus had been created in a laboratory in order to infect Black people. Another 20% believed that it could be true.[27] . . .

Folklorist Patricia A. Turner, in her book *I Heard It through the Grapevine: Rumor and Resistance in African-American Culture,* underscores why it is important not to ridicule but to pay attention to these strongly held theories abut genocide.[28] She argues that these rumors reveal much about what African Americans believe to be the state of their lives in this country. She contends that such views reflect Black beliefs that White Americans have historically been, and continue to be, ambivalent and perhaps hostile to the existence of Black people. Consequently, African-American attitudes toward biomedical research are not influenced solely by the Tuskegee Syphilis Study. African Americans' opinions about the value White society has attached to their lives should not be discounted. As Reverend Floyd Tompkins of Stanford University Memorial Church has said, "There is a sense in our community, and I think it shall be proved out, that if you are poor or you're a person of color, you were the guinea pig, and you continue to be the guinea pigs, and there is the fundamental belief that Black life is not valued like White life or like any other life in America."[29]

NOT JUST PARANOIA

Lorene Cary, in a cogent essay in *Newsweek,* expands on Reverend Tompkins' point. In an essay titled "Why It's Not Just Paranoia," she writes:

We Americans continue to value the lives and humanity of some groups more than the lives and humanity of others. That is not paranoia. It is our historical legacy and a present fact; it influences domestic and foreign policy and the daily interaction of millions of Americans. It influences the way we spend our public money and explains how we can read the staggering statistics on Black Americans' infant mortality, youth mortality, mortality in middle and old age, and not be moved to action.[30]

African Americans' beliefs that their lives are devalued by White society also influence their relationships with the medical profession. They perceive, at times correctly, that they are treated differently in the health care system solely because of their race, and such perceptions fuel mistrust of the medical profession. For example, a national telephone survey conducted in 1986 revealed that African Americans were more likely than Whites to report that their physicians did not inquire sufficiently about their pain, did not tell them how long it would take for prescribed medicine to work, did not explain the seriousness of their illness or injury, and did not discuss test and examination findings.[31] A 1994 study published in the *American Journal of Public Health* found that physicians were less likely to give pregnant Black women information about the hazards of smoking and drinking during pregnancy.[32]

The powerful legacy of the Tuskegee Syphilis Study endures, in part, because the racism and disrespect for Black lives that it entailed mirror Black people's contemporary experiences with the medical profession. The anger and frustration that many African Americans feel when they encounter the health care system can be heard in the words of Alicia Georges, a professor of nursing at Lehman College and a former president of the National Black Nurses Association, as she recalled an emergency room experience. "Back a few years ago, I was having excruciating abdominal pain, and I wound up at a hospital in my area," she recalled. "The first thing that they began to ask me was how many sexual partners I'd had. I was married and owned my own house. But immediately, in looking at me, they said,

'Oh, she just has pelvic inflammatory disease.'"[33] Perhaps because of her nursing background, Georges recognized the implications of the questioning. She had come face to face with the stereotype of Black women as sexually promiscuous. Similarly, the following story from the *Los Angeles Times* shows how racism can affect the practice of medicine:

When Althea Alexander broke her arm, the attending resident at Los Angeles County–USC Medical Center told her to "hold your arm like you usually hold your can of beer on Saturday night." Alexander who is Black, exploded. "What are you talking about? Do you think I'm a welfare mother?" The White resident shrugged: "Well aren't you?" Turned out she was an administrator at USC medical school.

This example graphically illustrates that health care providers are not immune to the beliefs and misconceptions of the wider community. They carry with them stereotypes about various groups of people.[34]

BEYOND TUSKEGEE

There is also a growing body of medical research that vividly illustrates why discussions of the relationship of African Americans and the medical profession must go beyond the Tuskegee Syphilis Study. These studies demonstrate racial inequities in access to particular technologies and raise critical questions about the role of racism in medical decision making. For example, in 1989 *The Journal of the American Medical Association* published a report that demonstrated racial inequities in the treatment of heart disease. In this study, White and Black patients had similar rates of hospitalization for chest pain, but the White patients were one third more likely to undergo coronary angiography and more than twice as likely to be treated by bypass surgery or angioplasty. The racial disparities persisted even after adjustments were made for differences in income.[35] Three years later, another study appearing in that journal reinforced these findings. It revealed that older Black patients on Medicare received coronary artery bypass grafts only about a fourth as often as comparable White patients. Disparities were greatest in the rural South, where White patients had the surgery seven times as often as Black patients. Medical factors did not fully explain the differences. This study suggests that an already-existing national health insurance program does not solve the access problems

of African Americans.[36] Additional studies have confirmed the persistence of such inequities.[37]

Why the racial disparities? Possible explanations include health problems that precluded the use of procedures, patient unwillingness to accept medical advice or to undergo surgery, and differences in severity of illness. However, the role of racial bias cannot be discounted, as the American Medical Association's Council on Ethical and Judicial Affairs has recognized. In a 1990 report on Black-White disparities in health care, the council asserted:

Because racial disparities may be occurring despite the lack of any intent or purposeful efforts to treat patients differently on the basis of race, physicians should examine their own practices to ensure that inappropriate considerations do not affect their clinical judgment. In addition, the profession should help increase the awareness of its members of racial disparities in medical treatment decisions by engaging in open and broad discussions about the issue. Such discussions should take place as part of the medical school curriculum, in medical journals, at professional conferences, and as part of professional peer review activities.[38]

The council's recommendation is a strong acknowledgement that racism can influence the practice of medicine. . . .

The Tuskegee Syphilis Study continues to cast its shadow over the lives of African Americans. For many Black people, it has come to represent the racism that pervades American institutions and the disdain in which Black lives are often held. But despite its significance, it cannot be the only prism we use to examine the relationship of African Americans with the medical and public health communities. The problem we must face is not just the shadow of Tuskegee but the shadow of racism that so profoundly affects the lives and beliefs of all people in this country.

NOTES

1. The most comprehensive history of the study is James H. Jones, *Bad Blood,* new and expanded edition (New York: Free Press, 1993).

2. "Remarks by the President in Apology for Study Done in Tuskegee," Press Release, the White House, Office of the Press Secretary, 16 May 1997.

3. "Final Report of the Tuskegee Syphilis Study Legacy Committee," Vanessa Northington Gamble, chair, and John C. Fletcher, co-chair, 20 May 1996.

4. Vanessa Northington Gamble, "A Legacy of Distrust: African Americans and Medical Research," *American Journal of Preventive Medicine* 9 (1993): 35–38; Shari Roan, "A Medical Imbalance," *Los Angeles Times,* 1 November 1994; Carol Stevens, "Research: Dis-

trust Runs Deep; Medical Community Seeks Solution," *The Detroit News,* 10 December 1995; Lini S. Kadaba, "Minorities in Research," *Chicago Tribune,* 13 September 1993; Robert Steinbrook, "AIDS Trials Shortchange Minorities and Drug Users," *Los Angeles Times,* 25 September 1989; Mark D. Smith, "Zidovudine: Does It Work for Everyone?" *Journal of the American Medical Association* 266 (1991): 2750–2751; Charlise Lyles, "Blacks Hesitant to Donate; Cultural Beliefs, Misinformation, Mistrust Make It a Difficult Decision," *The Virginian-Pilot,* 15 August 1994; Jeanni Wong, "Mistrust Leaves Some Blacks Reluctant to Donate Organs," *Sacramento Bee,* 17 February 1993; "Nightline," ABC News, 6 April 1994; Patrice Gaines, "Armed with the Truth in a Fight for Lives," *Washington Post,* 10 April 1994; Fran Henry, "Encouraging Organ Donation from Blacks," *Cleveland Plain Dealer,* 23 April 1994; G. Marie Swanson and Amy J. Ward, "Recruiting Minorities into Clinical Trials: Toward a Participant-Friendly System," *Journal of the National Cancer Institute* 87 (1995): 1747–1759; Dewayne Wickham, "Why Blacks Are Wary of White MDs," *The Tennessean,* 21 May 1997, 13A.

5. For example, see Stephen B. Thomas and Sandra Crouse Quinn, "The Tuskegee Syphilis Study, 1932 to 1972: Implications for HIV Education and AIDS Risk Education Programs in the Black Community," *American Journal of Public Health* 81 (1991): 1498–1505; Stephen B. Thomas and Sandra Crouse Quinn, "Understanding the Attitudes of Black Americans," in *Dimensions of HIV Prevention. Needle Exchange,* ed. Jeff Stryker and Mark D. Smith (Menlo Park, Calif.: Henry J. Kaiser Family Foundation, 1993), 99–128; and Stephen B. Thomas and Sandra Crouse Quinn, "The AIDS Epidemic and the African-American Community: Toward an Ethical Framework for Service Delivery," in *"It Just Ain't Fair": The Ethics of Health Care for African Americans,* ed. Annette Dula and Sara Goering (Westport, Conn.: Praeger, 1994), 75–88.

6. Thomas and Quinn, "The AIDS Epidemic and the African-American Community," 83.

7. Thomas and Quinn, "Understanding the Attitudes of Black Americans," 108–109; David L. Kirp and Ronald Bayer, "Needles and Races," *Atlantic,* July 1993, 38–42.

8. Lynda Richardson, "An Old Experiment's Legacy: Distrust of AIDS Treatment," *New York Times,* 21 April 1997, A1, A7.

9. Todd L. Savitt, "The Use of Blacks for Medical Experimentation and Demonstration in the Old South," *Journal of Southern History* 48 (1982): 331–348; David C. Humphrey, "Dissection and Discrimination: The Social Origins of Cadavers in America, 1760–1915," *Bulletin of the New York Academy of Medicine* 49 (1973): 819–827.

10. Harriet Martineau, *Retrospect of Western Travel,* vol. 1 (London: Saunders & Ottley; New York: Harpers and Brothers, 1838), 140, quoted in Humphrey, "Dissection and Discrimination," 819.

11. Theodore Dwight Weld, *American Slavery As It Is: Testimony of a Thousand Witnesses* (New York: American Anti-Slavery Society, 1839), 170, quoted in Savitt, "The Use of Blacks," 341.

12. F. N. Boney, "Doctor Thomas Hamilton: Two Views of a Gentleman of the Old South," *Phylon* 28 (1967); 288–292.

13. J. Marion Sims, *The Story of My Life* (New York: Appleton, 1889), 236–237.

14. Humphrey, "Dissection and Discrimination," 822–823.

15. A detailed examination of the campaign to establish Black hospitals can be found in Vanessa Northington Gamble, *Making a Place for Ourselves: The Black Hospital Movement, 1920–1945* (New York: Oxford University Press, 1995).

16. Eugene P. Link, "The Civil Rights Activities of Three Great Negro Physicians (1840–1940)," *Journal of Negro History* 52 (July 1969): 177.

17. "Seventh Annual Report of the Frederick Douglass Memorial Hospital and Training School" (Philadelphia, Pa.: 1902), 17.

18. H. M. Green, *A More or Less Critical Review of the Hospital Situation among Negroes in the United States* (n.d., circa 1930), 4–5.

19. For more in-depth discussion of the history of the Tuskegee Veterans Hospital, see Gamble, *Making a Place for Ourselves,* 70–104; Pete Daniel, "Black Power in the 1920's: The Case of Tuskegee Veterans Hospital," *Journal of Southern History* 36 (1970): 368–388; and Raymond Wolters, *The New Negro on Campus: Black College Rebellions of the 1920s* (Princeton, NJ: Princeton University Press, 1975), 137–191.

20. "Klan Halts March on Tuskegee," *Chicago Defender,* 4 August 1923.

21. Charles H. Garvin, "The 'New Negro' Physician," unpublished manuscript, n.d., box 1, Charles H. Garvin Papers, Western Reserve Historical Society Library, Cleveland, Ohio.

22. Ronald A. Taylor, "Conspiracy Theories Widely Accepted in U.S. Black Circles," *Washington Times,* 10 December 1991, A1; Frances Cress Welsing, *The Isis Papers: The Keys to the Colors* (Chicago: Third World Press, 1991), 298–299. Although she is not very well known outside of the African-American community, Welsing, a physician, is a popular figure within it. *The Isis Papers* headed for several weeks the best-seller list maintained by Black bookstores.

23. Jones, *Bad Blood,* 12.

24. For discussions of allegations of genocide in the implementation of these programs, see Robert G. Weisbord, "Birth Control and the Black American: A Matter of Genocide?" *Demography* 10 (1973): 571–590; Alex S. Jones, "Editorial Linking Blacks, Contraceptives Stirs Debate at Philadelphia Paper," *Arizona Daily Star,* 23 December 1990, F4; Doris Y. Wilkinson, "For Whose Benefit? Politics and Sickle Cell," *The Black Scholar* 5 (1974): 26–31.

25. Karen Grisby Bates, "Is It Genocide?" *Essence,* September 1990, 76.

26. Thomas and Quinn, "The Tuskegee Syphilis Study," 1499.

27. "The AIDS 'Plot' against Blacks," *New York Times,* 12 May 1992, A22.

28. Patricia A. Turner, *I Heard It Through the Grapevine: Rumor in African-American Culture* (Berkeley: University of California Press, 1993).

29. "Fear Creates Lack of Donor Organs among Blacks," *Weekend Edition,* National Public Radio, 13 March 1994.

30. Lorene Cary, "Why It's Not Just Paranoia: An American History of 'Plans' for Blacks," *Newsweek,* 6 April 1992, 23.

31. Robert J. Blendon, "Access to Medical Care for Black and White Americans: A Matter of Continuing Concern, *Journal of the American Medical Association* 261 (1989): 278–281.

32. M. D. Rogan et al., "Racial Disparities in Reported Prenatal Care Advice from Health Care Providers," *American Journal of Public Health* 84 (1994): 82–88.

33. Julie Johnson et al., "Why Do Blacks Die Young?" *Time,* 16 September 1992, 52.

34. Sonia Nazario, "Treating Doctors for Prejudice: Medical Schools Are Trying to Sensitize Students to 'Bedside Bias.'" *Los Angeles Times,* 20 December 1990.

35. Mark B. Wenneker and Arnold M. Epstein, "Racial Inequalities in the Use of Procedures for Patients with Ischemic Heart Disease in Massachusetts," *Journal of the American Medical Association* 261 (1989): 253–257.

36. Kenneth C. Goldberg et al., "Racial and Community Factors Influencing Coronary Artery Bypass Graft Surgery Rates for All 1986 Medicare Patients," *Journal of the American Medical Association* 267 (1992): 1473–1477.

37. John D. Ayanian, "Heart Disease in Black and White," *New England Journal of Medicine* 329 (1993): 656–658; J. Whittle et al., "Racial Differences in the Use of Invasive Cardiovascular Procedures in the Department of Veterans Affairs Medical System," *New England Journal of Medicine* 329 (1993): 621–627; Eric D. Peterson et al., "Racial Variation in Cardiac Procedure Use and Survival following Acute Myocardial Infarction in the Department of Veterans Affairs," *Journal of the American Medical Association* 271 (1994): 1175–1180; Ronnie D. Horner et al. "Theories Explaining Racial Differences in the Utilization of Diagnostic and Therapeutic Procedures for Cerebrovascular Disease," *Milbank Quarterly* 73 (1995): 443–462; Richard D. Moore et al., "Racial Differences in the Use of Drug Therapy for HIV Disease in an Urban Community," *New England Journal of Medicine* 350 (1994): 763–768.

38. Council on Ethical and Judicial Affairs, "Black-White Disparities in Health Care," *Journal of the American Medical Association* 263 (1990): 2346.

AMERICAN MEDICAL ASSOCIATION, COUNCIL ON ETHICAL AND JUDICIAL AFFAIRS

Gender Disparities in Clinical Decision Making

Recent evidence has raised concerns that women are disadvantaged because of inadequate attention to the research, diagnosis, and treatment of women's health care problems. In 1985, the US Public Health Service's Task Force on Women's Health Issues reported that the lack of research data on women limited understanding of women's health needs.[1]

One concern is that medical treatments for women are based on a male model, regardless of the fact that women may react differently to treatments than men or that some diseases manifest themselves differently in women than in men. The results of medical research on men are generalized to women without sufficient evidence of applicability to women.[2–4] For example, the original research on the prophylactic value of aspirin for coronary artery disease was derived almost exclusively from research on men, yet recommendations based on this research have been directed to the general populace.[4]

Some researchers attribute the lack of research on women to women's reproductive cycles. Women's menstrual cycles may constitute a separate variable affecting test results.[5] Also, researchers are reluctant to perform studies on women of childbearing age, because experimental treatments or procedures may affect their reproductive capabilities. However, the task force pointed out that it is precisely because medications and other therapeutic interventions have a differential effect on women according to their menstrual cycle that women should not be excluded from research.[6] Research on the use of antidepressant agents was initially conducted entirely on men, despite apparently higher rates of clinical depression in women.[6,7] Evidence is emerging that the effects of some antidepressants vary over the course of a woman's cycle, and as a result, a constant dosage of an antidepressant may be too high at some points in a woman's cycle, yet too low at others.[2,3]

In response to the task force, the National Institutes of Health promised to implement a policy ensuring that women would be included in study populations unless it would be scientifically inappropriate to do so.[4] However, in June 1990, the General Accounting Office reported that the National Institutes of Health had made little progress in implementing the policy and that many problems remained.[4]

Reprinted by permission of the publisher from *Journal of the American Medical Association* 266 (July 24/31, 1991), 559–562. Copyright © 1991, American Medical Association.

In addition to these general concerns raised by the task force about women's health, recent studies have examined whether a patient's gender inappropriately affects the access to and use of medical care. Three important areas in which evidence of gender disparities exists are (1) access to kidney transplantation, (2) diagnosis and treatment of cardiac disease, and (3) diagnosis of lung cancer. Other studies have also revealed gender-based differences in patterns of health care use. Although biological factors account for some differences between the sexes in the provision of medical care, these studies indicate that nonbiological or nonclinical factors may affect clinical decision making. There are not enough data to identify the exact nature of nonbiological or nonclinical factors. Nevertheless, the existence of these factors is a cause for concern that the medical community needs to address.

EVIDENCE OF DISPARITIES

GENDER DIFFERENCES IN HEALTH CARE USE

Some evidence indicates that, compared with men, women receive more health care services overall. In general, women have more physician visits per year and receive more services per visit.[8] Several studies have examined the issue of differences in health care use between men and women.[8-14] The results of these studies vary and some are contradictory. One of the most extensive studies on gender differences in the use of health care services found that when medical care differs for men and women (in approximately 30% to 40% of cases), the usual result is more care for women than for men. Women seem to receive more care even when both men and women report the same type of illness or complaint about their health.[8] Women undergo more examinations, laboratory tests, and blood pressure checks and receive more drug prescriptions and return appointments than men. However, the reasons for this are not clear.

Studies that have examined gender as a factor for receiving several major diagnostic or therapeutic interventions, however, suggest that women have less access than men to these interventions.

DISPARITIES IN PROVIDING MAJOR DIAGNOSTIC AND THERAPEUTIC INTERVENTIONS

Kidney Dialysis and Transplantation. Gender has been found to correlate with the likelihood that a patient with kidney disease will receive dialysis or a kidney transplant. In one study researchers analyzed the per-

centage of patients in the United States with end-stage renal disease who received dialysis.[15] Of men who needed dialysis, 37.3% were given dialysis, compared with 31.1% of women. Ninety percent of the difference resulted from the fact that younger people have a greater likelihood of receiving dialysis than older people.

Disparities based on gender are more pronounced for the likelihood of receiving a kidney transplant. An analysis of patient dialysis data from 1981 through 1985 indicated that women undergoing renal dialysis were approximately 30% less likely to receive a cadaver kidney transplant than men.[16] Another study, done during the period 1979 through 1985, showed that a female dialysis patient had only three-quarters the chance of a male patient to receive a renal transplant.[17] Controlling for age did not significantly reduce gender as a factor in the likelihood of receiving a transplant. Men were more likely to receive a transplant in every age category. The discrepancy between sexes was most pronounced in the group 46 to 60 years old, with women having only half the chance of receiving a transplant as men the same age.[18]

Diagnosis of Lung Cancer. Recent autopsy studies have revealed that in as many as a quarter of patients with lung cancer, a diagnosis is not made while they are alive.[18-20] A comparison between the population in which lung cancer is diagnosed and the population in which it is not diagnosed shows that a detection bias favors the ordering of diagnostic testing for lung cancer in patients who are smokers, have a recent or chronic cough, or are male.[20]

One study compared the rates of lung cancer detected at autopsy with the way cytologic studies of sputum were ordered in a hospital setting to detect lung cancer. Men and women have relatively equal rates of previously undiagnosed lung cancer detected during autopsy. In addition, other studies have shown that women and men with similar smoking practices are at essentially equivalent risk for lung cancer.[21] However, men were twice as likely to have cytologic studies of sputum ordered as women. Once smoking status and other medical considerations were taken into account, men still had 1.6 times the chance of having a cytologic test done.[20]

Catheterization for Coronary Bypass Surgery. Men seem to have cardiac catheterizations ordered at a rate disproportionately higher than women, regardless of each gender's likelihood of having coronary artery disease. A study done in 1987 showed that in a group of 390 patients, of those with abnormal exercise radionuclide scans, 40% of the male patients were referred for cardiac catheterization, while only 4% of the female patients were referred for further testing.[22] The study showed that once researchers controlled for the variables of abnormal test results, age, types of angina, presence of symptoms, and confirmed previous myocardial infarction, men were still 6.5 times more likely to be referred for catheterization than women, although men have only three times the likelihood of having coronary heart disease than women.

Of those patients whose nuclear scan test results ultimately were abnormal, women were more than twice as likely to have their symptoms attributed to somatic, psychiatric, or other noncardiac causes as men. For patients whose test scans were normal, men and women had a relatively equal chance of having their symptoms attributed to cardiac causes.

The authors concluded that the wide difference in referral rates between men and women could not be explained by gender-based differences in the accuracy of nuclear scans. Even after abnormal test results had been established, men were referred significantly more often than women. It is unlikely that the discrepancy results from a higher likelihood of referral in some types of nuclear scan abnormalities, since men had higher referral rates in every category of abnormality. Men were also more likely to be referred regardless of the probability of their having coronary artery disease before the nuclear scan.

POSSIBLE EXPLANATIONS

BIOLOGICAL DIFFERENCES BETWEEN THE SEXES

Differences in biological needs between male and female patients probably account for a large part of the differences in the use of health care services. The kind and number[23] of illnesses that are reported differ somewhat for women and men. Possibly, women get more care because they have more illnesses or because the types of illnesses they have require more overall care. Some figures show that the generally lower socioeconomic status of women may be associated with poorer health. Also, women tend to live longer than men and individuals of older ages may have more morbidities.[8]

However, real differences in morbidity and mortality between the sexes would not explain the fact that women seem to receive more care than men for the same type of complaint or illness.[8]

Real biological differences also cannot account for the gender disparities in rates of cardiac catheterization, kidney transplantation, or lung cancer diagnoses. For instance, the discrepancy in dialysis rates might be explained by the existence of coexisting diseases in women that lessen the potential effectiveness of dialysis. However, the Health Care Financing Administration reports that female patients receiving dialysis have a slightly better survival pattern than male patients.[24]

Also, biological differences between the sexes, such as the level of cytotoxic antibodies, number of complications after transplantation, or differences in the type of renal disease between men and women did not explain the disparity in the likelihood of receiving a kidney transplant.[17] It is unlikely that the difference reflects either patient or physician preference; successful transplantation is generally considered superior to lifetime dialysis by both patients and physicians.[16, 17]

The difference in sputum cytologic findings between male and female patients may reflect the historical association between male sex and cigarette smoking. Traditionally, more men than women have been smokers.[21] In fact, past demographic data showed that men were more likely to have lung cancer than women. Physicians, in turn, may view smoking and being male as independent risk factors for lung cancer and therefore tend to suspect cancer more readily in patients who either smoked or were men even though gender is not an independent risk factor.[21]

Differences in disease prevalence between men and women have been cited to explain the disparity in cardiac catheterization rates.[25] However, the difference in disease prevalence between men and women is 3:1, whereas the difference in catheterization rates was almost 7:1.[22, 26] Additionally, the similarities in use of antianginal drug treatment indicates that the patients were clinically comparable.[22]

Other evidence also suggests that women may be disadvantaged by inadequate attention to the manifestations of cardiovascular disease in women. There is some evidence that cardiovascular disease is not diagnosed or treated early enough in women. Studies show that women have a higher operative mortality rate for coronary bypass surgery[27, 28] and a higher mortality rate at the time of an initial myocardial infarction.[29–31] The higher mortality rates reflect the fact that cardiovascular disease is further advanced in women than men at both the time of surgery and the time of an initial heart attack.[29]

The lack of research done specifically on women may have resulted in a failure to develop diagnostic criteria and treatments that are appropriate for cardiovascular disease in women. Cardiovascular disease in women differs from the disease in men in several significant ways. One study showed that diabetes is a greater risk factor in women for morbidity and mortality from coronary heart disease than in men.[32] The same study also showed that the level of high-density lipoprotein cholesterol is a stronger predictor of heart disease in women than in men.[32] These differences between the sexes in the manifestation of cardiovascular disease may affect diagnostic and treatment indications for women. Yet, research on cardiovascular disease has concentrated almost entirely on men[3] despite the fact that cardiovascular disease is the leading cause of death in women in the United States.[2, 29] Also, tests traditionally used to detect cardiovascular disease in men, such as treadmill testing, are not as sensitive or specific for detecting cardiovascular disease in women as for men.[28]

SOCIETAL ATTITUDES MAY AFFECT DECISION MAKING IN THE HEALTH CARE CONTEXT

Data that suggest that a patient's gender plays an inappropriate role in medical decision making raise the question of possible gender bias in clinical decision making. Gender bias may not necessarily manifest itself as overt discrimination based on sex. Rather, social attitudes, including stereotypes, prejudices and other evaluations based on gender roles may play themselves out in a variety of subtle ways.

For instance, some evidence suggests that physicians are more likely to attribute women's health complaints to emotional rather than physical causes.[33-35] Women's concerns about their health and their greater use of health care services have been perceived to be due to "overanxiousness" about their health.[35] However, characterizing women's use patterns as a result of emotional excess or overuse risks providing inadequate care for women. For example, in the study of catheterization rates, attributing a disproportionate percentage of women's abnormal nuclear scan results to psychiatric or noncardiac causes for their symptoms may have compromised their care.[22]

Perceiving men's use practices as normal and attributing *over*anxiousness to women's concerns about

their health may be doing a disservice to both sexes. One study concluded that "women's greater interest in and concern with health matters and their greater attentiveness to bodily changes may be part of a set of behaviors that do contribute to women's lower mortality rates."[12] Men may tend to be "*under*anxious" about their health or to ignore symptoms or illnesses and, consequently, underuse health care. Statistics that show that men tend to have a lesser number but more severe types of health problems may reflect men's resistance to seeking care until a health problem has become acute.

Societal value judgments placed on gender or gender roles may also put women at a disadvantage in the context of receiving certain major diagnostic and therapeutic interventions, such as kidney transplantation and cardiac catheterization. A general perception that men's social role obligations or of their contributions to society are greater than women's may fuel these disparities.[9] For instance, altering one's work schedule to accommodate health concerns may be viewed as more difficult for men than women. Overall, men's financial contribution to the family may be considered more critical than women's. A kidney transplant is much less cumbersome than dialysis. Coronary bypass surgery, for which catheterization is a prerequisite, is a more efficient and immediate solution to the problem of coronary artery disease than continuous antianginal drug therapy. However, judgments based on evaluations of social worth or preconceptions about the probable roles of men and women are clearly inexcusable in the context of medical decision making.

ROLE OF THE MEDICAL PROFESSION IN EXAMINING GENDER DISPARITIES AND ELIMINATING BIASES

Available data do not conclusively demonstrate a connection between gender bias and gender disparities in the provision of health care. Designing a study that can control for the myriad social, economic, and cultural factors that might influence decision making in a clinical context has proved extraordinarily difficult.

Historically, societal perceptions regarding women's health status have often disadvantaged women. Throughout the mid-19th and well into the 20th century, women's perceived disposition toward both physical and mental illness was used as a rationale for keeping them from worldly spheres such as politics, science, medicine, and law. For women, behavior that violated expected gender-role norms was frequently attributed to various physical or mental illnesses[36, 37] and in turn often was treated in a variety of ways, including gynecological surgeries, such as hysterectomies and, occasionally, clitoridectomies.[38] Society and medicine have addressed and are working to remedy sex stereotypes and biases. Yet, many social and cultural attitudes that endorse sex-stereotyped roles for men and women remain in our society.

The medical community cannot tolerate any discrepancy in the provision of care that is not based on appropriate biological or medical indications. The US Public Health Service's Task Force on Women's Health Issues concluded that "[b]ecause health care is a legitimate concern of all people, the health professions are obligated to seek ways of ensuring that clinical decisions are based on science that adequately pertains to all people."[6] Insufficient research on women is not only discriminatory but may be dangerous; medical care or drug treatments that prove effective in men may not always be safely generalizable to women.[4] The influence that social attitudes and perceptions have had on health care in the past suggest that some biases could remain and affect modern medical care. Such attitudes and perceptions may disadvantage both women and men by reinforcing gender-based stereotypes or inhibiting access to care. Current evidence of possible discrepancies indicates a need for further scrutiny.

SUMMARY OF RECOMMENDATIONS

Physicians should examine their practices and attitudes for the influence of social or cultural biases that could affect medical care. Physicians must ensure that gender is not used inappropriately as a consideration in clinical decision making. Assessments of need based on presumptions about the relative worth of certain social roles must be avoided. Procedures and techniques that preclude or minimize the possibility of gender bias should be developed and implemented. A gender-neutral determination for kidney transplant eligibility should be used.

More medical research on women's health and women's health problems should be pursued. Results of medical testing done solely on men should not be generalized to women without evidence that results can be applied safely and effectively to both sexes. Research on health problems that affect both sexes should include male and female subjects. Sound medical and scientific reasons should be required for excluding women from medical tests and studies, such as that the proposed research does not or would not affect the health of women. An obvious example would be research on prostatic cancer. Also, further research into the possible causes of gender disparities should be conducted. The extent to which physician-patient interactions may be influenced by cultural and social conceptions of gender should be ascertained.

Finally, awareness of and responsiveness to sociocultural factors that could lead to gender disparities may be enhanced by increasing the number of female physicians in leadership roles and other positions of authority in teaching, research, and the practice of medicine.

NOTES

1. US Public Health Service. *Women's Health: Report of the Public Health Service Task Force on Women's Health Issues.* Washington, DC: US Dept of Health and Human Services; 1985;2.

2. Cotton P. Is there still too much extrapolation from data on middle-aged white men? *JAMA.* 1990;263:1049–1050.

3. Cotton P. Examples abound of gaps in medical knowledge because of groups excluded from scientific study. *JAMA.* 1990;263:1051–1052.

4. *Hearings Before the House Energy and Commerce Subcommittee on Health and the Environment,* 101st Congr, 1st Sess (1990) (testimony of Mark V. Nadel, associate director, US General Accounting Office).

5. Hamilton J, Parry B. Sex-related differences in clinical drug response: implications for women's health. *J Am Med Wom Assoc.* 1983;38:126–132.

6. Hamilton JA. Guidelines for avoiding methodological and policy-making biases in gender-related health research in Public Health Service. *Women's Health: Report of the Public Health Service Task Force on Women's Health Issues.* Washington, DC: US Department of Health and Human Services; 1985;2.

7. Raskin A. Age-sex differences in response to antidepressant drugs. *J Nerv Ment Dis.* 1974;159:120–130.

8. Verbrugge LM, Steiner RP. Physician treatment of men and women patients: sex bias or appropriate care? *Med Care.* 1981;19:609–632.

9. Marcus AC, Suman TE. Sex differences in reports of illness and disability: A preliminary test of the 'fixed role' hypothesis. *J Health Soc Behav.* 1981;22:174–182.

10. Gove WR, Hughes M. Possible causes of the apparent sex differences in physical health: an empirical investigation. *Am Social Rev.* 1979;44:126–146.

11. Cleary PD, Mechanic D, Greenley JR. Sex differences in medical care utilization: an empirical investigation. *J Health Soc Behav.* 1982;23:106–119.

12. Hibbard JH, Pope CR. Another look at sex differences in the use of medical care: illness orientation and the type of morbidities for which services are used. *Women Health.* 1986;11:21–36.

13. Armitage KJ, Schneiderman LF, Bass RA. Response of physicians to medical complaints in men and women. *JAMA.* 1979;241:2186.

14. Natanson CA. Illness and the feminine role: a theoretical review. *Soc Sci Med.* 1975;9:57–63.

15. Kjellstrand CM, Logan GM. Racial, sexual and age inequalities in chronic dialysis. *Nephron.* 1987;45:257–263.

16. Held PJ, Pauly MV, Bovbjerg RR, et al. Access to kidney transplantation. *Arch Intern Med.* 1988;148:2594–2600.

17. Kjellstrand CM. Age, sex, and race inequality in renal transplantation. *Arch Intern Med.* 1988;148:1305–1309.

18. McFarlane MJ, Feinstein AR, Wells CK. The 'epidemiologic necropsy': unexpected detections, demographic selections, and the changing rates of lung cancer. *JAMA.* 1987;258:331–338.

19. McFarlane MJ, Feinstein AR, Wells CK. Necropsy evidence of detection bias in the diagnosis of lung cancer. *Arch Intern Med.* 1986; 146:1695–1698.

20. Wells CK, Feinstein AR. Detection bias in the diagnostic pursuit of lung cancer. *Am J Epidemiol.* 1988;128:1016–1026.

21. Schoenberg JB, Wilcox HB, Mason TJ, et al. Variation in smoking-related lung cancer risk among New Jersey women. *Am J Epidemiol.* 1989;130:688–695.

22. Tobin JN, Wassertheil-Smoller S, Wexler JP, et al. Sex bias in considering coronary bypass surgery. *Ann Intern Med.* 1987; 107:19–25.

23. Verbrugge LM. Sex differentials in health. *Prevention.* 1982;97:417–437.

24. Eggers PW, Connerton R, McMullan M. The Medicare experience with end-stage renal disease: trends in incidence, prevalence, and survival. *Health Care Fin Rev.* 1984;5:69–88.

25. Karlin BG. Sex bias and coronary bypass surgery. *Ann Intern Med.* 1988;108:149.

26. Tobin JN, Wassertheil-Smoller S, Wexler JP, et al. Sex bias in considering coronary bypass surgery. *Ann Intern Med.* 1987; 107:19–25.

27. Khan SS, Nessim S, Gray R, Czer LS, Chaux A, Matloff J. Increased mortality of women in coronary artery bypass surgery: Evidence for referral bias. *Ann Intern Med.* 1990;112:561–567.

28. Wenger NK. Gender, coronary artery disease, and coronary bypass surgery. *Ann Intern Med.* 1990;112:557–558.

29. Wenger NK. Coronary disease in women. *Ann Rev Med.* 1985;36:285–294.

30. Fiebach NH, Viscoli CM, Horwitz RI. Differences between women and men in survival after myocardial infarction. *JAMA.* 1990;263:1092–1096.

31. Dittrich H, Gilpin E, Nicod P, Cali G, Henning H, Ross J. Acute myocardial infarction in women: influence of gender on mortality and prognosis variables. *Am J Cardiol.* 1988;62:1–7.

32. Lerner DJ, Kannel WB. Patterns of coronary heart disease morbidity and mortality in the sexes: a 26-year follow-up of the Framingham population. *Am Heart J.* 1986;111:383–390.

33. Bernstein B, Kane R. Physicians' attitudes toward female patients. *Med Care.* 1981;19:600–608.

34. Colameco S, Becker L, Simpson M. Sex bias in the assessment of patient complaints. *J Fam Pract.* 1983;16:1117–1121.

35. Savage WD, Tate P. Medical students' attitudes towards women: a sex-linked variable? *Med Educ.* 1983;17:159–164.

36. Waisberg J, Page P. Gender role nonconformity and perception of mental illness. *Women Health.* 1988;14:3–16.

37. Broverman IK, Broverman DM, Clarkson FE, et al. Sex-role stereotypes and clinical judgments of mental health. *J Consult Clin Psychol.* 1970;34:1–7.

38. Barker-Benfield B. 'The spermatic economy.' In: Gordon M, ed. *The American Family in Sociohistorical Perspective.* New York, NY: St Martin's Press; 1973.

CHRISTINE K. CASSEL AND BERNICE L. NEUGARTEN

The Goals of Medicine in an Aging Society

The unprecedented aging of our society has recently set off a vigorous debate about the appropriate use of expensive and extensive medical care for elderly persons. This debate involves very complex issues, which are too often and too easily oversimplified both in the media and in the professional literature. Some argue

Reprinted with permission of the publisher from Robert H. Binstock and Stephen G. Post, eds., *Too Old for Health Care? Controversies in Medicine, Law, Economics, and Ethics* (Baltimore: Johns Hopkins University Press, 1991), pp. 75–91.

that because the increases in longevity in the past two decades are largely the result of advances in medical technology, we can and should continue, by means of research and the implementation of new technologies, to push back the age barriers that presently create limits to good health and to length of life (e.g., Schneider, 1989). Others argue that there must be a natural end to the human life span, that old age is a reasonable and acceptable indicator of proximity to death, and that it is both unseemly and wasteful to keep augmenting medical technology in a struggle against the inevitability of death (e.g., Callahan, 1987).

In this [essay] we will examine the goals of medicine in light of the dramatic demographic and epidemiologic changes in our society. We do this in the hope of developing a framework within which the complex questions about appropriate medical care for patients of advanced age can be addressed most rationally, most effectively, and most humanely.

THE "STATE" OF MODERN MEDICINE

The decade of the 1970s saw the beginning of a reexamination of modern medicine. Many different and often conflicting voices were heard, as is true to the present day. Critics included John Knowles (1977), who edited an issue of the journal *Daedalus* entitled *Doing Better and Feeling Worse.* The title referred to the apparent difference between objective indicators of health, which showed improvement, and subjective reports from patients, which indicated increases in health-related complaints as well as growing dissatisfaction with physicians and hospitals.

Carlson's book *The End of Medicine* (1975) also was an indication of the introspection going on in the medical profession and the public examination of the practice of medicine and its role in our society. The title of the book suggested both a critique of the end(s), or the goal(s), of medicine, and a prediction that an oversized technocracy that has outgrown its human roots must inevitably decline and come to an end. Similar apocalyptic visions were popularized by Ivan Illich in his book *Medical Nemesis* (1976), which put forward the view of modern medicine as too narrowly focused on reductionist technical approaches to problems that would be better approached through social reforms or preventive practices. Howard Waitzkin, in *The Second Sickness* (1983), argued that perverse financial incentives were responsible for the imbalances described by Illich, Carlson, and others.

This reexamination of the goals of medicine and the proper place of medicine in society continued through the 1980s, but the themes became more focused. In the 1970s attention was concentrated on the role that unbridled technology has played in diminishing the humanism of medicine. In the 1980s, it was focused on the costs of that technology and on the ways to stem the steadily increasing expenditures (see Hiatt, 1987).

Today, increasing costs are often described as being closely linked to the increase in life expectancy, because older people use far greater amounts of medical care than do younger people. The increasing life expectancy of Americans is, at least in part, due to advances in medical care. Moreover, because today people seldom die prematurely, they need more medical care to help cope with the chronic diseases of senescence. The special interplay between advanced medical technologies and increasing life expectancy has led to even greater questioning of the goals of medicine. The issues of cost containment and the risks of dehumanized technology are often invoked to argue for setting limits on the use of medical interventions, especially for aged persons (e.g., Callahan, 1987; Callahan, 1990).

The goals of medicine in today's society must be examined in the context of medical technology and the rising costs of health care. Also, however, they must be reconsidered in light of the increasing longevity of the population, and the moral and ethical issues that underlie the practice of medicine.

THE INCREASE IN LIFE EXPECTANCY

Longevity has increased dramatically in this century, with average life expectancy almost doubling in the period from 1900 to 1965. During that period, two basic assumptions were made. The first was that most of the decline in mortality was due to advances in social conditions rather than to advances in medical treatment. Better sanitation, nutrition, education, and working conditions were largely responsible for the drop in premature deaths that occurred, historically, long before the advent of any specific life-saving medical discoveries, such as insulin or antibiotics.

The second assumption was that the genetically determined life span of the human species is probably about 75 years. It was recognized that a gap exists between maximum life span and average length of life. By the mid-1960s, however, as average life expectancy began to approach 70 years, it was assumed that the gap had been narrowed about as much as possible: that, in short, we had come close to maximizing life expectancy in this country.

Within a decade, however, the latter assumption was proved wrong, and the great demographic transition of the 1980s had begun. Life expectancy, after remaining stable for two decades, began to increase again. This transition has been described in extraordinary detail by demographers, epidemiologists, and health policy specialists (e.g., Olshansky and Ault, 1986).

The increase in longevity has not yet reached a plateau, nor has it ended. In fact, it is continuing at an unprecedented and unanticipated rate. Average life expectancy is now nearly 80 years for women and nearly 74 years for men, and mortality rates are declining most rapidly among the persons who are over 85. The latter group presently constitutes about 1 percent of the population, but it is projected to be over 2 percent in the next 20 years (U.S. Senate, Special Committee on Aging, et al., 1987). While still a small percentage, the numbers of people in this age group, now some 5 million, will increase to as many as 20 million in two decades. A sense of how dramatic this phenomenon has been can be seen in the U.S. Bureau of the Census publication *The Centenarians* (1988), which describes the growth in the number of persons over the age of 100, a number that jumped from 15,000 in 1980 to 25,000 only five years later, in 1985. At that rate, it is predicted that the number will reach 110,000 by the year 2000 and will perhaps be tripled 30 years later, in 2030.

The recent sharp increase in life expectancy is probably due much more to advances in medical treatment than was the increase seen before the mid-1960s. It is difficult to explain the latest gains as the reflection of new social advances, and even more difficult to imagine that a genetic or other biological change has occurred in the human species that would account for such a dramatic demographic transition in a period of only two decades. Instead, the single major factor often described is the decline in mortality from cardiovascular disease which has occurred in the past 20 years. There is some evidence to support the idea that preventive health measures, combined with advanced medical treatment, are probably responsible for the fact that the onset of severe or potentially fatal coronary disease now occurs at a much later age than it did 10 to 15 years ago. Clearly enough, more research is needed to identify the factors contributing to the drop in mortality rates.

ADDED LONGEVITY: GOOD OR BAD?

The gain in longevity among Americans has been a remarkable phenomenon, and it is probably the mark of an advanced industrialized civilization, for it has also appeared in other industrialized countries of the world. But is it a good thing? Are we to be pleased that people are living so much longer than we ever thought they would? How we answer such questions has a great deal to do with our understanding of society's response to the demographic transition, and it relates directly to the basic issue of the goals of medicine in an aging society.

One way of looking at the issue is by asking, as people reach such advanced old age, how healthy and happy are they? Today, the majority of persons over 65 report at least one chronic illness. Reported illness and impairment, however, do not necessarily result in disability. It is the number and the severity of functional disabilities that are the preferred measures of health status. Persons consider themselves in ill health primarily when an illness or impairment interferes with their activities of daily living, usually defined as the tasks related to personal care and to maintenance of the home environment. As might be anticipated, such health-related difficulties increase with advancing age, yet it is noteworthy that of persons aged 65 to 74, the most recent data show that more than 80 percent report no limitations in carrying out these daily activities. Of those aged 75 to 84, more than 70 percent report no such limitations, and even of those over age 85, half report no limitations (U.S. Senate, Special Committee on Aging, et al., 1987).

This is not to underestimate the problems of those persons who are significantly burdened by ill health or those who are dependent on others for their day-to-day care. It is instead to point out that only a minority of older persons, even at advanced older ages, are ill or disabled. National surveys have also found repeatedly that older people report high levels of life satisfaction, as high as or sometimes higher than the levels reported by younger people (Campbell et al., 1976; Harris et al., 1975; Harris et al., 1981).

Not only are old people as a group faring well, but of at least equal importance in the present context is the fact that, as individuals, people grow old in very different ways, and they become increasingly different from one another with the passage of years. Women age differently from men, and there are differences among racial, ethnic, and particularly socioeconomic groups. Added to this are the idiosyncratic sequences of events that accumulate over lifetimes to create increasing individual variation. The result is that older people are a very diverse group.

Although the prevalence of illness and disability increases with age in the second half of life, the association between age and health is far from perfect. Age is a good predictor of health status in statistical terms, but for any given individual, age is a poor predictor of physical, mental, or social competence. This finding has emerged repeatedly in systematic studies of performance in which a wide range of physiologic and psychological variables has been examined (Shock et al., 1984) and has come to be called a "superfact" in gerontological research (Maddox, 1986). . . .

The most optimistic analysts, exemplified by Fries (1980), predict that the overall health status of the elderly population will continue to improve, leading to a "compression of morbidity" in the last period of life. Others, exemplified by Brody and Schneider (1983), argue that an increase in life expectancy will lead to an increase in the average period of morbidity and dependency before death.

Recent studies that examine "active life expectancy" (e.g., Katz et al., 1983) attempt to forecast patterns of morbidity and disability, as well as length of life. In these studies, it appears that with advancing age, an increasing percentage of the remaining years of life is likely to be spent in a dependent or disabled state. For example, for persons who reach age 65, an average of 16.5 years of life remain. The forecast is that this period of 16-plus years will include, on average, 6 years (or 40 percent) spent in a state of disability and dependency. For persons who reach 85, it is projected that 7.5 years of life remain, a period that includes more than 4.5 years (or 60 percent) in a disabled state. These data support the prediction that the added years of life will be characterized by disability and dependency, and contradict the optimistic view that, as Fries predicts, most persons will stay healthy until about age 85, then die quickly.

It is the specter of disability, particularly mental impairment from chronic dementing diseases such as Alzheimer's disease, that is most frightening for older people and their families. Disability also creates the greatest need for long-term care, either in institutional or home settings. Alzheimer's disease, hip fracture, and other disorders that result in major loss of function increase exponentially after approximately age 75 to 80 (see Hing, 1987; Kane and Kane, 1990; Manton, 1990). This would suggest to some observers that it may be inappropriate to provide life-extending medical

care to individuals in their late seventies or older if the life that is extended is simply a life of disability and dependency. These averages, however, do not adequately describe the tremendous physiologic, psychological, and social variability among members of any age cohort, as mentioned above.

HEALTH CARE COSTS AND
THE APPROPRIATENESS OF TREATMENT

Many factors are contributing to the rise in health care costs, including general inflation, the rapid escalation of physicians' fees, and the mushrooming costs of hospital care, as well as the increase in the number of old people, with their needs for health care. . . . In this connection, it is important to note that a small proportion of older people, about 17 percent, account for over 60 percent of Medicare payments. This statistic confirms the fact that it is only a small fraction of older persons in any one year who are responsible [for] the high usage of medical services. It also is consistent with the observation that most old people are not very sick until the last year of their lives. One study showed that the 6 percent of Medicare beneficiaries who died during the year 1978 accounted for 28 percent of Medicare reimbursements in that year (Lubitz and Prihoda, 1984). Other studies of high-cost Medicare patients have shown that a considerable fraction of hospital costs are attributable to patients who die during their hospitalization or shortly after discharge (Scitovsky, 1984).

Such data have led to overly simplistic exhortations that old people, instead of irresponsibly consuming all these medical resources, should accept death and thus allow more resources to be used for the young (Callahan, 1987; Callahan, 1990; Lamm, 1987). Some commentators argue that investment in acute health care yields more potential years of life in the young than in the old, and thus it is a more prudential investment plan for society's health care dollars (Daniels, 1988).

Such statements raise fundamental moral questions about the value of human life. They also make misleading generalizations about the goals of most medical treatment, describing it as "life extension" rather than as providing comfort to the patient or enhancing the patient's functional status and quality of life. Just as it is difficult to generalize about the health status of "the elderly," it is equally difficult to generalize about the appropriate use of "medical technology." When the specific uses of the resources spent on patients in their last year of life are examined, it becomes clear that most such patients were functioning at a high level prior to their last illness. Furthermore, the large expenditures in the last year of life are much more likely to be for persons aged 65 to 80 than for persons aged 80 and over (Scitovsky, 1984).

In addition, physicians cannot predict at the onset of hospitalization which patients are likely to survive. As studies have suggested, half of the high-cost patients survive at reasonable levels of functional status for a year or more (Scitovsky, 1984). In other words, the high-cost Medicare patient has a 50:50 chance of meaningful survival. It would be difficult, on grounds of morality, to argue that for reasons of economy, not for medical reasons, all such patients should be allowed to die.

A basic question about the goals of medicine arises here. Persons in danger of dying are, by definition, persons who are extremely ill and are therefore likely to need extensive and expensive hospital care. It is not enough to look simply at the expenditures incurred for them; it may be quite appropriate to provide extensive hospital care for a person with a serious illness, especially if there is a reasonable likelihood of a successful outcome and if such care is consistent with the patient's values or expressed preferences.

The number of dollars spent does not necessarily reflect the appropriateness of any given medical intervention selected by the patient's physician. There is no doubt that life-extending technologies are sometimes used in treating elderly patients, as well as in treating some younger patients, where the prognosis does not warrant aggressive medical intervention and where the patients, if able to express their wishes, would probably refuse such treatment.

Physicians have learned a great deal from the new and emerging field of medical ethics about becoming aware of patients' preferences, which they elicit by encouraging the use of verbal or written "advance directives," or by holding discussions with family members who can report attitudes and values of the patient that might be relevant to making a decision to allow death to occur. Advance directives include legal instruments such as "living wills" and "durable powers of attorney for health care" (Kapp, 1989). They can also include conversations between the physician and the patient regarding the use or nonuse of life-sustaining treatments in the event of critical illness; in this case the patient's preferences are written down and become part of the medical record.

More and more physicians and hospitals are accepting the patient's right to die with dignity. More and more

hospitals have explicit policies for do-not-resuscitate orders (Miles and Cranford, 1982). More and more physicians and hospitals are accepting the concept of hospice care for patients who are not likely to regain any meaningful level of existence. More and more state supreme courts, in cases of hopeless illness, have decided in favor of the patient's or the family's petition for the withdrawal of life-sustaining medical treatment (Wanzer et al., 1989).

There is still room for progress in this area, however, for many physicians and other personnel in hospitals and nursing homes are still unduly worried about their legal liability in such situations. They may continue to use medically unwarranted and morally unacceptable medical treatment because of their fear of legal repercussions if treatment is discontinued. Such fear is largely unwarranted, for there are few instances of successful lawsuits brought against physicians for withholding or withdrawing life-sustaining measures when the patient and the family have been involved in the decision, and when the treatment adheres to stated institutional protocols (Miles and Gomez, 1989).

Nonetheless, in the litigious environment of the United States the physician or the medical institution can never be entirely immune from lawsuits. Physicians need to reassert their moral courage to advocate the course of treatment most consistent with caring medical practice and respect for the patient's wishes. Malpractice reform and increasing attention to statutes that encourage the use of advance directives would enhance the physician's likelihood of making sensible decisions regarding the care of hopelessly ill patients. It is most important that such decisions should continue to be based on the individual case, not on some sweeping policy or regulation, especially not on a policy that uses age as the decisive criterion for withholding intensive medical treatment.

For example, some families would want the physician to administer antibiotics to treat pneumonia in a parent with advanced Alzheimer's disease, even though the quality of that parent's life may be very low when assessed by others. The family may find simple physical caregiving to be meaningful to both the aged parent and the caretakers, and may not regard it as too burdensome, even in the home setting. At the same time, treatments such as cardiopulmonary resuscitation or mechanical ventilation, which are ordinarily used only in comparatively severe life-threatening episodes, may not be indicated for the same patient because the burdens of treatment for that patient would not be justified by the chances of success. In most such instances, the situation is seen by everyone concerned as offering no chance of the patient's recovery, and no disagreement arises. In other instances, families and physicians together come to such decisions. The decision reached depends on the patient's condition, the views of the patient and the family, and their relationship with the physician.

Decisions to withhold medical treatment are never easy, nor should they be. Struggling through the management of such cases should help physicians to become more sensitive to the needs of hopelessly ill patients, to the subtleties of clinical treatment decisions for the most frail elderly patients, and to the skills needed for communication with families who are under the stress of caring for a severely impaired relative.

WHAT ARE THE BASIC VALUES OF MEDICINE?

Concerns about health care expenditures have raised some fundamental questions about the goals of medicine. What is medical care for? Is it for prolonging the lives of the disabled, or is it only for prolonging the lives of those who can be functioning members of society? Is a person's functioning to be measured in terms of economic productivity, and is economic productivity the predominant value by which to judge human life? Should the criteria for medical treatment be different for patients who are financially covered by publicly funded programs such as Medicare and Medicaid than for patients who are privately insured and those who can pay out-of-pocket?

These issues arise not only in regard to elderly persons but also in regard to expenditures for the long-term care of disabled children and young adults. Such questions are now being raised increasingly often, especially with regard to intensive care for infants with severe birth defects. New developments in the care of AIDS patients, treatments that promise longer life expectancy but not complete recovery, will probably raise similar concerns.

In spite of these conflicting values—cost containment and patients' right to medical care—the basic values of medicine remain the same as before: the preservation of life, the relief of suffering, and respect for patients. Advances in medical technology have made the implementation of these values more complex, for in addition to problems of cost containment, the striving to save life often creates great emotional burdens for patients and families, and sometimes seems to conflict with a humanistic approach to patient care. The latter problem needs clarification if we are to understand the goals of modern medicine in an aging society.

It is useful to realize that policy controversies about the costs of medical care and about setting limits to medical interventions for old people center around two different models of medicine. Although these models are not necessarily mutually exclusive, and although, for some patients, the models may lead to identical modes of care, their primary goals are nevertheless clearly distinguishable.

THE "HEROIC" MODEL OF MEDICINE

The overriding goal of the heroic model of medicine is the extension of life. In this model, life itself is of irreducible value; and the goal for the medical researcher, as well as for the practicing physician, is to postpone death, regardless of the patient's quality of life and regardless of the cost of treatment. In its most simplistic form, the heroic model of medicine does not ask whether a death is premature, appropriate, or acceptable, but asks only how death, the enemy, can be held at bay. The physician experiences the death of a patient as a personal failure, and perhaps also as an unwelcome reminder of his or her own mortality.

The intoxicating successes of medical technology—such as routine cardiac monitoring and defibrillation, mechanical ventilation, and kidney dialysis—that appeared during the 1960s probably created a receptive environment for the growth and acceptance of this heroic model. Certainly this model did not exist in earlier periods of history, when the physician's role was as much to "abide with" families during the illness of a patient as to dramatically rescue the patient from death.

Perceptions of the inhumanity of highly technical medical care, especially in cases of terminal disease, have led to public expressions of frustration with the heroic model of medicine, especially by those who demand a right to "die with dignity." Researchers in thanatology (the study of death and dying) have examined why some physicians are unable to accept their own mortality and why other physicians can deal patiently and compassionately with their patients' deaths. Accordingly, thanatologists have suggested a range of educational and institutional changes to enable society to deal better with death and dying. One result has been the development of hospice care for patients with ter-

death and dying in the medical curriculum.

The heroic model of medicine has brought with it, of course, an emphasis on medical research, as symbolized by the growth of the U.S. National Institutes of Health, by the "wars" on cancer and on heart disease, and by the enthusiastic search for "cures." In medical training, however, this model has resulted in much less emphasis being placed on the management of chronic disease and on the treatment of the more common but not life-threatening problems that patients present, and more emphasis being placed on the diagnosis and treatment of less common but potentially curable disorders.

The heroic model has indeed won many heroic victories, and it is a glamorous and exciting model both for health care professionals and for the public at large. It is undeniable that the goal of a longer life and the fantasy of being rescued from death are attractive to most people. However, the heroic model cannot deal with uncertainty, with decline, or with death. It cannot encompass the wide range of clinical experience or the humility and compassion that are necessary for medical care in a society characterized by increasing longevity and increasing chronic illness.

THE HUMANISTIC MODEL OF MEDICINE

In the second model of medicine, the one called the "humanistic" model, the primary goal is the improvement of the quality of life. In this model, the physician is much more likely to accept the patient on the patient's own terms and to establish goals of treatment which improve or maintain that person's level of functioning and quality of life. The prolongation of the patient's life is not necessarily what the physician strives for if that is not the patient's goal.

One example of this humanistic model is seen in the palliative approach of hospice care, in which the aim is to control the patient's symptoms and to make the patient comfortable. The application of this model is fairly straightforward in the care of a patient who is suffering from a clearly terminal illness and whose life expectancy is measured in days or weeks. However, in the great majority of elderly patients, multiple chronic diseases are the rule. The distinction between treatment aimed at improving the quality of life for these persons and treatment aimed at life prolongation is not so clear. This is particularly true in patients of advanced old age.

The humanistic approach must extend to psychological, social, and other issues, and it often requires a multidisciplinary team approach. This is especially true in treating older people, because the health problems that cause them distress often cannot be dealt with simply by prescriptions or surgery. The old patient may require economic, psychological, and social support, possibly including improved transportation, suitable housing, education about nutrition, and more.

In the humanistic model, the physician seeks medical interventions that place a low burden on the patient and have a high likelihood of benefit. The physician is unlikely to subject a patient to a procedure or treatment that involves a great deal of pain, as, for example, in resuscitating a frail elderly patient where there is only a small likelihood of improvement in that patient's life after the treatment ends.

In many of the interventions that improve the quality of life, particularly in a very old person, the prolongation of life may be an inevitable side effect. A good example is when a physician recently prescribed a pacemaker for a 99-year-old woman who was experiencing attacks of fainting caused by cardiac arrhythmia. While it may be agreed that extraordinary efforts to prolong the patient's life would be unseemly, "contraindicated," or perhaps even rejected by the patient herself, nonetheless the implantation of a pacemaker will prevent her from continually fainting, and thus falling and risking a broken hip, with its likelihood of protracted disability. The goal of such treatment is palliative — to prevent falling and potential fracture — but the salutary effect that the pacemaker will have on her heart rhythm will undoubtedly extend her life.

The observation that treatments that improve life and those that extend life are often indistinguishable applies to almost any palliative measure, ranging from the administration of insulin to persons with diabetes and the administration of oxygen to persons who suffer from shortness of breath, to modern, technology-intensive treatments for heart failure or symptomatic malignancies.

A MODEL OF MEDICINE
FOR THE AGING SOCIETY

Why is it that we are seeking a principle by which to limit medical treatment? Is it not obvious to the clinician when a certain treatment is or is not indicated? Clearly, physicians themselves often feel at sea, particularly in the care of very old patients. Old people are a new population to be served, and how best to serve them is a question that has only recently been receiving attention in medical research and training (Cassel, 1987). The guidelines are not clear, and they become especially problematic in a society in which physicians are pressured to be the gatekeepers of society's wealth and to prevent the wasteful use of dollars on people who will not "benefit."

Who is to decide what it means for the patient to benefit? Must the patient's life also be of present benefit to society? One assumption often made in this discourse is that if we could identify the best-functioning elderly person, or perhaps the best-functioning person of any age, we could then produce proper guidelines and would then know to whom medical care should best be offered.

OPTIMAL CARE ONLY FOR THOSE WHO FUNCTION WELL?

Various indexes of functioning have been explored by investigators who believe that when the patient's quality of life is very low, it is appropriate to limit medical care, particularly life-extending medical care. Those who are arguing for the rationing of medical care for old people advocate such decisions in treating all older patients, even those who are not extremely ill or terminally ill, and the establishment of a general policy of this kind.

This would mean that over time medical care would be provided more often to old persons whose quality of life is relatively high—those who are often described as "aging successfully"—than to persons whose quality of life is low.

One problem is that, for many observers, the quality of life is defined in reductionist terms, as the level of functioning. In one notable instance, it has been defined in even more reductionist terms, as the level of physiologic functioning; in that instance, old persons who score high on tests of half a dozen physiologic functions are termed the "successful agers" (Rowe and Kahn, 1987).

If the level of functioning were to become, for policy makers, the criterion for determining the type of medical care to be provided, the outcome would be to give more medical care to those who are physically and mentally able, and less to those who are disabled. Not only would such a policy increase inequities in the allocation of health care, but it also raises other underlying ethical questions. Except for the most extremely ill

patients, about whom disagreements are rare, how and by whom shall the patient's quality of life be determined? At what point is any given type of medical care no longer warranted? Is it acceptable, on ethical grounds, to make such distinctions and then to act on them, in the interest of cost containment?

If such a policy mandating old-age-based rationing of medical care were to be implemented, it would represent a major departure from the prevailing goal of medicine in our society. Perhaps more importantly, however, for most persons in the society it would represent, on ethical grounds, too high a price for the society to pay.

OPTIMAL CARE FOR ALL PERSONS?

The goal of medicine our society has been pursuing to date is to provide medical care that enhances not only the level of functioning but also the quality of life for all persons. Today that goal focuses more sharply than before on the expectation that over time a larger and larger proportion of the population will age "successfully." However, to produce a population most of whose members are at high levels of functioning may not necessarily be the optimum, or even the preferred, goal for a society like our own.

We have been experiencing a tidal wave of improvement in health, which is most clearly shown by the dramatic rise in average life expectancy. Although not all subgroups in the population are experiencing the same rapid gains, still there is no disagreement that the population as a whole has benefited enormously. There is a price to be paid for this, however: the one implied by the metaphor "The rising tide lifts all boats equally." That is, the frail as well as the sturdy are being lifted. Although most people who survive to an advanced old age remain quite vigorous and independent, we shall never be without a certain number who, while they too are now surviving, do so with significant disability and with great need for both medical and social support.

In light of all the advantages of an increase in life expectancy, is the task of caring for those who are aging less than successfully too great a price for our society to pay? A related question is the one already suggested above, namely, whether our measures of success are too narrow. We have learned the sobering lessons of eugenics from a recent society in which only those persons who were regarded as the most highly functioning were allowed to survive. Equally sobering, in the present context, is the fact that the genocide practiced by the Nazis began with physician-supported "mercy killing" of persons who were retarded, mentally ill, or aged and infirm.

Whether or not our own society would move along the same downward path is debatable, but our medical successes have led some of us to view chronic disability and dependence, no matter what the cause, as simply undesirable, as a drain on our resources, or as our failure. These attitudes could lead to a harsh and unforgiving society, one that values only the healthy or only those who can pay their own way. It would be a regressive society, rather than one that reflects the successes of modern civilization. The civilized society allocates resources, both financial and emotional, for including in the life of the community those of its members who are less fortunate, and for providing care to them.

EMBRACING THE AGING SOCIETY

Some observers believe that caring for disabled elderly persons will be an unbearable burden on society and will enervate and destroy us. Perhaps, to the contrary, society will benefit if it is challenged by the need to care for the vulnerable and the frail. Society's vitality and productivity may be improved if it learns how to sustain the lessons of compassion and how best to care for those who need care—in so doing, developing attributes such as loyalty and trust—as well as how to increase community cohesion.

Caring for the disabled may lead, also, to the creation of institutions of medicine and health care which reflect the needs of the modern society—to provide more home care and long-term care, and to be more prudent in the use of expensive medical commodities of unproven value (Brook and Lohr, 1986). We might learn to cut costs by using governmental power to limit the profits generated by entrepreneurial pharmaceutical and medical equipment companies, and to discourage their marketing practices that lead to wasteful overutilization of high-priced therapeutic and diagnostic procedures. We might learn instead how to create policies and methods for the strict assessment of technological procedures. Modern technology is not an evil in itself, but its indiscriminate use is medically inappropriate and wasteful, for it often diverts resources that could be used for long-term or preventive care (see Hiatt, 1987, especially pp. 13–33).

The appropriateness of any technology or treatment must be decided separately for each individual patient. The physician's role is to understand the potential efficacy or lack of efficacy of a given treatment, and to recommend treatment consistent with the patient's condition and the patient's values, regardless of the patient's age, sex, skin color, or income level.

Medicine in today's world needs to embrace the changing society in which people are living so much longer, and to create a humane model of medical care that fits the new social realities. It should focus not on setting age limits for medical care but, rather, on adding opportunities for a continuing sense of the value of life, especially for the very old. In this approach one is neither nihilistic nor fatalistic about the chances of helping old as well as young people.

The complexity of modern medicine requires an integration of the heroic and the humanistic, the technologic and the psychosocial approaches to health. The welfare of the individual patient is the measure by which any medical intervention must be assessed. The aging of our society, and the critique of modern medicine it has engendered, can lead to a medical practice that is better for all patients, and therefore for the society at large. At the same time, it requires a careful examination of the complexities involved. Otherwise it could lead to discrimination against sick and disabled persons and to the dehumanization of our society.

REFERENCES

Brody, J.A., and Schneider, E.L. (1983). Aging, natural death, and the compression of morbidity: another view. *New England Journal of Medicine, 309,* 854–856.

Brook, R.H., and Lohr, K.N. (1986). Will we need to ration effective health care? *Issues in Science and Technology, 3*(1), 68–77.

Callahan, D. (1987). *Setting limits: medical goals in an aging society.* New York: Simon & Schuster.

Callahan, D. (1990). *What kind of life: the limits of medical progress.* New York: Simon & Schuster.

Campbell, A., Converse, P., and Rodgers, W. (1976). *The quality of American life.* New York: Russell Sage Foundation.

Carlson, R.J. (1975). *The end of medicine.* New York: John Wiley & Sons.

Cassel, C.K. (1987). Certification: another step for geriatric medicine. *Journal of the American Medical Association, 258,* 1518–1519.

Daniels, N. (1988). *Am I my parents' keeper? An essay on justice between the young and the old.* New York: Oxford University Press.

Fries, J.F. (1980). Aging, natural death, and the compression of morbidity. *New England Journal of Medicine, 303,* 130–135.

Harris, L., and Associates (1975). *The myth and reality of aging in America.* Washington, D.C.: National Council on the Aging.

Harris, L., and Associates (1981). *Aging in the eighties.* Washington, D.C.: National Council on the Aging.

Hiatt, H.H. (1987). *America's health in the balance.* New York: Harper & Row.

Hing, E. (1987). *Use of nursing homes by the elderly: preliminary data from the 1985 National Nursing Home Survey, Advance Data No. 135.* Hyattsville, Md: National Center for Health Statistics, May 14.

Illich, I. (1976). *Medical nemesis: the expropriation of health.* New York: Pantheon Books.

Kane, R.L., and Kane, R.A. (1990). Health care for older people: organizational and policy issues. In R.H. Binstock and L.K. George, eds, *Handbook of aging and the social sciences* (3rd ed.), pp. 415–437. San Diego: Academic Press.

Kapp, M. (1989). Medical treatments and the physician's legal duties. In C.K. Cassel and D. Reisenberg, eds., *Geriatric medicine* (2nd ed.), pp. 623–639. New York: Springer-Verlag.

Katz, S., Branch, L.G., Branson, M.H., Papsidero, J.A., Beck, J.C., and Greer, D.S. (1983). Active life expectancy. *New England Journal of Medicine, 309,* 1218–1224.

Knowles, J.H., ed. (1977). Doing better and feeling worse: health in the United States. *Daedalus: Journal of the American Academy of Arts and Sciences, 106*(1).

Lamm, R.D. (1987). Ethical health care for the elderly: are we cheating our children? In T.M. Smeeding, ed., *Should medical care be rationed by age?,* pp. xi–xv. Totowa, N.J.: Rowman & Littlefield.

Lubitz, J., and Prihoda, R. (1984). The uses and costs of Medicare services in the last two years of life. *Health Care Financing Review, 5*(3), 117–131.

Maddox, G. (1986). Dynamics of population aging: a changing, changeable profile. In *America's aging workforce: a Traveler's symposium,* pp. 30–37. Hartford, Conn.: Traveler's Insurance Co.

Manton, K.G. (1990). Mortality and morbidity. In R.H. Binstock and L.K. George, eds., *Handbook of aging and the social sciences* (3rd ed.), pp. 64–90. San Diego: Academic Press.

Miles, S.H., and Cranford, R. (1982). The do-not-resuscitate order in a teaching hospital. *Annals of Internal Medicine, 96,* 660–664.

Miles, S.H., and Gomez, C.F. (1989). *Protocols for elective use of life-sustaining treatments.* New York: Springer Publishing Co.

Olshansky, S.J., and Ault, B.A. (1986). The fourth stage of the epidemiologic transition: the age of delayed degenerative diseases. *Milbank Memorial Fund Quarterly/Health and Society, 64,* 355–391.

Rowe, J.W., and Kahn, R.L. (1987). Human aging: usual and successful. *Science, 237,* 143–149.

Schneider, E.L. (1989). Options to control the rising health care costs of older Americans. *Journal of the American Medical Association, 261,* 907.

Scitovsky, A.A. (1984). The high cost of dying: what do the data show? *Milbank Memorial Fund Quarterly/Health and Society, 62,* 591–608.

Shock, N.W., Greulich, R., Andres, R., Arenberg, D., Costa, P., Jr., Lakatta, E., and Tobin, J. (1984). *Normal human aging: the Baltimore longitudinal study of aging.* Washington, D.C.: U.S. Government Printing Office.

U.S. Bureau of the Census, Office of the Actuary (1988). *The centenarians.* Washington, D.C.: U.S. Government Printing Office.

U.S. Senate, Special Committee on Aging, in conjunction with the American Association of Retired Persons, the Federal Council on the Aging, and the U.S. Administration on Aging (1987). *Aging America: trends and projections.* Washington, D.C.: U.S. Government Printing Office.

Waitzkin, H. (1983). *The second sickness: contradictions of capitalist health care.* New York: Free Press.

Wanzer, S., Federman, D., Adelstein, S.J., Cassel, C., Cassem, E., Cranford, R., Hook, E., Lo, B., Mortel, C., Safar, P., Stone, A., and van Eys, J. (1989). The physician's responsibility toward hopelessly ill patients: a second look. *New England Journal of Medicine, 320,* 844–849.

N A N C Y   S .   J E C K E R

Caring for "Socially Undesirable" Patients

Mr. Bernard was a homeless man, aged 58. His medical history revealed alcohol abuse, seizure disorder, and two suicide attempts. Brought to the emergency room at a local hospital after being found "semicomatose," his respiratory distress led to his being in-

tubated and placed on a ventilator. The healthcare team suspected the patient ingested antifreeze. Transferred from the hospital to the intensive care unit (ICU) of the university hospital, his diagnosis was "high osmolar gap with high-anion gap metabolic acidosis, most likely secondary to ethylene glycol ingestion and renal insufficiency."

Noted on admission were minimal neurological function, absent corneal and pupillary responses, ab-

Reprinted with the permission of the author and the publisher from *Cambridge Quarterly of Healthcare Ethics* 5 (1996), 500–510. Copyright © 1996, Cambridge University Press.

sent doll's eyes, no response to pain, no spontaneous movement, and irregular breathing requiring placement on a ventilator. Ethanol infusion and dialysis were initiated. The patient continued to improve during six days in the ICU. On days one and two, he occasionally opened his eyes and showed positive corneal and pupillary responses. Following simple commands, such as closing his eyes and squeezing, occurred on day three. Extubation and removal from the ventilator happened on day four. However, to avoid aspiration, re-intubation remained a possibility.

The healthcare team discussed placing a DNR order in the patient's chart. Several residents felt that a unilateral decision to withhold resuscitation was justified and that continuing to treat Mr. Bernard was futile. During rounds, a resident stated that "somebody has to make the decision," but no explicit discussion of nonmedical considerations was acknowledged. No DNR order was written prior to the patient's transfer to a general medicine floor. An effort was made to contact someone from the local Mission (where the patient had stayed) to find out if the patient had any family members.

After transfer, the patient's respiratory status remained unstable and a high risk of aspiration was noted. A neurology consult was requested. The consult determined that the patient had "severe ischemic encephalopathy but some neurologic function is present . . . cannot rule out recovery and recommend checking EEG for prognostic purposes." A CT scan indicated bilateral basal ganglial and brainstem damage. The patients prognosis was guarded, yet uncertain.

A renal social worker requested an ethics consultation to address placing a DNR order. The same day the consultation took place, the patient was returned to the ICU after he coughed up blood and developed respiratory distress. He was emergently re-intubated, and the ICU nursing staff expressed anger that no DNR order had been written. The patient's daughter who resided in another state was reached by phone, and agreed to a DNR order based on the attending physician's recommendation.

The following day a medical student asked, "Why should we continue to treat this guy given the quality of life he had before he ever got here?" The student added that the patient was on Medicaid, and perhaps "society could find better ways to spend healthcare dollars." The attending physician responded, "We don't know what this man's life is like. Even if he lives under a bridge, he may help other people who live with him. Although he may be responsible for his condition, a

good society is a compassionate and forgiving society." Later, the attending pulled the residents aside and told them they were "doing good" and that there were times when physicians had to make rationing decisions when no one else will or can.[1]

This case raises concerns: (1) healthcare providers formed negative opinions about Mr. Bernard that appeared to influence how aggressively they treated the patient; (2) providers considered rationing and cost containment in an implicit manner; and (3) as a result of government, public officials, and ultimately society failing to put a more deliberate and just healthcare system in place, providers apparently felt compelled to act as society's agents.

A response to these concerns requires coming directly to grips with some difficult issues. First, are negative judgments about patients' social worth ever relevant to judging quality of life or evaluating the futility of a medical intervention? Second, are healthcare providers ever justified in rationing care on the basis of patients' perceived social worth? Finally, in the absence of a broader public mandate, in what manner should individuals and institutions allocate scarce healthcare resources?

I want to argue that healthcare providers should use medicine to benefit patients, not society. A corollary of this is that providers have no business implementing their own personal convictions about a just allocation of healthcare. In the absence of a broader public mandate, rationing and cost-containment decisions should be made at local and institutional levels only after a process of explicit discussion and deliberate choice among providers and patients.

SOCIAL WORTH, QUALITY OF LIFE, AND MEDICAL FUTILITY

It would be a serious mistake to assume that the case of Mr. Bernard is an anomaly, i.e., that medicine is largely immune from the sorts of values and prejudices pervasive in the larger society. Instead, there is every reason to suppose that whatever values we place on persons in the wider society will recur in the healthcare setting. How do members of society and, by extension, members of the healthcare field, make social worth assessments? Judgments that patients are "socially undesirable" can be usefully viewed as falling along a continuum. At one end are patients incarcerated for committing serious crimes, such as murder, rape, and assault, who require expensive and scarce healthcare resources, such as organ transplantation. A second group includes patients who engage in self-destructive behaviors, such as substance abuse or suicide attempts, and who threaten harm to others. Providers may call patients in this second group "difficult" if they are belligerent, noncompliant, foul-mouthed, or threaten violence. A final group harms neither themselves nor others, yet providers may judge these patients negatively because they lack financial means, relying on welfare to support themselves and their families. This last group of patients may be unemployed, live on the street, and lack the means to pay for food, transportation, medical prescriptions, or other basic needs. These circumstances may not only lead providers to form negative judgments about patients' social worth, but also may be thought to reduce patients' chances of benefiting from certain kinds of treatment. All three groups of patients may rely on public sources, such as Medicaid or the Federal Bureau of Prisons, to pay for care. Thus, the question of whether or not to limit scarce and expensive services to these patients implicitly involves the question of whether or not society should underwrite the cost of such care.

Mr. Bernard's situation locates toward the middle of this continuum. He had not injured or threatened harm to others; nor had he committed a crime for which he was being punished. However, Mr. Bernard had engaged in self-destructive behaviors, including suicide attempts, alcohol abuse, and related ingestion of antifreeze. Whether or not these actions were influenced by mental illness is unknown. The patient clearly lacked financial resources and lived on the street. For these and other reasons, the residents and medical students caring for Mr. Bernard may have considered him a financial "burden" to society, or thought that his homeless lifestyle was unlikely to result in any social benefits. It is unclear to what extent the attending physician, nurses, and social worker also formed negative judgments that influenced assessments of medical futility, recommendations for DNR, and concerns about health care costs.

In contrast to these kinds of cases are those in which we think patients have made, or will make, impressive social contributions. A continuum of positive social worth may include at one end patients who are uniquely able to benefit society. This includes a patient who possesses exceptional ability, e.g., the critically acclaimed artist, famous scientist, or Nobel prize author, as well as patients whose ordinary skills become exceptionally valuable under special circumstances, such as a natural disaster, a terrorist threat, or when a vessel is lost at sea. A middle group of patients makes less visible social contributions that benefit a smaller social circle. For instance, a caring parent helps offspring to mature and become well-adjusted adults; a gifted teacher inspires students to advance human knowledge; a good neighbor fosters a better community. A final set includes patients who have not yet made recognized benefits to society, but who hold out the promise of doing so in the future. For example, a newborn infant has a lifetime ahead to benefit society.[2]

These remarks make evident that social worth does not refer to any single criterion, but instead identifies a family of characteristics that we associate with positive and negative benefits to society. Moreover, judgments about patients' *social* worth differ in important respects from judgments about the *moral* worth of persons. To see that this is so, one need only consider that people with varying skills and abilities make different and unequal contributions to society, yet still may be thought to possess an equal moral worth and dignity.[3]

Just what light do these remarks shed on the question of whether or not social worth judgments are relevant to judging the futility of a medical intervention? To return to the case with which we began, if providers feel that Mr. Bernard's life will not make society better off, does it follow that life-sustaining interventions are futile? It may be tempting to draw this conclusion, but it should be clear upon reflection that it is entirely unwarranted. Whereas social worth evaluations consider benefits to society, futility judgments have to do with whether or not particular treatments hold out a reasonable prospect of benefiting individual patients. For example, when a physician judges that dialysis is futile for a particular patient, it is completely irrelevant to this judgment whether the patient is a renowned scientist or a homeless person, such as Mr. Bernard. Instead, all that matters to making a futility assessment is whether or not dialysis has a reasonable likelihood of conferring a minimal benefit on the patient. As soon as social worth judgments enter into medical decision making, our thinking has shifted from futility to other issues, such as rationing and the fair allocation of scarce healthcare resources.[4,5,6]

Those who doubt that a sharp conceptual line can be drawn between futility and social worth need only consider that creative geniuses who make enormous social contributions often lead tormented and unhappy lives, placing far less value than society does on their own continued existence. Likewise, those whom society considers a drain on its resources may find great pleasure in living. This shows that the *social* benefit we attribute to a patient, such as Mr. Bernard, is not the same thing as the benefit that the patient experiences from [continued] existence. Mr. Bernard may derive enormous satisfaction from living, quite independent of whether or not we believe his existence benefits society.

SOCIAL WORTH
AND HEALTHCARE RATIONING

If life-saving treatments, such as cardiopulmonary resuscitation and dialysis, are not futile for Mr. Bernard, this hardly settles the question of whether or not it is fair to allocate these treatments to him. The attending's comment that "there were times when physicians had to make rationing decisions when no one else will or can" had very little to do with futility and quite a bit to do with whether public healthcare dollars should be spent on patients who will not provide society any return on its investment.

HISTORICAL PERSPECTIVES

Should providers ever ration beneficial healthcare on the basis of patients' perceived social worth? To pose this question immediately throws open the door to its powerful history. I will deal briefly, and inadequately, with this history, using it primarily to frame contemporary ethical discussion of social worth against a larger backdrop. The recent historical context of rationing medicine according to social worth judgments began during the 1960s, when treatment for irreversible kidney failure first became available in Seattle, Washington and there were many more patients needing hemodialysis than equipment and personnel available to treat them.[7] An Admissions and Policy Committee, consisting of seven lay members, was convened and charged with the task of choosing among medically suitable candidates. The committee included a lawyer, minister, banker, housewife, state government official, labor leader, and surgeon. Before reaching the committee, candidates had already been screened by medical, financial, and social services to ensure that they could benefit from treatment, pay for it, and had the social support considered essential to coping with the demands of the medical regimen. When evaluating candidates, the committee reportedly took into account factors such as occupation, community service, family

circumstances, and educational background as a means of judging patients' social contributions.

The Seattle committee was harshly criticized for attempting to measure social worth. A common criticism was that the committee measured social worth in accordance with its own middle-class suburban value system. Although envisioned as representing a broad socioeconomic and occupational spectrum of the Seattle community, the committee was relatively homogeneous in terms of the education, occupation, socioeconomic class, and general social background of members.[8] Critics argued that its approach ruled out "creative nonconformists who rub the bourgeoisie the wrong way but who historically have contributed so much to the making of America."[9] They concluded, "The Pacific Northwest is no place for a Henry David Thoreau with bad kidneys."[9]

• • •

CONTEMPORARY PERSPECTIVES

. . . James Kilner has written that social worth is the least acceptable of all the . . . standards on which rationing might be based. According to Kilner, cases in which patients possess exceptional positive or negative social worth can best be dealt with by appealing to other criteria. For example, patients whom we think have a negative social worth can often be excluded on the basis of noncompliance with medical treatment or inadequate social support. Likewise, "many of the patients who would be most strongly favored by [a social worth] criterion can be granted priority on other, more widely accepted grounds, such as medical benefit, willingness [to accept treatment], and special responsibilities [to dependent family members]."[10]

Yet Kilner's approach, which putatively dispenses with social worth, in fact applies social worth standards in a covert fashion. The social worth judgment does not disappear; it is instead covered up by incorporating it into other, less controversial, criteria. The problem with Kilner's position is the same problem that plagues any covert method of rationing: it is not thought through, not applied consistently, not accountable to others, not decided democratically, and not insulated from arbitrary and invidious prejudice.

In contrast to Kilner, some bioethicists maintain that the explicit use of social worth is sometimes ethically warranted. Reflecting this approach, James Childress defends a random method as the best general approach to allocating scarce resources, while simultaneously recognizing the possibility of justifying exceptions to a random method based on a patient's positive social worth. He writes, "If [social worth] is used, a lay committee . . . would be called upon to deal with the alleged exceptions, since the doctors or others would in effect be appealing the outcome of chance . . . This lay committee would determine whether this patient was so indispensable at this time and place that he had to be saved even by sacrificing the values of random selection."[11] Childress and Beauchamp in the 1994 edition of their classic textbook, *Principles of Biomedical Ethics,* propose that social worth can become an "overriding" ethical consideration in "exceptional cases involving persons of critical social importance."[12]

Those who wish to retain the possibility of using social worth under exceptional circumstances often admit the difficulty of judging patients' social worth in the vast majority of cases, yet argue that it is possible to judge social worth in exceptional cases. In such cases, even if we cannot precisely determine patients' social worth, we can sometimes estimate it closely enough to produce more value than if such estimations were not made.

Proponents of social worth also appeal to the idea that society should be grateful to persons who go to great lengths to benefit others and the society. Such persons deserve to be recognized and appreciated for their efforts. By contrast, those who harm others and society, or actively break society's rules, are not on equal footing and do not merit equal consideration.

A further argument in support of applying social worth under exceptional circumstances holds that appeals to social worth can be essential to achieving important societal goals. A still controversial example of this view is the reported practice during World War II of using the scarce resource of penicillin to treat soldiers with venereal disease who could quickly return to battle, rather than soldiers with war injuries who were not in a position to return to battle.[13] Another example asks to imagine that

It is the eve of World War II, and you must decide between giving a life saving medical resource to a top diplomat . . . or some other person . . . The diplomat is the only one who has the personal connections to avert a war.[14]

A different interpretation of this argument sets as a goal maximizing the number of lives saved, and favors, e.g., giving priority to sailors on a crowded life boat to increase the chances of saving more people than would otherwise be saved.[15] Another version of this argument embraces as a goal maximizing society's return on its healthcare investment,[16] and contends that society gets more for its healthcare investment if it favors persons who contribute more to society.

Many contemporary bioethicists find the foregoing arguments unpersuasive. They are firmly committed to the idea that social worth never provides an ethically acceptable way of rationing scarce resources. Reflecting this stance, Gerald Winslow maintains that the best (most ethical) way for society to allocate scarce healthcare dollars is to place itself under a veil of ignorance.[17] Under such a veil, people would be ignorant of important information about themselves, including not only their health status and medical needs, but also their education, occupation, age, gender, class position or social status, natural assets and abilities, psychological propensities, and life plans.[18] Once we think about healthcare allocation from this perspective, Winslow argues, we have no choice but to reject social worth because we are forced to entertain the thought that we ourselves may be the person who will be judged as socially dispensable.

Even assuming rationing according to social worth were philosophically justified, critics claim that we should never actually use this standard because of our ignorance about how to do it right. Traditional yardsticks for measuring social worth, such as educational background, occupation, community service, and income or net worth, are crude measures of social value. Even in seemingly obvious cases, critics doubt that we possess the wisdom to judge social worth accurately. A publicly acclaimed scientist, for example, may have a dark side, such as engaging in domestic violence toward offspring, that will adversely affect generations to come. A convicted murderer may help would-be criminals to see the error of the path he chose. Or the greatness of a poet or playwright may be discovered only posthumously.

Critics also object to rationing based on social worth because it fails to meet society's responsibility to its most vulnerable members. This concern arises to the extent that those perceived as contributing less to society lack economic, educational, or social advantages throughout life. Even if society has no duty to help disadvantaged groups, rationing based on social worth may still be regarded as unethical if it worsens the plight of these groups.

A final argument against social worth claims that the use of social worth may buttress invidious prejudices that are widespread in society. Thus opponents worry that negative attitudes toward persons of nonwhite racial groups, persons with physical or mental disabilities, the elderly, women, or others, will systematically disadvantage such groups. Or they stress that social value is too often defined narrowly, in terms of economic productivity, thereby excluding persons who work outside the paid labor force, caring for small children or volunteering in the community.

As this review of the arguments shows, the question of whether or not social worth is ever ethically justified remains controversial. However, today's controversies differ from the historical debates. First, there is widespread agreement that the application of social worth can and did fall prey to various abuses. Moreover, the vast majority of ethicists who support social worth today do not favor using it as a general standard for allocating scarce resources. Hence, contemporary debates center on whether or not we are ethically justified in applying this standard under exceptional circumstances.

THE ROLE OF HEALTH PROFESSIONALS

Without resolving the question of whether or not rationing based on a patient's perceived social worth is ever ethically justified, let us assume for the purposes of argument that it sometimes is. This raises the further question, Who ought to interpret and apply social worth standards? Was the Seattle approach of forming a lay committee preferable to the approach of other dialysis centers operating during the 1960s that delegated selection to physicians? In a case such as Mr. Bernard's, are healthcare professionals ever justified in acting as "society's agents" and deciding if "society can find better ways to spend healthcare dollars"?

One answer to these questions holds that health professionals undertake a special responsibility to serve as their patients' advocates.[19] As a consequence, health professionals should not attempt to evaluate a patient's personal or social circumstances, such as ability to pay or perceived social worth, and use these as a basis for treatment decisions.[20, 21] To do so violates the special fiduciary obligations health professionals owe their patients. Reflecting this approach, the American Medical Association Council on Ethical and Judicial Affairs discourages physicians from invoking social worth as a basis for allocating healthcare, noting that

a social worth criterion is a marked departure from the traditional patient-centered orientation of the medical profession. Social worth considerations would destroy the public confidence in physicians' abilities to place patients' interests above broad social utility. Medicine should continue to concentrate on the best interest of patients and avoid evaluations of social worth.[22] . . .

Unlike health professionals, society must choose how to allocate the scarce healthcare resources at its disposal.[23] In the final analysis, it is society that must decide if social worth, or other nonmedical factors, should determine access to healthcare. When society shirks this responsibility, rationing occurs by default. Or, as in Mr. Bernard's case, healthcare providers and others who lack the ethical authority to make rationing decisions feel compelled to do so.

Once public policies for allocating healthcare are in place, health professionals are generally obligated to abide by such policies. In the case of Mr. Bernard, society has spoken (through the 1972 Medicare End-Stage Renal Disease Program) clearly and forcefully in favor of allocating public money to pay for kidney dialysis for all patients who stand to benefit, regardless of patients' social worth, ability to pay, or other nonmedical factors. To the extent that those caring for Mr. Bernard considered rationing dialysis on the basis of negative judgments about Mr. Bernard's social worth, they failed to respect society's choices. Rather than "acting as society's agents," they were in fact usurping society's legitimate role by taking matters into their own hands. Healthcare workers who disagree with public policies regarding cost containment or the allocation of scarce resources are not ethically authorized to exempt themselves from society's decisions. Although members of a healthcare team inevitably exercise discretion in applying broad policies to particular cases, abuse of discretionary authority clearly occurs when providers prevent the application of policies to their patients.[24-26]

RATIONING WITHOUT A CLEAR PUBLIC MANDATE

Although decisions about allocating scarce healthcare resources should ultimately rest with the wider society, in many instances society has not expressed its will through legal and political processes. As noted already, society has implemented a policy addressing the allocation of public funds to kidney dialysis. Yet in many other instances, society has not even begun to review healthcare priorities or debate how scarce healthcare dollars should be spent. Clearly, it will take time for this to occur; in some areas public policies governing the allocation of healthcare may never be forthcoming. Despite this, clinicians still must make decisions about caring for individual patients, and healthcare institutions still must determine how to allocate the resources at their disposal. In the absence of a broader public mandate, how can individuals and institutions make rationing decisions in a more just and public fashion? What role, if any, should the criterion of social worth have in these decisions? . . .

As the recent development of institutional review boards and ethics committees attests, a group or committee process can furnish a valuable cross-disciplinary forum for making ethical decisions. In the area of cost containment and associated rationing, use of institutional ethics committees carries distinct advantages. Unlike practitioners caring for individual patients, committees are in a position to recommend general allocation standards to be applied to all patients of a certain kind that are served by the institution. This contributes to fairness by ensuring that similar cases will be treated similarly. In contrast to bedside rationing, committee decisions tend to be explicitly formulated, publicly documented, and accountable to the institution's members. As Brock points out, "the ethics committee can help ensure that difficult and controversial ethical issues raised by . . . cost containment efforts are more fully and publicly aired, thereby increasing the overall legitimacy of the decision process."[27] Furthermore, the decisions of committees are more amenable than bedside decisions to incorporating diverse perspectives, including patients' and community representatives', as well as health professionals'. Finally, a group process can encourage critical thinking by providing a forum for reviewing and discussing ethical positions and arguments.

Although institutional ethics committee involvement in rationing has distinct advantages, committees should maintain independence, avoiding even the appearance of being coopted by the institution's financial or legal interests, by the prerogative of vocal or powerful members of the committee, or by the will of those who appoint committee members. Participating in developing rationing policies has the potential to tarnish a committee's reputation if it casts the impression that the committee is beholden to the institution's management. Likewise, publicly airing rationing decisions that were previously unacknowledged has the potential to create anger and resentment.

CONCLUSION

In closing, let us return to the questions raised at the beginning of this paper. First, *are negative judgments about Mr. Bernard's social worth relevant to recommending a course of treatment or judging the futility of medical interventions?* The answer is no. The basis for recommending a medical treatment plan is whether or not the plan will benefit the patient. Likewise, the medical futility of an intervention concerns whether or not a medical intervention holds out a minimal chance of benefiting the individual patient; it has nothing to do with whether or not the patient will, in turn, benefit society.

Second, *are healthcare providers themselves justified in making rationing decisions on the basis of Mr. Bernard's perceived social worth?* The answer is no. Any decision to apply social worth or other rationing standards should rest with society, not healthcare providers. If, in the future, society decides to implement social worth or other rationing criteria, healthcare providers are obligated to carry out these societal decisions. In the interim, the permissibility of using social worth as a basis for healthcare rationing, either as part of a general policy or in exceptional cases, should not be the decision of any individual practitioner.

Finally, *in the absence of a broader public mandate, in what manner should providers allocate scarce healthcare resources?* Healthcare institutions faced with resource and fiscal constraints should utilize cross-disciplinary groups to assist with inevitable cost containment and allocation decisions.

NOTES

1. This case is adapted from an unpublished case discussion prepared by Drs. Mark J. Bliton, Stuart G. Finder, and Richard M. Zaner; it is used with permission.

2. Jecker NS, Schneiderman LJ. Is Dying Young Worse than Dying Old? *Gerontologist* 1994;34(*1*): 66–72.

3. Darwall SL. Two Kinds of Respect. *Ethics* 1977;88(*1*): 36–49.

4. Jecker NS, Schneiderman LJ. Rationing and Futility. *American Journal of Medicine* 1992; 92: 189–96.

5. Schneiderman LJ, Jecker NS, Jonsen AR. Medical Futility: Its Meaning and Ethical Implications. *Annals of Internal Medicine* 1990; 112: 949–54.

6. Schneiderman LJ, Jecker NS. *Wrong Medicine.* Baltimore: Johns Hopkins University Press, 1995.

7. Alexander S. They Decide Who Lives, Who Dies. *Life Magazine.* November 9, 1962. 102–25.

8. Fox RC, Swazey, JP. *The Courage to Fail.* Chicago: University of Chicago Press, 1974.

9. Sanders D, Dukeminier J. Medical Advance and Legal Lag. *UCLA Law Review* 1968; 15: 357–413, at 378.

10. Kilner JF. *Who Lives, Who Dies?* New Haven: Yale University Press, 1990, p. 221.

11. Childress J. Who Shall Live When Not All Can Live? In: Veatch R, Branson R, Eds. *Ethics and Health Policy.* Cambridge, Massachusetts: Ballinger Publishing Company, 1976, p. 210.

12. Beauchamp T, Childress J. *Principles of Biomedical Ethics, 4th edition.* New York: Oxford University Press, 1994, p. 385.

13. Ramsey, P. *The Patient as Person.* New Haven: Yale University Press, 1970, pp. 257–58.

14. Basson MD. Choosing Among Candidates for Scarce Medical Resources. *Journal of Medicine and Philosophy* 1979; 4: 313–33.

15. Beauchamp T, Childress J. *Principles of Biomedical Ethics, 4th edition.* New York: Oxford University Press, 1994, pp. 384–86.

16. Rescher N. The Allocation of Exotic Medical Lifesaving Therapy. *Ethics* 1969; vol 69.

17. Winslow GR. *Triage and Justice.* Berkeley and Los Angeles: University of California Press, 1982.

18. Rawls J. *A Theory of Justice.* Cambridge, Massachusetts: Harvard University Press, 1971.

19. Levinsky N. The Doctor's Master. *New England Journal of Medicine* 1984; 311: 1573–75.

20. Schneiderman LJ, Jecker NS. Should a Criminal Receive a Heart Transplant? *Theoretical Medicine* 1996; 17(1): 33–44.

21. Schneiderman LJ, Jecker NS. A Different Kind of 'Prisoner's Dilemma.' *Cambridge Quarterly of Healthcare Ethics* 1995; 4: 531–34.

22. American Medical Association, Council on Ethical and Judicial Affairs. Ethical Considerations in the Allocation of Organs and Other Scarce Medical Resources Among Patients. *Archives of Internal Medicine* 1995; 155: 29–40, p. 32.

23. Jecker NS. Fidelity to Patients and Resource Constraints. In Campbell C, Ed., *Duties to Others.* Boston: Kluwer Academic Publishers, 1994: 293–308.

24. Morreim EH. Gaming the System. *Archives of Internal Medicine* 1991; 151: 443–7.

25. Morreim EH. Cost Containment: Challenging Fidelity and Justice. *Hastings Center Report* 1988; 18(6): 20–5.

26. Although identifying separate spheres of medical and social decisionmaking provides a helpful starting point, it is important to recognize the limits of this approach. On the one hand, social values inevitably spill over into healthcare decisions, and it would be misleading to characterize medical judgments as purely technical or value-free. One illustration of this is that the choice of how low the likelihood of benefit must be to qualify as futile depends upon a substantive value decision. Thus, the values that health professionals bring to bear in developing standards of care must ultimately be acceptable to the wider society. Social values also spill over into healthcare decision making because the determination of medical benefit may itself be affected by a patient's social, economic, or personal circumstances. For instance, a patient who lacks social or family support may be considered less likely to benefit from certain treatments compared to a patient from a "good home" who has the benefit of a parent or spouse who can provide around the clock support. Thus, a liver transplant candidate who lacks a supportive family may be considered less likely to benefit from transplant surgery.

27. Brock D. Ethics Committees and Cost Containment. *Hastings Center Report* 1990; 20(2): 29–31, p. 30.

PAUL CHODOFF

The Case for Involuntary Hospitalization of the Mentally Ill

I will begin this paper with a series of vignettes designed to illustrate graphically the question that is my focus: under what conditions, if any, does society have the right to apply coercion to an individual to hospitalize him against his will, by reason of mental illness?

Reprinted from *American Journal of Psychiatry,* 133 (May 1976) 496–501. Copyright 1976, the American Psychiatric Association. Reprinted by permission.

Case 1. A woman in her mid 50s, with no previous overt behavioral difficulties, comes to believe that she is worthless and insignificant. She is completely preoccupied with her guilt and is increasingly unavailable for the ordinary demands of life. She eats very little because of her conviction that the food should go to others whose need is greater than hers, and her physical condition progressively deteriorates. Although she will talk to others about herself, she insists that she is not sick, only bad. She refuses medication, and when hospitalization is suggested she also refuses that on the grounds that she would be taking up space that otherwise could be occupied by those who merit treatment more than she.

Case 2. For the past 6 years the behavior of a 42-year-old woman has been disturbed for periods of 3 months or longer. After recovery from her most recent episode she has been at home, functioning at a borderline level. A month ago she again started to withdraw from her environment. She pays increasingly less attention to her bodily needs, talks very little, and does not respond to questions or attention from those about her. She lapses into a mute state and lies in her bed in a totally passive fashion. She does not respond to other people, does not eat, and does not void. When her arm is raised from the bed it remains for several minutes in the position in which it is left. Her medical history and a physical examination reveal no evidence of primary physical illness.

Case 3. A man with a history of alcoholism has been on a binge for several weeks. He remains at home doing little else than drinking. He eats very little. He becomes tremulous and misinterprets spots on the wall as animals about to attack him, and he complains of "creeping" sensations in his body, which he attributes to infestation by insects. He does not seek help voluntarily, insists there is nothing wrong with him, and despite his wife's entreaties he continues to drink.

Case 4. Passersby and station personnel observe that a young woman has been spending several days at Union Station in Washington, D.C. Her behavior appears strange to others. She is finally befriended by a newspaper reporter who becomes aware that her perception of her situation is profoundly unrealistic and that she is, in fact, delusional. He persuades her to accompany him to St. Elizabeth's Hospital, where she is examined by a psychiatrist who recommends admission. She refuses hospitalization and the psychiatrist allows her to leave. She returns to Union Station. A few days later she is found dead, murdered, on one of the surrounding streets.

Case 5. A government attorney in his late 30s begins to display pressured speech and hyperactivity. He is too busy to sleep and eats very little. He talks rapidly, becomes irritable when interrupted, and makes phone calls all over the country in furtherance of his political ambitions, which are to begin a campaign for the presidency of the United States. He makes many purchases, some very expensive, thus running through a great deal of money. He is rude and tactless to his friends, who are offended by his behavior, and his job is in jeopardy. In spite of his wife's pleas he insists that he does not have the time to seek or accept treatment, and he refuses hospitalization. This is not the first such disturbance for this individual; in fact, very similar episodes have been occurring at roughly 2-year intervals since he was 18 years old.

Case 6. Passersby in a campus area observe two young women standing together, staring at each other, for over an hour. Their behavior attracts attention, and eventually the police take the pair to a nearby precinct station for questioning. They refuse to answer questions and sit mutely, staring into space. The police request some type of psychiatric examination but are informed by the city attorney's office that state law (Michigan) allows persons to be held for observation only if they appear obviously dangerous to themselves or others. In this case, since the women do not seem homicidal or suicidal, they do not qualify for observation and are released.

Less than 30 hours later the two women are found on the floor of their campus apartment, screaming and writhing in pain with their clothes ablaze from a self-made pyre. One woman recovers; the other dies. There is no conclusive evidence that drugs were involved.[1]

Most, if not all, people would agree that the behavior described in these vignettes deviates significantly from even elastic definitions of normality. However, it is clear that there would not be a similar consensus on how to react to this kind of behavior and that there is a considerable and increasing ferment about what attitude the organized elements of our society should take toward such individuals. Everyone has a stake in this important issue, but the debate about it takes place principally among psychiatrists, lawyers, the courts, and law enforcement agencies.

Points of view about the question of involuntary hospitalization fall into the following three principal groups: the "abolitionists," medical model psychiatrists, and civil liberties lawyers.

THE ABOLITIONISTS

Those holding this position would assert that in none of the cases I have described should involuntary hospitalization be a viable option because, quite simply, it should never be resorted to under any circumstances. As Szasz[2] has put it, "we should value liberty more highly than mental health no matter how defined" and "no one should be deprived of his freedom for the sake of his mental health." Ennis[3] has said that the goal "is nothing less than the abolition of involuntary hospitalization."

Prominent among the abolitionists are the "anti-psychiatrists," who, somewhat surprisingly, count in their ranks a number of well-known psychiatrists. For them mental illness simply does not exist in the field of psychiatry.[4] They reject entirely the medical model of mental illness and insist that acceptance of it relies on a fiction accepted jointly by the state and by psychiatrists as a device for exerting social control over annoying or unconventional people. The anti-psychiatrists hold that these people ought to be afforded the dignity of being held responsible for their behavior and required to accept its consequences. In addition, some members of this group believe that the phenomena of "mental illness" often represent essentially a tortured protest against the insanities of an irrational society.[5] They maintain that society should not be encouraged in its oppressive course by affixing a pejorative label to its victims.

Among the abolitionists are some civil liberties lawyers who both assert their passionate support of the magisterial importance of individual liberty and react with repugnance and impatience to what they see as the abuses of psychiatric practice in this field—the commitment of some individuals for flimsy and possibly self-serving reasons and their inhuman warehousing in penal institutions wrongly called "hospitals."

The abolitionists do not oppose psychiatric treatment when it is conducted with the agreement of those being treated. I have no doubt that they would try to gain the consent of the individuals described earlier to undergo treatment, including hospitalization. The psychiatrists in this group would be very likely to confine their treatment methods to psychotherapeutic efforts to influence the aberrant behavior. They would be unlikely to use drugs and would certainly eschew such somatic therapies as ECT [electroconvulsive therapy]. If efforts to enlist voluntary compliance with treatment

failed, the abolitionists would not employ any means of coercion. Instead, they would step aside and allow social, legal, and community sanctions to take their course. If a human being should be jailed or a human life lost as a result of this attitude, they would accept it as a necessary evil to be tolerated in order to avoid the greater evil of unjustified loss of liberty for others.[6]

THE MEDICAL MODEL PSYCHIATRISTS

I use this admittedly awkward and not entirely accurate label to designate the position of a substantial number of psychiatrists. They believe that mental illness is a meaningful concept and that under certain conditions its existence justifies the state's exercise, under the doctrine of *parens patriae,* of its right and obligation to arrange for the hospitalization of the sick individual even though coercion is involved and he is deprived of his liberty. I believe that these psychiatrists would recommend involuntary hospitalization for all six of the patients described earlier.

THE MEDICAL MODEL

There was a time, before they were considered to be ill, when individuals who displayed the kind of behavior I described earlier were put in "ships of fools" to wander the seas or were left to the mercies, sometimes tender but often savage, of uncomprehending communities that regarded them as either possessed or bad. During the Enlightenment and the early nineteenth century, however, these individuals gradually came to be regarded as sick people to be included under the humane and caring umbrella of the Judeo-Christian attitude toward illness. This attitude, which may have reached its height during the era of moral treatment in the early nineteenth century, has had unexpected and ambiguous consequences. It became overextended and partially perverted, and these excesses led to the reaction that is so strong a current in today's attitude toward mental illness.

However, reaction itself can go too far, and I believe that this is already happening. Witness the disastrous consequences of the precipitate dehospitalization that is occurring all over the country. To remove the protective mantle of illness from these disturbed people is to expose them, their families, and their communities to consequences that are certainly maladaptive and possibly irreparable. Are we really acting in accordance with their best interests when we allow them to "die with their rights on"[1] or when we condemn them to a "preservation of liberty which is actually so destructive as to constitute another form of imprisonment"?[7] Will they not suffer "if [a] liberty they cannot enjoy is made superior to a health that must sometimes be forced on them"?[8]

Many of those who reject the medical model out of hand as inapplicable to so-called "mental illness" have tended to oversimplify its meaning and have, in fact, equated it almost entirely with organic disease. It is necessary to recognize that it is a complex concept and that there is a lack of agreement about its meaning. Sophisticated definitions of the medical model do not require only the demonstration of unequivocal organic pathology. A broader formulation, put forward by sociologists and deriving largely from Talcott Parsons' description of the sick role,[9] extends the domain of illness to encompass certain forms of social deviance as well as biological disorders. According to this definition, the medical model is characterized not only by organicity but also by being negatively valued by society, by "non-voluntariness," thus exempting its exemplars from blame, and by the understanding that physicians are the technically competent experts to deal with its effects.[10]

Except for the question of organic disease, the patients I described earlier conform well to this broader conception of the medical model. They are all suffering both emotionally and physically, they are incapable by an effort of will of stopping or changing their destructive behavior, and those around them consider them to be in an undesirable sick state and to require medical attention.

Categorizing the behavior of these patients as involuntary may be criticized as evidence of an intolerably paternalistic and antitherapeutic attitude that fosters the very failure to take responsibility for their lives and behavior that the therapist should uncover rather than encourage. However, it must also be acknowledged that these severely ill people are not capable at a conscious level of deciding what is best for themselves and that in order to help them examine their behavior and motivation, it is necessary that they be alive and available for treatment. Their verbal message that they will not accept treatment may at the same time be conveying other more covert messages—that they are desperate and want help even though they cannot ask for it.[11]

Although organic pathology may not be the only determinant of the medical model, it is of course an important one and it should not be avoided in any discussion of mental illness. There would be no question that the previously described patient with delirium tremens is suffering from a toxic form of brain disease. There are a significant number of other patients who require involuntary hospitalization because of organic brain syndrome due to various causes. Among those who are not overtly organically ill, most of the candidates for involuntary hospitalization suffer from schizophrenia or one of the major affective disorders. A growing and increasingly impressive body of evidence points to the presence of an important genetic-biological factor in these conditions; thus, many of them qualify on these grounds as illnesses.

Despite the revisionist efforts of the anti-psychiatrists, mental illness *does* exist. It does not by any means include all of the people being treated by psychiatrists (or by nonpsychiatrist physicians), but it does encompass those few desperately sick people for whom involuntary commitment must be considered. In the words of a recent article, "The problem is that mental illness is not a myth. It is not some palpable falsehood propagated among the populace by power-mad psychiatrists, but a cruel and bitter reality that has been with the human race since antiquity."[12]

CRITERIA FOR INVOLUNTARY HOSPITALIZATION

Procedures for involuntary hospitalization should be instituted for individuals who require care and treatment because of diagnosable mental illness that produces symptoms, including marked impairment in judgment, that disrupt their intrapsychic and interpersonal functioning. All three of these criteria must be met before involuntary hospitalization can be instituted.

1. Mental Illness. This concept has already been discussed, but it should be repeated that only a belief in the existence of illness justifies involuntary commitment. It is a fundamental assumption that makes aberrant behavior a medical matter and its care the concern of physicians.

2. Disruption of Functioning. This involves combinations of serious and often obvious disturbances that are both intrapsychic (for example, the suffering of severe depression) and interpersonal (for example, withdrawal from others because of depression). It does not include minor peccadilloes or eccentricities. Furthermore, the behavior in question must represent symptoms of the mental illness from which the patient is suffering. Among these symptoms are actions that are imminently or potentially dangerous in a physical sense to self or others, as well as other manifestations of mental illness such as those in the cases I have described. This is not to ignore dangerousness as a criterion for commitment but rather to put it in its proper place as one of a number of symptoms of the illness. A further manifestation of the illness, and indeed, the one that makes involuntary rather than voluntary hospitalization necessary, is impairment of the patient's judgment to such a degree that he is unable to consider his condition and make decisions about it in his own interests.

3. Need for Care and Treatment. The goal of physicians is to treat and cure their patients; however, sometimes they can only ameliorate the suffering of their patients and sometimes all they can offer is care. It is not possible to predict whether someone will respond to treatment; nevertheless, the need for treatment and the availability of facilities to carry it out constitute essential preconditions that must be met to justify requiring anyone to give up his freedom. If mental hospital patients have a right to treatment, then psychiatrists have a right to ask for treatability as a front-door as well as a back-door criterion for commitment.[7] All of the six individuals I described earlier could have been treated with a reasonable expectation of return to a more normal state of functioning.

I believe that the objections to this formulation can be summarized as follows:

1. The whole structure founders for those who maintain that mental illness is a fiction.

2. These criteria are also untenable to those who hold liberty to be such a supreme value that the presence of mental illness per se does not constitute justification for depriving an individual of his freedom; only when such illness is manifested by clearly dangerous behavior may commitment be considered. For reasons to be discussed later, I agree with those psychiatrists[13, 14] who do not believe that dangerousness should be elevated to primacy above other manifestations of mental illness as a *sine qua non* for involuntary hospitalization.

3. The medical model criteria are "soft" and subjective and depend on the fallible judgment of psychiatrists. This is a valid objection. There is no reliable blood test for schizophrenia and no method for injecting grey cells into psychiatrists. A relatively small number of cases will always fall within a grey area that

will be difficult to judge. In those extreme cases in which the question of commitment arises, competent and ethical psychiatrists should be able to use these criteria without doing violence to individual liberties and with the expectation of good results. Furthermore, the possible "fuzziness" of some aspects of the medical model approach is certainly no greater than that of the supposedly "objective" criteria for dangerousness, and there is little reason to believe that lawyers and judges are any less fallible than psychiatrists.

4. Commitment procedures in the hands of psychiatrists are subject to intolerable abuses. Here, as Peszke said, "It is imperative that we differentiate between the principle of the process of civil commitment and the practice itself."[13] Abuses can contaminate both the medical and the dangerousness approaches, and I believe that the abuses stemming from the abolitionist view of no commitment at all are even greater. Measures to abate abuses of the medical approach include judicial review and the abandonment of indeterminate commitment. In the course of commitment proceedings and thereafter, patients should have access to competent and compassionate legal counsel. However, this latter safeguard may itself be subject to abuse if the legal counsel acts solely in the adversary tradition and undertakes to carry out the patient's wishes even when they may be destructive.

COMMENT

The criteria and procedures outlined will apply most appropriately to initial episodes and recurrent attacks of mental illness. To put it simply, it is necessary to find a way to satisfy legal and humanitarian considerations and yet allow psychiatrists access to initially or acutely ill patients in order to do the best they can for them. However, there are some involuntary patients who have received adequate and active treatment but have not responded satisfactorily. An irreducible minimum of such cases, principally among those with brain disorders and process schizophrenia, will not improve sufficiently to be able to adapt to even a tolerant society.

The decision of what to do at this point is not an easy one, and it should certainly not be in the hands of psychiatrists alone. With some justification they can state that they have been given the thankless job of caring, often with inadequate facilities, for badly damaged people and that they are now being subjected to criticism for keeping these patients locked up. No one really knows what to do with these patients. It may be that when treatment has failed they exchange their sick role for what has been called the impaired role,[15] which implies a permanent negative evaluation of them coupled with a somewhat less benign societal attitude. At this point, perhaps a case can be made for giving greater importance to the criteria for dangerousness and releasing such patients if they do not pose a threat to others. However, I do not believe that the release into the community of these severely malfunctioning individuals will serve their interests even though it may satisfy formal notions of right and wrong.

It should be emphasized that the number of individuals for whom involuntary commitment must be considered is small (although, under the influence of current pressures, it may be smaller than it should be). Even severe mental illness can often be handled by securing the cooperation of the patient, and certainly one of the favorable effects of the current ferment has been to encourage such efforts. However, the distinction between voluntary and involuntary hospitalization is sometimes more formal than meaningful. How "voluntary" are the actions of an individual who is being buffeted by the threats, entreaties, and tears of his family?

I believe, however, that we are at a point (at least in some jurisdictions) where, having rebounded from an era in which involuntary commitment was too easy and employed too often, we are now entering one in which it is becoming very difficult to commit anyone, even in urgent cases. Faced with the moral obloquy that has come to pervade the atmosphere in which the decision to involuntarily hospitalize is considered, some psychiatrists, especially younger ones, have become, as Stone[16] put it, "soft as grapes" when faced with the prospect of committing anyone under any circumstances.

THE CIVIL LIBERTIES LAWYERS

I use this admittedly inexact label to designate those members of the legal profession who do not in principle reject the necessity for involuntary hospitalization but who do reject or wish to diminish the importance of medical model criteria in the hands of psychiatrists. Accordingly, the civil liberties lawyers, in dealing with the problem of involuntary hospitalization, have enlisted themselves under the standard of dangerousness, which they hold to be more objective and capable of being dealt with in a sounder evidentiary manner than the medical model criteria. For them the question is not whether mental illness, even of disabling degree, is present, but only whether it has resulted in the probability of behavior dangerous to others or to self. Thus they would scrutinize the cases previously described for evidence of such dangerousness and would make the decision about involuntary hospitalization accordingly. They would probably feel that commitment is not indicated in most of these cases, since they were selected as illustrative of severe mental illness in which outstanding evidence of physical dangerousness was not present.

The dangerousness standard is being used increasingly not only to supplement criteria for mental illness but, in fact, to replace them entirely. The recent Supreme Court decision in *O'Connor v. Donaldson*[17] is certainly a long step in this direction. In addition, "dangerousness" is increasingly being understood to refer to the probability that the individual will inflict harm on himself or others in a specific physical manner rather than in other ways. This tendency has perhaps been carried to its ultimate in the *Lessard v. Schmidt* case[18] in Wisconsin, which restricted suitability for commitment to the "extreme likelihood that if the person is not confined, he will do immediate harm to himself or others." (This decision was set aside by the U.S. Supreme Court in 1974.) In a recent Washington, D.C., Superior Court case[19] the instructions to the jury stated that the government must prove that the defendant was likely to cause "substantial physical harm to himself or others in the reasonably foreseeable future."

For the following reasons, the dangerousness standard is an inappropriate and dangerous indicator to use in judging the conditions under which someone should be involuntarily hospitalized. Dangerousness is being taken out of its proper context as one among other symptoms of the presence of severe mental illness that should be the determining factor.

1. To concentrate on dangerousness (especially to others) as the sole criterion for involuntary hospitalization deprives many mentally ill persons of the protection and treatment that they urgently require. A psychiatrist under the constraints of the dangerousness rule, faced with an out-of-control manic individual whose frantic behavior the psychiatrist truly believes to be a disguised call for help, would have to say, "Sorry, I would like to help you but I can't because you haven't threatened anybody and you are not suicidal." Since psychiatrists are admittedly not very good at accurately predicting dangerousness to others, the evidentiary standards for commitment will be very stringent. This will result in mental hospitals becoming prisons for a

2. The attempt to differentiate rigidly (especially in regard to danger to self) between physical and other kinds of self-destructive behavior is artificial, unrealistic, and unworkable. It will tend to confront psychiatrists who want to help their patients with the same kind of dilemma they were faced with when justification for therapeutic abortion on psychiatric grounds depended on evidence of suicidal intent. The advocates of the dangerousness standard seem to be more comfortable with and pay more attention to the factor of dangerousness to others even though it is a much less frequent and much less significant consequence of mental illness than is danger to self.

3. The emphasis on dangerousness (again, especially to others) is a real obstacle to the right-to-treatment movement since it prevents the hospitalization and therefore the treatment of the population most amenable to various kinds of therapy.

4. Emphasis on the criterion of dangerousness to others moves involuntary commitment from a civil to a criminal procedure, thus, as Stone[14] put it, imposing the procedures of one terrible system on another. Involuntary commitment on these grounds becomes a form of preventive detention and makes the psychiatrist a kind of glorified policeman.

5. Emphasis on dangerousness rather than mental disability and helplessness will hasten the process of deinstitutionalization. Recent reports[20, 21] have shown that these patients are not being rehabilitated and reintegrated into the community, but rather, that the burden of custodialism has been shifted from the hospital to the community.

6. As previously mentioned, emphasis on the dangerousness criterion may be a tactic of some of the abolitionists among the civil liberties lawyers[22] to end involuntary hospitalization by reducing it to an unworkable absurdity.

DISCUSSION

It is obvious that it is good to be at liberty and that it is good to be free from the consequences of disabling and dehumanizing illness. Sometimes these two values are incompatible, and in the heat of the passions that are often aroused by opposing views of right and wrong, the partisans of each view may tend to minimize the importance of the other. Both sides can present their horror stories — the psychiatrists, their dead victims of the failure of the involuntary hospitalization process,

and the lawyers, their Donaldsons. There is a real danger that instead of acknowledging the difficulty of the problem, the two camps will become polarized, with a consequent rush toward extreme and untenable solutions rather than working toward reasonable ones.

The path taken by those whom I have labeled the abolitionists is an example of the barren results that ensue when an absolute solution is imposed on a complex problem. There are human beings who will suffer greatly if the abolitionists succeed in elevating an abstract principle into an unbreakable law with no exceptions. I find myself oppressed and repelled by their position, which seems to stem from an ideological rigidity which ignores that element of the contingent immanent in the structure of human existence. It is devoid of compassion.

The positions of those who espouse the medical model and the dangerousness approaches to commitment are, one hopes, not completely irreconcilable. To some extent these differences are a result of the vantage points from which lawyers and psychiatrists view mental illness and commitment. The lawyers see and are concerned with the failures and abuses of the process. Furthermore, as a result of their training, they tend to apply principles to classes of people rather than to take each instance as unique. The psychiatrists, on the other hand, are required to deal practically with the singular needs of individuals. They approach the problem from a clinical rather than a deductive stance. As physicians, they want to be in a position to take care of and to help suffering people whom they regard as sick patients. They sometimes become impatient with the rules that prevent them from doing this.

I believe we are now witnessing a pendular swing in which the rights of the mentally ill to be treated and protected are being set aside in the rush to give them their freedom at whatever cost. But is freedom defined only by the absence of external constraints? Internal physiological or psychological processes can contribute to a throttling of the spirit that is as painful as any applied from the outside. The "wild" manic individual without his lithium, the panicky hallucinator without his injection of fluphenazine hydrochloride and the understanding support of a concerned staff, the sodden alcoholic — are they free? Sometimes, as Woody Guthrie said, "Freedom means no place to go."

Today the civil liberties lawyers are in the ascendancy and the psychiatrists on the defensive to a degree that is harmful to individual needs and the public welfare. Redress and a more balanced position will not come from further extension of the dangerousness doctrine. I favor a return to the use of medical criteria by psychiatrists — psychiatrists, however, who have been chastened by the buffeting they have received and are quite willing to go along with even strict legal safeguards as long as they are constructive and not tyrannical.

NOTES

1. Treffert, D. A.: "The practical limits of patients' rights." *Psychiatric Annals* 5(4):91–96, 1971.

2. Szasz, T.: *Law, Liberty and Psychiatry.* New York, Macmillan Co., 1963.

3. Ennis, B.: *Prisoners of Psychiatry.* New York, Harcourt Brace Jovanovich, 1972.

4. Szasz, T.: *The Myth of Mental Illness.* New York, Harper & Row, 1961.

5. Laing, R.: *The Politics of Experience.* New York, Ballantine Books, 1967.

6. Ennis, B.: "Ennis on 'Donaldson.'" *Psychiatric News,* Dec. 3, 1975, pp. 4, 19, 37.

7. Peele, R., Chodoff, P., Taub, N.: "Involuntary hospitalization and treatability. Observations from the DC experience." *Catholic University Law Review* 23:744–753, 1974.

8. Michels, R.: "The right to refuse psychotropic drugs." *Hastings Center Report,* 3(3):10–11, 1973.

9. Parsons, T.: *The Social System.* New York, Free Press, 1951.

10. Veatch, R. M.: "The medical model: its nature and problems." *Hastings Center Studies* 1(3):59–76, 1973.

11. Katz, J.: "The right to treatment — an enchanting legal fiction?" *University of Chicago Law Review* 36:755–783, 1969.

12. Moore, M. S.: "Some myths about mental illness." *Arch Gen Psychiatry* 32:1483–1497, 1975.

13. Peszke, M. A.: "Is dangerousness an issue for physicians in emergency commitment?" *Am J Psychiatry* 132:825–828, 1975.

14. Stone, A. A.: "Comment on Peszke, M. A.: Is dangerousness an issue for physicians in emergency commitment?" *Ibid.,* 829–831.

15. Siegler, M., Osmond, H.: *Models of Madness, Models of Medicine.* New York, Macmillan Co., 1974.

16. Stone, A.: Lecture for course on The Law, Litigation, and Mental Health Services. Adelphi, Md., Mental Health Study Center, September 1974.

17. *O'Connor v. Donaldson,* 43 USLW 4929 (1975).

18. *Lessard v. Schmidt,* 349 F Supp 1078, 1092 (ED Wis 1972).

19. In re Johnnie Hargrove. Washington, D.C., Superior Court Mental Health number 506–575, 1975.

20. Rachlin, S., Pam, A., Milton, J.: "Civil liberties versus involuntary hospitalization." *Am J Psychiatry* 132:189–191, 1975.

21. Kirk, S. A., Therrien, M. E.: "Community mental health myths and the fate of former hospitalized patients." *Psychiatry* 38:209–217, 1975.

22. Dershowitz, A. A.: "Dangerousness as a criterion for confinement." *Bulletin of the American Academy of Psychiatry and the Law* 2:172–179, 1974.

SUGGESTED READINGS

GENERAL ISSUES

Ackerman, Terrence F., and Strong, Carson. *A Casebook of Medical Ethics.* New ed. New York: Oxford University Press, 1992.

Annas, George J. *Standard of Care: The Law of American Bioethics.* New York: Oxford University Press, 1993.

————. *Some Choice: Current Legal Issues in Medicine.* New York: Oxford University Press, 1998.

Bandman, Elsie L., and Bandman, Bertram. *Nursing Ethics Through the Life Span.* 3rd ed. Norwalk, CT: Appleton and Lange, 1995.

Bankowski, Zbigniew, and Bryant, John H. *Poverty, Vulnerability, the Value of Human Life and the Emergence of Bioethics.* Geneva: Council for International Organizations of Medical Sciences, 1995.

Beauchamp, Tom L., and Childress, James F. *Principles of Biomedical Ethics.* 4th ed. New York: Oxford University Press, 1994.

Benatar, Solomon R. "Just Healthcare beyond Individualism: Challenges for North American Bioethics." *Cambridge Quarterly for Healthcare Ethics* 6 (1997), 397–415.

Benjamin, Martin. "Nursing Ethics." In Becker, Lawrence C., and Becker, Charlotte B., eds., *Encyclopedia of Ethics.* New York: Garland, 1992, 915–17.

————, and Curtis, Joy. *Ethics in Nursing.* 3rd ed. New York: Oxford University Press, 1992.

Bloom, Samuel W. "Professional–Patient Relationship: II. Sociological Perspectives." In Reich, Warren Thomas, ed. *Encyclopedia of Bioethics.* Revised ed. New York: Simon and Schuster Macmillan, 1995, 2084–94.

Brock, Dan W., and Wartman, Steven A. "When Competent Patients Make Irrational Choices." *New England Journal of Medicine* 322 (1990), 1595–99.

Brody, Baruch. *Life and Death Decision Making.* New York: Oxford University Press, 1988.

Brody, Howard. *Ethical Decisions in Medicine.* 2nd ed. Boston: Little, Brown, 1981.

————. *The Healer's Power.* New Haven, CT: Yale University Press, 1992.

Campbell, Alastair *et al. Medical Ethics.* 2nd ed. New York: Oxford University Press, 1997.

Caplan, Arthur L. *If I Were a Rich Man Could I Buy a Pancreas? — And Other Essays on the Ethics of Health Care.* Bloomington, IN: Indiana University Press, 1992.

————. *Moral Matters: Ethical Issues in Medicine and the Life Sciences.* New York: Wiley, 1995.

————. *Am I My Brother's Keeper? The Ethical Frontiers of Biomedicine.* Bloomington, IN: Indiana University Press, 1997.

————. *Due Consideration: Controversy in the Age of Medical Miracles.* New York: Wiley, 1998.

Davis, Anne J. *et al. Ethical Dilemmas and Nursing Practice.* 4th ed. Norwalk, CT: Appleton-Century-Crofts, 1997.

Downie, R. S., ed. *Medical Ethics.* Brookfield, VT: Dartmouth Publishing Co., 1996.

Dubler, Nancy Neveloff, and Nimmons, David. *Ethics on Call: A Medical Ethicist Shows How to Take Charge of Life-and-Death Choices.* New York: Harmony Books, 1992.

Emanuel, Ezekiel J. *The Ends of Human Life: Medical Ethics in a Liberal Polity.* Cambridge, MA: Harvard University Press, 1991.

Engelhardt, H. Tristram, Jr. *The Foundations of Bioethics.* 2nd ed. New York: Oxford University Press, 1996.

Fulford, K. W. M.; Gillett, Grant R.; and Martin, Janet, eds. *Medicine and Moral Reasoning*. New York: Cambridge University Press, 1994.

Flack, Harley E., and Pellegrino, Edmund D., eds. *African-American Perspectives on Biomedical Ethics*. Washington, DC: Georgetown University Press, 1992.

Fry, Sara T., ed. "Nursing Ethics." *Journal of Medicine and Philosophy* 16 (1991), 231–359. Thematic issue.

———. *Ethics in Nursing Practice: A Guide to Ethical Decision Making*. Geneva: International Council of Nurses, 1994.

Gillon, Ranaan. *Philosophical Medical Ethics*. New York: Wiley, 1986.

———, and Lloyd, Ann, eds. *Principles of Healthcare Ethics*. New York: John Wiley & Sons, 1994.

Gorovitz, Samuel. *Drawing the Line: Life, Death, and Ethical Choices in an American Hospital*. New York: Oxford University Press, 1991.

Gregory, John. *John Gregory's Writings on Medical Ethics and Philosophy of Medicine*. Laurence B. McCullough, ed. Dordrecht: Kluwer Academic, 1998.

Hanna, Kathi E. *Biomedical Politics*. Washington, DC: National Academy Press, 1991.

Jecker, Nancy S.; Jonsen, Albert R.; and Pearlman, Robert A., eds. *Bioethics: An Introduction to the History, Methods, and Practice*. Sudbury, MA: Jones and Bartlett, 1997.

———; and Reich, Warren T. "Contemporary Ethics of Care." In Warren Thomas Reich, ed. *Encyclopedia of Bioethics*. Revised ed. New York: Simon & Schuster Macmillan, 1995, 336–44.

Jonsen, Albert R., and Jameton, Andrew. "History of Medical Ethics: V. The Americas. B. The United States in the Twentieth Century." In Warren Thomas Reich, ed. *Encyclopedia of Bioethics*. Revised ed. New York: Simon and Schuster Macmillan, 1995, 1616–32.

———. *The Birth of Bioethics*. New York: Oxford University Press, 1998.

———; Siegler, Mark; and Winslade, William J. *Clinical Ethics: A Practical Approach to Ethical Decisions in Clinical Medicine*. 4th ed. New York: McGraw-Hill, 1998.

———; Veatch, Robert M.; and Walters, LeRoy, eds. *Source Book in Bioethics: A Documentary History*. Washington, DC: Georgetown University Press, 1998.

Katz, Jay. *The Silent World of Doctor and Patient*. New York: Free Press, 1984.

Kass, Leon R. *Toward a More Natural Science: Biology and Human Affairs*. New York: Free Press, 1985.

Kennedy, Ian. *Treat Me Right: Essays in Medical Law and Ethics*. New York: Oxford University Press, 1988.

———, *Principles of Medical Law*. New York: Oxford University Press, 1998.

———, and Grubb, Andrew. *Medical Law: Text with Materials*. 2nd ed. London: Butterworths, 1994.

Levin, Betty Wolder, and Schiller, Nina Glick. "Social and Medical Decisionmaking: A Neglected Topic in Bioethics." *Cambridge Quarterly of Healthcare Ethics* 7 (1998), 41–56.

Macklin, Ruth. *Mortal Choices: Bioethics in Today's World*. New York: Pantheon Books, 1987.

———. *Enemies of Patients*. New York: Oxford University Press, 1993.

Mappes, Thomas A., and DeGrazia, David. *Biomedical Ethics*. 4th ed. New York: McGraw-Hill, 1996.

McCormick, Richard A. *How Brave a New World?* Expanded ed. Washington, DC: Georgetown University Press, 1985.

McCullough, Laurence B. *John Gregory and the Invention of Professional Medical Ethics and Profession of Medicine*. Dordrecht: Kluwer Academic, 1998.

———, Jones, James W.; and Brody, Baruch A. *Surgical Ethics*. New York: Oxford University Press, 1998.

Mechanic, David. "Changing Medical Organization and the Erosion of Trust." *Milbank Quarterly* 74 (1996): 171–89.

Moreno, Jonathan D. *Deciding Together: Bioethics and Moral Consensus*. New York: Oxford University Press, 1995.

Pellegrino, Edmund, and Thomasma, David. *For the Patient's Good: The Restoration of Beneficence in Health Care*. New York: Oxford University Press, 1988.

Pence, Gregory E. *Classic Cases in Medical Ethics*. 2nd ed. New York: McGraw-Hill, 1995.

Pence, Terry, and Cantrall, Janice, comps. *Ethics in Nursing: An Anthology*. New York: National League for Nursing, 1990.

Peterson, Lynn M., and Brennan, Troyen A. "Medical Ethics and Medical Injuries: Taking Our Duties Seriously." *Journal of Clinical Ethics* 1 (1990), 207–11.

Purtilo, Ruth B. "Professional-Patient Relationship: III. Sociological Perspectives." In Warren Thomas Reich, ed. *Encyclopedia of Bioethics*. Revised ed. New York: Simon and Schuster Macmillan, 1995, 2084–94.

Rothman, David J. *Strangers at the Bedside: A History of How Law and Bioethics Transformed Medical Decision Making*. New York: Basic Books, 1991.

———. *Beginnings Count: The Technological Imperative in American Health Care*. New York: Oxford University Press, 1997.

Ruddick, William. "Medical Ethics." In Lawrence C. Becker, and Charlotte B. Becker, eds. *Encyclopedia of Ethics*. New York: Garland, 1992, 778–81.

Sherwin, Susan. "Feminist and Medical Ethics: Two Different Approaches to Contextual Ethics." *Hypatia* 4 (1989), 57–72.

Silva, Mary Cipriano. *Ethical Decision Making in Nursing Administration*. Norwalk, CT: Appleton and Lange, 1990.

Sommerville, Ann. *Medical Ethics Today: Its Practice and Its Philosophy*. London: BMJ Publishing Group, 1993.

Starr, Paul. *The Social Transformation of American Medicine*. New York: Basic Books, 1982.

Veatch, Robert M. *A Theory of Medical Ethics*. New York: Basic Books, 1981.

———. *The Patient-Physician Relation: The Patient as Partner, Part 2*. Bloomington, IN: Indiana University Press, 1991.

———, ed. *Medical Ethics*. 2nd ed. Sudbury, MA: Jones and Bartlett, 1997.

———, and Fry, Sara T. *Case Studies in Nursing Ethics*. 2nd ed. Boston: Jones and Bartlett, 1995.

———, and Flack, Harley E. *Case Studies in Allied Health Ethics*. Upper Saddle River, NJ: Prentice Hall, 1997.

Warren, Virginia L. "Feminist Directions in Medical Ethics." *Hypatia* 4 (1989), 73–87.

White, Gladys B., ed. *Ethical Dilemmas in Contemporary Nursing Practice*. Washington, DC: American Nurses Publishing, 1992.

PROFESSIONAL CODES AND STATEMENTS

American College of Physicians, Ad Hoc Committee on Medical Ethics. *Ethics Manual*. 4th ed. Philadelphia: The College, 1998.

American Medical Association, Council on Ethical and Judicial Affairs. *Current Opinions with Annotations, 1996–1997 Edition.* Chicago: American Medical Association, 1996.

American Nurses Association. *Code for Nurses with Interpretive Statements.* Kansas City, MO: American Nurses Association, 1985.

American Psychiatric Association, Ethics Committee. *Opinions of the Ethics Committee on the Principles of Medical Ethics: With Annotations Especially Applicable to Psychiatry.* 1995 ed. Washington, DC: American Psychiatric Association, 1995.

Baker, Robert; Porter, Dorothy; and Porter, Roy, eds. *The Codification of Medical Morality: Historical and Philosophical Studies of the Formalization of Western Medical Morality in the Eighteenth and Nineteenth Centuries.* 2 vols. Dordrecht: Kluwer Academic Publishers, 1993.

Baylis, Françoise, and Downie, Jocelyn. *Codes of Ethics: Ethics Codes, Standards, and Guidelines for Professionals Working in a Health Care Setting in Canada.* Toronto: Department of Bioethics, Hospital for Sick Children, 1992.

Beauchamp, Tom L., and McCullough, Laurence B. *Medical Ethics: The Moral Responsibilities of Physicians.* Englewood Cliffs, NJ: Prentice-Hall, 1984.

British Medical Association. *Philosophy and Practice of Medical Ethics.* Revised ed. London: The Association, 1988.

Canadian Medical Association. *The Canadian Medical Association Code of Ethics.* Ottawa: The Association, April 1990.

Coughlin, Steven S., and Beauchamp, Tom L., eds. *Ethics and Epidemiology.* New York: Oxford University Press, 1996.

Gorlin, Rena A. *Codes of Professional Responsibility.* 3rd ed. Washington, DC: Bureau of National Affairs, 1994.

May, William F. "Code, Covenant, Contract, or Philanthropy." *Hastings Center Report* 5 (December 1975), 29–38.

Sharpe, Virginia A. "Why Do No Harm?" *Theoretical Medicine* 18 (March–June 1997), 197–215.

———, and Faden, Alan I. *Medical Harm: Historical, Conceptual, and Ethical Dimensions of Iatrogenic Illness.* New York: Cambridge University Press, 1998.

Spicer, Carol Mason, ed. "Appendix: Codes, Oaths, and Directives Related to Bioethics." In Warren Thomas Reich, ed. *Encyclopedia of Bioethics.* Revised ed. New York: Simon and Schuster Macmillan, 1995, 2599–2842.

———. "Appendix: Nature and Role of Codes and Other Ethics Directives." In Warren Thomas Reich, ed. *Encyclopedia of Bioethics.* Revised ed. New York: Simon and Schuster Macmillan, 1995, 2605–12.

Winslow, Gerald R. "From Loyalty to Advocacy: A New Metaphor for Nursing." *Hastings Center Report* 14 (June 1984), 32–39.

THE VIRTUES AND OBLIGATIONS OF PROFESSIONALS

Agich, George J. "Medicine as Business and Profession." *Theoretical Medicine* 11 (1990), 311–24.

Beauchamp, Tom L., and Childress, James F. *Principles of Biomedical Ethics.* 4th ed. New York: Oxford University Press, 1994. Chapters 7 and 8.

Bernal, Ellen W. "The Nurse as Patient Advocate." *Hastings Center Report* 22 (July–August 1992), 18–23.

Brennan, Troyen A. *Just Doctoring: Medical Ethics in the Liberal State.* Berkeley: University of California Press, 1991.

Caplan, Arthur L., ed. *When Medicine Went Mad: Bioethics and the Holocaust.* Totowa, NJ: Humana Press, 1992.

Carse, Alisa L. "The 'Voice of Care': Implications for Bioethical Education." *Journal of Medicine and Philosophy* 16 (1991), 5–28.

Childress, James F. "Conscience and Conscientious Actions in the Context of MCOs." *Kennedy Institute of Ethics Journal* 7 (1997): 403–11.

Churchill, Larry R. "Reviving a Distinctive Medical Ethic." *Hastings Center Report* 21 (January–February 1991), 25–31.

Daniels, Norman. "Why Saying No to Patients in the United States Is So Hard." *New England Journal of Medicine* 314 (1986), 1380–83.

Danis, Marion, and Churchill, Larry R. "Autonomy and the Common Weal." *Hastings Center Report* 21 (January–February 1991), 25–31.

Emmanuel, Ezekiel J., and Ezekiel, Linda L. "Four Models of the Physician-Patient Relationship." *Journal of the American Medical Association* 267 (1992), 2221–26.

Green, Ronald M. "Medical Joint-Venturing: An Ethical Perspective." *Hastings Center Report* 20 (July–August 1990), 22–26.

Jecker, Nancy S. "Integrating Medical Ethics with Normative Theory: Patient Advocacy and Social Responsibility." *Theoretical Medicine* 11 (1990), 125–39.

Johnson, G. Timothy. "Restoring Trust between Doctor and Patient." *New England Journal of Medicine* 322 (1990), 195–97.

May, William F. *The Patient's Ordeal.* Bloomington, IN: Indiana University Press, 1991.

———. *The Physician's Covenant: Images of the Healer in Medical Ethics.* Philadelphia: Westminster Press, 1983.

Pellegrino, Edmund D., and Thomasma, David C. *The Virtues in Medical Practice.* New York: Oxford University Press, 1993.

———. *The Christian Virtues in Medical Ethics.* Washington, DC: Georgetown University Press, 1996.

Pellegrino, Edmund D.; Veatch, Robert M.; and Langan, John P., eds. *Ethics, Trust, and the Professions: Philosophical and Cultural Aspects.* Washington: Georgetown University Press, 1991.

Ramsey, Paul. *The Patient as Person.* New Haven, CT: Yale University Press, 1970.

Shelp, Earl E., ed. *Virtue and Medicine: Explorations in the Character of Medicine.* Boston: Kluwer Academic Publishers, 1985.

Winslow, Betty J., and Winslow, Gerald R. "Integrity and Compromise in Nursing Ethics." *Journal of Medicine and Philosophy* 16 (1991), 307–23.

PATIENTS' RIGHTS AND RESPONSIBILITIES

Annas, George J. "Patients' Rights: I. Origin and Nature of Patients' Rights." In Warren Thomas Reich, ed. *Encyclopedia of Bioethics.* Revised ed. New York: Simon and Schuster Macmillan, 1995, 1925–27.

———. "Patients' Rights in Managed Care—Exit, Voice, and Choice." *New England Journal of Medicine* 337 (1997): 210–15.

———. *The Rights of Patients: The Basic ACLU Guide to Patient Rights.* 2nd ed. Totowa, NJ: Humana Press, 1992.

———. "Declaration on the Promotion of Patients' Rights in Europe." *European Journal of Health Law* 1 (1994), 279–91.

de Wachter, Maurice A. M. "The European Convention on Bioethics." *Hastings Center Report* 27 (January/February 1997), 12–23.

Dommel, F. William, Jr., and Alexander, Duane. "The Convention on Biomedicine and Human Rights of the Council of Europe." *Kennedy Institute of Ethics Journal* 7 (1997), 259–76.

Leenen, H. J. J. "Development of Patients' Rights and Instruments for the Promotion of Patients' Rights [Editorial]" *European Journal of Health Law* 3 (1996), 105–107.

———. "The Rights of Patients in Europe." *European Journal of Health Law* 1 (1994), 5–13.

———; Bevers, M. K. M. (Sjef); and Pinet, Genevieve. *The Rights of Patients in Europe: A Comparative Study.* Boston: Kluwer Law and Taxation Publishers, for the World Health Organization Regional Office for Europe, 1993.

Levinsky, Norman G. "Social, Institutional, and Economic Barriers to the Exercise of Patients' Rights." *New England Journal of Medicine* 334 (1996), 532–34.

The Patient's Charter. London: Scutari Press, 1995.

President's Advisory Commission of Consumer Protection and Quality in the Health Care Industry. *Quality First: Better Health Care for All Americans: Final Report to the President of the United States.* Washington, DC: U.S. Government Printing Office, 1998.

Promotion of the Rights of Patients in Europe: Proceedings of a WHO Consultation. The Hague and Boston: Kluwer Law International, 1995.

Rodwin, Marc A. "Patient Accountability and Quality of Care: Lessons from Medical Consumerism and the Patients' Rights, Women's Health and Disability Rights Movements." *American Journal of Law and Medicine* 20 (1994), 147–67.

Rosovsky, Lorne E. *The Canadian Patient's Book of Rights: A Consumer's Guide to Canadian Health Law.* Revised and updated. Toronto: Doubleday Canada, 1994.

Schyve, Paul M. "Patient Rights and Organization Ethics: the Joint Commission Perspective." *Bioethics Forum* 12 (Summer 1996), 13–20.

Silver, Melanie H. Wilson. "Patients' Rights in England and the United States of America: *The Patient's Charter* and the New Jersey Patient Bill of Rights: A Comparison." *Journal of Medical Ethics* 23 (1997), 213–30.

PROFESSIONALS AND SPECIFIC
PATIENT POPULATIONS

American Medical Association, Council on Ethical and Judicial Affairs. "Sexual Misconduct in the Practice of Medicine." *Journal of the American Medical Association* 266 (1991), 2741–45.

Agich, George J. *Autonomy and Long-Term Care.* New York: Oxford University Press, 1993.

Asch, Andrienne. "Disability: I. Attitudes and Social Perspectives." In Warren Thomas Reich, ed. *Encyclopedia of Bioethics.* Revised ed. New York: Simon and Schuster Macmillan, 1995, 602–08.

Binstock, Robert H., and Post, Stephen G., eds. *Too Old for Health Care? Controversies in Medicine, Law, Economics, and Ethics.* Baltimore: Johns Hopkins University Press, 1991.

Hilfiker, David. "Unconscious on a Corner. . ." *Journal of the American Medical Association* 258 (1987), 3155–56.

Jecker, Nancy S., ed. *Aging and Ethics: Philosophical Problems in Gerontology.* Clifton, NJ: Humana Press, 1991.

———, and Self, Donnie J. "Medical Ethics in the 21st Century: Respect for Autonomy in Care of the Elderly Patient." *Journal of Critical Care* 6 (1991), 46–51.

Kopelman, Loretta M., and Moskop, John C., eds. *Children and Health Care: Moral and Social Issues.* Boston: Kluwer Academic Publishers, 1989.

Lynn, Joanne. "Ethical Issues in Caring for Elderly Residents of Nursing Homes." *Primary Care* 13 (1986), 295–306.

McCullough, Laurence B., and Chervenak, Frank A. *Ethics in Obstetrics and Gynecology.* New York: Oxford University Press, 1994.

Miles, Steven H. "What Are We Teaching about Indigent Patients?" *Journal of the American Medical Association* 268 (1992), 2561–62.

Tong, Rosemarie. *Feminist Approaches to Bioethics: Theoretical Reflections and Practical Applications.* Boulder, CO: Westview Press, 1997.

Wicclair, Mark R. *Ethics and the Elderly.* New York: Oxford University Press, 1993.

Winick, Bruce J. *The Right to Refuse Mental Health Treatment.* Washington: American Psychological Association, 1997.

JOURNALS

American Journal of Law and Medicine
Bioethics
Cambridge Quarterly of Healthcare Ethics
Hastings Center Report
Journal of Clinical Ethics
Journal of Health Politics, Policy and Law
Journal of Law, Medicine and Ethics
Journal of Medical Ethics
Journal of Medicine and Philosophy
Kennedy Institute of Ethics Journal
Theoretical Medicine

BIBLIOGRAPHIES AND ENCYCLOPEDIAS
WITH BIBLIOGRAPHIES

Goldstein, Doris Mueller. *Bioethics: A Guide to Information Sources.* Detroit: Gale Research Company, 1982. See under "Bioethics," "Codes of Ethics," and "Professional-Patient Relationship."

Lineback, Richard H., ed. *Philosopher's Index.* Vols. 1– . Bowling Green, OH: Philosophy Documentation Center, Bowling Green State University. Issued quarterly. See under "Codes," "Nurses," "Physicians," "Rights," and "Therapy."

Reich, Warren Thomas, ed. *Encyclopedia of Bioethics.* Revised ed.. New York: Simon and Schuster Macmillan, 1995.

Walters, LeRoy, and Kahn, Tamar Joy, eds. *Bibliography of Bioethics.* Vols. 1– . Washington, DC: Kennedy Institute of Ethics, Georgetown University. Issued annually. See under "Medical Ethics," "Nursing Ethics," "Patient Care," "Patients' Rights," "Professional Ethics," and "Professional-Patient Relationship." (The information contained in the annual *Bibliography* can also be retrieved from BIOETHICSLINE, an online database of the National Library of Medicine).

WORLD WIDE WEB RESOURCES

National Library of Medicine: PubMed
   (*http://www.ncbi.nlm.nih.gov/PubMed/*)

National Library of Medicine: BIOETHICSLINE
   (*http://igm.nlm.nih.gov*)

University Microfilms: Periodical Abstracts
   (*http://www.umi.com/proquest*)

3.
The Management of Medical Information

INTRODUCTION

In Chapter 2 we examined professional obligations and patients' rights. In this chapter we extend this discussion to the presentation, communication, and confidentiality of information. The primary problems are (1) how to determine the conditions under which patients and related parties should have control over information about the patient's health status and (2) how professionals should manage and protect information in medical and research settings.

Several pioneers in the history of medical ethics have explored issues of justifiable nondisclosure and confidentiality. These include the authors of such classic historical documents as the Hippocratic writings (fifth to fourth century B.C.), the first *Code of Ethics* (1847) of the American Medical Association, and Thomas Percival's *Medical Ethics* (1803). In these traditional codes and writings, moral concerns for the autonomy of patients are uncommon. By contrast, a major feature of the contemporary discussion is whether respect for autonomy requires more disclosure, consultation, mutual decision making, and protection of confidential information than has traditionally been required.

TRUTH TELLING AND THE MANAGEMENT OF BAD NEWS

In modern medicine the nature and quality of the physician-patient relationship varies with prior contact, the mental or physical state of the patient, the manner in which the physician relates to the family, and problems with respect to patient-family interactions. The patient's right to know the truth and the physician's obligation to tell it are contingent on these and other factors in the relationship.

Most writers in the history of medical ethics have held that departures from the general principle of truth telling are justified when information disclosure itself carries serious risks for patients. They view truth telling as limited by the Hippocratic principle that they should do no harm to patients in difficult circumstances by revealing upsetting conditions. If disclosure of a diagnosis of cancer, for example, would cause the patient anxiety or lead to an act of self-destruction, they believe that medical ethics requires that the physician carefully monitor and, at times, withhold the information that could cause additional harm. A common thesis is that in cases in which risks of harm from nondisclosure are low and benefits of nondisclosure to the patient are substantial, a physician may legitimately deceive or underdisclose the truth, and sometimes lie.

Deception is sometimes said to be easier to justify than blatant lying, because deception does not necessarily threaten the relationship of trust. Underdisclosure and nondisclosure are also thought to be more easily justified than lying. Those who share this perspective argue that it is important not to conflate duties not to lie, not to deceive, and to disclose as if they were a single duty of veracity.

These justifications of nondisclosure seem especially plausible in cases in which bad news must be delivered to fragile patients or to strangers. Nevertheless, almost all authorities now agree that there is a strong duty of veracity in medicine because of respect for autonomous patients. Can these views about justified disclosure and justified nondisclosure be rendered consistent?

In the first essay in this chapter, David Thomasma explains both why truth telling is important and when truth telling rules might plausibly be overridden in the clinical setting. Thomasma defends the controversial thesis that "truth is a secondary good . . . [and] other primary values take precedence over the truth." Moreover, he says, "the only values that can trump the truth are recipient survival, community survival, and the ability to absorb the full impact of the truth at a particular time."

Using a very different analysis, Garry Sigman et al. analyze cases in which parents of children and adolescents request nondisclosure of a diagnosis. They use a case study to help identify specific clinical factors that will help persons decide about relevantly similar cases. They analyze disclosure duties, disease-specific factors, patient factors, and family factors — arguing for a context-specific approach to truth telling in which lying to the patient and hiding information may occasionally be justified in light of all the factors at work.

Despite the mitigating conditions mentioned by Thomasma and Sigman, many writers in contemporary bioethics believe that all intentional suppression of pertinent information violates a patient's autonomy rights and violates the fundamental duties of the health professional. Here the duty of veracity is derived from obligations of respect for the autonomy of persons. This thesis has been especially prominent in the recent literature on informed consent.

INFORMED CONSENT

It is now widely believed that the physician has a moral obligation not only to tell patients the truth, but to help them decide important matters that affect their health. This ability to make an educated decision is dependent upon the availability of truthful information and the patient's capacity to handle the information. For this reason it is often said that before a physician performs a medical procedure on a competent patient, he or she has an obligation to obtain the patient's informed consent and to engage in mutual decision making with the patient.

The practice of obtaining informed consent has its history predominantly in medicine and medical research, where the disclosure and the withholding of information are daily events. But the history of informed consent is not ancient. The term "informed consent" never appeared in any literature until the 1950s, and discussions of the concept as it is used today began only around 1972. As the idea of informed consent evolved, discussion of appropriate guidelines moved from a narrow focus on the physician's obligation to disclose information to the quality of a patient's or subject's understanding of information and right to authorize or refuse a biomedical intervention.

Prior to the 1950s, there was no firm ground in which a commitment to informed consent could take root. This is not to say that there is no relevant history of the physician's management of medical information in the encounter with patients. The major writings of prominent figures in ancient, medieval, and modern medicine contain a storehouse of information about commitments to disclosure and discussion in medical practice. However, with few exceptions, no serious consideration was given to issues of either consent or self-determination by patients and research subjects. Proper principles, practices, and virtues of "truthfulness" in disclosure were occasionally discussed, but the perspective was largely one of maximizing medical benefits by monitoring medical information. The central concern was how to make disclosures without harming patients by revealing their condition too abruptly and starkly. Withholding of information and even outright deception were tolerated in the effort to avoid harm.

Because of the considerable vagueness around the term "informed consent," some writers have been interested in analyzing the concept so that its meaning is as clear as possible.

If overdemanding criteria such as "full disclosure and complete understanding" are adopted, an informed consent becomes impossible to obtain. Conversely, if underdemanding criteria such as "the patient signed the form" are used, an informed consent becomes too easy to obtain and the term loses all moral significance. Many interactions between a physician and a patient or an investigator and a subject that have been called informed consents have been so labelled only because they rest on underdemanding criteria; they are inappropriately referred to as informed consents. For example, a physician's truthful disclosure to a patient has often been declared the essence of informed consent, as if a patient's silence following disclosure could add up to an informed consent.

Jay Katz has been at the forefront of this effort to analyze the concept of informed consent. He argues that "informed consent" and "shared decision making" should be treated as virtually synonymous terms. His basic moral conviction is that the primary goal of informed consent in medical care and in research is to enable potential subjects and patients to make autonomous decisions about whether to grant or refuse authorization for medical and research interventions.

Ruth Faden and Tom Beauchamp agree that there is a historical relationship between shared decision making and informed consent, but believe it is confusing to treat them as *synonymous*. They argue that decision making should be distinguished from a subject's or patient's act of knowledgeably *authorizing* the intervention, that is, giving an informed consent. The essence of an informed consent, on this analysis, is an autonomous authorization. Such an authorization requires more than merely acquiescing in, yielding to, or complying with an arrangement or a proposal made by a physician or investigator. A person gives an informed consent in this first sense if and only if the person, with substantial understanding and in substantial absence of control by others, intentionally authorizes a health professional to do something.

Informed consent has been widely analyzed in terms of the following elements: (1) disclosure, (2) comprehension, (3) voluntariness, (4) competence, and (5) consent. The idea is that one gives an informed consent to an intervention if and only if one receives a thorough disclosure about it; one comprehends the disclosure; one acts voluntarily; one is competent to act; and one consents to the intervention. But the widespread agreement that these conditions are necessary for an informed consent hides a considerable disagreement about how to explicate each one of these five conditions. In this chapter Katz and also Faden and Beauchamp concentrate on (1), (2), and (5).

One crucial question addressed in the readings on informed consent is whether a valid informed consent can be given if a patient or subject does *not* autonomously authorize an intervention. The authors in this chapter all appear to answer "No" to this question. Yet most of the "consents" obtained in health care institutions at the present time likely do not constitute autonomous authorizations, in the sense of autonomy discussed in Chapter 1. That is, it is doubtful that a patient substantially understands the circumstances, makes a decision absent coercion, and intentionally authorizes a professional to proceed with a medical or research intervention. This opens up a range of questions about the validity of the practices of consent currently at work in contemporary medicine and research.

Another problem addressed in these articles concerns adequate standards of disclosure in informed consent contexts. Legal history reveals an evolving legal doctrine of informed consent from a 1767 case to the 1972 *Canterbury v. Spence* case (and its aftermath). *Canterbury* was the first and most influential of the recent landmark informed consent cases. In *Canterbury,* surgery on the patient's back and a subsequent accident in the hospital led to further injuries and unexpected paralysis, the possibility of which had not yet been disclosed. Judge Spottswood Robinson's opinion focuses on the needs of the reasonable person and the right to self-determination. As for sufficiency of information, the court holds: "The patient's right of self-decision shapes the boundaries of the duty to reveal. That right can be effectively exercised only if the patient possesses enough information to enable an intelligent choice." Katz delivers a blistering attack on the development of these standards in the precedent legal cases, especially the *Canterbury* case.

Many have challenged whether any legal standard is adequate for clinical ethics (as distinct from a standard in law). Katz argues that no broad duty of disclosure follows from any legal standard now envisaged. If one takes this view, the alternative would seem to be a subjective standard that pays attention to how individual information needs can differ and the extent to which physicians must anticipate individual needs for information and counseling. Katz adopts this perspective as appropriate for ethics. However, critics of this view have objected that it is too onerous on the health care professional. They hold that the worthy ideal of informed consent is unrealistic under this standard, requiring much more discussion and disclosure than the medical system can afford or meaningfully provide.

In recent years the focus on informed consent has turned more toward the quality of consent. Much has been made of Katz's claim that the key to effective communication is to invite participation by patients or subjects in an exchange of information and dialogue. Asking questions, eliciting the concerns and interests of the patient or subject, and establishing a climate that encourages the patient or subject to ask questions seems to be more important for medical ethics than the full body of requirements of disclosed information in law.

In the final selection in this section, Robert Levine discusses why the Western model of informed consent is unsuitable in much of the remainder of the world, where he thinks the concept of "person" differs substantially from that in Western societies. Levine concludes that we would be better off if we used a procedural solution to these problems when they are encountered, rather than insisting on rules of obtaining consent. Levine's treatment also suggests how we might handle the growing problem of cultural diversity in Western nations when patients from non-Western countries present to health professionals.

PATIENT SELF-DETERMINATION AND ADVANCE DIRECTIVES

On December 1, 1991, the Patient Self-Determination Act — a federal law known as PSDA — went into effect in the United States. It was the first federal legislation regarding life-sustaining treatments and advance directives.

PSDA is linked directly to the history of informed consent. PSDA stresses the importance of patient and surrogate decision making about life-sustaining treatments and writing advance directives. The law requires health care facilities certified by Medicare or Medicaid to notify competent adult patients of the right to accept or refuse medical treatment and their right to execute an advance directive, under applicable state law. Five forms of action by institutions are required under this law:

1. Provide information to patients upon admission about rights under state law so that they may make decisions and formulate advance directives.
2. Document in patients' records whether an advance directive exists.
3. Maintain written policies, procedures, and records regarding advance directives and institutional obligations under law.
4. Comply with state laws regarding advance directives and various forms of education.
5. Be sure patients are not discriminated against because they have or have not created an advance directive.

This law fails to establish provisions about the quality of disclosure and understanding in the patient. By requiring only notification, the law follows the long-standing federal bias toward basic disclosure. However, the intent of the law is to allow patients to take control of their medical fate, on the grounds that their interests will ultimately be best served by making their own decisions, rather than having the decisions made for them. The right to refuse as well as the right to consent have become the core values that frame the provisions of this statute. These values, of course, are intimately tied to the moral values of respect for autonomy and to the legal values of self-determination in the common law that we have already examined.

Like the law of informed consent, the PSDA grows out of the conviction that there is more than the physician's conception of what is standard or good practice. There is also the patient's conception of what makes for a good life and a good death. This is especially important when choices are about the end of life, and even more important when those choices might be made by one party for another.

Susan Wolf and her coauthors consider the strengths and weaknesses of the PSDA in this chapter. They point to a number of concerns and maintain that we need to find ways to keep the PSDA from reducing the discussion of treatment options to a "bureaucratic process dominated by brochures and forms."

The final two articles in this section are focused on advance directives rather than the PSDA. In the first, Rebecca Dresser suggests that recent empirical evidence indicates that the significance of advance directives deserves reexamination. In light of data indicating that patients often desire to give broad decision making power to physicians and surrogates with respect to treatment options, Dresser proposes new directions for policy on how to treat seriously ill, incompetent patients.

Linda Emanuel et al. attempt to provide a practically oriented set of basic steps and skills for advance care planning. Their model of advance care planning *as a process* should be viewed as augmenting and updating (rather than replacing) executed advance-directive forms. They identify several steps of providing information, facilitating discussion, recording statements, reviewing directives, and implementing decisions. They believe that their model will minimize risks and maximize benefits for patients and health professionals alike.

THE MANAGEMENT OF CONFIDENTIAL INFORMATION

Unlike the notions of informed consent and advance directive, confidentiality has played a significant role since *ancient* codes of professional ethics, including the Hippocratic Oath. Here the physician vows: "What I may see or hear in the course of treatment or even outside of the treatment in regard to the life of men, . . . I will keep to myself."

But despite a venerable history and status in health care, Mark Siegler questions whether the venerable tradition of confidentiality is now a "decrepit" concept of more symbolic than real value. Siegler maintains that traditional medical confidentiality is a relic of the past that has been systematically compromised in the course of modern bureaucratic health care and data storage systems that allow informational access to a large number of persons. He and other critics argue that infringements of confidentiality have become routine parts of medical practice—the rule rather than the exception. Medical confidentiality, they say, lacks credibility and needs to be reconstructed into a more viable form if it is to be anything more than a myth.

In assessing these problems, we need to ask why we care so much about confidentiality and what would justify a practice of maintaining confidentiality in a profession where access to vital information may mean the difference between life and death. Two general types of justifications have been proposed for the confidentiality principle in health care relationships. The first type of justification appeals to the principle of respect for autonomy. This argument is that the health professional does not show proper respect for the patient's autonomy and privacy if he or she does not uphold the confidentiality of the professional–patient relationship. A variant of this approach asserts that there is an implied promise of confidentiality inherent in the professional–patient relationship, whether the professional explicitly recognizes the promise or not. In the absence of an explicit acknowledgement that confidentiality does *not* hold, the patient would always be entitled to assume that it does hold.

A second justification is that violations of confidentiality make patients unwilling to reveal sensitive information to health professionals. This unwillingness renders diagnosis and cure more difficult and, in the long run, is detrimental to the health of patients. The assumption is that the physicin–patient relationship rests on a basis of trust that would be imperiled if physicians were not under an obligation to maintain confidence.

This second justification appeals to the positive *consequences* of confidentiality, whereas the first looks to a moral violation that would be wrong irrespective of the kinds of consequences envisaged in the second. That is, the first set of arguments maintains that breaches of trust, broken promises, and failures to keep contractual obligations are themselves wrong, whereas the second argument looks not at what is intrinsically wrong but instead at whether the balance of the consequences supports maintaining confidentiality.

As we might expect, criticisms have been made of both arguments. Both have been challenged, for example, by those who believe that there is an overriding duty to warn persons who might be seriously harmed if confidentiality were maintained. The problem underlying this challenge is whether rules of confidentiality state an absolute duty. If not, there is an additional question as to the conditions under which it is permissible to reveal otherwise confidential information. Many who support a *firm* rule of confidentiality do not support an *absolute* rule, because they recognize a range of exceptions under which disclosure of clearly confidential information is permitted. One example of this problem is found in the contemporary discussion of the conditions under which confidential information about AIDS patients may be disclosed, especially when the disclosure constitutes a warning to others of imminent danger.

A now classic case of conflict between the obligation of confidentiality and the obligation to protect others from harm occurred in *Tarasoff v. Regents of the University of California.* In this case a patient confided to his psychologist that he intended to kill a third party. The psychologist then faced the choice of preserving the confidentiality of the patient or of infringing his right of confidentiality to warn a young woman that her life might be in danger. The court finds that health care professionals must weigh a peril to the public that a patient discloses in confidence against the disvalue of infringing confidentiality. However, this court and the courts generally have left open precisely *which duties* legitimately override obligations of confidentiality. Whatever the regional variations, almost every jurisdiction has recognized a core set of justified infringements of confidentiality. These requirements include the reporting of contagious diseases, child abuse, gunshot wounds, epilepsy (to a motor vehicle department), and the like.

Not all examples of the problem of confidentiality are so dramatic or socially significant. More troublesome and pervasive problems concern questions such as how much of a patient's medical record can be fed into a widely accessed "public" data bank, how much information about a patient's genetic makeup may be revealed to a sexual partner if there is a substantial likelihood of the couple's producing genetically handicapped children, how information about an irresponsible and publicly dangerous AIDS patient is to be handled, what information employers and insurance companies should and should not receive, and to whom in a family the full range of test results in genetic screening should be disclosed.

Some of these problems are considered in the final two selections in this chapter. First, Sir David Black explains that the duty of patient confidentiality is a valid norm of conduct, but not a categorical imperative or absolute obligation. Rather, it is a prima facie duty. He maintains that "the need to know" of other professionals on the health care team is one among several legitimate exceptions to the fiduciary duty of confidentiality.

In the final essay, Lawrence Gostin examines the emerging privacy issues surrounding the genetic discoveries of the Human Genome Project. Gostin points out that we want both to acquire voluminous data about the human genome and to protect the rights of individuals, families, and groups. Gostin argues that there is a sharp conflict between the need for genomic information and the need for privacy, and therefore that tradeoffs are inevitable.

T.L.B.

DAVID C. THOMASMA

Telling the Truth to Patients: A Clinical Ethics Exploration

REASONS FOR TELLING THE TRUTH

. . . In all human relationships, the truth is told for a myriad of reasons. A summary of the prominent reasons are that it is a right, a utility, and a kindness.

It is a right to be told the truth because respect for the person demands it. As Kant argued, human society would soon collapse without truth telling, because it is the basis of interpersonal trust, covenants, contracts, and promises.

The truth is a utility as well, because persons need to make informed judgments about their actions. It is a mark of maturity that individuals advance and grow morally by becoming more and more self-aware of their needs, their motives, and their limitations. All these steps toward maturity require honest and forthright communication, first from parents and later also from siblings, friends, lovers, spouses, children, colleagues, co-workers, and caregivers.[1]

Finally, it is a kindness to be told the truth, a kindness rooted in virtue precisely because persons to whom lies are told will of necessity withdraw from important, sometimes life-sustaining and life-saving relationships. Similarly, those who tell lies poison not only their relationships but themselves, rendering themselves incapable of virtue and moral growth.[2] . . .

OVERRIDING THE TRUTH

. . . Not all of us act rationally and autonomously at all times. Sometimes we are under sufficient stress that others must act to protect us from harm. This is called necessary paternalism. Should we become seriously ill, others must step in and rescue us if we are incapable of doing it ourselves. . . .

IN GENERAL RELATIONSHIPS

In each of the three main reasons why the truth must be told, as a right, a utility, and a kindness, lurk values that

From *Cambridge Quarterly of Healthcare Ethics* (1994), 3, 375–382. Copyright © 1994 Cambridge University Press. Reprinted with the permission of Cambridge University Press.

may from time to time become more important than the truth. When this occurs, the rule of truth telling is trumped, that is, overridden by a temporarily more important principle. The ultimate value in all instances is the survival of the community and/or the well-being of the individual. Does this mean for paternalistic reasons, without the person's consent, the right to the truth, the utility, and the kindness, can be shunted aside? The answer is "yes." The truth in a relationship responds to a multivariate complexity of values, the context for which helps determine which values in that relationship should predominate.

Nothing I have said thus far suggests that the truth may be treated in a cavalier fashion or that it can be withheld from those who deserve it for frivolous reasons. The only values that can trump the truth are recipient survival, community survival, and the ability to absorb the full impact of the truth at a particular time. All these are only temporary trump cards in any event. They only can be played under certain limited conditions because respect for persons is a foundational value in all relationships.

IN HEALTHCARE RELATIONSHIPS

It is time to look more carefully at one particular form of human relationship, the relationship between the doctor and the patient or sometimes between other healthcare providers and the patient.

Early in the 1960s, studies were done that revealed the majority of physicians would not disclose a diagnosis of cancer to a patient. Reasons cited were mostly those that derived from nonmaleficence. Physicians were concerned that such a diagnosis might disturb the equanimity of a patient and might lead to desperate acts. Primarily physicians did not want to destroy their patients' hope. By the middle 1970s, however, repeat studies brought to light a radical shift in physician attitudes. Unlike earlier views, physicians now emphasized patient autonomy and informed consent over paternalism. In the doctor-patient relation, this meant the majority of physicians stressed the patient's right to full disclosure of diagnosis and prognosis.

One might be tempted to ascribe this shift of attitudes to the growing patients' rights and autonomy movements in the philosophy of medicine and in public affairs. No doubt some of the change can be attributed to this movement. But also treatment interventions for cancer led to greater optimism about modalities that could offer some hope to patients. Thus, to offer them full disclosure of their diagnosis no longer was equivalent to a death sentence. Former powerlessness of the healer was supplanted with technological and pharmaceutical potentialities.

A more philosophical analysis of the reasons for a shift comes from a consideration of the goal of medicine. The goal of all healthcare relations is to receive/provide help for an illness such that no further harm is done to the patient, especially in that patient's vulnerable state.[3] The vulnerability arises because of increased dependency. Presumably, the doctor will not take advantage of this vulnerable condition by adding to it through inappropriate use of power or the lack of compassion. Instead, the vulnerable person should be assisted back to a state of human equality, if possible, free from the prior dependency.[4]

First, the goal of the healthcare giver–patient relation is essentially to restore the patient's autonomy. Thus, respect for the right of the patient to the truth is measured against this goal. If nothing toward that goal can be gained by telling the truth at a particular time, still it must be told for other reasons. Yet, if the truth would impair the restoration of autonomy, then it may be withheld on grounds of potential harm. Thus the goal of the healing relationship enters into the calculus of values that are to be protected.

Second, most healthcare relationships of an interventionist character are temporary, whereas relationships involving primary care, prevention, and chronic or dying care are more permanent. These differences also have a bearing on truth telling. During a short encounter with healthcare strangers, patients and healthcare providers will of necessity require the truth more readily than during a long-term relation among near friends. In the short term, decisions, often dramatically important ones, need to be made in a compressed period. There is less opportunity to maneuver or delay for other reasons, even if there are concerns about the truth's impact on the person.

Over a longer period, the truth may be withheld for compassionate reasons more readily. Here, the patient and physician or nurse know one another. They are more likely to have shared some of their values. In this context, it is more justifiable to withhold the truth temporarily in favor of more important long-term values, which are known in the relationship.

Finally, the goal of healthcare relations is treatment of an illness. An illness is far broader than its subset, disease. Illness can be viewed as a disturbance in the life of an individual, perhaps due to many nonmedical factors. A disease, by contrast, is a medically caused event that may respond to more interventionist strategies.[5]

Helping one through an illness is a far greater personal task than doing so for a disease. A greater, more enduring bond is formed. The strength of this bond may justify withholding the truth as well, although in the end "the truth will always out."

CLINICAL CASE CATEGORIES

The general principles about truth telling have been reviewed, as well as possible modifications formed from the particularities of the healthcare professional–patient relationship. Now I turn to some contemporary examples of how clinical ethics might analyze the hierarchy of values surrounding truth telling.

There are at least five clinical case categories in which truth telling becomes problematic: intervention cases, long-term care cases, cases of dying patients, prevention cases, and nonintervention cases.

INTERVENTION CASES

Of all clinically difficult times to tell the truth, two typical cases stand out. The first usually involves a mother of advanced age with cancer. The family might beg the surgeon not to tell her what has been discovered for fear that "Mom might just go off the deep end." The movie *Dad,* starring Jack Lemmon, had as its centerpiece the notion that Dad could not tolerate the idea of cancer. Once told, he went into a psychotic shock that ruptured standard relationships with the doctors, the hospital, and the family. However, because this diagnosis requires patient participation for chemotherapeutic interventions and the time is short, the truth must be faced directly. Only if there is not to be intervention might one withhold the truth from the patient for a while, at the family's request, until the patient is able to cope with the reality. A contract about the time allowed before telling the truth might be a good idea.

The second case is that of ambiguous genitalia. A woman, 19 years old, comes for a checkup because she plans to get married and has not yet had a period. She is very mildly retarded. It turns out that she has no vagina, uterus, or ovaries but does have an undescended testicle in her abdomen. She is actually a he. Should she be told this fundamental truth about herself? Those who argue for the truth do so on grounds that she will eventually find out, and more of her subsequent life will have been ruined by the lies and disingenuousness of others. Those who argue against the

truth usually prevail. National standards exist in this regard. The young woman is told that she has something like a "gonadal mass" in her abdomen that might turn into cancer if not removed, and an operation is performed. She is assisted to remain a female.

More complicated still is a case of a young Hispanic woman, a trauma accident victim, who is gradually coming out of a coma. She responds only to commands such as "move your toes." Because she is now incompetent, her mother and father are making all care decisions in her case. Her boyfriend is a welcome addition to the large, extended family. However, the physicians discover that she is pregnant. The fetus is about 5 weeks old. Eventually, if she does not recover, her surrogate decision makers will have to be told about the pregnancy, because they will be involved in the terrible decisions about continuing the life of the fetus even if it is a risk to the mother's recovery from the coma. This revelation will almost certainly disrupt current family relationships and the role of the boyfriend. Further, if the mother is incompetent to decide, should not the boyfriend, as presumed father, have a say in the decision about his own child?

In this case, revelation of the truth must be carefully managed. The pregnancy should be revealed only on a "need to know" basis, that is, only when the survival of the young woman becomes critical. She is still progressing moderately towards a stable state.

LONG-TERM CASES

Rehabilitation medicine provides one problem of truth telling in this category. If a young man has been paralyzed by a football accident, his recovery to some level of function will depend upon holding out hope. As he struggles to strengthen himself, the motivation might be a hope that caregivers know to be false, that he may someday be able to walk again. Yet, this falsehood is not corrected, lest he slip into despair. Hence, because this is a long-term relationship, the truth will be gradually discovered by the patient under the aegis of encouragement by his physical therapists, nurses, and physicians, who enter his life as near friends.

CASES OF DYING PATIENTS

Sometimes, during the dying process, the patient asks directly, "Doctor, am I dying?" Physicians are frequently reluctant to "play God" and tell the patient how many days or months or years they have left. This reluctance sometimes bleeds over into a less-than-forthright answer to the question just asked. A surgeon with whom I make rounds once answered this question posed by a terminally ill cancer patient by telling her that she did not have to worry about her insurance running out!

Yet in every case of dying patients, the truth can be gradually revealed such that the patient learns about dying even before the family or others who are resisting telling the truth. Sometimes, without directly saying "you are dying," we are able to use interpretative truth and comfort the patient. If a car driver who has been in an accident and is dying asks about other family members in the car who are already dead, there is no necessity to tell him the truth. Instead, he can be told that "they are being cared for" and that the important thing right now is that he be comfortable and not in pain. One avoids the awful truth because he may feel responsible and guilt ridden during his own dying hours if he knew that the rest of his family were already dead.

PREVENTION CASES

A good example of problems associated with truth telling in preventive medicine might come from screening. The high prevalence of prostate cancer among men over 50 years old may suggest the utility of cancer screening. An annual checkup for men over 40 years old is recommended. Latent and asymptomatic prostate cancer is often clinically unsuspected and is present in approximately 30% of men over 50 years of age. If screening were to take place, about 16.5 million men in the United States alone would be diagnosed with prostate cancer, or about 2.4 million men each year. As of now, only 120,000 cases are newly diagnosed each year. Thus, as Timothy Moon noted in a recent sketch of the disease, "a majority of patients with prostate cancer that is not clinically diagnosed will experience a benign course throughout their lifetime."[6]

The high incidence of prostate cancer coupled with a very low malignant potential would entail a whole host of problems if subjected to screening. Detection would force patients and physicians to make very difficult and life-altering treatment decisions. Among them are removal of the gland (with impotence a possible outcome), radiation treatment, and most effective of all, surgical removal of the gonads (orchiectomy). But why consider these rather violent interventions if the probable outcome of neglect will overwhelmingly be benign? For this reason the U.S. Preventive Services Task Force does not recommend either for or against screening for prostate cancer.[7] Quality-of-life issues would take precedence over the need to know.

NONINTERVENTION CASES

This last example more closely approximates the kind of information one might receive as a result of gene mapping. This information could tell you of the likelihood or probability of encountering a number of diseases through genetic heritage, for example, adult onset or type II diabetes, but could not offer major interventions for most of them (unlike a probability for diabetes).

Some evidence exists from recent studies that the principle of truth telling now predominates in the doctor–patient relationship. Doctors were asked about revealing diagnosis for Huntington's disease and multiple sclerosis, neither of which is subject to a cure at present. An overwhelming majority would consider full disclosure. This means that, even in the face of diseases for which we have no cure, truth telling seems to take precedence over protecting the patient from imagined harms.

The question of full disclosure acquires greater poignancy in today's medicine, especially with respect to Alzheimer's disease and genetic disorders that may be diagnosed in utero. There are times when our own scientific endeavors lack a sufficient conceptual and cultural framework around which to assemble facts. The facts can overwhelm us without such conceptual frameworks. The future of genetics poses just such a problem. In consideration of the new genetics, this might be the time to stress values over the truth.

CONCLUSION

Truth in the clinical relationship is factored in with knowledge and values.

First, truth is contextual. Its revelation depends upon the nature of the relationship between the doctor and patient and the duration of that relationship.

Second, truth is a secondary good. Although important, other primary values take precedence over the truth. The most important of these values is survival of the individual and the community. A close second would be preservation of the relationship itself.

Third, truth is essential for healing an illness. It may not be as important for curing a disease. That is why, for example, we might withhold the truth from the woman with ambiguous genitalia, curing her disease (having a gonad) in favor of maintaining her health (being a woman).

Fourth, withholding the truth is only a temporary measure. *In vino, veritas* it is said. The truth will eventually come out, even if in a slip of the tongue. Its revelation, if it is to be controlled, must always aim at the good of the patient for the moment.

At all times, the default mode should be that the truth is told. If, for some important reason, it is not to be immediately revealed in a particular case, a truth-management protocol should be instituted so that all caregivers on the team understand how the truth will eventually be revealed.

NOTES

1. Bok S. *Lying: Moral Choice in Public and Personal Life.* New York: Vintage Books, 1989.

2. Pellegrino ED, Thomasma DC. *The Virtues in Medical Practice.* New York: Oxford University Press, 1993.

3. Cassell E. The nature of suffering and the goals of medicine. *New England Journal of Medicine* 1982; 306(11):639–45.

4. See Nordenfelt L, issue editor. Concepts of health and their consequences for health care. *Theoretical Medicine* 1993; 14(4).

5. Moon TD. Prostate cancer. *Journal of the American Geriatrics Society* 1992; 40:622–7 (quote from 626).

6. See note 5. Moon. 1992; 40:622–7.

GARRY S. SIGMAN, JEROME KRAUT, AND JOHN LA PUMA

Disclosure of a Diagnosis to Children and Adolescents When Parents Object

Parents of children and adolescents occasionally request that the physician not disclose a diagnosis or prognosis to the young patient. Such a request creates an ethical dilemma for the practitioner: the conflict between a duty to respect parents' wishes as well as a duty to tell the truth to the child.

The authority of parents to direct the flow of information to the child and to organize and provide appropriate systems of emotional support is well recognized in pediatric care. Parents are regarded as moral agents for their children; pediatricians perceive that the integrity of the patient's family is necessary to sustain and nurture the child.

Still, parental authority cannot be absolute. A "best interest" standard that extends beyond parents' wishes is recognized in nontreatment decisions in severely ill neonates and children,[1] in relationship to the treatment

of children whose parents have religious objection to usual care,[2] and in relationship to the confidential care of adolescents.[3]

Several cases exploring the physicians' duties to tell the truth to children have been reported.[4-6] We attempt to advance the discussion by using an extraordinary case to identify the clinical circumstances that are important in the decision regarding truthful disclosure to children when parents object.

REPORT OF A CASE

The patient, aged 19 years, was first seen by her current physician, a specialist in the treatment of cystic fibrosis (CF) at age 9 years. After a normal pregnancy, labor, and delivery, the newborn developed irritability, vomiting, and frequent foul stools soon after discharge. At age 4 months, failure to thrive prompted a sweat test that was diagnostic for CF.

Both parents were born in Italy and moved to the United States as adults. The father, aged 48 years, owns a barber shop and is a postal worker. The mother, aged

Reprinted by permission of the publisher from American Journal of Diseases of Children: 147 (1993), 764–768. © 1993, American Medical Association.

39 years, cares for her family in the home. The now 6-year-old sister does not have CF.

The parents recall feeling devastated when told that CF is a lethal disease that usually results in early death. They said that nothing could be more horrible than their child knowing of her fatal disease. They agreed at the time of diagnosis that they would never tell her or her extended family of her disease and would not allow health care professionals to disclose the diagnosis and prognosis to their daughter. . . .

By age 15, the patient had grown into a normal-appearing teenager who did well in school and had a normal social life and good relationship with her parents. The physician felt increasingly guilty about participation in the nondisclosure, not because the patient was asking questions (she was not), but simply because she was getting older. In another conference, he and the social worker tried again to convince the parents to change their minds. The parents remained committed to their decision and made it clear that it was not negotiable. The parents agreed to counseling but did not see the benefits of telling their daughter her diagnosis and refused to make that a goal of counseling. They did not follow through with this treatment. . . .

Just after her 18th birthday, the patient developed another pulmonary exacerbation and was seen in the office prior to hospitalization. The physician explained the secrecy oath and the diagnosis and prognosis to the patient, with her parents present. Her mother tried to remove her daughter from the office, but the father gently calmed the mother and allowed the first discussion their daughter ever had about her disease. She reacted calmly and asked questions.

After the session the patient said that she had no idea that she had CF and had not felt the need to question her parents or physician. She thought she had allergies, asthma, and "weak lungs." The patient denied any anger toward her parents or the physician about the secrecy. She has had no further admissions, is doing well to date, understands her disease, and is involved in self-care . . .

ANALYZING DISCLOSURE DUTIES

If there is a moral justification for lying to the patient, or willfully hiding the truth, it must have a strength that overrides the principle of veracity, derived from basic human respect.[7(p31)] People deserve to be told the truth;

Clinical Factors to Be Considered Regarding Truthful Disclosure to Pediatric Patients

Physician factors
  Personal value system
  Societal, legal, and economic influences on medical decision making
  Professional codes of behavior

Disease-specific factors
  Natural history of disease
  Factors relating to provision of care
  Public health considerations

Patient factors
  Development and maturation
  Personality traits
  Psychiatric risk factors and symptoms

Family factors
  Cultural considerations
  Family dynamics and support mechanisms
  Family dysfunction and disease

and circumstances must be morally persuasive when considering deviating from this basic moral duty.

Physician factors, disease-specific factors, patient factors, and family factors are each important in the decision regarding disclosure to pediatric patients (Table). The strength of the individual factors will ultimately determine the "right" action for the physician regarding disclosure. The factors' relative importance is not implied by their order in the text; all or one may be important in individual cases. Indeed, the relative value of each clinical factor will be different in each case; each clinical decision is context specific. Decisions about disclosure must be made by considering the specific details of the case; they are decisions that must be made by a particular physician, regarding a particular disease, for and with a particular child from a particular family.

PHYSICIAN FACTORS

Physicians differ in their approaches to disclosure decisions. For example, individual differences exist in physicians' personal value systems. Some physicians view deception as therapeutic and therefore a justifiable alternative in certain clinical settings.[8] For them, truth telling is not a moral imperative, but a virtue with variable consequences for the patient's health.[9] For other physicians, any deception is wrong, no matter what the consequence. These physicians may consider nontruthful disclosure destructive of the physician's effectiveness with patients.[7(p238-241)] Even though they are unable to formally consent, the assent of children in medical decisions is increasingly recognized as morally and clinically important;[10] the lack of truthful disclosure would be antithetical to such a moral stance.

Internal personal values are derived from religious, social, and familial influences and affect physician attitudes regarding physician-assisted suicide,[11] withholding and withdrawing life-sustaining treatment,[12,13] and drug testing.[14] Some physicians find that, despite rational ethical arguments favoring certain decisions, they cannot make them because "it's against my conscience," an expression of personal values.

In addition, societal, economic, and legal phenomena also influence physicians' management of truthtelling dilemmas. Societal movements supporting individual rights and self-determination have become important and current during the last 25 years. Physicians have correspondingly altered their practices in favor of truthful disclosure, in recognition of patients' right of self-determination.[15,16]

Codes of professional behavior might influence physicians' ethical decisions. The American Medical Association's code of professional responsibility is not specific about truthful disclosure of diagnoses, although principle 2 of the preamble states, "A physician shall deal honestly with patients and colleagues."[17] The code's requirement for informed consent might be taken to apply to truthful disclosure, but the code does not address such issues regarding minors whose parents object to disclosure. To the best of our knowledge, the American Academy of Pediatrics has not published policies regarding truthful disclosure.

Suggesting that physicians differ on disclosure does not imply a moral relativism that leaves us unable to resolve any moral dilemmas. It does suggest that the medical profession, instead of mandating by code or standard of practice, has allowed decisions about disclosure to be left to each physician's assessment of the clinical circumstances.

DISEASE-SPECIFIC FACTORS

A strong argument for disclosure exists if a child's knowledge of the disease positively affects its course and prognosis. There are diseases in which self-care and survival would be impossible without a patient's knowledge of the disease and performance of daily self-care. Examples include diabetes mellitus, chronic renal failure, and severe CF.

Considering only physical aspects of disease does not address the question of whether knowing affects adjustment and prognosis. For CF, it appears that psychological adjustment to the disease is adequate for most adolescents and young adults who know their diagnosis and prognosis,[18-20] although gender differences in coping style have been reported. Girls have more difficulty integrating the presence of the disease with their self-concept.[21] Considering only adolescent identity formation and coping considerations, delay in learning of a CF diagnosis in a mild case may not be harmful in certain patients.

In addition, patients must know the facts of their disease to plan their lives. In CF, premature death and infertility (for most) are generally certain. Patients with CF should be made aware of the effects of the disease on reproduction, "when he or she is sexually and emotionally mature."[22] All young people who have a potential desire to procreate and who are sexually active should have access to genetic counseling. These facts about CF strengthen the need for a patient's decision making. A pediatrician might accede to parents who wish to raise a child in a particular way, but not to parents who usurp a child's future life decisions.

As with many chronic diseases, care for patients with CF is provided by a team approach. Nondisclosure, even if justified, cannot be carried out without a significant alteration in the normal patterns of team communication.[23] Such a "conspiracy" may have an effect on collective care givers that negatively impacts on morale and care provision. Medical education as well may be adversely affected if students and residents perceive that lying to the patient is okay as long as the parents insist.

Do patients with chronic diseases do better if they meet and interact with others with the disease? This cannot be empirically studied since this is standard for patients with CF. Nevertheless, a patient unable to attend a special disease of specialty-based clinic might be unable to take advantage of new diagnostic or treatment opportunities that are on the cutting edge.

The duty to disclose to the patient, despite parental objection, increases with the potential threat to the public health. While no such threats exist for CF, the diagnosis for youth who have human immunodeficiency virus infection, for example, cannot be hidden because of the potential for unwitting transmission.

This also applies to truthful disclosure of other chronic transmissible infections, such as hepatitis B or genital herpes simplex.

The duty to respect a patient by allowing him or her to make decisions is altered by the patient's inability to make such a decision. At young ages, children cannot do so and are dependent; parents are, of necessity, the primary decision makers. A parent's request to shield a young child from specific knowledge is less morally objectionable than such a request for a child or adolescent of greater maturity.

As a child matures, his or her ability and need to understand increases so that surrogate decision makers are less necessary.[24] As maturity progresses, an emerging adult takes on the moral authority to think, speak, and act for himself or herself.[25,26] The patient's advancing maturity confers an increasing duty to value the patient's right to know personal information above a parent's right to control that information.

The desire for self-determination and decision making varies among pediatric patients. These individual differences are a result of developmental maturity, personality factors, and environmental influences. Children differ in regard to the degree of control they believe that they have (and want) over their lives and their illnesses.[27]

Does a physician have a duty to disclose to a mature patient unrequested information? Just as it might be considered paternalistic on the part of parents to require secrecy, it is also paternalistic on the part of physicians to assume that truth is "good for the patient" if it is unrequested. The fact that patients do not ask does not mean that they do not desire more information. Families of patients with chronic diseases and fatal prognoses sometimes have unspoken agreements of silence about the prognosis; it is taboo to bring the reality of a child's impending death into the open.[28] This is recognized as a family defense mechanism and supports an emotional equilibrium in the family.[29]

An adolescent patient might emerge from a system of overwhelming family secrecy and demonstrate personal needs and desires if given a chance to speak confidentially to care givers. The physician must form a hypothesis about the patient's desire for autonomy in self-care and the ability to cope. It is a physician's duty to ask directly whether more information is requested. If the physician perceives that the patient wishes to achieve more control over decision making, helping the patient to become more autonomous is required. If the patient express no such wishes, the physician can respect the silence and allow others to decide, while making ongoing inquiries of the patient about his or her own desires.[30]

Finally, the patient's mental health must be considered. When a parent fears that the result of a disclosure might cause psychological harm, the physician should carefully consider the (generally remote) possibility of triggering psychiatric symptoms. Suicide has been reported in adolescents with chronic or fatal illnesses, but this is rare. Physicians should consider whether the history and examination demonstrate clinical features that might suggest a high risk for psychiatric symptoms when considering how, when, and whether disclosure should occur.[31]

Just as every patient is different, so is every family; cultural backgrounds and beliefs of families differ. Kleinman et al.[32] have written, "Illness behavior is a normative experience governed by cultural rules." Whether disclosure is right for a patient must be interpreted in light of a family's particular cultural background.[33,34] Otherwise, a physician might simply impose his or her own cultural value of "truth" or "autonomy" and thereby breach a boundary of paternalism. He or she might also do harm by upsetting a stable system of social support provided by the family.

The strength and consistency of parental authority differs between families, regardless of how it is derived. Families differ in how, when, and where they make decisions. Physicians must discern and respect unique decision-making practices in families when faced with dilemmas of disclosure and truth telling.

Family psychosocial dysfunction may account for the request of parents to not disclose a diagnosis. One or both parents may be delusional, guilt ridden, or otherwise unable to cope with a child's chronic illness. Psychiatric or psychological consultation may be helpful to determine whether the potential for harm to the child and the dysfunctional family member exists if their child is given information they wish him or her not to have.

CLINICAL FACTORS AND THE PRESENT CASE

The clinical factors described above apply specifically to the present case as follows:

The personal value system of the CF specialist in this case allowed him to care for the patient, even after deciding not to disclose the diagnosis. This decision was based on his belief that as long as the patient's medical needs were being met, the parents had a right to control medical information. No legal requirement mandated disclosure, and none was suggested by a professional code. The physician's personal reservations about adhering to the parents' demands were overridden by other factors.

DISEASE-SPECIFIC FACTORS

At the beginning of the patient's disease course, prognosis and care needs probably were not altered by her ignorance of the diagnosis. In practical terms, the only difference in her therapy would have been attending the CF clinic, taking pancreatic enzymes, and receiving more frequent chest physiotherapy. There will never be full scientific evidence to prove or disprove the long-term effectiveness of chest physiotherapy[35] since it is one of many treatment modalities that cannot be evaluated singly. It is generally accepted as standard therapy, so one must assume that the lack of it was a deficiency in the care of this patient. All other prescribed treatments were faithfully carried out by the parents, including the administration of medications when necessary.

It is not certain that the patient's treatment was of poorer quality than it would have been had she known about her disease. It cannot be shown that she suffered physically or psychologically by not knowing her diagnosis. For her parents, who did not accept the over-riding "right" of autonomy and self-determination of their daughter, it was difficult to accept the physician's argument that improved health would likely result if he told the patient her diagnosis. . . .

PATIENT FACTORS

Adolescent development and the maturing of cognitive processes created an increasing responsibility for the physician to seek out the patient's autonomous wishes. Even in her middle and late teenage years, however, she did not demonstrate initiative in discovering more than what she was told. Her lack of curiosity and general acceptance of all medical prescriptions suggested no desire to alter or rebel against the authority of her parents. A striving for independence and self-actualization did not appear as she aged, at least in regard to her

medical care. She questioned neither her parents nor the physician.

It is possible that the patient had perceived a "secret" that must not be discussed and wished to respect this boundary. She did not seem to challenge any such "taboo" and did not seem to seek help from the physician in challenging it. The long-term deception may have prevented her from expressing her choices and her physician from discerning them.

In summary, patient factors were significant in the final decision to disclose, but were not compelling early in the physician's involvement with her. Without evidence of patient psychopathology, the physician did not fear harming the patient by disclosure. The secrecy so firmly demanded by the parents prevented the physician from determining or even guessing what information the patient wanted.

FAMILY FACTORS

. . . The patient was aware of and respected a parent-dominated social structure in which parents made all medical and most nonmedical decisions for their children. Beyond the special characteristics of many first-generation Italian families, however, the persistence of the parents' refusal to tell their daughter the truth, the rigidity of their position, and their resistance to change as the daughter matured can be interpreted as an indication of a dysfunctional family process.[36] The parents unfortunately recognized neither a need for therapy nor any dysfunction in themselves or their daughter.

CONCLUSION

. . . The answer to the problem of disclosure depends on the clinical context that defines the patient's best interests and the physician's values and attitudes. Decisions about truth telling are context specific; they should be continually examined as the clinical situation changes. Patients' needs change with the natural history of their disease and as their developmental capabilities evolve. It is appropriate that models are developed for clinical ethics that embody this evolution.

NOTES

1. Walters JW. Approaches to ethical decision making in the neonatal intensive care unit. *AJDC.* 1988;142:825–830.

2. Ackerman TF. The limits of beneficence: Jehovah's Witness and childhood cancer. *Hasting Cent Rep.* 1980;10:13–18.

3. Forman EN, Ladd RE. Treating adolescents: when is a child an adult? In: *Ethical Dilemmas in Pediatrics: A Case Study Approach.* New York, NY: Springer Verlag NY Inc; 1991:111–128.

4. Leiken SL. An ethical issue in pediatric cancer care: nondisclosure of a fatal prognosis. *Pediatr Ann.* 1981;10:37–46.

5. Truth telling in pediatrics. In: Ganos D, Lipson RE, Warren G, Weil BJ, eds. *Difficult Decisions in Medical Ethics.* New York, NY: Alan B Liss Inc; 1983:171–196.

6. Higgs, R, ed. A father says, 'Don't tell my son the truth.' *J Med Ethics.* 1985;11:153–158.

7. Bok S. *Lying: Moral Choice in Public and Private Life.* New York, NY: Vintage Books; 1978.

8. Novack DH, Detering BJ, Arnold R, Forrow L, Ladinsky M, Pezzullo JC. Physicians' attitudes toward using deception to resolve difficult ethical problems. *JAMA.* 1989;261:2980–2985.

9. Pernick MS. Childhood death and medical ethics: an historical perspective on truth-telling in pediatrics. In: Ganos D, Lipson RE, Warren G, Weil BJ, eds. *Difficult Decisions in Medical Ethics.* New York, NY: Alan R Liss Inc; 1983:173–188.

10. Bartholome WG. A new understanding of consent in pediatric practice. *Pediatr Ann.* 1989;18:262–265.

11. Klagsbrun SC. Physician-assisted suicide: a double dilemma. *J Pain Symptom Manage.* 1991;6(special issue):325–328.

12. Paris J, Lantos J. The case of baby L. *N Engl J Med.* 1990;322:1012–1014.

13. Cranford RE. Helga Wanglie's ventilator. *Hastings Cent Rep.* 1991;21:23–24.

14. Linn LS, Yager J, Leake B. Professional vs personal factors related to physicians' attitudes toward drug testing. *J Drug Educ.* 1990;20:95–109.

15. Pellegrino ED, Thomasma DC. *For the Patient's Good.* New York, NY: Oxford University Press Inc; 1988:4.

16. Novack DH, Plumer R, Smith RL, Ochitill H, Morrow GR, Bennet JM. Changes in physicians' attitudes toward telling the cancer patient. *JAMA* 1979;241:897–900.

17. American Medical Association. *Principles of Medical Ethics and Current Opinions of the Council on Ethical and Judicial Affairs.* Chicago, Ill: American Medical Association; 1989:ix.

18. Kashani JH, Barbero GJ, Wifley DE, Morris DA, Sheppard JA. Psychological concomitants of cystic fibrosis in children and adolescents. *Adolescence.* 1988;23:873–880.

19. Mador JA, Smith DH. The psychological adaptation of adolescents with cystic fibrosis: a review of the literature. *J Adolesc Health Care.* 1988;10:136–142.

20. Shepard SL, Hovell MF, Harwood IR, et al. A comparative study of the psychosocial assets of adults with cystic fibrosis and their healthy peers. *Chest.* 1990;97:1310–1316.

21. Simmons R, Corey M, Cowen L, Keenan N, Robertson J, Levinson H. Emotional adjustment of early adolescents with cystic fibrosis. *Psychosom Med.* 1985;47:111–122.

22. Levine SB, Stern RC. Sexual function in cystic fibrosis. *Chest.* 1982;81:422–428.

23. Matthews LW, Droter D. Cystic fibrosis: A challenging long-term chronic disease. *Pediatr Clin North Am.* 1984;31:133–151.

24. Moreno JD. Treating the adolescent patient: an ethical analysis. *J Adolesc Health Care.* 1989;10:454–459.

25. Lantos JD, Miles SH. Autonomy in adolescent medicine. *J Adolesc Health Care.* 1989;10:460–466.

26. Chesler MA, Paris J, Barbarin OA. 'Telling' the child with cancer: parental choices to share information with ill children. *J Pediatr Psychol.* 1986; 2:497–515.

27. Sanger MS, Sandler-Howard K, Perrin EC. Concepts of illness and perception of control in healthy children and in children with chronic illnesses. *J Dev Behav Pediatr.* 1988;9:252–256.

28. Bluebond-Langer M. *The Private Worlds of Dying Children.* Princeton, NJ: Princeton University Press; 1978:198–230.

29. Silber TJ. Ethical considerations in the care of the chronically ill adolescent. In: Blum RW, ed. *Chronic Illness and Disabilities in Childhood and Adolescence.* Philadelphia, Pa: Grune & Stratton; 1984:17–27.

30. Childress JF. The place of autonomy in bioethics. *Hastings Cent Rep.* 1990;20:12–17.

31. Gunther MS. Acute-onset serious chronic organic illness in adolescence: some critical issues, *Adolesc Psychiatry.* 1985; 12:58–76.

32. Kleinman AM, Eisenberg L, Good B. Culture, illness and care: clinical lessons from anthropologic and cross-cultural research. *Ann Intern Medical.* 1978;88:251–258.

33. Surbone A. Truth telling to the patient. *JAMA.* 1992;268:1661–1662.

34. Pellegrino ED. Is truth telling to the patient a cultural artifact? *JAMA.* 1992;268:1734–1735.

35. MacLusky I, Levison H. Cystic fibrosis. In: Chernick V, Kendig EL, eds. *Kendig's Disorders of the Respiratory Tract in Children.* 5th ed. Philadelphia, Pa: WB Saunders Co; 1990:711.

36. Andolfi M, Angelo C, Menghi P, Nicolo-Carigliano AM. *Behind the Family Mask: Therapeutic Change in Rigid Family Systems.* New York, NY: Brunner/Mazel Publishers; 1983:13–14.

Informed Consent

UNITED STATES COURT OF APPEALS

Canterbury v. Spence

SPOTTSWOOD W. ROBINSON, III,
Circuit Judge

Suits charging failure by a physician adequately to disclose the risks and alternatives of proposed treatment are not innovations in American law. They date back a good half-century, and in the last decade they have multiplied rapidly. There is, nonetheless, disagreement among the courts and the commentators on many major questions, and there is no precedent of our own directly in point. For the tools enabling resolution of the issues on this appeal, we are forced to begin at first principles.

The root premise is the concept, fundamental in American jurisprudence, that "[e]very human being of adult years and sound mind has a right to determine what shall be done with his own body. . . ." True consent to what happens to one's self is the informed exercise of a choice, and that entails an opportunity to evaluate knowledgeably the options available and the risks attendant upon each. The average patient has little or no understanding of the medical arts, and ordinarily has only his physician to whom he can look for enlightenment with which to reach an intelligent decision. From these almost axiomatic considerations springs the need, and in turn the requirement, of a reasonable divulgence by physician to patient to make such a decision possible.

. . .

Once the circumstances give rise to a duty on the physician's part to inform his patient, the next inquiry is the scope of the disclosure the physician is legally

No. 22099, U.S. Court of Appeals, District of Columbia Circuit, May 19, 1972. 464 Federal Reporter, 2nd Series, 772.

obliged to make. The courts have frequently confronted this problem, but no uniform standard defining the adequacy of the divulgence emerges from the decisions. Some have said "full" disclosure,[1] a norm we are unwilling to adopt literally. It seems obviously prohibitive and unrealistic to expect physicians to discuss with their patients every risk of proposed treatment — no matter how small or remote — and generally unnecessary from the patient's viewpoint as well. Indeed, the cases speaking in terms of "full" disclosure appear to envision something less than total disclosure,[2] leaving unanswered the question of just how much.

The larger number of courts, as might be expected, have applied tests framed with reference to prevailing fashion within the medical profession. Some have measured the disclosure by "good medical practice," others by what a reasonable practitioner would have bared under the circumstances, and still others by what medical custom in the community would demand. We have explored this rather considerable body of law but are unprepared to follow it. The duty to disclose, we have reasoned, arises from phenomena apart from medical custom and practice. The latter, we think, should no more establish the scope of the duty than its existence. Any definition of scope in terms purely of a professional standard is at odds with the patient's prerogative to decide on projected therapy himself. That prerogative, we have said, is at the very foundation of the duty to disclose, and both the patient's right to know and the physician's correlative obligation to tell him are diluted to the extent that its compass is dictated by the medical profession.

In our view, the patient's right of self-decision shapes the boundaries of the duty to reveal. That right can be effectively exercised only if the patient possesses enough information to enable an intelligent choice. The scope of the physician's communications to the patient, then, must be measured by the patient's need, and that need is the information material to the decision. Thus the test for determining whether a particular peril must be divulged is its materiality to the patient's decision: all risks potentially affecting the decision must be unmasked. And to safeguard the patient's interest in achieving his own determination on treatment, the law must itself set the standard for adequate disclosure.

Optimally for the patient, exposure of a risk would be mandatory whenever the patient would deem it significant to his decision, either singly or in combination with other risks. Such a requirement, however, would summon the physician to second-guess the patient, whose ideas on materiality could hardly be known to the physician. That would make an undue demand upon medical practitioners, whose conduct, like that of others, is to be measured in terms of reasonableness. Consonantly with orthodox negligence doctrine, the physician's liability for nondisclosure is to be determined on the basis of foresight, not hindsight; no less than any other aspect of negligence, the issue of nondisclosure must be approached from the viewpoint of the reasonableness of the physician's divulgence in terms of what he knows or should know to be the patient's informational needs. If, but only if, the factfinder can say that the physician's communication was unreasonably inadequate is an imposition of liability legally or morally justified.

Of necessity, the content of the disclosure rests in the first instance with the physician. Ordinarily it is only he who is in a position to identify particular dangers; always he must make a judgment, in terms of materiality, as to whether and to what extent revelation to the patient is called for. He cannot know with complete exactitude what the patient would consider important to his decision, but on the basis of his medical training and experience he can sense how the average, reasonable patient expectably would react. Indeed, with knowledge of, or ability to learn, his patient's background and current condition, he is in a position superior to that of most others — attorneys, for example — who are called upon to make judgments on pain of liability in damages for unreasonable miscalculation.

From these considerations we derive the breadth of the disclosure of risks legally to be required. The scope of the standard is not subjective as to either the physi-

cian or the patient; it remains objective with due regard for the patient's informational needs and with suitable leeway for the physician's situation. In broad outline, we agreed that "[a] risk is thus material when a reasonable person, in what the physician knows or should know to be the patient's position, would be likely to attach significance to the risk or cluster of risks in deciding whether or not to forgo the proposed therapy."[3]

The topics importantly demanding a communication of information are the inherent and potential hazards of the proposed treatment, the alternatives to that treatment, if any, and the results likely if the patient remains untreated. The factors contributing significance to the dangerousness of a medical technique are, of course, the incidence of injury and the degree of the harm threatened. A very small chance of death or serious disablement may well be significant; a potential disability which dramatically outweighs the potential benefit of the therapy or the detriments of the existing malady may summon discussion with the patient.

There is no bright line separating the significant from the insignificant; the answer in any case must abide a rule of reason. Some dangers — infection, for example — are inherent in any operation; there is no obligation to communicate those of which persons of average sophistication are aware. Even more clearly, the physician bears no responsibility for discussion of hazards the patient has already discovered, or those having no apparent materiality to patients' decision on therapy. The disclosure doctrine, like others marking lines between permissible and impermissible behavior in medical practice, is in essence a requirement of conduct prudent under the circumstances. Whenever nondisclosure of particular risk information is open to debate by reasonable-minded men, the issue is for the finder of the facts.

Two exceptions to the general rule of disclosure have been noted by the courts. Each is in the nature of a physician's privilege not to disclose, and the reasoning underlying them is appealing. Each, indeed, is but a recognition that, as important as is the patient's right to know, it is greatly outweighed by the magnitudinous circumstances giving rise to the privilege. The first comes into play when the patient is unconscious or otherwise incapable of consenting, and harm from a failure to treat is imminent and outweighs any harm threatened by the proposed treatment. When a genuine emergency of that sort arises, it is settled that the impracticality of conferring with the patient dispenses with need for it. Even in situations of that character the physician should, as current law requires, attempt to secure a relative's consent if possible. But if time is too short to accommodate discussion obviously the physician should proceed with the treatment.

The second exception obtains when risk-disclosure poses such a threat of detriment to the patient as to become unfeasible or contraindicated from a medical point of view. It is recognized that patients occasionally become so ill or emotionally distraught on disclosure as to foreclose a rational decision, or complicate or hinder the treatment, or perhaps even pose psychological damage to the patient. Where that is so, the cases have generally held that the physician is armed with a privilege to keep the information from the patient, and we think it clear that portents of that type may justify the physician in action he deems medically warranted. The critical inquiry is whether the physician responded to a sound medical judgment that communication of the risk information would present a threat to the patient's well-being.

The physician's privilege to withhold information for therapeutic reasons must be carefully circumscribed, however, for otherwise it might devour the disclosure rule itself. The privilege does not accept the paternalistic notion that the physician may remain silent simply because divulgence might prompt the patient to forgo therapy the physician feels the patient really needs. That attitude presumes instability or perversity for even the normal patient, and runs counter to the foundation principle that the patient should and ordinarily can make the choice for himself. Nor does the privilege contemplate operation save where the patient's reaction to risk information, as reasonably foreseen by the physician, is menacing. And even in a situation of that kind, disclosure to a close relative with a view to securing consent to the proposed treatment may be the only alternative open to the physician.

NOTES

1. *E.g., Salgo v. Leland Stanford Jr. Univ. Bd. of Trustees,* 154 Cal. App. 2d 560, 317 P.2d 170, 181 (1975); *Woods v. Brumlop, supra* note 13 [in original text], 377 P.2d at 524–525.

2. See, Comment, Informed Consent in Medical Malpractice, 55 Calif. L. Rv. 1396, 1402–03 (1967).

3. Waltz and Scheuneman, Informed Consent to Therapy, 64, Nw. U.L. Rev. 628, 640 (1970).

JAY KATZ

Physicians and Patients: A History of Silence

Disclosure and consent, except in the most rudimentary fashion, are obligations alien to medical thinking and practice. Disclosure in medicine has served the function of getting patients to "consent" to what physicians wanted them to agree to in the first place. "Good" patients follow doctor's orders without question. Therefore, disclosure becomes relevant only with recalcitrant patients. Since they are "bad" and "ungrateful," one does not need to bother much with them. Hippocrates once said, "Life is short, the Art long, Opportunity fleeting, Experiment treacherous, Judgment difficult.

Reprinted by permission of the author.

The physician must be ready, not only to do his duty himself, but also to secure the cooperation of the patient, of the attendants and of externals." These were, and still are, the lonely obligations of physicians: to wrestle as best they can with life, art, opportunity, experiment and judgment. Sharing with patients the vagaries of available opportunities, however perilous or safe, or the rationale underlying judgments, however difficult or easy, is not part of the Hippocratic task. For doing that, the Art is too long and Life too short.

Physicians have always maintained that patients are only in need of caring custody. Doctors felt that in order to accomplish that objective they were obligated to attend to their patients' physical and emotional needs and to do so on their own authority, without consulting with their patients about the decisions that needed to be made. Indeed, doctors intuitively believed that such consultations were inimical to good patient care. The idea that patients may also be entitled to liberty, to sharing the burdens of decision with their doctors, was never part of the ethos of medicine. Being unaware of the idea of patient liberty, physicians did not address the possible conflict between notions of custody and liberty. When, however, in recent decades courts were confronted with allegations that professionals had deprived citizen-patients of freedom of choice, the conflict did emerge. Anglo-American law has, at least in theory, a long-standing tradition of preferring liberty over custody; and however much judges tried to side-step law's preferences and to side with physicians' traditional beliefs, the conflict remained and has ever since begged for a resolution. . . .

The legal doctrine remained limited in scope, in part, because judges believed or wished to believe that their pronouncements on informed consent gave legal force to what good physicians customarily did; therefore they felt that they could defer to the disclosure practices of "reasonable medical practitioners." Judges did not appreciate how deeply rooted the tradition of silence was and thus did not recognize the revolutionary, alien implications of their appeal for patient "self-determination." In fact, precisely because of the appeal's strange and bewildering novelty, physicians misinterpreted it as being more far-reaching than courts intended it to be.

Physicians did not realize how much their opposition to informed consent was influenced by suddenly encountering obligations divorced from their history, their clinical experience, or medical education. Had they appreciated that even the doctrine's modest appeal to patient self-determination represented a radical break with medical practices, as transmitted from teacher to student during more than two thousand years of recorded medical history, they might have been less embarrassed by standing so unpreparedly, so nakedly before this new obligation. They might then perhaps have realized that their silence had been until most recently a historical necessity, dictated not only by the inadequacy of medical knowledge but also by physicians' incapacity to discriminate between therapeutic effectiveness based on their actual physical interventions and benefits that must be ascribed to other causes. They might also have argued that the practice of silence was part of a long and venerable tradition that deserved not to be dismissed lightly. . . .

When I speak of silence I do not mean to suggest that physicians have not talked to their patients at all. Of course, they have conversed with patients about all kinds of matters, but they have not, except inadvertently, employed words to invite patients' participation in sharing the burden of making joint decisions. . . .

Judges have made impassioned pleas for patient self-determination, and then have undercut them by giving physicians considerable latitude to practice according to their own lights, exhorting them only to treat each patient with the utmost care. Judges could readily advance this more limited plea because generally doctors do treat their patients with solicitude. The affirmation of physicians' commitment to patients' physical needs, however, has failed to address physicians' lack of commitment to patients' decision making needs. These tensions have led judges to fashion a doctrine of informed consent that has secured for patients the right to better custody but not to liberty — the right to choose how to be treated. . . .

CANTERBURY V. SPENCE (1972)

Judge Robinson, of the D.C. Court of Appeals, who authored the . . . last landmark informed consent decision, also had good intentions. . . . The lesson to be learned from a study of *Canterbury* [is that]: The strong commitment to self-determination at the beginning of the opinion gets weaker as the opinion moves from jurisprudential theory to the realities of hospital and courtroom life. By the end, the opinion has only obscured the issue it intended to address: the nature of the relationship between the court's doctrine of informed consent, as ultimately construed, and its root premise of self-determination. . . .

Respect for the patient's right of self-determination on particular therapy demands a standard set by law for physicians rather than one which physicians may or may not impose upon themselves.

For this apparently bold move, *Canterbury* has been widely celebrated, as well as followed in many jurisdictions.

The new rule of law laid down in *Canterbury*, however, is far from clear. Judge Robinson, returning to basic principles of expert testimony, simply said that there is "no basis for operation of the special medical standard where the physician's activity does not bring his medical knowledge and skills peculiarly into play," and that ordinarily disclosure is not such a situation. But he left room for such situations by adding: "When medical judgment enters the picture and for that reason the special standard controls, prevailing medical practice must be given its *just due.*" He did not spell out the meaning of "*just due.*"

Both standards tend to confuse the need for *medical knowledge* to elucidate the risks of and alternatives to a proposed procedure in the light of professional experience with the need for *medical judgment* to establish the limits of appropriate disclosure to patients. The difference is crucial to the clarification of the law of informed consent. In *Natanson* and many subsequent cases, judges lumped the two together uncritically, relying solely on current medical practice to resolve the question of reasonableness of disclosure. In *Canterbury,* the distinction was formally recognized. The plaintiff was required to present expert evidence of the applicable medical knowledge, while the defendant had to raise the issue of medical judgment to limit disclosure in defense. But even *Canterbury* did not undertake a detailed judicial analysis of the nature of medical judgment required, precisely because judges were hesitant to make rules in an area that doctors strongly believed was solely the province of medicine.

In *Canterbury,* Dr. Spence claimed that "communication of that risk (paralysis) to the patient is not good medical practice because it might deter patients from undergoing needed surgery and might produce adverse psychological reactions which could preclude the success of the operation." Such claims will almost invariably be raised by physicians since they are derived from deeply held tenets of medical practice. Judge Robinson's enigmatic phrase of "just due" certainly suggests that the medical professional standard would be applicable in such a case, raising profound questions about the extent to which the novel legal standard has been swallowed up by the traditional and venerable medical standard.

In fact, medical judgment was given its "just due" twice. It could also be invoked under the "therapeutic privilege" not to disclose, which Judge Robinson retained as a defense to disclosure:

It is recognized that patients occasionally become so ill or emotionally distraught on disclosure as to foreclose a rational decision, or complicate or hinder the treatment, or perhaps even pose psychological damage to the patient. . . . The critical inquiry is whether the physician responded to a sound medical judgment that communication of the risk information would present a threat to the patient's well-being.

The therapeutic privilege not to disclose is merely a procedurally different way of invoking the professional standard of care. . . .

Since the court wished to depart from medical custom as the standard, it had to give some indication as to the information it expected physicians to disclose. The court said that "the test for determining whether a particular peril must be divulged is its materiality to the patient's decision: all risks potentially affecting the decision must be unmasked." It added that physicians must similarly disclose alternatives to the proposed treatment and the "results likely if the patient remains untreated."

But then the court chose to adopt an "objective" test for disclosure of risks and alternatives — what a [reasonable] *prudent* person in the patient's position would have decided if suitably informed" — and rejected a "subjective" test of materiality — "what an *individual* patient would have considered a significant risk." In opting for an "objective" standard, self-determination was given unnecessarily short shrift. The whole point of the inquiry was to safeguard the right of *individual* choice, even where it may appear idiosyncratic. Although law generally does not protect a person's right to be unreasonable and requires reasonably prudent conduct where injury to another may occur, it remains ambiguous about the extent to which prudence can be legally enforced where the potential injury is largely confined to the individual decision maker. For example, courts have split on the question of whether society may require the wearing of motorcycle helmets and whether an adult patient may be compelled to undergo unwanted blood transfusions.

The "objective" standard for disclosure contradicts the right of each individual to decide what will be done with his or her body. The belief that there is one "reasonable" or "prudent" response to every situation inviting medical intervention is nonsense, from the point of view of both the physician and the patient. The most cursory examination of medical practices demonstrates that what is reasonable to the internist may appear unreasonable to the surgeon or even to other internists and, more significantly, that the value preferences of physicians may not coincide with those of their patients. For example, doctors generally place a higher value on physical longevity than their patients do. But physical longevity is not the only touchstone of prudence. Why should not informed consent law countenance a wide range of potentially reasonable responses by patients to their medical condition based on other value preferences? . . .

Ascertaining patients' informational needs is difficult. Answers do not lie in guessing or "sensing" patients' particular concerns or in obliterating the "subjective" person in an "objective" mass of persons. The "objective" test of materiality only tempts doctors to introduce their own unwarranted subjectivity into the disclosure process. It would have been far better if the court had not committed itself prematurely to the labels "objective" and "subjective." Instead it should have considered more the patients' plight and required physicians to learn new skills: how to inquire openly about their patients' *individual* informational needs and patients' concerns, doubts, and misconceptions about treatment—its risks, benefits, and alternatives. Safeguarding self-determination requires assessing whether patients' informational needs have been satisfied by asking them whether they understand what has been explained to them. Physicians should not try to "second-guess" patients or "sense" how they will react. Instead, they need to explore what questions require further explanation. Taking such unaccustomed obligations seriously is not easy. . . .

SUMMING UP

The legal life of "informed consent," if quality of human life is measured not merely by improvements in physical custody but also by advancement of liberty, was over almost as soon as it was born. Except for the . . . law promulgated in a handful of jurisdictions and the more generally espoused dicta about "self-determination" and "freedom of choice," this is substantially true. Judges toyed briefly with the idea of patients' right to self-determination and largely cast it aside. . . .

Treatment decisions are extremely complex and require a more sustained dialogue, one in which patients are viewed as participants in medical decisions affecting their lives. This is not the view of most physicians, who believe instead that patients are too ignorant to make decisions on their own behalf, that disclosure increases patients' fears and reinforces "foolish" decisions, and that informing them about the uncertainties of medical interventions in many instances seriously undermines faith so essential to the success of therapy. Therefore, physicians asserted that they must be the ultimate decision makers. Judges did not probe these contentions in depth but were persuaded to refrain from interfering significantly with traditional medical practices.

I have not modified my earlier assessment of law's informed consent vision:

[T]he law of informed consent is substantially mythic and fairy tale-like as far as advancing patients' rights to self-decisionmaking is concerned. It conveys in its dicta about such rights a fairy tale-like optimism about human capacities for "intelligent" choice and for being respectful of other persons' choices; yet in its implementation of dicta, it conveys a mythic pessimism of human capacities to be choice-makers. The resulting tensions have had a significant impact on the law of informed consent which only has made a bow toward a commitment to patients' self-determination, perhaps in an attempt to resolve these tensions by a belief that it is "less important that this commitment be total than that we believe it to be there."

Whether fairy tale and myth can and should be reconciled more satisfactorily with reality remains to be seen. If judges contemplate such a reconciliation, they must acquire first a more profound understanding and appreciation of medicine's vision of patients and professional practice, of the capacities of physicians and patients for autonomous choice, and of the limits of professional knowledge. Such understanding cannot readily be acquired in courts of law, during disputes in which inquiry is generally constrained by claims and counter-claims that seek to assure victory for one side.

The call to liberty, embedded in the doctrine of informed consent, has only created an atmosphere in which freedom has the potential to survive and grow. The doctrine has not as yet provided a meaningful blueprint for implementing patient self-determination. The message . . . is this: Those committed to greater patient self-determination can, if they look hard enough, find inspiration in the common law of informed consent, and so can those, and more easily, who seek to perpetuate medical paternalism. Those who look for evidence of committed implementation will be sadly disappointed. The legal vision of informed consent, based on *self-determination,* is still largely a mirage. Yet a mirage, since it not only deceives but also can sustain hope, is better than no vision at all. . . .

RUTH R. FADEN AND TOM L. BEAUCHAMP

The Concept of Informed Consent

What is an informed consent? Answering this question is complicated because there are two common, entrenched, and starkly different meanings of "informed consent." That is, the term is analyzable in two profoundly different ways—not because of mere subtle differences of connotation that appear in different contexts, but because two different *conceptions* of informed consent have emerged from its history and are still at work, however unnoticed, in literature on the subject.

In one sense, which we label *sense₁*, "informed consent" is analyzable as a particular kind of action by individual patients and subjects: an autonomous authorization. In the second sense, *sense₂*, informed consent is analyzable in terms of the web of cultural and policy rules and requirements of consent that collectively form the social practice of informed consent in institutional contexts where *groups* of patients and subjects must be treated in accordance with rules, policies, and standard practices. Here, informed consents are not always *autonomous* acts, nor are they always in any meaningful respect *authorizations*.

SENSE₁: INFORMED CONSENT AS AUTONOMOUS AUTHORIZATION

The idea of an informed consent suggests that a patient or subject does more than express agreement with, acquiesce in, yield to, or comply with an arrangement or a proposal. He or she actively *authorizes* the proposal in the act of consent. John may *assent* to a treatment plan without authorizing it. The assent may be a mere submission to the doctor's authoritative order, in which case John does not call on his *own* authority in order to

From *A History and Theory of Informed Consent* by Ruth R. Faden and Tom L. Beauchamp. Copyright © 1986 by Oxford University Press, Inc. Reprinted by permission.

give permission, and thus does not authorize the plan. Instead, he acts like a child who submits, yields, or assents to the school principal's spanking and in no way gives permission for or authorizes the spanking. Just as the child merely submits to an authority in a system where the lines of authority are quite clear, so often do patients.

Accordingly, an informed consent in sense₁ should be defined as follows: An informed consent is an autonomous action by a subject or a patient that authorizes a professional either to involve the subject in research or to initiate a medical plan for the patient (or both). We can whittle down this definition by saying that an informed consent in sense₁ is given if a patient or subject with (1) substantial understanding and (2) in substantial absence of control by others (3) intentionally (4) authorizes a professional (to do intervention I).

All substantially autonomous acts satisfy conditions 1–3; but it does not follow from that analysis alone that all such acts satisfy 4. The fourth condition is what distinguishes informed consent as one *kind* of autonomous action. (Note also that the definition restricts the kinds of authorization to medical and research contexts.) A person whose act satisfies conditions 1–3 but who refuses an intervention gives an *informed refusal*.

The Problem of Shared Decisionmaking. This analysis of informed consent in sense₁ is deliberately silent on the question of how the authorizer and agent(s) being authorized *arrive at an agreement* about the performance of "I." Recent commentators on informed consent in clinical medicine, notably Jay Katz and the President's Commission, have tended to equate the idea of informed consent with a model of "shared decisionmaking" between doctor and patient. The President's

Commission titles the first chapter of its report on informed consent in the patient-practitioner relationship "Informed Consent as Active, Shared Decision Making," while in Katz's work "the idea of informed consent" and "mutual decisionmaking" are treated as virtually synonymous terms.[1]

There is of course an historical relationship in clinical medicine between medical decisionmaking and informed consent. The emergence of the legal doctrine of informed consent was instrumental in drawing attention to issues of decisionmaking as well as authority in the doctor-patient relationship. Nevertheless, it is a confusion to treat informed consent and shared decisionmaking as anything like *synonymous*. For one thing, informed consent is not restricted to clinical medicine. It is a term that applies equally to biomedical and behavioral research contexts where a model of shared decisionmaking is frequently inappropriate. Even in clinical contexts, the social and psychological dynamics involved in selecting medical interventions should be distinguished from the patient's *authorization*.

We endorse Katz's view that effective communication between professional and patient or subject is often instrumental in obtaining informed consents (sense$_1$), but we resist his conviction that the idea of informed consent entails that the patient and physician "share decisionmaking," or "reason together," or reach a consensus about what is in the patient's best interest. This is a manipulation of the concept from a too singular and defined moral perspective on the practice of medicine that is in effect a moral program for changing the practice. Although the patient and physician *may* reach a decision together, they need not. It is the essence of informed consent in sense$_1$ only that the patient or subject *authorizes autonomously;* it is a matter of indifference where or how the proposal being authorized originates.

For example, one might advocate a model of shared decisionmaking for the doctor-patient relationship without simultaneously advocating that every medical procedure requires the consent of patients. Even relationships characterized by an ample slice of shared decisionmaking, mutual trust, and respect would and should permit many decisions about routine and low-risk aspects of the patient's medical treatment to remain the exclusive province of the physician, and thus some decisions are likely always to remain subject ex-clusively to the physician's authorization. Moreover, in the uncommon situation, a patient could autonomously authorize the physician to make *all* decisions about medical treatment, thus giving his or her informed consent to an arrangement that scarcely resembles the sharing of decisionmaking between doctor and patient.

Authorization. In authorizing, one both assumes responsibility for what one has authorized and transfers to another one's authority to implement it. There is no informed consent unless one *understands* these features of the act and *intends* to perform that act. That is, one must understand that one is assuming responsibility and warranting another to proceed.

To say that one assumes responsibility does not quite locate the essence of the matter, however, because a *transfer* of responsibility as well as of authority also occurs. The crucial element in an authorization is that the person who authorizes uses whatever right, power, or control he or she possesses in the situation to endow another with the right to act. In so doing, the authorizer assumes some responsibility for the actions taken by the other person. Here one could either authorize *broadly* so that a person can act in accordance with general guidelines, or *narrowly* so as to authorize only a particular, carefully circumscribed procedure.

SENSE$_2$: INFORMED CONSENT AS EFFECTIVE CONSENT

By contrast to sense$_1$, sense$_2$, or *effective* consent, is a policy-oriented sense whose conditions are not derivable solely from analyses of autonomy and authorization, or even from broad notions of respect for autonomy. "Informed consent" in this second sense does not refer to *autonomous* authorization, but to a legally or institutionally *effective* (sometimes misleadingly called *valid*) authorization from a patient or a subject. Such an authorization is "effective" because it has been obtained through procedures that satisfy the rules and requirements defining a specific institutional practice in health care or in research.

The social and legal practice of requiring professionals to obtain informed consent emerged in institutional contexts, where conformity to operative rules was and still is the sole necessary and sufficient condition of informed consent. Any consent is an informed consent in sense$_2$ if it satisfies whatever operative rules apply to the practice of informed consent. Sense$_2$ requirements for informed consent typically do not focus on the autonomy of the act of giving consent (as sense$_1$ does), but rather on regulating the behavior of the *consent-seeker* and on establishing *procedures and rules* for the context of consent. Such requirements of professional behavior and procedure are obviously more readily monitored and enforced by institutions.

However, because formal institutional rules such as federal regulations and hospital policies govern whether an act of authorizing is effective, a patient or subject can autonomously authorize an intervention, and so give an informed consent in sense$_1$, and yet *not effectively authorize* that intervention in sense$_2$.

Consider the following example. Carol and Martie are nineteen-year-old, identical twins attending the same university. Martie was born with multiple birth defects, and has only one kidney. When both sisters are involved in an automobile accident, Carol is not badly hurt, but her sister is seriously injured. It is quickly determined that Martie desperately needs a kidney transplant. After detailed discussions with the transplant team and with friends, Carol consents to be the donor. There is no question that Carol's authorization of the transplant surgery is substantially autonomous. She is well informed and has long anticipated being in just such a circumstance. She has had ample opportunity over the years to consider what she would do were she faced with such a decision. Unfortunately, Carol's parents, who were in Nepal at the time of the accident, do not approve of her decision. Furious that they were not consulted, they decide to sue the transplant team and the hospital for having performed an unauthorized surgery on their minor daughter. (In this state the legal age to consent to surgical procedures is twenty-one.)

According to our analysis, Carol gave her informed consent in sense$_1$ to the surgery, but she did not give her informed consent in sense$_2$. That is, she autonomously authorized the transplant and thereby gave an informed consent in sense$_1$ but did not give a consent that was effective under the operative legal and institutional policy, which in this case required that the person consenting be a legally authorized agent. Examples of other policies that can define sense$_2$ informed consent (but not sense$_1$) include rules that consent be witnessed by an auditor or that there be a one-day waiting period between solicitation of consent and implementation of the intervention in order for the person's authorization to be effective. Such rules can and do vary, both within the United States by jurisdiction and institution, and across the countries of the world.

Medical and research codes, as well as case law and federal regulations, have developed models of informed consent that are delineated entirely in a sense$_2$ format, although they have sometimes attempted to justify the rules by appeal to something like sense$_1$. For example, disclosure conditions for informed consent are central to the history of "informed consent" in sense$_2$, because disclosure has traditionally been a *necessary* condition of effective informed consent (and sometimes a *sufficient* condition!). The legal doctrine of informed consent is primarily a law of disclosure; satisfaction of disclosure rules virtually consumes "informed consent" in law. This should come as no surprise, because the legal system needs a generally applicable informed consent mechanism by which injury and responsibility can be readily and fairly assessed in court. These disclosure requirements in the legal and regulatory contexts are not conditions of "informed consent" in sense$_1$; indeed disclosure may be entirely irrelevant to giving an informed consent in sense$_1$. If a person has an adequate *understanding* of relevant information without benefit of a disclosure, then it makes no difference whether someone *discloses* that information.

Other sense$_2$ rules besides those of disclosure have been enforced. These include rules requiring evidence of adequate comprehension of information and the aforementioned rules requiring the presence of auditor witnesses and mandatory waiting periods. Sense$_2$ informed consent requirements generally take the form of rules focusing on disclosure, comprehension, the minimization of potentially controlling influences, and competence. These requirements express the present-day mainstream conception in the federal government of the United States. They are also typical of international documents and state regulations, which all reflect a sense$_2$ orientation.

THE RELATIONSHIP BETWEEN SENSE$_1$ AND SENSE$_2$

A sense$_1$ "informed consent" can fail to be an informed consent in sense$_2$ by a lack of conformity to applicable rules and requirements. Similarly, an informed consent in sense$_2$ may not be an informed consent in sense$_1$. The rules and requirements that determine sense$_2$ consents need not result in autonomous authorizations at all in order to qualify as informed consents.

Such peculiarities in informed consent law have led Jay Katz to argue that the legal doctrine of "informed consent" bears a "name" that "promises much more than its construction in case law has delivered." He has argued insightfully that the courts have, in effect, imposed a mere duty to warn on physicians, an obligation confined to risk disclosures and statements of proposed interventions. He maintains that "This judicially imposed obligation must be distinguished from the *idea* of informed consent, namely, that patients have a decisive role to play in the medical decision-making process. The idea of informed consent, though alluded to also in case law, cannot be implemented, as courts have attempted, by only expanding the disclosure requirements." By their actions and declarations, Katz believes, the courts have made informed consent a "cruel hoax" and have allowed "the idea of informed consent . . . to wither on the vine."[2]

The most plausible interpretation of Katz's contentions is through the sense$_1$/sense$_2$ distinction. If a physician obtains a consent under the courts' criteria, then an informed consent (sense$_2$) has been obtained. But it does not follow that the courts are using the *right* standards, or *sufficiently rigorous* standards in light of a stricter autonomy-based model — or "idea" as Katz puts it — of informed consent (sense$_1$).[3] If Katz is correct that the courts have made a mockery of informed consent and of its moral justification in respect for autonomy, then of course his criticisms are thoroughly justified. At the same time, it should be recognized that people can proffer legally or institutionally effective authorizations under prevailing rules even if they fall far short of the standards implicit in sense$_1$.

Despite the differences between sense$_1$ and sense$_2$, a definition of informed consent need not fall into one or the other class of definitions. It may conform to both. Many definitions of informed consent in policy contexts reflect at least a strong and definite reliance on informed consent in sense$_1$. Although the conditions of sense$_1$ are not logically necessary conditions for sense$_2$, we take it as morally axiomatic that they *ought* to serve — and in fact have served — as the benchmark or model against which the moral adequacy of a definition framed for sense$_2$ purposes is to be evaluated. This position is, roughly speaking, Katz's position.

A defense of the moral viewpoint that policies governing informed consent in sense$_2$ *should* be formulated to conform to the standards of informed consent in sense$_1$ is not hard to express. The goal of informed consent in medical care and in research — that is, the purpose behind the obligation to obtain informed consent — is to enable potential subjects and patients to make autonomous decisions about whether to grant or refuse authorization for medical and research interventions. Accordingly, embedded in the reason for having the social institution of informed consent is the idea that institutional requirements for informed consent in sense$_2$ *should* be intended to maximize the likelihood that the conditions of informed consent in sense$_1$ will be satisfied.

A major problem at the policy level, where rules and requirements must be developed and applied in the aggregate, is the following: The obligations imposed to enable patients and subjects to make authorization decisions must be evaluated not only in terms of the demands of a set of abstract conditions of "true" or sense$_1$ informed consent, but also in terms of the impact of imposing such obligations or requirements on various institutions with their concrete concerns and priorities. One must take account of what is fair and reasonable to require of health care professionals and researchers, the effect of alternative consent requirements on efficiency and effectiveness in the delivery of health care and the advancement of science, and — particularly in medical care — the effect of requirements on the welfare of patients. Also relevant are considerations peculiar to the particular social context, such as proof, precedent, or liability theory in case law, or regulatory authority and due process in the development of federal regulations and IRB consent policies.

Moreover, at the sense$_2$ level, one must resolve not only which requirements will define effective consent; one must also settle on the rules stipulating the conditions under which effective consents must be obtained. In some cases, hard decisions must be made about whether requirements of informed consent (in sense$_2$) should be imposed at all, even though informed consent (in sense$_1$) *could* realistically and meaningfully be obtained in the circumstances and could serve as a model for institutional rules. For example, should there be any consent requirements in the cases of minimal risk medical procedures and research activities?

This need to balance is not a problem for informed consent in sense$_1$, which is not policy oriented. Thus, it is possible to have a *morally acceptable* set of requirements for informed consent in sense$_2$ that deviates considerably from the conditions of informed consent in sense₁. However, the burden of moral proof rests with those who defend such deviations since the primary moral justification of the obligation to obtain informed consent is respect for autonomous action.

NOTES

1. President's Commission, *Making Health Care Decisions,* Vol. 1, 15 and Jay Katz, *The Silent World of Doctor and Patient* (New York: The Free Press, 1984), 87 and "The Regulation of Human Research — Reflections and Proposals," *Clinical Research* 21 (1973):

758–91. Katz does not provide a sustained analysis of joint or shared decisionmaking, and it is unclear precisely how he would relate this notion to informed consent.

2. Jay Katz, "Disclosure and Consent," in A. Milunsky and G. Annas, eds., *Genetics and the Law II* (New York: Plenum Press, 1980), 122, 128.

3. We have already noted that Katz's "idea" of informed consent — as the active involvement of patients in the medical decision-making process — is different from our sense₁.

ROBERT J. LEVINE

Informed Consent: Some Challenges to the Universal Validity of the Western Model

INFORMED CONSENT

Informed consent holds a central place in the ethical justification of research involving human subjects. This position is signaled by the fact that it is the first-stated and , by far, the longest principle of the Nuremberg Code.[1]

I. The voluntary consent of the human subject is absolutely essential. This means that the person involved should have the legal capacity to give consent; should be so situated as to be able to exercise free power of choice, without the intervention of any element of force, fraud, deceit, duress, overreaching, or other ulterior form of constraint or coercion; and should have sufficient knowledge and comprehension of the elements of the subject matter involved as to enable him to make an understanding and enlightened decision. This latter element requires that before the acceptance of an affirmative decision by the experimental subject there should be made known to him the nature, duration, and purpose of the experiment; the method and means by which it is to be conducted; all inconveniences and hazards reasonably to be ex-

pected; and the effects upon his health or person which may possibly come from his participation in the experiment. . . .

The Nuremberg Code identifies four attributes of consent without which consent cannot be considered valid: consent must be "voluntary," "legally competent," "informed," and "comprehending." These four attributes stand essentially unchanged to this day. Although there has been extensive commentary on the meaning of each of these attributes and how they are to be interpreted in specific contexts, there has been no authoritative agreement reached that any of them may be omitted or that there should be any additional attribute elevated to the status of the original four. . . .

The National Commission grounded the requirement for informed consent in the ethical principle of respect for persons which it defined as follows:

Respect for persons incorporates at least two basic ethical convictions: First, that individuals should be treated as autonomous agents, and second, that persons with diminished autonomy and thus in need of protection are entitled to such protections.

The National Commission defined an "autonomous person" as ". . . an individual capable of deliberation

From Law, Medicine, and Health Care 19(1991): 207–213. Reprinted with the permission of the American Society of Law, Medicine & Ethics.

about personal goals and of acting under the direction of such deliberation." To show respect for autonomous persons requires that we leave them alone, even to the point of allowing them to choose activities that might be harmful, unless they agree or consent that we may do otherwise. We are not to touch them or to encroach upon their private spaces unless such touching or encroachment is in accord with their wishes. Our actions should be designed to affirm their authority and enhance their capacity to be self-determining; we are not to obstruct their actions unless they are clearly detrimental to others. We show disrespect for autonomous persons when we either repudiate their considered judgments or deny them the freedom to act on those judgments in the absence of compelling reasons to do so.

The National Commission's discussion of an autonomous person is consistent with the prevailing perception of the nature of the "moral agent" in Western civilization. A moral agent is an individual who is capable of forming a rational plan of life, capable of rational deliberation about alternative plans of action with the aim of making choices that are compatible with his or her life plan and who assumes responsibility for the consequences of his or her choices.

Although the National Commission did not cite either of the following sources as authoritative in developing its definition of respect for persons, it is clear to this observer that they found them influential: The first is the statement of the principle of respect for persons as articulated by the German philosopher, Immanuel Kant: "So act as to treat humanity, whether in thine own person or in that of any other, in every case as an end withal, never as a means only." A second influential statement is that of the American judge, Benjamin Cardozo: "Every human being of adult years and sound mind has the right to determine what will be done with his own body . . ."

. . . In the actual process of negotiating informed consent and in the reviews of plans for informed consent conducted by Institutional Review Boards (IRBs), there is a tendency to concentrate on the information to be presented to the prospective subject. Among the IRB's principal concerns are the following questions: Is there a full statement of each of the elements of informed consent? Is the information presented in a style of language that one could expect the prospective subject to understand? Implicit in this is a vision of informed consent as a two step process. First, informa-

tion is presented to the subject by the investigator. Secondly, the subject satisfies himself or herself that he or she understands, and based upon this understanding either agrees or refuses to participate in the research project. . . .

In the paper I presented at an earlier CIOMS conference[2] I concluded:

This brief survey of descriptions of relationships between health professionals and patients in three disparate cultures leads me to conclude that the informed consent standards of the Declaration of Helsinki are not universally valid. Imposition of these standards as they are now written will not accomplish their purposes; i.e., they will not guide physicians in their efforts to show respect for persons because they do not reflect adequately the views held in these cultures of the nature of the person in his or her relationship to society.

This conclusion was based on a review of observations of the doctor–patient relationship, subject–investigator relationship and perspectives on the nature of disease in three cultures: Western Africa, China, and a Central American Mayan Indian culture.

The concept of personhood as it exists in various cultures has been addressed in an excellent paper by Willy De Craemer.[3] De Craemer is a cross-cultural sociologist with extensive experience in the field in, among other places, Central Africa and Japan.

In this paper he makes it clear that the Western vision of the person is a minority viewpoint in the world. The majority viewpoint manifest in most other societies, both technologically developing (e.g., Central Africa) and technologically developed (e.g., Japan), does not reflect the American perspective of radical individualism. . . .

Although I commend to the readers' attention De Craemer's entire essay, I shall here excerpt some passages from his description of the Japanese vision of the person. I do this because Japan is unquestionably a highly developed society technologically as well as in other respects. Thus, it is less easy to dismiss its vision of the person as exotic, as could be done with some of the examples examined in my earlier paper: . . .

The special status that the Japanese accord to human relationships, with its emphasis on the empathic and solidary interdependence of many individuals, rather than on the autonomous independence of the individual person, includes within it several other core attributes. To begin with, the kind of reciprocity (*on*) that underlies human relationships means that both concretely and symbolically what anthropologist Marcel Mauss . . . termed "the theme of the gift" is one of its dominant motifs. A continuous, gift-exchange-structured flow of material and nonmaterial "goods" and "services" takes place between the members of the enclosed human nexus to which each individual belongs. Through a never-ending process of mutual giving, receiving, and repaying . . . a web of relations develops that binds donors and recipients together in diffuse, deeply personal, and overlapping creditor-debtor ways. Generalized benevolence is involved, but so is generalized obligation, both of which take into account another crucial parameter of Japanese culture: the importance attached to status, rank, and hierarchical order in interpersonal relationships, and to . . . "proper-place occupancy" within them. The triple obligation to give, receive, and repay are tightly regulated by this status-formalism and sense of propriety. . . .

It is not difficult to imagine how a research ethics committee in the Western world — particularly in the United States — would evaluate the custom of exchange of gifts — both material and immaterial — in a system that recognized the legitimacy of "status, rank, and hierarchical order." Attention would soon be focused on the problems of "conflicts of interest." Questions would be raised as to whether consent would be invalidated by "undue inducement," or what the Nuremberg Code calls "other ulterior form(s) of constraint or coercion." In my views, it is impossible to evaluate the meaning of cash payments, provision of free services, and other "inducements" without a full appreciation of the cultural significance of such matters.

It is against this backdrop that I have been asked by the CIOMS Conference Programme Committee to "provide a definition [of informed consent] which is widely applicable to different countries and cultures." Given that the purpose of informed consent is to show respect for persons, in recognition of the vastly different perspectives of the nature of "person," I cannot do this. Since I cannot provide a substantive definition of informed consent, I shall suggest a procedural approach to dealing with the problem.

As an American I am firmly committed to the Western vision of the person and deeply influenced by my experience with the American variant of this vision. . . .

Thus, it would not be prudent to trust an American to provide a universally applicable definition of informed consent. I suggest further, that it would not be prudent to rely on any person situated in any culture to provide a universally applicable definition of informed consent.

Before proceeding, I wish to comment on the continuing controversy on the topic of ethical justification of research that crosses national boundaries. There are those who contend that all research, wherever it is con-ducted, should be justified according to universally applicable standards; I refer to them as "universalists." Those opposed to the universalist position, whom I call "pluralists," accept some standards as universal, but argue that other standards must be adapted to accommodate the mores of particular cultures. Pluralists commonly refer to the universalist position as "ethical imperialism," while universalists often call that of their opponents, "ethical relativism."

Universalists correctly point out that most therapeutic innovations are developed in industrialized nations. Investigators from these countries may go to technologically developing countries to test their innovations for various reasons; some of these reasons are good and some of them are not (e.g., to save money and to take advantage of the less complex and sophisticated regulatory systems typical to technologically developing countries). Moreover, universalists observe that, once the innovations have been proved safe and effective, economic factors often limit their availability to citizens of the country in which they were tested. Requiring investigators to conform to the ethical standards of their own country when conducting research abroad is one way to restrain exploitation of this type. Universalists also point to the Declaration of Helsinki as a widely accepted universal standard for biomedical research that has been endorsed by most countries, including those labeled "technologically developing." This gives weight to their claim that research must be conducted according to universal principles. Furthermore, the complex regulations characteristic of technologically developed countries are, in general, patterned after the Declaration of Helsinki.

Marcia Angell, in a particularly incisive exposition of the universalists' position, suggests this analogy[4]

Does apartheid offend universal standards of justice, or does it instead simply represent the South African custom that should be seen as morally neutral? If the latter view is accepted, then ethical principles are not much more than a description of the mores of a society. I believe they must have more meaning than that. There must be a core of human rights that we would wish to see honored universally, despite local variations in their superficial aspects . . . The force of local custom or law cannot justify abuses of certain fundamental rights, and the right of self-determination, on which the doctrine of informed consent is based, is one of them.

Pluralists join with universalists in condemning economic exploitation of technologically developing countries and their citizens.[5] Unlike the universalists, however, they see the imposition of ethical standards for the conduct of research by a powerful country on a developing country as another form of exploitation. In their view, it is tantamount to saying, "No, you may not participate in this development of technology, no matter how much you desire it, unless you permit us to replace your ethical standards with our own." Pluralists call attention to the fact that the Declaration of Helsinki, although widely endorsed by the nations of the world, reflects a uniquely Western view of the nature of the person; as such it does not adequately guide investigators in ways to show respect for all persons in the world.

An example of pluralism may be found in the diversity of national policies regarding blind HIV-seroprevalence studies. The United States Centers for Disease Control are now conducting anonymous tests of leftover blood drawn for other purposes without notification in studies designed to "determine the level of HIV-seroprevalence in a nationwide sample of hospital patients and clients at family planning, sexually transmitted disease, tuberculosis, and drug treatment clinics. . . ." No personal identifiers are kept.[6] Although there seems to be widespread agreement among US commentators that such anonymous testing without notification is ethically justified, different judgments have been reached in other countries, most notably in the United Kingdom and in the Netherlands.[7] Who is to say which of these nations has the correct ethical perspective that should be made part of the "universal standard?"

The legitimacy of the pluralists' position is recognized implicitly in U.S. policy on whether research subjects are required to be informed of the results of HIV antibody testing.[8] In general, this policy requires that all individuals "whose test results are associated with personal identifiers must be informed of their own test results . . . individuals may not be given the option 'not to know' the result. . . ." This policy permits several narrowly defined exceptions. One of these provides that research "conducted at foreign sites should be carefully evaluated to account for cultural norms, the health resource capability and official health policies of the host country." Then "the reviewing IRB must consider if any modification to the policy is significantly justified by the risk/benefit evaluation of the research."

WHO/CIOMS Proposed International Guidelines provide specific guidance for the conduct of research in which an investigator or an institution in a technologically developed country serves as the "external sponsor" of research conducted in a technologically developing "host country."[9] In my judgment these guidelines strike a sensitive balance between the universalist and pluralist perspectives. They require that "the research protocol should be submitted to ethical review by the initiating agency. The ethical standards applied should be no less exacting than they would be for research carried out within the initiating country" (Article 28). They also provide for accommodation to the mores of the culture within the "host country." For example:

> Where individual members of a community do not have the necessary awareness of the implications of participation in an experiment to give adequately informed consent directly to the investigators, it is desirable that the decision whether or not to participate should be elicited through the intermediary of a trusted community leader. (Article 15).

The conduct of research involving human subjects must not violate any universally applicable ethical standards. Although I endorse certain forms of cultural relativism, there are limits to how much cultural relativism ought to be tolerated. Certain behaviors ought to be condemned by the world community even though they are sponsored by a nation's leaders and seem to have wide support of its citizens. For example, the Nuremberg tribunal appealed to universally valid principles in order to determine the guilt of the physicians (war criminals) who had conducted research according to standards approved by their nation's leaders.

I suggest that the principle of respect for persons is one of the universally applicable ethical standards. It is universally applicable when stated at the level of formality employed by Immanuel Kant: "So act as to treat humanity, whether in thine own person or in that of any other, in every case as an end withal, never as a means only." The key concept is that persons are never to be treated only or merely as means to another's ends. When one goes beyond this level of formality or abstraction, the principle begins to lose its universality. When one restates the principle of respect for persons in a form that reflects a peculiarly Western view of the person, it begins to lose its relevance to some people in Central Africa, Japan, Central America, and so on.

The Conference Programme Committee asked me to address the problem "of obtaining consent in cultures where non-dominant persons traditionally do not give consent, such as a wife." Having subscribed to the Western vision of the meaning of person, I believe that all persons should be treated as autonomous agents, wives included. Thus, I believe that we should show respect for wives in the context of research by soliciting their informed consent. But, if this is not permitted within a particular culture, would I exclude wives from participation in research?

Not necessarily. If there is a strong possibility either that the wife could benefit from participation in the research or that the class of women of which she is a representative could benefit (and there is a reasonable balance of risks and potential benefits), I would offer her an opportunity to participate. To do otherwise would not accomplish anything of value (e.g., her entitlement to self-determination); it would merely deprive her of a chance to secure the benefits of participation in the research. I would, of course, offer her an opportunity to decline participation, understanding that in some cultures she would consider such refusal "unthinkable."

. . . Finally, the Conference Programme Committee has asked me to consider "the special problems of obtaining consent when populations are uneducated or illiterate." Lack of education in and of itself presents no problems that are unfamiliar to those experienced with negotiating informed consent with prospective subjects. These are barriers to comprehension which are not generally insurmountable. Greater problems are presented by those who hold beliefs about health and illness that are inconsistent with the concepts of Western medicine. It may, for example, be difficult to explain the purpose of vaccination to a person who believes that disease is caused by forces that Western civilization dismisses as supernatural or magical.[10] The meaning of such familiar (in the Western world) procedures as blood-letting may be vastly different and very disturbing in some societies.[11] Problems with such explanations can, I believe, be dealt with best by local ethical review committees.

Illiteracy, in and of itself, presents no problems to the process of informed consent which, when conducted properly, entails talking rather than reading. Rather, it presents problems with the documentation of informed consent. The process of informed consent, designed to show respect for persons, fosters their interests by empowering them to pursue and protect their own interests. The consent form, by contrast, is an instrument designed to protect the interests of investigators and their institutions and to defend them against civil or criminal liability. If it is necessary to have such protection of investigators, subjects may be asked to make their mark on a consent document and a witness may be required to countersign and attest to the fact that the subject received the information.

A PROCEDURAL RESOLUTION

In "Proposal Guidelines for International Testing of Vaccines and Drugs Against HIV Infection and AIDS" (hereafter referred to as "Proposed HIV Guidelines"), reference is made to an ethical review system.[12] This system is based on that set forth in the WHO/CIOMS Proposed International Guidelines for Biomedical Research Involving Human Subjects. In the Proposed HIV Guidelines, there are suggestions for divisions of responsibility for ethical review. Here I shall elaborate how responsibilities should be divided for determining the adequacy of informed consent procedures.

This proposal presupposes the existence of an international standard for informed consent. I suggest that the standards for informed consent as set forth in the WHO/CIOMS Proposed International Guidelines and as elaborated in the Proposed HIV Guidelines, be recognized as the international standard for informed consent.

1. All plans to conduct research involving human subjects should be reviewed and approved by a research ethics committee (REC). Ideally the REC should be based in the community in which the research is to be conducted. However, as noted in CIOMS/WHO Proposed International Guidelines, under some circumstances regional or national committees may be adequate for these purposes. In such cases it is essential that regional or national committees have as members or consultants individuals who are highly familiar with the customs of the community in which the research is to be done.

The authority of the REC to approve research should be limited to proposals in which the plans for informed consent conform either to the international standard or to a modification of the international standard that has been authorized by a national ethical review body.

2. Proposals to employ consent procedures that do not conform to the international standard should be justified by the researcher and submitted for review and approval by a national ethical review body. Earlier in this paper I identified some conditions or circumstances that could justify such omissions or modifications.

The role of the national ethical review body is to authorize consent procedures that deviate from the international standard. The responsibility for review and approval of the entire protocol (with the modified consent procedure) remains with the REC. Specific details of consent procedures that conform to the international standard or to a modified version of the international standard approved by the national ethical review body should be reviewed and approved by the local ethical review committee.

3. There should be established an international ethical review body to provide advice, consultation and guidance to national ethical review bodies when such is requested by the latter.

4. In the case of externally sponsored research: Ethical review should be conducted in the initiating country. Although it may and should provide advice to the host country, its approval should be based on its finding that plans for informed consent are consistent with the international standard. If there has been a modification of consent procedures approved by the national ethical review body in the host country, the initiating country may either endorse the modification or seek consultation with the international review body.

NOTES

1. Reprinted in R.J. Levine: *Ethics and Regulation of Clinical Research.* Urban & Schwarzenberg, Baltimore & Munich, Second Edition, 1986.

2. R.J. Levine, "Validity of Consent Procedures in Technologically Developing Countries. In: *Human Experimentation and Medical Ethics.* Ed. by Z. Bankowski and N. Howard-Jones, Council for International Organizations of Medical Sciences, Geneva, 1982, pp. 16–30.

3. W. De Craemer, "A Cross-Cultural Perspective on Personhood," *Milbank Memorial Fund Quarterly* 61:19–34, Winter 1983.

4. M. Angell, "Ethical Imperialism? Ethics in International Collaborative Clinical Research." *New England Journal of Medicine* 319:1081–1083, 1988.

5. M. Barry, "Ethical Considerations of Human Investigation in Developing Countries: The AIDS Dilemma." *New England Journal of Medicine* 319:1083–1086, 1988; N.A. Christakis, "Responding to a Pandemic: International Interests in AIDS Control." *Daedalus* 118 (No. 2):113–114, 1989; and N.A. Christakis, "Ethical Design of an AIDS Vaccine Trial in Africa." *Hastings Center Report* 18 (No. 3):31–37, June/July, 1988.

6. M. Pappaioanou, et al., "The Family of HIV Seroprevalence Studies: Objectives, Methods and Uses of Sentinel Surveillance in the United States." *Public Health Reports* 105(2):113–119, 1990.

7. R. Bayer, L.H. Lumey, and L. Wan, "The American, British and Dutch Responses to Unlinked Anonymous HIV Seroprevalence Studies: An International Comparison." *AIDS* 4:283–290, 1990, reprinted in this issue of *Law, Medicine and Health Care,* 19:3–4.

8. R.E. Windom, Assistant Secretary for Health, policy on informing those tested about HIV serostatus, letter to PHS agency heads, Washington, DC, May 9, 1988.

9. Proposed International Guidelines for Biomedical Research Involving Human Subjects, A Joint Project of the World Health Organization and the Council for International Organizations of Medical Sciences, CIOMS, Geneva, 1982.

10. See De Craemer, *supra* note 3 and Levine, *supra* note 2.

11. A.J. Hall, "Public Health Trials in West Africa: Logistics and Ethics," *IRB: A Review of Human Subjects Research* 11 (No. 5):8–10, Sept/Oct 1989. See also Christakis, *supra* note 5.

12. R.J. Levine, and W.K. Mariner, "Proposed Guidelines for International Testing of Vaccines and Drugs Against HIV Infection and AIDS," prepared at the request of WHO, Global Programme on AIDS and submitted January 5, 1990.

Patient Self-Determination and Advance Directives

S U S A N   M .   W O L F ,   E T   A L .

Sources of Concern about the Patient Self-Determination Act

On December 1, 1991, the Patient Self-Determination Act of 1990 (PSDA)[1] went into effect. This is the first federal statute to focus on advance directives and the rights of adults to refuse life-sustaining treatment. The law applies to all health care institutions receiving Medicare or Medicaid funds, including hospitals, skilled-nursing facilities, hospices, home health and personal care agencies, and health maintenance organizations (HMOs).

The statute requires that the institution provide written information to each adult patient on admission (in the case of hospitals or skilled-nursing facilities), enrollment (HMOs), first receipt of care (hospices), or before the patient comes under an agency's care (home health or personal care agencies). The information provided must describe the person's legal rights in that state to make decisions concerning medical care, to refuse treatment, and to formulate advance directives, plus the relevant written policies of the institution. In addition, the institution must document advance directives in the person's medical record, ensure compliance with state law regarding advance directives, and avoid making care conditional on whether or not patients have directives or otherwise discriminating against them on that basis. Finally, institutions must maintain pertinent written policies and procedures and must provide staff and community education on advance directives. The states must help by preparing descriptions of the relevant law, and the Secretary of Health and Human Services must assist with the development of materials and conduct a public-education campaign. The Health Care Financing Administration has authority to issue regulations.

A goal of the statute is to encourage but not require adults to fill out advance directives — treatment directives (documents such as a living will stating the person's treatment preferences in the event of future incompetence), proxy appointments (documents such as a durable power of attorney appointing a proxy decision maker), or both. There is widespread agreement that directives can have many benefits.[2-5] These include improved communication between doctor and patient, increased clarity about the patient's wishes, and ultimately greater assurance that treatment accords with the patient's values and preferences. Yet few Americans have executed advance directives. Estimates range from 4 to 24 percent[6-8] (and Knox RA: personal communication).

A second goal of the PSDA is to prompt health professionals and institutions to honor advance directives. The U.S. Supreme Court's *Cruzan* decision suggests that advance directives are protected by the federal constitution.[9] The great majority of states and the District of Columbia also have specific statutes or judicial decisions recognizing treatment directives.[10] In addition, all states have general durable-power-of-attorney statutes, and most states further specify how this or another format can be used to appoint a proxy for health care decisions.[10] Patients thus have a right to use directives that are based in constitutional, statutory, and common law, and others must honor the recorded choices.[11] There is evidence, however, that advance directives are ignored or overridden one fourth of the time.[12]

Efforts to educate patients about directives and to educate health care professionals about their obligation to honor them thus seem warranted. But the PSDA has caused concern.[6,13,14] Implementation may result in

Reprinted by permission of the publisher from Susan M. Wolf, et al., "Sources of Concern about the Patient Self-Determination Act," *New England Journal of Medicine* 325, No. 23, December 5, 1991.

drowning patients in written materials on admission, insensitive and ill-timed inquiry into patients' preferences, and untrained bureaucrats attempting a job that should be performed by physicians. Indeed, one can favor directives yet oppose the PSDA because of these dangers. The question is how to accomplish the statute's positive underlying goals while minimizing the potential adverse effects.

The key to avoiding an insensitive and bureaucratic process is to ensure that physicians integrate discussions of directives into their ongoing dialogue with patients about current health status and future care. Many have urged that doctors do this.[4,6,15] Yet the literature shows that physicians still have reservations about advance directives,[6,12,13,16-19] and some remain reluctant to initiate discussion.[7,15,20,21] Only by forthrightly addressing these reservations can we successfully make directives part of practice, realize the potential benefits for all involved, and avoid implementing the PSDA in a destructive way.

Our multidisciplinary group—including physicians, a nurse, philosophers, and lawyers—convened to address those reservations in order to dispel doubts when appropriate and delineate continuing controversy where it exists.

RESERVATIONS ABOUT TREATMENT DIRECTIVES

Patients do not really want to discuss future incompetence and death, and so would rather not discuss advance directives. Future incompetence, serious illness, and death are not easy topics to discuss for either patients or physicians. Yet studies indicate that most patients want to discuss their preferences for future treatment[4,7,18,22] and that such discussion usually evokes positive reactions and an enhanced sense of control.[18,23]

Misconceptions nonetheless remain and may produce anxiety in some patients. Some people wrongly assume that treatment directives are used only to refuse treatments and thus shorten life.[24] But people use directives to request treatments as well.[4,25] Such a demand for treatment can raise important ethical problems later if the physician becomes concerned that the treatment may be medically inappropriate or futile for that patient. These problems are currently being debated.[26-29] Yet they are not peculiar to advance directives; they can arise whenever a patient or surrogate demands arguably inappropriate treatment. The point is that treatment directives are a way to express the patient's preferences for treatment, whatever they may be.

There are substantial advantages to both patients and doctors in discussing and formulating treatment directives. A discussion of future medical scenarios can reduce the uncertainty of patients and physicians, strengthen rapport, and facilitate decision making in the future.[16,23,30] Beyond their clinical advantages, directives are one way to fulfill the legal requirement in some states that there be "clear and convincing evidence" of the patient's wishes before life-sustaining treatment is withdrawn.[31,32] The state statutes on treatment directives also generally give physicians a guarantee of civil and criminal immunity when they withhold or withdraw life-sustaining treatment relying in good faith on a patient's directive.

Some debate remains, however, about when directives should first be discussed and with which patients.[4,21,33] The PSDA requires giving information to all adults when they first enter a relevant institution or receive care. This will involve some healthy patients and patients who are expected to return to good health after treatment for a reversible problem. Yet even healthy persons and young people wish to engage in advance planning with their physicians.[4]

Concern nonetheless persists about whether the time of admission or initial receipt of treatment is an appropriate moment to broach the topic of directives. Ideally, initial discussion should take place in the out-patient setting, before the patient experiences the dislocation that often attends inpatient admission. Many patients, however, will reach admission without the benefit of such discussion. If the discussion on admission is handled sensitively and as the first of many opportunities to discuss these matters with the physician and other care givers, admission is an acceptable time to begin the process. For patients who already have directives, admission is a logical time to check the directives in the light of their changed medical circumstances.

Discussion of advance directives takes too much time and requires special training and competence. The discussion of advance directives is an important part of the dialogue between doctor and patient about the patient's condition, prognosis, and future options. But the physician need not discharge this function alone. Others in the health care institution may play an important part in answering questions, providing information, or assisting with documents. The PSDA helpfully makes health care institutions and organizations responsible for the necessary staff education. However, because patients considering treatment directives need to understand their health status and treatment options, physicians have a central role.

Physicians may nonetheless harbor understandable concern about the amount of time that will be required to counsel each patient. An initial discussion of directives structured by a document describing alternative medical scenarios can be accomplished in 15 minutes,[4] but some will undoubtedly find that the initial discussion takes longer, and further discussion is also necessary in any case. Institutions may want to acquire brochures, videotapes, and other materials to help educate patients, and may enlist other personnel in coordinated efforts to assist patients. In addition, the PSDA requires institutions and organizations to engage in community education, which may reach patients before they are admitted. All these efforts promise to facilitate the discussion between doctor and patient.

Treatment directives are not useful, because patients cannot really anticipate what their preferences will be in a future medical situation and because patients know too little about life-support systems and other treatment options. The first part of this objection challenges the very idea of making decisions about medical situations that have not yet developed. Patients who make such decisions will indeed often be making decisions that are less fully informed than those of patients facing a current health problem.[6] Yet the decisions recorded in directives, even if imperfect, give at least an indication of what the patient would want. If the goal is to guide later treatment decisions by the patient's preferences, some indication is better than none.

The question, then, is not whether the decisions embodied in directives are just as informed as those made contemporaneously by a competent patient. It is instead whether the recorded decisions accurately indicate the patient's preferences as best he or she could know them when competent. The answer to that question depends largely on how skillful physicians are in explaining possible medical scenarios and the attendant treatment options. There are many spheres in which we ask people to anticipate the future and state their wishes — wills governing property and most contracts are examples. But in each case the quality of their decisions depends a good deal on the quality of the counseling they receive. It is incumbent on physicians to develop their skills in this regard. Several instruments have been described in the literature to help them communicate successfully with patients.[19,34,35] In addition, the patient's designation of a proxy can pro-

vide a person to work with the physician as the medical situation unfolds.

Good counseling by physicians is the best remedy for patients' ignorance about life-support systems, too. Patients need to understand these treatments in order to judge whether the expected burdens will outweigh the benefits in future medical circumstances. Yet a patient choosing in advance will usually have a less detailed understanding than a patient facing an immediate and specific decision, who may even try the treatment for a time to gain more information.[3] This too supports the wisdom of designating a proxy to work with the medical team.

Treatment-directive forms are too vague and open to divergent interpretations to be useful guides to treatment decisions later. Some forms do contain outmoded language. Terms such as "extraordinary" treatment and "heroic" care have been widely discredited as being overly vague[3,36] (even though "extraordinary" is used in some state laws[37]), and patients should be discouraged from using such generalities. Instead, patients who wish to use treatment directives should be encouraged to specify which treatments they wish to request or refuse, and the medical circumstances under which they want those wishes to go into effect. Although such specification has been challenged,[17] it is a more effective way for patients to communicate their wishes than a general refusal of life-sustaining treatment. The desire for a particular treatment may well vary according to diagnosis and prognosis[4,38] — for instance, artificial nutrition may be desired if the patient is conscious and has a reversible condition, but unwanted if the patient is in a persistent vegetative state. Another way to communicate wishes is for patients to state their preferred goals of treatment, depending on diagnosis[39] — for example, in case of terminal illness, provide comfort care only.

It is nonetheless almost impossible to write a directive that leaves no room for interpretation. Whatever language the patient uses, the goal is to try to determine the patient's intent. Often family members or other intimates can help. Even a vague directive will usually provide some guidance. Some patients will choose to avoid problems of interpretation and application by appointing a proxy and writing no treatment directive. The proxy can then work with the physician as circumstances unfold. Yet the proxy must still strive to choose as the patient would. If the patient has left a treatment directive or other statement of preferences, it will fall to the proxy to determine what the patient intended.

The incompetent patient's best interests should take precedence over even the most thoughtful choices of a patient while competent. Some people argue that the choices stated in a directive are sometimes less relevant than the current experience of the now incompetent patient.[40,41] In the vast majority of cases, this problem does not arise, because the patient's earlier decisions do not conflict with his or her best interests when incompetent. Yet some demented patients, in particular, may seem to derive continued enjoyment from life, although they have a directive refusing life-sustaining treatment. The argument for discounting the directive is that these patients are now such different people that they should not be bound by the choices of their earlier selves, they may no longer hold the values embodied in the directive, and they may appear to accept a quality of life they formerly deemed unacceptable.

Our group did not reach agreement on this argument for overriding some directives. Members who rejected it argued that it is essential that competent patients who record their wishes know those wishes will be followed later, a person's values and choices should govern even after loss of competence because he or she remains essentially the same person, and to recognize the proposed exception would invite widespread disregard of treatment directives. Although we did not resolve this controversy, we did agree on certain procedural safeguards. A treatment directive should not be overridden lightly. In cases in which this controversy arises, only the patient's appointed proxy, a court, or a court-appointed decision maker should be able to consider overriding the directive. Finally, physicians should specifically discuss with patients what the patients' preferences are in the event of dementia.

Even if a directive is valid in all other respects, it is not a reliable guide to treatment because patients may change their minds. Patients may indeed change their minds as their circumstances change. Physicians should therefore reexamine directives periodically with their patients. Data suggest, however, that there is considerable stability in patients' preferences concerning life-sustaining treatment.[16,42-44] In one study of hospitalized patients, 65 to 85 percent of choices did not change during a one-month period, the percentage depending on the illness scenario presented (kappa = 0.35 to 0.70,

where 0 represents random and 1 perfect agreement).[42] In another study there was 58 and 81 percent stability in patients' decisions over a six-month period when they were presented with two scenarios (kappa = 0.23 and 0.31).[43] Further research is necessary, but in any case, patients are always free to change or revoke earlier directives. Once a patient has lost competence and the physician can no longer check with the patient about treatment preferences, a directive becomes the most reliable guide to what the patient would want. Physicians cannot justifiably disregard directives because the patient might hypothetically have changed his or her mind.

RESERVATIONS ABOUT
PROXY APPOINTMENTS

Patients may appoint a proxy to make treatment decisions in the event of incompetence, using a durable power of attorney or other document. Some patients both appoint a proxy and execute a treatment directive. Proxy appointments raise some different sources of concern than treatment directives.

The appointed proxy may later seem to be the wrong surrogate decision maker. This concern may arise for one of several reasons. The proxy may have had no involvement in the patient's health planning and may not even realize that the patient has chosen him or her as proxy. To avoid this problem the physician should encourage the patient both to secure the proxy's acceptance of the appointment and to consider involving the proxy in the process of making decisions about future care. The proxy will then be prepared to discharge the function and will have some knowledge of the patient's wishes. The physician should also encourage the patient to tell family members and other intimates who the chosen proxy is, especially since some patients will prefer to designate a proxy from outside their families. This will reduce the chance of surprise and disagreement later.

Physicians may nonetheless encounter appointed proxies with little previous involvement in the patient's planning process and daily life. Yet a patient's designation of a proxy is an exercise in self-determination. The physician is bound to contact that person if the patient loses competence and the appointment goes into effect, rather than ignore the appointment and simply turn to someone else. There may be no further problems, because everyone may agree anyway on what course of treatment the patient would wish. But uncertainty or disagreement about the right choice of treatment may force the resolution of questions about who the most appropriate proxy is. If the medical team or the patient's relatives or other intimates have serious doubts about whether the designated proxy can fulfill the required functions, it is their responsibility to address these doubts through discussion. If the problem cannot be resolved in this way, they may need to seek judicial resolution and the appointment of an alternate.

Sometimes the designated proxy seems inappropriate not because the person is too remote but because the person is so involved that his or her own wishes and interests seem to govern, rather than the patient's. Family members and other intimates almost always have to deal with their own emotional and financial issues in serving as a proxy decision maker, and the mere existence of such issues does not disqualify them. Physicians and other members of the medical team have a responsibility to work with proxies, helping them to identify their own matters of concern, to separate those from the patient's, and to focus on the patient's wishes and interests in making decisions about treatment. Occasionally, the medical team will encounter a proxy who simply cannot do this. If efforts among the involved parties to remedy the problem fail, then care givers may have to seek judicial scrutiny and the appointment of another proxy.

Even a diligent proxy cannot tell what the patient wanted without an explicit treatment directive, so a proxy's choice should carry no particular weight. Family members, other intimates, and physicians often fail to select the same treatment the patient chooses when asked.[45-49] In one study there was 59 to 88 percent agreement, depending on the illness scenario the researchers posed (kappa $\leq$ 0.3 in all cases)[45]; in another study, agreement was 52 to 90 percent (kappa $\leq$ 0.4 in all cases).[49] Advising the proxy to choose as the patient would, rather than simply asking for a recommendation, seems to act as a partial corrective.[46]

These data should come as no surprise. Even a person's relatives and other intimates are not clairvoyant and may not share identical values. Moreover, proxies are not always adequately informed that their choices for the patient must be based on the patient's wishes and interests, even when those do not accord with the proxy's. Yet there is often no one better informed about the patient's past values and preferences than the proxy, and the patient in any case has manifested trust by appointing that person. Physicians should encourage patients not only to appoint a proxy, but also to provide instructions to guide the proxy. Physicians should also explicitly clarify for the proxy the primacy of the patient's wishes and interests.

The proxy may make a treatment choice contrary to the patient's treatment directive, claiming that the proxy appointment takes precedence over the directive. Some patients will appoint a proxy and leave no treatment directive or other instructions to limit the proxy's authority. Others will guide their proxy by writing a treatment directive or other record of preferences.[5] Problems may then arise if the proxy tries to override the preferences. The law in individual states often directly addresses the relation between proxy appointments and treatment directives.[50-53] In general, the proxy is ethically and legally bound to effectuate the patient's treatment choices. When the patient has failed to make explicit treatment choices, either in a treatment directive or orally, the proxy is bound to extrapolate from what is known of the patient's values and preferences to determine as best he or she can what the patient would want; this is typically labeled an exercise in "substituted judgment." If not enough is known of the patient's values and preferences to ground such a judgment, the proxy is bound to decide in the patient's best interests. A proxy's authority is thus governed by certain decision-making standards, and the proxy is obligated to honor the patient's wishes, whether stated in a treatment directive or elsewhere. One caveat has been noted: there is some disagreement over whether a proxy can override a treatment directive that seriously threatens an incompetent but conscious patient's best interests.

The proxy may make a decision with which the physician or institution disagrees. This is not a problem peculiar to appointed proxies or advance directives. Disagreement surfaces with some frequency between physicians and patients, families, other intimates, and proxies. As always, it is crucial for the physician to discuss the disagreement with the relevant decision maker, attempting to understand the source and resolve the matter. If resolution is elusive, others within the institution can sometimes assist. Judicial resolution is available if all else fails.

One source of disagreement deserves special mention. The proxy (or for that matter, the treatment directive itself) may state a treatment choice that the individual physician believes he or she cannot carry out as a matter of conscience or that violates the commitments and mission of the institution. There has been scholarly discussion[54,55] and some adjudication[56] of the circumstances under which institutions and physicians or other care givers can exempt themselves from carrying out treatment choices. Care givers and institutions are not free to impose unwanted treatment. The PSDA recognizes, however, that a number of states (such as New York) allow providers to assert objections of conscience.[57] Before a patient is admitted, institutions should give notice of any limitation on their willingness to implement treatment choices. Similarly, an individual physician should give as much notice as possible and should assist in the orderly transfer of the patient to a physician who can carry out those choices.

CONCLUSION

Advance directives have provoked a number of reservations. As the PSDA goes into effect, requiring discussion and implementation of directives, it will be essential to address physicians' further reservations as they arise.

Yet that necessary step will not be sufficient to ensure that the PSDA produces more benefit than harm. There is a risk that written advance directives may wrongly come to be viewed as the only way to make treatment decisions for the future. Physicians and other care givers may improperly begin to require an advance directive before treatment may be forgone for incompetent patients. To avoid this, staff education must include discussion of the various ways to decide about life-sustaining treatment and plan future care. Even under the PSDA, not all patients will use advance directives.

There is a further risk of confusion about the procedures and materials to use in implementing the PSDA. All personnel in the relevant institutions will need clarification of the step-by-step process to be followed with patients, the written materials to use, and how to resolve specific questions. The information conveyed to patients must be understandable, accurate in summarizing the patients' rights, and sensitively communicated. All staff members who are involved must be trained. Institutions must design appropriate protocols.

Finally, there is a risk that the PSDA will reduce the discussion of treatment options and directives to a bureaucratic process dominated by brochures and forms. To avoid this, the discussion of advance directives must be part of an ongoing dialogue between physician and patient about the patient's health status and future. Doctors must accept responsibility for initiating these discussions and conducting them skillfully. Such discussions should begin early in the patient's relationship with the doctor, and the content of directives should be reviewed periodically. Institutions and organizations should set up complementary systems to support this effort. The PSDA's requirements must become not a ceiling but a floor — a catalyst for broader innovation to integrate directives into good patient care.

Susan M. Wolf, J.D.

Philip Boyle, Ph.D.

Daniel Callahan, Ph.D.

Joseph J. Fins, M.D.

Bruce Jennings, M.A.

James Lindemann Nelson, Ph.D.

Jeremiah A. Barondess, M.D.

Dan W. Brock, Ph.D.

Rebecca Dresser, J.D.

Linda Emanuel, M.D., Ph.D.

Sandra Johnson, J.D.

John Lantos, M.D.

DaCosta R. Mason, J.D.

Mathy Mezey, Ed.D., R.N.

David Orentlicher, M.D., J.D.

Fenella Rouse, J.D.

NOTES

1. Omnibus Budget Reconciliation Act of 1990. Pub. L. No. 101–508 §§ 4206, 4751 (codified in scattered sections of 42 U.S.C., especially §§ 1395cc, 1396a (West Supp. 1991)).

2. President's Commission for the Study of Ethical Problems in Medicine and Biomedical and Behavioral Research. Making health care decisions: the ethical and legal implications of informed consent in the patient-practitioner relationship. Vol. 1. Report. Washington, D.C.: Government Printing Office, 1982.

3. Guidelines on the termination of life-sustaining treatment and the care of the dying. Bloomington, Ind.: Indiana University Press and the Hastings Center, 1987.

4. Emanuel LL, Barry MJ, Stoeckle JD, Ettelson LM, Emanuel EJ. Advance directives for medical care — a case for greater use. N Engl J Med 1991; 324:889–95.

5. Annas GJ. The health care proxy and the living will. N Engl J Med 1991;324:1210–3.

6. La Puma J, Orentlicher D, Moss RJ. Advance directives on admission: clinical implications and analysis of the Patient Self-Determination Act of 1990. JAMA 1991;266:402–5.

7. Gamble ER, McDonald PJ, Lichstein PR. Knowledge, attitudes, and behavior of elderly persons regarding living wills. Arch Intern Med 1991;151:277–80.

8. Knox RA. Poll: Americans favor mercy killing. Boston Globe, November 3, 1991:1, 22.

9. *Cruzan v. Director,* Mo. Dep't of Health, 110 S. Ct. 2841 (1990).

10. Society for the Right to Die. Refusal of treatment legislation: a state by state compilation of enacted and model statutes. New York: Society for the Right to Die, 1991.

11. Meisel A. The right to die. New York: John Wiley, 1989.

12. Danis M, Southerland LI, Garrett JM, et al. A prospective study of advance directives for life-sustaining care. N Engl J Med 1991;324:882–8.

13. White ML, Fletcher JC. The Patient Self-Determination Act: on balance, more help than hindrance. JAMA 1991;266:410–2.

14. Greco PJ, Schulman KA, Lavizzo-Mourey R, Hansen-Flaschen J. The Patient Self-Determination Act and the future of advance directives. Ann Intern Med 1991;115:639–43.

15. Teno J, Fleishman J, Brock DW, Mor V. The use of formal prior directives among patients with HIV-related diseases. J Gen Intern Med 1990;5:490–4.

16. Davidson KW, Hackler C, Caradine DR, McCord RS. Physicians' attitudes on advance directives. JAMA 1989;262:2415–9.

17. Brett AS. Limitations of listing specific medical interventions in advance directives. JAMA 1991;266:825–8.

18. Lo B, McLeod GA, Saika G. Patient attitudes to discussing life-sustaining treatment. Arch Intern Med 1986;146:1613–5.

19. Emanuel LL, Emanuel EJ. The medical directive: a new comprehensive advance care document. JAMA 1989;261:3288–93.

20. Kohn M, Menon G. Life prolongation: views of elderly outpatients and health care professionals. J Am Geriatr Soc 1988;36:840–4.

21. McCrary SV, Botkin JR. Hospital policy on advance directives: do institutions ask patients about living wills? JAMA 1989;262:2411–4.

22. Shmerling RH, Bedell SE, Lilienfeld A, Delbanco TL. Discussing cardiopulmonary resuscitation: a study of elderly outpatients. J Gen Intern Med 1988;3:317–21.

23. Finucane TE, Shumway JM, Powers RL, D'Alessandri RM. Planning with elderly outpatients for contingencies of severe illness: a survey and clinical trial. J Gen Intern Med 1988;3:322–5.

24. Ackerman F. Not everybody wants to sign a living will. New York Times. October 13, 1989:A32.

25. Molloy DW, Guyatt GH. A comprehensive health care directive in a home for the aged. Can Med Assoc J 1991;145:307–11.

26. Callahan D. Medical futility, medical necessity: the-problem-without-a-name. Hastings Cent Rep 1991;21(4):30–5.

27. Youngner SJ. Futility in context. JAMA 1990;264:1295–6.

28. Idem. Who defines futility? JAMA 1988;260:2094–5.

29. Lantos JD, Singer PA, Walker RM, et al. The illusion of futility in clinical practice. Am J Med 1989;87:81–4.

30. Emanuel LL. Does the DNR order need life-sustaining intervention? Time for comprehensive advance directives. Am J Med 1989;86:87–90.

31. Orentlicher D. The right to die after Cruzan. JAMA 1990;264:2444–6.

32. Weir RF, Gostin L. Decisions to abate life-sustaining treatment for non-autonomous patients: ethical standards and legal liability for physicians after Cruzan. JAMA 1990;264:1846–53.

33. Hardin SB, Welch HG, Fisher ES. Should advance directives be obtained in the hospital? A review of patient competence during hospitalizations prior to death. Clin Res 1991;39:626A. abstract.

34. Doukas DJ, McCullough LB. The values history: the evaluation of the patient's values and advance directives. J Fam Pract 1991;32:145–53.

35. Gibson JM. National values history project. Generations 1990;14:Suppl:51–64.

36. Eisendrath SJ, Jonsen AR. The living will: help or hindrance? JAMA 1983;249:2054–8.

37. North Carolina Gen. Stat. § 90–321(a)(2) (1991).

38. Forrow L, Gogel E, Thomas E. Advance directives for medical care. N Engl J Med 1991;325:1255.

39. Emanuel L. The health care directive: learning how to draft advance care documents. J Am Geriatr Soc 1991;39:1221–8.

40. Dresser RS. Advance directives, self-determination, and personal identity. In: Hackler C, Moseley R, Vawter DE, eds. Advance directives in medicine. New York: Praeger Publishers, 1989:155–70.

41. Buchanan AE, Brock DW. Deciding for others: the ethics of surrogate decision making. New York: Cambridge University Press, 1989:152–89.

42. Everhart MA, Pearlman RA. Stability of patient preferences regarding life-sustaining treatments. Chest 1990;97:159–64.

43. Silverstein MD, Stocking CB, Antel JP, Beckwith J, Roos RP, Siegler M. Amyotrophic lateral sclerosis and life-sustaining therapy: patients' desires for information, participation in decision making, and life-sustaining therapy. May Clin Proc 1991;66:906–13.

44. Emanuel LL, Barry MJ, Stoeckle JD, Emanuel EJ. A detailed advance care directive: practicality and durability. Clin Res 1990;38:738A. abstract.

45. Seckler AB, Meier DE, Mulvihill M, Paris BEC. Substituted judgement: how accurate are proxy predictions? Ann Intern Med 1991;115:92–8.

46. Tomlinson T, Howe K, Notman M, Rossmiller D. An empirical study of proxy consent for elderly persons. Gerontologist 1990;30:54–64.

47. Zweibel NR, Cassel CK. Treatment choices at the end of life: a comparison of decisions by older patients and their physician-selected proxies. Gerontologist 1989;29:615–21.

48. Ouslander JG, Tymchuk AJ, Rahbar B. Health care decisions among elderly long-term care residents and their potential proxies. Arch Intern Med 1989; 149:1367–72.

49. Uhlmann RF, Pearlman RA, Cain KC. Physicians' and spouses' predictions of elderly patients' resuscitation preferences. J Gerontol 1988;43:M115–M121.

50. Kansas Stat. Ann. § 58–629 (Supp. 1990).

51. Vermont Stat. Ann. tit. 14, §§ 3453, 3463 (Supp. 1991).

52. West Virginia Code § 16–30A–4 (Supp. 1991).

53. Wisconsin Stat. Ann. § 155.20 (1989–90).

54. Annas GJ. Transferring the ethical hot potato. Hastings Cent Rep 1987;17(1):20–1.

55. Miles SH, Singer PA, Siegler M. Conflicts between patients' wishes to forgo treatment and the policies of health care facilities. N Engl J Med 1989;321:48–50.

56. In re Jobes, 529 A.2d 434 (N.J. 1987).

57. New York Pub. Health Law § 2984 (McKinney Supp. 1991).

REBECCA DRESSER

Confronting the "Near Irrelevance" of Advance Directives

Joan M. Teno and her colleagues report a number of illuminating findings in "Do Formal Advance Directives Affect Resuscitation Decisions and the Use of Resources for Seriously Ill Patients?"—their study of a large group of patients who, in my view, could legitimately be labeled terminally ill (a predicted mortality rate of 50 percent or higher at six months, the remainder likely to die within a year or two). One might reasonably expect advance directives to be of great utility in guiding the care of patients in this group. But the SUPPORT (Study to Understand Prognoses and Preferences for Outcomes and Risks of Treatments) data contradict such expectations, leading the authors to conclude that formal advance directives were "nearly irrelevant" to decisions about how aggressively to treat these patients.

Teno *et al.* recount the following significant findings: (1) relatively few patients reported having formal advance directives; (2) only about 6 percent of these formal directives were noted in the patients' medical records; (3) having a directive did not influence patients' preferences about resuscitation; neither did it affect whether patients had a DNR order or whether a resuscitation effort was made at death; (4) although patients with directives more often reported having discussions with their physicians about resuscitation, these discussions were not noted in their records or acted on in any other official way; and (5) for patients who died during their initial hospitalization, costs of care were unaffected by the presence of advance directives.

Rebecca Dresser, JD, is Professor at the School of Law and at the Center for Biomedical Ethics of the School of Medicine, Case Western Reserve University, Cleveland.
From the *Journal of Clinical Ethics* 5 (1) 1994. Copyright © 1994 by *The Journal of Clinical Ethics*. All rights reserved.

These findings seriously challenge the current official preference for advance directives to guide decisions on life-sustaining treatment for incompetent patients. As such, the SUPPORT data on advance directives join a growing body of empirical and other work that undercuts the primary approach enshrined in most of the existing law and policy governing the care of seriously ill, incompetent patients. This work suggests a new emphasis and direction for the courts, legislators, and other officials charged with delineating the appropriate standards for decision making on behalf of incompetent patients.

PRACTICAL LIMITS ON ADVANCE DIRECTIVES

Formal advance directives have not caught on in the way that many bioethicists and policy makers expected they would. Current estimates are that relatively few people in the United States have completed formal advance directives.[1] It remains to be seen whether the Patient Self-Determination Act and other efforts by policy makers to increase these numbers will be effective. It appears that many elderly people do not make directives because they prefer and trust family members to act on their behalf in the event that they become incompetent.[2] Although we will probably see more directives accompany the aging of a generation more interested in and accustomed to participating in medical decision making, it would be surprising if the proportion of people with directives ever surpassed the one-fourth to one-half of the population who reportedly execute a property will.[3]

The inevitable need for interpretation of advance directives sets a further practical limit on them. Many advance directives include only very general, often undefined, statements on the acceptability of certain medical conditions and treatments. Proxy designations may not include any statement of substantive preferences. As a result, directives often are of limited assistance when dilemmas about specific treatment arise. Another barrier to the effectiveness of formal advance directives lies in the care system. Caregivers apparently often fail to record the existence of a directive and, thus, they fail to inform other caregivers of the directive's presence and content. And even when this is done, a directive may be overlooked or disregarded, based on a judgment that the directive refuses justified treatment or requests unjustified treatments.[4]

ETHICAL IMPLICATIONS

The data compiled by Teno and her colleagues indicate that formal advance directives play a relatively minor role in shaping decisions regarding the treatment of incompetent patients. It appears that future-oriented autonomy has little to do with how most questions about treatment are resolved. Indeed, the results of a study by Sehgal *et al.* suggest that even people who make the effort to complete formal directives do not necessarily want their future treatment determined by these documents. These authors found that 31 percent of subjects with relatively precise formal directives wanted their physicians and surrogate decision makers to have "complete leeway" to override their directives, and the majority wanted physicians and surrogates to have at least some leeway to override their directives.[5] These findings undermine the claim that a failure to attend to or comply with a patient's formal advance directive necessarily constitutes a violation of that patient's earlier exercise of self-determination.

Moreover, advance directives fail to address one of the most important issues facing healthcare decision makers today. Patients do not have an absolute right to receive life-sustaining interventions. For example, the American Heart Association has delineated three categories of patients from whom resuscitation efforts should be withheld or terminated, based on the medical judgment that there is no chance of survival.[6] Whether there are other categories of patients from whom resuscitation and other life-prolonging measures may be withheld without the involvement of the patients or their surrogate decision makers is now being debated.[7]

NEW DIRECTIONS FOR POLICY

The findings that Teno and her colleagues present, together with the results of other recent empirical studies on advance directives, signal the need to turn elsewhere for guidance on how aggressively to treat seriously ill, incompetent patients. Because advance directives are relatively rare, usually vague, and frequently uninformed by the realities of the patient's current status, directives cannot (and, apparently, do not) resolve dilemmas at the bedside of most incompetent patients. The recent emphasis on advance directives in law and healthcare policy has, in some respects, done a disservice to most real patients and their families and caregivers, for it has provided little substantive guidance on how to proceed in many cases in which directives are absent, unclear, or otherwise problematic. The major alternatives to the advance-directive standard, which consists of the substituted-judgment and best-interest standards, remain vague and relatively indeterminate, with courts interpreting them in differing ways.

Happily, there are signs that this situation is beginning to change. Almost half the states now have laws officially recognizing the authority of family members to decide on behalf of their relatives.[8] There is also increasing legal recognition of the need to formulate standards to govern the care of patients who failed to register their preferences while competent.[9]

A great deal of work remains, however. Policy makers need to clarify the range of discretion families and other surrogate decision makers have in deciding to forgo life-sustaining treatment. When is a decision to withhold or withdraw so unreasonable that it should be overridden? When is a surrogate's insistence on continued treatment properly disregarded on grounds that it imposes unjustified burdens on the incompetent patient or, alternatively on grounds that the financial costs of such treatment are too high, and the benefits to the patient too small, to require caregivers to comply? Commentators have begun to explore these and related issues in greater detail.[10] I encourage clinical ethicists and others to concentrate more on developing and refining defensible standards of treatment that can supplement and substitute for the existing, but elusive, ideal of the advance directive.

NOTES

1. L. Emanuel, "Advance Directives: What Have We Learned So Far?" *The Journal of Clinical Ethics* 4 (1993): 8–16.

2. D. High, "A New Myth about Families of Older People?" *Gerontologist* 31 (1991): 611–18.

3. J. Menikoff, G. Sachs, and M. Siegler, "Beyond Advance Directives: Health Care Surrogate Laws," *New England Journal of Medicine* 327 (1992): 1165–69; Emanuel, "Advance Directives."

4. M. Danis *et al.,* "A Prospective Study of Advance Directives for Life-Sustaining Care," *New England Journal of Medicine* 324 (1991): 882–88.

5. A. Sehgal *et al.* "How Strictly Do Dialysis Patients Want Their Advance Directives Followed?" *Journal of the American Medical Association* 267 (1992): 59–63.

6. Conference on Cardiopulmonary Resuscitation and Emergency Cardiac Care, "Ethical Considerations in Resuscitation," *Journal of the American Medical Association* 268 (1992): 2282–88.

7. See, for example, R. Truog, A. Brett, and J. Frader, "The Problem with Futility," *New England Journal of Medicine* 326 (1992): 1560–64.

8. Menikoff, Sachs, and Siegler, "Beyond Advance Directives."

9. See, for example, *In re Conroy,* 486 A.2d 1209 (N.J. 1985).

10. L. Emanuel and E. Emanuel, "Decisions at the End of Life: Guided by Communities of Patients," *Hastings Center Report* 23, no. 5 (1993): 6–14; R. Dresser, "Missing Persons: Legal Perceptions of Incompetent Patients," *Rutgers Law Review* (forthcoming, 1994).

LINDA A. EMANUEL, MARION DANIS, ROBERT A. PEARLMAN, AND PETER A. SINGER

Advance Care Planning as a Process: Structuring the Discussions in Practice

A PROCESS OF ADVANCE PLANNING

FACILITATING A STRUCTURED DISCUSSION

The structured discussion should be aimed at framing the issues, and tentatively identifying wishes. It need not aim to resolve all issues or come to final determination of all prior wishes. Neither should it aim to be a deep personal revelation seeking perfect knowledge of the patient's core self; this is unrealistic and unnecessary. Nevertheless, this step is the core of all advanced planning processes.

The skills required of the professional for this stage are those of communicating pertinent medical understanding and of supportive elicitation of the patient's wishes, as in most ideal informed consent discussions. Specific training sessions may be needed to acquire the information, skills, and judgment involved in this critical part of the process of advance planning because, unlike most medical decisions, in this case patients' preferences are cast forward into future scenarios.

Initial Decisions About the Mode of Advance Planning. An early part of the discussion may focus on whether proxy designation, instructional directives, or both are most suitable for the particular patient. Most patients should be advised to combine the two forms of planning so that the proxy may be guided by the patient's stated prior wishes. Thus, the conversation might continue as follows:

"Ms/r. X, I suggest we start by considering a few examples as a way of getting to know your thinking. I will use examples that I use for everyone."

If, in the physician's judgment, a particular patient proves not competent to make prior directives, he or she might nevertheless be competent to designate a proxy decision-maker. In such a case the conversation might go rather differently. For example, the physician might proceed as follows:

"These decisions may be hard to think about when they are not even relevant right now. You have had a long and trusting relationship with Ms/r. Y. You might even

From *The American Geriatrics Society* 43 (1995), 440–446. Reprinted by permission.

have had discussions like this before with her/him. Would you want to give Ms/r. Y, or someone else you trust, the authority to make decisions for you in case of need?"

Understanding the Patient's Goals for Treatment in a Range of Scenarios. When instructional directives are suitable, we believe that the physician should help the patient articulate abstract values, goals of treatment, and concrete examples of treatment preferences in order to provide all the major components of decision-making. Discussions can be well structured by going through an illustrative predrafted document together; this approach can prevent long confusing and overwhelming encounters. With such structuring, this portion of advance planning can be informative, accessible to patients with a wide range of educational levels, and still quite brief. Many documents that can be used for structuring discussions are available; however, a properly validated document should be chosen to maximize the chance that patients are accurately representing their wishes.

Scenarios representative of the range of prognosis and of the range of disability usually encountered in circumstances of incompetence should be presented to the patient. The physician might start like this:

"So, let's try to imagine several circumstances. We will go through four and then perhaps another one or two. First imagine you were in a coma with no awareness. Assume there was a chance that you might wake up and be yourself again, but it wasn't likely. Some people would want us to withdraw treatment and let them die, others would want us to attempt everything possible, and yet others would want us to try to restore health but stop treatment and allow death if it was not working. What do you think you would want?"

After a standard set of scenarios, tailored scenarios can be considered. When a patient has a serious diagnosis with a predictable outcome involving incompetence that is not covered in the standard document, the physician might continue:

"We should also consider the situations that your particular illness can cause; that way you can be sure we will do what you want. For sure, all people are different and you may never face these circumstances. Nevertheless, let's imagine . . ."

While illness scenarios may be difficult for people to imagine, we suggest that preferences arrived at without illness scenarios are unlikely to be accurate or realistic wishes; a treatment preference without a specified illness circumstance is meaningless.

A patient considering illness scenarios also may be able to articulate which states, if any, are greatly feared and/or are felt to be *worse than death* for them. So, for example, the physician may go on:

"People often think about circumstances they have seen someone in or heard about in the news. Some may seem worse than death. Do you have such concerns?"

When a range of scenarios have been considered it is often possible to go back and identify the scenario(s) in which the patient's goals changed from "treat" to "don't treat." This can provide a useful personal threshold to guide the physician and proxy later. The physician may also use it to check back at the time with the patient that his or her wishes are properly reflected, saying, for example:

"Well, we've gone through several scenarios now. It seems to me that you feel particularly strongly about . . . Indeed, you move from wanting intervention to wanting to be allowed to die in peace at the point when . . . Do I speak for you correctly if I say that your personal threshold for deciding to let go is . . . ?"

Raising Specific Examples and Asking About General Values. In any scenario after the patient's response about goals, specific examples may be used:

"So, let us take an example to be sure I understand you, not only in general but also in specific. Say you were in a coma with a very small chance of recovery, and you had pneumonia; to cure the pneumonia we would have to put you on a breathing machine. Would you want us to use the breathing machine and try to cure; allow the pneumonia to cause death; or perhaps try the treatment, withdrawing the breathing machine if you did not get better?"

Checking and specifying a patient's views by providing concrete examples may be a useful way to reduce the incidence of clinically unrealistic choices by patients. So, for example, a patient who declines intubation but wants resuscitation may need more information on resuscitation and a suggestion as to how his or her wishes may be translated into a clinically reasonable decision.

The preceding discussion about goals for treatment and specific choices may be usefully combined with an open ended question about the patient's reasons for particular decisions and the *values* that pertain to such decisions.

"I think you have given a good picture of particular decisions you would want. Can you also say something about the values or beliefs that you hold? Understanding your more general views can be an important part of getting specific decisions right."

Patients' statements might refer to their wish to act in accord with the positions of their religious denomination, or to their views on the sanctity of life or dignity of death, or they might articulate their disposition to take a chance or to favor a secure choice.

Including the Proxy. The proxy, if already known at this point, should be encouraged to attend this discussion. Much understanding of the patient's wishes can be gained from hearing this part of the process. The clinician can guide the proxy to adopt a listening role; the proxy may ask clarifying questions but should avoid biasing the patient's expressions. Sometimes the proxy can be following the conversation with a pre-drafted document in hand, noting down the patient's statements. The ground can be set for future discussions between any of the patient, physician, and proxy. The proxy becomes part of the working team, and future interactions between proxy and physician, if the patient does become incompetent, are likely to go more smoothly than they might without such prior discussions.

At this stage, the advance directive should be, at most, pencilled in. The tentative draft can be taken home by the patient for further reflection and review with other involved parties, such as the proxy, family, friends, or pastor. This step can be a useful mechanism for dealing with difference among the parties ahead of time. The structured discussion should be brief and followed by a subsequent meeting when a directive may be finalized. Physicians will initially take longer in these interviews, but with training in the requisite skills and with experience, time will be reduced.

COMPLETING AN ADVISORY DIRECTIVE
AND RECORDING IT

. . . The professional's main required skill here is to ascertain whether the patient has reached resolution and is ready to articulate well considered preferences. Any facet of the first two steps not yet complete should be completed at this step. Even if a patient has reached resolution, there should be a reminder that advance directives can be revised if his/her wishes are changed.

If the proxy has not been present at previous stages, the physician should particularly encourage the proxy to enter the process at this point. The proxy should again be encouraged to adopt a listening and clarifying role, avoiding undue influence on the patient. It can be helpful for the physician to co-sign the document at this stage to endorse physician involvement and to document the primary physician for ease of future follow up.

REVIEWING AND UP-DATING DIRECTIVES

Along with other regular check-ups and screening tests, patients should be told to expect periodic review of their directives. The clinician may re-introduce the topic.

"Ms/r. X, a year has gone by since we completed your advance care plans, and in that time a lot has happened. People do sometimes change their wishes so let's review the wishes you wrote down a year ago."

Competent people are often known to change their minds about all matters, whether they are of great import or not. Reasonable but imperfect consistency has also been found in advance planning decisions by competent individuals. Physicians should be aware of this and should review directives with the patient periodically. Physicians should check which decisions a patient maintains and which are changed. Changed positions should prompt the physician to pay particular attention to the source of change; some changes will be well reasoned, and others will be markers for misunderstandings that need to be clarified. Some people will be generally changeable; the physician should address this observation to the patient, inquiring after the reason. If supportive guidance and education do not permit the patient to reach reasonable stability in his or her advance directives, more emphasis must be placed on proxy decision-making for the patient. The physician will often be able to come to this decision jointly with the patient and proxy:

"Your choices changed on several decisions both times when we reviewed your statement, even though we have discussed the issues a lot. You have already said that you want Ms/r. Y to be your proxy. Would you prefer to give these decisions over to Ms/r. Y to decide according to what she/he thinks would be in your best interests?"

Some changed decisions may occur after the onset of incompetence. There is continuing debate on how to deal with such circumstances. The physician should be careful to evaluate the exact nature of the patient's incompetence; some patients will be globally incompetent while others will be competent to make some decisions and incompetent for other decisions. The role of the proxy and possibly a further adjudicating party may be crucial in such circumstances.

The skills that physicians require for this portion of advance planning are not as yet matched by detailed understanding of how patients might make or can be encouraged to make valid and enduring decisions, or the type of circumstances that tend to prompt changes. It is reasonable to expect that researchers will continue to study how best to elicit patient's enduring and valid wishes.

APPLICATION OF PRIOR DIRECTIVES
TO ACTUAL CIRCUMSTANCES

Clinicians will require both interpersonal and interpretive skills in this difficult final step. Patients will often end up in need of decisions that are not accurately specified in their advance directive. The physicians and proxy, then, must work from the information they have to make a good guess as to what the patient would have wanted. Knowledge of the patient's values, goals, choices in a range of scenarios, and thresholds for withholding or withdrawing specific interventions can all be helpful. Choices in scenarios can often provide very accurate predictors.

The spirit as much as the letter of the directive should be the focus of the physician and the proxy. Documents that are given as an advisory statement rather than a legal imperative are less likely to lead to blind application of irrelevant decisions. So, for example, if a patient has a poorly drafted document stating only that he or she does not want to be on a respirator, the physicians should try to clarify what circumstances this preference applies to; the patient may have intended the statement to apply to circumstances of hopeless prognosis, but may actually be facing a reversible life threatening illness. The physicians and proxy would need to "override" the simple statement in order to honor the true wishes of the patient in such a case; they would be interpreting simple statements to match presumed true wishes, not trumping the patient's wishes. The full responsibility of this interpretive process and the risks of misusing it in parentalistic judgments should be clear to the physician and proxy.

When the physician writes orders for the incompetent patient's care they should be as detailed as the advance directive permits. Thus a "Do Not Resuscitate" order can usually be supplemented with orders such as "evaluate and treat infection," "do not intubate," "pro-

vide full comfort care," and so forth. They can be gathered together in a series of orders altogether intended to translate the directive into doctors orders. Life threatening illness often prompts a change in health care facility or attending physician and will, therefore, entail transfer of advance directives from the physician who has guided the process to a new physician. At a minimum, physicians, patients, proxies, and institutions should all be aware of the need to transfer advance care documents with the patient to the new facility and physician. However, transmittal of accurate portrayals of a patient's wishes will rarely be adequately completed by simply passing on a document; whenever possible, the earlier physician should remain available as a key resource as the patient's prior wishes are brought to bear on specific decisions. It is likely that the physician and proxy who have undertaken the entire process of advance planning with the patient will have a more accurate sense of the patient's actual wishes than those who were simply presented with a document after patient incompetence has already occurred. Those who attempt substituted judgments in the absence of specific patient guidance are known to have discrepancies in their decisions compared with the wishes of the patient, and it is reasonable to assume that explicit communication on the matter should reduce the gap.

Decision-making, especially when there is a proxy involved, is a collaborative matter. The physician and the proxy have distinct roles that should be understood. The physician's role is to diagnose the condition and convey information, opinions, and judgment, and then to discuss them with the proxy, as would ordinarily occur with the patient. The proxy's role is to attempt substituted judgments and speak for the patient wherever possible, or to make best interest judgments as a second best approach if there is no way of surmising what the patient would have wanted. Unless the patient or the local state statutes say otherwise, the proxy should take on the "voice" of the patient and assume equal levels of authority—nor more or less—that would have been the patient's.

FURTHER CONCERNS

ARE ADVANCED DIRECTIVES FOR EVERYONE?

Time constraints and other practical considerations may lead physicians to target their sicker and older patients. However, younger and healthier patients are often quite interested in the approach. Furthermore, advance planning for those who suffer an accident or sudden illness may be most helpful. Advance planning may be considered as a branch of preventive medicine.

There will be a proportion of patients who should not be advised to undertake advance care planning. For example, there are people with no one they wish to choose as a proxy who also have limited ability to imagine future hypothetical situations. Others might find the notion so dissonant with the type of care relationship they want that they do not wish to consider the process. This latter group of patients should still have sufficient discussion to permit understanding of how decisions get made in the absence of directives. For example, the different powers of proxy and next of kin should be clear, as should the occasional role of a guardian ad lidum, and the limited ability of substituted decisions to match the patient's prior wishes in the absence of guidance from the patient. Neither physician nor patient should allow themselves the assumption that this is a topic they need not even raise. If the patient and physician are explicitly content with the hitherto more traditional approaches to decision-making at the end of life, this is acceptable.

A considerable proportion of people have no primary care physician or health professional, and the only educational materials that reach them will be through the public media. Some of these people are able to have a physician; they should seek out a physician for the purposes of advance planning if they wish to undertake it. They should be aware that many directives are highly dependent on medical knowledge and understanding of the individual patient's medical circumstances; decisions made in the absence of medical expertise may be inaccurate reflections of the person's true preferences.

People who face limited access to the health care system should not be discouraged from advance care planning if they are inclined toward it. However, people who complete directives without talking to a physician should be encouraged to discuss their views in as much depth as possible with their next-of-kin or proxy so that ultimately someone will be able to discuss with a physician how the patient's known prior wishes relate to actual circumstances and treatment decisions. Publicly provided information or work sheets to guide persons and their proxy in such discussions can be helpful.

WHEN AND WHERE SHOULD ADVANCE DIRECTIVES BE DISCUSSED?

Advanced care planning should ideally be initiated in the outpatient setting, where such discussions are known to be well received. Then, when the topic is raised on admission to the hospital, as required by the Patient Self Determination Act, it is likely to be less threatening. Inquiry can be continued to an indepth inpatient discussion in selected cases. For example, it is appropriate with patients who are at risk of needing life-sustaining intervention soon, and discussions in this setting can be well conducted, providing guidance and welcome coordination of goals and expectations for all concerned. Although judgment of need for such intervention is known to be difficult, physicians may be guided in part by published criteria. For those with a completed directive, review during an admission may also be advisable. Other patients with a good prognosis who want to complete directives should first be advised of the merits of deferring the process to an outpatient setting. While there is little data on the question, we fear that those patients who complete directives for the first time in the hospital setting risk making more unstable decisions because of the emotional turbulence of the moment. For those who do complete a directive for the first time during hospital admission, review of the directives after health has stabilized may be particularly important.

TIME CONSTRAINTS

No step in the process of advance care planning needs to take longer than standard doctor-patient encounters. Furthermore, advance care planning probably reduces difficult and time-consuming decisions made in the absence of such planning and should, therefore, be understood as a wise investment of time. Like any other clinical process, skill and experience will make the planning process more time-efficient.

WHAT IS THE ROLE FOR NONPHYSICIAN HEALTHCARE PROFESSIONALS?

Decision-making for incompetent patients has always been among the central tasks of the physician. We regard the facilitation of a structured discussion as the central step in the process of advance planning and, therefore, as particularly dependent on physician involvement. Nevertheless, time constraints and the different communication styles of physicians will make it inevitable that some, and perhaps many, physicians will not include all the steps of advance planning in the routine activities that are the core of good doctoring. Thus, there is likely to be a need for other healthcare professionals to engage in the process of advance planning. Some facilities may form interdisciplinary source groups or consult services that will be available to physicians or patients who seek extra help. Other facilities may train nursing staff in advance planning. Social workers may have a role in facilitating communication around these difficult concepts. However, we view it as essential that the physician, who must ultimately take responsibility for life-sustaining treatment decisions, communicate with the patient at some point and at least check with the patient for possible misunderstandings unrealistic expectations, or wishes for treatment that the physician would find contrary to standards of medical practice or contrary to his or her conscience. Omission of this step risks discovery of advance directives which have internal inconsistencies or other major problems when it is too late to correct the problem. If the physician cannot participate in this step of advance planning, then another appropriate point may be at the next step of completing a signed advisory statement.

HELPING PROXIES UNDERSTAND THEIR ROLE

The proxy will need to distinguish his or her emotional and personal motives from concerns appropriate to their role as a proxy. Some will have emotional connections with the patient or personal views of their own that will drive them toward more aggressive intervention; others may have monetary or other concerns which may cause a conflict of interest and motivate them toward less aggressive intervention than the patient would have wanted. The physician should be sensitive to these and related possibilities and be able to help the proxy disentangle and understand the relevant motivations, both during the planning process and when making actual decisions. Complex or destructive cases may require further professional counseling and support. Together, the physician and proxy should deliberate the various therapeutic options available. The goal is to avoid any need for one party to assert authority over the other and to achieve consensus instead.

RISKS OF PLACING THE ADVANCE DIRECTIVE
IN THE PATIENT'S CHART

Concerns have arisen about how to record the statement in such a fashion that it is least likely to result in inappropriate care and most likely to be available when it becomes relevant. Advance directives placed in hospital records may run the same risk as "Do Not Resuscitate" orders, which are known to sometimes result in inappropriate cessation of other therapies. Education of health professionals on the matter is clearly necessary. Detailed doctors orders can help too. In addition, sections in the medical records for advance directives may be prominently stamped with a statement to the effect that prior directives are (1) intended as an extension of patient autonomy beyond *wishlessness,* (2) may be for the purposes of requesting as well as declining treatment, and (3) have no relevance to care before incompetence.

Copies of the advisory statement and statutory document are best kept not only by the physician but also the proxy and any other person likely to be in early contact in the event of changed medical circumstances. The physician's copy should be recorded as part of the patient's medical records.

DEALING WITH LEGAL CONCERNS

Advance planning statements with physicians should be considered as advisory statements rather than adversarial challenges. (We use the term "advisory statement" in order to distinguish planning devices from narrower statutory documents, which have different legal purposes.) Physicians should make it clear to patients that the advisory statement is the area where medical counsel is most relevant and that the advisory statement is one of the best means of expressing their wishes. An advisory statement can be considered a portrait of a patient's wishes, a profile that should be interpreted to fit with whatever circumstances ultimately pertain. Such a statement can be interpreted with the flexibility needed to meet the complexities of medical decision-making and uncertainties of human decision-making.

Clinicians should be reassured that it has been well argued that such advisory statements will be honored under Common, Statutory, or Constitutional Law, even if they are not part of a statutory document. We nevertheless urge health care professionals to be less concerned with legal issues and more concerned with the medical task of translating a patient's deepest wishes into sound medical decisions. Usually, an advisory statement does not need to raise legal issues because its primary purpose is to provide a valid description of the patient's wishes. However, points of legal concern such as whether living will and proxy statutes in other states are significantly different, may require legal expertise; in such a case the physician should avoid offering unauthorized legal advice and refer to a lawyer.

Physicians may encourage simultaneous use of statutory documents, i.e., predrafted statements designed for specific state statutes, because this is what gives physicians most legal immunity from prosecution when the physician carries out the patient's or proxy's directions. Some statutory documents may contain an advisory section. If not, the advisory and statutory documents may be combined or filed together.

The Management of Confidential Information

CALIFORNIA SUPREME COURT

Tarasoff v. Regents of the University of California

TOBRINER, Justice

On October 27, 1969, Prosenjit Poddar killed Tatiana Tarasoff. Plaintiffs, Tatiana's parents, allege that two months earlier Poddar confided his intention to kill Tatiana to Dr. Lawrence Moore, a psychologist employed by the Cowell Memorial Hospital at the University of California at Berkeley. They allege that on Moore's request, the campus police briefly detained Poddar, but released him when he appeared rational. They further claim that Dr. Harvey Powelson, Moore's superior, then directed that no further action be taken to detain Poddar. No one warned plaintiffs of Tatiana's peril. . . .

We shall explain that defendant therapists cannot escape liability merely because Tatiana herself was not their patient. When a therapist determines, or pursuant to the standards of his profession should determine, that his patient presents a serious danger of violence to another, he incurs an obligation to use reasonable care to protect the intended victim against such danger. The discharge of this duty may require the therapist to take one or more of various steps, depending upon the nature of the case. Thus it may call for him to warn the intended victim or others likely to apprise the victim of the danger, to notify the police, or to take whatever other steps are reasonably necessary under the circumstances. . . .

1. PLAINTIFFS' COMPLAINTS
Plaintiffs, Tatiana's mother and father, filed separate but virtually identical second amended complaints. The issue before us on this appeal is whether those complaints now state, or can be amended to state, causes of action against defendants. We therefore begin by setting forth the pertinent allegations of the complaints.

Plaintiffs' first cause of action, entitled "Failure to Detain a Dangerous Patient," alleges that on August 20, 1969, Poddar was a voluntary outpatient receiving therapy at Cowell Memorial Hospital. Poddar informed Moore, his therapist, that he was going to kill an unnamed girl, readily identifiable as Tatiana, when she returned home from spending the summer in Brazil.

---

131 California Reporter 14. Decided July 1, 1976. All footnotes and numerous references in the text of the decision and a dissent have been omitted.

Moore, with the concurrence of Dr. Gold, who had initially examined Poddar, and Dr. Yandell, assistant to the director of the department of psychiatry, decided that Poddar should be committed for observation in a mental hospital. Moore orally notified Officers Atkinson and Teel of the campus police that he would request commitment. He then sent a letter to Police Chief William Beall requesting the assistance of the police department in securing Poddar's confinement.

Officers Atkinson, Brownrigg, and Halleran took Poddar into custody, but, satisfied that Poddar was rational, released him on his promise to stay away from Tatiana. Powelson, director of the department of psychiatry at Cowell Memorial Hospital, then asked the police to return Moore's letter, directed that all copies of the letter and notes that Moore had taken as therapist be destroyed, and "ordered no action to place Prosenjit Poddar in 72-hour treatment and evaluation facility."

Plaintiffs' second cause of action, entitled "Failure to Warn On a Dangerous Patient," incorporates the allegations of the first cause of action, but adds the assertion that defendants negligently permitted Poddar to be released from police custody without "notifying the parents of Tatiana Tarasoff that their daughter was in grave danger from Prosenjit Poddar." Poddar persuaded Tatiana's brother to share an apartment with him near Tatiana's residence; shortly after her return from Brazil, Poddar went to her residence and killed her. . . .

2. PLAINTIFFS CAN STATE A CAUSE OF ACTION AGAINST DEFENDANT THERAPISTS FOR NEGLIGENT FAILURE TO PROTECT TATIANA

The second cause of action can be amended to allege that Tatiana's death proximately resulted from defendants' negligent failure to warn Tatiana or others likely to apprise her of her danger. Plaintiffs contend that as amended, such allegations of negligence and proximate causation, with resulting damages, establish a cause of action. Defendants, however, contend that in the circumstances of the present case they owed no duty of care to Tatiana or her parents and that, in the absence of such duty, they were free to act in careless disregard of Tatiana's life and safety. . . .

In the landmark case of *Rowland v. Christian* (1968), Justice Peters recognized that liability should be imposed "for an injury occasioned to another by his want of ordinary care or skill" as expressed in section 1714 of the Civil Code. Thus, Justice Peters, quoting from *Heaven v. Pender* (1883) stated: "'whenever one person is by circumstances placed in such a position with regard to another . . . that if he did not use ordinary care and skill in his own conduct . . . he would cause danger of injury to the person or property of the other, a duty arises to use ordinary care and skill to avoid such danger.'"

We depart from "this fundamental principle" only upon the "balancing of a number of considerations"; major ones "are the foreseeability of harm to the plaintiff, the degree of certainty that the plaintiff suffered injury, the closeness of the connection between the defendant's conduct and the injury suffered, the moral blame attached to the defendant's conduct, the policy of preventing future harm, the extent of the burden to the defendant and consequences to the community of imposing a duty to exercise care with resulting liability for breach, and the availability, cost and prevalence of insurance for the risk involved."

The most important of these considerations in establishing duty is foreseeability. As a general principle, a "defendant owes a duty of care to all persons who are foreseeably endangered by his conduct, with respect to all risks which make the conduct unreasonably dangerous."

As we shall explain, however, when the avoidance of foreseeable harm requires a defendant to control the conduct of another person, or to warn of such conduct, the common law has traditionally imposed liability only if the defendant bears some special relationship to the dangerous person or to the potential victim. Since the relationship between a therapist and his patient satisfies this requirement, we need not here decide whether foreseeability alone is sufficient to create a duty to exercise reasonable care to protect a potential victim of another's conduct. . . .

A relationship of defendant therapists to either Tatiana or Poddar will suffice to establish a duty of care; as explained in section 315 of the Restatement Second of Torts, a duty of care may arise from either "(a) a special relation . . . between the actor and the third person which imposes a duty upon the actor to control the third person's conduct, or (b) a special relation . . . between the actor and the other which gives to the other a right of protection." . . .

The courts hold that a doctor is liable to persons infected by his patient if he negligently fails to diagnose a contagious disease, or, having diagnosed the illness, fails to warn members of the patient's family.

Since it involved a dangerous mental patient, the decision in *Merchants Nat. Bank & Trust Co. of Fargo v. United States* (1967) comes closer to the issue. The Veterans Administration arranged for the patient to work on a local farm, but did not inform the farmer of the man's background. The farmer consequently permitted the patient to come and go freely during nonworking hours; the patient borrowed a car, drove to his wife's residence and killed her. Notwithstanding the lack of any "special relationship" between the Veterans Administration and the wife, the court found the Veterans Administration liable for the wrongful death of the wife.

In their summary of the relevant rulings Fleming and Maximov conclude that the "case law should dispel any notion that to impose on the therapists a duty to take precautions for the safety of persons threatened by a patient, where due care so requires, is in any way opposed to contemporary ground rules on the duty relationship. On the contrary, there now seems to be sufficient authority to support the conclusion that by entering into a doctor-patient relationship the therapist becomes sufficiently involved to assume some responsibility for the safety, not only of the patient himself, but also of any third person whom the doctor knows to be threatened by the patient." (Fleming & Maximov, *The Patient or His Victim: The Therapist's Dilemma* [1974] 62 Cal.L.Rev. 1025, 1030.)

Defendants contend, however, that imposition of a duty to exercise reasonable care to protect third persons is unworkable because therapists cannot accurately predict whether or not a patient will resort to violence. In support of this argument amicus representing the American Psychiatric Association and other professional societies cites numerous articles which indicate that therapists, in the present state of the art, are unable reliably to predict violent acts; their forecasts, amicus claims, tend consistently to overpredict violence, and indeed are more often wrong than right. Since predictions of violence are often erroneous, amicus concludes, the courts should not render rulings that predicate the liability of therapists upon the validity of such predictions. . . .

We recognize the difficulty that a therapist encounters in attempting to forecast whether a patient presents a serious danger of violence. Obviously we do not require that the therapist, in making that determination, render a perfect performance; the therapist need only exercise "that reasonable degree of skill, knowledge, and care ordinarily possessed and exercised by members of [that professional specialty] under similar circumstances." Within the broad range of reasonable practice and treatment in which professional opinion and judgment may differ, the therapist is free to exercise his or her own best judgment without liability; proof, aided by hindsight, that he or she judged wrongly is insufficient to establish negligence.

In the instant case, however, the pleadings do not raise any question as to failure of defendant therapists to predict that Poddar presented a serious danger of violence. On the contrary, the present complaints allege that defendant therapists did in fact predict that Poddar would kill, but were negligent in failing to warn.

Amicus contends, however, that even when a therapist does in fact predict that a patient poses a serious danger of violence to others, the therapist should be absolved of any responsibility for failing to act to protect the potential victim. In our view, however, once a therapist does in fact determine, or under applicable professional standards reasonably should have determined, that a patient poses a serious danger of violence to others, he bears a duty to exercise reasonable care to protect the foreseeable victim of that danger. While the discharge of this duty of due care will necessarily vary with the facts of each case, in each instance the adequacy of the therapist's conduct must be measured against the traditional negligence standard of the rendition of reasonable care under the circumstances. As explained in Fleming and Maximov, *The Patient or His Victim: The Therapist's Dilemma* (1974) 62 Cal.L.Rev. 1025, 1967: ". . . the ultimate question of resolving the tension between the conflicting interests of patient and potential victim is one of social policy, not professional expertise. . . . In sum, the therapist owes a legal duty not only to his patient, but also to his patient's would-be victim and is subject in both respects to scrutiny by judge and jury." . . .

The risk that unnecessary warning may be given is a reasonable price to pay for the lives of possible victims that may be saved. We could hesitate to hold that the therapist who is aware that his patient expects to attempt to assassinate the President of the United States would not be obligated to warn the authorities because the therapist cannot predict with accuracy that his patient will commit the crime.

Defendants further argue that free and open communication is essential to psychotherapy, that "Unless a patient . . . is assured that . . . information [revealed to him] can and will be held in utmost confidence, he will be reluctant to make the full disclosure upon which diagnosis and treatment . . . depends." The giving of a warning, defendants contend, constitutes a breach of trust which entails the revelation of confidential communications.

We recognize the public interest in supporting effective treatment of mental illness and in protecting the rights of patients to privacy, and the consequent public importance of safeguarding the confidential character of psychotherapeutic communication. Against this interest, however, we must weigh the public interest in safety from violent assault. . . .

We realize that the open and confidential character of psychotherapeutic dialogue encourages patients to express threats of violence, few of which are ever executed. Certainly a therapist should not be encouraged routinely to reveal such threats; such disclosures could seriously disrupt the patient's relationship with his therapist and with the persons threatened. To the contrary, the therapist's obligations to his patient require that he not disclose a confidence unless such disclosure is necessary to avert danger to others, and even then that he do so discretely, and in a fashion that would preserve the privacy of his patient to the fullest extent compatible with the prevention of the threatened danger.

The revelation of a communication under the above circumstances is not a breach of trust or a violation of professional ethics; as stated in the Principles of Medical Ethics of the American Medical Association (1957), section 9: "A physician may not reveal the confidence entrusted to him in the course of medical attendance . . . *unless he is required to do so by law or unless it becomes necessary in order to protect the welfare of the individual or of the community.*" (Emphasis added.) We conclude that the public policy favoring protection of the confidential character of patient–psychotherapist communications must yield to the extent to which disclosure is essential to avert danger to others. The protective privilege ends where the public peril begins. . . .

For the foregoing reasons, we find that plaintiffs' complaints can be amended to state a cause of action against defendants Moore, Powelson, Gold, and Yandell and against the Regents as their employer, for breach of a duty to exercise reasonable care to protect Tatiana.

• • •

CLARK, Justice (dissenting).

Until today's majority opinion, both legal and medical authorities have agreed that confidentiality is essential to effectively treat the mentally ill, and that imposing a duty on doctors to disclose patient threats to potential victims would greatly impair treatment. Further, recognizing that effective treatment and society's safety are necessarily intertwined, the Legislature has already decided effective and confidential treatment is preferred over imposition of a duty to warn.

The issue of whether effective treatment for the mentally ill should be sacrificed to a system of warnings is, in my opinion, properly one for the Legislature, and we are bound by its judgment. Moreover, even in the absence of clear legislative direction, we must reach the same conclusion because imposing the majority's new duty is certain to result in a net increase in violence. . . .

Overwhelming policy considerations weigh against imposing a duty on psychotherapists to warn a potential victim against harm. While offering virtually no benefit to society, such a duty will frustrate psychiatric treatment, invade fundamental patient rights and increase violence.

The importance of psychiatric treatment and its need for confidentiality have been recognized by this court. "It is clearly recognized that the very practice of psychiatry vitally depends upon the reputation in the community that the psychiatrist will not tell." (Slovenko, *Psychiatry and a Second Look at the Medical Privilege* (1960) 6 Wayne L.Rev. 175, 188.)

Assurance of confidentiality is important for three reasons.

DETERRENCE FROM TREATMENT

First, without substantial assurance of confidentiality, those requiring treatment will be deterred from seeking assistance. It remains an unfortunate fact in our society that people seeking psychiatric guidance tend to become stigmatized. Apprehension of such stigma — apparently increased by the propensity of people considering treatment to see themselves in the worst possible light—creates a well-recognized reluctance to seek aid. This reluctance is alleviated by the psychiatrist's assurance of confidentiality.

FULL DISCLOSURE

Second, the guarantee of confidentiality is essential in eliciting the full disclosure necessary for effective treatment. The psychiatric patient approaches treatment with conscious and unconscious inhibitions against revealing his innermost thoughts. "Every person, however well-motivated, has to overcome resistances to therapeutic exploration. These resistances seek support from every possible source and the possibility of disclosure would easily be employed in the service of resistance." (Goldstein & Katz, 36 Conn. Bar J. 175, 179.) Until a patient can trust his psychiatrist not to violate their confidential relationship, "the unconscious psychological control mechanism of repression will prevent the recall of past experiences." (Butler, *Psychotherapy and Griswold: Is Confidentiality a Privilege or a Right?* (1971) 3 Conn.L.Rev. 599, 604.)

SUCCESSFUL TREATMENT

Third, even if the patient fully discloses his thoughts, assurance that the confidential relationship will not be breached is necessary to maintain his trust in his psychiatrist—the very means by which treatment is effected. "[T]he essence of much psychotherapy is the contribution of trust in the external world and ultimately in the self, modelled upon the trusting relationship established during therapy." (Dawidoff, *The Malpractice of Psychiatrists,* 1966 Duke L.J. 696, 704.) Patients will be helped only if they can form a trusting relationship with the psychiatrist. All authorities appear to agree that if the trust relationship cannot be developed because of collusive communication between the psychiatrist and others, treatment will be frustrated.

Given the importance of confidentiality to the practice of psychiatry, it becomes clear the duty to warn imposed by the majority will cripple the use and effectiveness of psychiatry. Many people, potentially violent—yet susceptible to treatment—will be deterred from seeking it; those seeking it will be inhibited from making revelations necessary to effective treatment; and, forcing the psychiatrist to violate the patient's trust will destroy the interpersonal relationship by which treatment is effected.

VIOLENCE AND CIVIL COMMITMENT

By imposing a duty to warn, the majority contributes to the danger to society of violence by the mentally ill and greatly increases the risk of civil commitment—the total deprivation of liberty—of those who should not be confined. The impairment of treatment and risk of improper commitment resulting from the new duty to warn will not be limited to a few patients but will extend to a large number of the mentally ill. Although under existing psychiatric procedures only a relatively few receiving treatment will ever present a risk of violence, the number making threats is huge, and it is the latter group—not just the former—whose treatment will be impaired and whose risk of commitment will be increased.

Both the legal and psychiatric communities recognize that the process of determining potential violence in a patient is far from exact, being fraught with complexity and uncertainty. In fact precision has not even been attained in predicting who of those having already committed violent acts will again become violent, a task recognized to be of much simpler proportions.

This predictive uncertainty means that the number of disclosures will necessarily be large. As noted above, psychiatric patients are encouraged to discuss all thoughts of violence, and they often express such thoughts. However, unlike this court, the psychiatrist does not enjoy the benefit of overwhelming hindsight in seeing which few, if any, of his patients will ultimately become violent. Now, confronted by the majority's new duty, the psychiatrist must instantaneously calculate potential violence from each patient on each visit. The difficulties researchers have encountered in accurately predicting violence will be heightened for the practicing psychiatrist dealing for brief periods in his office with heretofore nonviolent patients. And, given the decision not to warn or commit must always be made at the psychiatrist's civil peril, one can expect most doubts will be resolved in favor of the psychiatrist protecting himself.

MARK SIEGLER

Confidentiality in Medicine — A Decrepit Concept

Medical confidentiality, as it has traditionally been understood by patients and doctors, no longer exists. This ancient medical principle, which has been included in every physician's oath and code of ethics since Hippocratic times, has become old, worn-out, and useless; it is a decrepit concept. Efforts to preserve it appear doomed to failure and often give rise to more problems than solutions. Psychiatrists have tacitly acknowledged the impossibility of ensuring the confidentiality of medical records by choosing to establish a separate, more secret record. The following case illustrates how the confidentiality principle is compromised systematically in the course of routine medical care.

A patient of mine with mild chronic obstructive pulmonary disease was transferred from the surgical intensive-care unit to a surgical nursing floor two days after an elective cholecystectomy. On the day of transfer, the patient saw a respiratory therapist writing in his medical chart (the therapist was recording the results of an arterial blood gas analysis) and became concerned about the confidentiality of his hospital records. The patient threatened to leave the hospital prematurely unless I could guarantee that the confidentiality of his hospital record would be respected.

This patient's complaint prompted me to enumerate the number of persons who had both access to his hospital record and a reason to examine it. I was amazed to learn that at least 25 and possibly as many as 100 health professionals and administrative personnel at our university hospital had access to the patient's record and that all of them had a legitimate need, indeed a professional responsibility, to open and use that chart. These persons included 6 attending physicians (the primary physician, the surgeon, the pulmonary

consultant, and others); 12 house officers (medical, surgical, intensive-care unit, and "covering" house staff); 20 nursing personnel (on three shifts); 6 respiratory therapists; 3 nutritionists; 2 clinical pharmacists; 15 students (from medicine, nursing, respiratory therapy, and clinical pharmacy); 4 unit secretaries; 4 hospital financial officers; and 4 chart reviewers (utilization review, quality assurance review, tissue review, and insurance auditor). It is of interest that this patient's problem was straightforward, and he therefore did not require many other technical and support services that the modern hospital provides. For example, he did not need multiple consultants and fellows, such specialized procedures as dialysis, or social workers, chaplains, physical therapists, occupational therapists, and the like.

Upon completing my survey I reported to the patient that I estimated that at least 75 health professionals and hospital personnel had access to his medical record. I suggested to the patient that these people were all involved in providing or supporting his health care services. They were, I assured him, working for him. Despite my reassurances the patient was obviously distressed and retorted, "I always believed that medical confidentiality was part of a doctor's code of ethics. Perhaps you should tell me just what you people mean by 'confidentiality'!"

TWO ASPECTS OF MEDICAL CONFIDENTIALITY

CONFIDENTIALITY AND THIRD-PARTY INTERESTS

Previous discussions of medical confidentiality usually have focused on the tension between a physician's responsibility to keep information divulged by patients secret and a physician's legal and moral duty, on occasion, to reveal such confidences to third parties, such as families, employers, public-health authorities, or police

Reprinted by permission of *New England Journal of Medicine*, Vol. 307. © 1982 Massachusetts Medical Society.

authorities. In all these instances, the central question relates to the stringency of the physician's obligation to maintain patient confidentiality when the health, well-being, and safety of identifiable others or of society in general would be threatened by a failure to reveal information about the patient. The tension in such cases is between the good of the patient and the good of others.

CONFIDENTIALITY AND THE PATIENT'S INTEREST

As the example above illustrates, further challenges to confidentiality arise because the patient's personal interest in maintaining confidentiality comes into conflict with his personal interest in receiving the best possible health care. Modern high-technology health care is available principally in hospitals (often, teaching hospitals), requires many trained and specialized workers (a "health-care team"), and is very costly. The existence of such teams means that information that previously had been held in confidence by an individual physician will now necessarily be disseminated to many members of the team. Furthermore, since health-care teams are expensive and few patients can afford to pay such costs directly, it becomes essential to grant access to the patient's medical record to persons who are responsible for obtaining third-party payment. These persons include chart reviewers, financial officers, insurance auditors, and quality-of-care assessors. Finally, as medicine expands from a narrow, disease-based model to a model that encompasses psychological, social, and economic problems, not only will the size of the health-care team and medical costs increase, but more sensitive information (such as one's personal habits and financial condition) will now be included in the medical record and will no longer be confidential.

The point I wish to establish is that hospital medicine, the rise of health-care teams, the existence of third-party insurance programs, and the expanding limits of medicine will appear to be responses to the wishes of people for better and more comprehensive medical care. But each of these developments necessarily modifies our traditional understanding of medical confidentiality.

THE ROLE OF CONFIDENTIALITY
IN MEDICINE

Confidentiality serves a dual purpose in medicine. In the first place, it acknowledges respect for the patient's sense of individuality and privacy. The patient's most personal physical and psychological secrets are kept confidential in order to decrease a sense of shame and vulnerability. Secondly, confidentiality is important in improving the patient's health care—a basic goal of medicine. The promise of confidentiality permits people to trust (i.e., have confidence) that information revealed to a physician in the course of a medical encounter will not be disseminated further. In this way patients are encouraged to communicate honestly and forthrightly with their doctors. This bond of trust between patient and doctor is vitally important both in the diagnostic process (which relies on an accurate history) and subsequently in the treatment phase, which often depends as much on the patient's trust in the physician as it does on medications and surgery. These two important functions of confidentiality are as important now as they were in the past. They will not be supplanted entirely either by improvements in medical technology or by recent changes in relations between some patients and doctors toward a rights-based, consumerist model.

POSSIBLE SOLUTIONS
TO THE CONFIDENTIALITY PROBLEM

First of all, in all nonbureaucratic, noninstitutional medical encounters—that is, in the millions of doctor–patient encounters that take place in physician's offices, where more privacy can be preserved—meticulous care should be taken to guarantee that patients' medical and personal information will be kept confidential.

Secondly, in such settings as hospitals or large-scale group practices, where many persons have opportunities to examine the medical record, we should aim to provide access only to those who have "a need to know." This could be accomplished through such administrative changes as dividing the entire record into several sections—for example, a medical and financial section—and permitting only health professionals access to the medical information.

The approach favored by many psychiatrists—that of keeping a psychiatric record separate from the general medical record—is an understandable strategy but one that is not entirely satisfactory and that should not be generalized. The keeping of separate psychiatric records implies that psychiatry and medicine are different undertakings and thus drives deeper the wedge between them and between physical and psychological illness. Furthermore, it is often vitally important for internists or surgeons to know that a patient is being seen by a psychiatrist or is taking a particular medication. When separate records are kept, this information may not be available. Finally, if generalized, the practice of keeping a separate psychiatric record could lead to the unacceptable consequence of having a separate record for each type of medical problem.

Patients should be informed about what is meant by "medical confidentiality." We should establish the distinction between information about the patient that generally will be kept confidential regardless of the interest of third parties and information that will be exchanged among members of the health-care team in order to provide care for the patient. Patients should be made aware of the large number of persons in the modern hospital who require access to the medical record in order to serve the patient's medical and financial interests.

Finally, at some point most patients should have an opportunity to review their medical record and to make informed choices about whether their entire record is to be available to everyone or whether certain portions of the record are privileged and should be accessible only to their principal physician or to others designated explicitly by the patient. This approach would rely on traditional informed-consent procedural standards and might permit the patient to balance the personal value of medical confidentiality against the personal value of high-technology, team health care. There is no reason that the same procedure should not be used with psychiatric records instead of the arbitrary system now employed, in which everything related to psychiatry is kept secret.

AFTERTHOUGHT: CONFIDENTIALITY AND INDISCRETION

There is one additional aspect of confidentiality that is rarely included in discussions of the subject. I am referring here to the wanton, often inadvertent, but avoidable exchanges of confidential information that occur frequently in hospital rooms, elevators, cafeterias, doctors' offices, and at cocktail parties. Of course, as more people have access to medical information

about the patient the potential for this irresponsible abuse of confidentiality increases geometrically.

Such mundane breaches of confidentiality are probably of greater concern to most patients than the broader issues of whether their medical records may be entered into a computerized data bank or whether a respiratory therapist is reviewing the results of an arterial blood gas determination. Somehow, privacy is violated and a sense of shame is heightened when intimate secrets are revealed to people one knows or is close to — friends, neighbors, acquaintances, or hospital roommates — rather than when they are disclosed to an anonymous bureaucrat sitting at a computer terminal in a distant city or to a health professional who is acting in an official capacity.

I suspect that the principles of medical confidentiality, particularly those reflected in most medical codes of ethics, were designed principally to prevent just this sort of embarrassing personal indiscretion rather than to maintain (for social, political, or economic reasons) the absolute secrecy of doctor–patient communications. In this regard, it is worth noting that Percival's Code of Medical Ethics (1803) includes the following admonition: "Patients should be interrogated concerning their complaint in a tone of voice which cannot be overheard."* We in the medical profession frequently neglect these simple courtesies.

CONCLUSION

The principle of medical confidentiality described in medical codes of ethics and still believed in by patients no longer exists. In this respect, it is a decrepit concept. Rather than perpetuate the myth of confidentiality and invest energy vainly to preserve it, the public and the profession would be better served if they devoted their attention to determining which aspects of the original principle of confidentiality are worth retaining. Efforts could then be directed to salvaging those.

---

*Leake CD, ed. Percival's medical ethics. Baltimore: Williams & Wilkins, 1927.

SIR DOUGLAS BLACK

Absolute Confidentiality?

Since I have been allotted, and been glad to accept, the ostensibly negative role of denying that confidentiality in the doctor-patient relationship is absolute, I must pre-empt possible misunderstanding by emphasizing my adherence to two important positive positions, which may be summarily expressed thus:

1. The doctor-patient relationship is both so important and so potentially fragile as to require the support of a clear ethical framework, understood and accepted implicitly or even explicitly by both doctor and patient.
2. I accept both the general value of stated ethical principles, and in particular the validity of the principles indicated by the terms 'autonomy, beneficence, non-maleficence, and justice'.

What then can be my grounds for questioning the absolute character of what is undoubtedly a major ethical requirement in the relationships between doctors and patients? The detailed arguments and instances which I see as supporting these grounds should, of course, form the content of this chapter, but it may make the nature of my argument clearer if even at this early stage I indicate its general course in the form of three summary propositions:

1. The statement of an ethical position can be valid, valuable, and generally acceptable, without its having the qualities of universality in acceptance and application which would justify its designation as 'absolute'.
2. There are likely to be 'legitimate exceptions' in the practical application of ethical principles,

even those which are soundly based and generally accepted.
3. There are practical situations, both in clinical medicine and in public health medicine, where two or even more agreed ethical principles would appear to be in conflict, in the sense that action dictated by one of them would be incompatible with courses of action dictated by the other or others.

... The first definition of absolute given in *Chambers 20th-century dictionary* (1983) is 'free from limits, restrictions, or conditions', which I take to be the common usage. Later on there is another definition, qualified by '(*philos*)', which reads 'existing in and by itself without necessary relation to anything else' — a usage which certainly could not be relevant to practical medical ethics. But could even the first, less 'free-standing', definition be sensibly applied to the type of proposition commonly made in medical ethics?

At the (commonly accepted) risk of putting words into the mouths of hypothetical others, I suppose a deontologist might argue that some such propositions might rank as 'categorical imperatives', in the sense that they would be willed by all intelligences; and might give 'Thou shalt not kill' as an example. But even in relation to that precept, and among those intelligences to which we can obtain limited access by observing their behaviour and actions, there is a disturbing lack of unanimity, with deviance all too overtly expressed by terrorists, by other murderers, and more legitimately perhaps by agents of the state — and of course the different ethical standards of different countries and societies indicate that there is no escape from individual aberration by resort to organized collectivity.

There have, of course, been attempts, still within a deontological framework, and without rushing to naked utilitarianism, to escape from the difficulty imposed by the extreme variability of observed human behaviour, often accompanied by bizarre attempts at justification, such as the Nazi defence of slaying the mentally handicapped, even before they embarked on wholesale murder on racial grounds. For example, a distinction has been made between *prima facie ethical principles* (which should prevail in the absence of conflicting obligations); and *absolute duty* (which presumably must govern conduct without exception, and which seems difficult to exemplify.[1] Another approach recognizes the general validity of moral principles, but would resolve such conflicts as may arise between them by having set them in a hierarchical or *lexical ordering,* such that the 'higher' principles be satisfied before observing those 'lower' in the imposed order.[2]

In the later, more pragmatic, sections of this chapter I shall be illustrating what I believe to be justifiable transgressions of the general principle of confidentiality of information given in the context of health care by patients to doctors, and indeed to other 'health care professionals', to use the accepted if somewhat cumbrous phrase used to denote the many groups other than doctors who give a professional service related to health. If confidentiality in these situations were indeed 'absolute', all such transgressions would be illegitimate and immoral; and it would obviously be wrong even to discuss them without having attained a prior conviction that confidentiality is not in fact 'absolute'. That is certainly my own belief; it may be an intuitive one, though I have laboured in preceding paragraphs to give it some groundwork in theory.

Those who, like myself, have a mistrust of absolutes, or to put it more simply are chary of the words 'always' and 'never' in our ethical discourse, are quite likely to be considered as ethical reprobates by those who take the opposite view. Let me therefore lay it on the line that I believe in the formulation and study of ethical principles and of the practical precepts which may flow from them; and that they represent a norm of proper conduct, deviations from which require to be justified. To go further in the specific matter of confidentiality, it has both historical acceptance going back to the ancient world; and a very strong ethical base. . . . Release of personal health information supplied by patients is a breach of their *autonomy,* unless of course they have given specific informed consent. The dissemination of health information, whether by careless leakage or deliberate malice, offends against the principle of *non-maleficence.* Further, confidentiality of health information is compatible in almost all circumstances with the principles of beneficence and of justice; although later I shall hope to produce instances in which the need for beneficence or for justice may override the obligation to maintain the confidentiality of personal health information. . . .

WHAT CONSTITUTES A BREACH OF CONFIDENTIALITY?

Not every disclosure of personal health information represents a breach of confidentiality. With one important proviso, any disclosure of information can be legitimated by the patient's consent to the disclosure. The proviso is, of course, that of *adequately informed consent.* This means that, for any disclosure of importance, the patient must know what is to be disclosed, the purpose of the disclosure, the person or persons to whom the disclosure is to be made, and that his consent is 'specific', i.e. he is sanctioning, unless otherwise agreed, *one* disclosure of a *specified part* of his record. These are the strict requirements, perhaps more easily stated than fulfilled, and of such gravamen that they may be strictly appropriate to areas in which possible damage or hurt to the patient may be foreseen. But in any matter of possible moment the necessary rigour of consent should be judged by the patient, whose trust or ignorance is not something to be abused.

Legitimation by adequately informed consent is the most valid guarantee that a disclosure does not constitute a breach of confidentiality. But of course it is now the rule rather than the exception that health care is provided not by an isolated doctor, but by a team of health professionals, and also in many cases social workers. Transfers of information are a necessary part of the care of any major episode of illness; and it would be unrealistic to subject each such transfer to the formal sanctions of informed consent. In actual practice the assumption is made that the patient in his own interests would agree to transfer of information relevant to his care and hopefully cure; this assumption of what may be called *implied consent* is pragmatically useful, if not even necessary in the interests of reasonable efficiency. It is, however, ethically and perhaps even legally frail, in that it could be construed as a derogation from the patient's autonomy. There is one safeguard which should certainly be applied to pragmatic transfers of personal health information, that they should be made only to those who require the information to enable them to serve the patient's own interests — it is this which constitutes the criterion known as the *right to know*.

It is transfer of personal health information without the consent of the patient to those who do not need to know such information for purposes of legitimate health or social care, which constitutes a breach of confidentiality. A deliberate breach of this kind, with malicious intent, is a serious ethical offence, and may also be a criminal act. Consideration of the numbers of people who may, quite legitimately, become possessed of health information about a patient, must arouse some concern about leakage of information, not through malice, but through inattention to proper reticence, or to carelessness in the handling of records. The important safeguard here lies in professional adherence to codes of confidentiality, and to similar obligations laid on other employees as part of their terms and conditions of service.

CONFIDENTIALITY IN A CLINICAL SETTING

. . . At the level of ethical principle, doctors in general would assent to the sentence in the Hippocratic oath which says, 'Whatever I see or hear, professionally or privately, which ought not to be divulged, I will keep secret and tell no one.' But it should be noted that this obligation comes well short of the absolute secrecy attributed to the clergy in the confessional; the phrase 'which ought not be divulged' leaves room for the exercise of professionally informed ethical judgment. Freedom commonly opens the way to error, and the particular temptation here is to act according to our own ethical preconceptions, rather than to discover the patient's own judgment of what should or should not be told. Of course, common sense has to enter, in the recognition that in the majority of clinical settings no particular problems are likely to arise, particularly if for sound pragmatic reasons we assume that if a patient agrees, at our suggestion, to see a colleague for a further opinion, he will not simply agree, but will positively expect that we will pass on information about his state of health. Such an assumption comes naturally to me, as a doctor who practised in a hospital setting, and dealt with general medical problems in which the help of a colleague was often needed, and in relation to which 'stigmatization' was not a likely issue. Even so, from time to time things would come to light with a bearing on life insurance, on fitness for employment,

on disease communicable in various ways, or even on an accident associated with previous treatment. . . .

As I hinted, perhaps somewhat obliquely, at the beginning of this section, the attitudes and consent behaviour of doctors in relation to confidentiality are likely to be affected by the type of practice in which they are engaged. My own perspective as a general physician may well be different from that of an occupational physician, who has a degree of responsibility to an employer as well as to a patient; and even more different from that of a venereologist, whose access to patients is critically dependent on perception by the prospective patient that confidentiality will be absolute. This emphasis on absolute confidentiality has largely dictated the conventional wisdom on the ethical dilemmas posed by AIDS; but I personally share the view expressed in a statement made in relation to AIDS by the General Medical Council in 1988, that 'most doctors are now prepared to regard these conditions as similar in principle to other infections and life-threatening conditions, and are willing to apply established principles in approaching their diagnosis and management, rather than treating them as medical conditions quite distinct from all others' . . . I would be prepared, in the face of absolute refusal by the patient, to divulge to a spouse, with the promise of appropriate counselling, that her partner had AIDS; and I support the action of surgeons in testing patients for HIV, when there is a risk that they might pass on the virus to other patients — just as I would see it as the surgeon's duty to notify an infection which he had acquired. I think I am consistent at any rate with the thrust of this chapter in considering the principle of autonomy not as absolute, but capable in the right circumstances of having to yield place to the principle of non-maleficence.

CONFIDENTIALITY AND SOCIETY

Although considerations of confidentiality are of the utmost importance in clinical settings, such settings are so much a relationship between individuals, some of them idiosyncratic by nature or as a result of illness, that the general principles by which they are undoubtedly informed are not easily extracted from the complex scene for demonstration purposes. However, society, or rather the agents acting on its behalf, quite rightly ask for a more formal definition of principles and of practical safeguards. . . .

In these matters the general principle, and also the public expectation, is that when an individual provides or a doctor elicits information on that individual's state of health, such information will not be divulged. To do so would breach the *prima facie* principle of *autonomy*. I suggested . . . that departures from conduct apparently dictated by *prima facie* ethical principles could be justified either by the recognition of *legitimate exceptions,* or by *conflict between principles.*

LEGITIMATE EXCEPTIONS

The most obvious of these is when a patient voluntarily abrogates his own autonomy, by giving free informed consent to the release of health information contained in his record. When information is to be used for other than clinical purposes — e.g. for insurance, welfare or housing — the patient's consent should have been preceded by explanation of the possible consequences of release of his personal health information to the authority concerned. A less important gloss, at least in most cases, on the release of information legitimated by consent is that a patient can abrogate his own autonomy but not, without the other's consent, someone else's. For example, if the record includes a family history attributing to relatives a condition which they might not wish generally known, their consent should formally be obtained to disclosure of that part of the record. Common sense might suggest, however, that sensitive matter of this kind is not frequent, and that when it does occur it may be less cumbrous to delete that part of the record than to go through a formal consent procedure with a distant relative.

It was suggested earlier that, in a clinical context, those looking after the patient in various ways could have legitimate access to his record either in whole or in necessary part; and more debatably perhaps that such transfers might be legitimated by the consent implied in having had recourse to health care. But when we go outside the clinical field the possibility of release on a 'right to know' basis is limited in two particular ways, which can be expressed in the form of questions which should be answered before the information is released:

Who needs to know?

How much of the record is needed?

On the first of these questions, it is the *need* to know, and not just the *wish* to know, which confers the *right.* When the disclosure is made in the interests of the patient, his consent should still be sought. Even so, the transfer of information should still be made to a responsible individual, not broadcast to an institution. On the second question, it is often preferable to make

a specific disclosure appropriate to the particular need, than to adopt the inherently sloppy course of sending unedited material. To go back for an illustration to the clinical field, I have on occasion seen patients referred from other hospitals bringing with them their entire notes and X-rays, but no summary of the specific problem at issue. I felt sad for the patient sitting there while I ploughed through this material; but I fell short of my duty of *agape* to the referring registrar.

These are but examples of possible legitimate exceptions to the principle of confidentiality of health information. In any material case their legitimacy should rest on a considered decision, taken in the interests of the patient. But there are also cases of conflict between the interests of individuals, between individuals and society, and even conflict between principles themselves.

CONFLICT BETWEEN PRINCIPLES

It is a matter of common observation that one man's autonomy may be at another's expense; banal examples in the health field are in the 'freedom' to transmit colds, or to smoke in public. Some such conflicts of interest reflect discordance not simply in the application of a principle, but between principles themselves. As examples, I will discuss first the conflict between 'autonomy' and 'benevolence', using as illustration the possible constraints on research; and then the conflict between 'autonomy' and 'non-maleficence', illustrating it by legal pressures to use health information in the detection or prevention of crime.

RESEARCH

In order to avoid an argument tangential to the main theme, let me join the good company of Thomas Jefferson, and say that 'I hold it to be a self-evident truth' that it is desirable to increase knowledge by carrying out research; and it is further beneficial if the results of such research can be applied to the prevention and cure of illness. Clinical research has its ethical problems, soluble in the main by truly informed consent; but they are not particularly those arising from disclosing information, rather perhaps arising from withholding it. But one very important branch of research is based on the use of records, with as a rule no direct interview between researcher and subject in which explanation can be given and consent sought. The academic and practical values of epidemiological studies are not in question; argument focuses on how the patient's right of confidentiality can be secured. One extreme position, strongly held by nursing organizations, is that any access to records must be preceded by explicit informed consent given by the patient; in other words, complete preservation of autonomy, at whatever cost to research or its possible fruits. There are not, of course, any advocates of the theoretical other extreme, which would be research without consent and without safeguards. The middle position, taken by the majority of the IPWG, is that any proposal for epidemiological study of records should be submitted to a research ethics committee; and that the results should be published in such a way that no individual patient could be identified — 'anonymized publication', in the jargon. Much valuable epidemiological research is based in part on death certificates, for example the effect of smoking on heart disease and lung cancer; a rigid stipulation of 'consent' would prevent such research.

LAW ENFORCEMENT

The principle of 'non-maleficence' would seem to favour the arrest of criminals and the detection of crime; but the criminal himself might see things rather differently, especially if health information volunteered by him for another purpose was made instrumental in his pursuit. Absolute 'autonomy' would preclude the use of such information — would indeed preclude either arrest or prevention. On the other hand — and not fancifully — rigid devotees of law and order have happily suggested that the immigration officer or the tax inspector might get some useful information from clinical records. But I think most people might see this as a matter of degree, giving the preference to autonomy for trivial offences, but becoming skewed to non-maleficence in case of terrorism or other serious crime. But in the practical world two specific problems arise, how to define 'serious crime'; and who is to make the disclosure. . . .

Formal disclosures to the police of health information are not a daily occurrence, but authorities must have a mechanism for deciding on them. In family practice the onus is presumably on the individual doctor; and in hospital the doctor in charge of the patient is the first choice; but he or she may not always be available in an emergency, and it may then be necessary to fall back on an administrative arrangement — which should not, however, be the first choice, as administrators, however strong their personal integrity, are under no professional constraint, and have not got the traditions of confidentiality which medical training and practice should inculcate.

Where a doctor finds himself possessed of information which may be relevant to the detection or prevention of serious crime, he can as a rule make his decision as a free agent. But there are quite a number of statutory provisions which may variously require, permit, or prevent disclosure; and in some of these contexts the requirement is on the health authority, with or in some cases without the necessary awareness of the doctor. A doctor may also be ordered by a court of law to disclose health information on his patient, and he is then under a legal obligation to do so. It is unlikely, but not impossible, that a legal requirement would be in flagrant conflict with personal or professional ethics; but if it were, the damage to personal integrity would have to be balanced against the penalty likely to be imposed by the court.

RECAPITULATION

Doctors and other health workers should not divulge personal health information given them by patients. This is a norm of conduct, not a categorical ethical imperative. Disclosures can be legitimated by the informed consent of the patient, and by the 'need to know' of other health professionals directly involved in the care of that patient. For information to go outside the health care field and into society generally, stringent safeguards are needed; but even so, other ethical principles in particular contexts may take precedence over the principle of confidentiality based on autonomy. There are also statutory and legal constraints to be taken into account.

NOTES

1. Ross, W. D. 1930. *The right and the good.* Oxford University Press, Oxford.

2. Rawls, J. 1976. *A theory of justice.* Oxford University Press, Oxford.

LAWRENCE O. GOSTIN

Genetic Privacy

Human genomic information is invested with enormous power in a scientifically motivated society. Genomic information has the capacity to produce a great deal of good for society. It can help identify and understand the etiology and pathophysiology of disease. In so doing, medicine and science can expand the ability to prevent and ameliorate human malady through genetic testing, treatment, and reproductive counseling.

Genomic information can just as powerfully serve less beneficent ends. Information can be used to discover deeply personal attributes of an individual's life. That information can be used to invade a person's private sphere, to alter a person's sense of self- and family identity, and to affect adversely opportunities in education, employment, and insurance. Genomic information can also affect families and ethnic groups that share genetic similarities.

It is sometimes assumed that significant levels of privacy can coexist with widespread collection of genomic information. Understandably, we want to advance all valid interests — both collective and individual. We want to believe that we can continue to acquire and use voluminous data from the human genome while also protecting individual, family, and group privacy. This article demonstrates that no such easy resolution of the conflict between the need for genomic information and the need for privacy exists. Because absolute privacy cannot realistically be achieved while collecting genetic data, we confront a hard choice: Should we sharply limit the systematic collection of genomic information to achieve reasonable levels of privacy? Or, is the value of genomic information so important to the achievement of societal aspirations for

health that the law ought not promise absolute or even significant levels of privacy, but rather that data be collected and used in orderly and just ways, consistent with the values of individuals and communities? As I argue, the law at present neither adequately protects privacy nor ensures fair information practices. Moreover, the substantial variability in the law probably impedes the development of an effective genetic information system.

In earlier articles, I scrutinized the meaning and boundaries of health information privacy.[1] Here, I build on that work by examining a particular aspect of health information — genetic privacy. . . . This is well-tread territory; what I hope to bring to the literature is a conceptual structure relating to the acquisition and use of genomic information. First, the methods of collection and use of genomic data must be understood and its public purposes evaluated. Second, the privacy implications of genomic information must be measured. To what extent are genomic data the same as, or different from, other health information? Third, an examination of the current constitutional and statutory law must be undertaken to determine whether existing safeguards are adequate to protect the privacy and security of genomic data. Finally, proposals for balancing societal needs for genomic information and claims for privacy by individuals and families must be generated.

GENETIC INFORMATION INFRASTRUCTURE

I define the *genetic information infrastructure* as the basic, underlying framework of collection, storage, use, and transmission of genomic information (including human tissue and extracted DNA) to support all essential functions in genetic research, diagnosis, treatment, and reproductive counseling. Despite the technical problems and the cost, several governmental and private

From the *Journal of Law, Medicine & Ethics,* 23 (1995): 320–30. Reprinted with the permission of the American Society of Law, Medicine & Ethics and Professor Gostin.

committees have proposed automation of health data, including genomic information. Several conceptual and technological innovations are likely to accelerate the automation of health records: patient-based longitudinal clinical records, which include genetic testing and screening information; unique identifiers and the potential to link genomic information to identifiable persons; and genetic data bases for clinical, research, and public health purposes.

LONGITUDINAL CLINICAL RECORDS: TESTING AND SCREENING

The health care system is moving toward patient-based longitudinal health records. These records, held in electronic form, contain all data relevant to the individual's health collected over a lifetime. What is foreseen is a single record for every person in the United States, continually expanded from prebirth to death, and accessible to a wide range of individuals and institutions.[2]

Genetic testing and screening are likely to become an important part of longitudinal clinical records. The principal forms include: fetal (prenatal), newborn, carrier, and clinical (primary care) screening.[3] Prenatal screening seeks to identify disease in the fetus. Prenatal diagnosis of birth defects often involves genetic analysis of amniotic fluid, blood, or other tissues. Prenatal diagnostic methods are used for genetic diseases including Down syndrome, Tay-Sachs, sickle cell, and thalassemia major (Cooley's anemia). Newborn screening often focuses on detection of inborn errors of metabolism. Phenylketonuria (PKU) was the first condition subject to newborn screening; other inborn defects often screened at birth are galactosemia, branched-chain ketonuria, and homocystinuria.[4] Carrier screening seeks to identify heterozygotes for genes for recessive disease. Carrier testing has been used for such conditions as Tay-Sachs, cystic fibrosis (CF), and sickle cell.

The Human Genome Initiative has advanced to the point where it is not possible to conceive of an ever-expanding ability to detect genetic causes of diseases in individuals and populations. Testing for predispositions to disease represents one of the most important developments. For example, testing for predispositions to Huntington's disease, colon cancer, heart disease, and Alzheimer's disease are currently possible or expected.[5] . . . Genetic methods to identify elevated risk for multi-factorial diseases are also likely. It may be possible, for example, to identify individuals at risk for such conditions as schizophrenia, manic depression, and alcohol or drug dependency.

Clinical records could potentially be linked to many other sources of genomic information: (i) a lucrative commercial market in self-testing, which is growing even before scientists regard test-kits as reliable (for example, testing for genetic predictors of breast cancer),[6] (ii) workplace screening, through which employers can determine an employee's current and future capacity to perform a job or to burden pension or health care benefit plans (such testing may occur despite some legal restrictions under disability discrimination statutes),[7] (iii) screening to determine eligibility for health, life, and disability insurance which is likely when tests are more cost-effective, (iv) testing in the criminal justice system, which will increase as more courts recognize the probative value of genomic data,[8] and (v) testing for a wide variety of public purposes (for instance, to prevent fraud in collection of welfare or other social benefits, to identify family ties in adoption, and to adjudicate paternity suits).[9] Automated health information systems hold the capacity electronically to link information collected for these and other purposes. Data from several sources can be compared and matched; and different configurations of data can reveal new understandings about the individual.

It is thus possible to conceive of a genetic information system that contains a robust account of the past, present, and future health of each individual, ranging from genetic fetal abnormalities and neonate carrier states, to current and future genetic conditions at different points in one's life. Genetic data can even explain causes of morbidity and mortality after death; for example, genetic technologies were used to determine whether Abraham Lincoln had Marfan's disease.[10] As will become apparent below, such genetic explanations of morbidity and mortality provide an expansive understanding of the attributes not only of the individual, but also of her family (ancestors as well as current and future generations) and possibly of whole populations.

UNIQUE IDENTIFIERS AND POTENTIAL LINKS TO IDENTIFIABLE PERSONS

Health data can be collected and stored in identifiable or nonidentifiable forms. Data raise different levels of privacy concerns, depending on whether they can be linked to a specific person. The most serious privacy concerns are raised where genomic data are directly linked to a known individual. For reasons of efficiency, many health plans in the private and public sector are considering the use of unique identifiers. These identifiers would be used for a variety of health, administrative, financial, statistical, and research purposes. The identifier would facilitate access to care and reimbursement for services rendered. Some envisage using the social security number (SSN) as the unique identifier, which is controversial because the SSN is linked to data from the Internal Revenue Service, Department of Defense, debt collectors, the Medical Information Bureau, credit card companies, and so forth.

Where data are collected or held in nonidentifiable form, they pose few problems of privacy. Because anonymous data are not personally linked, they cannot reveal intimate information that affect individual privacy rights. Epidemiological data, including health statistics, are frequently collected in this form. This enables investigators or public health personnel to collect a great deal of information, usually without measurable burdens on privacy interests. The obvious question arises whether genomic data can also be collected in nonidentifiable form. Genomic data that are not linked to identified individuals can significantly reduce, but do not eliminate, privacy concerns. Genomic data are qualitatively different from other health data because they are inherently linked to one person. While non-genetic descriptions of any given patient's disease and treatment could apply to many other individuals, genomic data are unique. But, although the ability to identify a named individual in a large population simply from genetic material is unlikely, the capacity of computers to search multiple data bases provides a potential for linking genomic information to that person. It follows that nonlinked genomic data do not assure anonymity and that privacy and security safeguards must attach to any form of genetic material. It is, therefore, a concern that even the strict genetic privacy statutes that have been introduced in Congress exempt "personal genetic records maintained anonymously for research purposes only."[11] Minimally, such statutes must require that privacy and security arrangements ensure that these "anonymous" data are never linked to identified persons.

GENETIC DATA BASES

Data bases collect, store, use, and transfer vast amounts of health information, often in electronic or automated form. The technology exists to transfer data among data bases, to match and reconfigure information, and to seek identifying characteristics of individuals and populations. Data bases hold information on numerous subjects including medical cost reimbursements, hospital discharges, health status, research, and specific diseases. A growing number of data bases also contain genetic information. Genetic research usually requires only DNA, sources of which include not only solid tissue, but also blood, saliva, and any other nucleated cells. Reilly defines DNA banking as "the long-term storage of cells, transformed cell lines, or extracted DNA for subsequent retrieval and analysis"; it is "the indefinite storage of information derived from DNA analysis, such as linkage profiles of persons at risk for Huntington Disease or identify profiles based on analysis with a set of probes and enzymes."[12]

Genetic data bases are held in both the private and public sector for clinical, research, and public health purposes. The National Institutes of Health (NIH), for example, maintains a genetic data base for cancer research, while private universities, such as the University of Utah human tissue repository, conduct genetic research. Commercial companies offer genetic banking as a service to researchers or individuals.[13] Genetic data bases are also created to support non-health-related functions, such as identification of remains of soldiers,[14] detection, prosecution, and post-conviction supervision through "DNA fingerprinting" of persons engaging in criminal conduct,[15] and identification of blood lines in paternity and child disputes.[16]

One problematic source of information is previously stored tissues samples. Stored samples may be regarded as inchoate data bases because the technology exists to extract from them considerable current and future health data.[17] The public health and research communities have shown increasing interest in using existing tissue samples for genetic testing and for creating new genetic data bases. From a privacy perspective, this interest raises a serious problem: any consent that was obtained when that tissue was originally extracted would not meet current informed consent standards because the donor could not have envisaged future genetic applications.

The most prominent example of an inchoate genetic data base is the Guthrie spot program, whereby dried blood spots are taken from virtually all newborns throughout the United States. All states screen newborns for PKU, congenital hyperthyroidism, and other genetic defects. The genetic composition of Guthrie spots remains stable for many years and, if frozen, can be held indefinitely. A recent survey found that three-quarters of the states store their Guthrie cards, with thirteen storing them for more than five years. Of them, several store these cards indefinitely; and a number of other states have expressed an intention to do so.[18] Only two require parental consent for the blood spot.

Perhaps the most ambitious public or private effort to create a data base with both genetic and nongenetic applications is the National Health and Nutrition Examination Survey (NHANES) conducted by several federal agencies.[19] NHANES has collected comprehensive health status data in patient-identifiable form on some 40,000 Americans in eighty-one counties in twenty-six states. About 500 pieces of data are collected from each subject, ranging from sociodemographics, diet, bone density, and blood pressure, to risk status, drug use, and sexually transmitted diseases (STDs). Additionally, NHANES tests and stores biological samples for long-term follow-up and statistical research.

NHANES provides a classic illustration of a massive collection of highly personal and sensitive information that has enduring societal importance. These data pose a significant risk of privacy invasion, but they are critical to understanding health problems in the population.

CLINICAL AND PUBLIC HEALTH BENEFITS OF GENOMIC INFORMATION

Americans seem enamored with the power of genomic information. It is often thought capable of explaining much that is human: personality, intelligence, appearance, behavior, and health.[20] Genetic technologies generated from scientific assessment are commonly believed always to be accurate and highly predictive. These beliefs are highly exaggerated; for instance, personal attributes are influenced by social, behavioral, and environmental factors.

A person's genetic diary, moreover, is highly complex, with infinite possibilities of genetic influence. Ample evidence exists that the results of genetic-based diagnosis and prognosis are uncertain. The sensitivity of genetic testing is limited by the known mutations in a target population. For example, screening can detect only 75 percent of CF chromosomes in the U.S. population. Approximately one of every two couples from the general population identified by CF screening as "at-risk" will be falsely labeled.[21] Predicting the nature, severity, and course of disease based on a genetic marker is an additional difficulty. For most genetic diseases, the onset data, severity of symptoms, and efficacy of treatment and management vary greatly.

Nonetheless, the force of genomic information, even if exaggerated, is powerful. Genomic information is highly beneficial for health care decisions regarding prevention, treatment, diet, lifestyle, and reproductive choices. In particular, collection of genomic data can provide the following benefits to individuals and to society.

Enhanced patient choice. Genetic testing can enhance autonomous decision making by providing patients with better information. Genomic data, for example, can provide information about carrier states, enabling couples to make more informed reproductive choices; about disabilities of the fetus, guiding decisions about abortion or fetal treatment; about markers for future disease, informing lifestyle decisions; and about current health status, providing greater options for early treatment. Some may not agree that genetic information used for these purposes is inherently good, for the information could be used to increase selective abortion to "prevent" the births of babies with genetic disabilities.

Clinical benefit. Often a disconnection exists between the ability of science to detect disease and its ability to prevent, treat, or cure it. Scientific achievement in identifying genetic causes of disease must be tempered by a hard look at scientifically possible methods of intervention. As discussed below, if the possible stigma or discrimination associated with the disease is great, and science remains powerless to prevent or treat it, the potential benefits may outweigh harms. Despite this caveat, the Human Genome Initiative holds the current or potential ability to achieve a great deal of good for patients.

Couples can decide to change their plans for reproduction based on information disclosed in genetic counseling, thus reducing the chance of a child born with disease. Detection of metabolic abnormalities can empower a person to control their diet and lifestyle to prevent the onset of symptomatology. Identification of enhanced risk for multifactorial diseases, such as certain cancers or mental illness, could help people avoid exposure to particular occupational or environmental toxins or stresses.[22] Finally, medicine is increasing its ability to treat genetic conditions. Wivel and Walters discuss several categories of human genetic intervention: somatic cell gene therapy involving correction of genetic defects in any human cells except germ or reproductive cells; germ-line modification involving correction or prevention of genetic deficiencies through the transfer of properly functioning genes into reproductive cells; and use of somatic and/or germ-line modifications to effect selected physical and mental characteristics, with the aim of influencing such features as physical appearance or physical abilities (in the patient or in succeeding generations).[23] While use of germ-line therapy, particularly when designed to enhance human capability, is highly charged, most people agree that the ability to prevent and treat genetic disease offers patients a chance for health and well-being that would not be possible absent genetic intervention. Clinical applications of genetic technologies are also possible in other areas; for example, scientists have reported progress in transplanting animal organs into humans. Insertion of human genes into animals would render their organs more suitable for transplantation into humans without substantial tissue rejection.[24]

Improved research. Despite substantial progress in the Human Genome Initiative, a great deal more must be understood about the detection, prevention, and treatment of genetic disease. Genetic research holds the potential for improving diagnosis, counseling, and treatment for persons with genetic conditions or traits. Research can help determine the frequency and distribution of genetic traits in various populations, the interconnections between genotypes and phenotypes, and the safety and efficacy of various genetic interventions.

Genetic data bases, containing DNA and/or stored tissue, could make this kind of research less expensive by reducing the costs of collecting and analyzing data, more trustworthy by increasing the accuracy of the data, and more generalizable to segments of the population by assuring the completeness of the data.

Protection of public health. While traditional genetic diagnosis, treatment, and research is oriented toward the individual patient, genetic applications can also benefit the public health. There is considerable utility in using population-based data to promote community health. Genomic data can help track the incidence, patterns, and trends of genetic carrier states or disease in populations. Carefully planned surveillance or epidemiological activities facilitate rapid identification of health needs. This permits reproductive counseling, testing, health education, and treatment resources to be better targeted, and points the way for future research. For example, recent epidemiological research of DNA samples from Eastern European Jewish women found that nearly 1 percent contained a specific gene mutation that may predispose them to breast and ovarian cancer. This finding offered the first evidence from a large study that an alteration in the gene, BRCA1, is present at measurable levels not only in families at high risk for disease, but also in a specific group of the general population. Certainly, evidence of enhanced risk of disease in certain populations, such as sickle cell in African Americans or Tay-Sachs in Ashkenazi Jews, may foster discrimination against these groups. At the same time, population-based genetic findings support other clinical studies to evaluate the risk to populations bearing the mutation or to determine whether BRCA1 testing should be offered to particular ethnic groups as part of their routine health care.

PRIVACY IMPLICATIONS OF GENOMIC DATA

The vision of a comprehensive genetic information system described above is technologically feasible, and a well-functioning system would likely achieve significant benefits for individuals, families, and populations. However, to decide whether to continue to accumulate vast amounts of genomic information, it is necessary to measure the probable effects on the privacy of these groups. The diminution in privacy entailed in genetic information systems depends on the sensitive nature of the data, as well as on the safeguards against unauthorized disclosure of the information.

GENOMIC DATA AND HARMS OF DISCLOSURE

Privacy is not simply the almost inexhaustible opportunities for access to data; it is also the intimate nature of those data and the potential harm to persons whose privacy is violated. Health records contain much information with multiple uses: demographic information; financial information; information about disabilities, special needs, and other eligibility criteria for government benefits; and medical information. This information is frequently sufficient to provide a detailed profile of the individual and that person's family. Traditional medical records, moreover, are only a subset of records containing personal information held by social services, immigration, and law enforcement.

Genomic data can personally identify an individual and his/her parents, siblings, and children, and provide a current and future health profile with far more scientific accuracy than other health data. The features of a person revealed by genetic information are fixed — unchanging and unchangeable. Although some genomic data contain information that is presently indecipherable, they may be unlocked by new scientific understanding; but such discoveries could raise questions about improper usage of stored DNA samples. Finally, societies have previously sought to control the gene pool through eugenics. This practice is particularly worrisome because different genetic characteristics occur with different frequencies in racial and ethnic populations.

The combination of emerging computer and genetic technologies poses particularly compelling privacy concerns. Scientists have the capacity to store a million DNA fragments on one silicon microchip.[25] While this technology can markedly facilitate research, screening, and treatment of genetic conditions, it may also permit a significant reduction in privacy through its capacity to store and decipher unimaginable quantities of highly sensitive data.

A variety of underlying harms to patients may result from unwanted disclosures of these sensitive genomic data. A breach of privacy can result in economic harms, such as loss of employment, insurance, or housing. It can also result in social or psychological harms. Disclosure of some conditions can be stigmatizing, and can cause embarrassment, social isolation, and a loss of self-esteem. These risks are especially great when the perceived causes of the health condition include drug or alcohol dependency, mental illness, mental retardation, obesity, or other genetically linked conditions revealed by a person's DNA. Even though genomic information can be unreliable or extraordinarily complicated to decipher, particularly with multifactorial disease or other complicated personal characteristics (for instance, intelligence), public perceptions attribute great weight to genetic findings and simply aggravate the potential stigma and discrimination.

Maintaining reasonable levels of privacy is essential to the effective functioning of the health and public health systems. Patients are less likely to divulge sensitive information to health professionals, such as family histories, if they are not assured that their confidences will be respected. The consequence of incomplete information is that patients may not receive adequate diagnosis and treatment. Persons at risk of genetic disease may not come forward for the testing, counseling, or treatment. Informational privacy, therefore, not only protects patients' social and economic interests, but also their health and the health of their families and discrete populations.

LEGAL PROTECTION OF GENETIC PRIVACY AND SECURITY OF HEALTH INFORMATION

One method of affording some measure of privacy protection is to furnish rigorous legal safeguards. Current legal safeguards are inadequate, fragmented, and inconsistent, and contain major gaps in coverage. Significant theoretical problems also exist.

CONSTITUTIONAL RIGHT TO PRIVACY

A considerable literature has emerged on the existence and extent of a constitutional right to informational privacy independent of the Fourth Amendment prohibition on unreasonable searches and seizures. To some, judicial recognition of a constitutional right to informational privacy is particularly important because the government is an important collector and disseminator of information. Citizens, it is argued, should not have to rely on government to protect their privacy interests. Rather, individuals need protection from government itself, and an effective constitutional remedy is the surest method to prevent unauthorized government acquisition or disclosure of personal information. The problem with this approach is that the Constitution does not expressly provide a right to privacy, and the Supreme Court has curtailed constitutional protection both for decisional and informational privacy.[26] . . .

The right to privacy under the Constitution is, of course, limited to state action. As long as the federal or a state government itself collects information or requires other entities to collect it, state action will not be a central obstacle. However, collection and use of genomic data by private or quasi-private health data organizations, health plans, researchers, and insurers remains unprotected by the Constitution, particularly in light of an absence of government regulation or genetic data banking.

LEGISLATING HEALTH INFORMATION PRIVACY: THEORETICAL CONCERNS

Legislatures and agencies have designed a number of statutes and regulations to protect privacy. A full description and analysis of the legislation and regulation is undertaken elsewhere.[27] The Department of Health and Human Services described this body of legislation as "a morass of erratic law."[28] The law is fragmented, highly variable, and, at times, weak; the legislation treats some kinds of data as super-confidential, while providing virtually no protection for other kinds.

Health data are frequently protected as part of the physician-patient relationship. However, data collected in our information age is based only in small part on this relationship. Many therapeutic encounters in a managed care context are not with a primary care physician. Patients may see various nonphysician health professionals. Focusing legal protection on a single therapeutic relationship within this information environment is an anachronistic vestige of an earlier and simpler time in medicine. Moreover, the health record, as I pointed out, contains a substantial amount of information gathered from numerous primary and secondary sources. Patients' health records not only are kept in the office of a private physician or of a health plan, but also are kept by government agencies, regional health data base organizations, or information brokers. Data bases maintained in each of these settings will be collected and transmitted electronically, reconfigured, and linked.

Rules enforcing informational privacy in health care place a duty on the entity that possesses the information. Thus, the keeper of the record—whether private physician's office, a hospital, or a hospital maintenance organization—holds the primary duty to maintain the confidentiality of the data. The development of electronic health care networks permitting standardized patient-based information to flow nationwide, and perhaps worldwide, means that the current privacy protection system, which focuses on requiring the institution to protect its records, needs to be reconsidered. Our past thinking assumed a paper or automated record created and protected by the provider. We must now envision a patient-based record that anyone in the system can call up on a screen. Because location has less meaning in an electronic world, protecting privacy requires attaching protection to the health record itself, rather than to the institution that generates it.

GENETIC PRIVACY LEGISLATION

. . . Existing and proposed genetic-specific privacy statutes are founded on the premise that genetic information is sufficiently different from other health information to justify special treatment. Certainly, genomic data present compelling justifications for privacy protection: the sheer breadth of information discoverable; the potential to unlock secrets that are currently unknown about the person; the unique quality of the information enabling certain identification of the individual; the stability of DNA rendering distant future applications possible; and the generalizability of the data to families, genetically related communities, and ethnic and racial populations.

It must also be observed that genetic-specific privacy statutes could create inconsistencies in the rules governing dissemination of health information. Under genetic-specific privacy statutes, different standards would apply to data held by the same entity, depending on whether genetic analysis had been used. The creation of strict genetic-specific standards may significantly restrain the dissemination of genomic data (even to the point of undermining legitimate health goals), while nongenomic data receive insufficient protection. Arguments that genomic data deserve special protection must reckon with the fact that other health conditions raise similar sensitivity issues (for examples, HIV infection, tuberculosis, STDs, and mental illnesses). Indeed, carving out special legal protection for sensitive data may be regarded as inherently faulty, because the desired scope of privacy encompassing a health condition varies from individual to individual. Some patients may be just as sensitive about prevalent nongenetic or multifactorial diseases like cancer and heart disease as they are about diseases with a unique genetic component. Even if it could be argued that most diseases will one day be found to be, at least in part, genetically caused, this will still raise questions about why purely viral or bacterial diseases should receive less, or different, protection.

Finally, adoption of different privacy and security rules for genomic data could pose practical problems in our health information infrastructure. The flow of medical information is rarely restricted to particular diseases or conditions. Transmission of electronic data for purposes of medical consultation, research, or public health is seldom limited to one kind of information. Requiring hospitals, research institutions, health departments, insurers, and others to maintain separate privacy and security standards (and perhaps separate record systems) for genomic data may not be wise or practical. A more thoughtful solution would be to adopt a comprehensive federal statute on health information privacy, with explicit language applying privacy and security standards to genomic information. If genomic data were insufficiently protected by these legal standards, additional safeguards could be enacted.

UNIFORM STANDARDS FOR ACQUISITION AND DISCLOSURE OF HEALTH INFORMATION

I previously proposed uniform national standards for the acquisition and disclosure of health information. Below, I briefly describe those standards and outline how they would apply equally to genomic data.

Substantive and procedural review. Many see the collection of health data as an inherent good. Even if the social good to be achieved is not immediately apparent, it is always possible that some future benefit could accrue. But despite optimism in the power of future technology, the diminution in privacy attributable to the collection of health data demands that the acquisition of information serve some substantial interest. The burden rests on the collector of information not merely to assert a substantial public interest, but also to demonstrate that it would be achieved. Information should only be collected under the following conditions: (1) the need for the information is substantial; (2) the collection of the data would actually achieve the objective; (3) the purpose could not be achieved without the collection of identifiable information; and (4) the data would be held only for a period necessary to meet the valid objectives. Thus, collectors of genomic information would have to justify the collection and the use of the information, and they would have to show why collection of tissue or DNA is necessary to achieve the purpose.

The collection of large amounts of health information, such as a tissue or a DNA repository, not only requires a substantive justification, but also warrants procedural review. Decisions to create health data bases, whether by government or private sector, ought to require procedural review. Some mechanism for independent review by a dispassionate expert body would provide a forum for examination of the justification for the data collection, the existence of thoughtful consent procedures, and the maintenance of adequate privacy and security.

Autonomy to control personal data. If a central ethical value behind privacy is respect for personal autonomy, then individuals from whom data are collected

must be afforded the right to know about and to approve the uses of those data. Traditional informed consent requires that a competent person have adequate information to make a genuinely informed choice. However, a few objective standards have been developed to measure the adequacy of consent. To render consent meaningful, the process must incorporate clear content areas: how privacy and security will be maintained; the person's right of ownership of, and control over, the data; specific instructions on means of access, review, and correction of records; the length of time that the information will be stored and the circumstances when it would be expunged; authorized third-party access to the data; and future secondary uses. If secondary uses of those data go beyond the scope of the original consent (for example, use of human tissue to create cell lines or disclosure to employers or insurers) additional consent must be sought.

Right to review and correct personal data. A central tenet of fair information practices is that individuals have the right to review data about themselves and to correct or amend inaccurate or incomplete records. This right respects a person's autonomy, while assuring the integrity of data. Individuals cannot meaningfully control the use of personal data unless they are fully aware of their contents and can assess the integrity of the information. Individuals can also help determine if the record is accurate and complete. Health data can only achieve essential societal purposes if they are correct and reasonably comprehensive. One method, therefore, of ensuring the reliability of health records to provide a full and fair procedure to challenge the accuracy of records and to make corrections. Thus, persons must be fully aware of the tissue and genetic material that is collected and stored. Moreover, they must be fully informed about the *content* and *meaning* of any genetic analysis — past, current, or future. For instance, if an individual consents to the collection of tissue for epidemiological research on breast cancer, he/she would be entitled to see and correct any information derived from that tissue. If, in the future, the tissue were used to predict, say, dementia in the patient, he/she would have to consent and would also have the right to see and correct any new information derived from that particular genetic analysis.

Use of data for intended purposes. Entities that possess information have obligations that go beyond their own needs and interests. In some sense, they hold the information on behalf of the individual and, more generally, for the benefit of all patients in the health system. A confidence is reposed in a professional who possesses personal information for the benefit of others. They have an obligation to use health information only for limited purposes; to disclose information only for purposes for which the data were obtained; to curtail disclosure to the minimum necessary to accomplish the purpose; and to maintain an accounting of any disclosure.

The idea of seeing holders of information as trustees has special force with genomic data. Because DNA might unlock the most intimate secrets of human beings and holds the potential for unethical uses, those who possess it must meet the highest ethical standards.

CONCLUSION

The human genome retains enormous appeal in the United States. Americans, enamored with the power of science, often turn to genetic technology for easy answers to perplexing medical and social questions. This exaggerated perception is problematic. Genomic information can wield considerable influence, affecting the decisions of health care professionals, patients and their families, employers, insurers, and the justice system. How does society control this information without stifling the real potential for human good that it offers? The answer to this question must be in recognizing that trade-offs are inevitable. Permitting the Human Genome Initiative to proceed unabated will have costs in personal privacy. While careful security safeguards will not provide complete privacy, the public should be assured that genomic information will be treated in an orderly and respectful manner and that individual claims of control over those data will be adjudicated fairly.

NOTES

1. L.O. Gostin, "Health Information Privacy," *Cornell Law Review,* 80 (1995): 451–528.

2. L.O. Gostin et al., "Privacy and Security of Personal Information in a New Health Care System," *JAMA,* 270 (1993): 2487–93.

3. P.T. Rowley, "Genetic Screening: Marvel or Menace?," *Science,* 225 (1984): 138–44.

4. Id.

5. B.S. Wilfond and K. Nolan, "National Policy Development for the Clinical Application of Genetic Diagnostic Techniques: Lessons from Cystic Fibrosis," *JAMA,* 270 (1993): 2948–54.

6. G. Kolata, "Tests to Assess Risks for Cancer Raising Questions," *New York Times,* Mar. 27, 1995, at A1; and E. Tanouye, "Gene Testing for Cancer to be Widely Available, Raising Thorny Questions, *Wall Street Journal,* Dec. 14, 1995, at B1.

7. L. Gostin, "Genetic Discrimination: The Use of Genetically Based Diagnostic and Prognostic Tests by Employers and Insurers," *American Journal of Law & Medicine,* XII (1991): 109–44.

8. C. Ezzell, "Panel Oks DNA Fingerprints in Court Cases," *Science News,* 141 (1992): at 261; and G. Kolata, "Chief Says Panel Backs Courts' Use of a Genetic Test," *New York Times,* Apr. 15, 1992, at A1.

9. S.M. Suter, "Whose Genes Are These Anyway? Familial Conflicts Over Access to Genetic Information," *Michigan Law Review,* 91 (1993): 1854–908.

10. W.E. Leary, "A Search for Lincoln's DNA," *New York Times,* Feb. 10, 1991, at 1.

11. H.R. 5612, Cong. 101, Sess. 2 (Sept. 13, 1990).

12. P.R. Reilly, letter, "DNA Banking," *American Journal of Human Genetics,* 51 (1992): at 32–33.

13. Id.

14. Deputy Secretary of Defense Memorandum No. 47803 (Dec. 16, 1991).

15. E.D. Shapiro and M. L. Weinberg, "DNA Data Banking: The Dangerous Erosion of Privacy," *Cleveland State Law Review,* 38 (1990): 455–86 (many states authorize the banking of DNA usually for convicted sex offenders; the FBI is establishing a computerized DNA data bank); Burk, *supra* note 3; and Note, "The Advent of DNA Databanks: Implications for Information Privacy," *American Journal of Law & Medicine,* XVI (1990): 381–98.

16. Suter, *supra* note 9.

17. J.E. McEwen and P.R. Reilly, "Stored Guthrie Cards as DNA 'Banks'," *American Journal of Human Genetics,* 55 (1994): 196–200.

18. Id.

19. Department of Health and Human Services, *National Health and Nutrition Examination Survey III* (1994).

20. D. Nelkin and S. Lindee, *The DNA Mystique: The Gene as a Cultural Icon* (New York: W.H. Freeman, 1995); D. Nelkin, "The Double-Edged Helix," *New York Times,* Feb. 4, 1994, at A23; and R. Weiss, "Are We More Than the Sum of Our Genes?," *Washington Post Health,* Oct. 3, 1995, at 10.

21. N. Fost, "The Cystic Fibrosis Gene: Medical and Social Implication for Heterozygote Detection," *JAMA,* 263 (1990): 2777–83.

22. P. Reilly, "Rights, Privacy, and Genetic Screening," *Yale Journal of Biology & Medicine,* 64 (1991): 43–45.

23. N.A. Wivel and L. Walters, "Germ-Line Gene Modification and Disease Prevention: Some Medical and Ethical Perspectives," *Science,* 262 (1993): 533–38.

24. P.J. Hilts, "Gene Transfers Offer New Hope for Interspecies Organ Transplants," *New York Times,* Oct. 19, 1993, at A1.

25. R.T. King Jr., "Soon, a Chip Will Test Blood for Diseases," *Wall Street Journal,* Oct. 25, 1994, at B1.

26. *Webster v. Reproductive Health Servs.,* 492 U.S. 490 (1989); *Bowers v. Hardwick,* 478 U.S. 186 (1986); and *Paul v. Davis,* 424 U.S. 693 (1976).

27. Gostin, *supra* note 1, at 499–508.

28. Workgroup for Electronic Data Interchange, *Obstacles to EDI in the Current Health Care Infrastructure* (Washington, D.C.: DHHS, 1992): app. 4, at iii.

SUGGESTED READINGS

TRUTH TELLING AND THE MANAGEMENT
OF BAD NEWS

Asai, Atsushi. "Should Physicians Tell Patients the Truth?" *Western Journal of Medicine* 163 (1995), 36–39.

Bok, Sissela. *Lying: Moral Choice in Public and Private Life.* New York: Pantheon Books, 1978.

Beauchamp, Tom L. "Looking Back and Judging our Predecessors." *Kennedy Institute of Ethics Journal* 6 (1996), 251–70.

Buckman, R. F. *How to Break Bad News.* Baltimore: Johns Hopkins University Press, 1992.

Burack, Jeffrey H.; Back, Anthony L.; and Pearlman, Robert A. "Provoking Nonepileptic Seizures: The Ethics of Deceptive Diagnostic Testing." *Hastings Center Report* 27 (Jul.–Aug. 1997), 24–33.

Cabot, Richard C. "The Use of Truth and Falsehood in Medicine," as edited by Jay Katz from the 1909 version. *Connecticut Medicine* 42 (1978), 189–94.

De Deyn, P. P., and D'Hooge, R. "Placebos in Clinical Practice and Research," *Journal of Medical Ethics* 22 (1996), 140–46.

Erde, Edmund L.; Drickamer, Margaret A.; and Lachs, Mark S. "Should Patients with Alzheimer's Disease Be Told Their Diagnosis?" *New England Journal of Medicine* 326 (Apr. 2, 1992), 947–51.

Gillon, Raanan. "Is There an Important Moral Distinction for Medical Ethics Between Lying and Other Forms of Deception?" *Journal of Medical Ethics* 19 (1993), 131–32.

Hattori, Hiroyuki, *et al.* "The Patient's Right to Information in Japan—Legal Rules and Doctor's Opinions." *Social Science and Medicine* 32 (1991), 1007–16.

Jackson, Jennifer. "Telling the Truth." *Journal of Medical Ethics* 17 (1991), 5–9.

Novack, Dennis, *et al.* "Physicians' Attitudes Toward Using Deception to Resolve Difficult Ethical Problems." *Journal of the American Medical Association* 261 (May 26, 1989), 2980–85.

Orona, Celia J.; Koenig, Barbara A.; and Davis, Anne J. "Cultural Aspects of Nondisclosure." *Cambridge Quarterly of Healthcare Ethics* 3 (1994), 338–46.

Potter, Nancy. "Discretionary Power, Lies, and Broken Trust." *Theoretical Medicine* 17 (1996), 329–52.

Ptacek, J. T., and Eberhardt, Tara L. "Breaking Bad News: A Review of the Literature." *Journal of the American Medical Association* 276 (Aug. 14, 1996), 496–502.

Siminoff, L. A.; Fetting, J. H.; and Abeloff, M. D. "Doctor–Patient Communication about Breast Cancer Adjuvant Therapy." *Journal of Clinical Oncology* 7 (1989), 1192–1200.

Spece, Roy G.; Shimm, David S.; and Buchanan, Allen E., eds. *Conflicts of Interest in Clinical Practice and Research.* New York: Oxford University Press, 1996.

Weir, Robert. "Truthtelling in Medicine." *Perspectives in Biology and Medicine* 24 (Autumn 1980), 95–112.

INFORMED CONSENT

American Psychiatric Association. Council on Psychiatry and Law. "American Psychiatric Association Resource Document on Principles of Informed Consent in Psychiatry." *Journal of the American Academy of Psychiatry and the Law* 25 (1997), 121–25.

American Society of Human Genetics. "ASHG Report: Statement on Informed Consent for Genetic Research." *American Journal of Human Genetics* 59 (1996), 471–74.

Applebaum, Paul S.; Lidz, Charles W.; and Meisel, Alan. *Informed Consent: Legal Theory and Clinical Practice.* New York: Oxford University Press, 1987.

Beauchamp, Tom L., and Childress, James F. *Principles of Biomedical Ethics.* 4th ed. New York: Oxford University Press, 1994, Chap. 3.

Bok, Sissela. "Informed Consent in Tests of Patient Reliability." *Journal of the American Medical Association* 267 (February 26, 1992), 1118–19.

———. "Shading the Truth in Seeking Informed Consent." *Kennedy Institute of Ethics Journal* 5 (1995), 1–17.

Buchanan, Allen E., and Brock, Dan W. *Deciding for Others: The Ethics of Surrogate Decision Making.* Cambridge: Cambridge University Press, 1989.

Cocking, Dean, and Oakley, Justin. "Medical Experimentation, Informed Consent and Using People." *Bioethics* 8 (1994), 293–311.

Davis, Vivianne de Vahl. "How Informed Is Informed Consent?" *Bulletin of Medical Ethics* 76 (1992), 13–18.

Faden, Ruth. "Informed Consent and Clinical Research." *Kennedy Institute of Ethics Journal* 6 (1996), 356–59.

———, and Beauchamp, Tom L. *A History and Theory of Informed Consent.* New York: Oxford University Press, 1986.

Fan, Ruiping. "Self-Determination vs. Family-Determination: Two Incommensurable Principles of Autonomy." *Bioethics* 11 (1997), 309–22.

Geller, Gail; Strauss, Misha; Bernhardt, Barbara A.; and Holtzman, Neil A. "'Decoding' Informed Consent: Insights from Women Regarding Breast Cancer Susceptibility Testing." *Hastings Center Report* 27 (1997), 28–33.

Geller, Gail, *et al.* "Genetic Testing for Susceptibility to Adult-Onset Cancer: The Process and Content of Informed Consent." *Journal of the American Medical Association* 277 (May 14, 1997), 1467–74.

Gunderson, Martin. "Justifying a Principle of Informed Consent: A Case Study in Autonomy-based Ethics." *Public Affairs Quarterly* 4 (1990), 249–65.

Gunderson, Martin; Mayo, David; and Rhame, Frank. "Routine HIV Testing of Hospital Patients and Pregnant Women: Informed Consent in the Real World." *Kennedy Institute of Ethics Journal* 6 (1996), 161–82.

Hewlett, Sarah. "Consent to Clinical Research—Adequately Voluntary or Substantially Influenced?" *Journal of Medical Ethics* 22 (1996), 232–37.

Katz, Jay. *The Silent World of Doctor and Patient.* New York: Free Press, 1984.

———. "Informed Consent—A Fairy Tale?: Law's Vision." *University of Pittsburgh Law Review* 39 (1977), 137–74.

Lidz, Charles W., *et al. Informed Consent: A Study of Decisionmaking in Psychiatry.* New York: Guilford Press, 1984.

Meisel, Alan, and Kuczewski, Mark. "Legal and Ethical Myths About Informed Consent." *Archives of Internal Medicine* 156 (December 9–23, 1996), 2521–26.

Merz, Jon F., and Fischoff, Baruch. "Informed Consent Does Not Mean Rational Consent." *The Journal of Legal Medicine* 11 (1990), 321–50.

President's Commission for the Study of Ethical Problems in Medicine and Biomedical and Behavioral Research. Vols. 1–3. *Making Health Care Decisions.* Washington: Government Printing Office, 1982.

Veatch, Robert M. *The Patient as Partner: A Theory of Human-Experimentation Ethics.* Bloomington, IN: Indiana University Press, 1987. Chaps. 3 and 12.

Wear, Stephen. *Informed Consent.* Boston: Kluwer, 1993.

PATIENT SELF-DETERMINATION
AND ADVANCE DIRECTIVES

Ackerman, Terrence F. "Forsaking the Spirit for the Letter of the Law: Advance Directives in Nursing Homes." *Journal of the American Geriatrics Society* 45 (1997), 114–16.

Advance Directives Seminar Group. "Advance Directives: Are They an Advance?" *Canadian Medical Association Journal* 146 (January 15, 1992), 127–34.

Brock, Dan. "A Proposal for the Use of Advance Directives in the Treatment of Incompetent Mentally Ill Persons." *Bioethics* 7 (1993), 247–56.

———. "What Is the Moral Authority of Family Members to Act as Surrogates for Incompetent Patients? " *Milbank Quarterly* 74 (1996), 599–618.

Cattorini, Paolo, and Reichlin, Massimo. "Persistent Vegetative State: A Presumption to Treat." *Theoretical Medicine* 18 (1997) 263–81.

Celesia, Gastone G. "Persistent Vegetative State: Clinical and Ethical Issues." *Theoretical Medicine* 18 (1997), 221–36.

Emanuel, Linda. "Advance Directives: What Have We Learned So Far?" *The Journal of Clinical Ethics* 4 (1993), 8–16.

Engel, John D., *et al.* "The Patient Self-Determination Act and Advance Directives: Snapshots of Activities in a Tertiary Health Care Center." *Journal of Medical Humanities* 18 (1997), 193–208.

King, Nancy. *Making Sense of Advance Directives.* Dordrecht: Kluwer Academic Publishers, 1991.

May, Thomas. "Reassessing the Reliability of Advance Directives." *Cambridge Quarterly of Healthcare Ethics* 6 (1997), 325–38.

Olick, Robert. "Approximating Informed Consent and Fostering Communication: The Anatomy of an Advance Directive." *Journal of Clinical Ethics* 2 (1991), 181–95.

Teno, Joan M., and Lynn, Joanne, *et al.* "Do Formal Advance Directives Affect Resuscitation Decisions and the Use of Resources for Seriously Ill Patients?" *Journal of Clinical Ethics* 5 (1994), 23–30 [with following Commentary].

Sehgal, A., *et al.* "How Strictly Do Dialysis Patients Want Their Advance Directives Followed? *Journal of the American Medical Association* 267 (January 1, 1992), 59–63.

Omnibus Budget Reconciliation Act of 1990. Public Law 101–508 (Nov. 5, 1990). §§ 4206, 4751. See 42 USC, scattered sections.

Welie, Jos V. M. "The Patient Self-Determination Act: A Legal Solution for a Moral Dilemma." *Cambridge Quarterly of Healthcare Ethics* 1 (1992), 75–79.

CONFIDENTIALITY AND PRIVACY

Allen, Anita. *Uneasy Access: Privacy for Women in a Free Society.* Totowa, NJ: Rowman and Allanheld, 1987.

Bayer, Ronald, and Toomey, Kathleen E. "HIV Prevention and the Two Faces of Partner Notification." *American Journal of Public Health* 82 (Aug. 1992), 1158–64.

Beauchamp, Tom L., and Childress, James F. *Principles of Biomedical Ethics.* 4th ed. New York: Oxford University Press, 1994, Chaps. 3 and 7.

Beck, James C., ed. *Confidentiality Versus the Duty to Protect: Foreseeable Harm in the Practice of Psychiatry.* Washington: American Psychiatry Press, Inc., 1990.

Bok, Sissela. *Secrets: On the Ethics of Concealment and Revelation.* New York: Pantheon Books, 1983.

Ford, Carol A., *et al.* "Influence of Physician Confidentiality Assurances on Adolescents' Willingness to Disclose Information and Seek Future Health Care: A Randomized Controlled Trial." *Journal of the American Medical Association* 278 (1997), 1029–34.

Gostin, Lawrence O. "Health Information Privacy." *Cornell Law Review* 80 (1995), 451–528.

———. *et al.* "Privacy and Security of Personal Information in a New Health Care System." *Journal of the American Medical Association* 270 (Nov. 24, 1993), 2487–93.

Gillon, Raanan. "Confidentiality." *British Medical Journal* 291 (December 7, 1985), 1634–36.

Kottow, Michael H. "Medical Confidentiality: an Intransigent and Absolute Obligation." *Journal of Medical Ethics* 12 (1986), 117–22.

Powers, Madison. "Privacy and the Control of Genetic Information." In Mark S. Frankel and Albert Teich, eds., *The Genetic Frontier: Ethics, Law, and Policy.* Washington: AAAS, 1994, 77–100.

Roback, Howard B., *et al.* "Confidentiality Dilemmas in Group Psychotherapy with Substance-Dependent Physicians." *American Journal of Psychiatry* 153 (1996), 1250–60.

Schoeman, Ferdinand D., ed. *Philosophical Dimensions of Privacy: An Anthology.* New York: Cambridge University Press, 1984.

Turkington, Richard C.; Trubow, George B.; and Allen, Anita L., eds. *Privacy: Cases and Materials.* Houston: John Marshall Publishing Co., 1992.

Veatch, Robert M. "Consent, Confidentiality, and Research" [editorial]. *New England Journal of Medicine* 336 (March 20, 1997), 869–70.

Weiss, Barry D. "Confidentiality Expectations of Patients, Physicians, and Medical Students." *Journal of the American Medical Association* 247 (1982), 2695–97.

BIBLIOGRAPHIES AND ENCYCLOPEDIAS
WITH BIBLIOGRAPHIES

Bioethicsline: Computer Retrieval Service.

Encyclopedia of Bioethics, ed. Warren Reich, 2d ed., New York: Macmillan, 1995.

Encyclopedia of Ethics, ed. Lawrence Becker and Charlotte Becker. New York: Garland Publishing Inc., 1992.

Lineback, Richard H., ed. *Philosopher's Index.* Vols. 1– . Bowling Green, OH: Philosophy Documentation Center, Bowling Green State University. Issued Quarterly.

Walters, LeRoy, and Kahn, Tamar Joy, eds. *Bibliography of Bioethics.* Vols. 1– . New York: Free Press. Issued annually.

4.

Abortion and Maternal-Fetal Relations

INTRODUCTION

Despite the legality of abortion in many western nations, questions of its ethical and legal acceptability continue to be widely debated. In this chapter contemporary ethical and legal issues about both abortion and maternal-fetal relations will be examined.

THE PROBLEM OF MORAL JUSTIFICATION

An abortion might be desired for many reasons: psychological trauma, pregnancy caused by rape, the inadvertent use of fetus-deforming drugs, genetic predisposition to disease, prenatally diagnosed birth defects, and many personal and family reasons such as the financial burden or intrusiveness of a child. These reasons explain why an abortion is often viewed as a desirable way to extricate a woman or a family from an undesired circumstance. But an *explanation* of this sort does not answer the problem of *justification:* What reasons, if any, are sufficient to justify the act of aborting a human fetus?

Some contend that abortion is never acceptable or, at most, is permissible only if it is necessary to bring about some great moral good such as saving a pregnant woman's life. This view is commonly called the conservative theory of abortion because it emphasizes conserving life. Traditionally, Roman Catholics have been exponents of the conservative approach, but they are by no means its only advocates. The case for this point of view is presented in this chapter by Don Marquis, who does not rely on any form of religious claim to defend his views. The opposite conclusion is that abortion is always permissible, whatever the state of fetal development. This outlook is commonly termed the liberal theory of abortion because it emphasizes freedom of choice and the right of a woman to make decisions that affect her body. Mary Anne Warren defends this approach in this chapter.

Many writers defend theories intermediate between liberal and conservative approaches. They hold that abortion is ethically permissible up to a specified stage of fetal development or for some moral reasons that are believed to be sufficient to warrant abortions under special circumstances. Baruch Brody discusses possible intermediate theories leaning toward conservatism, while Judith Thomson's essay suggests an intermediate theory that leans toward liberalism.

THE ONTOLOGICAL STATUS OF THE FETUS

Recent controversies about abortion focus on ethical problems of our obligations to fetuses and on what rights, if any, fetuses possess. A more basic issue, some say, concerns the kind of entities fetuses are. Following current usage, this problem is one of *ontological status.* An account of the kind of entities fetuses are will determine their status and will have important implications for the issues of our obligations to fetuses and their rights.

Several layers of questions may be distinguished about ontological status: (1) Is the fetus an individual organism? (2) Is the fetus biologically a human being? (3) Is the fetus psychologically a human being? and (4) Is the fetus a person? It is widely agreed that one attributes a more significant status to the fetus by granting that it is fully a human being (biologically and psychologically), rather than merely saying that it is an individual organism, and that one enhances its status still further by attributing personhood to the fetus.

Many are willing to concede that an individual life begins at fertilization but not willing to concede that there is a psychological human being or a person at fertilization. Others claim that the fetus is human biologically and psychologically at fertilization but not a person. Still others grant full personhood at fertilization. Those who espouse these views sometimes differ because they define one or the other of these terms differently. Many differences, however, derive from theoretical disagreements about what constitutes life, humanity, or personhood.

THE CONCEPT OF HUMANITY

The concept of human life has long been at the center of the abortion discussion. It is a confusing concept, because "human life" can take two very different meanings. On the one hand, it can mean *biological human life,* that group of biological characteristics that set the human species apart from nonhuman species. On the other hand, "human life" can be used to mean *life that is distinctively human* — that is, a life characterized by psychological rather than biological properties. For example, the ability to use symbols, to imagine, to love, and to perform higher intellectual skills are among the most distinctive human properties. Having these properties implies that one is a human being.

A simple example illustrates the differences between these two senses: Some infants with extreme disabilities die shortly after birth. They are born of human parents, and they are biologically human. However, they never exhibit any distinctively human psychological traits, and (in many cases) have no potential to do so. For these individuals it is not possible to make human life in the biological sense human in the psychological sense. We do not differentiate these two aspects of life in discourse about any other animal species. We do not, for example, speak of making feline life more distinctively feline. But we do meaningfully speak of making human life more human, and this usage makes sense because of the dual meaning just mentioned.

In discussions of abortion, it is important to be clear about which meaning is being employed when using the expression "the taking of human life."

THE CONCEPT OF PERSONHOOD

The concept of personhood may or may not be different from either the biological sense or the psychological sense of "human life." That is, one might claim that what it means to be a person is simply to have some properties that make an organism human in one or both of these senses. However, most writers have suggested a list of more demanding criteria for being a person. A list of conditions for being a person, similar to the following, is advanced by Warren and several other recent writers:

1. Self-consciousness
2. Freedom to act and the capacity to engage in purposeful sequences of actions
3. Having reasons for actions and the ability to appreciate reasons for acting
4. Ability to communicate with other persons using a language
5. Capacity to make moral judgments
6. Rationality

Sometimes it is said by those who propose such a list that in order to be a person, an individual need only satisfy one of the aforementioned criteria — for example, bona fide linguistic behavior (4) — but need not also satisfy the other conditions (2–3, 5–6). Others say that all of these conditions must be satisfied. Nonetheless, there is now a broad consensus that more than one of the above criteria is necessary to qualify as a person. It allegedly follows that fetuses, newborns, profoundly brain-damaged persons, and most if not all animals fail the cognitive criteria, and so do not have the moral standing conferred by the category of person. These creatures might gain moral protections in some other way, but no metaphysical, biological, or status-conferring category provides them with moral protection on this account. However, the dominant and prior question is whether any list approximating (1)–(6) is acceptable. Marquis, Brody, and Thomson tend not to view the core problems of abortion as turning on the acceptance or rejection of any such list.

The problem of ontological status is further complicated by a factor related to the biological development of the fetus. It is important to specify the point of development at which an entity achieves the status of a human or a person. Locating the crucial point of development is a central task in Brody's essay and also in the opinions in *Roe v. Wade* and *Planned Parenthood v. Casey* of the U.S. Supreme Court.

One polar position is that the fetus never satisfies any of the criteria mentioned above and therefore has *no ontological status* (of any moral importance). Warren defends this view. The opposite position is that the fetus always has *full ontological status* in regard to all of the significant measures of status. Marquis supports a version of this view, to the effect that the loss of a future to the fetus (if killed) is as great a loss as that suffered by an adult human who is killed. There are many intermediate positions, which all draw the line somewhere between the extremes of conception and birth. For example, the line may be drawn at quickening or viability, or when brain waves are first present, as Brody argues.

THE MORAL STATUS OF THE FETUS

The notion of "moral status" has been explicated in several ways. In a weak sense, this term refers to a standing, grade, or rank of moral importance or of moral value. In a stronger and more common sense, "status" means to have rights, or the functional equivalent of rights, in the form of having protected interests and being positioned to make valid claims (or to have them asserted on one's behalf). Thus, having moral status is to qualify under some range of moral protections. If fetuses have *full moral status* then they possess the same rights as those who have been born. Brody holds this thesis for at least some periods of fetal development, and Marquis's analysis suggests it for all periods. By contrast, many writers hold that fetuses have only a *partial moral status* and therefore only a partial set of rights; and some maintain that fetuses possess no moral status and therefore no rights, as Warren maintains. If Warren's account is accepted, then the fetus has no more right to life than a body cell or a tumor, and an abortion is no more morally objectionable than surgery to remove the tumor. But if the full-status view is accepted, fetuses possess the rights possessed by human beings, and an abortion is as objectionable as any common killing of an innocent person.

Theories of moral status are often directly linked with theories of ontological status. A typical conservative thesis is that because the line between the human and the nonhuman is properly drawn at conception, the fetus has full ontological status and, therefore, full moral status. A typical liberal claim is that the line between the human and the nonhuman must be drawn at birth; the fetus has no significant ontological status and, therefore, no moral status. Some liberals argue that even though the fetus is biologically human, it nonetheless is not human in an ontologically significant sense and, therefore, has no significant moral status.

This claim is usually accompanied by the thesis that only persons have a significant onto-logical status, and because fetuses are not persons they have no moral status (see Warren).

Moderates use a diverse mixture of arguments, which sometimes do and sometimes do not combine an ontological account with a moral one. Typical of moderate views is the claim that the line between the human and the nonhuman or the line between persons and nonpersons should be drawn at some point between conception and birth. Therefore, the fetus has no significant moral status during some stages of growth but does have significant moral status beginning at some later stage. For example, the line may be drawn at viability, with the result that the fetus is given either full moral status or partial moral status at via-bility. Some legal strategies adopted to protect the rights of the pregnant woman in the opin-ions in U.S. Supreme Court cases involved a similar although not identical premise about the role of viability.

PROBLEMS OF CONFLICTING RIGHTS

If either the liberal or the conservative view of the moral status of the fetus is adopted, the problem of morally justifying abortion may seem straightforward. If one holds that a fetus does not have human rights, abortions do not seem morally reprehensible and are pruden-tially justified just as other surgical procedures are. In contrast, if one accepts that a fetus at any stage of development is a human life with full moral status, then the equation "abortion is murder" seems to follow. By this reasoning abortion is never justified under any condi-tions or at least it can be permitted only if it is an instance of "justified homicide."

However, establishing a position on abortion is not this straightforward. Even on a con-servative theory there may be cases of justified abortion. For example, it has been argued by some conservatives that a pregnant woman may legitimately abort the fetus in "self-defense" if both will die unless the life of the fetus is terminated. In order to claim that abortion is always wrong, one must justify the claim that the fetus's "right to life" always overrides the pregnant woman's rights to life and liberty. Even if the conservative theory is construed so that human fetuses have equal rights, these rights may not always override all other moral rights. Here a proponent of this theory confronts the problem of conflicting rights: The unborn possess some rights (including a right to life) and pregnant women also possess rights (including a right to life). Those who possess the rights have a (prima facie) moral claim to be treated in accordance with their rights. But what happens when their rights conflict?

This problem is no less problematic for moderate theories of the moral status of the fetus. These theories provide moral grounds against arbitrary termination of fetal life (the fetus has some claim to protection against the actions of others), yet do not grant to the fetus (at least in some stages) the same rights to life possessed by persons. Accordingly, advocates of these theories are faced with the problem of specifying which rights should take precedence. Does the woman's right to decide what happens to her body justify abortion? Does pregnancy resulting from rape justify abortion? Does self-defense justify abortion? Does psychologi-cal damage justify abortion? Does knowledge of a grossly deformed fetus justify abortion? And further, does the fetus have a right to a "minimum quality of life," that is, to protection against wrongful life? Some of these issues about conflicting rights are raised by Thomson, who is then criticized by both Brody and Warren.

LEGAL ISSUES

The 1973 U.S. Supreme Court case of *Roe v. Wade* addressed the social problem of how abortion legislation may and may not be formulated in the attempt to protect the fetus against abortion. In the opinion of the court, the majority held that the right to privacy implicit in the Fourteenth Amendment is broad enough to encompass a woman's decision to have an abortion. This right overrides all other concerns until the fetus reaches the point of viability. After that point, the Court finds that states have a legitimate interest in protecting the life of the fetus, even if offering that protection directly competes with the woman's interest in liberty.

The Court's conception of a solution to the social problem of abortion has increasingly come under attack, both from external critics and internally from Supreme Court justices who have filed dissenting opinions. O'Connor presented an early version of these justices' views in the case of *City of Akron v. Akron Center for Reproductive Health.* She attacked the framework of *Roe,* maintaining that the Court's reasoning is not sufficient to justify its fundamental analytical framework of "stages" of pregnancy. She also argued that the state's compelling interests in maternal and fetal health will change as medical technology changes. O'Connor envisioned the following possibility: As the point of viability is pushed back by technological advancement, the point at which abortion is legally allowed must also be pushed back; as medical practices improve, the need to protect maternal health will also be reduced. She concluded that the *Roe* framework is unworkable and "on a collision course with itself."

In *Planned Parenthood v. Casey,* which appears in this chapter, O'Connor and two other justices join hands in reaffirming the essential holding in *Roe* that a woman has a legal right to seek an abortion prior to fetal viability, but they strip *Roe* of what they consider its untenable parts, especially the "trimester" conception of three stages of pregnancy. They argue that an undue burden test should be used rather than the trimester framework in evaluating any legal restrictions placed on access to abortion prior to viability. They then defend certain restrictions as not constituting undue burdens, including requirements of informed consent, parental notification and consent, and a 24-hour waiting period. However, they argue that a spousal notification provision does place an undue burden on a woman, and they therefore declare it legally invalid.

The history of Supreme Court decisions in Canada is also discussed in this chapter by Susan Dwyer. She provides a useful orientation to legal-moral issues in both Canada and the United States in the opening selection in the legal section.

MATERNAL-FETAL RELATIONSHIPS AND RIGHTS

We earlier encountered the problem of conflicting rights when the fetus's rights and the pregnant woman's rights conflict. Under the assumption that both have rights, we discussed whose rights should prevail if the woman seeks an abortion. Now we extend this discussion beyond abortion to problems of maternal-fetal relationships that arise not from the desire to end pregnancy, but from the condition of pregnancy itself.

In order to protect the fetus, various laws and court decisions have attempted to restrict or otherwise control the behavior of pregnant women and, in some cases, women who may become pregnant. In several historic law cases, U.S. courts held that women cannot legitimately be excluded from employment while pregnant merely because they are pregnant. Far more untested in the courts are circumstances in which corporations, municipalities, states, and institutions such as hospitals have adopted laws and policies that involve the coercion, detention, or incarceration of pregnant women for alcohol and drug abuse during pregnancy. In a few cases, physicians or courts have imposed or attempted to impose surgical and other medical interventions on women who do not consent to the procedures. Remedies include forced surgical procedures such as cesarean sections, forced medication such as penicillin, and incarceration to reduce the threat of harm. The motives are sometimes paternalistic—to protect the women—but in virtually all cases there is a motive to protect the fetus.

No one doubts that pregnant women have moral obligations to protect the fetus from harm, but do other persons gain a right to limit the liberty of pregnant women when they fail to live up to this obligation? Two areas of controversy have centered on (1) what constitutes a risk of harm to the fetus that is sufficiently grave to justify limitation of the woman's liberty, and (2) what constitutes a legitimate reason for the woman not to take steps to prevent harm. Regarding the first question, in some cases the possibility of harm is remote, whereas in other cases it is virtually certain that harm will occur. Regarding the second question, women sometimes have reasons for their actions that are elsewhere recognized as valid grounds for refusing treatment, such as religious beliefs that lead to refusing a surgical intervention requiring blood transfusions.

These two problems are parts of the larger question, "What constitutes a sufficient reason for legal coercion of pregnant women?" Many believe that it is fundamentally wrong to transform any *moral* obligation to prevent harm to or promote the health of the fetus into a *legal* obligation that allows institutions and courts to coerce pregnant women. Several reasons have been offered in support of this view. One is the right of all competent persons to refuse medical interventions, and another is that an action is normally made a legal violation only if one person has actually caused harm to another, not because there is merely a risk that harm may be caused. These reasons may be connected to arguments about negative consequences that will occur if laws restrict a pregnant woman's liberty. For example, some writers argue (1) that women who are most likely to harm a fetus by their behavior will be the first to stay away from prenatal care (where their abuse must by law be reported), thereby increasing rather than decreasing risk to the fetus; (2) that women will become skeptical and distrustful of their physicians; and (3) that society and the fetus will be worse off rather than better off by placing pregnant women in correctional facilities, which typically offer poor health care. Here the argument is that the negative consequences of these policies outweigh the positive consequences.

Persons who defend rights of fetuses are unpersuaded by arguments that weight the social consequences of public policies. They regard the fetus no less than the woman as a patient to be helped, and they see fetal abuse as a violation of rights and a cause of avoidable deaths and serious birth defects. These violations, they argue, are wrong irrespective of the consequences, and should be declared legal no less than moral wrongs. From their perspective, to prosecute a woman who abuses a fetus or to remove a child at birth from the woman's care is justifiable in order to protect the fetus or the newborn from harm.

The opening selection dealing with these issues—the U.S. Supreme Court opinion in *Automobile Workers v. Johnson Controls, Inc.*—illustrates one facet of these problems, and the one that has been most decisively handled in the courts. The problem in this case emerged in the 1980s, when it was reported in leading newspapers that fertile women workers were, in increasing numbers, electing to undergo voluntary sterilization rather than give up high-paying jobs involving exposure to chemicals that are potentially harmful to a developing fetus. This disclosure precipitated discussion of a new civil rights issue: Is a company unjustifiably discriminating against a woman in order to protect her unborn child?

At issue in *Johnson Controls* was a corporation's Fetal Protection Program. It held that women must be excluded unless they can prove sterility and that women of childbearing capacity would not be hired for positions that exposed them to unacceptable lead contamination or for positions from which they could transfer to such jobs. The reason for corporate policies excluding women from hazardous workplaces is straightforward: Of the thousands of toxic substances listed by the National Institute of Occupational Safety and Health (NIOSH), over fifty are animal mutagens (that is, they cause chromosomal damage to either the ova or the sperm cells), and roughly five hundred are animal teratogens (that is, they can cause deformations in a developing fetus). Corporations sought to protect the fetus against these effects of chemicals in the workplace by banning pregnant and potentially pregnant women from jobs with exposure to known mutagens and teratogens.

However, the U.S. Supreme Court found that employers cannot legally adopt fetal protection policies that exclude women of childbearing age from a hazardous workplace, because such policies involve illegal sex discrimination. As a result of this decision, most U.S. corporations no longer have policies to protect fetuses that involve the actual exclusion of women, although prior to 1990 policies of exclusion had been the industry standard. Instead, corporations now simply notify employees of potential harm. Still at issue is whether these notification policies adequately protect the fetus.

The next two articles involve the most common and most publicized area of maternal-fetal relations: forced cesarean sections. In the case of *In re A. C.,* a 28-year old, terminally ill woman named Angela Carder was forced under court order to undergo a cesarean section in a failed attempt to save her 26-½-week-old fetus. Her premature infant was born, but died within three hours. The patient had agreed to a cesarean at 28 weeks, but not at 26-½. The family wanted her to be allowed to die in peace, but the hospital requested legal intervention, and a court allowed an emergency cesarean to be performed. The patient had expressly, though perhaps incompetently, refused to consent to the intervention. At the critical time of the decision in the case, testimony indicated that the patient was too heavily medicated to be able to respond to questions, and that the medication could not be reduced without threatening to reduce her survival time.

However, on April 26, 1990, the District of Columbia Court of Appeals held that the trial judge was in error in authorizing the cesarean. The appellate court vacated the decision of the lower court, holding that there had been an incorrect weighing of Carder's interests against the state's interests in her fetus, and also an error in attempting to determine if Carder was competent. *In re A. C.* has been viewed as especially important because it broke with a judicial trend of ordering women to submit to cesarean sections at the request of physicians. However, the court left unaddressed many questions about a woman's rights in pregnancy when her behavior presents substantial risk to the fetus.

In the final two selections in this section, Nancy Rhoden and John Seymour discuss these moral and legal problems of maternal-fetal relations. Rhoden takes the view that courts should not order cesarean deliveries against a woman's will even if the woman is acting in a morally improper way and there will be tragic consequences to the fetus. Seymour provides a framework within which to consider decisions to withhold consent to cesarean sections when harm would likely be caused to the fetus. Seymour argues for a model of the maternal-fetal relationship that emphasizes the "shared needs and interdependence of the woman and her fetus." Analysis of this model leads to the conclusion that the basic decision maker is the pregnant woman, but that the fetus has independent interests that the law should recognize.

These maternal-fetal circumstances present difficult choices for health care centers and clinicians. If both the woman and the fetus are patients, clinicians will have to decide who the primary patient is, as well as whose rights have priority. "When does the fetus become a significant patient?" is a question that looks very much like the question "When does the fetus gain significant status?" Problems of ontological and moral status, then, underlie moral problems of maternal-fetal relationships no less than moral problems of abortion.

T. L. B.

DON MARQUIS

Why Abortion Is Immoral

The view that abortion is, with rare exceptions, seriously immoral has received little support in the recent philosophical literature. No doubt most philosophers affiliated with secular institutions of higher education believe that the anti-abortion position is either a symptom of irrational religious dogma or a conclusion generated by seriously confused philosophical argument. The purpose of this essay is to undermine this general belief. This essay sets out an argument that purports to show, as well as any argument in ethics can show, that abortion is, except possibly in rare cases, seriously immoral, that it is in the same moral category as killing an innocent adult human being. . . .

[A] necessary condition of resolving the abortion controversy is a more theoretical account of the wrongness of killing. After all, if we merely believe, but do not understand, why killing adult human beings such as ourselves is wrong, how could we conceivably show that abortion is either immoral or permissible?

II.

In order to develop such an account, we can start from the following unproblematic assumption concerning our own case: It is wrong to kill *us*. Why is it wrong? Some answers can be easily eliminated. It might be said that what makes killing us wrong is that a killing brutalizes the one who kills. But the brutalization consists of being inured to the performance of an act that is hideously immoral; hence, the brutalization does not explain the immorality. It might be said that what makes killing us wrong is the great loss others would

experience due to our absence. Although such hubris is understandable, such an explanation does not account for the wrongness of killing hermits, or those whose lives are relatively independent and whose friends find it easy to make new friends.

A more obvious answer is better. What primarily makes killing wrong is neither its effect on the murderer nor its effect on the victim's friends and relatives, but its effect on the victim. The loss of one's life deprives one of all the experiences, activities, projects, and enjoyments that would otherwise have constituted one's future. Therefore, killing someone is wrong, primarily because the killing inflicts (one of) the greatest possible losses on the victim. To describe this as the loss of life can be misleading, however. The change in my biological state does not by itself make killing me wrong. The effect of the loss of my biological life is the loss to me of all those activities, projects, experiences, and enjoyments which would otherwise have constituted my future personal life. These activities, projects, experiences, and enjoyments are either valuable for their own sakes or are means to something else that is valuable for its own sake. Some parts of my future are not valued by me now, but will come to be valued by me as I grow older and as my values and capacities change. When I am killed, I am deprived both of what I now value which would have been part of my future personal life, but also what I would come to value. Therefore, when I die, I am deprived of all of the value of my future. Inflicting this loss on me is ultimately what makes killing me wrong. This being the case, it would seem that what makes killing *any* adult human being prima facie seriously wrong is the loss of his or her future.

Fron the *Journal of Philosophy,* 86(4): 183–202, April 1989. Reprinted by permission.

How should this rudimentary theory of the wrongness of killing be evaluated? It cannot be faulted for deriving an 'ought' from an 'is,' for it does not. The analysis assumes that killing me (or you, reader) is prima facie seriously wrong. The point of the analysis is to establish which natural property ultimately explains the wrongness of the killing, given that it is wrong. A natural property will ultimately explain the wrongness of killing, only if (1) the explanation fits with our intuitions about the matter and (2) there is no other natural property that provides the basis for a better explanation of the wrongness of killing. This analysis rests on the intuition that what makes killing a particular human or animal wrong is what it does to that particular human or animal. What makes killing wrong is some natural effect or other of the killing. Some would deny this. For instance, a divine-command theorist in ethics would deny it. Surely this denial is, however, one of those features of divine-command theory which renders it so implausible.

The claim that what makes killing wrong is the loss of the victim's future is directly supported by two considerations. In the first place, this theory explains why we regard killing as one of the worst of crimes. Killing is especially wrong, because it deprives the victim of more than perhaps any other crime. In the second place, people with AIDS or cancer who know they are dying believe, of course, that dying is a very bad thing for them. They believe that the loss of a future to them that they would otherwise have experienced is what makes their premature death a very bad thing for them. A better theory of the wrongness of killing would require a different natural property associated with killing which better fits with the attitudes of the dying. What could it be?

The view that what makes killing wrong is the loss to the victim of the value of the victim's future gains additional support when some of its implications are examined. In the first place, it is incompatible with the view that it is wrong to kill only beings who are biologically human. It is possible that there exists a different species from another planet whose members have a future like ours. Since having a future like that is what makes killing someone wrong, this theory entails that it would be wrong to kill members of such a species. Hence, this theory is opposed to the claim that only life that is biologically human has great moral worth, a claim which many anti-abortionists have seemed to adopt. This opposition, which this theory

has in common with personhood theories, seems to be a merit of the theory.

In the second place, the claim that the loss of one's future is the wrong-making feature of one's being killed entails the possibility that the futures of some actual nonhuman mammals on our own planet are sufficiently like ours that it is seriously wrong to kill them also. Whether some animals do have the same right to life as human beings depends on adding to the account of the wrongness of killing some additional account of just what it is about my future or the futures of other adult human beings which makes it wrong to kill us. No such additional account will be offered in this essay. Undoubtedly, the provision of such an account would be a very difficult matter. Undoubtedly, any such account would be quite controversial. Hence, it surely should not reflect badly on this sketch of an elementary theory of the wrongness of killing that it is indeterminate with respect to some very difficult issues regarding animal rights.

In the third place, the claim that the loss of one's future is the wrong-making feature of one's being killed does not entail, as sanctity of human life theories do, that active euthanasia is wrong. Persons who are severely and incurably ill, who face a future of pain and despair, and who wish to die will not have suffered a loss if they are killed. It is, strictly speaking, the value of a human's future which makes killing wrong in this theory. This being so, killing does not necessarily wrong some persons who are sick and dying. Of course, there may be other reasons for a prohibition of active euthanasia, but that is another matter. Sanctity-of-human-life theories seem to hold that active euthanasia is seriously wrong even in an individual case where there seems to be good reason for it independently of public policy considerations. This consequence is most implausible, and it is a plus for the claim that the loss of a future of value is what makes killing wrong that it does not share this consequence.

In the fourth place, the account of the wrongness of killing defended in this essay does straightforwardly entail that it is prima facie seriously wrong to kill children and infants, for we do presume that they have futures of value. Since we do believe that it is wrong to kill defenseless little babies, it is important that a theory of the wrongness of killing easily account for this. Personhood theories of the wrongness of killing, on the other hand, cannot straightforwardly account for the wrongness of killing infants and young children. Hence, such theories must add special ad hoc accounts of the wrongness of killing the young. The plausibility of such ad hoc theories seems to be a function of how desperately one wants such theories to work. The claim that the primary wrong-making feature of a killing is the loss to the victim of the value of its future accounts for the wrongness of killing young children and infants directly; it makes the wrongness of such acts as obvious as we actually think it is. This is a further merit of this theory. Accordingly, it seems that this value of a future-like-ours theory of the wrongness of killing shares strengths of both sanctity-of-life and personhood accounts while avoiding weaknesses of both. In addition, it meshes with a central intuition concerning what makes killing wrong.

The claim that the primary wrong-making feature of a killing is the loss to the victim of the value of its future has obvious consequences for the ethics of abortion. The future of a standard fetus includes a set of experiences, projects, activities, and such which are identical with the futures of adult human beings and are identical with the futures of young children. Since the reason that is sufficient to explain why it is wrong to kill human beings after the time of birth is a reason that also applies to fetuses, it follows that abortion is prima facie seriously morally wrong.

This argument does not rely on the invalid inference that, since it is wrong to kill persons, it is wrong to kill potential persons also. The category that is morally central to this analysis is the category of having a valuable future like ours; it is not the category of personhood. The argument to the conclusion that abortion is prima facie seriously morally wrong proceeded independently of the notion of person or potential person or any equivalent. Someone may wish to start with this analysis in terms of the value of a human future, conclude that abortion is, except perhaps in rare circumstances, seriously morally wrong, infer that fetuses have the right to life, and then call fetuses "persons" as a result of their having the right to life. Clearly, in this case, the category of person is being used to state the *conclusion* of the analysis rather than to generate the *argument* of the analysis.

The structure of this anti-abortion argument can be both illuminated and defended by comparing it to what appears to be the best argument for the wrongness of the wanton infliction of pain on animals. This latter argument is based on the assumption that it is prima facie wrong to inflict pain on me (or you, reader). What is the natural property associated with the infliction of pain which makes such infliction wrong? The obvious answer seems to be that the infliction of pain causes suffering and that suffering is a misfortune. The suffering caused by the infliction of pain is what makes the wanton infliction of pain on me wrong. The wanton infliction of pain on other adult humans causes suffering. The wanton infliction of pain on animals causes suffering. Since causing suffering is what makes the wanton infliction of pain wrong and since the wanton infliction of pain on animals causes suffering, it follows that the wanton infliction of pain on animals is wrong.

This argument for the wrongness of the wanton infliction of pain on animals shares a number of structural features with the argument for the serious prima facie wrongness of abortion. Both arguments start with an obvious assumption concerning what it is wrong to do to me (or you, reader). Both then look for the characteristic or the consequence of the wrong action which makes the action wrong. Both recognize that the wrong-making feature of these immoral actions is a property of actions sometimes directed at individuals other than postnatal human beings. If the structure of the argument for the wrongness of the wanton infliction of pain on animals is sound, then the structure of the argument for the prima facie serious wrongness of abortion is also sound, for the structure of the two arguments is the same. The structure common to both is the key to the explanation of how the wrongness of abortion can be demonstrated without recourse to the category of person. In neither argument is that category crucial.

This defense of an argument for the wrongness of abortion in terms of a structurally similar argument for the wrongness of the wanton infliction of pain on animals succeeds only if the account regarding animals is the correct account. Is it? In the first place, it seems plausible. In the second place, its major competition is Kant's account. Kant believed that we do not have direct duties to animals at all, because they are not persons. Hence, Kant had to explain and justify the wrongness of inflicting pain on animals on the grounds that "he who is hard in his dealings with animals becomes hard also in his dealing with men."[1] The problem with Kant's account is that there seems to be no reason for accepting this latter claim unless Kant's account is rejected. If the alternative to Kant's account is accepted, then it is easy to understand why someone who is indifferent to inflicting pain on animals is also indifferent to inflicting pain on humans, for one is indifferent to what makes inflicting pain wrong in both cases. But, if Kant's account is accepted, there is no intelligible reason why one who is hard in his dealings with animals (or crabgrass or stones) should also be hard in his dealings with men. After all, men are persons: animals are no more persons than crabgrass or stones. Persons are Kant's crucial moral category. Why, in short, should a Kantian accept the basic claim in Kant's argument?

Hence, Kant's argument for the wrongness of inflicting pain on animals rests on a claim that, in a world of Kantian moral agents, is demonstrably false. Therefore, the alternative analysis, being more plausible anyway, should be accepted. Since this alternative analysis has the same structure of the anti-abortion argument being defended here, we have further support for the argument for the immorality of abortion being defended in this essay.

Of course, this value of a future-like-ours argument, if sound, shows only that abortion is prima facie wrong, not that it is wrong in any and all circumstances. Since the loss of the future to a standard fetus, if killed, is, however, at least as great a loss as the loss of the future to a standard adult human being who is killed, abortion, like ordinary killing, could be justified only by the most compelling reasons. The loss of one's life is almost the greatest misfortune that can happen to one. Presumably abortion could be justified in some circumstances, only if the loss consequent on failing to abort would be at least as great. Accordingly, morally permissible abortions will be rare indeed unless, perhaps, they occur so early in pregnancy that a fetus is not yet definitely an individual. Hence, this argument should be taken as showing that abortion is presumptively very seriously wrong, where the presumption is very strong — as strong as the presumption that killing another adult human being is wrong.

III.

How complete an account of the wrongness of killing does the value of a future-like-ours account have to be in order that the wrongness of abortion is a consequence? This account does not have to be an account of the necessary conditions for the wrongness of killing. Some persons in nursing homes may lack valuable human futures, yet it may be wrong to kill them for other reasons. Furthermore, this account does not obviously have to be the sole reasons killing is wrong where the victim did have a valuable future. This analysis claims only that, for any killing where the victim did have a valuable future like ours, having that future by itself is sufficient to create the strong presumption that the killing is seriously wrong.

One way to overturn the value of a future-like-ours argument would be to find some account of the wrongness of killing which is at least as intelligible and which has different implications for the ethics of abortion. Two rival accounts possess at least some degree of plausibility. One account I based on the obvious fact that people value the experience of living and wish for that valuable experience to continue. Therefore, it might be said, what makes killing wrong is the discontinuation of that experience for the victim. Let us call this the *discontinuation account.* Another rival account is based upon the obvious fact that people strongly desire to continue to live. This suggests that what makes killing us so wrong is that it interferes with the fulfillment of a strong and fundamental desire, the fulfillment of which is necessary for the fulfillment of any other desires we might have. Let us call this the *desire account.*

Consider first the desire account as a rival account of the ethics of killing which would provide the basis for rejecting the anti-abortion position. Such an account will have to be stronger than the value of a future-like-ours account of the wrongness of abortion if it is to do the job expected of it. To entail the wrongness of abortion, the value of a future-like-ours account has only to provide a sufficient, but not a necessary, condition for the wrongness of killing. The desire account, on the other hand, must provide us also with a necessary condition for the wrongness of killing in order to generate a pro-choice conclusion on abortion. The reason for this is that presumably the argument from the desire account moves from the claim that what makes killing wrong is interference with a very strong desire to the claim that abortion is not wrong because the fetus lacks a strong desire to live. Obviously, this inference fails if someone's having the desire to live is not a necessary condition of its being wrong to kill that individual.

One problem with the desire account is that we do regard it as seriously wrong to kill persons who have little desire to live or who have no desire to live or, indeed, have a desire not to live. We believe it is seriously wrong to kill the unconscious, the sleeping, those who are tired of life, and those who are suicidal. The value-of-a-human-future account renders standard morality intelligible in these cases; these cases appear to be incompatible with the desire account.

The desire account is subject to a deeper difficulty. We desire life, because we value the good of this life. The goodness of life is not secondary to our desire for it. If this were not so, the pain of one's own premature death could be done away with merely by an appropriate alteration in the configuration of one's desires. This is absurd. Hence, it would seem that it is the loss of the goods of one's future, not the interference with the fulfillment of a strong desire to live, which accounts ultimately for the wrongness of killing.

It is worth noting that, if the desire account is modified so that it does not provide a necessary, but only a sufficient, condition for the wrongness of killing, the desire account is compatible with the value of a future-like-ours account. The combined accounts will yield an anti-abortion ethic. This suggests that one can retain what is intuitively plausible about the desire account without a challenge to the basic argument of this paper.

It is also worth noting that, if future desires have moral force in a modified desire account of the wrongness of killing, one can find support for an anti-abortion ethic even in the absence of a value of a future-like-ours account. If one decides that a morally relevant property, the possession of which is sufficient to make it wrong to kill some individual, is the desire at some future time to live — one might decide to justify one's refusal to kill suicidal teenagers on these grounds, for example — then, since typical fetuses will have the desire in the future to live, it is wrong to kill typical fetuses. Accordingly, it does not seem that a desire account of the wrongness of killing can provide a justification of a pro-choice ethic of abortion which is nearly as adequate as the value of a human-future justification of an anti-abortion ethic.

The discontinuation account looks more promising as an account of the wrongness of killing. It seems just as intelligible as the value of a future-like-ours account, but it does not justify an anti-abortion position. Obviously, if it is the continuation of one's activities, experiences, and projects, the loss of which makes killing wrong, then it is not wrong to kill fetuses for that reason, for fetuses do not have experiences, activities, and projects to be continued or discontinued. Accordingly, the discontinuation account does not have the

anti-abortion consequences that the value of a future-like-ours account has. Yet, it seems as intelligible as the value of a future-like-ours account, for when we think of what would be wrong with our being killed, it does seem as if it is the discontinuation of what makes our lives worthwhile which makes killing us wrong.

Is the discontinuation account just as good an account as the value of a future-like-ours account? The discontinuation account will not be adequate at all, if it does not refer to the *value* of the experience that may be discontinued. One does not want the discontinuation account to make it wrong to kill a patient who begs for death and who is in severe pain that cannot be relieved short of killing. (I leave open the question of whether it is wrong for other reasons.) Accordingly, the discontinuation account must be more than a bare discontinuation account. It must make some reference to the positive value of the patient's experiences. But, by the same token, the value of a future-like-ours account cannot be a bare future account either. Just having a future surely does not itself rule out killing the above patient. This account must make some reference to the value of the patient's future experiences and projects also. Hence, both accounts involve the value of experiences, projects, and activities. So far we still have symmetry between the accounts.

The symmetry fades, however, when we focus on the time period of the value of the experiences, etc., which has moral consequences. Although both accounts leave open the possibility that the patient in our example may be killed, this possibility is left open only in virtue of the utterly bleak future for the patient. It makes no difference whether the patient's immediate past contains intolerable pain, or consists in being in a coma (which we can imagine is a situation of indifference), or consists in a life of value. If the patient's future is a future of value, we want our account to make it wrong to kill the patient. If the patient's future is intolerable, whatever his or her immediate past, we want our account to allow killing the patient. Obviously, then, it is the value of that patient's future which is doing the work in rendering the morality of killing the patient intelligible.

This being the case, it seems clear that whether one has immediate past experiences or not does not work in the explanation of what makes killing wrong. The addition the discontinuation account makes to the value of a human future account is otiose. Its addition to the value-of-a-future account plays no role at all in rendering intelligible the wrongness of killing. Therefore, it can be discarded with the discontinuation account of which it is a part.

IV.

The analysis of the previous section suggests that alternative general accounts of the wrongness of killing are either inadequate or unsuccessful in getting around the anti-abortion consequences of the value of a future-like-ours argument. A different strategy for avoiding these anti-abortion consequences involves limiting the scope of the value of a future argument. More precisely, the strategy involves arguing that fetuses lack a property that is essential for the value-of-a-future argument (or for any anti-abortion argument) to apply to them.

One move of this sort is based upon the claim that a necessary condition of one's future being valuable is that one values it. Value implies a valuer. Given this one might argue that, since fetuses cannot value their futures, their futures are not valuable to them. Hence, it does not seriously wrong them deliberately to end their lives.

This move fails, however, because of some ambiguities. Let us assume that something cannot be of value unless it is valued by someone. This does not entail that my life is of no value unless it is valued by me. I may think, in a period of despair, that my future is of no worth whatsoever, but I may be wrong because others rightly see value—even great value—in it. Furthermore, my future can be valuable to me even if I do not value it. This is the case when a young person attempts suicide, but is rescued and goes on to significant human achievements. Such young people's futures are ultimately valuable to them, even though such futures do not seem to be valuable to them, at the moment of attempted suicide. A fetus's future can be valuable to it in the same way. Accordingly, this attempt to limit the anti-abortion argument fails. . . .

V.

In this essay, it has been argued that the correct ethic of the wrongness of killing can be extended to fetal life and used to show that there is a strong presumption that any abortion is morally impermissible. If the ethic of killing adopted here entails, however, that contraception is also seriously immoral, then there would appear to be a difficulty with the analysis of this essay.

But this analysis does not entail that contraception is wrong. Of course, contraception prevents the actualization of a possible future of value. Hence, it follows from the claim that futures of value should be maxi-mized that contraception is prima facie immoral. This obligation to maximize does not exist, however; furthermore, nothing in the ethics of killing in this paper entails that it does. The ethics of killing in this essay would entail that contraception is wrong only if something were denied a human future of value by contraception. Nothing at all is denied such a future by contraception, however.

Candidates for a subject of harm by contraception fall into four categories: (1) some sperm or other, (2) some ovum or other, (3) a sperm and an ovum separately, and (4) a sperm and an ovum together. Assigning the harm to some sperm is utterly arbitrary, for no reason can be given for making a sperm the subject of harm rather than an ovum. Assigning the harm to some ovum is utterly arbitrary, for no reason can be given for making an ovum the subject of harm rather than a sperm. One might attempt to avoid these problems by insisting that contraception deprives both the sperm and the ovum separately of a valuable future like ours. On this alternative, too many futures are lost. Contraception was supposed to be wrong, because it deprived us of one future of value, not two. One might attempt to avoid this problem by holding that contraception deprives the combination of sperm and ovum of a valuable future like ours. But here the definite article misleads. At the time of contraception, there are hundreds of millions of sperm, one (released) ovum and millions of possible combinations of all of these. There is no actual combination at all. Is the subject of the loss to be a merely possible combination? Which one? This alternative does not yield an actual subject of harm either. Accordingly, the immorality of contraception is not entailed by the loss of a future-like-ours argument simply because there is no nonarbitrarily identifiable subject of the loss in the case of contraception.

VI.

The purpose of this essay has been to set out an argument for the serious presumptive wrongness of abortion subject to the assumption that the moral permissibility of abortion stands or falls on the moral status of the fetus. Since a fetus possesses a property, the possession of which in adult human beings is sufficient to make killing an adult human being wrong, abortion is wrong. This way of dealing with the problem of abortion seems superior to other approaches to the ethics of abortion, because it rests on an ethics of killing which is close to self-evident, because the crucial morally relevant property clearly applies to fetuses, and because the argument avoids the usual equivocations on 'human life', 'human being', or 'person'. The argument rests neither on religious claims nor on Papal dogma. It is not subject to the objection of "speciesism." Its soundness is compatible with the moral permissibility of euthanasia and contraception. It deals with our intuitions concerning young children.

Finally, this analysis can be viewed as resolving a standard problem—indeed, *the* standard problem—concerning the ethics of abortion. Clearly, it is wrong to kill adult human beings. Clearly, it is not wrong to end the life of some arbitrarily chosen single human cell. Fetuses seem to be like arbitrarily chosen human cells in some respects and like adult humans in other respects. The problem of the ethics of abortion is the problem of determining the fetal property that settles this moral controversy. The thesis of this essay is that the problem of the ethics of abortion, so understood, is solvable.

NOTES

1. "Duties to Animals and Spirits," in *Lectures on Ethics,* Louis Infeld, trans. (New York: Harper, 1963), p. 239.

JUDITH JARVIS THOMSON

A Defense of Abortion[1]

Most opposition to abortion relies on the premise that the fetus is a human being, a person, from the moment of conception. The premise is argued for, but, as I think, not well. Take, for example, the most common argument. We are asked to notice that the development of a human being from conception through birth into childhood is continuous; then it is said that to draw a line, to choose a point in this development and say "before this point the thing is not a person, after this point it is a person" is to make an arbitrary choice, a choice for which in the nature of things no good reason can be given. It is concluded that the fetus is, or anyway that we had better say it is, a person from the moment of conception. But this conclusion does not follow. Similar things might be said about the development of an acorn into an oak tree, and it does not follow that acorns are oak trees, or that we had better say they are. Arguments of this form are sometimes called "slippery slope arguments"—the phrase is perhaps self-explanatory—and it is dismaying that opponents of abortion rely on them so heavily and uncritically.

I am inclined to agree, however, that the prospects for "drawing a line" in the development of the fetus look dim. I am inclined to think also that we shall probably have to agree that the fetus has already become a human person well before birth. Indeed, it comes as a surprise when one first learns how early in its life it begins to acquire human characteristics. By the tenth week, for example, it already has a face, arms and legs, fingers and toes; it has internal organs, and brain activity is detectable.[2] On the other hand, I think that the premise is false, that the fetus is not a person from the moment of conception. A newly fertilized ovum, a newly implanted clump of cells, is no more a person than an acorn is an oak tree. But I shall not discuss any of this. For it seems to me to be of great interest to ask what happens if, for the sake of argument, we allow the premise. How, precisely, are we supposed to get from there to the conclusion that abortion is morally impermissible? Opponents of abortion commonly spend most of their time establishing that the fetus is a person, and hardly any time explaining the step from there

Reprinted with permission of the publisher from *Philosophy and Public Affairs,* Vol. 1, No. 1 (1971), pp. 47–66. Copyright © 1971 by Princeton University Press.

to the impermissibility of abortion. Perhaps they think the step too simple and obvious to require much comment. Or perhaps instead they are simply being economical in argument. Many of those who defend abortion rely on the premise that the fetus is not a person, but only a bit of tissue that will become a person at birth; and why pay out more arguments than you have to? Whatever the explanation, I suggest that the step they take is neither easy nor obvious, that it calls for closer examination than it is commonly given, and that when we do give it this closer examination we shall feel inclined to reject it.

I propose, then, that we grant that the fetus is a person from the moment of conception. How does the argument go from here? Something like this, I take it. Every person has a right to life. So the fetus has a right to life. No doubt the mother has a right to decide what shall happen in and to her body; everyone would grant that. But surely a person's right to life is stronger and more stringent than the mother's right to decide what happens in and to her body, and so outweighs it. So the fetus may not be killed; an abortion may not be performed.

It sounds plausible. But now let me ask you to imagine this. You wake up in the morning and find yourself back to back in bed with an unconscious violinist. A famous unconscious violinist. He has been found to have a fatal kidney ailment, and the Society of Music Lovers has canvassed all the available medical records and found that you alone have the right blood type to help. They have therefore kidnapped you, and last night the violinist's circulatory system was plugged into yours, so that your kidneys can be used to extract poisons from his blood as well as your own. The director of the hospital now tells you, "Look, we're sorry the Society of Music Lovers did this to you—we would never have permitted it if we had known. But still, they did it, and the violinist now is plugged into you. To unplug you would be to kill him. But never mind, it's only for nine months. By then he will have recovered from his ailment, and can safely be unplugged from you." Is it morally incumbent on you to accede to this situation? No doubt it would be very nice of you if you did, a great kindness. But do you *have* to accede to it? What if it were not nine months, but nine years? Or longer still? What if the director of the hospital says, "Tough luck, I agree, but you've now got to stay in bed, with the violinist plugged into you, for the rest of your life. Because remember this. All persons have a right to life, and violinists are persons. Granted you have a right to

decide what happens in and to your body, but a person's right to life outweighs your right to decide what happens in and to your body. So you cannot ever be unplugged from him." I imagine you would regard this as outrageous, which suggests that something really is wrong with that plausible-sounding argument I mentioned a moment ago.

In this case, of course, you were kidnapped; you didn't volunteer for the operation that plugged the violinist into your kidneys. Can those who oppose abortion on the ground I mentioned make an exception for a pregnancy due to rape? Certainly. They can say that persons have a right to life only if they didn't come into existence because of rape; or they can say that all persons have a right to life, but that some have less of a right to life than others, in particular, that those who came into existence because of rape have less. But these statements have a rather unpleasant sound. Surely the question of whether you have a right to life at all, or how much of it you have, shouldn't turn on the question of whether or not you are the product of a rape. And in fact the people who oppose abortion on the ground I mentioned do not make this distinction, and hence do not make an exception in case of rape.

Nor do they make an exception for a case in which the mother has to spend the nine months of her pregnancy in bed. They would agree that would be a great pity, and hard on the mother; but all the same, all persons have a right to life, the fetus is a person, and so on. I suspect, in fact, that they would not make an exception for a case in which, miraculously enough, the pregnancy went on for nine years, or even the rest of the mother's life.

Some won't even make an exception for a case in which continuation of the pregnancy is likely to shorten the mother's life; they regard abortion as impermissible even to save the mother's life. Such cases are nowadays very rare, and many opponents of abortion do not accept this extreme view. All the same, it is a good place to begin: a number of points of interest come out in respect to it.

1. Let us call the view that abortion is impermissible even to save the mother's life "the extreme view." I want to suggest first that it does not issue from the argument I mentioned earlier without the addition of some fairly powerful premises. Suppose a woman has become pregnant, and now learns that she has a cardiac condition such that she will die if she carries the baby

to term. What may be done for her? The fetus, being a person, has a right to life, but as the mother is a person too, so has she a right to life. Presumably they have an equal right to life. How is it supposed to come out that an abortion may not be performed? If mother and child have an equal right to life, shouldn't we perhaps flip a coin? Or should we add to the mother's right to life her right to decide what happens in and to her body, which everybody seems to be ready to grant—the sum of her rights now outweighing the fetus's right to life?

The most familiar argument here is the following. We are told that performing the abortion would be directly killing[3] the child, whereas doing nothing would not be killing the mother, but only letting her die. Moreover, in killing the child, one would be killing an innocent person, for the child has committed no crime, and is not aiming at his mother's death. And then there are a variety of ways in which this might be continued. (a) But as directly killing an innocent person is always and absolutely impermissible, an abortion may not be performed. Or, (b) as directly killing an innocent person is murder, and murder is always and absolutely impermissible, an abortion may not be performed.[4] Or, (c) as one's duty to refrain from directly killing an innocent person is more stringent than one's duty to keep a person from dying, an abortion may not be performed. Or, (d) if one's only options are directly killing an innocent person or letting a person die, one must prefer letting the person die, and thus an abortion may not be performed.[5]

Some people seem to have thought that these are not further premises which must be added if the conclusion is to be reached, but that they follow from the very fact that an innocent person has a right to life.[6] But this seems to me to be a mistake, and perhaps the simplest way to show this is to bring out that while we must certainly grant that innocent persons have a right to life, the theses in (a) through (d) are all false. Take (b), for example. If directly killing an innocent person is murder, and thus is impermissible, then the mother's directly killing the innocent person inside her is murder, and thus is impermissible. But it cannot seriously be thought to be murder if the mother performs an abortion on herself to save her life. It cannot seriously be said that she *must* refrain, that she *must* sit passively by and wait for her death. Let us look again at the case of you and the violinist. There you are, in bed with the violinist, and the director of the hospital says to you,

"It's all most distressing, and I deeply sympathize, but you see this is putting an additional strain on your kidneys, and you'll be dead within the month. But you *have* to stay where you are all the same. Because unplugging you would be directly killing an innocent violinist, and that's murder, and that's impermissible." If anything in the world is true, it is that you do not commit murder, you do not do what is impermissible, if you reach around to your back and unplug yourself from that violinist to save your life.

The main focus of attention in writings on abortion has been on what a third party may or may not do in answer to a request from a woman for an abortion. This is in a way understandable. Things being as they are, there isn't much a woman can safely do to abort herself. So the question asked is what a third party may do, and what the mother may do, if it is mentioned at all, is deduced, almost as an afterthought, from what it is concluded that third parties may do. But it seems to me that to treat the matter in this way is to refuse to grant to the mother that very status of person which is so firmly insisted on for the fetus. For we cannot simply read off what a person may do from what a third party may do. Suppose you find yourself trapped in a tiny house with a growing child. I mean a very tiny house, and a rapidly growing child—you are already up against the wall of the house and in a few minutes you'll be crushed to death. The child on the other hand won't be crushed to death; if nothing is done to stop him from growing he'll be hurt, but in the end he'll simply burst open the house and walk out a free man. Now I could well understand it if a bystander were to say, "There's nothing we can do for you. We cannot choose between your life and his, we cannot be the ones to decide who is to live, we cannot intervene." But it cannot be concluded that you too can do nothing, that you cannot attack it to save your life. However innocent the child may be, you do not have to wait passively while it crushes you to death. Perhaps a pregnant woman is vaguely felt to have the status of house, to which we don't allow the right of self-defense. But if the woman houses the child, it should be remembered that she is a person who houses it.

I should perhaps stop to say explicitly that I am not claiming that people have a right to do anything whatever to save their lives. I think, rather, that there are drastic limits to the right of self-defense. If someone threatens you with death unless you torture someone else to death, I think you have not the right, even to save your life, to do so. But the case under consideration here is very different. In our case there are only two people in-volved, one whose life is threatened, and one who threatens it. Both are innocent: the one who is threat-ened is not threatened because of any fault, the one who threatens does not threaten because of any fault. For this reason we may feel that we bystanders cannot intervene. But the person threatened can.

In sum, a woman surely can defend her life against the threat to it posed by the unborn child, even if doing so involves its death. And this shows not merely that the theses in (a) through (d) are false; it shows also that the extreme view of abortion is false, and so we need not canvass any other possible ways of arriving at it from the argument I mentioned at the outset.

2. The extreme view could of course be weakened to say that while abortion is permissible to save the mother's life, it may not be performed by a third party, but only by the mother herself. But this cannot be right either. For what we have to keep in mind is that the mother and the unborn child are not like two tenants in a small house which has, by an unfortunate mistake, been rented to both: the mother *owns* the house. The fact that she does adds to the offensiveness of deducing that the mother can do nothing from the supposition that third parties can do nothing. But it does more than this: it casts a bright light on the supposition that third parties can do nothing. Certainly it lets us see that a third party who says "I cannot choose between you" is fooling himself if he thinks this is impartiality. If Jones has found and fastened on a certain coat, which he needs to keep him from freezing, but which Smith also needs to keep him from freezing, then it is not impartiality that says "I cannot choose between you" when Smith owns the coat. Women have said again and again "This body is *my* body!" and they have reason to feel angry, reason to feel that it has been like shouting into the wind. Smith, after all, is hardly likely to bless us if we say to him, "Of course it's your coat, anybody would grant that it is. But no one may choose between you and Jones who is to have it."

We should really ask what it is that says "no one may choose" in the face of the fact that the body that houses the child is the mother's body. It may be simply a failure to appreciate this fact. But it may be some-thing more interesting, namely, the sense that one has a right to refuse to lay hands on people, even where it would be just and fair to do so, even where jus-tice seems to require that somebody do so. Thus justice might call for somebody to get Smith's coat back from Jones, and yet you have a right to refuse to be the one

to lay hands on Jones, a right to refuse to do physical violence to him. This, I think, must be granted. But then what should be said is not "no one may choose," but only "*I* cannot choose," and indeed not even this, but "*I* will not *act*," leaving it open that somebody else can or should, and in particular that anyone in a posi-tion of authority, with the job of securing people's rights, both can and should. So this is no difficulty. I have not been arguing that any given third party must accede to the mother's request that he perform an abor-tion to save her life, but only that he may.

I suppose that in some views of human life the mother's body is only on loan to her, the loan not being one which gives her any prior claim to it. One who held this view might well think it impartiality to say "I can-not choose." But I shall simply ignore this possibility. My own view is that if a human being has any just, prior claim to anything at all, he has a just, prior claim to his own body. And perhaps this needn't be argued for here anyway, since, as I mentioned, the arguments against abortion we are looking at do grant that the woman has a right to decide what happens in and to her body.

But although they do grant it, I have tried to show that they do not take seriously what is done in grant-ing it. I suggest the same thing will reappear even more clearly when we turn away from cases in which the mother's life is at stake, and attend, as I propose we now do, to the vastly more common cases in which a woman wants an abortion for some less weighty reason than preserving her own life.

3. Where the mother's life is not at stake, the argu-ment I mentioned at the outset seems to have a much stronger pull. "Everyone has a right to life, so the un-born person has a right to life." And isn't the child's right to life weightier than anything other than the mother's own right to life, which she might put for-ward as ground for an abortion?

This argument treats the right to life as if it were un-problematic. It is not, and this seems to me to be pre-cisely the source of the mistake.

For we should now, at long last, ask what it comes to, to have a right to life. In some views having a right to life includes having a right to be given at least the bare minimum one needs for continued life. But sup-pose that what in fact *is* the bare minimum a man needs for continued life is something he has no right at all to be given. If I am sick unto death, and the only thing that will save my life is the touch of Henry Fonda's cool hand on my fevered brow, then all the same, I have no right to be given the touch of Henry Fonda's cool hand on my fevered brow. It would be frightfully nice of him to fly in from the West Coast to provide it. It would be less nice, though no doubt well meant, if my friends flew out to the West Coast and carried Henry Fonda back with them. But I have no right at all against anybody that he should do this for me. Or again, to return to the story I told earlier, the fact that for continued life that violinist needs the continued use of your kidneys does not establish that he has a right to be given the continued use of your kidneys. He certainly has no right against you that *you* should give him continued use of your kidneys. For nobody has any right to use your kidneys unless you give him such a right; and nobody has the right against you that you shall give him this right — if you do allow him to go on using your kidneys, this is a kindness on your part, and not something he can claim from you as his due. Nor has he any right against anybody else that they should give him continued use of your kidneys. Certainly he had no right against the Society of Music Lovers that *they* should plug him into you in the first place. And if you now start to unplug yourself, having learned that you will otherwise have to spend nine years in bed with him, there is nobody in the world who must try to prevent you, in order to see to it that he is given something he has a right to be given.

Some people are rather stricter about the right to life. In their view, it does not include the right to be given anything, but amounts to, and only to, the right not to be killed by anybody. But here a related difficulty arises. If everybody is to refrain from killing that violinist, then everybody must refrain from doing a great many different sorts of things. Everybody must refrain from slitting his throat, everybody must refrain from shooting him — and everybody must refrain from unplugging you from him. But does he have a right against everybody that they shall refrain from unplugging you from him? To refrain from doing this is to allow him to continue to use your kidneys. It could be argued that he has a right against us that we should allow him to continue to use your kidneys. That is, while he had no right against us that we should give him the use of your kidneys, it might be argued that he anyway has a right against us that we shall not now intervene and deprive him of the use of your kidneys. I

shall come back to third-party interventions later. But certainly the violinist has no right against you that *you* shall allow him to continue to use your kidneys. As I said, if you do allow him to use them, it is a kindness on your part, and not something you owe him.

The difficulty I point to here is not peculiar to the right to life. It reappears in connection with all the other natural rights; and it is something which an adequate account of rights must deal with. For present purposes it is enough just to draw attention to it. But I would stress that I am not arguing that people do not have a right to life — quite to the contrary, it seems to me that the primary control we must place on the acceptability of an account of rights is that it should turn out in that account to be a truth that all persons have a right to life. I am arguing only that having a right to life does not guarantee having either a right to be given the use of or a right to be allowed continued use of another person's body — even if one needs it for life itself. So the right to life will not serve the opponents of abortion in the very simple and clear way in which they seem to have thought it would.

4. There is another way to bring out the difficulty. In the most ordinary sort of case, to deprive someone of what he has a right to is to treat him unjustly. Suppose a boy and his small brother are jointly given a box of chocolates for Christmas. If the older boy takes the box and refuses to give his brother any of the chocolates, he is unjust to him, for the brother has been given a right to half of them. But suppose that, having learned that otherwise it means nine years in bed with that violinist, you unplug yourself from him. You surely are not being unjust to him for you gave him no right to use your kidneys, and no one else can have given him any such right. But we have to notice that in unplugging yourself, you are killing him; and violinists, like everybody else, have a right to life, and thus in the view we were considering just now, the right not to be killed. So here you do what he supposedly has a right you shall not do, but you do not act unjustly to him in doing it.

The emendation which may be made at this point is this: the right to life consists not in the right not to be killed, but rather in the right not to be killed unjustly. This runs a risk of circularity, but never mind: it would enable us to square the fact that the violinist has a right to life with the fact that you do not act unjustly toward him in unplugging yourself, thereby killing him. For if you do not kill him unjustly, you do not violate his right to life, and so it is no wonder you do him no injustice.

But if this emendation is accepted, the gap in the argument against abortion stares us plainly in the face: It is by no means enough to show that the fetus is a person, and to remind us that all persons have a right to life—we need to be shown also that killing the fetus violates its right to life, i.e., that abortion is unjust killing. And is it?

I suppose we may take it as a datum that in a case of pregnancy due to rape the mother has not given the unborn person a right to the use of her body for food and shelter. Indeed, in what pregnancy could it be supposed that the mother has given the unborn person such a right? It is not as if there were unborn persons drifting about the world, to whom a woman who wants a child says "I invite you in."

But it might be argued that there are other ways one can have acquired a right to the use of another person's body than by having been invited to use it by that person. Suppose a woman voluntarily indulges in intercourse, knowing of the chance it will issue in pregnancy, and then she does become pregnant; is she not in part responsible for the presence, in fact the very existence, of the unborn person inside her? No doubt she did not invite it in. But doesn't her partial responsibility for its being there itself give it a right to the use of her body?[7] If so, then her aborting it would be more like the boy's taking away the chocolates, and less like your unplugging yourself from the violinist—doing so would be depriving it of what it does have a right to, and thus would be doing it an injustice.

And then, too, it might be asked whether or not she can kill it even to save her own life: If she voluntarily called it into existence, how can she now kill it, even in self-defense?

The first thing to be said about this is that it is something new. Opponents of abortion have been so concerned to make out the independence of the fetus, in order to establish that it has a right to life, just as its mother does, that they have tended to overlook the possible support they might gain from making out that the fetus is *dependent* on the mother, in order to establish that she has a special kind of responsibility for it, a responsibility that gives it rights against her which are not possessed by any independent person—such as an ailing violinist who is a stranger to her.

On the other hand, this argument would give the unborn person a right to its mother's body only if her pregnancy resulted from a voluntary act, undertaken in full knowledge of the chance a pregnancy might result from it. It would leave out entirely the unborn person whose existence is due to rape. Pending the availability of some further argument, then, we would be left with the conclusion that unborn persons whose existence is due to rape have no right to the use of their mothers' bodies, and thus that aborting them is not depriving them of anything they have a right to and hence is not unjust killing.

And we should also notice that it is not at all plain that this argument really does go even as far as it purports to. For there are cases and cases, and the details make a difference. If the room is stuffy, and I therefore open a window to air it, and a burglar climbs in, it would be absurd to say, "Ah, now he can stay, she's given him a right to the use of her house—for she is partially responsible for his presence there, having voluntarily done what enabled him to get in, in full knowledge that there are such things as burglars, and that burglars burgle." It would be still more absurd to say this if I had had bars installed outside my windows, precisely to prevent burglars from getting in, and a burglar got in only because of a defect in the bars. It remains equally absurd if we imagine it is not a burglar who climbs in, but an innocent person who blunders or falls in. Again, suppose it were like this: people-seeds drift about in the air like pollen, and if you open your windows, one may drift in and take root in your carpets or upholstery. You don't want children, so you fix up your windows with fine mesh screens, the very best you can buy. As can happen, however, and on very, very rare occasions does happen, one of the screens is defective; and a seed drifts in and takes root. Does the person-plant who now develops have a right to the use of your house? Surely not—despite the fact that you voluntarily opened your windows, you knowingly kept carpets and upholstered furniture, and you knew that screens were sometimes defective. Someone may argue that you are responsible for its rooting, that it does have a right to your house, because after all you *could* have lived out your life with bare floors and furniture, or with sealed windows and doors. But this won't do— for by the same token anyone can avoid a pregnancy due to rape by having a hysterectomy, or anyway by never leaving home without a (reliable!) army.

It seems to me that the argument we were looking at can establish at most that there are *some* cases in which the unborn person has a right to the use of its mother's body, and therefore *some* cases in which abortion is unjust killing. There is room for much discussion and argument as to precisely which, if any. But I think we should sidestep this issue and leave it open, for at any rate the argument certainly does not establish that all abortion is unjust killing.

5. There is room for yet another argument here, however. We surely must all grant that there may be cases in which it would be morally indecent to detach a person from your body at the cost of his life. Suppose you learn that what the violinist needs is not nine years of your life, but only one hour. All you need do to save his life is to spend one hour in that bed with him. Suppose also that letting him use your kidneys for that one hour would not affect your health in the slightest. Admittedly you were kidnapped. Admittedly you did not give anyone permission to plug him into you. Nevertheless it seems to me plain you *ought* to allow him to use your kidneys for that hour — it would be indecent to refuse.

Again, suppose pregnancy lasted only an hour, and constituted no threat to life or health. And suppose that a woman becomes pregnant as a result of rape. Admittedly she did not voluntarily do anything to bring about the existence of a child. Admittedly she did nothing at all which would give the unborn person a right to the use of her body. All the same it might well be said, as in the newly emended violinist story, that she *ought* to allow it to remain for that hour — that it would be indecent in her to refuse.

Now some people are inclined to use the term "right" in such a way that it follows from the fact that you ought to allow a person to use your body for the hour he needs, that he has a right to use your body for the hour he needs, even though he has not been given that right by any person or act. They may say that it follows also that if you refuse, you act unjustly toward him. This use of the term is perhaps so common that it cannot be called wrong; nevertheless it seems to me to be an unfortunate loosening of what we would do better to keep a tight rein on. Suppose that box of chocolates I mentioned earlier had not been given to both boys jointly, but was given only to the older boy. There he sits, stolidly eating his way through the box, his small brother watching enviously. Here we are likely to say "You ought not to be so mean. You ought to give your brother some of those chocolates." My own view is that it just does not follow from the truth of this that the brother has any right to any of the chocolates. If the boy refuses to give his brother any, he is greedy, stingy,

callous — but not unjust. I suppose that the people I have in mind will say it does follow that the brother has a right to some of the chocolates, and thus that the boy does act unjustly if he refuses to give his brother any. But the effect of saying this is to obscure what we should keep distinct, namely the difference between the boy's refusal in this case and the boy's refusal in the earlier case, in which the box was given to both boys jointly, and in which the small brother thus had what was from any point of view clear title to half.

A further objection to so using the term "right" that from the fact that A ought to do a thing for B, it follows that B has a right against A that A do it for him, is that it is going to make the question of whether or not a man has a right to a thing turn on how easy it is to provide him with it; and this seems not merely unfortunate, but morally unacceptable. Take the case of Henry Fonda again. I said earlier that I had no right to the touch of his cool hand on my fevered brow, even though I needed it to save my life. I said it would be frightfully nice of him to fly in from the West Coast to provide me with it, but that I had no right against him that he should do so. But suppose he isn't on the West Coast. Suppose he has only to walk across the room, place a hand briefly on my brow — and lo, my life is saved. Then surely he ought to do it, it would be indecent to refuse. Is it to be said "Ah well, it follows that in this case she has a right to the touch of his hand on her brow, and so it would be an injustice in him to refuse"? So that I have a right to it when it is easy for him to provide it, though no right when it's hard? It's rather a shocking idea that anyone's right should fade away and disappear as it gets harder and harder to accord them to him.

So my own view is that even though you ought to let the violinist use your kidneys for the one hour he needs, we should not conclude that he has a right to do so — we would say that if you refuse, you are, like the boy who owns all the chocolates and will give none away, self-centered and callous, indecent in fact, but not unjust. And similarly, that even supposing a case in which a woman pregnant due to rape ought to allow the unborn person to use her body for the hour he needs, we should not conclude that he has a right to do so; we should conclude that she is self-centered, callous, indecent, but not unjust, if she refuses. The complaints are no less grave; they are just different. However, there is no need to insist on this point. If anyone does wish to deduce "he has a right" from "you ought," then all the same he must surely grant that there are cases in which it is not morally required of you that you allow that violinist to use your kidneys, and in which he does not have a right to use them, and in which you do not do him an injustice if you refuse. And so also for mother and unborn child. Except in such cases as the unborn person has a right to demand it — and we were leaving open the possibility that there may be such cases — nobody is morally *required* to make large sacrifices, of health, of all other interests and concerns, of all other duties and commitments, for nine years, or even for nine months, in order to keep another person alive.

6. We have in fact to distinguish between two kinds of Samaritan: the Good Samaritan and what we might call the Minimally Decent Samaritan. The story of the Good Samaritan, you will remember, goes like this:

> A certain man went down from Jerusalem to Jericho, and fell among thieves, which stripped him of his raiment, and wounded him, and departed, leaving him half dead.
>
> And by chance there came down a certain priest that way; and when he saw him, he passed by on the other side.
>
> And likewise a Levite, when he was at the place, came and looked on him, and passed by on the other side.
>
> But a certain Samaritan, as he journeyed, came where he was; and when he saw him he had compassion on him.
>
> And went to him, and bound up his wounds, pouring in oil and wine, and set him on his own beast, and brought him to an inn, and took care of him.
>
> And on the morrow, when he departed, he took out two pence, and gave them to the host, and said unto him, "Take care of him; and whatsoever thou spendest more, when I come again, I will repay thee."
>
> (Luke 10:30–35)

The Good Samaritan went out of his way, at some cost to himself, to help one in need of it. We are not told what the options were, that is, whether or not the priest and the Levite could have helped by doing less than the Good Samaritan did, but assuming they could have, then the fact they did nothing at all shows they were not even Minimally Decent Samaritans, not because they were not Samaritans, but because they were not even minimally decent.

These things are a matter of degree, of course, but there is a difference, and it comes out perhaps most clearly in the story of Kitty Genovese, who, as you will remember, was murdered while thirty-eight people watched or listened, and did nothing at all to help her. A Good Samaritan would have rushed out to give di-

rect assistance against the murderer. Or perhaps we had better allow that it would have been a Splendid Samaritan who did this, on the ground that it would have involved a risk of death for himself. But the thirty-eight not only did not do this, they did not even trouble to pick up a phone to call the police. Minimally Decent Samaritanism would call for doing at least that, and their not having done it was monstrous.

After telling the story of the Good Samaritan, Jesus said, "Go, and do thou likewise." Perhaps he meant that we are morally required to act as the Good Samaritan did. Perhaps he was urging people to do more than is morally required of them. At all events it seems plain that it was not morally required of any of the thirty-eight that he rush out to give direct assistance at the risk of his own life, and that it is not morally required of anyone that he give long stretches of his life — nine years or nine months — to sustaining the life of a person who has no special right (we were leaving open the possibility of this) to demand it.

Indeed, with one rather striking class of exceptions, no one in any country in the world is *legally* required to do anywhere near as much as this for anyone else. The class of exceptions is obvious. My main concern here is not the state of the law in respect to abortion, but it is worth drawing attention to the fact that in no state in this country is any man compelled by law to be even a Minimally Decent Samaritan to any person; there is no law under which charges could be brought against the thirty-eight who stood by while Kitty Genovese died. By contrast, in most states in this country women are compelled by law to be not merely Minimally Decent Samaritans, but Good Samaritans to unborn persons inside them. This doesn't by itself settle anything one way or the other, because it may well be argued that there should be laws in this country — as there are in many European countries — compelling at least Minimally Decent Samaritanism.[8] But it does show that there is a gross injustice in the existing state of the law. And it shows also that the groups currently working against liberalization of abortion laws, in fact working toward having it declared unconstitutional for a state to permit abortion, had better start working for the adoption of Good Samaritan laws generally, or earn the charge that they are acting in bad faith.

I should think, myself, that Minimally Decent Samaritan laws would be one thing, Good Samaritan laws quite another, and in fact highly improper. But we are not here concerned with the law. What we should ask is not whether anybody should be compelled by law to be a Good Samaritan, but whether we must accede to a situation in which somebody is being compelled — by nature, perhaps — to be a Good Samaritan. We have, in other words, to look now at third-party interventions. I have been arguing that no person is morally required to make large sacrifices to sustain the life of another who has no right to demand them, and this even where the sacrifices do not include life itself; we are not morally required to be Good Samaritans or anyway Very Good Samaritans to one another. But what if a man cannot extricate himself from such a situation? What if he appeals to us to extricate him? It seems to me plain that there are cases in which we can, cases in which a Good Samaritan would extricate him. There you are, you were kidnapped, and nine years in bed with that violinist lie ahead of you. You have your own life to lead. You are sorry, but you simply cannot see giving up so much of your life to the sustaining of his. You cannot extricate yourself, and ask us to do so. I should have thought that — in light of his having no right to the use of your body — it was obvious that we do not have to accede to your being forced to give up so much. We can do what you ask. There is no injustice to the violinist in our doing so.

7. Following the lead of the opponents of abortion, I have throughout been speaking of the fetus merely as a person, and what I have been asking is whether or not the argument we began with, which proceeds only from the fetus's being a person, really does establish its conclusion. I have argued that it does not.

But of course there are arguments and arguments, and it may be said that I have simply fastened on the wrong one. It may be said that what is important is not merely the fact that the fetus is a person, but that it is a person for whom the woman has a special kind of responsibility issuing from the fact that she is its mother. And it might be argued that all my analogies are therefore irrelevant — for you do not have that special kind of responsibility for that violinist, Henry Fonda does not have that special kind of responsibility for me. And our attention might be drawn to the fact that men and women both *are* compelled by law to provide support for their children.

I have in effect dealt (briefly) with this argument in section 4 above; but a (still briefer) recapitulation now may be in order. Surely we do not have any such "special responsibility" for a person unless we have assumed it, explicitly or implicitly. If a set of parents do not try to prevent pregnancy, do not obtain an abortion, and then at the time of birth of the child do not put it out for adoption, but rather take it home with them, then they have assumed responsibility for it, they have given it rights, and they cannot *now* withdraw support from it at the cost of its life because they now find it difficult to go on providing for it. But if they have taken all reasonable precautions against having a child, they do not simply by virtue of their biological relationship to the child who comes into existence have a special responsibility for it. They may wish to assume responsibility for it, or they may not wish to. And I am suggesting that if assuming responsibility for it would require large sacrifices, then they may refuse. A good Samaritan would not refuse — or anyway, a Splendid Samaritan, if the sacrifices that had to be made were enormous. But then so would a Good Samaritan assume responsibility for that violinist; so would Henry Fonda, if he is a Good Samaritan, fly in from the West Coast and assume responsibility for me.

8. My argument will be found unsatisfactory on two counts by many of those who want to regard abortion as morally permissible. First, while I do argue that abortion is not impermissible, I do not argue that it is always permissible. There may well be cases in which carrying the child to term requires only Minimally Decent Samaritanism of the mother, and this is a standard we must not fall below. I am inclined to think it a merit of my account precisely that it does *not* give a general yes or a general no. It allows for and supports our sense that, for example, a sick and desperately frightened fourteen-year-old schoolgirl, pregnant due to rape, may *of course* choose abortion, and that any law which rules this out is an insane law. And it also allows for and supports our sense that in other cases resort to abortion is even positively indecent. It would be indecent in the woman to request an abortion, and indecent in a doctor to perform it, if she is in her seventh month and wants the abortion just to avoid the nuisance of postponing a trip abroad. The very fact that the arguments I have been drawing attention to treat all cases of abortion, or even all cases of abortion in which the mother's life is not at stake, as morally on a par ought to have made them suspect at the outset.

Secondly, while I am arguing for the permissibility of abortion in some cases, I am not arguing for the right to secure the death of the unborn child. It is easy to confuse these two things in that up to a certain point in the life of the fetus it is not able to survive outside the mother's body; hence removing it from her body guarantees its death. But they are importantly different. I have argued that you are not morally required to spend nine months in bed, sustaining the life of that violinist; but to say this is by no means to say that if, when you unplug yourself, there is a miracle and he survives, you then have a right to turn around and slit his throat. You may detach yourself even if this costs him his life; you have no right to be guaranteed his death, by some other means, if unplugging yourself does not kill him. There are some people who will feel dissatisfied by this feature of my argument. A woman may be utterly devastated by the thought of a child, a bit of herself, put out for adoption and never seen or heard of again. She may therefore want not merely that the child be detached from her, but more, that it die. Some opponents of abortion are inclined to regard this as beneath contempt—thereby showing insensitivity to what is surely a powerful source of despair. All the same, I agree that the desire for the child's death is not one which anybody may gratify, should it turn out to be possible to detach the child alive.

At this place, however, it should be remembered that we have only been pretending throughout that the fetus is a human being from the moment of conception. A very early abortion is surely not the killing of a person, and so is not dealt with by anything I have said here.

NOTES

1. I am very much indebted to James Thomson for discussion, criticism, and many helpful suggestions.

2. Daniel Callahan, *Abortion: Law, Choice and Morality* (New York, 1970), p. 373. This book gives a fascinating survey of the available information on abortion. The Jewish tradition is surveyed in David M. Feldman, *Birth Control in Jewish Law* (New York, 1968), Part 5; the Catholic tradition in John T. Noonan, Jr., "An Almost Absolute Value in History," in *The Morality of Abortion,* ed. John T. Noonan, Jr. (Cambridge, Mass., 1970).

3. The term "direct" in the arguments I refer to is a technical one. Roughly, what is meant by "direct killing" is either killing as an end in itself, or killing as a means to some end, for example, the end of saving someone else's life. See note 6, below, for an example of its use.

4. Cf. *Encyclical Letter of Pope Pius XI on Christian Marriage,* St. Paul Editions (Boston, n.d.), p. 32: "however much we may pity the mother whose health and even life is gravely imperiled in the performance of the duty allotted to her by nature, nevertheless what could ever be a sufficient reason for excusing in any way the direct murder of the innocent? This is precisely what we are dealing with here." Noonan (*The Morality of Abortion,* p. 43) reads this as follows: "What cause can ever avail to excuse in any way the direct killing of the innocent? For it is a question of that."

5. The thesis in (d) is in an interesting way weaker than those in (a), (b), and they rule out abortion even in cases in which both mother and child will die if the abortion is not performed. By contrast, one who held the view expressed in (d) could consistently say that one needn't prefer letting two persons die to killing one.

6. Cf. the following passage from Pius XII, *Address to the Italian Catholic Society of Midwives:* "The baby in the maternal breast has the right to life immediately from God. — Hence there is no man, no human authority, no science, no medical eugenic, social, economic or moral 'indication' which can establish or grant a valid juridical ground for a direct deliberate disposition of an innocent human life, that is a disposition which looks to its destruction either as an end or as a means to another end perhaps in itself not illicit. — The baby, still not born, is a man in the same degree and for the same reason as the mother" (quoted in Noonan, *The Morality of Abortion,* p. 45).

7. The need for a discussion of this argument was brought home to me by members of the Society for Ethical and Legal Philosophy, to whom this paper was originally presented.

8. For a discussion of the difficulties involved, and a survey of the European experience with such laws, see *The Good Samaritan and the Law,* ed. James M. Ratcliffe (New York, 1966).

BARUCH BRODY

The Morality of Abortion

THE WOMAN'S RIGHT TO HER BODY

It is a common claim that a woman ought to be in control of what happens to her body to the greatest extent possible, that she ought to be able to use her body in ways that she wants to and refrain from using it in ways that she does not want to. This right is particularly pressed where certain uses of her body have deep and lasting effects upon the character of her life, personal, social, and economic. Therefore, it is argued, a woman should be free either to carry her fetus to term, thereby using her body to support it, or to abort the fetus, thereby not using her body for that purpose.

In some contexts in which this argument is advanced, it is clear that it is not addressed to the issue of the morality of abortion at all. Rather, it is made in opposition to laws against abortion on the ground that the choice to abort or not is a moral decision that should belong only to the mother. But that specific direction of the argument is irrelevant to our present purposes; I will consider it [later] when I deal with the issues raised by laws prohibiting abortions. For the moment, I am concerned solely with the use of this principle as a putative ground tending to show the permissibility of abortion, with the claim that because it is the woman's body that carries the fetus and upon which the fetus depends, she has certain rights to abort the fetus that no one else may have.

We may begin by remarking that it is obviously correct that, as carrier of the fetus, the mother has it within her power to choose whether or not to abort the fetus.

From *Abortion and the Sanctity of Human Life: A Philosophical View* (Cambridge, Mass.: MIT Press, 1975), pp. 26–32, 37–39, 44–47, 123–129, 131, and "Fetal Humanity and the Theory of Essentialism," in *Philosophy and Sex*, Robert Baker and Frederick Elliston, eds. (Buffalo, NY: Prometheus Books, 1975), pp. 348–352. (Some parts of these essays were later revised by Professor Brody.) Reprinted by permission.

And, as an autonomous and responsible agent, she must make this choice. But let us notice that this in no way entails either that whatever choice she makes is morally right or that no one else has the right to evaluate the decision that she makes.

. . .

At first glance, it would seem that this argument cannot be used by anyone who supposes, as we do for the moment, that there is a point in fetal development from which time on the fetus is a human being. After all, people do not have the right to do anything whatsoever that may be necessary for them to retain control over the uses of their bodies. In particular, it would seem wrong for them to kill another human being in order to do so.

In a recent article,[1] Professor Judith Thomson has, in effect, argued that this simple view is mistaken. How does Professor Thomson defend her claim that the mother has a right to abort the fetus, even if it is a human being, whether or not her life is threatened and whether or not she has consented to the act of intercourse in which the fetus is conceived? At one point,[2] discussing just the case in which the mother's life is threatened, she makes the following suggestion:

In [abortion], there are only two people involved, one whose life is threatened and one who threatens it. Both are innocent: the one who is threatened is not threatened because of any fault, the one who threatens does not threaten because of any fault. For this reason, we may feel that we bystanders cannot intervene. But the person threatened can.

But surely this description is equally applicable to the following case: *A* and *B* are adrift on a lifeboat, *B* has a disease that he can survive, but *A*, if he contracts it, will die, and the only way that *A* can avoid that is by killing *B* and pushing him overboard. Surely, *A* has no right to do this. So there must be some special reason why the mother has, if she does, the right to abort the fetus.

There is, to be sure, an important difference between our lifeboat case and abortion, one that leads us to the heart of Professor Thomson's argument. In the case that we envisaged, both *A* and *B* have equal rights to be in the lifeboat, but the mother's body is hers and not the fetus's and she has first rights to its use. The primacy of these rights allows an abortion whether or not her life is threatened. Professor Thomson summarizes this argument in the following way:[3]

I am arguing only that having a right to life does not guarantee having either a right to be given the use of, or a right to be allowed continued use of, another person's body — even if one needs it for life itself.

One part of this claim is clearly correct. I have no duty to *X* to save *X*'s life by giving him the use of my body (or my life savings, or the only home I have, and so on), and *X* has no right, even to save his life, to any of those things. Thus, the fetus conceived in the laboratory that will perish unless it is implanted into a woman's body has in fact no right to any woman's body. But this portion of the claim is irrelevant to the abortion issue, for in abortion of the fetus that is a human being the mother must kill *X* to get back the sole use of her body, and that is an entirely different matter.

This point can also be put as follows: . . . we must distinguish the taking of *X*'s life from the saving of *X*'s life, even if we assume that one has a duty not to do the former and to do the latter. Now that latter duty, if it exists at all, is much weaker than the first duty; many circumstances may relieve us from the latter duty that will not relieve us from the former one. Thus, I am certainly relieved from my duty to save *X*'s life by the fact that fulfilling it means the loss of my life savings. It may be noble for me to save *X*'s life at the cost of everything I have, but I certainly have no duty to do that. And the same observation may be made about cases in which I can save *X*'s life by giving him the use of my body for an extended period of time. However, I am not relieved of my duty not to take *X*'s life by the fact that fulfilling it means the loss of everything I have and not even by the fact that fulfilling it means the loss of my life. . . .

At one point in her paper, Professor Thomson does consider this objection. She has previously imagined the following case: a famous violinist, who is dying from a kidney ailment, has been, without your consent, plugged into you for a period of time so that his body can use your kidneys:

Some people are rather stricter about the right to life. In their view, it does not include the right to be given anything, but amounts to, and only to, the right not to be killed by anybody. But here a related difficulty arises. If everybody is to refrain from killing that violinist, then everybody must refrain from doing a great many different sorts of things . . . everybody must refrain from unplugging you from him. But does he have a right against everybody that they shall refrain from unplugging you from him? To refrain from doing this is to allow him to continue to use your kidneys . . . certainly the violinist has no right against you that you shall allow him to continue to use your kidneys.

Applying this argument to the case of abortion, we can see that Professor Thomson's argument would run as follows:

a. Assume that the fetus's right to life includes the right not to be killed by the woman carrying him.
b. But to refrain from killing the fetus is to allow him the continued use of the woman's body.
c. So our first assumption entails that the fetus's right to life includes the right to the continued use of the woman's body.
d. But we all grant that the fetus does not have the right to the continued use of the woman's body.
e. Therefore, the fetus's right to life cannot include the right not to be killed by the woman in question.

And it is also now clear what is wrong with this argument. When we granted that the fetus has no right to the continued use of the woman's body, all that we meant was that he does not have this right merely because the continued use saves his life. But, of course, there may be other reasons why he has this right. One would be that the only way to take the use of the woman's body away from the fetus is by killing him, and that is something that neither she nor we have the right to do. So, I submit, the way in which Assumption d is true is irrelevant, and cannot be used by Professor Thomson, for Assumption d is true only in cases where the saving of the life of the fetus is at stake and not in cases where the taking of his life is at stake.

I conclude therefore that Professor Thomson has not established the truth of her claims about abortion, primarily because she has not sufficiently attended to the distinction between our duty to save X's life and our duty not to take it. Once one attends to that distinction, it would seem that the mother, in order to regain control over her body, has no right to abort the fetus from the point at which it becomes a human being.

It may also be useful to say a few words about the larger and less rigorous context of the argument that the woman has a right to her own body. It is surely true that one way in which women have been oppressed is by their being denied authority over their own bodies. But it seems to me that, as the struggle is carried on for meaningful amelioration of such oppression, it ought not to be carried so far that it violates the steady responsibilities all people have to one another. Parents may not desert their children, one class may not oppress another, one race or nation may not exploit another. For parents, powerful groups in society, races or nations in ascendancy, there are penalties for refraining from these wrong actions, but those penalties can in no way be taken as the justification for such wrong actions. Similarly, if the fetus is a human being, the penalty of carrying it cannot, I believe, be used as the justification for destroying it.

. . .

THE MODEL PENAL CODE CASES

All of the arguments that we have looked at so far are attempts to show that there is something special about abortion that justifies its being treated differently from other cases of the taking of human life. We shall now consider claims that are confined to certain special cases of abortion: the case in which the mother has been raped, the case in which bearing the child would be harmful to her health, and the case in which having the child may cause a problem for the rest of her family (the latter case is a particular case of the societal argument). In addressing these issues, we shall see whether there is any point to the permissibility of abortions in some of the cases covered by the Model Penal Code[4] proposals.

When the expectant mother has conceived after being raped, there are two different sorts of considerations that might support the claim that she has the right to take the life of the fetus. They are the following:

(A) the woman in question has already suffered immensely from the act of rape and the physical and/or psychological aftereffects of that act. It would be particularly unjust, the argument runs, for her to have to live through an unwanted pregnancy owing to that act of rape. Therefore, even if we are at a stage at which the fetus is a human being, the mother has the right to abort it; (B) the fetus in question has no right to be in that woman. It was put there as a result of an act of aggression upon her by the rapist, and its continued presence is an act of aggression against the mother. She has a right to repel that aggression by aborting the fetus.

The first argument is very compelling. We can all agree that a terrible injustice has been committed on the woman who is raped. The question that we have to consider, however, is whether it follows that it is morally permissible for her to abort the fetus. We must make that consideration reflecting that, however unjust the act of rape, it was not the fetus who committed or commissioned it. The injustice of the act, then, should in no way impinge upon the rights of the fetus, for it is innocent. What remains is the initial misfortune of the mother (and the injustice of her having to pass through the pregnancy, and, further, to assume responsibility of at least giving the child over for adoption or assuming the burden of its care). However unfortunate that circumstance, however unjust, the misfortune and the injustice are not sufficient cause to justify the taking of the life of an innocent human being as a means of mitigation.

It is at this point that Argument B comes in, for its whole point is that the fetus, by its mere presence in the mother, is committing an act of aggression against her, one over and above the one committed by the rapist, and one that the mother has a right to repel by abortion. But . . . (1) the fetus is certainly innocent (in the sense of not responsible) for any act of aggression against the mother and . . . (2) the mere presence of the fetus in the mother, no matter how unfortunate for her, does not constitute an act of aggression by the fetus against the mother. Argument B fails then at just that point at which Argument A needs its support, and we can therefore conclude that the fact that pregnancy is the result of rape does not give the mother the right to abort the fetus.

We turn next to the case in which the continued existence of the fetus would threaten the mental and/or physical health but not necessarily the life of the mother. Again, . . . the fact that the fetus's continued existence poses a threat to the life of the mother does not justify her aborting it.* It would seem to be true, a fortiori, that the fact that the fetus's continued existence poses a threat to the mental and/or physical health of the mother does not justify her aborting it either.

We come finally to those cases in which the continuation of the pregnancy would cause serious problems for the rest of the family. There are a variety of cases that we have to consider here together. Perhaps the health of the mother will be affected in such a way that she cannot function effectively as a wife and mother during, or even after, the pregnancy. Or perhaps the expenses incurred as a result of the pregnancy would be utterly beyond the financial resources of the family. The important point is that the continuation of the pregnancy raises a serious problem for other innocent people involved besides the mother and the fetus, and it may be argued that the mother has the right to abort the fetus to avoid that problem.

By now, the difficulties with this argument should be apparent. We have seen earlier that the mere fact that the continued existence of the fetus threatens to harm the mother does not, by itself, justify the aborting of the fetus. Why should anything be changed by the fact that the threatened harm will accrue to the other members of the family and not to the mother? Of course, it would be different if the fetus were committing an act of aggression against the other members of the family. But, once more, this is certainly not the case.

We conclude, therefore, that none of these special circumstances justifies an abortion from that point at which the fetus is a human being.

· · ·

*Ed. note: Professor Brody provided a lengthy argument to this effect in a chapter not here excerpted. His summary of that argument is as follows: "Is it permissible, as an act of killing a pursuer, to abort the fetus in order to save the mother? The first thing that we should note is that Pope Pius's objection to aborting the fetus as a permissible act of killing a pursuer is mistaken. His objection is that the fetus shows no knowledge or intention in his attempt to take the life of the mother, that the fetus is, in a word, innocent. But that only means that the condition of guilt is not satisfied, and we have seen that its satisfaction is not necessary."

"Is, then, the aborting of the fetus, when necessary to save the life of the mother, a permissible act of killing a pursuer? It is true that in such cases the fetus is a danger to the mother. But it is also clear that the condition of attempt is not satisfied. The fetus has neither the beliefs nor the intention to which we have referred. Furthermore, there is on the part of the fetus no action that threatens the life of the mother. So not even the condition of action is satisfied. It seems to follow, therefore, that aborting the fetus could not be a permissible act of killing a pursuer."

FETAL HUMANITY AND BRAIN FUNCTION

The question which we must now consider is the question of fetal humanity. Some have argued that the fetus is a human being with a right to life (or, for convenience, just a human being) from the moment of conception. Others have argued that the fetus only becomes a human being at the moment of birth. Many positions in between these two extremes have also been suggested. How are we to decide which is correct?

The analysis which we will propose here rests upon certain metaphysical assumptions which I have defended elsewhere. These assumptions are: (a) the question is when has the fetus acquired all the properties essential (necessary) for being a human being, for when it has, it is a human being; (b) these properties are such that the loss of any one of them means that the human being in question has gone out of existence and not merely stopped being a human being; (c) human beings go out of existence when they die. It follows from these assumptions that the fetus becomes a human being when it acquires all those characteristics which are such that the loss of any one of them would result in the fetus's being dead. We must, therefore, turn to the analysis of death.

· · ·

We will first consider the question of what properties are essential to being human if we suppose that death and the passing out of existence occur only if there has been an irreparable cessation of brain function (keeping in mind that that condition itself, as we have noted, is a matter of medical judgment). We shall then consider the same question on the supposition that [Paul] Ramsey's more complicated theory of death (the modified traditional view) is correct.

According to what is called the brain-death theory, as long as there has not been an irreparable cessation of brain function the person in question continues to exist, no matter what else has happened to him. If so, it seems to follow that there is only one property—leaving aside those entailed by this one property—that is essential to humanity, namely, the possession of a brain that has not suffered an irreparable cessation of function.

Several consequences follow immediately from this conclusion. We can see that a variety of often advanced claims about the essence of humanity are false. For example, the claim that movement, or perhaps just the ability to move, is essential for being human is false. A human being who has stopped moving, and even one who has lost the ability to move, has not therefore stopped existing. Being able to move, and a fortiori moving, are not essential properties of human beings and therefore are not essential to being human. Similarly, the claim that being perceivable by other human beings is essential for being human is also false. A human being who has stopped being perceivable by other humans (for example, someone isolated on the other side of the moon, out of reach even of radio communication) has not stopped existing. Being perceivable by other human beings is not an essential property of human beings and is not essential to being human. And the same point can be made about the claims that viability is essential for being human, that independent existence is essential for being human, and that actual interaction with other human beings is essential for being human. The loss of any of these properties would not mean that the human being in question had gone out of existence, so none of them can be essential to that human being and none of them can be essential for being human.

Let us now look at the following argument: (1) A functioning brain (or at least, a brain that, if not functioning, is susceptible of function) is a property that every human being must have because it is essential for being human. (2) By the time an entity acquires that property, it has all the other properties that are essential for being human. Therefore, when the fetus acquires that property it becomes a human being. It is clear that the property in question is, according to the brain-death theory, one that is had essentially by all human beings. The question that we have to consider is whether the second premise is true. It might appear that its truth does follow from the brain-death theory. After all, we did see that the theory entails that only one property (together with those entailed by it) is essential for being human. Nevertheless, rather than relying solely on my earlier argument, I shall adopt an alternative approach to strengthen the conviction that this second premise is true: I shall note the important ways in which the fetus resembles and differs from an ordinary human being by the time it definitely has a functioning brain (about the end of the sixth week of development). It shall then be evident, in light of our theory of essentialism, that none of these differences

involves the lack of some property in the fetus that is essential for its being human.

Structurally, there are few features of the human being that are not fully present by the end of the sixth week. Not only are the familiar external features and all the internal organs present, but the contours of the body are nicely rounded. More important, the body is functioning. Not only is the brain functioning, but the heart is beating sturdily (the fetus by this time has its own completely developed vascular system), the stomach is producing digestive juices, the liver is manufacturing blood cells, the kidney is extracting uric acid from the blood, and the nerves and muscles are operating in concert, so that reflex reactions can begin.

What are the properties that a fetus acquires after the sixth week of its development? Certain structures do appear later. These include the fingernails (which appear in the third month), the completed vocal chords (which also appear then), taste buds and salivary glands (again, in the third month), and hair and eyelashes (in the fifth month). In addition, certain functions begin later than the sixth week. The fetus begins to urinate (in the third month), to move spontaneously (in the third month), to respond to external stimuli (at least in the fifth month), and to breathe (in the sixth month). Moreover, there is a constant growth in size. And finally, at the time of birth the fetus ceases to receive its oxygen and food through the placenta and starts receiving them through the mouth and nose.

I will not examine each of these properties (structures and functions) to show that they are not essential for being human. The procedure would be essentially the one used previously to show that various essentialist claims are in error. We might, therefore, conclude, on the supposition that the brain-death theory is correct, that the fetus becomes a human being about the end of the sixth week after its development.

There is, however, one complication that should be noted here. There are, after all, progressive stages in the physical development and in the functioning of the brain. For example, the fetal brain (and nervous system) does not develop sufficiently to support spontaneous motion until some time in the third month after conception. There is, of course, no doubt that that stage of development is sufficient for the fetus to be human. No one would be likely to maintain that a spontaneously moving human being has died; and similarly, a spontaneously moving fetus would seem to have become human. One might, however, want to claim that the fetus does not become a human being until the point of spontaneous movement. So then, on the supposition that the brain-death theory of death is correct, one ought to conclude that the fetus becomes a human being at some time between the sixth and twelfth week after its conception.

But what if we reject the brain-death theory, and replace it with its equally plausible contender, Ramsey's theory of death? According to that theory — which we can call the brain, heart, and lung theory of death — the human being does not die, does not go out of existence, until such time as the brain, heart and lungs have irreparably ceased functioning naturally. What are the essential features of being human according to this theory?

Actually, the adoption of Ramsey's theory requires no major modifications. According to that theory, what is essential to being human, what each human being must retain if he is to continue to exist, is the possession of a functioning (actually or potentially) heart, lung, or brain. It is only when a human being possesses none of these that he dies and goes out of existence; and the fetus comes into humanity, so to speak, when he acquires one of these.

On Ramsey's theory, the argument would now run as follows: (1) The property of having a functioning brain, heart, or lungs (or at least organs of the kind that, if not functioning, are susceptible of function) is one that every human being must have because it is essential for being human. (2) By the time that an entity acquires that property it has all the other properties that are essential for being human. Therefore, when the fetus acquires that property it becomes a human being. There remains, once more, the problem of the second premise. Since the fetal heart starts operating rather early, it is not clear that the second premise is correct. Many systems are not yet operating, and many structures are not yet present. Still, following our theory of essentialism, we should conclude that the fetus becomes a human being when it acquires a functioning heart (the first of the organs to function in the fetus).

There is, however, a further complication here, and it is analogous to the one encountered if we adopt the brain-death theory: When may we properly say that the fetal heart begins to function? At two weeks, when occasional contractions of the primitive fetal heart are present? In the fourth to fifth week, when the heart, although incomplete, is beating regularly and pumping blood cells through a closed vascular system, and when the tracings obtained by an ECG exhibit the classical elements of an adult tracing? Or after the end of the seventh week, when the fetal heart is functionally complete and "normal"?

We have not reached a precise conclusion in our study of the question of when the fetus becomes a human being. We do know that it does so some time between the end of the second week and the end of the third month. But it surely is not a human being at the moment of conception and it surely is one by the end of the third month. Though we have not come to a final answer to our question, we have narrowed the range of acceptable answers considerably.

[In summary] we have argued that the fetus becomes a human being with a right to life some time between the second and twelfth week after conception. We have also argued that abortions are morally impermissible after that point except in rather unusual circumstances. What is crucial to note is that neither of these arguments appeal to any theological considerations. We conclude, therefore, that there is a human-rights basis for moral opposition to abortions.

• • •

LAW AND SOCIETY IN A DEMOCRACY

Before turning to such considerations, however, we must first examine several important assertions about law and society that, if true, would justify the joint assertion of the principles that abortion is murder but nevertheless should be or remain legal. The first is the assertion that citizens of a pluralistic society must forgo the use of the law as a method of enforcing what are their private moralities. It might well be argued that in our pluralistic society, in which there are serious disagreements about the status of the fetus and about the rightness and wrongness of abortion in consequence, it would be wrong (or inappropriate) to legislate against abortion.

Such assertions about a pluralistic society are difficult to evaluate because of their imprecision. So let us first try to formulate some version of them more carefully. Consider the following general principle: Principle [1]. When the citizens of a society strongly disagree about the rightness and wrongness of a given action, and a considerable number think that such an action is right (or, at least, permissible), then it is wrong (or inappropriate) for that society to prohibit that action by law, even if the majority of citizens believe such an action to be wrong.

There are a variety of arguments that can be offered in support of the principle. One appeals to the right of the minority to follow its own conscience rather than being compelled to follow the conscience of the majority. That right has a theoretical political justification, but it also is practically implicit in the inappropriateness in the members of the majority imposing this kind of enforcement upon the minority that would be opposed were they the minority and were the enforcement being imposed upon them. Another argument appeals to the detrimental consequences to a society of the sense on the part of a significant minority that the law is being used by the majority to coerce. Such considerations make it seem that a principle like [1] is true.

If Principle [1] is true, it is easy to offer a defense of the joint assertion of the principles that abortion is murder but nevertheless should be or remain legal. All we need are the additional obvious assumptions that the citizens of our society strongly disagree about the morality of abortion and that at least a significant minority of individuals believe that there are many cases in which abortion is permissible. From these assumptions and Principle [1] it follows that abortions should be or remain legal even if they are murders.

The trouble with this argument is that it depends upon Principle [1]. I agree that, because of the considerations mentioned already, something like Principle [1] must be true. But Principle [1] as formulated is much too broad to be defensible. Consider, after all, a society in which a significant number of citizens think that it is morally permissible, and perhaps even obligatory, to kill Blacks or Jews, for example, because they are seen as being something less than fully human. It would seem to follow from Principle [1] that the law should not prohibit such actions. Surely this consequence of Principle [1] is wrong. Even if a pluralistic society should forgo passing many laws out of deference to the views of those who think that the actions that would thereby be prevented are not wrong, there remain some cases in which the force of the law should be applied because of the evil of the actions it is intended to prevent. If such actions produce very harmful results and infringe upon the rights of a sufficiently large number of individuals, then the possible benefits that may be derived from passing and enforcing a law preventing those actions may well override the rights of the minority (or even of the majority) to follow its conscience.

Principle [1] must therefore be modified as follows: Principle [2]. When the citizens of a society strongly disagree about the rightness and wrongness of a given action, and a considerable number think that such an action is right (or, at least, permissible), then it is wrong (or inappropriate) for that society to prohibit that action by law, even if the majority of citizens believe such an action to be wrong, unless the action in question is so evil that the desirability of legal prohibition outweighs the desirability of granting to the minority the right to follow its own conscience.

Principle [2] is, of course, rather vague. In particular, its last clause needs further clarification. But Principle [2] is clear enough for us to see that it cannot be used to justify the joint assertibility of the principles that abortion is murder but should nevertheless be or remain legal. Principle [2], conjoined with the obvious truths that the citizens of our society strongly disagree about the rightness and wrongness of abortion and that a significant number of citizens believe that, in certain circumstances, the right (or, at least, a permissible) thing to do is to have an abortion, does not yield the conclusion that abortion should be or remain legal if abortion is murder. After all, if abortion is murder, then the action in question is the unjustifiable taking of a human life and may well fall under the last clause of Principle [2]. The destruction of a fetus may not be unlike the killing of a Black or Jew. They may all be cases of the unjust taking of a human life.

•   •   •

THE DECISION IN *ROE V. WADE*

Two decisions were announced by the [United States Supreme] Court on January 22 [1973]. The first (*Roe v. Wade*) involved a challenge to a Texas law prohibiting all abortions not necessary to save the life of the mother. The second (*Doe v. Bolton*) tested a Georgia law incorporating many of the recommendations of the Model Penal Code as to the circumstances under which abortion should be allowed (in the case of rape and of a defective fetus, as well as when the pregnancy threatens the life or health of the mother), together with provisions regulating the place where abortions can be performed, the number of doctors that must concur, and other factors.

Of these two decisions, the more fundamental was *Roe v. Wade*. It was in this case that the Court came to grips with the central legal issue, namely, the extent to which it is legitimate for the state to prohibit or regulate abortion. In *Doe v. Bolton*, the Court was more concerned with subsidiary issues involving the legitimacy of particular types of regulations.

The Court summarized its decision in *Roe v. Wade* as follows:[5]

(a) For the stage prior to approximately the end of the first trimester/three months the abortion decision and its effectuation must be left to the medical judgment of the pregnant woman's attending physician.

(b) For the stage subsequent to approximately the end of the first trimester, the state, in promoting its interest in the health of the mother, may, if it chooses, regulate the abortion procedure in ways that are reasonably related to maternal health.

(c) For the stage subsequent to viability, the state, in promoting its interest in the potentiality of human life, may, if it chooses, regulate, and even proscribe, abortion except where it is necessary, in appropriate medical judgment, for the preservation of the life or health of the mother.

In short, the Court ruled that abortion can be prohibited only after viability and then only if the life or health of the mother is not threatened. Before viability, abortions cannot be prohibited, but they can be regulated after the first trimester if the regulations are reasonably related to maternal health. This last clause is taken very seriously by the Court. In *Doe v. Bolton*, instances of regulation in the Georgia code were found unconstitutional on the ground that they were not reasonably related to maternal health.

How did the Court arrive at this decision? In Sections V and VII of the decision, it set out the claims on both sides. Jane Roe's argument was summarized in these words:[6]

The principal thrust of appellant's attack on the Texas statutes is that they improperly invade a right, said to be possessed by the pregnant woman, to choose to determine her pregnancy.

On the other hand, the Court saw as possible legitimate interests of the state the regulation of abortion, like other medical procedures, so as to ensure maximum safety for the patient and the protection of prenatal life. At this point in the decision, the Court added the following very significant remark:[7]

Logically, of course, a legitimate state interest in this area need not stand or fall on acceptance of the belief that life begins at conception or at some other point prior to live birth. In assessing the state's interest, recognition may be given to the less rigid claim that as long as at least potential life is in-

volved, the state may assert interests beyond the protection of the pregnant woman alone.

In Sections VIII to X, the Court stated its conclusion. It viewed this case as one presenting a conflict of interests, and it saw itself as weighing these interests. It began by agreeing that the woman's right to privacy did encompass her right to decide whether or not to terminate her pregnancy. But it argued that this right is not absolute, since the state's interests must also be considered:[8]

We therefore conclude that the right of personal privacy includes the abortion decision, but that this right is not unqualified and must be considered against important state interests in regulation.

The Court had no hesitation in ruling that the woman's right can be limited after the first trimester because of the state's interest in preserving and protecting maternal health. But the Court was less prepared to agree that the woman's right can be limited because of the state's interest in protecting prenatal life. Indeed, the Court rejected Texas's strong claim that life begins at conception, and that the state therefore has a right to protect such life by prohibiting abortion. The first reason advanced for rejecting that claim was phrased in this way:[9]

We need not resolve the difficult question of when life begins. When those trained in the respective disciplines of medicine, philosophy, and theology are unable to arrive at any consensus, the judiciary, at this point in the development of man's knowledge, is not in a position to speculate as to the answer.

Its second reason was that[10]

In areas other than criminal abortion, the law has been reluctant to endorse any theory that life, as we recognize it, begins before live birth or to accord legal rights to the unborn except in narrowly defined situations and except when the rights are contingent upon live birth.

The Court accepted the weaker claim that the state has an interest in protecting the potential of life. But when does that interest become compelling enough to enable the state to prohibit abortion? The Court said:[11]

. . . the compelling point is at viability. This is so because the fetus then has the capacity of meaningful life outside the mother's womb. State regulation protective of fetal life after viability thus has both logical and biological justifications. If the state is interested in protecting fetal life after viability, it may go so far as to proscribe abortion during that period except where it is necessary to preserve the life or health of the mother.

THE COURT ON POTENTIAL LIFE

I want to begin by considering that part of the Court's decision that allows Texas to proscribe abortions after viability so as to protect its interest in potential life. I note that it is difficult to evaluate that important part of the decision because the Court had little to say in defense of it other than the paragraph just quoted.

There are three very dubious elements of this ruling:

1. Why is the state prohibited from proscribing abortions when the life or health of the mother is threatened? Perhaps the following argument may be offered in the case of threat to maternal life: the mother is actually alive but the fetus is only potentially alive, and the protection of actual life takes precedence over the protection of potential life. Even if we grant this argument, why is the state prevented from prohibiting abortion when only maternal health is threatened? What is the argument against the claim that protecting potential life takes precedence in that case?

2. Why does the interest in potential life become compelling only when the stage of viability is reached? The Court's whole argument for this claim is[12]

This is so because the fetus then presumably has the capacity of meaningful life outside the mother's womb.

There is, no doubt, an important type of potential for life, the capacity of meaningful life outside the mother's womb, that the fetus acquires only at the time of viability. But there are other types of potential for life that it acquires earlier. At conception, for example, the fertilized cell has the potential for life in the sense that it will, in the normal course of events, develop into a human being. A six-week-old fetus has the potential for life in the stronger sense that all of the major organs it needs for life are already functioning. Why then does the state's interest in protecting potential life become compelling only at the point of viability? The Court failed to answer that question.

3. It can fairly be said that those trained in the respective disciplines of medicine, philosophy, and the-

ology are unlikely to be able to arrive at any consensus on the question of when the fetus becomes potentially alive and when the state's interest in protecting this potential life becomes compelling enough to outweigh the rights of the mother. Why then did not the Court conclude, as it did when it considered the question of fetal humanity, that the judiciary cannot rule on such a question?

In pursuit of this last point, we approach the Court's more fundamental arguments against prohibiting abortion before viability.

THE COURT ON ACTUAL LIFE

The crucial claim in the Court's decision is that laws prohibiting abortion cannot be justified on the ground that the state has an interest in protecting the life of the fetus who is a human being. The Court offered two reasons for this claim: that the law has never yet accorded the fetus this status, and that the matter of fetal humanity is not one about which it is appropriate for the courts to speculate.

The first of the Court's reasons is not particularly strong. Whatever force we want to ascribe to precedent in the law, the Court has in the past modified its previous decisions in light of newer information and insights. In a matter as important as the conflict between the fetus's right to life and the rights of the mother, it would have seemed particularly necessary to deal with the issues rather than relying upon precedent.

In its second argument, the Court did deal with those issues by adopting the following principle:

1. It is inappropriate for the Court to speculate about the answer to questions about which relevant professional specialists cannot arrive at a consensus. This principle seems irrelevant. The issue before the Court was whether the Texas legislature could make a determination in light of the best available evidence and legislate on the basis of it. Justice White, in his dissent, raised this point:[13]

The upshot is that the people and legislatures of the fifty states are constitutionally disentitled to weigh the relative importance of the continued existence and development of the fetus on the one hand against the spectrum of possible impacts on the mother on the other hand.

This objection could be met, however, if we modified the Court's principle in the following way:

2. It is inappropriate for a legislature to write law upon the basis of its best belief when the relevant pro-

fessional specialists cannot agree that that belief is correct.

On the basis of such a principle, the Court could argue that Texas had no right to protect by law the right of the fetus to life, thereby acknowledging it to be a human being with such a right, because the relevant specialists do not agree that the fetus has that right. As it stands, however, Principle 2 is questionable. In a large number of areas, legislatures regularly do (and must) act upon issues upon which there is a wide diversity of opinion among professional specialists. So Principle 2 has to be modified to deal with only certain cases, and the obvious suggestion is:

3. It is inappropriate for the legislature, on the ground of belief, to write law in such a way as to violate the basic rights of some individuals, when professional specialists do not agree that that belief is correct.

This principle could be used to defend the Court's decision. But is there any reason to accept it as true? Two arguments for this principle immediately suggest themselves: (a) If the relevant professional specialists do not agree, then there cannot be any proof that the answer in question is the correct one. But a legislature should not infringe the rights of people on the basis of unproved belief. (b) When the professional specialists do not agree, there must be legitimate and reasonable alternatives of belief, and we ought to respect the rights of believers in each of these alternatives to act on their own judgments.

· · ·

We have already discussed . . . the principles that lie behind these arguments. We saw . . . that neither of these arguments, as applied to abortion, is acceptable if the fetus is a human being. To employ these arguments correctly, the Court must presuppose that the fetus is not a human being. And that, of course, it cannot do, since the aim of its logic is the view that courts and legislatures, at least at this juncture, should remain neutral on the issue of fetal humanity.

There is a second point that should be noted about Principles 1 to 3. There are cases in which, by failing to deal with an issue, an implicit, inevitable decision is in fact reached. We have before us such a case. The Court was considering Texas's claim that it had the right to prohibit abortion in order to protect the fetus. The Court conceded that if the fetus had a protectable

right to life, Texas could prohibit abortions. But when the Court concluded that it (and, by implication, Texas) could not decide whether the fetus is a human being with the right to life, Texas was compelled to act as if the fetus had no such right that Texas could protect. Why should Principles like 1 to 3 be accepted if the result is the effective endorsement of one disputed claim over another?[14]

There is an alternative to the Court's approach. It is that each of the legislatures should consider the vexing problems surrounding abortions, weigh all of the relevant factors, and write law on the basis of its conclusions. The legislature would, undoubtedly, have to consider the question of fetal humanity, but, I submit, the Court is wrong in supposing that there is a way in which that question can be avoided.

· · ·

CONCLUSION

The Supreme Court has ruled, and the principal legal issues in this country are, at least for now, resolved. I have tried to show, however, that the Court's ruling was in error, that it failed to grapple with the crucial issues surrounding the laws prohibiting abortion. The serious public debate about abortion must, and certainly will, continue.

NOTES

1. J. Thomson, "A Defense of Abortion," *Philosophy and Public Affairs,* Vol. 1 (1971), pp. 47–66.

2. Ibid., p. 53.

3. Ibid., p. 56.

4. On the Model Penal Code provisions, see American Law Institute, *Model Penal Code:* Tentative Draft No. 9 (1959).

5. *Roe v. Wade, 41 LW* 4229.

6. *Roe, 41 LW* 4218.

7. *Roe, 41 LW* 4224.

8. *Roe, 41 LW* 4226.

9. *Roe, 41 LW* 4227.

10. *Roe, 41 LW* 4228.

11. *Roe, 41 LW* 4228–4229.

12. Ibid.

13. *Roe, 41 LW* 4246.

14. This argument is derived from one used (for very different purposes) by William James in *The Will to Believe,* reprinted in William James, *The Will to Believe and Other Essays on Popular Philosophy* (New York: Dover, 1956), pp. 1–31.

MARY ANNE WARREN

On the Moral and Legal Status of Abortion

We will be concerned with both the moral status of abortion, which for our purposes we may define as the act which a woman performs in voluntarily terminating, or allowing another person to terminate, her pregnancy, and the legal status which is appropriate for this act. I will argue that, while it is not possible to produce a satisfactory defense of a woman's right to obtain an abortion without showing that a fetus is not a human being, in the morally relevant sense of that term, we ought not to conclude that the difficulties involved in determining whether or not a fetus is human make it impossible to produce any satisfactory solution to the problem of the moral status of abortion. For it is possible to show that, on the basis of intuitions which we may expect even the opponents of abortion to share, a fetus is not a person, and hence not the sort of entity to which it is proper to ascribe full moral rights.

Of course, while some philosophers would deny the possibility of any such proof,[1] others will deny that there is any need for it, since the moral permissibility of abortion appears to them to be too obvious to require proof. But the inadequacy of this attitude should be evident from the fact that both the friends and the foes of abortion consider their position to be morally self-evident. Because proabortionists have never adequately come to grips with the conceptual issues surrounding abortion, most, if not all, of the arguments which they advance in opposition to laws restricting access to abortion fail to refute or even weaken the traditional antiabortion argument, i.e., that a fetus is a human being, and therefore abortion is murder.

These arguments are typically of one of two sorts. Either they point to the terrible side effects of the restrictive laws, e.g., the deaths due to illegal abortions, and the fact that it is poor women who suffer the most as a result of these laws, or else they state that to deny a woman access to abortion is to deprive her of her right to control her own body. Unfortunately, however, the fact that restricting access to abortion has tragic side effects does not, in itself, show that the restrictions are unjustified, since murder is wrong regardless of the consequences of prohibiting it; and the appeal to the right to control one's body, which is generally construed as a property right, is at best a rather feeble argument for the permissibility of abortion. Mere ownership does not give me the right to kill innocent people whom I find on my property, and indeed I am apt to be held responsible if such people injure themselves while on my property. It is equally unclear that I have any moral right to expel an innocent person from my property when I know that doing so will result in his death.

Furthermore, it is probably inappropriate to describe a woman's body as her property, since it seems natural to hold that a person is something distinct from her property, but not from her body. Even those who would object to the identification of a person with his body, or with the conjunction of his body and his mind, must admit that it would be very odd to describe, say, breaking a leg, as damaging one's property, and much more appropriate to describe it as injuring one*self.* Thus it is probably a mistake to argue that the right to obtain an abortion is in any way derived from the right to own and regulate property.

But however we wish to construe the right to abortion, we cannot hope to convince those who consider abortion a form of murder of the existence of any such right unless we are able to produce a clear and convincing refutation of the traditional antiabortion argument, and this has not, to my knowledge, been done. With respect to the two most vital issues which that argument involves, i.e., the humanity of the fetus and its implication for the moral status of abortion, confusion has prevailed on both sides of the dispute.

Reprinted from *The Monist,* Vol. 57, No. 1 (January 1973) with the permission of the publisher. Copyright © 1973, *The Monist.*

Thus, both proabortionists and antiabortionists have tended to abstract the question of whether abortion is wrong to that of whether it is wrong to destroy a fetus, just as though the rights of another person were not necessarily involved. This mistaken abstraction has led to the almost universal assumption that if a fetus is a human being, with a right to life, then it follows immediately that abortion is wrong (except perhaps when necessary to save the woman's life), and that it ought to be prohibited. It has also been generally assumed that unless the question about the status of the fetus is answered, the moral status of abortion cannot possibly be determined.

Two recent papers, one by B. A. Brody,[2] and one by Judith Thomson,[3] have attempted to settle the question of whether abortion ought to be prohibited apart from the question of whether or not the fetus is human. Brody examines the possibility that the following two statements are compatible: (1) that abortion is the taking of innocent human life, and therefore wrong; and (2) that nevertheless it ought not to be prohibited by law, at least under the present circumstances.[4] Not surprisingly, Brody finds it impossible to reconcile these two statements since, as he rightly argues, none of the unfortunate side effects of the prohibition of abortion is bad enough to justify legalizing the *wrongful* taking of human life. He is mistaken, however, in concluding that the incompatibility of (1) and (2), in itself, shows that "the legal problem about abortion cannot be resolved independently of the status of the fetus problem" (p. 369).

What Brody fails to realize is that (1) embodies the questionable assumption that if a fetus is a human being, then of course abortion is morally wrong, and that an attack on *this* assumption is more promising, as a way of reconciling the humanity of the fetus with the claim that laws prohibiting abortion are unjustified, than is an attack on the assumption that if abortion is the wrongful killing of innocent human beings then it ought to be prohibited. He thus overlooks the possibility that a fetus may have a right to life and abortion still be morally permissible, in that the right of a woman to terminate an unwanted pregnancy might override the right of the fetus to be kept alive. The immorality of abortion is no more demonstrated by the humanity of the fetus, in itself, than the immorality of killing in self-defense is demonstrated by the fact that the assailant is a human being. Neither is it demonstrated by the *innocence* of the fetus, since there may be situa-

tions in which the killing of innocent human beings is justified.

It is perhaps not surprising that Brody fails to spot this assumption, since it has been accepted with little or no argument by nearly everyone who has written on the morality of abortion. John Noonan is correct in saying that "the fundamental question in the long history of abortion is, How do you determine the humanity of a being?"[5] He summarizes his own antiabortion argument, which is a version of the official position of the Catholic Church, as follows:

. . . it is wrong to kill humans, however poor, weak, defenseless, and lacking in opportunity to develop their potential they may be. It is therefore morally wrong to kill Biafrans. Similarly, it is morally wrong to kill embryos.[6]

Noonan bases his claim that fetuses are human upon what he calls the theologians' criterion of humanity: that whoever is conceived of human beings is human. But although he argues at length for the appropriateness of this criterion, he never questions the assumption that if a fetus is human then abortion is wrong for exactly the same reason that murder is wrong.

Judith Thomson is, in fact, the only writer I am aware of who has seriously questioned this assumption; she has argued that, even if we grant the antiabortionist his claim that a fetus is a human being, with the same right to life as any other human being, we can still demonstrate that, in at least some and perhaps most cases, a woman is under no moral obligation to complete an unwanted pregnancy.[7] Her argument is worth examining, since if it holds up it may enable us to establish the moral permissibility of abortion without becoming involved in problems about what entitles an entity to be considered human, and accorded full moral rights. To be able to do this would be a great gain in the power and simplicity of the proabortion position, since, although I will argue that these problems can be solved at least as decisively as can any other moral problem, we should certainly be pleased to be able to avoid having to solve them as part of the justification of abortion.

On the other hand, even if Thomson's argument does not hold up, her insight, i.e., that it requires *argument* to show that if fetuses are human then abortion is properly classified as murder, is an extremely valuable one. The assumption she attacks is particularly invidious, for it amounts to the decision that it is appropriate, in deciding the moral status of abortion, to leave the rights of the pregnant woman out of consideration entirely, except possibly when her life is threatened. Obviously, this will not do; determining what moral rights, if any, a fetus possesses is only the first step in determining the moral status of abortion. Step two, which is at least equally essential, is finding a just solution to the conflict between whatever rights the fetus may have, and the rights of the woman who is unwillingly pregnant. While the historical error has been to pay far too little attention to the second step, Ms. Thomson's suggestion is that if we look at the second step first we may find that a woman has a right to obtain an abortion *regardless* of what rights the fetus has.

Our own inquiry will also have two stages. In Section I, we will consider whether or not it is possible to establish that abortion is morally permissible even on the assumption that a fetus is an entity with a full-fledged right to life. I will argue that in fact this cannot be established, at least not with the conclusiveness which is essential to our hopes of convincing those who are skeptical about the morality of abortion, and that we therefore cannot avoid dealing with the question of whether or not a fetus really does have the same right to life as a (more fully developed) human being.

In Section II, I will propose an answer to this question, namely, that a fetus cannot be considered a member of the moral community, the set of beings with full and equal moral rights, for the simple reason that it is not a person, and that it is personhood, and not genetic humanity, i.e., humanity as defined by Noonan, which is the basis for membership in this community. I will argue that a fetus, whatever its stage of development, satisfies none of the basic criteria of personhood, and is not even enough *like* a person to be accorded even some of the same rights on the basis of this resemblance. Nor, as we will see, is a fetus's *potential* personhood a threat to the morality of abortion, since, whatever the rights of potential people may be, they are invariably overridden in any conflict with the moral rights of actual people.

I

We turn now to Professor Thomson's case for the claim that even if a fetus has full moral rights, abortion is still morally permissible, at least sometimes, and for some reasons other than to save the woman's life. Her argument is based upon a clever, but I think faulty, analogy. She asks us to picture ourselves waking up one day, in bed with a famous violinist. Imagine that you have been kidnapped, and your bloodstream hooked up to that of the violinist, who happens to have an ailment which will certainly kill him unless he is permitted to share your kidneys for a period of nine months. No one else can save him, since you alone have the right type of blood. He will be unconscious all that time, and you will have to stay in bed with him, but after the nine months are over he may be unplugged, completely cured, that is, provided that you have cooperated.

Now then, she continues, what are your obligations in this situation? The antiabortionist, if he is consistent, will have to say that you are obligated to stay in bed with the violinist: for all people have a right to life, and violinists are people, and therefore it would be murder for you to disconnect yourself from him and let him die (p. 49). But this is outrageous, and so there must be something wrong with the same argument when it is applied to abortion. It would certainly be commendable of you to agree to save the violinist, but it is absurd to suggest that your refusal to do so would be murder. His right to life does not obligate you to do whatever is required to keep him alive; nor does it justify anyone else in forcing you to do so. A law which required you to stay in bed with the violinist would clearly be an unjust law, since it is no proper function of the law to force unwilling people to make huge sacrifices for the sake of other people toward whom they have no such prior obligation.

Thomson concludes that, if this analogy is an apt one, then we can grant the antiabortionist his claim that a fetus is a human being, and still hold that it is at least sometimes the case that a pregnant woman has the right to refuse to be a Good Samaritan towards the fetus, i.e., to obtain an abortion. For there is a great gap between the claim that *x* has a right to life, and the claim that *y* is obligated to do whatever is necessary to keep *x* alive, let alone that he ought to be forced to do so. It is *y*'s duty to keep *x* alive only if he has somehow contracted a *special* obligation to do so; and a woman who is unwillingly pregnant, e.g., who was raped, has done nothing which obligates her to make the enormous sacrifice which is necessary to preserve the conceptus.

This argument is initially quite plausible, and in the extreme case of pregnancy due to rape it is probably conclusive. Difficulties arise, however, when we try to specify more exactly the range of cases in which abortion is clearly justifiable even on the assumption that the fetus is human. Professor Thomson considers it a virtue of her argument that it does not enable us to conclude that abortion is *always* permissible. It would, she says, be "indecent" for a woman in her seventh month to obtain an abortion just to avoid having to postpone a trip to Europe. On the other hand, her argument enables us to see that "a sick and desperately frightened schoolgirl pregnant due to rape may *of course* choose abortion, and that any law which rules this out is an insane law" (p. 65). So far, so good; but what are we to say about the woman who becomes pregnant not through rape but as a result of her own carelessness, or because of contraceptive failure, or who gets pregnant intentionally and then changes her mind about wanting a child? With respect to such cases, the violinist analogy is of much less use to the defender of the woman's right to obtain an abortion.

Indeed, the choice of a pregnancy due to rape, as an example of a case in which abortion is permissible even if a fetus is considered a human being, is extremely significant; for it is only in the case of pregnancy due to rape that the woman's situation is adequately analogous to the violinist case for our intuitions about the latter to transfer convincingly. The crucial difference between a pregnancy due to rape and the *normal* case of an unwanted pregnancy is that in the normal case we cannot claim that the woman is in no way responsible for her predicament; she could have remained chaste, or taken her pills more faithfully, or abstained on dangerous days, and so on. If on the other hand, you are kidnapped by strangers, and hooked up to a strange violinist, then you are free of any shred of responsibility for the situation, on the basis of which it would be argued that you are obligated to keep the violinist alive. Only when her pregnancy is due to rape is a woman clearly just as nonresponsible.[8]

Consequently, there is room for the antiabortionist to argue that in the normal case of unwanted pregnancy a woman has, by her own actions, assumed responsibility for the fetus. For if *x* behaves in a way which he could have avoided, and which he knows involves, let us say, a 1 percent chance of bringing into existence a human being, with a right to life, and does so knowing that if this should happen then that human being will perish unless *x* does certain things to keep him alive, then it is by no means clear that when it does happen *x* is free of any obligation to what he knew in advance would be required to keep that human being alive.

The plausibility of such an argument is enough to show that the Thomson analogy can provide a clear and persuasive defense of a woman's right to obtain an abortion only with respect to those cases in which the woman is in no way responsible for her pregnancy, e.g., where it is due to rape. In all other cases, we would almost certainly conclude that it was necessary to look carefully at the particular circumstances in order to determine the extent of the woman's responsibility, and hence the extent of her obligation. This is an extremely unsatisfactory outcome, from the viewpoint of the opponents of restrictive abortion laws, most of whom are convinced that a woman has a right to obtain an abortion regardless of how and why she got pregnant.

Of course a supporter of the violinist analogy might point out that it is absurd to suggest that forgetting her pill one day might be sufficient to obligate a woman to complete an unwanted pregnancy. And indeed it *is* absurd to suggest this. As we shall see, the moral right to obtain an abortion is not in the least dependent upon the extent to which the woman is responsible for her pregnancy. But unfortunately, once we allow the assumption that a fetus has full moral rights, we cannot avoid taking this absurd suggestion seriously. Perhaps we can make this point more clear by altering the violinist story just enough to make it more analogous to a normal unwanted pregnancy and less to a pregnancy due to rape, and then seeing whether it is still obvious that you are not obligated to stay in bed with the fellow.

Suppose, then, that violinists are peculiarly prone to the sort of illness the only cure for which is the use of someone else's bloodstream for nine months, and that because of this there has been formed a society of music lovers who agree that whenever a violinist is stricken they will draw lots and the loser will, by some means, be made the one and only person capable of saving him. Now then, would you be obligated to cooperate in curing the violinist if you had voluntarily joined this society, knowing the possible consequences, and then your name had been drawn and you had been kidnapped? Admittedly, you did not promise ahead of time that you would, but you did deliberately place yourself in a position in which it might happen that a human life would be lost if you did not. Surely this is at least a prima facie reason for supposing that you have an obligation to stay in bed with the violinist. Suppose that you had gotten your name drawn deliberately;

surely *that* would be quite a strong reason for thinking that you had such an obligation.

It might be suggested that there is one important disanalogy between the modified violinist case and the case of an unwanted pregnancy, which makes the woman's responsibility significantly less, namely, the fact that the fetus *comes into existence* as the result of the woman's actions. This fact might give her a right to refuse to keep it alive, whereas she would not have had this right had it existed previously, independently, and then as a result of her actions become dependent upon her for its survival.

My own intuition, however, is that x has no more right to bring into existence, either deliberately or as a foreseeable result of actions he could have avoided, a being with full moral rights (*y*), and then refuse to do what he knew beforehand would be required to keep that being alive, than he has to enter into an agreement with an existing person, whereby he may be called upon to save that person's life, and then refuse to do so when so called upon. Thus, *x*'s responsibility for *y*'s existence does not seem to lessen his obligation to keep *y* alive, if he is also responsible for *y*'s being in a situation in which only he can save him.

Whether or not this intuition is entirely correct, it brings us back once again to the conclusion that once we allow the assumption that a fetus has full moral rights it becomes an extremely complex and difficult question whether and when abortion is justifiable. Thus the Thomson analogy cannot help us produce a clear and persuasive proof of the moral permissibility of abortion. Nor will the opponents of the restrictive laws thank us for anything less; for their conviction (for the most part) is that abortion is obviously *not* a morally serious and extremely unfortunate, even though sometimes justified act, comparable to killing in self-defense or to letting the violinist die, but rather is closer to being a morally neutral act, like cutting one's hair.

The basis of this conviction, I believe, is the realization that a fetus is not a person, and thus does not have a full-fledged right to life. Perhaps the reason why this claim has been so inadequately defended is that it seems self-evident to those who accept it. And so it is, insofar as it follows from what I take to be perfectly obvious claims about the nature of personhood, and about the proper grounds for ascribing moral rights, claims which ought, indeed, to be obvious to both the friends and foes of abortion. Nevertheless, it is worth examining these claims, and showing how they demonstrate the moral innocuousness of abortion, since this apparently has not been adequately done before.

II

The question which we must answer in order to produce a satisfactory solution to the problem of the moral status of abortion is this: How are we to define the moral community, the set of beings with full and equal moral rights, such that we can decide whether a human fetus is a member of this community or not? What sort of entity, exactly, has the inalienable rights to life, liberty, and the pursuit of happiness? Jefferson attributed these rights to all *men,* and it may or may not be fair to suggest that he intended to attribute them *only* to men. Perhaps he ought to have attributed them to all human beings. If so, then we arrive, first, at Noonan's problem of defining what makes a being human, and second, at the equally vital question which Noonan does not consider, namely, What reason is there for identifying the moral community with the set of all human beings, in whatever way we have chosen to define that term?

ON THE DEFINITION OF "HUMAN"

One reason why this vital second question is so frequently overlooked in the debate over the moral status of abortion is that the term "human" has two distinct, but not often distinguished, senses. This fact results in a slide of meaning, which serves to conceal the fallaciousness of the traditional argument that since (1) it is wrong to kill innocent human beings, and (2) fetuses are innocent human beings, then (3) it is wrong to kill fetuses. For if "human" is used in the same sense in both (1) and (2) then, whichever of the two senses is meant, one of these premises is question-begging. And if it is used in two different senses, then of course the conclusion doesn't follow.

Thus, (1) is a self-evident moral truth,[9] and avoids begging the question about abortion, only if "human being" is used to mean something like "a full-fledged member of the moral community." (It may or may not also be meant to refer exclusively to members of the species *Homo sapiens.*) We may call this the *moral* sense of "human." It is not to be confused with what we will call the *genetic* sense, i.e., the sense in which *any* member of the species is a human being, and no member of any other species could be. If (1) is acceptable only if the moral sense is intended, (2) is non-question-begging only if what is intended is the genetic sense.

In "Deciding Who Is Human," Noonan argues for the classification of fetuses with human beings by pointing to the presence of the full genetic code, and the potential capacity for rational thought (p. 135). It is clear that what he needs to show, for his version of the traditional argument to be valid, is that fetuses are human in the moral sense, the sense in which it is analytically true that all human beings have full moral rights. But, in the absence of any argument showing that whatever is genetically human is also morally human, and he gives none, nothing more than genetic humanity can be demonstrated by the presence of the human genetic code. And, as we will see, the *potential* capacity for rational thought can at most show that an entity has the potential for *becoming* human in the moral sense.

DEFINING THE MORAL COMMUNITY

Can it be established that genetic humanity is sufficient for moral humanity? I think that there are very good reasons for not defining the moral community in this way. I would like to suggest an alternative way of defining the moral community, which I will argue for only to the extent of explaining why it is, or should be, self-evident. The suggestion is simply that the moral community consists of all and only *people,* rather than all and only human beings;[10] and probably the best way of demonstrating its self-evidence is by considering the concept of personhood, to see what sorts of entity are and are not persons, and what the decision that a being is or is not a person implies about its moral rights.

What moral characteristics entitle an entity to be considered a person? This is obviously not the place to attempt a complete analysis of the concept of personhood, but we do not need such a fully adequate analysis just to determine whether and why a fetus is or isn't a person. All we need is a rough and approximate list of the most basic criteria of personhood, and some idea of which, or how many, of these an entity must satisfy in order to properly be considered a person.

In searching for such criteria, it is useful to look beyond the set of people with whom we are acquainted, and ask how we would decide whether a totally alien being was a person or not. (For we have no right to assume that genetic humanity is necessary for personhood.) Imagine a space traveler who lands on an unknown planet and encounters a race of beings utterly unlike any he has ever seen or heard of. If he wants to be sure of behaving morally toward these beings, he has to somehow decide whether they are people, and

hence have full moral rights, or whether they are the sort of thing which he need not feel guilty about treating as, for example, a source of food.

How should he go about making this decision? If he has some anthropological background he might look for such things as religion, art, and the manufacturing of tools, weapons, or shelters, since these factors have been used to distinguish our human from our prehuman ancestors, in what seems to be closer to the moral than the genetic sense of "human." And no doubt he would be right to consider the presence of such factors as good evidence that the alien beings were people, and morally human. It would, however, be overly anthropocentric of him to take the absence of these things as adequate evidence that they were not, since we can imagine people who have progressed beyond, or evolved without ever developing, these cultural characteristics.

I suggest that the traits which are most central to the concept of personhood, or humanity in the moral sense, are, very roughly, the following:

1. Consciousness (of objects and events external and/or internal to the being), and in particular the capacity to feel pain;
2. Reasoning (the *developed* capacity to solve new and relatively complex problems);
3. Self-motivated activity (activity which is relatively independent of either genetic or direct external control);
4. The capacity to communicate, by whatever means, messages of an indefinite variety of types, that is, not just with an indefinite number of possible contents, but on indefinitely many possible topics;
5. The presence of self-concepts, and self-awareness, either individual or racial, or both.

Admittedly, there are apt to be a great many problems involved in formulating precise definitions of these criteria, let alone in developing universally valid behavioral criteria for deciding when they apply. But I will assume that both we and our explorer know approximately what (1)–(5) mean, and that he is also able to determine whether or not they apply. How, then, should he use his findings to decide whether or not the alien beings are people? We needn't suppose that an entity must have *all* of these attributes to be properly considered a person; (1) and (2) alone may well be sufficient for personhood, and quite probably (1)–(3) are sufficient. Neither do we need to insist that any one of these criteria is *necessary* for personhood, although once again (1) and (2) look like fairly good candidates for necessary conditions, as does (3), if "activity" is construed so as to include the activity of reasoning.

All we need to claim, to demonstrate that a fetus is not a person, is that any being which satisfies *none* of (1)–(5) is certainly not a person. I consider this claim to be so obvious that I think anyone who denied it, and claimed that a being which satisfied none of (1)–(5) was a person all the same, would thereby demonstrate that he had no notion at all of what a person is — perhaps because he had confused the concept of a person with that of genetic humanity. If the opponents of abortion were to deny the appropriateness of these five criteria, I do not know what further arguments would convince them. We would probably have to admit that our conceptual schemes were indeed irreconcilably different, and that our dispute could not be settled objectively.

I do not expect this to happen, however, since I think that the concept of a person is one which is very nearly universal (to people), and that it is common to both proabortionists and antiabortionists, even though neither group has fully realized the relevance of this concept to the resolution of their dispute. Furthermore, I think that on reflection even the antiabortionists ought to agree not only that (1)–(5) are central to the concept of personhood, but also that it is a part of this concept that all and only people have full moral rights. The concept of a person is in part a moral concept; once we have admitted that *x* is a person we have recognized, even if we have not agreed to respect, *x*'s right to be treated as a member of the moral community. It is true that the claim that *x* is a *human being* is more commonly voiced as part of an appeal to treat *x* decently than is the claim that *x* is a person, but this is either because "human being" is here used in the sense which implies personhood, or because the genetic and moral senses of "human" have been confused.

Now if (1)–(5) are indeed the primary criteria of personhood, then it is clear that genetic humanity is neither necessary nor sufficient for establishing that an entity is a person. Some human beings are not people, and there may well be people who are not human beings. A man or woman whose consciousness has been permanently obliterated but who remains alive is a human being which is no longer a person; defective human beings, with no appreciable mental capacity,

are not and presumably never will be people; and a fetus is a human being which is not yet a person, and which therefore cannot coherently be said to have full moral rights. Citizens of the next century should be prepared to recognize highly advanced, self-aware robots or computers, should such be developed, and intelligent inhabitants of other worlds, should such be found, as people in the fullest sense, and to respect their moral rights. But to ascribe full moral rights to an entity which is not a person is as absurd as to ascribe moral obligations and responsibilities to such an entity.

FETAL DEVELOPMENT AND THE RIGHT TO LIFE

Two problems arise in the application of these suggestions for the definition of the moral community to the determination of the precise moral status of a human fetus. Given that the paradigm example of a person is a normal adult being, then (1) How like this paradigm, in particular how far advanced since conception, does a human being need to be before it begins to have a right to life by virtue, not of being fully a person as of yet, but of being *like* a person? and (2) To what extent, if any, does the fact that a fetus has the *potential* for becoming a person endow it with some of the same rights? Each of these questions requires some comment.

In answering the first question, we need not attempt a detailed consideration of the moral rights of organisms which are not developed enough, aware enough, intelligent enough, etc., to be considered people, but which resemble people in some respects. It does seem reasonable to suggest that the more like a person, in the relevant aspects, a being is, the stronger is the case for regarding it as having a right to life, and indeed the stronger its right to life is. Thus we ought to take seriously the suggestion that, insofar as "the human individual develops biologically in a continuous fashion . . . the rights of a human person might develop in the same way."[11] But we must keep in mind that the attributes which are relevant in determining whether or not an entity is enough like a person to be regarded as having some of the same moral rights are no different from those which are relevant to determining whether or not it is fully a person—i.e., are not different from (1)–(5)—and that being genetically human, or having recognizably human facial and other physical features, or detectable brain activity, or the capacity to survive outside the uterus, are simply not among these relevant attributes.

Thus it is clear that even though a seven- or eight-month fetus has features which make it apt to arouse in us almost the same powerful protective instinct as is commonly aroused by a small infant, nevertheless it is not significantly more personlike than is a very small embryo. It is *somewhat* more personlike; it can apparently feel and respond to pain, and it may even have a rudimentary form of consciousness, insofar as its brain is quite active. Nevertheless, it seems safe to say that it is not fully conscious, in the way that an infant of a few months is, and that it cannot reason, or communicate messages of indefinitely many sorts, does not engage in self-motivated activity, and has no self-awareness. Thus, in the *relevant* respects, a fetus, even a fully developed one, is considerably less personlike than is the average mature mammal, indeed the average fish. And I think that a rational person must conclude that if the right to life of a fetus is to be based upon its resemblance to a person, then it cannot be said to have any more right to life than, let us say, a newborn guppy (which also seems to be capable of feeling pain), and that a right of that magnitude could never override a woman's right to obtain an abortion, at any stage of her pregnancy.

There may, of course, be other arguments in favor of placing legal limits upon the stage of pregnancy in which an abortion may be performed. Given the relative safety of the new techniques of artificially inducing labor during the third trimester, the danger to the woman's life or health is no longer such an argument. Neither is the fact that people tend to respond to the thought of abortion in the later stages of pregnancy with emotional repulsion, since mere emotional responses cannot take the place of moral reasoning in determining what ought to be permitted. Nor, finally, is the frequently heard argument that legalizing abortion, especially late in the pregnancy, may erode the level of respect for human life, leading, perhaps to an increase in unjustified euthanasia and other crimes. For this threat, if it is a threat, can be better met by educating people to the kinds of moral distinctions which we are making here than by limiting access to abortion (which limitation may, in its disregard for the rights of women, be just as damaging to the level of respect for human rights).

Thus, since the fact that even a fully developed fetus is not personlike enough to have any significant right to life on the basis of its person-likeness shows that no legal restrictions upon the stage of pregnancy in which an abortion may be performed can be justified on the grounds that we should protect the rights of the older fetus; and since there is no other apparent justification for such restrictions, we may conclude that they are entirely unjustified. Whether or not it would be *indecent*

(whatever that means) for a woman in her seventh month to obtain an abortion just to avoid having to postpone a trip to Europe, it would not, in itself, be *immoral,* and therefore it ought to be permitted.

POTENTIAL PERSONHOOD AND THE RIGHT TO LIFE

We have seen that a fetus does not resemble a person in any way which can support the claim that it has even some of the same rights. But what about its *potential,* the fact that if nurtured and allowed to develop naturally it will very probably become a person? Doesn't that alone give it at least some right to life? It is hard to deny that the fact that an entity is a potential person is a strong prima facie reason for not destroying it; but we need not conclude from this that a potential person has a right to life, by virtue of that potential. It may be that our feeling that it is better, other things being equal, not to destroy a potential person is better explained by the fact that potential people are still (felt to be) an invaluable resource, not to be lightly squandered. Surely, if every speck of dust were a potential person, we would be much less apt to conclude that every potential person has a right to become actual.

Still, we do not need to insist that a potential person has no right to life whatever. There may well be something immoral, and not just imprudent, about wantonly destroying potential people, when doing so isn't necessary to protect anyone's rights. But even if a potential person does have some prima facie right to life, such a right could not possibly outweigh the right of a woman to obtain an abortion, since the rights of any actual person invariably outweigh those of any potential person, whenever the two conflict. Since this may not be immediately obvious in the case of a human fetus, let us look at another case.

Suppose that our space explorer falls into the hands of an alien culture, whose scientists decide to create a few hundred thousand or more human beings, by breaking his body into its component cells, and using these to create fully developed human beings, with, of course, his genetic code. We may imagine that each of these newly created men will have all of the original man's abilities, skills, knowledge, and so on, and also have an individual self-concept, in short that each of them will be a bona fide (though hardly unique) person. Imagine that the whole project will take only seconds, and that its chances of success are extremely high, and that our explorer knows all of this, and also knows that these people will be treated fairly. I maintain that in such a situation he would have every right to escape if he could, and thus to deprive all of these potential people of their potential lives; for his right to life outweighs all of theirs together, in spite of the fact that they are all genetically human, all innocent, and all have a very high probability of becoming people very soon, if only he refrains from action.

Indeed, I think he would have a right to escape even if it were not his life which the alien scientists planned to take, but only a year of his freedom, or, indeed, only a day. Nor would he be obligated to stay if he had gotten captured (thus bringing all these people-potentials into existence) because of his own carelessness, or even if he had done so deliberately, knowing the consequences. Regardless of how he got captured, he is not morally obligated to remain in captivity for *any* period of time for the sake of permitting any number of potential people to come into actuality, so great is the margin by which one actual person's right to liberty outweighs whatever rights to life even a hundred thousand potential people have. And it seems reasonable to conclude that the rights of a woman will outweigh by a similar margin whatever right to life a fetus may have by virtue of its potential personhood.

Thus, neither a fetus's resemblance to a person, nor its potential for becoming a person provides any basis whatever for the claim that it has any significant right to life. Consequently, a woman's right to protect her health, happiness, freedom, and even her life,[12] by terminating an unwanted pregnancy will always override whatever right to life it may be appropriate to ascribe to a fetus, even a fully developed one. And thus, in the absence of any overwhelming social need for every possible child, the laws which restrict the right to an abortion, or limit the period of pregnancy during which an abortion may be performed, are a wholly unjustified violation of a woman's most basic moral and constitutional rights.[13]

POSTSCRIPT ON INFANTICIDE

Since the publication of this [essay], many people have written to point out that my argument appears to justify not only abortion, but infanticide as well. For a new-born infant is not significantly more person-like than an advanced fetus, and consequently it would seem that if the destruction of the latter is permissible so too must be that of the former. Inasmuch as most people, regardless of how they feel about the morality of abor-

tion, consider infanticide a form of murder, this might appear to represent a serious flaw in my argument.

Now, if I am right in holding that it is only people who have a full-fledged right to life, and who can be murdered, and if the criteria of personhood are as I have described them, then it obviously follows that killing a new-born infant isn't murder. It does *not* follow, however, that infanticide is permissible, for two reasons. In the first place, it would be wrong, at least in this country and in this period of history, and other things being equal, to kill a new-born infant, because even if its parents do not want it and would not suffer from its destruction, there are other people who would like to have it, and would, in all probability, be deprived of a great deal of pleasure by its destruction. Thus, infanticide is wrong for reasons analogous to those which make it wrong to wantonly destroy natural resources, or great works of art.

Secondly, most people, at least in this country, value infants and would much prefer that they be preserved, even if foster parents are not immediately available. Most of us would rather be taxed to support orphanages than allow unwanted infants to be destroyed. So long as there are people who want an infant preserved, and who are willing and able to provide the means of caring for it, under reasonably humane conditions, it is, *certeris paribus,* wrong to destroy it.

But, it might be replied, if this argument shows that infanticide is wrong, at least at this time and in this country, doesn't it also show that abortion is wrong? After all, many people value fetuses, are disturbed by their destruction, and would much prefer that they be preserved, even at some cost to themselves. Furthermore, as a potential source of pleasure to some foster family, a fetus is just as valuable as an infant. There is, however, a crucial difference between the two cases: so long as the fetus is unborn, its preservation, contrary to the wishes of the pregnant woman, violates her rights to freedom, happiness, and self-determination. Her rights override the rights of those who would like the fetus preserved, just as if someone's life or limb is threatened by a wild animal, his right to protect himself by destroying the animal overrides the rights of those who would prefer that the animal not be harmed.

The minute the infant is born, however, its preservation no longer violates any of its mother's rights, even if she wants it destroyed, because she is free to put it up for adoption. Consequently, while the moment of birth does not mark any sharp discontinuity in the degree to which an infant possesses the right to life, it does mark the end of its mother's right to determine its fate. Indeed, if abortion could be performed without killing the fetus, she would never possess the right to have the fetus destroyed, for the same reasons that she has no right to have an infant destroyed.]

On the other hand, it follows from my argument that when an unwanted or defective infant is born into a society which cannot afford and/or is not willing to care for it, then its destruction is permissible. This conclusion will, no doubt, strike many people as heartless and immoral; but remember that the very existence of people who feel this way, and who are willing and able to provide care for unwanted infants, is reason enough to conclude that they should be preserved.

NOTES

1. For example, Roger Wertheimer, who in "Understanding the Abortion Argument" (*Philosophy and Public Affairs*, 1, No. 1 [Fall, 1971], 67–95), argues that the problem of the moral status of abortion is insoluble, in that the dispute over the status of the fetus is not a question of fact at all, but only a question of how one responds to the facts.

2. B. A. Brody, "Abortion and the Law," *The Journal of Philosophy*, 68, No. 12 (June 17, 1971), 357–69.

3. Judith Thomson, "A Defense of Abortion," *Philosophy and Public Affairs*, 1, No. 1 (Fall, 1971), 47–66.

4. I have abbreviated these statements somewhat, but not in a way which affects the argument.

5. John Noonan, "Abortion and the Catholic Church: A Summary History," *Natural Law Forum*, 12 (1967), 125.

6. John Noonan, "Deciding Who Is Human," *Natural Law Forum*, 13 (1968), 134.

7. "A Defense of Abortion."

8. We may safely ignore the fact that she might have avoided getting raped, e.g., by carrying a gun, since by similar means you might likewise have avoided getting kidnapped, and in neither case does the victim's failure to take all possible precautions against a highly unlikely event (as opposed to reasonable precautions against a rather likely event) mean that he is morally responsible for what happens.

9. Of course, the principle that it is (always) wrong to kill innocent human beings is in need of many other modifications, e.g., that it may be permissible to do so to save a greater number of other innocent human beings, but we may safely ignore these complications here.

10. From here on, we will use "human" to mean genetically human, since the moral sense seems closely connected to, and perhaps derived from, the assumption that genetic humanity is sufficient for membership in the moral community.

11. Thomas L. Hayes, "A Biological View," *Commonweal*, 85 (March 17, 1967), 677–78; quoted by Daniel Callahan, in *Abortion, Law, Choice, and Morality* (London: Macmillan & Co., 1970).

12. That is, insofar as the death rate, for the woman, is higher for childbirth than for early abortion.

13. My thanks to the following people, who were kind enough to read and criticize an earlier version of this paper: Herbert Gold, Gene Glass, Anne Lauterbach, Judith Thomson, Mary Mothersill, and Timothy Binkley.

Legal Issues of Abortion

SUSAN DWYER

A Short Legal History of Abortion in the United States and Canada

The problem of abortion is as much a public policy issue as it is a moral issue. . . .

In both the United States and Canada, any law regarding abortion must pass constitutional scrutiny; that is, the restrictions on abortion embodied in the legis-

From Susan Dwyer and Joel Feinberg, eds., *The Problem of Abortion*, 3rd ed. Copyright © 1997 Wadsworth Publishing Co. Reprinted by permission.

lation must not illegitimately infringe women's rights. Again, matters would be somewhat more straightforward if the right to abortion were enumerated in either the U.S. Bill of Rights or in the Canadian Charter of Rights and Freedoms, but it is not. When confronted with the problem of abortion, the Supreme Court in each country has had to grapple with complex jurisprudential questions. The two sections that follow provide a brief overview of judicial discussion about abortion in the United States and in Canada. . . .

Blackmun's approach [in *Roe v. Wade*] was to employ the so-called trimester framework. The majority in *Roe* held that the state cannot interfere with a woman's right to choose abortion during the first trimester of her pregnancy (that is, during the first twelve weeks) but that the state's interest in protecting maternal health becomes compelling during the second trimester, so some restrictions on second-trimester abortion are permissible. The state's interest in protecting potential human life was said to become compelling during the third trimester, so the Court held that the state can prohibit abortion in the final twelve weeks of pregnancy. It is important to note that the Court did not address the question of when human life begins. However, it did argue that the fetus is not a person in the sense of *person* relevant to the Fourteenth Amendment, which specifies in part that no "State [shall] deprive any person of life, liberty, or property, without due process of law."

The immediate effect of *Roe* was to overturn forty-six of the fifty states' laws governing abortion. Public, political, and academic reaction was swift. Pro-life forces began to organize against liberal abortion laws. Only eight days after the announcement of the *Roe* decision, Maryland Republican representative Lawrence J. Hogan introduced the first of several suggested constitutional amendments, proposing that the fetus be declared a Fourteenth Amendment person from the moment of conception. The debate engendered by *Roe* has not subsided. Throughout the 1980s, vigorous lobbying began to restrict the use of public funds to support abortion services and counseling. In addition, a candidate's stand on abortion has been, for better or worse, a central factor in recent presidential campaigns and in the ratification of Supreme Court and surgeon-general nominees.

For a variety of reasons, *Roe* is a controversial decision. It has been criticized from the political Right and the political Left, by feminists and nonfeminists. Two lines of criticism are worth focusing on. First is the complaint that the Court overstepped its authority to engage in judicial *review;* some argue that the Court's decision in *Roe* amounted to judicial law*making*. The second criticism is motivated by concerns about the implications of the fact that *Roe* grounds a woman's right to choose an abortion in the right of privacy. Let us look at each in turn.

Abortion has always been a divisive issue. And some critics of *Roe* have argued that, when no explicit guidance is offered by the Constitution, the resolution of such issues should be left to individual legislatures. By effectively invalidating the vast majority of existing state legislation on abortion, the Court appeared to foreclose the opportunity for individual states to decide the matter for themselves. . . .

More recently, Mary Ann Glendon and Ruth Bader Ginsburg, both of whom favor women's access to abortion, have argued that such access would have been better secured had the Court not decided *Roe* the way it did, but rather, left the abortion question to individual states.

The second line of criticism that bears mention here concerns the idea that abortion is an issue of privacy. The criticism actually takes two different forms, depending on whether it is advanced as part of a pragmatic argument or as part of a constitutional argument. Quite aside from the question of whether there is a constitutional right of privacy, feminist critics of *Roe* have argued that framing women's right to choose abortion in terms of privacy seriously distorts the meaning of an unwanted pregnancy in women's lives and, moreover, has negative consequences for women's access to abortion. Some worry that the language of privacy and personal choice is easily appropriated by those opposed to abortion, and others have argued that casting abortion as a privacy issue isolates abortion from other issues of reproductive health.[1] Rosalind Petchesky argues that interpreting abortion as a matter of privacy renders the right to abortion a "mere legality . . . [and one that] is perfectly compatible with a wide range of constraints on abortion *access* . . . Legality assures women neither material means nor moral support and political legitimization in their abortion decisions."[2] Petchesky's complaint is arguably borne out by the Supreme Court's subsequent decisions upholding the prohibition of federal funding for abortion services and counseling.[3] The Court has argued that the denial of public funding for abortion does not infringe the right guaranteed by *Roe*. In *Harris v. McRae,* for example, Justice Powell writes: "Although the government may not place obstacles in the path of a woman's exercise of her freedom of choice, it need not remove those not of its own creation. Indigency falls in the latter category."

Other pro-choice critics of *Roe* have argued that privacy was the wrong *constitutional* strategy for assessing abortion legislation. Rather, they claim, the question should be addressed in terms of sex equality. Matters here are complex, because it is very difficult to say when the law may take sex-based differences into account and when it may not. Moreover, when sex-based differences have been enshrined in law, the effect has generally been detrimental for women's equality. Nonetheless, women and men do differ in terms of the respective reproductive capacities; only women become pregnant. Because pregnancy carries a significant set of burdens and risks, this biological difference between women and men arguably implicates equality concerns. For example, when a law prohibits women from choosing abortion, it imposes a burden on women that they need not, as a matter of course, bear. In other words, when women alone are denied the ability to control their reproductive lives, they fail to enjoy the equal protection of the law.

Sylvia Law has suggested the following equality approach to law governing aspects of reproductive biology. For any particular piece of legislation, we should "consider whether the state can meet the burden of showing that [such a law] . . . either (1) has no significant impact in perpetuating the oppression of women or culturally imposed sex role constraints on individual freedom or (2) is the best means for meeting a compelling state interest."[4] Applied to abortion, then, the relevant test of a law restricting abortion would require that, in the first instance, the Court examine whether the restrictions in question serve to perpetuate women's oppression. Any legislation that bans abortion outright would fail this test, because in denying pregnant women's ability to make independent moral decisions and by impairing women's capacity for self-determination, such a law would serve to perpetuate women's oppression. Certain restrictions embodied in a more liberal abortion law would also fail Law's test—for example, spousal consent and notification provisions—but others, like record-keeping provisions, might pass.

The equality approach sketched here appears to be consistent with the Supreme Court's recognition in *Roe* and subsequent decisions that the state has a legitimate interest in protecting fetal life, at least postviability, for it is arguable that a restriction on third-trimester abortion, except when it is necessary to save the life of the pregnant woman, would be the best means for the state to meet its compelling interest in protecting fetal life. But while an equality approach to the legal problem of abortion might deliver results similar to those of the privacy approach adopted by the Court,

advocates of the former stress the superiority of their account on the grounds that it best mirrors the reality surrounding decisions about reproduction.

While the reasoning in *Roe* has been criticized by academics, women's access to abortion, which many thought had been secured by *Roe,* has been under attack socially and politically. The Hyde Amendment, passed by Congress in 1976, forbade the use of Medicaid funds for abortion: in 1980, President Ronald Reagan promised to appoint justices to the Supreme Court who would overrule *Roe;* and in 1988, the so-called gag rule that prevented staff at any federally funded clinic from discussing abortion with their patients, even when the woman's life was endangered by the pregnancy, was introduced by executive order through the Health and Human Services Department.[5] Over the years, several states have introduced legislation imposing a variety of restrictions on a woman's right to choose abortion. Examples of these measures are: a spousal notification requirement; a mandatory twenty-four-hour waiting period; mandatory counseling about fetal development and abortion; and a parental consent requirement for minors.

In evaluating the constitutionality of these restrictions, the Court has distinguished between legislation that places obstacles in the path of women seeking abortion and legislation that merely realizes the state's refusal to facilitate abortion. Since *Roe,* the Court has emphasized states' legitimate interests in protecting the potentiality of human life and has ruled that states may make a value judgment favoring childbirth over abortion and implement this judgment by allocating funds differentially, effectively paying for live births and not paying for abortion. In its 1989 *Webster* decision, the Court upheld a Missouri statute that prohibits the use of public facilities for the purpose of performing abortions, disallows the use of public funds for abortion, and requires physicians to establish whether any fetus of twenty weeks or older is viable. The *Webster* decision, whether or not it was explicitly intended as such by the Court, was widely interpreted as a sign that states could permissibly legislate a variety of restrictions on abortion. Certainly, many states reacted this way.[6] For example, Louisiana declared all abortion illegal except when the life of the woman is in danger or in cases of rape and incest, provided the violation is rapidly reported to the police. Pennsylvania instituted a mandatory twenty-four-hour waiting period, counseling, and a spousal notification requirement. By contrast, fearing that *Webster* signaled the imminent overruling of *Roe,* other states (for example, New York, New Jersey, and Florida) looked to their state constitutions to justify liberal access to abortion.

Despite the significant criticisms leveled at *Roe* since 1973, that decision has not been overturned. In the Court's most recent important decision concerning abortion (*Planned Parenthood of Southeastern Pennsylvania v. Casey* [1992]), a plurality—consisting of Justices Kennedy, Souter, and O'Connor—reaffirmed what they called the central holding in *Roe,* namely, that the state has an interest in protecting and preserving both maternal and fetal health and life, that the state may not unduly interfere with the right of a woman to choose to have an abortion prior to viability, and that the state may prohibit abortion after viability if it allows for exceptions when the pregnancy threatens the woman's life or health. In the second part of its opinion, the plurality in *Casey* essentially rejected the trimester framework developed in *Roe* and argued that the appropriate standard for assessing the constitutionality of restrictions on abortion should be whether the legislation constitutes an undue burden for a woman seeking an abortion. On this ground, the Court upheld a range of provisions, including mandatory counseling by a physician followed by a twenty-four-hour waiting period. However, it invalidated Pennsylvania's requirement that a married woman notify her spouse before obtaining an abortion. Arguing that many women are vulnerable to physical and psychological violence at the hands of their husbands, the Court deemed that this provision imposes an undue burden on married women seeking abortions. . . .

CANADA

In sharp contrast with the United States, the Canadian Supreme Court has considered the abortion issue only four times in recent history. The earliest statutory prohibition against attempting to procure an abortion is the 1869 "Act respecting Offences against the Person," which made the abortion of a "quick fetus" a crime punishable by life imprisonment. This prohibition entered the Canadian Criminal Code in 1892, and the provision survived (relatively unaltered) as part of the Code until 1969. In that year, under pressure from the medical community, the relevant section of the Code (section 251)

was amended to allow for therapeutic exceptions to the outright ban on abortion. The revised section 251 set out the conditions under which an abortion would be legal: the procedure had to be carried out by a licensed medical practitioner in an accredited or approved hospital on the written advice of a three-member therapeutic abortion committee to the effect that the continuation of the pregnancy endangered the pregnant woman's life or health. The new law clearly made some abortions legal, but it did not make access to abortion uniform across the country. Hospitals were not required by law to establish therapeutic abortion committees, so many women were unable even to make the necessary requests. More important, whether a pregnant woman could undergo an abortion was wholly contingent upon the committee's assessment of the threat the pregnancy posed to her health or life; a pregnant woman could not represent her case to such committees.

Dr. Henry Morgentaler has been, perhaps, *the* pivotal figure in the judicial history of the problem of abortion in Canada.[7] For nearly two decades, Morgentaler directly defied the criminal provisions against abortion, opening clinics in several provinces. He was charged several times under section 251 and spent time in jail. The immediately relevant aspect of Morgentaler's story concerns the results of his appeal to the Canadian Supreme Court in 1988. This case represents the first time the Supreme Court considered that abortion question in the context of the Canadian Charter of Rights and Freedoms, which came into effect in 1982. Prior to the adoption of the Charter, courts could strike down only that legislation that violated the separation-of-powers doctrine under the British North American Act. But with the Charter in place, legislation can be challenged on the grounds that it unjustifiably infringes on Canadians' rights as articulated in that document.

At issue in *R. v. Morgentaler* was whether the abortion provision of the Criminal Code violates women's rights to security of the person as expressed in section 7 of the Charter. Section 7 reads:

> Everyone has the right to life, liberty and security of the person and the right not to be deprived thereof except in accordance with the principles of fundamental justice.

Judicial review of legislation challenged on Charter grounds involves two steps. First, the Court decides whether the impugned legislation does in fact infringe some right guaranteed in the Charter. Second, if this is so, the Court must determine whether that infringement is justified under section 1 of the Charter, which reads:

The Canadian Charter of Rights and Freedoms guarantees the rights and freedoms set out in it subject to reasonable limits prescribed by law as can be demonstrably justified in a free and democratic society.

This so-called section 1 analysis is somewhat similar to the notion of strict scrutiny employed by the U.S. Supreme Court. A piece of impugned legislation will survive section 1 analysis only if it can be demonstrated (1) that the objective of the legislation relates to substantial governmental concerns; (2) that the measures adopted to meet that objective are rationally connected to the objective in question (that is, are not arbitrary or unfair, but based on rational considerations); and (3) that the measures taken to meet the objective minimally impair the right at stake.[8]

In *Morgentaler*, the majority agreed that section 251 did indeed infringe on a pregnant woman's right to security of the person. Focusing on the requirement for therapeutic abortion committees, the Court declared that "forcing a woman, by threat of criminal sanction, to carry a foetus to term unless she meets certain criteria unrelated to her own priorities and aspirations, is a profound interference with a woman's body and thus a violation of security of the person." (32) While the Court ruled that the section 251 provisions unjustifiably infringed a woman's security of the person, it clearly established that not all restrictions on abortion would do so. Justice Bertha Wilson was explicit that section 1 allows for the imposition of reasonable limits on a woman's section 7 right. In particular, she suggested that abortion legislation that is sensitive to the developmental facts of pregnancy — for example, legislation that adopts a permissive attitude toward early-term abortions and a more restrictive attitude toward late-term abortions — would probably be constitutional.

The Supreme Court's decision in *R. v. Morgentaler* invalidated the only abortion law in Canada, and subsequent attempts by Parliament to introduce new legislation have been unsuccessful. The current situation, then, is one in which there is no abortion law in Canada. Nonetheless, access to and funding for abortion is not uniform across the country. With respect to the future of the legal status of abortion in Canada, several things are worth noting. First, the Canadian Supreme Court did not explicitly declare, as the U.S. Supreme Court did in *Roe*, that the right to abortion is a fundamental right. Second, the Court expressly said that the state has a legitimate interest in protecting fetal life: "[The] protection of the fetus is and . . . always has been, a valid objective in Canadian criminal law" (113); the Court also suggested that an abortion law somewhat less restrictive than section 251 would pass constitutional scrutiny. Third, the Court has never directly considered the question of the fetus' juridical personality, that is, the question of whether the fetus is included in the term *everyone* in section 7. One anti-abortion campaigner, Joseph Borowski, sought to challenge section 251 on the grounds that in allowing therapeutic abortions at all it violated fetus' rights to security of the person, but section 251 had already been invalidated by the time the Court considered Borowski's appeal. Finally, it is arguable whether the *Morgentaler* decision is one that feminist advocates of choice would or should support. Unlike its counterpart in the United States, the Canadian Supreme Court did not speak of the right of privacy in overturning the abortion provisions. But in her remarks in *Morgentaler*, Justice Bertha Wilson stressed the connections among personal dignity, autonomy, and the existence of an essentially private sphere around each individual into which the state cannot trespass and implied that the decision to have an abortion is a private one for women. Thus, some of the pragmatically motivated feminist concerns, discussed above, about framing the legal problem of abortion in terms of privacy arise again. Construing pregnancy and abortion as issues of private choice encourages the belief that childbearing and childrearing are also entirely private matters. A possible consequence of this attitude is that existing social policies that support childbearing and childrearing may no longer be seen as justified. However, the Charter does appear to embody the resources to launch a sex-equality defense of liberal abortion laws, so it will be interesting to see how the Canadian Supreme Court addresses the question of abortion on future occasions.

NOTES

1. See, for example, Christine Overall, *Human Reproduction: Principles, Practices, Policies* (Toronto: Oxford University Press, 1993).

2. Rosalind Petchesky, *Abortion and Woman's Choice*, rev. ed. (Boston: Northeastern University Press, 1990), xxiv.

3. These cases include *Beal v. Doe* (1977); *Maher v. Roe* (1977); and *Harris v. McRae* (1980). See also *Webster v. Reproductive Health Services* (1989), in which the Court argued that the prohibition on the use of state hospitals for abortion does not impair a woman's ability to choose abortion. See the Annotated Chronology of U.S. and Canadian Supreme Court cases for details. For an argument explicitly linking privacy to the funding decisions, see Catharine A. MacKinnon, "Privacy v. Equality: Beyond *Row v. Wade,*" in *Feminism Unmodified* (Cambridge, Mass.: Harvard University Press, 1987).

4. Sylvia Law, "Rethinking Sex and the Constitution," *University of Pennsylvania Law Review* 132 (1984): 955–1040, 1016–1017. See also Sally Markowitz, "Abortion and Feminism," in this volume, pp. 194–202.

5. The Supreme Court upheld the constitutionality of the gag rule in *Rust v. Sullivan* (1991). In January, 1993, President Clinton signed an executive order overturning the gag rule and four other restrictions on abortion established and upheld during the Reagan and Bush administrations.

6. In 1990, no fewer than 465 abortion-related bills were introduced by state legislatures, representing a threefold increase over the previous year. See "State Legislation on Reproductive Health in 1990: What Was Proposed and Enacted," *Family Planning Perspectives,* March–April, 1992.

7. See F. L. Morton, *Morgentaler v. Borowski: Abortion, the Charter and the Courts* (Toronto: McCleland and Steward, 1992).

8. See *R. v. Oakes* [1986] 1. S.C.R. 103.

UNITED STATES SUPREME COURT

Roe v. Wade: Majority Opinion and Dissent

[MR. JUSTICE BLACKMUN delivered the opinion of the Court.]

It is . . . apparent that at common law, at the time of the adoption of our Constitution, and throughout the major portion of the nineteenth century, abortion was viewed with less disfavor than under most American statutes currently in effect. Phrasing it another way, a woman enjoyed a substantially broader right to terminate a pregnancy than she does in most states today. At least with respect to the early stage of pregnancy, and very possibly without such a limitation, the opportunity to make this choice was present in this country well into the nineteenth century. Even later, the law continued for some time to treat less punitively an abortion procured in early pregnancy. . . .

Three reasons have been advanced to explain historically the enactment of criminal abortion laws in the nineteenth century and to justify their continued existence.

It has been argued occasionally that these laws were the product of a Victorian social concern to discourage illicit sexual conduct. Texas, however, does not advance this justification in the present case, and it appears that no court or commentator has taken the argument seriously. . . .

A second reason is concerned with abortion as a medical procedure. When most criminal abortion laws were first enacted, the procedure was a hazardous one for the woman. This was particularly true prior to the development of antisepsis. Antiseptic techniques, of course, were based on discoveries by Lister, Pasteur, and others first announced in 1867, but were not generally accepted and employed until about the turn of the century. Abortion mortality was high. Even after 1900, and perhaps until as late as the development of antibiotics in the 1940s, standard modern techniques such as dilation and curettage were not nearly so safe as they are today. Thus it has been argued that a state's real concern in enacting a criminal abortion law was to protect the pregnant woman, that is, to restrain her from submitting to a procedure that placed her life in serious jeopardy.

Modern medical techniques have altered this situation. Appellants and various *amici* refer to medical data indicating that abortion in early pregnancy, that is, prior to the end of first trimester, although not without its

Reprinted from 410 *United States Reports* 113; decided January 22, 1973.

risk, is now relatively safe. Mortality rates for women undergoing early abortions, where the procedure is legal, appear to be as low as or lower than the rates for normal childbirth. Consequently, any interest of the state in protecting the woman from an inherently hazardous procedure, except when it would be equally dangerous for her to forgo it, has largely disappeared. Of course, important state interests in the area of health and medical standards do remain. The state has a legitimate interest in seeing to it that abortion, like any other medical procedure, is performed under circumstances that insure maximum safety for the patient. This interest obviously extends at least to the performing physician and his staff, to the facilities involved, to the availability of after-care, and to adequate provision for any complication or emergency that might arise. The prevalence of high mortality rates at illegal "abortion mills" strengthens, rather than weakens, the state's interest in regulating the conditions under which abortions are performed. Moreover, the risk to the woman increases as her pregnancy continues. Thus the state retains a definite interest in protecting the woman's own health and safety when an abortion is performed at a late stage of pregnancy.

The third reason is the state's interest — some phrase it in terms of duty — in protecting prenatal life. Some of the argument for this justification rests on the theory that a new human life is present from the moment of conception. The state's interest and general obligation to protect life then extends, it is argued, to prenatal life. Only when the life of the pregnant mother herself is at stake, balanced against the life she carries within her, should the interest of the embryo or fetus not prevail. Logically, of course, a legitimate state interest in this area need not stand or fall on acceptance of the belief that life begins at conception or at some other point prior to live birth. In assessing the state's interest, recognition may be given to the less rigid claim that as long as at least *potential* life is involved, the state may assert interests beyond the protection of the pregnant woman alone.

Parties challenging state abortion laws have sharply disputed in some courts the contention that a purpose of these laws, when enacted, was to protect prenatal life. Pointing to the absence of legislative history to support the contention, they claim that most state laws were designed solely to protect the woman. Because medical advances have lessened this concern, at least with respect to abortion in early pregnancy, they argue that with respect to such abortions the laws can no longer be

justified by any state interest. There is some scholarly support for this view of original purpose. The few states courts called upon to interpret their laws in the late nineteenth and early twentieth centuries did focus on the state's interest in protecting the woman's health rather than in preserving the embryo and fetus. . . .

The Constitution does not explicitly mention any right of privacy. In a line of decisions, however, going back perhaps as far as *Union Pacific R. Co. v. Botsford* (1891), the Court has recognized that a right of personal privacy, or a guarantee of certain areas or zones of privacy, does exist under the Constitution. In varying contexts the Court or individual Justices have indeed found at least the roots of that right in the First Amendment, . . . in the Fourth and Fifth Amendments, . . . in the penumbras of the Bill of Rights, . . . in the Ninth Amendment, . . . or in the concept of liberty guaranteed by the first section of the Fourteenth Amendment. . . . These decisions make it clear that only personal rights that can be deemed "fundamental" or "implicit in the concept of ordered liberty" . . . are included in this guarantee of personal privacy. They also make it clear that the right has some extension to activities relating to marriage, . . . procreation, . . . contraception, . . . family relationships, . . . and child rearing and education. . . .

This right of privacy, whether it be founded in the Fourteenth Amendment's concept of personal liberty and restrictions upon state action, as we feel it is, or, as the District Court determined, in the Ninth Amendment's reservation of rights to the people, is broad enough to encompass a woman's decision whether or not to terminate her pregnancy. . . .

Appellants and some *amici* argue that the woman's right is absolute and that she is entitled to terminate her pregnancy at whatever time, in whatever way, and for whatever reason she alone chooses. With this we do not agree. Appellants' arguments that Texas either has no valid interest at all in regulating the abortion decision, or no interest strong enough to support any limitation upon the woman's sole determination, is unpersuasive. The Court's decisions recognizing a right of privacy also acknowledge that some state regulation in areas protected by that right is appropriate. As noted above, a state may properly assert important interests in safeguarding health, in maintaining medical standards, and in protecting potential life. At some point in pregnancy, these respective interests become sufficiently compelling to sustain regulation of the factors that govern the abortion decision. The privacy rights involved, therefore, cannot be said to be absolute. . . .

We therefore conclude that the right of personal privacy includes the abortion decision, but that this right is not unqualified and must be considered against important state interests in regulation.

We note that those federal and state courts that have recently considered abortion law challenges have reached the same conclusion. . . .

Although the results are divided, most of these courts have agreed that the right of privacy, however based, is broad enough to cover the abortion decision; that the right, nonetheless, is not absolute and is subject to some limitations; and that at some point the state interests as to protection of health, medical standards, and prenatal life, become dominant. We agree with this approach. . . .

The appellee and certain *amici* argue that the fetus is a "person" within the language and meaning of the Fourteenth Amendment. In support of this they outline at length and in detail the well-known facts of fetal development. If this suggestion of personhood is established, the appellant's case, of course, collapses, for the fetus's right to life is then guaranteed specifically by the Amendment. The appellant conceded as much on reargument. On the other hand, the appellee conceded on reargument that no case could be cited that holds that a fetus is a person within the meaning of the Fourteenth Amendment. . . .

All this, together with our observation, *supra,* that throughout the major portion of the nineteenth century prevailing legal abortion practices were far freer than they are today, persuades us that the word "person," as used in the Fourteenth Amendment, does not include the unborn. . . . Indeed, our decision in *United States v. Vuitch* (1971), inferentially is to the same effect, for we there would not have indulged in statutory interpretation favorable to abortion in specified circumstances if the necessary consequence was the termination of life entitled to Fourteenth Amendment protection.

. . . As we have intimated above, it is reasonable and appropriate for a state to decide that at some point in time another interest, that of health of the mother or that of potential human life, becomes significantly involved. The woman's privacy is no longer sole and any right of privacy she possesses must be measured accordingly.

Texas urges that, apart from the Fourteenth Amendment, life begins at conception and is present throughout pregnancy, and that, therefore, the state has a compelling interest in protecting that life from and after conception. We need not resolve the difficult question of when life begins. When those trained in the respective disciplines of medicine, philosophy, and theology are unable to arrive at any consensus, the judiciary, at this point in the development of man's knowledge, is not in a position to speculate as to the answer.

It should be sufficient to note briefly the wide divergence of thinking on this most sensitive and difficult question. There has always been strong support for the view that life does not begin until live birth. This was the belief of the Stoics. It appears to be the predominant, though not the unanimous, attitude of the Jewish faith. It may be taken to represent also the position of a large segment of the Protestant community, insofar as that can be ascertained; organized groups that have taken a formal position on the abortion issue have generally regarded abortion as a matter for the conscience of the individual and her family. As we have noted, the common law found greater significance in quickening. Physicians and their scientific colleagues have regarded that event with less interest and have tended to focus either upon conception or upon live birth or upon the interim point at which the fetus becomes "viable," that is, potentially able to live outside the mother's womb, albeit with artificial aid. Viability is usually placed at about seven months (28 weeks) but may occur earlier, even at 24 weeks. . . .

In areas other than criminal abortion the law has been reluctant to endorse any theory that life, as we recognize it, begins before live birth or to accord legal rights to the unborn except in narrowly defined situations and except when the rights are contingent upon live birth. . . . In short, the unborn have never been recognized in the law as persons in the whole sense.

In view of all this, we do not agree that, by adopting one theory of life, Texas may override the rights of the pregnant woman that are at stake. We repeat, however, that the state does have an important and legitimate interest in preserving and protecting the health of the pregnant woman, whether she be a resident of the state or a nonresident who seeks medical consultation and treatment there, and that it has still *another* important and legitimate interest in protecting the potentiality of human life. These interests are separate and distinct. Each grows in substantiality as the woman approaches term and, at a point during pregnancy, each becomes "compelling."

With respect to the state's important and legitimate interest in the health of the mother, the "compelling" point, in the light of present medical knowledge, is at approximately the end of the first trimester. This is so because of the now established medical fact . . . that until the end of the first trimester mortality in abortion is less than mortality in normal childbirth. It follows that, from and after this point, a state may regulate the abortion procedure to the extent that the regulation reasonably relates to the preservation and protection of maternal health. Examples of permissible state regulation in this area are requirements as to the qualifications of the person who is to perform the abortion; as to the licensure of that person; as to the facility in which the procedure is to be performed, that is, whether it must be a hospital or may be a clinic or some other place of less-than-hospital status; as to the licensing of the facility; and the like.

This means, on the other hand, that, for the period of pregnancy prior to this "compelling" point, the attending physician, in consultation with his patient, is free to determine, without regulation by the state, that in his medical judgment the patient's pregnancy should be terminated. If that decision is reached, the judgment may be effectuated by an abortion free of interference by the state.

With respect to the state's important and legitimate interest in potential life, the "compelling" point is at viability. This is so because the fetus then presumably has the capability of meaningful life outside the mother's womb. State regulation protective of fetal life after viability thus has both logical and biological justifications. If the state is interested in protecting fetal life after viability, it may go so far as to proscribe abortion during that period except when it is necessary to preserve the life or health of the mother. . . .

To summarize and repeat:

1. A state criminal abortion statute of the current Texas type, that excepts from criminality only a *life-saving* procedure on behalf of the mother, without regard to pregnancy stage and without recognition of the other interests involved, is violative of the Due Process Clause of the Fourteenth Amendment.

(a) For the stage prior to approximately the end of the first trimester, the abortion decision and its effectuation must be left to the medical judgment of the pregnant woman's attending physician.

(b) For the stage subsequent to approximately the end of the first trimester, the state, in promoting its interest in the health of the mother, may, if it chooses, regulate the abortion procedure in ways that are reasonably related to maternal health.

(c) For the stage subsequent to viability the state, in promoting its interest in the potentiality of human life, may, if it chooses, regulate, and even proscribe, abortion except where it is necessary, in appropriate medical judgment, for the preservation of the life or health of the mother.

2. The state may define the term "physician" . . . to mean only a physician currently licensed by the state, and may proscribe any abortion by a person who is not a physician as so defined.

. . . The decision leaves the state free to place increasing restrictions on abortion as the period of pregnancy lengthens, so long as those restrictions are tailored to the recognized state interests. The decision vindicates the right of the physician to administer medical treatment according to his professional judgment up to the points where important state interests provide compelling justifications for intervention. Up to those points the abortion decision in all its aspects is inherently, and primarily, a medical decision, and basic responsibility for it must rest with the physician. If an individual practitioner abuses the privilege of exercising proper medical judgment, the usual remedies, judicial and intraprofessional, are available. . . .

[MR. JUSTICE WHITE, with whom Mr. Justice Rehnquist joins, dissenting.]

At the heart of the controversy in these cases are those recurring pregnancies that pose no danger whatsoever to the life or health of the mother but are, nevertheless, unwanted for any one or more of a variety of reasons—convenience, family planning, economics, dislike of children, the embarrassment of illegitimacy, etc. The common claim before us is that for any one of such reasons, or for no reason at all, and without asserting or claiming any threat to life or health, any woman is entitled to an abortion at her request if she is able to find a medical advisor willing to undertake the procedure.

The Court for the most part sustains this position: During the period prior to the time the fetus becomes viable, the Constitution of the United States values the convenience, whim, or caprice of the putative mother more than the life or potential life of the fetus; the Constitution, therefore, guarantees the right to an abortion as against any state law or policy seeking to protect the fetus from an abortion not prompted by more compelling reasons of the mother.

With all due respect, I dissent. I find nothing in the language or history of the Constitution to support the Court's judgment. The Court simply fashions and announces a new constitutional right for pregnant mothers and, with scarcely any reason or authority for its action, invests that right with sufficient substance to override most existing state abortion statutes. The upshot is that the people and the legislatures of the 50 states are constitutionally disentitled to weigh the relative importance of the continued existence and development of the fetus, on the one hand, against a spectrum of possible impacts on the mother, on the other hand. As an exercise of raw judicial power, the Court perhaps has authority to do what it does today; but in my view its judgment is an improvident and extravagant exercise of the power of judicial review that the Constitution extends to this Court.

The Court apparently values the convenience of the pregnant mother more than the continued existence and development of the life or potential life that she carries. Whether or not I might agree with that marshaling of values, I can in no event join the Court's judgment because I find no constitutional warrant for imposing such an order of priorities on the people and legislatures of the states. In a sensitive area such as this, involving as it does issues over which reasonable men may easily and heatedly differ, I cannot accept the Court's exercise of its clear power of choice by interposing a constitutional barrier to state efforts to protect human life and by investing mothers and doctors with the constitutionally protected right to exterminate it. This issue, for the most part, should be left with the people and to the political processes the people have devised to govern their affairs.

It is my view, therefore, that the Texas statute is not constitutionally infirm because it denies abortions to those who seek to serve only their convenience rather than to protect their life or health. Nor is this plaintiff, who claims no threat to her mental or physical health, entitled to assert the possible rights of those women whose pregnancy assertedly implicated their health. This, together with *United States v. Vuitch,* 402 U.S. 62 (1971), dictates reversal of the judgment of the District Court.

UNITED STATES SUPREME COURT

Planned Parenthood of Southeastern Pennsylvania v. Robert P. Casey, et al., etc.

[June 29, 1992]

[JUSTICE O'CONNOR, JUSTICE KENNEDY, and JUSTICE SOUTER announced the judgment of the Court and delivered the opinion of the Court.]

I

Liberty finds no refuge in a jurisprudence of doubt. Yet 19 years after our holding that the Constitution protects

Slip Opinion, Docket No. 91–744, 29 June 1992.

a woman's right to terminate her pregnancy in its early stages, *Roe v. Wade,* 410 U.S. 113 (1973), that definition of liberty is still questioned. Joining the respondents as *amicus curiae,* the United States, as it has done in five other cases in the last decade, again asks us to overrule *Roe.* . . .

At issue in these cases are five provisions of the Pennsylvania Abortion Control Act of 1982 as amended in 1988 and 1989. . . . The Act requires that a woman seeking an abortion give her informed consent prior to the abortion procedure, and specifies that she be provided with certain information at least 24 hours before the abortion is performed. For a minor to obtain an abortion, the Act requires the informed consent of one of her parents, but provides for a judicial bypass option if the minor does not wish to or cannot obtain a parent's consent. Another provision of the Act requires that, unless certain exceptions apply, a married woman seeking an abortion must sign a statement indicating that she has notified her husband of her intended abortion. The Act exempts compliance with these three requirements in the event of a "medical emergency," which is defined in § 3203 of the Act. In addition to the above provisions regulating the performance of abortions, the Act imposes certain reporting requirements on facilities that provide abortion services. . . .

We find it imperative to review once more the principles that define the rights of the woman and the legitimate authority of the State respecting the termination of pregnancies by abortion procedures.

After considering the fundamental constitutional questions resolved by *Roe,* principles of institutional integrity, and the rule of *stare decisis,* we are led to conclude this: the essential holding of *Roe v. Wade* should be retained and once again reaffirmed.

It must be stated at the outset and with clarity that *Roe*'s essential holding, the holding we reaffirm, has three parts. First is a recognition of the right of the woman to choose to have an abortion before viability and to obtain it without undue interference from the State. Before viability, the State's interests are not strong enough to support a prohibition of abortion or the imposition of a substantial obstacle to the woman's effective right to elect the procedure. Second is a confirmation of the State's power to restrict abortions after fetal viability, if the law contains exceptions for pregnancies which endanger a woman's life or health. And third is the principle that the State has legitimate interests from the outset of the pregnancy in protecting the health of the woman and the life of the fetus that may become a child. These principles do not contradict one another; and we adhere to each.

II

Constitutional protection of the woman's decision to terminate her pregnancy derives from the Due Process Clause of the Fourteenth Amendment. It declares that no State shall "deprive any person of life, liberty, or property, without due process of law." The controlling word in the case before us is "liberty." . . .

It is a promise of the Constitution that there is a realm of personal liberty which the government may not enter. We have vindicated this principle before. Marriage is mentioned nowhere in the Bill of Rights and interracial marriage was illegal in most States in the 19th century, but the Court was no doubt correct in finding it to be an aspect of liberty protected against state interference by the substantive component of the Due Process Clause. . . .

In *Griswold,* we held that the Constitution does not permit a State to forbid a married couple to use contraceptives. That same freedom was later guaranteed, under the Equal Protection Clause, for unmarried couples. See *Eisenstadt v. Baird,* 405 U.S. 438 (1972). Constitutional protection was extended to the sale and distribution of contraceptives in *Carey v. Population Services International, supra.* It is settled now, as it was when the Court heard arguments in *Roe v. Wade,* that the Constitution places limits on a State's right to interfere with a person's most basic decisions about family and parenthood. . . .

The inescapable fact is that adjudication of substantive due process claims may call upon the Court in interpreting the Constitution to exercise that same capacity which by tradition courts always have exercised: reasoned judgment. Its boundaries are not susceptible of expression as a simple rule. That does not mean we are free to invalidate state policy choices with which we disagree; yet neither does it permit us to shrink from the duties of our office. . . .

It should be recognized, moreover, that in some critical respects the abortion decision is of the same character as the decision to use contraception, to which *Griswold v. Connecticut, Eisenstadt v. Baird,* and *Carey v. Population Services International,* afford constitutional protection. We have no doubt as to the correctness of those decisions. They support the reasoning in *Roe* relating to the woman's liberty because they involve personal decisions concerning not only the meaning of procreation but also human responsibility and respect for it. As with abortion, reasonable people will have differences of opinion about these matters. One view is based on such reverence for the wonder of creation that any pregnancy ought to be welcomed and carried to full term no matter how difficult it will be to provide for the child and ensure its well-being. Another is that the inability to provide for the nurture and care of the infant is a cruelty to the child and an anguish to the parent. These are intimate views with infinite variations, and their deep, personal character underlay our decisions in *Griswold, Eisenstadt,* and *Carey.* The same concerns are present where the woman confronts the reality that, perhaps despite her attempts to avoid it, she has become pregnant. . . .

III

. . . No evolution of legal principle has left *Roe*'s doctrinal footings weaker than they were in 1973. No development of constitutional law since the case was decided has implicitly or explicitly left *Roe* behind as a mere survivor of obsolete constitutional thinking. . . .

The *Roe* Court itself placed its holding in the succession of cases most prominently exemplified by *Griswold v. Connecticut,* 381 U.S. 479 (1965), see *Roe,* 410 U.S., at 152–153. When it is so seen, *Roe* is clearly in no jeopardy, since subsequent constitutional developments have neither disturbed, nor do they threaten to diminish, the scope of recognized protection accorded to the liberty relating to intimate relationships, the family, and decisions about whether or not to beget or bear a child. . . .

[However], time has overtaken some of *Roe*'s factual assumptions: advances in maternal health care allow for abortions safe to the mother later in pregnancy than was true in 1973, see *Akron I, supra,* at 429, n. 11, and advances in neonatal care have advanced viability to a point somewhat earlier. . . . But these facts go only to the scheme of time limits on the realization of competing interests, and the divergences from the factual premises of 1973 have no bearing on the validity of *Roe*'s central holding, that viability marks the earliest point at which the State's interest in fetal life is constitutionally adequate to justify a legislative ban on nontherapeutic abortions. The soundness or unsoundness of that constitutional judgment in no sense turns on whether viability occurs at approximately 28 weeks, as was usual at the time of *Roe,* at 23 to 24 weeks, as it sometimes does today, or at some moment even slightly earlier in pregnancy, as it may if fetal respiratory capacity can somehow be enhanced in the future. Whenever it may occur, the attainment of viability may continue to serve as the critical fact, just as it has done since *Roe* was decided; which is to say that no change in *Roe*'s factual underpinning has left its central holding obsolete, and none supports an argument for overruling it. . . .

. . . Liberty must not be extinguished for want of a line that is clear. And it falls to us to give some real substance to the woman's liberty to determine whether to carry her pregnancy to full term.

We conclude the line should be drawn at viability, so that before that time the woman has a right to choose to terminate her pregnancy. We adhere to this principle for two reasons. First . . . is the doctrine of *stare decisis.* Any judicial act of line-drawing may seem somewhat arbitrary, but *Roe* was a reasoned statement, elaborated with great care. We have twice reaffirmed it in the face of great opposition. . . .

The second reason is that the concept of viability, as we noted in *Roe,* is the time at which there is a realistic possibility of maintaining and nourishing a life outside the womb, so that the independent existence of a second life can in reason and all fairness be the object of state protection that now overrides the rights of the woman. See *Roe v. Wade,* 410 U.S., at 163. Consistent with other constitutional norms, legislatures may draw lines which appear arbitrary without the necessity of offering a justification. But courts may not. We must justify the lines we draw. And there is no line other than viability which is more workable. To be sure, as we have said, there may be some medical developments that affect the precise point of viability, but this is an imprecision within tolerable limits given that the medical community and all those who must apply its discoveries will continue to explore the matter. The viability line also has, as a practical matter, an element of fairness. In some broad sense it might be said that a woman who fails to act before viability has consented to the State's intervention on behalf of the developing child.

The woman's right to terminate her pregnancy before viability is the most central principle of *Roe v. Wade.* It is a rule of law and a component of liberty we cannot renounce.

On the other side of the equation is the interest of the State in the protection of potential life. The *Roe* Court recognized the State's "important and legitimate interest in protecting the potentiality of human life." *Roe, supra,* at 162. The weight to be given this state interest, not the strength of the woman's interest, was the difficult question faced in *Roe.* We do not need to say whether each of us, had we been Members of the Court when the valuation of the State interest came before it as an original matter, would have concluded, as the *Roe* Court did, that its weight is insufficient to justify a ban on abortions prior to viability even when it is subject to certain exceptions. The matter is not before us in the first instance, and coming as it does after nearly 20 years of litigation in *Roe*'s wake we are satisfied that the immediate question is not the soundness of *Roe*'s resolution of the issue, but the precedential force that must be accorded to its holding. And we have concluded that the essential holding of *Roe* should be reaffirmed.

Yet it must be remembered that *Roe v. Wade* speaks with clarity in establishing not only the woman's liberty but also the State's "important and legitimate interest in potential life." *Roe, supra,* at 163. That portion of the decision in *Roe* has been given too little acknowledgement and implementation by the Court in its subsequent cases. . . .

Roe established a trimester framework to govern abortion regulations. Under this elaborate but rigid construct, almost no regulation at all is permitted during the first trimester of pregnancy; regulations designed to protect the woman's health, but not to further the State's interest in potential life, are permitted during the second trimester; and during the third trimester, when the fetus is viable, prohibitions are permitted provided the life or health of the mother is not at stake. *Roe v. Wade, supra,* at 163–166. Most of our cases since *Roe* have involved the application of rules derived from the trimester framework. . . .

The trimester framework no doubt was erected to ensure that the woman's right to choose not become so subordinate to the State's interest in promoting fetal life that her choice exists in theory but not in fact. We do not agree, however, that the trimester approach is necessary to accomplish this objective. A framework of this rigidity was unnecessary and in its later interpretation sometimes contradicted the State's permissible exercise of its powers.

Though the woman has a right to choose to terminate or continue her pregnancy before viability, it does not at all follow that the State is prohibited from taking steps to ensure that this choice is thoughtful and informed. Even in the earliest stages of pregnancy, the State may enact rules and regulations designed to encourage her to know that there are philosophic and social arguments of great weight that can be brought to bear in favor of continuing the pregnancy to full term and that there are procedures and institutions to allow adoption of unwanted children as well as a certain degree of state assistance if the mother chooses to raise the child herself. . . .

Numerous forms of state regulation might have the incidental effect of increasing the cost or decreasing the availability of medical care, whether for abortion or any other medical procedure. The fact that a law which serves a valid purpose, one not designed to strike at the right itself, has the incidental effect of making it more difficult or more expensive to procure an abortion cannot be enough to invalidate it. Only where state regulation imposes an undue burden on a woman's ability to make this decision does the power of the State reach into the heart of the liberty protected by the Due Process Clause. . . .

These considerations of the nature of the abortion right illustrate that it is an overstatement to describe it as a right to decide whether to have an abortion "without interference from the State," *Planned Parenthood of Central Mo. v. Danforth,* 428 U.S. 52, 61 (1976). All abortion regulations interfere to some degree with a woman's ability to decide whether to terminate her pregnancy. . . .

Roe v. Wade was express in its recognition of the State's "important and legitimate interest[s] in preserving and protecting the health of the pregnant woman [and] in protecting the potentiality of human life." 410 U.S., at 162. The trimester framework, however, does not fulfill *Roe*'s own promise that the State has an interest in protecting fetal life or potential life. *Roe* began the contradiction by using the trimester framework to forbid any regulation of abortion designed to advance that interest before viability. *Id.,* at 163. Before viability, *Roe* and subsequent cases treat all governmental attempts to influence a woman's decision on behalf of the potential life within her as unwarranted. This treatment is, in our judgment, incompatible with the recognition that there is a substantial state interest in potential life throughout pregnancy. Cf. *Webster,* 492 U.S., at 519 (opinion of Rehnquist, C. J.); *Akron I, supra,* at 461 (O'Connor, J., dissenting).

The very notion that the State has a substantial interest in potential life leads to the conclusion that not all regulations must be deemed unwarranted. Not all burdens on the right to decide whether to terminate a pregnancy will be undue. In our view, the undue burden standard is the appropriate means of reconciling the State's interest with the woman's constitutionally protected liberty. . . .

A finding of an undue burden is a shorthand for the conclusion that a state regulation has the purpose or effect of placing a substantial obstacle in the path of a woman seeking an abortion of a nonviable fetus. A statute with this purpose is invalid because the means chosen by the State to further the interest in potential life must be calculated to inform the woman's free choice, not hinder it. . . . That is to be expected in the application of any legal standard which must accommodate life's complexity. We do not expect it to be otherwise with respect to the undue burden standard. We give this summary:

(a) To protect the central right recognized by *Roe v. Wade* while at the same time accommodating the State's profound interest in potential life, we will employ the undue burden analysis as explained in this opinion. An undue burden exists, and therefore a provision of law is invalid, if its purpose or effect is to place a substantial obstacle in the path of a woman seeking an abortion before the fetus attains viability.

(b) We reject the rigid trimester framework of *Roe v. Wade*. To promote the State's profound interest in potential life, throughout pregnancy the State may take measures to ensure that the woman's choice is informed, and measures designed to advance this interest will not be invalidated as long as their purpose is to persuade the woman to choose childbirth over abortion. These measures must not be an undue burden on the right.

(c) As with any medical procedure, the State may enact regulations to further the health or safety of a woman seeking an abortion. Unnecessary health regulations that have the purpose or effect of presenting a substantial obstacle to a woman seeking an abortion impose an undue burden on the right.

(d) Our adoption of the undue burden analysis does not disturb the central holding of *Roe v. Wade,* and we reaffirm that holding. Regardless of whether exceptions are made for particular circumstances, a State may not prohibit any woman from making the ultimate decision to terminate her pregnancy before viability.

(e) We also reaffirm *Roe*'s holding that "subsequent to viability, the State in promoting its interest in the potentiality of human life may, if it chooses, regulate, and even proscribe, abortion except where it is necessary, in appropriate medical judgment, for the preservation of the life or health of the mother." *Roe v. Wade,* 410 U.S., at 164–165.

These principles control our assessment of the Pennsylvania statute, and we now turn to the issue of the validity of its challenged provisions.

V

The Court of Appeals applied what it believed to be the undue burden standard and upheld each of the provisions except for the husband notification requirement. We agree generally with this conclusion, but refine the undue burden analysis in accordance with the principles articulated above. . . . . . .

B

We next consider the informed consent requirement. 18 Pa. Cons. Stat. Ann. § 3205. Except in a medical emergency, the statute requires that at least 24 hours before performing an abortion a physician inform the woman of the nature of the procedure, the health risks of the abortion and of childbirth, and the "probable gestational age of the unborn child." The physician or a qualified nonphysician must inform the woman of the availability of printed materials published by the State describing the fetus and providing information about medical assistance for childbirth, information about child support from the father, and a list of agencies which provide adoption and other services as alternatives to abortion. An abortion may not be performed unless the woman certifies in writing that she has been informed of the availability of these printed materials and has been provided them if she chooses to view them.

Our prior decisions establish that as with any medical procedure, the State may require a woman to give her written informed consent to an abortion. . . .

In *Akron I,* 462 U.S. 416 (1983), we invalidated an ordinance which required that a woman seeking an abortion be provided by her physician with specific information "designed to influence the woman's informed choice between abortion or childbirth." *Id.,* at 444. As we later described the *Akron I* holding in *Thornburgh v. American College of Obstetricians and Gynecologists,* 476 U.S., at 762, there were two purported flaws in the Akron ordinance: the information was designed to dissuade the woman from having an abortion and the ordinance imposed "a rigid requirement that a specific body of information be given in all cases, irrespective of the particular needs of the patient. . . ." *Ibid.* . . .

In attempting to ensure that a woman apprehend the full consequences of her decision, the State furthers the legitimate purpose of reducing the risk that a woman may elect an abortion, only to discover later, with devastating psychological consequences, that her decision was not fully informed. If the information the State requires to be made available to the woman is truthful and not misleading, the requirement may be permissible.

We also see no reason why the State may not require doctors to inform a woman seeking an abortion of the availability of materials relating to the consequences to the fetus, even when those consequences have no direct relation to her health. An example illustrates the point. We would think it constitutional for the State to require that in order for there to be informed consent to a kidney transplant operation the recipient must be supplied with information about risks to the donor as well as risks to himself or herself. . . .

Whether the mandatory 24-hour waiting period is nonetheless invalid because in practice it is a substantial obstacle to a woman's choice to terminate her pregnancy is a closer question. The findings of fact by the District Court indicate that because of the distances many women must travel to reach an abortion provider, the practical effect will often be a delay of much more than a day because the waiting period requires that a woman seeking an abortion make at least two visits to the doctor. The District Court also found that in many instances this will increase the exposure of women seeking abortions to "the harassment and hostility of anti-abortion protestors demonstrating outside a clinic." 744 F. Supp., at 1351. As a result, the District Court found that for those women who have the fewest financial resources, those who must travel long distances, and those who have difficulty explaining their whereabouts to husbands, employers, or others, the 24-hour waiting period will be "particularly burdensome." . . .

We are left with the argument that the various aspects of the informed consent requirement are unconstitutional because they place barriers in the way of abortion on demand. Even the broadest reading of *Roe,* however, has not suggested that there is a constitutional right to abortion on demand. See, *e.g., Doe v. Bolton,* 410 U.S., at 189. Rather, the right protected by *Roe* is a right to decide to terminate a pregnancy free of undue interference by the State. Because the informed consent requirement facilitates the wise exercise of that right it cannot be classified as an interfer-

ence with the right *Roe* protects. The informed consent requirement is not an undue burden on that right.

C

Section 3209 of Pennsylvania's abortion law provides, except in cases of medical emergency, that no physician shall perform an abortion on a married woman without receiving a signed statement from the woman that she has notified her spouse that she is about to undergo an abortion. The woman has the option of providing an alternative signed statement certifying that her husband is not the man who impregnated her; that her husband could not be located; that the pregnancy is the result of spousal sexual assault which she has reported; or that the woman believes that notifying her husband will cause him or someone else to inflict bodily injury upon her. A physician who performs an abortion on a married woman without receiving the appropriate signed statement will have his or her license revoked, and is liable to the husband for damages. . . .

The American Medical Association (AMA) has published a summary of the recent research in this field, which indicates that in an average 12-month period in this country, approximately two million women are the victims of severe assaults by their male partners. In a 1985 survey, women reported that nearly one of every eight husbands had assaulted their wives during the past year. The AMA views these figures as "marked underestimates," because the nature of these incidents discourages women from reporting them, and because surveys typically exclude the very poor, those who do not speak English well, and women who are homeless or in institutions or hospitals when the survey is conducted. According to the AMA, "[r]esearchers on family violence agree that the true incidence of partner violence is probably *double* the above estimates; or four million severely assaulted women per year. Studies suggest that from one-fifth to one-third of all women will be physically assaulted by a partner or ex-partner during their lifetime." AMA Council on Scientific Affairs, Violence Against Women 7 (1991) (emphasis in original). Thus on an average day in the United States, nearly 11,000 women are severely assaulted by their male partners. Many of these incidents involve sexual assault. . . . In families where wife-beating takes place, moreover, child abuse is often present as well. . . .

In well-functioning marriages, spouses discuss important intimate decisions such as whether to bear a child. But there are millions of women in this country who are the victims of regular physical and psychological abuse at the hands of their husbands. Should these women become pregnant, they may have very good reasons for not wishing to inform their husbands of their decision to obtain an abortion. Many may have justifiable fears of physical abuse, but may be no less fearful of the consequences of reporting prior abuse to the Commonwealth of Pennsylvania. Many may have a reasonable fear that notifying their husbands will provoke further instances of child abuse; these women are not exempt from § 3209's notification requirement. . . . If anything in this field is certain, it is that victims of spousal sexual assault are extremely reluctant to report the abuse to the government; hence, a great many spousal rape victims will not be exempt from the notification requirement imposed by § 3209.

The spousal notification requirement is thus likely to prevent a significant number of women from obtaining an abortion. It does not merely make abortions a little more difficult or expensive to obtain; for many women, it will impose a substantial obstacle. We must not blind ourselves to the fact that the significant number of women who fear for their safety and the safety of their children are likely to be deterred from procuring an abortion as surely as if the Commonwealth had outlawed abortion in all cases. . . .

This conclusion is in no way inconsistent with our decisions upholding parental notification or consent requirements. See, *e.g., Akron II.* Those enactments, and our judgment that they are constitutional, are based on the quite reasonable assumption that minors will benefit from consultation with their parents and that children will often not realize that their parents have their best interests at heart. We cannot adopt a parallel assumption about adult women. . . .

Our cases establish, and we reaffirm today, that a State may require a minor seeking an abortion to obtain the consent of a parent or guardian, provided that there is an adequate judicial bypass procedure. See, *e.g., Akron II.* Under these precedents, in our view, the one-parent consent requirement and judicial bypass procedure are constitutional. . . .

VI

Our Constitution is a covenant running from the first generation of Americans to us and then to future generations. It is a coherent succession. Each generation must learn anew that the Constitution's written terms embody ideas and aspirations that must survive more ages than one. We accept our responsibility not to retreat from interpreting the full meaning of the covenant in light of all of our precedents. We invoke it once again to define the freedom guaranteed by the Constitution's own promise, the promise of liberty.

• • •

The judgment in No. 91–902 is affirmed. The judgment in No. 91–744 is affirmed in part and reversed in part, and the case is remanded for proceedings consistent with this opinion, including consideration of the question of severability.

It is so ordered.

Maternal–Fetal Relationships and Rights

UNITED STATES SUPREME COURT

Automobile Workers v. Johnson Controls, Inc.

[March 20, 1991]

JUSTICE BLACKMUN delivered the opinion of the Court.

In this case we are concerned with an employer's gender-based fetal-protection policy. May an employer exclude a fertile female employee from certain jobs because of its concern for the health of the fetus the woman might conceive?

I

Respondent Johnson Controls, Inc., manufactures batteries. In the manufacturing process, the element lead is a primary ingredient. Occupational exposure to lead entails health risks, including the risk of harm to any fetus carried by a female employee.

Before the Civil Rights Act of 1964, 78 Stat. 241, became law, Johnson Controls did not employ any woman in a battery-manufacturing job. In June 1977, however, it announced its first official policy concerning its employment of women in lead-exposure work. . . .

Johnson Controls "stopped short of excluding women capable of bearing children from lead exposure," *id.,* at 138, but emphasized that a woman who expected to have a child should not choose a job in which she would have such exposure. The company also required a woman who wished to be considered for employment to sign a statement that she had been advised of the risk of having a child while she was exposed to lead. . . .

Five years later, in 1982, Johnson Controls shifted from a policy of warning to a policy of exclusion. Between 1979 and 1983, eight employees became pregnant while maintaining blood lead levels in excess of 30 micrograms per deciliter. Tr. of Oral Arg. 25, 34.

Supreme Court Reporter 111, 1196–1217. March 20, 1991.

This appeared to be the critical level noted by the Occupational Health and Safety Administration (OSHA) for a worker who was planning to have a family. See 29 CFR § 1910.1025 (1989). The company responded by announcing a broad exclusion of women from jobs that exposed them to lead:

". . . [I]t is [Johnson Controls'] policy that women who are pregnant or who are capable of bearing children will not be placed into jobs involving lead exposure or which could expose them to lead through the exercise of job bidding, bumping, transfer or promotion rights." App. 85–86.

The policy defined "women . . . capable of bearing children" as "[a]ll women except those whose inability to bear children is medically documented." *Id.,* at 81. It further stated that an unacceptable work station was one where, "over the past year," an employee had recorded a blood lead level of more than 30 micrograms per deciliter or the work site had yielded an air sample containing a lead level in excess of 30 micrograms per cubic meter. *Ibid.*

II

In April 1984, petitioners filed in the United States District Court for the Eastern District of Wisconsin a class action challenging Johnson Controls' fetal-protection policy as sex discrimination that violated Title VII of the Civil Rights Act of 1964, as amended, 42 U. S. C. § 2000e *et seq.* Among the individual plaintiffs were petitioners Mary Craig, who had chosen to be sterilized in order to avoid losing her job. . . .

III

The bias in Johnson Controls' policy is obvious. Fertile men, but not fertile women, are given a choice as to whether they wish to risk their reproductive health for a particular job. Section 703(a) of the Civil Rights Act of 1964, 78 Stat. 255, as amended, 42 U. S. C. § 2000e-2(a), prohibits sex-based classifications in terms and conditions of employment, in hiring and discharging decisions, and in other employment decisions that adversely affect an employee's status. Respondent's fetal-protection policy explicitly discriminates against women on the basis of their sex. The policy excludes women with childbearing capacity from lead-exposed jobs and so creates a facial classification based on gender. Respondent assumes as much in its brief before this Court. Brief for Respondent 17, n. 24.

Nevertheless, the Court of Appeals assumed, as did the two appellate courts who already had confronted the issue, that sex-specific fetal-protection policies do not involve facial discrimination. . . .

. . . The court assumed that because the asserted reason for the sex-based exclusion (protecting women's unconceived offspring) was ostensibly benign, the policy was not sex-based discrimination. That assumption, however, was incorrect.

First, Johnson Controls' policy classifies on the basis of gender and childbearing capacity, rather than fertility alone. Respondent does not seek to protect the unconceived children of all its employees. Despite evidence in the record about the debilitating effect of lead exposure on the male reproductive system, Johnson Controls is concerned only with the harms that may befall the unborn offspring of its female employees. . . . Johnson Controls' policy is facially discriminatory because it requires only a female employee to produce proof that she is not capable of reproducing.

Our conclusion is bolstered by the Pregnancy Discrimination Act of 1978 (PDA), 92 Stat. 2076, 42 U. S. C. § 2000e(k), in which Congress explicitly provided that, for purposes of Title VII, discrimination "on the basis of sex" includes discrimination "because of or on the basis of pregnancy, childbirth, or related medical conditions." "The Pregnancy Discrimination Act has now made clear that, for all Title VII purposes, discrimination based on a woman's pregnancy is, on its face, discrimination because of her sex." *Newport News Shipbuilding & Dry Dock Co. v. EEOC,* 462 U. S. 669, 684 (1983). In its use of the words "capable of bearing children" in the 1982 policy statement as the criterion for exclusion, Johnson Controls explicitly classifies on the basis of potential for pregnancy. Under

the PDA, such a classification must be regarded, for Title VII purposes, in the same light as explicit sex discrimination. Respondent has chosen to treat all its female employees as potentially pregnant; that choice evinces discrimination on the basis of sex. . . .

The beneficence of an employer's purpose does not undermine the conclusion that an explicit gender-based policy is sex discrimination under § 703(a) and thus may be defended only as a BFOQ [bona fide occupational qualification].

The enforcement policy of the Equal Employment Opportunity Commission accords with this conclusion. On January 24, 1990, the EEOC issued a Policy Guidance in the light of the Seventh Circuit's decision in the present case. . . .

In sum, Johnson Controls' policy "does not pass the simple test of whether the evidence shows 'treatment of a person in a manner which but for that person's sex would be different.'" . . .

IV

Under § 703(e)(1) of Title VII, an employer may discriminate on the basis of "religion, sex, or national origin in those certain instances where religion, sex, or national origin is a bona fide occupational qualification reasonably necessary to the normal operation of that particular business or enterprise." 42 U. S. C. § 2000e-2(e)(1). We therefore turn to the question whether Johnson Controls' fetal-protection policy is one of those "certain instances" that come within the BFOQ exception. . . .

The PDA's amendment to Title VII contains a BFOQ standard of its own: unless pregnant employees differ from others "in their ability or inability to work," they must be "treated the same" as other employees "for all employment-related purposes." 42 U. S. C. § 2000e(k). This language clearly sets forth Congress' remedy for discrimination on the basis of pregnancy and potential pregnancy. Women who are either pregnant or potentially pregnant must be treated like others "similar in their ability . . . to work." *Ibid.* In other words, women as capable of doing their jobs as their male counterparts may not be forced to choose between having a child and having a job. . . .

V

We have no difficulty concluding that Johnson Controls cannot establish a BFOQ. Fertile women, as far as appears in the record, participate in the manufacture of batteries as efficiently as anyone else. Johnson Controls' professed moral and ethical concerns about the welfare of the next generation do not suffice to establish a BFOQ of female sterility. Decisions about the welfare of future children must be left to the parents who conceive, bear, support, and raise them rather than to the employers who hire those parents. Congress has mandated this choice through Title VII, as amended by the Pregnancy Discrimination Act. Johnson Controls has attempted to exclude women because of their reproductive capacity. Title VII and the PDA simply do not allow a woman's dismissal because of her failure to submit to sterilization.

Nor can concerns about the welfare of the next generation be considered a part of the "essence" of Johnson Controls' business. . . .

Johnson Controls argues that it must exclude all fertile women because it is impossible to tell which women will become pregnant while working with lead. This argument is somewhat academic in light of our conclusion that the company may not exclude fertile women at all; it perhaps is worth noting, however, that Johnson Controls has shown no "factual basis for believing that all or substantially all women would be unable to perform safely and efficiently the duties of the job involved." *Weeks v. Southern Bell Tel. & Tel. Co.,* 408 F. 2d 228, 235 (CA5 1969), quoted with approval in *Dothard,* 433 U. S., at 333. Even on this sparse record, it is apparent that Johnson Controls is concerned about only a small minority of women. Of the eight pregnancies reported among the female employees, it has not been shown that any of the babies have birth defects or other abnormalities. The record does not reveal the birth rate for Johnson Controls' female workers but national statistics show that approximately nine percent of all fertile women become pregnant each year. The birthrate drops to two percent for blue collar workers over age 30. See Becker, 53 U. Chi. L. Rev., at 1233. Johnson Controls' fear of prenatal injury, no matter how sincere, does not begin to show that substantially all of its fertile women employees are incapable of doing their jobs. . . .

It is no more appropriate for the courts than it is for individual employers to decide whether a woman's reproductive role is more important to herself and her family than her economic role. Congress has left this choice to the woman as hers to make.

The judgment of the Court of Appeals is reversed and the case is remanded for further proceedings consistent with this opinion.

It is so ordered.

DISTRICT OF COLUMBIA COURT OF APPEALS

In Re A. C.

On Hearing en Banc
TERRY, ASSOCIATE JUDGE:

This case comes before the court for the second time. In *In re A. C.,* 533 A.2d 611 (D.C.1987), a three-judge motions division denied a motion to stay an order of the trial court which had authorized a hospital

District of Columbia Court of Appeals. 573 A.2d 1235 (D.C. App. 1990).

to perform a caesarean section on a dying woman in an effort to save the life of her unborn child. The operation was performed, but both the mother and the child died. A few months later, the court ordered the case heard en banc and vacated the opinion of the motions division. *In re A. C.,* 539 A.2d 203 (D.C.1988). Although the motions division recognized that, as a practical matter, it "decided the entire matter when [it] denied the stay," 533 A.2d at 613, the en banc court has nevertheless heard the full case on the merits.

We are confronted here with two profoundly difficult and complex issues. First, we must determine who has the right to decide the course of medical treatment for a patient who, although near death, is pregnant with a viable fetus. Second, we must establish how that decision should be made if the patient cannot make it for herself—more specifically, how a court should proceed when faced with a pregnant patient, *in extremis,* who is apparently incapable of making an informed decision regarding medical care for herself and her fetus. We hold that in virtually all cases the question of what is to be done is to be decided by the patient—the pregnant woman—on behalf of herself and the fetus. If the patient is incompetent or otherwise unable to give an informed consent to a proposed course of medical treatment, then her decision must be ascertained through the procedure known as substituted judgment. Because the trial court did not follow that procedure, we vacate its order and remand the case for further proceedings.

This case came before the trial court when George Washington University Hospital petitioned the emergency judge in chambers for declaratory relief as to how it should treat its patient, A.C., who was close to death from cancer and was twenty-six and one-half weeks pregnant with a viable fetus. After a hearing lasting approximately three hours, which was held at the hospital (though not in A.C.'s room), the court ordered that a caesarean section be performed on A.C. to deliver the fetus. Counsel for A.C. immediately sought a stay in this court, which was unanimously denied by a hastily assembled division of three judges. *In re A. C.,* 533 A.2d 611 (D.C.1987). The caesarean was performed, and a baby girl, L.M.C., was delivered. Tragically, the child died within two and one-half hours, and the mother died two days later.

Counsel for A.C. now maintain that A.C. was competent and that she made an informed choice not to have the caesarean performed. Given this view of the facts, they argue that it was error for the trial court to weigh the state's interest in preserving the potential life of a viable fetus against A.C.'s interest in having her decision respected. They argue further that, even if the substituted judgment procedure had been followed, the evidence would necessarily show that A.C. would not have wanted the caesarean section. . . .

A.C. was first diagnosed as suffering from cancer at the age of thirteen. In the ensuing years she underwent major surgery several times, together with multiple radiation treatments and chemotherapy. A.C. married when she was twenty-seven, during a period of remission, and soon thereafter she became pregnant. . . .

On Tuesday, June 9, 1987, when A.C. was approximately twenty-five weeks pregnant, she went to the hospital for a scheduled check-up. Because she was experiencing pain in her back and shortness of breath, an x-ray was taken, revealing an apparently inoperable tumor which nearly filled her right lung. On Thursday, June 11, A.C. was admitted to the hospital as a patient. By Friday her condition had temporarily improved, and when asked if she really wanted to have her baby, she replied that she did.

Over the weekend A.C.'s condition worsened considerably. Accordingly, on Monday, June 15, members of the medical staff treating A.C. assembled, along with her family, in A.C.'s room. The doctors then informed her that her illness was terminal, and A.C. agreed to palliative treatment designed to extend her life until at least her twenty-eighth week of pregnancy. The "potential outcome [for] the fetus," according to the doctors, would be much better at twenty-eight weeks than at twenty-six weeks if it were necessary to "intervene." A.C. knew that the palliative treatment she had chosen presented some increased risk to the fetus, but she opted for this course both to prolong her life for at least another two weeks and to maintain her own comfort. When asked if she still wanted to have the baby, A.C. was somewhat equivocal, saying "something to the effect of 'I don't know, I think so.'" As the day moved toward evening, A.C.'s condition grew still worse, and at about 7:00 or 8:00 p.m. she consented to intubation to facilitate her breathing.

The next morning, June 16, the trial court convened a hearing at the hospital . . . and the District of Columbia was permitted to intervene for the fetus as *parens patriae.* The court heard testimony . . . that the chances of survival for a twenty-six-week fetus delivered at the hospital might be as high as eighty percent, but that this particular fetus, because of the mother's medical history, had only a fifty to sixty percent chance of survival. . . .

Regarding A.C.'s ability to respond to questioning and her prognosis, Dr. Louis Hamner, another treating obstetrician, testified that A.C. would probably die within twenty-four hours "if absolutely nothing else is done. . . . As far as her ability to interact, she has been heavily sedated in order to maintain her ventilatory function. She will open her eyes sometimes when you are in the room, but as far as her being able to . . . carry on a meaningful-type conversation . . . at this point, I don't think that is reasonable." . . .

There was no evidence before the court showing that A.C. consented to, or even contemplated, a caesarean section before her twenty-eighth week of pregnancy. There was, in fact, considerable dispute as to whether she would have consented to an immediate caesarean delivery at the time the hearing was held. A.C.'s mother opposed surgical intervention, testifying that A.C. wanted "to live long enough to hold that baby" and that she expected to do so, "even though she knew she was terminal." Dr. Hamner testified that, given A.C.'s medical problems, he did not think she would have chosen to deliver a child with a substantial degree of impairment. . . .

After hearing this testimony and the arguments of counsel, the trial court made oral findings of fact. It found, first, that A.C. would probably die, according to uncontroverted medical testimony, "within the next twenty-four to forty-eight hours"; second, that A.C. was "pregnant with a twenty-six and a half week viable fetus who, based upon uncontroverted medical testimony, has approximately a fifty to sixty percent chance to survive if a caesarean section is performed as soon as possible"; third, that because the fetus was viable, "the state has [an] important and legitimate interest in protecting the potentiality of human life"; and fourth, that there had been some testimony that the operation "may very well hasten the death of [A.C.]," but that there had also been testimony that delay would greatly increase the risk to the fetus and that "the prognosis is not great for the fetus to be delivered postmortem. . . ." Most significantly, the court found:

> The court is of the view that it does not clearly know what [A.C.'s] present views are with respect to the issue of whether or not the child should live or die. . . .

Having made these findings of fact and conclusions of law, the court ordered that a caesarean section be performed to deliver A.C.'s child.

The court's decision was then relayed to A.C., who had regained consciousness. When the hearing reconvened later in the day, Dr. Hamner told the court:

> I explained to her essentially what was going on. . . . I said it's been deemed we should intervene on behalf of the baby by caesarean section and it would give it the only possible chance of it living. Would you agree to this procedure? *She said yes.* I said, do you realize that you may not survive the

surgical procedure? *She said yes.* And I repeated the two questions to her again [and] asked her did she understand. *She said yes.* [Emphasis added.]

When the court suggested moving the hearing to A.C.'s bedside, Dr. Hamner discouraged the court from doing so, but he and Dr. Weingold, together with A.C.'s mother and husband, went to A.C.'s room to confirm her consent to the procedure. . . .

[A.C.] then seemed to pause for a few moments and then very clearly mouthed words several times, *I don't want it done. I don't want it done.*

[Dr. Weingold testified:]

> I would obviously state the obvious and that is this is an environment in which, from my perspective as a physician, this would not be an informed consent one way or the other. She's under tremendous stress with the family on both sides, but I'm satisfied that I heard clearly what she said. . . .

Dr. Weingold later qualified his opinion as to A.C.'s ability to give an informed consent, stating that he thought the environment for an informed consent was non-existent because A.C. was in intensive care, flanked by a weeping husband and mother. . . .

After hearing this new evidence, the court found that it was "still not clear what her intent is" and again ordered that a caesarean section be performed. A.C.'s counsel sought a stay in this court, which was denied. *In re A. C.,* 533 A.2d 611, 613 (D.C.1987). The operation took place, but the baby lived for only a few hours, and A.C. succumbed to cancer two days later. . . .

It has been suggested that fetal cases are different [from other duty-to-aid cases] because a woman who "has chosen to lend her body to bring [a] child into the world" has an enhanced duty to assure the welfare of the fetus, sufficient even to require her to undergo caesarean surgery. Robertson, *Procreative Liberty,* 69 Va.L.Rev. at 456. Surely, however, a fetus cannot have rights in this respect superior to those of a person who has already been born. . . .

This court has recognized as well that, above and beyond common law protections, the right to accept or forego medical treatment is of constitutional magnitude. . . .

What we distill from the [precedent] cases is that every person has the right, under the common law and the Constitution, to accept or refuse medical treatment. This right of bodily integrity belongs equally to persons who are competent and persons who are not. Further, it matters not what the quality of a patient's life may be; the right of bodily integrity is not extinguished simply because someone is ill, or even at death's door. To protect that right against intrusion by others — family members, doctors, hospitals, or anyone else, however well-intentioned — we hold that a court must determine the patient's wishes by any means available, and must abide by those wishes unless there are truly extraordinary or compelling reasons to override them. . . .

From the record before us, we simply cannot tell whether A.C. was ever competent, after being sedated, to make an informed decision one way or the other regarding the proposed caesarean section. The trial court never made any finding about A.C.'s competency to decide. Undoubtedly, during most of the proceedings below, A.C. was incompetent to make a treatment decision; that is, she was unable to give an informed consent based on her assessment of the risks and benefits of the contemplated surgery. . . .

We have no reason to believe that, if competent, A.C. would or would not have refused consent to a caesarean. We hold, however, that without a competent refusal from A.C. to go forward with the surgery, and without a finding through substituted judgment that A.C. would not have consented to the surgery, it was error for the trial court to proceed to a balancing analysis, weighing the rights of A.C. against the interests of the state. . . .

The court should also consider previous decisions of the patient concerning medical treatment, especially when there may be a discernibly consistent pattern of conduct or of thought. . . . Thus in a case such as this it would be highly relevant that A.C. had consented to intrusive and dangerous surgeries in the past, and that she chose to become pregnant and to protect her pregnancy by seeking treatment at the hospital's high-risk pregnancy clinic. It would also be relevant that she accepted a plan of treatment which contemplated caesarean intervention at the twenty-eighth week of pregnancy, even though the possibility of a caesarean during the twenty-sixth week was apparently unforeseen. On the other hand, A.C. agreed to a plan of palliative treatment which posed a greater danger to the fetus than would have been necessary if she were unconcerned about her own continuing care. Further, when A.C. was informed of the fatal nature of her illness, she was equivocal about her desire to have the baby.

Courts in substituted judgment cases have also acknowledged the importance of probing the patient's value system as an aid in discerning what the patient would choose. We agree with this approach. . . . Most people do not foresee what calamities may befall them; much less do they consider, or even think about, treatment alternatives in varying situations. The court in a substituted judgment case, therefore, should pay special attention to the known values and goals of the incapacitated patient, and should strive, if possible, to extrapolate from those values and goals what the patient's decision would be. . . .

After reviewing the transcript of the hearing and the court's oral findings, it is clear to us that the trial court did not follow the substituted judgment procedure. . . .

The court did not go on, as it should have done, to make a finding as to what A.C. would have chosen to do if she were competent. Instead, the court undertook to balance the state's and L.M.C.'s interests in surgical intervention against A.C.'s perceived interest in not having the caesarean performed.

After A.C. was informed of the court's decision, she consented to the caesarean; moments later, however, she withdrew her consent. The trial court did not then make a finding as to whether A.C. was competent to make the medical decision or whether she had made an informed decision one way or the other. Nor did the court then make a substituted judgment for A.C. Instead, the court said that it was "still not clear what her intent is" and again ordered the caesarean.

It is that order which we must now set aside. What a trial court must do in a case such as this is to determine, if possible, whether the patient is capable of making an informed decision about the course of her medical treatment. If she is, and if she makes such a decision, her wishes will control in virtually all cases. . . .

Accordingly, we vacate the order of the trial court and remand the case for such further proceedings as may be appropriate. We note, in doing so, that the trial court's order allowing the hospital to perform the caesarean section was presumptively valid from the date it was entered until today. What the legal effect of that order may have been during its lifetime is a matter on which we express no opinion here.

Vacated and remanded.

BELSON, ASSOCIATE JUDGE, concurring in part and dissenting in part:

I agree with much of the majority opinion, but I disagree with its ultimate ruling that the trial court's order must be set aside, and with the narrow view it takes of the state's interest in preserving life and the unborn child's interest in life. . . .

The state's interest in preserving human life and the viable unborn child's interest in survival are entitled, I think, to more weight than I find them assigned by the majority when it states that "in virtually all cases the decision of the patient . . . will control." Majority opinion at 1252. I would hold that in those instances, fortunately rare, in which the viable unborn child's interest in living and the state's parallel interest in protecting human life come into conflict with the mother's decision to forgo a procedure such as a caesarean section, a balancing should be struck in which the unborn child's and the state's interests are entitled to substantial weight.

It was acknowledged in *Roe v. Wade,* 410 U.S. 113, 93 S.Ct. 705, 35 L.Ed.2d 147 (1973), that the state's interest in potential human life becomes compelling at the point of viability. Even before viability, the state has an "important and legitimate interest in protecting the potentiality of human life." . . .

We are dealing with the situation that exists when a woman has carried an unborn child to viability. When the unborn child reaches the state of viability, the child becomes a party whose interests must be considered. . . .

[In] *Bonbrest v. Kotz,* 65 F.Supp. 138 (D.D.C. 1946) . . . the court . . . stated:

It has, if viable, its own bodily form and members, manifests all the anatomical characteristics of individuality, possesses its own circulatory, vascular and excretory systems and is capable *now* of being ushered into the visible world.

Id. at 141 (footnote omitted).

Bonbrest proved to be a landmark case. In *Greater Southeast Hospital v. Williams,* 482 A.2d 394 (D.C. 1984), this court noted that "every jurisdiction in the United States has followed *Bonbrest* in recognizing a cause of action for prenatal injury, at least when the injury is to a viable infant later born alive." *Id.* at 396. We went on to hold in *Greater Southeast Hospital* that a viable unborn child *is a person* within the coverage of the wrongful death statute, D.C.Code § 16-2701 (1981):

Inherent in our adoption of *Bonbrest* is the recognition that a viable fetus is an independent person with the right to be free of prenatal injury. The liability for prenatal injury recognized in *Bonbrest* arises at the time of the injury. If a viable fetus is a "person injured" at the time of the injury, then perforce the fetus is a "person" when he dies of those injuries, and it can make no difference in liability under the wrongful death and survival statutes whether the fetus dies of the injuries just prior to or just after birth. . . .

A viable unborn child is a *person* at common law who has legal rights that are entitled to the protection of the courts. In a case like the one before us, the unborn child is a patient of both the hospital and any treating physician, and the hospital or physician may be liable to the child for the child's prenatal injury or death if caused by their negligence. . . .

The balancing test should be applied in instances in which women become pregnant and carry an unborn child to the point of viability. This is not an unreasonable classification because, I submit, a woman who carries a child to viability is in fact a member of a unique category of persons. Her circumstances differ fundamentally from those of other potential patients for medical procedures that will aid another person, for example, a potential donor of bone marrow for transplant. This is so because she has undertaken to bear another human being, and has carried an unborn child to viability. Another unique feature of the situation we address arises from the singular nature of the dependency of the unborn child upon the mother. A woman carrying a viable unborn child is not in the same category as a relative, friend, or stranger called upon to donate bone marrow or an organ for transplant. Rather, the expectant mother has placed herself in a special class of persons who are bringing another person into existence, and upon whom that other person's life is totally dependent. Also, uniquely, the viable unborn child is literally captive within the mother's body. No other potential beneficiary of a surgical procedure on another is in that position.

For all of these reasons, a balancing becomes appropriate in those few cases where the interests we are discussing come into conflict. To so state is in no sense to fail to recognize the extremely strong interest of each individual person, including of course the expectant mother, in her bodily integrity, her privacy, and, where involved, her religious beliefs.

Thus, I cannot agree with the conclusion of the majority opinion that while we "do not quite foreclose the possibility that a conflicting state interest may be so compelling that the patient's wishes must yield . . . we anticipate that such cases will be extremely rare and truly exceptional." Majority opinion at 1252. While it is, fortunately, true that such cases will be rare in the sense that such conflicts between mother and viable unborn child are rare, I cannot agree that in cases where a viable unborn child is in the picture, it would be extremely rare, within that universe, to require that the mother accede to the vital needs of the viable unborn child. . . .

I next address the sensitive question of how to balance the competing rights and interests of the viable unborn child and the state against those of the rare expectant mother who elects not to have a caesarean section necessary to save the life of her child. The indisputable view that a woman carrying a viable child has an extremely strong interest in her own life, health, bodily integrity, privacy, and religious beliefs necessarily requires that her election be given correspondingly great weight in the balancing process. In a case, however, where the court in an exercise of a substituted judgment has concluded that the patient would probably opt against a caesarean section, the court should vary the weight to be given this factor in proportion to the confidence the court has in the accuracy of its conclusion. Thus, in a case where the indicia of the incompetent patient's judgment are equivocal, the court should accord this factor correspondingly less weight. The appropriate weight to be given other factors will have to be worked out by the development of law in this area, and cannot be prescribed in a single court opinion. Some considerations obviously merit special attention in the balancing process. One such consideration is any danger to the mother's life or health, physical or mental, including the relatively small but still significant danger that necessarily inheres in any cae-

sarean delivery, and including especially any danger that exceeds that level. The mother's religious beliefs as they relate to the operation would appear to deserve inclusion in the balancing process.

On the other side of the analysis, it is appropriate to look to the relative likelihood of the unborn child's survival. . . . The child's interest in being born with as little impairment as possible should also be considered. This may weigh in favor of a delivery sooner rather than later. The most important factor on this side of the scale, however, is life itself, because the viable unborn child that dies because of the mother's refusal to have a caesarean delivery is deprived, entirely and irrevocably, of the life on which the child was about to embark.

. . . Also to be considered in the balance was the rather minimal, but nevertheless undisputable, additional risk that caesarean delivery presented for the mother.

Turning to the interest of the unborn child in living and the parallel interest of the state in protecting that life, the evidence indicated that the child had a fifty to sixty percent chance of survival and a less than twenty percent chance of entering life with a serious handicap such as cerebral palsy or mental retardation. The evidence also showed that a delay in delivering the child would have increased the likelihood of a handicap. In view of the record before Judge Sullivan, and on the basis that there had been no plain error in not applying the sort of substituted judgment analysis that we for the first time mandate in today's ruling, I think it cannot be said that he abused his discretion in the way he struck the balance between the considerations that favored the procedure and those that went against it.

For the reasons stated above, I would affirm.

NANCY K. RHODEN

Cesareans and Samaritans

Until recently, if one asked the proverbial person on the street to list maternal-fetal conflicts, he or she would have mentioned abortion and, when pressed to continue, looked at the questioner blankly. Now, however, the populace is becoming aware of a host of maternal-fetal conflicts. Indeed, mother-and-child, long a somewhat romanticized unity, are increasingly being treated by physicians, courts, and the media as potential adversaries, locked in battle on the rather inconvenient battleground of the woman's belly.

Some of these newly publicized conflicts — pregnant women abusing drugs or alcohol, or continuing to work in occupations hazardous to fetal health — are not all that new: the hazards of various substances have been known for years. Other of the conflicts are new, inasmuch as doctors could not recommend Cesareans or other procedures for the fetus' benefit until they could detect fetal problems during or before labor. But probably what is most unprecedented is that now, suddenly, physicians are seeking court intervention to protect these imperiled fetuses — intervention that, inevitably, constitutes a significant intrusion into the woman's conduct during pregnancy or birth.

This essay will discuss just one of the proliferating array of maternal-fetal conflicts — the question whether courts should have the power to authorize doctors to perform Cesarean deliveries against the woman's will. Doctors typically seek these orders when they believe, based on diagnostic techniques, that vaginal delivery risks death or neurological damage to the fetus. (In some cases, vaginal delivery is a risk for the woman as well.) Women who refuse most commonly do so based on religious beliefs opposed to surgery, though they may refuse because they fear surgery, do not believe the doctor's prognoses, or whatever. . . .

The position I will defend is that courts should not order competent women to have Cesareans, despite the potentially tragic consequences to the fetus. This is

Law, Medicine & Health Care 15(3) Fall, 1987, pp. 118–125. Reprinted by permission of the publisher.

neither an easy position nor a fully satisfactory one. Indeed, it is the sort of hard-line civil libertarian position that I ordinarily find oversimplified in bioethics issues. Yet I believe that it is the morally and legally correct position — albeit merely the "least worst" one — because these orders (1) impose an unparalleled intrusion upon pregnant women; (2) undermine the teachings of the informed consent doctrine that only the individual being subjected to a procedure can assess its risks and benefits; and (3) contain within them the seeds of widespread and pernicious usurpation of women's choices during obstetrical care.

JUSTIFICATIONS FOR NONCONSENSUAL CESAREANS

ABORTION LAW

In the cases of which I am aware, every judge but one who has ruled on an application for nonconsensual Cesarean delivery has granted the request. Interestingly, *Roe v. Wade,*[1] which has stood firmly for a woman's right to privacy and right to make her own decisions about pregnancy, is the case most commonly invoked by courts to justify these orders.[2] Under *Roe,* women must be allowed to choose abortion prior to fetal viability (subject to state regulation to protect the mother's health in the second trimester). But once a fetus is capable of independent life outside the womb, albeit with artificial aid, the state's interest in potential life becomes compelling.[3] Then the state can prohibit abortion, unless it is necessary to protect the woman's life or health. Courts invoking *Roe* to support nonconsensual Cesarean delivery reason that since states can prohibit the intentional termination of fetal life after viability, they can likewise protect viable fetuses by preventing vaginal delivery when it will have the same effect as abortion.[4]

At first glance this analysis appears attractive. Attempting a vaginal delivery when responsible medical opinion says that surgical delivery is necessary for the fetus may cause a stillbirth or, perhaps worse, profound neurological damage to the child. These consequences are clearly ones that states have an interest in preventing. But the fact that states have an interest in preventing certain consequences does not mean that any and all action to prevent such consequences is constitutional. For example, states have an interest in preventing use of illicit drugs, and they can make such conduct criminal. But this doesn't mean that they can take any and all other steps to prevent drug use, such as ordering random strip searches at airports (though the way things are going, we may soon see random urine samples). Similarly, the Court in *Roe* said that in the third trimester, the state can even "go so far as to proscribe abortion,"[5] unless the woman's health is at stake. That the state can go this far, prohibiting intentional fetal destruction, doesn't necessarily mean that it can go even farther, and mandate major surgery to protect and preserve the fetus' life. There is a quantum leap in logic between prohibiting destruction and requiring surgical preservation that courts and commentators relying on abortion law have ignored.

In fact, if one reads *Roe* and its progeny more closely, it becomes apparent that court-ordered Cesareans violate *Roe*'s constitutional schema. *Roe* emphasizes that even after the fetus is viable, the woman's life and health come first. If her health is threatened by her pregnancy even after the fetus is viable, she must be allowed to abort.[6] In *Colautti v. Franklin,*[7] the Supreme Court discussed the primacy of maternal health even more specifically. It invalidated a statute that required doctors performing post-viability abortions to use the technique least harmful to the fetus, unless another technique was necessary for the woman's health. Among other infirmities, this statute impermissibly implied that the more hazardous technique had to be *indispensable* to the woman's health, and suggested that doctors could be required to make trade-offs between her health and additional percentage points of the fetus' survival.[8] Abortion law makes clear that such trade-offs cannot be required.

Thus a state could not, under *Colautti,* require that all abortions after viability be done by hysterotomy, a surgical technique that is basically a mini-Cesarean, on the grounds that this is safest for the fetus. A state could not require this because such a technique is less safe for the woman. It may not be immediately apparent that this proscription of compulsory maternal-fetal trade-offs in late abortion applies to the Cesarean dilemma. Yet this becomes quite clear when one realizes that after a fetus is viable, the methods of abortion and of premature delivery simply merge. Although the Supreme Court in *Roe* and subsequent cases has spoken of post-viability abortion, doctors have historically thought of late terminations necessitated by a health problem on the woman's part as premature deliveries — deliveries that may put the fetus at great risk but that are not specifically intended to destroy it. In other words, post-viability terminations of pregnancy are simply inductions of labor, just as might be done at full term.

Once we recognize this, we see that what the Court says about third-trimester abortion should apply to delivery methods as well. When that yardstick is applied, it yields the conclusion that a state clearly could not enact a statute requiring Cesarean over vaginal delivery to protect the fetus. Inasmuch as surgical delivery involves approximately four times the maternal mortality rate of vaginal delivery, such a statute would impermissibly mandate trade-offs between maternal and fetal health. The state could not statutorily mandate surgical delivery even in those cases where the fetus' health was seriously threatened by vaginal delivery, because the mother's health will still almost always be somewhat threatened by surgical delivery. Likewise, it violates the Constitution for courts to authorize nonconsensual Cesarean delivery in individual cases, since it seems clear that courts should not issue orders in individual cases that, if generalized in the form of a statute, would be unconstitutional.

THE CHILD NEGLECT/FETAL NEGLECT ANALOGY

Despite the strong argument that nonconsensual Cesareans are at odds with the teachings of *Roe* and other Supreme Court abortion cases, it may be objected that in rejecting maternal-fetal trade-offs, the Supreme Court was thinking only about abortions, not about full-term deliveries. Given the state's strong interest in preservation of life, why, one might ask, must doctors stand by while a baby who could be fine if delivered surgically dies or suffers irreversible brain damage? Whatever abortion law says, should women really have a right to make this potentially lethal choice, when the risk to them is quite minimal?

Courts and commentators have frequently relied on the law of child neglect to argue that harmful choices such as these are not the woman's to make.[9] Parents, of course, cannot refuse needed medical care for their children, even if the provision of such care violates their most cherished religious beliefs. Likewise, it is often argued, pregnant women cannot refuse care necessary for their fetus' well-being. To do so is the prenatal equivalent of child neglect (and, according to this theory, taking substances such as heroin while one is pregnant is the prenatal equivalent of child abuse).

There's a simple charm to this notion that if parents cannot deny care to a child, neither can a pregnant woman deny it to a fetus, at least to a fetus that is fully formed and clearly viable. When analyzed, however, this notion is far from charming. It has far-reaching and very alarming implications, and it is far less simple than it appears. Child neglect is, of course, the failure to perform one's legal duties to one's children. The term "fetal neglect" implies that there are legally enforceable duties to fetuses. But while parents have historically owed a whole panoply of duties to their children, women have not heretofore been held to have legally enforceable duties to fetuses. . . .

Obviously, "fetal neglect" proponents recognize the *fact* of the fetus' internal location. They then draw the analogy with child neglect by stating that this difference in location is the only difference between a fetus and a child. True, it is (at least for very late-term fetuses). But in terms of what a state must do to end "fetal neglect" as opposed to ending child neglect, this "slight disanalogy" is like the difference between night and day. Children can simply be treated, in opposition to parental demands. But "fetal neglect" cannot be remedied without, as it were, "breaching the maternal barrier" — restraining and physically invading the woman. . . .

THE STATE'S INTEREST IN THE WELL-BEING OF THIRD PARTIES

Competent persons can refuse medical treatment, even when it means their death. Their rights to privacy and bodily integrity are increasingly respected, even though the state has interests, such as in preserving life, that are arrayed against virtually all treatment refusals. In other words, while the state's interests are neither negligible nor forgotten, the patients' privacy rights trump them. But most refusals do not have a direct and devastating effect upon third parties. How do we weigh the individual's right to refuse in these cases against the state's interest in preserving a third party's life — an interest that puts these cases in a class by themselves?

Courts have not taken the interests of third parties lightly, even when the goal was to preserve their emotional welfare rather than to protect them from physical harm. Some courts have overridden treatment refusals by parents of dependent children (usually Jehovah's Witnesses refusing blood transfusions), on the grounds that the parent should not be allowed to orphan his or her child.[10] It can readily be argued that if a parent's privacy right can be overridden to spare his child emotional or financial loss, surely it can be overridden to prevent a stillbirth or a birth injury that may cause profound impairment. The only problem with this argument is that these cases are, in my opinion, clearly wrong. Although the practice is frowned upon, parents can abandon their children by putting them in foster care or even up for adoption; some parents de facto abandon their children by, for example, divorcing and leaving the jurisdiction; and parents take health risks, such as hang gliding, sky diving, or joining the U.S. army, that could potentially result in their children being orphaned. Why, in the one sphere of medical treatment, should they be required to violate their faith and adhere to medical orthodoxy? I see no good reason why here, but not elsewhere, parenthood should obliterate personal autonomy. . . .

Having recognized that the true analogue to imposed Cesareans is nonconsensual surgery sought to benefit a third party, we now confront a significant dearth of caselaw. One reason is that there are few fact patterns in which a medical procedure performed on A will save B. Another reason is that compelling A to undergo risks so as to save B has always been considered beyond the reaches of state authority. . . .

In this country there is no general duty to rescue. There are exceptions, which include a special relationship between the parties such as that of innkeeper and guest, common carrier and passenger, and, most importantly, parent and child.[11] But even when a special relationship gives rise to a duty to rescue, there is still no duty to undertake *risky* rescues.[12] Nor is there such a duty in countries where there is a general duty to rescue.[13] It is easy to see that a demand for someone's kidney falls under the law of rescue (Samaritan law) and goes far beyond what is ever required of potential rescuers. In the one case on point, *McFall v. Shimp*,[14] a man dying of aplastic anemia asked the court to mandate that his cousin donate bone marrow to save him. The court called the relative's refusal to donate morally reprehensible, but held that for the law to "sink its teeth into the jugular vein or neck of one of its members and suck from it sustenance for *another* member, is revolting to our hard-wrought concepts of jurisprudence.

Such would raise the spectre of the swastika and the Inquisition, reminiscent of the horrors this portends."[15] Although there are no *McFall*-type cases involving parent–child donation, I think we can say with a fair degree of certainty that the outcome would and should be the same. Parents have a duty to rescue their children — i.e., to be basic Good Samaritans — but they have no duty to be "Splendid Samaritans,"[16] embarking upon rescues that risk their life or health.

THE ILLEGITIMACY OF INTERPERSONAL RISK–BENEFIT COMPARISONS

If what a court does in mandating a Cesarean is no different from mandating a bone marrow transfusion to save a dying relative, it clearly exceeds the state's legitimate authority. While the two seem equivalent to me, they certainly haven't seemed so to most of the courts that have considered requests for nonconsensual Cesareans. For various reasons, court-ordered Cesareans strike many people as legitimate, while court-ordered bone marrow transfusions or kidney donations (a more equivalent intrusion), even from parent to child, seem outrageous. These reasons are important and cannot be ignored — they are what makes this situation so agonizing. However, I will try to show that while these reasons go to the woman's conduct, the appropriate question concerns the nature of the *state's* conduct. When we look to it, all nonconsensual risks imposed on one person to save another are equally illegitimate.

The Cesarean cases unquestionably *feel* different from cases or hypotheticals involving forced intrusions on parents to save children. For one thing, the woman is going to give birth anyway, and if she just does it surgically instead of vaginally the baby will probably be fine. Cesareans are common and relatively safe, and the potential harm from delivering the baby vaginally is very serious. Moreover, it seems to some that women who choose not to abort thereby assume certain obligations to their fetuses, a by no means unreasonable suggestion. Finally, pregnancy simply is a unique situation. A dying relative, even a child, is a separate, independent person. However dire his need, he is not a tiny, helpless, totally dependent creature.

Emotional responses should certainly not be disregarded in bioethics. But neither should they necessarily rule. Physicians understandably become very uncomfortable when a woman appears ready to risk her fetus' life and health for the sake of her religious faith, and they feel even stronger when her reasons appear less weighty. Indeed, trivial reasons for running this risk may justify our casting moral aspersions on the woman's conduct. Despite the uniqueness of pregnancy, however, and despite the strength or weakness of the woman's reason for refusal (assuming she is competent), what the *state* does when it orders a compulsory Cesarean is no different from what it does when it orders compulsory bone marrow or kidney "donation," and what the state does is wrong.

The most significant feature of decisions ordering Cesareans is that the court, explicitly or implicitly, finds that the potential harm to the fetus overrides the woman's rights to privacy, autonomy, and bodily integrity, and justifies imposing a physical harm upon her (because surgery is a harm even if it has no untoward consequences). The court, in other words, takes two people, looks at the potential consequences of a bad situation, and says that the probably severe harm to X warrants imposing a lesser physical harm on Y. The legitimacy of this argument depends upon the assumption that a third party can step in and weigh the risks of surgery for someone who has competently chosen to forego them, and can then order that these risks be run. This is an assumption that has always been rejected in American jurisprudence, and that, if accepted, has far-reaching and extraordinarily frightening implications.

There is something special about the body. In theory, we can all recognize that everyone's body is equally special. But in practice, somehow our own seems far more special than anyone else's. It is very easy for us to say, as objective third parties, that a patient really should have needed surgery, because its risks are minute — perhaps only 1 in 10,000. But when we are thinking about that same surgery for ourselves, the minuteness of that chance may somehow seem less pertinent than the ghastly thought that we might be that one. This different attitude toward low statistical risks when run by a group of strangers and when run by oneself explains the old saying, "Minor surgery is surgery performed on somebody else." Perhaps this difference also explains why even countries with general duties to rescue never require risky rescues. While cowardice may not be admired, it is too human a quality to be formally punished by law.

Needless to say, a court can contemplate surgery for a pregnant woman only as a third-party bystander, albeit a careful and concerned bystander. It can assess the objective risks of surgery to the woman and the corresponding benefits to the fetus. But its ability truly to understand the situation is radically limited. . . .

In ordering surgery, the court is thus rendering objective a determination that cannot rightfully be anything but subjective. Although it is doing so for the best of reasons, its action nonetheless denies to a disturbing extent the woman's uniqueness and individuality. It denies her special fears or her special spiritual reasons for rejecting surgery and "leaving things in the hands of God." When it subjugates her views about having her body invaded (or about interfering with Providence) to its assessment of the "right" action based on potential consequences, it is making an interpersonal risk–benefit comparison and holding that she must run the risk to prevent the greater risk to the baby. Objectively, this may well be the proper assessment. But decisions about major surgery on unconsenting adults simply are not delegated to third parties, and delegating this one is no different from delegating a decision about bone marrow extraction or kidney transplant. I can think of no other instance where a state feels it has the authority to compare the risks faced by one individual to those faced by the other. The court compromises its integrity in making these orders, because whether it realizes it or not, it is treating the woman as a means — a vehicle for rescuing an imperiled fetus — and not as an end in herself.

Two disturbing potential scenarios will help illustrate why a nonconsensual Cesarean is inevitably a wrong against the woman. First, imagine surgery has been authorized, and the woman struggles to try to avoid it. In the case at North Central Bronx, doctors repeatedly asked what they should do if this occurred. Should they hold her down and anesthetize her? Some proponents of intervention would characterize this as merely a practical problem in enforcement — some injunctions being easier to enforce than others. Yet this is much more than a mere enforcement issue. It illustrates the violence lurking here, whether or not it is ever actually committed. The court is at one remove from the violence, because its role is limited to issuing the order. Nonetheless, the court has authorized an act of violence against the woman, even if the violence is obscured by her cowed compliance in the face of judicial power.

Second, imagine that the highly unexpected happens, and the woman is killed or injured by the surgery. Although this is exceedingly unlikely, its possibility raises an interesting moral issue. The court cannot, of course, be held legally responsible for this harm, nor can the doctors, assuming they were not negligent. Yet the court would be, it seems, morally responsible, because it chose to subject the woman to this risk. There is no comparison between the state's responsibility under this scenario and its responsibility if the woman's refusal is upheld and the baby is harmed. If the baby suffers, the woman is causally responsible (assuming surgery would have prevented the harm) and in some cases, at least, will be morally to blame. But the state won't be implicated, because the state does not normally intervene in a person's medical decisions. In other words, a private wrong will have occurred. But if the state has the hubris to intervene in what is ordinarily a private (albeit potentially tragic) choice, it takes on the moral responsibility for the outcome as well. Although the chances of maternal injury are low, the moral risk is great, and this possibility should make courts think twice before mandating surgery.

SOME ADDITIONAL SOCIAL CONCERNS

For purposes of analyzing nonconsensual Cesareans, I have been assuming that the physicians' predictions of harm to the infant are correct. In any individual case, of course, the doctor's alarm is most likely warranted — although it is interesting to note that in *Jefferson, Headley,* and *Jeffries,* the women delivered vaginally and the infants were fine. But when we think of mandatory Cesareans not simply as individual cases but as a social policy, we must recognize that some of the operations will be unnecessary. This is because the tools upon which doctors rely to diagnose problems during pregnancy or labor detect abnormally high risks, but do not necessarily distinguish cases in which the risks will materialize from those in which they will not.

Some tools and diagnoses are better than others. For example, ultrasonography is highly reliable in detecting placenta previa, and diagnosis of complete placenta previa reliably dictates Cesarean delivery. But even here prediction is not 100-percent accurate: both Ms. Jefferson and Ms. Jeffries, who were diagnosed as having complete placenta previa, delivered vaginally. Other tools are as likely to be wrong as right. . . .

Physicians should be risk-averse and reluctant to gamble with the lives of babies, and fears of legal liability naturally enhance these traits. However, technological limitations combined with a cautious, risk-averse approach virtually ensure that some of the Cesareans doctors recommend will turn out not to have been required. While the vast majority of women would far rather risk an unnecessary operation than an impaired infant, it is not so clear that, given the technological limitations, it is irrational or immoral to take a different approach to risk. At any rate, mandatory Cesareans will mean that the judicial system requires this risk-averse approach, and forces pregnant women as a group to run some unnecessary risks to ensure healthy babies.

Although it might be suggested that courts can distinguish truly risky situations from only somewhat risky ones, this suggestion unfortunately puts more faith in the judicial system than it deserves, at least in these types of cases. The doctors bringing them will undoubtedly believe that surgery is necessary. The courts will have little choice but to accept the doctor's assessment — especially since in the typical Cesarean case the woman is either not present at all (and of course not represented by counsel) or represented by an attorney appointed only hours or days before and patently incapable of presenting contrary medical evidence even if it could be obtained. These cases have thus far been very one-sided, and given the time constraints will almost surely continue to be so. This may account in part for the fact that most courts have issued the orders. It is interesting to note that in the Pamela Rae Stewart case, where Ms. Stewart was criminally prosecuted for prenatal conduct that allegedly caused her child to be born with brain damage and then to die, there was for once a two-sided debate. Here the American Civil Liberties Union came to Ms. Stewart's defense, and all charges against her were dismissed.[17]

Another social consequence of mandatory Cesareans might well be harm to the babies themselves. When the court authorized nonconsensual surgery for Ms. Jeffries, she went into hiding and could not be found even by a police search. When the court authorized the surgery for Ms. Headley, she avoided the hospital by having a home birth with a lay midwife. If women with unorthodox religious beliefs know that their beliefs will not be honored, they may avoid physicians during delivery or even during their entire pregnancy, thus placing their babies at greatly increased risk. Presumably the informed consent doctrine would dictate that physicians tell women, early on in prenatal care, that they will not honor their religious beliefs if their fetus is endangered. This disclosure, however, will only serve to make such women avoid prenatal care (much as the reporting of drug abuse will make pregnant drug users avoid doctors and hospitals). Hence as a general social policy, mandatory fetal protection will have questionable success in protecting fetuses.

CONCLUSION

Emotionally compelling cases often make bad law. It is very hard for physicians and judges to resist the urge to save fetuses threatened by what appears to be the irrational conduct of the mother. The benevolence they feel is deeply rooted and deserves our respect. Unfortunately, mandatory rescue of the fetus requires an imposition upon the mother that goes far beyond what our society has imposed, or should impose, on others. Our historical restraint regarding such impositions has strong constitutional and ethical bases. Technology threatens this restraint, by making mandatory intervention possible. But technology cannot change the ethical principles that make mandatory intervention wrong.

NOTES

1. 410 U.S. 113 (1973).

2. *Jefferson v. Griffin Spalding County Hospital Authority,* 274 S.E.2d 457 (Ga. 1981); *North Central Bronx Hospital Authority v. Headley,* No. 1992-85 (N.Y. Sup. Ct. Jan. 6, 1986), slip op. at 5; In re Unborn Baby Kenner, No. 79-JN-83 (Colo. Juv. Ct. Mar. 6, 1979), slip op. at 6–9.

3. 410 U.S. at 163–64.

4. *North Central Bronx Hospital Authority v. Headley,* No. 1992-85 (N.Y. Sup. Ct. Jan. 6, 1986); In re Unborn Baby Kenner, No. 79-JN-83 (Colo. Juv. Ct. Mar. 6, 1979).

5. 410 U.S. at 163–64.

6. Id.

7. 439 U.S. 379 (1979).

8. Id. at 400.

9. See, e.g., *Jefferson v. Griffin Spalding County Hospital Authority,* 274 S.E.2d 457 (Ga. 1981).

10. See In re President and Directors of Georgetown College, Inc., 331 F.2d 1000, 1008 (D.C. Cir.), *reh. denied en banc,* 331 F.2d 1010, *cert. denied* 377 U.S. 978 (1964); *Powell v. Columbian [sic] Presbyterian Medical Center,* 267 N.Y.S.2d 450 (Misc. 2d 1965). Cf. In re Osborne, 294 A.2d 372 (D.C. 1972).

11. Prosser W, Keeton W, The law of torts, 5th ed., St. Paul: West Publishing Co., 1984, §56, 376–377.

12. See, e.g., Vt. Stat. Ann. tit.12, §519(a) (1973); Minn. Stat. Ann. §604.05.01 (West Supp. 1986).

13. European countries, which generally do require rescue, exempt physically hazardous rescues. See, e.g., Code Penal, art. 63 (Fr.).

14. 10 Pa. D. & C.3d 90 (1978).

15. Id. at 92 (emphasis in original).

16. This terminology is from Judith Jarvis Thomson's famous article defending abortion on the grounds that requiring a woman to continue a pregnancy is requiring her to be a "Splendid Samaritan," a requirement not imposed on anyone else in society. See Thomson JJ, A defense of abortion, Philosophy & Public Affairs 1971, 1(1): 47–66, 48–52.

17. *People v. Stewart,* No. M508197 (San Diego Mun. Ct. Feb. 26, 1987).

JOHN SEYMOUR

A Pregnant Woman's Decision to Decline Treatment: How Should the Law Respond?*

In 1993 the Australian Medical Association commissioned an inquiry into fetal welfare and the law. One question specifically raised by this inquiry was how the law should respond when a pregnant woman declines medical intervention which her medical adviser believes to be in her best interests or in the best interests of her fetus. While the problem can occur in a number of different situations, in this article the focus will be on a woman's decision not to consent to a caesarean section. The legal issues which arise when such a decision has been taken have recently attracted a good deal of attention; in particular, there is the question whether there are any circumstances in which a court may override the woman's wishes. In a much publicised 1992 decision, the Family Division of the English High Court made an order authorising the performance of a caesarean section in spite of the woman's decision, to withhold her consent to the procedure. More recently, the United States Supreme Court has indicated that such an order should not be made. Further, the problem has arisen, but ultimately not been confronted, in Australia. In New South Wales there was a case in which a woman initially withheld consent to a caesarean section and a judge of the Family Court of Australia indicated that he was prepared to hear an application for an order authorising the performance of the operation. The matter did not reach the court as the woman subsequently decided to give her consent. Cases of this kind may arise in the future. When they do, it is important that the issues which they pose should be clearly identified.

The purpose of this article is to provide a framework within which to consider the question whether there are any circumstances in which a compulsory caesarean section should be performed. What will be identified are several different ways of examining the relationship between the pregnant woman and her fetus. There is now much theoretical analysis — particularly feminist analysis — which illuminates the nature of this relationship. In the context of a possible caesarean section, there are two opposing views. On the one hand is the view that the fetus is a sufficiently distinct entity to have interests which the law should protect and that if the woman's decision to decline the procedure is manifestly putting the fetus at risk, legal intervention should be possible to permit the operation to be carried out. On the other hand is the view that since the fetus is part of the woman's body it does not have interests which the law should recognise by intervening to authorise the operation. One of the central arguments of this article is that each of these views is an oversimplification.

The development of this argument requires a consideration of three different models of the maternal–fetal relationship. Before these are discussed, however, it must be emphasised that none of them necessarily involves a denial of the woman's rights. Clearly the pregnant woman has a right to life: it would be unacceptable to permit a woman to be killed so that her fetus will survive. Similarly, she has the right to personal autonomy and self-determination. She also has the right to bodily integrity and from this it follows that the inquiry must begin with the presumption that she has the right to refuse to consent to medical treatment. She also has the right to freedom of religion. This is relevant because many of the reported cases involving refusal of medical treatment arose because of the women's

*From the *Journal of Law and Medicine* 2 (1) 1994, 27–37. Reprinted by permission.

religious objections to the proposed treatment. Recognition of the woman's rights must, therefore, be our starting-point. As Gallagher has noted: "Given the very geography of pregnancy, questions as to the status of the fetus must follow, not precede, an examination of the rights of the woman within whose body and life the fetus exists.[1] The pregnant woman's rights are, therefore, not in dispute. What is problematic, however, is whether these rights are absolute and whether in certain circumstances they may be overridden. It is this question which necessitates a close examination of the relationship between a pregnant woman and her fetus.

The three models of this relationship which will be considered here are as follows. The woman and her fetus can be seen as one entity; on this analysis, the fetus is no more than a part of the woman's body. Alternatively, the woman and her fetus can be regarded as separate entities. Between these two extremes is the view that the woman and her fetus are separate but indivisibly linked. Each of these models will be outlined and some of their implications explored.

PART OF THE WOMAN'S BODY

Although much of the relevant literature discusses this model, it is difficult to find many commentators who have unequivocally adopted it. One who has done so is Rothman: "[T]he baby is not planted within the mother, but flesh of her flesh, part of her."[2] While such a statement may seem straightforward, semantic problems arise when we scrutinise it closely. In one sense, of course, the assertion is incontrovertible: clearly a fetus is a part of a woman's body in the sense that it is contained within that body. This use of language is the same as that employed when we describe a room as part of a house. In contrast with such a description, it is possible to treat the fetus as no more than a body part, with the result that woman and fetus are seen as one entity. It is, therefore, difficult to determine quite what is meant by the statement that the fetus is part of the woman's body. Perhaps it means no more than that the fetus has no separate, independent existence. If so, the result is not a distinctive model: the statement is simply a denial of the separate-entities model (discussed below). Alternatively, the claim that a fetus is part of a woman's body may indicate that the fetus is to be regarded as a body part. It is to this interpretation which we must now turn.

There are obvious deficiencies in this model. These deficiencies are concisely outlined by MacKinnon, a leading feminist author. She asserts emphatically: "[T]he fetus is not a body part." As she points out, unlike a body part, the fetus is the result of a social (that is, sexual) relationship. . . .

One other comment should be made about the single-entity model. Although systematic research is lacking (and should be undertaken), anecdotal evidence suggests that the single-entity model does not accord with many women's experience of pregnancy. A pregnant woman will often refer to "the baby" moving or kicking. Similarly, when displaying an ultrasound picture, a pregnant woman will frequently point to the baby's hand or feet. This is not the action of someone talking about a body part. It seems clear, therefore, that the body-part model should be rejected on the ground that it oversimplifies a complex relationship. The pregnant woman and her fetus are more than one entity.

SEPARATE ENTITIES

SEPARATENESS AND RIGHTS LANGUAGE

The view that woman and fetus are separate entities has been urged by many obstetricians. For example, it has been remarked: "The care of a pregnant woman involves two patients, the mother and the fetus."[3] . . . [T]here are many other titles of books and journal articles which indicate an acceptance of the separateness of the fetus. One implication of this is the possibility of employing two physicians, one for the fetus and another for the pregnant woman.[4] Further, in the United States, there have been cases in which mother and fetus have been represented by separate lawyers.

The separate-entities model of the relationship between woman and fetus has been reinforced by recent developments in medicine. The growth of ultrasound imaging, amniocentesis, fetal heart monitoring and in utero therapy and surgery can be seen as contributing to the notion of the fetus as a separate entity. All of these enable the fetus to be separately treated.

If the fetus is a separate entity, questions will arise as to whether it possesses rights. It is important to appreciate how use of the language of rights is an inseparable consequence of the adoption of the separate-entities model. This model entails viewing the pregnant woman and the fetus as two beings in a single body, with the result that each has a full complement of rights. To acknowledge the rights of the fetus is to emphasise its separate existence: there must be a distinct entity by or on behalf of which the rights may be asserted. Rights discourse is thus a product of the separate-entities model. As Olsen has observed, resort to rights rhetoric portrays individuals as "separated owners of their respective bundles of rights".[5]

Before these rights are discussed, it is necessary to make one general point about rights language. This language is often unhelpful. It is frequently used in an uncritical, polemic manner. On examination, it is common to find that a statement that a particular entity "has" certain rights is no more than an assertion by the writer that the entity's interests should be protected. In some circumstances, the claim is accurate. As noted earlier, a woman has a right to bodily integrity which the law will protect. In contrast is the claim made by some commentators . . . that all children have a "right" to be born healthy. While there would probably be no disagreement with the view that, in a perfect world, all children should be born healthy, commitment to this ideal is not the same as asserting that every fetus has the "right" to this outcome. What looks like a factual statement turns out to be the expression of a value judgment. Bennett has drawn attention to just how quickly a desire to ensure the birth of a healthy child can be translated into an assertion that a fetus has an "interest" and this, in turn, is transformed first into a moral "right" and then into a legal "right".[6] The distinction between statements which accurately identify legally protected rights and those which embody personal value judgments should not be overlooked.

SOME POSTULATED RIGHTS OF THE FETUS

The rights of the woman have been discussed earlier in this article. It is now necessary to consider the possibility that the fetus possesses rights which may be asserted against the mother. One commentator has argued that a fetus should be entitled to all the rights and legal protections conferred on a child:

> "Since the unborn child has health needs and vulnerabilities analogous to those of children, and since between the child when unborn and after birth there is continuity in all essential respects, then it would seem logical and just to assign to parents duties to their unborn children analogous (when applicable) to those they have to their children, and to recognise in unborn children analogous rights (when applicable) to those already granted to children."[7]

Such a claim seems to go too far, for to confer on the fetus "analogous" rights to those enjoyed by a child is to blur the issue and to ignore the unique status of the fetus. Whatever one's reservations about the concept of fetal rights, no attempt to define them will be satisfactory if the special nature of the fetus is ignored. The fetus should not be equated with a child.

An alternative approach, which would have particular implications for the woman, would be the recognition of a right "to be born healthy". This has been explicitly accepted in a Canadian decision[8] and in the United States a similar concept has been expressed as the right "to begin life with a sound mind and body".[9] The ramifications of the recognition of such a right would be far-reaching. For our purposes, the most important of these would be that the fetus would have an independent entitlement to antenatal care, to medical treatment (such as in utero surgery), to appropriate intervention to ensure a safe birth, and to intervention designed to control the mother's behaviour during pregnancy. Can a right to be born healthy be unreservedly accepted? One commentator has argued that it cannot: to assert such a right on behalf of a fetus is to claim "considerably more than is acknowledged for those already born, whether children or adults".[10] On this, however, views will differ and the following analysis will proceed on the basis that the fetus may possess some rights which might conflict with the recognised rights of the pregnant woman.

CONFLICT

It is clear that if the fetus has a right to protection in certain circumstances, this may conflict with the rights possessed by the mother. This is a direct consequence of the adoption of the separate-entities model, which postulates the existence of individual right-holders. An individualistic perspective is an oppositional perspective: one set of rights must be pitted or, at least, weighed against the other.[11] . . . If there is a conflict between the rights of the fetus and those of the pregnant woman, one must "win" and the other must "lose". This is a troubling notion, because in situations where the rights of the fetus prevail, this will inevitably lead to the diminution of some of those rights (identified earlier in the article) which a pregnant woman, in common with all competent adults, enjoys.

The more the individuality of the fetus is stressed, the less the individuality of the woman is recognised. . . . Consequently, the adoption of the separate-entities model can be seen as reducing the woman to no more than a "container", "incubator" or "life support machine" with the result that she is devalued and her interests disregarded.[12] Some of the recent feminist literature regards this attitude as being reinforced by the use of ultrasound imaging:

> "Feminist critics emphasise the degrading impact fetal-imaging techniques have on the pregnant woman. She now becomes the 'maternal environment', the 'site' of the fetus, a passive spectator in her own pregnancy."[13]

Similarly, in Karpin's view, the use of ultrasound techniques can result in the woman being "technoculturally constructed as a passive container for the fetus".[14] In short, the new technology is regarded as reinforcing the tendency of medical personnel to see the woman and her fetus as two separate entities.

If, because of this development, the fetus is more likely to be regarded as a separate entity requiring protection, control will inevitably be exercised over the woman. Karpin has identified a process of "wresting control of the 'endangered' fetus from the woman and removing it to a place of masculine scrutiny and control—the clinic, the laboratory, and, if need be, the courtroom".[15] Ascribing rights to the fetus, and taking action to protect those rights, will of necessity result in the rights of the mother being ignored. As Rowland has observed:

> "That fetal rights threaten and in fact supersede women's autonomy is most clearly shown in the occurrence of coerced caesarean section where women have been legally constrained to have the operation on the grounds that the fetus required it."[16]

Such analysis underlines the political implications of the debate about the way in which the relationship between a woman and her fetus is defined. The use of rights language can mask the reality of the control of pregnant women, even where this consequence is not intentional. Adoption of the two-entities model can thus be seen as another device to ensure the continuance of women's subordination. As MacKinnon argues, the choice of model plays a very important part in this process: "[T]he social organization of reproduction is a major bulwark of women's social inequality."[17] . . .

The argument so far is that the ascription of rights to the fetus in the context of its relationship with the woman simultaneously generates conflict, devalues the woman, and subjects her to control. Further, the rights analysis which is the product of the separate-entities model can also be criticised on the ground that it pro-vides an inadequate conceptual tool. It embodies one world view to the exclusion of another. . . . For the purposes of this article, it is unnecessary to comment on this analysis. At this stage, the important point is to explain these differing perceptions and to stress the significance of the concepts of connectedness and interdependence. The rights analysis which is the corollary of the separate-entities model ignores these and is therefore incomplete. This is not to suggest, however, that a world view emphasising interdependence precludes the assertion of rights in appropriate circumstances. Ultimately, what is needed is a synthesis which gives equal weight to rights and those responsibilities which are inherent in a sense of connection.

Appreciation of the significance of the concepts of connectedness and interdependence reveals further deficiencies in the separate-entities model. As has been noted, this model rests on a theory which provides only a partial account of the complex nature of pregnancy. It is partial in the sense that it places all the emphasis on separation and individual rights, and therefore presents an oversimplified picture. Further, the conflict which is implicit in this model in the context of the relationship between the fetus and the pregnant woman devalues the woman, with a consequent ignoring of her rights. Nor is the separate-entities model an accurate depiction of the special status of the fetus. It is clear that, while it is at some stage capable of becoming separate, the fetus is not separate from the mother. The fetus exhibits the potential for separation only.

The model also pays insufficient attention to the views of women. With regard to women's views, it is only necessary to refer to the notions of connectedness and interdependence which have been explained above: "For the law to ascribe rights to the foetus which must then be balanced against a woman's rights is . . . a completely inaccurate depiction of how women think about being pregnant. . . ."[18] The concepts of connectedness and interdependence will be further examined below. These can be seen as holding the key to the understanding of women's experience of pregnancy.

INDIVISIBLY LINKED

The third model needs less discussion, since it grows directly out of the rejection of the first two models. Its key feature is the emphasis which it places on the shared needs and interdependence of the woman and her fetus. As might be expected, "connectedness, mutuality, and reciprocity"[19] are regarded as crucial factors. There is, however, no simple way of explaining the third model. Perhaps the best we can do is to refer to Karpin's concept of "Not-One-But-Not-Two".[20] Ruddick and Wilcox spell out some of the implications of this model:

"Mother-and-child is a complex, both bodily and morally: just as we cannot easily say whether pregnancy involved two bodies or only one (in a special expanding state), just so we cannot easily say whether pregnancy involves two sets of overlapping interests or only one set (in a special expanding state). If we allow that there are two sets, then we must recognize that they are mutually dependent to an unusual degree."[21]

The importance of this analysis is its recognition of the possibility of two sets of overlapping interests possessed by two entities which are peculiarly interdependent. This avoids the objectionable features of a model built on separate entities with conflicting rights, while at the same time allowing for a fetus to be treated as having some interests which the law can protect.

It is, however, necessary to distinguish between two versions of the third model. If it is conceded that there are some circumstances in which a fetus has identifiable interests, a further question must be asked. Given the special nature of the mother-fetus relationship, who should be responsible for articulating those interests? Two answers are possible. It might still be argued that a third person should be able to articulate — and take action to protect — the rights of the fetus. Alternatively, it can be asserted that only the mother should be empowered to articulate the rights of the fetus.

The former version (articulation by a third party) reflects the view that, although the relationship between mother and fetus is a special one, there is still the possibility of a conflict between their interests. In this version, while it is conceded that normally the woman will act in the best interests of the fetus, there will be a small number of cases in which a third party should intervene to protect the fetus. On examination, it is apparent that this form of the third model is simply another way of stating the two-entities model. It preserves the possibility of conflict between mother and fetus and of overriding the wishes of the mother. It thus does not reflect an appreciation of the special relationship between mother and fetus. "Not-One-But-Not-Two" in fact becomes two.

The second version (that it is only the mother who should be in a position to articulate the rights of the fetus) attempts to reflect the special nature of the relationship, but places all control in the hands of the woman. While adoption of this model recognises that she is under a moral obligation to take into account the interests of the fetus, it leads ultimately to the conclusion that it is she who determines what those interests are. It is important to understand the full implications of this result. The mother will be in a position to decide not only how the interests of the fetus are to be protected but also whether they will be protected. An inescapable conclusion of the adoption of the second version of the model is that it enables the woman to elect to ignore the interests of the fetus.

SOME IMPLICATIONS

It has been suggested that the single-entity and separate-entities models should be rejected. Before moving on to a consideration of the implications of adopting the third model, it is worth pausing to ask how the first two would be employed to determine how to deal with the problem which arises when a woman declines to consent to a caesarean section. Under the single-entity model, there is no problem, since there is no sufficiently distinct entity whose interests may require compulsory intervention against the woman's wishes. Under the separate-entities model, the interests of one (the woman) must be balanced against the interests of the other (the fetus). This paves the way for the woman's decision not to consent to a caesarean section to be overridden if the interests of the fetus are thought to outweigh those of the mother.

Adoption of the third model — at least in its second version — prevents this outcome. The central principle embodied in this model is that, although the fetus has interests which the law should recognise, in no circumstances should these interests be permitted to override those of the mother. The pregnant woman is thus placed in the same position as any other competent adult. Since all competent adults have the right to refuse treatment, the pregnant woman must be the one to decide whether or not to consent to a caesarean section.

If this analysis is accepted, it will be necessary for the Australian law to make it clear that no court has jurisdiction to authorise a caesarean section when a competent and properly advised woman has refused her consent to the procedure. This might best be done by State statutes which provide that it is unlawful for a medical practitioner to perform such a procedure on a pregnant woman in the face of an informed refusal.

Although the problem is a difficult one, such an outcome seems most in accord with current and developing law in Australia. This law recognises, and is likely in the future to place increased emphasis on, individual autonomy. While prediction is difficult, it seems reasonable to suppose that the state's willingness to intervene in individuals' lives will diminish, rather than increase. Rejection of the view that medical treatment should be imposed on unwilling adults is consistent with this prediction. Further, the idea of a doctor compulsorily treating a patient is a disturbing one and may not be accepted by the medical profession. The doctor-patient relationship depends on trust; this relationship would be impaired if it is known that the doctor can invoke the coercive machinery of the law. Indeed, pregnant women may be discouraged from seeking medical advice if court action by the doctor is a possible outcome. In the long run, this would cause more harm to the health of pregnant women and their babies than would occasional failures to intervene in situations in which medical advice is rejected.

It is necessary, however, to confront the full implications of the recognition of the woman's autonomy. As already noted, she must bear responsibility for the consequences of her decision. Whether this should be limited to moral responsibility only, or whether there are some circumstances in which legal liability should attach to the woman, is a question which cannot be fully explored here. If a baby is born damaged, and the necessary causal connection can be established between this outcome and the rejection of medical advice, should the child be able to sue the mother? One way of answering this question would be to recommend that the woman be immune from legal action in such a situation; the argument here would be that an intra-family tort action would be destructive of family relationships and, if successful, would result in the artificial redistribution of money within the family.

It is also important to clarify the doctor's position, once the properly advised woman decides to withhold her consent to a caesarean section. Should the doctor who is unhappy with the patient's decision be free to decline to continue providing treatment? Equally important for the medical profession, the law should make it clear — and if there is any doubt, statutory provisions should be enacted — that a doctor who continues to provide competent treatment should not be liable to any damages claim by the mother or child if the

child is born damaged. The corollary of the assertion by the patient of her autonomy and right to decide about treatment should be the lifting of legal liability from the doctor's shoulders. Finally, one qualification must be added to the autonomy principle. The patient's decision-making power should not be such as to permit her to insist on the provision of treatment of which the doctor disapproves and which is inconsistent with good medical practice.

One further comment must be made about the model on which the foregoing analysis has been based. In legal terms, the appeal of the "Not-One-But-Not-Two" model is that it allows greater flexibility than the first or second models. The model enables women's views to be taken into account without ignoring the claims of the fetus for appropriate recognition of its distinctive characteristics. It thus permits the fetus in some circumstances to be viewed as an entity possessing interests which the law can accommodate and seek to protect, while at the same time not ignoring the woman's claims. In short, the model acknowledges the needs of the fetus, but allows its special relationship with the mother to be taken into account. The practical importance of this result is that it provides a basis upon which legal action can be taken on behalf of the fetus in some situations but not in others. . . .

The importance of such an outcome is that it permits more sensitive answers to many of the questions posed by any inquiry into fetal welfare and the law. The principle advanced above is that, while a fetus has interests capable of being recognised by the law, these interests should not be enforced in such a way as to override the interests of the mother. As has been shown, this provides a basis on which to deal with the problem of a woman's decision not to consent to a caesarean section. Adoption of the third model implies that her right to refuse should be respected. Reliance on the model would, however, allow for different conclusions in other situations. The view that a fetus does not possess rights which justify the overriding of a woman's rejection of medical advice need not necessarily lead to the conclusion that it lacks rights which may be enforced at the expense of other persons. If a fetus has recognisable interests and suffers injury, for example by a criminal assault, by a road accident or by environmental pollution, there is no reason why, when the child is born, that child should not sue the person who caused the injury.

It is when these possibilities are considered that the flexibility of the "Not-One-But-Not-Two" model becomes apparent. Unlike the first two models, it does not demand an "all-or-nothing" approach to the problem of identifying fetal interests. Further, the foregoing analysis demonstrates how important it is to appreciate that an inquiry into the nature of the fetus should not be confined to an examination of the pregnant woman's relationship to it. A definition of the fetus which satisfactorily explains the relationship between the fetus and the woman may not be appropriate to explain the relationship between the fetus and the outside world. The task of understanding the nature of the fetus does not begin and end with an analysis of this relationship. The aim must be a definition of a fetus which is appropriate not only in the context of its relationship with the woman, but also in broader contexts.

NOTES

1. J Gallagher, "Fetus as Patient" in S Cohen and N Taub (eds), *Reproductive Laws for the 1990s* (Humana Press Clifton, NJ, 1989), pp 187–188.

2. B K Rothman, *Recreating Motherhood: Ideology and Technology in a Patriarchal Society* (Norton, NY, 1989), p 161.

3. W A Bowes and B Selgestad, "Fetal Versus Maternal Rights: Medical and Legal Perspectives" (1981) 58 *Obstetrics and Gynecology* 209 at 209.

4. J L Lenow, "The Fetus as a Patient: Emerging Rights as a Person?" (1983) 9 *American Journal of Law and Medicine* 1 at 17.

5. F Olsen, "Statutory Rape: A Feminist Critique of Rights Analysis" (1984) 63 Texas LR 387 at 393.

6. B Bennett, "Pregnant Women and the Duty to Rescue: A Feminist Response to the Fetal Rights Debate" (1991) (1) *Law in Context* 70 at 86.

7. E W Keyserlingk, *The Unborn Child's Right to Prenatal Care. A Comparative Law Perspective* (McGill University, Montreal, 1984), p 103.

8. *Re Brown* (1976) 21 *Reports of Family Law* 315 at 323.

9. *Smith v. Brennan* 157 A 2d 497 at 503 (NJ Sup Ct 1960).

10. Keyserlingk, op cit n 20, p 82.

11. C Bell, "Case Note: Planned Parenthood of Southeastern Pennsylvania, et al. v Robert P Casey, et al." (1993) 1 *Feminist Legal Studies* 91 at 97; and S Noonan, "Theorizing Connection" (1992) 30 Alberta LR 719 at 722.

12. G L Annas, "Pregnant Women as Fetal Containers" (1986) 16(6) *Hastings Center Report* 13 at 14.

13. R P Petchesky, "Fetal Images: The Power of Visual Culture in the Politics of Reproduction" (1987) 13 *Feminist Studies* 263 at 277. See also Rothman, op cit n 6, pp. 113–115.

14. I Karpin, "Legislating the Female Body: Reproductive Technology and the Reconstructed Woman" (1992) 3 *Columbia Journal of Gender and Law* 325 at 333.

15. Ibid at 333–334.

16. R Rowland, *Living Laboratories: Woman and Reproductive Technologies* (Indiana University Press, Bloomington, 1992), p 123.

17. C A MacKinnon, "Reflections on Sex Equality under Law" (1991) 100 Yale LJ 1281 at 1319. Compare Oakley: "[H]ow reproduction is managed and controlled is inseparable from how women are managed and controlled": A Oakley, *Subject Women* (Robertson, Oxford, 1981), p 206.

18. D Greschner, "Abortion and Democracy for Women: A Critique of Tremblay v. Daigle" (1990) 35 McGill LJ 633 at 652–653.

19. K De Gama, "A Brave New World? Rights Discourse and the Politics of Reproductive Autonomy" (1993) 20 *Journal of Law and Society* 114 at 115.

20. Karpin, op cit n 30, at 329.

21. W Ruddick and W Wilcox, "Operating on the Fetus" (1982) 12(5) *Hastings Center Report* 10 at 13.

SUGGESTED READINGS

American College of Obstetricians and Gynecologists. Committee on Ethics. "Patient Choice: Maternal–Fetal Conflict." *Committee Opinion,* 55 (October 1987).

American Medical Association. Board of Trustees. "Legal Interventions during Pregnancy: Court-ordered Medical Treatments and Legal Penalties for Potentially Harmful Behavior by Pregnant Women." *Journal of the American Medical Association* 264 (November 1990), 2663–70.

Brandt, Richard B. "The Morality of Abortion." *The Monist* 36 (1972), 503–26.

Brock, Dan W. "Taking Human Life." *Ethics* 95 (1985), 851–65.

Brody, Baruch A. "Abortion and the Sanctity of Human Life." *American Philosophical Quarterly* 10 (1973), 133–40.

Callahan, Daniel. *Abortion: Law, Choice and Morality.* New York: Macmillan, 1970.

Callahan, Daniel, and Callahan, Sidney, eds. *Abortion: Understanding Differences.* New York: Plenum Press, 1984.

Callahan, Joan. "Ensuring a Stillborn: the Ethics of Fetal Lethal Injection in Late Abortion." *Journal of Clinical Ethics* 6 (1995), 254–63.

Chervenak, Frank A., and McCullough, Laurence B. "Inadequacies with the ACOG and AAP Statements on Managing Ethical Conflict During the Intrapartum period." *Journal of Clinical Ethics* 2 (Spring 1991), 23–24.

Clinics in Perinatology 14 (1987), 329–43. Special issue on "Maternal–Fetal Relations." See essays by Strong, Carson, and Murray, Thomas H.

Colker, Ruth. *Abortion and Dialogue: Prochoice, Prolife, and American Law.* Bloomington and Indianapolis: Indiana University Press, 1992.

Connery, John R. *Abortion: The Development of the Roman Catholic Perspective.* Chicago: Loyola University Press, 1977.

Cudd, Ann E. "Sensationalized Philosophy: A Reply to Marquis's 'Why Abortion is Immoral.'" *Journal of Philosophy* 87 (1990), 262–64.

Davis, Michael. "Fetuses, Famous Violinists, and the Right to Continued Aid." *Philosophical Quarterly* 33 (1983), 259–78.

Davis, Nancy (Ann). "Abortion and Self-Defense." *Philosophy & Public Affairs* 13 (1984), 175–207.

———. "The Abortion Debate: The Search for Common Ground. Part 1." *Ethics* 103 (1993): 516–39.

———. "The Abortion Debate: The Search for Common Ground. Part 2." *Ethics* 103 (1993): 731–78.

Dore, Clement. "Abortion, Some Slippery Slope Arguments and Identity over Time." *Philosophical Studies* 55 (1989), 279–91.

Druker, Dan. *Abortion Decisions of the Supreme Court, 1973–1989.* Jefferson, NC: McFarland & Company, Inc., 1990.

Dworkin, Ronald. *Life's Dominion: An Argument About Abortion, Euthanasia and Individual Freedom.* New York: Alfred A. Knopf, Inc., 1993.

Ely, John Hart. "The Wages of Crying Wolf: A Comment on *Roe v. Wade.*" *Yale Law Journal* 82 (1973), 920–49.

Engelhardt, H. Tristram. *The Foundations of Bioethics.* New York: Oxford University Press, 1986. Chap. 6.

English, Jane. "Abortion and the Concept of a Person." *Canadian Journal of Philosophy* 5 (1975), 233–43.

Fagot-Largeault, Anne. "Abortion and Arguments from Potential." In Raanan Gillon, ed., *Principles of Health Care Ethics.* Chichester: Wiley, 1994, 577–86.

Feinberg, Joel, ed. *The Problem of Abortion,* 2d ed. Belmont, CA: Wadsworth Publishing Company, 1984.

Finnis, John. "Abortion and Health Care Ethics." In Raanan Gillon, ed., *Principles of Health Care Ethics.* Chichester: Wiley, 1994, 547–57.

———. "The Rights and Wrongs of Abortion: A Reply to Judith Thomson." *Philosophy & Public Affairs* 2 (1973), 117–45.

Fleming, Lorette. "The Moral Status of the Fetus: A Reappraisal." *Bioethics* 1 (1987), 15–34.

Fletcher, John C. "Abortion Politics, Science, and Research Ethics: Take Down the Wall of Separation." *Journal of Contemporary Health Law & Policy* 8 (1992), 95–121.

Foot, Philippa. "The Problem of Abortion and the Doctrine of Double Effect." *The Oxford Review* 5 (1967), 59–70.

Gert, Heather J. "Viability." *International Journal of Philosophical Studies* 3 (1995), 133–42.

Ginsburg, Ruth Bader. "Some Thoughts on Autonomy and Equality in Relation to *Roe v. Wade.*" *North Carolina Law Review* 63 (1985), 375–86.

Goldberg, Susan. "Medical Choices During Pregnancy: Whose Decision Is It, Anyway?" *Rutgers Law Review* 41 (1989), 591–623.

Hare, R. M. "Abortion and the Golden Rule." *Philosophy & Public Affairs* 4 (1975), 201–22.

Hasnas, John. "From Cannibalism to Caesareans: Two Conceptions of Fundamental Rights." *Northwestern University Law Review* 89 (1995), 900–941.

Hursthouse, Rosalind. *Beginning Lives.* Oxford: Basil Blackwell, 1987.

———. "Virtue Theory and Abortion." *Philosophy & Public Affairs* 20 (1991), 223–46.

Johnsen, Dawn. "A New Threat To Pregnant Women's Autonomy." *Hastings Center Report* 17 (August 1987), 33–40.

Jordan, James M. "Incubating for the State: The Precarious Autonomy of Persistently Vegetative and Brain-Dead Pregnant Women." *Georgia Law Review* 22 (1988), 1103–65.

Kamm, Frances M. *Creation and Abortion.* New York: Oxford University Press, 1992.

King, Patricia A. "The Juridical Status of the Fetus: A Proposal for Legal Protection of the Unborn." *Michigan Law Review* 77 (1979), 1647–87.

Kluge, Eike-Henner W. "When Caesarean Section Operations Imposed by a Court Are Justified." *Journal of Medical Ethics* 14 (1988), 206–11.

Loewy, Arnold H. "Why *Roe v. Wade* Should Be Overruled." *North Carolina Law Review* 67 (1989), 939–48.

Mackenzie, Catriona. "Abortion and Embodiment." *Australasian Journal of Philosophy* 70 (1992), 136–55.

Macklin, Ruth. "Antiprogestin Drugs: Ethical Issues." *Law, Medicine and Health Care* 20 (1992), 215–19.

Mahowald, Mary B. "Is There Life After *Roe v. Wade?*" *Hastings Center Report* 19 (1989), 22–29.

Mathieu, Deborah. *Preventing Prenatal Harm: Should the State Intervene?* Boston: Kluwer Academic, 1991.

McMahan, Jeff. "The Right to Choose an Abortion." *Philosophy & Public Affairs* 22 (1993), 331–48.

Noonan, John T., Jr., ed. *The Morality of Abortion: Legal and Historical Perspectives.* Cambridge, MA: Harvard University Press, 1970.

Overall, Christine. "Mother/Fetus/State Conflicts." *Health Law in Canada* 9 (1989), 101–03, 122.

Pojman, Louis P., and Beckwith, Francis J., eds. *The Abortion Controversy.* Boston: Jones and Bartlett Publishers, 1994.

Purdy, Laura M. "Are Pregnant Women Fetal Containers?" *Bioethics* 4 (1990), 273–91.

Quinn, Warren. "Abortion: Identity and Loss." *Philosophy & Public Affairs* 13 (1984), 24–54.

Regan, Tom, ed. *Matters of Life and Death.* 3d ed. New York: Random House, 1992.

Rhoden, Nancy K. "The Judge in the Delivery Room: The Emergence of Court-Ordered Cesareans." *California Law Review* 74 (1986), 1951–2030.

———. "A Compromise on Abortion." *Hastings Center Report* 19 (1989), 32–37.

Rubin, Eva R., ed. *The Abortion Controversy: A Documentary History.* Westport, CT: Greenwood Press, 1994.

Solomon, Renee I. "Future Fear: Prenatal Duties Imposed by Private Parties." *American Journal of Law and Medicine* 17 (1991), 411–34.

Smith, Holly. "Intercourse and Moral Responsibility for the Fetus." In W. B. Bondeson, et al., eds. *Abortion and the Status of the Fetus.* Dordrecht: D. Reidel, 1983.

Stein, Ellen J. "Maternal–fetal Conflict: Reformulating the Equation." In Grubb, Andrew, ed. *Challenges in Medical Care.* New York: Wiley, 1992, 91–108.

Strong, Carson. "Fetal Tissue Transplantation: Can It Be Morally Insulated From Abortion?" *Journal of Medical Ethics* 17 (1991), 70–76.

Sumner, L. W. *Abortion and Moral Theory.* Princeton, NJ: Princeton University Press, 1981.

Thompson, Elizabeth. "Criminalization of Maternal Conduct During Pregnancy: Decisionmaking Model for Lawmakers." *Indiana Law Journal* 64 (1988–89), 357–74.

Thomson, Judith Jarvis. "Rights and Deaths." *Philosophy & Public Affairs* 2 (1973), 146–55.

Tooley, Michael. *Abortion and Infanticide.* Oxford: Oxford University Press, 1983.

Tribe, Laurence H. *Abortion: The Clash of Absolutes.* New York: Norton, 1990

Warren, Mary Anne. "Abortion." In Singer, Peter, ed. *A Companion to Ethics.* Cambridge, MA: Blackwell Reference, 1991, 303–14.

Warren, Mary Ann. "The Moral Significance of Birth." *Hypatia* 4 (1989), 46–65.

Wing, Kenneth R. "Speech, Privacy, and the Power of the Purse: Lessons from the Abortion 'Gag Rule' Case." *Journal of Health Politics, Policy and Law* 17 (1992), 163–75.

Wolf-Devine, Celia. "Abortion and the 'Feminine Voice'." *Public Affairs Quarterly* 3 (1989), 81–87.

Women's Health Issues 1 (Fall 1990). Special issue on "Maternal–Fetal Relations."

Zaitchik, Alan. "Viability and the Morality of Abortion." *Philosophy & Public Affairs* 10 (1981), 18–26.

BIBLIOGRAPHIES AND ENCYCLOPEDIAS
WITH BIBLIOGRAPHIES

Bioethicsline: Computer Retrieval Service.

Encyclopedia of Bioethics, ed. Warren Reich, 2d ed., New York: Macmillan, 1995.

Encyclopedia of Ethics, ed. Lawrence Becker and Charlotte Becker. New York: Garland Publishing Inc., 1992.

Lineback, Richard H., eds. *Philosopher's Index.* Vols. 1– . Bowling Green, OH: Philosophy Documentation Center, Bowling Green State University. Issued Quarterly. Also CD Rom.

Walters, LeRoy, and Kahn, Tamar Joy, eds. *Bibliography of Bioethics.* Vols. 1– . Washington, DC: Kennedy Institute of Ethics.

5.
Euthanasia and Assisted Suicide

INTRODUCTION

There is no stronger or more enduring prohibition in medicine than the rule against killing or prematurely causing the death of patients. Yet many arguments in the current literature on medical ethics suggest a need to reform both the law and medical practice. Several questions are addressed in this chapter about withholding and withdrawing treatment, as well as about killing and letting die.

REFUSAL OF TREATMENT AND THE RIGHT TO DIE

The subject of the first section of this chapter is refusal of treatment by a patient or duly authorized representative of the patient, usually when a patient is seriously or terminally ill. The major question is, "Under what conditions, if any, is it permissible for patients, health professionals, and surrogate decisionmakers to forgo treatment with the foreknowledge that the patient will die?"

Refusals by Competent Persons. From the standpoint of a competent patient, or a competent person thinking ahead to future status, this question might be phrased as follows: "What kinds of treatment should I accept, and what kinds of treatment should I refuse in particular circumstances?" For third parties — whether family members or friends or health providers — the question is usually formulated as, "What types of treatment should be started (or continued), and what kinds of treatment should be withheld (or withdrawn) for the sake of this patient on whose behalf I am deciding or making recommendations about treatment?"

It is now generally agreed, in both law and ethics, that a competent patient has the right to forgo treatment at any time, including the right to refuse medical nutrition and hydration. However, competent persons sometimes exercise their rights in a way inconsistent with the commitments of a family or a health care institution — a problem that arises in the case of Elizabeth Bouvia in this chapter. Bouvia suffered from cerebral palsy that left her with virtually no motor function in her limbs or skeletal muscles, but she was unaffected cognitively. The court asserts that patients have a moral and constitutional right to refuse treatment even if its exercise creates a "life-threatening condition" of which physicians disapprove. This opinion urges courts and physicians to protect this right so that physicians can assist patients in bringing about the end of their lives in dignity and comfort. In a particularly vigorous concurring opinion, Associate Justice Compton exhorts physicians to rethink their traditional objections to *assisting* such patients to die.

Refusals by Formerly Competent Persons. Several celebrated legal cases have centered on formerly competent patients, the best known case being that of Nancy Cruzan. The 25-year-old Ms. Cruzan was in a persistent vegetative state for over three years. Her parents then petitioned for permission to remove the feeding tube, knowing that, with such action, their daughter would die. A lower court's authorization of termination of treatment was reversed by the Missouri Supreme Court, which ruled that no one may order an end to life-sustaining treatment for an incompetent person in the absence of a valid living will or clear and convincing evidence of the patient's wishes.

This decision was appealed to the United States Supreme Court, which handed down its decision in 1990. The majority opinion holds that a state may constitutionally require "clear and convincing evidence" wherever surrogates claim to represent a patient's desires about continuing or refusing life-sustaining treatment. The majority insists that its findings rest on a judgment by society that it is better to err in preserving life in a vegetative state than to err through a decision that leads directly to death. The dissenting justices express a particularly vigorous disagreement with this majority opinion. Justices Brennan, Marshall, and Blackmun find that "Nancy Cruzan has a fundamental right to be free of unwanted artificial nutrition and hydration"—a direct challenge to the line of argument in the majority opinion.

The essays by Lawrence Gostin and John Robertson respond, in diverse ways, to this Supreme Court opinion. Gostin argues that the state has no bona fide interests in preserving the life of a persistent vegetative state (PVS) patient and that all of the burden must be borne by the family. Gostin would have us focus more on whether an abuse is occurring by a family's decisions than on whether the patient has stated some prior preference about treatments of this type. He believes the Court's opinion does little to protect the interests of these patients, while doing much to harm those interests. He finds the "clear and convincing evidence" criterion far too strenuous. Gostin presents alternatives that could displace the ruling in *Cruzan*.

In the next article, John Robertson argues that the Supreme Court's decision violates no constitutional right of Nancy Cruzan or of her family, because the protected liberty interest in refusing medical treatment can only be exercised by competent patients, not by either incompetent patients or surrogates. Robertson even argues that sustaining PVS patients never harms them because they do not "have interests that can be harmed"; Cruzan's right to refuse treatment is not being denied, because she has not refused treatment. Robertson agrees with the Court that a state can maintain strict standards of the sort Missouri envisages and that, in any event, states should have wide discretion in setting these standards.

KILLING, LETTING DIE, AND VOLUNTARY EUTHANASIA

Physicians and nurses have long worried that if they withdraw treatment and a patient dies, they will be accused of killing the patient and subject to criminal liability. They hold a parallel concern that if they acknowledge the refusal by patients who withdraw or withhold treatment, they thereby assist in the suicide. Typical cases involve persons suffering from a terminal illness or mortal injury and who, as a consequence, refuse a therapy without which they will die, but with which their life can be extended.

The Distinction between Killing and Letting Die. In the past, physicians, lawyers, and moral philosophers have routinely construed forgoing treatment as letting die, not killing. Courts and many writers in ethics explain that the cause of death should not be categorized as either suicide or homicide when an individual forgoes life-sustaining treatment because an underlying disease or injury is the cause of death. They argue that medical technology—for example, a respirator—only delays the natural course of the disease or injury. When the technology is removed, a "natural death" occurs; natural conditions continue as though the technology had never been initiated. Because the cause of death is disease or injury, not the physician's, surrogate's, or patient's action, it is not homicide or suicide.

However, this way of distinguishing killing and letting die has proven difficult to explicate. In its ordinary language meaning, *killing* is any form of deprivation or destruction of life, including animal and plant life. Neither in ordinary language nor in law does the word "killing" entail a wrongful act or a crime, even if human persons are killed (unlike "murder," which does entail criminal wrongfulness). In ordinary language, *killing* represents a family of ideas whose central condition is direct causation of another's death, whereas *allowing to die* represents another family of ideas whose central condition is intentional avoidance of causal intervention so that a natural death is caused by a disease or injury. But a person can be killed by intentionally letting him or her die of a "natural" condition when the death should have been prevented. Is this circumstance a killing, a letting die, or both? Even if an act is properly classified as a killing, is it morally impermissible?

Killing is justified under some conditions (for example, in cases of self-defense), and we cannot confidently assert without examining particular cases whether a killing was justified or unjustified. As Dan Brock suggests in his essay, to correctly apply the label "killing" or the label "letting die" to a set of events will not determine whether an action is acceptable or unacceptable. For example, mercy killing at the request of a seriously ill and suffering patient is not obviously wrong. Nothing about either killing or letting die entails a judgment about the wrongness or rightness of either type of action.

Several readings in this chapter address this issue. James Rachels argues that the cessation of treatment in terminal cases is an "intentional termination of the life of one human being by another" and, more generally, that letting a patient die is an action, not merely an omission. He questions whether a clear and morally useful distinction between killing and allowing to die is available. Rachels also holds that if it is morally permissible to intentionally allow a patient to die, then acting directly to terminate a patient's life would be justified if it would cause less suffering to the patient than intentionally allowing him or her to die.

By contrast, Beauchamp and Childress argue that killing may not be justified even if it causes less suffering for some patients, because the act might violate a justified rule prohibiting such actions. The rule would be justified public policy if seriously harmful consequences might occur by abandoning the killing/letting die distinction in law. Beauchamp and Childress agree with Rachels that nothing about either killing or allowing to die entails wrongness or rightness, and they also agree that whether *an act* of either killing or letting die is justified or unjustified depends on the morally relevant features of the case at hand. Their thesis is that it may be appropriate for law and professional societies to prohibit such actions even if the act itself is not morally wrong.

Voluntary Active Euthanasia. These questions about killing and letting die are generally treated in bioethics as problems of either euthanasia or physician-assisted suicide. Euthanasia is the act or practice of ending a person's life in order to release the person from an incurable disease, intolerable suffering, or undignified death. Originally, *euthanasia* was derived from two Greek roots meaning "good death." Today the term is used to refer to painlessly causing death or failing to prevent death from natural causes for merciful reasons.

Two main subtypes of euthanasia are commonly distinguished: active and passive. Using this distinction, four subtypes of euthanasia can be represented schematically as follows:

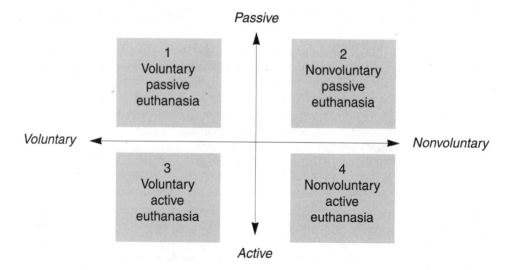

If a person requests the termination of his or her life, the action is called voluntary euthanasia. If the person is not mentally competent to make an informed request, the action is called nonvoluntary euthanasia. Both forms should be distinguished from involuntary euthanasia, in which a person capable of making an informed request has not done so. Involuntary euthanasia has been universally condemned.

The center of recent ethical controversy has been over voluntary active euthanasia (VAE). Supporters of VAE argue that there are cases in which respect for the rights of patients obligates society to respect the decisions of those who elect euthanasia. If competent patients have a legal and moral right to refuse treatment that brings about their deaths, they ask, why is there not a similar right to arrange for death by an active means? Proponents of VAE primarily emphasize circumstances in which a condition has become overwhelmingly burdensome for a patient, pain management for the patient is inadequate, and only a physician seems capable of bringing relief.

The right to assistance in the form of voluntary active euthanasia has until very recently never been recognized in law or in codes of medical ethics. Codes of medical and research ethics from the Hippocratic corpus to today's major professional codes strictly prohibit mercy killing, even if a patient has a good reason for wanting to die. Although courts have often defended the autonomy of patients in cases of *passive* euthanasia, the courts have never allowed voluntary active euthanasia. In opposition, judicial opinions cite a principle of respect for life, according to which human life has value in itself that deserves respect.

Those, such as David Thomasma in the present chapter, who support medical traditions and are opposed to killing, often appeal to either (1) professional role obligations that prohibit bringing about death or (2) the social consequences that would result from changing these traditions. The first argument is straightforward: Killing patients is inconsistent with the roles of nursing, caregiving, and healing. The second argument is more complex and has come to be the centerpiece of discussion. This argument is referred to as the wedge argument or the slippery slope argument, and proceeds roughly as follows: Although particular acts of active killing are sometimes morally justified, the social consequences of sanctioning practices of killing would run serious risks of abuse and misuse and, on balance, would cause more harm than benefit. The argument is not that these negative consequences will occur immediately, but that they will grow incrementally over time. Although society might start by carefully restricting the number of patients who qualify for assistance in suicide or homicide, these restrictions would be revised and expanded over time, with an ever-increasing risk of unjustified killing. Unscrupulous persons would learn how to abuse the system, just as they do with methods of tax evasion.

Slippery slope arguments are discussed in this chapter in the essays by several authors, including Brock, Thomasma, Beauchamp and Childress, and the Judicial Council of the American Medical Association. The success or failure of these arguments depends on speculative predictions of a progressive erosion of moral restraints. If massively dire consequences will flow from the legal legitimation of assisted suicide or voluntary active euthanasia, then slippery slope arguments are supported, and it would appear that such practices should be legally prohibited. But how accurate is the evidence that such dire consequences will occur? Is there a sufficient reason to think that we cannot maintain control over public policy? Are our methods of monitoring so frail that we cannot adequately control such practices? These are among the primary questions asked in the current debate about euthanasia.

PHYSICIAN-ASSISTED SUICIDE

Physician-assisted suicide is a patient's voluntary suicide with the assistance of a physician. Unlike voluntary active euthanasia, physician-assisted suicide does not entail that the person who dies be acutely suffering or terminally ill, though these conditions are usually the reasons for electing suicide. The persons who die are themselves the ultimate cause of death; the physician merely assists.

Physician-assisted suicide can be difficult to distinguish from treatment withdrawals with physician assistance. Like typical suicides, patients who refuse a treatment after a trial period often intend to end their lives because of their grim prospects, not because they seek death as an end in itself. In each case death is self-produced, whether by a lethal poison or by disconnecting a respirator.

It has generally been held in professional medical ethics — for example, in the policy statements of the American Medical Association — that a *request* for assistance in dying by a competent patient does not have the same authority and obligatory force in law and morals as a *refusal* of treatment and therefore does not justify an action of physician-assisted suicide. However, this conclusion is controversial. An alternative view is that whether physicians are either morally permitted or morally required to honor requests for direct assistance that will lead to death depends on the nature of the request, the nature of the patient–physician relationship, and the nature of the physician's prior commitments. A physician with a broad set of professional commitments to help patients die has made a moral commitment that differs from the commitment made by a physician who draws the line in opposition to all forms of euthanasia and assistance in suicide.

One of the most critical questions for acts of killing in medicine is whether an act of assisting persons in bringing about their deaths causes them a loss, or, rather, provides a benefit. If a person chooses death and sees that event as a personal benefit, then helping that person bring about death may neither harm nor wrong the person and may provide a benefit or at least fulfill the person's last important goal. On the one hand, avoidance of intentionally causing the death of patients is a deep and primitive restraint encouraged by the many reservations society has long had about killing innocent persons. To change this perspective would seem to be sweeping and dangerous. On the other hand, if physicians can benefit patients in ways other than by healing and palliation, should they be restricted by law or morals from doing so? This question is the centerpiece of the contemporary discussion about physician–assisted suicide.

A widely discussed case about assisted suicide involves physician Timothy Quill, who reports his relationship with a leukemia patient in this chapter. Quill prescribed the barbiturates desired by a 45-year-old woman who had refused treatment. She had been his patient for many years, and members of her family had, as a group, come to a decision with the counsel of the physician. Many believe that Quill's actions were justified because: (1) the patient was competent and acting voluntarily; (2) there was an ongoing patient–physician relationship; (3) there was mutual and informed decision making by patient and physician; (4) there was a critical and probing discussion before the decision; (5) there had been a consideration of and rejection of alternatives; (6) there was a repeated request for assistance in dying by the patient; (7) there would be unbearable suffering from the patient's perspective; (8) and a means was used that was as painless as possible.

Nonetheless, some critics have found the action by Quill unsettling and unjustified. Quill's act violated a New York State law against assisted suicide, thereby exposing him to criminal liability. His act also opened up the possibility of misconduct charges from the New York State Health Department. (A grand jury in Rochester, New York, where the events occurred, declined to indict him, apparently because jurors sympathized with his motives and possibly his action). In effect, Quill was acting as a civil disobedient, against established canons of physician ethics.

One moral problem is whether physicians are justified in performing such actions; a second is whether public policies that legalize these acts are justified. It is one thing to justify particular acts of assisting a person in suicide, another to justify general practices or policies sanctioned by law. To maintain a viable practice that avoids undesirable consequences, it may be necessary to prohibit some acts that would not be wrong were it not for their far-reaching social consequences. Particular acts of assisted suicide may in particular circumstances be humane, compassionate, and in everyone's best interest, but a social policy that authorizes such acts in medicine, it is often argued, would weaken moral restraints that we cannot easily replace, threatening practices that provide a basis of trust between patients and health-care professionals. Thus, the focus of discussion is often on whether society can legalize assisted suicide without jeopardizing the lives of the vulnerable.

In some legal jurisdictions, any deliberate aiding, advising, or encouraging of suicide is illegal. But there is increasing pressure to reform these laws, so that physicians are allowed to play a more extensive role in facilitation. A major initiative was accepted by the majority of citizens in the state of Oregon. Ballot Measure 16 was approved by voters in November 1994, allowing physicians to prescribe lethal drugs for terminally ill patients who wished to escape unbearable suffering. Under the provisions of "The Oregon Death with Dignity Act," which is reprinted in this chapter, physicians are legally allowed to prescribe death-inducing drugs for terminally ill patients (so declared by two physicians) who wish to escape unbearable suffering and three times request a physician's prescription for lethal drugs.

This Oregon legislation was ultimately upheld as a result of the important 1997 U.S. Supreme Court decisions of *Vacco v. Quill* and *Washington v. Glucksberg,* which are reprinted in this chapter. The Supreme Court reviewed two decisions in circuit courts that endorsed a constitutional right to limited physician-assisted suicide. The decisions of these lower courts were reversed in law by the Supreme Court decision, which found that there are no constitutional rights to physician aid-in-dying, but that each state may set its own policy. This simple decision had the effect of clearing the way for a right to physician-assisted death to be enacted by individual states. Its consequences were realized almost immediately in Oregon, where voters reaffirmed Measure 16, passed three years previously.

This Oregon vote allowing a limited form of physician-assisted suicide and the Supreme Court opinion leaving the issue up to the states reflect the new frontier of the social and legal acceptance of expanded autonomy rights to control one's death. The cutting-edge has now shifted from *refusal* of treatment to *request* for aid in dying.

An alternative to physician-assisted suicide is proposed in three of the next four articles in this chapter. In the first, the Council on Ethical and Judicial Affairs of the American Medical Association argues that physician-assisted suicide threatens the core of the medical profession's ethical integrity. The Council argues that physician-assisted suicide cannot properly be viewed as an extension of the right to refuse treatment, is no part of the physician's role, and opens the door to policies that carry far greater social risks than now exist.

In the second article, Bernat, Gert, and Mogielnicki argue that no one is constrained to stay alive, because every patient can refuse hydration and nutrition, which will ultimately cause death. They point out that all patients have a right to refuse treatment so as to bring about death. All patients therefore already have the power to control their own destinies, and there is no need to rush to physician-assisted suicide or voluntary active euthanasia. These authors maintain that the key questions in these debates turn on whether a competent patient has rationally refused treatment; if someone rationally refuses nutrition and hydration, they will die. What makes something a case of letting a competent person die is the patient's refusal, not an "inaction" or "omission" by the physician. Therefore, the distinction between killing and letting die should be retained, but should be based on patients' requests and patients' refusals: Dying by starvation is, on this analysis, a case of letting die, not of killing, despite the fact that the physician assists the patient during the dying process.

The two concluding articles in the chapter exhibit the sharply different opinions surrounding these issues at the present time. F. M. Kamm argues for the permissibility of both euthanasia and physician-assisted suicide. She discusses (1) whether death can be a benefit, (2) the status of a right to choose the end of one's life, (3) whether a doctor has a duty to relieve suffering even if it foreseeably makes the doctor a killer, and (4) whether a patient can waive the right to live, thereby releasing others from the duty not to kill him or her. Kamm believes that a patient would sometimes do no wrong in intending or causing his or her own death. She concludes that if it is permissible to treat persons in their best interests when we foresee that the treatment will rapidly cause death, then it is permissible to intentionally kill or assist in killing someone when the death is in the person's best interest.

In the final essay of this section, Leon Kass raises questions about both the coherence and the consequences of the frequently asserted right to die. Noting that the language of rights was introduced into political discourse by Hobbes and Locke, Kass argues that the right to die betrays the excessive individualism of its intellectual forebears. Kass questions whether the right-to-die notion applies equally well to contexts in which treatment is refused with uncertain consequences and to situations where treatment is refused in order to achieve the result of the patient's death. The author also suspects that the right to die is at times cynically asserted on behalf of others by bright and healthy people who fervently hope that the unproductive, the incurable, and the repulsive will die sooner rather than later.

Refusal of Treatment

CALIFORNIA COURT OF APPEALS, SECOND DISTRICT

Bouvia v. Superior Court

OPINION AND ORDER FOR A PEREMPTORY
WRIT OF MANDATE
BEACH, Associate Justice

Petitioner, Elizabeth Bouvia, a patient in a public hospital seeks the removal from her body of a nasogastric tube inserted and maintained against her will and without her consent by physicians who so placed it for the purpose of keeping her alive through involuntary forced feeding....

The trial court denied petitioner's request for the immediate relief she sought. It concluded that leaving the tube in place was necessary to prolong petitioner's life, and that it would, in fact, do so. With the tube in place petitioner probably will survive the time required to prepare for trial, a trial itself and an appeal, if one proved necessary. The real party physicians also assert, and the trial court agreed, that physically petitioner tolerates the tube reasonably well and thus is not in great physical discomfort....

FACTUAL BACKGROUND

Petitioner is a 28-year-old woman. Since birth she has been afflicted with and suffered from severe cerebral palsy. She is quadriplegic. She is now a patient at a public hospital maintained by one of the real parties in interest, the County of Los Angeles.... Petitioner's physical handicaps of palsy and quadriplegia have progressed to the point where she is completely bedridden. Except for a few fingers of one hand and some slight head and facial movements, she is immobile.

Reprinted from the *California Reporter,* 225 Cal.Rptr. 297 (Cal. App. 2 Dist.).

She is physically helpless and wholly unable to care for herself. She is totally dependent upon others for all of her needs. These include feeding, washing, cleaning, toileting, turning, and helping her with elimination and other bodily functions. She cannot stand or sit upright in bed or in a wheelchair. She lies flat in bed and must do so the rest of her life. She suffers also from degenerative and severely crippling arthritis. She is in continual pain. Another tube permanently attached to her chest automatically injects her with periodic doses of morphine which relieves some, but not all of her physical pain and discomfort.

She is intelligent, very mentally competent. She earned a college degree. She was married but her husband has left her. She suffered a miscarriage. She lived with her parents until her father told her that they could no longer care for her. She has stayed intermittently with friends and at public facilities. A search for a permanent place to live where she might receive the constant care which she needs has been unsuccessful. She is without financial means to support herself and, therefore, must accept public assistance for medical and other care.

She has on several occasions expressed the desire to die. In 1983 she sought the right to be cared for in a public hospital in Riverside County while she intentionally "starved herself to death." A court in that county denied her judicial assistance to accomplish that goal. She later abandoned an appeal from that ruling. Thereafter, friends took her to several different facilities, both public and private, arriving finally at her present location....

Petitioner must be spoon fed in order to eat. Her present medical and dietary staff have determined that she is not consuming a sufficient amount of nutrients. Petitioner stops eating when she feels she cannot orally swallow more, without nausea and vomiting. As she cannot now retain solids, she is fed soft liquid-like food. Because of her previously announced resolve to starve herself, the medical staff feared her weight loss might reach a life-threatening level. Her weight since admission to real parties' facility seems to hover between 65 and 70 pounds. Accordingly, they inserted the subject tube against her will and contrary to her express written instruction. . . .

THE RIGHT TO REFUSE MEDICAL TREATMENT

"[A] person of adult years and in sound mind has the right, in the exercise of control over his own body, to determine whether or not to submit to lawful medical treatment." (*Cobbs v. Grant* (1972) 8 Cal.3d 229, 242, 104 Cal.Rptr, 505, 502 P.2d 1.) It follows that such a patient has the right to refuse *any* medical treatment, even that which may save or prolong her life. (*Barber v. Superior Court* (1983) 147 Cal. App.3d 1006, 195 Cal.Rptr. 484; *Bartling v. Superior Court* (1984) 163 Cal.App.3d 186, 209 Cal.Rptr. 220.) In our view the foregoing authorities are dispositive of the case at bench. Nonetheless, the County and its medical staff contend that for reasons unique to this case, Elizabeth Bouvia may not exercise the right available to others. Accordingly, we again briefly discuss the rule in the light of real parties' contentions.

The right to refuse medical treatment is basic and fundamental. It is recognized as a part of the right of privacy protected by both the state and federal constitutions. . . . Its exercise requires no one's approval. It is not merely one vote subject to being overridden by medical opinion.

In *Barber v. Superior Court, supra,* 147 Cal.App.3d 1006, 195 Cal.Rptr. 484, we considered this same issue although in a different context. Writing on behalf of this division, Justice Compton thoroughly analyzed and reviewed the issue of withdrawal of life-support systems beginning with the seminal case of the *Matter of Quinlan* (N.J. 1976) 355 A.2d 647, *cert. den.* 429 U.S. 922, 97 S.Ct. 319, 50 L.Ed.2d 289, and continuing on to the then recent enactment of the California Natural Death Act (Health & Saf. Code. §§ 7185–7195). His opinion clearly and repeatedly stresses the fundamental underpinning of its conclusion, i.e., the patient's right to decide: 147 Cal.App.3d at page 1015, 195 Cal.Rptr. 484, "In this state a clearly recognized legal right to control one's own medical treatment predated the Nat-

ural Death Act. A long line of cases, approved by the Supreme Court in *Cobbs v. Grant* (1972) 8 Cal.3d 229 [104 Cal.Rptr. 505, 502 P.2d 1] . . . have held that where a doctor performs treatment in the absence of an informed consent, there is an actionable battery. The obvious corollary to this principle is that *"a competent adult patient has the legal right to refuse medical treatment."* . . .

Bartling v. Superior Court, supra, 163 Cal.App.3d 186, 209 Cal.Rptr. 220, was factually much like the case at bench. Although not totally identical in all respects, the issue there centered on the same question here present: i.e., "May the patient refuse even life continuing treatment?" Justice Hastings, writing for another division of this court, explained: "In this case we are called upon to decide whether a competent adult patient, with serious illness which are probably incurable but have not been diagnosed as terminal, has the right, over the objection of his physicians and the hospital, to have life-support equipment disconnected despite the fact that withdrawal of such devices will surely hasten his death." (At p. 189, 209 Cal.Rptr. 220.) . . .

The description of Mr. Bartling's condition fits that of Elizabeth Bouvia. The holding of that case applies here and compels real parties to respect her decision even though she is not "terminally" ill. . . .

THE CLAIMED EXCEPTIONS TO THE PATIENT'S RIGHT TO CHOOSE ARE INAPPLICABLE

. . . At bench the trial court concluded that with sufficient feeding petitioner could live an additional 15 to 20 years; therefore, the preservation of petitioner's life for that period outweighed her right to decide. In so holding the trial court mistakenly attached undue importance to the *amount of time* possibly available to petitioner, and failed to give equal weight and consideration for the *quality* of that life; an equal, if not more significant, consideration.

All decisions permitting cessation of medical treatment or life-support procedures to some degree hastened the arrival of death. In part, at least, this was permitted because the quality of life during the time remaining in those cases had been terribly diminished. In Elizabeth Bouvia's view, the quality of her life has been diminished to the point of hopelessness, uselessness, unenjoyability and frustration. She, as the patient, lying helplessly in bed, unable to care for herself, may consider her existence meaningless. . . .

Here Elizabeth Bouvia's decision to forego medical treatment or life-support through a mechanical means belongs to her. It is not a medical decision for her physicians to make. Neither is it a legal question whose soundness is to be resolved by lawyers or judges. It is not a conditional right subject to approval by ethics committees or courts of law. It is a moral and philosophical decision that, being a competent adult, is hers alone. . . .

Here, if force fed, petitioner faces 15 to 20 years of a painful existence, endurable only by the constant administrations of morphine. Her condition is irreversible. There is no cure for her palsy or arthritis. Petitioner would have to be fed, cleaned, turned, bedded, toileted by others for 15 to 20 years! Although alert, bright, sensitive, perhaps even brave and feisty, she must lie immobile, unable to exist except through physical acts of others. Her mind and spirit may be free to take great flights but she herself is imprisoned and must lie physically helpless subject to the ignominy, embarrassment, humiliation, and dehumanizing aspects created by her helplessness. We do not believe it is the policy of this State that all and every life must be preserved against the will of the sufferer. It is incongruous, if not monstrous, for medical practitioners to assert their right to preserve a life that someone else must live, or, more accurately, endure, for "15 to 20 years." We cannot conceive it to be the policy of this State to inflict such an ordeal upon anyone.

It is, therefore, immaterial that the removal of the nasogastric tube will hasten or cause Bouvia's eventual death. Being competent she has the right to live out the remainder of her natural life in dignity and peace. It is precisely the aim and purpose of the many decisions upholding the withdrawal of life-support systems to accord and provide a large measure of dignity, respect and comfort as possible to every patient for the remainder of his days, whatever be their number. This goal is not to hasten death, though its earlier arrival may be an expected and understood likelihood. . . .

It is not necessary to here define or dwell at length upon what constitutes suicide. Our Supreme Court dealt with the matter in the case of *In re Joseph G.* (1983) 34 Cal.3d 429, 194 Cal.Rptr. 163, 667 P.2d 1176, wherein declaring that the State has an interest in preserving and recognizing the sanctity of life, it observed that it is a crime to aid in suicide. But it is significant that the instances and the means there discussed all involved

affirmative, assertive, proximate, direct conduct such as furnishing a gun, poison, knife, or other instrumentality or usable means by which another could physically and immediately inflict some death-producing injury upon himself. Such situations are far different than the mere presence of a doctor during the exercise of his patient's constitutional rights.

This is the teaching of *Bartling* and *Barber.* No criminal or civil liability attaches to honoring a competent, informed patient's refusal of medical service.

We do not purport to establish what will constitute proper medical practice in all other cases or even other aspects of the care to be provided petitioner. We hold only that her right to refuse medical treatment even of the life-sustaining variety, entitles her to the immediate removal of the nasogastric tube that has been involuntarily inserted into her body. The hospital and medical staff are still free to perform a substantial, if not the greater part of their duty, i.e., that of trying to alleviate Bouvia's pain and suffering.

Petitioner is without means to go to a private hospital and, apparently, real parties' hospital as a public facility was required to accept her. Having done so it may not deny her relief from pain and suffering merely because she has chosen to exercise her fundamental right to protect what little privacy remains to her. . . .

IT IS ORDERED

Let a peremptory writ of mandate issue commanding the Los Angeles Superior Court immediately upon receipt thereof, to make and enter a new and different order granting Elizabeth Bouvia's request for a preliminary injunction, and the relief prayed for therein; in particular to make an order (1) directing real parties in interest forthwith to remove the nasogastric tube from petitioner, Elizabeth Bouvia's, body, and (2) prohibiting any and all of the real parties in interest from replacing or aiding in replacing said tube or any other or similar device in or on petitioner without her consent. . . .

COMPTON, ASSOCIATE JUSTICE, CONCURRING OPINION

I have no doubt that Elizabeth Bouvia wants to die; and if she had the full use of even one hand, could probably find a way to end her life — in a word — commit suicide. In order to seek the assistance which she needs in ending her life by the only means she sees available — starvation — she has had to stultify her position before this court by disavowing her desire to end her life in such a fashion and proclaiming that she will eat all that she can physically tolerate. Even the majority opinion here must necessarily "dance" around the issue.

Elizabeth apparently has made a conscious and informed choice that she prefers death to continued existence in her helpless and, to her, intolerable condition. I believe she has an absolute right to effectuate that decision. This state and the medical profession instead of frustrating her desire, should be attempting to relieve her suffering by permitting and in fact assisting her to die with ease and dignity. The fact that she is forced to suffer the ordeal of self-starvation to achieve her objective is in itself inhumane.

The right to die is an integral part of our right to control our own destinies so long as the rights of others are not affected. That right should, in my opinion, include the ability to enlist assistance from others, including the medical profession, in making death as painless and quick as possible. . . .

UNITED STATES SUPREME COURT

Cruzan v. Director, Missouri Department of Health

ARGUED D CEMBER 6, 1989.
DECIDED JUNE 25, 1990.

OPINION OF THE COURT

CHIEF JUSTICE REHNQUIST delivered the opinion of the Court.

Petitioner Nancy Beth Cruzan was rendered incompetent as a result of severe injuries sustained during an automobile accident. Co-petitioners Lester and Joyce Cruzan, Nancy's parents and co-guardians, sought a court order directing the withdrawal of their daughter's artificial feeding and hydration equipment after it became apparent that she had virtually no chance of recovering her cognitive faculties. The Supreme Court of Missouri held that because there was no clear and convincing evidence of Nancy's desire to have life-sustaining treatment withdrawn under such circumstances, her parents lacked authority to effectuate such a request. . . .

She now lies in a Missouri state hospital in what is commonly referred to as a persistent vegetative state: generally, a condition in which a person exhibits motor reflexes but evinces no indications of significant cognitive function.[1] The State of Missouri is bearing the cost of her care.

After it had become apparent that Nancy Cruzan had virtually no chance of regaining her mental facilities her parents asked hospital employees to terminate the artificial nutrition and hydration procedures. All agree that such a removal would cause her death. The employees refused to honor the request without court approval. The parents then sought and received authorization from the state trial court for termination. The court found that a person in Nancy's condition had a fundamental right under the State and Federal Constitutions to refuse or direct the withdrawal of "death prolonging procedures." App to Pet for Cert A99. The court also found that Nancy's "expressed thoughts at age twenty-five in somewhat serious conversation with a housemate friend that if sick or injured she would not wish to continue her life unless she could live at least halfway normally suggest that given her present condition she would not wish to continue with her nutrition and hydration." Id., at A97–A98.

The Supreme Court of Missouri reversed by a divided vote. The court recognized a right to refuse treatment embodied in the common-law doctrine of informed consent, but expressed skepticism about the

From *United States* [*Supreme Court*] *Reports* 497 (1990), 261–357 (excerpts). Some footnotes and references omitted.

application of that doctrine in the circumstances of this case. *Cruzan v. Harmon,* 760 SW2d 408, 416–417 (Mo 1988) (en banc). The court also declined to read a broad right of privacy into the State Constitution which would "support the right of a person to refuse medical treatment in every circumstance," and expressed doubt as to whether such a right existed under the United States Constitution. Id., at 417–418. It then decided that the Missouri Living Will statue, Mo Rev Stat § 459.010 et seq. (1986), embodied a state policy strongly favoring the preservation of life. 760 SW2d, at 419–420. The court found that Cruzan's statements to her roommate regarding her desire to live or die under certain conditions were "unreliable for the purpose of determining her intent," id., at 424, "and thus insufficient to support the co-guardians claim to exercise substituted judgment on Nancy's behalf." Id., at 426. It rejected the argument that Cruzan's parents were entitled to order the termination of her medical treatment, concluding that "no person can assume that choice for an incompetent in the absence of the formalities required under Missouri's Living Will statutes or the clear and convincing, inherently reliable evidence absent here." Id., at 425. The court also expressed its view that "[b]road policy questions bearing on life and death are more properly addressed by representative assemblies" than judicial bodies. Id., at 426. . . .

[The] notion of bodily integrity has been embodied in the requirement that informed consent is generally required for medical treatment. Justice Cardozo, while on the Court of Appeals of New York, aptly described this doctrine: "Every human being of adult years and sound mind has a right to determine what shall be done with his own body; and a surgeon who performs an operation without his patient's consent commits an assault, for which he is liable in damages." *Schloendorff v. Society of New York Hospital,* 211 NY 125, 129–30, 105 NE 92, 93 (1914). The informed consent doctrine has become firmly entrenched in American tort law. . . .

The common-law doctrine of informed consent is viewed as generally encompassing the right of a competent individual to refuse medical treatment. Beyond that, [court] decisions demonstrate both similarity and diversity in their approach to decision of what all agree is a perplexing question with unusual strong moral and ethical overtones. State courts have available to them for decision a number of sources — state constitutions, statutes, and common law — which are not available to us. In this Court, the question is simply and starkly whether the United States Constitution prohibits Missouri from choosing the rule of decision which it did. This is the first case in which we have been squarely presented with the issue of whether the United States Constitution grants what is in common parlance referred to as a "right to die." . . .

The Fourteenth Amendment provides that no State shall "deprive any person of life, liberty, or property, without due process of law." The principle that a competent person has a constitutionally protected liberty interest in refusing unwanted medical treatment may be inferred from our prior decisions. . . .

But determining that a person has a "liberty interest" under the Due Process Clause does not end the inquiry; "whether respondent's constitutional rights have been violated must be determined by balancing his liberty interests against the relevant state interests." *Youngberg v. Romeo,* 457 US 307, 321 (1982). See also *Mills v. Rogers,* 457 US 291, 299 (1982).

Petitioners insist that under the general holdings of our cases, the forced administration of life-sustaining medical treatment, and even of artificially delivered food and water essential to life, would implicate a competent person's liberty interest. . . . The dramatic consequences involved in refusal of treatment would inform the inquiry as to whether the deprivation of the interest is constitutionally permissible. But for purposes of this case, we assume that the United States Constitution would grant a competent person a constitutionally protected right to refuse lifesaving hydration and nutrition.

Petitioners go on to assert that an incompetent person should possess the same right in this respect as is possessed by a competent person. . . .

The difficulty with petitioners' claim is that in a sense it begs the question: an incompetent person is not able to make an informed and voluntary choice to exercise a hypothetical right to refuse treatment or any other right. Such a "right" must be exercised for her, if at all, by some sort of surrogate. Here, Missouri has in effect recognized that under certain circumstances a surrogate may act for the patient in electing to have hydration and nutrition withdrawn in such a way as to cause death, but it has established a procedural safeguard to assure that the action of the surrogate conforms as best it may to the wishes expressed by the patient while competent. Missouri requires that evidence of the incompetent's wishes as to the withdrawal of treatment be proved by clear and convincing evidence.

The question, then, is whether the United States Constitution forbids the establishment of this procedural requirement by the State. We hold that it does not.

Whether or not Missouri's clear and convincing evidence requirement comports with the United States Constitution depends in part on what interests the State may properly seek to protect in this situation. Missouri relies on its interest in the protection and preservation of human life, and there can be no gainsaying this interest. . . .

But in the context presented here, a State has more particular interests at stake. The choice between life and death is a deeply personal decision of obvious and overwhelming finality. We believe Missouri may legitimately seek to safeguard the personal element of this choice through the imposition of heightened evidentiary requirements. It cannot be disputed that the Due Process Clause protects an interest in life as well as an interest in refusing life-sustaining medical treatment. Not all incompetent patients will have loved ones available to serve as surrogate decision makers. And even where family members are present "[t]here will, of course, be some unfortunate situations in which family members will not act to protect a patient." . . . Finally, we think a State may properly decline to make judgments about the "quality" of life that a particular individual may enjoy, and simply assert an unqualified interest in the preservation of human life to be weighed against the constitutionally protected interests of the individual.

In our view, Missouri has permissibly sought to advance these interests through the adoption of a "clear and convincing" standard of proof to govern such proceedings. "The function of a standard of proof, as that concept is embodied in the Due Process Clause and in the realm of factfinding, is to 'instruct the factfinder concerning the degree of confidence our society thinks he should have in the correctness of factual conclusions for a particular type of adjudication.' " . . .

There is no doubt that statutes requiring wills to be in writing, and statutes of frauds which require that a contract to make a will be in writing, on occasion frustrate the effectuation of the intent of a particular decedent, just as Missouri's requirement of proof in this case may have frustrated the effectuation of the not-fully-expressed desires of Nancy Cruzan. But the Constitution does not require general rules to work faultlessly; no general rule can. . . .

The Supreme Court of Missouri held that in this case the testimony adduced at trial did not amount to clear and convincing proof of the patient's desire to have hy-

dration and nutrition withdrawn. In so doing, it reversed a decision of the Missouri trial court which had found that the evidence "suggest[ed]" Nancy Cruzan would not have desired to continue such measures, App to Pet for Cert A98, but which had not adopted the standard of "clear and convincing evidence" enunciated by the Supreme Court. The testimony adduced at trial consisted primarily of Nancy Cruzan's statements made to a housemate about a year before her accident that she would not want to live should she face life as a "vegetable," and other observations to the same effect. The observations did not deal in terms with withdrawal of medical treatment or of hydration and nutrition. We cannot say that the Supreme Court of Missouri committed constitutional error in reaching the conclusion that it did. . . .

No doubt is engendered by anything in this record but that Nancy Cruzan's mother and father are loving and caring parents. If the States were required by the United States Constitution to repose a right of "substituted judgment" with anyone, the Cruzans would surely qualify. But we do not think the Due Process Clause requires the State to repose judgment on these matters with anyone but the patient herself. Close family members may have a strong feeling — a feeling not at all ignoble or unworthy, but not entirely disinterested, either — that they do not wish to witness the continuation of the life of a loved one which they regard as hopeless, meaningless, and even degrading. But there is no automatic assurance that the view of close family members will necessarily be the same as the patient's would have been had she been confronted with the prospect of her situation while competent. All of the reasons previously discussed for allowing Missouri to require clear and convincing evidence of the patient's wishes lead us to conclude that the State may choose to defer only to those wishes, rather than confide the decision to close family members.

The judgment of the Supreme Court of Missouri is affirmed.

SEPARATE OPINIONS

JUSTICE O'CONNOR, concurring.

[T]he Court does not today decide the issue whether a State must also give effect to the decisions of a surrogate decisionmaker. . . . In my view, such a duty may well be constitutionally required to protect the patient's liberty interest in refusing medical treatment. Few individuals provide explicit oral or written instructions regarding their intent to refuse medical treatment should they become incompetent.[1] States which decline to consider any evidence other than such instructions may frequently fail to honor a patient's intent. Such failures might be avoided if the State considered an equally probative source of evidence: the patient's appointment of a proxy to make health care decisions on her behalf. Delegating the authority to make medical decisions to a family member or friend is becoming a common method of planning for the future. . . .

Today's decision, holding only that the Constitution permits a State to require clear and convincing evidence of Nancy Cruzan's desire to have artificial hydration and nutrition withdrawn, does not preclude a future determination that the Constitution requires the States to implement the decisions of a patient's duly appointed surrogate. Nor does it prevent States from developing other approaches for protecting an incompetent individual's liberty interest in refusing medical treatment. As is evident from the Court's survey of state court decisions, . . . no national consensus has yet emerged on the best solution for this difficult and sensitive problem. Today we decide only that one State's practice does not violate the Constitution; the more challenging task of crafting appropriate procedures for safeguarding incompetents' liberty interests is entrusted to the "laboratory" of the States, *New State Ice Co. v. Liebmann,* 285 US 262, 311 (1932) (Brandeis, J., dissenting), in the first instance.

Justice Brennan, with whom Justice Marshall and Justice Blackmun join, dissenting.

A grown woman at the time of the accident, Nancy had previously expressed her wish to forgo continuing medical care under circumstances such as these. Her family and her friends are convinced that this is what she would want. A guardian ad litem appointed by the trial court is also convinced that this is what Nancy would want. See 760 SW2d at 444 (Higgins, J., dissenting from denial of rehearing). Yet the Missouri Supreme Court, alone among state courts deciding such a question, has determined that an irreversibly vegetative patient will remain a passive prisoner of medical technology—for Nancy, perhaps for the next 30 years. . . . Because I believe that Nancy Cruzan has a fundamental right to be free of unwanted artificial nutrition and hydration, which right is not outweighed by any interests of the State, and because I find that the improperly biased procedural obstacles imposed by the Missouri Supreme Court impermissibly burden that right, I respectfully dissent. Nancy Cruzan is entitled to choose to die with dignity. . . .

I

The starting point for our legal analysis must be whether a competent person has a constitutional right to avoid unwanted medical care. Earlier this Term, this Court held that the Due Process Clause of the Fourteenth Amendment confers significant liberty interest in avoiding unwanted medical treatment. *Washington v. Harper,* 108 L Ed 2d 178 (1990). Today, the Court concedes that our prior decisions "support the recognition of a general liberty interest in refusing medical treatment." The Court, however, avoids discussing either the measure of that liberty interest or its application by assuming, for purposes of this case only, that a competent person has a constitutionally protected liberty interest in being free of unwanted artificial nutrition and hydration. . . .

The right to be free from medical attention without consent, to determine what shall be done with one's own body, *is* deeply rooted in this Nation's traditions, as the majority acknowledges. . . . This right has long been "firmly entrenched in American tort law" and is securely grounded in the earliest common law. . . . "'Anglo-American law starts with the premise of thoroughgoing self determination. It follows that each man is considered to be master of his own body, and he may, if he be of sound mind, expressly prohibit the performance of lifesaving surgery, or other medical treatment.'" *Natanson v. Kline,* 186 Kan 393, 406–407, 350 P2d 1093, 1104 (1960). . . .

No material distinction can be drawn between the treatment to which Nancy Cruzan continues to be subject—artificial nutrition and hydration—and any other medical treatment. . . .

Artificial delivery of food and water is regarded as medical treatment by the medical profession and the Federal Government. According to the American Academy of Neurology, "[t]he artificial provision of nutrition and hydration is a form of medical treatment . . . analogous to other forms of life-sustaining treatment, such as the use of the respirator. When a patient is unconscious, both a respirator and an artificial feeding device serve to support or replace normal bodily functions that are compromised as a result of the patient's illness." . . .

A

The right to be free from unwanted medical attention is a right to evaluate the potential benefit of treatment and its possible consequences according to one's own values and to make a personal decision whether to subject oneself to the intrusion. For a patient like Nancy Cruzan, the sole benefit of medical treatment is being kept metabolically alive. . . .

There are also affirmative reasons why someone like Nancy might choose to forgo artificial nutrition and hydration under these circumstances. Dying is personal. And it is profound. For many, the thought of an ignoble end, steeped in decay, is abhorrent. A quiet, proud death, bodily integrity intact, is a matter of extreme consequence. "In certain, thankfully rare, circumstances the burden of maintaining the corporeal existence degrades the very humanity it was meant to serve." *Brophy v. New England Sinai Hospital, Inc.* 398 Mass 417, 434, 497 NE2d 626, 635–636 (1986). . . .

Such conditions are, for many, humiliating to contemplate, as is visiting a prolonged and anguished vigil on one's parents, spouse, and children. A long, drawn-out death can have a debilitating effect on family members. . . .

B

Although the right to be free of unwanted medical intervention, like other constitutionally protected interests, may not be absolute, no State interest could outweigh the rights of an individual in Nancy Cruzan's position. Whatever a State's possible interests in mandating life-support treatment under other circumstances, there is no good to be obtained here by Missouri's insistence that Nancy Cruzan remain on life-support systems if it is indeed her wish not to do so. Missouri does not claim, nor could it, that society as a whole will be benefited by Nancy's receiving medical treatment. No third party's situation will be improved and no harm to others will be averted. Cf, nn 6 and 8, supra.

The only state interest asserted here is a general interest in the preservation of life. But the State has no legitimate general interest in someone's life, completely abstracted from the interest of the person living that life, that could outweigh the person's choice to avoid medical treatment. . . . Thus, the State's general interest in life must accede to Nancy Cruzan's particularized and intense interest in self-determination in her choice of medical treatment. There is simply nothing

legitimately within the State's purview to be gained by superseding her decision.

Moreover, there may be considerable danger that Missouri's rule of decision would impair rather than serve any interest the State does have in sustaining life. Current medical practice recommends use of heroic measures if there is a scintilla of a chance that the patient will recover, on the assumption that the measures will be discontinued should the patient improve. When the President's Commission in 1982 approved the withdrawal of life support equipment from irreversibly vegetative patients, it explained that "[a]n even more troubling wrong occurs when a treatment that might save life or improve health is not started because the health care personnel are afraid that they will find it very difficult to stop the treatment if, as is fairly likely, it proves to be of little benefit and greatly burdens the patient." President's Commission 75. . . .

III

Missouri may constitutionally impose only those procedural requirements that serve to enhance the accuracy of a determination of Nancy Cruzan's wishes or are at least consistent with an accurate determination. The Missouri "safeguard" that the Court upholds today does not meet that standard. The determination needed in this context is whether the incompetent person would choose to live in a persistent vegetative state on life-support or to avoid this medical treatment. Missouri's rule of decision imposes a markedly asymmetrical evidentiary burden. Only evidence of specific statements of treatment choice made by the patient when competent is admissible to support a finding that the patient, now in a persistent vegetative state, would wish to avoid further medical treatment. Moreover, this evidence must be clear and convincing. No proof is required to support a finding that the incompetent person would wish to continue treatment. . . .

Even more than its heightened evidentiary standard, the Missouri court's categorical exclusion of relevant evidence dispenses with any semblance of accurate factfinding. The court adverted to no evidence supporting its decision, but held that no clear and convincing, inherently reliable evidence had been presented to show that Nancy would want to avoid further treatment. In doing so, the court failed to consider statements Nancy had made to family members and a close friend. The court also failed to consider testimony from Nancy's mother and sister that they were certain that Nancy would want to discontinue artificial nutrition and hydration, even after the court found that Nancy's family was loving and without malignant motive. See 760 SW2d, at 412. The court also failed to consider the conclusions of the guardian ad litem, appointed by the trial court, that there was clear and convincing evidence that Nancy would want to discontinue medical treatment and that this was in her best interests. Id., at 444 (Higgins, J., dissenting from denial of rehearing); Brief for Respondent Guardian Ad Litem 2–3. The court did not specifically define what kind of evidence it would consider clear and convincing, but its general discussion suggests that only a living will or equivalently formal directive from the patient when competent would meet this standard. Seed 760 SW2d, at 424–425. . . .

The Missouri Court's disdain for Nancy's statements in serious conversations not long before her accident, for the opinions of Nancy's family and friends as to her values, beliefs and certain choice, and even for the opinion of an outside objective factfinder appointed by the State evinces a disdain for Nancy Cruzan's own right to choose. The rules by which an incompetent person's wishes are determined must represent every effort to determine those wishes. The rule that the Missouri court adopted and that this Court upholds, however, skews the result away from a determination that as accurately as possible reflects the individual's own preferences and beliefs. It is a rule that transforms human beings into passive subjects of medical technology. . . .

That Missouri and this Court may truly be motivated only by concern for incompetent patients makes no matter. As one of our most prominent jurists warned us decades ago: "Experience should teach us to be most on our guard to protect liberty when the government's purposes are beneficent. . . . The greatest dangers to liberty lurk in insidious encroachment by men of zeal, well meaning but without understanding." *Olmstead v. United States,* 277 US 438, 479 (1928) (Brandeis, J., dissenting).

I respectfully dissent.

NOTE

1. See 2 President's Commission for the Study of Ethical Problems in Medicine and Biomedical and Behavioral Research, Making Health Care Decisions 241–242 (1982) (36% of those surveyed gave instructions regarding how they would like to be treated if they ever became too sick to make decisions: 23% put those instructions in writing) (Lou Harris Poll, September 1982); American Medical Association Surveys of Physicians and Public Opinion on Health Care Issues 29–30 (1988) (56% of those surveyed had told family members their wishes concerning the use of life-sustaining treatment if they entered an irreversible coma; 15% had filled out a living will specifying those wishes).

L A W R E N C E   O .   G O S T I N

Life and Death Choices after *Cruzan*

The state interests used by the court to justify denial of Nancy Cruzan's right to decline artificial feeding are hardly persuasive. The state interest in preserving the life of a person in PVS is purely theoretical. The state's authority to preserve "life" has become a magical concept, often driven by blind ideology rather than by any thoughtful appreciation of the unique characteristics of human life. When an individual has no meaningful interaction with her environment, no recognition of familiar persons or objects, nor any human feelings or experience of any kind, the state's interest in life is a mere abstraction.

To assert an interest in the outcome of a decision to abate life-sustaining treatment requires some demonstrable burden. All of the burden is borne by the family who suffers from the refusal of the law to allow a de-

Law, Medicine & Health Care, 19, nos. 1–2 (1991): 9–12. Reprinted with the permission of the American Society of Law, Medicine & Ethics and Professor Gostin.

cision to dignify a natural death process. Whether the burden of continued life is measured by emotional suffering, by economic cost,[1] or by any other standard, it is not society, the medical profession, or the state that has to pay the cost. The family must live with the consequences.

The right of a person in PVS to be allowed to die is now well grounded in biomedical ethics. What greater purpose could a moral right to liberty — or a constitutional right to privacy — achieve than to reject unwarranted state intrusion into such an intimate moment as death? The essence of the right to liberty (or privacy) is that the decision is deeply personal and critically important in the ordering of a patient's life. It is a decision which uniquely involves the individual, and in which the outcome matters little to third parties — no one else is harmed by the decision, affected by it, or is properly interested. A family's decision to abate treatment of a loved one in PVS is supremely a private decision.

No one doubts the validity of the state interests in preventing abuse by a surrogate and in ensuring accurate fact finding. But these interests are not reasonably achieved by requiring clear and convincing evidence of the incompetent patient's prior wishes. Some review process, perhaps by a hospital ethics committee, to ensure that the diagnosis of PVS is reliable and that the family is properly motivated may be appropriate. The state can reasonably ensure that surrogates do not abuse their authority, not by removing their power of substitute judgment as occurred in *Cruzan,* but by ensuring that they are not unduly motivated by economic or other personal benefit.

Nor does a clear and convincing standard best ensure accurate fact finding. Justice Brennan's dissent in *Cruzan* explains the markedly asymmetrical evidentiary burden of the Missouri rule. All of the burden rests on the incompetent patient and her family to prove unequivocally that she would not want to be treated. The proxy must adduce specific statements by the patient that foresaw the precise technological shackles she now endures. The state, on the other hand, need not submit any proof to support a finding that the patient would want to continue treatment.

The fact is that the Supreme Court has removed an entire class of people from the protection of the federal constitution. The Court accepted a high evidentiary standard that only a few previously foresighted non-autonomous patients will be able to meet. The *Cruzan* opinion does not constitutionally protect the never-autonomous (e.g., the severely mentally retarded and young children who cannot express any view); the once-autonomous who failed to express a view about their future treatment; and the once-autonomous who expressed views insufficiently exact to meet the rigorous clear and convincing evidence standard. . . .

The *Cruzan* decision shows how far out of touch the Supreme Court has become with regard to how people think and behave. The overwhelming majority of people do not anticipate the circumstances of their death with the exactness required under a clear and convincing evidence standard and do not plan their lives by creating formal legal instruments.[2] Even if a person dwells on the remote possibility of loss of cognition, she may not marshal the formal evidence of her preferences or may not be sufficiently precise in enunciating the exact medical circumstances under which treatment should be abated.[3] When a person tells a family member or close friend that she does not want her life sustained artificially, she is "express[ing] her wishes in the only terms familiar to her, and . . . as clearly as a lay person should be asked to express them."[4]

What is more important, the Court creates a presumption that a person would want technological support to sustain an unconscious, non-purposeful life. Exactly the opposite presumption is warranted. When asked, very few people would choose to be kept physically alive when all conscious life is over.

Finally, the Court reasons that since *some* family members are improperly motivated, *all* family members may be precluded from making substitute decisions in the absence of a durable power or other legally sufficient evidence of intent. Again, most people prefer close relatives or friends who know them well to make proxy decisions. Patients certainly do not wish to have their family's hands tied because they neglected to execute the proper legal instrument.

The insistence on "clear and convincing evidence" imposes a particular burden on persons without sufficient education or means. Legal formalities in drafting adequate advance directives or complying with statutory requirements can be complicated and vary from state to state. Those who are poor, illiterate, or have inadequate access to legal or other advice simply will be foreclosed from exercising their rights. . . .

One obvious method of ensuring that a person's wishes are respected after *Cruzan* is to provide assistance in complying with state evidentiary requirements in writing a power of attorney and/or an advance directive. State agencies could publish and distribute simple advance directive forms. Alternatively, states could fund charitable or community organizations to provide forms and advice in completing them. . . .

Some states may still fail to recognize the constitutional importance of advance directives. We can expect to see future federal court cases under the constitutional theory that durable powers of attorney have binding force even in restrictive states like Missouri. Justice O'Connor's concurrence opens the door to the argument that durable powers give patients a constitutional right to have the decisions of their proxies respected.

While states should make every effort to encourage persons to prepare advance directives, the greater challenge is to devise legal mechanisms to respect patient choices with a minimum of legal formality. State legislatures have a number of policy options. First, the state could establish a low threshold of proof. A person's desire to have treatment abated could be demonstrated by a preponderance of evidence (i.e., the balance of evidence)—not merely by legal instrument, but by informal communication. . . .

Second, states could create a presumption favoring substitute decisions by family members. By relying primarily on family evaluation of a patient's statements and values, states could at once avoid the burden of a lengthy process of judicial review, and designate the proxy decision-maker most likely to be intimately familiar with the patient. Only in cases where the family has a conflict of interest or is divided itself would an alternative process of evaluation be necessary. . . .

Third, states could enact laws which require health care facilities to inform patients of the right to make an advance directive and to record their treatment preferences. Reasonable opportunities for persons to reflect on treatment alternatives arise when they are admitted to a hospital, nursing home, or hospice, or even when they apply for health insurance, Medicaid, or Medicare. . . .

The federal Patient Self-Determination Act, enacted within the Omnibus Budget Reconciliation Act of 1990, provides a good illustration of a "routine offering" requirement.[5] The Act requires health care providers, as a condition of the receipt of Medicare or Medicaid dollars, to provide written information at the time of admission about the patient's rights under state law to accept or refuse medical treatment and to formulate advance directives. Health care providers will be responsible for documenting in each person's medical record whether she has executed an advance directive. States are required to develop a written description of state law on advance directives, and health care providers must undertake public education programs for staff and the community on the subject of advance directives.

A wide chasm exists between people's desires to express their wishes and their failure to draft written advance directives.[6] The most probable reason is that people are simply not asked. "Routine offering" statutes will ensure that, long after Cruzan has been forgotten by most citizens, patients will be informed of their rights and provided assistance in exercising them.

Experience dictates that even considerable efforts to encourage patients to plan for their deaths are not always successful. . . . In the absence of known preferences, the state should assume that individuals would wish to be treated in their best interests and would trust their families to make decisions on their behalf. Decisions to abate treatment, therefore, could be made by loved ones in the cases in which this would best serve the patient's interests.

Life and death choices across the country could sink to such a low level that people would be required to deliberatively marshall their legal evidence in the fear that their government will fail to respect their wishes and privacy with regard to medical treatments. Alternatively, states can enact creative laws to encourage meaningful dialogue with family and physicians on final care, assist people in making clear and simple statements of their preferences, and adopt legal presumptions about the closeness of family life which best reflect the value systems and behavior of most Americans.

NOTES

1. The Supreme Court, however, was careful to observe that in Nancy Cruzan's case the state was paying for the costs of her continued treatment. The Court did not indicate, however, that it would have altered its decisions if the family were bearing the financial burden.

2. S.V. McCrary and J.R. Botkin, "Hospital Policy on Advance Directives," *Journal of the American Medical Association* 1989, 262:2411–14; L. Emanuel and E. Emanuel, "The Medical Directive: A New Comprehensive Advance Care Document," *Journal of the American Medical Association* 1989, 261:3288.

3. *Cruzan v. Director,* Missouri Department of Health, 110 S.Ct. 2841 (1990).

4. *In re O'Connor,* 72 N.Y.2d 517, 551 (1988) (Simons J, dissenting).

5. The implementation date of the Act is December 1, 1991.

6. J.C. Danforth, "Opening Statement to Subcommittee on Medicare and Long-term Care of the Committee on Finance Hearing on the Patient Self-Determination Act," July 20, 1990.

JOHN A. ROBERTSON

Cruzan: No Rights Violated

Cruzan was correctly decided. Not because persons in persistent vegetative state should be sustained indefinitely, but because sustaining them does not violate their own or their family's constitutional rights.

Gastrostomy feeding of Nancy Cruzan does not harm her. A permanently vegetative patient does not have interests that can be harmed. Even critics of the decision agree that she does not feel pain and is unaware of her situation. Thus she cannot be harmed by medical treatment. The state is not violating her right to refuse treatment because, in her present condition, she has not refused treatment. Indeed, she is incapable of refusing.

Nor does treatment violate a right to decline treatment in advance. If such a right exists, it is a right to choose — to direct — that treatment not occur. A state could violate such a right only if the person when competent had clearly directed that no treatment occur. Surmising that the person probably would have refused, or that nontreatment is consistent with her previous values does not itself establish a violation of the right to decide in advance. Inferences that the patient would have issued such a directive are not evidence that the directive was issued. To trump a state law mandating treatment, the patient must have in fact issued a directive against treatment.

The nub of *Cruzan* is this: May the state require that the past directive be clearly established if treatment is to be withheld on the basis of that directive? The Supreme Court correctly says yes. Surely a state may require reliable evidence that a past directive was knowingly made. Requiring that it be written or otherwise explicitly made is not an undue burden on persons who wish to issue directives against medical care when incompetent.

What if clear evidence of a past directive is lacking (as often occurs)? Treatment in the case does not violate a right to direct future care, for there is no evidence that the patient so directed. Nor does it violate a present right to refuse treatment when the patient lacks the capacity to refuse. Since the patient is comatose treatment would not violate any other constitutional interest.

One could argue that an incompetent patient has a right to have a proxy decide for the patient on the basis of her previous values. But that claim cannot be based on the comatose patient's current interests (there are none), nor on a past exercise of autonomy, for no directive against treatment has been issued. Surely there is no constitutional right to be treated "like one once was" now that one is so radically different.

The claim in *Cruzan* thus becomes the family's right to decide the matter because of the impact of continued treatment on their own, not Nancy's interests. Does family privacy, recognized by the Court to include decisions about having children and how they are reared, include the right to terminate medical treatment that is not harming (or helping) their daughter? Parents have never had the right to deny their children medical care that the state deems necessary. For example, parents are free to terminate their custody of handicapped newborns but not necessarily to terminate treatment. The Supreme Court should not expand family privacy when harm to the comatose ward from the disputed treatment does not exist.

Critics of *Cruzan* ignore these important distinctions, and fallaciously conclude that an undesirable state policy is necessarily unconstitutional. Treating Nancy over her parents' objections may be unwise, but it does not follow that anyone's constitutional rights are thereby violated.

From the *Hastings Center Report* 20 (September/October 1990), pp. 8–9. Reproduced by permission. © The Hastings Center.

In some respects, however, *Cruzan* is a significant victory for a constitutional "right to die." The competent patient's right to refuse treatment has been explicitly recognized (though called a liberty interest rather than a fundamental right). Logical development of this interest could extend beyond refusing medical treatment to suicide, assisted suicide, and consensual active euthanasia. The right to be free of state mandated medical intrusions could be taken to require that a competent person also be free of state interference with his or her other efforts to end the bodily burdens of disease.

The Court also seems prepared to accept a right to make explicit directives concerning treatment when incompetent. Such an extension, however, does not necessarily follow. The interest in being free of present bodily burdens that underlies the right to refuse treatment does not exist when one is issuing a directive about a hypothetical future state in which one's interests will be drastically altered from how they appear to the now competent person. There are no bodily burdens being imposed at the time the directive is issued. There may be none when the directive would take effect.

Moreover, recognizing a constitutional right to make binding directives against medical treatment would logically lead to constitutionalizing a whole range of prior directives, from living wills and testamentary dispositions to surrogate mother contracts and agreements to dispose of frozen embryos. If autonomy gives the right to refuse treatment in advance, why should it not give the right to consent to termination of child custody or abortion in advance as well? The fact that the person is competent when these future situations occur should not matter — it is the prior exercise of autonomy that is the claimed right. Indeed, since other persons will have relied on prior reproductive directives, the case for enforcing them is even stronger.

The Court in *Cruzan* rightfully leaves states wide discretion to resolve difficult questions of life and death decisionmaking. Missouri, like most other states, *should* permit the family to stop Nancy's treatment and their own ordeal. But Missouri violates no constitutional rights in choosing otherwise.

Voluntary Active Euthanasia

JAMES RACHELS

Active and Passive Euthanasia

The distinction between active and passive euthanasia is thought to be crucial for medical ethics. The idea is that it is permissible, at least in some cases, to withhold treatment and allow a patient to die, but it is never permissible to take any direct action designed to kill the patient. This doctrine seems to be accepted by most doctors, and it was endorsed in a statement adopted by the House of Delegates of the American Medical Association on December 4, 1973:

The intentional termination of the life of one human being by another — mercy killing — is contrary to that for which the medical profession stands and is contrary to the policy of the American Medical Association.

The cessation of the employment of extraordinary means to prolong the life of the body when there is irrefutable evidence that biological death is imminent is the decision of the patient and/or his immediate family. The advice and judg-

Reprinted with permission from *The New England Journal of Medicine*, Vol. 292, No. 2 (January 9, 1975), pp. 78–80.

However, a strong case can be made against this doctrine. In what follows I will set out some of the relevant arguments, and urge doctors to reconsider their views on this matter.

To begin with a familiar type of situation, a patient who is dying of incurable cancer of the throat is in terrible pain, which can no longer be satisfactorily alleviated. He is certain to die within a few days, even if present treatment is continued, but he does not want to go on living for those days since the pain is unbearable. So he asks the doctor for an end to it, and his family joins in the request.

Suppose the doctor agrees to withhold treatment, as the conventional doctrine says he may. The justification for his doing so is that the patient is in terrible agony, and since he is going to die anyway, it would be wrong to prolong his suffering needlessly. But now notice this. If one simply withholds treatment, it may take the patient longer to die, and so he may suffer more than he would if more direct action were taken and a lethal injection given. This fact provides strong reason for thinking that, once the initial decision not to prolong his agony has been made, active euthanasia is actually preferable to passive euthanasia, rather than the reverse. To say otherwise is to endorse the option that leads to more suffering rather than less, and is contrary to the humanitarian impulse that prompts the decision not to prolong his life in the first place.

Part of my point is that the process of being "allowed to die" can be relatively slow and painful, whereas being given a lethal injection is relatively quick and painless. Let me give a different sort of example. In the United States about one in 600 babies is born with Down's syndrome. Most of these babies are otherwise healthy — that is, with only the usual pediatric care, they will proceed to an otherwise normal infancy. Some, however, are born with congenital defects such as intestinal obstructions that require operations if they are to live. Sometimes, the parents and the doctor will decide not to operate, and let the infant die. Anthony Shaw describes what happens then.

> When surgery is denied [the doctor] must try to keep the infant from suffering while natural forces sap the baby's life away. As a surgeon whose natural inclination is to use the scalpel to fight off death, standing by and watching a salvageable baby die is the most emotionally exhausting experience I know. It is easy at a conference, in a theoretical discussion, to decide that such infants should be allowed to die. It is altogether different to stand by in the nursery and watch as dehydration and infection wither a tiny being over hours and days. This is a terrible ordeal for me and the hospital staff — much more so than for the parents who never set foot in the nursery.[1]

I can understand why some people are opposed to all euthanasia, and insist that such infants must be allowed to live. I think I can also understand why other people favor destroying these babies quickly and painlessly. But why should anyone favor letting "dehydration and infection wither a tiny being over hours and days"? The doctrine that says that a baby may be allowed to dehydrate and wither, but may not be given an injection that would end its life without suffering, seems so patently cruel as to require no further refutation. The strong language is not intended to offend, but only to put the point in the clearest possible way.

My second argument is that the conventional doctrine leads to decisions concerning life and death made on irrelevant grounds.

Consider again the case of the infants with Down's syndrome who need operations for congenital defects unrelated to the syndrome to live. Sometimes there is no operation, and the baby dies, but when there is no such defect, the baby lives on. Now, an operation such as that to remove an intestinal obstruction is not prohibitively difficult. The reason why such operations are not performed in these cases is, clearly, that the child has Down's syndrome and the parents and doctor judge that because of that fact it is better for the child to die.

But notice that this situation is absurd, no matter what view one takes of the lives and potentials of such babies. If the life of such an infant is worth preserving, what does it matter if it needs a simple operation? Or, if one thinks it better that such a baby should not live on, what difference does it make that it happens to have an unobstructed intestinal tract? In either case, the matter of life and death is being decided on irrelevant grounds. It is the Down's syndrome, and not the intestines, that is the issue. The matter should be decided, if at all, on that basis, and not be allowed to depend on the essentially irrelevant question of whether the intestinal tract is blocked.

What makes this situation possible, of course, is the idea that when there is an intestinal blockage, one can "let the baby die," but when there is no such defect there is nothing that can be done, for one must not "kill" it. The fact that this idea leads to such results as deciding life or death on irrelevant grounds is another good reason why the doctrine should be rejected.

One reason why so many people think that there is an important moral difference between active and passive euthanasia is that they think killing someone is morally worse than letting someone die. But is it? Is killing, in itself, worse than letting die? To investigate this issue, two cases may be considered that are exactly alike except that one involves killing whereas the other involves letting someone die. Then, it can be asked whether this difference makes any difference to the moral assessments. It is important that the cases be exactly alike, except for this one difference, since otherwise one cannot be confident that it is this difference and not some other that accounts for any variation in the assessments of the two cases. So, let us consider this pair of cases:

In the first, Smith stands to gain a large inheritance if anything should happen to his six-year-old cousin. One evening while the child is taking his bath, Smith sneaks into the bathroom and drowns the child, and then arranges things so that it will look like an accident.

In the second, Jones also stands to gain if anything should happen to his six-year-old cousin. Like Smith, Jones sneaks in planning to drown the child in his bath. However, just as he enters the bathroom Jones sees the child slip and hit his head, and fall face down in the water. Jones is delighted; he stands by, ready to push the child's head back under if it is necessary, but it is not necessary. With only a little thrashing about, the child drowns all by himself, "accidentally," as Jones watches and does nothing.

Now Smith killed the child, whereas Jones "merely" let the child die. That is the only difference between them. Did either man behave better, from a moral point of view? If the difference between killing and letting die were in itself a morally important matter, one should say that Jones's behavior was less reprehensible than Smith's. But does one really want to say that? I think not. In the first place, both men acted from the same motive, personal gain, and both had exactly the same end in view when they acted. It may be inferred from Smith's conduct that he is a bad man, although that judgment may be withdrawn or modified if certain further facts are learned about him—for example, that he is mentally deranged. But would not the very same thing be inferred about Jones from his conduct? And would not

the same further considerations also be relevant to any modification of this judgment? Moreover, suppose Jones pleaded, in his own defense, "After all, I didn't do anything except just stand there and watch the child drown. I didn't kill him; I only let him die." Again, if letting die were in itself less bad than killing, this defense should have at least some weight. But it does not. Such a "defense" can only be regarded as a grotesque perversion of moral reasoning. Morally speaking, it is no defense at all.

Now it may be pointed out, quite properly, that the cases of euthanasia with which doctors are concerned are not like this at all. They do not involve personal gain or the destruction of normal healthy children. Doctors are concerned only with cases in which the patient's life is of no further use to him, or in which the patient's life has become or will soon become a terrible burden. However, the point is the same in these cases: the bare difference between killing and letting die does not, in itself, make a moral difference. If a doctor lets a patient die, for humane reasons, he is in the same moral position as if he had given the patient a lethal injection for humane reasons. If his decision was wrong—if, for example, the patient's illness was in fact curable—the decision would be equally regrettable no matter which method was used to carry it out. And if the doctor's decision was the right one, the method used is not in itself important.

The AMA policy statement isolates the crucial issue very well; the crucial issue is "the intentional termination of the life of one human being by another." But after identifying this issue, and forbidding "mercy killing," the statement goes on to deny that the cessation of treatment is the intentional termination of a life. This is where the mistake comes in, for what is the cessation of treatment, in these circumstances, if it is not "the intentional termination of the life of one human being by another"? Of course it is exactly that, and if it were not, there would be no point to it.

Many people will find this judgment hard to accept. One reason, I think, is that it is very easy to conflate the question of whether killing is, in itself, worse than letting die, with the very different question of whether most actual cases of killing are more reprehensible than most actual cases of letting die. Most actual cases of killing are clearly terrible (think, for example, of all the murders reported in the newspapers), and one hears of such cases every day. On the other hand, one hardly ever hears of a case of letting die, except for the actions of doctors who are motivated by humanitarian reasons.

So one learns to think of killing in a much worse light than of letting die. But this does not mean that there is something about killing that makes it in itself worse than letting die, for it is not the bare difference between killing and letting die that makes the difference in these cases. Rather, the other factors — the murderer's motive of personal gain, for example, contrasted with the doctor's humanitarian motivation — account for different reactions to the different cases.

I have argued that killing is not in itself any worse than letting die; if my contention is right, it follows that active euthanasia is not any worse than passive euthanasia. What arguments can be given on the other side? The most common, I believe, is the following:

"The important difference between active and passive euthanasia is that, in passive euthanasia, the doctor does not do anything to bring about the patient's death. The doctor does nothing, and the patient dies of whatever ills already afflict him. In active euthanasia, however, the doctor does something to bring about the patient's death: he kills him. The doctor who gives the patient with cancer a lethal injection has himself caused his patient's death; whereas if he merely ceases treatment, the cancer is the cause of the death."

A number of points needs to be made here. The first is that it is not exactly correct to say that in passive euthanasia the doctor does nothing, for he does do one thing that is very important: he lets the patient die. "Letting someone die" is certainly different, in some respects, from other types of action — mainly in that it is a kind of action that one may perform by way of not performing certain other actions. For example, one may let a patient die by way of not giving medication, just as one may insult someone by way of not shaking his hand. But for any purpose of moral assessment, it is a type of action nonetheless. The decision to let a patient die is subject to moral appraisal in the same way that a decision to kill him would be subject to moral appraisal: it may be assessed as wise or unwise, compassionate or sadistic, right or wrong. If a doctor deliberately let a patient die who was suffering from a routinely curable illness, the doctor would certainly be to blame for what he had done, just as he would be to blame if he had needlessly killed the patient. Charges against him would then be appropriate. If so, it would be no defense at all for him to insist that he didn't "do anything." He would have done something very serious indeed, for he let his patient die.

Fixing the cause of death may be very important from a legal point of view, for it may determine whether criminal charges are brought against the doctor. But I do not think that this notion can be used to show a moral difference between active and passive euthanasia. The reason why it is considered bad to be the cause of someone's death is that death is regarded as a great evil — and so it is. However, if it has been decided that euthanasia — even passive euthanasia — is desirable in a given case, it has also been decided that in this instance death is no greater an evil than the patient's continued existence. And if this is true, the usual reason for not wanting to be the cause of someone's death simply does not apply.

Finally, doctors may think that all of this is only of academic interest — the sort of thing that philosophers may worry about but that has no practical bearing on their own work. After all, doctors must be concerned about the legal consequences of what they do, and active euthanasia is clearly forbidden by the law. But even so, doctors should also be concerned with the fact that the law is forcing upon them a moral doctrine that may well be indefensible, and has a considerable effect on their practices. Of course, most doctors are not now in the position of being coerced in this matter, for they do not regard themselves as merely going along with what the law requires. Rather, in statements such as the AMA policy statement that I have quoted, they are endorsing this doctrine as a central point of medical ethics. In that statement, active euthanasia is condemned not merely as illegal but as "contrary to that for which the medical profession stands," whereas passive euthanasia is approved. However, the preceding considerations suggest that there is really no moral difference between the two, considered in themselves (there may be important moral differences in some cases in their *consequences,* but, as I pointed out, these differences may make active euthanasia, and not passive euthanasia, the morally preferable option). So, whereas doctors may have to discriminate between active and passive euthanasia to satisfy the law, they should not do any more than that. In particular, they should not give the distinction any added authority and weight by writing it into official statements of medical ethics.

NOTE

1. A. Shaw, "Doctor, Do We Have a Choice?" *The New York Times Magazine,* January 30, 1972, p. 54.

TOM L. BEAUCHAMP AND JAMES F. CHILDRESS

Rachels on Active and Passive Euthanasia

James Rachels contends that killing is not, in itself, worse than letting die; the "bare difference" between acts of killing and acts of letting die is not in itself a morally relevant difference.[1] We agree with Rachels that the acts in his two cases are equally reprehensible because of the agents' motives and actions, and we agree that killing as a type of act is in itself no different *morally* than allowing to die as a type of act. However, we do not accept his conclusion that his examples and arguments show that the distinction between killing and letting die and passive and active euthanasia are morally irrelevant in the formulation of public policy. We also do not agree that his cases demonstrate what he claims.

PROBLEMS IN RACHELS'S ANALYSIS

First, Rachels's cases and the cessations of treatment envisioned by the AMA are markedly disanalogous. In some cases of unjustified acts, including both of Rachels's examples, we are not interested in moral distinctions between killing and letting die (per se). As Richard Trammell points out, some examples have a "masking" or "sledgehammer" effect; the fact that "one cannot distinguish the taste of two wines when both are mixed with green persimmon juice, does not imply that there is no distinction between the wines."[2] Because Rachels's examples involve two morally unjustified acts by agents whose motives and intentions are despicable, it is not surprising that some other features of their situations, such as killing and letting die, are not morally compelling considerations in the circumstances.

Second, Smith and Jones are morally responsible and morally blameworthy for the deaths of their respective cousins, even if Jones, who allowed his cousin to drown, is not causally responsible. The law might find only Smith, who killed his cousin, guilty of homicide (because of the law's theory of proximate cause), but morality condemns both actions alike because of the agents' commissions and omissions. We find Jones's actions reprehensible because he should have rescued the child. Even if he had no other special duties to the child, there is an affirmative obligation of beneficence in such a case.

Third, the point of the range of cases envisioned by the AMA is consistent with Rachels's arguments, though he thinks them inconsistent. The AMA's central claim is that the physician is always morally prohibited from killing patients but is not morally bound to preserve life in all cases. According to the AMA, the physician has a right and perhaps a duty to stop treatment if and only if three conditions are met: (1) the life of the body is being preserved by extraordinary means, (2) there is irrefutable evidence that biological death is imminent, and (3) the patient or the family consents. Whereas Rachels's cases involve two unjustified actions, one of killing and the other of letting die, the AMA statement distinguishes cases of unjustified killing from cases of justified letting die. The AMA statement does not claim that the moral difference is entirely predicated on the distinction between killing and letting die. It also does not imply that the bare difference between (passive) letting die and (active) killing is the major difference or a morally sufficient difference to distinguish the justified from the unjustified cases. The point is only that the justified actions in medicine are confined to letting die (passive euthanasia).

The AMA statement holds that "mercy killing" in medicine is unjustified in all circumstances, but it holds neither that letting die is right in all circumstances nor that killing outside medicine is always wrong. For an act that results in an earlier death for the patient to be justified, it is necessary that it be an act of letting die, but this condition is not sufficient to justify the act; nor is the bare fact of an act's being a killing sufficient to make the act wrong. This AMA declaration is meant to control conduct exclusively in the context of the physician–patient relationship. The rationale for the prohibition is not stated, but the scope of the prohibition is quite clear.

Even if the distinction between killing and letting die is morally irrelevant in many cases, it does not follow that it is morally irrelevant in all contexts. Although we quite agree that Rachels does effectively undermine all attempts to rest moral judgments about ending life on the "bare difference" between killing and letting die, his target may nonetheless be made of straw. Many philosophers and theologians have argued that there are independent moral, religious, and other reasons both for defending the distinction and for prohibiting killing while authorizing allowing to die in some circumstances or based on some motives.

HOW AND WHERE TO DEFEND THE DISTINCTION BETWEEN KILLING AND LETTING DIE

Even if there are sufficient reasons in some cases to warrant mercy killing, there may also be good reasons to retain the distinction between killing and letting die and to maintain our current practices and policies against killing *in medicine,* albeit with some clarifications and modifications.

Acts and Practices. The most important arguments for the distinction between killing and letting die depend on a distinction between acts and practices.[3] It is one thing to justify an act; it is another to justify a general practice. Many beliefs about principles and consequences are applied to rules rather than directly to acts. For example, we might justify a rule of confidentiality because it encourages people to seek therapy and because it promotes respect for persons and their privacy, although such a rule might lead to undesirable results in particular cases where confidentiality should not be maintained.

Likewise, a rule that prohibits "active killing" while permitting some range of "allowed deaths" may be justifiable, even if it excludes some particular acts of killing that in themselves are justifiable. For example, suppose the rule prohibits killing a patient who suffers from terrible pain, who will die within three weeks, and who

rationally asks for a merciful assisted death. In order to maintain a viable practice that expresses our principles and avoids seriously undesirable consequences, it may be necessary to prohibit such acts of killing, even though (viewed in isolation) such acts are morally justified. Thus, although particular *acts* of killing may be humane and compassionate, a *policy* or *practice* that authorizes killing in medicine — in even a few cases — might create a grave risk of harm in many cases and a risk that we find it unjustified to assume.

The prohibition of killing even for "mercy" expresses principles and supports practices that provide a basis of trust between patients and health-care professionals. When we trust these professionals, we expect them to ask our consent and to do us no harm without a prospect of correlative benefit. The prohibition of killing is an attempt to promote a solid basis for trust in the role of caring for patients and protecting them from harm. This prohibition is both instrumentally and symbolically important, and its removal could weaken a set of practices and restraints that we cannot easily replace.

Wedge or Slippery Slope Arguments. This last argument — an incipient wedge or slippery slope argument — is plausible but needs to be stated carefully. Because of the widespread misuses of such arguments in biomedical ethics, there is a tendency to dismiss them whenever they are offered. However, they are defensible in some cases. They force us to consider whether unacceptable harms may result from attractive and apparently innocent first steps. Legitimation of acts such as active voluntary euthanasia run the risk of leading to other acts or practices that are morally objectionable even if some individual acts of this type are acceptable in themselves. The claim made by those who defend these arguments is that accepting the act in question would cross a line that has already been drawn against killing; and once that line has been crossed, it will not be possible to draw it again to preclude unacceptable acts or practices.

However, wedge arguments of some types may not be as damaging as they may seem at first. As Rachels correctly contends, "there obviously are good reasons for objecting to killing patients in order to get away for the weekend — or for even more respectable purposes, such as securing organs for transplantation — which do not apply to killing in order to put the patient out of extreme agony."[4] In other words, the counterreply is that relevant distinctions can be drawn, and we are not subject to uncontrollable implications from general principles. Some versions of the wedge argument therefore do not assist supporters of the distinction between killing and letting die as much as they might suppose.

Indeed, the argument can be used against them: If it is morally defensible to allow patients to die under conditions X, Y, and Z, then it is morally defensible to kill them under those same conditions. If it is in their best interests to die, it is (prima facie) irrelevant how death is brought about. Rachels makes a similar point when he argues that reliance on the distinction between killing and letting die may lead to decisions about life and death made on irrelevant grounds—such as whether the patient will or will not die without certain forms of treatment—instead of being made in terms of the patient's best interests.

In the now famous Johns Hopkins Hospital case, an infant with Down syndrome and duodenal atresia was placed in a back room and died eleven days later of dehydration and starvation. This process of dying, which senior physicians had recommended against, was ex-tremely difficult for all the parties involved, particularly the nurses. If decision makers legitimately determine that a patient would be better off dead (we think the parties mistakenly came to this conclusion in this case), how could an act of killing violate the patient's interests if the patient will not die when artificial treatment is discontinued? A morally irrelevant factor would be allowed to dictate the outcome.

The lack of empirical evidence to determine the adequacy of slippery slope arguments is unfortunate, but it is not a sufficient reason to reject them. Some arguments of this form should be taken with the utmost seriousness. They force us to think carefully about whether unacceptable harm is likely to result from attractive and apparently innocent first steps.

NOTES

1. James Rachels, "Active and Passive Euthanasia," *New England Journal of Medicine* 292 (1975): 78–80.

2. Richard L. Trammell, "Saving Life and Taking Life," *Journal of Philosophy* 72 (1975): 131–37.

3. This distinction and our arguments are indebted to John Rawls, "Two Concepts of Rules," *Philosophical Review* 64 (1955): 3–32.

4. James Rachels, "Medical Ethics and the Rule against Killing: Comments on Professor Hare's Paper," in *Philosophical Medical Ethics*, ed. Spicker and Engelhardt, p. 65.

DAN W. BROCK

Voluntary Active Euthanasia

From "Voluntary Active Euthanasia," *Hastings Center Report* 22, No. 2 (March/April 1992), pp. 10–22 (edited). Reprinted by permission of the publisher.

. . . In the recent bioethics literature some have endorsed physician-assisted suicide but not euthanasia. Are they sufficiently different that the moral arguments for one often do not apply to the other? A paradigm case of physician-assisted suicide is a patient's ending his or her life with a lethal dose of a medication requested of and provided by a physician for that purpose. A paradigm case of voluntary active euthanasia is a physician's administering the lethal dose, often because the patient is unable to do so. The only difference that need exist between the two is the person who actually administers the lethal dose—the physician or the patient. In each, the physician plays an active and necessary causal role.

In physician-assisted suicide the patient acts last (for example, Janet Adkins herself pushed the button after Dr. Kevorkian hooked her up to his suicide machine), whereas in euthanasia the physician acts last by performing the physical equivalent of pushing the button. In both cases, however, the choice rests fully with the patient. In both the patient acts last in the sense of retaining the right to change his or her mind until the point at which the lethal process becomes irreversible. How could there be a substantial moral difference between the two based only on this small difference in the part played by the physician in the causal process resulting in death? Of course, it might be held that the moral difference is clear and important—in euthanasia the physician kills the patient whereas in physician-assisted suicide the patient kills him- or herself. But this is misleading at best. In assisted suicide the physician and patient together kill the patient. To see this, suppose a physician supplied a lethal dose to a patient with the knowledge and intent that the patient will wrongfully administer it to another. We would have no difficulty in morality or the law recognizing this as a case of joint action to kill for which both are responsible.

If there is no significant, intrinsic moral difference between the two, it is also difficult to see why public or legal policy should permit one but not the other; worries about abuse or about giving anyone dominion over the lives of others apply equally to either. As a result, I will take the arguments evaluated below to apply to both and will focus on euthanasia.

My concern here will be with *voluntary* euthanasia only—that is, with the case in which a clearly competent patient makes a fully voluntary and persistent request for aid in dying. Involuntary euthanasia, in which a competent patient explicitly refuses or opposes receiving euthanasia, and nonvoluntary euthanasia, in which a patient is incompetent and unable to express his or her wishes about euthanasia, will be considered here only as potential unwanted side-effects of permitting voluntary euthanasia. I emphasize as well that I am concerned with *active* euthanasia, not withholding or withdrawing life-sustaining treatment, which some commentators characterize as "passive euthanasia." . . .

THE CENTRAL ETHICAL ARGUMENT FOR VOLUNTARY ACTIVE EUTHANASIA

The central ethical argument for euthanasia is familiar. It is that the very same two fundamental ethical values supporting the consensus on patient's rights to decide about life-sustaining treatment also support the ethical permissibility of euthanasia. These values are individual self-determination or autonomy and individual well-being. By self-determination as it bears on euthanasia, I mean people's interest in making important decisions about their lives for themselves according to their own values or conceptions of a good life, and in being left free to act on those decisions. Self-determination is valuable because it permits people to form and live in accordance with their own conception of a good life, at least within the bounds of justice and consistent with others doing so as well. In exercising self-determination people take responsibility for their lives and for the kinds of persons they become. A central aspect of human dignity lies in people's capacity to direct their lives in this way. The value of exercising self-determination presupposes some minimum of decisionmaking capacities or competence, which thus limits the scope of euthanasia supported by self-determination; it cannot justifiably be administered, for example, in cases of serious dementia or treatable clinical depression.

Does the value of individual self-determination extend to the time and manner of one's death? Most people are very concerned about the nature of the last stage of their lives. This reflects not just a fear of experiencing substantial suffering when dying, but also a desire to retain dignity and control during this last period of life. Death is today increasingly preceded by a long period of significant physical and mental decline, due in part to the technological interventions of modern medicine. Many people adjust to these disabilities and find meaning and value in new activities and ways. Others find the impairments and burdens in the last stage of their lives at some point sufficiently great to make life no longer worth living. For many patients near death, maintaining the quality of one's life, avoiding great suffering, maintaining one's dignity, and insuring that others remember us as we wish them to become of paramount importance and outweigh merely extending one's life. But there is no single, objectively correct answer for everyone as to when, if at all, one's life becomes all things considered a burden and unwanted. If self-determination is a fundamental value, then the great variability among people on this question makes it especially important that individuals control the manner, circumstances, and timing of their dying and death.

The other main value that supports euthanasia is individual well-being. It might seem that individual well-being conflicts with a person's self-determination when the person requests euthanasia. Life itself is commonly taken to be a central good for persons, often valued for its own sake, as well as necessary for pursuit of all other goods within a life. But when a competent patient decides to forgo all further life-sustaining treatment then the patient, either explicitly or implicitly, commonly decides that the best life possible for him or her with treatment is of sufficiently poor quality that it is worse than no further life at all. Life is no longer considered a benefit by the patient, but has now become a burden. The same judgment underlies a request for euthanasia: continued life is seen by the patient as no longer a benefit, but now a burden. Especially in the often severely compromised and debilitated states of many critically ill or dying patients, there is no objective standard, but only the competent patient's judgment of whether continued life is no longer a benefit. . . .

Most opponents do not deny that there are some cases in which the values of patient self-determination and well-being support euthanasia. Instead, they commonly offer two kinds of arguments against it that on their view outweigh or override this support. The first kind of argument is that in any individual case where considerations of the patient's self-determination and well-being do support euthanasia, it is nevertheless always ethically wrong or impermissible. The second kind of argument grants that in some individual cases euthanasia may *not* be ethically wrong, but maintains nonetheless that public and legal policy should never permit it. The first kind of argument focuses on features of any individual case of euthanasia, while the second kind focuses on social or legal policy. In the next section I consider the first kind of argument.

EUTHANASIA IS THE DELIBERATE KILLING OF AN INNOCENT PERSON

The claim that any individual instance of euthanasia is a case of deliberate killing of an innocent person is, with only minor qualifications, correct. Unlike forgoing life-sustaining treatment, commonly understood as allowing to die, euthanasia is clearly killing, defined as depriving of life or causing the death of a living being. While providing morphine for pain relief at doses where the risk of respiratory depression and an earlier death may be a foreseen but unintended side effect of treating the patient's pain, in a case of euthanasia the patient's death is deliberate or intended even if in both the physician's ultimate end may be respecting the patient's wishes. If the deliberate killing of an innocent person is wrong, euthanasia would be nearly always impermissible.

In the context of medicine, the ethical prohibition against deliberately killing the innocent derives some of its plausibility from the belief that nothing in the currently accepted practice of medicine is deliberate killing. Thus, in commenting on the "It's Over, Debbie" case, four prominent physicians and bioethicists could entitle their paper "Doctors Must Not Kill."[1] The belief that doctors do not in fact kill requires the corollary belief that forgoing life-sustaining treatment, whether by not starting or by stopping treatment, is allowing to die, not killing. Common though this view is, I shall argue that it is confused and mistaken.

Why is the common view mistaken? Consider the case of a patient terminally ill with ALS disease. She is completely respirator dependent with no hope of ever being weaned. She is unquestionably competent but finds her condition intolerable and persistently requests to be removed from the respirator and allowed to die. Most people and physicians would agree that the patient's physician should respect the patient's wishes and remove her from the respirator, though this will certainly cause the patient's death. The common understanding is that the physician thereby allows the patient to die. But is that correct?

Suppose the patient has a greedy and hostile son who mistakenly believes that his mother will never decide to stop her life-sustaining treatment and that even if she did her physician would not remove her from the respirator. Afraid that his inheritance will be dissipated by a long and expensive hospitalization, he enters his mother's room while she is sedated, extubates her, and she dies. Shortly thereafter the medical staff discovers what he has done and confronts the son. He replies, "I didn't kill her, I merely allowed her to die. It was her ALS disease that caused her death." I think this would rightly be dismissed as transparent sophistry—the son went into his mother's room and deliberately killed her. But, of course, the son performed just the same physical actions, did just the same thing, that the physician would have done. If that is so, then doesn't the physician also kill the patient when he extubates her? . . .

I have argued elsewhere that this alternative account is deeply problematic, in part because it commits us to accepting that what the greedy son does is to allow to die, not kill. Here, I want to note two other reasons why the conclusion that stopping life support is killing is resisted.

The first reason is that killing is often understood, especially within medicine, as unjustified causing of death; in medicine it is thought to be done only accidentally or negligently. It is also increasingly widely accepted that a physician is ethically justified in stopping life support in a case like that of the ALS patient. But if these two beliefs are correct, then what the physician does cannot be killing, and so must be allowing to die. Killing patients is not, to put it flippantly, understood to be part of physicians' job description. What is mistaken in this line of reasoning is the assumption that all killings are *unjustified* causings of death. Instead, some killings are ethically justified, including many instances of stopping life support.

Another reason for resisting the conclusion that stopping life support is often killing is that it is psychologically uncomfortable. Suppose the physician had stopped the ALS patient's respirator and had made the son's claim, "I didn't kill her, I merely allowed her to die. It was her ALS disease that caused her death." The clue to the psychological role here is how naturally the "merely" modifies "allowed her to die." The characterization as allowing to die is meant to shift felt responsibility away from the agent—the physician—and to the lethal disease process. Other language common in death and dying contexts plays a similar role; "letting nature take its course" or "stopping prolonging the dying process" both seem to shift responsibility from the physician who stops life support to the fatal disease process. However psychologically helpful these conceptualizations may be in making the difficult responsibility of a physician's role in the patient's death bearable, they nevertheless are confusions. Both physicians and family members can instead be helped to understand that it is the patient's decision and consent to stopping treatment that limits their responsibility for the patient's death and that shifts that responsibility to the patient. . . .

Suppose both my arguments are mistaken. Suppose that killing is worse than allowing to die and that withdrawing life support is not killing, although euthanasia is. Euthanasia still need not for that reason be morally wrong. To see this, we need to determine the basic principle for the moral evaluation of killing persons. What is it that makes paradigm cases of wrongful killing wrongful? One very plausible answer is that killing denies the victim something that he or she values greatly—continued life or a future. Moreover, since continued life is necessary for pursuing any of a person's plans and purposes, killing brings the frustration of all of these plans and desires as well. In a nutshell, wrongful killing deprives a person of a valued future, and of all the person wanted and planned to do in that future.

A natural expression of this account of the wrongness of killing is that people have a moral right not to be killed. But in this account of the wrongness of killing, the right not to be killed, like other rights, should be waivable when the person makes a competent decision that continued life is no longer wanted or a good, but is instead worse than no further life at all. In this view, euthanasia is properly understood as a case of a person having waived his or her right not to be killed.

This rights view of the wrongness of killing is not, of course, universally shared. Many people's moral views about killing have their origins in religious views that human life comes from God and cannot be justifiably destroyed or taken away, either by the person whose life it is or by another. But in a pluralistic society like our own with a strong commitment to freedom of religion, public policy should not be grounded in religious beliefs which many in that society reject. I turn now to the general evaluation of public policy on euthanasia.

WOULD THE BAD CONSEQUENCES OF EUTHANASIA OUTWEIGH THE GOOD?

The argument against euthanasia at the policy level is stronger than at the level of individual cases, though even here I believe the case is ultimately unpersuasive, or at best indecisive. The policy level is the place where the main issues lie, however, and where moral considerations that might override arguments in favor of euthanasia will be found, if they are found anywhere. It is important to note two kinds of disagreement about the consequences for public policy of permitting euthanasia. First, there is empirical or factual disagreement about what the consequences would be. This disagreement is greatly exacerbated by the lack of firm data on the issue. Second, since on any reasonable assessment there would be both good and bad consequences, there are moral disagreements about the relative importance of different effects. In addition to these two sources of disagreement, there is also no single, well-specified policy proposal for legalizing euthanasia on which policy assessments can focus. But without such specification, and especially without explicit procedures for protecting against well-intentioned misuse and ill-intentioned abuse, the consequences for policy are largely speculative. Despite these difficulties, a preliminary account of the main likely good and bad consequences is possible. This should help clarify where better data or more moral analysis and argument are needed, as well as where policy safeguards must be developed.

POTENTIAL GOOD CONSEQUENCES
OF PERMITTING EUTHANASIA

What are the likely good consequences? First, if euthanasia were permitted it would be possible to respect the self-determination of competent patients who want it, but now cannot get it because of its illegality. . . .

One important factor substantially affecting the number of persons who would seek euthanasia is the extent to which an alternative is available. The widespread acceptance in the law, social policy, and medical practice of the right of a competent patient to forgo life-sustaining treatment suggests that the number of competent persons in the United States who would want euthanasia if it were permitted is probably relatively small.

A second good consequence of making euthanasia legally permissible benefits a much larger group. Polls have shown that a majority of the American public believes that people should have a right to obtain euthanasia if they want it.[2] No doubt the vast majority of those who support this right to euthanasia will never in fact come to want euthanasia for themselves. Nevertheless, making it legally permissible would reassure many people that if they ever do want euthanasia they would be able to obtain it. This reassurance would supplement the broader control over the process of dying given by the right to decide about life-sustaining treatment. . . .

A third good consequence of the legalization of euthanasia concerns patients whose dying is filled with severe and unrelievable pain or suffering. When there is a life-sustaining treatment that, if forgone, will lead relatively quickly to death, then doing so can bring an end to these patients' suffering without recourse to euthanasia. For patients receiving no such treatment, however, euthanasia may be the only release from their otherwise prolonged suffering and agony. This argument from mercy has always been the strongest argument for euthanasia in those cases to which it applies.[3]

The importance of relieving pain and suffering is less controversial than is the frequency with which patients are forced to undergo untreatable agony that only euthanasia could relieve. If we focus first on suffering caused by physical pain, it is crucial to distinguish pain that *could* be adequately relieved with modern methods of pain control, though it in fact is not, from pain that is relievable only by death.[4] For a variety of reasons, including some physicians' fear of hastening the patient's death, as well as the lack of a publicly accessible means for assessing the amount of the patient's pain, many patients suffer pain that could be, but is not, relieved.

Specialists in pain control, as for example the pain of terminally ill cancer patients, argue that there are very few patients whose pain could not be adequately controlled, though sometimes at the cost of so sedating them that they are effectively unable to interact with other people or their environment. Thus, the argument from mercy in cases of physical pain can probably be met in a large majority of cases by providing adequate measures of pain relief. This should be a high priority, whatever our legal policy on euthanasia — the relief of pain and suffering has long been, quite properly, one of the central goals of medicine. Those cases in which pain could be effectively relieved, but in fact is not, should only count significantly in favor of legalizing euthanasia if all reasonable efforts to change pain management techniques have been tried and have failed.

Dying patients often undergo substantial psychological suffering that is not fully or even principally the result of physical pain.[5] The knowledge about how to relieve this suffering is much more limited than in the case of relieving pain, and efforts to do so are probably more often unsuccessful. If the argument from mercy is extended to patients experiencing great and unrelievable psychological suffering, the numbers of patients to which it applies are much greater.

One last good consequence of legalizing euthanasia is that once death has been accepted, it is often more humane to end life quickly and peacefully, when that is what the patient wants. Such a death will often be seen as better than a more prolonged one. People who suffer a sudden and unexpected death, for example by dying quickly or in their sleep from a heart attack or stroke, are often considered lucky to have died in this way. We care about how we die in part because we care about how others remember us, and we hope they will remember us as we were in "good times" with them and not as we might be when disease has robbed us of our dignity as human beings. . . .

POTENTIAL BAD CONSEQUENCES
OF PERMITTING EUTHANASIA

Some of the arguments against permitting euthanasia are aimed specifically against physicians, while others are aimed against anyone being permitted to perform it. I shall first consider one argument of the former sort. Permitting physicians to perform euthanasia, it is said, would be incompatible with their fundamental moral and professional commitment as healers to care for patients and to protect life. Moreover, if euthanasia by physicians became common, patients would come to fear that a medication was intended not to treat or care, but instead to kill, and would thus lose trust in their physicians. This position was forcefully stated in a paper by Willard Gaylin and his colleagues:

> The very soul of medicine is on trial . . . This issue touches medicine at its moral center; if this moral center collapses, if physicians become killers or are even licensed to kill, the profession—and, therewith, each physician—will never again be worthy of trust and respect as healer and comforter and protector of life in all its frailty.

These authors go on to make clear that, while they oppose permitting anyone to perform euthanasia, their special concern is with physicians doing so:

> We call on fellow physicians to say that they will not deliberately kill. We must also say to each of our fellow physicians that we will not tolerate killing of patients and that we shall take disciplinary action against doctors who kill. And we must say to the broader community that if it insists on tolerating or legalizing active euthanasia, it will have to find nonphysicians to do its killing.[6]

If permitting physicians to kill would undermine the very "moral center" of medicine, then almost certainly physicians should not be permitted to perform euthanasia. But how persuasive is this claim? Patients should not fear, as a consequence of permitting *voluntary* active euthanasia, that their physicians will substitute a lethal injection for what patients want and believe is part of their care. If active euthanasia is restricted to cases in which it is truly voluntary, then no patient should fear getting it unless she or he has voluntarily requested it. (The fear that we might in time also come to accept nonvoluntary, or even involuntary, active euthanasia is a slippery slope worry I address below.) Patients' trust of their physicians could be increased, not eroded, by knowledge that physicians will provide aid in dying when patients seek it. . . .

A second bad consequence that some foresee is that permitting euthanasia would weaken society's commitment to provide optimal care for dying patients. We live at a time in which the control of health care costs has become, and is likely to continue to be, the domi-

nant focus of health care policy. If euthanasia is seen as a cheaper alternative to adequate care and treatment, then we might become less scrupulous about providing sometimes costly support and other services to dying patients. Particularly if our society comes to embrace deeper and more explicit rationing of health care, frail, elderly, and dying patients will need to be strong and effective advocates for their own health care and other needs, although they are hardly in a position to do this. We should do nothing to weaken their ability to obtain adequate care and services.

This second worry is difficult to assess because there is little firm evidence about the likelihood of the feared erosion in the care of dying patients. There are at least two reasons, however, for skepticism about this argument. The first is that the same worry could have been directed at recognizing patients' or surrogates' rights to forgo life-sustaining treatment, yet there is no persuasive evidence that recognizing the right to refuse treatment has caused a serious erosion in the quality of care of dying patients. The second reason for skepticism about this worry is that only a very small proportion of deaths would occur from euthanasia if it were permitted. In the Netherlands, where euthanasia under specified circumstances is permitted by the courts, though not authorized by statute, the best estimate of the proportion of overall deaths that result from it is about 2 percent.[7] Thus, the vast majority of critically ill and dying patients will not request it, and so will still have to be cared for by physicians, families, and others. Permitting euthanasia should not diminish people's commitment and concern to maintain and improve the care of these patients.

A third possible bad consequence of permitting euthanasia (or even a public discourse in which strong support for euthanasia is evident) is to threaten the progress made in securing the rights of patients or their surrogates to decide about and to refuse life-sustaining treatment.[8] This progress has been made against the backdrop of a clear and firm legal prohibition of euthanasia, which has provided a relatively bright line limiting the dominion of others over patients' lives. It has therefore been an important reassurance to concerns about how the authority to take steps ending life might be misused, abused, or wrongly extended.

Many supporters of the right of patients or their surrogates to refuse treatment strongly oppose euthanasia, and if forced to choose might well withdraw their support of the right to refuse treatment rather than accept euthanasia. Public policy in the last fifteen years has generally let life-sustaining treatment decisions be made in health care settings between physicians and patients or their surrogates, and without the involvement of the courts. However, if euthanasia is made legally permissible greater involvement of the courts is likely, which could in turn extend to a greater court involvement in life-sustaining treatment decisions. Most agree, however, that increased involvement of the courts in these decisions would be undesirable, as it would make sound decisionmaking more cumbersome and difficult without sufficient compensating benefits.

As with the second potential bad consequence of permitting euthanasia, this third consideration too is speculative and difficult to assess. The feared erosion of patients' or surrogates' rights to decide about life-sustaining treatment, together with greater court involvement in those decisions, are both possible. However, I believe there is reason to discount this general worry. The legal rights of competent patients and, to a lesser degree, surrogates of incompetent patients to decide about treatment are very firmly embedded in a long line of informed consent and life-sustaining treatment cases, and are not likely to be eroded by a debate over, or even acceptance of, euthanasia. It will not be accepted without safeguards that reassure the public about abuse, and if that debate shows the need for similar safeguards for some life-sustaining treatment decisions they should be adopted there as well. In neither case are the only possible safeguards greater court involvement, as the recent growth of institutional ethics committees shows.

The fourth potential bad consequence of permitting euthanasia has been developed by David Velleman and turns on the subtle point that making a new option or choice available to people can sometimes make them worse off, even if once they have the choice they go on to choose what is best for them.[9] Ordinarily, people's continued existence is viewed by them as given, a fixed condition with which they must cope. Making euthanasia available to people as an option denies them the alternative of staying alive by default. If people are offered the option of euthanasia, their continued existence is now a choice for which they can be held responsible and which they can be asked by others to justify. We care, and are right to care, about being able to justify ourselves to others. To the extent that our society is unsympathetic to justifying a severely depen-

dent or impaired existence, a heavy psychological burden of proof may be placed on patients who think their terminal illness or chronic infirmity is not a sufficient reason for dying. Even if they otherwise view their life as worth living, the opinion of others around them that it is not can threaten their reason for living and make euthanasia a rational choice. Thus the existence of the option becomes a subtle pressure to request it.

This argument correctly identifies the reason why offering some patients the option of euthanasia would not benefit them. Velleman takes it not as a reason for opposing all euthanasia, but for restricting it to circumstances where there are "unmistakable and overpowering reasons for persons to want the option of euthanasia," and for denying the option in all other cases. But there are at least three reasons why such restriction may not be warranted. First, polls and other evidence support that most Americans believe euthanasia should be permitted (though the recent defeat of the referendum to permit it in the state of Washington raises some doubt about this support). Thus, many more people seem to want the choice than would be made worse off by getting it. Second, if giving people the option of ending their life really makes them worse off, then we should not only prohibit euthanasia, but also take back from people the right they now have to decide about life-sustaining treatment. The feared harmful effect should already have occurred from securing people's right to refuse life-sustaining treatment, yet there is no evidence of any such widespread harm or any broad public desire to rescind that right. Third, since there is a wide range of conditions in which reasonable people can and do disagree about whether they would want continued life, it is not possible to restrict the permissibility of euthanasia as narrowly as Velleman suggests without thereby denying it to most persons who would want it; to permit it only in cases in which virtually everyone would want it would be to deny it to most who would want it.

A fifth potential bad consequence of making euthanasia legally permissible is that it might weaken the general legal prohibition of homicide. This prohibition is so fundamental to civilized society, it is argued, that we should do nothing that erodes it. If most cases of stopping life support are killing, as I have already argued, then the court cases permitting such killing have already in effect weakened this prohibition. However, neither the courts nor most people have seen these cases as killing and so as challenging the prohibition of homicide. The courts have usually grounded patients' or their surrogates' rights to refuse life-sustaining treatment in rights to privacy, liberty, self-determination, or bodily integrity, not in exceptions to homicide laws.

Legal permission for physicians or others to perform euthanasia could not be grounded in patients' rights to decide about medical treatment. Permitting euthanasia would require qualifying, at least in effect, the legal prohibition against homicide, a prohibition that in general does not allow the consent of the victim to justify or excuse the act. Nevertheless, the very same fundamental basis of the right to decide about life-sustaining treatment—respecting a person's self-determination—does support euthanasia as well. Individual self-determination has long been a well-entrenched and fundamental value in the law, and so extending it to euthanasia would not require appeal to novel legal values or principles. That suicide or attempted suicide is no longer a criminal offense in virtually all states indicates an acceptance of individual self-determination in the taking of one's own life analogous to that required for voluntary active euthanasia. The legal prohibition (in most states) of assisting in suicide and the refusal in the law to accept the consent of the victim as a possible justification of homicide are both arguably a result of difficulties in the legal process of establishing the consent of the victim after the fact. If procedures can be designed that clearly establish the voluntariness of the person's request for euthanasia, it would under those procedures represent a carefully circumscribed qualification on the legal prohibition of homicide. Nevertheless, some remaining worries about this weakening can be captured in the final potential bad consequence, to which I will now turn.

This final potential bad consequence is the central concern of many opponents of euthanasia and, I believe, is the most serious objection to a legal policy permitting it. According to this "slippery slope" worry, although active euthanasia may be morally permissible in cases in which it is unequivocally voluntary and the patient finds his or her condition unbearable, a legal policy permitting euthanasia would inevitably lead to active euthanasia being performed in many other cases in which it would be morally wrong. To prevent those other wrongful cases of euthanasia we should not permit even morally justified performance of it.

Slippery slope arguments of this form are problematic and difficult to evaluate.[10] From one perspective, they are the last refuge of conservative defenders of the status quo. When all the opponent's objections to the wrongness of euthanasia itself have been met, the opponent then shifts ground and acknowledges both that it is not in itself wrong and that a legal policy which resulted only in its being performed would not be bad. Nevertheless, the opponent maintains, it should still not be permitted because doing so would result in its being performed in other cases in which it is not voluntary and would be wrong. In this argument's most extreme form, permitting euthanasia is the first and fateful step down the slippery slope to Nazism. Once on the slope we will be unable to get off.

Now it cannot be denied that it is *possible* that permitting euthanasia could have these fateful consequences, but that cannot be enough to warrant prohibiting it if it is otherwise justified. A similar *possible* slippery slope worry could have been raised to securing competent patients' rights to decide about life support, but recent history shows such a worry would have been unfounded. It must be relevant how likely it is that we will end with horrendous consequences and an unjustified practice of euthanasia. How *likely* and *widespread* would the abuses and unwarranted extensions of permitting it be? By abuses, I mean the performance of euthanasia that fails to satisfy the conditions required for voluntary active euthanasia, for example, if the patient has been subtly pressured to accept it. By unwarranted extensions of policy, I mean later changes in legal policy to permit not just voluntary euthanasia, but also euthanasia in cases in which, for example, it need not be fully voluntary. Opponents of voluntary euthanasia on slippery slope grounds have not provided the data or evidence necessary to turn their speculative concerns into well-grounded likelihoods.

It is at least clear, however, that both the character and likelihood of abuses of a legal policy permitting euthanasia depend in significant part on the procedures put in place to protect against them. I will not try to detail fully what such procedures might be, but will just give some examples of what they might include:

1. The patient should be provided with all relevant information about his or her medical condition, current prognosis, available alternative treatments, and the prognosis of each.
2. Procedures should ensure that the patient's request for euthanasia is stable or enduring (a brief waiting period could be required) and fully voluntary (an advocate for the patient might be appointed to ensure this).

3. All reasonable alternatives must have been explored for improving the patient's quality of life and relieving any pain or suffering.
4. A psychiatric evaluation should ensure that the patient's request is not the result of a treatable psychological impairment such as depression.[11]

These examples of procedural safeguards are all designed to ensure that the patient's choice is fully informed, voluntary, and competent, and so a true exercise of self-determination. Other proposals for euthanasia would restrict its permissibility further—for example, to the terminally ill—a restriction that cannot be supported by self-determination. Such additional restrictions might, however, be justified by concern for limiting potential harms from abuse. At the same time, it is important not to impose procedural or substantive safeguards so restrictive as to make euthanasia impermissible or practically infeasible in a wide range of justified cases.

These examples of procedural safeguards make clear that it is possible to substantially reduce, though not to eliminate, the potential for abuse of a policy permitting voluntary active euthanasia. Any legalization of the practice should be accompanied by a well-considered set of procedural safeguards together with an ongoing evaluation of its use. Introducing euthanasia into only a few states could be a form of carefully limited and controlled social experiment that would give us evidence about the benefits and harms of the practice. Even then firm and uncontroversial data may remain elusive, as the continuing controversy over what has taken place in the Netherlands in recent years indicates.[12]

THE SLIP INTO NONVOLUNTARY ACTIVE EUTHANASIA

While I believe slippery slope worries can largely be limited by making necessary distinctions both in principle and in practice, one slippery slope concern is legitimate. There is reason to expect that legalization of voluntary active euthanasia might soon be followed by strong pressure to legalize some nonvoluntary euthanasia of incompetent patients unable to express their own wishes. Respecting a person's self-determination and recognizing that continued life is not always of value to a person can support not only voluntary active euthanasia, but some nonvoluntary euthanasia as well. These are the same values that ground competent pa-

tients' right to refuse life-sustaining treatment. Recent history here is instructive. In the medical ethics literature, in the courts since Quinlan, and in norms of medical practice, that right has been extended to incompetent patients and exercised by a surrogate who is to decide as the patient would have decided in the circumstances if competent.[13] It has been held unreasonable to continue life-sustaining treatment that the patient would not have wanted just because the patient now lacks the capacity to tell us that. Life-sustaining treatment for incompetent patients is today frequently forgone on the basis of a surrogate's decision, or less frequently on the basis of an advance directive executed by the patient while still competent. The very same logic that has extended the right to refuse life-sustaining treatment from a competent patient to the surrogate of an incompetent patient (acting with or without a formal advance directive from the patient) may well extend the scope of active euthanasia. The argument will be, Why continue to force unwanted life on patients just because they have now lost the capacity to request euthanasia from us? . . .

Even if voluntary active euthanasia should slip into nonvoluntary active euthanasia, with surrogates acting for incompetent patients, the ethical evaluation is more complex than many opponents of euthanasia allow. Just as in the case of surrogates' decisions to forgo life-sustaining treatment for incompetent patients, so also surrogates' decisions to request euthanasia for incompetent persons would often accurately reflect what the incompetent person would have wanted and would deny the person nothing that he or she would have considered worth having. Making nonvoluntary active euthanasia legally permissible, however, would greatly enlarge the number of patients on whom it might be performed and substantially enlarge the potential for misuse and abuse. As noted above, frail and debilitated elderly people, often demented or otherwise incompetent and thereby unable to defend and assert their own interests, may be especially vulnerable to unwanted euthanasia.

For some people, this risk is more than sufficient reason to oppose the legalization of voluntary euthanasia. But while we should in general be cautious about inferring much from the experience in the Netherlands to what our own experience in the United States might be, there may be one important lesson that we can learn from them. One commentator has noted that in the Netherlands families of incompetent patients have less authority than do families in the United States to act as surrogates for incompetent patients in making decisions to forgo life-sustaining treatment.[14] From the Dutch perspective, it may be we in the United States who are *already* on the slippery slope in having given surrogates broad authority to forgo life-sustaining treatment for incompetent persons. In this view, the more important moral divide, and the more important with regard to potential for abuse, is not between forgoing life-sustaining treatment and euthanasia, but instead between voluntary and nonvoluntary performance of either. If this is correct, then the more important issue is ensuring the appropriate principles and procedural safeguards for the exercise of decisionmaking authority by surrogates for incompetent persons in *all* decisions at the end of life. This may be the correct response to slippery slope worries about euthanasia. . . .

NOTES

1. Willard Gaylin, Leon R. Kass, Edmund D. Pellegrino, and Mark Siegler, "Doctors Must Not Kill," *JAMA* 259 (1988): 2139–40.

2. P. Painton and E. Taylor, "Love or Let Die," *Time,* 19 March 1990, pp. 62–71; *Boston Globe*/Harvard University Poll, *Boston Globe,* 3 November 1991.

3. James Rachels, *The End of Life* (Oxford: Oxford University Press, 1986).

4. Marcia Angell, "The Quality of Mercy," *NEJM* 306 (1982): 98–99; M. Donovan, P. Dillon, and L. Mcguire, "Incidence and Characteristics of Pain in a Sample of Medical-Surgical Inpatients," *Pain* 30 (1987): 69–78.

5. Eric Cassell, *The Nature of Suffering and the Goals of Medicine* (New York: Oxford University Press, 1991).

6. Gaylin et al., "Doctors Must Not Kill."

7. Paul J. Van der Maas et al., "Euthanasia and Other Medical Decisions Concerning the End of Life," *Lancet* 338 (1991): 669–674.

8. Susan M. Wolf, "Holding the Line on Euthanasia," Special Supplement, *Hastings Center Report* 19, no. 1 (1989): 13–15.

9. My formulation of this argument derives from David Velleman's statement of it in his commentary on an earlier version of this paper delivered at the American Philosophical Association Central Division meetings; a similar point was made to me by Elisha Milgram in discussion on another occasion.

10. Frederick Schauer, "Slippery Slopes," *Harvard Law Review* 99 (1985): 361–83; Wibren van der Burg, "The Slippery Slope Argument," *Ethics* 102 (October 1991): 42–65.

11. There is evidence that physicians commonly fail to diagnose depression. See Robert I. Misbin, "Physicians Aid in Dying," *NEJM* 325 (1991): 1304–7.

12. Richard Fenigsen, "A Case against Dutch Euthanasia," Special Supplement, *Hastings Center Report* 19, no. 1 (1989): 22–30.

13. Allen E. Buchanan and Dan W. Brock, *Deciding for Others: The Ethics of Surrogate Decisionmaking* (Cambridge: Cambridge University Press, 1989).

14. Margaret P. Battin, "Seven Caveats Concerning the Discussion of Euthanasia in Holland," *American Philosophical Association Newsletter on Philosophy and Medicine* 89, no. 2 (1990).

DAVID C. THOMASMA

When Physicians Choose to Participate in the Death of Their Patients

Physicians have long aided their patients in dying in an effort to ease human suffering. It is only in the nineteenth and twentieth centuries that the prolongation of life has taken on new meaning due to the powers now available to physicians, through new drugs and high technology interventions. Whereas earlier physicians and patients could readily acknowledge that nothing further could be done, today that judgment is problematic.

From the *Journal of Law, Medicine & Ethics,* 24 (1996): 183–97. Reprinted with the permission of the American Society of Law, Medicine & Ethics and the author.

Most often, aiding the dying took the form of not doing anything further to prolong life. Morally, this act of restraint was not difficult, because few options could have been considered. However, some physicians, rarely, would help patients die either by hastening death directly or by increasing pain control with the risk of hastening death, the so-called double effect. When directly hastening death, physicians either directly caused the death of the patient through euthanasia, or supplied the means to the patients to bring about death with or without encouragement to use these means. The latter is physician-assisted suicide (PAS). . . .

ETHICAL ANALYSIS

Public debate about PAS too often focuses on the strategic questions, and less so on the ethical issues. Before rushing to legalize PAS, we must understand more fully the implications of such a broad social policy as it would affect those who suffer, both the patients and the families.

AUTONOMY AND CONTROL OF ONE'S LIFE

The first ethical question about PAS has nothing to do with the physician, but with the patient. Can and should individuals have control over their own lives to such an extent that suicide be morally permitted? At one time, suicide was proscribed by all U.S. states. The origin of this proscription was religious and secular. The religious basis of the laws against suicide arose from the belief that life is a gift of God, and that only God can take it back. Persons who committed suicide were buried at crossroads, not in church cemeteries. This represented a widespread superstition that persons who committed suicide were "troubled," and that if the devil were passing over the grave site to claim that troubled soul, he would see the cross in the crossroads and leave the person alone. The secular basis of a proscription against suicide in Anglo-Saxon law seems to have arisen from England's chronic underpopulation. To commit suicide, then, was to deprive the king of an able-bodied person to fight the wars.

These reasons no longer carry the same weight. The motives and circumstances surrounding suicide are sufficiently understood that persons who do commit suicide are given religious burials, and that the laws against suicide have been repealed. Nonetheless, some moral opprobrium, and its attendant embarrassment for the family, still exists about the practice. Attempted suicide is still viewed as caused by depression or a mental disorder, and our interventionist efforts are oriented to helping such people. Erring on the side of life stems from ancient beliefs that life is sacred. Jean-Marie Meyer notes:

[F]rom the very early years of mankind, life and death have been understood, experienced or celebrated in funeral rites as instruments by which to come into contact with God or the gods. This contact has been seen by social communi-

ties as a process which transforms human realities and endows them with something which is divine and sacred.[1]

Once the religious conviction about the source of life and death is eroded, we are left with the view, articulated by Tristam Engelhardt, that the individual controls his/her own life, and that one's primary ethical duty is to respect self-determination.[2] Most often, religious convictions lead to opposition to PAS and euthanasia because of a different conception of human nature.[3] The secular, autonomy-based view of human life, however, places the burden of continued existence squarely on the shoulders of the individual.

Although people commit suicide for different reasons, debilitating and chronic illnesses increasingly lead many to choose to end their lives. (This is usually done in the context of care—in a nursing home or by a member of a family who supports the individual. When this happens, care givers may think that they were responsible, because their care obviously was judged insufficient to surmount the growing depression of their loved one or patient. This is not usually true.)

The individual who makes a rational judgment that his/her life is no longer worth living may do so out of fear of the physical or financial burdens of illness or of social rejection. In his eighties, increasingly upset over his growing incapacities and public criticism of his work with autistic children (especially claims that he had been abusive), Bruno Bettelheim asphyxiated himself by tying a plastic bag over his head. For some, this would represent a failure of the proper care. For others, it represents the triumph of the human spirit over terrible circumstances. . . .

MERCY

When a physician chooses to help a patient die, he/she does so from a profound commitment to compassion, care, and humility. Although pain can be controlled (though frequently it is not), suffering cannot. It cannot be removed entirely, but it can be assuaged by suffering with patients, and not abandoning them. A strong criticism by the Dutch of the American opponents of PAS is that they would, instead of offering assistance, abandon patients at the end of life. Indeed, proponents of PAS and euthanasia argue that attending to patients at this critical time is a special virtue of the modern physician.

The mercy argument is used by both opponents and proponents of PAS. Opponents argue that authentic mercy is compassion for the patient amid suffering that cannot and perhaps should not be entirely removed. On the other hand, Margaret Battin has constructed an argument in favor of PAS and euthanasia from the standpoint of mercy. She claims that care givers have two duties to the dying: not to prolong suffering any further, and to act to end pain and suffering already occurring.[4] In her view, a commitment to care leads physicians to employ the technology and interventions available, to try to eliminate pain and to assuage the suffering of dying. For Battin, choosing to participate in the death of patients is a major demonstration that the physician cares.

One survey suggests that one in ten primary care physicians has taken actions that directly cause a patient's death. It is not clear whether such actions occurred while increasing pain control (the double effect).[5] Most ethicists and physicians would agree that the intention of such an act is to treat the patient's pain and suffering, to reduce it no matter what the consequences. Such an intention is moral and ethical.

Yet surveys surprisingly reveal that physicians, were laws to change, would prefer euthanasia to PAS. Why this is so is unclear—perhaps because PAS is less direct, less "honest," than direct euthanasia, perhaps because shared decision making in PAS is too messy and threatening. Along the same lines, Alexander Capron is concerned that PAS may more readily lead to abuse than euthanasia, even if legalized and regulated, because the physician is more emotionally distant and physically removed from the patient who takes the overdose of drugs.[6]

PAS AND THE DOCTOR–PATIENT RELATIONSHIP

The most important feature of the American bioethics debate today is the growing awareness of the inadequacy of the autonomy assumption, especially as these bioethicists encounter their international colleagues. The doctor–patient relationship has been dominated by the Hippocratic ethic, which stresses the knowledge of the physician and frank paternalism in relation to the patient. In fact, Hippocratism explicitly ruled out abortion, euthanasia, and PAS at a time when such actions were quite popular among other schools of physicians in ancient Greece. The Hippocratic Oath then should be seen as an effort by reform-minded physicians, a revolutionary minority, to determine how medicine should be properly practiced. As Nigel Cameron argues, Hippocratic medicine rejected pre-Hippocratic ethics based on relief-of-suffering ethic and replaced it with a sanctity-of-life ethic.[7]

Physicians today understand their role as a balance between relief of suffering and nonharm. This is clear in a report on a meeting between Dr. Kevorkian and a committee of the Michigan State Medical Society.[8] Kevorkian's ideas received little credence from the assembled physicians, including his notion that, because certain procedures for assisting in dying are clearly medical, and because they have been performed for centuries by people in power, they can be considered ethical. Yet Howard Brody, who chaired that committee, said that Kevorkian "impressed many people in the room by his presentation."[9] Absolutization of the patient's autonomy is a subject of growing tension. Concerns about libertarian assumptions implied by this emphasis have led many thinkers to counter autonomy with the need for beneficence and for the balance provided by the four-principled approach of Tom Beauchamp and James Childress.[10]

Serious concern arises about the impact on the community when physicians get involved in voluntary active euthanasia.[11] Kass articulates what is owed to a dying patient by the physician. He argues that humanity is owed humanity, not just "humaneness" (that is, being merciful by killing the patient). He argues that the very reason we are compelled to put animals out of their misery is that they are *not* human; thus they require from us some measure of humaneness. By contrast, human beings demand humanity itself. This thesis, in turn, rests on the relationship between the healer and the ill as constituted, essentially, "even if only tacitly, [on] the desire of both to promote the wholeness of the one who is ailing."[12]

Studies have shown that physicians do not evaluate whether a patient is dying solely on the basis of biomedical data. They also take into account the important features of human interaction, and the dynamic between therapeutically available interventions and the possible outcome.[13] Such interactive concerns tend to present counterpressures to straightforward honoring of patient wishes with respect to euthanasia requests. Needless to say, fears about litigation also contribute to reluctance to honor patient requests, even for pain medication.

The temptation to employ technology rather than to give of oneself in the process of healing is a "technological fix." The fix is much easier to conceptualize and implement than truly human engagement. The training and skills of modern health professionals overwhelmingly foster use of technological fixes. . . .

VULNERABLE POPULATIONS

Many opponents of PAS are concerned that the vulnerable populations, the debilitated, and the elderly will be pressured to choose PAS if it is legalized. They often cite the Nazi experience. Proponents object that the United States is different from Nazi Germany, that the warnings are not valid. Most Americans would react with dismay, even anger, to the Nazi parallel.

Yet the greatest danger is to ignore lessons of history. Some of the factors shaping today's debate are similar to those that shaped the discussion in Nazi Germany leading to social programs to kill the vulnerable and weak.[14] The movement to legalize euthanasia was widely discussed, as it is in the United States today. It was from the arguments of mercy that Adolf Hitler signed a law granting certain designated physicians permission to kill patients (*Gnadentod*) judged "incurably sick by medical examination."[15] This law is not far from Kevorkian's suggestion that only certain, trained physicians — obitiarists — carry out euthanasia for those who request it.[16] Nazi law was focused on the mentally retarded and the mentally ill, however, in an effort to "catch up" to other governments that eliminated the "unfit," the United States included.

Attitudes of superiority and of devaluing individual lives creep into our own thinking as well. They creep in while we ration health care. Although we intend to minimize suffering and maximize the common good, individuals in high numbers face neglect. That said, it is important to recognize that focus on the voluntariness of euthanasia in all discussions and debate can ensure avoidance of mercy killing. What the Nazis did was not euthanasia, but murder for the "good" of the state. If quality of life judgments and social utility judgments are held in check by our cultural and historical memory, then we can provide a humane treatment for suffering not only at the end of life but also throughout it. But we must find a compassionate and just vision of equality in our health care system before PAS and euthanasia are implemented.

THE RULE AGAINST KILLING

The broader debate about PAS exposes contradictions in our attitudes and behavior about the "rule against killing." This ancient rule is embedded in Western civilization, such that only strictly controlled killing is permitted, that is, killing in self-defense, in war, and in capital punishment.[17] Strict control has to do with the moral rules by which the rule against killing is temporarily and on a case-by-case basis suspended. For example, the just war theory details the particular circumstances under which a person suspends ordinary rules against killing. Why, however, does society permit killing in self-defense in a "just war" or in capital punishment, but not permit mercy killing or participation in the rational suicide of a patient by providing the means?

One answer comes from the Nazi backdrop of mercy killing. There is serious and just concern that physicians will tilt toward mercy killing, as Nazi physicians did. This objection to suspending the rule against killing represents a conflation of the reflections on how physicians in Germany could have supported Nazi initiatives, especially those of "biological purity." As Elie Wiesel agonizes: "That doctors participated in the planning, execution, and justification of the concentration camp massacres is bad enough, but it went beyond medicine. Like the cancer of immorality, it spread into every area of spiritual, cultural, and intellectual endeavor. Thus, the meaning of what happened transcended its own immediate limits."[18] George Annas and Michael Grodin ask explicitly: "How could physician healers turn into murderers? This is among the most profound questions in medical ethics."[19] . . .

As Americans discuss euthanasia and PAS, as the practice of euthanasia spreads around the world, and as attention to genetic therapies increases, what "good" will infuse virtues in medical practice? Rational discussion in academic literature is not enough to provide the proper checks and balances on physicians. Training in the virtues, as Wiesel has noted, does not guarantee a good outcome; mores and social standards in conjunction with that training may. This is why the virtues in medical practice must be coupled with a principle-based ethics. Further, neither one nor both guarantees good behavior. Only critically reflective medical ethics and self-critical individuals of good character can offer hope that medical miscarriages are not repeated in the PAS debate.

INTENTIONALITY AND RELEVANT DISTINCTIONS

Consider the problem of intention. Among elements to be examined in ethics are the act itself, the motives or intentions of the agent, the consequences, and the duties, values, ethical principles, and virtues involved. The notion of intention has permitted us to distinguish between active and passive euthanasia, such that passive euthanasia does not carry the moral freight that active does. In passive euthanasia, one does not intend the death of the patient, but the relief of suffering. Thus we speak of not prolonging dying, of letting nature take its course, of permitting a patient's disease to bring about his/her death. It is not, strictly speaking, euthanasia. In active or direct euthanasia, the intention is to bring about the death, even if it is seen as a means for relieving suffering, and then one executes this intention through direct action.

Once we abandon the notion that one should never intend the death of another person, the distinction between active and passive euthanasia vanishes, as does its moral significance. If it is morally appropriate to intend the death of patients, then assisting in their suicide appears to be a weaker solution than directly giving them an injection.

These realities contribute to the problem of maintaining purity of intention. For many years some ethicists have argued that there is no moral distinction between killing and letting die. Yet a distinction exists from the point of view of intention. If one intends to kill directly by action, then withholding or withdrawing care or actively killing the patient makes no moral difference, because the intention is that death is a good thing, and one's actions are meant to bring about that death as a means of relieving suffering. If, however, one intends only to relieve suffering, and death is a by-product of that decision through the use of higher doses of pain medication, then a morally relevant distinction arises between killing and letting die.

Physicians today are not concerned about the mercy killing of vulnerable populations, as the Nazis were. Instead, they are concerned about individuals who have made a judgment that life is no longer useful. In such instances, as James Rachels has argued, little moral difference exists between allowing the patient to die by the underlying disease process for human reasons and directly ending the patient's life for humane reasons (presumably, too, providing the means for the patients to end his/her life).[20] Cessation of treatment, if intended to end a person's life, is permitted under most circumstances. Yet, how does this differ from direct killing for the same humane reasons? If there is little or no moral difference between the two actions, then PAS would make moral sense. As Judge Breck noted in one case against Dr. Kevorkian, there is no

legal distinction between a doctor withdrawing life support and a doctor injecting a patient with lethal drugs. "In both cases, the physician is causing death to occur."[21] This thinking is like that found in the appellate court decisions.

ARGUMENTS FOR AND AGAINST PAS

A summary of the best arguments for and against PAS may now be offered.

ARGUMENTS IN FAVOR OF PAS

One, a goal of medicine is to address the suffering of patients.[22] As that suffering increases, duties arise to provide adequate pain control and to be concerned for the values of the patient in other areas that affect suffering. When pain or suffering becomes intractable, and the patient repeatedly requests termination of life, then the physician has a duty from both the goal of medicine and from a wider responsibility of care to provide relief through a lethal dose of medication.

Two, responsibility for technology exists. Persons used to die at home without much medical intervention, because little could be done. They died before the onset of major metastases or other effects of terminal illness. Usually they died from infection. Today, as a result of efforts to obtain greater quality of life during a terminal illness, people live longer but suffer more intense pain near the end. Physicians who have helped the patient gain some additional time, through interventions such as chemotherapy, must then take responsibility for those interventions and help patients to die peacefully.

Three, physicians ought to respect individual autonomy. If rational suicide is possible, not only among the dying but also among persons of advanced age, then request for PAS should be honored,[23] assuming proper precautions are taken, principally and even solely on the basis of an individual's assessment of the quality of his/her own life. Yet the physician must still evaluate the request and approve it.

Four, concern for misuse of the powers of life and death is appropriate. Given twentieth-century history, proper precautions must be established. But these procedures do not represent an insurmountable hurdle. The Dutch criteria by which physicians are not prosecuted for assisting the dying of their patients (even though this assistance is illegal)[24] can be legalized in the United States and elsewhere. Although PAS is an extraordinary and irreversible treatment, Drs. Timothy Quill, Christine Cassel, and Diane Meier have noted that "it is not idiosyncratic, selfish, or indicative of a psychiatric disorder for people with an incurable illness to want some control over how they die."[25] They propose the following clinical criteria, which closely parallel the Dutch.

- The patient has an incurable condition associated with severe and unrelenting suffering. The patient understands this condition, the prognosis, and the types of comfort care available.
- The patient's suffering is certified by the primary physician as not due to inadequate comfort care.
- The patient clearly and repeatedly requests to die, on his/her own initiative.
- The physician ensures that the patient's judgment is not distorted.
- Assisted suicide must be carried out only in the context of a meaningful doctor-patient relationship.
- Consultation with a second physician is required to ensure that the patient's request is voluntary and rational, that the diagnosis is adequate, and that all other avenues of comfort care have been exhausted.
- Clear documentation of each condition is required.

In England, in response to the Cox case, Tim Helme and Nicola Padfield proposed that a patient or nearest relative be able to apply for euthanasia or assistance. The doctor may register his intent to act, and disputes can be resolved through "euthanasia tribunals."[26]

Five, PAS has a long history. It need not be considered a new or even experimental idea. Today, because of public exposure, not only of the issue, but also of the physicians who support aid-in-dying, legalization is necessary.

Six, the argument that all respect for life is grounded in religious values about the sanctity of life, stewardship of life, and limits on human autonomy assumes that religious values rule out taking the lives of patients. This argument is flawed. The diversity of religious arguments about euthanasia and assisted suicide reflects pluralistic viewpoints, even within the same traditions.[27] For example, against the argument that one cannot take one's own life because it is a gift from God, a theological argument can be constructed that one cannot take one's life *irresponsibly,* but can still honor one's relationship with God by acting responsibly to end one's life.

Seven, there is no need to force someone to participate in PAS. Indeed, the strongest argument in favor of legalization is that strict controls, like those in Australia, render the practice difficult and keep social checks on fascination with death. Further, even those who are opposed to PAS should recognize the right of others to request help from doctors who are willing to provide it, because this is the earmark of a decent, liberal democratic society.[28]

ARGUMENTS AGAINST PAS

One, no matter what society encourages or permits, physicians ought not to kill on principle. As Willard Gaylin, Leon Kass, Mark Siegler, and Edmund Pellegrino have argued, "[A]t least since the Oath of Hippocrates, Western medicine has regarded the killing of patients, even on request, as a profound violation of the deepest meaning of the medical vocation. . . . Neither legal tolerance nor the best bedside manner can ever make medical killing medically ethical."[29] This argument forms the basis of the AMA's decision to rule out any "intentional termination of the life of one human being by another."[30]

Two, once the habit of taking dominion over the lives of others is formed, a slippery slope will develop in hard times, such that physicians will become more insistent in their role in assisting suicide and urge suicide on patients who have become not only depressed but also burdens to themselves and to others.

As a corollary, physicians tend to become messianic about their role, such that gradual abuse may creep in under the guise of social, public, physician, and peer pressure to end one's life. In addition, judicial case-by-case review of now legal acts may not provide the same sort of weight that the Dutch method of judicial review of illegal acts does.

Three, the doctor–patient relationship itself depends on trust, and if the public begins to distrust the medical profession, then the profession itself will suffer irreparable harm.

Four, at the very time patients' rights movements have sought to curtail physical control over individuals, society is considering permitting such physicians to have the ultimate power of life and death. It is ironic that efforts to legalize and gain professional acceptance of euthanasia and assisted suicide, under the mantle of patient autonomy, have actually led to a significant expansion of the powers of the physician.[31]

Five, given the moral, political, social, and care giver ramifications, have all possible alternatives for supporting the dying been exhausted?[32] Efforts can still be made to use better means for controlling pain and addressing suffering. Much common ground still remains for individuals on both sides of the issue to develop models for better care of the dying, without violating the ancient proscriptions against killing.

Six, the argument that legalization would proceed in any case is specious, because as Pellegrino argues, "right and wrong, good and evil, are not decided by votes unless one subscribes to a theory of morality totally subservient to societal mores."[33]

Seven, changing the law to permit PAS is a "sea change," in the words of Daniel Callahan, because we have never in history "maintained that suicide is good — we have only looked upon it as sad."[34] To alter this commitment to value life is to neglect the real issue of controlling pain and addressing suffering.

CONCLUSION: TERMINAL CARE AND A WAY OUT

Brody notes that the dispute between supporters of and objectors to PAS will not be resolved on philosophical grounds. I agree that the arguments seem evenly balanced. Proponents and opponents must live with the tensions this creates. Brody argues that PAS should be seen as a compassionate response to a medical failure, rather than as a practice to be prohibited or to be established as general policy.[35] We should not rush to legalize such acts in place of care of the terminally ill.

The Dutch use the expression *medical decisions at the end of life* to include PAS and euthanasia. This is unusual nomenclature, which emphasizes their conviction that such actions are medical decisions, done in consultation with patients.[36] The expression also stresses the importance of considering PAS and euthanasia only within the context of a thorough and committed program of terminal care. Providing death as an escape from intractable suffering is seen as the last kind act of personal engagement with the dying person. It is done usually by a general practitioner who knows the patient very well, or by a hospital physician who has been involved throughout the dying patient's treatment. Physicians must know the patients' values very well. And the act itself is still illegal, and may remain so, meaning that judicial review can occur in all cases.

Over 75 percent of Americans favor some form of aid-in-dying.[37] One of the significant political and ethical movements of our time has been the rise of patient rights. In part this movement stems from a desire to check the power of the modern medical establishment.

The most important point, however, is that our society should make a major effort to help persons more completely during their dying by providing proper terminal care based on the principles of hospice. This will require a thorough educational program where professional schools teach about dying. Because denial of death is such a powerful force in a technologically equipped hospital environment, a terminal care program in that setting has no chance to succeed without education.

Without such terminal care programs, Americans may opt for PAS and euthanasia in the absence of a personal commitment to care for the dying. This lack of commitment may represent the care givers' fear of the pain that death causes. Given the moral, professional, and social problems with PAS, it may be better to encourage physicians to be more engaged with the dying patient, to develop medical training programs for caring for the dying, and to train thoroughly all who care for dying patients in the art of pain control. Further, society should guarantee terminal care for all citizens, so that none need fear bankrupting their families during the dying process.

In sum, a good social policy would develop the rights of the terminally ill to supportive and palliative care. One cannot easily justify taking lives on the one hand while neglecting the suffering of dying persons on the other. Doctors belong with their patients to the end, to help them die well. Physicians regularly recoil from dying, and, as Dr. Steven Miles has pointed out, "often underdiagnose and undertreat pain or depression, either of which may be part of why a patient may choose to die."[38] A project of the American Board of Internal Medicine seeks to remedy this situation."[39] Almost 2.5 million people die each year in the United States but only 250,000 receive hospice care.[40] Quill only supported PAS when he realized that for a few patients palliative care does not work. As the Dutch have already realized, in the end it is not pain that leads people to request PAS or euthanasia, it is consciousness itself.[41]

Humility is difficult to cultivate in any circumstance; it is more so for physicians today, given the powerful life-prolonging resources available. These resources have advanced during the past ten years from temporary to quasi-permanent life support, from organ-system support to total systemic support. Employing this technology subtly leads to the assumption of God-like powers over life and death. To avoid this assumption and to cultivate proper humility means that today's ethical challenges should not be to curtail use of technology, but to direct and shepherd it to good human ends.[42]

One way to avoid physician involvement in assisted suicide, then, is for physicians to certify that all means at their disposal have been tried to palliate the dying person, and that despite all efforts to convince that person otherwise, the patient persists in requesting assisted suicide. In effect, this certification would allow for obtaining lethal doses of medication such that the person may, without doctor supervision, perhaps with skilled care of another sort, self-deliver.

NOTES

1. J.-M. Meyer, "The Sacredness of Life in Pagan Philosophy," *Dolentium Hominum*, 11, no. 31 (1996): at 56.

2. H.T. Engelhardt Jr., *Bioethics and Secular Humanism* (Philadelphia: Trinity Press International, 1992). See also R. Brandt, "The Morality and Rationality of Suicide," in J. Rachels, ed., *Moral Problems* (New York: Harper and Row, 1975): 363–87.

3. H. Jochemsen, *Euthanasia: A Christian Evaluation* (Oxford: Latimer House Studies #49, 1995).

4. M.P. Battin, "Euthanasia: The Fundamental Issues," in M.P. Battin, *Least Worst Death: Essays in Bioethics on the End of Life* (New York: Oxford University Press, 1994): at 101–29. Unlike Alexander Capron, Battin thinks that assisted suicide is a better first option than euthanasia, because it depends so thoroughly on the patient's own assessment of the relationship between suffering and continued existence or death. She would reserve euthanasia for those who choose it ahead of time but are no longer able to request it near the time of death.

5. D.C. Thomasma and G.C. Graber, *Euthanasia: Toward an Ethical Social Policy* (New York Continuum Publishing, 1990).

6. A. Capron, "Legalizing Physician-Aided Death," *Cambridge Quarterly of Healthcare Ethics*, 5, no. 1 (1996): 10–23, esp. 17–18.

7. N.M. deS. Cameron, *The New Medicine: Life and Death After Hippocrates* (Wheaton: Crossway Books, 1992).

8. Anonymous, "Missouri and Kevorkian Continue to Provoke Controversy," *Hospital Ethics*, 8, no. 6 (1992): 9.

9. Id.

10. E.D. Pellegrino and D.C. Thomasma, *For the Patient's Good: The Restoration of Beneficence in Health Care* (New York: Oxford University Press, 1988); and E. Loewy, "Beneficence in Trust," *Hastings Center Report*, 19, no. 1 (1989): 42–43; and T. Beauchamp and J. Childress, *Principles of Biomedical Ethics* (New York: Oxford University Press, 3d ed., 1994).

11. W. Gaylin et al., "Doctors Must Not Kill," *JAMA*, 259 (1988): 2139–40.

12. L. Kass, "Arguments Against Active Euthanasia by Doctors Found at Medicine's Core," *Kennedy Institute of Ethics Newsletter*, 3 (1989): 1–3, 6.

13. J. Muller and B. Koenig, "On the Boundary of Life and Death: The Definition of Dying by Medical Residents," in M. Lock and D. Gordon, eds., *Biomedicine Examined* (Dordrecht: Kluwer Academic, 1988): 351–74.

14. D.C. Thomasma, "The Ethics of Caring for Vulnerable Individuals," in *Reflections on Ethics* (Washington, D.C.: American Speech-Language-Hearing Association, 1990): 39–45.

15. R.N. Proctor, "Nazi Doctors, Racial Medicine, and Human Experimentation," in G.J. Annas and M.A. Grodin, eds., *The Nazi Doctors and the Nuremberg Code* (New York: Oxford University Press, 1992): at 23.

16. J. Kevorkian, *Presciption—Medicide: The Goodness of Planned Death* (Buffalo: Prometheus Books, 1991).

17. J.F. Kilner, A.B. Miller, and E.D. Pellegrino, eds., *Dignity and Dying: A Christian Appraisal* (Grand Rapids: W.B. Eerdmans, 1996).

18. E. Wiesel, "Preface," in G. J. Annas and M. A. Grodin, eds., *The Nazi Doctors and the Nuremberg Code* (New York: Oxford University Press, 1992): at vii.

19. G.J. Annas and M.A. Grodin, "Introduction," in G.J. Annas and M.A. Grodin, eds., *The Nazi Doctors and the Nuremberg Code* (New York: Oxford University Press, 1992): at 3.

20. J. Rachels, "Active and Passive Euthanasia," *N. Engl. J. Med.*, 292 (1975): 78–80.

21. Id.

22. E. Cassell, "The Nature of Suffering and the Goals of Medicine," *N. Engl. J. Med.*, 306 (1982): 639–45.

23. M. Kohl, "Altruistic Humanism and Voluntary Beneficent Euthanasia," *Issues in Law & Medicine*, 8 (1992): 331–42.

24. P. Admiraal, "Justifiable Active Euthanasia in the Netherlands," in R.M. Baird and S.E. Rosenbaum, eds., *Euthanasia: The Moral Issues* (Buffalo: Prometheus Books, 1989): 125–28.

25. T.E. Quill, C.K. Cassel, and D.E. Meier, "Care of the Hopelessly Ill: Proposed Clinical Criteria for Physician-Assisted Suicide," *N. Engl. J. Med.*, 327 (1992): note 8.

26. T. Helme and N. Padfield, "Safeguarding Euthanasia," *New Law Journal*, Oct. 2 (1992): 1335–36.

27. C.S. Campbell, "Religious Ethics and Active Euthanasia in a Pluralistic Society," *Kennedy Institute of Ethics Journal*, 2 (1992): 253–77.

28. J. Bresnahan, "Observations on the Rejection of Physician-Assisted Suicide: A Roman Catholic Perspective," *Christian Bioethics: Non-Ecumenical Studies in Medical Morality*, 1 (1995): 256–84.

29. Gaylin et al., *supra* note 11.

30. House of Delegates of the American Medical Association, Dec. 4, 1973, as quoted in Rachels, *supra* note 5, at 97.

31. J.V.M. Welie, "The Medical Exception: Physicians, Euthanasia and the Dutch Criminal Law," *Journal of Medicine and Philosophy*, 17 (1992): 419–37. See the objections raised to PAS and euthanasia in Newsletter of Evangelical Churches, "Legalized Physician-Assisted Suicide," *Discernment*, 1, no. 3 (1992): 1–4.

32. C.S. Campbell, "'Aid-in-Dying' and the Taking of Human Life," *Journal of Medical Ethics*, 18 (1992): 128–34.

33. E.D. Pellegrino, "Euthanasia and Physician Assisted Suicide," in J.F. Kilner, A.B. Miller, and E.D. Pellegrino, eds., *Dignity and Dying: A Christian Appraisal* (Grand Rapids: W.B. Eerdmans, 1996): at 117.

34. As quoted in P. Wilkes and S.L. Carter, "The Case Against Doctor-Assisted Suicide—The Next Pro-Lifers," *New York Times Magazine*, July 21, 1996, at 22.

35. H. Brody, "Assisted Death—A Compassionate Response to a Medical Failure," *N. Engl. J. Med.,* 327 (1992): 1384–88.

36. D.C. Thomasma, "Models of the Doctor–Patient Relationship and the Ethics Committee, Part Two," *Cambridge Quarterly of Healthcare Ethics,* 3, no. 1 (1993): 10–26.

37. H. Kuhse and P. Singer, "Euthanasia: A Survey of Nurses' Attitudes and Practices." *Australian Nurses Journal,* 21, no. 8 (1992): 21–22. . . .

38. S.H. Miles, "Physicians and Their Patients' Suicides," *JAMA,* 271 (1994): at 1786.

39. American Board of Internal Medicine, *Caring for the Dying: Identification and Promotion of Physician Competency. Parts One and Two, Narratives and Educational Resource Development* (Philadelphia: American Board of Internal Medicine, 1996).

40. J. Wilson Ross, "Review: The Future of Dying," *Western Bioethics News,* July (1996): at 4.

41. B.C. Witsenburg, "Dood op Verzoek" ("Death on Request"), *Medisch Contact,* 50 (1995): 1293–94.

42. D.C. Thomasma, *Human Life in the Balance* (Louisville: Westminster Press, 1990).

Physician-Assisted Suicide

TIMOTHY E. QUILL

Death and Dignity: A Case of Individualized Decision Making

Diane was feeling tired and had a rash. A common scenario, though there was something subliminally worrisome that prompted me to check her blood count. Her hematocrit was 22, and the white-cell count was 4.3 with some metamyelocytes and unusual white cells. I wanted it to be viral, trying to deny what was staring me in the face. Perhaps in a repeated count it would disappear. I called Diane and told her it might be more serious than I had initially thought—that the test needed to be repeated and that if she felt worse, we might have to move quickly. When she pressed for the possibilities, I reluctantly opened the door to leukemia. Hearing the word seemed to make it exist. "Oh, shit!" she said. "Don't tell me that." Oh, shit! I thought, I wish I didn't have to.

Diane was no ordinary person (although no one I have ever come to know has been really ordinary). She was raised in an alcoholic family and had felt alone for much of her life. She had vaginal cancer as a young woman. Through much of her adult life, she had struggled with depression and her own alcoholism. I had come to know, respect, and admire her over the previous eight years as she confronted these problems and gradually overcame them. She was an incredibly clear, at times brutally honest, thinker and communicator. As she took control of her life, she developed a strong sense of independence and confidence. In the previous 3½ years, her hard work had paid off. She was completely abstinent from alcohol, she had established much deeper connections with her husband, college-age son, and several friends, and her business and her artistic work were blossoming. She felt she was really living fully for the first time.

Not surprisingly, the repeated blood count was abnormal, and detailed examination of the peripheral-blood smear showed myelocytes. I advised her to come into the hospital, explaining that we needed to do a bone marrow biopsy and make some decisions relatively rapidly. She came to the hospital knowing what we would find. She was terrified, angry, and sad. Although we knew the odds, we both clung to the thread of possibility that it might be something else.

Reprinted by permission of the publisher from Timothy E. Quill, "Death and Dignity: A Case of Individualized Decision Making," *New England Journal of Medicine* 324, No. 10 (March 7, 1991), pp. 691–94.

The bone marrow confirmed the worst: acute myelomonocytic leukemia. In the face of this tragedy, we looked for signs of hope. This is an area of medicine in which technological intervention has been successful, with cures 25 percent of the time — long-term cures. As I probed the costs of these cures, I heard about induction chemotherapy (three weeks in the hospital, prolonged neutropenia, probable infectious complications, and hair loss; 75 percent of patients respond, 25 percent do not). For the survivors, this is followed by consolidation chemotherapy (with similar side effects; another 25 percent die, for a net survival of 50 percent). Those still alive, to have a reasonable chance of long-term survival, then need bone marrow transplantation (hospitalization for two months and whole-body irradiation, with complete killing of the bone marrow, infectious complications, and the possibility for graft-versus-host disease — with a survival of approximately 50 percent, or 25 percent of the original group). Though hematologists may argue over the exact percentages, they don't argue about the outcome of no treatment — certain death in days, weeks, or at most a few months.

Believing that delay was dangerous, our oncologist broke the news to Diane and began making plans to insert a Hickman catheter and begin induction chemotherapy that afternoon. When I saw her shortly thereafter, she was enraged at his presumption that she would want treatment, and devastated by the finality of the diagnosis. All she wanted to do was go home and be with her family. She had no further questions about treatment and in fact had decided that she wanted none. Together we lamented her tragedy and the unfairness of life. Before she left, I felt the need to be sure that she and her husband understood that there was some risk in delay, that the problem was not going to go away, and that we needed to keep considering the options over the next several days. We agreed to meet in two days.

She returned in two days with her husband and son. They had talked extensively about the problem and the options. She remained very clear about her wish not to undergo chemotherapy and to live whatever time she had left outside the hospital. As we explored her thinking further, it became clear that she was convinced she would die during the period of treatment and would suffer unspeakably in the process (from hospitalization, from lack of control over her body, from the side ef-

fects of chemotherapy, and from pain and anguish). Although I could offer support and my best effort to minimize her suffering if she chose treatment, there was no way I could say any of this would not occur. In fact, the last four patients with acute leukemia at our hospital had died very painful deaths in the hospital during various stages of treatment (a fact I did not share with her). Her family wished she would choose treatment but sadly accepted her decision. She articulated very clearly that it was she who would be experiencing all the side effects of treatment and that odds of 25 percent were not good enough for her to undergo so toxic a course of therapy, given her expectations of chemotherapy and hospitalization and the absence of a closely matched bone marrow donor. I had her repeat her understanding of the treatment, the odds, and what to expect if there were no treatment. I clarified a few misunderstandings, but she had a remarkable grasp of the options and implications.

I have been a longtime advocate of active, informed patient choice of treatment or nontreatment, and of a patient's right to die with as much control and dignity as possible. Yet there was something about her giving up a 25 percent chance of long-term survival in favor of almost certain death that disturbed me. I had seen Diane fight and use her considerable inner resources to overcome alcoholism and depression, and I half expected her to change her mind over the next week. Since the window of time in which effective treatment can be initiated is rather narrow, we met several times that week. We obtained a second hematology consultation and talked at length about the meaning and implications of treatment and nontreatment. She talked to a psychologist she had seen in the past. I gradually understood the decision from her perspective and became convinced that it was the right decision for her. We arranged for home hospice care (although at that time Diane felt reasonably well, was active, and looked healthy), left the door open for her to change her mind, and tried to anticipate how to keep her comfortable in the time she had left.

Just as I was adjusting to her decision, she opened up another area that would stretch me profoundly. It was extraordinarily important to Diane to maintain control of herself and her own dignity during the time remaining to her. When this was no longer possible, she clearly wanted to die. As a former director of a hospice program, I know how to use pain medicines to keep patients comfortable and lessen suffering. I explained the philosophy of comfort care, which I strongly believe in. Although Diane understood and appreciated this, she had known of people lingering in what was called relative comfort, and she wanted no part of it. When the time came, she wanted to take her life in the least painful way possible. Knowing of her desire for independence and her decision to stay in control, I thought this request made perfect sense. I acknowledged and explored this wish but also thought that it was out of the realm of currently accepted medical practice and that it was more than I could offer or promise. In our discussion, it became clear that preoccupation with her fear of a lingering death would interfere with Diane's getting the most out of the time she had left until she found a safe way to ensure her death. I feared the effects of a violent death on her family, the consequences of an ineffective suicide that would leave her lingering in precisely the state she dreaded so much, and the possibility that a family member would be forced to assist her, with all the legal and personal repercussions that would follow. She discussed this at length with her family. They believed that they should respect her choice. With this in mind, I told Diane that information was available from the Hemlock Society that might be helpful to her.

A week later she phoned me with a request for barbiturates for sleep. Since I knew that this was an essential ingredient in a Hemlock Society suicide, I asked her to come to the office to talk things over. She was more than willing to protect me by participating in a superficial conversation about her insomnia, but it was important to me to know how she planned to use the drugs and to be sure that she was not in despair or overwhelmed in a way that might color her judgment. In our discussion, it was apparent that she was having trouble sleeping, but it was also evident that the security of having enough barbiturates available to commit suicide when and if the time came would leave her secure enough to live fully and concentrate on the present. It was clear that she was not despondent and that in fact she was making deep, personal connections with her family and close friends. I made sure that she knew how to use the barbiturates for sleep, and also that she knew the amount needed to commit suicide. We agreed to meet regularly, and she promised to meet with me before taking her life, to ensure that all other avenues had been exhausted. I wrote the prescription with an uneasy feeling about the boundaries I was exploring—spiritual, legal, professional, and personal.

Yet I also felt strongly that I was setting her free to get the most out of the time she had left, and to maintain dignity and control on her own terms until her death.

The next several months were very intense and important for Diane. Her son stayed home from college, and they were able to be with one another and say much that had not been said earlier. Her husband did his work at home so that he and Diane could spend more time together. She spent time with her closest friends. I had her come into the hospital for a conference with our residents, at which she illustrated in a most profound and personal way the importance of informed decision making, the right to refuse treatment, and the extraordinarily personal effects of illness and interaction with the medical system. There were emotional and physical hardships as well. She had periods of intense sadness and anger. Several times she became very weak, but she received transfusions as an outpatient and responded with marked improvement of symptoms. She had two serious infections that responded surprisingly well to empirical courses of oral antibiotics. After three tumultuous months, there were two weeks of relative calm and well-being, and fantasies of a miracle began to surface.

Unfortunately, we had no miracle. Bone pain, weakness, fatigue, and fevers began to dominate her life. Although the hospice workers, family members, and I tried our best to minimize the suffering and promote comfort, it was clear that the end was approaching. Diane's immediate future held what she feared the most—increasing discomfort, dependence, and hard choices between pain and sedation. She called up her closest friends and asked them to come over to say goodbye, telling them that she would be leaving soon. As we had agreed, she let me know as well. When we met, it was clear that she knew what she was doing, that she was sad and frightened to be leaving, but that she would be even more terrified to stay and suffer. In our tearful goodbye, she promised a reunion in the future at her favorite spot on the edge of Lake Geneva, with dragons swimming in the sunset.

Two days later her husband called to say that Diane had died. She had said her final goodbyes to her husband and son that morning, and asked them to leave her alone for an hour. After an hour, which must have seemed an eternity, they found her on the couch, lying very still and covered by her favorite shawl. There was no sign of struggle. She seemed to be at peace. They called me for advice about how to proceed. When I arrived at their house, Diane indeed seemed peaceful. Her husband and son were quiet. We talked about what a remarkable person she had been. They seemed to have no doubts about the course she had chosen or about their cooperation, although the unfairness of her illness and the finality of her death were overwhelming to us all.

I called the medical examiner to inform him that a hospice patient had died. When asked about the cause of death, I said, "acute leukemia." He said that was fine and that we should call a funeral director. Although acute leukemia was the truth, it was not the whole story. Yet any mention of suicide would have given rise to a police investigation and probably brought the arrival of an ambulance crew for resuscitation. Diane would have become a "coroner's case," and the decision to perform an autopsy would have been made at the discretion of the medical examiner. The family or I could have been subject to criminal prosecution, and I to professional review, for our roles in support of Diane's choices. Although I truly believe that the family and I gave her the best care possible, allowing her to define her limits and directions as much as possible, I am not sure the law, society, or the medical profession would agree. So I said "acute leukemia" to protect all of us, to protect Diane from an invasion into her past and her body, and to continue to shield society from the knowledge of the degree of suffering that people often undergo in the process of dying. Suffering can be lessened to some extent, but in no way eliminated or made benign, by the careful intervention of a competent, caring physician, given current social constraints.

Diane taught me about the range of help I can provide if I know people well and if I allow them to say what they really want. She taught me about life, death, and honesty and about taking charge and facing tragedy squarely when it strikes. She taught me that I can take small risks for people that I really know and care about. Although I did not assist in her suicide directly, I helped indirectly to make it possible, successful, and relatively painless. Although I know we have measures to help control pain and lessen suffering, to think that people do not suffer in the process of dying is an illusion. Prolonged dying can occasionally be peaceful, but more often the role of the physician and family is limited to lessening but not eliminating severe suffering.

I wonder how many families and physicians secretly help patients over the edge into death in the face of such severe suffering. I wonder how many severely ill or dying patients secretly take their lives, dying alone in despair. I wonder whether the image of Diane's final aloneness will persist in the minds of her family, or if they will remember more the intense, meaningful months they had together before she died. I wonder whether Diane struggled in that last hour, and whether the Hemlock Society's way of death by suicide is the most benign. I wonder why Diane, who gave so much to so many of us, had to be alone for the last hour of her life. I wonder whether I will see Diane again, on the shore of Lake Geneva at sunset, with dragons swimming on the horizon.

The Oregon Death with Dignity Act

ALLOWS TERMINALLY ILL ADULTS TO OBTAIN PRESCRIPTION FOR LETHAL DRUGS

Question. Shall law allow terminally ill adult patients voluntary informed choice to obtain physician's prescription for drugs to end life?

Summary. Adopts law. Allows terminally ill adult Oregon residents voluntary informed choice to obtain physician's prescription for drugs to end life. Removes criminal penalties for qualifying physician-assisted suicide. Applies when physicians predict patient's death within 6 months. Requires:

15-day waiting period;

2 oral, 1 written request;

second physician's opinion;

counseling if either physician believes patient has mental disorder, impaired judgment from depression.

Person has choice whether to notify next of kin. Health care providers immune from civil, criminal liability for good faith compliance.

SECTION 1: GENERAL PROVISIONS

§ 1.01 DEFINITIONS

The following words and phrases, whenever used in this Act, shall have the following meanings:

1. "Adult" means an individual who is 18 years of age or older.
2. "Attending physician" means the physician who has primary responsibility for the care of the patient and treatment of the patient's terminal disease.
3. "Consulting physician" means a physician who is qualified by specialty or experience to make a professional diagnosis and prognosis regarding the patient's disease.
4. "Counseling" means a consultation between a state licensed psychiatrist or psychologist and a patient for the purpose of determining whether the patient is suffering from a psychiatric or psychological disorder, or depression causing impaired judgment.
5. "Health care provider" means a person licensed, certified, or otherwise authorized or permitted by the law of this State to administer health care in the ordinary course of business or practice of a profession, and includes a health care facility.
6. "Incapable" means that in the opinion of a court or in the opinion of the patient's attending physician or consulting physician, a patient lacks the ability to make and communicate health care decisions to health care providers, including communication through persons familiar with the patient's manner of communicating if those persons are available. Capable means not incapable.
7. "Informed decision" means a decision by a qualified patient, to request and obtain a prescription to end his or her life in a humane and dignified manner, that is based on an appreciation of the relevant facts and after being fully informed by the attending physician of:
   (a) his or her medical diagnosis;
   (b) his or her prognosis;
   (c) the potential risks associated with taking the medication to be prescribed;
   (d) the probable result of taking the medication to be prescribed;
   (e) the feasible alternatives, including, but not limited to, comfort care, hospice care and pain control.
8. "Medically confirmed" means the medical opinion of the attending physician has been confirmed by a consulting physician who has examined the patient and the patient's relevant medical records.

9. "Patient" means a person who is under the care of a physician.

10. "Physician" means a doctor of medicine or osteopathy licensed to practice medicine by the Board of Medical Examiners for the State of Oregon.

11. "Qualified patient" means a capable adult who is a resident of Oregon and has satisfied the requirements of this Act in order to obtain a prescription for medication to end his or her life in a humane and dignified manner.

12. "Terminal disease" means an incurable and irreversible disease that has been medically confirmed and will, within reasonable medical judgment, produce death within six (6) months.

SECTION 2: WRITTEN REQUEST FOR MEDICATION TO END ONE'S LIFE IN A HUMANE AND DIGNIFIED MANNER

§ 2.01 WHO MAY INITIATE A WRITTEN REQUEST FOR MEDICATION

An adult who is capable, is a resident of Oregon, and has been determined by the attending physician and consulting physician to be suffering from a terminal disease, and who has voluntarily expressed his or her wish to die, may make a written request for medication for the purpose of ending his or her life in a humane and dignified manner in accordance with this Act.

§ 2.02 FORM OF THE WRITTEN REQUEST

1. A valid request for medication under this Act shall be in substantially the form described in Section 6 of this Act, signed and dated by the patient and witnessed by at least two individuals who, in the presence of the patient, attest that to the best of their knowledge and belief the patient is capable, acting voluntarily, and is not being coerced to sign the request.

2. One of the witnesses shall be a person who is not:
   (a) A relative of the patient by blood, marriage or adoption;
   (b) A person who at the time the request is signed would be entitled to any portion of the estate of the qualified patient upon death under any will or by operation of law; or

   (c) An owner, operator or employee of a health care facility where the qualified patient is receiving medical treatment or is a resident.

3. The patient's attending physician at the time the request is signed shall not be a witness.

4. If the patient is a patient in a long term care facility at the time the written request is made, one of the witnesses shall be an individual designated by the facility and having the qualifications specified by the Department of Human Resources by rule.

SECTION 3: SAFEGUARDS

§ 3.01 ATTENDING PHYSICIAN RESPONSIBILITIES

The attending physician shall:

1. Make the initial determination of whether a patient has a terminal disease, is capable, and has made the request voluntarily;

2. Inform the patient of:
   (a) his or her medical diagnosis;
   (b) his or her prognosis;
   (c) the potential risks associated with taking the medication to be prescribed;
   (d) the probable result of taking the medication to be prescribed;
   (e) the feasible alternatives, including, but not limited to, comfort care, hospice care and pain control.

3. Refer the patient to a consulting physician for medical confirmation of the diagnosis, and for a determination that the patient is capable and acting voluntarily;

4. Refer the patient for counseling if appropriate pursuant to Section 3.03;

5. Request that the patient notify next of kin;

6. Inform the patient that he or she has an opportunity to rescind the request at any time and in any manner, and offer the patient an opportunity to rescind at the end of the 15-day waiting period pursuant to Section 3.06;

7. Verify, immediately prior to writing the prescription for medication under this Act, that the patient is making an informed decision;

8. Fulfill the medical record documentation requirements of Section 3.09;

9. Ensure that all appropriate steps are carried out in accordance with this Act prior to writing a prescription for medication to enable a qualified pa-

tient to end his or her life in a humane and dignified manner.

§ 3.02 CONSULTING PHYSICIAN CONFIRMATION

Before a patient is qualified under this Act, a consulting physician shall examine the patient and his or her relevant medical records and confirm, in writing, the attending physician's diagnosis that the patient is suffering from a terminal disease, and verify that the patient is capable, is acting voluntarily and has made an informed decision.

§ 3.03 COUNSELING REFERRAL

If in the opinion of the attending physician or the consulting physician a patient may be suffering from a psychiatric or psychological disorder, or depression causing impaired judgment, either physician shall refer the patient for counseling. No medication to end a patient's life in a humane and dignified manner shall be prescribed until the person performing the counseling determines that the patient is not suffering from a psychiatric or psychological disorder, or depression causing impaired judgment.

§ 3.04 INFORMED DECISION

No person shall receive a prescription for medication to end his or her life in a humane and dignified manner unless he or she has made an informed decision as defined in Section 1.01(7). Immediately prior to writing a prescription for medication under this Act, the attending physician shall verify that the patient is making an informed decision.

§ 3.05 FAMILY NOTIFICATION

The attending physician shall ask the patient to notify next of kin of his or her request for medication pursuant to this Act. A patient who declines or is unable to notify next of kin shall not have his or her request denied for that reason.

§ 3.06 WRITTEN AND ORAL REQUESTS

In order to receive a prescription for medication to end his or her life in a humane and dignified manner, a qualified patient shall have made an oral request and a written request, and reiterate the oral request to his or her attending physician no less than fifteen (15) days after making the initial oral request. At the time the qualified patient makes his or her second oral request,

the attending physician shall offer the patient an opportunity to rescind the request.

§ 3.07 RIGHT TO RESCIND REQUEST

A patient may rescind his or her request at any time and in any manner without regard to his or her mental state. No prescription for medication under this Act may be written without the attending physician offering the qualified patient an opportunity to rescind the request.

§ 3.08 WAITING PERIODS

No less than fifteen (15) days shall elapse between the patient's initial oral request and the writing of a prescription under this Act. No less than 48 hours shall elapse between the patient's written request and the writing of a prescription under the Act.

§ 3.09 MEDICAL RECORD DOCUMENTATION REQUIREMENTS

The following shall be documented or filed in the patient's medical record:

1. All oral requests by a patient for medication to end his or her life in a humane and dignified manner;
2. All written requests by a patient for medication to end his or her life in a humane and dignified manner;
3. The attending physician's diagnosis and prognosis, determination that the patient is capable, acting voluntarily and has made an informed decision;
4. The consulting physician's diagnosis and prognosis, and verification that the patient is capable, acting voluntarily and has made an informed decision;
5. A report of the outcome and determinations made during counseling, if performed;
6. The attending physician's offer to the patient to rescind his or her request at the time of the patient's second oral request pursuant to Section 3.06; and
7. A note by the attending physician indicating that all requirements under this Act have been met and indicating the steps taken to carry out the request, including a notation of the medication prescribed.

§ 3.10 RESIDENCY REQUIREMENTS

Only requests made by Oregon residents, under this Act, shall be granted.

§ 3.11 REPORTING REQUIREMENTS

1. The Health Division shall annually review a sample of records maintained pursuant to this Act.
2. The Health Division shall make rules to facilitate the collection of information regarding compliance with this Act. The information collected shall not be a public record and may not be made available for inspection by the public.
3. The Health Division shall generate and make available to the public an annual statistical report of information collected under Section 3.11(2) of this Act.

§ 3.12 EFFECT ON CONSTRUCTION OF WILLS, CONTRACTS, AND STATUTES

1. No provision in a contract, will or other agreement, whether written or oral, to the extent the provision would affect whether a person may make or rescind a request for medication to end his or her life in a humane and dignified manner, shall be valid.
2. No obligation owing under any currently existing contract shall be conditioned or affected by the making or rescinding of a request, by a person, for medication to end his or her life in a humane and dignified manner.

§ 3.13 INSURANCE OR ANNUITY POLICIES

The sale, procurement, or issuance of any life, health, or accident insurance or annuity policy or the rate charged for any policy shall not be conditioned upon or affected by the making or rescinding of a request, by a person, for medication to end his or her life in a humane and dignified manner. Neither shall a qualified patient's act of ingesting medication to end his her life in a humane and dignified manner have an effect upon a life, health, or accident insurance or annuity policy.

§ 3.14 CONSTRUCTION OF ACT

Nothing in this Act shall be construed to authorize a physician or any other person to end a patient's life by lethal injection, mercy killing or active euthanasia. Actions taken in accordance with this Act shall not, for any purpose, constitute suicide, assisted suicide, mercy killing or homicide, under the law.

SECTION 4: IMMUNITIES AND LIABILITIES

§ 4.01 IMMUNITIES

Except as provided in Section 4.02:

1. No person shall be subject to civil or criminal liability or professional disciplinary action for participating in good faith compliance with this Act. This includes being present when a qualified patient takes the prescribed medication to end his or her life in a humane and dignified manner.
2. No professional organization or association, or health care provider, may subject a person to censure, discipline, suspension, loss of license, loss of privileges, loss of membership or other penalty for participating or refusing to participate in good faith compliance with this Act.
3. No request by a patient for or provision by an attending physician of medication in good faith compliance with the provisions of this Act shall constitute neglect for any purpose of law or provide the sole basis for the appointment of a guardian or conservator.
4. No health care provider shall be under any duty, whether by contract, by statute or by any other legal requirement to participate in the provision to a qualified patient of medication to end his or her life in a humane and dignified manner. If a health care provider is unable or unwilling to carry out a patient's request under this Act, and the patient transfers his or her care to a new health care provider, the prior health care provider shall transfer, upon request, a copy of the patient's relevant medical records to the new health care provider.

§ 4.02 LIABILITIES

1. A person who without authorization of the patient willfully alters or forges a request for medication or conceals or destroys a rescission of that request with the intent or effect of causing the patient's death shall be guilty of a Class A felony.
2. A person who coerces or exerts undue influence on a patient to request medication for the purpose of ending the patient's life, or to destroy a rescission of such a request, shall be guilty of a Class A felony.
3. Nothing in this Act limits further liability for civil damages resulting from other negligent conduct or intentional misconduct by any person.

4. The penalties in this Act do not preclude criminal penalties applicable under other law for conduct which is inconsistent with the provisions of this Act.

any other section of this Act which can be given full effect without the invalid section or application.

SECTION 5: SEVERABILITY

§ 5.01 SEVERABILITY

Any section of this Act being held invalid as to any person or circumstance shall not affect the application of

SECTION 6: FORM OF THE REQUEST

§ 6.01 FORM OF THE REQUEST

A request for medication as authorized by this act shall be in substantially the [boxed] form.

REQUEST FOR MEDICATION TO END MY LIFE IN A HUMANE AND DIGNIFIED MANNER

I, _____, am an adult of sound mind.

I am suffering from _____, which my attending physician has determined is a terminal disease and which has been medically confirmed by a consulting physician.

I have been fully informed of my diagnosis, prognosis, the nature of medication to be prescribed and potential associated risks, the expected result, and the feasible alternatives, including comfort care, hospice care and pain control.

I request that my attending physician prescribe medication that will end my life in a humane and dignified manner.

INITIAL ONE:

_____ I have informed my family of my decision and taken their opinions into consideration.

_____ I have decided not to inform my family of my decision.

_____ I have no family to inform of my decision.

I understand that I have the right to rescind this request at any time.

I understand the full import of this request and I expect to die when I take the medication to be prescribed.

I make this request voluntarily and without reservation, and I accept full moral responsibility for my actions.

Signed: _____

Dated: _____

DECLARATION OF WITNESSES

We declare that the person signing this request:

    (a) Is personally known to us or has provided proof of identity;

    (b) Signed this request in our presence;

    (c) Appears to be of sound mind and not under duress, fraud or undue influence;

    (d) Is not a patient for whom either of us is attending physician.

_____ Witness 1/Date

_____ Witness 2/Date

NOTE: one witness shall not be a relative (by blood, marriage or adoption) of the person signing this request, shall not be entitled to any portion of the person's estate upon death and shall not own, operate or be employed at a health care facility where the person is a patient or resident. If the patient is an inpatient at a health care facility, one of the witnesses shall be an individual designated by the facility.

UNITED STATES SUPREME COURT

Dennis C. Vacco, Attorney General of New York, et al.,
Petitioners v. Timothy E. Quill et al.

On Writ of Certiorari to the United States
Court of Appeals for the Second Circuit

[June 26, 1997]

CHIEF JUSTICE REHNQUIST delivered the opinion of the Court.

In New York, as in most States, it is a crime to aid another to commit or attempt suicide, but patients may refuse even lifesaving medical treatment. The question presented by this case is whether New York's prohibition on assisting suicide therefore violates the Equal Protection Clause of the Fourteenth Amendment. We hold that it does not. . . .

The Equal Protection Clause commands that no State shall "deny to any person within its jurisdiction the equal protection of the laws." This provision creates no substantive rights. . . . Instead, it embodies a general rule that States must treat like cases alike but may treat unlike cases accordingly. . . .

On their faces, neither New York's ban on assisting suicide nor its statutes permitting patients to refuse medical treatment treat anyone differently than anyone else or draw any distinction between persons. *Everyone,* regardless of physical condition, is entitled, if competent, to refuse unwanted lifesaving medical treatment; *no one* is permitted to assist a suicide. Generally speaking, laws that apply evenhandedly to all "unquestionably comply" with the Equal Protection Clause. . . .

The Court of Appeals, however, concluded that some terminally ill people — those who are on life-support systems — are treated differently than those who are not,

in that the former may "hasten death" by ending treatment, but the latter may not "hasten death" through physician-assisted suicide. 80 F. 3d, at 729. This conclusion depends on the submission that ending or refusing lifesaving medical treatment "is nothing more nor less than assisted suicide." *Ibid.* Unlike the Court of Appeals, we think the distinction between assisting suicide and withdrawing life-sustaining treatment, a distinction widely recognized and endorsed in the medical profession and in our legal traditions, is both important and logical; it is certainly rational. . . .

The distinction comports with fundamental legal principles of causation and intent. First, when a patient refuses life-sustaining medical treatment, he dies from an underlying fatal disease of pathology; but if a patient ingests lethal medication prescribed by a physician, he is killed by that medication. . . .

Furthermore, a physician who withdraws, or honors a patient's refusal to begin, life-sustaining medical treatment purposefully intends, or may so intend, only to respect his patient's wishes and "to cease doing useless and futile or degrading things to the patient when [the patient] no longer stands to benefit from them." Assisted Suicide in the United States, Hearing before the Subcommittee on the Constitution of the House Committee on the Judiciary, 104th Cong., 2d Sess., 368 (1996) (testimony of Dr. Leon R. Kass). The same is true when a doctor provides aggressive palliative care; in some cases, painkilling drugs may hasten a patient's death, but the physician's purpose and intent is, or may be, only to ease his patient's pain. A doctor who assists a suicide, however, "must, necessarily and indubitably, intend primarily that the patient be made dead." *Id.,* at 367. Similarly, a patient who commits suicide with a doctor's aid necessarily has the specific intent to end his or her own life, while a patient who refuses or discontinues treatment might not. . . .

The law has long used actors' intent or purpose to distinguish between two acts that may have the same result. See, *e.g., United States v. Bailey,* 444 U.S. 394, 403–406 (1980) ("[T]he . . . common law of homicide often distinguishes . . . between a person who knows that another person will be killed as the result of his conduct and a person who acts with the specific purpose of taking another's life"). . . . M. Hale, 1 Pleas of the Crown 412 (1847) ("If A., with an intent to prevent gangrene beginning in his hand doth without any advice cut off his hand, by which he dies, he is not thereby *felo de se* for tho it was a voluntary act, yet it was not with an intent to kill himself"). Put differently, the law distinguishes actions taken "because of" a given end from actions taken "in spite of" their unintended but foreseen consequences. *Feeney,* 442 U.S., at 279; *Compassion in Dying v. Washington,* 79 F. 3d 790, 858 (CA9 1996) (Kleinfeld, J., dissenting) ("When General Eisenhower ordered American soldiers onto the beaches of Normandy, he knew that he was sending many American soldiers to certain death. . . . His purpose, though, was to . . . liberate Europe from the Nazis").

Given these general principles, it is not surprising that many courts, including New York courts, have carefully distinguished refusing life-sustaining treatment from suicide. See, *e.g., Fosmire v. Nicoleau,* 75 N.Y. 2d 218, 227, and n. 2, 551 N.E. 2d 77, 82, and n. 2 (1990) ("[M]erely declining medical . . . care is not considered a suicidal act").[1] In fact, the first state-court decision explicitly to authorize withdrawing lifesaving treatment noted the "real distinction between the self-infliction of deadly harm and a self-determination against artificial life support." *In re Quinlan,* 70 N.J. 10, 43, 52. . . .

Similarly, the overwhelming majority of state legislatures have drawn a clear line between assisting suicide and withdrawing or permitting the refusal of unwanted lifesaving medical treatment by prohibiting the former and permitting the latter. And "nearly all states expressly disapprove of suicide and assisted suicide either in statutes dealing with durable powers of attorney in health-care situations, or in 'living will' statutes." *Kevorkian,* 447 Mich., at 478–479, and nn. 53–54, 527

N.W 2d, at 731–732, and nn. 53–54. Thus, even as the States move to protect and promote patients' dignity at the end of life, they remain opposed to physician-assisted suicide. . . .

This Court has also recognized, at least implicitly, the distinction between letting a patient die and making that patient die. In *Cruzan v. Director, Mo. Dept. of Health,* 497 U.S. 261, 278 (1990), we concluded that "[t]he principle that a competent person has a constitutionally protected liberty interest in refusing unwanted medical treatment may be inferred from our prior decisions," and we assumed the existence of such a right for purposes of that case, *id.,* at 279. But our assumption of a right to refuse treatment was grounded not, as the Court of Appeals supposed, on the proposition that patients have a general and abstract "right to hasten death," 80 F, 3d at 727–728, but on well established, traditional rights to bodily integrity and freedom from unwanted touching, *Cruzan,* 497 U.S., at 278–279; *id.,* at 287–288. (O'CONNOR, J., concurring). In fact, we observed that "the majority of States in this country have laws imposing criminal penalties on one who assists another to commit suicide." *Id.,* at 280. *Cruzan* therefore provides no support for the notion that refusing life-sustaining medical treatment is "nothing more nor less than suicide."

For all these reasons, we disagree with respondents' claim that the distinction between refusing lifesaving medical treatment and assisted suicide is "arbitrary" and "irrational." Brief for Respondents 44. Granted, in some cases, the line between the two may not be clear, but certainty is not required, even were it possible. Logic and contemporary practice support New York's judgment that the two acts are different, and New York may therefore, consistent with the Constitution, treat them differently. By permitting everyone to refuse unwanted medical treatment while prohibiting anyone from assisting a suicide, New York law follows a longstanding and rational distinction.

New York's reasons for recognizing and acting on this distinction — including prohibiting intentional killing and preserving life; preventing suicide; maintaining physicians' role as their patients' healers; protecting vulnerable people from indifference, prejudice, and psychological and financial pressure to end their lives; and avoiding a possible slide towards euthanasia — are discussed in greater detail in our opinion in *Glucksberg, ante.* These valid and important public interests easily satisfy the constitutional requirement that a legislative classification bear a rational relation to some legitimate end.

The judgment of the Court of Appeals is reversed.

It is so ordered.

1. Thus, the Second Circuit erred in reading New York law as creating a "right to hasten death"; instead, the authorities cited by the court recognize a right to refuse treatment, and nowhere equate the exercise of this right with suicide. *Schloendorff v. Society of New York Hospital,* 211 N.Y. 125, 129–130, 105 N.E. 92, 93 (1914), which contains Justice Cardozo's famous statement that "[e]very human being of adult years and sound mind has a right to determine what shall be done with his own body," was simply an informed-consent case. . . .

UNITED STATES SUPREME COURT

Washington, et al., Petitioners v. Harold Glucksberg et al.
On Writ of Certiorari to the United States
Court of Appeals for the Ninth Circuit

[June 26, 1997]

CHIEF JUSTICE REHNQUIST delivered the opinion of the Court.

The question presented in this case is whether Washington's prohibition against "caus[ing]" or "aid[ing]" a suicide offends the Fourteenth Amendment to the United States Constitution. We hold that it does not. . . .

In almost every State—indeed, in almost every western democracy—it is a crime to assist a suicide. The States' assisted-suicide bans are not innovations. Rather, they are longstanding expressions of the States' commitment to the protection and preservation of all human life. . . . Indeed, opposition to and condemnation of suicide—and, therefore, of assisting suicide—are consistent and enduring themes of our philosophical, legal, and cultural heritages. . . .

Because of advances in medicine and technology, Americans today are increasingly likely to die in institutions, from chronic illnesses. President's Comm'n for the Study of Ethical Problems in Medicine and Biomedical and Behavioral Research, Deciding to Forego Life-Sustaining Treatment 16–18 (1983). Public concern and democratic action are therefore sharply focused on how best to protect dignity and independence at the end of life, with the result that there have been many significant changes in state laws and in the attitudes these laws reflect. . . .

Thus, the States are currently engaged in serious, thoughtful examinations of physician-assisted suicide and other similar issues. For example, New York State's Task Force on Life and the Law—an ongoing, blue-ribbon commission composed of doctors, ethicists, lawyers, religious leaders, and interested laymen—was convened in 1984 and commissioned with "a broad mandate to recommend public policy on issues raised by medical advances." New York Task Force vii. . . .

Attitudes toward suicide itself have changed . . . but our laws have consistently condemned, and continue to prohibit, assisting suicide. Despite changes in medical technology and notwithstanding an increased emphasis on the importance of end-of-life decision-making, we have not retreated from this prohibition. Against this backdrop of history, tradition, and practice, we now turn to respondents' constitutional claim.

II

The Due Process Clause guarantees more than fair process, and the "liberty" it protects includes more than the absence of physical restraint. . . . The Clause also provides heightened protection against government interference with certain fundamental rights and liberty interests. . . . We have . . . assumed, and strongly suggested, that the Due Process Clause protects the traditional right to refuse unwanted lifesaving medical treatment. *Cruzan,* 497 U.S., at 278–279.

But we "ha[ve] always been reluctant to expand the concept of substantive due process because guideposts for responsible decisionmaking in this unchartered area are scarce and open-ended." *Collins,* 503 U.S., at 125. By extending constitutional protection to an asserted right or liberty interest, we, to a great extent, place the matter outside the arena of public debate and legislative action. . . .

Our established method of substantive-due-process analysis has two primary features: First, we have regularly observed that the Due Process Clause specially protects those fundamental rights and liberties which are, objectively, "deeply rooted in this Nation's history and tradition," *id.,* at 503 (plurality opinion); . . . Second, we have required in substantive-due-process cases a "careful description" of the asserted fundamental liberty interest. . . .

The Washington statute at issue in this case prohibits "aid[ing] another person to attempt suicide," Wash. Rev. Code §9A.36.060(1) (1994), and, thus, the question before us is whether the "liberty" specially protected by the Due Process Clause includes a right to commit suicide which itself includes a right to assistance in doing so.

We now inquire whether this asserted right has any place in our Nation's traditions. Here, as discussed above . . . we are confronted with a consistent and almost universal tradition that has long rejected the asserted right . . .

Respondents contend, however, that the liberty interest they assert *is* consistent with this Court's substantive-due-process line of cases, if not with this Nation's history and practice. Pointing to *Casey* and *Cruzan,* respondents read our jurisprudence in this area as reflecting a general tradition of "self-sovereignty," Brief of Respondents 12, and as teaching that the "liberty" protected by the Due Process Clause includes "basic and intimate exercises of personal autonomy," *id.,* at 10; see *Casey,* 505 U.S., at 847 ("It is a promise of the Constitution that there is a realm of personal liberty which the government may not enter"). According to respondents, our liberty jurisprudence, and the broad, individualistic principles it reflects, protects the "liberty of competent, terminally ill adults to make end-of-

life decisions free of undue government interference." Brief for Respondents 10. . . .

The decision to commit suicide with the assistance of another may be just as personal and profound as the decision to refuse unwanted medical treatment, but it has never enjoyed similar legal protection. Indeed, the two acts are widely and reasonably regarded as quite distinct. See *Quill v. Vacco, post,* at 5–13. In *Cruzan* itself, we recognized that most States outlawed assisted suicide — and even more do today — and we certainly gave no intimation that the right to refuse unwanted medical treatment could be somehow transmuted into a right to assistance in committing suicide. 497 U.S., at 280. . . .

[O]ur decisions lead us to conclude that the asserted "right" to assistance in committing suicide is not a fundamental liberty interest protected by the Due Process Clause. The Constitution also requires, however, that Washington's assisted-suicide ban be rationally related to legitimate government interests. . . . This requirement is unquestionably met here. As the court below recognized, 79 F. 3d, at 816–817,[1] Washington's assisted-suicide ban implicates a number of state interests.[2] . . .

First, Washington has an "unqualified interest in the preservation of human life." *Cruzan,* 497 U.S., at 282. The State's prohibition on assisted suicide, like all homicide laws, both reflects and advances its commitment to this interest. . . .

The State also has an interest in protecting the integrity and ethics of the medical profession. In contrast to the Court of Appeals' conclusion that "the integrity of the medical profession would [not] be threatened in any way by [physician-assisted suicide]," 79 F. 3d, at 827, the American Medical Association, like many other medical and physicians' groups, has concluded that "[p]hysician-assisted suicide is fundamentally incompatible with the physician's role as healer." American Medical Association, Code of Ethics §2.211 (1994); see Council on Ethical and Judicial Affairs, Decisions Near the End of Life, 267 JAMA 2229, 2233 (1992) ("[T]he societal risks of involving physicians in medical interventions to cause patients' deaths is too great"); New York Task Force 103–109 (discussing physicians' views). And physician-assisted suicide could, it is argued, undermine the trust that is essential to the doctor–patient relationship by blurring the time-honored line between healing and harming. . . .

Next, the State has an interest in protecting vulnerable groups — including the poor, the elderly, and disabled persons—from abuse, neglect, and mistakes. The Court of Appeals dismissed the State's concern that disadvantaged persons might be pressured into physician-assisted suicide as "ludicrous on its face." 79 F. 3d, at 825. We have recognized, however, the real risk of subtle coercion and undue influence in end-of-life situations. *Cruzan,* 497 U.S., at 281. Similarly, the New York Task Force warned that "[l]egalizing physician-assisted suicide would pose profound risks to many individuals who are ill and vulnerable. . . . The risk of harm is greatest for the many individuals in our society whose autonomy and well-being are already compromised by poverty, lack of access to good medical care, advanced age, or membership in a stigmatized social group." New York Task Force 120. . . .

Finally, the State may fear that permitting assisted suicide will start it down the path to voluntary and perhaps even involuntary euthanasia. . . .

We need not weigh exactly the relative strengths of these various interests. They are unquestionably important and legitimate, and Washington's ban on assisted suicide is at least reasonably related to their promotion and protection. We therefore hold that Wash. Rev. Code §9A.36.060(1) (1994) does not violate the Fourteenth Amendment, either on its face or "as applied to competent, terminally ill adults who wish to hasten their deaths by obtaining medication prescribed by their doctors." 79 F. 3d, at 838.

· · ·

Throughout the Nation, Americans are engaged in an earnest and profound debate about the morality, legality, and practicality of physician-assisted suicide. Our holding permits this debate to continue, as it should in a democratic society. The decision of the en banc Court of Appeals is reversed, and the case is remanded for further proceedings consistent with this opinion.

It is so ordered.

JUSTICE STEVENS, concurring in the judgments. . . .

A State, like Washington, that has authorized the death penalty and thereby has concluded that the sanctity of human life does not require that it always be preserved, must acknowledge that there are situations in which an interest in hastening death is legitimate. Indeed, not only is that interest sometimes legitimate, I am also convinced that there are times when it is entitled to constitutional protection.

· · ·

The state interests supporting a general rule banning the practice of physician-assisted suicide do not have the same force in all cases. . . . That interest not only justifies—it commands—maximum protection of every individual's interest in remaining alive, which in turn commands the same protection for decisions about whether to commence or to terminate life-support systems or to administer pain medication that may hasten death. Properly viewed, however, this interest is not a collective interest that should always outweigh the interests of a person who because of pain, incapacity, or sedation finds her life intolerable, but rather, an aspect of individual freedom. . . .

Although as a general matter the State's interest in the contributions each person may make to society outweighs the person's interest in ending her life, this interest does not have the same force for a terminally ill patient faced not with the choice of whether to live, only of how to die. Allowing the individual, rather than the State, to make judgments " 'about the "quality" of life that a particular individual may enjoy.' " *ante,* at 25 (quoting *Cruzan,* 497 U.S., at 282), does not mean that the lives of terminally-ill, disabled people have less value than the lives of those who are healthy, see *ante,* at 28. Rather, it gives proper recognition to the individual's interest in choosing a final chapter that accords with her life story, rather than one that demeans her values and poisons memories of her. . . .

Similarly, the State's legitimate interests in preventing suicide, protecting the vulnerable from coercion and abuse, and preventing euthanasia are less significant in this context. I agree that the State has a compelling interest in preventing persons from committing suicide because of depression, or coercion by third parties. But the State's legitimate interest in preventing abuse does not apply to an individual who is not victimized by abuse, who is not suffering from depression, and who makes a rational and voluntary decision to seek assistance in dying. . . .

Relatedly, the State and *amici* express the concern that patients whose physical pain is inadequately treated will be more likely to request assisted suicide. Encouraging the development and ensuring the availability of adequate pain treatment is of utmost importance; palliative care, however, cannot alleviate all pain and suffering. . . . An individual adequately informed of the care alternatives thus might make a rational choice for assisted suicide. For such an individual, the State's interest in preventing potential abuse and mistake is only minimally implicated.

The final major interest asserted by the State is its interest in preserving the traditional integrity of the medical profession. The fear is that a rule permitting physicians to assist in suicide is inconsistent with the perception that they serve their patients solely as healers. But for some patients, it would be a physician's refusal to dispense medication to ease their suffering and make their death tolerable and dignified that would be inconsistent with the healing role. . . . For doctors who have long-standing relationships with their patients, who have given their patients advice on alternative treatments, who are attentive to their patient's individualized needs, and who are knowledgeable about pain symptom management and palliative care options, see Quill, Death and Dignity, A Case of Individualized Decision Making, 324 New England J. of Med. 691–694 (1991), heeding a patient's desire to assist in her suicide would not serve to harm the physician–patient relationship. Furthermore, because physicians are already involved in making decisions that hasten the death of terminally ill patients—through termination of life support, withholding of medical treatment, and terminal sedation—there is in fact significant tension between the traditional view of the physician's role and the actual practice in a growing number of cases. . . .

I agree that the distinction between permitting death to ensue from an underlying fatal disease and causing it to occur by the administration of medication or other means provides a constitutionally sufficient basis for the State's classification. Unlike the Court, however, . . . I am not persuaded that in all cases there will in fact be a significant difference between the intent of the physicians, the patients or the families in the two situations.

There may be little distinction between the intent of a terminally-ill patient who decides to remove her life-support and one who seeks the assistance of a doctor in ending her life; in both situations, the patient is seeking to hasten a certain, impending death. The doctor's intent might also be the same in prescribing lethal medication as it is in terminating life support. A doctor who fails to administer medical treatment to one who is dying from a disease could be doing so with an intent to harm or kill that patient. Conversely, a doctor who prescribes lethal medication does not necessarily intend the patient's death—rather that doctor may seek simply to ease the patient's suffering and to com-

ply with her wishes. The illusory character of any differences in intent or causation is confirmed by the fact that the American Medical Association unequivocally endorses the practice of terminal sedation—the administration of sufficient dosages of pain-killing medication to terminally ill patients to protect them from excruciating pain even when it is clear that the time of death will be advanced. The purpose of terminal sedation is to ease the suffering of the patient and comply with her wishes, and the actual cause of death is the administration of heavy doses of lethal sedatives. This same intent and causation may exist when a doctor complies with a patient's request for lethal medication to hasten her death.

Thus, although the differences the majority notes in causation and intent between terminating life-support and assisting in suicide support the Court's rejection of the respondents' facial challenge, these distinctions may be inapplicable to particular terminally ill patients and their doctors. Our holding today in *Vacco v. Quill* that the Equal Protection Clause is not violated by New York's classification, just like our holding in *Washington v. Glucksberg* that the Washington statue is not invalid on its face, does not foreclose the possibility that some applications of the New York statute may impose an intolerable intrusion on the patient's freedom.

There remains room for vigorous debate about the outcome of particular cases that are not necessarily resolved by the opinions announced today. How such cases may be decided will depend on their specific facts. In my judgment, however, it is clear that the so-called "unqualified interest in the preservation of human life," *Cruzan,* 497 U.S., at 282, *Glucksberg, ante,* at 24, is not itself sufficient to outweigh the interest in liberty that may justify the only possible means of preserving a dying patient's dignity and alleviating her intolerable suffering. . . .

JUSTICE O'CONNOR, concurring.*

Death will be different for each of us. For many, the last days will be spent in physical pain and perhaps the despair that accompanies physical deterioration and a loss of control of basic bodily and mental functions.

*JUSTICE GINSBURG concurs in the Court's judgments substantially for the reasons stated in this opinion. JUSTICE BREYER joins this opinion except insofar as it joins the opinions of the Court.

Some will seek medication to alleviate that pain and other symptoms.

The Court frames the issues in this case as whether the Due Process Clause of the Constitution protects a "right to commit suicide, which itself includes a right to assistance in doing so," . . . and concludes that our Nation's history, legal traditions, and practices do not support the existence of such a right. I join the Court's opinions because I agree that there is no generalized right to "commit suicide." But respondents urge us to address the narrower question whether a mentally competent person who is experiencing great suffering has a constitutionally cognizable interest in controlling the circumstances of his or her imminent death. I see no need to reach that question in the context of the facial challenges to the New York and Washington laws at issue here. . . . The parties and *amici* agree that in these States a patient who is suffering from a terminal illness and who is experiencing great pain has no legal barriers to obtaining medication, from qualified physicians, to alleviate that suffering, even to the point of causing unconsciousness and hastening death. . . . In this light, even assuming that we would recognize such an interest, I agree that the State's interests in protecting those who are not truly competent or facing imminent death, or those whose decisions to hasten death would not truly be voluntary, are sufficiently weighty to justify a prohibition against physician-assisted suicide. . . .

Every one of us at some point may be affected by our own or a family member's terminal illness. There is no reason to think the democratic process will not strike the proper balance between the interests of terminally ill, mentally competent individuals who would seek to end their suffering and the State's interests in protecting those who might seek to end life mistakenly or under pressure. As the Court recognizes, States are presently undertaking extensive and serious evaluation of physician-assisted suicide and other related issues. . . . In such circumstances, "the . . . challenging task of crafting appropriate procedures for safeguarding . . . liberty interests is entrusted to the 'laboratory' of the States . . . in the first instance." *Cruzan v. Director, Mo. Dept. of Health,* 497 U.S. 261, 292 (1990) (O'CONNOR, J., concurring) (citing *New State Ice Co. v. Liebmann,* 285 U.S. 262, 311 (1932)).

In sum, there is no need to address the question whether suffering patients have a constitutionally cognizable interest in obtaining relief from the suffering that they may experience in the last days of their lives. There is no dispute that dying patients in Washington and New York can obtain palliative care, even when doing so would hasten their deaths. The difficulty in defining terminal illness and the risk that a dying patient's request for assistance in ending his or her life might not be truly voluntary justifies the prohibitions on assisted suicide we uphold here.

NOTES

1. The court identified and discussed six state interests: (1) preserving life; (2) preventing suicide; (3) avoiding the involvement of third parties and use of arbitrary, unfair, or undue influence; (4) protecting family members and loved ones; (5) protecting the integrity of the medical profession; and (6) avoiding future movement toward euthanasia and other abuses. 79 F. 3d, at 816–832.

2. Respondents also admit the existence of these interests, Brief for Respondents 28–39, but contend that Washington could better promote and protect them through regulation, rather than prohibition, of physician-assisted suicide. Our inquiry, however, is limited to the question whether the State's prohibition is rationally related to legitimate state interests.

AMERICAN MEDICAL ASSOCIATION, COUNCIL ON ETHICAL AND JUDICIAL AFFAIRS

Physician-Assisted Suicide

INTRODUCTION

Physician-assisted suicide presents one of the greatest contemporary challenges to the medical profession's ethical responsibilities. Proposed as a means toward more humane care of the dying, assisted suicide threatens the very core of the medical profession's ethical integrity.

While the Council of Ethical and Judicial Affairs has long-standing policy opposing euthanasia, it did not expressly address the issue of assisted suicide until its June 1991 report, Decisions Near the End of Life. In that report, the Council concluded that physician-assisted suicide is contrary to the professional role of physicians and that therefore physicians "must not . . . participate in assisted suicide." Previously, the Council had issued reports rejecting the use of euthanasia. In June 1977, the Council stated that "mercy killings or euthanasia — is contrary to public policy, medical tradition, and the most fundamental measures of human value and worth." Similarly, in June 1988, the Council reaffirmed "its strong opposition to 'mercy killing.'" . . .

DEFINITIONS

Assisted suicide occurs when a physician provides a patient with the medical means and/or the medical knowledge to commit suicide. For example, the physician could provide sleeping pills and information about the lethal dose, while aware that the patient is contemplating suicide. In physician-assisted suicide, the patient performs the life-ending act, whereas in euthanasia, the physician administers the death-causing drug or other agent.

Assisted suicide and euthanasia should not be confused with the provision of a palliative treatment that may hasten the patient's death ("double effect"). The intent of the palliative treatment is to relive pain and suffering, not to end the patient's life, but the patient's death is a possible side effect of the treatment. It is ethically acceptable for a physician to gradually increase the appropriate medication for a patient, realizing that the medication may depress respiration and cause death.

Assisted suicide also must be distinguished from withholding or withdrawing life-sustaining treatment, in which the patient's death occurs because the patient or the patient's proxy, in consultation with the treating physician, decides that the disadvantages of treatment outweigh its advantages and therefore that treatment is refused.

ETHICAL CONSIDERATIONS

1. INAPPROPRIATE EXTENSION OF THE RIGHT TO REFUSE TREATMENT

In granting patients the right to refuse life-sustaining medical treatment, society has acknowledged the right of patients to self-determination on matters of their medical care even if the exercise of that self-determination results in the patient's death. Because any medical treatment offers both benefits and detriments, and people attach different values to those benefits and detriments, only the patient can determine whether the advantages of treatment outweigh the disadvantages. As the Council has previously concluded, "[t]he principle of patient autonomy requires that physicians must respect the decision to forgo life-sustaining treatment of a patient who possesses decision-making capacity."

Although a patient's choice of suicide also represents an expression of self-determination, there is a fundamental difference between refusing life-sustaining treatment and demanding a life-ending treatment. The right of self-determination is a right to accept or refuse offered interventions, but not to decide what should be offered. The right to refuse life-sustaining treatment does not automatically entail a right to insist that others take action to bring on death.

When a life-sustaining treatment is declined, the patient dies primarily because of an underlying disease. The illness is simply allowed to take its natural course. With assisted suicide, however, death is hastened by the taking of a lethal drug or other agent. Although a physician cannot force a patient to accept a treatment against the patient's will, even if the treatment is life-sustaining, it does not follow that a physician ought to provide a lethal agent to the patient. The inability of physicians to prevent death does not imply that physicians are free to help cause death.

For a number of reasons, the medical profession has rejected assisted suicide as fundamentally inconsistent with the professional role of physicians as healers. Indeed, according to the Hippocratic Oath, physicians shall "give no deadly drug to any, though it be asked of [them], nor will [they] counsel such." Physicians serve patients not because patients exercise self-determination but because patients are in need. Therefore, a patient may not insist on treatments that are inconsistent with sound medical practices. Rather, physicians provide treatments that are designated to make patients well, or as well as possible. The physician's role is to affirm life, not hasten its demise.

Permitting assisted suicide would compromise the physician's professional role also because it would involve physicians in making inappropriate value judgments about the quality of life. Indeed, with the refusal of life-sustaining treatment, society does not limit the right to refuse treatment only to patients who meet a specific standard of suffering. With refusal of treatment, the state recognizes that the patient (or the patient's proxy) alone can decide that there no longer is a meaningful quality of life.

Objections to causing death also underlie religious views on assisted suicide. Most of the world's major religions oppose suicide in all forms and do not condone physician assisted suicide even in cases of suffering or imminent death. In justification of their position, religions generally espouse common beliefs about the sanctity of human life, the appropriate interpretation of suffering, and the subordination of individual autonomy to a belief in God's will or sovereignty.

2. THE PHYSICIAN'S ROLE

The relief of suffering is an essential part of the physician's role as healer, and some patients seek assisted suicide because they are suffering greatly. Suffering is a complex process that may exist in one or several forms, including pain, loss of self-control and independence, a sense of futility, loss of dignity and fear of dying. It is incumbent upon physicians to discuss and identify the elements contributing to the patient's suffering and address each appropriately. The patient, and family members as well, should participate with the physician to ensure that measures to provide comfort will be given the patient in a timely fashion.

One of the greatest concerns reported by patients facing a terminal illness or chronic debilitation is the fear that they will be unable to receive adequate relief for their pain. Though there is some basis for this fear in a small number of cases, for most patients pain can be adequately controlled. Inadequate pain relief is only rarely due to the unavailability of effective pain control medications; more often, it may be caused by reluctance on the part of physicians to use these medications aggressively enough to sufficiently alleviate the patient's pain. Further efforts to educate physicians about advanced pain management techniques, both at the undergraduate and graduate levels, are necessary to overcome any shortcomings in this area.

Pain control medications should be employed in whatever dose necessary, and by whatever route necessary, to fully relieve the patient's pain. The patient's treatment plan should be tailored to meet the particular patient's needs. Some patients will request less pain control in order to remain mentally lucid; others may need to be sedated to the point of unconsciousness. Ongoing discussions with the patient, if possible, or with the patient's family or surrogate decisionmaker will be helpful in identifying the level of pain control necessary to relieve the patient's suffering in accordance with the patient's treatment goals. Techniques of patient controlled analgesia (PCA) enhance the sense of control of terminally ill patients, and, for this reason, are particularly effective. Often, it is the loss of control, rather than physical pain, that causes the most suffering for dying patients.

The first priority for the care of patients facing severe pain as a result of a terminal illness or chronic condition should be the relief of their pain. Fear of addiction to pain medications should not be a barrier to the adequate relief of pain. Nor should physicians be concerned about legal repercussions or sanctions by licensing boards. The courts and regulatory bodies readily distinguish between use of narcotic drugs to relieve pain in dying patients and use in other situations. Indeed, it is well accepted both ethically and legally that the pain medications may be administered in whatever necessary dose to relieve the patient's suffering, even if the medication has the side effect of causing addiction or of causing death through respiratory depression.

Relieving the patient's psychosocial and other suffering is as important as relieving the patient's pain. When the treatment goals for a patient in the end stages of a terminal illness shift from curative efforts to comfort care, the level of physician involvement in the patient's care should in no way decrease. Patients in these circumstances must be managed "in a setting of [the patient's] own choosing, as free as possible from pain and other burdensome symptoms, and with the optimal psychological and spiritual support of family and friends." Because the loss of control may be the greatest fear of dying patients, all efforts should be made to maximize the patient's sense of control.

Accomplishing these goals requires renewed efforts from physicians, nurses, family members and other sources of psychological and spiritual support. Often, the patient's despair with his or her quality of life can be relieved by psychiatric intervention. Seriously ill patients contemplating suicide may develop a renewed desire to live as a result of counseling and/or antidepressant medications. When requests for assisted suicide occur, it is important to provide the patient with an evaluation by a health professional with expertise in psychiatric aspects of terminal illness.

The hospice movement has made great strides in providing comfort care to patients at the end of life. In hospice care, the patient's symptoms, including pain, are aggressively treated to make the patient as comfortable as possible, but efforts to extend the patient's life are usually not pursued. Hospice patients are often cared for at home, or, if their condition requires care to be delivered in an institutional setting, intrusive medical technology is kept to a minimum. The provision of a humane, low technology environment in which to spend their final days can go far in alleviating patients' fears of an undignified, lonely, technologically dependent death.

Physicians must not abandon or neglect the needs of their terminally ill patients. Indeed, the desire for sui-

cide is a signal to the physician that more intensive efforts to comfort and care for the patient are needed. Physicians, family and friends can help patients near the end of life by their presence and by their loving support. Patients may feel obligated to die in order to spare their families the emotional and financial burden of their care or to spare limited societal resources for other health care needs. While patients may rationally and reasonably be concerned about the burden on others, physicians and family members must reassure patients that they are under no obligation to end their lives prematurely because of such concerns.

In some cases, terminally ill patients voluntarily refuse food or oral fluids. In such cases, patient autonomy must be respected and forced feeding or aggressive parental rehydration should not be employed. Emphasis should be placed on renewed efforts at pain control, sedation and other comfort care for the associated discomfort.

3. "SLIPPERY SLOPE" CONCERNS

Permitting assisted suicide opens the door to policies that carry far greater risks. For example, if assisted suicide is permitted, then there is a strong argument for allowing euthanasia. It would be arbitrary to permit patients who have the physical ability to take a pill to end their lives, but not let similarly suffering patients die if they require the lethal drug to be administered by another person. Once euthanasia is permitted, however, there is a serious risk of involuntary death. Given the acceptance of withdrawal of life-sustaining treatment by proxies for incompetent patients, it would be easy for society to permit euthanasia for incompetent patients by proxy.

The Dutch experience with euthanasia demonstrates the risks of sanctioning physician assisted suicide. In the Netherlands, there are strict criteria for the use of euthanasia that are similar to the criteria proposed for assisted suicide in the United States. In the leading study of euthanasia in the Netherlands, however, researchers found that, in about 28 percent of cases of euthanasia or physician-assisted suicide, the strict criteria were not fulfilled, suggesting that some patients' lives were ended prematurely or involuntarily. In a number of cases, the decision to end the patient's life was made by a surrogate decisionmaker since the patient had lost decisionmaking capacity by the time the decision to employ euthanasia was made.

RECOMMENDATIONS

In lieu of Resolution 3 (A-93) the Council on Ethical and Judicial Affairs recommends that the following statements be adopted:

1. Physician-assisted suicide is fundamentally inconsistent with the physician's professional role.
2. It is critical that the medical profession redouble its efforts to ensure that dying patients are provided optimal treatment for their pain and other discomfort. The use of more aggressive comfort care measures, including greater reliance on hospice care, can alleviate the physical and emotional suffering the dying patients experience. Evaluation and treatment by a health professional with expertise in the psychiatric aspects of terminal illness can often alleviate the suffering that leads a patient to desire assisted suicide.
3. Physicians must resist the natural tendency to withdraw physically and emotionally from their terminally ill patients. When the treatment goals for a patient in the end stages of a terminal illness shift from curative efforts to comfort care, the level of physician involvement in the patient's care should in no way decrease.
4. Requests for physician-assisted suicide should be a signal to the physician that the patient's needs are unmet and further evaluation to identify the elements contributing to the patient's suffering is necessary. Multidisciplinary intervention, including specialty consultation, pastoral care, family counseling and other modalities, should be sought as clinically indicated.
5. Further efforts to educate physicians about advance pain management techniques, both at the undergraduate and graduate levels, are necessary to overcome any shortcomings in this area. Physicians should recognize that courts and regulatory bodies readily distinguish between use of narcotic drugs to relieve pain in dying patients and use in other situations.

JAMES L. BERNAT, BERNARD GERT, AND R. PETER MOGIELNICKI

Patient Refusal of Hydration and Nutrition: An Alternative to Physician-Assisted Suicide or Voluntary Active Euthanasia

Public and scholarly debates on legalizing physician-assisted suicide (PAS) and voluntary active euthanasia (VAE) have increased dramatically in recent years.[1-5] These debates have highlighted a significant moral controversy between those who regard PAS and VAE as morally permissible and those who do not. Unfortunately, the adversarial nature of this controversy has led both sides to ignore an alternative that avoids moral controversy altogether and has fewer associated practical problems in its implementation. In this article, we suggest that educating chronically and terminally ill patients about the feasibility of patient refusal of hydration and nutrition (PRHN) can empower them to control their own destiny without requiring physicians to reject the taboos on PAS and VAE that have existed for millennia. To be feasible, this alternative requires confirmation of the preliminary scientific evidence that death by starvation and dehydration need not be accompanied by suffering.

DEFINITIONS

Before proceeding, we will define several terms. Patients are *competent* to make a decision about their

Reprinted by permission of the publisher from Archives of Internal Medicine 153 (December 1993), 2723–2728. © 1993, American Medical Association.

health care if they have the capacity to understand and appreciate all the information necessary to make a rational decision. Patient competence, freedom from coercion, and the receipt of adequate information from the physician are the elements of valid (informed) consent or refusal of treatment.[6,7]

A decision is *rational* if it does not produce harm to the patient (e.g., death, pain, or disability) without an adequate reason (e.g., to avoid suffering an equal or greater harm). It is rational to rank harms in different ways. For example, it is rational to rank immediate death as worse than several months of suffering from a terminal disease; it is also rational to rank the suffering as worse than immediate death. We count as irrational only those rankings that result in the person suffering great harm and that would be rejected as irrational by almost everyone in the person's culture or subculture.[6,7]

Physician-assisted suicide occurs when the physician provides the necessary medical means for the patient to commit suicide, but death is not the direct result of the physician's act. In PAS, a physician accedes to the rational *request* of a competent patient to be provided with the necessary medical means for the patient to commit suicide. A suicide is *physician-assisted* if the physician's participation is a necessary but not sufficient component to the suicide. For example, a physician who complies with a dying patient's request to write a prescription for 100 pentobarbital tablets that the patient plans to swallow at a later time to commit suicide would be performing PAS.

Voluntary active euthanasia ("killing") occurs when a physician accedes to the rational *request* of a competent patient for some act by the physician to cause the death of the patient, which usually follows immediately on its completion. The physician's act in VAE is both necessary and sufficient to produce the patient's death. For example, a physician who complies with a dying patient's request to kill him mercifully with a lethal intravenous injection of pentobarbital sodium would be performing VAE.

Voluntary passive euthanasia ("letting die") occurs when a physician abides by the rational *refusal* of treatment by a competent patient with the knowledge that doing so will result in the patient dying sooner than if the physician had overruled the patient's refusal and had started or continued treatment. For example, when a physician complies with the refusal of a ventilator-dependent patient with motor neuron disease to receive further mechanical ventilatory support, and the patient dies as the result of extubation, this act is an example

of voluntary passive euthanasia. Providing medical treatment to alleviate the pain and discomfort that normally accompanies extubation neither alters the fact that the physician is letting the patient die nor makes the act PAS. *Patient refusal of hydration and nutrition* is an example of voluntary passive euthanasia.

There are critical differences in the morality and legality of these acts. Physician-assisted suicide is legally prohibited in many jurisdictions, and there is a current controversy about whether it is moral. Voluntary active euthanasia is classified as criminal homicide and hence is strictly illegal in nearly every jurisdiction. Like PAS, its morality remains controversial. By contrast, there is no disagreement that physicians are morally and legally prohibited from overruling the rational refusal of therapy by a competent patient even when they know that death will result. There is also no disagreement that physicians are allowed to provide appropriate treatment for the pain and suffering that may accompany such refusals. In other words, physicians are morally and legally *required* to respect the competent patient's rational refusal of therapy, and they are morally and legally allowed to provide appropriate treatment for the pain and suffering involved. Physicians also are morally and legally required to abide by such refusals given as advance directives.[8]

CONFUSION CONCERNING KILLING VS LETTING DIE

Three areas of terminologic confusion that have clouded clear thinking about the morality of physician involvement in the care of the dying patient are (1) requests vs refusals by patients, (2) acts vs omissions by physicians, and (3) "natural" vs other causes of death.

PATIENTS' REQUESTS VS REFUSALS

Physicians are morally and legally required to honor a competent patient's rational *refusal* of therapy.[9-11] This requirement arises from the moral and legal prohibition against depriving a person of freedom and from the liberty-based right of a person to be left alone. In the medical context, it requires that the patient provide valid consent before any medical tests or treatments may be performed.

The moral and legal requirement to honor a refusal does not extend, however, to honoring a patient's *request* for specific therapy or other acts. Physicians should honor such requests or refuse to honor them on the basis of their professional judgment about the legal, moral, or medical appropriateness of doing so. A common example of the exercise of this freedom is physicians' refusal to prescribe requested narcotics in situations in which they judge narcotics to be inappropriate. . . .

The distinction between requests and refusals has a critical importance in understanding the distinction between voluntary passive euthanasia (letting die) and VAE (killing). Patient *refusals* must be honored when they represent the rational decisions of competent patients even when physicians know death will result. There is no moral requirement to honor patient *requests* when physicians know death will result and there may be legal prohibitions against doing so.

PHYSICIANS' ACTS VS OMISSIONS

Some philosophers have misunderstood the definitions of VAE (killing) and passive euthanasia (letting die, including PRHN) and their moral significance by basing the distinction between killing and letting die on the distinction between acts and omissions.[12,13] In so doing, they have followed many physicians who have concentrated solely on what they themselves do (acts) or do not do (omissions) in distinguishing between killing and letting die. This way of distinguishing between killing and letting die creates a false moral distinction between a physician turning off intravenous feeding (act) and not replacing the intravenous solution container when it is empty (omission). When the distinction between killing and letting die is made in this way, it undermines legitimate medical and legal practice that permits allowing to die and does not permit killing.

This mistaken narrow focus on what the physician does or does not do without taking into account the larger context in which the physician acts or does not act can lead to the mistaken conclusion that PAS and VAE are really no different from voluntary passive euthanasia or "letting die." Recognition of the key role of whether or not the action is in response to the *patient's request* or the *patient's refusal* casts the issue in a clearer light.

As a matter of medical and legal practice, on the basis of a rational refusal of a competent patient, it is permitted either not to begin ventilatory therapy or to stop it; not to start treatment with antibiotics or to discontinue antibiotics; and not to start artificial hydration and nutrition or to cease them. All of these acts and omissions are morally and legally permitted when they result from a rational refusal by a competent patient. Indeed, it is misleading to say that these acts are morally and legally permitted, for they are morally and legally *required.* It is the rational refusal by a competent patient that is decisive here, not whether the physician acts or omits acting. It is the patient's refusal that makes the physician's acts and omissions "letting die" rather than "killing." Whether honoring this refusal requires the physician to act or omit acting is irrelevant. That is why those who base the distinction between killing and letting die on the distinction between acts and omissions mistakenly conclude that no morally relevant distinction exists.

'NATURAL' VS OTHER CAUSES OF DEATH

The term *natural,* as in "death by natural causes," has been another source of confusion. *Natural* is often used as a word of praise or, more generally, as a way of condoning something that otherwise would be considered unacceptable. Thus, voluntary passive euthanasia is often presented as acceptable because it allows the patient to "die a natural death." Because the death was caused by the disease process, no person is assigned responsibility for the death. The freedom from responsibility for the patient's death is psychologically helpful for the physician. To make some state laws authorizing advance directives more acceptable to the public, they even have been labeled "natural death acts."

When death results from lack of hydration and nutrition, however, it is less plausible to say that "the death was caused by the disease process." Thus, someone must be assigned responsibility for the patient's death, and physicians wish to avoid this responsibility. A partial explanation for the misuse of technology to prolong dying unjustifiably may be an attempt by physicians to avoid this psychological responsibility. Physicians who recognize that patients have the authority to refuse any treatment, including hydration and nutrition, are more likely to avoid unjustified feelings of responsibility for their deaths.

Just as it is erroneous to think that the distinction between acts and omissions has any moral relevance, so it is erroneous to think that anything morally significant turns on the use of the terms *natural* or *cause.* What is morally significant is that the terminally ill patient is competent and has made a rational decision to refuse further treatment. Indeed, it is not even important whether what the patient has refused counts as treatment. If the patient has refused, the physician has no moral or legal authority to overrule that refusal. It is morally and legally irrelevant whether or not the resulting death is considered natural.

PATIENT REFUSAL OF HYDRATION AND NUTRITION

We maintain that a preferable alternative to legalization of PAS and VAE is for physicians to educate patients that they may refuse hydration and nutrition and that physicians will help them do so in a way that minimizes suffering. Chronically or terminally ill patients who wish to gain more control over their deaths can then refuse to eat and drink and refuse enteral or parenteral feedings or hydration. The failure of the present debate to include this alternative may be the result of the confusion discussed above, an erroneous assumption that thirst and hunger remain strong drives in terminal illness, and a misconception that failure to satisfy these drives causes intractable suffering. . . .

It is the consensus of experienced physicians and nurses that terminally ill patients dying of dehydration or lack of nutrition do not suffer if treated properly. In fact, maintaining physiologic hydration and adequate nutrition is difficult in most seriously ill patients because intrinsic thirst and hunger are usually diminished or absent. . . .

However, if the distinction between killing and letting die is based as it should be on patients' requests vs patients' refusals, these latter considerations lose their force. Now the crucial consideration becomes the degree of suffering associated with lack of hydration and nutrition. If the associated suffering is trivial, PRHN clearly has major advantages over PAS or VAE. Only if this suffering is unmanageable does the choice become more difficult. Scientific studies and anecdotal reports both suggest that dehydration and starvation in the seriously ill do not cause significant suffering. Physicians and particularly nurses have written many observational pieces describing peaceful and apparently comfortable deaths by starvation and dehydration.[14–16] Lay observers have corroborated these reports. . . .[17]

A handful of laboratory studies and clinical trials are consistent with these older observational comments, but the picture is far from complete. Starvation is known to produce increased levels of acetoacetate, β-hydroxybutyrate, and acetone.[18] Other ketones (methyl butyl ketone and methyl heptyl ketone) have been shown to have an anesthetic action on isolated squid axons.[19] Depriving male Wistar rats of water and food for periods ranging from 24 to 72 hours has been shown to increase the levels of some endogenous opioids in the hypothalamus, although levels elsewhere in the brain and other organs decrease.[20] Healthy elderly men (over 65 years old) have been demonstrated to experience reduced thirst and associated symptoms during a 24-hour period of water deprivation and, when given ad libitum access to water to correct their dehydration, do so much more slowly than young healthy men.[21]

Observational data on the experience of terminally ill patients dying of dehydration have been recorded most recently in the hospice literature. This evidence suggests that the overwhelming majority of hospice deaths resulting from lack of hydration and nutrition can be managed such that the patients remain comfortable.[14, 22–25] In a 1990 survey of 826 members of the (US) Academy of Hospice Physicians, 89% of hospice nurses and 86% of hospice physicians reported that their terminal patients who died by cessation of hydration and nutrition had peaceful and comfortable deaths.[26]

Taken in toto, the anecdotal reports, laboratory studies, and the observations of nurses and physicians who care for terminally ill patients suggest that lack of hydration and nutrition does not cause unmanageable suffering in terminally ill patients and may even have an analgesic effect. Clinical experience with severely ill patients suggests that the major symptom of dry mouth can be relieved by ice chips, methyl cellulose, artificial saliva, or small sips of water insufficient to reverse progressive dehydration.

BENEFITS OF PRHN OVER PAS AND VAE

Unlike PAS and VAE, PRHN is recognized by all as consistent with current medical, moral, and legal practices. It does not compromise public confidence in the medical profession because it does not require physicians to assume any new role or responsibility that could alter their roles of healer, caregiver, and counselor. It places the proper emphasis on the duty of physicians to care for dying patients, because these patients need care and comfort measures during the dying period. It encourages physicians to engage in educational discussions with patients and families about dying and the desirability of formulating clear advance directives.

Legalization of PAS or VAE would likely create unintended and harmful social pressures and expectations. Many elderly or chronically ill patients could feel "the duty to die." They would request euthanasia not on the basis of personal choice but because they believed that their families considered them a burden and expected them to agree to be killed. Furthermore, patients might sense pressure from their physicians to consider VAE as an alternative and agree because the physicians must know what is best for them.[27] The meaning of "voluntary" euthanasia thus could become corrupted, causing the elderly and chronically ill to become victimized.

Unlike the "duty to die" resulting from legalizing PAS or VAE, it is unlikely that patients choosing to die by PRHN would feel as much social pressure or expectations from family members to die earlier because of the duration of the process and the opportunity therein for reconsideration and family interaction. Furthermore, it is much less likely that there would be pressure from physicians or other health professionals. Additionally, the several-day interval before unconsciousness ensues from PRHN would permit time for appropriate mourning and good-byes to family and friends.

Physicians may experience psychological stress about the patient's refusal of hydration and nutrition. Their moral and legal obligation to respect the treatment refusal should absolve some of the physician's discomfort. Physicians can seek no such solace in PAS or VAE because even if both were legalized, they would not be required. Physicians acceding to requests for PAS or VAE, even if it were legal, do so without legal or moral force compelling them to do so. This underscores the essential difference between passive euthanasia and PAS or VAE. It also lays bare the distress to be expected by physicians should they become involved with PAS or VAE in that they always will do so without an accompanying moral mandate.

Legalization of PAS or VAE would require the creation of a network of cumbersome legal safeguards to protect patients from abuse and misunderstanding or miscommunication. Despite such bureaucratic efforts, these would remain a risk that the practice of voluntary euthanasia would extend to involuntary cases, as has been alleged in the Dutch experience where VAE, although officially illegal, is permitted if physicians follow a series of judicial guidelines.[28, 29] Furthermore, the safeguards would require the insinuation of courts, lawyers, and bureaucrats between the patient–family and the physician. The new legal requirements could have the effect of delaying the patient's death and generating unnecessary administrative complexity and expense.

Unlike PAS and VAE, PRHN is lawful already in most jurisdictions. Indeed, refusal of hydration and nutrition is listed as an option in commonly drafted advance directives in the United States. Communication errors, misunderstandings, and abuse are less likely with PRHN than with PAS or VAE and thus are less likely to result in an unwanted earlier death. The patient who refuses hydration and nutrition clearly demonstrates the seriousness and consistency of his or her desire to die. The seven-day interval before the patient becomes unconscious provides time to reconsider the decision and for the family to accept that dying clearly represents the patient's wish. Furthermore, the process can begin immediately without first requiring legal approvals or other bureaucratic interventions. Thus, it may allow the patient to die faster than PAS or VAE, given the delays intrinsic to bureaucratic process.

THE PHYSICIAN'S ROLE IN PRHN

The current interest in legalizing PAS and VAE misplaces the emphasis of physicians' duties to their dying patients. Physicians should be more concerned about providing patients optimal terminal care than killing them or helping them kill themselves. Legalizing PAS would make it unnecessary for physicians to strive to maximize comfort measures in terminally ill patients and unnecessary for society to support research to improve the science of palliation. By comparison, PRHN appropriately encourages the physician to attend to the medical treatment of dying patients.

The physician's traditional role has been summarized as "to cure sometimes, to relieve often, and to comfort always."[30] With PRHN, the physician can concentrate his or her energy on the last two of these three challenging tasks. In the modern era, this involves a number of important pragmatic matters worthy of review. . . .

There needs to be societal acceptance that physicians have a moral duty to respect the rational wishes of competent, chronically ill but not terminally ill patients who wish to die by PRHN or other valid refusals of therapy. There is no reason why such patients should not have the same rights as the terminally ill to refuse life-sustaining therapies including hydration and nutrition. The American Academy of Neurology recently published a position statement asserting that chronically ill patients with severe paralysis and intact cognition, whether terminally ill or not, have the right to refuse life-sustaining therapy, including hydration and nutrition.[31,32] . . .

1. Crigger BJ, ed. Dying well? a colloquy on euthanasia and assisted suicide. *Hastings Cent Rep.* 1992;22: 6–55.

2. Campbell CS, Crigger BJ, eds. Mercy, murder, and morality: perspectives on euthanasia. *Hastings Cent Rep.* 1989;19(suppl 1): 1–32.

3. Pellegrino ED. Doctors must not kill. *J Clin Ethics.* 1992; 3:95–102.

4. Quill TE, Cassel CK, Meier DE. Care of the hopelessly ill: proposed clinical criteria for physician-assisted suicide. *N Engl J Med.* 1992;327:1380–1384.

5. Brody H. Assisted death: a compassionate response to a medical failure. *N Engl J Med.* 1992;327:1384–1388.

6. Culver CM, Gert B. Basic ethical concepts in neurologic practice. *Semin Neurol.* 1984;4:1–8.

7. Gert B, Culver CM. Moral theory in neurologic practice. *Semin Neurol.* 1984;4:9–14.

8. Gert B, Culver CM. Distinguishing between active and passive euthanasia. *Clin Geriatr Med.* 1986;2:29–36.

9. Culver CM, Gert B. *Philosophy in Medicine: Conceptual and Ethical Issues in Medicine and Psychiatry.* New York, NY: Oxford University Press; 1982:20–64.

10. Gert B. *Morality: A New Justification of the Moral Rules.* New York, NY: Oxford University Press; 1988:282–303.

11. Meisel A. Legal myths about terminating life support. *Arch Intern Med.* 1991;151:1497–1502.

12. Rachels J. Active and passive euthanasia. *N Engl J Med.* 1975;292:78–80.

13. Brock DW. Voluntary active euthanasia. *Hastings Cent Rep.* 1992;22:10–22.

14. Andrews M, Levine A. Dehydration in the terminal patient: perception of hospice nurses. *Am J Hospice Care.* 1989;3:31–34.

15. Zerwekh J. The dehydration question. *Nursing.* 1983;13: 47–51.

16. Printz LA. Terminal dehydration, a compassionate treatment. *Arch Intern Med.* 1992;152:697–700.

17. Nearing H. *Loving and Leaving the Good Life.* Post Mills, Vt: Chelsea Green Publishing Co; 1992.

18. Owen O, Caprio S, Reichard G, et al. Ketosis of starvation: a revisit and new perspectives. *Clin Endocrinol Metab.* 1983;12: 359–379.

19. Elliott JR, Haydon DA, Hendry BM. Anaesthetic action of esters and ketones: evidence for an interaction with the sodium channel protein in squid axons. *J Physiol.* 1984;354:407–418.

20. Majeed NH, Lason W, Prewlocka B, et al. Brain and peripheral opioid peptides after changes in ingestive behavior. *Neuroendocrinology.* 1986;42:267–272.

21. Phillips PA, Rolls BJ, Ledingham JGG, et al. Reduced thirst after water deprivation in healthy elderly men. *N Engl J Med.* 1984;311:753–759.

22. Miller RJ, Albright PG. What is the role of nutritional support and hydration in terminal cancer patients? *Am J Hospice Care.* 1989;6:33–38.

23. Cox SS. Is dehydration painful? *Ethics Med.* 1987;12:1–2.

24. Lichter I, Hunt E. The last 48 hours of life. *J Palliat Care.* 1990;6:7–15.

25. Miller RJ. Hospice care as an alternative to euthanasia. *Law Med Health Care.* 1992;20:127–132.

26. Miller RJ. Nutrition and hydration in terminal disease. *J Palliat Care.* In press.

27. Kamisar Y. Some non-religious views against proposed 'mercy-killing' legislation. *Minn Law Rev.* 1958;42:969–1042.

28. Benrubi GI. Euthanasia: the need for procedural safeguards. *N Engl J Med.* 1992;326:197–199.

29. Van der Maas PJ, van Delden JJM, Pijnenborg L, Looman CWN. Euthanasia and other medical decisions concerning the end of life. *Lancet.* 1991;338:669–674.

30. Strauss MB, ed. *Familiar Medical Quotations.* Boston, Mass: Little Brown & Co; 1968:410.

31. American Academy of Neurology. Position statement, certain aspects of the care and management of profoundly and irreversibly paralyzed patients with retained consciousness and cognition. *Neurology.* 1993;53:222–223.

32. Bernat JL, Cranford RE, Kittredge FL Jr, Rosenberg RN. Competent patients with advanced states of permanent paralysis have the right to forgo life-sustaining therapy. *Neurology.* 1993;43: 224–225.

The Right To Die

F . M . K A M M

A Right to Choose Death?

. . . [T]he debate about the right to choose death may appear to present a stand-off between people who endorse life's intrinsic value, and those who think life's value depends on the interests, judgments, and choices of the person whose life it is.

This picture of irreconcilable moral conflict is, I believe, too despairing about the powers of moral argument. To make headway, however, we may need to pay closer attention to the complexities of cases and the specific moral terrain they occupy: to think about people on medication, being treated by physicians, sometimes relying on technical means to stay alive, trying to decide how to live out what remains of their lives. I will explore this terrain in *moral,* not legal, terms: I will be asking you to consult your moral judgments about cases, and follow out the implications of those judgments. Though this moral argument bears on constitutional argument and on appropriate legislation, I will not propose laws or rules for judges, doctors, or hospital administrators to consult, or worry about slippery slopes created by legally hard cases. The moral landscape affords firmer footing, and does not, I will suggest, permit a blanket ban on euthanasia and physician-assisted suicide: Though both involve intentionally ending human lives, both are sometimes morally permissible. I will conclude by discussing a different argument for such permissibility offered by a distinguished group of moral philosophers in a recent *amicus* brief to the Supreme Court.

An earlier version of this paper was given as a talk at the Plenary Session of the American Academy of Forensic Sciences in New York, in February 1997.

From Boston Review (Summer 1997) 20–23.

I. LOGICAL TROUBLES?

Before getting to the issue of moral permissibility, we need to overcome a preliminary hurdle. I said that euthanasia and physician-assisted suicide are intended to benefit the patient. Some may object that these ideas make no sense. How is it possible for death to benefit the person who dies? Death eliminates the person — how can we produce a benefit if we eliminate the potential beneficiary?

To see how, consider the parallel question about death as a harm: Can a person be harmed by her own death even though death means that she is no longer around to suffer the harm? Suppose Schubert's life would have included even greater musical achievement had he not died so young. Because musical achievement is an important good, Schubert had a less good life overall than he would have had if he lived longer. But living a less good life is a harm. By excluding those achievements, then, Schubert's death harmed him: it prevented the better life. Now come back to the original concern about how death might be a benefit. Suppose a person's life would go on containing only misery and pain with no compensating goods. That person will be better off living a shorter life containing fewer such uncompensated-for bad things rather than a longer one containing more of them. But living a better life is a benefit. By interfering with the important bads, the person's death benefits him; it prevents the worse life.

It is possible, in short, to benefit a person by ending his life. The concept of euthanasia is, therefore, at least not simply logically confused; similarly for the idea that physician-assisted suicide may be aimed at the good of the patient. But conceptual coherence does not imply moral permissibility. So let's turn now to the moral question: Is it ever morally permissible to benefit a person by hastening his death, even when he requests it?

II. A RIGHT TO CHOOSE

Suppose a doctor is treating a terminally ill patient in severe pain. Suppose, too, that the pain can only be managed with morphine, but that giving the morphine is certain to hasten the patient's death. With the patient's consent, the doctor may nevertheless give the morphine. Why so? Because, in this particular case, the greater good for the patient is relief of pain, and the lesser evil is loss of life: after all, the patient is terminally ill, and in severe pain, so life would end soon anyway and is not of very good quality. So the patient is overall benefited by having a shorter pain-free life rather than a longer, even more painful life. (Notice that this could be true even if the morphine put the patient in a deep unconscious state from which he never awoke, so that he never consciously experienced pain-free time.)

In giving morphine to produce pain relief, the doctor foresees with certainty (let's assume) that the patient will die soon. Still, death is a side-effect of the medication, not the doctor's goal or reason for giving it: the doctor, that is, is not *intending* the patient's death, and would give the medication even if he thought death would not result. (If I have a drink to soothe my nerves and foresee a hangover, it does not follow that I intend the hangover.) Because the intended death is not present, we don't yet have a case of euthanasia or physician-assisted suicide. At the same time, in giving morphine for pain relief, the doctor is not simply letting the patient die as the disease runs its course; he administers a drug which causes death. So I think this should be understood as a case of killing, even though the doctor does not intend the death. (In other cases we have no trouble seeing that it is possible to kill without intending death: consider a driver who runs someone over while speeding.)

Now suppose the morphine loses its power to reduce the intensity of the patient's pain, but that administering it would still shorten the patient's life and thus limit the duration of his pain. Suppose, too, that the patient requests the morphine; fully aware of its effects, he wants to take it so that it will end his pain by killing him. In short, we now have a case of *morphine for death* rather than *morphine for pain relief.* Is it still morally permissible to give the morphine? Some people say that we may not kill in this case. They do not deny that relief of pain is still the greater good and

death the lesser evil: they know that the consequences are essentially the same as in the case of morphine for pain relief. The problem, they say, lies in a difference of intent. In the case of giving morphine for pain relief, we intend the pain relief, and merely foresee the death; but in the case of giving morphine for death, we intend the death (which is the lesser evil): we would not give the morphine if we did not expect the death. But some people think it is impermissible to act with the intent to produce an evil. They support what is called the *Doctrine of Double Effect,* according to which there is a large moral difference between acting with the foresight that one's conduct will have some evil consequence and acting with the intent to produce that same evil (even as part of or means to a greater good). So whereas killing the patient by giving morphine for pain relief is permissible, killing the patient by giving morphine for death is impermissible.

The distinction between intending an evil and merely foreseeing it sometimes makes a moral difference. But does it provide a reason to refrain from performing euthanasia or assisting in suicide? I think not. On many occasions already, doctors (with a patient's consent) *intend the lesser evil* to a person in order *to produce his own greater good.* For example, a doctor may intentionally amputate a healthy leg (the lesser evil) in order to get at and remove a cancerous tumor, thereby saving the patient's life (the greater good). Or, he may intentionally cause blindness in a patient if seeing would somehow, for example, destroy the patient's brain, or cause him to die. Furthermore, he may intentionally cause someone pain, thereby acting contrary to a duty to relieve suffering, if this helps to save the person's life. The duty to save life sometimes just outweighs the other duty. Why then is it impermissible for doctors to intend death when it is the lesser evil, in order to produce the greater good of no pain; why is it morally wrong to benefit the patient by giving her a shorter, less painful life rather than having her endure a longer, more painful one? Recall that in the case of morphine for pain relief, it was assumed that death would be the lesser evil and pain relief the greater good. That was one reason we could give the morphine. Why is it wrong, then, for doctors sometimes to act against a duty to preserve life in order to relive pain, just as they could sometimes act against a duty not to intend pain in order to save a life?

To summarize, I have constructed a three-step argument for physician-assisted suicide and euthanasia. Assuming patient consent:

1. We may permissibly cause death as a side effect if it relieves pain, because sometimes death is a lesser evil and pain relief a greater good.
2. We may permissibly intend other lesser evils to the patient, for the sake of her greater good.
3. Therefore, when death is a lesser evil, it is sometimes permissible for us to intend death in order to stop pain.

Thus, suppose we accept that it is sometimes permissible to *knowingly* shorten a life by giving pain-relieving medication, and agree, too, that it is sometimes permissible for a doctor to *intend* a lesser evil in order to produce a greater good. How, then, can it be wrong to *intentionally* shorten a life when that will produce the greater good?[1]

I don't expect that everyone will immediately find this argument compelling. I suspect that many—including some who are inclined to agree with the conclusion—will feel that death is different, so to speak. While they agree that we may intend pain, if it is a lesser evil, in order to save a life, they think it is impermissible to intentionally hasten death in order to relieve pain. I will address this concern later. But first I want to add another set of considerations that support euthanasia and physician-assisted suicide.

III. AN ARGUMENT FOR DUTY

According to the three-step argument, a doctor is *permitted* to give morphine for pain relief, even though he knows it will expedite the patient's death, if death is the lesser evil. But I think we can say more. Suppose, as I have stipulated, that giving morphine is the only way for a doctor to relieve a patient's suffering. A doctor, I assume, has a duty to relieve a patient's suffering. I conclude that the doctor has a *duty* to relieve suffering by giving the morphine, if the patient requests this. He cannot refuse to give the morphine on the ground that he will be a killer if he does.

If doctors have a duty to relieve pain, and even being a killer does not override this duty when the patient requests morphine for pain relief, then perhaps they also have a duty, not merely a permission, to kill their patients, or aid in their being killed, intending their deaths

in order to relieve suffering. Now we have a new argument. Assuming patient consent:

1. There is a duty to treat pain even if it foreseeably makes one a killer, when death is the lesser evil and no pain is the greater good.
2. There is a duty to intend the other lesser evils (e.g., amputation) for a patient's own greater good.
3. There is a duty to kill the patient, or assist in his being killed, intending his death when this is the lesser evil and pain relief the greater good.

I think this argument, too, is compelling, but will concentrate here on the case for permissibility.

IV. IS KILLING SPECIAL?

As I indicated earlier, a natural rejoinder to the three-step argument for euthanasia and physician-assisted suicide is to emphasize that "death is different." But how precisely is it different, and why is the difference morally important?

Perhaps it will be said, simply, that the doctor who intends the death of his patient is *killing*. Even if intending a lesser evil for a greater good is often permissible, it might be condemned when it involves killing. Killing, it might be said, is not on a par with other lesser evils.

But this does not suffice to upset the three-step argument. For giving a lethal injection of morphine to relieve pain also involves killing and we approve of giving the morphine. To be sure, a patient's right to life includes a right not to be killed. But that right gives us a protected option whether to live or die, an option with which others cannot legitimately interfere; it does not give one a duty to live. If a patient decides to die, he is waiving his right to live. By waiving his right, he releases others (perhaps a specific other person) from a duty not to kill him, at least insofar as that duty stems from his right to live.[2] The duty not to kill him may also stem from their duty not to harm him, even if he so wishes; but I have stipulated that the doctor is to kill only when death is the lesser evil.

A more compelling version of the objection is, however, waiting in the wings. This one points not merely to the fact of killing, but to intentional killing. It claims that there is something distinctive about intending death, and that this distinction makes a large moral difference. In particular, acting with the intention to bring about death as a lesser evil requires that we treat ourselves or other persons as available to be used for achieving certain goods — in particular, the reduction of suffering. In euthanasia and physician-assisted suicide, we intentionally terminate a being with a rational nature — a being that judges, aims at goals, and evaluates how to act.[3] We have no such intention to use a person as a mere means when we aim at such lesser evils as destruction of a leg. Indeed, one of the things that seems odd about killing someone only if he is capable of voluntarily deciding in a reasonable way to end his life is that one is thereby ensuring that what is destroyed is a reasoning, thinking being, and therefore a being of great worth. This will not be so if the person is unconscious or vegetative or otherwise no longer functioning as a rational being. Obviously, people take control of their lives and devote their rational natures to the pursuit of certain goals within those lives; but, it is claimed, when this is appropriate, they do not aim to interfere with or destroy their personhood but set it in one direction or another.

The idea that there are limits on what we may do to ourselves as persons derives from Immanuel Kant. In his moral writings, Kant said that rational humanity, as embodied in ourselves and others, is — and should be treated as — *an end in itself, and not a mere means* to happiness or other goals. The fact that one is a judging, aiming, evaluating rational agent has worth in itself. To have this value as a person is more like an honor to us (Kant called it "dignity") than a benefit that answers to some interest of ours. Thus my life may have worth, even if my life is not a benefit to me (and my death would benefit me) because goods *other than* being a person are outweighed by bads. The worth of my life is not measured solely by its worth to me in satisfying my desires, or its worth to others in satisfying theirs. According to Kant, then, it is wrong for others to treat me as a mere means for their ends, but equally wrong for me to treat myself as a mere means for my own ends: As others should respect my dignity as a person by not using me merely as a means for their purposes, I should have proper regard for my own dignity as a person, and not simply use myself as a means for my own purposes. But that is precisely what I do when I aim at my own death as a way to eliminate pain. So I ought not to pursue that aim, and therefore ought not to consent to a morphine injection aiming at death, or give one to a patient who has consented.

Before assessing this Kantian argument, I want to justify focusing it on intentional killing rather than other ways of intentionally contributing to a death. Consider a patient who intends his own death and therefore wants life support of any sort removed. Suppose, for the sake of argument, that we disapprove of this intention. Suppose, too, that we disapprove of a doctor's agreeing to remove treatment because he also intends this patient's death. But while we may disapprove of the intentions and conduct, acting on that disapproval would require us to *force* life support on the patient, and he has a right that we not do this. Our opposition to his intentions and the doctor's is trumped by our opposition to forced invasion of the patient. So we permit the patient and doctor to act — to remove treatment — intending death. Consider, in contrast, a patient who intends his own death and, therefore, requests a lethal injection or pills. Suppose, once more, that we disapprove of this intention. Acting on our opposition would require us to refrain from invading him with a lethal injection or refuse the pills. But it seems clear that the right not to be invaded with treatment against one's will is stronger than the right simply to be invaded (with a lethal injection) or given pills. So the fact that we must terminate treatment, even when the patient and doctor intend the patient's death, does not show that it is permissible to kill the patient or assist him in killing when he and his doctor intend his death. Correspondingly, an objection to intentional killing need not imply an objection to terminating treatment for someone who intends his own death.[4]

I turn now to the Kantian-style argument against aiming at one's death (or aiming at another's death with his consent). In assessing this argument, we must distinguish three different ways in which one may treat a person as a mere means:

1. Calculating the worth of living on in a way which gives insufficient weight to the worth of being a person.
2. Treating the nonexistence of persons as a means to a goal (e.g., no pain).
3. Using persons in order to bring about their own end.

The first idea is that being a person has worth in itself and is not merely a means to an overall balance of other goods over evils in the person's life. On this interpretation, we treat persons as a mere means if we give inadequate weight in our decisions to the value of our existence as persons; if we do, then death may seem a lesser evil. But even when there are few goods in life besides the capacity to be a rational agent, the loss of life — and therefore the loss of that capacity — may still be a greater evil than pain.

Though I do not doubt that this idea has force, it can equally well be given as a reason for not terminating a course of treatment, even when one merely foresees one's death. Because this way of treating a person as a mere means does not distinguish the *morality of intending death* from the *morality of merely foreseeing death,* it cannot be used to explain why intentional killing in particular is impermissible.[5] . . .

What, then, about the second and third interpretations of the idea of using persons as mere means? To see the difference between them, consider an analogy: My radio is a device for getting good sounds and filtering out bad sounds. It is a means to a balance of good sounds over bad ones. Suppose it stops performing well, that it only produces static, but cannot be turned off. I can wait until its batteries run down and not replace them, or I can smash it now, thus using the radio itself to stop the noise it produces. Either way, I would see its death as I saw its life, as a means to a better balance of good over bad sounds. While I have always seen my radio as a mere means to an end if I smash it, I use it as a means to its end (termination): This is sense (3).[6] If I let the radio run down, intending its demise, but do not smash it — I see it wasting away and do not replace its parts — then I do not see it as a means to its own end, but I do see *its end as a means* to a better balance of sounds. This is sense (2).

Active suicide is analogous to smashing the radio: the person uses himself as a means to his own death. Some people find this complete taking control of one's life particularly morally inappropriate, perhaps because they think our bodies belong to God and that we have no right to achieve the goal of our own death by manipulating a "tool" that is not ours (or intending that others manipulate it). This objection is not present if — here we have sense (2) — we terminate medical assistance with the intention that the system run down, aiming at its death. For then we achieve the goal of death by interfering with what is ours (the medication), not God's. Here we have another reason why someone may object to killing but not to terminating treatment, even if accompanied by the intention that the system run down; unlike intentional killing, terminating treatment does not involve using persons to bring about

their own end. Some say, though, that this way of using persons as means is also more objectionable than merely foreseeing the death. They say that if we terminate medical assistance, intending death, we do not merely treat our life as a means to greater good over bad, but treat *our death (the end of our life)* as a means to greater good over bad.

How much weight, then, should be placed on the second and third senses of "using a person as a means"? Should they really stand in our way? I believe not. It cannot be argued, at least in secular moral terms, that one's body belongs to someone else and that one cannot, therefore, use it as a means to achieve death. Notice also that if your body belonged to someone else, it isn't clear why you should be permitted to use it by administering morphine to stop your pain when you merely foresee that this will destroy the body. We aren't usually permitted to treat other people's property in this way either. Nor does it seem that treating one's death as available for one's purposes (i.e., being rid of pain) is necessarily a morally inappropriate attitude to take to oneself — so long as there is not failure to properly value the importance of just being a person. If this is right, then, at least sometimes, a patient would do no wrong in intending or causing his death. At least sometimes, a doctor who helped him by giving pills would also do no wrong merely because he killed, or assisted killing, aiming at death.

The strongest case for such conduct can be made, I believe, if the overriding aim is to end physical pain. The need to do this may be rare with modern techniques of pain control, but still the patient has a "disjunctive" right: either to adequate pain control or the assistance in suicide of a willing doctor. Psychological suffering which is a reaction to one's knowledge or beliefs about a state of affairs is a weaker case. The test I suggest here is: Would we give a drug to treat psychological suffering if we *foresaw* that it would rapidly kill as a side effect? If not, then giving pills to a patient intending that they kill him in order to end psychological suffering would not be permissible. This same test can be applied to other reasons that might be offered for seeking death by euthanasia or physician-assisted suicide. For example, would we allow a patient to use a drug that will rapidly cause death (rather than a safer one) if it will save him money? If not, then we may not perform euthanasia or physician-assisted suicide to stop the drain on his family finances. Would we give a demented patient a drug that unraveled the tangled neurons that caused his dementia but which we foresaw would rapidly kill him as a side effect? If not, then why should we be permitted to give him pills, intending his death? Of course, the application of this test may yield positive responses rather than negative ones to these questions. . . .

NOTES

1. I first presented this argument in *Creation and Abortion* (New York: Oxford University Press, 1992), pp. 33–35, and again in *Morality, Mortality,* Vol. II (New York: Oxford University Press, 1996), pp. 194–98.

2. Notice that this waiver seems to be morally necessary even when the doctor wishes to give morphine that will kill as a foreseen side effect. This means doctors should get permission for giving the morphine for pain relief as well as for giving it to deliberately kill. (I do not believe they always do so.)

3. We also terminate human life considered independently of whether it is the life of a rational being. It may seem harder to justify destroying a person than a human life that lacks qualities required for personhood — for example, a functioning brain. But I will assume that one could substitute "human life" for "person" in the argument I give against intentional killing and in my response to that argument.

4. In contrast, suppose that a patient who intends his own death is also suffering great pain that only morphine will stop. He asks for the morphine, not because it will stop the pain, but because he knows it will kill him. If it would not kill him, he would not ask for it. Does he have a right that the doctor give him the morphine? If he does, then the doctor is not at liberty to refuse simply because of the *patient's intention,* any more than he could refuse to terminate treatment because of the patient's intention. Indeed we might not be permitted to interfere with the doctor's giving morphine in this case even if he gave it only because *he* intended death. I owe this case to Timothy Hall.

5. Kant thought we had a duty to actively preserve rational humanity and hence we should not too lightly do what we foresee will lead to its end. Still, he allows that we may sometimes engage in conduct though we foresee it will result in our deaths, but we may never aim at our deaths.

6. If I see someone else destroy it and do not interfere, I may be intending its use as a means to its own end, though I do not myself use it.

LEON R. KASS

Is There a Right to Die?

It has been fashionable for some time now and in many aspects of American public life for people to demand what they want or need as a matter of rights. During the past few decades we have heard claims of a right to health or health care, a right to education or employment, a right to privacy (embracing also a right to abort or to enjoy pornography, or to commit suicide or sodomy), a right to clean air, a right to dance naked, a right to be born, and a right not to have been born. Most recently we have been presented with the ultimate new rights claim, a "right to die."

This claim has surfaced in the context of changed circumstances and burgeoning concerns regarding the end of life. Thanks in part to the power of medicine to preserve and prolong life, many of us are fated to end our once-flourishing lives in years of debility, dependence, and disgrace. Thanks to the respirator and other powerful technologies that can, all by themselves, hold comatose and other severely debilitated patients on this side of the line between life and death, many who would be dead are alive only because of sustained mechanical intervention. Of the 2.2 million annual deaths in the United States, 80 percent occur in health care facilities; in roughly 1.5 million of these cases, death is preceded by some explicit decision about stopping or not starting medical treatment. Thus, death in America is not only medically managed, but its timing is also increasingly subject to deliberate choice. It is from this background that the claims of a right to die emerge.

I do not think that the language and approach of rights are well suited either to sound personal decision-making or to sensible public policy in this very difficult and troubling matter. In most of the heartrending end-of-life situations, it is hard enough for practical

From *Hastings Center Report* 23 (January–February 1993), 34–40, 41–43. © 1993, Leon R. Kass. Reprinted by permission of the author.

wisdom to try to figure out what is morally right and humanly good, without having to contend with intransigent and absolute demands of a legal or moral right to die. And, on both philosophical and legal grounds, I am inclined to believe that there can be no such thing as a *right* to die—that the notion is groundless and perhaps even logically incoherent. Even its proponents usually put "right to die" in quotation marks, acknowledging that it is at best a misnomer.

Nevertheless, we cannot simply dismiss this claim, for it raises important and interesting practical and philosophical questions. Practically, a right to die is increasingly asserted and gaining popular strength; increasingly, we see it in print without the quotation marks. The former Euthanasia Society of America, shedding the Nazi-tainted and easily criticized "E" word, changed its name to the more politically correct Society for the Right to Die before becoming Choice In Dying. End-of-life cases coming before the courts, nearly always making their arguments in terms of rights, have gained support for some sort of "right to die." The one case to be decided by a conservative Supreme Court, the *Cruzan* case, has advanced the cause. . . .

The voter initiatives to legalize physician-assisted suicide and euthanasia in Washington and California were narrowly defeated, in part because they were badly drafted laws; yet the proponents of such practices seem to be winning the larger social battle over principle. According to several public opinion polls, most Americans now believe that "if life is miserable, one has the right to get out, actively and with help if necessary." Though the burden of philosophical proof for establishing new rights (especially one as bizarre as a "right to die") should always fall on the proponents, the social burden of proof has shifted to those who would oppose the voluntary choice of death through assisted suicide. Thus it has become politically necessary—and at the same time exceedingly difficult—to make principled arguments about why doctors must not kill, about why euthanasia is not the proper human response to human finitude, and about why there is no right to die, natural or constitutional. This is not a merely academic matter: our society's willingness and ability to protect vulnerable life hang in the balance.

An examination of "right to die" is even more interesting philosophically. It reveals the dangers and the limits of the liberal—that is, rights-based—political philosophy and jurisprudence to which we Americans

are wedded. As the ultimate new right, grounded neither in nature nor in reason, it demonstrates the nihilistic implication of a new ("postliberal") doctrine of rights, rooted in the self-creating will. And as liberal society's response to the bittersweet victories of the medical project to conquer death, it reveals in pure form the tragic meaning of the entire modern project, both scientific and political.

The claim of a right to die is made only in Western liberal societies—not surprisingly, for only in Western liberal societies do human beings look first to the rights of individuals. Also, only here do we find the high-tech medicine capable of keeping people from dying when they might wish. Yet the claim of a right to die is also a profoundly strange claim, especially in a liberal society founded on the primacy of the right to life. We Americans hold as a self-evident truth that governments exist to secure inalienable rights, first of all, to self-preservation; now we are being encouraged to use government to secure a putative right of self-destruction. A "right to die" is surely strange and unprecedented, and hardly innocent. Accordingly, we need to consider carefully what it could possibly mean, why it is being asserted, and whether it really exists—that is, whether it can be given a principled grounding or defense.

A *RIGHT* TO DIE

Though the major ambiguity concerns the substance of the right—namely, to die—we begin by reminding ourselves of what it means, in general, to say that someone has a right to something. I depart for now from the original notion of *natural* rights, and indeed abstract altogether from the question of the source of rights. I focus instead on our contemporary usage, for it is only in contemporary usage that this current claim of a right to die can be understood.

A right, whether legal or moral, is not identical to a need or a desire or an interest or a capacity. I may have both a need and a desire for, and also an interest in, the possessions of another, and the capacity or power to take them by force or stealth—yet I can hardly be said to have a right to them. A right, to begin with, is a species of liberty. Thomas Hobbes, the first teacher of rights, held a right to be a *blameless* liberty. Not everything we are free to do, morally or legally, do we have a right to do: I may be at liberty to wear offensive perfumes or to sass my parents or to engage in unnatural sex, but it does not follow that I have a right to do so. Even the decriminalization of a once-forbidden act does not yet establish a legal right, not even if I can give reasons for doing it. Thus, the freedom to take my life — "I have inclination, means, reasons, opportunity, and you cannot stop me, and it is not against the law" — does not suffice to establish the *right* to take my life. A true right would be at least a blameless or permitted liberty, at best a praiseworthy or even rightful liberty, to do or not to do, without anyone else's interference or opposition.

Historically, the likelihood of outside interference and opposition was in fact the necessary condition for the assertion of rights. Rights were and are, to begin with, *political* creatures, the first principles of liberal politics. The rhetoric of claiming rights, which are in principle always absolute and unconditional, performs an important function of defense, but only because the sphere of life in which they are asserted is limited. Rights are asserted to protect, by deeming them blameless or rightful, certain liberties that others are denying or threatening to curtail. Rights are claimed to defend the safety and dignity of the individual against the dominion of tyrant, king, or prelate, and against those high-minded moralizers and zealous meddlers who seek to save man's soul or to preserve his honor at the cost of his life and liberty.

To these more classical, negative rights against interference with our liberties, modern thought has sought to add certain so-called welfare rights — rights that entitle us to certain opportunities or goods to which, it is argued, we have a rightful claim on others, usually government, to provide. The rhetoric of welfare rights extends the power of absolute and unqualified claims beyond the goals of defense against tyranny and beyond the limited sphere of endangered liberties; for these reasons their legitimacy as rights is often questioned. Yet even these ever-expanding lists of rights are not unlimited. I cannot be said to have a right to be loved by those who I hope will love me, or a right to become wise. There are many good things that I may rightfully possess and enjoy, but to which I have no claim if they are lacking. Most generally, then, having a right means having a *justified* claim against others that they act in a fitting manner: either that they refrain from interfering or that they deliver what is justly owed. It goes without saying that the mere assertion of a claim or demand, or the stipulation of a right, is insufficient to establish it; making a claim and actually having a rightful claim to make are not identical. In considering an alleged right to die, we must be careful to look for a *justifiable* liberty or claim, and not merely a desire, interest, power, or demand.

Rights seem to entail obligations: one person's right, whether to noninterference or to some entitled good or service, necessarily implies another person's obligation. It will be important later to consider what obligations on others might be entailed by enshrining a right to die.

A RIGHT *TO DIE*

Taken literally, a right to die would denote merely a right to the inevitable; the certainty of death for all that lives is the touchstone of fated inevitability. Why claim a right to what is not only unavoidable, but is even, generally speaking, an evil? Is death in danger of losing its inevitability? Are we in danger of bodily immortality? Has death, for us, become a good to be claimed rather than an evil to be shunned or conquered?

Not exactly and not yet, though these questions posed by the literal reading of "right to die" are surely germane. They hint at our growing disenchantment with the biomedical project, which seeks, in principle, to prolong life indefinitely. It is the already available means to sustain life for prolonged periods — not indefinitely, but far longer than is in many cases reasonable or desirable — that has made death so untimely late as to seem less than inevitable, that has made death, when it finally does occur, appear to be a blessing.

For we now have medical "treatments" (that is, interventions) that do not treat (that is, cure or ameliorate) specific diseases, but do nothing more than keep people alive by sustaining vital functions. The most notorious such device is the respirator. Others include simple yet still artificial devices for supplying food and water and the kidney dialysis machine for removing wastes. And, in the future, we shall have the artificial heart. These devices, backed by aggressive institutional policies favoring their use, are capable of keeping people alive, even when comatose, often for decades. The "right to die," in today's discourse, often refers to — and certainly is meant to embrace — a right to refuse such life-sustaining medical treatment.

But the "right to die" usually embraces also something more. The ambiguity of the term blurs over the difference in content and intention between the already well-established common-law right to refuse surgery or other unwanted medical treatments and hospitalization and the newly alleged "right to die." The former permits the refusal of therapy, even a respirator, even if it means accepting an increased risk of death. The latter permits the refusal of therapy, such as renal dialysis or the feeding tube, *so that* death *will* occur. The former seems more concerned with choosing how to live while dying; the latter seems mainly concerned with a choice *for death*. In this sense the claimed "right to die" is not a misnomer.

Still less is it a misnomer when we consider that some people who are claiming it demand not merely the discontinuance of treatment but positive assistance in bringing about their deaths. Here the right to die embraces the (welfare!) right to a lethal injection or an overdose of pills administered by oneself, by one's physician, or by someone else. This "right to die" would better be called a right to assisted suicide or a right to be mercifully killed — in short, a right *to become dead,* by assistance if necessary.

This, of course, looks a lot like a claim to a right to commit suicide, which need not have any connection to the problems of dying or medical technology. Some people in fact argue that the "right to die" through euthanasia or medically assisted suicide grows not from a right to refuse medical treatment but rather from this putative right to commit suicide (suicide is now decriminalized in most states). There does seem to be a world of moral difference between submitting to death (when the time has come) and killing yourself (in or out of season), or between permitting to die and causing death. But the boundary becomes fuzzy with the alleged right to refuse food and water, artificially delivered. Though few proponents of a right to die want the taint of a general defense of suicide (which though decriminalized remains in bad odor), they in fact presuppose its permissibility and go well beyond it. They claim not only a right to attempt suicide but a right to succeed, and this means, in practice, a *right to the deadly assistance of others*. It is thus certainly proper to understand the "right to die" in its most radical sense, namely, as a right to become or to be made dead, by whatever means.

This way of putting the matter will not sit well with those who see the right to die less as a matter of life and death, more as a matter of autonomy or dignity. For them the right to die means the right to continue, despite disability, to exercise control over one's own destiny. It means, in one formulation, not the right to become dead, but the right to choose the manner, the timing, and the circumstances of one's death, or the right to choose what one regards as the most humane or dignified way to finish out one's life. Here the right

to die means either the right to self-command or the right to death with dignity — claims that would oblige others, at a minimum, to stop interfering, but also, quite commonly, to "assist self-command" or to "provide dignity" by participating in bringing one's life to an end, according to plan. In the end, these proper and high-minded demands for autonomy and dignity turn out in most cases to embrace also a right to become dead, with assistance if necessary.

This analysis of current usage shows why one might be properly confused about the meaning of the term "right to die." In public discourse today, it merges all the aforementioned meanings: right to refuse treatment even if, or so that, death may occur; right to be killed or to become dead; right to control one's own dying; right to die with dignity; right to assistance in death. Some of this confusion inheres in the term; some of it is deliberately fostered by proponents of all these "rights," who hope thereby to gain assent to the more extreme claims by merging them with the more modest ones. Partly for this reason, however, we do well to regard the "right to die" at its most radical — and I will do so in this essay — as a right to become dead, by active means and if necessary with the assistance of others. In this way we take seriously and do justice to the novelty and boldness of the claim, a claim that intends to go beyond both the existing common-law right to refuse unwanted medical treatment and the so-called right to commit suicide all by oneself. (The first right is indisputable, the second, while debatable, will not be contested in this essay. What concerns us here is those aspects of the "right to die" that go beyond a right to attempt suicide and a right to refuse treatment.)

Having sought to clarify the meaning of "right to die," we face next the even greater confusion about who it is that allegedly has such a right. Is it only those who are "certifiably" terminally ill and irreversibly dying, with or without medical treatment? Also those who are incurably ill and severely incapacitated, although definitely not dying? Everyone, mentally competent or not? Does a senile person have a "right to die" if he is incapable of claiming it for himself? Do I need to be able to claim *and act* on such a right in order to have it, or can proxies be designated to exercise my right to die on my behalf? If the right to die is essentially an expression of my autonomy, how can anyone else exercise it for me?

Equally puzzling is the question, Against whom or what is a right to die being asserted? Is it a liberty right mainly against those officious meddlers who keep me from dying — against those doctors, nurses, hospitals, right-to-life groups, and district attorneys who interfere either with my ability to die (by machinery and hospitalization) or with my ability to gain help in ending my life (by criminal sanctions against assisting suicide)? If it is a right to become dead, is it not also a welfare right claimed against those who do not yet assist — a right demanding also the provision of the poison that I have permission to take? (Compare the liberty right to seek an abortion with the welfare right to obtain one.) Or is it, at bottom, a demand asserted also *against nature,* which has dealt me a bad hand by keeping me alive, beyond my wishes and beneath my dignity, and alas without terminal illness, too senile or enfeebled to make matters right?

The most radical formulations, whether in the form of "a right to become dead" or "a right to control my destiny" or "a right to dignity," are, I am convinced, the complaint of human pride against what our tyrannical tendencies lead us to experience as "cosmic injustice, directed against me." Here the ill-fated demand a right not to be ill-fated; those who want to die, but cannot, claim a right to die, which becomes, as Harvey Mansfield has put it, a tort claim against nature. It thus becomes the business of the well-fated to correct nature's mistreatment of the ill-fated *by making them dead.* Thus would the same act that was only yesterday declared a crime against humanity become a mandated act, not only of compassionate charity but of compensatory justice!

WHY ASSERT A RIGHT TO DIE?

Before proceeding to the more challenging question of the existence and ground of a "right to die," it would be useful briefly to consider why such a right is being asserted, and by whom. Some of the reasons have already been noted in passing:

- fear of prolongation of dying due to medical intervention; hence, a right to refuse treatment or hospitalization, even if death occurs as a result;
- fear of living too long, without fatal illness to carry one off; hence, a right to assisted suicide;
- fear of the degradations of senility and dependence; hence, a right to death with dignity;
- fear of loss of control; hence, a right to choose the time and manner of one's death.

Equally important for many people is the fear of becoming a burden to others — financial, psychic, social. Few parents, however eager or willing they might be to stay alive, are pleased by the prospect that they might thereby destroy their children's and grandchildren's opportunities for happiness. Indeed, my own greatest weakening on the subject of euthanasia is precisely this: I would confess a strong temptation to remove myself from life to spare my children the anguish of years of attending my demented self and the horrible likelihood that they will come, hatefully to themselves, to resent my continued existence. Such reasons in favor of death might even lead me to think I had a *duty* to die — they do not, however, establish for me any right to become dead.[1]

But the advocates of a "right to die" are not always so generous. On the contrary, much dishonesty and mischief are afoot. Many people have seen the advantage of using the language of individual rights, implying voluntary action, to shift the national attitudes regarding life and death, to prepare the way for the practice of terminating "useless" lives.[2]

Many who argue for a right to die mean for people not merely to have it but to exercise it with dispatch, so as to decrease the mounting socioeconomic costs of caring for the irreversibly ill and dying. In fact, most of the people now agitating for a "right to die" are themselves neither ill nor dying. Children looking at parents who are not dying fast enough, hospital administrators and health economists concerned about cost-cutting and waste, doctors disgusted with caring for incurables, people with eugenic or aesthetic interests who are repelled by the prospect of a society in which the young and vigorous expend enormous energy to keep alive the virtually dead — all these want to change our hard-won ethic in favor of life.

But they are either too ashamed or too shrewd to state their true intentions. Much better to trumpet a right to die, and encourage people to exercise it. These advocates understand all too well that the present American climate requires one to talk of rights if one wishes to have one's way in such moral matters. Consider the analogous use of arguments for abortion rights by organizations which hope thereby to get women — especially the poor, the unmarried, and the nonwhite — to exercise their "right to choose," to do their supposed duty toward limiting population growth and the size of the underclass.

This is not to say that all reasons for promoting a "right to die" are suspect. Nor do I mean to suggest that it would never be right or good for someone to elect to die. But it might be dangerous folly to circumvent the grave need for prudence in these matters by substituting the confused yet absolutized principle of a "right to die," especially given the mixed motives and dangerous purposes of some of its proponents.

Truth to tell, public discourse about moral matters in the United States is much impoverished by our eagerness to transform questions of the right and the good into questions about individual rights. Partly, this is a legacy of modern liberalism, the political philosophy on which the genius of the American republic mainly rests. But it is augmented by American self-assertion and individualism, increasingly so in an age when family and other mediating institutions are in decline and the naked individual is left face to face with the bureaucratic state.

But the language of rights gained a tremendous boost from the moral absolutism of the 1960s, with the discovery that the nonnegotiable and absolutized character of all rights claims provides the most durable battering ram against the status quo. Never mind that it fuels resentments and breeds hatreds, that it ignores the consequences to society, or that it short-circuits a political process that is more amenable to working out a balanced view of the common good. Never mind all that: go to court and demand your rights. And the courts have been all too willing to oblige, finding or inventing new rights in the process.

These sociocultural changes, having nothing to do with death and dying, surely are part of the reason we are now confronted with vociferous claims of a right to die. These changes are also part of the reason why, despite its notorious difficulties, a right to die is the leading moral concept advanced to address these most complicated and delicate human matters at the end of life. Yet the reasons for the assertion, even if suspect, do not settle the question of truth, to which, at long last, we finally turn. Let us examine whether philosophically . . . we can truly speak of a right to die.

IS THERE A RIGHT TO DIE?

Philosophically speaking, it makes sense to take our bearings from those great thinkers of modernity who are the originators and most thoughtful exponents of our rights-based thinking. They above all are likely to have understood the purpose, character, grounds, and limits for the assertion of rights. If a newly asserted right, such as the right to die, cannot be established on the natural or rational ground for rights offered by these thinkers, the burden of proof must fall on the proponents of novel rights, to provide a new yet equally solid ground in support of their novel claims.

If we start at the beginning, with the great philosophical teachers of natural rights, the very notion of a right to die would be nonsensical. As we learn from Hobbes and from John Locke, all the rights of man, given by nature, presuppose our self-interested attachment to our own lives. All natural rights trace home to the primary right to life, or better, the right to self-preservation—itself rooted in the powerful, self-loving impulses and passions that seek our own continuance, and asserted first against deadly, oppressive policies or against those who might insist that morality requires me to turn the other cheek when my life is threatened. Mansfield summarizes the classical position elegantly:

> Rights are given to men by nature, but they are needed because men are also subject to nature's improvidence. Since life is in danger, men's equal rights would be to life, to the liberty that protects life, and to the pursuit of the happiness with which life, or a tenuous life, is occupied.
>
> In practice, the pursuit of happiness will be the pursuit of property, for even though property is less valuable than life or liberty, it serves as guard for them. Quite apart from the pleasures of being rich, having secure property shows that one has liberty secure from invasion either by the government or by others; and secure liberty is the best sign of a secure life.[3]

Because death, my extinction, is the evil whose avoidance is the condition of the possibility of my having any and all of my goods, my right to secure my life against death—that is, my rightful liberty to self-preservative conduct—is the bedrock of all other rights and of all politically relevant morality. Even Hans Jonas, writing to defend "the right to die," acknowledges that it stands alone, and concedes that "every other right ever argued, claimed, granted, or denied can be viewed as an extension of this primary right [to life], since every particular right concerns the exercise of some faculty of life, the access to some necessity of life, the satisfaction of some aspiration of life."[4] It is obvious that one cannot found on this rock any right to die or right to become dead. Life loves to live, and it needs all the help it can get.

This is not to say that these early modern thinkers were unaware that men might tire of life or might come to find existence burdensome. But the decline in the will to live did not for them drive out or nullify the right to life, much less lead to a trumping new right, a right to die. For the right to life is a matter of nature, not will. Locke addresses and rejects a natural right to suicide, in his discussion of the state of nature:

But though this be a state of liberty, yet it is not a state of license; though man in that state has an uncontrollable liberty to dispose of his person or possessions, yet he has not liberty to destroy himself, or so much as any creature in his possession, but where some nobler use than its bare preservation calls for it. The state of nature has a law of nature to govern it, which obliges everyone; and reason, which is that law, teaches all mankind who will but consult it, that, being all equal and independent, no one ought to harm another in his life, health, liberty, or possessions.[5]

Admittedly, the argument here turns explicitly theological — we are said to be our wise Maker's property. But the argument against a man's willful "quitting of his station" seems, for Locke, to be a corollary of the natural inclination and right of self-preservation.

Some try to argue, wrongly in my view, that Locke's teaching on property rests on a principle of self-ownership, which can then be used to justify self-destruction: since I own my body and my life, I may do with them as I please. As this argument has much currency, it is worth examining in greater detail. Locke does indeed say something that seems at first glance to suggest self-ownership:

Though the earth and all inferior creatures be common to all men, *yet every man has a property in his own person;* this nobody has a right to but himself. The labor of his body and the work of his hands we may say are properly his.[6]

But the context defines and constricts the claim. Unlike the property rights in the fruits of his labor, the property a man has in his own person is inalienable: a man cannot transfer title to himself by selling himself into slavery. The "property in his own person" is less a metaphysical statement declaring self-ownership, more a political statement denying ownership by another. This right removes each and every human being from the commons available to all human beings for appropriation and use. My body and my life are my property *only in the limited sense* that they are *not yours.* They are different from my alienable property — my house, my car, my shoes. My body and my life, while mine to use, are not mine to dispose of. In the deepest sense, my body is nobody's body, not even mine.[7]

Even if one continues, against reason, to hold to strict self-ownership and self-disposability, there is a further argument, one that is decisive. Self-ownership might enable one at most to justify *attempting* suicide; it cannot justify a right to succeed or, more important, a right to the assistance of others. The designated potential assistant-in-death has neither a natural duty nor a natural right to become an actual assistant-in-death, and the liberal state, instituted above all to protect life, can never countenance such a right to kill, even on request. A right to become dead or to be made dead cannot be sustained on classical liberal grounds.

Later thinkers in the liberal tradition, including those who prized freedom above preservation, also make no room for a "right to die." Jean-Jacques Rousseau's complaints about the ills of civil society centered especially and most powerfully on the threats to life and limb from a social order whose main purpose should have been to protect them.[8] And Immanuel Kant, for whom rights are founded not in nature but in reason, holds that the self-willed act of self-destruction is simply self-contradictory.

It seems absurd that a man can injure himself (*volenti non fit injuria* [Injury cannot happen to one who is willing]). The Stoic therefore considered it a prerogative of his personality as a wise man to walk out of his life with an undisturbed mind whenever he liked (as out of a smoke-filled room), not because he was afflicted by actual or anticipated ills, but simply because he could make use of nothing more in this life. And yet this very courage, this strength of mind — of not fearing death and of knowing of something which man can prize more highly than his life — ought to have been an ever so much greater motive for him not to destroy himself, a being having such authoritative superiority over the strongest sensible incentives; consequently, it ought to have been a motive for him not to deprive himself of life.

Man cannot deprive himself of his personhood so long as one speaks of duties, thus so long as he lives. That man ought to have the authorization to withdraw himself from all obligation, i.e., to be free to act as if no authorization at all were required for this withdrawal, involves a contradiction. To destroy the subject of morality in his own person is tantamount to obliterating from the world, as far as he can, the very existence of morality itself; but morality is, nevertheless, an end in itself. Accordingly, to dispose of oneself as a mere means to some end of one's own liking is to degrade the humanity in one's person (*homo noumenon*), which, after all, was entrusted to man (*homo phænomenon*) to preserve.[9]

It is a heavy irony that it should be autonomy, the moral notion that the world owes mainly to Kant, that is now invoked as the justifying ground of a right to die. For Kant, autonomy, which literally means self-legislation, requires acting in accordance with one's true self—that is, with one's rational will determined by a universalizable, that is, rational, maxim. Being autonomous means not being a slave to instinct, impulse, or whim, but rather doing as one ought, as a rational being. But autonomy has now come to mean "doing as you please," compatible no less with self-indulgence than with self-control. Herewith one sees clearly the triumph of the Nietzschean self, who finds reason just as enslaving as blind instinct and who finds his true "self" rather in unconditioned acts of pure creative will.

Yet even in its willful modern meaning, "autonomy" cannot ground a right to die. First, one cannot establish on this basis a right to have *someone else's* assistance in committing suicide—a right, by the way, that would impose an obligation on someone else and thereby restrict *his* autonomy. Second, even if my choice for death were "reasonable" and my chosen assistant freely willing, my autonomy cannot ground *his* right to kill me, and, hence, it cannot ground my right to become dead. Third, a liberty right to an assisted death (that is, a right against interference) can at most approve assisted suicide or euthanasia for the mentally competent and alert—a restriction that would prohibit effecting the deaths of the mentally incompetent or co-matose patients who have not left explicit instructions regarding their treatment. It is, by the way, a long philosophical question whether all such instructions must be obeyed, for the person who gave them long ago may no longer be "the same person" when they become relevant. Can my fifty-three-year-old self truly prescribe today the best interests for my seventy-five-year-old and senile self?

In contrast to arguments presented in recent court cases, it is self-contradictory to assert that a proxy not chosen by the patient can exercise the patient's rights of autonomy. Can a citizen have a right to vote that would be irrevocably exercised "on his behalf," and in the name of his autonomy, by the government?[10] Finally, if autonomy and dignity lie in the free exercise of will and choice, it is at least paradoxical to say that our autonomy licenses an act that puts our autonomy permanently out of business.

It is precisely this paradox that appeals to the Nietzschean creative self, the bearer of so many of this century's "new rights." As Mansfield brilliantly shows, the creative ones are not bound by normality or good sense:

> Creative beings are open-ended. They are open-ended in fact and not merely in their formal potentialities. Such beings do not have interests; for who can say what is in the interest of a being that is becoming something unknown? Thus the society of new rights is characterized by a loss of predictability and normality: no one knows what to expect, even from his closest companions.[11]

The most authentic self-creative self revels in the unpredictable, the extreme, the perverse. He does not even flinch before self-contradiction; indeed, he can display the triumph of his will most especially in self-negation. And though it may revolt us, who are we to deny him this form of self-expression? Supremely tolerant of the rights of others to their own eccentricities, we avert our glance and turn the other moral cheek. Here at last is the only possible philosophical ground for a right to die: arbitrary will, backed by moral relativism. Which is to say, no ground at all.

• • •

THE TRAGIC MEANING OF "RIGHT TO DIE"

The claim of a "right to die," asserted especially against physicians bent on prolonging life, clearly exposes certain deep difficulties in the foundations of modern society. Modern liberal, technological society rests especially upon two philosophical pillars raised first in the seventeenth century, at the beginning of the modern era: the preeminence of the human individual, embodied in the doctrine of natural rights as espoused first by Hobbes and Locke; and the idea of mastery of nature, attained through a radically new science of nature as proposed by Francis Bacon and René Descartes.

Both ideas were responses to the perceived partial inhospitality of nature to human need. Both encouraged man's opposition to nature, the first through the flight from the state of nature into civil society for the purpose of safeguarding the precarious rights to life and liberty; the second through the subduing of nature for the purpose of making life longer, healthier, and more commodious. One might even say that it is especially an opposition to death that grounds these twin responses. Politically, the fear of violent death at the hands of warring men requires law and legitimate authority to secure natural rights, especially life. Technologically, the fear of death as such at the hands of unfriendly nature inspires a bolder approach, namely, a scientific medicine to wage war against disease and even against death itself, ultimately with a promise of bodily immortality.

Drunk on its political and scientific successes, modern thought and practice have abandoned the modest and moderate beginnings of political modernity. In civil society the natural rights of self-preservation, secured through active but moderate self-assertion, have given way to the non-natural rights of self-creation and self-expression; the new rights have no connection to nature or to reason, but appear as the rights of the untrammeled will. The "self" that here asserts itself is not a natural self, with the predictable interests given it by a universal human nature with its bodily needs, but a uniquely individuated and self-made self. Its authentic selfhood is demonstrated by its ability to say no to the needs of the body, the rules of society, and the dictates of reason. For such a self, self-negation through suicide and the right to die can be the ultimate form of self-assertion.

In medical science, the unlimited battle against death has found nature unwilling to roll over and play dead. The successes of medicine so far are partial at best and the victory incomplete, to say the least. The welcome triumphs against disease have been purchased at the price of the medicalized dehumanization of the end of life: to put it starkly, once we lick cancer and stroke, we can all live long enough to get Alzheimer's disease. And if the insurance holds out, we can die in the intensive care unit, suitably intubated. Fear of the very medical power we engaged to do battle against death now leads us to demand that it give us poison.

Finally, both the triumph of individualism and our reliance on technology (not only in medicine) and on government to satisfy our new wants-demanded-as-rights have weakened our more natural human associations—especially the family, on which we all need to rely when our pretense to autonomy and mastery is eventually exposed by unavoidable decline. Old age and death have been taken out of the bosom of family life and turned over to state-supported nursing homes and hospitals. Not the clergyman but the doctor (in truth, the nurse) presides over the end of life, in sterile surroundings that make no concessions to our finitude. Both the autonomous will and the will's partner in pride, the death-denying doctor, ignore the unavoidable limits on will and technique that nature insists on. Failure to recognize these limits now threatens the entire venture, for rebellion against the project through a "right

to die" will only radicalize its difficulties. Vulnerable life will no longer be protected by the state, medicine will become a death-dealing profession, and isolated individuals will be technically dispatched to avoid the troubles of finding human ways to keep company with them in their time of ultimate need.

•   •   •

Nothing I have said should be taken to mean that I believe life should be extended under all circumstances and at all costs. Far from it. I continue, with fear and trembling, to defend the practice of allowing to die while opposing the practice of deliberately killing—despite the blurring of this morally bright line implicit in the artificial food and water cases, and despite the slide toward the retailing of death that continues on the sled of a right to refuse treatment. I welcome efforts to give patients as much choice as possible in how they are to live out the end of their lives. I continue to applaud those courageous patients and family members and those conscientious physicians who try prudently to discern, in each case, just what form of treatment or nontreatment is truly good for the patient, even if it embraces an increased likelihood of death. But I continue to insist that we cannot serve the patient's good by deliberately eliminating the patient. And if we have no right to do this to another, we have no right to have others do this to ourselves. There is, when all is said and done, no defensible right to die.

A CODA: ABOUT RIGHTS

The rhetoric of rights still performs today the noble, time-honored function of protecting individual life and liberty, a function now perhaps even more necessary than the originators of such rhetoric could have imagined, given the tyrannical possibilities of the modern bureaucratic and technologically competent state. But with the claim of a "right to die," as with so many of the novel rights being asserted in recent years, we face an extension of this rhetoric into areas where it no longer relates to that protective function, and beyond the limited area of life in which rights claims are clearly appropriate and indeed crucial. As a result, we face a number of serious and potentially dangerous distortions in our thought and in our practice. We distort our understanding of rights and weaken their respectability in their proper sphere by allowing them to be invented—without ground in nature or in reason—in response to moral questions that lie outside the limited domain of rights. We distort our understanding of moral deliberation and the moral life by reducing all complicated questions of right and good to questions of individual rights. We subvert the primacy and necessity of prudence by pretending that the assertion of rights will produce the best — and most moral — results. In trying to batter our way through the human condition with the bludgeon of personal rights, we allow ourselves to be deceived about the most fundamental matters: about death and dying, about our unavoidable finitude, and about the sustaining interdependencies of our lives.

Let us, by all means, continue to deliberate about whether and when and why it might make sense for someone to give up on his life, or even actively to choose death. But let us call a halt to all this dangerous thoughtlessness about rights. Let us refuse to talk any longer about a "right to die."

NOTES

1. For my "generosity" to succeed, I would, of course, have to commit suicide without assistance and without anyone's discovering it — i.e., well before I were demented. I would not want my children to believe that I suspected them of being incapable of loving me through my inevitable decline. There is another still more powerful reason for resisting this temptation: is it not unreasonably paternalistic of me to try to order the world so as to free my children from the usual intergenerational experiences, ties, obligations, and burdens? What principle of family life am I enacting and endorsing with my "altruistic suicide"?

2. Here is a recent example from a professor of sociology who objected to my condemnation of Derek Humphry's *Final Exit:*

Is Mr. Kass absolutely opposed to suicide? Would he have dissuaded Hitler? Would he disapprove of suicide by Pol Pot? . . . If we would welcome suicide by certain figures on limited occasions, should we prolong the lives of people who lived useless, degrading or dehumanized lives; who inflicted these indignities upon others; or who led vital lives but were reduced to uselessness and degradation by incurable disease? (*Commentary,* May 1992, p. 12).

3. Harvey C. Mansfield, Jr., "The Old Rights and the New: Responsibility vs. Self-Expression," in *Old Rights and New,* ed. Robert A. Licht (Washington: American Enterprise Institute, 1993), in press.

4. Hans Jonas, "The Right to Die," *Hastings Center Report* 8, no. 4 (1978): 31–36, at 31.

5. John Locke, *Second Treatise on Civil Government,* ch. 2, "Of the State of Nature," para. 6.

6. Locke, *Second Treatise,* ch. 5, "Of Property," para. 27. Emphasis added.

7. Later, in discussing the extent of legislative power, Locke denies to the legislative, though it be the supreme power in every commonwealth, arbitrary power over the individual and, in particular, power to destroy his life. "For nobody can transfer to another more power than he has in himself; and nobody has an absolute arbitrary power over himself or over any other to destroy his own life, or take away the life or property of another." *Second Treatise,* ch. 9, "Of the

Extent of the Legislative Power," para. 135. Because the state's power derives from the people's power, the person's lack of arbitrary power over himself is the ground for restricting the state's power to kill him.

8. See, for example, Rousseau, *Discourse on the Origin and Foundations of Inequality among Men,* note 9, especially paragraphs four and five.

9. Immanuel Kant, *The Metaphysical Principles of Virtue,* trans. James Ellington (Indianapolis: Bobbs-Merrill, 1964), pp. 83–84. My purpose in citing Kant here is not to defend Kantian morality — and I am not myself a Kantian — but simply to show that the thinker who thought most deeply about rights in relation to *reason* and *autonomy* would have found the idea of a "right to die" utterly indefensible on these grounds.

10. The attempt to ground a right to die in the so-called right to privacy fails for the same reasons. A right to make independent judgments regarding one's body in one's private sphere, free of governmental inference, cannot be the basis of the right of someone else, appointed by or protected by government, to put an end to one's bodily life.

11. Mansfield, "The Old Rights and the New." This permanent instability of "the self" defeats the main benefit of a rights-based politics, which knows how to respect individual rights precisely because they are understood to be rooted in a common human nature, with reliable common interests, both natural and rational. The self-determining self, because it is variable, also turns out to be an embarrassment for attempts to respect prior acts of self-determination, as in the case of living wills. For if the "self" is truly constantly being recreated, there is no reason to honor today "its" prescriptions of yesterday, for the two selves are not the same.

SUGGESTED READINGS

Admiraal, Pieter V. "Euthanasia in the Netherlands: Justifiable Euthanasia." *Issues in Law & Medicine* 3 (Spring 1988), 361–70, and also *The Euthanasia Review* 3 (Fall–Winter 1990), 107–18.

American Academy of Pediatrics. Policy Statement. "Ethics and the Care of Critically Ill Infants and Children." *Pediatrics* 98 (July 1996), 149–52.

American Geriatrics Society. Public Policy Committee. "Voluntary Active Euthanasia." *Journal of the American Geriatrics Society* 39 (August 1991), 826.

American Medical Association. Council on Ethical and Judicial Affairs. "Euthanasia: Report C." In *Proceedings of the House of Delegates.* Chicago: American Medical Association, June 1988, 258–60; *Current Opinions,* § 2.20, 1989; "Decisions Near the End of Life." *Report B.* Adopted by the House of Delegates (1991), 11–15; and "Decisions Near the End of Life." *Journal of the American Medical Association* 267 (April 1992), 2229–33.

American Neurological Association. Committee on Ethical Affairs. "Persistent Vegetative State: Report." *Annals of Neurology* 33 (April 1993), 386–90.

Angell, Marcia. "The Supreme Court and Physician-Assisted Suicide — the Ultimate Right." *New England Journal of Medicine* 336 (1997), 50–53.

Annas, George J., and Grodin, Michael. eds. *The Nazi Doctors and the Nuremberg Code.* New York: Oxford University Press, 1992.

Anonymous. "It's Over, Debbie." *Journal of the American Medical Association* 259 (1988), 258–72.

Battin, Margaret. "Voluntary Euthanasia and the Risks of Abuse: Can We Learn Anything from the Netherlands?" *Law, Medicine & Health Care* 20 (Spring–Summer 1992), 135.

————. "Euthanasia: The Way We Do It, the Way They Do It." *Journal of Pain and Symptom Management* 6 (July 1991), 298–305.

Beauchamp, Tom L., ed. *Intending Death: The Ethics of Assisted Suicide and Euthanasia.* Upper Saddle River, NJ: Prentice-Hall, 1996.

Beauchamp, Tom L. and Veatch, Robert, eds. *Ethical Issues in Death and Dying.* Upper Saddle River, NJ: Prentice-Hall, 1997.

————, and Childress, James F. *Principles of Biomedical Ethics.* 4th ed. New York: Oxford University Press, 1994, Chap. 4.

Bender, Leslie. "A Feminist Analysis of Physician-Assisted Dying and Voluntary Active Euthanasia." *Tennessee Law Review* 59 (Spring 1992), 519–46.

Bleich, J. D. "Life as an Intrinsic Rather than Instrumental Good: The 'Spiritual' Case Against Euthanasia." *Issues in Law and Medicine* 9 (Fall 1993), 139–49.

Brock, Dan W. "Death and Dying." In Veatch, Robert M., ed. *Medical Ethics.* 2d ed. Boston: Jones and Bartlett Publishers, 1997.

————. *Life and Death: Philosophical Essays in Biomedical Ethics.* New York: Cambridge University Press, 1993.

Brody, Baruch A. *Suicide and Euthanasia: Historical and Contemporary Themes.* Dordrecht, Holland: Kluwer Academic Publishers, 1989.

Callahan, Daniel. "Pursuing a Peaceful Death." *Hastings Center Report* 23 (1993), 32–38.

————. *The Troubled Dream of Life: Living with Mortality.* New York: Simon and Schuster, 1993.

Caplan, Arthur and Blank, Robert H., eds. *Compassion: Government Intervention in the Treatment of Critically Ill Newborns.* Totowa, NJ: Humana Press, 1992.

Cassel, Christine K. "Physician-Assisted Suicide: Are We Asking the Right Questions?" *Second Opinion* 18 (October 1992), 95–98.

————, and Meier, D. E. "Morals and Moralism in the Debate Over Euthanasia and Assisted Suicide." *New England Journal of Medicine* 323 (1990), 750–52.

Conwell, Yeates and Craine, Eric D. "Rational Suicide and the Right to Die." *New England Journal of Medicine* 325 (1991), 1100–1102.

Doerflinger, Richard. "Assisted Suicide: Pro-Choice or Anti-Life?" *Hastings Center Report* 19 (1989), S10–S12.

Dworkin, Ronald. *Life's Dominion: An Argument About Abortion, Euthanasia, and Individual Freedom.* New York: Knopf, 1993.

Foot, Philippa. "Euthanasia." *Philosophy & Public Affairs* 6 (1977), 85–112.

Gert, Bernard; Culver, Charles M.; and Clouser, K. Danner, *Bioethics: A Return to Fundamentals.* New York: Oxford, 1997, chs. 11–12.

Glover, Jonathan. *Causing Death and Saving Lives.* New York: Penguin Books, 1977.

Gomez, Carlos. *Regulating Death: Euthanasia and the Case of the Netherlands.* New York: Free Press, 1991.

Gostin, Lawrence O. "Drawing a Line Between Killing and Letting Die: The Law, and Law Reform, on Medically Assisted Dying." *Journal of Law, Medicine and Ethics* 21 (Spring 1993), 94–101.

The Hastings Center. "Guidelines on the Termination of Life-Sustaining Treatment and the Care of the Dying." In *Guidelines on the Termination of Life-Sustaining Treatment and the Care of the Dying.* Briarcliff Manor, NY: The Hastings Center, 1987, 26–29, 30–31.

The Journal of Medicine and Philosophy 17 (1992). Special issue on the "Cruzan Case."

Kadish, Sanford H. "Authorizing Death." In Coleman, Jules, and Buchanan, Allen, eds. *Harm's Way.* Cambridge: Cambridge University Press, 1993.

Kamisar, Yale. "When Is There a Constitutional 'Right to Die'? When Is There No Constitutional 'Right to Live'?" *Georgia Law Review* 25 (1991), 1203–42.

Kevorkian, Jack. *Prescription: Medicide—The Goodness of Planned Death.* Buffalo, NY: Prometheus Books, 1991.

Koop, C. Everett, and Grant, Edward R. "The 'Small Beginnings' of Euthanasia." *Journal of Law, Ethics & Public Policy* 2 (1986), 607–32.

Kuhse, Helga and Singer, Peter. *Should the Baby Live?* Oxford: Oxford University Press, 1985.

Law, Medicine, and Health Care 17 (1989). Special issue on the "Linares Case."

Leenen, H. J. J., and Ciesielski-Carlucci, Chris. *Force majeure (Legal Necessity): Justification for Active Termination of Life in the Case of Severely Handicapped Newborns after Forgoing Treatment." *Cambridge Quarterly of Healthcare Ethics* 2 (Summer 1993), 271–74.

Lifton, Robert J. *The Nazi Doctors: Medical Killing and the Psychology of Genocide.* New York: Basic Books, 1986.

Lynn, Joanne, ed. *By No Extraordinary Means.* Bloomington, IN: Indiana University Press, 1986.

Macklin, Ruth. "Which Way Down the Slippery Slope? Nazi Medical Killing and Euthanasia Today." In Caplan, Arthur L., ed. *When Medicine Went Mad: Bioethics and the Holocaust.* Totowa, NJ: Humana Press, 1992, 173–200, 343–45.

Meier, Diane E. "Physician-Assisted Dying: Theory and Reality. *Journal of Clinical Ethics* 3 (Spring 1992), 35–37.

Meisel, Alan. *The Right to Die.* New York: John Wiley and Sons, 1989, § 5.10.

————. "The Legal Consensus about Forgoing Life-Sustaining Treatment: Its Status and Its Prospects." *Kennedy Institute of Ethics Journal* 2 (December 1992), 309–45.

McMillan, Richard C.; Engelhardt, H. Tristram, Jr.; and Spicker, Stuart F., eds. *Euthanasia and the Newborn: Conflicts Regarding Saving Lives.* Dordrecht: D. Reidel, 1987.

Miller, Franklin G., and Fletcher, John C. "The Case for Legalized Euthanasia." *Perspectives in Biology and Medicine* 36 (Winter 1993), 159–76.

Miller, Franklin G., et al. "Regulating Physician-Assisted Death." *The New England Journal of Medicine* 331 (1994), 119–23.

Misbin, Robert I. "Physicians' Aid in Dying." *New England Journal of Medicine* 325 (1991), 1307–11.

New York State Task Force on Life and the Law. *When Death Is Sought: Assisted Suicide and Euthanasia in the Medical Context.* New York: New York State Task Force, 1994.

Orentlicher, David. "The Legalization of Physician Assisted Suicide: A Very Modest Revolution." *Boston College Law Review* 28 (1997), 443–75.

————. "Physician-Assisted Dying: The Conflict with Fundamental Principles of American Law." In Blank, Robert H., and Bonnicksen, Andrea L., eds. *Medicine Unbound.* New York: Columbia University Press, 1994.

President's Commission for the Study of Ethical Problems in Medicine and Biomedical and Behavioral Research. *Deciding to Forego Life-Sustaining Treatment.* Washington: U.S. Government Printing Office, 1983.

Quill, Timothy E. *Death and Dignity: Making Choices and Taking Charge*. New York: W. W. Norton, 1993.

————, et al. "Care of the Hopelessly Ill: Proposed Clinical Criteria for Physician-Assisted Suicide." *New England Journal of Medicine* 327 (1992), 1380–84.

Rachels, James. *The End of Life: Euthanasia and Morality*. Oxford: Oxford University Press, 1986.

Regan, Tom, ed. *Matters of Life and Death*. 3d ed. New York: Random House, 1992.

Robertson, John. "Cruzan and the Constitutional Status of Non-Treatment Decisions for Incompetent Patients." *Georgia Law Review* 25 (1991), 1139–1202.

Rosenblum, Victor G., and Forsythe, Clarke D. "The Right to Assisted Suicide: Protection of Autonomy or an Open Door to Social Killing?" *Issues in Law & Medicine* 6 (1990), 3–31.

Schaffner, Kenneth F. "Recognizing the Tragic Choice: Food, Water, and the Right to Assisted Suicide." *Critical Care Medicine* 16 (October 1988), 1063–68.

Schneiderman, Lawrence J. "Is It Morally Justifiable *Not* to Sedate this Patient before Ventilator Withdrawal?" *Journal of Clinical Ethics* 2 (1991), 129–30.

Siegler, Mark, and Weisbard, Alan J. "Against the Emerging Stream: Should Fluids and Nutritional Support Be Discontinued?" *Archives of Internal Medicine* 145 (1985), 129–32.

Thomasma, David C., and Graber, Glenn C. *Euthanasia: Toward an Ethical Social Policy*. New York: Continuum Publishing Co., 1990.

Truog, Robert D., and Berde, Charles B. "Pain, Euthanasia, and Anesthesiologists." *Anesthesiology* 78 (February 1993), 353–60.

van Delden, Johannes J. M., et al. "The Remmelink Study: Two Years Later." *Hastings Center Report* 23 (1993), 24–27.

van der Maas, Paul J., et al. "Euthanasia and Other Medical Decisions Concerning the End of Life." *The Lancet* 338 (1991), 669–74.

Wanzer, S. H., et al. "The Physician's Responsibility Toward Hopelessly Ill Patients: A Second Look." *New England Journal of Medicine* 320 (1989), 844–49.

Weir, Robert F. *Ethical Issues in Death and Dying*. 2d ed. New York: Columbia University Press, 1986.

Wolf, Susan. "Holding the Line on Euthanasia." *Hastings Center Report* 19 (1989), S13–S15.

REFERENCE AND BIBLIOGRAPHICAL WORKS

Bailey, Don V. *The Challenge of Euthanasia: An Annotated Bibliography on Euthanasia and Related Subjects*. Lanham, MD: University Press of America, 1990.

Bioethicsline: Computer Retrieval Service.

Buehler, David A. "CQ Sources: Suicide and Euthanasia." [Bibliography]. *Cambridge Quarterly of Healthcare Ethics* 2 (Winter 1993), 77–80.

Encyclopedia of Bioethics, ed. Warren Reich, 2d ed., New York: Macmillan, 1995.

Encyclopedia of Ethics. ed. Lawrence Becker and Charlotte Becker. New York: Garland Publishing Inc., 1992.

Farberow, Norman L. *Bibliography on Suicide and Suicide Prevention, 1897–1957, 1958–1970*. DHEW Publication No. (HSM) 72-9080. Rockville, MD: National Institutes of Mental Health. Washington, DC: U.S. Government Printing Office, 1972.

Johnson, Gretchen L. *Voluntary Euthanasia: A Comprehensive Bibliography*. Los Angeles: Hemlock Society, 1987.

Lineback, Richard H., ed. *Philosopher's Index*. Vols. 1– . Bowling Green, OH: Philosophy Documentation Center, Bowling Green State University. Issued Quarterly. Also CD Rom.

Walters, LeRoy, and Kahn, Tamar Joy, eds. *Bibliography of Bioethics*. Vols. 1– . New York: Free Press. Issued annually.

6.
Justice in the Distribution of Health Care

INTRODUCTION

Health care costs continue to rise dramatically throughout the world. These costs have been subjected to intense study by many government reviews, most of which agree that payment policies have fuelled unacceptable increases in expenditures for health care services. The basic *economic problem* about health care is how to control costs and efficiently distribute resources in order to satisfy human needs and desires. The basic *ethical problem* is how to structure a health care system that fairly distributes resources and provides equitable access to health care. These ethical and economic problems are often intertwined in the formation of health policy.

The proper role of government is often at the center of health policy discussions. Most members of society agree that government is constituted to protect citizens against risks from the environment, risks from external invasion, risks from crime, risks from fire, risks from highway accidents, and the like. But the idea that health care should be similarly provided as a government service has long been controversial, and even if the government has an obligation to provide health care, there are limits to what government can and should do.

THE ALLOCATION OF HEALTH CARE RESOURCES

Many public policy and private corporate decisions aim at allocating resources fairly and efficiently. To allocate is to distribute goods and services among the alternative possibilities for their use. This distribution need not be made by government officials. For example, the free market distributes goods and services through exchanges made by free agents acting in their own interests.

When the decision is social or governmental, rather than individual, decisions fall into two broad types: macroallocation and microallocation. In macroallocation, social decisions are made about how much will be expended for health care resources, as well as how it will be distributed. These decisions are taken by Congress, state legislatures, health organizations, private foundations, and health insurance companies. At the microallocation level, decisions are made by particular institutions or health professionals concerning who shall obtain available resources—for example, which of several potential patients will be admitted to the last available bed in the intensive care unit. This chapter emphasizes issues of fairness in systems of macroallocation.

Two primary considerations are involved in macroallocation decisions about health care and research: (1) What percentage of the total available resources should be allotted to biomedical research and clinical practice, which compete for funding with other social projects such as defense, education, transportation, and the like? (2) How much budgeted to biomedicine should go to each specific area—for example, how much to cancer research, to preventive medicine, and to the production of technology for treatment facilities? An example of the second problem is whether funding for *preventive* medicine should take priority over funding for *crisis* medicine. From one perspective, the prevention of disease by improvements in unsanitary environments and dissemination of health information is cheaper and more efficient in raising health levels and saving lives than are kidney dialysis, heart transplantation, and intensive care units. From another perspective, a concentrated preventive approach seems morally unsatisfactory if it leads to neglecting needy persons who could directly benefit from available resources.

These problems of macroallocation are handled differently by competing systems of distribution. Which among these systems is the fairest?

DISTRIBUTIVE JUSTICE IN REDISTRIBUTING RESOURCES

In Chapter 1 we surveyed theories of justice. We can now examine how these theories might be used to gauge the justice of health care systems, including macroallocation and microallocation decisions in those systems.

Egalitarian Theory.   In Chapter 1 we noted that John Rawls's *A Theory of Justice* has been a particularly influential work on social justice in the egalitarian tradition. Rawls argues that a social arrangement is a communal effort to advance the good of all in the society. Because inequalities of birth, historical circumstance, and natural endowment are undeserved, persons in a cooperative society should aim to correct them by making the unequal situation of naturally disadvantaged members more equal. Evening out disabilities in this way is, Rawls claims, a fundamental part of our shared conception of justice. His recognition of a positive societal obligation to eliminate or reduce barriers that prevent fair opportunity and that correct or compensate for various disadvantages has clear implications for discussions of justice in health care.

Rawls's analysis of justice deeply influenced the article in this chapter by Robert Veatch, who begins with the Rawlsian model of justice and then proposes two separate uses of egalitarian theory for health care. He believes that those individuals who are worst off in a society (that is, are at the minimum level) should be guaranteed access to a certain level of health care. In this way, the society improves the conditions of the least fortunate by increasing their level of care.

Utilitarian Theory.   One need not be an egalitarian to believe in an equitable social system that redistributes resources to improve the health care needs of all citizens. Utilitarians believe that society has an obligation to assist its members by preventing harms such as sickness and also that we are morally blameworthy if we do nothing at all. Utilitarians argue that *justice* is the name for the most paramount and stringent forms of social obligation created by the principle of utility. In the distribution of health care, utilitarians commonly view justice as involving trade-offs and partial allocations that strike a balance. In devising a system of public funding for health care, we must balance public and private benefit, predicted cost savings, the probability of failure, the magnitude of risks, and the like.

No author in this chapter explicitly defends a utilitarian system of distribution for health care. However, the article by the President's Commission for the Study of Ethical Problems adopts roughly the utilitarian approach. To the commission, society has an obligation to ensure equitable access to health care for all citizens, because of the special importance of relieving suffering and preventing premature death. It contends that creators of a health care distribution system must balance the issues of social responsibility, individual responsibility, and social resources. The commission report opts for a two-tiered system of health care in which those who wish to purchase more than is provided by the social scheme of insurance are free to do so at personal expense.

Libertarian Theory. A perennial problem concerning the distribution of health care is whether justice requires any explicit distribution plan for health care. Robert Nozick has raised the following question about our shared conception of justice:

> Hearing the term "distribution," most people presume that some thing or mechanism uses some principle or criterion to give out a supply of things. . . . So it is an open question, at least, whether *re-distribution* should take place; whether we should do again what has already been done once.[1]

In Chapter 1 we examined the libertarian theory of justice, for which Nozick is a spokesperson. These free-market theorists explicitly reject the conclusion that egalitarian and utilitarian patterns of distribution represent an appropriate normative ideal for distributing health care. People may be equal in many morally significant respects, but *justice* does not demand the collection and redistribution of economic resources, such as the tax dollars, that are required to fund government-distributed health care goods and services. For a libertarian, there is no pattern of just distribution in addition to free-market procedures of acquiring property, legitimately transferring that property, and providing rectification for those who had property illegitimately extracted or otherwise were illegitimately obstructed in the free market.

A libertarian prefers a system in which health care insurance is privately and voluntarily purchased by individual or group initiative. In this system no one has had property coercively extracted by the state in order to benefit someone else. This libertarian theory is defended in this chapter by H. Tristram Engelhardt, Jr., who relies heavily on the principle of rights of free choice rather than a substantive principle of justice. Engelhardt argues that a theory of justice should work to protect our right not to be coerced; it should not propound a doctrine intended to regulate society through redistributive arrangements. Use of the tax code to effect social goals such as saving lives with advanced medical technologies is a matter of social *choice,* not social justice. Some disadvantages created by ill health, Engelhardt argues, should be viewed as merely *unfortunate,* whereas injury and illness caused by another person are correctly viewed as *unfair.* From this perspective, one will call a halt to the demands of justice where one draws the distinction between the unfair (and therefore obligatory in justice to correct) and the merely unfortunate.

THE RIGHT TO HEALTH CARE

These debates about justice and fair macroallocation have implications for claims about a right to health care. If this right exists, national allocations for health care would presumably be based on justice rather than on charity, compassion, or benevolence. Critics of the view that there is a right to health care respond that failures to allocate health care resources may be uncharitable, lacking in compassion, and even stingy — and therefore morally condemnable — yet not violations of anyone's rights. These critics themselves may view a governmental system as seriously inadequate and still find no fault in not recognizing a *right* to health care.

Positions in contemporary ethics on the right to health care range from a denial of rights to strong egalitarian rights for all citizens. Typically utilitarians argue that the principle of utility determines whether a right to health care is supportable; egalitarians attempt to derive a right to health care from a principle of equality, such as fair equality of opportunity; and libertarians deny that there are any welfare rights, including rights to health care.

In this context a "right" is understood as an *entitlement* to some measure of health care; rights are contrasted with privileges, ideals, and acts of charity. In many nations there is a firmly established legal right to health care goods and services for all citizens. The prevailing legal view in the United States, by contrast, is that even if there are solid moral reasons for the enactment of a right to health care and no constitutional constraints against it, there is no *constitutional* right to health care. In 1965 Congress created Medicare to provide coverage for health care costs in populations that could not afford adequate coverage, especially the elderly. Medicare conferred a right to health care on a particularly vulnerable population and thereby stimulated discussion of whether all citizens have, or at least should have, a right to health care under similar conditions of need. There is no realistic legal basis to support such claims, but is there a moral basis?

It is often asked whether there is a right to a "decent minimum" of health care. These proponents assert that each person should have equal access to an adequate (though not maximal) level of health care for all available types of services. The distribution proceeds on the basis of need, and needs are met by fair access to adequate services. Better services, such as luxury hospital rooms and expensive but optional dental work, can then be made available for purchase at personal expense by those who are able to and wish to do so.

However, the basic level of care to which all are entitled may have to be *funded* by multiple funding systems, not merely by a government agency. Many designs for a universal health insurance rely not on government but rather on managed competition with a mixed public and private sponsorship. One might try to locate some variety of insurance for all persons who do not already qualify for a public program such as Medicare and Medicaid.

The President's Commission and Allen Buchanan argue that we have no *right* to this decent minimum of care but that there is nonetheless a social *obligation* to provide it. Engelhardt concludes that there is no right and no social obligation, although a society may freely choose to enact such a policy. From this perspective and Buchanan's, if needs are unfortunate they may still be ameliorated by benevolence or compassion; but only if they are unfair does the obligation of justice justify compensation to the disadvantaged by using state force to tax and redistribute resources. Maleficently or negligently caused setbacks to health are *unfair,* but other setbacks to health are merely matters of *misfortune.*

In light of this problem of a criterion of unfairness, the implications of the Rawlsian approach and the demands of the fair opportunity rule remain uncertain in biomedical ethics and health policy. However, Rawlsians like Veatch hold out for a different conclusion. Veatch defends a right stronger than the right to a decent minimum. He proposes the distribution of health care based on the individual's health care needs, by using the yardstick of an "equal right to health care." The result is that "people have a right to needed health care to provide an opportunity for a level of health equal as far as possible to the health of other people." This application of the principle of justice to health care would result in a health care delivery system with only one class of services available, rather than a two-tiered system.

Even if one does not support either moral rights to health care or political obligations to supply it, one can still support legal entitlements to health care on grounds of charity, beneficence, or a sense of moral excellence in a community. Many appeals other than those to moral rights can be used to defend public distributions that confer legal rights, as Buchanan and the President's Commission in effect note. These appeals may also support a system of required contributions on grounds that it is the best system for those willing to cooperate and that it will be socially efficient.

UNIVERSAL ACCESS AND MANAGED CARE

Many problems about justice in health care start with how to pay for and distribute limited social resources. The overarching problem in health policy is, "How can a health policy provide adequate and fairly distributed care to all subscribers at an affordable price?" Many current problems stem from unequal resources and unequal access to care. Others stem from the advent of a system in which much of the health care is distributed through managed care and price competition.

Several obstacles stand in the way of a more efficient, fair, and comprehensive system of access to health care in the U.S. system. Roughly forty million U.S. citizens annually lack all health care coverage, largely because of the high cost of health insurance and a system in which access is generally obtained through an employer-based health plan. All but the most affluent citizens need some form of insurance to meet actual or potential health care needs, which are often unpredictable in onset, catastrophic if unmet, and too expensive for an individual's resources. Although more than two thousand dollars per person and over 12 percent of the gross national product are spent annually for health care in the United States, the poor and the uninsured often cannot afford or find access to even minimally adequate care. A small group of citizens turns out to be uninsurable, because they cannot pass physical examinations, present the kind of medical histories required for insurance, or are excluded because of their occupation.

There is also a problem of underinsurance for over 20 million U.S. citizens who have seriously inadequate coverage. Costs require limiting coverage even in employer-based plans, and many exclusionary clauses deny access for types of treatment, as well as for specific diseases, injuries, or organ systems. A few people are both uninsured and underinsured. They experience gaps in insurance coverage that cannot be bridged because they move quickly from job to job or suffer from temporary but lengthy layoffs. More than a million laborers lose their insurance for some period of time during the year while they are unemployed, and more than 25 percent of the entire U.S. population changes insurance, with a resulting coverage gap, during the course of each year.

In the face of rapid rises in health care costs, the situation in U.S. health care is increasingly referred to as a "crisis." One generic issue concerns how to design or structure our basic health care institutions and forms of distribution for maximum coverage and efficiency. Various approaches produce different programs of health care services, who will have access to them, who may and should deliver those services, and how the services will be funded and distributed.

Each author in the second section of this chapter has a vision of how to handle these and other questions about access to health care. Equitable and efficient access to care is the highest item on their agenda. Some approaches make direct appeals to the *right* to health care and some invoke one or more *theories* of justice; others make only an indirect appeal to rights and theories. Because there is neither a social consensus nor a paramount theory of justice at the present time, we should expect public policies to oscillate, now using the premises of one approach, later emphasizing another.

In the first article of this section, Ezekiel Emanuel and Nancy Dubler attempt to provide a normative standard for evaluating systems of health care. Their concern is primarily with managed care and the preservation of a proper patient–physician relationship. They recognize that there is little chance of realizing an "ideal physician–patient relationship" for most Americans, and maintain that managed care has good outcomes in some regions, but also has the potential of undermining ideals of the patient–physician relationship.

In the second article, Lawrence Gostin is concerned with the buying and selling of health care as a commodity and the failure to provide universal coverage in the United States. He argues that the prevention of disease or disability and the promotion of health justifies the government in constructing a system of universal coverage. In light of the fact that many people receive insufficient and inequitable access to medical services, Gostin argues for considerably greater equity (not equality) so that health care is distributed more fairly.

David Orentlicher, in the final selection in this section, focuses on concerns for the patient–physician relationship that would arise under significant health care reform, especially reform that created universal or near-universal coverage. He is particularly concerned about the elimination of independence in the patient's choice of physician and insurance and about the threat to physician loyalty from health care reform.

RATIONING AND THE OREGON PLAN

Ethics and health policy have recently seen a rise in the language of *rationing* health care resources. This term often suggests financially stringent and critical circumstances that require social decisions to include some citizens while excluding others. However, the original meaning of rationing did not suggest austerity or an emergency. It meant a form of allowance, share, or portion, as when food is divided into rations in the military. Only recently has it been tied to limited resources and crisis management. If insurance coverage or ability to pay is a way of eliminating those who are uninsured from access to health care, then much of the U.S.'s health care system involves rationing by level of personal resources. There are many other forms of rationing, including forms of government reimbursement to hospitals, various forms of cost containment, restricting the elderly to some forms of care, and methods for disseminating new medical technologies.

Many now believe that the most important task of democratic political procedures for macroallocation is to establish priorities that distinguish the most important and the least important goals of a health care system. Determining which categories of injury, illness, or disease (if any) should receive a priority ranking in the allocation of public resources is a vital aspect of health policy. In trying to determine priorities among medical needs, policymakers justifiably take into account factors of various diseases such as communicability, frequency, cost, pain and suffering, and prospects for rehabilitation. It might be appropriate, for instance, to concentrate less on killer diseases, such as some forms of cancer, and more on widespread disabling diseases, such as arthritis.

A closely watched attempt to implement this strategy while extending health care to a wider set of citizens has taken place in the state of Oregon, which has been at the forefront of rationing decisions in the United States. Faced with skyrocketing costs and a restive population demanding more efficient and fairer access to quality health care, Oregon established a state committee in 1989 charged to rank hundreds of medical procedures for Medicaid, from most to least important, based in part on data about quality of well-being. State officials sought to extend coverage to a larger percentage of its citizens through its allocated Medicaid funds, and to do so both efficiently and fairly. The goal was to fund as many top priority-ranked services as possible.

In 1990, Oregon's Health Services Commission issued a list of 1,600 ranked medical procedures that formed the initial centerpiece of the plan. Procedures were ranked according to their respective costs and likely results on the patient's quality of well-being. A quality of life approach was used from the outset. This approach helps rank procedures by considering both the change in quality of life offered by the treatment to the average patient and its associated effect on the quality of life. Because the data collected for the ranking of treatments focus on how a treatment changes the quality of life for the average patient receiving it, and not on the quality of life at a given point in time after treatment, patients are not penalized for having serious debilitating diseases or injuries. The system was designed to ensure that the very sick are not discriminated against. (The elderly, the blind, and the disabled are excluded from the ranking scheme.)

Oregon's plan is the first proposal for systematic allocation and rationing of health care funds in the United States. As such, it may mark the beginning of a new era in American medical care that brings it closer to the more systematic approaches adopted in other countries. In sacrificing high-cost operations that only benefit a few patients, in favor of a minimal level of health care for all residents, Oregon has at least implicitly relied on a theory of justice in making its determinations. The sensitive issue of who will suffer a setback under the Oregon plan has proved troublesome to resolve.

These problems are treated in the final three selections in this chapter. In the first, Norman Daniels discusses troublesome questions about fairness in rationing. He focuses on four general rationing problems that he thinks remain unresolved in bioethics and that also plague Oregon's rationing plan. In the course of a reply to Daniels, Leonard M. Fleck argues in the second selection that our national efforts at health reform ought to be informed by several lessons that can be learned from Oregon. Specifically, he thinks that we can learn that rationing is inevitable and that it must be public and visible. The kind of hidden rationing that occurs in the present system therefore must be eliminated.

Finally, Dan Brock raises the more particular question of whether prioritizing and rationing health care discriminate against the disabled. He begins with a case study of the Oregon reform plan, which takes him to questions about the general fairness of the methodology and ranking system used in Oregon. His larger question is whether this methodology and other rationing schemes wrongly discriminate against persons with disabilities. Brock thinks we have largely ignored these kinds of questions because we have clung to the illusions that we neither do nor should ration beneficial care and therefore that prioritization is unnecessary. In his view, prioritization is absolutely essential.

T.L.B.

NOTE

1. Robert Nozick, *Anarchy, State, and Utopia* (New York: Basic Books, 1974), pp. 149–50.

Just Health Care and the Right to Health Care

PRESIDENT'S COMMISSION FOR THE STUDY OF ETHICAL PROBLEMS IN MEDICINE AND BIOMEDICAL AND BEHAVIORAL RESEARCH

Securing Access to Health Care

The President's Commission was mandated to study the ethical and legal implications of differences in the availability of health services. In this Report to the President and Congress, the Commission sets forth an ethical standard: access for all to an adequate level of care without the imposition of excessive burdens. It believes that this is the standard against which proposals for legislation and regulation in this field ought to be measured. . . .

In both their means and their particular objectives, public programs in health care have varied over the years. Some have been aimed at assuring the productivity of the work force, others at protecting particularly vulnerable or deserving groups, still others at manifesting the country's commitment to equality of opportunity. Nonetheless, most programs have rested on a common rationale: to ensure that care be made accessible to a group whose health needs would otherwise not be adequately met.

The consequence of leaving health care solely to market forces — the mechanism by which most things are allocated in American society — is not viewed as acceptable when a significant portion of the population lacks access to health services. Of course, government financing programs, such as Medicare and Medicaid as

From *Securing Access to Health Care,* Vol. 1. Washington, D.C.: U.S. Government Printing Office, 1983.

well as public programs that provide care directly to veterans and the military and through local public hospitals, have greatly improved access to health care. These efforts, coupled with the expanded availability of private health insurance, have resulted in almost 90% of Americans having some form of health insurance coverage. Yet the patchwork of government programs and the uneven availability of private health insurance through the workplace have excluded millions of people. The Surgeon General has stated that "with rising unemployment, the numbers are shifting rapidly. We estimate that from 18 to 25 million Americans — 8 to 11 percent of the population — have no health-insurance coverage at all." Many of these people lack effective access to health care, and many more who have some form of insurance are unprotected from the severe financial burdens of sickness. . . .

[W]hile people have some ability — through choice of life-style and through preventive measures — to influence their health status, many health problems are beyond their control and are therefore undeserved. Besides the burdens of genetics, environment, and chance, individuals become ill because of things they do or fail to do — but it is often difficult for an individual to choose to do otherwise or even to know with enough specificity and confidence what he or she ought to do to remain healthy. Finally, the incidence and severity of ill health is distributed very unevenly among people.

Basic needs for housing and food are predictable, but even the most hardworking and prudent person may suddenly be faced with overwhelming needs for health care. Together, these considerations lend weight to the belief that health care is different from most other goods and services. In a society concerned not only with fairness and equality of opportunity but also with the redemptive powers of science, there is a felt obligation to ensure that some level of health services is available to all.

There are many ambiguities, however, about the nature of this societal obligation. What share of health costs should individuals be expected to bear, and what responsibility do they have to use health resources prudently? Is it society's responsibility to ensure that every person receives care or services of as high quality and as great extent as any other individual? Does it require that everyone share opportunities to receive all available care or care of any possible benefit? If not, what level of care is "enough"? And does society's obligation include a responsibility to ensure both that care is available and that its costs will not unduly burden the patient?

The resolution of such issues is made more difficult by the spectre of rising health care costs and expenditures. Americans annually spend over 270 million days in hospitals, make over 550 million visits to physicians' offices, and receive tens of millions of X-rays. Expenditures for health care in 1981 totaled $287 billion — an average of over $1225 for every American. Although the finitude of national resources demands that trade-offs be made between health care and other social goods, there is little agreement about which choices are most acceptable from an ethical standpoint. . . . The Commission attempts to lay an ethical foundation for evaluating both current patterns of access to health care and the policies designed to address remaining problems in the distribution of health care resources. . . .

THE CONCEPT OF EQUITABLE ACCESS TO HEALTH CARE

The special nature of health care helps to explain why it ought to be accessible, in a fair fashion, to all. But if this ethical conclusion is to provide a basis for evaluating current patterns of access to health care and proposed health policies, the meaning of fairness or equity in this context must be clarified. The concept of equitable access needs definition in its two main aspects: the level of care that ought to be available to all and the

extent to which burdens can be imposed on those who obtain these services.

ACCESS TO WHAT?

"Equitable access" could be interpreted in a number of ways: equality of access, access to whatever an individual needs or would benefit from, or access to an adequate level of care.

Equity as Equality. It has been suggested that equity is achieved either when everyone is assured of receiving an equal quantity of health care dollars or when people enjoy equal health. The most common characterization of equity as equality, however, is as providing everyone with the same level of health care. In this view, it follows that if a given level of care is available to one individual it must be available to all. If the initial standard is set high, by reference to the highest level of care presently received, an enormous drain would result on the resources needed to provide other goods. Alternatively, if the standard is set low in order to avoid an excessive use of resources, some beneficial services would have to be withheld from people who wished to purchase them. In other words, no one would be allowed access to more services or services of higher quality than those available to everyone else, even if he or she were willing to pay for those services from his or her personal resources.

As long as significant inequalities in income and wealth persist, inequalities in the use of health care can be expected beyond those created by differences in need. Given people with the same pattern of preferences and equal health care needs, those with greater financial resources will purchase more health care. Conversely, given equal financial resources, the different patterns of health care preferences that typically exist in any population will result in a different use of health services by people with equal health care needs. Trying to prevent such inequalities would require interfering with people's liberty to use their income to purchase an important good like health care while leaving them free to use it for frivolous or inessential ends. Prohibiting people with higher incomes or stronger preferences for health care from purchasing more care than everyone else gets would not be feasible, and would probably result in a black market for health care.

Equity as Access Solely According to Benefit or Need. Interpreting equitable access to mean that everyone must receive all health care that is of any benefit to them also has unacceptable implications. Unless health is the only good or resources are unlimited, it would be irrational for a society — as for an individual — to make a commitment to provide whatever health care might be beneficial regardless of cost. Although health care is of special importance, it is surely not all that is important to people. . . .

"[N]eed" could be even more expansive in scope than "benefit." Philosophical and economic writings do not provide any clear distinction between "needs" and "wants" or "preferences." Since the term means different things to different people, "access according to need" could become "access to any health service a person wants." Conversely, need could be interpreted very narrowly to encompass only a very minimal level of services — for example, those "necessary to prevent death."

Equity as an Adequate Level of Health Care. Although neither "everything needed" nor "everything beneficial" nor "everything that anyone else is getting" are defensible ways of understanding equitable access, the special nature of health care dictates that everyone have access to *some* level of health care: enough care to achieve sufficient welfare, opportunity, information, and evidence of interpersonal concern to facilitate a reasonably full and satisfying life. That level can be termed "an adequate level of health care." The difficulty of sharpening this amorphous notion into a workable foundation for health policy is a major problem in the United States today. This concept is not new; it is implicit in the public debate over health policy and has manifested itself in the history of public policy in this country. In this [essay], the Commission attempts to demonstrate the value of the concept, to clarify its content, and to apply it to the problems facing health policymakers.

Understanding equitable access to health care to mean that everyone should be able to secure an adequate level of care has several strengths. Because an adequate level of care may be less than "all beneficial care" and because it does not require that all needs be satisfied, it acknowledges the need for setting priorities within health care and signals a clear recognition that society's resources are limited and that there are other goods besides health. Thus, interpreting equity as access to adequate care does not generate an open-ended obligation. One of the chief dangers of interpretations of equity that require virtually unlimited resources for health care is that they encourage the view that equitable access is an impossible ideal. Defining equity as an adequate level of care for all avoids an impossible commitment of resources without falling into the opposite error of abandoning the enterprise of seeking to ensure that health care is in fact available for everyone.

In addition, since providing an adequate level of care is a limited moral requirement, this definition also avoids the unacceptable restriction on individual liberty entailed by the view that equity requires equality. Provided that an adequate level is available to all, those who prefer to use their resources to obtain care that exceeds that level do not offend any ethical principle in doing so. Finally, the concept of adequacy, as the Commission understands it, is society-relative. The content of adequate care will depend upon the overall resources available in a given society, and can take into account a consensus of expectations about what is adequate in a particular society at a particular time in its historical development. This permits the definition of adequacy to be altered as societal resources and expectations change.

With What Burdens? It is not enough to focus on the care that individuals receive; attention must be paid to the burdens they must bear in order to obtain it — waiting and travel time, the cost and availability of transport, the financial cost of the care itself. Equity requires not only that adequate care be available to all, but also that these burdens not be excessive.

If individuals must travel unreasonably long distances, wait for unreasonably long hours, or spend most of their financial resources to obtain care, some will be deterred from obtaining adequate care, with adverse effects on their health and well-being. Others may bear the burdens, but only at the expense of their ability to meet other important needs. If one of the main reasons for providing adequate care is that health care increases welfare and opportunity, then a system that required large numbers of individuals to forego food, shelter, or educational advancement in order to obtain care would be self-defeating and irrational.

The concept of acceptable burdens in obtaining care, as opposed to excessive ones, parallels in some respects the concept of adequacy. Just as equity does not require equal access, neither must the burdens of obtaining adequate care be equal for all persons. What is crucial is that the variations in burdens fall within an acceptable range. As in determining an adequate level of care, there is no simple formula for ascertaining when the burdens of obtaining care fall within such a range. . . .

A SOCIETAL OBLIGATION

Society has a moral obligation to ensure that everyone has access to adequate care without being subject to excessive burdens. In speaking of a societal obligation the Commission makes reference to society in the broadest sense — the collective American community. The community is made up of individuals, who are in turn members of many other, overlapping groups, both public and private: local, state, regional, and national units; professional and workplace organizations; religious, educational, and charitable organizations; and family, kinship, and ethnic groups. All these entities play a role in discharging societal obligations.

The Commission believes it is important to distinguish between society, in this inclusive sense, and government as one institution among others in society. Thus the recognition of a collective or societal obligation does not imply that government should be the only or even the primary institution involved in the complex enterprise of making health care available. It is the Commission's view that the societal obligation to ensure equitable access for everyone may best be fulfilled in this country by a pluralistic approach that relies upon the coordinated contributions of actions by both the private and public sectors.

Securing equitable access is a societal rather than a merely private or individual responsibility for several reasons. First, while health is of special importance for human beings, health care — especially scientific health care — is a social product requiring the skills and efforts of many individuals; it is not something that individuals can provide for themselves solely through their own efforts. Second, because the need for health care is both unevenly distributed among persons and highly unpredictable and because the cost of securing care may be great, few individuals could secure adequate care without relying on some social mechanism for sharing the costs. Third, if persons generally deserved their health conditions or if the need for health care were fully within the individual's control, the fact that some lack adequate care would not be viewed as an inequity. But differences in health status, and hence differences in health care needs, are largely undeserved because they are, for the most part, not within the individual's control. . . .

WHO SHOULD ENSURE THAT SOCIETY'S OBLIGATION IS MET?

THE LIMITATIONS OF RELYING UPON THE GOVERNMENT

Although the Commission recognizes the necessity of government involvement in ensuring equity of access, it believes that such activity must be carefully crafted and implemented in order to achieve its intended purpose. Public concern about the inability of the market and of private charity to secure access to health care for all has led to extensive government involvement in the financing and delivery of health care. This involvement has come about largely as a result of ad hoc responses to specific problems; the result has been a patchwork of public initiatives at the local, state, and Federal level. These efforts have done much to make health care more widely available to all citizens, but . . . they have not achieved equity of access.

To a large extent, this is the result of a lack of consensus about the nature of the goal and the proper role of government in pursuing it. But to some degree, it may also be the product of the nature of government activity. In some instances, government programs (of all types, not just health-related) have not been designed well enough to achieve the purposes intended or have been subverted to serve purposes explicitly not intended.

In the case of health care, it is extremely difficult to devise public strategies that, on the one hand, do not encourage the misuse of health services and, on the other hand, are not so restrictive as to unnecessarily or arbitrarily limit available care. There is a growing concern, for example, that government assistance in the form of tax exemptions for the purchase of employment-related health insurance has led to the overuse of many services of only very marginal benefit. Similarly, government programs that pay for health care directly (such as Medicaid) have been subject to fraud and abuse by both beneficiaries and providers. . . .

A RIGHT TO HEALTH CARE?

Often the issue of equitable access to health care is framed in the language of rights. Some who view health care from the perspective of distributive justice argue that the considerations discussed in this [essay] show not only that society has a moral obligation to provide equitable access, but also that every individual has a moral right to such access. The Commission has chosen not to develop the case for achieving equitable access through the assertion of a right to health care. Instead it has sought to frame the issues in terms of the special nature of health care and of a society's moral obligation to achieve equity, without taking a position on whether the term "obligation" should be read as entailing a moral right. The Commission reaches this conclusion for several reasons: first, such a right is not legally or constitutionally recognized at the present time; second, it is not a logical corollary of an ethical obligation of the type the Commission has enunciated; and third, it is not necessary as a foundation for appropriate governmental actions to secure adequate health care for all.

Legal Rights. Neither the Supreme Court nor any appellate court has found a constitutional right to health or to health care. However, most Federal statutes and many state statutes that fund or regulate health care have been interpreted to provide statutory rights in the form of entitlements for the intended beneficiaries of the program or for members of the group protected by the regulatory authority. As a consequence, a host of legal decisions have developed significant legal protections for program beneficiaries. . . .

Moral Obligations and Rights. The relationship between the concept of a moral right and that of a moral obligation is complex. To say that a person has a moral right to something is always to say that it is that person's due, that is, he or she is morally entitled to it. In contrast, the term "obligation" is used in two different senses. All moral rights imply corresponding obligations, but, depending on the sense of the term that is being used, moral obligations may or may not imply corresponding rights. In the broad sense, to say that society has a moral obligation to do something is to say that it ought morally to do that thing and that failure to do it makes society liable to serious moral criticism. This does not, however, mean that there is a corresponding right. For example, a person may have a moral obligation to help those in need, even though the needy cannot, strictly speaking, demand that person's aid as something they are due.

The government's responsibility for seeing that the obligation to achieve equity is met is independent of the existence of a corresponding moral right to health care. There are many forms of government involvement, such as enforcement of traffic rules or taxation to support national defense, to protect the environment, or to promote biomedical research, that do not presuppose corresponding moral rights but that are nonetheless legitimate and almost universally recognized as such. In a democracy, at least, the people may assign to government the responsibility for seeing that important collective obligations are met, provided that doing so does not violate important moral rights.

As long as the debate over the ethical assessment of patterns of access to health care is carried on simply by the assertion and refutation of a "right to health care," the debate will be incapable of guiding policy. At the very least, the nature of the right must be made clear and competing accounts of it compared and evaluated. Moreover, if claims of rights are to guide policy they must be supported by sound ethical reasoning and the connections between various rights must be systematically developed, especially where rights are potentially in conflict with one another. At present, however, there is a great deal of dispute among competing theories of rights, with most theories being so abstract and inadequately developed that their implications for health care are not obvious. Rather than attempt to adjudicate among competing theories of rights, the Commission has chosen to concentrate on what it believes to be the more important part of the question: what is the nature of the societal obligation, which exists whether or not people can claim a corresponding right to health care, and how should this societal obligation be fulfilled?

MEETING THE SOCIETAL OBLIGATION

HOW MUCH CARE IS ENOUGH?

Before the concept of an adequate level of care can be used as a tool to evaluate patterns of access and efforts to improve equity, it must be fleshed out. Since there is no objective formula for doing this, reasonable people can disagree about whether particular patterns and policies meet the demands of adequacy. The Commission does not attempt to spell out in detail what adequate care should include. Rather it frames the terms in which those who discuss or critique health care issues can consider ethics as well as economics, medical science, and other dimensions.

Characteristics of Adequacy. First, the Commission considers it clear that health care can only be judged adequate in relation to an individual's health condition.

To begin with a list of techniques or procedures, for example, is not sensible: a CT scan for an accident victim with a serious head injury might be the best way to make a diagnosis essential for the appropriate treatment of that patient; a CT scan for a person with headaches might not be considered essential for adequate care. To focus only on the technique, therefore, rather than on the individual's health and the impact the procedure will have on that individual's welfare and opportunity, would lead to inappropriate policy.

Disagreement will arise about whether the care of some health conditions falls within the demands of adequacy. Most people will agree, however, that some conditions should not be included in the societal obligation to ensure access to adequate care. A relatively uncontroversial example would be changing the shape of a functioning, normal nose or retarding the normal effects of aging (through cosmetic surgery). By the same token, there are some conditions, such as pregnancy, for which care would be regarded as an important component of adequacy. In determining adequacy, it is important to consider how people's welfare, opportunities, and requirements for information and interpersonal caring are affected by their health condition.

Any assessment of adequacy must consider also the types, amounts, and quality of care necessary to respond to each health condition. It is important to emphasize that these questions are implicitly comparative: the standard of adequacy for a condition must reflect the fact that resources used for it will not be available to respond to other conditions. Consequently, the level of care deemed adequate should reflect a reasoned judgment not only about the impact of the condition on the welfare and opportunity of the individual but also about the efficacy and the cost of the care itself in relation to other conditions and the efficacy and cost of the care that is available for them. Since individual cases differ so much, the health care professional and patient must be flexible. Thus adequacy, even in relation to a particular health condition, generally refers to a range of options.

The Relationship of Costs and Benefits. The level of care that is available will be determined by the level of resources devoted to producing it. Such allocation should reflect the benefits and costs of the care provided. It should be emphasized that these "benefits," as well as their "costs," should be interpreted broadly, and not restricted only to effects easily quantifiable in monetary terms. Personal benefits include improvements in individuals' functioning and in their quality of life, and the reassurance from worry and the provision of information that are a product of health care. Broader social benefits should be included as well, such as strengthening the sense of community and the belief that no one in serious need of health care will be left without it. Similarly, costs are not merely the funds spent for a treatment but include other less tangible and quantifiable adverse consequences, such as diverting funds away from other socially desirable endeavors including education, welfare, and other social services.

There is no objectively correct value that these various costs and benefits have or that can be discovered by the tools of cost/benefit analysis. Still, such an analysis, as a recent report of the Office of Technology Assessment noted, "can be very helpful to decision-makers because the process of analysis gives structure to the problem, allows an open consideration of all relevant effects of a decision, and forces the explicit treatment of key assumptions."[1] But the valuation of the various effects of alternative treatments for different conditions rests on people's values and goals, about which individuals will reasonably disagree. In a democracy, the appropriate values to be assigned to the consequences of policies must ultimately be determined by people expressing their values through social and political processes as well as in the marketplace.

Approximating Adequacy. The intention of the Commission is to provide a frame of reference for policy-makers, not to resolve these complex questions. Nevertheless, it is possible to raise some of the specific issues that should be considered in determining what constitutes adequate care. It is important, for example, to gather accurate information about and compare the costs and effects, both favorable and unfavorable, of various treatment or management options. The options that better serve the goals that make health care of special importance should be assigned a higher value. As already noted, the assessment of costs must take two factors into account: the cost of a proposed option in relation to alternative forms of care that would achieve the same goal of enhancing the welfare and opportunities of the patient, and the cost of each proposed option in terms of foregone opportunities to apply the same resources to social goals other than that of ensuring equitable access.

Furthermore, a reasonable specification of adequate care must reflect an assessment of the relative importance of many different characteristics of a given form of care for a particular condition. Sometimes the problem is posed as: What *amounts* of care and what *quality* of care? Such a formulation reduces a complex problem to only two dimensions, implying that all care can readily be ranked as better or worse. Because two alternative forms of care may vary along a number of dimensions, there may be no consensus among reasonable and informed individuals about which form is of higher overall quality. It is worth bearing in mind that adequacy does not mean the highest possible level of quality or strictly equal quality any more than it requires equal amounts of care; of course, adequacy does require that everyone receive care that meets standards of sound medical practice.

Any combination of arrangements for achieving adequacy will presumably include some health care delivery settings that mainly serve certain groups, such as the poor or those covered by public programs. The fact that patients receive care in different settings or from different providers does not itself show that some are receiving inadequate care. The Commission believes that there is no moral objection to such a system so long as all receive care that is adequate in amount and quality and all patients are treated with concern and respect. . . .

NOTE

1. Office of Technology Assessment, U.S. Congress, *The Implications of Cost-Effectiveness Analysis of Medical Technology. Summary,* U.S. Government Printing Office, Washington (1980), p. 8.

ROBERT M. VEATCH

Justice, the Basic Social Contract, and Health Care

The principle that each person's welfare should count equally is crucial if the community generated is to be a moral community. The moral community is one of impartiality. If the community employed an impartial perspective to draw up the basic principles or practices for the society, the principles would be generated without reference to individual talents, skills, abilities, or good fortune. Another way of formulating this condition is to say that the basic principles or practices established must meet the test of reversibility. That is, they must be acceptable to one standing on either the giving or the receiving end of a transaction.[1] The general notion is that the contractors must take equal account of all persons. It is only by such an abandonment of an egoistic perspective that common social intercourse is possible. As Plato wrote in Book I of the Republic, "the unjust

are incapable of common action . . . and [the] utterly unjust, they would have been utterly incapable of action."

The most intriguing contractual theory of ethics that makes this commitment to impartiality or reversibility is that espoused by John Rawls.[2] In his version of social contract theory, Rawls asks us to envision ourselves in what he calls the original position. He does not pretend that such a position exists or ever could exist. Rather, it is a device for making "vivid to ourselves the restrictions that it seems reasonable to impose on arguments for principles of justice, and therefore on these principles themselves."[3] The restrictions on the original position are that no one should be advantaged or disadvantaged in the choice of principles either by natural fortune or social circumstances. Persons in the original position are equal. To help us imagine such a situation, he asks us to impose what he calls a "veil of ignorance," under which "no one knows his place in society, his class position or social status, nor

From *A Theory of Medical Ethics,* © 1981. Reprinted by permission of the Kennedy Institute of Ethics.

does any one know his fortune in the distribution of natural assets and abilities, his intelligence, strength, and the like."[4]

From that position one can derive impartially a set of principles or practices that provide the moral foundations for a society. Even if we cannot discover a universal basis for ethical decisions, perhaps we can create a community that accepts rules such as respect for freedom and the impartial consideration of interests; that is, one that adopts the moral point of view and thereby provides a common foundation for deciding what is ethical. Those who take this view believe it possible to generate some commonly agreed upon principles or practices for a society. The creation of a contractual framework could then provide a basis for making medical ethical decisions that would be commonly recognized as legitimate. . . .

There is . . . a moral community constituted symbolically by the metaphor of the contract or covenant. There is a convergence between the vision of people coming together to discover a preexisting moral order — an order that takes equally into account the welfare of all — and the vision of people coming together to invent a moral order that as well takes equally into account the welfare of all. The members of the moral community thus generated are bound together by bonds of mutual loyalty and trust. There is a fundamental equality and reciprocity in the relationship, something missing in the philanthropic condescension of professional code ethics. . . .

THE MAXIMIN THEORY

Some say that reasonable people considering alternative policies or principles for a society would not opt to maximize the aggregate benefits that exist in the society. Rather, they say that at least for basic social practices that determine the welfare of members of the moral community, they would opt for a strategy that attempts to assure fundamentally that the least well off person would do as well as possible. . . .

The implication is that those having the greatest burden have some claim on the society independent of whether responding to their needs is the most efficient way of producing the greatest net aggregate benefit. Holders of this view say that the commitment of a principle of justice is to maximize not net aggregate benefit, but the position of the least advantaged members of the society. If the principle of justice is a right-making characteristic of actions, a principle that reasonable peo-

ple would accept as part of the basic social contract independent of the principle of beneficence, it probably incorporated some moral notion that the distribution of benefits and burdens counts as well as the aggregate amount of them. One plausible alternative is to concentrate, insofar as we are concerned about justice, on the welfare of the least well off. This is part of those principles of justice defended by Rawls as derived from his version of social contract theory. . . .

Since Rawls's scheme is designed to provide insights into only the basic practices and social institutions, it is very hard to discern what the implications are for specific problems of resource distribution such as the allocation of health care resources. Some have argued that no direct implications can be read from the Rawlsian principles. That seems, however, to overstate the case. At the least, basic social practices and institutional arrangements must be subject to the test of the principles of justice.

It appears, then, that this view will not justify inequalities in the basic health care institutions and practices simply because they produce the greatest net aggregate benefit. Its notion of justice, concentrating on improving the lot of the least advantaged, is much more egalitarian in this sense than the utilitarian system. It would distribute health care resources to the least well off rather than just on the aggregate amount of benefit.

There is no obvious reason why our hypothetical contractors articulating the basic principles for a society would favor a principle that maximized aggregate utility any more than one that maximized minimum utility. Our contract model, as an epistemological device for discovering the basic principles, views them, after all, as committed to the moral point of view, as evaluating equally the welfare of each individual from a veil of ignorance, to use the Rawlsian language. This perspective retains the notion of individuals as identifiable, unique personalities, as noncommensurable human beings, rather than simply as components of an aggregate mass. Faced with a forced choice, it seems plausible that one would opt for maximizing the welfare of individuals, especially the least well-off individuals, rather than maximizing the aggregate.

Nevertheless, the interpretation of justice that attempts to maximize the minimum position in the society (and is hence sometimes called the "maximin" position), still permits inequalities and even labels them as just. What, for example, of basic health care institutional arrangements that systematically single out elites with unique natural talents for developing medical skill and services and gives these individuals high salaries as incentives to serve the interests of the least well off? What if a special health care system were institutionalized to make sure these people were always in the best of health, were cared for first in catastrophies, and were inconvenienced least by the normal bureaucratic nuisances of a health care system?

It is conceivable that such an institutional arrangement would be favored by reasonable people taking the moral point of view. They could justify the special gains that would come to the elites by the improved chances thus created for the rest of the population (who would not have as great a gain as the favored ones, but would at least be better off than if the elite were not so favored). The benefits, in lesser amounts, would trickle down in this plan to the consumers of health care so that all, or at least the least advantaged, would gain. The gap between the elite of the health profession and the masses could potentially increase by such a social arrangement, but at least all would be better off in absolute terms.

So it is conceivable that reasonable people considering equally both the health professionals and the masses would favor such an arrangement, but it is not obvious. Critics of the Rawlsian principles of justice say that in some cases alternative principles of distribution would be preferred. Brian Barry, for example, argues that rational choosers would look not just at the welfare of the least advantaged, but also at the average or aggregate welfare of alternative policies.[5] On the other hand, Barry and many others suggest that in some circumstances, rational choosers might opt for the principle that would maximize equality of outcome.[6] At most, considering the institutionalization of advantages for a health care elite, they would be supported as a prudent sacrifice of the demands of justice in order to serve some other justifiable moral end.

From this perspective, favoring elites with special monetary and social incentives in order to benefit the poor might be a prudent compromise.[7] It might mediate between the demands that see justice as requiring equality of outcome (subject to numerous qualifications) and the demands of the principle of beneficence requiring maximum efficiency in producing good con-

sequences. If that is the case, though, then there is still a fourth interpretation of the principle of justice that must be considered, one that is more radically egalitarian than the maximin strategy.

THE EGALITARIAN THEORY

Those who see the maximin strategy as a compromise between the concern for justice and the concern for efficient production of good consequences must feel that justice requires a stricter focus on equality than the maximin understanding of the principle of justice. The maximin principle is concerned about the distribution of benefits. It justifies inequalities only if they benefit the least well off. But it does justify inequalities — and it does so in the name of justice.

Rawls recognizes that there is an important difference between a right action and a just or a fair action. Fairness is a principle applying to individuals along with beneficence, noninjury, mutual respect, and fidelity. The list is not far removed from the basic principles I have identified. But, given this important difference between what is right in this full, inclusive sense and what is fair, if one is convinced that incentives and advantages for medical elites are justified, why would one claim that the justification is one based on the principle of fairness? One might instead maintain that they are right on balance because they are a necessary compromise with the principle of fairness (or justice) in order to promote efficiently the welfare of a disadvantaged group. It is to be assumed, given the range of basic principles in an ethical system, that conflicts will often emerge so that one principle will be sacrificed, upon occasion, for the sake of another.

The egalitarian understanding of the principle of justice is one that sees justice as requiring (subject to certain important qualifications) equality of net welfare for individuals.[8] . . .

Everyone, according to the principle of egalitarian justice, ought to end up over a lifetime with an equal amount of net welfare (or, as we shall see shortly, a chance for that welfare). Some may have a great deal of benefit offset by large amounts of unhappiness or disutility, while others will have relatively less of both. What we would call "just" under this principle is a basic social practice or policy that contributes to the same extent to greater equality of outcome (subject to restrictions to be discussed). I am suggesting that reasonable people who are committed to a contract model for discovering, inventing, or otherwise articulating the basic principles will want to add to their list the notion that one of the right-making characteristics of a society would be the equality of welfare among the members of the moral community.

THE EQUALITY OF PERSONS

The choice of this interpretation of the principle of justice will depend upon how the contractors understand the commitment to the moral point of view — the commitment to impartiality that takes the point of view of all equally into account. We certainly are not asserting the equality of ability or even the equality of the merit of individual claims. . . .

If this is what is meant by the moral point of view, taking into account equally the individuality of each member of the community, then in addition to the right-making characteristics or principles of beneficence, promise keeping, autonomy, truth telling, and avoiding killing, the principle of justice as equality of net welfare must be added to the list. The principle might be articulated as affirming that people have a claim on having the total net welfare in their lives equal insofar as possible to the welfare in the lives of others.

Of course, no reasonable person, even an egalitarian, is going to insist upon or even desire that all the features of people's lives be identical.[9] It seems obvious that the most that anyone would want is that the total net welfare for each person be comparable. . . .

If this egalitarian understanding of the principle of justice would be acceptable to reasonable people taking the moral point of view, it provides a solution to the dilemma of the tension between focusing exclusively on the patient and opening the doors to considerations of social consequences such as in classical utilitarianism. The principle of justice provides another basis for taking into account a limited set of impacts on certain other parties. If the distribution of benefits as well as the aggregate amount is morally relevant, then certain impacts on other parties may be morally more relevant than others. A benefit that accrues to a person who is or predictably will be in a least well-off group would count as a consideration of justice while a benefit of equal size that accrued to other persons not in the least well-off group would not. The hypothetical benefits of a Nazi-type experiment would not accrue to a least well-off group (while the harms of the experiment presumably would). They are thus morally different from, in fact diametrically opposed to, a redistribution scheme that produced benefits for only the least advantaged group.

EQUALITY AND ENVY

Critics of the egalitarian view of justice have argued that the only way to account for such a position is by attributing it to a psychology of envy.[10] Freud accounted for a sense of justice in this way.[11] They feel the only conceivable reason to strive for equality is the psychological explanation that the less well off envy the better off, and they hold that contractors take that psychological fact into account. Since they believe that envy is not an adequate justification for a commitment to equal outcome, they opt instead for an alternative theory of justice. . . .

The egalitarian holds that there is something fundamentally wrong with gross inequalities, with gross differences in net welfare. The problem is encountered when people of unequal means must interact, say, when representatives of an impoverished community apply to an elite foundation for funds to support a neighborhood health program. There is no way that real communication can take place between the elites of the foundation and the members of the low-income community. It is not simply that the poor envy the foundation executives or that the executives feel resentful of the poor. Rather, as anyone who has been in such a relationship knows, the sense of community is fractured. Not only do the less well off feel that they cannot express themselves with self-respect, but the elites realize that there is no way the messages they receive can be disentangled from the status and welfare differentials. Neither can engage in any true interaction. A moral relationship is virtually impossible. . . .

THE IMPLICATIONS OF THE EGALITARIAN FORMULA

It turns out that incorporating health care into this system of total welfare will be extremely difficult. Let us begin, temporarily, therefore, by considering a simpler system dealing only with food, clothing, and shelter. Fairness could mean, according to the egalitarian formula, that each person had to have an equal amount of each of these. No reasonable person, however, would find that necessary or attractive. Rather, what the egalitarian has in mind with his concept of justice is that the net of welfare, summed across all three of these goods, be as similar as possible. We could arbitrarily fix the amount of resources in each category, but nothing seems wrong with permitting people to trade some food for clothing, or clothing for shelter. If one person preferred a large house and minimal food and could find someone with the opposite tastes, nothing seems wrong with permitting a trade. The assumption is that the need of people for food, clothing, and shelter is about the same in everybody and that marginal utilities in the trades will be about the same. If so, then permitting people to trade around would increase the welfare of each person without radically distorting the equality of net overall welfare. Up to this point, then, the egalitarian principle of justice says that it is just (though not necessarily right) to strive in social practices for equality of net welfare. . . .

For health care and education, however, the situation is much different. Here it is reasonable to assume that human needs vary enormously. Nothing could be more foolish than to distribute health care or even the money for health care equally. The result would be unequal overall well-being for those who were unfortunate in the natural lottery for health, objectively much worse off than others. If the goal of justice is to produce a chance for equal, objective net welfare, then the starting point for consideration of health care distribution should be the need for it. Education (or the resources to buy education) initially would be distributed in the same way. The amount added to the resources for food, clothing, and shelter should then be in proportion to an "unhealthiness status index" plus another amount proportional to an "educational needs index."

However, that proposal raises two additional questions: Should people be permitted to use the resources set aside for health care in some other way? And who should bear the responsibility if people have an opportunity to be healthy and do not take advantage of it?

THE CASE FOR AN EQUAL RIGHT TO HEALTH CARE

Even for the egalitarian it is not obvious why society ought to strive for an equal right to health care. Certainly it ought not to be interested in obtaining the same amount of health care for everyone. To do so would require forcing those in need of great amounts of care to go without or those who have the good fortune to be healthy to consume uselessly. But it is not even obvious that we should end up with a right to health care equal in proportion to need, though that is the conclusion that many, especially egalitarians, are reaching. . . .

Is there any reason to believe that health care is any more basic than, say, food or protection from the ele-

ments? All are absolutely essential to human survival, at least up to some minimum for subsistence. All are necessary conditions for the exercise of liberty, self-respect, or any other functioning as part of the human moral community. Furthermore, while the bare minimum of health care is as necessary as food and shelter, in all cases these may not really be "necessities" at the margin. If trades are to be tolerated between marginal food and clothing, is there any reason why someone placing relatively low value on health care should not be permitted to trade, say, his annual checkups for someone else's monthly allotment of steak dinners? Or, if we shall make trading easier by distributing money fairly rather than distributing rations of these specific goods, is there any reason why, based on an "unhealthiness index," we could not distribute a fair portion of funds for health care as well as for other necessities? Individuals could then buy the health care (or health care insurance) that they need, employing individual discretion about where their limit for health care is in comparison with steak dinners. Those at a high health risk would be charged high amounts for health care (or high premiums for insurance), but those costs would be exactly offset by the money supplement based on the index.

Perhaps we cannot make a case for equal access to health care on the basis that it is more fundamental than other goods. There may still be reasons, though, why reasonable people would structure the basic institutions of society to provide a right to equal health care in the sense I am using the term, that is a right equal in proportion to need.

Our response will depend somewhat upon whether we are planning a health care distribution for a just world or one with the present inequities in the distribution of net welfare. . . .

But obviously we do not live in a perfectly just world. The problem becomes more complex. How do we arrange the health care system, which all would agree is fundamental to human well-being at least at some basic level, in order to get as close as possible to equality of welfare as the outcome? Pragmatic considerations may, at this point, override the abstract, theoretical argument allowing trades of health care for other goods even at the margin.

Often defenders of free-market and partial free-market solutions to the allocation of health care resources assume that if fixed in-kind services such as health care are not distributed, money will be. . . .

There is a more subtle case for an equal right to health care (in proportion to need) in an unfair world.

Bargaining strengths are likely to be very unequal in a world where resources are distributed unfairly. Those with great resources, perhaps because of natural talents or naturally occurring good health or both, are in an invincible position. The needy, for example those with little earning power because of congenital health problems, may be forced to use what resources they have in order to buy immediate necessities, withholding on health care investment; particularly preventive health care and health insurance, while gambling that they will be able to survive without those services.

It is not clear what our moral response should be to those forced into this position of bargainers from weakness. If the just principle of distribution were Pareto optimality (where bargains were acceptable, regardless of the weaknesses of the parties, provided all gained in the transaction), we would accept the fact that some would bargain from weakness and be forced to trade their long-term health care needs for short-term necessities. If the principle of justice that reasonable people would accept taking the moral point of view, however, is something like the maximin position or the egalitarian position, then perhaps such trades of health care should be prohibited. The answer will depend on how one should behave in planning social policies in an unjust world. The fact that resources are not distributed fairly generates pressures on the least well off (assuming they act rationally) to make choices they would not have to make in a more fair world. If unfairness in the general distribution of resources is a given, we are forced into a choice between two unattractive options: We could opt for the rule that will permit the least well off to maximize their position under the existing conditions or we could pick the rule that would arrange resources as closely as possible to the way they would be arranged in a just world. In our present, unjust society distributing health care equally is a closer approximation to the way it would be distributed in a just society than giving a general resource like money or permitting trades. . . .

I see justice not just as a way to efficiently improve the lot of the least well off by permitting them trades (even though those trades end up increasing the gap between the haves and the have-nots). That might be efficient and might preserve autonomy, but it would not be justice. If I were an original contractor I would cast my vote in favor of the egalitarian principle of justice, applying it so that there would be a right to health care equal in proportion to health care need. The principle of justice for health care could, then, be stated as follows: People have a right to needed health care to provide an opportunity for a level of health equal as far as possible to the health of other people.

The principle of justice for health care is a pragmatic derivative from the general principle of justice requiring equality of objective net welfare. The result would be a uniform health care system with one class of service available for all. Practical problems would still exist, especially at the margins. The principle, for example, does not establish what percentage of total resources would go for health care. The goal would be to arrange resources so that health care needs would, in general, be met about as well as other needs. This means that a society would rather arbitrarily set some fixed amount of the total resources for health care. Every nation currently spends somewhere between five and ten percent of its gross national product (GNP) in this area, with the wealthier societies opting for the higher percentages. Presumably the arbitrary choice would fall in that range.

With such a budget fixed, reasonable people will come together to decide what health care services can be covered under it. The task will not be as great as it seems. The vast majority of services will easily be sorted into or out of the health care system. Only a small percentage at the margin will be the cause of any real debate. The choice will at times be arbitrary, but the standard applied will at least be clear. People should have services necessary to give them a chance to be as close as possible to being as healthy as other people. Those choices will be made while striving to emulate the position of original contractors taking the moral point of view. The decision-making panels will not differ in task greatly from the decision makers who currently sort health care services in and out of insurance coverage lists. However, panels will be committed to a principle of justice and will take the moral point of view, whereas the self-interested insurers try to maximize profits or efficiency or a bargaining position against weak, unorganized consumers.

NOTES

1. Kurt Baier, *The Moral Point of View: A Rational Basis of Ethics* (New York: Random House, 1965), p. 108.

2. John Rawls, *A Theory of Justice* (Cambridge, Mass.: Harvard University Press, 1971).

3. Ibid., p. 18.

4. Ibid., p. 12; cf. pp. 136–42.

5. Brian Barry, *The Liberal Theory of Justice: A Critical Examination of the Principal Doctrines in "A Theory of Justice" by John*

Rawls (Oxford: Clarendon Press, 1973), p. 109; see also Robert L. Cunningham, "Justice: Efficiency or Fairness?" *Personalist* 52 (Spring 1971): 253–81.

6. Barry, *The Liberal Theory;* idem. "Reflections on 'Justice as Fairness,'" in *Justice and Equality,* ed. H. Bedau (Englewood Cliffs, N.J.: Prentice-Hall, 1971), pp. 103–115; Bernard Williams, "The Idea of Equality," reprinted in Bedau, *Justice and Equality,* pp. 116–137; Christopher Ake, "Justice as Equality," *Philosophy and Public Affairs* 5 (Fall 1975): 69–89; Robert M. Veatch, "What Is 'Just' Health Care

Delivery?" in *Ethics and Health Policy,* ed. R. M.Veatch and R. Branson (Cambridge, Mass.: Ballinger, 1976), pp. 127–153.

7. Barry, "Reflections," p. 113.

8. See Ake, "Justice as Equality," for a careful development of the notion.

9. Hugo A. Bedau, "Radical Egalitarianism," in *Justice and Equality,* ed. H. A. Bedau, p. 168.

10. Rawls, *A Theory of Justice,* p. 538, note 9.

11. Sigmund Freud, *Group Psychology and the Analysis of the Ego,* rev. ed., trans. James Strachey (London: Hogarth Press, 1959), pp. 51f. (as cited in Rawls, *A Theory of Justice,* p. 439).

ALLEN E. BUCHANAN

The Right to a Decent Minimum of Health Care

THE ASSUMPTION THAT THERE IS A RIGHT TO A DECENT MINIMUM

A consensus that there is (at least) a right to a decent minimum of health care pervades recent policy debates and much of the philosophical literature on health care. Disagreement centers on two issues. Is there a more extensive right than the right to a decent minimum of health care? What is included in the decent minimum to which there is a right?

PRELIMINARY CLARIFICATION OF THE CONCEPT

Different theories of distributive justice may yield different answers both to the question 'Is there a right to a decent minimum?' and to the question 'What comprises the decent minimum?' The justification a particular theory provides for the claim that there is a right to a decent minimum must at least cohere with the justifications it provides for other right-claims. Moreover, the character of this justification will determine, at least in part, the way in which the decent minimum is specified, since it will include an account of the nature and significance of health-care needs. To the ex-

tent that the concept of a decent minimum is theory-dependent, then, it would be naive to assume that a mere analysis of the concept of a decent minimum would tell us whether there is such a right and what its content is. Nonetheless, before we proceed to an examination of various theoretical attempts to ground and specify a right to a decent minimum, a preliminary analysis will be helpful.

Sometimes the notion of a decent minimum is applied not to health care but to health itself, the claim being that everyone is entitled to some minimal level, or welfare floor, of health. I shall not explore this variant of the decent minimum idea because I think its implausibility is obvious. The main difficulty is that assuring any significant level of health for all is simply not within the domain of social control. If the alleged right is understood instead as the right to everything which can be done to achieve some significant level of health for all, then the claim that there is such a right becomes implausible simply because it ignores the fact that in circumstances of scarcity the total social expenditure on health must be constrained by the need to allocate resources for other goods.

Though the concept of a right is complex and controversial, for our purposes a partial sketch will do. To say that person A has a right to something, X, is first of all to say that A is entitled to X, that X is due to him or

From President's Commission, *Securing Access to Health Care,* Vol. II. Washington, D.C. U.S. Government Printing Office, 1983.

her. This is not equivalent to saying that if A were granted X it would be a good thing, even a morally good thing, or that X is desired by or desirable for A. Second, it is usually held that valid right-claims, at least in the case of basic rights, may be backed by sanctions, including coercion if necessary (unless doing so would produce extremely great disutility or grave moral evil), and that (except in such highly exceptional circumstances) failure of an appropriate authority to apply the needed sanctions is itself an injustice. Recent rights-theorists have also emphasized a third feature of rights, or at least of basic rights or rights in the strict sense: valid right-claims 'trump' appeals to what would maximize utility, whether it be the utility of the right-holder, or social utility. In other words, if A has a right to X, then the mere fact that infringing A's right would maximize overall utility or even A's utility is not itself a sufficient reason for infringing it.[1] Finally, a universal (or general) right is one which applies to all persons, not just to certain individuals or classes because of their involvement in special actions, relationships, or agreements.

The second feature — enforceability — is of crucial importance for those who assume or argue that there is a universal right to a decent minimum of health care. For, once it is granted that there is such a right and that such a right may be enforced (absent any extremely weighty reason against enforcement), the claim that there is a universal right provides the moral basis for using the coercive power of the state to assure a decent minimum for all. Indeed, the surprising absence of attempts to justify a coercively backed decent minimum policy by arguments that do *not* aim at establishing a universal right suggests the following hypothesis: advocates of a coercively backed decent minimum have operated on the assumption that such a policy must be based on a universal right to a decent minimum. The chief aim of this article is to show that this assumption is false.

I think it is fair to say that many who confidently assume there is a (universal) right to a decent minimum of health care have failed to appreciate the significance of the first feature of our sketch of the concept of a right. It is crucial to observe that the claim that there is a right to a decent minimum is much stronger than the claim that everyone *ought* to have access to such a minimum, or that if they did it would be a good thing, or that any society which is capable, without great sacrifice, of providing a decent minimum but fails to do so is deeply

morally defective. None of the latter assertions implies the existence of a right, if this is understood as a moral entitlement which ought to be established by the coercive power of the state if necessary. . . .

THE ATTRACTIONS OF THE IDEA OF A DECENT MINIMUM

There are at least three features widely associated with the idea of a right to a decent minimum which, together with the facile consensus that vagueness promotes, help explain its popularity over competing conceptions of the right to health care. First, it is usually, and quite reasonably, assumed that the idea of a decent minimum is to be understood in a society-relative sense. Surely it is plausible to assume that, as with other rights to goods or services, the content of the right must depend upon the resources available in a given society and perhaps also upon a certain consensus of expectations among its members. So the first advantage of the idea of a decent minimum, as it is usually understood, is that it allows us to adjust the level of services to be provided as a matter of right to relevant social conditions and also allows for the possibility that as a society becomes more affluent the floor provided by the decent minimum should be raised.

Second, the idea of a decent minimum avoids the excesses of what has been called the strong equal access principle, while still acknowledging a substantive universal right. According to the strong equal access principle, everyone has an equal right to the best health-care services available. Aside from the weakness of the justifications offered in support of it, the most implausible feature of the strong equal access principle is that it forces us to choose between two unpalatable alternatives. We can either set the publicly guaranteed level of health care lower than the level that is technically possible or we can set it as high as is technically possible. In the former case, we shall be committed to the uncomfortable conclusion that no matter how many resources have been expended to guarantee equal access to that level, individuals are forbidden to spend any of their resources for services not available to all. Granted that individuals are allowed to spend their after-tax incomes on more frivolous items, why shouldn't they be allowed to spend it on health? If the answer is that they should be so allowed, as long as this does not interfere with the provision of an adequate package of health-care services for everyone, then we have retreated from the strong equal access principle to something very like the principle of a decent minimum. If, on the other hand, we set the level of services guaranteed for all so high as to eliminate the problem of persons seeking extra care beyond this level, this would produce a huge drain on total resources, foreclosing opportunities for producing important goods other than health care.

So both the recognition that health care must compete with other goods and the conviction that beyond some less than maximal level of publicly guaranteed services individuals should be free to purchase additional services point toward a more limited right than the strong access principle asserts. Thus, the endorsement of a right to a decent minimum may be more of a recognition of the implausibility of the stronger right to equal access than a sign of any definite position on the content of the right to health care.

A third attraction of the idea of a decent minimum is that since the right to health care must be limited in scope (to avoid the consequences of a strong equal access right), it should be limited to the 'most basic' services, those normally 'adequate' for health, or for a 'decent' or 'tolerable' life. However, although this aspect of the idea of a decent minimum is useful because it calls attention to the fact that health-care needs are heterogeneous and must be assigned some order of priority, it does not itself provide any basis for determining which are most important.

THE NEED FOR A SUPPORTING THEORY

In spite of these attractions, the concept of a right to a decent minimum of health care is inadequate as a moral basis for a coercively backed decent minimum policy in the absence of a coherent and defensible theory of justice. Indeed, when taken together they do not even imply that there is a right to a decent minimum. Rather, they only support the weaker conditional claim that if there is a right to health care, then it is one that is more limited than a right of strong equal access, and is one whose content depends upon available resources and some scheme of priorities which shows certain health services to be more basic than others. It appears, then, that a theoretical grounding for the right to a decent minimum of health care is indispensable. . . .

My suggestion is that the combined weight of arguments from special (as opposed to universal) rights to

health care, harm-prevention, prudential arguments of the sort used to justify public health measures, and two arguments that show that effective charity shares features of public goods (in the technical sense) is sufficient to do the work of an alleged universal right to a decent minimum of health care.

ARGUMENTS FROM SPECIAL RIGHTS

The right-claim we have been examining (and find unsupported) has been a *universal* right-claim: one that attributes the same right to all persons. *Special* right-claims, in contrast, restrict the right in question to certain individuals or groups.

There are at least three types of arguments that can be given for special rights to health care. First, there are arguments from the requirements of rectifying past or present institutional injustices. It can be argued, for example, that American blacks and native Americans are entitled to a certain core set of health-care services owing to their history of unjust treatment by government or other social institutions, on the grounds that these injustices have directly or indirectly had detrimental effects on the health of the groups in question. Second, there are arguments from the requirements of compensation to those who have suffered unjust harm or who have been unjustly exposed to health risks by the assignable actions of private individuals or corporations — for instance, those who have suffered neurological damage from the effects of chemical pollutants.

Third, a strong moral case can be made for special rights to health care for those who have undergone exceptional sacrifices for the good of society as a whole — in particular those whose health has been adversely affected through military service. The most obvious candidates for such compensatory special rights are soldiers wounded in combat.

ARGUMENTS FROM THE PREVENTION OF HARM

The content of the right to a decent minimum is typically understood as being more extensive than those traditional public health services that are usually justified on the grounds that they are required to protect the citizenry from certain harms arising from the interactions of persons living together in large numbers. Yet such services have been a major factor — if not *the* major factor — in reducing morbidity and mortality rates. Examples include sanitation and immunization. The moral justification of such measures, which constitute an important element in a decent minimum of health care, rests upon the widely accepted Harm (Prevention) Principle, not upon a right to health care.

The Harm Prevention argument for traditional public health services, however, may be elaborated in a way that brings them closer to arguments for a universal right to health care. With some plausibility one might contend that once the case has been made for expending public resources on public health measures, there is a moral (and perhaps Constitutional) obligation to achieve some standard of *equal protection* from the harms these measures are designed to prevent. Such an argument, if it could be made out, would imply that the availability of basic public health services should not vary greatly across different racial, ethnic, or geographic groups within the country.

PRUDENTIAL ARGUMENTS

Prudent arguments for health-care services typically emphasize benefits rather than the prevention of harm. It has often been argued, in particular, that the availability of certain basic forms of health care make for a more productive labor force or improve the fitness of the citizenry for national defense. This type of argument, too, does not assume that individuals have moral rights (whether special or universal) to the services in question.

It seems very likely that the combined scope of the various special health-care rights discussed above, when taken together with harm prevention and prudential arguments for basic health services and an argument from equal protection through public health measures, would do a great deal toward satisfying the health-care needs which those who advocate a universal right to a decent minimum are most concerned about. In other words, once the strength of a more pluralistic approach is appreciated, we may come to question the popular dogma that policy initiatives designed to achieve a decent minimum of health care for all must be grounded in a universal moral right to a decent minimum. This suggestion is worth considering because it again brings home the importance of the methodological difficulty encountered earlier. Even if, for instance, there is wide consensus on the considered judgment that the lower health prospects of inner city blacks are not only morally unacceptable but an injustice, it does not follow that this injustice consists of the infringement of a universal right to a decent minimum of health care. Instead, the injustice might lie in the failure to rectify past injustices or in the failure to achieve public health arrangements that meet a reasonable standard of equal protection for all.

TWO ARGUMENTS FOR ENFORCED BENEFICENCE

The pluralistic moral case for a legal entitlement to a decent minimum of health care (in the absence of a universal moral right) may be strengthened further by non-rights-based arguments from the principle of beneficence.[2] The possibility of making out such arguments depends upon the assumption that some principles may be justifiably enforced even if they are not principles specifying valid right-claims. There is at least one widely recognized class of such principles requiring contribution to the production of 'public goods' in the technical sense (for example, tax laws requiring contribution to national defense). It is characteristic of public goods that each individual has an incentive to withhold his contribution to the collective goal even though the net result is that the goal will not be achieved. Enforcement of a principle requiring all individuals to contribute to the goal is necessary to overcome the individual's incentive to withhold contribution by imposing penalties for his own failure to contribute and by assuring him that others will contribute. There is a special subclass of principles whose enforcement is justified not only by the need to overcome the individual's incentive to withhold compliance with the principle but also to ensure that individuals' efforts are appropriately *coordinated*. For example, enforcing the rule of the road to drive only on the right not only ensures a joint effort toward the goal of safe driving but also coordinates individuals' efforts so as to make the attainment of that goal possible. Indeed, in the case of the 'rule of the road' a certain kind of coordinated joint effort is the public good whose attainment justifies enforcement. But regardless of whether the production of a public good requires the solution of a coordination problem or not, there may be no *right* that is the correlative of the coercively backed obligation specified by the principle. There are two arguments for enforced beneficence, and they each depend upon both the idea of coordination and on certain aspects of the concept of a public good.

Both arguments begin with an assumption reasonable libertarians accept: there is a basic moral obligation of charity or beneficence to those in need. In a society that has the resources and technical knowledge to improve health or at least to ameliorate important health defects, the application of this requirement of beneficence includes the provision of resources for at least certain forms of health care. If we are sincere, we will be concerned with the efficacy of our charitable or beneficent impulses. It is all well and good for the libertarian to say that voluntary giving *can* replace the existing array of government entitlement programs, but this *possibility* will be cold comfort to the needy if, for any of several reasons, voluntary giving falters.

Social critics on the left often argue that in a highly competitive acquisitive society such as ours it is naive to think that the sense of beneficence will win out over the urgent promptings of self-interest. One need not argue, however, that voluntary giving fails from weakness of the will. Instead one can argue that even if each individual recognizes a moral duty to contribute to the aid of others and is motivationally capable of acting on that duty, some important forms of beneficence will not be forthcoming because each individual will rationally conclude that he should not contribute.

Many important forms of health care, especially those involving large-scale capital investment for technology, cannot be provided except through the contributions of large numbers of persons. This is also true of the most important forms of medical research. But if so, then the beneficent individual will not be able to act effectively, in isolation. What is needed is a coordinated joint effort.

First argument. There are many ways in which I might help others in need. Granted the importance of health, providing a decent minimum of health care for all, through large-scale collective efforts, will be a more important form of beneficence than the various charitable acts A, B, and C, which I might perform *independently,* that is, whose success does not depend upon the contributions of others. Nonetheless, if I am rationally beneficent I will reason as follows: either enough others will contribute to the decent minimum project to achieve this goal, even if I do not contribute to it; or not enough others will contribute to achieve a decent minimum, even if I do contribute. In either case, my contribution will be wasted. In other words, granted the scale of the investment required and the virtually negligible size of my own contribution, I can disregard the minute possibility that my contribution might make the difference between success and failure. But if so, then the rationally beneficent thing for me to do is not to waste my contribution on the project of ensuring a decent minimum but instead to undertake an independent act of beneficence; A, B, or C—where I know my efforts will be needed and efficacious. But if everyone, or

even many people, reason in this way, then what we each recognize as the most effective form of beneficence will not come about. Enforcement of a principle requiring contributions to ensuring a decent minimum is needed.

The first argument is of the same form as standard public goods arguments for enforced contributions to national defense, energy conservation, and many other goods, with this exception. In standard public goods arguments, it is usually assumed that the individual's incentive for not contributing is self-interest and that it is in his interest not to contribute because he will be able to partake of the good, if it is produced, even if he does not contribute. In the case at hand, however, the individual's incentive for not contributing to the joint effort is not self-interest, but rather his desire to maximize the good he can do for others with a given amount of his resources. Thus if he contributes but the goal of achieving a decent minimum for all would have been achieved without his contribution, then he has still failed to use his resources in a maximally beneficent way relative to the options of either contributing or not to the joint project, even though the goal of achieving a decent minimum is attained. The rationally beneficent thing to do, then, is not to contribute, even though the result of everyone's acting in a rationally beneficent way will be a relatively ineffective patchwork of small-scale individual acts of beneficence rather than a large-scale, coordinated effort.

Second argument. I believe that ensuring a decent minimum of health care for all is more important than projects A, B, or C, and I am willing to contribute to the decent minimum project, but only if I have assurance that enough others will contribute to achieve the threshold of investment necessary for success. Unless I have this assurance, I will conclude that it is less than rational—and perhaps even morally irresponsible—to contribute my resources to the decent minimum project. For my contribution will be wasted if not enough others contribute. If I lack assurance of sufficient contributions by others, the rationally beneficent thing for me to do is to expend my 'beneficence budget' on some less-than-optimal project A, B, or C, whose success does not depend on the contribution of others. But without enforcement, I cannot be assured that enough others will contribute, and if others reason as I do, then what we all believe to be the most effective form of beneficence will not be forthcoming. Others may fail to contribute either because the promptings of self-interest overpower their sense of beneficence, or because they reason as I did in the First Argument, or for some other reason.

Both arguments conclude that an enforced decent minimum principle is needed to achieve coordinated joint effort. However, there is this difference. The Second Argument focuses on the *assurance problem,* while the first does not. In the Second Argument all that is needed is the assumption that rational beneficence requires assurance that enough others will contribute. In the First Argument the individual's reason for not contributing is not that he lacks assurance that enough others will contribute, but rather that it is better for him not to contribute regardless of whether others do or not.

Neither argument depends on an assumption of conflict between the individual's moral motivation of beneficence and his inclination of self-interest. Instead the difficulty is that in the absence of enforcement, individuals who strive to make their beneficence most effective will thereby fail to benefit the needy as much as they might.

A standard response to those paradoxes of rationality known as public goods problems is to introduce a coercive mechanism which attaches penalties to noncontribution and thereby provides each individual with the assurance that enough others will reciprocate so that his contribution will not be wasted and an effective incentive for him to contribute even if he has reason to believe that enough others will contribute to achieve the goal without his contribution. My suggestion is that the same type of argument that is widely accepted as a justification for enforced principles requiring contributions toward familiar public goods provides support for a coercively backed principle specifying a certain list of health programs for the needy and requiring those who possess the needed resources to contribute to the establishment of such programs, even if the needy have no *right* to the services those programs provide. Such an arrangement would serve a dual function: it would coordinate charitable efforts by focusing them on one set of services among the indefinitely large constellation of possible expressions of beneficence, and it would ensure that the decision to allocate resources to these services will become effective. . . .

NOTES

1. Ronald Dworkin, *Taking Rights Seriously* (Cambridge, MA: Harvard University Press, 1977), pp. 184–205.

2. For an exploration of various arguments for a duty of beneficence and an examination of the relationship between justice and beneficence, in general and in health care, see Allen E. Buchanan, "Philosophical Foundations of Beneficence," *Beneficence and Health Care,* ed. Earl E. Shelp (Dordrecht, Holland: Reidel Publishing Co., 1982).

H . T R I S T R A M   E N G E L H A R D T ,   J R .

Rights to Health Care, Social Justice, and Fairness in Health Care Allocations: Frustrations in the Face of Finitude

The imposition of a single-tier, all-encompassing health care system is morally unjustifiable. It is a coercive act of totalitarian ideological zeal, which fails to recognize the diversity of moral visions that frame interests in health care, the secular moral limits of state authority, and the authority of individuals over themselves and their own property. It is an act of secular immorality.

A basic human secular moral right to health care does not exist—not even to a "decent minimum of health care." Such rights must be created.

The difficulty with supposed right to health care, as well as with many claims regarding justice or fairness in access to health care, should be apparent. Since the secular moral authority for common action is derived from permission or consent, it is difficult (indeed, for a large-scale society, materially impossible) to gain moral legitimacy for the thoroughgoing imposition on health care of one among the many views of beneficence and justice. There are, after all, as many accounts of beneficence, justice, and fairness as there are major religions.

Most significantly, there is a tension between the foundations of general secular morality and the various particular positive claims founded in particular visions of beneficence and justice. It is materially impossible both to respect the freedom of all and to achieve their long-range best interests. . . .

Rights to health care constitute claims on services and goods. Unlike rights to forbearance, which require others to refrain from interfering, which show the unity of the authority to use others, rights to beneficence are

rights grounded in particular theories or accounts of the good. For general authority, they require others to participate actively in a particular understanding of the good life or justice. Without an appeal to the principle of permission, to advance such rights is to claim that one may press others into labor or confiscate their property. Rights to health care, unless they are derived from special contractual agreements, depend on particular understandings of beneficence rather than on authorizing permission. They may therefore conflict with the decisions of individuals who may not wish to participate in, and may indeed be morally opposed to, realizing a particular system of health care. Individuals always have the secular moral authority to use their own resources in ways that collide with fashionable understandings of justice or the prevailing consensus regarding fairness.

HEALTH CARE POLICY: THE IDEOLOGY OF EQUAL, OPTIMAL CARE

It is fashionable to affirm an impossible commitment in health care delivery, as, for example, in the following four widely embraced health care policy goals, which are at loggerheads:

1. The best possible care is to be provided for all.
2. Equal care should be guaranteed.
3. Freedom of choice on the part of health care provider and consumer should be maintained.
4. Health care costs are to be contained.

One cannot provide the best possible health care for all and contain health care costs. One cannot provide equal health care for all and respect the freedom of in-

From *Foundations of Bioethics,* 2d ed., by H. Tristram Engelhardt, Jr. Reprinted by permission of Oxford University Press, 1996.

dividuals peaceably to pursue with others their own visions of health care or to use their own resources and energies as they decide. For that matter, one cannot maintain freedom in the choice of health care services while containing the costs of health care. One may also not be able to provide all with equal health care that is at the same time the very best care because of limits on the resources themselves. That few openly address these foundational moral tensions at the roots of contemporary health care policy suggests that the problems are shrouded in a collective illusion, a false consciousness, an established ideology within which certain facts are politically unacceptable.

These difficulties spring not only from a conflict between freedom and beneficence, but from a tension among competing views of what it means to pursue and achieve the good in health care (e.g., is it more important to provide equal care to all or the best possible health care to the least-well-off class?). . . .

Only a prevailing collective illusion can account for the assumption in U.S. policy that health care may be provided (1) while containing costs (2) without setting a price on saving lives and preventing suffering when using communal funds and at the same time (3) ignoring the morally unavoidable inequalities due to private resources and human freedom. This false consciousness shaped the deceptions central to the Clinton health care proposal, as it was introduced in 1994. It was advanced to support a health care system purportedly able to provide all with (1) the best of care and (2) equal care, while achieving (3) cost containment, and still (4) allowing those who wish the liberty to purchase fee-for-service health care.[1] While not acknowledging the presence of rationing, the proposal required silent rationing in order to contain costs by limiting access to high-cost, low-yield treatments that a National Health Board would exclude from the "guaranteed benefit package."[2] In addition, it advanced mechanisms to slow technological innovation so as further to reduce the visibility of rationing choices.[3] One does not have to ration that which is not available. There has been a failure to acknowledge the moral inevitability of inequalities in health care due to the limits of secular governmental authority, human freedom, and the existence of private property, however little that may be. There was also the failure to acknowledge the need to ration health care within communal programs if costs are to be contained. It has been ideologically unacceptable to recognize these circumstances. . . .

JUSTICE, FREEDOM, AND INEQUALITY

Interests in justice as beneficence are motivated in part by inequalities and in part by needs. That some have so little while others have so much properly evokes moral concerns of beneficence. Still, . . . the moral authority to use force to set such inequalities aside is limited. These limitations are in part due to the circumstance that the resources one could use to aid those in need are already owned by other people. One must establish whether and when inequalities and needs generate rights or claims against others.

THE NATURAL AND SOCIAL LOTTERIES

"Natural lottery" is used to identify changes in fortune that result from natural forces, not directly from the actions of persons. The natural lottery shapes the distribution of both naturally and socially conditioned assets. The natural lottery contrasts with the social lottery, which is used to identify changes in fortune that are not the result of natural forces but the actions of persons. The social lottery shapes the distribution of social and natural assets. The natural and social lotteries, along with one's own free decisions, determine the distribution of natural and social assets. The social lottery is termed a lottery, though it is the outcome of personal actions, because of the complex and unpredictable interplay of personal choices and because of the unpredictable character of the outcomes, which do not conform to an ideal pattern, and because the outcomes are the results of social forces, not the immediate choices of those subject to them.

All individuals are exposed to the vicissitudes of nature. Some are born healthy and by luck remain so for a long life, free of disease and major suffering. Others are born with serious congenital or genetic diseases, others contract serious crippling fatal illnesses early in life, and yet others are injured and maimed. Those who win the natural lottery will for most of their lives not be in need of medical care. They will live full lives and die painless and peaceful deaths. Those who lost the natural lottery will be in need of health care to blunt their sufferings and, where possible, to cure their diseases and to restore function. There will be a spectrum of losses, ranging from minor problems such as having teeth with cavities to major tragedies such as developing childhood leukemia, inheriting Huntington's chorea, or developing amyelotrophic lateral sclerosis.

These tragic outcomes are the deliverances of nature, for which no one, without some special view of accountability or responsibility, is responsible (unless, that is, one recognizes them as the results of the Fall or as divine chastisements). The circumstance that individuals are injured by hurricanes, storms, and earthquakes is often simply no one's fault. When no one is to blame, no one may be charged with the responsibility of making whole those who lose the natural lottery on the ground of accountability for the harm. One will need an argument dependent on a particular sense of fairness to show that the readers of this volume should submit to the forcible redistribution of their resources to provide health care for those injured by nature. It may very well be unfeeling, unsympathetic, or uncharitable not to provide such help. One may face eternal hellfires for failing to provide aid.[4] But it is another thing to show in general secular moral terms that individuals owe others such help in a way that would morally authorize state force to redistribute their private resources and energies or to constrain their free choices with others. To be in dire need does not by itself create a secular moral right to be rescued from that need. The natural lottery creates inequalities and places individuals at disadvantage without creating a straightforward secular moral obligation on the part of others to aid those in need.

Individuals differ in their resources not simply because of outcomes of the natural lottery, but also due to the actions of others. Some deny themselves immediate pleasures in order to accumulate wealth or to leave inheritances; through a complex web of love, affection, and mutual interest, individuals convey resources, one to another, so that those who are favored prosper and those who are ignored languish. Some as a consequence grow wealthy and others grow poor, not through anyone's malevolent actions or omissions, but simply because they were not favored by the love, friendship, collegiality, and associations through which fortunes develop and individuals prosper. In such cases there will be neither fairness nor unfairness, but simply good and bad fortune.

In addition, some will be advantaged or disadvantaged, made rich, poor, ill, diseased, deformed, or disabled because of the malevolent and blameworthy actions and omissions of others. Such will be unfair circumstances, which just and beneficent states should try to prevent and to rectify through legitimate police protection, forced restitution, and charitable programs.

Insofar as an injured party has a claim against an injurer to be made whole, not against society, the outcome is unfortunate from the perspective of society's obligations and obligations of innocent citizens to make restitution. Restitution is owed by the injurer, not society or others. There will be outcomes of the social lottery that are on the one hand blameworthy in the sense of resulting from the culpable actions of others, though on the other hand a society has no obligation to rectify them. The social lottery includes the exposure to the immoral and unjust actions of others. Again, one will need an argument dependent on a particular sense of fairness to show that the readers of this volume should submit to the forcible redistribution of their resources to provide health care to those injured by others.

When individuals come to purchase health care, some who lose the natural lottery will be able at least in part to compensate for those losses through their winnings at the social lottery. They will be able to afford expensive health care needed to restore health and to regain function. On the other hand, those who lose in both the natural and the social lottery will be in need of health care, but without the resources to acquire it.

THE RICH AND THE POOR: DIFFERENCES IN ENTITLEMENTS

If one owns property by virtue of just acquisition or just transfer, then one's title to that property will not be undercut by the tragedies and needs of others. One will simply own one's property. On the other hand, if one owns property because such ownership is justified within a system that ensures a beneficent distribution of goods (e.g., the achievement of the greatest balance of benefits over harms for the greatest number or the greatest advantage for the least-well-off class), one's ownership will be affected by the needs of others. . . . Property is in part privately owned in a strong sense that cannot be undercut by the needs of others. In addition, all have a general right to the fruits of the earth, which constitutes the basis for a form of taxation as rent to provide fungible payments to individuals, whether or not they are in need. Finally, there are likely to be resources held in common by groups that may establish bases for their distribution to meet health care concerns. The first two forms of entitlement or ownership exist unconstrained by medical or other needs. The last form of entitlement or ownership, through the decision of a community, may be conditioned by need.

The existence of any amount of private resources can be the basis for inequalities that secular moral authority may not set aside. Insofar as people own things, they will have a right to them, even if others need them. Because the presence of permission is cardinal, the test of whether one must transfer one's goods to others will not be whether such a redistribution will not prove onerous or excessive for the person subjected to the distribution, but whether the resources belong to that individual. Consider that you may be reading this book next to a person in great need. The test of whether a third person may take resources from you to help that individual in need will not be whether you will suffer from the transfer, but rather whether you have consented — at least this is the case if the principle of permission functions in general secular morality. . . . The principle of permission is the source of authority when moral strangers collaborate, because they do not share a common understanding of fairness or of the good. As a consequence, goal-oriented approaches to the just distribution of resources must be restricted to commonly owned goods, where there is authority to create programs for their use.

Therefore, one must qualify the conclusions of the 1983 American President's Commission for the Study of Ethical Problems that suggest that excessive burdens should determine the amount of tax persons should pay to sustain an adequate level of health care for those in need.[5] Further, one will have strong grounds for morally condemning systems that attempt to impose an all-encompassing health care plan that would require "equality of care [in the sense of avoiding] the creation of a tiered system [by] providing care based only on differences of need, not individual or group characteristics."[6] Those who are rich are always at secular moral liberty to purchase more and better health care.

DRAWING THE LINE BETWEEN
THE UNFORTUNATE AND THE UNFAIR

How one regards the moral significance of the natural and social lotteries and the moral force of private ownership will determine how one draws the line between circumstances that are simply unfortunate and those that are unfortunate and in addition unfair in the sense of constituting a claim on the resources of others.

Life in general, and health care in particular, reveal circumstances of enormous tragedy, suffering, and deprivation. The pains and sufferings of illness, disability, and disease, as well as the limitations of deformity, call on the sympathy of all to provide aid and give comfort. Injuries, disabilities, and diseases due to the forces of nature are unfortunate. Injuries, disabilities, and diseases due to the unconsented-to actions of oth-

ers are unfair. Still, outcomes of the unfair actions of others are not necessarily society's fault and are in this sense unfortunate. The horrible injuries that come every night to the emergency rooms of major hospitals may be someone's fault, even if they are not the fault of society, much less that of uninvolved citizens. Such outcomes, though unfair with regard to the relationship of the injured with the injurer, may be simply unfortunate with respect to society and other citizens (and may licitly be financially exploited). One is thus faced with distinguishing the difficult line between acts of God, as well as immoral acts of individuals that do not constitute a basis for societal retribution on the one hand, and injuries that provide such a basis on the other.

A line must be created between those losses that will be made whole through public funds and those that will not. Such a line was drawn in 1980 by Patricia Harris, the then secretary of the Department of Health, Education, and Welfare, when she ruled that heart transplantations should be considered experimental and therefore not reimbursable through Medicare.[7] To be in need of a heart transplant and not have the funds available would be an unfortunate circumstance but not unfair. One was not eligible for a heart transplant even if another person had intentionally damaged one's heart. From a moral point of view, things would have been different if the federal government had in some culpable fashion injured one's heart. So, too, if promises of treatment had been made. For example, to suffer from appendicitis or pneumonia and not as a qualifying patient receive treatment guaranteed through a particular governmental or private insurance system would be unfair, not simply unfortunate.

Drawing the line between the unfair and the unfortunate is unavoidable because it is impossible in general secular moral terms to translate all needs into rights, into claims against the resources of others. One must with care decide where the line is to be drawn. To distinguish needs from mere desires, one must endorse one among the many competing visions of morality and human flourishing. One is forced to draw a line between those needs (or desires) that constitute claims on the aid of others and those that do not. The line distinguishing unfortunate from unfair circumstances justifies by default certain social and economic inequalities in the sense of determining who, if any one, is obliged in general secular immorality to remedy such circumstances or achieve equality. Is the request of an individual to have life extended through a heart transplant at great cost, and perhaps only for a few years, a desire for an inordinate extension of life? Or is it a need to be secure against a premature death? . . . Outside a particular view of the good life, needs do not create rights to the services or goods of others.[8] Indeed, outside of a particular moral vision there is no canonical means for distinguishing desires from needs.

There is a practical difficulty in regarding major losses at the natural and social lotteries as generating claims to health care: attempts to restore health indefinitely can deplete societal resources in the pursuit of ever-more incremental extensions of life of marginal quality. A relatively limited amount of food and shelter is required to preserve the lives of individuals. But an indefinite amount of resources can in medicine be committed to the further preservation of human life, the marginal postponement of death, and the marginal alleviation of human suffering and disability. Losses at the natural lottery with regard to health can consume major resources with little return. Often one can only purchase a little relief, and that only at great costs. Still, more decisive than the problem of avoiding the possibly overwhelming costs involved in satisfying certain health care desires (e.g., postponing death for a while through the use of critical care) is the problem of selecting the correct content-full account of justice in order canonically to distinguish between needs and desires and to translate needs into rights.

BEYOND EQUALITY: AN EGALITARIANISM OF ALTRUISM VERSUS AN EGALITARIANISM OF ENVY

The equal distribution of health care is itself problematic, a circumstance recognized in *Securing Access to Health Care,* the 1983 report of the President's Commission.[9] The difficulties are multiple:

1. Although in theory, at least, one can envisage providing all with equal levels of decent shelter, one cannot restore all to or preserve all in an equal state of health. Many health needs cannot be satisfied in the same way one can address most needs for food and shelter.
2. If one provided all with the same amount of funds to purchase health care or the same amount of services, the amount provided would be far too much for some and much too little for others

who could have benefited from more investment in treatment and research.
3. If one attempts to provide equal health care in the sense of allowing individuals to select health care only from a predetermined list of available therapies, or through some managed health care plan such as accountable (to the government) health care plans or regional health alliances, which would be provided to all so as to prevent the rich from having access to better health care than the poor, one would have immorally confiscated private property and have restricted the freedom of individuals to join in voluntary relationships and associations.

That some are fortunate in having more resources is neither more nor less arbitrary or unfair than some having better health, better looks, or more talents. In any event, the translation of unfortunate circumstances into unfair circumstances, other than with regard to violations of the principle of permission, requires the imposition of a particular vision of beneficence or justice.

The pursuit of equality faces both moral and practical difficulties. If significant restrictions were placed on the ability to purchase special treatment with one's resources, one would need not only to anticipate that a black market would inevitably develop in health care services, but also acknowledge that such a black market would be a special bastion of liberty and freedom of association justified in general secular moral terms. . . .

CONFLICTING MODELS OF JUSTICE: FROM CONTENT TO PROCEDURE

John Rawls's *A Theory of Justice* and Robert Nozick's *Anarchy, State, and Utopia* offer contrasting understandings of what should count as justice or fairness. They sustain differing suggestions regarding the nature of justice in health care. They provide a contrast between justice as primarily structural, a pattern of distributions that is amenable to rational disclosure, versus justice as primarily procedural, a matter of fair negotiation.[10] In *A Theory of Justice* Rawls forwards an expository device of an ahistorical perspective from which to discover the proper pattern for the distribution of resources, and therefore presumably for the distribution of health care resources. In this understanding, it is assumed that societally based entitlements have moral priority. Nozick, in contrast, advances a historical account of just distributions within which justice depends on what individuals have agreed to do with and for each other. Nozick holds that individually based entitlements are morally prior to societally based entitlements. In contrast with Rawls, who argues that one can discover a proper pattern for the allocation of resources, Nozick argues that such a pattern cannot be discovered and that instead one can only identify the characteristics of a just process for fashioning rights to health care. . . .

The differences between Nozick of *Anarchy, State, and Utopia* and Rawls of *A Theory of Justice* express themselves in different accounts of entitlements and ownership, and in different understandings of nonprincipled fortune and misfortune. For Rawls, one has justifiable title to goods if such a title is part of a system that ensures the greatest benefit to the least advantaged, consistent with a just-savings principle, and with offices and positions open to all under conditions of fair equality and opportunity, and where each person has an equal right to the most extensive total system of equal basic liberties compatible with a similar system of liberty for all. In contrast, for Nozick, one simply owns things: "Things come into the world already attached to people having entitlements over them."[11] If one really owns things, there will be freedom-based limitations on principles of distributive justice. One may not use people or the property without their permission or authorization. The needs of others will not erase one's property rights. The readers of this book should consider that they may be wearing wedding rings or other jewelry not essential to their lives, which could be sold to buy antibiotics to save identifiable lives in the third world. Those who keep such baubles may in part be acting in agreement with Nozick's account and claiming that "it is my right to keep my wedding ring for myself, even though the proceeds from its sale could save the lives of individuals in dire need."

Nozick's account requires a distinction between someone's secular moral rights and what is right, good, or proper to do. At times, selling some (perhaps all) of one's property to support the health care of those in need will be the right thing to do, even though one has a secular moral right to refuse to sell. This contrast derives from the distinction Nozick makes between *freedom as a side constraint,* as the very condition for the possibility of a secular moral community, and *freedom as one value among others.* This contrast can be understood as a distinction between those claims of justice based on the very possibility of a moral community, versus those claims of justice that turn on interests

in particular goods and values, albeit interests recognized in the original position. . . .

This contrast between Rawls and Nozick can be appreciated more generally as a contrast between two quite different principles of justice, each of which has strikingly different implications for the allocation of health care resources.

1. Freedom- or permission-based justice is concerned with distributions of goods made in accord with the notion of the secular moral community as a peaceable social structure binding moral strangers, members of diverse concrete moral communities. Such justice will therefore require the consent of the individuals involved in a historical nexus of justice-regarding institutions understood in conformity with the principle of permission. The principle of beneficence may be pursued only within constraints set by the principle of permission.

2. Goals-based justice is concerned with the achievement of the good of individuals in society, where the pursuit of beneficence is not constrained by a strong principle of permission, but driven by some particular understanding of morality, justice, or fairness. Such justice will vary in substance as one attempts, for example, to (a) give each person an equal share; (b) give each person what that person needs; (c) give each person a distribution as a part of a system designed to achieve the greatest balance of benefits over harms for the greatest number of persons; (d) give each person a distribution as a part of a system designed to maximize the advantage of the least-well-off class with conditions of equal liberty for all and of fair opportunity.

Allocations of health care in accord with freedom- or permission-based justice must occur within the constraint to respect the free choices of persons, including their exercise of their property rights. Allocations of health care in accord with goals-based justice will need to establish what it means to provide a just pattern of health care, and what constitutes true needs, not mere desires, and how to rank the various health goals among themselves and in comparison with nonhealth goals. Such approaches to justice in health care will require a way of ahistorically discovering the proper pattern for the distribution of resources.

Permission-based and goals-based approaches to justice in health care contrast because they offer competing interpretations of the maxim, "Justitia est constans et perpetua voluntas jus suum cuique tribuens" (Justice is the constant and perpetual will to render everyone his due).[12] A permission-based approach holds that justice is first and foremost giving to each the right to be respected as a free individual as the source of secular moral authority, in the disposition of personal services and private goods: that which is due (*ius*) to individuals is respect of their authority over themselves and their possessions. In contrast, a goals-based approach holds that justice is receiving a share of the goods, which is fair by an appeal to a set of ahistorical criteria specifying what a fair share should be, that is, what share is due to each individual. Since there are various senses of a fair share (e.g., an equal share, a share in accordance with the system that maximizes the balance of benefits over harms, etc.), there will be various competing senses of justice in health care under the rubric of goals-based justice. . . .

THE MORAL INEVITABILITY OF A MULTITIER HEALTH CARE SYSTEM

. . . In the face of unavoidable tragedies and contrary moral intuitions, a multitiered system of health care is in many respects a compromise. On the one hand, it provides some amount of health care for all, while on the other hand allowing those with resources to purchase additional or better services. It can endorse the use of communal resources for the provision of a decent minimal or basic amount of health care for all, while acknowledging the existence of private resources at the disposal of some individuals to purchase better basic as well as luxury care. While the propensity to seek more than equal treatment for oneself or loved ones is made into a vicious disposition in an egalitarian system, a multitier system allows for the expression of individual love and the pursuit of private advantage, though still supporting a general social sympathy for those in need. Whereas an egalitarian system must suppress the widespread human inclination to devote private resources to the purchase of the best care for those whom one loves, a multitier system can recognize a legitimate place for the expression of such inclinations. A multitier system (1) should support individual providers and consumers against attempts to interfere in their free association and their use of their own resources, though (2) it may allow positive rights to health care to be created for individuals who have not been advantaged by the social lottery.

The serious task is to decide how to define and provide a decent minimum or basic level of care as a floor of support for all members of society, while allowing money and free choice to fashion special tiers of services for the affluent. In addressing this general issue of defining what is to be meant by a decent minimum basic level or a minimum adequate amount of health care, the American President's Commission in 1983 suggested that in great measure content is to be created rather than discovered by democratic processes, as well as by the forces of the market. "In a democracy, the appropriate values to be assigned to the consequences of policies must ultimately be determined by people expressing their values through social and political processes as well as in the marketplace."[13] The Commission, however, also suggested that the concept of adequacy could in part be discovered by an appeal to that amount of care that would meet the standards of sound medical practice. "Adequacy does require that everyone receive care that meets standards of sound medical practice."[14] But what one means by "sound medical practice" is itself dependent on particular understandings within particular cultures. Criteria for sound medical practice are as much created as discovered. The moral inevitability of multiple tiers of care brings with it multiple standards of proper or sound medical practice and undermines the moral plausibility of various obiter dicta concerning the centralized allocation of medical resources. . . .

Concepts of adequate care are not discoverable outside of particular views of the good life and of proper medical practice. In nations encompassing diverse moral communities, an understanding of what one will mean by an adequate level or a decent minimum of health care will need to be fashioned, if it can indeed be agreed to, through open discussion and by fair negotiation. . . .

NOTES

1. The White House Domestic Policy Council, *The President's Health Security Plan* (New York: Times Books, 1993).

2. The White House Domestic Policy Council, *The President's Health Security Plan*, p. 43.

3. Innovation would be discouraged as drug prices are subject to review as reasonable. The White House Domestic Policy Council, *The President's Health Security Plan*, p. 45.

4. In considering how to respond to the plight of the impecunious, one might consider the story Jesus tells of the rich man who

fails to give alms to "a certain beggar named Lazarus, full of sores, who was laid at his gate, desiring to be fed with the crumbs which fell from the rich man's table" (Luke 16:20–21). The rich man, who was not forthcoming with alms, was condemned eternally to a hell of excruciating torment.

5. President's Commission for the Study of Ethical Problems in Medicine and Biomedical and Behavioral Research, *Securing Access to Health Care* (Washington, D.C.: U.S. Government Printing Office, 1983), vol. 1, pp. 43–46.

6. The White House Domestic Policy Council, "Ethical Foundations of Health Reform," in *The President's Health Security Plan*, p. 11.

7. H. Newman, "Exclusion of Heart Transplantation Procedures from Medicare Coverage." *Federal Register* 45 (Aug. 6, 1980): 52296. See also H. Newman, "Medicare Program: Solicitation of Hospitals and Medical Centers to Participate in a Study of Heart Transplants," *Federal Register* 46 (Jan. 22, 1981): 7072–75.

8. The reader should understand that the author holds that almsgiving is one of the proper responses to human suffering (in addition to being an appropriate expression of repentance, an act of repentance to which surely the author is obligated). It is just that the author acknowledges the limited secular moral authority of the state to compel charity coercively.

9. President's Commission, *Securing Access to Health Care*, vol. 1, pp. 18–19.

10. John Rawls, *A Theory of Justice* (Cambridge, Mass.: Harvard University Press, 1971), and Robert Nozick, *Anarchy, State, and Utopia* (New York: Basic Books, 1974).

11. Nozick, *Anarchy, State, and Utopia*, p. 160.

12. Flavius Petrus Sabbatius Justinianus, *The Institutes of Justinian*, trans. Thomas C. Sandars (1922; repr. Westport, Conn,: Greenwood Press, 1970), 1.1, p. 5.

13. President's Commission, *Securing Access to Health Care*, vol. 1, p. 37.

14. Ibid.

Managed Care and Universal Access

EZEKIEL J. EMANUEL AND NANCY NEVELOFF DUBLER

Preserving the Physician–Patient Relationship in the Era of Managed Care

. . .

THE IDEAL PHYSICIAN–PATIENT RELATIONSHIP

To evaluate the effects of managed care, we need to delineate an ideal conception of the physician–patient relationship.[1] This ideal establishes the normative standard for assessing the effect of the current health care system as well as changes in the system. Although patients receive health care from a diverse number of

Reprinted by permission of the publisher from the *Journal of the American Medical Association*, 273 (1995), 323–29.

providers, and the use of nonphysician providers, such as nurse practitioners, physician assistants, and nurse midwives, is likely to increase with more emphasis on primary care and managed care, we chose to concentrate on the physician–patient relationship. The reasons for this focus are many: physicians outnumber nonphysician providers; most Americans continue to receive their health care from physicians rather than nonphysician providers; there have been many more years, indeed, centuries, for reflection on the elements that constitute the ideal physician–patient relationship, while the ethical guidelines and legal rulings on nonphysician provider–patient relationships are more recent and have not been as exhaustively developed; and there is substantially more empirical research on the physician–patient relationship with which to formulate educated projections. Where relevant, we explore how relationships between physicians and non-physician providers might affect interactions with patients. . . . [M]uch has been written by physicians, ethicists, and lawyers about what constitutes the ideal physician–patient relationship.[2] . . .

It is . . . important to recognize that this ideal evolves over time. Traits admired decades ago may no longer be revered, while other traits have become more prominent. For instance, paternalism might have been the accepted norm previously, but today respect for patient autonomy is widely agreed to be a core facet of the ideal physician–patient relationship. In addition, the ideal may not describe actual physician–patient relationships. Physicians may not recognize or may fail to fulfill their duties, or adverse practice conditions may interfere with the realization of the ideal. Nevertheless, the fundamental elements of the ideal physician–patient relationship seem to be enduring and define the goal toward which we aspire. We measure our achievement by the ideal even when we fall short.

We suggest that the fundamental elements of the ideal physician–patient relationship that are embodied in our intuitions and common to ethical analyses and legal standards can be expressed as six C's: choice, competence, communication, compassion, continuity, and (no) conflict of interest. While many people emphasize the importance of trust in the physician–patient relationship, we believe trust is the culmination of realizing the six C's, not an independent element. . . .

CHOICE

. . . Four critical dimensions of . . . choice are (1) choice of practice type and setting, (2) choice of primary care physician, (3) choice of a specialist or special facility in an emergency or for a special condition, and (4) choice among treatment alternatives.[3] . . .

COMPETENCE

. . . Competence entails four elements. Physicians must possess (1) a good fund of knowledge that is kept current with developing practices; (2) good technical skills to perform diagnostic and therapeutic procedures; (3) good clinical judgment to differentiate important signs and symptoms from secondary ones, to

know what diagnostic tests to utilize in what order, and to select the most appropriate therapies; and (4) an understanding of their own limitations and a willingness to consult specialists or other health care providers as required by the situation. . . .

COMMUNICATION

. . . [G]ood communication means that physicians listen to and understand the patient and communicate their understanding. This entails understanding the patient's symptoms, the patient's values, the effect of the disease on the patient's life, family, job, and other pursuits, and any other health-related concerns the patient deems important. In addition, patients should be able to tell their physicians what kind of information they want and do not want to know. For example, some patients with cancer prefer not to know their prognosis or a detailed delineation of the side effects of treatment alternatives. . . .

Good communication skills also mean that physicians are capable of explaining to patients, in clear and comprehensible language, the nature of their disease, the diagnostic and therapeutic treatment alternatives available, and how these alternatives are likely to fulfill or undermine the patients' values. In this sense, physicians offer advice and direction that guide their patients through the issues raised by their illness and possible treatments. . . .

COMPASSION

Patients not only want technically proficient physicians, they also want empathic physicians.[4] Empathy from their physician enables patients to feel supported during times of great stress. . . . Sometimes physicians see the need to help patients reconsider and revise their values, overcome their feelings, and place their experiences in a larger perspective. But these efforts are all undertaken with the intention of demonstrating compassion for the patient.

CONTINUITY

. . . The establishment of an ideal physician–patient relationship requires a significant investment of time. . . . If patients are frequently forced to change physicians, it is hard for them to develop a deep and understanding relationship. . . .

Relationships that endure over time may be more efficient. Knowing a patient means that a physician more easily identifies therapies appropriate for the personality and capabilities of the patient. The physician will know what support services the patient can draw on. Similarly, patients are more likely to accept recommendations to "wait and see" or to delay expensive diagnostic testing from a physician in whom they have confidence by virtue of having established a trusting relationship. . . .

(NO) CONFLICT OF INTEREST

We expect that a physician's primary concern will be his or her patient's well-being, even though physicians may have obligations that conflict. Attending to the well-being of one patient may conflict with caring for another patient. Similarly, it is well recognized that caring for a patient may conflict with — and even be superseded by — the need to protect the interests of a third party. Nevertheless, we do expect that the physician's care of a patient and concern for the patient's well-being will take precedence over the physician's own personal interests, especially financial interests. . . .

THE PHYSICIAN–PATIENT RELATIONSHIP IN THE ERA OF MANAGED CARE

Despite the lack of comprehensive health care system reform legislation, significant changes are occurring without legislative and governmental regulation, driven predominantly by the increased efforts of employers to reduce health care costs. These changes include more managed care, increased use of primary care physicians and generalists rather than specialists, increased use of nonphysician providers, emphasis on preventive measures, greater commitment to the care of children and intensive quality assessment. Although it is impossible to predict the precise concrete manifestations and effects of all these changes, it is possible to provide some educated reflections on their probable implications for the physician–patient relationship. . . . Because the health care system is so complex, the changes may not always tend in a coherent direction; some aspects may enhance a particular element of the physician–patient relationship while others undermine it. It is often difficult to know which tendency will dominate in practice, and so we try to outline the potential trends in both directions. . . .

POTENTIAL IMPROVEMENTS

With some expansion of managed care, the range of choice for many insured Americans could also increase. Americans who live in regions without significant managed care penetration, such as the South, will soon have the option of care in a managed care setting. In addition, other Americans could now have several managed care plans as well as fee-for-service options to choose from. However, if managed care expands too much, it may threaten to eliminate fee-for-service practitioners in a region altogether, as it appears to be doing in northern California and Minnesota. Under such circumstances, patients' choice of practice setting, even for well-insured Americans, could be effectively reduced.

Managed care may also provide the insured with a wider range of treatment alternatives. For example, by removing financial barriers, managed care plans should give enrollees more effective choice over utilizing preventive interventions, such as screening tests. Indeed, studies consistently demonstrate greater use of preventive tests and procedures among managed care enrollees.[5-7] In addition, many managed care plans contain benefits packages that include services not currently covered by many insurance programs. Indeed, pediatric patients may significantly benefit from the coverage of vaccinations, small co-payments for well-child visits, and coverage of dental visual services for children.

Managed care plans are increasingly attempting to develop quality measures; they are trying to use these quality measures for routine assessments of performance and to provide the public with the performance results based on these quality indicators. While such extensive efforts at quality assessment in medicine have never before been undertaken and there is skepticism that these measures will be reliable and valid, if this effort is successful, many Americans will have a rigorous and systematic mechanism to evaluate the competence of their health plans and physicians.[8,9]

Besides closer monitoring of quality other changes could improve physicians' competence and their communication with patients. The pressure created by cost controls, the resource-based relative value scale, and managed care has resulted in trends to improve reimbursement for primary care and to train more generalists. Although these initiatives are untested, they could increase the number of generalists, prompt the retraining of specialists in general medicine, and decrease the excessive reliance on specialists with their tendency toward higher use of diagnostic tests and technical interventions without notable effect on traditional health status measures.[10,11] In addition, managed care's increased emphasis on primary care will accelerate the trend toward greater use of nurse practitioners, physician assistants, and midwives and teams composed of physicians and nonphysician providers. While the transition to such a team approach could not be accomplished instantaneously, and while it would require changing habits and increased communications among health care providers, research demonstrates that, when it is well implemented, it can improve patient care, communication, and satisfaction.[12-14] With such multidisciplinary teams, several providers are knowledgeable about the patient's condition and available to the patient, enhancing communication and continuity of care.[12,13] By increasing the number of providers for a patient, this team approach may increase the chances that patients with different cultural backgrounds might establish rapport and understanding with a provider.[12,13]

POTENTIAL THREATS

There are aspects of managed care, especially under significant cost controls and price competition, with the potential to undermine, or preclude the realization of, the ideal physician–patient relationship. The spread of managed care is being promoted by big employers and corporations; it is closely linked to price competition—if not outright managed competition—which has ramifications for almost every facet of the ideal physician–patient interaction.

First, to hold down costs, many insurance companies and managed care organizations may try to select enrollees who are likely to use fewer and cheaper services ("cherry pick") through selective marketing, increased use of exclusions, modifications of benefits offered, and other techniques. In the absence of significant health insurance regulatory reform legislation or universal coverage, such techniques could mean that more Americans will be unable to afford health insurance or effectively barred from coverage. Indeed, recent statistics suggest that the ranks of the uninsured are growing.[15] In turn, this deprives more Americans of the ideal physician–patient relationship. In addition, without insurance reform legislation to ensure transportability of health coverage when people change jobs, a significant number of Americans could be forced either to forgo coverage for periods of time or to change managed care plans with each job change. Given that 7 million Americans change jobs or become employed each month, there could be significant disruption of choice, communication, and continuity.

Second, to restrain costs, a growing number of employers are restricting patient choice in all its facets. An increasing number of employers are offering only one health care plan; other employers are requiring their workers to enroll in a particular managed care plan or select a physician from a precertified list; still others are requiring their workers to pay substantially more for the opportunity to see a physician of their choosing outside their managed care panel; and still others are discouraging workers from selecting higher priced health plans. Some employers are even reverting to an old practice of hiring their own "company" physicians.[16] Through these and other techniques, a growing, albeit unknown, number of insured Americans are having their choice limited mainly by employers. These practices may seriously disrupt, or require patients to abandon, longstanding relationships with physicians. In addition, in some instances, especially in managed care settings, patient choice of specialists, specialty facilities, and particular treatments is being eroded.

Increasingly, managed care plans will compete for employers' contracts and subscribers on the basis of price. Yet there is no guarantee that the cheapest plan this year will be the cheapest plan during the next enrollment period. Indeed, if price competition is effective, the cheapest plan should change from year to year.[17] In such a price-competitive marketplace, employers may switch health care plans from year to year and patients may be forced to choose between continuing with their current physician and managed care plan at a higher price or switching to the cheaper plan. While patients may appear to opt for discontinuous care rather than pay more, the cost pressures—which fall disproportionately on those with lower incomes—hardly make such choices voluntary. A recent study demonstrates a direct linear relationship between a lower family income and willingness to switch to cheaper health care plans. The importance of such decisions lies in the reason for change of physician.[17] Change is harmful if it is imposed on patients explicitly or implicitly by financial incentives and interrupts continuity. When the patient, however, decides to switch physicians, continuity of care has been outweighed in the patient's mind by other factors, such as competence or communication. Consequently, significant price competition, while not engendered by managed care, is certainly exacerbated by it and could have an adverse effect on both patient choice of practice type and physician and continuity of care.[17]

A third threat to choice in the physician–patient relationship comes from the potential financial failure of managed care plans. If price competition is effective, inefficient plans will lose in the marketplace and close. Plan failure could pose a serious threat to patient choice and continuity of care, especially if the collapse happens between enrollment periods. Under such conditions, patients may be randomly assigned to other managed care plans. Or, their former physician may become affiliated with a plan that they are unable to join. Another threat to the physician–patient relationship may occur when managed care plans "deselect" a physician. In such circumstances, patients cannot choose that physician unless they are willing to go out of the plan. More important, patients who have been receiving care from that physician may be forced to switch to another physician in the managed care panel, again undermining patient choice and continuity of care.

Managed care also poses potential threats to competence. Its greater emphasis on the provision of primary care could adversely affect competence. Since specialists are more expensive than generalists, cost considerations foster a tendency to have generalists or even nonphysicians manage conditions that are best handled by specialists. For example, follow-up of cancer patients may be shifted from oncologists to primary care physicians. And there is some suggestion that these changes lead to fewer follow-up visits and less monitoring of the progress of disease in the managed care setting. In addition, since time spent with specialists is expensive, there may be a tendency to use medications or other less expensive interventions in place of consultations with specialists. Similarly, given the current shortage of generalists, there is already a movement to retrain specialist physicians as generalists. Since there are no standards for the amount and type of education needed for retraining, these retrained specialists may lack the breadth of knowledge, skills, and experience necessary to be competent primary care providers. Assessments of quality outcomes may be insensitive to these threats to competence.[18]

There are worries about the development of quality indicators. We lack quality indicators for most aspects of medical care. In addition, many quality indicators require risk adjustments for severity of illness that cannot be, or currently are not being performed.[18,19] It will take significant time and resources to develop reliable and validated quality indicators and risk adjustors for medical procedures. Yet the demand for these indica-

tors could result in a rush to implementation without proper pretesting and validation. Mistakes related to the imperative to release of Medicare hospital mortality data as a quality measure before they were properly adjusted may be repeated on an even larger scale.[20–23] Use of faulty quality information could damage attempts to improve the competence of physicians, undermine patient trust, and cause patients to switch physicians unnecessarily.

Communication in the physician–patient relationship could be undermined by practice efficiencies necessitated by intensified price competition and financial pressures on managed care plans. Productivity requirements may translate into pressure on physicians to see more patients in shorter time periods, reducing the time to discuss patient values, alternative treatments, or the impact of a therapy on the patient's overall life.[24,25] Such changes have been tried by managed care plans in the competitive Boston, Mass, health care market.[26] Compressing physician–patient interactions into short time periods in the name of productivity could curtail, if not eliminate, productive communication and compassion. A recent survey of patients in managed care plans showed that the physician spent less time with the patient and offered less explanation of care compared with those in traditional fee-for-service settings.[3] Similarly, to reduce costs, managed care plans might restrict telephone calls to the patient's primary care physician. Currently some plans limit patients' calls to their physicians to 1-hour time periods in the day. In addition, incentives might be put into place to encourage patients to talk with or see physicians or nonphysician providers with whom they are unfamiliar or who are not of their choosing. All of these cost-saving mechanisms could easily inhibit physician–patient communication and continuity of care.

A further problem may arise in the competition among managed care plans to lure subscribers. They are likely to use advertising with implicit if not explicit promises of higher quality or more wide-ranging services. Such advertisements could easily create high expectations on the part of patients. Simultaneously, however, to control costs plans will require physicians to be efficient in their personal time allocation as well as in their ordering of tests and use of other services. This could easily create a conflict between patient expectations and physician restrictions, undermining good communication, compassion, and trust.

Finally, while there has been significant attention on conflict of interest in fee-for-service practice, there has been much less effort to investigate and address conflict of interest in managed care. Physician decision making may account for as much as 75% of health care costs. In the setting of significant price competition, managed care plans trying to reduce costs will therefore try to influence physician decision making, especially to reduce the use of medical services. Managed care plans have already tried various mechanisms to try to reduce physician use of health care resources for their patients, including providing bonuses to physicians who order few tests and basing a percentage of physicians' salaries on volume and test ordering standards. Such conflicts of interest may proliferate with increased price competition, the need for managed care plans to reduce costs, and the absence of governmental regulation.

CONCLUSIONS

The physician–patient relationship is the cornerstone for achieving, maintaining, and improving health. The structure of financing and regulation should be designed to foster and support an ideal relationship between the physician and the patient. Clearly, the current system incompletely realizes this ideal even for many well-insured Americans, and trends within the current system threaten to make this ideal even more elusive.

Managed care offers some advantages in realizing the ideal physician–patient relationship. For many Americans, increased use of managed care may secure choice, especially for preventive services, possibly expand continuity in their relationship with physicians, and implement a systematic assessment of quality and competence. But the expansion of managed care, in an environment that encourages competition and makes financial pressures intense and omnipresent, could promote serious impediments to realizing the ideal physician–patient relationship. Some practical steps that might diminish these impediments include (1) using global budgets instead of price competition among managed care plans for cost control; (2) prohibiting all schemes that use salary incentives or bonuses tied to physician test ordering patterns; (3) restricting expensive advertising by managed care plans by capping their promotion budgets; (4) requiring managed care plans to have a board of patients and physicians to approve policies regarding length of office visits and telephone calls; (5) creating an independent review board to assess the reliability and validity of all quality indicators before they are approved or required for use by managed care plans; (6) implementing insurance reform legislation to ensure mobility of insurance with job changes and purchasing of coverage by individuals; and (7) providing universal coverage to enable otherwise uninsured patients to have an opportunity for an ideal physician–patient relationship. As changes in our health care system develop, we must find ways, such as these, to encourage fiscal prudence without undermining the fundamental elements of the ideal physician–patient relationship.

NOTES

1. Weber, M. The fundamental concepts of sociology. In: Parsons T, ed. *The Theory of Social and Economic Organizations.* New York, NY: The Free Press, 1947:87–157.

2. Szasz, TS, Hollender, MH. The basic models of the doctor–patient relationship. *Arch Intern Med.* 1956;97:585–592.

3. Blendon, RJ, Knox, RA, Brodie, M, Benson, JM, Chervinsky, G. Americans compare managed care, Medicare, and fee for service. *J Am Health Policy.* 1994;4:42–47.

4. Spiro, H, McCrea-Curnen, MG, Peschel, I, St. James, D, eds. *Empathy and the Practice of Medicine.* New Haven, Conn: Yale University Press; 1993:chaps 1–3, 8, 9, 13–16.

5. Bernstein, AB, Thompson, GB, Harlan, LC. Differences in rates of cancer screening by usual source of medical care: data from the 1987 National Health Interview Survey. *Med Care.* 1991;29:196–209.

6. Retchin, SM, Brown, B. The quality of ambulatory care in Medicare health maintenance organizations. *Am J Public Health.* 1990;80:411–415.

7. Udvarhelyi, IS, Jennison, K, Phillips, RS, Epstein, AM. Comparison of the quality of ambulatory care for fee-for-service and prepaid patients. *Ann Intern Med.* 1991;327:424–429.

8. Laffel, G, Berwick, DM. Quality in health care. *JAMA.* 1992;268:407–409.

9. Kritchevsky, SB, Simmons, BP. Continuous quality improvement: concepts and applications for physician care. *JAMA.* 1991;266:1817–1823

10. Greenfield, S, Nelson, EC, Zubkoff, M, et al. Variations in resource utilization among medical specialties and systems of care. *JAMA.* 1992;267:1624–1630

11. Schroeder, SA, Sandy, LG. Specialty distribution of U.S. physicians—the invisible driver of health care costs. *N Engl J Med.* 1993;328:961–963.

12. *Nurse Practitioners, Physicians' Assistants, and Certified Nurse Midwives: Policy Analysis.* Washington, DC: Office of Technology Assessment; 1986.

13. Freund, C. Research in support of nurse practitioners. In: Mezey M, McGivern D, eds. *Nurses and Nurse Practitioners: The Evolution to Advance Practice.* New York, NY: Springer Publishing Co. Inc.; 1993.

14. Kavesh, W. Physician and nurse-practitioner relationships. In: Mezey, M, McGivern, D, eds. *Nurses and Nurse Practitioners: The Evolution to Advanced Practice.* New York, NY: Springer Publishing Co. Inc.; 1993.

15. Pear, R. Health insurance percentage is lowest in four Sun Belt states. *New York Times.* October 6, 1994:A16.

16. Pasternak, J. In-house doctors give some firms a health care remedy. *Los Angeles Times.* July 11, 1993:A1.

17. Emanuel, EJ, Brett, AS. Managed competition and the physician–patient relationship. *N Engl J Med.* 1993;329:879–882.

18. Salem-Schatz, S, Moore, G, Rucker, M, Pearson, SD. The case for case-mix adjustment in practice profiling: when good apples look bad. *JAMA.* 1994;272:871–874.

19. McNeil, BJ, Pederson, SH, Gatsonis, C. Current issues in profiling quality care. *Inquiry.* 1992;29:298–307.

20. Green, J, Passman, LJ, Wintfield, N. Analyzing hospital mortality: the consequences of diversity in patient mix. *JAMA.* 1991;265:1849–1853.

21. Burke, M. HCFA's Medicare mortality data: the controversy continues. *Hospitals.* 1992:118, 120, 122.

22. Greenfield, S, Aronow, HU, Elashoff, RM, Wantanabe, D. Flaws in mortality data: the hazards of ignoring comorbid disease. *JAMA.* 1988;260:2253–2255.

23. Robinson, ML. Limitations of mortality data confirmed: studies. *Hospitals.* 1988;62:23–24.

24. Baker, LC, Cantor, JC. Physician satisfaction under managed care. *Health Aff (Millwood).* 1993;12(suppl):258–270.

25. Jellinek, MS, Nurcombe, B. Two wrongs don't make a right: managed care, mental health, and the marketplace. *JAMA.* 1993;270:1737–1739.

26. Knox, RA, Stein, C. HMO doctors want boss out in dispute on patient load. *Boston Globe.* November 21, 1991:1, 27.

LAWRENCE O. GOSTIN

Securing Health or Just Health Care? The Effect of the Health Care System on the Health of America

. . . Given the emphasis on financial costs and personal burdens, it is not surprising that political debate and academic discourse on health care reform focused so intensely on market structures and the economic effects on major segments of commercial society. Consequently, the linguistics of health care reform was market-oriented: managed competition, small and large insurance markets, employer mandates, tax credits and other market incentives. The overarching concern was the economic impact on the predominate players in the market: large employers, small businesses, insurers, and health care providers.

Manifestly, the effects of reform on the buying and selling of health care as a commodity, and its economic effects on American business (including the business of health care) are weighty concerns. It is not misguided, then, that so much focus was placed on the effects of health care reform on the economy. Yet, it is striking that so little attention was given to a still more fundamental value — the effect of the health care system on the health of individuals and populations. It is my thesis that promotion of the health of the population is the most important objective of health care reform; that reasonable levels of resource allocation are warranted to achieve this purpose; and that the adverse effects on the economy, American business, and citizens are as high, or higher, under the status quo than they would be if government assured universal coverage for health care. . . .

I. THE PREEMINENCE OF THE VALUE OF HEALTH

. . . In this article, I make no claim to a right to health. The government cannot be expected to take responsibility for assuring the health of each member of the population, and the concept of a right to health is too broad to have legal meaning. Nor do I claim a constitutional right to any level of health care that a person may want. An unfettered constitutional right to health care is not currently tenable. Further, the government could not be expected to respond to all demands and preferences for health care, irrespective of the cost or effectiveness.

Saint Louis University Law Journal 39(1): 7–43, Fall 1994. Reprinted by permission.

My claim is simply that the prevention of disease or disability and the promotion of health, within reasonable resource constraints, provides the preeminent justification for the government to act for the welfare of society. In determining the allocation of resources in society, the transcending public value must be based upon improved health outcomes for the population, based upon objective measures of morbidity and mortality. Despite marked increases in spending for personal medical services and advances in bio-medical technology, the decade 1980–90 showed little improvement in numerous objective health indicators such as maternal and child health, nutrition, sexually transmitted diseases, and occupational health and safety. Health promotion is measured not only by increased longevity or life extension. Rather, health promotion is measured by improvement in the quality of life, "compression" of morbidity and suffering, and extension of *active* or well-functioning life expectancy.

The very purpose of government is to attain through collective action human goods that individuals acting alone could not realistically achieve. Chief among those human goods is the assurance of the conditions under which people can be healthy. While the government cannot assure health, it can, within the reasonable limits of its resources, organize its activities in ways that best prevent illness and disability, and promotes health among its population. . . .

II. THE IMPORTANCE OF UNIVERSAL ACCESS TO HEALTH CARE SERVICES

It is not necessary to demonstrate which is the more fundamental governmental activity — public health or personal medical services. What is important is that both are essential to the health of individuals and populations, and both systems are functioning badly. Consequently, an assessment of the inadequacies in the personal health care system shows many people receiving insufficient and inequitable access to medical services.

Most countries with advanced economies in the world concentrate their resources in one health insurance system that provides universal coverage to their populations.[1] The United States, however, provides a fragmented array of private and public programs that results in a substantial portion of the population without health insurance coverage or with highly inadequate coverage. The American public, while purporting to support universal coverage,[2] appears highly ambivalent about whether health insurance is a social good, of which the costs should be borne collectively, or an economic enterprise that effectively should be governed by market forces.[3]

Whatever vision of health care that the public may prefer, the system itself has become market-oriented. By the nature of markets those who are unable or unwilling to pay the price of the commodity are left out. Not being included in a commodities market that trades in durable goods and services may be justified on economic grounds, but exclusion from the market in health care presents profoundly different considerations.

The number and profile of those who have been left out of the health insurance market, juxtaposed with current national health expenditures, is illuminating. The United States spent approximately $900 billion dollars on health care in 1993.[4] This represented approximately 14% of the nation's gross domestic product.[5] Health care expenditures are expected to reach $1.7 trillion, between 16% and 18% of the gross domestic product, by the end of the decade if effective controls are not instituted.[6]

Despite the inordinate national expenditures on health care, many Americans lack health insurance. At any given time during the last year, approximately 37 to 40 million people were without health insurance,[7] about 15–18% of all children and adults.[8] While different methods of counting the uninsured have allowed critics of health care reform to obfuscate its true dimensions, any dispassionate assessment reveals a considerable and enduring national problem.[9] Thus, while the census reported 33.5 million uninsured in 1992 based on monthly averages, others calculated that 50[10] to 58 million[11] lacked health insurance for at least one month in that year.

It is suggested by market-oriented analysts that the alleged 37 million uninsured is a "big lie"[12] that "wilts under analysis."[13] These analysts claim that the chronically uninsured amount to fewer than 10 million, and that the number of uninsured persons could be reduced dramatically by introducing medical savings accounts.[14] These claims are based on data suggesting that the median spell length of persons without insurance is six months, and that 70% of all spells end within nine months.[15] However, a deeper examination of the pool of uninsured persons demonstrates the intransigence and severity of the problem. At least 28% of all uninsured spells last for more than one year, and

15–18% last more than two years. For over 20 million people in 1993, being without health insurance was not a temporary or transient phase in their lives.[16] Professor Swartz, the scholar who originally reported these insurance data, concludes that the point-in-time estimate of 37 million uninsured actually refers to at least 21 million long-term uninsured plus nearly 16 million with spells lasting less than one year.[17] . . .

The uninsured are not the only persons in the population with difficulties in obtaining access to health care. An additional 20 million people are thought to be underinsured. Under-insurance is a concept that is hard to define or quantify. Persons may have inadequate access to health care because of insufficient overall insurance coverage (e.g., capitations on coverage based on limits on cost or hospital stays); exemptions for certain conditions (e.g., pre-existing coverage, waiting periods, mental health or childbirth services); or low reimbursement schedules for the payment of physicians, which results in denials of service (e.g., Medicaid patients in certain geographic areas or seeking certain kinds of services). . . .

The demographics of the uninsured population reveal the deep interconnections between the absence of health insurance and socio-economic status, race, and age. The uninsured population is disproportionately poor or near-poor, African-American or Hispanic, young, and unemployed.[18] . . .

There is certainly an inter-connectedness to each of the primary barriers to access — financial, structural, personal and cultural. It is clear, however, that without dismantling financial barriers, access to health care will continue to be highly adequate; the Institute of Medicine recently "reaffirmed that lack of health care coverage is, to a great extent, a good proxy for access."[19]

It is commonly believed that patients without health insurance are not so much denied access, but are diverted to emergency rooms and other public clinics for their care. It is, therefore, important to inquire whether the absence of insurance leads to delayed or insufficient access of such seriousness that it actually affects health outcomes. The data show that lack of access is closely associated not only with under-utilization of services but, more importantly, with poorer health outcomes.[20] Although health insurance coverage is not the sole determinant of health status, it is a key factor. . . .

Those who reject the view that health is the foremost objective of a health care system may instead prefer to focus attention to the finance system, administrative efficiency, or a favorable cost-benefit ratio. Health care is only one of many possible goods that government can provide. It is, therefore, not unreasonable to suggest that if health care could be provided more efficiently and less expensively, government could spend on other worthwhile social programs such as housing, poverty, hunger, or education.

As explained previously, the expenditure on health care in the United States represents approximately 14% of the nation's gross domestic product.[21] Health care expenditures are expected to reach $1.7 trillion, between sixteen and eighteen percent of the gross domestic product, by the end of the decade if effective controls are not instituted.[22] These figures stand in stark contrast to the percentage of the gross national product (GNP) that is devoted to health care in countries that offer their citizens virtually universal health coverage such as Canada, Germany, Great Britain, and Japan; these countries devote from 5.8% to 8.7% of their GNP to health care.[23] In 1990, while the United Kingdom, Japan, and Germany spent between $909 and $1,287 on each person for health care, the United States spent $2,566;[24] for every $1 per capita spent in England, the United States spends $3 per capita.[25] The high per capita expenditures on health care in the United States relative to other countries is not all spent on personal care services. It is estimated that 19% to 24% of health care expenditures goes toward administrative expenses, including those of the nation's insurance companies.[26]

In summary, whether the U.S. health care system is measured in terms of infant mortality or life expectancy, utilization rates, or cost effectiveness, it appears to lag well behind other developed countries in North America and Europe.

III. INEQUITABLE ACCESS TO HEALTH CARE

There is another perspective on how to measure the quality of a health care system. All else held constant, it is possible to argue that if health care resources are distributed equitably, the system provides consistent and fair benefits for all citizens. Some may even be willing to sacrifice certain benefits of health care to achieve greater equity. If a society does very well in health outcomes for some of its citizens, say those who are in higher socioeconomic classes and within majority racial populations, and others do very poorly, is that society worth emulating? Under Rawlsian theory, if individuals could not pre-determine whether they would be born into a favored or the disfavored class, most people would choose to be in a country that provides roughly equal access to health care for all classes.[27]. . .

A. SCRUTINY OF THE "EQUITY" PRINCIPLE

Before examining the substantial disparities in access to health care and health status among various classes in the United States, it is necessary to ask two interrelated questions: what ethical values support the claim of equity in the distribution of health services, and what exactly is the equity claim being made? To many, it is not intuitively obvious that equity is a principle that deserves general recognition in society. Americans are prepared to tolerate significant and pervasive inequalities in wealth and in the distribution of most social goods. A theory of equity in health care must provide an account of why health care deserves special treatment, unless the advocate is prepared to defend a considerably broader view of distributive justice for all goods and services.

One theory of equity in health care . . . relies on the special importance of health care in providing a necessary condition for the fulfillment of human opportunity. Professor Daniels observes that pain and disability, limitation of function, and premature loss of life all restrict human opportunities.[28] If it is accepted that a certain level of health services is a precondition to affording human beings reasonable life opportunities, then some equitable access to those services is warranted.

Government is prepared to provide a public education to all children of school age. Access to education is presumably justified by the importance of education in furnishing fair opportunities for all children, irrespective of their social or economic class. Like education, a certain level of health care is essential to a person's ability to pursue life's opportunities on some roughly equitable basis. Health care, at least in some fundamental ways, is as important to equal opportunity as education. While health care does not provide opportunities by facilitating basic knowledge and skill, it does so by enabling the person to function mentally and physically in the application of that knowledge and skill.

More equitable access to health care is supported by collective, as well as individual goods. Health care does not only enable individuals to gain life opportunities

for themselves, it also allows individuals to contribute to society. A healthy population, like an educated population, is much more likely to be socially and economically productive, and less dependent. A multi-tiered system of health care, in which those in the lower tiers receive clearly inferior and lower-quality services, perpetuates inequalities among individuals and groups. These inequalities occur not only in attaining health but, indirectly, in attaining status, acceptance, and livelihood in society. As various inequalities among individuals and groups expand, society must deal with the consequences of social unrest, alienation, and dissatisfaction. Strikingly disparate standards of health care for different social, economic and racial groups, then, is unjust for individuals who lose indispensable life opportunities and harmful for society generally which loses much productive activity and risks greater disaffection among major segments of the population.

Professor Daniels makes the following claim to equity in health care: "*if* an acceptable theory of justice includes a principle providing for fair equality of opportunity, then health care institutions should be among those governed by it."[29] But to suggest that health care institutions ought to be governed by the principle of fair equality of opportunity, is not the same as stating precisely the claim being made. For reasons explained earlier, no claim to health, let alone equal health, is feasible since the vast variabilities in health are to a great extent biologically, socially, and behaviorally determined. Nor do I make a claim for *equal* health care or even equal access to health care. Such a claim would not only require a fundamental redistribution of health care resources, but also would require restrictions on discretionary spending. Very few health care systems in developed countries restrict access to private health insurers, providers, and technology for people who can afford them, irrespective of the fact that these amenities are effectively inaccessible to the poor or near poor. Even in education, families are not restricted in their access to private educational opportunities of many kinds that are of better quality than public education. Nor is public education itself equal in quality, but is often superior in more affluent neighborhoods.

Rather than defending the broad re-distributive agenda implied in the principle of *equality* so that health care must be the same, I urge the modest claim of greater *equity,* so that health care is distributed more fairly. I do not even expect society to achieve anywhere near complete equity in the sense that health care is distributed in a totally impartial or unbiased way. But it is reasonable to expect society to set a goal of a more equitable system by reducing inordinately wide disparities in health care. The claim of equitable or fair access applies especially to those health services that most effectively help prevent illness, disease, disability, and premature death, and which best care for and treat persons in ill-health.

B. DISPARITIES IN ACCESS
TO HEALTH CARE AMONG POPULATIONS

Access to health care is measured by the use of health services, the quality of those services, and health outcomes. The test of equity involves a determination of whether there are systematic differences in access, and whether these differences result from financial or other barriers to health care. Using these objective measures of equitable access to health care, researchers have been able to demonstrate persistent and sometimes remarkable differences among groups in the United States.

There is a powerful and growing literature on inequitable access to health care. On each of the three dimensions just discussed — use, quality, and health outcomes — considerable data exist to demonstrate significant differences among groups based upon their personal, social, and economic status. The disparities in access to care are particularly sharp and enduring for persons with low socioeconomic status (the poor or near poor, the uninsured, and those in public programs such as Medicaid) and persons in minority racial and ethnic groups.

The relationships between low socioeconomic status and poor health are deep and enduring. In 1991, there were 35.7 million persons below the official poverty level,[30] accounting for 14.2% of the population.[31] If alternative methods of valuation were used that excluded non-cash benefits such as Medicaid and food stamps, there would have been 54.8 million persons in official poverty, accounting for 21.8% of the population.[32] From 1977 to 1990, the poorest 20% of the population suffered a 15% loss in real income, while the wealthiest one percent had a 110% after-tax rise in income.[33] . . .

The subgroups that are over-represented in the poverty population are precisely those groups that are most affected by lack of health insurance and poor health. In 1991, nearly one-third (32.7%) of all African-Americans and more than one quarter of Hispanics (28.7%) were living under the poverty line.[34] One half

of the nation's poor were either children or the elderly.[35] One-fourth of all children and one half of all African-American children were below the poverty line.[36]

Health disparities between poor people and those with higher incomes are almost universal for all dimensions of health. . . .

The association between economic disadvantage and ill-health is manifested most strongly in strikingly poor pregnancy outcomes (e.g., prematurity, low birth weight, birth defects) and higher infant mortality; the limitations in life activities due to ill health; and elevated mortality rates. Low income people have death rates that are twice the rates for people with incomes above the poverty level.

Compared to other groups in society, African-Americans and other racial and ethnic minorities are three times more likely to live in poverty and to lack health insurance. They also are subject to discrimination in health care. The effects of these burdens are borne out by poorer utilization of services, outcomes, and health status "virtually across the board." . . .

IV. HEALTH CARE AND MARKETS

• • •

A. THE APPLICABILITY OF MARKET THEORY TO
HEALTH CARE

Competition is widely thought to be an effective mechanism for lowering the price and increasing the quality of goods and services in the marketplace. The question, however, is whether competition is an appropriate theory, or the marketplace is the appropriate approach, to the cost effective allocation of health care services. Competition in health care can occur at least on two levels — health care plans can compete for subscribers, and individual providers can compete in offering service to patients. Each level of competition presents its own set of opportunities for reducing cost and its own set of theoretical and practical problems.

Competition among health care plans, which is the organizing theory behind managed competition, is vehemently put forward as a strategy for cost containment. Managed competition remains a proposal constructed in theory, not practice. No health care system outside of the United States has demonstrated the worth of managed competition in promoting quality and constraining medical inflation.

The theory of managed competition assumes that a sufficient number of health care plans exist to sustain competition in the market. A study by one of managed competition's original proponents suggests that populations large enough to support three or more competing health plans exist only in middle-sized to large metropolitan areas.[37] Professor Kronick and his colleagues assume that a minimum of three competing health plans is necessary for the system to work effectively, however, no empirical evidence exists to rely on this number to foster competition. Would players in the market truly compete or would they collude to maintain prices? What economic conditions and/or antitrust arrangements would have to exist to ensure genuine competition? . . .

Predicting the economic effects of managed competition on national health spending is fraught with complexity. Managed competition is not based on empirical evidence, and since the elements of proposals are diverse, it is exceedingly difficult to determine the probable economic effects. Estimates of the economic impact of managed competition on national health care expenditures vary significantly, "rang[ing] from *increased spending* of $47.9 billion in 1993 to *decreased spending* of $21.8 billion in 1994."[38] Given the totality of the evidence, competition among health care plans has theoretical potential for impeding the rise in health care spending, but the potential is unproven and would be unlikely to produce significant reductions in national health expenditures.

Would greater competition among health care plans help achieve the primary good of increased access or equity? Managed competition theorists argue that the savings from their program might be used to fund subsidies for increased access, but no assurance exists as to when, or if, savings would occur. Even if savings do occur, much of the economic benefit will accrue to the private sector; it is unclear to what extent, if any, government would benefit or whether government would use any cost savings to subsidize health care for the poor. Competition at the level of the health plan, in and of itself, promises little to increase access to health services for the currently uninsured or under-insured.

Competition can also occur at the level of the individual provider who competes in offering services to patients. The implicit assumption behind competition is that consumers purchase health care in the same way they buy durable goods or personal services. Good reasons exist, however, for believing that consumers view health care rather differently than most other goods and services. Health services are unique because they can relieve unremitting pain or suffering, restore normal functioning, or prevent premature death. If a medical service could provide a small chance of an improved quality of life or a longer life, most people would be prepared to pay an inordinate price for the service. It is precisely because health is a preeminent human value that markets cannot determine the worth of medical services to individuals in need of care.

Additionally, when persons become ill they are more appropriately seen in the subservient position of a patient rather than of an educated consumer. Patients who are suffering seldom are able to make the clear-headed economic judgments society expects of consumers in the marketplace. They are unable to accurately assess the quality of the "product" or to make reasoned judgments about alternatives.

Even if it were accurately assumed that the market would behave as theorized when buying and selling health services, the result of a well functioning market would be the opposite of that which is desirable. The essential characteristic of the marketplace is that it allocates goods and services on the basis of the ability to pay rather than on the basis of the need for the service. The market, therefore, excludes those who are unable to afford the service being sold. Seen in this way, it is not surprising that the U.S. health care system has exhibited two notable trends, both harmful to the social fabric — steadily increasing prices and greater numbers of persons unable to afford medical services. If it is true that health care is a precious and sought after commodity, the demand for services would be expected to rise. As demand increases, so should price. It would be similarly expected that individuals in poorer income groups would have a decreasing ability to purchase the product as the price rises. Since poverty is often associated with poorer health for a variety of environmental, nutritional and behavioral reasons, those who need the service most would be least likely to afford access.

Free market scholars acknowledge that the market has not worked efficiently. Rather than abandoning the idea, they choose to "fix" the health services market through greater deregulation. The results of these efforts, however, are likely to exacerbate existing problems precisely because inaccessibility and inequity are inherent concerns with competition in all markets. . . .

At least from the time of President Truman to the present day, reform of the health care system at the national level has been very much a part of the public and scholarly discourse in the United States. Yet comprehensive reform of the health care system has become, for now and the immediate future, unattainable. The country appears caught in a paradox. We value the choice and quality in the current health care system, but recognize the harm to the economy of escalating costs and the harm to the social fabric from inadequate access and inequitable distribution of services. . . .

Those in our society who tolerate significant numbers of their fellow men, women, and children going without health care coverage have a burden of carefully explaining the values that underlie their position and demonstrating why they take precedence over the health of the wider community.

NOTES

1. John K. Iglehart, *The American Health Care System,* 326 NEW ENGL J. MED. 962, 962 (1992).

2. *See, e.g.,* Robert J. Blendon et al., *The American Public and the Critical Choices for Health Reform,* 271 JAMA 1540 (1994).

3. Iglehart, *supra* note 1, at 962.

4. *See* Sally T. Burner et al., *National Health Expenditures Projections Through 2030,* 11 HEALTH CARE FINANCE REV. at 1, 14, 20 (1992) (estimates).

5. OFFICE OF TECHNOLOGY ASSESSMENT, U.S. CONGRESS, UNDERSTANDING ESTIMATES OF NATIONAL HEALTH EXPENDITURES UNDER HEALTH REFORM 1 (1994) [hereinafter UNDERSTANDING ESTIMATES].

6. *See* id. at 1–3 (figures 1–2); Sally T. Sonnenfield et al., *Projections of National Health Expenditures Through the Year 2000,* HEALTH CARE FINANCE REV., Fall 1991, at 1, 4, 22. *See also* CONGRESSIONAL BUDGET OFFICE, PROJECTIONS OF NATIONAL HEALTH EXPENDITURES 14 (1992) [hereinafter HEALTH EXPENDITURES] (table).

7. Sarah C. Snyder, *Who Are the Medically Uninsured in the United States?, STAT. BULL.,* 20, 21 (1994) (38.9 million had no private or public health insurance during 1992); BNA, *Number of Uninsured Persons Increases to 36.6 million in 1991,* Daily Labor Rep., Jan. 12, 1993, *available in* LEXIS, BNA Library, DLABRT File.

8. Emily Friedman, *The Uninsured: From Dilemma to Crisis,* 265 JAMA 2491, 2491 (1991).

9. *See How Many Americans Are Uninsured?,* 111 ARCHIVES OF OPHTHALMOLOGY 309, 309 (1993) (number of uninsured Americans varies with the method of surveying, giving a variety of numbers).

10. BUREAU OF THE CENSUS, U.S. DEP'T OF COMMERCE, HEALTH INSURANCE COVERAGE: 1987-1990: SELECTED DATA FROM THE SURVEY OF INCOME AND PROGRAM PARTICIPATION 3 (1992); Friedman, *supra* note 59, at 2491 (noting that 63.6 million lacked insurance for at least one month from 1986 to 1988).

11. FAMILIES USA FOUNDATION, HALF OF US: FAMILIES PRICED OUT OF HEALTH PROTECTION 3 (1993).

12. Alan Reynolds, *Another Big Lie,* FORBES, June 22, 1992, at 241, 241.

13. *Medical Reform Simplified,* WALL ST., J., Oct. 18, 1993, at A16.

14. See id.

15. Katherine Swartz & Timothy McBride, *Spells with Health Insurance: Distributions of Durations and Their Link to Point-in-Time Estimates of the Uninsured,* 27 INQUIRY 281, 283 (1990).

16. Katherine Swartz, *Dynamics of People Without Health Insurance: Don't Let the Numbers Fool You,* 271 JAMA 64, 65 (1994) (estimating that at least 21 million people were uninsured all of 1992).

17. id..

18. Howard E. Freeman et al., Abstract, *Uninsured Working-age Adults: Characteristics and Consequences,* 265 JAMA 2474, 2474 (1991) (noting that "the uninsured are most likely to be poor or near poor, Hispanic, young, unmarried and unemployed.")

19. *See* COMMISSION ON MONITORING ACCESS TO PERSONAL HEALTH CARE SERVICES, INSTITUTE OF MEDICINE, ACCESS TO HEALTH CARE IN AMERICA 2 (Michael Millman ed., 1993) at 17 (hereinafter ACCESS TO HEALTH CARE] (noting that population-based strategies in such areas as the environment, pollutants, health education, occupational health, and injury control could potentially "save more lives and have a greater impact on quality of life than programs to extend health services.").

20. Id. at 3 (indicators that measure health outcomes suggest that low income persons with no health insurance experience profoundly different health outcomes).

21. UNDERSTANDING ESTIMATES, *supra* note 5, at 1.

22. Id. at 1–3 (figures 1–2); Sally T. Sonnenfield, *supra* note 6 at 1, 4, 22. *See also* HEALTH EXPENDITURES, *supra* note 6, at 14 (table).

23. George J. Schieber et al., *Health Care Systems in Twenty-Four Countries,* 10 HEALTH AFF. 22, 24 (Fall 1991). *See* Timothy S. Jost & Sandra J. Tanenbaum, *Selling Cost Containment,* 19 AM. J. L., & MED. 95, 96–97 (1993).

24. *See generally* ORGANIZED FOR ECONOMIC AND COMMUNITY DEVELOPMENT, HEALTH DATA: COMPARATIVE ANALYSIS OF HEALTH CARE SYSTEMS (1991) [hereinafter COMPARATIVE ANALYSIS]: William C. Hsiao, *Comparing Health Care Systems: What Nations Can Learn from One Another,* 17 J. HEALTH POL., POL'Y & L. 613, 626–29 (1992).

25. Victor R. Fuchs, *The Best Health Care System in the World?,* 268 JAMA 916, 917 (1992).

26. Steffie Woolhandler & David U. Himmelstein, *The Deteriorating Administrative Efficiency of the U.S. Health Care System,* 324 NEW ENG. J. MED. 1253, 1255–56 (1991).

27. *See* JOHN RAWLS, A THEORY OF JUSTICE 95–100 (1971).

28. *See generally* Norman Daniels, *Health-Care Needs and Distributive Justice,* 10 PHIL., & PUB. AFF. 146 (1981); Norman Daniels, *Health Care Needs and Distributive Justice,* in IN SEARCH OF EQUITY: HEALTH NEEDS AND THE HEALTH CARE SYSTEM 1 (Ronald Bayer et al. eds., 1983); Norman Daniels, JUST HEALTH CARE (1985).

29. Norman Daniels, *Health Care Needs and Distributive Justice,* in IN SEARCH OF EQUITY: HEALTH NEEDS AND THE HEALTH CARE SYSTEM 115 (Ronald Bayer et al. eds., 1983). (emphasis added).

30. The poverty line was set in 1993 at the low level of $11,890 for a family of three. This leaves many families living just above the

poverty line who have difficulty affording housing, food, and clothing. *See* Victor W. Sidel et al., *The Resurgence of Tuberculosis in the United States: Societal Origins and Societal Responses,* 21 J. L., MED. & ETHICS 303, 307 (1993).

31. *See* Eleanor Baugher, *Poverty,* in BUREAU OF THE CENSUS, U.S. DEP'T OF COMMERCE, POPULATION PROFILE OF THE UNITED STATES 1993, at 28 (1994).

32. Id. at 29.

33. Sidel, *supra* note 30, at 308 (citing STEFFIE WOOLHANDLER & DAVID U. HIMMELSTEIN, THE NATIONAL HEALTH PROGRAM CHARTBOOK 24 (1992)).

34. BUREAU OF THE CENSUS, U.S. DEP'T OF COMMERCE, POPULATION PROFILE OF THE UNITED STATES 1993, at 29 (1994).

35. Id.

36. Sidel, *supra* note 30, at 307.

37. Richard Kronick et al., *The Marketplace in Health Care Reform: The Demographic Limitations of Managed Competition,* 328 NEW ENG. J. MED. 148 (1993).

38. OFFICE OF TECHNOLOGY ASSESSMENT, U.S. CONGRESS, AN INCONSISTENT PICTURE: A COMPILATION OF ANALYSES OF ECONOMIC IMPACTS OF COMPETING APPROACHES TO HEALTH CARE REFORM BY EXPERTS AND STAKEHOLDERS 34 (1993) (emphasis added).

DAVID ORENTLICHER

Health Care Reform and The Patient–Physician Relationship

INTRODUCTION

Health Care Reform would greatly benefit the patient–physician relationship. With universal or near-universal coverage, many millions more patients would establish relationships with primary care physicians. As a result, these patients would have better access to preventive health measures. There also would be earlier detection of diseases like hypertension, diabetes, and cancer so that treatment could be instituted earlier with greater effectiveness and at a lower cost.

Nevertheless, health care reform also would pose important concerns for the patient–physician relationship. This Article will focus on these concerns. In Part I, the risk of greater discontinuities in the patient–physician relationship will be reviewed. . . . In Part II, threats to the traditional dedication of physicians to the needs of their patients are discussed. . . .

I. DISCONTINUITIES IN THE PATIENT–PHYSICIAN RELATIONSHIP

• • •

THE THREAT TO CONTINUITY FROM HEALTH CARE REFORM

Health care reform threatens continuity in the patient–physician relationship because it is driving the U.S.

Health Matrix: Journal of Law-Medicine 5 (1995), 141–180. Reprinted by permission.

health care system more toward insurance provided by prepaid, comprehensive health plans like health maintenance organizations (HMOs) away from insurance provided by traditional, fee-for-service plans like Blue Cross-Blue Shield. In doing so, reform is eliminating the independence of the patient's choice of physician from the patient's choice of insurance. . . .

The linkage between patients' choice of an HMO and their choice of physicians increases the likelihood of discontinuities in the patient–physician relationship for several reasons. First, when patients initially choose to receive care from an HMO, they may find that some or none of their current physicians are on the HMO's panel. Consequently, patients may have to sever existing relationships with their physicians and receive their care from different physicians. Second, if patients become dissatisfied with their HMO and decide to switch to a different HMO, they also will have to switch to the new HMO's panel of physicians. Third, patients may be satisfied with their choice of HMO and the physicians from whom they receive care but find that one or more of their physicians transfer to a competing HMO. The patients then must choose between following the physician(s) who move(s) or staying with the physician(s) who remain(s) with their current HMO. Fourth, patients may receive their health care as a benefit of employment and find that their employers no longer offer the current HMO as an option. To retain the employers' contribution to the cost of the health insurance, patients may have to switch to other insurance plans.

In sum, to the extent that health care reform results in a shift in health insurance from fee-for-service plans to prepaid, comprehensive care plans, patients are more likely to find that they are unable to maintain long-standing relationships with their physicians. As a result, they will be unable to realize the benefits from such relationships.

RESPONDING TO THE RISK OF DISCONTINUITIES

How should society respond to the risk of greater discontinuities in patient–physician relationships from the shift toward prepaid, comprehensive health care plans? While some consider this risk an important argument in favor of a Canadian-style health care system in which patients are free to seek care from any physician and the government reimburses the physician for the care provided, the concern about discontinuities in the patient–physician relationship cannot alone settle the debate between managed competition and single-payer care given all of the other advantages and disadvantages of managed competition and single-payer systems. There are many ways within a system of HMO-style care in which discontinuities can be limited. For example, many HMOs allow patients to seek care from physicians outside of their panel as long as the patient pays a somewhat higher copayment for the outside physician services. Under such a system, patients could maintain some independence between their choice of insurers and their choice of physicians.

II. DIVISION OF THE PHYSICIAN'S FIDUCIARY DUTY OF LOYALTY

. . .

THE IMPORTANCE OF THE PHYSICIAN'S DUTY OF LOYALTY

Traditionally, the patient–physician relationship has been viewed as a fiduciary relationship in which the physician owes the patient a fundamental duty to place the patient's interests first, above not only the physician's personal interests but also the interests of other patients.[1] This duty of loyalty arises primarily from the unequal relationship between patients and physicians. . . .

The duty of loyalty underlies a wide range of ethical obligations of physicians. Physicians must maintain the confidentiality of their patients' disclosures, care for patients who are too poor to pay for their care,

and care for the sick even when doing so exposes them to personal health risks.

To be sure, there have always been conflicts of interest that divide physicians' loyalty to patients. Fee-for-service medicine encourages physicians to order unnecessary tests or perform unnecessary operations that not only may cause economic harm to their patients, but also may cause physical harm if complications ensue. Similarly, when physicians assume responsibility for the care of multiple patients, they often may find that more than one patient requires attention at a given time. As a result, physicians may delay attending to one patient while providing care to another patient. Nevertheless, these conflicts have not seriously undermined patient trust in physicians. Indeed, surveys by the Gallup poll taken over the past fifteen years have consistently found that the public has greater trust in physicians than almost all other professionals.[2]

THE THREAT TO PHYSICIAN LOYALTY FROM HEALTH CARE REFORM

While conflicts of interest that divide the physician's duty of loyalty are not new, they are likely to be accentuated under health care reform. . . .

1. Balancing the Needs of Individual Patients with the Needs of Other Patients. [Physicians will be required] to balance the needs of individual patients with those of other patients and the needs of society. As efforts intensify to contain health care costs, there necessarily will be coverage for fewer medical services. Even if wasted health care spending could be eliminated, it still would not be possible to fund all useful medical care. Some treatments will provide so little benefit that their benefit will not justify their cost; other treatments will be so costly that their benefit also will not justify their cost. Accordingly, society needs to devise some methods for choosing when treatment will be covered and when it will not be covered. . . .

Rationing decisions could be made by the individual health care plans. Currently, for example, health care insurers make decisions about the extent to which they will cover experimental treatments like bone marrow transplantation for metastatic breast cancer. However, these organizations . . . could fail to address the bulk of rationing decisions, leaving the decisions by default to individual physicians. Physicians may be given the instruction to provide care only when it is medically necessary. When treating patients, physicians would have to consider whether additional treatment would provide sufficient benefit or whether the resources should be conserved for other patients.

Even if the government and health plans take an active role in resolving allocation questions, there will still be a good deal of decision making left for physicians. It will take some time to assess the value of a particular treatment and decide whether it should be covered. It took Oregon several years and millions of dollars to develop its rationing plan for Medicaid benefits, and even that rationing plan, despite its complexity, leaves many questions unanswered. . . .

2. Financial Incentives to Encourage Cost-Conscious Practices by Physicians. Recent legislative proposals have not informed us how physicians would be guided, but we can easily deduce how they would be guided from the emphasis on having health care provided by HMOs and other managed care plans. Managed care plans rely heavily on personal financial incentives for physicians to encourage greater cost consciousness among physicians when making treatment decisions. For example, the plans often compensate physicians with capitation fees or a salary. With a capitation fee, since the physicians earn a fixed amount of money per patient, physicians cannot increase their income by providing more services to their patients, as with fee-for-service care. Similarly, physicians paid by salary have no financial incentive to provide more services. Rather, when their income is fixed by capitation or salary, physicians have an incentive to provide fewer services and free up more time for leisure or other activities.

In addition to incentives for physicians to limit their own services, managed care plans typically employ incentives for physicians to limit their use of diagnostic tests, referrals to other physicians, hospital care, or other ancillary services. For example, managed care plans often pay bonuses to physicians, with the amount of the bonus increasing as the plans' expenditures for patient care decrease. Managed care plans often withhold a fixed percentage of physician compensation until the end of the year to cover any shortfalls in the funds budgeted for expenditures on patient care. If there is no shortfall, or the shortfall can be covered by part of the withheld fees, the remaining withheld fees are returned to the physicians.

Financial incentives may be common, but they are nevertheless controversial. They not only impel physicians to balance the needs of their patients with the needs of other patients, they also accentuate the conflict between patient needs and the personal financial interests of physicians. In other words, there is not only a dual loyalty but a triple loyalty.

The concerns with incentives to limit care are significant. Physicians may be tempted to cut corners or start viewing as elective those treatments that were previously considered necessary.[3] Physicians also might delay or omit diagnostic tests or therapeutic procedures, or they might assume responsibility for care that should be referred to more expert and more expensive specialists.[4] Even in the absence of actual physical harm to patients, incentives to limit care may compromise the trust that patients place in their physicians. If patients realize that their physicians are being pressured with financial rewards to economize on care, then patients will likely wonder whether treatment is being withheld because it is unnecessary or because their physicians have financial reasons to withhold the care. . . .

Financial incentives to withhold services are also problematic because their effects may not be apparent to patients. When physicians recommend an invasive diagnostic test, surgery, or some other course of action, patients may choose to seek a second opinion before undertaking the risks and costs of the action. However, when physicians do not offer an intervention, patients may have no idea that a diagnostic or treatment option was withheld and therefore not realize that a second opinion might be appropriate.

Nevertheless, there are several reasons why incentives to limit care may not compromise the quality of medical care. First, while physicians are motivated by financial concerns, they also are strongly devoted to other values and goals, in particular, to enhancing the health of their patients. Physicians clearly seek financial gain, but it is not clear that they would sacrifice the welfare of their patients to do so.

Second, the threat of malpractice liability provides a strong deterrent to the withholding of necessary care. Physicians already are prone to practice defensive medicine—their perception of the risk of a malpractice lawsuit is up to three times the actual risk of suit.[5] Hospitals and health care plans are also at risk from physician malpractice and therefore have strong incentives to monitor quality of care and ensure that appropriate care is not withheld by physicians.

Third, it is possible that financial incentives to limit care will lead to care with fewer complications and more efficient utilization of health care resources. For example, because delays in intervention can allow a disease to develop or progress and become more costly to treat, incentives to limit care may actually result in more aggressive efforts to ensure that patients receive preventive and therapeutic services as early as possible. If physicians are penalized for high health care costs, they are more likely to try to prevent high costs from materializing. . . .

While there are theoretical arguments both in support of and in opposition to the claim that incentives to limit care will compromise physician decision making, the experience with incentives to expand services suggests that incentives to limit care will likely influence physician behavior. A number of studies have indicated that financial incentives to prescribe x-rays, physical therapy, or other medical services result in increased use of the services. If incentives to expand services result in greater use of those services and possibly overtreatment of patients, then it arguably follows that incentives to limit care will result in lower use of those services and possibly undertreatment.

It does not necessarily follow, however, that incentives to limit services will result in inadequate care. If . . . the harm to patient health is greater when necessary treatment is withheld than when unnecessary treatment is provided, physicians are less likely to be influenced by incentives to limit care than by incentives to expand care. With incentives to limit care, physician concerns with patient welfare will be a stronger countervailing force. When physicians are uncertain whether to offer additional tests or treatments, concerns about protecting patient health may overcome the pull from any incentives to limit care and result in the physicians offering the extra tests or procedures.

Moreover, the existence of health care insurance makes it likely that physician practices have been affected more by incentives to expand care than they would be by incentives to limit care. The primary harm from excessive care is financial, but the current system of health care insurance dilutes the financial harm to patients from overuse of services. . . .

1. Eliminate Financial Incentives that Have a High Potential for Abuse. Commentators have identified several characteristics of financial incentives that are important indicators of whether physicians are being given too strong an incentive to limit care. These char-

acteristics include: (a) the amount of financial risk borne by the physicians, (b) whether incentives are tied to the performance of physicians individually or as a group, and (c) the length of time over which physician performance is measured.[6]

a. Amount of Financial Risk Shifted

Health insurers may shift financial risk to physicians in a number of ways. A percentage of physician fees may be withheld until the end of the year to cover deficits in the fund for expenditures on diagnostic tests, referral services, hospital care, or other ancillary care. Withheld funds can be used to cover a narrow range of services like diagnostic tests and referrals to specialists or to cover the full range of ancillary services. As the breadth of services covered by the withheld funds increases, the amount of risk shifted to physicians increases. Risk also may be shifted by varying the fee paid for a particular service from month to month depending upon the extent to which services are utilized. . . .

b. Number of Physicians Sharing the Risk

If physician incentive payments are based solely on each physician's own treatment decisions, there is a strong incentive to limit services for each patient. Every additional medical service will have a direct effect on the physician's income. When payments are based on the performance of a group of physicians, on the other hand, the strength of the incentive is diminished. . . .

Basing the incentives on a group of physicians is useful for two other reasons. First, when physicians are placed at risk together, they have a collective incentive to ensure that their colleagues are practicing in a cost-effective manner.[7] Second, if incentive payments are based on a large group of physicians, the payments will necessarily be based on the costs incurred by a large pool of patients. When the patient pool is small, there is a risk that treatment costs will be skewed by an unrepresentative group of patients that have unusually high needs for medical care. The larger the patient pool, the more likely that its treatment costs will not be skewed but will reflect average costs.

c. Length of Time for Measuring Performance

The strength of a financial incentive also varies with the frequency of incentive payments. If payments are made monthly rather than yearly, the physician receives rapid feedback on the economic consequences of treatment decisions and is therefore likely to be more sensitive to those consequences. When incentives are calculated monthly, there also is less of an opportunity for the costs of cases that are above average to be offset by the costs of cases that are below average. Accordingly, there is a stronger incentive not to incur unusually high expenses in any one case.

In its proposed rules, HCFA permits less of a physician's income to be put at risk if incentive payments are made more frequently than once a year. If payments are made once a year, up to 30% of a physician's income may be placed at risk; if payments are made more frequently than once a year, up to 20% of a physician's income may be placed at risk.[8]

2. Eliminate the Incentives Entirely. Limiting the kinds of incentives that can be offered is an important step; however, some commentators argue that it is not sufficient just to eliminate only the most dangerous incentives. They observe that there is no objective method for defining "too dangerous" an incentive, and the definition chosen may fall short of that needed to protect patient welfare. While prohibiting the more serious incentives would lower the risk to patients, it would not eliminate the risk. Further, the risk to patient trust may depend as much on the existence of incentives to limit care and the divided loyalties they create as on their magnitude. Even relatively moderate incentives can cause patients to question their physicians' commitment to patient needs. Accordingly, these commentators advocate the elimination of financial incentives to limit care entirely, on the grounds that they pose too great a threat to patient welfare and that alternative measures to contain costs can be utilized.

There are several problems with this view. First, as to the argument that the risk to patient trust depends as much on the existence of incentives as on their magnitude, all compensation systems reward physicians either for providing too much care, as with fee-for-service, or for providing too little care, as with capitation fees or salary. As commentators have noted for decades, the traditional fee-for-service system leads to a good deal of unnecessary medical care, and such care can be not only economically injurious to patients but also detrimental to their health if one of the inherent risks of medical care materializes. Paying physicians on a salaried

basis would remove their incentive to overserve their patients, but it would leave them with an incentive to underserve them. By seeing fewer patients, scheduling fewer follow-up visits, and performing fewer procedures, salaried physicians can free up more time for alternative activities, such as consulting, research, or leisure, without losing any income. It simply is not possible to have a compensation scheme that avoids all incentives for physicians to provide inappropriate care to their patients. It may be possible to reduce the magnitude of the conflict of interest between a physician's personal financial interests and patient welfare, but there will always be some conflict of interest.

Second, as to the argument that costs can be controlled without using financial incentives to limit care, while prohibition of incentives to limit care would limit the risk to patient welfare, it is not clear that alternative measures to contain costs are sufficiently effective. For example, health care plans have used educational interventions to modify physician use of services. These interventions include efforts to improve physician awareness of the costs of and medical indications for tests, procedures, and treatments and to provide feedback to the physicians regarding their expenditures for patient care and the medical appropriateness of their practices. . . .

3. Balancing Ethical Concerns with Cost Constraints. . . . [T]he need to contain health care costs will inevitably require physicians to exercise their own discretion to decide when potentially beneficial diagnostic tests or therapeutic procedures should be withheld from their patients. While to some extent decisions about which tests or procedures will be withheld from which patients can be made by the public, acting through their government or their private health care plans, in many cases, society will have to rely on physician discretion. This is so for two reasons: developing rationing guidelines takes a good deal of time and money, and it simply is not possible to create guidelines for every medical decision that might arise. Although placing physicians in the role of rationers of health care divides their duty of loyalty to their patients, it is not possible to avoid dividing the loyalty. Accordingly, physicians will have to become more cost-conscious in their decision making.

. . . [I]f society wishes to change physician behavior so that physicians become more cost-conscious in their decision making, it must employ mandates or financial incentives. Education alone does not work. . . .

4. Deciding Between Fixed Budgets and Personal Financial Incentives for Physicians. From an ethical standpoint, the fixed budget approach is preferable. Although it forces physicians to balance the needs of each patient against those of other patients, it does not create an additional conflict between patient needs and the physicians' personal interests. In other words, physicians have a dual loyalty, but not the triple loyalty that exists with financial incentives to limit care.

Fixed budgets have other important benefits. They force society to confront directly the fact that there are competing demands for its resources and that hard choices have to be made among those demands. The public is better served by an open process for deciding how many resources will be devoted to health care and how many to other social services.

Fixed budgets also assure physicians that, if they conserve resources when treating one patient, more resources will be available for other, more deserving patients. Conversely, if physicians do not conserve resources, fewer resources will be available for later, more deserving patients. Currently, many commentators argue that because there is no guarantee that resources saved on one patient will be available for other patients or that spending resources on one patient will deplete the resources available for other patients, physicians must not withhold potentially beneficial care from one patient on the ground that the saved resources would be better used elsewhere. If we adopt a closed system with a fixed budget, it is inevitable that treating one patient will affect the resources available for other patients.

The primary objection to fixed budgets is that they are politically difficult to achieve. Medicare and Medicaid costs have far exceeded the levels projected when they were first enacted. Further, in the recent health care reform debate, the idea of budget caps did not survive very long. In Oregon, where the legislature has adopted a fixed budget, the funding level was so generous that little cost savings were realized. While fixed budgets arouse fierce political opposition, personal financial incentives for physicians are readily accepted politically and are already widespread.

CONCLUSION

Whether the result of legislation or private initiative, health care reform would pose serious threats to the patient–physician relationship. With its emphasis on managed care arrangements that link the patient's choice of insurer with the patient's choice of physicians, reform would increase the likelihood of discontinuities in patient care. With its greater responsibility for physicians to make individual rationing decisions, reform would also increasingly divide the loyalty of physicians to their patients.

There is no ideal solution to these problems. Linking the patients' choice of insurance to their choice of physicians is an important measure for containing health care costs. Similarly, while hard rationing decisions are also necessary if health care costs are to be contained, there is no way to remove all of those decisions from physicians.

Despite the lack of an ideal solution, the harmful effects of reform can be mitigated. If health care plans include an option for patients to use physicians outside of their plan at a higher cost, then there would not be as much disruption of patient–physician relationships. In addition, if fixed budgets rather than financial incentives were used to ensure that physicians limit their use of health care resources, then rationing decisions would be influenced much less by the physicians' personal financial interests.

NOTES

1. Edmund D. Pellegrino, *Rationing Health Care: The Ethics of Medical Gatekeeping,* 2 J. CONTEMP. HEALTH L. & POL'Y 23, 25 (1986) (discussing the origins and history of the ethical duty of physicians to act on behalf of patients).

2. Leslie McAneny, *Honesty and Ethics Poll: Pharmacists Retain Wide Lead as Most Honorable Profession,* L.A. TIMES SYNDICATE, July 29, 1993, *available in* Gallup Poll News Service.

3. Pellegrino, *supra* note 1, at 31.

4. Id.

5. Ann G. Lawthers et al., *Physicians' Perceptions of the Risk of Being Sued,* 17 J. HEALTH POL. POL'Y & L. 463, 468–69 (1992) (reporting results by physician specialty).

6. PHYSICIAN PAYMENT REVIEW COMM'N, *supra* note 19, at 287–88. U.S. GENERAL ACCOUNTING OFFICE. MEDICARE: PHYSICIAN INCENTIVE PAYMENTS BY PREPAID HEALTH PLANS COULD LOWER QUALITY OF CARE, GAO/HRD-89-29, at 23 (Dec. 1988).

7. PHYSICIAN PAYMENT REVIEW COMM'N. ANNUAL REPORT TO CONGRESS 275–81 (1989).

8. Medicare and Medicaid Programs, Requirements for Physician Incentive Plans in Prepaid Health Care Organizations, 57 Fed. Reg. 59,024, 59,032.

NORMAN DANIELS

Rationing Fairly: Programmatic Considerations

Despite its necessity, rationing raises troublesome questions about fairness. We ration in situations in which losers, as well as winners, have plausible claims to have their needs met. When we knowingly and deliberately refrain from meeting some legitimate needs, we had better have justification for the distributive choices we make. Not surprisingly, health planners and legislators appeal to bioethicists for help, asking what justice requires here. Can we help them? I think we are not ready to yet, and I will support this claim by noting four general rationing problems that we remain unsure how to solve, illustrating how they plague Oregon's rationing plan.

Before turning to the four problems, I want to make several preliminary remarks. First, philosophers (including me) have traditionally underestimated the importance of rationing, thinking of it as a peripheral, not central problem. Since we simply cannot afford, for example, to educate, treat medically, or protect legally people in all the ways their needs for these goods require or the accepted distributive principles seem to demand, rationing is clearly pervasive, not peripheral.

Rationing decisions share three key features. First, the goods we often must provide — legal services, health care, educational benefits — are not divisible without loss of benefit, unlike money. We thus cannot avoid unequal or "lumpy" distributions. Meeting the educational, health care or legal needs of some people, for example, will mean that the requirements of others will go unsatisfied. Second, when we ration, we deny benefits to some individuals who can plausibly claim

they are owed them in principle. They can cite an accepted principle of distributive justice that governs their situation and should protect them. Third, the general distributive principles appealed to by claimants as well as by rationers do not by themselves provide adequate reasons for choosing among claimants: they are too schematic. This point was driven home to me by the way in which my "fair equality of opportunity" account of just health care (Daniels 1985, 1988) fails to yield specific solutions to the rationing problems I shall survey. Finally, even the best work in the general theory of justice has not squarely faced the problems raised by the indeterminacy of distributive principles. Rawls (1971), for example, suggests that the problem of fleshing out the content of principles of distributive justice is ultimately procedural, falling to the legislature. Perhaps, but the claim that we must in general turn to a fair democratic procedure should not be an assumption, but the conclusion, either of a general argument or of a failed search for appropriate moral constraints on rationing. If however, there are substantive principles governing rationing, then the theory of justice is incomplete in a way we have not noticed. This point cuts across the debates between proponents of "local justice" (Walzer 1983; Elster 1992) and "global justice" (Rawls 1971; Gauthier 1986), and between liberalism and communitarianism (cf. Emanuel 1991; Daniels 1992).

FOUR UNSOLVED RATIONING PROBLEMS: ILLUSTRATIONS FROM OREGON

THE FAIR CHANCES/BEST OUTCOMES PROBLEM

Before seeing how the fair chances/best outcomes problem arises in Oregon's macrorationing plan, consider its more familiar microrationing form: Which of

Bioethics 7 (1993), 224–233. Copyright © 1993 Basil Blackwell Ltd.

several equally needy individuals should get a scarce resource, such as a heart transplant? Suppose, for example, that Alice and Betty are the same age, have waited on queue the same time, and that each will live only one week without a transplant. With the transplant, however, Alice is expected to live two years and Betty twenty. Who should get the transplant (cf. Kamm 1989)? Giving priority to producing best outcomes, a priority built into some point systems for awarding organs, would mean that Betty gets the organ and Alice dies (assuming persistent scarcity of organs, as Brock (1988) notes). But Alice might complain, "Why should I give up my only chance at survival — and two years of survival is not insignificant — just because Betty has a chance to longer? It is not fair that I give up everything that is valuable to me just so Betty can have more of what is valuable to her." Alice demands a lottery that gives her an equal chance with Betty.

Some people agree with Alice's complaint and agree with her demand for a lottery. Few would agree with her, however, if she had very little chance at survival; more would agree if her outcomes were only somewhat worse than Betty's. Still, at the level of intuitions, there is much disagreement about when and how much to favor best outcomes. Brock (1988), like Broome (1987) proposes breaking this deadlock by giving Alice and Betty chances proportional to the benefits they can get (e.g., by assigning Alice one side of a ten sided die). Kamm (1989, 1993) notes that Brock's proposal must be amended once we allow differences in urgency or need among patients. She favors assigning multiplicative weights to the degree of need or urgency. Then, the neediest might end up with no chance to receive a transplant if their outcomes were very poor, but, compared to Brock's "proportional chances" proposal, they would have greater opportunity to get an organ if their outcomes were reasonably high. Both Brock's and Kamm's suggestions seem ad hoc. That there is some force to each of Alice's and Betty's demands does not, as Brock would have it, mean the force is clearly equal; similarly, assigning weights to more factors, as Kamm does, seems to add an element of precision lacking in our intuitions about these cases. Our intuitions may fall short of giving us clear, orderly principles here.

We might try to break the deadlock at the level of intuitions by appealing to more theoretical considerations. For example, we might respond to Alice that she already has lost a "natural" lottery; she might have been the one with twenty years expected survival, but it turned out to be Betty instead. After the fact, how-ever, Alice is unlikely to agree that there were no prior differences in access to care and so on. To undercut Alice's demand for a new lottery, we would have to persuade her that the proper perspective for everyone to adopt is *ex ante,* not *ex post* information about her condition (cf Menzel 1989). But what should Alice know about herself *ex ante*? If Alice knows about her family history of heart disease, she might well not favor giving complete priority to best outcomes. Perhaps Alice should agree it is reasonable to adopt more radical *ex ante* position, one that denies her all information about herself, a thick "veil of ignorance." Controversy persists. Behind such a veil, some would argue that it would be irrational to forego the greater expected payoff that would result from giving priority to best outcomes. Citing Rawls's adoption of a maximin strategy, Kamm (1993) argues against such "gambling" behind the veil. Alternatively, she appeals to Scanlon (1982): if Alice would "reasonably regret" losing to Betty, then she should not be held to a scheme that favors best outcomes. Unclear about our intuitions, we are also stymied by a controversy at the deepest theoretical levels.

The best outcomes problem arises in macrorationing as well. Consider HSS Secretary Louis Sullivan's (1992) recent refusal to grant a Medicaid waiver to Oregon's rationing plan. Sullivan's main criticism of the Oregon plan is that in preferring treatments that provide greater net benefits the plan discriminates against the disabled. The clearest example of such discrimination would be this: Two groups of patients, both in need of a treatment that can give them a net benefit of a given magnitude; because one group has a disability, e.g., difficulty walking, that would not be affected by the treatment, we deny them the treatment. Neither Sullivan nor the NLC give an example, even hypothetical, of how this situation could arise in the Oregon scheme. The denial of coverage for aggressive treatment of very low birthweight (<500 gr) neonates, which they do cite as an example of discrimination, is not an appropriate example, because the denial is premised on the lack of benefit produced by aggressive treatment of such neonates.

Consider an example suggestive of the Oregon scheme. Suppose two treatments, T1 and T2, can benefit different groups of patients, G1 and G2 as follows. T1 preserves life for G1's (or provides some other major benefit), but it does not restore a particular function, such as walking, to G1s. T2 not only preserves life for G2s (or provides some other major benefit), but it also enables them to walk again. The Oregon Health Service Commission ranks T2 as a more important service than T1 because it produces a greater net benefit (I ignore the OTA (1991) argument that net benefit is not a major contributor to rank). Sullivan says that it is discriminatory to deny G1s T1, even though a single person would clearly consider relative benefit in deciding between T1 and T2.

The Sullivan/NLCMDD objection can, with charity, be interpreted as a version of Alice's complaint that favoring best outcomes denies her a fair chance at a benefit. Interpreted this way, the Sullivan/NLCMDD objection is that we cannot rule out giving G1s any chance at the benefit treatment would bring them simply because G2s would benefit more from the use of our limited resources. In effect, they seem to be saying we should give no weight to best outcomes. As I noted earlier, this extreme position does not seem to match our intuitions in the microrationing case. But neither does the alternative extreme position, that we must always give priority to better outcomes. The point is that a rationing approach that ranks services by net benefit, whether it turns out to be Oregon's scheme or simply Hadorn's (1991) alternative proposal, thus carries with it unsolved moral issues. To justify ranking by net benefit we must be prepared to address those underlying issues.

THE PRIORITIES PROBLEM

Oregon's (intended) methodology of ranking by net benefit also ignores the moral issues I group here as the priorities problem. Suppose that two treatment condition pairs give equal net benefits. (Remember, this [does] not generally mean they produce the same health outcomes, only the same net benefits). Then the OHSC should rank them equal in importance. But now suppose that people with C1 are more seriously impaired by their disease or disability than people with C2. Though T1 and T2 produce equivalent net gains in benefit, people with C2 will end up better off than people with C1, since they started out better off. Nothing in the method of ranking treatment/condition pairs by net benefit responds to this difference between C1s and C2s. Nevertheless, most of us would judge it more important to give services to C1s than it is to give them to C2s under these conditions. We feel at least some inclination to help those worse off than those better off.

For example, if C1s after treatment were no better off than C2s before treatment, we are more strongly inclined to give priority to the worse off. Our concern to respect that priority might decline if the effect of treating C1s but not C2s is that C1s end up better off than C2s. How troubled we would be by this outcome might depend on how great the new equality turned out to be, or on how significant the residual impairment of C2s was.

Suppose now that there is greater net benefit from giving T2 to C2s than there is from giving T1 to C1s. If C1s are sufficiently worse off to start with than T2s, and if C1s end up worse off or not significantly better off than C2s, then our concern about priorities may compel us to forego the greater net benefit that results from giving T2 to C2s. But how much priority we give to the worst off still remains unclear. If we can only give a very modest improvement to the worst off, but we must forego a very significant improvement to those initially better off, then we may overrule our concern for the worst off. Our intuitions do not pull us toward a strict priority for the worst off.

Just what the structure of our concern about priority is, however, remains unclear. The unsolved priorities problem not only affects a methodology that ranks by net benefit or by net QLY's. It affects cost/benefit and cost/effectiveness rankings, including Eddy's (1991a) "willingness to pay" methodology. So too does the aggregation problem, to which I now briefly turn.

THE AGGREGATION PROBLEM

In June of 1990, the Oregon Health Services Commission released a list of treatment/condition pairs ranked by a cost/benefit calculation. Critics were quick to seize on rankings that seemed completely counter-intuitive. For example, as Hadorn noted (1991), toothcapping was ranked higher than appendectomy. The reason was simple: an appendectomy cost about $4,000, many times the cost of capping a tooth. Simply aggregating the net medical benefit of many capped teeth yielded a net benefit greater than that produced by one appendectomy.

Eddy (1991b) points out that our intuitions in these cases are largely based on comparing treatment/condition pairs for their importance on a one:one basis. One appendectomy is more important than one toothcapping because it saves a life rather than merely reduces pain and preserves dental function. But our intuitions are much less developed when it comes to making one:many comparisons (though we can establish indifference curves that capture trades we are willing to make; cf.

Nord 1992). When does saving more lives through one technology mean we should forego saving fewer through another? The complex debate about whether "numbers count" has a bearing on rationing problems. How many legs should we be willing to forego saving in order to save one life? How many eyes? How many teeth? Can we aggregate *any* small benefits, or only those that are in some clear way significant, when we want to weigh these benefits against clearly significant benefits (e.g. saving a life) to a few? Kamm (1987, 1993) argues persuasively that we should not favor saving one life and curing a sore throat over saving a different life, because curing a sore throat is not a "competitor" with saving a life. She also argues that benefits that someone is morally not required to sacrifice in order to save another's life also have significant standing and can be aggregated. If we are not required to sacrifice an arm in order to save someone's life, then we can aggregate arms saved and weigh them against lives saved. She suggests that our judgments about aggregation differ if we are in contexts where saving lives rather than inducing harms (positive vs. negative duties) are at issue.

Kamm shows that we are not straightforward aggregators of all benefits and that our moral views are both complex and difficult to explicate in terms of well-ordered principles. These views are not compatible with the straightforward aggregation (sum ranking) that is presupposed by the dominant methodologies derived from welfare economics. Yet we do permit, indeed require, some forms of aggregation. Our philosophical task is to specify which principles governing aggregation have the strongest justification. If it appears there is no plausible, principled account of aggregation, then we have strong reason to rely instead on fair procedures and an obligation to give any of them.

THE DEMOCRACY PROBLEM

When Sullivan rejected Oregon's application for a Medicaid waiver, he complained that the methodology for assessing net medical benefit drew on biased or discriminatory public attitudes toward disabilities. Adapting Kaplan's (Kaplan and Anderson 1990) "quality of wellbeing" scale for use in measuring the benefit of medical treatments, Oregon surveyed residents, asking them to judge on a scale of 0 (death) to 100 (perfect health) what the impact would be of having to live the rest of one's life with some physical or mental impairment or symptom; for example, wearing eyeglasses was rated 95 out of 100, for a weighting of −0.05.

Many of these judgments seem downright bizarre, whether or not they reflect bias. For example, having to wear eyeglasses was rated slightly worse than the −0.046 weighting assigned to not being able to drive a car or use public transportation or the −0.049 assigned to having to stay at a hospital or nursing home. Other weightings clearly reflected cultural attitudes and possibly bias: having trouble with drugs or alcohol was given the second most negative weighting (−0.455) of all conditions, much worse than, for example, having a bad burn over large areas of your body (−0.372) or being so impaired that one needs help to eat or go to the bathroom (−0.106). Having to use a walker or wheelchair under your own control was weighted as much worse (−0.373) than having losses of consciousness from seizures, blackouts or coma (−0.114).

Claiming that people who experience a disabling condition, like being unable to walk, tend to give less negative ratings to them than people who have experienced them, Sullivan argued Oregon was likely to underestimate the benefit of a treatment that left people with such disabilities. Excluding such treatments would thus be the result of public bias.[1] His complaint carries over to other methodologies, e.g., Eddy's (1991) willingness-to-pay approach and the use of QLY's in cost-effectiveness or cost-benefit analyses.

Sullivan's complaint raises an interesting question: Whose judgments about the effects of a condition should be used? Those who do not have a disabling condition may suffer from cultural biases, overestimating the impact of disability. But those who have the condition may rate it as less serious because they have modified their preferences, goals, and values in order to make a "healthy adjustment" to their condition. Their overall dissatisfaction—tapped by these methodologies—may not reflect the impact that would be captured by a measure more directly attuned to the range of capabilities they retain. Still, insisting on the more objective measure has a high political cost and may even seem paternalistic.

Sullivan simply assumes that we must give priority to the judgments made by those experiencing the condition, but that is not so obvious. Clearly, there is something attractive about the idea, embedded in all these methodologies, of assessing the relative impact of conditions on people by asking them what they think about that impact (cf. Menzel 1992). Should we give people what they actually want? Or should we give them what they should want, correcting for various defects in their judgment? What corrections to expressed preferences are plausible?

The democracy problem arises at another level in procedures that purport to be directly democratic. The Oregon plan called for the OHSC to respect "community values" in its ranking of services. Because prevention and family planning services were frequently discussed in community meetings, the OHSC assigned the categories including those services very high ranking. Consequently, in Oregon, vasectomies are ranked more important than hip replacements. Remember the priority and aggregation problems: it would seem more important to restore mobility to someone who cannot walk than to improve the convenience of birth control through vasectomy in several people. But, assuming that the Commissioners properly interpreted the wishes of Oregonians, that is not what Oregonians wanted the rankings to be. Should we treat this as error? Or must we abide by whatever the democratic process yields?

Thus far I have characterized the problem of democracy as a problem of error: a fair democratic process, or a methodology that rests in part on expressions of preferences, leads to judgments that deviate from either intuitive or theoretically based judgments about the relative importance of certain health outcomes or services. The problem is how much weight to give the intuitive or theoretically based judgments as opposed to the expressed preferences. The point should be put in another way as well. Should we in the end think of the democratic process as a matter of pure procedural justice? If so, then we have no way to correct the judgment made through the process, for what it determines to be fair is what counts as fair. Or should we really consider the democratic process as an impure and imperfect form of procedural justice? Then it is one that can be corrected by appeal to some prior notion of what constitutes a fair outcome of rationing. I suggest that we do not yet know the answer to this question, and we will not be able to answer it until we work harder at providing a theory of rationing.

CONCLUSION

I conclude with a plea against provincialism. The four problems I illustrated have their analogues in the rationing of goods other than health care. To flesh out a principle that says "people are equal before the law" will involve decisions about how to allocate legal services among all people who can make plausible claims to need them by citing that principle. Similarly, to give content to a principle that assumes equal educational opportunity will involve decisions about resource allocation very much like those involved in rationing health care. Being provincial about health care rationing will prevent us from seeing the relationships among these rationing problems. Conversely, a rationing theory will have greater force if it derives from consideration of common types of problems that are independent of the kinds of goods whose distribution is in question. I am suggesting that exploring a theory of rationing in this way is a prolegomenon to serious work in "applied ethics."

REFERENCES

Brock, Dan. 1988. "Ethical Issues in Recipient Selection for Organ Transplantation." In D. Mathieu (ed.) *Organ Substitution Technology: Ethical, Legal, and Public Policy Issues.* Boulder: Westview. pp. 86–99.

Broome, John. 1987. "Fairness and the Random Distribution of Goods." (unpublished manuscript).

Capron, Alexander. 1992. "Oregon's Disability: Principles or Politics?" *Hastings Center Report* 22: 6 (November-December): 18–20.

Daniels, Norman. 1985. *Just Health Care.* Cambridge: Cambridge University Press.

Daniels, Norman. 1988. *Am I My Parents' Keeper? An Essay on Justice Between the Young and the Old.* New York: Oxford University Press.

Daniels, Norman. 1992. "Liberalism and Medical Ethics," *Hastings Center Report.* 22: 6 (November-December): 41–3.

Eddy, D. 1991a. "Rationing by Patient Choice," *JAMA* 265: 1 (January 2): 105–08.

Eddy, D. 1991b. "Oregon's Methods: Did Cost-Effectiveness Analysis Fail?" *JAMA* 266: 15 (October 16): 2135–41.

Elster, John. 1992. *Local Justice: How Institutions Allocate Scarce Goods and Necessary Burdens.* New York: Russel Sage.

Emanuel, Ezekiel. 1991. *The Ends of Human Life: Medical Ethics in a Liberal Polity.* Cambridge, MA: Harvard University Press.

Gauthier, D. 1986. *Morals By Agreement.* Oxford: Oxford University Press.

Hadorn, David. 1992. "The Problem of Discrimination in Health Care Priority Setting," *JAMA* 268: 11 (16 September): 1454–59.

Kamm, Frances. 1987. "Choosing Between People: Commonsense Morality and Doctors' Choices," *Bioethics* 1: 255–71.

Kamm, Frances. 1989. "The Report of the US Task Force on Organ Transplantation: Criticisms and Alternatives," *Mount Sinai Journal of Medicine* 56: 207–20.

Kamm, Frances. 1993. *Morality and Mortality, Vol. 1.* Oxford: Oxford University Press.

Kaplan, R.M. Anderson, J.P. 1990. "The General Health Policy Model: An Integrated Approach." In B. Spilker (ed.) *Quality of Life Assessments in Clinical Trials.* New York: Raven Press.

Menzel, Paul. 1989. *Strong Medicine.* New York: Oxford University Press.

Menzel, Paul. 1992. "Oregon's Denial: Disabilities and Quality of Life," *Hastings Center Report* 22: 6 (November-December): 21–25.

National Legal Center for the Medically Dependent and Disabled. 1991. Letter to Representative Christopher H. Smith.

Nord, Eric. 1992. "The Relevance of Health State After Treatment in Prioritising Between Different Patients," *Journal of Medical Ethics.* (forthcoming).

Office of Technology Assessment. 1991. *Evaluation of the Oregon Medicaid Proposal.* U.S. Congress (final draft in press).

Oregon Health Services Commission. 1991. *Prioritization of Health Services: A Report to the Governor and Legislature.*

Rawls, John. 1971. *A Theory of Justice.* Cambridge, MA: Harvard University Press.

Scanlon, Thomas. 1982. "Contractualism and Utilitarianism." In Amartya Sen and Bernard Williams, eds. *Utilitarianism and Beyond,* pp. 103–28. Cambridge: Cambridge University Press.

Sullivan, Louis. 1992. Press Release (August 3, 1992). Health and Human Services Press Office.

Walzer, Michael. 1983. *Spheres of Justice.* New York: Basic.

NOTE:

1. The OTA (1991) notes that men gave dismenorhea a greater negative weight than women. The effect of this weighting is that greater net benefit, and thus higher rank accrues to treating dismenorhea if we include the judgments of men than if we counted only the judgments of women.

L E O N A R D   M .   F L E C K

Just Caring: Oregon, Health Care Rationing, and Informed Democratic Deliberation

What does it mean to be a just and caring society when we have only limited resources and virtually unlimited health care needs that must be met? This is the problem of health care rationing. This is *the* central problem of health reform for the foreseeable future. Oregon has taken the lead in addressing this problem. Health care rationing is a ubiquitous phenomenon, though few recognize that, because rationing is accomplished for the most part in invisible ways that effectively hide the practice from critical scrutiny.

What is distinctive of Oregon is that its citizens chose to make explicit, visible, systematic rationing decisions that would be a product of democratic deliberations that were morally and rationally justifiable. For its efforts Oregon has been subjected to intense moral and political criticism, claiming that it is the politically weak, sick poor who will bear the burden of health care rationing. . . .

I. IS THE OREGON RATIONING PLAN FAIR?

We begin with two preliminary claims. First, the problems of health reform in general, and health care rationing in particular, are fundamentally moral and political problems, and only secondarily economic or organizational problems. . . . Health care services are not simply commodities in the market, like VCRs, that can be justifiably distributed in accord with individual ability to pay. As Daniels has argued, access to needed and effective health care is essential to protecting fair equality of opportunity in our society. Thus, health care ought to be thought of as a public good, as a public interest, and hence, as a legitimate object of public policy.

Our second preliminary claim is that *justice,* not beneficence, is the fundamental moral value that ought to govern the debates about health reform options. . . . What I have in mind is a Rawlsian, moderately egalitarian contractarian conception of justice congruent with our liberal democratic commitments. . . (Rawls, 1993). However, there are morally distinctive features of health care that require the articulation of a conception of "health care justice" (Fleck, 1989b). In this essay our goal is to articulate some considered judgments of just health care rationing.

Oregon sought to achieve two health policy objectives simultaneously: (1) expand access to needed health care for the uninsured, and (2) control health care costs for the state. . . . What is noteworthy is that these policies were justified by a very explicit appeal to moral principles. John Kitzhaber, physician-president

Journal of Medicine and Philosophy 19 (1994), 367–388 © Swets & Zeitlinger Publishers. Used with permission.

of the Oregon Senate, has listed eight publicly approved principles behind this legislation (Kitzhaber, 1990). The first of these required "universal access for the state's citizens to a basic level of health care" while the fourth asserted that it is "the obligation of society to provide sufficient resources to finance a basic level of care for those who cannot pay for it themselves" (Kitzhaber, 1990).

Note that it is not *equal access* to health care that Oregon feels morally obligated to guarantee to the poor and uninsured. For Oregon the poor and uninsured do not have a moral claim to a middle class standard of care, but to *basic care*. There are *limits* to society's obligation to assure access to needed health care because, according to Oregon's eighth principle, "allocations for health care must be part of a broader allocation policy which recognizes that health can only be maintained if investments in a number of related areas are balanced" (Kitzhaber, 1990). These include housing, education, and highways, all of which are important public goods, all of which have legitimate claims on public resources, but none of which have unlimited claims on these resources. Granting this, how can we determine fairly and rationally what will count as basic health care that must be guaranteed to all citizens?

Oregon's response to our question was that there was no perfectly objective, uniquely rational, or indisputably fair way of answering it. At bottom, however, this was a process question that would have to be resolved through open, democratic dialogue whose outcome would be shaped both by social value judgments and medical information. The goal of the dialogue would be a prioritization of health services, a ranking of 709 medical-condition/treatment pairs, from those that were most effective in addressing a given medical problem and yielding substantial benefit at a reasonable cost, to those that were marginally effective at best and yielded only small benefits at often unreasonable costs.

Though the public dialogue initially shaped this prioritization process, the ultimate responsibility for the final rankings fell to a Commission comprised of eleven individuals. Then the legislature chose a funding level. The legislature was barred from tinkering with the rankings. All the services above that line constituted the basic package of health services guaranteed to all citizens in Oregon; the services below the line would

not be funded. Morally speaking, services below the line did not represent futile or medically inappropriate or non-beneficial care. Rather, they represented marginally beneficial care, where the benefits were very uncertain or relatively small, especially in relationship to costs. This is health care rationing.

The well-known case of Coby Howard put a human face on the practice of rationing. Howard's death came about when it did and as it did because of a deliberate social choice not to fund bone marrow transplants. Middle class children in Oregon in the same medical circumstances as Coby did receive bone marrow transplants paid for by their parents' health insurance. Is it morally right that middle class children should have an opportunity for survival denied to poor *children*? . . .

II. THE INESCAPABILITY OF HEALTH CARE RATIONING

It is by now a truism that escalating health care costs are socially problematic. However, rising costs do not, of themselves, yield the conclusion that rationing is necessary, morally or politically, as a policy response. There are compelling reasons for resisting rationing as a cost containment strategy if there are other viable cost containment approaches. Rationing seems morally objectionable because: (1) needed, potentially beneficial health care is directly denied an identifiable individual; (2) the denial of these benefits is coercively imposed, not freely chosen; (3) the benefits that they are denied may be very substantial, such as life itself, and often irreplaceable and uncompensatable; (4) the individuals denied these benefits are sick and vulnerable; (5) the denial of benefits to individuals will appear to be arbitrary because the primary reason for the denial will be economic; (6) the ultimate source of the rationing decision disadvantaging this individual will be government, and government is supposed to protect equally the rights of all; and (7) the proximate source of the rationing decision will often be an individual's personal physician, ideally a loyal and uncompromised advocate for that individual.

The above paragraph represents the first premise in the anti-rationing argument. The second premise is that there are alternative ways of effectively controlling health costs that do not have the morally objectionable features associated with rationing. The unholy trinity of waste, fraud, and abuse are usually cited, and proposed remedies include: more effective utilization review (Angell, 1985), better technology assessment, banning self-referral by physicians (Rodwin, 1993), and reducing administrative waste (Himmelstein and Wool-handler, 1994). This list fairly represents premise two in the anti-rationing argument, which concludes that rationing is unnecessary given all these morally legitimate, barely tried alternatives to health care cost containment.

Note that critics of rationing construe the concept very narrowly. The most critical defining features seem to be that an identified individual is denied needed health care through a coercive government policy, and this seems to violate the social values of compassion and respect for individual liberty.

One implication of this narrow construal of rationing is that it will appear to be conceptually inappropriate to speak of "rationing by ability to pay." Markets distribute by ability to pay, but this seems to be done in a wholly impartial, mechanical manner that is wholly indifferent to the welfare of any identified individual. However, this is a dodge. One of the features of markets is that they do diffuse responsibility for bad outcomes, often creating the impression that these outcomes are a product of chance and the workings of specific markets. . . .

Angell (1985), Brown (1991) and Relman (1991a; 1991b) imagine that more rational and efficient overall management of health care system and the use of health services will result in cost containment without rationing. Health planning, technology assessment, utilization review and practice protocols are recommended to control health costs without the objectionable moral consequences associated with rationing. Yet all these cost containment methods will in various circumstances result in "preventable" deaths and harms. But these deaths and harms will be mixed so thoroughly with non-preventable, natural deaths and harms from assorted medical problems that they will all appear equally fated and equally unfortunate, whereas death or harm to someone like Coby Howard that is the product of an explicit rationing decision will appear to be uncaring and unjust and preventable. Is this in fact a morally correct judgment? I do not believe it is.

Implicit rationing is, first, a pervasive feature of our approaches to health care cost containment, and it is at least as morally problematic as Oregon's explicit approach to health care rationing. Second, that there are *identifiable* individuals who are the "victims" of health care rationing is morally and conceptually irrelevant. Here I disagree with Hadorn (1991b). What is concep-

tually essential to rationing is that someone makes a judgment regarding kinds of health care that are judged to be non-costworthy and marginally beneficial. Once that judgment is made there will always be individuals who will bear the consequences of that decision. Third, there is nothing intrinsically immoral about any rationing decision. The real moral question is whether a particular individual has a just claim to the health care that he will be denied. But, fourth, what is presumptively morally problematic about *implicit* forms of rationing is that all manner of arbitrary, discriminatory, and clearly unjust rationing decisions can be effectively hidden from moral scrutiny by anyone, including the individuals who are the victims of these choices. Hence, for its commitment to explicit rationing Oregon deserves moral commendation, not condemnation. Fifth, Oregon did make a moral mistake in the Coby Howard case, for it represented piecemeal, uncoordinated rationing, which will always be morally difficult to justify. Oregon's subsequent efforts at rationing and priority setting in a more comprehensive, rational, systematic fashion are immune to such criticism. But the many forms of implicit rationing that are pervasive features of most of our current approaches to health care cost containment continue to be morally objectionable because they are piecemeal and uncoordinated. This reflects our highly fragmented approach to health care financing, which both permits and encourages irresponsible cost-shifting. . . .

III. OREGON AND HEALTH CARE RATIONING: KEY MORAL LESSONS

We will draw eleven key moral lessons from Oregon's experience with health care rationing, explicate them, then respond to the moral criticisms directed at Oregon's efforts.

Lesson One: Rationing decisions made in a piecemeal, uncoordinated fashion are very likely to be arbitrary and unjust. Fair rationing decisions must be a product of comprehensive, systematic, rational deliberation. This is the main lesson of the Coby Howard case. Rationing decisions always imply trade-offs. Health resources will be denied to some health needs because there are other health needs that have a stronger just claim to those resources. When rationing is done systematically and explicitly, then we know what trade-offs we have endorsed, and those trade-offs are open to rational and moral assessment.

Lesson Two: Rationing decisions made publicly are open to critical assessment and correction, and are more likely to be just. Oregon was not the first state to permit the denial of life-sustaining medical care to a Medicaid patient. This is surely a routine occurrence in Medicaid programs and for patients who are without health insurance (Hadley, 1991; Lurie, 1984). But denials are effected subtly and are essentially hidden from the public scrutiny, as well as scrutiny by the patient himself which means there is ample opportunity for invidious discrimination.

Lesson Three: The whole process of health reform and health rationing must be guided by explicit moral considerations, such as health care justice, and only secondarily be economic or managerial or organizational considerations. There are thousands of children and adults like Coby Howard, whose lives are threatened by a deadly illness and whose lives could be prolonged if they had access to some expensive life-prolonging medical technology, such as a bone marrow transplant. Whether they have a just claim to that technology will not be settled by an economic equation or organizational theory or more clinical data. We need to address that issue directly as a moral problem. Further, allocational problems caused by advancing medical technology are not an oddity in our health care system; they are at the heart of twentieth-century technological medicine.

Lesson Four: Fair rationing decisions ought to be a product of informed democratic decisionmaking processes that include all who will be affected by the decision.

Lesson Five: If all who will be affected by rationing decisions have a fair opportunity to shape these decisions, then these rationing decisions will be freely self-imposed, which is an essential feature of just rationing decisions.

Lesson Six: Stable community membership over the course of a life is essential to preserving the fairness of the rationing process. Individuals cannot have the option of enjoying the benefits of health reform in a given community only to exit the community when the burdens of rationing fall upon them.

Lessons four through six comprise our "principle of community" for health care rationing. All of us as citizens must take responsibility for health reform; experts alone will not do. Expert knowledge is essential for intelligent rationing decisions, but expert knowledge is not a suitable replacement for public moral judgment and public moral responsibility for fair rationing judgments.

Moreover, rationing decisions are more likely to be fair if they are decisions that are self-imposed rather than being imposed by some (healthy individuals) on others (sick and vulnerable individuals). Note that for a liberal society embedded in this principle of community must be a principle of autonomy with respect to health care rationing: just rationing decisions must be freely self-imposed. These two principles must be inextricably linked with one another as a practical matter and as a moral matter. . . .

What the Oregon approach recognizes is that a budget for meeting health needs must be communally agreed to. As noted earlier, there is no perfectly objective way of identifying health needs because there are value considerations necessarily bound up with that determination, and because emerging medical technologies are constantly adding "new" health needs. This means there is no perfectly objective way of determining that communal health budget. That will require a balancing judgment that takes into account other important social needs. In a democratic society all should have the opportunity to participate in the making of that balancing judgment since all will be affected by the results of that judgment.

In order for such impartial circumstances to yield actually fair health priorities and rationing protocols all who have a voice in shaping those protocols and priorities must be ongoing members of that community so that all are more or less equally at risk of having to accept the burdens of rationing. . . .

Lesson Seven: Justice requires that there be limits that health care makes on total societal resources, and that these limits be expressed in the form of hard budgets. The moral virtue of hard budgets is that they make clear and visible the trade-offs that must be made among competing health needs.

Lesson Eight: Hard budgets give structure and coherence to a process of prioritizing health needs/services.

A process of prioritizing that is explicit, rationally determined, and freely agreed to protects fairness against special pleading.

Lesson Nine: Those who are least well off healthwise have presumptively stronger moral claims to needed health resources so long as they are able to benefit sufficiently from those resources, and so long as their health needs are fairly judged as being of sufficiently high priority from the larger social perspective embodied in the prioritization process. No individual has a right to unlimited health care; and no individual has a moral right to have their health needs met at the expense of the more just (higher priority) health claims of others.

Lesson Ten: Physicians are more likely to protect their own moral integrity as loyal advocates of their patients' best interests and as fair rationers of societal resources if they make their rationing decisions within the framework of a fixed global budget and a system of health priorities that have been freely agreed to by all who are part of that health care system. This is the perspective that allows physicians to be just and compassionate to patients over the course of their life.

Lesson Eleven: Equity and efficiency must be achieved together. We will not have fair or effective or affordable or stable health reform if we attempt to maximize either of these social values at the expense of the other.

Oregon is less than a perfect exemplar of the moral lessons regarding just health care rationing sketched above. The most frequently voiced criticism of Oregon is that the poor were exploited to achieve health reform. That is, Oregon committed itself to achieving nearly universal access to health care and hoped to pay for it by imposing a rationing system on the poor, that is, those who were least well off. The objective was clearly laudable, but the means to the objective were unjust (Daniels, 1991, p. 2232). I have defended Oregon on this point at some length (Fleck, 1990c). I argue that this policy choice must be assessed from the perspective of non-ideal justice. More precisely, Oregon can justifiably argue that the poor as a class are better off under the reform proposal than they are under the current Medicaid program, which covers only 58% of the poor. All the poor can now be assured access to a basic package of health services. It is also morally relevant that rational poor persons, suitably informed, would autonomously choose this reform package over the current Medicaid program.

Daniels readily concedes that Oregon has achieved a more equitable health care system. However, he adds that "even greater reductions in inequality are possible if other groups sacrifice instead of Medicaid recipients. It is unfair for current Medicaid recipients to bear a burden that others could bear much better, especially since inequality would then be even further reduced" (1991, pp. 2232–33). Better-off Oregonians, for example, could pay more taxes in support of the Medicaid program. Indeed, an actual attempt was made to cover all state employees with the same benefit package and rationing protocols as the Medicaid population, but that measure was soundly defeated in the state legislature. Morally, this outcome is bothersome. Moreover, it is not consistent with the principle of community discussed above, since it appears that the healthy and powerful are imposing rationing protocols on the sick and poor, who are not in a fair bargaining position. . . .

IV. JUSTICE, RATIONING, AND DEMOCRATIC DELIBERATION

We now turn to a consideration of rational democratic deliberation as an approach to health care rationing. There are two criticisms of this process I will address. First, the poor were not fairly represented in the democratic forums in Oregon integral to priority-setting and were the ones who ended up having to bear the risks and burdens of rationing. Prima facie, this looks like a morally insensitive middle class majority imposing its will on the politically weak, sick poor.

This first criticism can be addressed if the following conditions are met: (1) We must all belong to one or another Accountable Health Plan. . . . Alternatively, we must all belong to the same single-payer health care system, where "all belong" means that there is no potentially morally objectionable sorting of individuals according to socio-economic status or health status. (2) Belonging to the plan must mean that there is a single health budget to purchase all health services for plan members. (3) We must know the budget cannot cover all likely demands for health services. (4) We must limit demands on the budget through a priority-setting process and mutually agreed upon rationing protocols that apply equally to all members of the plan. (5) We must be largely ignorant of our future health care needs, which is largely true for most of us most of the time. If these conditions are met, then the likelihood is that the rationing protocols and health priorities that emerge from a rationally informed process of democratic deliberation will be "just enough" or "fair enough." This is to concede that there will be future individuals who will die "prematurely" because they will have been denied the only medical intervention that promised them some additional opportunity for prolonged life for no better reason than that it was the informed and impartial judgment of the community that the benefits promised by these interventions were too small, too costly, and too uncertain. The essential fairness of the process is secure because any member of that community, given the right circumstances, could be the individual denied particular interventions.

A second critical objection is the democracy problem (Daniels, 1993). Democracy is about respecting expressed preferences. Daniels points out that Oregonians in community meetings were very concerned about assured access to family planning services. As a result vasectomies were rated more highly in the priority setting process than hip replacements for the elderly. Daniels asks whether we must abide by whatever the democratic process yields? If we see this as a matter of pure procedural justice, then there is no correcting of results that seem counter-intuitive. But if it can be corrected by an appeal to some prior notion of what counts as a fair rationing outcome, then we might wonder what the point of the democratic process is.

Yet another rationing problem is the "fair chances/ best outcome" problem (Daniels, 1993, p. 225), which I see as related to the democracy problem. Daniels borrows the following example from Frances Kamm (1989). Alice and Betty are both in need of a liver transplant; both are the same age and have waited the same period of time for a transplant; both will be dead in a week without the transplant. With the transplant Alice will live only two years while Betty will live twenty. Who should get the transplant? We get the best outcome, maximum number of quality-adjusted life years saved, by saving Betty. But Alice wants a lottery, in effect arguing that each has an equal right to life, however long the rest of their life might be. Both have reasonable and morally compelling considerations on their side. Oregon's democratic deliberations favored the net benefit approach. The critical issue is whether Alice has a moral right to be aggrieved as this result.

Has she been harmed in a morally significant sense, and does this undermine the moral authority of the democratic deliberative process for yielding just results?

In responding I want to sketch a somewhat idealized version of just rational democratic deliberation. We begin with the assumption that no matter how fine-grained a conception of health care justice we develop, it will never be fine-grained enough to generate a uniquely correct complete set of just rationing protocols. There are innumerable reasonable, morally permissible trade-offs that might be made in articulating some set of rationing protocols. I will refer to this moral space as "the domain of the just democratic decisionmaking." Again, within this space we have no reason to believe that we could identify something that could justifiably be called the "most just" set of rationing protocols possible for our society. Many possible trade-off patterns will be "just enough," all things considered, especially when we recall that there are other values besides justice that are a legitimate part of the overall moral equation.

There are two critical conditions that elicit and justify the need for a democratic deliberative process of decisionmaking. The first is that we cannot simply allow individual liberty to resolve this particular rationing decision. For if we did allow medical or administrative or consumer discretion to be ultimately determinative, the result would be the potential for arbitrary or discriminatory results that would be unjust. . . .

Our second condition for appealing to the rational democratic deliberative process is that there are these plural choice possibilities, all of which have prima facie moral and political legitimacy, but none of which are unequivocally superior from a moral, political, or rational perspective. This is the situation we are faced with regard to Alice and Betty. A good case can be made for going with a decision rule that might favor a lottery in this situation, or going with net benefits. There are any number of very complex decisions rules we might adopt, especially if we vary morally relevant case facts, such as the ages of the individuals, the gap between likelihood of survival for each, morally permissible quality of life consideration, and so on. What is morally important is that whatever decision rule we adopt through the democratic deliberative process is one that is applied consistently over time to all members of that society/health plan. So long as that decision rule is in place and was, in fact, approved by both Alice and Betty (or their democratic representatives) at some prior point in time when they did not know that their future medical circumstances, neither one will have just cause for moral complaint, no matter what the outcome. Again, one of the other assumptions we have to work with is that individual participants in this democratic process are ongoing members of this community so that the trade-offs they agree to, some specific distribution of benefits and burdens, or benefits and risks, is a distribution that they are imposing on themselves. That is, in many cases of rationing, say, with reference to the health care needs of the elderly (our future elderly selves), the distribution of benefits and burdens do not occur simultaneously with respect to any individual. It would clearly be unfair for a younger individual to derive the benefits of rationing health care for the elderly, then have the option of exiting that health plan as an older person to escape the risks/burdens of rationing for the elderly.

Two other large points must be made with respect to understanding the moral and political legitimacy of rational democratic decisionmaking. The first is that this "democratic space" should be thought of as being bounded and structured by principles of health care justice. These principles have emerged and will emerge through the same process of moral discourse that has generated medical ethics as we know it today. These principles should be thought of as having a status akin to constitutional principles, which is to say that any proposed rationing protocol that violated one of these principles would have to be rejected.

Among such principles, I would include: (1) a Publicity Principle, aimed at eliminating invisible rationing; (2) a Fair Equality of Opportunity Principle; (3) an Equality Principle, the intent of which is to assure each citizen equal moral consideration; (4) an Autonomy Principle: (5) a Just Maximizing Principle; (6) Need-Identification Principles, to distinguish health needs from health preferences; (7) Priority-Setting Principles; and (8) a Neutrality Principle aimed at protecting the liberal character of our society with respect to choosing health services in our benefit package. . . .

In concluding, Oregon failed to meet important requirements of just democratic decisionmaking. But it was an instructive failure. Oregon should not be thought of as being morally culpable for its failures; we however, would be morally culpable if we failed to learn the lessons of Oregon.

REFERENCES

Aaron, H.: 1992, 'The Oregon experiment', in *Rationing America's Medical Care: The Oregon Plan and Beyond,* M. Strosberg *et al.* (eds.), The Brookings Institution, Washington, D.C., pp. 107–11.

Angell, M.: 1985, 'Cost containment and the physician', *Journal of the American Medical Association* 254, 1203–07.

Brown, L.: 1991, 'The national politics of Oregon's rationing plan', *Health Affairs* 10 (Summer), 28–51.

Daniels, N.: 1991, 'Is the Oregon rationing plan fair?' *Journal of the American Medical Association* 265, 2232–35.

Daniels, N.: 1993, 'Rationing fairly: programmatic considerations', *Bioethics 7,* 224–33.

Fleck, L. M.: 1990c, 'The Oregon medicaid experiment: is it just enough?', *Business and Professional Ethics Journal 9* (Fall) 201–17.

Hadley, J. *et al.*: 1991, 'Comparison of uninsured and privately insured hospital patients: condition on admission, resource use, and outcome', *Journal of the American Medical Association* 265, 274–78.

Hadorn, D. C.: 1991a, 'Oregon priority-seeting exercise: quality of life and public policy', *The Hastings Center Report* 19 (May/June), S11–16.

Hadorn, D. C.: 1991b, 'Setting health care priorities in Oregon: cost-effectiveness meets the rule of rescue', *Journal of the American Medical Association* 265, 2218–25.

Himmelstein, D. U. and Woolhandler, S.: 1994, *The National Health Program Book: A Source Guide for Advocates,* Common Courage Press, Monroe, Maine.

Kamm, F.: 1993, *Morality, Mortality: Death and Whom to Save From It,* Volume 1, Oxford University Press, Oxford, England.

Kitzhaber, J.: 1990, 'Rationing health care: the Oregon model', *The Center Report,* The Center for Public Policy and contemporary Issues (Denver) 2 (Winter), 3–4.

Lurie, N. *et al.*: 1984, 'Termination from Medi-Cal—does it affect health?', *The New England Journal of Medicine* 311, 480–84.

Oregon Health Services Commission: 1991, *Prioritization of Health Services: A Report to the Governor and the Legislature,* Salem, Oregon.

Rawls, J.: 1993, *Political Liberalism,* Columbia University Press, New York.

Relman, A.: 1991a, 'Is rationing inevitable?', *The New England Journal of Medicine* 322, 1809–10.

Relman, A.: 1991b, 'The trouble with rationing', *The New England Journal of Medicine* 323, 911–12.

Rodwin, M.: 1993, *Money, Medicine, and Morals,* Oxford University Press, Oxford, England.

DAN W. BROCK

Justice and the ADA: Does Prioritizing and Rationing Health Care Discriminate against the Disabled?

INTRODUCTION: HEALTH-CARE RATIONING IN OREGON

. . . The Oregon reform plan is intended to respond to the two central issues of health-care reform generally in the United States—controlling the growth of health-care costs and extending access to health care to all citizens. In public policy debates about how to achieve these goals, it has been increasingly recognized that we cannot provide all beneficial care to everyone, without regard to how great the costs and how small the benefits of particular services. (This is not to say, however, that supporters of health-care reform plans will readily and publicly acknowledge that their plans will limit or ration health care.) It is not economically rational to ignore the opportunity costs of providing low-benefit/high-cost health care when there are higher-benefit uses to which resources devoted to that care could be put. It is also unjust to expend resources in health care without regard to the costs of the benefits produced when the result is overutilization of health care and an inability to meet fully other public responsibilities required by justice, such as the education of children.

Typical measures in the past to limit the growth of costs in the Medicaid program, the principal public program to extend access to health care to the poor in the United States, have included tightening eligibility requirements to the point where now well over one half of the people living below the federal poverty level nationwide are ineligible for Medicaid on income grounds. Those still covered by Medicaid are eligible at least in theory, for a relatively generous package of benefits, although it often remains difficult in practice to secure

services because of the program's very low levels of reimbursement to health-care providers. In 1989, the state of Oregon proposed to make a more rational and fair use of limited resources devoted to health care for the poor by bringing everyone in the state living below the federal poverty level into its Medicaid program; the income eligibility level for Medicaid in Oregon was then approximately 60 percent of the federal poverty level. To make this extension of benefits possible within resource constraints, Oregon's program would also explicitly limit the services that would be covered and reimbursed by Medicaid. Instead of "rationing people" in or out of the program, Oregon proposed to bring in all citizens living below the poverty level and to "ration services" by providing the same health-care services to all participants.

The Oregon Basic Health Services Act of 1989 established the Oregon Health Services Commission (OHSC), charged with prioritizing all forms of health-care services. . . . Oregon largely abandoned a cost-benefit analysis and prioritization of different services in favor of a relative-benefit analysis and prioritization.

To perform this prioritization required two distinct steps. First, an expected outcome for a patient had to be associated with each treatment/condition pair; this was an empirical determination which would ideally rest on outcome studies and data, although the OHSC found that the necessary data often either did not exist or were extremely limited. Second, a relative value had to be assigned to the different expected outcomes; this was an evaluative determination, and was done largely on the basis of telephone surveys of a random selection of Oregon citizens. Adapting the Quality of Well-Being Scale (QWB) developed by Robert Kaplan and John Anderson, citizens were asked how much particular

Social Philosophy and Policy 12 (1995), 159–185. Copyright © 1995. Reprinted by permission of Cambridge University Press.

impairments of health or quality of life — described in terms of "physical or emotional symptoms and of different degrees of impairment in mobility, physical activity, and social activity" — would reduce quality of life (the citizens polled did not themselves have the impairments they were asked about).[1] This enabled the OHSC to assign a relative value to different outcome states of treatments, and then to calculate the net benefit for each of 709 treatment/condition pairs. The OHSC then made further "by hand" adjustments of the resultant ranking where its members believed the ranking reflected mistakes from inadequate data about outcomes, or from other sources. It was this ranking of treatment/condition pairs, based on their expected benefits and reflecting the valuations of outcomes obtained from Oregon citizens in the telephone poll, that Oregon used in applying to the Health Care Financing Administration (HCFA), the federal agency that administers the Medicaid program, for waivers of certain federal Medicaid requirements — waivers that were necessary for Oregon to put its new program into effect.

I take the Oregon prioritization to be a paradigmatic attempt to make more rational use of health-care resources in the face of explicit acknowledgment of resource scarcity. The QWB scale is one among a number of measures that have been developed by health-policy analysts for making comparative assessments of the benefits of different health-care services and programs; another is quality-adjusted life years (QALYs), a measure of the number of years of life extension, adjusted for differences in the quality of life of those years, provided by different health-care services or programs.[2] While the various measures differ in detail, my concern here is with the central feature they all share — recognition that the relative benefits of health-care services can be assessed in terms of their effects in extending patients' lives and improving or protecting the quality of their lives or their well-being. These measures also make explicit at the policy level an often implicit notion of "medical need" — a notion that physicians use at the clinical level when they make rough assessments of the relative importance of patients' needs for health-care services based on the degree of gain in length and quality of life that specific services are expected to provide. Thus, both at the level of health policy and at the level of clinical medicine, when health-care services must be prioritized, it is typically assumed that the prioritization should be in terms of their relative benefits to patients (I set aside, for now, the relevance of costs).

Virtually all prominent proposals for national health-care reform in the United States seek to rein in the growth of health-care costs without explicit rationing of care, which is considered by most political analysts to be so controversial that it must be avoided, in name if not in fact. Unlike these national reform plans, the Oregon plan is the most explicit, and certainly the most widely publicized, program in the United States to openly prioritize and ration health-care services; as a result, from the time when it was initially proposed, the Oregon plan has drawn much attention and criticism.[3] Probably the most common criticism has been that the plan is a case of "us" rationing "them" — that is, of middle- and upper-class Oregonians placing limits on the health-care services available to the poor, limits the middle and upper classes do not and likely would not accept for themselves. This is a serious criticism, although its force has been mitigated to a degree by the intent of the plan's proponents ultimately to bring nearly all Oregonians under the same benefit package and limits in the future. This issue did not figure into the Bush administration's response to Oregon's waiver request, however, and it will not be my concern here.

Instead, then Secretary of Health and Human Services Louis Sullivan surprised most who were following the fate of the Oregon plan by denying the waiver request in 1992 on the ground that the plan was in violation of the Americans with Disabilities Act (ADA) because it would unjustly and illegally discriminate against disabled and handicapped persons.[4] The ADA went into effect as federal law in 1990 to "establish a clear and comprehensive prohibition of discrimination on the basis of disability."[5] This act includes separate titles prohibiting discrimination on the basis of disability in employment, public services, transportation, and public accommodations. Since it prohibits discrimination on the basis of disability in both public and private services programs, in health care "it applies to programs provided by the government, benefits provided by employers, and services provided by physicians."[6] The precise legal implications for the Oregon plan (as well as for other forms of health-care prioritizing and rationing) of the ADA and other legislation protecting disabled persons are both complex and controversial, and I shall not explore them here. My concern will be with the moral issues. . . . I shall argue that there are serious (and surprisingly complex and controversial) issues of moral and political philosophy, and specifically of justice, underlying this challenge to Oregon's priority setting and to health-care rationing more generally. What is at stake are the broad issues with which I began this essay, issues regarding what treatment disabled persons are due on ground of justice, and more specifically, how they should be treated in the prioritization of claims on scarce resources in public programs. I shall identify three more-general problems of justice that are part of the specific issue of justice to the disabled: first, the conflict between maximizing benefits and ensuring fair chances; second, the problem of compensation for handicaps; third, what I call the perspective problem—whether we should use the perspective of a nondisabled person or a disabled person in evaluating the quality of life of disabled persons for purposes of resource allocation. . . .

[M]y concern will be with the methodology and raking Oregon initially submitted to the Department of Health and Human Services, a ranking which prioritized services on the basis of their relative effects on length and quality of life. It is this methodology which allows us to pose most sharply the question of whether a relative-benefit, or cost-benefit, prioritization and rationing of health-care services wrongly discriminates against persons with disabilities. . . .

DO DISADVANTAGES OF THE DISABLED IN PRIORITIZING HEALTH CARE CONSTITUTE UNJUST DISCRIMINATION?

How did Oregon avoid the conflict with the ADA in order to secure the federal waivers needed under Medicaid law? Recall that Oregon, quite plausibly, prioritized not treatments, but treatment/condition pairs. A particular treatment can appear more than once on the list of prioritized services, because when given to patients in significantly different conditions it can have substantially different expected benefits. One example in the original list of 709 treatment/condition pairs that attracted the attention of disability-rights organizations, and was specifically criticized by Health and Human Services Secretary Sullivan in his initial denial of Oregon's request for Medicaid wavers, is the medical treatment of low-birth-weight newborns. The secretary specifically noted that ranking at number twenty-two the treatment of newborns over twenty-three weeks gestation, while ranking next to last at number 708 the treatment of newborns under twenty-three weeks gestation, raised concerns under the ADA. His

letter did not make the precise nature of the concern clear, but it appears to be that differentiation in the ranking between otherwise similar patients, either on the basis of a disabling condition or on the basis of a likely resultant disability from treatment, would violate the ADA. Oregon's apparently ad hoc response was to combine treatment of all premature newborns with birth-weights below twenty-five hundred grams; this new combined category received a ranking of number forty, presumably reflecting the much larger number of newborns between five hundred and twenty-five hundred grams (most of whom will have good outcomes) than below five hundred grams (nearly all of whom will have very poor outcomes).

Although this new combined category removed the putative discrimination on grounds of disability to which the secretary had objected, it is important to understand that combining the two groups of premature newborns was flatly in conflict with Oregon's methodology of ranking treatments in terms of their benefits for patients in particular conditions. What that methodology requires, and what Oregon did at other places in its ranking, was to *differentiate,* not *combine,* treatment/condition pairs when the same treatment produces substantially different overall benefits for patients in different conditions. The separation of newborns under and over twenty-three weeks gestation in the earlier ranking was the result of correctly following that methodology. More generally, in any of the kinds of cases that I have discussed, in which the presence of a disability pre- or post-treatment causes an important reduction in the benefits provided to the patient by that treatment, the methodology in principle requires separation into more than one treatment/condition pair, with the resulting disadvantage to patients with the disability. The methodology will frequently be in conflict with the ADA so long as the ADA is understood as barring appeal to "quality of life" and "ability to function," which, Secretary Sullivan indicated, "place importance on 'restored' health and functional 'independence' and thus expressly value a person without a disability more highly than a person with a disability in the allocation of medical treatment."[7]

In two of the most detailed and explicit defenses of Oregon's plan against the charge that it wrongly discriminates against people with disabilities, David Hadorn and Paul Menzel both acknowledge that using quality of life and ability to function to evaluate treatment outcomes does sometimes disadvantage persons with disabilities, but they argue in effect that we must accept that result as the cost of a rational priority-setting process. . . . The Oregon methodology of prioritizing by relative benefit is incompatible with a prohibition on giving weight to quality of life and ability to function in assessing the relative benefits of treatment outcomes. Moreover, if the methodology is openly employed at the policy level in prioritizing health-care services, it will be difficult at the clinical level to convince physicians that they should not take similar account of quality of life and ability to function in recommendations about treatment for individual patients, with the result that patients with disabilities do not receive treatments that do go to nondisabled patients.

Menzel, too, bites the bullet in accepting that priority setting cannot avoid disadvantaging the disabled:

Quality of life considerations as well as likelihood of medical success sometimes do get associated with disabilities (though not *only* with disabilities). Such considerations must not be seen as biased against persons with disabilities just because they catch disabilities in their net. They ought to be regarded as inconsistent with the ADA only if we would reject them as legitimate considerations at all were they not sometimes to deny care to persons with disabilities. This is a tough distinction for many to accept, for it means that even with the ADA, particular disabled individuals will end up disadvantaged. It is, however, a distinction utterly essential to maintain if we are going to have any significant rationing at all. . . . Rationing that considers quality of life must be allowed to go forward even if at times it happens to disadvantage persons with disabilities. Indeed, it is questionable whether we could ever devise a system of priority setting that was not informed in some measure by assessments of quality of life.[8]

In this view, quality-of-life considerations are inconsistent with the ADA only if we would systematically reject them, quite apart from their sometimes resulting in disadvantages to disabled persons. Menzel is correct, I believe, when he says that the conflict between rational prioritizing by relative benefit and disadvantaging the disabled is ineliminable. Such prioritizing does seem to place less value on the lives of the disabled, and on some treatments provided to disabled patients as opposed to otherwise similar nondisabled patients.

A measure of benefits like QALYs will, in certain cases, favor a nondisabled person over an otherwise similar disabled person. But perhaps it does not follow from this that the use of that measure unjustly devalues disabled people's lives, despite the disadvantage the disabled are placed at by this method of prioritizing. Perhaps this disadvantage no more unjustly devalues

the lives of, or discriminates against, the disabled than giving a scarce intensive-care-unit bed to a more critically ill patient, rather than to another patient who can be managed with less risk without intensive care, discriminates against the less ill patient. Giving preference in circumstances of scarcity to patients for whom treatment will do the most good or prevent the greatest harm does not imply that the person who is thereby favored is judged of greater value, or that the patient who is not favored has been the subject of unjust discrimination.

This defense of relative-benefit prioritizing seems least convincing in the case of life-sustaining treatment. Though it is the lesser benefit from treatment, not an explicit judgment that disabled people and their lives are of less value, that is the basis for the priority, it is precisely the lower quality of the disabled person's life (which is produced by his disability) that makes the life-sustaining treatment for him less beneficial. A significantly disabled life is life of fewer QALYs, other things being equal, than a nondisabled person's life. Moreover, this is not an implication only of the QALY measure, since no plausible measure of treatment benefits could entirely ignore effects on quality of life. This prioritization does seem to imply that it is a less good outcome if the disabled person survives than if the nondisabled person survives, because the disabled person has a less good life. . . .

THE PERSPECTIVE PROBLEM — NORMAL OR DISABLED?

. . . It is unclear to what extent Oregon's prioritized list was affected by this difference in evaluations of the quality of life of disabled persons, but that is not my concern here. Rather, my question is how we should resolve this issue of perspective for the purpose of priority setting. . . .

The deeper theoretical . . . problem concerns determining the correct evaluative standpoint for estimating the effect of a particular disability on quality of life. Here is the problem as I see it. Assume that both the nondisabled person and the disabled person have the same correct beliefs about what differences in functional capacities exist between a nondisabled person and, say, a person who is unable to walk, and assume as well that the result noted by Secretary Sullivan still obtains — "as compared to persons who have the disabilities in question, persons without disabilities systematically undervalue the quality of life of those with disabilities." The question then is what degree of reduction in quality of life the disability creates. Why should there be any difference in the perspectives of nondisabled and disabled persons on quality of life with a disability, once any stereotypes and false beliefs have been removed? The nondisabled person is being asked to evaluate the degree to which he believes his quality of life would be reduced by the disability. The natural way to do so is by estimating the degree to which his ability successfully to pursue his aims, ends, and activities, or to carry out his plan of life, would be decreased by having the disability. Why would this evaluation by a nondisabled person be different from that of the person who actually has the disability?

A disabled person will likely have adjusted his plan of life to accommodate his disability in two respects. First, he will have given up the aims and activities that are not much more difficult or impossible as a result of his disability, and substituted new aims that he can now achieve, but that he would likely have considered less valuable before becoming disabled. As a result of this change in his life-plan and values, the degree to which he successfully achieves his aims will likely be higher than the nondisabled person *correctly* judges his would be if he were disabled but still retained his original life-plan and values. The second accommodation of the disabled person to his condition is in his subjective satisfaction or happiness with his life. Individuals who suffer serious disability often come to accept their limitations in function in a way that makes possible a higher level of satisfaction or happiness than the nondisabled person correctly expects that he would have, given his current aims and expectations, if he suffered that same disability. In the extreme case of complete accommodation to the disability, disabled persons may have sufficiently changed their aims and values so as to have as high a degree of success (or even higher) in pursuing their new aims as they had with their old aims before becoming disabled, and to have as high a level of satisfaction or happiness (or even higher) as they had before becoming disabled. Should we then say that the disability has produced no reduction in their quality of life? What is the correct value of the quality of life with the disability?

Two points needed underlining. The nondisabled person is correct about how his quality of life would decline judged from his current aims and values. The

disabled person is also correct that his quality of life is not less, judged from his current aims and values, which he has adapted to accommodate his disability. The standpoint of the nondisabled person seems correct for the evaluation of how bad it would be for him to become disabled, and thus for determining the value of health care that protects against that disability, or restores function after he has been disabled but before he has adjusted to his new condition. On the other hand, the perspective of the disabled person seems correct, for example, about the evaluation of treatment that preserves his life, or about the increase in quality of life that restoring him to normal function would bring about. The two different standpoints yield conflicting evaluations of the quality of life with a given disability, whereas either a relative-benefit or cost-benefit methodology for prioritizing treatments requires that a determinate value be assigned to the quality of life with a given limitation in function. . . .

Another related aspect of the complexity of the perspective problem is the degree to which quality of life in various impaired states should be evaluated on objective or subjective grounds. By "objective grounds," I have in mind here the degree to which normal human function is in fact impaired by disease. An objective evaluation requires the specification of a range of normal human functions, giving a rough weighting to the different functions according to their role and importance in carrying out normal human life-plans, and from this constructing a scale or measure of overall functional capacity. Some such objective evaluation of functional capacity will be appropriate, for example, if we want to measure the degree of opportunity, or impairment of opportunity, an individual has in pursuing a normal range of life-plans in her society.

By "subjective grounds," I have in mind the degree to which a particular individual's quality of life or well-being is impaired by disease. Subjective grounds will differ from objective grounds in at least two respects. First, the degree to which disease impairs an individual's quality of life — and, in turn, the degree of benefit from treatment that prevents that disease and impairment — should be measured principally in terms of the effects of the disease and treatment on that particular individual's pursuit of her own specific life-plan. The standard is the particular individual's life-plan, not a general range of normal human life-plans. Second, a part of an individual's quality of life or well-being is the subjective satisfaction or happiness she has with how well the pursuit of her life-plan is going. An individual's subjective satisfaction or happiness is to some degree independent of her success in pursing her aims, and thus neither of these subjective grounds of quality of life can serve as a surrogate for the other. Because of this partial independence, the relative weight to be given to these two subjective grounds in overall quality-of-life judgments is important, but also ethically controversial. Some appeal to these subjective grounds seems unavoidable if we are concerned with the relative benefits of medical treatments on the quality of life of the individuals who receive the treatments. It is unavoidable as well if we are to take account of the different impacts that particular health-care services can have on the lives of nondisabled and disabled persons. And it is the use of these subjective grounds which gives rise to what I have called the perspective problem. . . .

CONCLUSION

Both in health policy and in the clinical care of patients, we have been able largely to ignore the issues about justice and the disabled that I have discussed in this essay, because we have clung to the illusions that we neither do nor should limit access to beneficial care, and that prioritizing care is therefore unnecessary. Instead, both physicians and third-party payers have generally used a standard of "medical necessity" and accepted that all medically necessary care should be provided and funded. Very roughly, "medically necessary care" has been understood to be any and all care that makes a significant contribution to the effective treatment of a patient's disease, but with little if any regard to its cost. Cost-effectiveness has generally entered in only when the same or comparable benefits could be obtained with less costly means. Under this standard of medical necessity, the additional medical needs of disabled persons should receive all effective treatment, without regard to whether there are more beneficial uses of resources for nondisabled as well as disabled persons either within or outside the area of health care. The illusion in the United States that it is possible to provide to everyone all beneficial care, no matter how small the benefit and how high the cost, will continue to erode as the health-care system is transformed by both private and governmental efforts to control costs. All health-care systems always have and always will confront resource limits. Open, fair, and accountable prioritization in the use of health-care resources is desirable to the extent that it contributes to

creating a health-care system that is more economically rational and more just. That prioritization will force us to confront the issues I have discussed here, and others, in order to clarify our moral responsibilities to disabled persons; and we have seen that these issues concerning the disabled turn out to raise deep and difficult, more general issues about just health-care prioritizing and rationing.[9]

NOTES

1. Robert Kaplan and John Anderson, "A General Health Policy Model: Update and Applications," *Health Services Research,* vol. 23 (1988), pp. 203–35.

2. See Dan W. Brock, "Quality of Life Measures in Health Care and Medical Ethics," in *The Quality of Life,* ed. A. Sen and M. Nussbaum (Oxford: Oxford University Press, 1993).

3. Norman Daniels, "Is the Oregon Rationing Plan Fair?" *Journal of the American Medical Association,* vol. 265 (1991), pp. 2232–35.

4. Unpublished letter from Secretary of Health and Human Services Louis W. Sullivan to Governor Barbara Roberts of Oregon, August 3, 1992.

5. Public Law 101–336, July 26, 1990, 104 Stat. 327, 42 USC 12101–12213, 47 USC 225 and 611.

6. David Orentlicher, "Rationing and the Americans with Disabilities Act," *Journal of the American Medical Association,* vol. 271 (1994), pp. 308–14. Orentlicher provides a comprehensive legal analysis of the likely application of the ADA (and other legislation protecting the disabled) to a variety of forms of health-care rationing.

7. Sullivan, unpublished letter.

8. Paul T. Menzel, "Oregon's Denial: Disabilities and Quality of Life," *Hastings Center Report,* vol. 22, no. 6 (1992), pp. 21–25.

9. See Norman Daniels, "Rationing Fairly: Programmatic Considerations," *Bioethics,* vol. 7, nos. 2 and 3 (1993), pp. 224–33; and Dan W. Brock, "Some Unresolved Issues in Priority-Setting of Mental Health Services," in *What Price Mental Health? The Ethics and Politics of Setting Priorities,* ed. P. Boyle (Washington, DC: Georgetown University Press, 1995).

SUGGESTED READINGS

Benatar, Solomon R. "Health Care Reform in the New South Africa." *New England Journal of Medicine* 336 (March 20, 1997), 891–95.

Binstock, Robert H., and Post, Stephen G., eds. *Too Old for Health Care?: Controversies in Medicine, Law, Economics, and Ethics.* Baltimore: Johns Hopkins University Press, 1991, 92–119.

Blank, Robert. *Rationing Medicine.* New York: Columbia University Press, 1988.

Bole, Thomas J., and Bondeson, William B., eds. *Rights to Health Care.* Boston: Kluwer Academic Publishers, 1991.

Brock, Dan W. "Justice, Health Care, and the Elderly." *Philosophy & Public Affairs* 18 (1989), 297–312.

Buchanan, Allen. "Health-Care Delivery and Resource Allocation." In Veatch, Robert M., ed. *Medical Ethics,* 2d ed. Boston: Jones and Bartlett, 1997, 321–61.

Callahan, Daniel. *Setting Limits: Medical Goals in an Aging Society.* New York: Simon & Schuster, 1987.

———. "Rationing Medical Progress: The Way to Affordable Health Care." *New England Journal of Medicine* 322 (June 21, 1990), 1810–13.

———. *What Kind of Life: The Limits of Medical Progress.* New York: Simon & Schuster, 1990.

Capron, Alexander Morgan. "Oregon's Disability: Principles or Politics?" *Hastings Center Report* 22 (November-December 1992), 18–20.

Cassel, Christine K., and Purtilo, Ruth B. "Justice and the Allocation of Health Care Resources." In Cassel, Christine K., et al., eds. *Geriatric Medicine.* 2d ed. New York: Springer-Verlag, 1990, 615–22.

Churchill, Larry M. *Self-Interest and Universal Health Care: Why Well-Insured Americans Should Support Coverage for Everyone.* Cambridge, MA: Harvard University Press, 1994.

Daniels, Norman. *Am I My Parent's Keeper? An Essay on Justice Between the Young and the Old.* New York: Oxford University Press, 1988.

Daniels, Norman; Light, Donald W.; and Caplan, Ronald L. *Benchmarks of Fairness for Health Care Reform.* New York: Oxford University Press, 1996.

Daniels, Norman. "Insurability and the HIV Epidemic: Ethical Issues in Underwriting." *Milbank Quarterly* 68 (1990), 497–525.

———. *Just Health Care.* New York: Cambridge University Press, 1985.

———. "National Health-Care Reform." In Veatch, Robert M., ed. *Medical Ethics.* Boston: Jones and Bartlett, 1997, 415–41.

———. *Seeking Fair Treatment: From the AIDS Epidemic to National Health Care Reform.* New York: Oxford University Press, 1995.

DeGrazia, David. "Why the United States Should Adopt a Single-Payer System of Health Care Finance." *Kennedy Institute of Ethics Journal* 6 (1996), 145–60.

Dougherty, Charles J. "And Still the Only Advanced Nation With Universal Health Coverage." *Hastings Center Report* 27 (Jul.-Aug. 1997), 39–41.

———. *Back to Reform: Values, Markets, and the Health Care System.* New York: Oxford University Press, 1996.

———. "Setting Health Care Priorities: Oregon's Next Steps." *Hastings Center Report* 21 (May-June 1991), S1–S10.

Eddy, David M. "The Individual vs. Society: Resolving the Conflict." *Journal of the American Medical Association* 265 (May 8, 1991), 2399–2401, 2405–06.

Emanuel, Ezekiel J. *The Ends of Human Life: Medical Ethics in a Liberal Polity.* Cambridge, MA: Harvard University Press, 1991.

———. and Emanuel, Linda L. "Preserving Community in Health Care." *Journal of Health Politics, Policy, and Law* 22 (1997), 147–84.

Engelhardt, H. Tristram. "Freedom and Moral Diversity: The Moral Failures of Health Care in the Welfare State." *Social Philosophy & Policy* 14 (1997), 180–96.

Fleck, Leonard M. "Justice, HMOs, and the Invisible Rationing of Health Care Resources." *Bioethics* 4 (1990), 97–120.

Garland, Michael J. "Justice, Politics, and Community: Expanding Access and Rationing Health Services in Oregon." *Law, Medicine and Health Care* 20 (1992), 67–81.

———. "Oregon's Contribution to Defining Adequate Health Care." In Audrey R. Chapman, ed., *Health Care Reform: A Human Rights Approach.* Washington: Georgetown University Press, 1994, 211–32.

Goold, Susan D. "Allocating Health Care: Cost-Utility Analysis, Informed Democratic Decision Making, or the Veil of Ignorance?" *Journal of Health Politics, Policy and Law* 21 (1996), 69–98.

Hadorn, David. C. "The Problem of Discrimination in Health Care Priority Setting." *Journal of the American Medical Association* 268 (September 16, 1992), 1454–59.

Hall, Mark A. *Making Medical Spending Decisions: The Law, Ethics, and Economics of Rationing Mechanisms.* New York: Oxford University Press, 1997.

Halligan, Caitlin J. "'Just What the Doctor Ordered': Oregon's Medicaid Rationing Process and Public Participation in Risk Regulation." *The Georgetown Law Journal* 83 (1995), 2697–2725.

Health Affairs 10 (1991). Special issue on "Rationing."

Jones, Gary E. "The Right to Health Care and the State." *Philosophical Quarterly* 33 (1983), 278–87.

Journal of the American Geriatrics Society 40 (1992). Special issue on "Ethics and Rationing."

Journal of Medicine and Philosophy 19 (Aug. 1994). Special issue on the Oregon Health Plan.

Kapp, Marshall B. "Rationing Health Care: Will It Be Necessary? Can It Be Done Without Age or Disability Discrimination?" *Issues in Law & Medicine* 5 (1989), 337–51.

Kaveny, M. Cathleen. "Distributive Justice in the Era of the Benefit Package: The Dispute over the Oregon Basic Health Services Act." In Kevin William Wildes, ed., *Critical Choices and Critical Care.* Boston: Kluwer, 1995, 163–85.

Kitzhaber, John A. "The Oregon Health Plan: A Process for Reform." *Annals of Emergency Medicine* 23 (February 1994), 330–33.

Lomasky, Loren E. "Medical Progress and National Health Care." *Philosophy & Public Affairs* 10 (1981), 65–88.

Mechanic, David. "Dilemmas in Rationing Health Care Services: The Case for Implicit Rationing." *British Medical Journal* 310 (1995), 1655–59.

———. *From Advocacy to Allocation: The Evolving American Health Care System.* New York: Free Press, 1986.

Menzel, Paul T. "Equality, Autonomy, and Efficiency: What Health Care System Should We Have?" *Journal of Medicine & Philosophy* 17 (1992), 33–57.

———. "At Law-Oregon's Denial: Disabilities and Quality of Life." *Hastings Center Report* 22 (November-December 1992), 21–25.

———. *Medical Costs, Moral Choices.* New Haven, CT: Yale University Press, 1983.

———. *Strong Medicine: The Ethical Rationing of Health Care.* New York: Oxford University Press, 1990.

Moreno, Jonathan D. "Recapturing Justice in the Managed Care Era." *Cambridge Quarterly of Healthcare Ethics* 5 (1996), 493–99.

Nelson, Robert M., and Drought, Theresa. "Justice and the Moral Acceptability of Rationing Medical Care: The Oregon Experiment." *Journal of Medicine and Philosophy* 17 (1992), 97–117.

Powers, Madison. "Justice and the Market for Health Insurance." *Kennedy Institute of Ethics Journal* 1 (1991), 307–23.

President's Commission for the Study of Ethical Problems in Medicine and Biomedical and Behavioral Research. *Securing Access to Health Care.* Vols. I–III. Washington: U.S. Government Printing Office, 1983.

Reinhardt, Uwe E. "Reforming the Health Care System: The Universal Dilemma." *American Journal of Law and Medicine* 19 (1993), 21–36.

Relman, Arnold S. "The Trouble with Rationing." *New England Journal of Medicine* 323 (September 27, 1990), 911–13.

Sass, Hans-Martin, and Massey, Robert U., eds. *Health Care Systems: Moral Conflicts in European and American Public Policy.* Boston: Kluwer Academic, 1988.

Veatch, Robert M. *The Foundations of Justice: Why the Retarded and the Rest of Us Have Claims to Equality.* New York: Oxford University Press, 1986.

———. "Should Basic Care Get Priority? Doubts About Rationing the Oregon Way." *Kennedy Institute of Ethics Journal* 1 (1991), 187–206.

———. "Single Payers and Multiple Lists: Must Everyone Get the Same Coverage in a Universal Health Plan?" *Kennedy Institute of Ethics Journal* 7 (1997), 153–69.

Weinstein, Milton C., and Stason, William B. "Allocating Resources: The Case of Hypertension." *Hastings Center Report* 7 (October 1977), 24–29.

Yarborough, Mark. "The Private Health Insurance Industry: The Real Barrier to Healthcare Access? *Cambridge Quarterly of Healthcare Ethics* 3 (1994), 99–107.

BIBLIOGRAPHIES AND ENCYCLOPEDIAS WITH BIBLIOGRAPHIES

Bioethicsline: Computer Retrieval Service.

Encyclopedia of Bioethics, ed. Warren Reich, 2d ed., New York: Macmillan, 1995.

Encyclopedia of Ethics, ed. Lawrence Becker and Charlotte Becker. New York: Garland Publishing Inc., 1992.

Leatt, Peggy, et al. *Perspectives on Physician Involvement in Resource Allocation and Utilization Management: An Annotated Bibliography.* Toronto: University of Toronto, 1991.

Lineback, Richard H., ed. *Philosopher's Index.* Vols. 1– . Bowling Green, OH: Philosophy Documentation Center, Bowling Green State University. Issued Quarterly.

Walters, LeRoy, and Kahn, Tamar Joy, eds. *Bibliography of Bioethics.* Vols. 1– . New York: Free Press. Issued annually.

Part V

BIOMEDICAL RESEARCH AND TECHNOLOGY

7.
Research Involving Human and Animal Subjects

CONCEPTUAL QUESTIONS

The definition of "research" can perhaps best be approached by considering the concepts of "therapy" and "research". In the biomedical and behavioral fields, "therapy" refers to a class of activities designed solely to benefit an individual or the members of a group. Therapy may take several forms: It may be a treatment for a disease, diagnostic procedures, or even preventive measures. In contrast, "research" refers to a class of scientific activities designed to develop or contribute to generalizable knowledge. Examples of research could include a study of alternative methods for training pigeons, a comparison of two drugs for treating AIDS, or a review of patient charts in an effort to detect a correlation between smoking and lung cancer.

With research, two subtypes involving human or animal subjects can be identified. In the first, often designated as *clinical research,* research is combined with the diagnosis, treatment, or prevention of illness in the research subjects themselves. It is research aimed directly toward discovering better methods of diagnosing or treating the condition from which human or animal patients are suffering or toward preventing disease in susceptible humans or animals. A study of a new polio vaccine in children at risk for contracting polio would be an example of such research. Randomized clinical trials are an important subtype of clinical research.

In the second type, research is unrelated (or at least not directly related) to an illness or susceptibility of the subjects involved. For example, healthy human volunteers can be involved in studies that examine how long a new drug remains in the bodies of people who receive a certain dose of the drug. Similarly, healthy nonhuman animals are frequently involved in research that aims to understand disease processes in human beings. Thus, coronary arteries may be obstructed in canine subjects so that researchers can better understand what happens to the human heart in a myocardial infraction (heart attack). There is no simple or widely accepted term that applies to all the various kinds of nonclinical research.

One category of research, at first glance, seems to straddle the line between clinical and nonclinical research. It is research on human patients that is unrelated to diagnosing or treating the patients' illnesses. This type of research deserves special mention because it was a prominent feature in the Tuskegee syphilis study and in the human radiation experiments conducted by the U.S. Atomic Energy Commission. In terms of the distinctions developed in the preceding paragraphs, this kind of research should be categorized as nonclinical because it is not designed to benefit the patients being studied — even though the research may be conducted in a clinic.

A BRIEF HISTORY OF HUMAN AND ANIMAL RESEARCH

Systematic research on living animals is a relatively recent phenomenon in the history of science. The first important results of animal research were achieved in the seventeenth century when William Harvey demonstrated the circulation of the blood and Robert Hooke explored the mechanism of respiration.[1] Both researchers employed living animals in their work. Similar physiological research continued during the eighteenth century but achieved special prominence in nineteenth-century France, especially in the pioneering studies of François Magendie and his student, Claude Bernard.[2] Late in life Bernard wrote an extended defense of animal research (often called "vivisection" by its critics) in the book entitled *An Introduction to the Study of Experimental Medicine*.[3] During the twentieth century basic physiological research involving animals has continued, even as new modes of applied research in animals have been developed—for example, innovations in surgical technique and the preclinical testing of drugs and biological agents such as vaccines.

Systematic research in human beings is also a relatively recent phenomenon. One of the earliest well-documented studies was Dr. Zabdiel Boylston's attempt, during the early years of the eighteenth century, to protect Boston's children against smallpox through inoculation. Boylston's feasibility study, conducted in 1703, involved inoculating his son and two of his slaves with small doses of infectious material.[4] Toward the end of the century, in 1789, Edward Jenner attempted to immunize several children against smallpox by using swinepox and cowpox injections. His own son and several orphan children were among the first subjects.[5] In the same century but on a different subject, Scottish-born physician James Lind demonstrated in a small clinical trial that citrus fruits prevented scurvy in sailors.[6]

The involvement of human subjects in research has increased steadily since 1800. During the nineteenth century the French physiological approach that had produced such striking results in animal studies was also applied to human beings. Once again, Claude Bernard was a pioneer.[7] Bernard's countrymen, Pierre Louis and Louis Pasteur, also made important contributions to biomedical knowledge, as Leon Eisenberg notes in his essay in this chapter. At the turn of the century, U.S. Army Major Walter Reed recruited more than a dozen human volunteers in his effort to demonstrate that yellow fever was transmitted through the bites of mosquitoes.[8] Large-scale clinical trials are primarily a post-World-War-II phenomenon, with Sir Bradford Hill's 1948 randomized study of streptomycin in the treatment of pulmonary tuberculosis being one of the first clear examples.[9]

RESEARCH INVOLVING HUMAN SUBJECTS

THE MORAL JUSTIFICATION

In the literature on human research, including codes of research ethics, surprisingly little attention is paid to the general justification for involving human subjects in research. This silence at the most general level of justification is particularly striking when one considers that the traditional ethic of medicine has been exclusively a patient-benefit ethic. The motto *primum non nocere* (do no harm) has generally been interpreted to mean, "Do nothing that is not intended for the direct benefit of the patient." One must ask, then, whether good reasons can be given for deviating in any way from therapy, as that term was defined in the previous section.

The primary argument in favor of human research appeals to the principle of beneficence (as described in Chapter 1). It asserts that the social benefits to be gained from such research are substantial and that the harms resulting from the cessation of such investigations would be exceedingly grave. In his essay in this chapter, Leon Eisenberg advances such claims. He notes that the therapeutic value of many reputed "therapies" is in fact unknown; indeed, these treatments may be no more useful than the bloodletting technique so much in vogue during the eighteenth and nineteenth centuries. On this view, the only alternative to a per-petual plague of medically induced illness is the vigorous pursuit of biomedical research, including research involving human subjects.

A second approach to the justification of human research is based on a joint appeal to the principles of beneficence and justice. According to this view, beneficence requires that each of us make at least a modest positive contribution to the good of our fellow citizens or so-ciety as a whole. If our participation in research promises significant benefit to others, at little or no risk to ourselves, then such participation may be a duty of beneficence. In addi-tion, if we fail to fulfill this modest duty while most of our contemporaries perform it, we may be acting unjustly by not performing our fair share of a communal task. Eisenberg ad-vances a qualified version of this argument.

The justice argument can be further elaborated by reference to the past. Every person currently alive is the beneficiary of earlier human subjects' involvement in research. To be more specific, the willingness of past human volunteers to take part in studies of antibiotics (such as penicillin) and vaccines (such as polio vaccine) has contributed to the health of us all. Accordingly, it seems unfair for us to reap the benefits of such already-performed re-search without making a similar contribution to the alleviation of disability and disease for future generations.

Several commentators on the moral justification of research involving human subjects have vigorously contested both the beneficence and justice approaches to the general justi-fication of human research. In answer to the consequential argument advanced by Eisen-berg, they assert that while human research generally contributes to medical progress, most research involving human subjects is not *essential* to the well-being or survival of the human species. These critics, most notably Hans Jonas,[10] have also rejected the thesis that there is a general moral duty to participate in biomedical research. On this view, there is no injustice involved in people's not volunteering to take part in the production of general-izable knowledge. Non-participants in research are simply being less altruistic than their fellow-citizens who volunteer for this type of community service.[11]

Within the past decade, a paradigm shift has occurred in the debate about the moral jus-tification of research involving human subjects. The view that participation in clinical re-search entails a sacrifice for human subjects has been replaced, or at least complemented, by the notion that participation in many kinds of clinical trials is, on balance, beneficial to the subjects themselves. The development of new therapies for AIDS and HIV infection was the first context in which this new emphasis appeared. More recently, commentators on the ethics of human research have called for expanded access by women, including pregnant women, and children to clinical trials.[12]

CONTROLLED CLINICAL TRIALS

Even if one accepts that research involving human subjects is morally justifiable in princi-ple, there remains a more specific question: Under what circumstances is a controlled clin-ical trial morally permissible? Benjamin Freedman's essay, "Equipoise and the Ethics of Clinical Research," wrestles with the answer to this question. Equipoise is a "state of un-certainty about the relative merits of [Treatments] A and B." Freedman argues that the pre-dominant notion of equipoise, which he calls theoretical equipoise, sets too stringent a standard. This concept of equipoise can be disturbed at any time by new data and is subject to the idiosyncratic views of particular clinicians. As a preferred alternative, Freedman pro-poses "clinical equipoise," which he defines as a state in which "[t]here is no consensus within the expert clinical community about the comparative merits of the alternatives to be tested." If clinical equipoise exists, Freedman asserts, the design and initiation of a controlled clinical trial to compare the alternatives is morally justified. He further stipulates that the trial should be designed in such a way that its results are likely to resolve the preexisting dispute among expert clinicians.

PAST ABUSES OF HUMAN RESEARCH SUBJECTS

The current chapter recounts or alludes to four examples of gross abuses committed against human subjects during the course of the twentieth century. The first instance — the Tuskegee syphilis study — was more a study in the natural history of disease in African-American men than an experiment in the strict sense. In the second example, the judges who pronounced the verdict in the Nuremberg trial (1946–1947) responded to inhumane and often-lethal experiments conducted on unconsenting subjects confined to Nazi concentration camps. A third example of unethical research is much less well known. During the 1930s and 1940s, Japanese soldiers who occupied China and Manchuria — in collaboration with physicians and scientists — deliberately exposed hapless civilians from the occupied regions to a panoply of infectious diseases. Finally, the United States government sponsored several thousand human radiation experiments, many of them performed on unsuspecting human subjects, during the years between 1944 and 1974. These studies were first described in detail by a presidential advisory committee in 1995.

RESEARCH INVOLVING ANIMALS

The first question to be clarified in any discussion of animal research is: Which animals are to be included within the scope of consideration? Books and articles on the ethics of animal research have devoted attention to this question. One can usually infer from these writings that nonhuman mammals — such as monkeys, dogs, and rats — are to be included in the protected group. Indeed, Tom Regan explicitly limits his argument to "all species of mammalian animals." A somewhat broader class would be all vertebrates, that is, mammals plus birds, reptiles, amphibians, and fish. In the discussion that follows, it is assumed that the term "animals" refers to nonhuman vertebrates.

Statistics from two countries that closely monitor the use of animals in research may serve to make the notion of animal research more concrete. In the United Kingdom, 2.8 million research procedures involving animals were performed in 1993. Rodents were the research subjects in 86 percent of the cases; fish comprised another 5 percent of the subjects.[13] Data from Canada indicate that in 1992 2,115,006 animals were used in scientific research, testing, and education. Of these animals, approximately 930,000, or 44 percent, were rats and mice. Scientific research accounted for 86 percent of the total use of animals.[14]

Two primary ethical issues can be identified in the animal research debate: (1) the consequences of the research and (2) the moral status of animals. Proponents of animal research usually advance arguments that appeal rather straightforwardly to the principle of beneficence. The weak form of the argument can be formulated as follows: Good consequences are achieved through the use of animals in research. A somewhat stronger thesis is that at least some of these good consequences can be achieved *only* by means of animal research, that is, no alternative (nonhuman) means to the desired end exist. In his essay in this chapter, Carl Cohen defends this stronger thesis.

Critics of animal research can also appeal to the principle of beneficence. In response to the weak form of the proponents' argument, the critics urge that alternatives to animal research be more vigorously explored and actively employed. The strong form of the proponents' argument presents a more formidable challenge, however. If animal research is the only means for achieving a desirable consequence, the critic can respond by insisting on a conscientious weighing of research benefits against harm to animals. Reformers such as Andrew Rowan recommend the use of precisely this kind of calculus. In contrast, Tom Regan rejects any weighing or balancing of harms done to animals for any purpose other than benefiting the individual animals themselves on grounds that the moral rights of (at least) mammalian animals always trump possible benefits to humans. In other words, if proper respect for animal rights "means that there are some things we cannot learn, then so be it."

A complicating factor in any effort to assess consequences is the problem of animal sentience, or sensitivity to pain. The notion of sentience raises both conceptual and empirical issues. A broad construal of the concept of sentience might conceivably include primitive "avoidance" reactions to aversive stimuli, for example, a paramecium's response to a toxic chemical or a rabbit's reaction to cold. However, a narrower construal of sentience might require the presence of anticipatory or retrospective psychological states such as fear or regret. Even if one were able to agree on a definition of sentience, there would remain the formidable empirical problem of measuring exactly how much pain is being inflicted upon, or in some sense being experienced by, animal subjects.

The second major issue in the animal research debate is the moral status of animals. This issue closely parallels the problem of personhood and the question of fetal status. Regan argues that some animals have rights because they are conscious beings that have interests in certain kinds of welfare. According to Regan, mammalian animals can even be said to have a certain kind of autonomy. Cohen vigorously disputes Regan's thesis that nonhuman animals have, or can have, moral rights. In contrast, Rowan adopts a mediating position, eschewing the language of rights and arguing for an approach that accords increasing status to animals as they exhibit more refined types of sentience and, especially, self-awareness.

CODES AND GUIDELINES

The codes and guidelines reprinted in this chapter illustrate a gradual evolution in standards for the proper conduct of research involving human and animal subjects. The central affirmation of the Nuremberg Code, that the voluntary consent of every human subject is a *sine qua non* for the subject's participation, has gradually been supplemented by other important considerations. For example, the Declaration of Helsinki adds the distinction between research involving patients and research involving healthy volunteers. Helsinki also advocates prior review of research protocols by an "independent committee," as well as making explicit provision for participation in research by legally incompetent persons. The CIOMS guidelines for human and animal research illustrate the global character of research with both human and animal subjects and the substantial international consensus that exists, especially on the ethics of human research. In addition, the 1993 CIOMS guidelines are attentive to the issues that may arise when human research is conducted in Third World settings.

In the essay that concludes the first section of this chapter, Baruch Brody illustrates both the extent and limits of ethical agreement on research ethics. For research involving competent adult human subjects, Brody discovers near-unanimity on ethical standards throughout the world. Ethical guidelines for research involving animals reveal areas of disagreement, while the views of various nations and expert advisory groups on research with preimplantation human embryos are sharply divided. Brody notes that conflicting presuppositions about the moral, and even metaphysical, status of animals and early human embryos underlie at least some of the disagreements about research involving these two types of subjects.

L. W.

NOTES

1. Baruch A. Brody, *The Ethics of Biomedical Research: An International Perspective* (New York: Oxford University Press, 1998), p. 12.

2. Ibid.

3. Claude Bernard, *An Introduction to the Study of Experimental Medicine,* translated from the French by H. C. Greene (New York: Dover Publications, 1957).

4. Gert H. Brieger, "Human Experimentation: History," in Warren T. Reich, ed. *Encyclopedia of Bioethics* (New York: Free Press, 1978), p. 686.

5. Albert R. Jonsen, *The Birth of Bioethics* (New York: Oxford University Press, 1998), p. 126.

6. Brieger, op. cit., p. 686.

7. Jonsen, op. cit., p. 127.

8. Brieger, op. cit., pp. 687–88.

9. Brody, op. cit., p. 140.

10. Hans Jonas, "Philosophical Reflections on Experimenting with Human Subjects," *Daedalus* 98 (Spring 1969), pp. 219–47.

11. Ibid., pp. 223–24, 231–33.

12. See, for example, Anna C. Mastroianni, Ruth Faden, and Daniel Federman, eds., *Women and Health Research: Ethical and Legal Issues of Including Women in Clinical Studies* (2 vols.; Washington, DC: National Academy Press, 1994).

13. "Home Office Reports a Further Decline in Experiments on Animals," *Veterinary Record* (February 25, 1995), pp. 182–83; cited by Brody, *op. cit.,* pp. 13, 361.

14. Canadian Council on Animal Care, "Scientific Use of Animals in Canada," *Resource,* supplement to the issue of Spring 1994; cited by Brody, *ibid.*

Codes and Guidelines

The Nuremberg Code (1947)

The great weight of the evidence before us is to the effect that certain types of medical experiments on human beings, when kept within reasonably well-defined bounds, conform to the ethics of the medical profession generally. The protagonists of the practice of human experimentation justify their views on the basis that such experiments yield results for the good of society that are unprocurable by other methods or means of study. All agree, however, that certain basic principles must be observed in order to satisfy moral, ethical and legal concepts.

1. The voluntary consent of the human subject is absolutely essential.

This means that the person involved should have legal capacity to give consent; should be so situated as to be able to exercise free power of choice, without the intervention of any element of force, fraud, deceit, duress, overreaching, or other ulterior form of constraint or coercion; and should have sufficient knowledge and comprehension of the elements of the subject matter involved as to enable him to make an understanding and enlightened decision. This latter element requires that before the acceptance of an affirmative decision by the experimental subject there should be made known to him the nature, duration, and purpose of the experiment; the method and means by which it is to be conducted; all inconveniences and hazards reasonably to be expected; and the effects upon his health or person which may possibly come from his participation in the experiment.

The duty and responsibility for ascertaining the quality of the consent rests upon each individual who initiates, directs or engages in the experiment. It is a personal duty and responsibility which may not be delegated to another with impunity.

2. The experiment should be such as to yield fruitful results for the good of society, unprocurable by other methods or means of study, and not random and unnecessary in nature.

3. The experiment should be so designed and based on the results of animal experimentation and a knowledge of the natural history of the disease or other problems under study that the anticipated results will justify the performance of the experiment.

4. The experiment should be so conducted as to avoid all unnecessary physical and mental suffering and injury.

5. No experiment should be conducted where there is an *a priori* reason to believe that death or disabling injury will occur; except perhaps, in those experiments where the experimental physicians also serve as subjects.

6. The degree of risk to be taken should never exceed that determined by the humanitarian importance of the problem to be solved by the experiment.

7. Proper preparations should be made and adequate facilities provided to protect the experimental subject against even remote possibilities of injury, disability, or death.

8. The experiment should be conducted only by scientifically qualified persons. The highest degree of skill and care should be required through all stages of the experiment of those who conduct or engage in the experiment.

9. During the course of the experiment the human subject should be at liberty to bring the experiment to an end if he has reached the physical or mental state where continuation of the experiment seems to him to be impossible.

10. During the course of the experiment the scientist in charge must be prepared to terminate the experiment at any stage, if he has probable cause to believe, in the exercise of the good faith, superior skill and careful judgment required of him that a continuation of the experiment is likely to result in injury, disability, or death to the experimental subject.

From *Trials of War Criminals Before the Nuremberg Military Tribunals Under Control Council Law No. 10.* Vol. II, Nuremberg, October 1946–April 1949.

World Medical Association, Declaration of Helsinki (1996)*

Recommendations Guiding Physicians in Biomedical Research Involving Human Subjects

INTRODUCTION

It is the mission of the physician to safeguard the health of the people. His or her knowledge and conscience are dedicated to the fulfillment of this mission.

The Declaration of Geneva of the World Medical Association binds the physician with the words, "The health of my patient will be my first consideration," and the International Code of Medical Ethics declares that, "A physician shall act only in the patient's interest when providing medical care which might have the effect of weakening the physical and mental condition of the patient."

The purpose of biomedical research involving human subjects must be to improve diagnostic, therapeutic and prophylactic procedures and the understanding of the aetiology and pathogenesis of disease.

In current medical practice most diagnostic, therapeutic or prophylactic procedures involve hazards. This applies especially to biomedical research.

Medical progress is based on research which ultimately must rest in part on experimentation involving human subjects.

In the field of biomedical research a fundamental distinction must be recognized between medical research in which the aim is essentially diagnostic or therapeutic for a patient, and medical research, the essential object of which is purely scientific and without implying direct diagnostic or therapeutic value to the person subjected to the research.

---

*Adopted by the 18th World Medical Assembly, Helsinki, Finland, 1964, and amended by the 29th World Medical Assembly, Tokyo, Japan, 1975; 35th World Medical Assembly, Venice, Italy, 1983; 41st World Medical Assembly, Hong Kong, 1989; and the 48th General Assembly, Somerset West, Republic of South Africa, 1996.

Reprinted with permission from the World Medical Association.

Special caution must be exercised in the conduct of research which may affect the environment, and the welfare of animals used for research must be respected.

Because it is essential that the results of laboratory experiments be applied to human beings to further scientific knowledge and to help suffering humanity, the World Medical Association has prepared the following recommendations as a guide to every physician in biomedical research involving human subjects. They should be kept under review in the future. It must be stressed that the standards as drafted are only a guide to physicians all over the world. Physicians are not relieved from criminal, civil and ethical responsibilities under the laws of their own countries.

I. BASIC PRINCIPLES

1. Biomedical research involving human subjects must conform to generally accepted scientific principles and should be based on adequately performed laboratory and animal experimentation and on a thorough knowledge of the scientific literature.

2. The design and performance of each experimental procedure involving human subjects should be clearly formulated in an experimental protocol which should be transmitted for consideration, comment and guidance to a specially appointed committee independent of the investigator and the sponsor provided that this independent committee is in conformity with the laws and regulations of the country in which the research experiment is performed.

3. Biomedical research involving human subjects should be conducted only by scientifically qualified persons and under the supervision of a clinically competent medical person. The responsibility for the human subject must always rest with a medically qualified

person and never rest on the subject of the research, even though the subject has given his or her consent.

4. Biomedical research involving human subjects cannot legitimately be carried out unless the importance of the objective is in proportion to the inherent risk to the subject.

5. Every biomedical research project involving human subjects should be preceded by careful assessment of predictable risks in comparison with foreseeable benefits to the subject or to others. Concern for the interests of the subject must always prevail over the interests of science and society.

6. The right of the research subject to safeguard his or her integrity must always be respected. Every precaution should be taken to respect the privacy of the subject and to minimize the impact of the study on the subject's physical and mental integrity and on the personality of the subject.

7. Physicians should abstain from engaging in research projects involving human subjects unless they are satisfied that the hazards involved are believed to be predictable. Physicians should cease any investigation if the hazards are found to outweigh the potential benefits.

8. In publication of the results of his or her research, the physician is obliged to preserve the accuracy of the results. Reports of experimentation not in accordance with the principles laid down in this Declaration should not be accepted for publication.

9. In any research on human beings, each potential subject must be adequately informed of the aims, methods, anticipated benefits and potential hazards of the study and the discomfort it may entail. He or she should be informed that he or she is at liberty to abstain from participation in the study and that he or she is free to withdraw his or her consent to participation at any time. The physician should then obtain the subject's freely-given informed consent, preferably in writing.

10. When obtaining informed consent for the research project the physician should be particularly cautious if the subject is in a dependent relationship to him or her or may consent under duress. In that case the informed consent should be obtained by a physician who is not engaged in the investigation and who is completely independent of this official relationship.

11. In case of legal incompetence, informed consent should be obtained from the legal guardian in accordance with national legislation. Where physical or mental incapacity makes it impossible to obtain in-

formed consent, or when the subject is a minor, permission from the responsible relative replaces that of the subject in accordance with national legislation. Whenever the minor child is in fact able to give a consent, the minor's consent must be obtained in addition to the consent of the minor's legal guardian.

12. The research protocol should always contain a statement of the ethical considerations involved and should indicate that the principles enunciated in the present Declaration are complied with.

II. MEDICAL RESEARCH COMBINED WITH PROFESSIONAL CARE
(Clinical Research)

1. In the treatment of the sick person, the physician must be free to use a new diagnostic and therapeutic measure, if in his or her judgment it offers hope of saving life, reestablishing health or alleviating suffering.

2. The potential benefits, hazards and discomfort of a new method should be weighed against the advantages of the best current diagnostic and therapeutic methods.

3. In any medical study, every patient — including those of a control group, if any — should be assured of the best proven diagnostic and therapeutic method. This does not exclude the use of inert placebo in studies where no proven diagnostic or therapeutic method exists.

4. The refusal of the patient to participate in a study must never interfere with the physician-patient relationship.

5. If the physician considers it essential not to obtain informed consent, the specific reasons for this proposal should be stated in the experimental protocol for transmission to the independent committee (I,2).

6. The physician can combine medical research with professional care, the objective being the acquisition of new medical knowledge, only to the extent that medical research is justified by its potential diagnostic or therapeutic value for the patient.

III. NON-THERAPEUTIC BIOMEDICAL RESEARCH INVOLVING HUMAN SUBJECTS
(Non-Clinical Biomedical Research)

1. In the purely scientific application of medical research carried out on a human being, it is the duty of

the physician to remain the protector of the life and health of that person on whom biomedical research is being carried out.

2. The subjects should be volunteers—either healthy persons or patients for whom the experimental design is not related to the patient's illness.

3. The investigator or the investigating team should discontinue the research if in his/her or their judgment it may, if continued, be harmful to the individual.

4. In research on man, the interest of science and society should never take precedence over considerations related to the well-being of the subject.

COUNCIL FOR INTERNATIONAL ORGANIZATIONS OF MEDICAL SCIENCES (CIOMS) IN COLLABORATION WITH THE WORLD HEALTH ORGANIZATION (WHO)

International Ethical Guidelines for Biomedical Research Involving Human Subjects (1993)

• • •

GENERAL ETHICAL PRINCIPLES

All research involving human subjects should be conducted in accordance with three basic ethical principles, namely respect for persons, beneficence and justice. It is generally agreed that these principles, which in the abstract have equal moral force, guide the conscientious preparation of proposals for scientific studies. In varying circumstances they may be expressed differently and given different moral weight, and their application may lead to different decisions or courses of action. The present guidelines are directed at the application of these principles to research involving human subjects.

Respect for persons incorporates at least two fundamental ethical considerations, namely:

a) respect for autonomy, which requires that those who are capable of deliberation about their per-

Reprinted from Z. Bankowski and R. J. Levine, eds., *Ethics and Research on Human Subjects: International Guidelines* (Geneva: CIOMS, 1993), pp. 1–45 (excerpts). Reprinted with the permission of CIOMS.

sonal choices should be treated with respect for their capacity for self-determination; and

b) protection of persons with impaired or diminished autonomy, which requires that those who are dependent or vulnerable be afforded security against harm or abuse.

Beneficence refers to the ethical obligation to maximize benefits and to minimize harms and wrongs. This principle gives rise to norms requiring that the risks of research be reasonable in the light of the expected benefits, that the research design be sound, and that the investigators be competent both to conduct the research and to safeguard the welfare of the research subjects. Beneficence further proscribes the deliberate infliction of harm on persons; this aspect of beneficence is sometimes expressed as a separate principle, **nonmaleficence** (do no harm).

Justice refers to the ethical obligation to treat each person in accordance with what is morally right and proper, to give each person what is due to him or her. In the ethics of research involving human subjects the principle refers primarily to **distributive justice,**

which requires the equitable distribution of both the burdens and the benefits of participation in research. Differences in distribution of burdens and benefits are justifiable only if they are based on morally relevant distinctions between persons; one such distinction is vulnerability. "Vulnerability" refers to a substantial incapacity to protect one's own interests owing to such impediments as lack of capability to give informed consent, lack of alternative means of obtaining medical care or other expensive necessities, or being a junior or subordinate member of a hierarchical group. Accordingly, special provisions must be made for the protection of the rights and welfare of vulnerable persons.

PREAMBLE

The term "research" refers to a class of activities designed to develop or contribute to generalizable knowledge. Generalizable knowledge consists of theories, principles or relationships, or the accumulation of information on which they are based, that can be corroborated by accepted scientific methods of observation and inference. In the present context "research" includes both medical and behavioural studies pertaining to human health. Usually "research" is modified by the adjective "biomedical" to indicate that the reference is to health-related research.

Progress in medical care and disease prevention depends upon an understanding of physiological and pathological processes or epidemiological findings, and requires at some time research involving human subjects. The collection, analysis and interpretation of information obtained from research involving human beings contribute significantly to the improvement of human health.

Research involving human subjects includes that undertaken together with patient care (clinical research) and that undertaken on patients or other subjects, or with data pertaining to them, solely to contribute to generalizable knowledge (non-clinical biomedical research). Research is defined as "clinical" if one or more of its components is designed to be diagnostic, prophylactic or therapeutic for the individual subject of the research. Invariably, in clinical research, there are also components designed not to be diagnostic, prophylactic or therapeutic for the subject; examples include the administration of placebos and the performance of laboratory tests in addition to those required to serve the purposes of medical care. Hence the term "clinical research" is used here rather than "therapeutic research."

Research involving human subjects includes:

- studies of a physiological, biochemical or pathological process, or of the response to a specific intervention — whether physical, chemical or psychological — in healthy subjects or patients;
- controlled trials of diagnostic, preventive or therapeutic measures in larger groups of persons, designed to demonstrate a specific generalizable response to these measures against a background of individual biological variation;
- studies designed to determine the consequences for individuals and communities of specific preventive or therapeutic measures; and
- studies concerning human health-related behaviour in a variety of circumstances and environments.

Research involving human subjects may employ either observation or physical, chemical or psychological intervention; it may also either generate records or make use of existing records containing biomedical or other information about individuals who may or may not be identifiable from the records or information. The use of such records and the protection of the confidentiality of data obtained from those records are discussed in *International Guidelines for Ethical Review of Epidemiological Studies* (CIOMS, 1991).

Research involving human subjects includes also research in which environmental factors are manipulated in a way that could affect incidentally-exposed individuals. Research is defined in broad terms in order to embrace field studies of pathogenic organisms and toxic chemicals under investigation for health-related purposes.

Research involving human subjects is to be distinguished from the practice of medicine, public health and other forms of health care, which is designed to contribute directly to the health of individuals or communities. Prospective subjects may find it confusing when research and practice are to be conducted simultaneously, as when research is designed to obtain new information about the efficacy of a drug or other therapeutic, diagnostic or preventive modality.

Research involving human subjects should be carried out only by, or strictly supervised by, suitably qualified and experienced investigators and in accordance with a protocol that clearly states: the aim of the research; the reasons for proposing that it involve human subjects; the nature and degree of any known risks to the subjects; the sources from which it is proposed to recruit subjects; and the means proposed for ensuring that subjects' consent will be adequately informed and voluntary. The protocol should be scientifically and ethically appraised by one or more suitably constituted review bodies, independent of the investigators.

New vaccines and medicinal drugs, before being approved for general use must be tested on human subjects in clinical trials; such trials . . . constitute a substantial part of all research involving human subjects. . . .

THE GUIDELINES

INFORMED CONSENT OF SUBJECTS

Guideline 1: Individual Informed Consent. For all biomedical research involving human subjects, the investigator must obtain the informed consent of the prospective subject or, in the case of an individual who is not capable of giving informed consent, the proxy consent of a properly authorized representative.

• • •

Guideline 2: Essential Information for Prospective Research Subjects. Before requesting an individual's consent to participate in research, the investigator must provide the individual with the following information, in language that he or she is capable of understanding:

- that each individual is invited to participate as a subject in research, and the aims and methods of the research;
- the expected duration of the subject's participation;
- the benefits that might reasonably be expected to result to the subject or to others as an outcome of the research;
- any foreseeable risks or discomfort to the subject, associated with participation in the research;
- any alternative procedures or courses of treatment that might be as advantageous to the subject as the procedure or treatment being tested;
- the extent to which confidentiality of records in which the subject is identified will be maintained;
- the extent of the investigator's responsibility, if any, to provide medical services to the subject;
- that therapy will be provided free of charge for specified types of research-related injury;
- whether the subject or the subject's family or dependents will be compensated for disability or death resulting from such injury; and

- that the individual is free to refuse to participate and will be free to withdraw from the research at any time without penalty or loss of benefits to which he or she would otherwise be entitled.

• • •

Guideline 3: Obligations of Investigators Regarding Informed Consent. The investigator has a duty to:

- communicate to the prospective subject all the information necessary for adequately informed consent;
- give the prospective subject full opportunity and encouragement to ask questions;
- exclude the possibility of unjustified deception, undue influence and intimidation;
- seek consent only after the prospective subject has adequate knowledge of the relevant facts and of the consequences of participation, and has had sufficient opportunity to consider whether to participate;
- as a general rule, obtain from each prospective subject a signed form as evidence of informed consent; and
- renew the informed consent of each subject if there are material changes in the conditions or procedures of the research.

• • •

Guideline 4: Inducement to Participate. Subjects may be paid for inconvenience and time spent, and should be reimbursed for expenses incurred, in connection with their participation in research; they may also receive free medical services. However, the payments should not be so large or the medical services so extensive as to induce prospective subjects to consent to participate in the research against their better judgment ("undue inducement"). All payments, reimbursements and medical services to be provided to research subjects should be approved by an ethical review committee.

• • •

Guideline 5: Research Involving Children. Before undertaking research involving children, the investigator must ensure that:

- children will not be involved in research that might equally well be carried out with adults;
- the purpose of the research is to obtain knowledge relevant to the health needs of children;
- a parent or legal guardian of each child has given proxy consent;

- the consent of each child has been obtained to the extent of the child's capabilities;
- the child's refusal to participate in research must always be respected unless according to the research protocol the child would receive therapy for which there is no medically-acceptable alternative;
- the risk presented by interventions not intended to benefit the individual child-subject is low and commensurate with the importance of the knowledge to be gained; and
- interventions that are intended to provide therapeutic benefit are likely to be at least as advantageous to the individual child-subject as any available alternative.

• • •

Guideline 6: Research Involving Persons with Mental or Behavioral Disorders. Before undertaking research involving individuals who by reason of mental or behavioral disorders are not capable of giving adequately informed consent, the investigator must ensure that:

- such persons will not be subjects of research that might equally well be carried out on persons in full possession of their mental faculties;
- the purpose of the research is to obtain knowledge relevant to the particular health needs of persons with mental or behavioural disorders;
- the consent of each subject has been obtained to the extent of that subject's capabilities, and a prospective subject's refusal to participate in non-clinical research is always respected;
- in the case of incompetent subjects, informed consent is obtained from the legal guardian or other duly authorized person;
- the degree of risk attached to interventions that are not intended to benefit the individual subject is low and commensurate with the importance of the knowledge to be gained; and
- interventions that are intended to provide therapeutic benefit are likely to be at least as advantageous to the individual subject as any alternative.

• • •

Guideline 7: Research Involving Prisoners. Prisoners with serious illness or at risk of serious illness should not arbitrarily be denied access to investigational drugs, vaccines or other agents that show promise of therapeutic or preventive benefit.

• • •

Guideline 8: Research Involving Subjects in Underdeveloped Communities. Before undertaking research involving subjects in underdeveloped communities, whether in developed or developing countries, the investigator must ensure that:

- persons in underdeveloped communities will not ordinarily be involved in research that could be carried out reasonably well in developed communities;
- the research is responsive to the health needs and the priorities of the community in which it is to be carried out;
- every effort will be made to secure the ethical imperative that the consent of individual subjects be informed; and
- the proposals for the research have been reviewed and approved by an ethical review committee that has among its members or consultants persons who are thoroughly familiar with the customs and traditions of the community.

• • •

Guideline 9: Informed Consent in Epidemiological Studies. For several types of epidemiological research individual informed consent is either impracticable or inadvisable. In such cases the ethical review committee should determine whether it is ethically acceptable to proceed without individual informed consent and whether the investigator's plans to protect the safety and respect the privacy of research subjects and to maintain the confidentiality of the data are adequate.

• • •

SELECTION OF RESEARCH SUBJECTS

Guideline 10: Equitable Distribution of Burdens and Benefits. Individuals or communities to be invited to be subjects of research should be selected in such a way that the burdens and benefits of the research will be equitably distributed. Special justification is required for inviting vulnerable individuals and, if they are selected, the means of protecting their rights and welfare must be particularly strictly applied.

• • •

Guideline 11: Selection of Pregnant or Nursing (Breastfeeding) Women as Research Subjects. Pregnant or nursing women should in no circumstances be the subjects of non-clinical research unless the research carries no more than minimal risk to the fetus or nursing infant and the object of the research is to obtain new knowledge about pregnancy or lactation. As a general rule, pregnant or nursing women should not be subjects of any clinical trials except such trials as are designed to protect or advance the health of pregnant or nursing women or fetuses or nursing infants, and for which women who are not pregnant or nursing would not be suitable subjects.

• • •

CONFIDENTIALITY OF DATA

Guideline 12: Safeguarding Confidentiality. The investigator must establish secure safeguards of the confidentiality of research data. Subjects should be told of the limits to the investigators' ability to safeguard confidentiality and of the anticipated consequences of breaches of confidentiality.

• • •

COMPENSATION OF RESEARCH SUBJECTS
FOR ACCIDENTAL INJURY

Guideline 13: Right of Subjects to Compensation. Research subjects who suffer physical injury as a result of their participation are entitled to such financial or other assistance as would compensate them equitably for any temporary or permanent impairment or disability. In the case of death, their dependents are entitled to material compensation. The right to compensation may not be waived.

• • •

REVIEW PROCEDURES

Guideline 14: Constitution and Responsibilities of Ethical Review Committees. All proposals to conduct research involving human subjects must be submitted for review and approval to one or more independent ethical and scientific review committees. The investigator must obtain such approval of the proposal to conduct research before the research is begun.

• • •

EXTERNALLY SPONSORED RESEARCH

Guideline 15: Obligations of Sponsoring and Host Countries. Externally sponsored research entails two ethical obligations:

- An external sponsoring agency should submit the research protocol to ethical and scientific review according to the standards of the country of the sponsoring agency, and the ethical standards applied should be no less exacting than they would be in the case of research carried out in that country.
- After scientific and ethical approval in the country of the sponsoring agency, the appropriate authorities of the host country, including a national or local ethical review committee or its equivalent, should satisfy themselves that the proposed research meets their own ethical requirements.

• • •

REFERENCE

CIOMS. 1991. *International Guidelines for Ethical Review of Epidemiological Studies.* Geneva.

COUNCIL FOR INTERNATIONAL ORGANIZATIONS OF MEDICAL SCIENCES

International Guiding Principles for Biomedical Research Involving Animals (1985)

PREAMBLE

Experimentation with animals has made possible major contributions to biological knowledge and to the welfare of man and animals, particularly in the treatment and prevention of diseases. Many important advances in medical science have had their origins in basic biological research not primarily directed to practical ends as well as from applied research designed to investigate specific medical problems. There is still an urgent need for basic and applied research that will lead to the discovery of methods for the prevention and treatment of diseases for which adequate control methods are not yet available — notably the noncommunicable diseases and the endemic communicable diseases of warm climates.

Past progress has depended, and further progress in the foreseeable future will depend, largely on animal experimentation which, in the broad field of human medicine, is the prelude to experimental trials on human beings of, for example, new therapeutic, prophylactic, or diagnostic substances, devices, or procedures.

There are two international ethical codes intended principally for the guidance of countries or institutions that have not yet formulated their own ethical requirements for human experimentation: The Tokyo revision of the *Declaration of Helsinki* of the World Medical Association (1975); and the *Proposed International Guidelines for Biomedical Research Involving Human Subjects* of the Council for International Organizations

Reprinted from Council for International Organizations of Medical Sciences, *International Guiding Principles for Biomedical Research Involving Animals* (Geneva: CIOMS, 1985), pp. 17–19. Reprinted with the permission of CIOMS.

of Medical Sciences and the World Health Organization (1982). These codes recognize that while experiments involving human subjects are a *sine qua non* of medical progress, they must be subject to strict ethical requirements. In order to ensure that such ethical requirements are observed, national and institutional ethical codes have also been elaborated with a view to the protection of human subjects involved in biomedical (including behavioural) research.

A major requirement both of national and international ethical codes for human experimentation, and of national legislation in many cases, is that new substances or devices should not be used for the first time on human beings unless previous tests on animals have provided a reasonable presumption of their safety.

The use of animals for predicting the probable effects of procedures on human beings entails responsibility for their welfare. In both human and veterinary medicine animals are used for behavioural, physiological, pathological, toxicological, and therapeutic research and for experimental surgery or surgical training and for testing drugs and biological preparations. The same responsibility toward the experimental animals prevails in all of these cases.

Because of differing legal systems and cultural backgrounds there are varying approaches to the use of animals for research, testing, or training in different countries. Nonetheless, their use should be always in accord with humane practices. The varying approaches in different countries to the use of animals for biomedical purposes, and the lack of relevant legislation or of formal self-regulatory mechanisms in some, point to the need for international guiding principles elaborated as a result of international and interdisciplinary consultations.

The guiding principles proposed here provide a framework for more specific national or institutional provisions. They apply not only to biomedical research but also to all uses of vertebrate animals for other biomedical purposes, including the production and testing of therapeutic, prophylactic, and diagnostic substances, the diagnosis of infections and intoxications in man and animals, and to any other procedures involving the use of intact live vertebrates.

BASIC PRINCIPLES

I. The advancement of biological knowledge and the development of improved means for the protection of the health and well-being both of man and of animals require recourse to experimentation on intact live animals of a wide variety of species.

II. Methods such as mathematical models, computer simulation and *in vitro* biological systems should be used wherever appropriate.

III. Animal experiments should be undertaken only after due consideration of their relevance for human or animal health and the advancement of biological knowledge.

IV. The animals selected for an experiment should be of an appropriate species and quality, and the minimum number required to obtain scientifically valid results.

V. Investigators and other personnel should never fail to treat animals as sentient, and should regard their proper care and use and the avoidance or minimization of discomfort, distress, or pain as ethical imperatives.

VI. Investigators should assume that procedures that would cause pain in human beings cause pain in other vertebrate species, although more needs to be known about the perception of pain in animals.

VII. Procedures with animals that may cause more than momentary or minimal pain or distress should be performed with appropriate sedation, analgesia, or anesthesia in accordance with accepted veterinary practice. Surgical or other painful procedures should not be performed on unanesthetized animals paralysed by chemical agents.

VIII. Where waivers are required in relation to the provisions of article VII, the decisions should not rest solely with the investigators directly concerned but should be made, with due regard to the provisions of articles IV, V, and VI, by a suitably constituted review body. Such waivers should not be made solely for the purpose of teaching or demonstration.

IX. At the end of, or, when appropriate, during an experiment, animals that would otherwise suffer severe or chronic pain, distress, discomfort, or disablement that cannot be relieved should be painlessly killed.

X. The best possible living conditions should be maintained for animals kept for biomedical purposes. Normally the care of animals should be under the supervision of veterinarians having experience in laboratory animal science. In any case, veterinary care should be available as required.

XI. It is the responsibility of the director of an institute or department using animals to ensure that investigators and personnel have appropriate qualifications or experience for conducting procedures on animals. Adequate opportunities shall be provided for in-service training, including the proper and humane concern for the animals under their care. . . .

BARUCH A. BRODY

Research Ethics: International Perspectives

In recent years, bioethics has increasingly become an international area of inquiry, with major contributions being made not only in North America but also in Europe and in the Pacific Rim countries. This general observation is particularly true for research ethics. Little attention has been paid, however, to this internationalization of bioethics in general and research ethics in particular, and there are few studies comparing what has emerged in the different countries.

I have recently completed a book-length comparative study[1] of the official policies in various countries on a wide variety of issues in the ethics of research on subjects. It reveals that there is a wide variation ranging from substantial international agreement on some issues to major disagreement on other issues. An important question about the foundations of bioethics emerges: What makes some issues more amenable to the development of an international consensus in official national policies than other issues?

In this paper, I will briefly review three examples of issues in research ethics: research on competent adult subjects, research on animals, and research on embryos shortly after fertilization. I will show the existence of a broad consensus about principles in national policies on the first issue, of some disagreement about principles combined with substantial agreement on most principles in national policies on the second issue, and of total disagreement about fundamental principles among national policies on the third issue. I will also offer a hypothesis to explain the difference between these three areas, a hypothesis that relates this difference to certain traditional claims in cultural anthropology about cultural differences on ethical issues.

Reprinted with the permission of the publisher from *Cambridge Quarterly of Healthcare Ethics* 6 (1997), 376–384. Copyright © 1997 Cambridge University Press.

RESEARCH ON COMPETENT ADULT SUBJECTS: AN INTERNATIONAL CONSENSUS

The regulation of research on competent adult subjects grew out of a response to the horrors of German and Japanese research in World War II. It also grew out of a recognition that there were continuing real, even if more modest, abuses in research activities in democratic countries in the post World War II period.

Extensive international and national policies have been developed. The Declaration of Helsinki, first issued in 1964 but modified several times since then, represents the most important international response, although mention must also be made of the influential 1982 guidelines (modified in important ways in 1993) from the World Health Organization-Council for International Organizations of Medical Sciences. In the United States, there exist regulations from the National Institutes of Health (NIH) and the Food and Drug Administration (FDA) from the early 1980s combined with the federal Common Rule of 1991.[2] In Canada, there exist 1978 guidelines, revised in 1987, from the Medical Research Council.[3] Europe contributed in 1990 two major multinational guidelines, the Recommendation of the Committee of Ministers of the Council of Europe[4] and the Guidelines on Good Clinical Trials from the Commission of the European Union.[5] These are supplemented by important national guidelines in Europe, including British reports (from the Royal College of Physicians in 1990, from the British Medical Association in 1993, and from the National Health Service in 1993),[6] French legislation (the 1988 Huriet-Serusclat Act, modified and supplemented several times in the 1990s),[7] German legislation (the 1994 Amendment to the German Drug Law,)[8] Swiss Guidelines (from the Swiss Academy of Medical Sciences in 1984), and the common Nordic Guidelines of 1989.[9]

The National Medical and Research Council of Australia updated its earlier guidelines in 1992, as did the New Zealand Department of Health in 1991.[10]

It is possible to describe a consensus of basic principles embodied in all of this material. One basic and universal principle is the procedural principle that research on competent adult subjects needs to be articulated in a protocol that is approved in advance by a committee that is independent of researchers. Two other basic and universal principles are substantive: informed voluntary consent of the subjects must be obtained and the research protocol must minimize risks and must involve a favorable risk-benefit ratio. Other principles often mentioned are the protection of confidentiality and the equitable, nonexploitative selection of subjects.

This is not to say that there exist no disagreements in this area of research ethics. They do exist. Among the questions that have provoked some disagreement are the following: (1) What should be the composition of the independent review group? How much public representation should there be on that group? How can its independence from the researchers best be maintained? (2) Are there any occasions in which such research can be conducted without informed consent? What about emergency research when the subjects are temporarily incapable of consenting and surrogate consent cannot be obtained? What about research being conducted in societies in which individual informed consent would be culturally inappropriate? (3) How should informed voluntary consent be obtained and documented? Are some inducements to participate so great that they interfere with the voluntariness of the subject's choice? What information must be provided for the consent to be properly informed? Must the consent always be in writing? (4) Given that there will always be risks associated with the research process, what arrangements should be made to compensate those who suffer from their participation? (5) Are there groups of competent adult subjects (e.g., prisoners) who are vulnerable to exploitation in the research process and who must be protected from this exploitation? If so, how should they be protected? Alternatively, are there groups of competent adult subjects (e.g., women) who have been unfairly denied the benefits of participation in research and who are entitled to the elimination of that injustice? If so, what is the best way to eliminate it?

As one reviews this list of questions and others that have been raised, it is clear that their existence in no way challenges the broad international consensus about the ethical principles governing research on competent adult subjects. Most of them are disagreements about the details of how the principles of the consensus should be carried out; their existence presupposes the consensus rather than challenges it.

The only exception to this generalization are the issues raised under (2), the questions about the exceptions to informed consent. But even there, those who would allow emergency research without consent usually confine that exception to cases in which it is reasonable to suppose that the subjects would consent if they could. And those who allow for cultural exceptions to the informed consent requirement often say that this is justified because the subjects, as members of the cultural community in question, would neither expect nor want, if they could even understand, the insistence upon individual informed consent. In an important sense, then, they are arguing that the exceptions really are based on the values embodied in the normal requirement for informed consent. The critics of these exceptions are, of course, equally committed to the values in question, and do not see how they can be realized by making exceptions. At a deep level, then, this disagreement still presupposes the principles of the consensus.

I am not claiming that research practice in any country is fully in accord with the principles of the international consensus nor am I claiming that all the countries in question have been equally, even if imperfectly, successful in carrying out these principles. All I am claiming is that there exists in this area a remarkable consensus about principles in both national and international regulatory policies. We shall soon see that not all areas of research ethics have realized a similar consensus.

RESEARCH ON ANIMALS: SOME INTERNATIONAL DISAGREEMENT

The regulation of the use of animals in research, which dates back to the British Act of 1876, predates the regulation of research using human subjects. It too arose as a response to abuses. In the case of animal research, it was opposition both to the public demonstrations by Magendie and Bernard on live animals of their physiological findings and to the perceived insensitivity of researchers in physiology to the pain experienced by their research subjects. As the use of live animals for research has increased, and the concern about animal interests and rights has also increased, extensive regulatory schemes have emerged in many countries.

The Council for International Organizations of Medical Sciences issued in 1985 a set of international guiding principles for biomedical research involving animals. The basic framework for much of the regulation in Europe, incorporating in many ways the international guiding principles, is provided by a 1986 directive from the Council of the European Communities (now the European Union). It is implemented in Great Britain by the Animals (Scientific Procedures) Act of 1986, in Germany by the 1986 Law on Animal Protection, in France by the 1987 decree on Animal Experimentation, and in Sweden by the 1988 Animal Protection Law. All of these recent European national policies replace and strengthen earlier policies.[11] In the same time period, the United States regulatory scheme was strengthened by 1986 regulations from the National Institutes of Health and by the 1985 Animal Welfare Act enforced by the Department of Agriculture.[12] The Canadian system of regulation dates back to the 1968 formation of the Canadian Council on Animal Care.[13] Finally, animal research in Australia is governed by a Code of Practice whose fifth edition was issued in 1990. While not quite as extensive as the national policies governing the use of human subjects, these national policies certainly represent an extensive effort deserving careful comparative analysis.

It is once more possible to describe a consensus of basic principles embodied in all of this material. Procedurally, all of these regulatory schemes involve some process for review of animal research by an external body that is independent of the researchers. Substantively, all of these regulatory schemes reject the human dominion view that maintains that animal interests may be totally disregarded as well as the animal equality view that maintains that animal interests and/or the rights of animals count as much as the interests of human beings. Put otherwise, they are schemes designed to minimize the burdens on animals while permitting human beings to continue to obtain the benefits from experimentation on [animal] subjects. They do this by mandating (1) improving the conditions in which animals used for research live, (2) lessening suffering in the actual research process (e.g., by the use, where possible, of analgesics and/or anesthesia), and (3) minimizing the number of animals used in research.

This is not to say that there are no disagreements in this area of research ethics. Among the issues about

which official regulatory schemes disagree are the following: (a) Which animals should be protected by the regulatory schemes? Should they extend to all vertebrates? Should the protection of some vertebrates be given higher priority? Should a preference be shown for conducting research on animals bred for that purpose? Should any invertebrates be protected? (b) Should independent review and monitoring be conducted by governmental agencies or by review processes created by the institutions doing the research? Should research protocols be reviewed in advance? (c) Just how much expense must be incurred to improve research animal living conditions? Must attention be paid to psychological and emotional well-being or is it sufficient that physical needs be appropriately met? (d) Are there research protocols that involve so much unalleviable suffering that they should not be conducted regardless of the potential benefits?

As one reviews this list of issues, it is clear that their existence in no way challenges the existence of a broad international consensus on the principles governing research on animals. They presuppose the existence of the consensus and the attempt to resolve them is an attempt to elaborate on the meaning of the principles structuring the international consensus.

There is, however, one disagreement among the regulatory schemes that does involve a fundamental disagreement about principles. The 1986 British Act requires that the regulatory authority, in deciding whether to issue a license authorizing the conduct of a particular research project, must "weigh the likely adverse effects on the animals concerned against the benefit likely to accrue as a result of the programme to be specified in the license." I call this type of position a balancing position. On this position, animal interests count sufficiently, even if not equally with human interests, that they can outweigh human interests in the conduct of the research; in such cases, the research is not allowed. This should be differentiated from the human priority position that attempts to minimize animal suffering by modifying the conduct of the research but that does not allow that concern with animal suffering to prevent the research being conducted. As far as I can see, some of the European regulations (Great Britain, Switzerland, perhaps Germany) and the Australian regulations accept the balancing position, while the rest of the European regulations (following the Directive of the Council of the European Communities) do so at least in research involving severe pain or distress. On the other hand, the North American regulations, by making no reference to balancing judgments, seem to accept the human priority position.

This type of disagreement does represent a disagreement about fundamental principles; its existence means that there is a less than complete international consensus about the principles governing animal research.

What is this disagreement really about? It is a disagreement about the moral status of animals. The human dominion view gives animals no moral standing while the animal equality view gives animals the same moral standing as human beings. The various regulatory schemes, rejecting these two extreme positions, give animals some moral standing, but they disagree about what that standing is. For the human priority position, human interests take lexical priority over animal interests, so we do the research we need, while limiting animal suffering to the extent that we can. For the balancing position, there is no such lexical priority. As a result, if animal losses are sufficiently great, they can outweigh human gains. This is a subtle, but very real, difference in principle. When its implications are carefully explored, I believe it will become clear that this difference has substantial implications for what types of research on animals may be conducted.

It would be interesting to see whether these differences have already appeared in the actual conduct of research on animals in the different countries. For now, however, it suffices to say that the international consensus on principles is less than complete in this area of research ethics.

RESEARCH ON PREIMPLANTATION ZYGOTES: A COMPLETE LACK OF CONSENSUS

The development of regulations on preimplantation zygotes did not arise as a response to specific abuses; instead, it is nearly contemporaneous with the development of a new technology, in vitro fertilization, that makes such research possible. Such research could be conducted on 'spare zygotes', created to produce a pregnancy but not implanted; such zygotes would otherwise be disposed of or frozen for use in future attempts to create a pregnancy. Alternatively, such research could be conducted on zygotes specifically created for use in research (analogously to animals bred for use in research).

Two radically different approaches have developed in official regulatory schemes, a permissive approach

and a restrictive approach. The permissive approach allows for such research subject to various restrictions, some of which are themselves matters of controversy. The restrictive approach prohibits all, or at least nearly all, such research. The permissive approach was adopted by Victoria in its 1984 Infertility (Medical Procedures) Act, by Great Britain in its 1990 Human Fertilization and Embryology Act,[14] and by Canada in a 1993 report of the Canadian Royal Commission on New Reproductive Technologies.[15] A number of other European countries have adopted it. It was recommended in the United States by an NIH advisory panel in 1994.[16] The restrictive approach was adopted by Germany in its 1990 Embryo Protection Law,[17] by France in its 1994 Bioethics statute,[18] by Norway in a 1990 report of its National Committee for Medical Research Ethics,[19] and by Victoria in a 1995 statute which repealed the 1984 statute.[20] The European Parliament of the Council of Europe adopted a restrictive approach in 1989 and insisted in 1995 that Article 15 of the proposed European Bioethics convention drop the provision allowing for such research in those countries that approve it.[21] In the United States, the advisory panel's report has not been implemented, and Congress has temporarily banned federal funding for such research.

The following are the main components of the permissive position: (a) it allows for research on preimplantation zygotes after consent without commercial inducements has been obtained from the donor and after an independent review board has approved the research; (b) it sets a time limit after fertilization on the conduct of such research. The Australian time limit is 7–14 days after fertilization, corresponding to the time [during] which implantation occurs. The British and Canadian time limit is 14 days, corresponding to the time at which the primitive streak appears and further division into two embryos is not possible. The NIH advisory panel allowed for some cases of research until 17–21 days, corresponding to the time of the beginning of the closure of the neural tube; (c) with the exception of the 1984 Victoria statute, it allows for the creation of zygotes for use in research, either because the emergence of freezing as a successful technique has limited the supply of spare zygotes or because some types of research (e.g., research on the safety of new drugs to induce ovulation) require the use of such zygotes; (d) it bans some types of research, most commonly cross-species research and research on postcloning transfer of zygotes. The NIH panel, responding to important feminist concerns, also banned research on preimplantation gender selection.

It is of interest to note that several versions of the permissive position were specifically advocated by their proponents as attempts to fashion a compromise between those who advocated a ban on preimplantation zygote research and those who would be far more permissive. This is the explicit motivation of some of the recommendations in the Canadian report. It has also been advocated by some of the members of the NIH advisory panel. In light of the widespread adoption of the restrictive position, it is clear that this attempt to fashion a moral compromise as a basis for a regulatory consensus has not been successful.

There are a number of features of the restrictive position that need to be emphasized: (1) Not all preimplantation research is prohibited. Therapeutic research, designed to improve the likelihood of the zygote's developing normally, followed by an attempt to implant the zygote is explicitly allowed in the French statute and implicitly allowed for in the Norwegian report and the new Victorian statute, which only prohibit destructive research. This exception covers, of course, only a small portion of the research that has been proposed. (2) The basis of the opposition to preimplantation research is expressed in different terms in different sources. Some see the prohibition of nontherapeutic research on preimplanted zygotes as the protection of the rights of a human being with full rights deserving of protection. Some see this prohibition as an expression of respect for the value of human life in general. Some see it as an implementation of the principle of protecting the vulnerable from exploitation. (3) Particular opposition is expressed to the creation of zygotes for research purposes. This is very different from the case of research on animals, where the breeding of animals for use in research is seen as morally preferable.

Enough has been said to demonstrate that this is an area of research ethics in which official national policies are in sharp disagreement with each other. The only type of research that nearly every policy will permit is the very limited case of therapeutic research designed to improve the outcome for the particular zygote in question once it is implanted.

A HYPOTHESIS

In our examination of official policies in three areas of research ethics, we have found a significant international consensus in one area, a subtle but important disagreement in a second area, and major fundamental

disagreements in a third area. In my forthcoming book, I demonstrate that this type of difference extends to other areas of research ethics; the extent of consensus in official policies is highly variable.

Can we explain this variability? A full explanation would require examining all of the different areas of research ethics, and that lies beyond the scope of this paper. For now, I would like to examine the differences demonstrated in this paper to see what can explain them.

There is a feature found in the case of research on animals and research on preimplantation zygotes that may explain why there is more disagreement in those areas. In both of those cases, there is continuing disagreement about the moral status of the subjects on which the research is conducted. Such disagreement is not found in the case of research on competent adult human subjects. My suggestion is that disagreements about the moral status of entities are harder to resolve than other moral disagreements and that it is this difficulty which explains the lack of an international consensus.

There is a long history of disagreement about the moral status of animals, about whether we are morally required to consider their interests. Some, such as Descartes, denied that they had the feelings which are prerequisites of having interests. On that account, we obviously do not need to consider their interests; in that way, they have no moral status. Others, such as Kant, did not deny them the requisite feelings, but did deny them moral status anyway. This is not to say that Kant allowed for wanton cruelty to animals. But he opposed such practices only because they hardened our feelings and might lead to indifference to human suffering. Since the rise of utilitarianism, with its emphasis on the moral significance of suffering, there has been more of a commitment to the moral status of animals, more of a commitment to the view that animal interests in avoiding suffering must be considered. Still, in a world in which animals are consumed for food after being produced in confining conditions, the animal equality position on the significance of animals interests is unlikely to be the basis for official policies; animals are not accorded that degree of moral status. So animals are treated as having a real but subordinate moral status; their interests count but not as much as human interests. This leaves room for considerable disagreement about the exact moral significance of protecting animal interests; it is just this type of disagreement that is reflected in the difference between the official policies that do and the policies that do not incorporate the balancing approach.

There is an equally long history of controversy about the moral status of zygotes, embryos, and fetuses, a controversy that is complicated when one considers the preimplantation status of preimplantation zygotes. There are those who would accord no moral status to any of these entities until birth (or even afterwards). At the other extreme, there are those who argue that such entities have full moral status from the moment of conception, even in vitro. Naturally, many in-between positions exist as well. Of particular importance is the view that the moral status of such entities is sufficiently close to the moral status of postbirth humans that a failure to respect the interests of these pre-birth entities would seriously damage the basic respect for human life which is central to civilized societies. The permissive policies represent an attempt to fashion a national policy that is an adequate compromise between these views; the proponents of the restrictive policy insist that the compromises proposed are inadequate. This fundamental disagreement results in fundamentally different official policies.

Why are such disagreements so difficult to resolve? Earlier in this century, Edward Westermarck pointed out in his studies of ethical differences among societies[22] that the differences were not primarily about the content of the accepted moral rules; rather, they were primarily differences about the scope of the rules. Societies differed primarily over who was accorded moral status, about who was protected by the accepted moral rules. Some extended those rules only to favored groups within the society, others to all members of the society, others to larger groups (perhaps even to all human beings). The process of extending the scope is hard to justify rationally. It seems to involve an emotional recognition of similarities, rather than any rational argumentation. Think of how Huck Finn comes to recognize Jim as a fellow human being. Naturally, different individuals and/or different societies may not share in these recognitions. To be sure, some philosophical systems offer a systematic approach to the question of the scope of their moral principles. Classical utilitarianism, with its view that all who can experience pleasure and pain count, is the most clear-cut example. But official policies are rarely based upon philosophical systems. Not surprisingly, then, official policies are likely to vary when questions of moral status are involved.

I am not claiming that all fundamental differences between official policies in research ethics are due to differences in social attitudes toward the moral status of the subjects involved. Such a claim would have to be evaluated in light of a more comprehensive examination of all of the areas of research ethics. All that I am claiming is that this factor helps explain the variability [and] the extent of the differences in the three areas we have examined.

One final thought. Some might believe that a comparative study of official policies on research ethics would be a technical exploration of legal technicalities. I hope that this paper helps to undercut such a belief. The issues of research ethics are related to fundamental moral and metaphysical questions, and answers to those questions (even when they are not part of systematic theories) help shape official policies. A comparative study of those policies sheds much light upon how different societies answer those questions differently.

NOTES

1. Brody B. *Ethics of Biomedical Research: An International Perspective.* New York: Oxford University Press, 1998.

2. The NIH regulations are found in 45 *CFR* 46 and the FDA in 21 *CFR* 50. The Federal Common Rule was published in the 18 June 1991 issue of the *Federal Register,* pp. 28002–32.

3. Medical Research Council of Canada. *Guidelines on Research Involving Human Subjects.* Ottawa: Medical Research Council of Canada, 1987.

4. European guidance on medical research. *Bulletin of Medical Ethics* 1990;(56):9–10.

5. Guidelines in good clinical trials. *Bulletin of Medical Ethics* 1990;(60):18–23.

6. Foster CG. *Manual for Research Ethics Committees.* London: King's College, 1993.

7. Gromb S. *Le droit de l'experimentation sur l'homme.* Paris: Litec, 1992.

8. Graf HP, Cole D. Ethics committee authorization in Germany. *Journal of Medical Ethics* 1995;(21):229–33.

9. Nordic Council of Medicines. *Good Clinical Trial Practice: Nordic Guidelines.* Uppsala: Nordic Council on Medicines, 1989.

10. McNeil P. *The Ethics and Politics of Human Experimentation.* Cambridge: Cambridge University Press, 1993.

11. The European and the Australian material is conveniently collected in *Animals and their Legal Rights.* Washington (DC): Animal Welfare Institute, 1990.

12. The best source for the complex U.S. laws and regulations is Office for Protection from Research Risks. *Institutional Animal Care and Use Committee Guidebook.* Washington (DC): National Institutes of Health, 1992.

13. *Guide to the Care and Use of Experimental Animals.* Ottawa: Canadian Council on Animal Care, 1993.

14. *Public General Acts* no. 2 (1990) 1471–1509.

15. *Proceed with Caution.* Ottawa: Minister of Government Services, 1993.

16. *Report of the Human Embryo Research Panel.* Washington (DC): National Institutes of Health, 1994.

17. *International Digest of Health Legislation* 1991:42;60–4.

18. *International Digest of Health Legislation* 1994:45;479.

19. *Research on Fetuses.* Oslo: National Committee for Medical Research Ethics, 1990.

20. A good discussion of the old and the new Victoria legislation is found in New Victoria IVF law changes pioneering legislation. *Monash Bioethics Review* 1995:14(3):6.

21. Rogers A, deBousingen DD. *Bioethics in Europe.* Strasbourg: Council of Europe Press, 1995.

22. Westermarck E. *Ethical Relativity.* [Westport, CT:] Greenwood Press: 1970 [1932].

Ethical Issues in Human Research

LEON EISENBERG

The Social Imperatives of Medical Research

Peculiar to this time[1] is the need to restate a proposition that, a decade ago, would have been regarded as self-evident, namely, that fostering excellence in medical research is in the public interest. Contemporary news accounts and learned journals alike have announced as exposé what always has been true: that doctors are fallible, that researchers are not all noble, and that what appeared to be true in the light of yesterday's evidence proves false by tomorrow's. The sins committed in the name of medical research are stressed in entire disproportion to the human gains that continue to flow from the enterprise. That a significant amount of funded research will inevitably fail to yield the expected answers is taken as a sign of boondoggling, because the nature of science is not understood. We are asked for guarantees of absolute safety as if this were an attainable goal.

Some of the specific criticism has been just and instructive, some of it merely misinformed, some of it completely irrelevant. A constructive response to the criticism of medical research would have been easier

had not distrust been aroused at the same time by the misapplications of technical knowledge (the spread of weapons systems, wire tapping, computerization, nuclear wastes) and the use of technical devices by government against its own people. Those of us who argue for the necessity of scientific research in medicine are too often regarded as if we were indifferent to misuses of it and as though we were apologists for the Establishment. I know of no remedy other than to redouble our effort to explain the nature and the justification of well-designed medical research, the calculus of risk and benefit that is an integral part of it, and the design of methods to maximize its potential for gain. If we permit it to be circumscribed with a bureaucracy of regulation so cumbersome as to impede its progress, we incur a risk to society from the restriction of medical science that will far outweigh the aggregate risk to all the subjects in experimental studies.

MEDICAL PRACTICE AND MEDICAL RESEARCH

One source of misunderstanding is the confusion of what is usual and customary in medical practice with

From *Science* 198 (December 16, 1977), 1105–1110. Copyright © 1977 by the American Association for the Advancement of Science. Reprinted with permission of the author and the publisher.

what is safe and useful. The critics of research are often exquisitely aware of the dangers in an experiment (indeed, the responsible investigator is at pains to spell them out as precisely as he or she can). At the same time, these critics, surprisingly naive about the extent to which medical practice rests on custom rather than evidence, fail to appreciate the necessity for controlled trials to determine whether what is traditional does harm rather than good.

Consider, for example, the fact that about 1 million tonsillectomies and adenoidectomies are done each year in the United States; T and A's make up 30 percent of all surgery on children. Set aside budgetary considerations, even though the outlay—about $500 million—represents a significant "opportunity cost" in resources lost to more useful medical care.[2] During the 1950s, T and A's resulted in some 200 to 300 deaths per year.[3] Current mortality has been estimated at one death per 16,000 operations.[4] Yet this procedure (whose origins are lost in antiquity) continues at epidemic rates though there is no evidence that it is effective[5] except for a few uncommon conditions.[6] Doctors disagree so widely about the "indications" for T and A that within one state (Vermont) there is a fivefold variation by area of residence in the probability that a person will have his or her tonsils removed by age 20.[7] Thus, we have a procedure of dubious value employed at high frequency despite significant mortality and dollar costs. Why? It is done because doctors and parents believe in it; having become usual and customary, it is not subject to the systematic scrutiny of an experimental design.

Compare the human cost from this single routine and relatively minor procedure to the risk to human subjects in nontherapeutic and therapeutic research. Cardon and his colleagues[8] surveyed investigators conducting research on 133,000 human subjects over the past 3 years. In nontherapeutic research, which involved some 93,000 subjects, there was not one fatality, there was only one instance of permanent disability (0.001 percent), and there were 37 cases of temporary disability (0.04 percent). In therapeutic research (that is, clinical research carried out on sick people who stood to benefit directly from the knowledge gained), among 39,000 patients, 43 died (0.1 percent) and 13 suffered permanent disability (0.03 percent). (Most of the deaths were of patients on cancer chemotherapy.) The risk to experimental subjects in nontherapeutic research is comparable to the rates for accidental injury in the general population (when one makes appropriate calculation for days of risk per year). Tonsillectomy, a relatively minor surgical procedure, produces more deaths per 100,000 each year than the total from all nontherapeutic research! If we add into our calculation the deaths resulting from major surgical procedures that may be performed more often than is warranted—for example, the current rate of 647 hysterectomies per 100,000 females projects to loss of the uterus for half the female population by age 65[9]—and from excessive and injudicious prescription of powerful drugs, it becomes clear that the gain in public safety from exacting scrutiny of medical practice by means of controlled trials would far outweigh any possible gain from the most restrictive approach to medical research. Let me not be misunderstood: I do not deny the necessity for surveillance of the ethics of the research community; the point I stress is that medical research, applied to medical practice, stands alone in its ability to avert unnecessary human suffering and death.

THE SOURCES OF MEDICAL ERROR

Among the reasons given for the persistence of medical error are venality on the part of physicians, professional incompetence, and lack of commitment to the public weal. There are venal physicians; we need look no further than the exposure of Medicaid mills to find them. But that hardly accounts for the overprescription of surgery when we recognize that surgery is performed on physicians' families even more often than it is on the general public[10]; physicians as consumers follow the advice they proffer as providers. There are incompetent doctors, and we still lack adequate methods for weeding them out; but anesthetic and surgical deaths occur in the best of hands because of the risks inherent in the procedures. Not all doctors are actuated by the public interest, but this hardly explains what concerns us about physician behavior. Although these factors contribute to wrongheadedness in medical practice, a far more important source is simply the doctor's conviction that what he or she does is for the patient's welfare. When good evidence is lacking, the best and most dedicated of us do wrong in the utter conviction of being right.

BLOODLETTING AS PANACEA

Let me offer a historical illustration from the career of a man with many admirable qualities, a leading U.S. physician of the late 18th century. Benjamin Rush was uncommon among his peers in having a university degree in medicine (from Edinburgh); he was appointed professor of chemistry at the College of Philadelphia (soon to become the Medical School of the University of Pennsylvania, the first medical school in America) and later professor of the institute and practices of medicine. He was among the most steadfast of patriots, a signer of the Declaration of Independence, a member of the Pennsylvania delegation that voted to adopt the Constitution of the United States, and a founder of the first antislavery society.[11] His book *Medical Inquiries and Observations upon the Diseases of the Mind* was the first comprehensive American treatise on mental illness.[12] Thus, we have a physician with as good an education as his time could provide, a leading member of the faculty of the premier school of medicine, and a man dedicated to the public interest.

In 1793, a severe epidemic of yellow fever fell upon the city of Philadelphia.[13] It is estimated that more than one-third of its population of 50,000 fled the city and that more than 4,000 lives were lost. Panic beset the medical community, and doctors were among those who took flight to escape the pestilence. From illness and defection at the height of the epidemic, only three physicians were available to treat more than 6,000 patients. Rush dispatched his wife and children to the safety of the countryside and remained behind to fulfill his medical responsibility.

Rush was an adherent of the Brunonian system of medicine, according to which febrile illnesses resulted from an excess of stimulation and a corresponding excitement of the blood. In keeping with this theory, he ministered to his patients by vigorous bleeding and purging, the latter to "divert the force of the fever to [the bowels] and thereby save the liver and brains from a fatal and dangerous congestion." Rush went from patient to patient, letting blood copiously and purging with vigor. His desperate remedies, contemporary critics contended, were more dangerous than the disease, a criticism history has borne out.

His beliefs were not something he reserved for others. He himself was taken with a violent fever. He instructed his assistant to bleed him "plentifully" and give him "a dose of the mercurial medicine." From illness and treatment combined, he almost died; his convalescence was prolonged. That he did recover persuaded him that his methods were correct. Thus, when the epidemic subsided, he wrote: "Never before did I experience such sublime joy as I now felt on contemplating the success of my remedies. . . . The conquest

of a formidable disease was through the triumph of a principle in medicine."[14] Neither dedication so great that he risked his life to minister to others, nor willingness to treat himself as he treated others, nor yet the best education to be had in his day was sufficient to prevent Rush from committing grievous harm in the name of doing good. Convinced of the correctness of his theory of medicine and lacking a means for the systematic study of treatment outcome, he attributed each new instance of improvement to the efficacy of his treatment and each new death that occurred despite it to the severity of the disease.

INTRODUCTION OF THE NUMERICAL METHOD

Bloodletting continued to be a widely used medical remedy until the middle of the 19th century. According to Osler,[15] it was finally abandoned because of the introduction into American medicine of the "numerical method" of the French physician Pierre Charles Alexandre Louis. Louis had been disenchanted with his medical education and his experience as a practitioner. He withdrew from practice to devote himself to study. As one contemporary commented:[15]

He consecrated the whole of his time and talent to rigorous, impartial observation. All private practice was relinquished and he allowed no considerations of personal emolument to interfere with the resolution he had formed. For some time, his extreme minuteness in inquiry and accuracy of description were the subjects of sneering and ridicule, and "to what end?" was not infrequently and tauntingly asked.

One result of his study, an essay on bloodletting, appeared in Paris in 1835.[16] Within a year, it was translated into English by G. C. Putnam.[17] In a preface to the volume James Jackson, physician to the Massachusetts General Hospital, wrote:[18]

If anything may be regarded as settled in the treatment of diseases, it is that bloodletting is useful in the class of diseases called inflammatory; and especially in inflammation of the thoracic viscera. To this general opinion or belief on this subject, M. Louis gives support by his observations; but the result of these observations is that the benefits derived from bleeding in the diseases, which he has here examined, are not so great and striking as they had been represented by many teachers. If the same methods should be obtained by others, after making observations as rigorous as M. Louis, many of us will be forced to modify our former opinions. . . . The author does not pretend that the questions, here discussed, are decided forever. He makes a valuable contribution to the evidence, on which they must be decided; he points out the mode, in which this evidence should be collected, and in which its material should be analyzed; seeking truth only, he calls on others to adduce facts, which, being gathered from various quarters, may show us, with a good degree of exactness, the precise value of the remedy in question.

Louis himself began his monograph with the comment:[19]

The results of my researches on the effects of bloodletting in inflammation are so little in accord with the general opinion, that it is not without a degree of hesitation I have decided to publish them. After having analyzed the facts, which relate to them, for the first time, I thought myself deceived, and began my work anew; but having again from this new analysis, obtained the same results, I could no longer doubt their correctness.

He was led to conclude:

We infer that bloodletting has had very little influence on the progress of pneumonitis . . . ; that its influence has not been more evident in the cases bled copiously and repeatedly, than in those bled only once and to a small amount; that we do not at once arrest inflammations, as it too often finally imagined; that, in cases where it appears to be otherwise, it is undoubtedly owing, either to an error in diagnosis, or to the fact that the bloodletting was practiced at an advanced period of the disease, when it had nearly run its course.

Yet, so strong was the power of authority, that he was moved to comment:[20]

I will add that bloodletting, notwithstanding its influence is limited, should not be neglected in inflammations which are severe and are seated in an important organ.

Louis's precise observations, his stress on the importance of studying series of cases, and his insistence on reexamining standard belief were to have an enormous influence. Many American physicians went to Paris to become his pupils and returned to these shores persuaded of the value of his method. Insofar as it can be said that any single contribution led to the abandonment on this continent of bloodletting as a panacea, it was Louis's numerical method. It had its roots in the earlier applications of elementary statistics to public health and became far more powerful as a method when the concepts of probability statistics were applied to its simple tabulations.[21] From these beginnings stems much of the progress in medical science.

IMPORTANCE OF CLINICAL DESCRIPTION AND CLASSIFICATION

I have thus far stressed the contributions of the controlled clinical trial[22] to the provision of more effective remedies and to the elimination of harmful ones. But before physicians can treat, they must be able to discriminate disorders one from another. Here, careful delineation of disease patterns, both immediate and longitudinal, and attention to ways in which patients resemble and differ from each other provide the necessary groundwork for identifying the underlying pathophysiology. The process begins with the report of a puzzling and hitherto undescribed group of cases. Initially attention is directed at differentiating the new syndrome from superficially similar conditions. Some decades pass during which doctors disagree on the diagnosis and include or exclude a penumbra of cases which markedly affect the reported outcome. Next a fundamental pathogenic lesion is discovered, and confirmed by other workers, to be present in "typical" cases. As the mechanism of the disease is clarified, the disease itself is redefined in terms of the underlying pathology. Now new and variant clinical forms can be identified, cases that would not have met the original criteria. Let me illustrate this by an example from hematology.

In 1925 Cooley and Lee separated out from the group of childhood anemias (known as von Jaksch's anemia) five cases with hepatosplenomegaly, skin pigmentation, thick bones, and oddly shaped red cells with decreased osmotic fragility. Cooley's anemia was renamed thalassemia in 1932 by Whipple and Bradford, who noted that the children came from families of Mediterranean origin. The genetic basis of thalassemia was established by Wintrobe in 1940 in a paper which distinguished thalassemia minor (the heterozygous state) from thalassemia major (the homozygous state). Fifteen years later Kunkel discovered the normal minor hemoglobin component hemoglobin A_2 and found it to be elevated in individuals with thalassemia minor.[23] A subsequent explosion of research on the hemoglobin molecule has led to the recognition of some 50 combinations of genetic errors which can produce the clinical picture of thalassemia. . . .

Hand in hand with the controlled clinical trial and with the continuing search for diagnostic precision must go fundamental research in basic biology. Much of our armamentarium for the treatment and prevention of disease is at the level of what Lewis Thomas[24] has called "halfway technology," measures which, though useful, only partly reverse the disease process, are costly, and are toxic. Consider the situation this nation faced not long ago in coping with poliomyelitis. Each year it took 2,000 lives and left 3,000 persons with severe paralysis. The hospital cost for acute and chronic care, the iron lung, the wet pack, and physiotherapy exceeded $1 billion a year. For an investment of $40 million in the basic research which led to Ender's method of cultivating the polio virus in the chick embryo, and not more than several hundred million dollars for applied technology and population trials, an enormous human and financial loss has been averted.[25]

The psychiatrist today is in the position of the pediatrician a generation ago. Chemotherapy aborts acute psychotic episodes, but recurrence is common, permanent disability frequent, and drug toxicity considerable. We have strong evidence for familial predisposition but cannot specify modes of inheritance or what is inherited, or distinguish the potential patient before illness occurs. The hope of prevention must rest upon increased support for fundamental research in neurobiology, genetics, and epidemiology.[26] The problem is not a gap in the application of knowledge but a gap in knowledge itself.

Basic research does not begin and end with molecular biology. Vaccination provides a model for infectious diseases and perhaps even for neoplasms; it is simply irrelevant to behavior-linked health problems: the consequences of smoking, overeating, drinking, drugging, and reckless driving. Belloc and Breslow have shown that seven personal health habits sum to a powerful prediction of morbidity[27] and mortality[28] for middle-aged adults. To recognize that cultural patterns, social forces, and idiosyncratic personal behaviors have major effects on health[29] is not equivalent to knowing how to alter them. It does, however, argue for the urgency of research in the social as well as the biological sciences if physicians are to learn how to intervene effectively.[30]

THE RESTRICTION OF RISK AND THE RISK OF RESTRICTION

Health will be held hazard to custom until the current preoccupation with the dangers of research is placed in the appropriate context: namely, weighing in the very same scales the dangers of not doing research. Surveillance of research ethics requires simultaneous assessment of the scientific and the ethical soundness of the protocols themselves. "A poorly or improperly designed study involving human subjects—one that could not possibly yield scientific facts (that is, reproducible observations) relevant to the question under study—is by definition unethical."[31] Commendation for a high rate of rejection of research proposals implies that the proper goal for a research review committee is blocking human studies. To the contrary, the systematic imposition of impediments to significant therapeutic research is itself unethical because an important benefit is being denied to the community.

This is not a call for unrestricted rights for medical researchers. If I do not accept the view that medical researchers are worse than lawyers or philosophers, I will not argue that they are better. They are simply human; that is to say, fallible. As in the case of all professional activity, social controls are necessary. But in establishing those controls, it is necessary to weigh fully the possible resultant losses. The decision not to do something poses as many ethical quandaries as the decision to do it. Not to act is to act.[32]

Important ethical issues in medical research have been overlooked in the preoccupation with ethical absolutes. Consider, for example, the clear social class bias in the likelihood of being a subject in a medical experiment. For that there can be no justification. Even if risk in research be inevitable, inequity in exposure because of caste or class need not be. The patients on whom clinical research is most often done are clinic patients, those who by reason of economic circumstance and education are the least able to assert their rights against medical authority.

It was not long ago, to our shame, that this practice was explicitly justified on the ground that the poor paid society back for the "privilege" of receiving charitable care by being suitable clinical material for research and teaching. Few would defend that position in so callous a way today. Yet the practice continues, less by plan than by fallout from our two-track medical care system. Researchers are located in teaching hospitals. Teaching hospitals are a major medical resource for the poor. The poor become the patients on whom studies are done because of their convenience as a study population and our insensitivity to the injustice of the practice. It is not enough to say that we now offer explanation and choice and obtain informed consent. Indeed, we do. But the quality of consent is not the same when the social position of doctor and patient are disparate as it is when they are more nearly equals.

Enhancing the human quality of the community in which we live is the responsibility of every citizen; one way to meet that responsibility is by sharing in the risks of the search to diminish human suffering. Richard Titmuss[33] has pointed to the health benefits to the United Kingdom from a public policy based on a voluntary blood donor system [but see Sapolsky and Finkelstein for a contrary view[34]]. I suggest that there will be moral gain as well as health gain to the United States to the extent that we succeed in creating a community of shared responsibility for health research.

INFORMED CONSENT IN THE ABSENCE OF INFORMATION

What does "informed" consent mean in the real world of medical practice? When risks are specifiable so that it is possible to make a rational decision by weighing alternatives, it is clearly the physician's duty to inform the patient fully. That has long been a hallmark of good medical practice and sound clinical investigation; it is no contemporary discovery. But what does "informed" mean when what is available to the physician, let alone the patient, is not information but noise? In what sense is there a choice to be made between treatment A and treatment B if there is no proof that either works or that one is superior to the other? What right have I lost if, in a national health scheme, I am assigned to a randomized trial without being asked my preference, when that preference can only be capricious? The very justification for a randomized trial is that there is insufficient information to permit a rational, that is, informed, choice. In a free society we will reserve the right for any citizen to opt out. But when we respect the privilege to be guided by superstition, astrology, or simple orneriness, let us drop the adjective "informed" and speak only of "consent."

DO WE NEED MEDICAL RESEARCH?

A major undercurrent in the criticism of medical research is a growing belief that it is basically irrelevant to contemporary human needs. The argument runs something like this: what doctors do has only marginal effects on health; anyway, what researchers learn, when it does

add to knowledge, doesn't get into practice; besides, from a higher moral view, what really matters is learning to live with the existential realities of pain and dying and not to permit technical iatrogenesis to alienate man from his nature.[35] To what extent is this credible?

There is good evidence for the proposition that the increase in longevity over the past century in industrialized nations has been principally the result of social forces: better nutrition, better hygiene, and changed behavior.[36] An instructive example is the striking decline in mortality from tuberculosis over the last 100 years, with only a small additional decrement visible after the introduction of streptomycin. But there is no assurance that further social change will eliminate the residual cases. Moreover, chemotherapy is decisive in the treatment of the tuberculosis that is still with us; the lack of a prominent effect on aggregate mortality statistics reflects the lesser prevalence of the disease as a public health problem, not the ineffectiveness of treatment. But the major defect of the proposition, as a general indictment of medical care, is at a more fundamental level. Doctors, at best, postpone death; death itself is inevitable. Most of what doctors do is to mitigate discomfort and pain and to enhance function in the presence of chronic disease, an effect that is not registered in mortality tables.[37] Sole reliance on longevity and mortality leaves unmeasured the benefits most patients consult doctors for and the major benefits they have always derived from them.[38] Morbidity rates, and the consequent demand for medical resources,[39] cannot be predicted from mortality data.[40]

The second theme, the failure to translate research into practice, . . . is grossly exaggerated. Lag undoubtedly occurs in the transfer of medical skills from highly specialized centers to rural areas; the much more troublesome problem is the indiscriminate introduction into practice of new drugs and surgical innovations well before their indications and limitations are clear, often in such ways as to compromise their usefulness. The major barriers to the treatment of life-threatening disease stem not from failing to use what we know but from not knowing what to use.

Eighty percent of the deaths in this country are caused by cardiovascular, neoplastic, cerebrovascular, and renal disease.[24] For the very great majority of the specific disorders within these categories the treatments we have are only palliatives. Palliatives are important, and certainly they should be distributed fairly; but the most evenhanded and prompt distribution of all available remedies would have only a small effect on death rates. As to resource allocation, the percentage of the health dollar (well under 2 percent) devoted to applied and basic medical research in toto is so small a part of total health costs that complete diversion of those funds would have negligible effects on health care delivery. The one clear result would be to end all prospect for improving the quality of the care delivered.

The idea that pain and dying are integral parts of man's fate, though put forth as a truism, is in fact a theological view of the human condition.[35] To comprehend its meaning, it is necessary to ask: How much pain? Death at what age? Whose pain and whose death? By what standards: today's or a century ago's, white American or black American, Indian or African? Perhaps, with a life expectancy exceeding the Biblical threescore and ten, affluent white Americans can afford the luxury of wondering whether medical research makes much sense in view of the risks and costs it entails. That is, we can if we mistake our fate for man's fate, ourselves for all of humankind.

A THIRD WORLD PERSPECTIVE ON RESEARCH

The armchair view of medical research as fun and games undergoes radical transformation from the standpoint of the third world, where infant mortality may be as high as 20 percent and life expectancy no more than 30 years. "People are sick because they are poor, they become poorer because they are sick and they become sicker because they are poorer."[41] Six infectious diseases that are almost unknown on our shores plague Africa, Asia, and Latin America: Malaria afflicts an estimated quarter billion; the mosquito that spreads it is becoming resistant to the standard pesticides and the plasmodium to chloroquin. Trypanosomiasis afflicts perhaps 20 million; we lack effective weapons against either the vector or the parasite; the treatment in use can be more dangerous than the disease. Leishmaniasis claims some 12 million; there is no known treatment. Filariasis and onchocerciasis infect 300 million; treatment is ineffective. Schistosomiasis afflicts 250 million; as nations attempt to improve their agricultural productivity through irrigation, the snail vector multiplies. Finally, there are 12 to 15 million lepers in the world; the current treatment requires 7 years; drug-resistant lepra bacilli have begun to appear.

In the face of all this, there is a clear moral imperative in developed nations for medical research in tropical diseases, to seek to permit two-thirds of the world's population to share in the freedom from pain and un-

timely death we have achieved for ourselves. In the forceful words of Barry Bloom:[41]

Discourse about medicine and ethics has focused almost entirely on problems of a wealthy society, and relatively little attention has been given to those affecting the vast majority of people in the world. There is a preponderant concern with individualism and individual rights, most recently reflected in the enormous preoccupation with death and dying. Imagine the impact of the anguished disquisitions about the Karen Quinlan case on the reader in Bangladesh or Upper Volta. The public agitation over "pulling the plug" on a single machine seems almost perverse when juxtaposed against the unmet health needs, the desperate struggle for survival of millions of people around the globe. I do not deny that there are serious problems of individual liberty at stake or that the Quinlan case may serve as a model for delimiting the role of the family, physician, or state in authorizing medical treatment for those unable to speak for themselves. But when the model so fills the horizon as to obscure the reality, then all perspective is lost.

•   •   •

M. PASTEUR'S RESEARCH

Because science is incomplete, reason imperfect, and both can be put to damaging uses, some would abandon science and reason in favor of mysticism, hermeneutics, and transcendental rapture. It is not knowledge but ignorance that assures misery. It is not science but its employment for inhuman purposes that threatens our survival. The fundamental ethical questions of science are political questions:[42] Who shall control its products? For what purposes shall they be employed?

Four years after the community protests against the dangers of [Louis Pasteur's] research, the citizens of France, by public subscriptions in gratitude for his contribution to human welfare, erected the Pasteur Institute. In the ceremony of dedication, Pasteur, overcome by his feelings, asked his son to read his remarks, which concluded:[43]

Two opposing laws seem to be now in contest. The one, a law of blood and of death, ever imagining new means of destruction, forces nations always to be ready for battle. The other, a law of peace, work and health, ever evolving means of delivering man from the scourges which beset him. The one seeks violent conquests, the other the relief of humanity. The one places a single life above all victories, the other sacrifices hundreds of thousands of lives to the ambition of a single individual. The law of which we are the instruments strives even in the midst of carnage to cure the wounds due to the law of war. Treatment by our antiseptic methods may save the lives of thousands of soldiers. Which of these two laws will ultimately prevail, God alone knows. But this we may assert: that French science will have tried, by obeying the law of Humanity, to extend the frontiers of life.

NOTES.

1. A. Etzioni and C. Nunn, *Daedalus* 103, 191 (1974).

2. H. H. Hiatt, *N. Engl. J. Med.* 293, 235 (1975).

3. H. Bakwin, *J. Pediatr.* 52, 339 (1958).

4. L. W. Pratt, *Trans. Am. Acad. Ophthalmol. Otolaryngol.* 74, 1146 (1970).

5. W. Shaikh, E. Vayda, W. Feldman, *Pediatrics* 57, 401 (1976).

6. C. Guilleminault, F. L. Eldridge, F. B. Simons, W. C. Dement, *ibid.* 58, 23 (1976).

7. J. Wennberg and A. Gittelsohn, *Science* 182, 1102 (1973).

8. P. V. Cardon, F. W. Dommel, R. R. Trumble, *N. Engl. J. Med.* 295, 650 (1976).

9. J. Bunker, V. C. Donahue, P. Cole, M. Notman, ibid., p. 264.

10. J. Bunker and B. Brown, ibid., 290, 1051 (1974).

11. G. W. Corner, *The Autobiography of Benjamin Rush* (Princeton Univ. Press, Princeton, N.J., 1948).

12. B. Rush, *Medical Inquiries and Observations, Upon the Diseases of the Mind* (Kimber & Richardson, Philadelphia, 1812; reprinted by Hafner, New York, 1962).

13. W. S. Middleton, *Ann. Med. Hist.* 10, 434 (1928).

14. Ibid., p. 442.

15. W. Osler, *Bull. Johns Hopkins Hosp.* 8, 161 (1897).

16. W. J. Gaines and H. G. Langford, *Arch. Intern. Med.* 106, 571 (1960).

17. P. C. A. Louis, *Researches on the Effects of Bloodletting in Some Inflammatory Diseases and on the Influence of Tartarized Antimony and Vesication in Pneumonitis,* translated by C. G. Putnam with preface and appendix by J. Jackson (Hilliard, Gray, Boston, 1836).

18. Ibid., pp. v–vi

19. Ibid., p. 1.

20. Ibid., p. 22.

21. G. Rosen, *Bull. Hist. Med.* 29, 27 (1955).

22. A. L. Cochrane, *Effectiveness and Efficiency: Random Reflections on Health Services* (Nuffield Provincial Hospitals Trust, London, 1972).

23. D. J. Weatherall, *Johns Hopkins Med. J.* 139, 194 (1976).

24. L. Thomas, *Daedalus* 106, 35 (1977).

25. H. H. Fudenberg, *J. Invest. Dermatol.* 61, 321 (1973).

26. L. Eisenberg, *Bull. N.Y. Acad. Med.* 51, 118 (1975).

27. N. B. Belloc and L. Breslow, *Prev. Med.* 1, 409 (1972).

28. ____, ibid. 2, 67 (1973).

29. L. Eisenberg, *N. Engl. J. Med.* 296, 903 (1977).

30. A. Kleinman, L. Eisenberg, B. Good, *Ann. Intern. Med.* 88, 251 (1978).

31. D. D. Rutstein, *Daedalus* 98, 523 (1969).

32. L. Eisenberg, *J. Child Psychol. Psychiatr.* 16, 93 (1975).

33. R. Titmuss, *The Gift Relationship: From Human Blood to Social Policy* (Pantheon, New York, 1971).

34. H. M. Sapolsky and S. N. Finkelstein, *Public Interest* (Winter 1977), p. 15.

35. I. Illich, *Medical Nemesis: The Expropriation of Health* (Calder & Boyars, London, 1975).

36. T. McKeown, *The Role of Medicine: Dream, Mirage or Nemesis?* (Nuffield Provincial Hospitals Trust, London, 1976).

37. W. McDermott, *Daedalus* 106, 135 (1977).

38. L. Eisenberg, in *Research and Medical Practice* (Ciba Foundation Symposium 44, Elsevier/Excerpta Medica/North-Holland, Amsterdam, 1976), pp. 3–23.

39. A. Barr and R. F. L. Logan, *Lancet* 1977-I, 994 (1977).

40. D. P. Forster, ibid., p. 997.

41. B. R. Bloom, *Hastings Center Rep.* 6, 9 (1976).

42. L. Eisenberg, *J. Med. Philos.* 1, 318 (1976).

43. R. Vallery-Radot, *The Life of Pasteur* (Doubleday, Page, Garden City, N.Y., 1923), p. 444.

BENJAMIN FREEDMAN

Equipoise and the Ethics of Clinical Research

There is widespread agreement that ethics requires that each clinical trial begin with an honest null hypothesis.[1,2] In the simplest model, testing a new treatment B on a defined patient population P for which the current accepted treatment is A, it is necessary that the clinical investigator be in a state of genuine uncertainty regarding the comparative merits of treatments A and B for population P. If a physician knows that these treatments are not equivalent, ethics requires that the superior treatment be recommended. Following Fried, I call this state of uncertainty about the relative merits of A and B "equipoise."[3]

Equipoise is an ethically necessary condition in all cases of clinical research. In trials with several arms, equipoise must exist between all arms of the trial; otherwise the trial design should be modified to exclude the inferior treatment. If equipoise is disturbed during the course of a trial, the trial may need to be terminated and all subjects previously enrolled (as well as other patients within the relevant population) may have to be offered the superior treatment. It has been rigorously argued that a trial with a placebo is ethical only in investigating conditions for which there is no known treatment[2]; this argument reflects a special application of the requirement for equipoise. Although equipoise has commonly been discussed in the special context of the ethics of randomized clinical trials,[4,5] it is important to recognize it as an ethical condition of all controlled clinical trials, whether or not they are randomized, placebo-controlled, or blinded.

The recent increase in attention to the ethics of research with human subjects has highlighted problems associated with equipoise. Yet, as I shall attempt to show, contemporary literature, if anything, minimizes those difficulties. Moreover, there is evidence that concern on the part of investigators about failure to satisfy the requirements for equipoise can doom a trial as a result of the consequent failure to enroll a sufficient number of subjects.

The solutions that have been offered to date fail to resolve these problems in a way that would permit clinical trials to proceed. This paper argues that these problems are predicated on a faulty concept of equipoise itself. An alternative understanding of equipoise as an ethical requirement of clinical trials is proposed, and its implications are explored.

Many of the problems raised by the requirement for equipoise are familiar. Shaw and Chalmers have written that a clinician who "knows, or has a good reason to believe," that one arm of the trial is superior may not ethically participate.[6] But the reasoning or preliminary results that prompt the trial (and that may themselves be ethically mandatory)[7] may jolt the investigator (if not his or her colleagues) out of equipoise before the trial begins. Even if the investigator is undecided between A and B in terms of gross measures such as mortality and morbidity, equipoise may be disturbed because evident differences in the quality of life (as in the case of two surgical approaches) tip the balance.[3-5,8] In either case, in saying "we do not know" whether A or B is better, the investigator may create a false impression in prospective subjects, who hear him or her as saying "no evidence leans either way," when the investigator means "no controlled study has yet had results that reach statistical significance."

Late in the study — when P values are between 0.05 and 0.06 — the moral issue of equipoise is most readily apparent,[9,10] but the same problem arises when the

Reprinted by permission of the publisher from Benjamin Freedman, "Equipoise and the Ethics of Clinical Research," *New England Journal of Medicine* 317 (1987), 141–45.

earliest comparative results are analyzed.[11] Within the closed statistical universe of the clinical trial, each result that demonstrates a difference between the arms of the trial contributes exactly as much to the statistical conclusion that a difference exists as does any other. The contribution of the last pair of cases in the trial is no greater than that of the first. If, therefore, equipoise is a condition that reflects equivalent evidence for alternative hypotheses, it is jeopardized by the first pair of cases as much as by the last. The investigator who is concerned about the ethics of recruitment after the penultimate pair must logically be concerned after the first pair as well.

Finally, these issues are more than a philosopher's nightmare. Considerable interest has been generated by a paper in which Taylor et al.[12] describe the termination of a trial of alternative treatments for breast cancer. The trial foundered on the problem of patient recruitment, and the investigators trace much of the difficulty in enrolling patients to the fact that the investigators were not in a state of equipoise regarding the arms of the trial. With the increase in concern about the ethics of research and with the increasing presence of this topic in the curricula of medical and graduate schools, instances of the type that Taylor and her colleagues describe are likely to become more common. The requirement for equipoise thus poses a practical threat to clinical research.

RESPONSES TO THE PROBLEMS OF EQUIPOISE

The problems described above apply to a broad class of clinical trials, at all stages of their development. Their resolution will need to be similarly comprehensive. However, the solutions that have so far been proposed address a portion of the difficulties, at best, and cannot be considered fully satisfactory.

Chalmers' approach to problems at the onset of a trial is to recommend that randomization begin with the very first subject.[11] If there are no preliminary, uncontrolled data in support of the experimental treatment B, equipoise regarding treatments A and B for the patient population P is not disturbed. There are several difficulties with this approach. Practically speaking, it is often necessary to establish details of administration, dosage, and so on, before a controlled trial begins, by means of uncontrolled trials in human subjects. In addition, as I have argued above, equipoise from the in-

vestigator's point of view is likely to be disturbed when the hypothesis is being formulated and a protocol is being prepared. It is then, before any subjects have been enrolled, that the information that the investigator has assembled makes the experimental treatment appear to be a reasonable gamble. Apart from these problems, initial randomization will not, as Chalmers recognizes, address disturbances of equipoise that occur in the course of a trial.

Data-monitoring committees have been proposed as a solution to problems arising in the course of the trial.[13] Such committees, operating independently of the investigators, are the only bodies with information concerning the trial's ongoing results. Since this knowledge is not available to the investigators, their equipoise is not disturbed. Although committees are useful in keeping the conduct of a trial free of bias, they cannot resolve the investigators' ethical difficulties. A clinician is not merely obliged to treat a patient on the basis of the information that he or she currently has, but is also required to discover information that would be relevant to treatment decisions. If interim results would disturb equipoise, the investigators are obliged to gather and use that information. Their agreement to remain in ignorance of preliminary results would, by definition, be an unethical agreement, just as a failure to call up the laboratory to find out a patient's test results is unethical. Moreover, the use of a monitoring committee does not solve problems of equipoise that arise before and at the beginning of a trial.

Recognizing the broad problems with equipoise, three authors have proposed radical solutions. All three think that there is an irresolvable conflict between the requirement that a patient be offered the best treatment known (the principle underlying requirement for equipoise) and the conduct of clinical trials; they therefore suggest that the "best treatment" requirement be weakened.

Schafer has argued that the concept of equipoise, and the associated notion of the best medical treatment, depends on the judgment of patients rather than of clinical investigators.[14] Although the equipoise of an investigator may be disturbed if he or she favors B over A, the ultimate choice of treatment is the patient's. Because the patient's values may restore equipoise, Schafer argues, it is ethical for the investigator to proceed with a trial when the patient consents. Schafer's strategy is directed toward trials that test treatments with known and divergent side effects and will probably not be useful in trials conducted to test efficacy or unknown side effects. This approach, moreover, confuses the ethics of competent medical practice with those of consent. If we assume that the investigator is a competent clinician, by saying that the investigator is out of equipoise, we have by Schafer's account said that in the investigator's professional judgment one treatment is therapeutically inferior—for that patient, in that condition, given the quality of life that can be achieved. Even if a patient would consent to an inferior treatment, it seems to me a violation of competent medical practice, and hence of ethics, to make the offer. Of course, complex issues may arise when a patient refuses what the physician considers the best treatment and demands instead an inferior treatment. Without settling that problem, however, we can reject Schafer's position. For Schafer claims that in order to continue to conduct clinical trials, it is ethical for the physician to offer (not merely accede to) inferior treatment.

Meier suggests that "most of us would be quite willing to forego a modest expected gain in the general interest of learning something of value."[15] He argues that we accept risks in everyday life to achieve a variety of benefits, including convenience and economy. In the same way, Meier states, it is acceptable to enroll subjects in clinical trials even though they may not receive the best treatment throughout the course of the trial. Schafer suggests an essentially similar approach.[5,14] According to this view, continued progress in medical knowledge through clinical trials requires an explicit abandonment of the doctor's fully patient-centered ethic.

These proposals seem to be frank counsels of desperation. They resolve the ethical problems of equipoise by abandoning the need for equipoise. In any event, would their approach allow clinical trials to be conducted? I think this may fairly be doubted. Although many people are presumably altruistic enough to forgo the best medical treatment in the interest of the progress of science, many are not. The numbers and proportions required to sustain the statistical validity of trial results suggest that in the absence of overwhelming altruism, the enrollment of satisfactory numbers of patients will not be possible. In particular, very ill patients, toward whom many of the most important clinical trials are directed, may be disinclined to be altruistic. Finally, as the study by Taylor et al.[12] reminds us, the problems of equipoise trouble investigators as well as patients. Even if patients are prepared to dispense with the best treatment, their physicians, for reasons of ethics and professionalism, may well not be willing to do so.

Marquis has suggested a third approach. "Perhaps what is needed is an ethics that will justify the conscription of subjects for medical research," he has written. "Nothing less seems to justify present practice."[4] Yet, although conscription might enable us to continue present practice, it would scarcely justify it. Moreover, the conscription of physician investigators, as well as subjects, would be necessary, because, as has been repeatedly argued, the problems of equipoise are as disturbing to clinicians as they are to subjects. Is any less radical and more plausible approach possible?

THEORETICAL EQUIPOISE VERSUS CLINICAL EQUIPOISE

The problems of equipoise examined above arise from a particular understanding of that concept, which I will term "theoretical equipoise." It is an understanding that is both conceptually odd and ethically irrelevant. Theoretical equipoise exists when, overall, the evidence on behalf of two alternative treatment regimens is exactly balanced. This evidence may be derived from a variety of sources, including data from the literature, uncontrolled experience, considerations of basic science and fundamental physiologic processes, and perhaps a "gut feeling" or "instinct" resulting from (or superimposed on) other considerations. The problems examined above arise from the principle that if theoretical equipoise is disturbed, the physician has, in Schafer's words, a "treatment preference"—let us say, favoring experimental treatment B. A trial testing A against B requires that some patients be enrolled in violation of this treatment preference.

Theoretical equipoise is overwhelmingly fragile; that is, it is disturbed by a slight accretion of evidence favoring one arm of the trial. In Chalmers' view, equipoise is disturbed when the odds that A will be more successful than B are anything other than 50 percent. It is therefore necessary to randomize treatment assignments beginning with the very first patient, lest equipoise be disturbed. We may say that theoretical equipoise is balanced on a knife's edge.

Theoretical equipoise is most appropriate to one-dimensional hypotheses and causes us to think in those terms. The null hypothesis must be sufficiently simple and "clean" to be finely balanced: Will A or B be superior in reducing mortality or shrinking tumors or lowering fevers in population P? Clinical choice is commonly more complex. The choice of A or B depends on some combination of effectiveness, consistency, minimal or relievable side effects, and other factors. On close examination, for example, it sometimes appears that even trials that purport to test a single hypothesis in fact involve a more complicated, portmanteau measure — e.g., the "therapeutic index" of A versus B. The formulation of the conditions of theoretical equipoise for such complex, multidimensional clinical hypotheses is tantamount to the formulation of a rigorous calculus of apples and oranges.

Theoretical equipoise is also highly sensitive to the vagaries of the investigator's attention and perception. Because of its fragility, theoretical equipoise is disturbed as soon as the investigator perceives a difference between the alternatives — whether or not any genuine difference exists. Prescott writes, for example, "It will be common at some stage in most trials for the survival curves to show visually different survivals," short of significance but "sufficient to raise ethical difficulties for the participants."[16] A visual difference, however, is purely an artifact of the research methods employed: when and by what means data are assembled and analyzed and what scale is adopted for the graphic presentation of data. Similarly, it is common for researchers to employ interval scales for phenomena that are recognized to be continuous by nature — e.g., five-point scales of pain or stages of tumor progression. These interval scales, which represent an arbitrary distortion of the available evidence to simplify research, may magnify the differences actually found, with a resulting disturbance of theoretical equipoise.

Finally, as described by several authors, theoretical equipoise is personal and idiosyncratic. It is disturbed when the clinician has, in Schafer's words, what "might even be labeled a bias or a hunch," a preference of a "merely intuitive nature."[14] The investigator who ignores such a hunch, by failing to advise the patient that because of it the investigator prefers B to A or by recommending A (or a chance of random assignment to A) to the patient, has violated the requirement for equipoise and its companion requirement to recommend the best medical treatment.

The problems with this concept of equipoise should be evident. To understand the alternative, preferable interpretation of equipoise, we need to recall the basic reason for conducting clinical trials: there is a current or imminent conflict in the clinical community over what treatment is preferred for patients in a defined population P. The standard treatment is A, but some evidence suggests that B will be superior (because of its effectiveness or its reduction of undesirable side effects, or for some other reason). (In the rare case when the first evidence of a novel therapy's superiority would be entirely convincing to the clinical community, equipoise is already disturbed.) Or there is a split in the clinical community, with some clinicians favoring A and others favoring B. Each side recognizes that the opposing side has evidence to support its position, yet each still thinks that overall its own view is correct. There exists (or, in the case of a novel therapy, there may soon exist) an honest, professional disagreement among expert clinicians about the preferred treatment. A clinical trial is instituted with the aim of resolving this dispute.

At this point, a state of "clinical equipoise" exists. There is no consensus within the expert clinical community about the comparative merits of the alternatives to be tested. We may state the formal conditions under which such a trial would be ethical as follows: at the start of the trial, there must be a state of clinical equipoise regarding the merits of the regimens to be tested, and the trial must be designed in such a way as to make it reasonable to expect that, if it is successfully concluded, clinical equipoise will be disturbed. In other words, the results of a successful clinical trial should be convincing enough to resolve the dispute among clinicians.

A state of clinical equipoise is consistent with a decided treatment preference on the part of the investigators. They must simply recognize that their less-favored treatment is preferred by colleagues whom they consider to be responsible and competent. Even if the interim results favor the preference of the investigators, treatment B, clinical equipoise persists as long as those results are too weak to influence the judgment of the community of clinicians, because of limited sample size, unresolved possibilities of side effects, or other factors. (This judgment can necessarily be made only by those who know the interim results — whether a data-monitoring committee or the investigators.)

At the point when the accumulated evidence in favor of B is so strong that the committee or investigators believe no open-minded clinician informed of the results would still favor A, clinical equipoise has been disturbed. This may occur well short of the original schedule for the termination of the trial, for unexpected reasons. (Therapeutic effects or side effects may be much stronger than anticipated, for example, or a definable subgroup within population P may be recognized for which the results demonstrably disturb clinical equipoise.) Because of the arbitrary character of human judgment and persuasion, some ethical problems regarding the termination of a trial will remain. Clinical equipoise will confine these problems to unusual or extreme cases, however, and will allow us to cast persistent problems in the proper terms. For example, in the face of a strong established trend, must we continue the trial because of others' blind fealty to an arbitrary statistical benchmark?

Clearly, clinical equipoise is a far weaker—and more common—condition than theoretical equipoise. Is it ethical to conduct a trial on the basis of clinical equipoise, when theoretical equipoise is disturbed? Or, as Schafer and others have argued, is doing so a violation of the physician's obligation to provide patients with the best medical treatment?[4,5,14] Let us assume that the investigators have a decided preference for B but wish to conduct a trial on the grounds that clinical (not theoretical) equipoise exists. The ethics committee asks the investigators whether, if they or members of their families were within population P, they would not want to be treated with their preference, B? An affirmative answer is often thought to be fatal to the prospects for such a trial, yet the investigators answer in the affirmative. Would a trial satisfying this weaker form of equipoise be ethical?

I believe that it clearly is ethical. As Fried has emphasized,[3] competent (hence, ethical) medicine is social rather than individual in nature. Progress in medicine relies on progressive consensus within the medical and research communities. The ethics of medical practice grants no ethical or normative meaning to a treatment preference, however powerful, that is based on a hunch or on anything less than evidence publicly presented and convincing to the clinical community. Persons are licensed as physicians after they demonstrate the acquisition of this professionally validated knowledge, not after they reveal a superior capacity for guessing. Normative judgments of their behavior—e.g., malpractice actions—rely on a comparison with what is done by the community of medical practitioners. Failure to follow a "treatment preference" not shared by this community and not based on information that would convince it could not be the basis for an allegation of legal or ethical malpractice. As Fried states: "[T]he conception of what is good medicine is the product of a professional consensus." By definition, in a state of clinical equipoise, "good medicine" finds the choice between A and B indifferent.

In contrast to theoretical equipoise, clinical equipoise is robust. The ethical difficulties at the beginning and end of a trial are therefore largely alleviated. There remain difficulties about consent, but these too may be diminished. Instead of emphasizing the lack of evidence favoring one arm over another that is required by theoretical equipoise, clinical equipoise places the emphasis in informing the patient on the honest disagreement among expert clinicians. The fact that the investigator has a "treatment preference," if he or she does, could be disclosed; indeed, if the preference is a decided one, and based on something more than a hunch, it could be ethically mandatory to disclose it. At the same time, it would be emphasized that this preference is not shared by others. It is likely to be a matter of chance that the patient is being seen by a clinician with a preference for B over A, rather than by an equally competent clinician with the opposite preference.

Clinical equipoise does not depend on concealing relevant information from researchers and subjects, as does the use of independent data-monitoring committees. Rather, it allows investigators, in informing subjects, to distinguish appropriately among validated knowledge accepted by the clinical community, data on treatments that are promising but are not (or, for novel therapies, would not be) generally convincing, and mere hunches. Should informed patients decline to participate because they have chosen a specific clinician and trust his or her judgment—over and above the consensus in the professional community—that is no more than the patients' right. We do not conscript patients to serve as subjects in clinical trials.

THE IMPLICATIONS OF CLINICAL EQUIPOISE

The theory of clinical equipoise has been formulated as an alternative to some current views on the ethics of human research. At the same time, it corresponds closely to a preanalytic concept held by many in the research and regulatory communities. Clinical equipoise serves, then, as a rational formulation of the approach of many toward research ethics; it does not so much change things as explain why they are the way they are.

Nevertheless, the precision afforded by the theory of clinical equipoise does help to clarify or reformulate some aspects of research ethics; I will mention only two.

First, there is a recurrent debate about the ethical propriety of conducting clinical trials of discredited treatments, such as Laetrile.[17] Often, substantial political pressure to conduct such tests is brought to bear by adherents of quack therapies. The theory of clinical equipoise suggests that when there is no support for a treatment regimen within the expert clinical community, the first ethical requirement of a trial—clinical equipoise—is lacking; it would therefore be unethical to conduct such a trial.

Second, Feinstein has criticized the tendency of clinical investigators to narrow excessively the conditions and hypotheses of a trial in order to ensure the validity of its results.[18] This "fastidious" approach purchases scientific manageability at the expense of an inability to apply the results to the "messy" conditions of clinical practice. The theory of clinical equipoise adds some strength to this criticism. Overly "fastidious" trials, designed to resolve some theoretical question, fail to satisfy the second ethical requirement of clinical research, since the special conditions of the trial will render it useless for influencing clinical decisions, even if it is successfully completed.

The most important result of the concept of clinical equipoise, however, might be to relieve the current crisis of confidence in the ethics of clinical trials. Equipoise, properly understood, remains an ethical condition for clinical trials. It is consistent with much current practice. Clinicians and philosophers alike have been premature in calling for desperate measures to resolve problems of equipoise.

NOTES

1. Levine RJ. Ethics and regulation of clinical research. 2d ed. Baltimore: Urban & Schwarzenberg, 1986.

2. Idem. The use of placebos in randomized clinical trials. IRB: Rev Hum Subj Res 1985; 7(2):1–4.

3. Fried C. Medical experimentation: personal integrity and social policy. Amsterdam: North-Holland Publishing, 1974.

4. Marquis D. Leaving therapy to chance. Hastings Cent Rep 1983; 13(4):40–7.

5. Schafer A. The ethics of the randomized clinical trial. N Engl J Med 1982; 307:719–24.

6. Shaw LW, Chalmers TC. Ethics in cooperative clinical trials. Ann NY Acad Sci 1970; 169:487–95.

7. Hollenberg NK, Dzau VJ, Williams GH. Are uncontrolled clinical studies ever justified? N Engl J Med 1980; 303:1067.

8. Levine RJ, Lebacqz K. Some ethical considerations in clinical trials. Clin Pharmacol Ther 1979; 25:728–41.

9. Klimt CR, Canner PL. Terminating a long-term clinical trial. Clin Pharmacol Ther 1979; 25:641–6.

10. Veatch RM. Longitudinal studies, sequential designs and grant renewals: what to do with preliminary data. IRB: Rev Hum Subj Res 1979; 1(4):1–3.

11. Chalmers T. The ethics of randomization as a decision-making technique and the problem of informed consent. In: Beauchamp TL, Walters L, eds. Contemporary issues in bioethics. Encino, Calif.: Dickenson, 1978:426–9.

12. Taylor KM, Margolese RG, Soskolne CL. Physicians' reasons for not entering eligible patients in a randomized clinical trial of surgery for breast cancer. N Engl J Med 1984; 310:1363–7.

13. Chalmers TC. Invited remarks. Clin Pharmacol Ther 1979; 25:649–50.

14. Schafer A. The randomized clinical trial: for whose benefit? IRB: Rev Hum Subj Res 1985; 7(2):4–6.

15. Meier P. Terminating a trial—the ethical problem. Clin Pharmacol Ther 1979; 25:633–40.

16. Prescott RJ. Feedback of data to participants during clinical trials. In: Tagnon HJ, Staquet MJ, eds. Controversies in cancer: design of trials and treatment. New York: Masson Publishing, 1979: 55–61.

17. Cowan DH. The ethics of clinical trials of ineffective therapy. IRB: Rev Hum Subj Res 1981; 3(5):10–1.

18. Feinstein AR. An additional basic science for clinical medicine. II. The limitations of randomized trials. Ann Intern Med 1983; 99:544–50.

Past Abuses of Human Research Subjects

GREGORY E. PENCE

The Tuskegee Study

The Tuskegee study of syphilis began during the great depression—around 1930—and lasted for 42 years. Because of its long time span . . . some historical background is important for understanding the many issues raised by the Tuskegee research.

THE MEDICAL ENVIRONMENT: SYPHILIS

Syphilis is a chronic, contagious bacterial disease, often venereal and sometimes congenital. Its first symptom is a chancre; after this chancre subsides, the disease spreads silently for a time but then produces an outbreak of secondary symptoms such as fever, rash, and swollen lymph glands. Then the disease becomes latent for many years, after which it may reappear with a variety of symptoms in the nervous or circulatory systems. Today, syphilis is treated with penicillin or other antibiotics; but this treatment has been possible only since about 1946, when penicillin first became widely available.

Until relatively recently, then, the common fate of victims of syphilis—kings and queens, peasants and slaves—was simply to suffer the sequelae once the first symptoms had appeared. Victims who suffered this inevitable progress included Cleopatra, King Herod of Judea, Charlemagne, Henry VIII of England, Napoleon Bonaparte, Frederick the Great, Pope Sixtus IV, Pope Alexander VI, Pope Julius II, Catherine the Great, Christopher Columbus, Paul Gauguin, Franz Schubert, Albrecht Dürer, Johann Wolfgang von Goethe, Friedrich Nietzsche, John Keats, and James Joyce.[1]

It is generally believed that syphilis was brought to Europe from the new world during the 1490s, by Christopher Columbus's crews, but the disease may have appeared in Europe before that time. In any case, advances in transportation contributed greatly to the spread of syphilis. . . . For hundreds of years, syphilis was attributed to sin and was associated with prostitutes, though attempts to check its spread by expelling prostitutes failed because their customers were disregarded. Efforts to eradicate it by quarantine also failed.

In the eighteenth century, standing professional armies began to be established, and with them came a general acceptance of high rates of venereal disease. It is estimated, for instance, that around the year 1900, one-fifth of the British army had syphilis or gonorrhea.

Between 1900 and 1948, and especially during the two world wars, American reformers mounted what was called a *syphilophobia* campaign: the Social Hygiene Movement or Purity Crusade. Members of the campaign emphasized that syphilis was spread by prostitutes, and held that it was rapidly fatal; as an alternative to visiting a prostitute, they advocated clean, active sports (in today's terms, "Just say no"). According to the medical historian Allan Brandt, there were two splits resulting from disagreements within this reform movement: once during World War I, when giving out condoms was controversial; and later during World War II, when giving out penicillin was at issue. In each of these conflicts, reformers whose basic intention was to reduce the physical harm of syphilis were on one side, whereas those who wanted to reduce illicit behavior were on the other side.[2]

The armed services during the world wars took a pragmatic position. Commanders who needed healthy troops overruled the moralists and ordered the release of condoms in the first war and penicillin in the second—and these continued to be used by returning troops after each war.

The spirochete (bacterium) which causes syphilis was discovered by Fritz Schaudinn in 1906. Syphilis is, classically, described in three stages:

- *Primary syphilis* — In this first stage, spirochetes mass and produce a primary lesion causing a *chancre* (pronounced "SHANK-er"). During the primary stage, syphilis is highly infectious.
- *Secondary syphilis* — In the second stage, spirochetes disseminate from the primary lesion throughout the body, producing systemic and widespread lesions, usually in internal organs and other internal sites. Externally, however — after the initial chancre subsides — syphilis spreads silently during a "latent" period lasting from 1 to 30 years, although secondary symptoms such as fever, rash, and swollen glands may appear. During the secondary stage, the symptoms of syphilis vary so widely that it is known as the "great imitator."
- *Tertiary syphilis* — In the third stage, chronic destructive lesions cause major damage to the cardiac system, the neurological system, or both, partly because immune responses decrease with age. During the tertiary stage, syphilis may produce paresis (slight or incomplete paralysis), gummas (gummy or rubbery tumors), altered gait, blindness, or lethal narrowing of the aorta.

Beginning in the sixteenth century, mercury — a heavy metal — was the common treatment for syphilis; it was applied to the back as a paste and absorbed through the skin. During the nineteenth century, this treatment alternated with bismuth, another heavy metal administered the same way. Neither mercury nor bismuth killed the spirochetes, though either could ameliorate symptoms.

In 1909, after the spirochete of syphilis had been identified, two researchers — a German, Paul Ehrlich, and a Japanese, S. Hata — tried 605 forms of arsenic and finally discovered what seemed to be a "magic bullet" against it: combination 606 of heavy metals including arsenic. Ehrlich called this *salvarsan* and patented it; the generic name is arsphenamine.[3] Salvarsan was administered as an intramuscular injection. After finding that it cured syphilis in rabbits, Ehrlich injected it into men with syphilis. (According to common practice, none of the men was asked to consent.)

At first, salvarsan seemed to work wonders, and during 1910 Ehrlich was receiving standing ovations at medical meetings. Later, however, syphilis recurred, fatally, in some patients who had been treated with salvarsan; furthermore, salvarsan itself apparently killed some patients. Ehrlich maintained that the drug had not been given correctly, but he also developed another form, neosalvarsan, which was less toxic and could be given more easily. Neosalvarsan also was injected intramuscularly — ideally, in 20 to 40 dosages given over 1 year.

Though better than salvarsan, neosalvarsan was (as described by a physician of the time) used erratically, and "generally without rhyme or reason — an injection now and then, possibly for a symptom, [for] some skin lesion, or when the patient had a ten-dollar bill."[4] It was also expensive. Moreover, neither salvarsan nor neosalvarsan was a "magic bullet" for patients with tertiary syphilis.

Another researcher, Caesar Boeck in Norway, took a different approach: from 1891 to 1910, he studied the natural course of untreated syphilis in 1,978 subjects. Boeck, a professor of dermatology at the University of Oslo, believed that heavy metals removed only the symptoms of syphilis rather than its underlying cause; he also thought that these metals suppressed what is today recognized as the immune system. He therefore decided that not treating patients at all might be an improvement over treatment with heavy metals.

In 1929, Boeck's student and successor, J. E. Bruusgaard, selected 473 of Boeck's subjects for further evaluation, in many cases examining their hospital charts.[5] This method had an obvious bias, since the more severely affected of Boeck's subjects would be most likely to have hospital records. Despite this bias, however, Bruusgaard was surprised to find that in 65 percent of these cases, either the subjects were externally symptom-free or there was no mention in their charts of the classic symptoms of syphilis. Of the subjects who had had syphilis for more than 20 years, 73 percent were asymptomatic.

Bruusgaard's findings contradicted the message of the syphilophobia campaign: they indicated that syphilis was not universally fatal, much less rapidly so. These results also suggested the possibility that some people with syphilis spirochetes would never develop any symptoms of the disease.

When the Tuskegee study began in 1932, Boeck's and Bruusgaard's work was the only existing study of the natural course of untreated syphilis.

In the 1930s, American medicine was, and had long been, widely racist—certainly by our present standards and to some extent even by the standards of the time. For at least a century before the Tuskegee study began, most physicians condescended to African American patients, held stereotypes about them, and sometimes used them as subjects of nontherapeutic experiments.

The historian Todd Savitt, for example, has described how in the 1800s, J. Marion Sims, a pioneer in American gynecology, practiced techniques for closing vesical-vaginal fistulas on slave women.[6] John Brown, a former slave who wrote a book about his life under slavery, described how a physician in Georgia kept him in an open-pit oven to produce sunburns and to try out different remedies.

The best known account of the racial background of the Tuskegee study is James Jones's *Bad Blood* (1981; the significance of the title will become apparent below).[7] In the late nineteenth century, the United States was swept by social Darwinism, a popular corruption of Darwin's theory of evolution by natural selection. . . . Some whites predicted on this basis that the Negro race (to use the term then current) would be extinct by 1900: their idea was that Darwin's "survival of the fittest" implied a competition which Negroes would lose. (It bears repeating that this is a misconception and misapplication of Darwin's actual theory.) According to Jones, this popular belief was shared by white physicians, who thought that it was confirmed by defects in African Americans' anatomy and therefore became obsessed with the details of such presumed defects. Although comparable defects in white patients went unreported, defects in black patients were described in great detail in medical journals and became the basis for sweeping conclusions; to take one example, genital development and brain development were said to vary inversely.

In addition to social Darwinism, physicians shared many of the popular stereotypes of African Americans; well into the twentieth century, physicians often simply advanced such stereotypes as "facts." The following example appeared in *Journal of the American Medical Association* in 1914:

The negro springs from a southern race, and as such his sexual appetite is strong; all of his environments stimulate this appetite, and as a general rule his emotional type of religion certainly does not decrease it.[8]

African Americans were also seen as dirty, shiftless, promiscuous, and incapable of practicing personal hygiene. Around the turn of the century, a physician in rural Georgia wrote, "Virtue in the negro race is like 'angels' visits'—few and far between. In a practice of sixteen years in the South, I have never examined a virgin over fourteen years of age."[9] In 1919, a medical professor in Chicago wrote that African American men were like bulls or elephants in *furor sexualis,* unable to refrain from copulation when in the presence of females.[10]

Ideas about syphilis reflected this racial environment. For white physicians at the time when the Tuskegee study began, syphilis was a natural consequence of the innately low character of African Americans, who were described by one white physician as a "notoriously syphilis-soaked race."[11] Moreover, it was simply assumed that African American men would not seek treatment for venereal disease.

The historian Allan Brandt has suggested that in the United States during the early 1900s, it was a rare white physician who was not a racist—and that this would have remained the case throughout many years of the Tuskegee study. He writes, "There can be little doubt that the Tuskegee researchers regarded their subjects as less than human."[12]

DEVELOPMENT OF THE TUSKEGEE CASE

A "STUDY IN NATURE" BEGINS

Studies in nature were distinguished from experiments in 1865 by a famous experimenter and physiologist, Claude Bernard: in an experiment, some factor is manipulated, whereas a *study in nature* merely observes what would happen anyway. For a century before the Tuskegee study, medicine considered it crucially important to discover the natural history of a disease and therefore relied extensively on studies in nature.

The great physician William Osler had said, "Know syphilis in all its manifestations and relations, and all others things clinical will be added unto you."[13] As late as 1932, however, the natural history of syphilis had not been conclusively documented (the only existing study, as noted above, was that of Boeck and Bruusgaard), and there was uncertainty about the inexorability of its course. The United States Public Health Service (USPHS) believed that a study in nature of syphilis was necessary because physicians needed to know its natural sequence of symptoms and final outcomes in order to recognize key changes during its course. This perceived need was one factor in the Tuskegee research.

A second factor was simply that USPHS found what it considered an opportunity for such a study. Around 1929, there were several counties in the United States where venereal disease was extraordinarily prevalent, and a philanthropical organization—the Julius Rosenwald Foundation in Philadelphia—started a project to eradicate it. With help from USPHS, the foundation originally intended to treat with neosalvarsan all syphilitics in six counties with rates of syphilis above 20 percent. In 1930, the foundation surveyed African American men in Macon County, Alabama, which was then 82 percent black; this was the home of the famous Tuskegee Institute. The survey found the highest rate of syphilis in the nation: 36 percent. The foundation planned a demonstration study in which these African American syphilitics would be treated with neosalvarsan, and it did treat or partially treat some of the 3,694 men who had been identified as having syphilis (estimates of how many received treatment or partial treatment range from less than half to 95 percent). However, 1929 was the year when the great depression began; as it ground on, funds for philanthropy plummeted, and the Rosenwald Foundation pulled out of Tuskegee, hoping that USPHS would continue the treatment program. (Funds available for public health were also dropping, though: USPHS would soon see its budget lowered from over $1 million before the depression to less than $60,000 in 1935.)

In 1931, USPHS repeated the foundation's survey in Macon County, testing 4,400 African American residents; USPHS found a 22 percent rate of syphilis in men, and a 62 percent rate of congenital syphilis. In this survey, 399 African American men were identified who had syphilis of several years' duration but had never been treated by the Rosenwald Foundation or in any other way. It was the identification of these 399 untreated men that USPHS saw as an ideal opportunity for a study in nature of syphilis. The surgeon general suggested that they should be merely observed rather than treated: this decision would become a moral crux of the study.

It is important to reemphasize that the USPHS research—it was undertaken in cooperation with the Tuskegee Institute and is called the *Tuskegee study* for that reason—was a study in nature. The Tuskegee physicians saw themselves as ecological biologists, simply observing what occurred regularly and naturally. In 1936, a paper in *Journal of the American Medical Association* by the surgeon general and his top assistants described the 1932–1933 phase of the Tuskegee study as "an unusual opportunity to study the untreated syphilitic patient from the beginning of the disease to the death of the infected person." It noted specifically that the study consisted of "399 syphilitic Negro males who had never received treatment."[14]

There are also two important points to emphasize about the subjects of the Tuskegee study. First, at the outset the 399 syphilitic subjects had *latent syphilis,* that is, secondary syphilis; most of them were probably in the early latent stage. During this stage, syphilis is largely noninfectious during sexual intercourse, although it can be passed easily through a blood transfusion (or, in a pregnant woman, through the placenta). However, latent or secondary syphilis (as noted above) has extremely variable symptoms and outcomes; and external lesions, which can be a source of infection during sex, do sometimes appear.

Second, these 399 syphilitic subjects were not divided into the typical experimental and control or "treatment" and "not treatment" groups: they were all simply to be observed. There was, however, another group of "controls," consisting of about 200 age-matched men who did not have syphilis. (Originally, there was also a third group, consisting of 275 syphilitic men who had been treated with small amounts of arsphenamine; these subjects were followed for a while but were dropped from the study in 1936—perhaps because funds were lacking, or perhaps because the researchers were by then interested only in the "study in nature" group.)

THE MIDDLE PHASE: "BAD BLOOD"

The Tuskegee study was hardly a model of scientific research or scientific method; and even on its own terms, as a study in nature, it was carried out rather haphazardly. Except for an African American nurse, Eunice Rivers, who was permanently assigned to the study, there was no continuity of medical personnel. There was no central supervision; there were no written protocols; no physician was in charge. Names of the subjects were not housed at any one location or facility. Most worked as sharecroppers or as small farmers and simply came into the town of Tuskegee when

Eunice Rivers told them to do so (she would drive them into town in her car, a ride that several subjects described as making them feel important).

There were large gaps in the study. The "federal doctors," as the subjects called them, returned only every few years. Visits are documented in 1939 and then not again until 1948; 7 years passed between visits in 1963 and 1970. Only the nurse, Eunice Rivers, remained to hold the shaky study together. When the physicians did return to Tuskegee after a gap, they found it difficult to answer their own questions because the records were so poor.

Still, there were some rudimentary procedures. The physicians wanted to know, first, if they had a subject in the study group; and second, if so, how far his syphilis had progressed. To determine the progress of the disease, spinal punctures (called *taps*) were given to 271 of the 399 syphilitic subjects. In a spinal tap, a 10-inch needle is inserted between two vertebrae into the cerebrospinal fluid and a small amount of fluid is withdrawn—a delicate and uncomfortable process. The subjects were warned to lie very still, lest the needle swerve and puncture the fluid sac, causing infection and other complications.

Subjects were understandably reluctant to leave their farms, travel for miles over back roads to meet the physicians, and then undergo these painful taps, especially when they had no pressing medical problem. For this reason, the physicians offered inducements: free transportation, free hot lunches, free medicine for any disease other than syphilis, and free burials. (The free burials were important to poor subjects, who often died without enough money for even a pauper's grave; but USPHS couldn't keep this promise itself after its budget was reduced and had to be rescued by the Milbank Memorial Fund.) In return for these "benefits," the physicians got not only the spinal taps but, later, autopsies to see what damage syphilis had or had not done.

There seems no doubt that the researchers also resorted to deception. Subjects were told that they had "bad blood" and that the spinal taps were "treatment" for it; moreover, the researchers sensationalized the effects of untreated "bad blood." USPHS sent the subjects the following letter, under the imposing letterhead "Macon County Health Department," with the subheading "Alabama State Board of Health and U.S. Public Health Service Cooperating with Tuskegee Institute" (all of which participated in the study):

Dear Sir:
Some time ago you were given a thorough examination and since that time we hope you have gotten a great deal of treatment for bad blood. You will now be given your last chance to get a second examination. This examination is a very special one and after it is finished you will be given a special treatment if it is believed you are in a condition to stand it.[15]

The "special treatment" mentioned was simply the spinal tap for neurosyphilis, a diagnostic test. The subjects were instructed to meet the public health nurse for transportation to "Tuskegee Institute Hospital for this free treatment." The letter closed in capitals:

REMEMBER THIS IS YOUR LAST CHANCE
FOR SPECIAL FREE TREATMENT.
BE SURE TO MEET THE NURSE.

To repeat, the researchers never treated the subjects for syphilis. In fact, during World War II, the researchers contacted the local draft board and prevented any eligible subject from being drafted—and hence from being treated for syphilis by the armed services. Although penicillin was developed around 1941–1943 and was widely available by 1946, the subjects in the Tuskegee study never received it, even during the 1960s or 1970s. However, as will be discussed below, it is not clear how much the subjects with late noninfectious syphilis were harmed by not getting penicillin.

THE FIRST INVESTIGATIONS

In 1966, Peter Buxtun, a recent college graduate, had just been hired by USPHS as a venereal disease investigator in San Francisco. After a few months, he learned of the Tuskegee study and began to question and criticize the USPHS officials who were still running it.[16] By this time, the physicians supervising the study and its data collection had been moved to the newly created Centers for Disease Control (CDC) in Atlanta. CDC officials were annoyed by Buxtun's questions about the morality of the study; later in 1966, having invited him to Atlanta for a conference on syphilis, they harangued him and tried to get him to be silent. He expected to be fired from USPHS; he was not, though, and he continued to press CDC for 2 more years.

By 1969, Buxtun's inquiries and protests led to a meeting of a small group of physicians at CDC to consider the Tuskegee study. The group consisted of

William J. Brown (Director of Venereal Diseases at CDC), David Sencer (Director of CDC), Ira Meyers (Alabama's State Health Officer from 1951 to 1986), Sidney Olansky (a physician at Emory Hospital who was knowledgeable about the early years of the study and had been in charge of it in 1951), Lawton Smith (an ophthalmologist from the University of Miami), and Gene Stollerman (chairman of medicine at the University of Tennessee). In general, this group avoided Buxtun's questions about the morality of the study and focused on whether continuing the study would harm the subjects. Meyers said of the Tuskegee subjects, "I haven't seen this group, but I don't think they would submit to treatment" if they were told what was going on.[17] Smith (the ophthalmologist) pressed hardest for continuing the study; only Stollerman repeatedly opposed continuing it, on both moral and therapeutic grounds. At the end, the committee overrode Stollerman and voted to continue the study.

Also in 1969, Ira Meyers told the physicians in the Macon County Medical Society about the Tuskegee study. These physicians did not object to the study; in fact, they were given a list of all the subjects and agreed not to give antibiotics to any subjects for any condition, if a subject came to one of their offices. It should be noted that although this medical society had been all-white in the 1930s, during the 1960s its membership was almost entirely African American.

In 1970, a monograph on syphilis was published, sponsored by the American Public Health Association, to give useful information to public health officials and venereal disease (VD) control officers. This monograph stated that treatment for late benign syphilis should consist of "6.0 to 9.0 million units of benzathine penicillin G given 3.0 million units at sessions seven days apart."[18] The first author listed on the monograph is William J. Brown, head of CDC's Tuskegee section from 1957 to 1971. Brown had been on the CDC panel in 1969 (when the monograph was probably written) and had argued for continuing the Tuskegee study, in which, of course, subjects with late benign syphilis received *no* penicillin.

THE STORY BREAKS

In July of 1972, Peter Buxtun, who had then been criticizing the Tuskegee research for 6 years and was disappointed by CDC's refusal to stop it, mentioned the Tuskegee study to a friend who was a reporter for the

Associated Press (AP) on the west coast. Another AP reporter—Jean Heller, on the east coast—was assigned to the story, and on the morning of July 26, 1972, her report appeared on front pages of newspapers nationwide.[19]

Heller's story described a medical study run by the federal government in Tuskegee, Alabama, in which poor, uneducated African American men had been used as "guinea pigs." After noting the terrible effects of tertiary syphilis, the story said that in 1969 a CDC study of 276 of the untreated subjects had proved that at least 7 subjects died "as a direct result of syphilis."

Heller's story had an immediate effect. (It might have made even more of an impact, but it was competing with a political story which broke the same day—a report that the Democratic candidate for vice president, Thomas Eagleton, had received shock therapy for depression.) Some members of Congress were amazed to learn of the Tuskegee study, and Senator William Proxmire called it a "moral and ethical nightmare."

CDC, of course, responded. J. D. Millar, chief of Venereal Disease Control, said that the study "was never clandestine," pointing to 15 published articles in medical and scientific journals over a 30-year span. Millar also maintained that the subjects had been informed that they could get treatment for syphilis at any time. "Patients were not denied drugs," he said; "rather, they were not offered drugs." He also tried to emphasize that "the study began when attitudes were much different on treatment and experimentation."[20]

The public and the press, however, scorned Millar's explanations. One political cartoon, for instance, showed a frail African American man being studied under a huge microscope by a white man in a white coat with a sign in the background: "This is a NO-TREATMENT study by your Public Health Service."[21] Another cartoon showed ragged African American men walking past tombstones; the caption read: "Secret Tuskegee Study—free autopsy, free burial, plus $100 bonus." Another showed a white physician standing near the body of an African American man, partially covered by a sheet; the chart at the foot of the hospital bed on which the body lay read "Ignore this syphilis patient (experiment in progress)"; in the background, a skeptical nurse holding a syringe asked, "*Now* can we give him penicillin?"

CDC and USPHS had always feared a "public relations problem" if the Tuskegee study became generally known, and now they had one. So did the Macon County Medical Society: when its president told the *Montgomery Advertiser* that the members had voted to identify remaining subjects and given them "appropriate therapy," USPHS in Atlanta flatly contradicted him, retorting that the local physicians — African American physicians — had accepted the Tuskegee study. The society then acknowledged that it had agreed to continuation of the study but had not agreed to withhold treatment from subjects who came to the offices of its members, whereupon USPHS documented the physicians' agreement to do exactly that.

THE AFTERMATH

Almost immediately after Heller's story appeared, Congress commissioned a special panel to investigate the Tuskegee study and issue a report. (The report was supposed to be ready by December 31, 1972; as we will see, however, it was late.)

Also almost at once, senators Sparkman and Allen of Alabama (both Democrats) sponsored a federal bill to give each of the Tuskegee subjects $25,000 in compensation. The southern African American electorate had been instrumental in electing these two senators and many southern members of Congress in the 1960s and 1970s, as well as presidents Kennedy and Johnson.

On November 16, 1972, Casper Weinberger, Secretary of Health, Education, and Welfare (HEW), officially terminated the Tuskegee study. At that time, CDC estimated that 28 of the original syphilitic group had died of syphilis during the study; after the study was ended, the remaining subjects received penicillin.

In February and March 1973, Senator Edward Kennedy's Subcommittee on Health of the Committee on Labor and Public Welfare held hearings on the Tuskegee study. Two of the Tuskegee subjects, Charles Pollard and Lester Scott, testified; one of them appeared to have been blinded by late-stage syphilis. These two men revealed more about the study: Pollard said they had not been told that they had syphilis; both said they thought "bad blood" meant something like low energy. Kennedy strongly condemned the study and proposed new regulations for medical experimentation.

In April 1973, the investigatory panel that had been commissioned when the Tuskegee story broke finally issued its report, which did not prove to be very useful. Moreover, for some reason this panel had met behind closed doors, and thus reporters had not been able to cover it.[22]

On July 23, 1973, Fred Gray, representing some of the Tuskegee subjects, filed a class-action suit against the federal government. Gray, a former Alabama legislator (in 1970, he had become the first African American Democrat elected in Alabama since Reconstruction), had been threatening to sue for compensation since Heller's story first broke, hoping for a settlement. He presented the suit as an issue of race, suing only the federal government and omitting the Tuskegee Institute, Rivers, the Tuskegee hospitals, and the Macon County Medical Society.

Eventually, the Justice Department decided that it couldn't win the suit in federal court, since the trial would have been held in nearby Montgomery, in the court of Frank Johnson, a liberal Alabama judge who had desegregated southern schools and upgraded mental institutions. Therefore, in December 1974 the government settled out of court.

According to the settlement, "living syphilitics" (subjects alive on July 23, 1973) received $37,500 each; "heirs of deceased syphilitics," $15,000 (since some children might have congenital syphilis); "living controls," $16,000; heirs of "deceased controls," $5,000. (Controls and their descendants were compensated because they had been prevented from getting antibiotics during the years of the study.) Also, the federal government agreed to provide free lifetime medical care for Tuskegee subjects, their wives, and their children. By September 1988, the government had paid $7.5 million for medical care for Tuskegee subjects. At that time, 21 of the original syphilitic subjects were still alive — each of whom had had syphilis for at least 57 years.[23] In addition, 41 wives and 19 children had evidence of syphilis and were receiving free medical care.

By the time this settlement was reached, more than 18 months had passed since Jean Heller's first story, and the Tuskegee issue was no longer front-page news: even the *New York Times* was giving it only an occasional short paragraph or two on inside pages. The issue was, after all, complicated; ethical standards had changed over the long course of the Tuskegee research; and, as noted above, the special panel commissioned to evaluate the study had met in secret. The public, therefore, had more or less forgotten about the Tuskegee study.

NOTES

1. Molly Selvin, "Changing Medical and Societal Attitudes toward Sexually Transmitted Diseases: A Historical Overview," in King K. Holmes et al., eds., *Sexually Transmitted Diseases,* McGraw-Hill, New York, 1984, pp. 3–19.

2. Allan Brandt, "Racism and Research: The Case of the Tuskegee Syphilis Study," *Hastings Center Report,* vol. 8, no. 6, December 1978, pp. 21–29.

3. Paul de Kruif, *Microbe Hunters,* Harcourt Brace, New York, 1926, p. 323.

4. R. H. Kampmeier, "The Tuskegee Study of Untreated Syphilis" (editorial), *Southern Medical Journal,* vol. 65, no. 10, October 1972, pp. 1247–1251.

5. J. E. Bruusgaard, "Über das Schicksal der nicht spezifisch behandelten Luetiker" ("Fate of Syphilitics Who Are Not Given Specific Treatment") *Archives of Dermatology of Syphilis,* vol. 157, April 1929, pp. 309–332.

6. Todd Savitt, *Medicine and Slavery: The Disease and Health of Blacks in Antebellum Virginia,* University of Illinois Press, Champaign, 1978.

7. James Jones, *Bad Blood,* Free Press, New York, 1981.

8. H. H. Hazen, "Syphilis in the American Negro," *Journal of the American Medical Association,* vol. 63, August 8, 1914, p. 463.

9. Jones, op. cit., p. 74

10. Ibid.

11. Ibid.

12. Brandt, op. cit.

13. Quoted in E. Ramont, "Syphilis in the AIDS Era," *New England Journal of Medicine,* vol. 316, no. 25, June 18, 1987, pp. 600–601.

14. R. A. Vonderlehr, T. Clark, and J. R. Heller, "Untreated Syphilis in the Male Negro," *Journal of the American Medical Association,* pp. 107, no. 11, September 12, 1936.

15. Archives of National Library of Medicine; quoted in Jones, op. cit., p. 127.

16. Jones, op. cit., pp. 190–193.

17. Quoted ibid., p. 196.

18. W. J. Brown et al., *Syphilis and Other Venereal Diseases,* Harvard University Press, Cambridge, Mass., 1970, p. 34.

19. Jean Heller, "Syphilis Victims in the United States Study Went Untreated for 40 Years," *New York Times,* July 26, 1972, pp. 1, 8.

20. Ibid., p. 8.

21. Jones, op. cit., insert following p. 48.

22. Tuskegee Syphilis Study Ad Hoc Panel to Department of Health, Education, and Welfare, *Final Report,* Superintendent of Documents, Washington, D.C., 1973.

23. David Tase, "Tuskegee Syphilis Victims, Kin May Get $1.7 Million in Fiscal 1989," Associated Press, September 11, 1988.

SHELDON H. HARRIS

Factories of Death

The Manchurian village of Beiyinhe in 1933 was a nondescript community of perhaps twenty to thirty families. It was one of several tiny villages that collectively the locals called "Zhong Ma City." The inhabitants were simple illiterate peasants trying to produce sufficient food for themselves and to earn a few coins to purchase a necessity.

There was nothing special about Beiyinhe. Manchuria was dotted with thousands of tiny hamlets similar in composition to Beiyinhe. However, it did have one thing in its favor. Beiyinhe was located on the Beiyin River and adjacent to the Northeastern Lafa-Harbin Railroad line. It was only 2 *li* (less than one kilometer) from the railroad station. Harbin, Heilongjiang province's principal city, was little more than 100 kilometers north of the town. By train, Harbin could be reached in less than one and one half hours.[1]

From *Factories of Death: Japanese Biological Warfare, 1932–45, and the American Cover-Up* by Sheldon H. Harris, pp. 13–14, 39, 62–69, 76–82, 189, 242–243, 245, 250. Copyright © 1994 Routledge. Reprinted by permission.

One day in either July or August 1932,[2] several Japanese officers, along with supporting troops, roared into Beiyinhe, and ordered everyone to pack their belongings and to be prepared to leave the village within three days. Those who did not obey the orders would be killed on evacuation day, and their homes and belongings would be burned. The villagers, aware of the brutality of the Japanese occupation, complied reluctantly with the order.

The officer in charge of the Beiyinhe operation was a young major whom the Chinese called Zhijiang Silang, but who is better known as Ishii Shiro. Major Ishii had recently been posted to Manchuria. He was anxious to put into practice some novel ideas he had developed on modern warfare, and, he believed, what better place could there be to experiment with these concepts than in Manchuria, Japan's newest colony? Consequently, he is reported to have written to his superiors in Tokyo in late 1932 that "due to your great help we have already achieved a great deal in our bacteria research. It is time we start to experiment. We appeal to be sent to Manchukuo to develop new weapons."[3]

There were many miscreants who share responsibility for Japan's chemical and biological warfare programs. In fact, so many members of Japan's scientific establishment, along with virtually every military leader of note, either participated in chemical or biological warfare research, or supported these projects with men, money, and material, that it is difficult today to apportion exact blame or responsibility. But there is no doubt that the person most responsible for converting Manchuria into one huge biological warfare [BW] laboratory during the Japanese occupation was the young Army doctor, Major Ishii Shiro.

. . .

The Ping Fan project was an enormously complex and expensive undertaking. In reality, Ishii controlled a huge fiefdom in Ping Fan. He employed thousands of Chinese workers, both unskilled and craftsmen, in the construction and maintenance of his death factory. Many Japanese scientists and technicians were brought to Ping Fan to work on various scientific projects under Ishii's direction. Hundreds of other Japanese served there in clerical and technical support roles. Delicate and intricate equipment, much of it coming from Europe and the United States, and costing tens of thousands of yen, was purchased for the facility.[4]

It was such a huge project that even arrogant Japanese administrators were forced to invent a cover story for Ping Fan. They were usually so contemptuous of, or indifferent to, Chinese public opinion, that the normal procedure was to ignore it. But Ping Fan was simply too large to ignore. Consequently, as an artifice, the local population was informed by Ishii's subordinates that the Japanese were constructing a lumber mill within the compound. And with the exquisite sarcastic "humor" for which Ishii and his colleagues were famous, they referred among themselves to their human subjects as *maruta,* or logs.[5]

. . .

Human experimentation followed three separate tracks. The most important of these were the laboratory experiments conducted at Ping Fan, at Anda and at the other Ishii Unit branches in Manchuria and occupied China. A second path was open-air experiments on humans at Anda that were conducted to discover the effectiveness of . . . prototype delivery systems. . . . And, finally, there were the field tests in which both civilian populations and military contingents were subject to pathogenic exposure.

Hundreds, if not thousands, of experiments were conducted on humans in the underground laboratories that were a characteristic of all the BW research installations constructed under Ishii's master plans. *Marutas* were dragged from their cells in buildings 7 and 8, or their smaller counterparts in the branch units, and led into the underground testing facilities. Here scientists injected victims with pathogens of differing dosages in order to determine the appropriate quantity of a specific germ to administer to individuals or to a general population. Tests were conducted on the "logs" with separate properties to learn whether certain foods, fabrics, tools, or utensils could be used as germ carriers. Human subjects were forced to eat different foods laced with specific germs. These included chocolates filled with anthrax, and cookies containing plague bacteria.[6] Other subjects were given various fluids (tea, coffee, milk, water, beer, spirits, etc.) to drink, with each liquid containing some specific dose of a pathogen.

Ishii found produce was a valuable conduit for spreading disease, and experimented with a number of viruses injected into different vegetables and fruits. Most of the fruit and vegetable studies were conducted at the Army Medical College in Tokyo under the direction of one of Ishii's brightest disciples, Naito Ryoichi.[7] Naito focused most of his research on "fugu toxin," which he obtained from the livers of blowfish. He reported success with developing a concentrate of toxin sufficient to kill mice, and he believed that he could secure excellent results for man if he were given enough time. However, the "degree of concentration" required to be effective with humans "was not obtained, and further efforts were interrupted by B-29 raids" over Tokyo in November 1944, and "ceased altogether with destruction, by fire, of the Army Medical College in April, 1945."[8]

Each laboratory at Ping Fan contained a large bulletin board that was displayed prominently on one wall. A technician recorded on the board every day data such as: "Specific date; 3 *maruta,* numbers so and so, were given injections of so and so, x cc; we need x number of hearts, or x number of livers, etc."[9] Laboratory technicians would then go to either building 7 or 8, order guards to provide the number of "logs" needed for the next experiment, and prepare the laboratory to receive victims. Some of the tests involved hanging "material" (humans) upside down, in order to determine the time necessary for a person to choke to death.

Other experiments were conducted in which air was injected into the subjects to test the rate of onset of embolisms. Horse urine was injected into human kidneys in still other experiments. Mitomo Kazuo later recalled one experiment conducted in late August 1944, in which he

> put as much as a gram of heroin into some porridge to an arrested Chinese citizen . . . about thirty minutes later he lost consciousness and remained in that state until he died 15–16 hours later. . . . On some prisoners I experimented 5–6 times, testing the action of Korean bindweed, heroin, bactal and castor-oil seeds. . . . I was also present when gendarmes shot three prisoners on whom I had performed experiments.[10]

Some of the tests conducted by "scientists" and "medical doctors" defy imagination today.

"Logs" generally lasted a few weeks before either they succumbed to the experiments, or they were "sacrificed" because they were no longer viable test material. A few somehow remained alive for four to six months, but no longer. There was always a ready supply of fresh replacements.[11] Pathologists inherited the dead *maruta* almost immediately after the conclusion of the test. They would wheel the dead into one of the autopsy rooms, and would go to work by making a large "y"-shaped incision on the "material," and then performing the normal autopsy. After all tests were completed, the pathologists directed orderlies and guards to dispose of the carcasses in one of the several nearby crematoria.

Experiments covered every conceivable approach to spreading disease, and to prevention. A typical laboratory experiment with cholera was conducted in May and June 1940. Twenty prisoners, all between the ages of twenty and thirty, and in good health, were selected for the test. Eight persons were given cholera vaccine injections produced with ultrasonic equipment. Eight others were injected with cholera vaccine manufactured by a conventional method. Four experimentees were not inoculated. Twenty days later, all the victims were forced to drink copious quantities of cholera-infected milk. The four who received no immunization contracted cholera and died. Several of those tested who received conventional cholera injections also became ill and died. The eight who were vaccinated with ultrasonic cholera vaccine showed no cholera symptoms. A similar test with plague vaccines produced comparable results. Ishii then ordered his Vac-

cine Squad, renamed the "A Team" in 1940, to work only with ultrasonically produced vaccines.[12]

Ishii, Kitano, [Masaii], and the other Unit 731 researchers did not trumpet their activities throughout the scientific world, but neither did they shrink from publicly sharing some of their findings. They just disguised the human experimentation aspect. Researchers published or read more than one hundred scientific papers, both during the heyday of Unit 731's operation as well as in the postwar period. When dealing with humans, the researchers referred to experiments with "monkeys," or "Manchurian monkeys;" animal experiments were labeled with the animals' proper subspecies, such as "long-tailed monkey," "Taiwan monkey," or "Formosan monkey."[13] In "Japanese medical society," their human experiments "were known; that is, [were] an open secret."[14]

Under a cloak of immunity from possible prosecution, the "open secret" became detailed fact in 1946 and 1947. By that time, Unit 731 scientists did not have to resort to deceptive animal terms in describing their work to American scientists eager to gain precious information concerning human BW experiments. Perhaps they were not totally candid with the Americans, but they did provide them with specific details of some of their previous work in the course of lengthy interviews, and in written reports to investigators. The data were allegedly reconstructed from memory, since all records in Manchuria were supposedly destroyed during the Japanese retreat in 1945. However, the documents themselves suggest strongly that many of 731's records survived.[15]

Dugway, Utah, is approximately 10,000 miles from Ping Fan. Yet, here in the barren, windswept desert of western Utah is a United States Army chemical and biological warfare base which houses some of the remnants of Japanese BW research.[16] Among the many facilities to be found at Dugway Proving Grounds, a restricted research center that stretches over 840,911 acres of Utah desert, is a technical library that receives all the latest scientific publications that relate to CW and BW research, as well as general publications.[17] It also stores materials that other research centers no longer want, but that may contain useful intelligence for investigators. Tucked away in an unmarked box in the technical library are more than twenty reports compiled by American scientists from their postwar interviews with Ishii, Kitano, and other surviving Unit 731 authorities. This box contains also three extraordinary autopsy reports that cover glanders, plague, and anthrax. The autopsy reports range in length from 350 pages to more than 800 pages. Each autopsy report contains hundreds of pastel-colored artist drawings of human organs in various states of disintegration. At one time, these reports were designated as Top Secret, but advances in BW research make the findings obsolete, if not arcane. They were declassified in 1978.

At least two dozen BW scientists were interviewed, and the topics ranged from aerosols to typhus. The purpose of the exchanges was to "obtain information necessary to clarify reports submitted by Japanese personnel on the subject of B. W. . . . To examine human pathological material. . . . To obtain protocols necessary for understanding the significance of the pathological material."[18] What follows is a representative selection of the data Unit 731 researchers provided:

Dr Futagi Hideo, in reporting on his experiments with tuberculosis, noted that in human tests with the Calmette bacillus (BCG) "All subjects recovered in this series," but in tests with the Cl Tuberculosis Hominis, "all doses produced military tuberculosis which was fatal within 1 month in those injected with 10.0 and 1.0 mg. The others were severely ill, lived longer but probably died later." In another test, "death at 1 month occurred following a stormy course with fever immediately post-injection." Futagi experimented with Manchurian children and achieved positive tuberculin results. He received the "original stock" of tuberculum germs from a "natural case. Virulence was maintained by passage through guinea pigs."[19] Dr Futagi Hideo's experiments were particularly hideous because tuberculosis is not an effective BW strategy. Usually it is too slow to have a BW impact. It is reasonable to conclude, therefore, that these experiments were carried out for purely academic purposes at the expense of the lives of those subjects tested.

Dr Tabei Kanau worked on typhoid experiments from 1938 until he was transferred in 1943. During that five-year period he tested perhaps several hundred subjects with different strains and dosages of typhoid germs. Some strains were mixed with sucrose, while others were stirred into milk. In one experiment, "Deaths occurred in 2 cases and 3 committed suicide." In another

One subject was exposed to a bomb burst containing buckshot mixed with 10 mg bacilli and 10 gm of clay. The buckshot had grooves which were impregnated with the bacteria-clay mixture. Bomb burst 1 meter from the rear of the subject. He developed symptoms of typhoid fever with positive laboratory signs. Laboratory infections occurred in 2 Japanese investigators who seemed to be much sicker than Manchurians

although none died. It was the impression of Dr. Tabei that Manchurians had more natural resistance than Japanese.[20]

Kitano dealt with many diseases, some of which were exotic, while others were of the common garden variety. His findings on songo fever, tick encephalitis, and typhus were especially welcomed by the Americans. They now could secure data on tick encephalitis that involved injecting mouse brain suspension in humans. One man, according to Kitano's protocol, "produced symptoms after an incubation of 7 days. Highest temperatures was 39.8°C. This subject was sacrificed when fever was subsiding, about the 12th day." Another "received similar mouse brain emulsion i. n. in a dose of 1.0 cc. After an incubation period of 10 days the same symptoms appeared." The manifestations of the disease were grim:

Fever is the first change. When the fever begins to subside, motor paralysis appears in the upper extremities, neck, face, eyelids, and respiratory muscles. There are no significant sensor changes. No paralysis is observed in the tongue, muscles of deglutition or lower extremities. After recovery, paralysis may be permanent. . . . Kitano observed it longer than 6 months.[21]

Ishii, as usual, was the star. He was interviewed on his work with human subjects that related to botulism, brucellosis, gas gangrene, glanders, influenza, meningococcus, plague, smallpox, tetanus, and tularemia.[22] Some of his findings were detailed, and covered many typescript pages. Others were as brief as: "Tularemia, Experiments in M were conducted with 10 subjects who were injected s.c. All developed fever lasting as long as 6 months. None died or were sacrificed."[23]

At least thirty-five reports involving human experiments were submitted by the Japanese scientists interviewed,[24] detailing tests conducted upon 801 "logs" plus 30 suicides.[25] This was remarkable, since the interviews took place within slightly more than a one-month period, November–December, in late 1947. Material obtained in such a limited time frame was a fraction of the information Japanese BW researchers realized in China and Manchuria, but even this paltry amount delighted their American counterparts. The Japanese apologetically acknowledged that they maintained autopsy reports on slightly less than 1000 sacrificed persons. Moreover, they regretted that "adequate material" for only 403[26] cases was still available.[27]

This, too, was a patent understatement of the true facts, but American scientists rejoiced at their good fortune.

After completing a brief mission to Japan in November 1947, Edwin V. Hill, M.D., Chief, Basic Sciences, Camp Detrick, Maryland, observed, "Evidence gathered in this investigation has greatly supplemented and amplified previous aspects of this field." The data gathered by enemy scientists was secured "at the expenditure of many millions of dollars and years of work. . . . Such information could not be obtained in our own laboratories because of scruples attached to human experimentation." However, thanks to the Japanese, Hill observed the "data were secured with a total outlay of ¥250,000 to date, a mere pittance by comparison with the actual cost of the studies." Hill noted also that "the pathological material which has been collected constitutes the only material evidence of the nature of these experiments."[28]

The toll of sacrificed *maruta* was much greater than the figures provided to United States investigators. At the 1949 trial of Japanese prisoners in Khabarovsk, USSR, Major General Kawashima Kiyoshi, former head of Unit 731's First, Third, and Fourth Sections, testified that "I can say that the number of prisoners of Detachment 731 who died from the effects of experiments in infecting them with severe infectious diseases was no less than about 600 per annum."[29] Kawashima was stationed at Ping Fan from 1941 until the end of the war. Scholars, using Kawashima's figure of 600 deaths annually, concluded that 3000 people were killed in the BW experiments.[30]

Three thousand deaths is a gross underestimate of the actual number of men, women, and children slaughtered. It does not take into consideration those killed prior to 1941. Ishii, it must be remembered, began human experiments in Harbin in 1932. Hundreds, perhaps thousands, were destroyed during the Beiyinhe venture. Others were killed at Ping Fan from 1938 until Kawashima's arrival there in 1941. Still others were exterminated in the branch camps at Anda, Hailar, Linkow, Sunyu, and Dairen. Many more were murdered in Canton,[31] Peking (Beijing),[32] and, most probably, Shanghai and Singapore (Unit 9420).[33] At least 5000–6000 humans were annihilated in BW death factories not directly under Ishii's control (Mukden, Nanking, and Changchun) during the Japanese rampage in China. Nor does the count include the tens of thousands massacred in August 1945 in order to prevent their falling into the hands of the advancing Soviet or Chinese troops.[34]

• • •

The city of Anda lies directly due north of Harbin, roughly two hours by train from Ping Fan. Today it is a fairly prosperous community of 200,000 inhabitants that sits astride the Daqing oilfield. China's largest known petroleum deposit. From 1939 until 1945 Anda achieved another sort of distinction. Then little more than an expanse of empty pastureland interspersed with a handful of villages, Anda was the remote site for Unit 731's proving ground. When a new procedure appeared promising in the Ping Fan laboratory, it was submitted to further tests at Anda. Invariably, humans were used throughout the testing procedure, either in underground laboratories similar to those at Ping Fan, or, more frequently, in above-ground open-air trials. . . .

Scores of tests were conducted with hundreds of human guinea pigs at Anda during the Ishii-Kitano reign. Although there is no exact count of the number of proving-ground casualties, the scope of the enterprise can be gauged from some data disclosed during the postwar Soviet investigation of Japanese BW activities. For example, in the course of the annual inspection of the Anda facility in 1945, a probationary officer in the Quartermaster Corps was asked by a civilian employee for permission to discard some worn blankets. This request offers an important clue for a tally of sacrificed humans, since each year obsolete or worn equipment was replaced with new supplies, if the inspector gave his approval. The probationary officer noticed that "Dried blood was visible on them. These blankets were extremely tattered." There were some eighty badly frayed and blood-encrusted blankets in the pile shown to the quartermaster. When asked to account for the ragged condition of the blankets, the civilian employee replied that they "were used to protect the bodies of experimentees while experiments were being performed on them."[35] It is reasonable to conclude, therefore, that more than eighty persons were killed at the Anda proving grounds yearly during the period it existed.

Anda dealt with the usual laundry list of pathogens. It appears, though, that special emphasis was placed on testing the possibilities of plague,[36] anthrax and frostbite.[37] As early as June 1941, Anda tested plague-infested flea bombs on humans. Between ten and fifteen captives were fastened to stakes in the ground in one trial, and then an airplane dropped more than ten bombs on the site. The results are unknown, but they must have been promising, since other tests followed that summer.

In the next experiment, fifteen humans were fastened to stakes in the ground. "Flags and smoke signals were used to guide the planes." The planes took off from Ping Fan, and once over the site, dropped at least "two dozen bombs, which burst at about 100 or 200 meters from the ground." The fleas dispersed, and after waiting a sufficient length of time for the fleas to infect the prisoners, the victims were disinfected and taken back to Ping Fan for observation. Unfortunately, the tests were unsuccessful, disappointing the Colonel in charge of the experiment. He told a colleague that "the experiment did not yield good results." Evidently, the explosive force of the bombs' blasts caused excessively high temperatures, which in turn made the fleas "very sluggish."[38] Shrapnel bombs simply did not prove to be effective plague-dispersal vessels.[39]

Anthrax experiments were conducted periodically at Anda throughout 1943 and 1944. In general, scientists worked with ten *maruta* in each test. The head of Ping Fan's anthrax production team visited Anda on several occasions in 1943 and 1944 to supervise experiments, and observed that the *maruta* tested "looked like Chinese." They, too, as with the plague "logs," were tied to stakes in the ground. Then anthrax-filled bombs were exploded nearby. The anthrax expert did note with some professional pride that "some of the experimentees were infected with anthrax and, as I learned later, they died."[40] Nevertheless, experiments at Anda with anthrax were disappointing. Unit 731 experts failed to develop a viable anthrax delivery system by the end of the war.[41]

Since most germ bomb experiments ended in failure, Unit 731 scientists in 1944 conducted experiments with plague germ contamination through the respiratory tract. They hoped to develop a technique that would prove to be a feasible venue for BW. Accordingly, ten *maruta* were brought to Anda, and, as usual, were tied to stakes in the ground. Each *maruta* was stationed a prescribed number of meters away from his fellow "log." Test tubes filled with an emulsion of plague germs which were bred from the lymph, spleen, and hearts of plague-infected rats were scattered among the *maruta* at predetermined distances. The scientists arranged for the test tubes to burst, and their contents were distributed among the experimentees. The plague emulsion broke into tiny droplets which

eventually were inhaled by the test subjects. Despite the hopes of the scientists involved in developing this technique, the test ended in failure. Still other respiratory trace experiments were conducted throughout 1944 and 1945, but they, too, ended in failure.[42]

•   •   •

. . . [Beginning in 1939,] Ishii expanded his field test operations to encompass all of Manchuria and both occupied and free China. From late 1939 through 1942, Unit 731 operatives conducted many tests against both enemy military forces and civilian populations. The logistics required for such extensive trials were so great that Ishii must have received approval to move forward from both the Kwantung Army leaders and area commanders of Japan's invading China forces. Logic suggests strongly that the top War Ministry officials in Tokyo were kept apprised of his operations, and approved them. They were so far-reaching that the devastation and carnage he unleashed brought an outcry from too many sources in China to be refuted as nothing more than lying Kuomintang propaganda.

The tests covered a host of insidious but imaginative artifices. Manchurian water wells were laced with typhoid germs that were remarkably effective killers. It is estimated that more than 1000 wells in and around Harbin were contaminated with typhoid bacilli in 1939 and 1940. Casualties ranged from single deaths to limited outbreaks of typhoid, which devastated entire villages. Mrs. Ada Pivo, a native of Harbin, remembered the day her eldest sister died of typhoid fever. The sister belonged to a Harbin Jewish Zionist youth group that went on a field trip in early summer 1940. The day was extremely warm, and on their return home, some of the forty-odd youngsters, thirteen to fifteen years old, bought bottles of lemonade in downtown Harbin. All children who drank the lemonade, which was bottled locally, and contained well-drawn water, contracted typhoid fever and subsequently died. The attending doctors traced the typhoid outbreak to the contaminated lemonade.[43]

Ishii, working with his Changchun counterpart,[44] caused a cholera outbreak in the Manchukuon capital. He descended upon the city in 1940, informed local authorities that cholera was moving in on their community, and that the general population must be inoculated. What he did not tell them was that the "vaccine" he intended to use was a solution containing cholera germs. Innocent people were lined up, given an injection, and possibly some liquid to drink or some contaminated food to eat. In any event, a cholera epidemic spread through metropolitan Changchun shortly after.[45]

In July 1942, Ishii led a BW expedition to Nanking, where he linked forces with local BW death factory personnel. Jointly, they distributed typhoid and paratyphoid germs from metal flasks and glass bottles, dumping the bacteria into wells, marshes, and houses of ordinary citizens. They could afford to be lavish with their dispensation, since Ishii brought along 130 kilograms of paratyphoid "A" and anthrax germs, and an unknown quantity of typhoid, all produced at Ping Fan.[46] Epidemics broke out in the region shortly afterwards, much to the delight of the researchers.

The Nanking trip yielded other benefits as well. Ishii, during his visit to the city, provided special treats for Chinese prisoners of war held in two nearby camps. In addition, he prepared an unusual delicacy for local youngsters, chocolates filled with anthrax bacteria.[47] Three thousand POWs were given, as a special holiday favor, dumplings that had been injected with either typhoid or paratyphoid. The prisoners were then released and sent home, where they acted as unwitting agents for spreading disease. The children gorged themselves on chocolates, with the unavoidable resulting side effects.

Sweet cakes, infused with typhoid and paratyphoid bacteria, were still another Ishii confectionery delight that he used in the Nanking expedition. Japanese soldiers were given 300–400 of the sweet cakes and ordered to leave them near fences and by trees. The idea was to create an impression that the soldiers forgot to take the food with them in the midst of a hasty retreat. It was expected that the local population, always short of food, would be delighted with the opportunity to feast on Japanese provisions. Inevitably, an outbreak of disease occurred shortly after the sweet cakes were ingested. Researchers concluded that "paratyphoid had proved to be the most effective"[48] of the pathogens tested.

In other field tests, Unit 731 saboteurs released, into densely populated areas, rats that were carrying plague-infested fleas. Researchers anticipated that the plague rats would breed with the local rat population, resulting in outbreaks of massive plague epidemics. Unit 731 men found also that germs implanted into expressly modified fountain pens and walking sticks were an effective method for disseminating BW. The germ-encrusted devices were dropped along dirt paths and paved roads, where either the curious or the needy would take them home. An epidemic would develop (plague generally), Japanese soldiers would rush to the affected area, order all villagers to evacuate, and then proceed to torch the villages in order to prevent outsiders from discovering what really took place. These sabotage techniques were so successful that Sir Joseph Needham, the great British scientist stationed in China at the time, noted:

In the beginning, I felt great doubt about its credibility, but I believe now that the information collected by the Chinese Military Medical Bureau clearly indicates that the Japanese forces have been scattering and are continuing to scatter plague invested fleas in several areas.[49]

Massive BW testing actually commenced with an attack upon an innocent population in July 1940. Two months earlier, Ishii dispatched from Ping Fan a heavily guarded train. Its destination was Hangchow (Hangzhou), the beautiful holiday resort favored by Shanghai's wealthy. The train's cargo was 70 kilograms of typhoid bacterium, 50 kilos of cholera germs, and 5 kilos of plague-infested fleas. The BW target was Ning Bo, a community south of Hangchow. Ning Bo was an important Treaty Port in the nineteenth century, and the birth place of Chiang Kai Shek.[50] For the next five months, Ning Bo and its environs were subjected to a series of BW attacks.

The methods for spreading disease in Ning Bo varied. Ishii and his researchers devised a host of delivery systems they planned to test on the simple residents of the area. Pathogens were dumped into water reservoirs, ponds, and individual residential water wells. Infected grains of wheat and millet were disseminated by aerial spraying in early October. Later that month, Ishii personally directed the scattering of contaminated wheat and cotton in and around Ning Bo. On 26 November, specially equipped Unit 731 aircraft flew over nearby Jin Hua county, dropping bombs which, on impact, gave off smoke-like objects that later turned a light yellow color.

The final results were that, as a consequence of the five-month campaign, cholera, typhus, and plague spread throughout Ning Bo and at least five surrounding counties. It is known that more than 1000 persons became ill with one or another of the Ishii-produced diseases, and that over 500 people succumbed.[51] Most alarming is that the diseases Ishii unleashed in summer and fall 1940 had long-term effects. Plague ravaged Ning Bo and nearby communities in 1941, 1946, and 1947. Casualties were high.[52]

* * *

All tests on humans, BW as well as the specialized non-BW experiments, were recorded carefully by the Unit 731 scientist or technician in charge of a specific project. The data compiled, both on paper and on film, indicate that Ishii's and Kitano's men recorded every conceivable reaction the human subjects developed during the course of the experiment, until the subject either perished from the effects of the tests, or was no longer a useful specimen and, therefore, was sacrificed. The records accumulated were of enormous quantity, and would prove alluring to both Soviet and American scientists and intelligence authorities in the heyday of the Cold War.

* * *

By the end of 1947, if not earlier, the [American] authorities amassed enormous quantities of data suggesting strongly that a number of Japanese scientists — both military and civilian — had conducted BW experiments that involved the use of human guinea pigs. Much of their work constituted blatant human rights violations as defined by the charters governing both the Nuremburg and the Tokyo war crimes trials. The principals (Ishii, Wakamatsu, Kitano, et al.) tried to wriggle their way out from prosecution for their past conduct by lies, deceptions, evasions, and pleas of ignorance during repeated questioning. Still, some of their responses inadvertently damaged their cause. In addition, testimony by former colleagues convincingly branded them as being war criminals. So much evidence was compiled over a two-year investigation, linking the leaders to violations of international law, that any prosecutor could have taken their cases to the proper authorities and secured indictments and probable convictions. All that was required for such a scenario to take place was the desire of responsible officials to see justice done.

Unfortunately for Ishii's victims, the United States military had other priorities. The dominant American view in Tokyo was that the former commander of Ping Fan was too important a figure to be subjected to the criteria used for determining the issue of prosecuting an individual for war crimes. This attitude perhaps was best expressed by Lt. Colonel Robert McQuail of Army Intelligence (G-2). In a "Summary of Information" that McQuail prepared for his office in early Jan-

uary 1947, he noted that "A Confidential Informant claims that Ishii had his assistants inject bubonic plague bacilli into the bodies of some Americans in Mukden, Manchuria, as an experiment." McQuail, instead of being horrified, commented matter-of-factly that "Naturally, the results of these experiments are of the highest intelligence value."[53] Intelligence value, not war crimes, would be the dominant factor in all discussions concerning the Japanese BW experts.

NOTES

1. The account of the Beiyinhe facility is based on an interview I conducted with Mr Han Xiao, Deputy Director of the Unit 731 Memorial Museum in Ping Fan, Manchuria, 8 June 1989, and the following publications: Han Xiao and Zhou Deli, "Record of Actual Events of the Bacterial Factory in Ping Fan," *People's China,* vol. 3 (1971), translated by Ms Wang Qing Ling; Han Xiao, "Bacterial Factory in Beiyinhe, Zhong Ma City," *Harbin Historical Chronicle,* vol. 1 (1984), pp. 80–83, translated by Ms Lu Cheng; Dong Zhen Yu, "Kwantung Army Number 731," *Historical Material on Jilin History,* ed. by Jilin Branch of the Committee on Culture and History (Changchun), 1987, pp. 47–77, translated by Ms Wang Qing Ling.

2. The Chinese authorities are a little hazy on the exact date.

3. Quoted in Dong, "Kwantung Army Number 731" [see note 1].

4. Interview with John W. Powell, Jr., 28 February 1989.

5. Interview with Mr. Hao Yun Feng, Professor of Welding, Harbin Institute of Technology, 24 April 1984. Mr. Hao, a native of the Ping Fan area, was a teenager during Ping Fan's peak period of operation. He barely avoided being drafted to work in Ping Fan before the end of the war.

6. *Materials on the Trial of Former Servicemen of the Japanese Army Charged with Manufacturing and Employing Bacteriological Weapons* (Moscow: Foreign Languages Publishing House, 1950), p. 286; hereafter referred to as *Khabarovsk Trial.* Anthrax is not naturally transmitted in the fashion described at the Khabarovsk trial, and possibly it cannot infect via this route. The defendant testifying may have meant to name another disease that could be distributed in food. However, it should be remembered that Ishii's group was testing all possibilities shotgun style, and may have attempted to spread anthrax in the manner described above.

7. Lt. Colonel Naito would play an important role in the postwar United States interrogation of Japanese BW scientists. He ostensibly collaborated fully with the Americans. Once freed of the threat of war crimes prosecution, Naito would go on to an illustrious career in the "ethical drug" industry in the three decades after 1945.

8. Thompson, Arvo T., "Report on Japanese Biological Warfare (BW) Activities, 31 May 1946," Army Service Forces, Camp Detrick, Frederick, Md., p. 17, Fort Detrick Library Archives. Hereafter referred to as Thompson Report.

9. Dong, "Kwantung Army Number 731."

10. *Khabarovsk Trial,* p. 80.

11. Ibid

12. Han Xiao, "Compliation of Camp 731 Fascist Savage Acts," *Unforgettable History* (Harbin, 1985), translated by Ms Lu Cheng....

13. See, as representative examples, [the] citations in footnotes 34, 35, 36, 37, 38, [in] Tsuneishi, Kei-ichi, "The Research Guarded by Military Secrecy — The Isolation of the E.H.F. Virus in [the]

Japanese Bilogical Warfare Unit." *Historia Scientarium,* No. 30 (Tokyo), 1986, pp. 88–90; see also Tsuneishi, Kei-ichi, *The Germ Warfare Unit That Disappeared: Kwantung Army's 731st Unit* (Tokyo: Kai-mei-sha Publishers, 1981), pp. 164–165 in the English translation kindly furnished me by Mr Norman Covert. All citations hereafter are from the English translation, and the title will be cited as *The Germ Warfare Unit That Disappeared;* Morimura, Seiichi, *The Devil's Gluttony* (Tokyo: Kadokawa Shoten, Tokyo, 1983), vol. 3, Chapter 4.

14. Tsuneishi, "Research Guarded by Military Secrecy," p. 89.

15. See Thompson Report, pp. 11–12.

16. I want to thank United States Representative Wayne Owens (Dem., Utah) for his help in enabling me to visit Dugway Proving Grounds in November 1989.

17. Typescript copy, "Dugway Proving Grounds History" (1987), provided by the Dugway Proving Grounds Public Information Office.

18. Edwin V. Hill to General Alden C. Waitt, 12 December 1947, Folder 56–5365, Dugway Proving Grounds Technical Library (hereafter cited as Dugway Library).

19. "Tuberculosis," Interview with Dr Hideo Futagi, 15 November 1947, Document 020, AA, Dugway Library. Futagi's data are unusual, since it usually takes a longer period of incubation for tuberculosis to have an impact on a subject.

20. "Typhoid," Interview with Dr. Tabei, 24 November 1947, Document 022, AC, Dugway Library.

21. "Tick Encephalitis," Information Furnished by Drs Yukio Kashara and Masaji Kitano, Document 019, Dugway Library.

22. Edwin V. Hill to General Alden C. Waitt, 12 December 1947, Dugway Library.

23. "Tularemia," Interview with Dr Shiro Ishii, 22 November 1947, Document 021, Dugway Library.

24. I have been unable to locate fifteen, or possibly more, reports allegedly submitted to American authorities. These documents may still be in other military archives, protected under some cloak of secrecy.

25. *Tulsa* (Okla.) *Tribune,* 29 February 1984, p. 13 A.

26. The Hill memo to General Waitt gives the figure as 401, but a tally of the data in his memo indicated that the correct figure is 403.

27. Only the three autopsy reports referred to earlier are in the Dugway Technical Library. Others no doubt exist, but their location at present is unknown.

28. Hill to General Alden C. Waitt, 12 December 1947, Dugway Library.

29. *Khabarovsk Trial,* p. 57. Kawashima committed suicide shortly before he was due to be repatriated to Japan in 1956. See the NHK Television documentary, *Modern History Scoop,* 13, 14 April 1992.

30. See, for representative statements, Tsuneishi, *The Germ Warfare Unit That Disappeared,* passim; Morimura, *Devil's Gluttony,* vol. 1; *Japan Times* (Tokyo), 1 August 1982, p. 1; and Pitter, C. and Yamamoto, R., *Gene Wars; Military Control over the New Genetic Technologies* (New York: Beach Books, William Morrow, 1988), p. 87.

31. At present, little is known of the Canton operation, except for the unit's designation, Unit 8604 (called Bo Zi in Chinese, or "Wave Unit"), and that it was housed until 1944 on a site that is today Sun Yat Sen University. Information provided me by Mr. Han Xiao in an interview on 10 June 1991.

32. The North China Army established Unit 1855 in Peking in 1938. The 2000-man unit was housed near the Temple of Heaven in Peking, and was headed by a Colonel Nishimura Yeni, who was a surgeon. Unit 1855 reported directly to Ishii. There is currently no published material in China on Unit 1855. However, a key authority estimates that the unit killed at least 1000 persons in experiments from 1938 until 1945. Information provided me by Mr. Han Xiao in an interview conducted on 10 June 1991.

33. At present, there is no concrete evidence concerning a purported BW unit in Shanghai. However, Kitano worked there from early 1945 until Japan's surrender. There are other tantalizing bits of information suggesting a Shanghai BW operation, but at the moment no substantial body of data has surfaced. For Singapore, see the Singapore *Straits Times,* 19 September 1991, pp. 1, 3; 25 September 1991, p. 1; 11 November 1991, pp. 1, 3; and Sidhu, H., *The Bamboo Fortress: True Singapore War Stories* (Singapore: Native Publications, 1991), pp. 160–184.

34. It was previously noted that Chinese authorities discovered a mass grave in Hailar containing more than ten thousand bodies. These people were killed in the closing days of the war. Many came from the BW facility in Hailar. Interview with Mr E. Er Dun in Hailar, 14 June 1991.

35. *Khabarovsk Trial,* p. 371.

36. "*Question:* What germs were tested most frequently on the proving ground? *Answer:* Plague germs." *Khabarovsk Trial,* p. 259.

37. See the discussion on pp. 28, 34, 69–71 for frostbite tests. [not reprinted]

38. *Khabarovsk Trial,* pp. 57, 259.

39. Tsuneishi, *The Germ Warfare Unit That Disappeared,* p. 133.

40. *Khabarovsk Trial,* p. 67.

41. Tsuneishi, *The Germ Warfare Unit That Disappeared,* pp. 130–133.

42. Ibid., pp. 131–132.

43. Interview with Mrs. Ada Pivo of Encino, California, 7 February 1989.

44. See Chapter 7. [not reprinted]

45. Han, "Compilation of Camp 731 Fascist Savage Acts."

46. *Khabarovsk Trial,* p. 66–67.

47. Ibid., pg. 286. . . .

48. Ibid. pp., 354–355.

49. Quoted in Tsuneishi, *The Germ Warfare Unit That Disappeared,* p. 148.

50. Chiang was born in a village near Ning Bo in 1887. See Spence, Jonathan D., *The Search for Modern China* (New York: W. W. Norton, 1990), p. 276–277.

51. Han Xiao and Zhou Deli, "Record of Actual Events of the Biological Factory in Ping Fan," *People's China,* vol. 3, 1971.

52. Ibid.

53. Summary of Information, Subject Ishii, Shiro. 10 Jan 47, Document 41, US Army Intelligence and Security Command Archive, Fort Meade, Md.

ADVISORY COMMITTEE ON HUMAN RADIATION EXPERIMENTS

Final Report: Executive Summary (1995)

THE CREATION OF THE ADVISORY COMMITTEE

On January 15, 1994, President Clinton appointed the Advisory Committee on Human Radiation Experiments. The President created the Committee to investigate reports of possible unethical experiments funded by the government decades ago.

The members of the Advisory Committee were fourteen private citizens from around the country: a representative of the general public and thirteen experts in bioethics, radiation oncology and biology, nuclear medicine, epidemiology and biostatistics, public health, history of science and medicine, and law. . . .

The controversy surrounding the plutonium experiments and others like them brought basic questions to the fore: How many experiments were conducted or sponsored by the government, and why? How many were secret? Was anyone harmed? What was disclosed to those subjected to risk, and what opportunity did they have for consent? By what rules should the past be judged? What remedies are due those who were wronged or harmed by the government in the past? How well do federal rules that today govern human experimentation work? What lessons can be learned for application to the future? . . .

THE PRESIDENT'S CHARGE

The President directed the Advisory Committee to uncover the history of human radiation experiments during the period 1944 through 1974. It was in 1944 that the first known human radiation experiment of inter-

From United States, Advisory Committee on Human Radiation Experiments, *Final Report: Executive Summary and Guide to Final Report* (Washington, DC: U.S. Government Printing Office, 1995), pp. 3–19.

est was planned, and in 1974 that the Department of Health, Education and Welfare adopted regulations governing the conduct of human research, a watershed event in the history of federal protections for human subjects.

In addition to asking us to investigate human radiation experiments, the President directed us to examine cases in which the government had intentionally released radiation into the environment for research purposes. He further charged us with identifying the ethical and scientific standards for evaluating these events, and with making recommendations to ensure that whatever wrongdoing may have occurred in the past cannot be repeated.

We were asked to address human experiments and intentional releases that involved radiation. The ethical issues we addressed and the moral framework we developed are, however, applicable to all research involving human subjects. . . .

THE COMMITTEE'S APPROACH

. . . As we began our search into the past, we quickly discovered that it was going to be extremely difficult to piece together a coherent picture. Many critical documents had long since been forgotten and were stored in obscure locations throughout the country. Often they were buried in collections that bore no obvious connection to human radiation experiments. There was no easy way to identify how many experiments had been conducted, where they took place, and which government agencies had sponsored them. Nor was there a quick way to learn what rules applied to these experiments for the period prior to the mid-1960s. With the assistance of hundreds of federal officials and agency staff, the Committee retrieved and reviewed hundreds of thousands of government documents. Some of the most important documents were secret and were declassified at our request. Even after this extraordinary effort, the historical record remains incomplete. Some potentially important collections could not be located and were evidently lost or destroyed years ago.

Nevertheless, the documents that were recovered enabled us to identify nearly 4,000 human radiation experiments sponsored by the federal government between 1944 and 1974. In the great majority of cases, only fragmentary data was locatable; the identity of subjects and the specific radiation exposures involved were typically unavailable. Given the constraints of information, even more so than time, it was impossible for the Committee to review all these experiments, nor could we evaluate the experiences of countless individual subjects. We thus decided to focus our investigation on representative case studies reflecting eight different categories of experiments that together addressed our charge and priorities. These case studies included:

- experiments with plutonium and other atomic bomb materials
- the Atomic Energy Commission's program of radioisotope distribution
- nontherapeutic research on children
- total body irradiation
- research on prisoners
- human experimentation in connection with nuclear weapons testing
- intentional environmental releases of radiation
- observational research involving uranium miners and residents of the Marshall Islands

In addition to assessing the ethics of human radiation experiments conducted decades ago, it was also important to explore the current conduct of human radiation research. Insofar as wrongdoing may have occurred in the past, we needed to examine the likelihood that such things could happen today. We therefore undertook three projects:

- A review of how each agency of the federal government that currently conducts or funds research involving human subjects regulates this activity and oversees it.
- An examination of the documents and consent forms of research projects that are today sponsored by the federal government in order to develop insight into the current status of protections for the rights and interests of human subjects.

- Interviews of nearly 1,900 patients receiving outpatient medical care in private hospitals and federal facilities throughout the country. We asked them whether they were currently, or had been, subjects of research, and why they had agreed to participate in research or had refused.

THE HISTORICAL CONTEXT

Since its discovery 100 years ago, radioactivity has been a basic tool of medical research and diagnosis. In addition to the many uses of the x ray, it was soon discovered that radiation could be used to treat cancer and that the introduction of "tracer" amounts of radioisotopes into the human body could help to diagnose disease and understand bodily processes. At the same time, the perils of overexposure to radiation were becoming apparent.

During World War II the new field of radiation science was at the center of one of the most ambitious and secret research efforts the world has known—the Manhattan Project. Human radiation experiments were undertaken in secret to help understand radiation risks to workers engaged in the development of the atomic bomb.

Following the war, the new Atomic Energy Commission used facilities built to make the atomic bomb to produce radioisotopes for medical research and other peacetime uses. This highly publicized program provided the radioisotopes that were used in thousands of human experiments conducted in research facilities throughout the country and the world. This research, in turn, was part of a larger postwar transformation of biomedical research through the infusion of substantial government monies and technical support.

The intersection of government and biomedical research brought with it new roles and new ethical questions for medical researchers. Many of these researchers were also physicians who operated within a tradition of medical ethics that enjoined them to put the interests of their patients first. When the doctor also was a researcher, however, the potential for conflict emerged between the advancement of science and the advancement of the patient's well-being.

Other ethical issues were posed as medical researchers were called on by government officials to play new roles in the development and testing of nuclear weapons. For example, as advisers they were asked to provide human research data that could reassure officials about the effects of radiation, but as scientists they were not always convinced that human research could provide scientifically useful data. Similarly, as scientists, they came from a tradition in which research results were freely debated. In their capacity as advisers to and officials of the government, however, these researchers found that the openness of science now needed to be constrained.

None of these tensions were unique to radiation research. Radiation represents just one of several examples of the exploration of the weapons potential of new scientific discoveries during and after World War II. Similarly, the tensions between clinical research and the treatment of patients were emerging throughout medical science, and were not found only in research involving radiation. Not only were these issues not unique to radiation, but they were not unique to the 1940s and 1950s. Today society still struggles with conflicts between the openness of science and the preservation of national security, as well as with conflicts between the advancement of medical science and the rights and interests of patients.

KEY FINDINGS

HUMAN RADIATION EXPERIMENTS

- Between 1944 and 1974 the federal government sponsored several thousand human radiation experiments. In the great majority of cases, the experiments were conducted to advance biomedical science; some experiments were conducted to advance national interests in defense or space exploration; and some experiments served both biomedical and defense or space exploration purposes. As noted, in the great majority of cases only fragmentary data are available.

- The majority of human radiation experiments identified by the Advisory Committee involved radioactive tracers administered in amounts that are likely to be similar to those used in research today. Most of these tracer studies involved adult subjects and are unlikely to have caused physical harm. However, in some nontherapeutic tracer studies involving children, radioisotope exposures were associated with increases in the potential lifetime risk for developing thyroid cancer that would be considered unacceptable today. The Advisory Committee also identified several studies in which patients died soon after receiving external radiation or radioisotope doses in the therapeutic range that were associated with acute radiation effects.

- Although the AEC, the Defense Department and the National Institutes of Health recognized at an early date that research should proceed only with the consent of the human subject, there is little evidence of rules or practices of consent except in research with healthy subjects. It was commonplace during the 1940s and 1950s for physicians to use patients as subjects of research without their awareness or consent. By contrast, the government and its researchers focused with substantial success on the minimization of risk in the conduct of experiments, particularly with respect to research involving radioisotopes. But little attention was paid during this period to issues of fairness in the selection of subjects.

- Government officials and investigators are blameworthy for not having had policies and practices in place to protect the rights and interests of human subjects who were used in research from which the subjects could not possibly derive direct medical benefit. To the extent that there was reason to believe that research might provide a direct medical benefit to subjects, government officials and biomedical professionals are less blameworthy for not having had such protections and practices in place.

INTENTIONAL RELEASES

- During the 1944–1974 period, the government conducted several hundred intentional releases of radiation into the environment for research purposes. Generally, these releases were not conducted for the purpose of studying the effects of radiation on humans. Instead they were usually conducted to test the operation of weapons, the safety of equipment, or the dispersal of radiation into the environment.

- For those intentional releases where dose reconstructions have been undertaken, it is unlikely that members of the public were directly harmed solely as a consequence of these tests. However, these releases were conducted in secret and despite continued requests from the public that stretch back well over a decade, some information about them was made public only during the life of the Advisory Committee.

URANIUM MINERS

- As a consequence of exposure to radon and its daughter products in underground uranium mines, at least several hundred miners died of lung cancer and surviving miners remain at elevated risk. These men, who were the subject of government study as they mined uranium for use in weapons manufacturing, were subject to radon exposures well in excess of levels known to be hazardous. The government failed to act to require the reduction of the hazard by ventilating the mines, and it failed to adequately warn the miners of the hazard to which they were being exposed.

SECRECY AND THE PUBLIC TRUST

- The greatest harm from past experiments and intentional releases may be the legacy of distrust they created. Hundreds of intentional releases took place in secret, and remained secret for decades. Important discussion of the policies to govern human experimentation also took place in secret. Information about human experiments was kept secret out of concern for embarrassment to the government, potential legal liability, and worry that public misunderstanding would jeopardize government programs.
- In a few instances, people used as experimental subjects and their families were denied the opportunity to pursue redress for possible wrongdoing because of actions taken by the government to keep the truth from them. Where programs were legitimately kept secret for national security reasons, the government often did not create or maintain adequate records, thereby preventing the public, and those most at risk, from learning the facts in a timely and complete fashion.

CONTEMPORARY HUMAN SUBJECTS RESEARCH

- Human research involving radioisotopes is currently subjected to more safeguards and levels of review than most other areas of research involving human subjects. There are no apparent differences between the treatment of human subjects of radiation research and human subjects of other biomedical research.
- Based on the Advisory Committee's review, it appears that much of human subjects research poses only minimal risk of harm to subjects. In our review of research documents that bear on human subjects issues, we found no problems or only minor problems in most of the minimal-risk studies we examined.
- Our review of documents identified examples of complicated, higher-risk studies in which human subjects issues were carefully and adequately addressed and that included excellent consent forms. In our interview project, there was little evidence that patient-subjects felt coerced or pressured by investigators to participate in research. We interviewed patients who had declined offers to become research subjects, reinforcing the impression that there are often contexts in which potential research subjects have a genuine choice.
- At the same time, however, we also found evidence suggesting serious deficiencies in aspects of the current system for the protection of the rights and interests of human subjects. For example, consent forms do not always provide adequate information and may be misleading about the impact of research participation on people's lives. Some patients with serious illnesses appear to have unrealistic expectations about the benefits of being subjects in research.

CURRENT REGULATIONS ON SECRECY IN HUMAN RESEARCH AND ENVIRONMENTAL RELEASES

- Human research can still be conducted in secret today, and under some conditions informed consent in secret research can be waived.
- Events that raise the same concerns as the intentional releases in the Committee's charter could take place in secret today under current environmental laws. . . .

KEY RECOMMENDATIONS

APOLOGIES AND COMPENSATION

The government should deliver a personal, individualized apology and provide financial compensation to those subjects of human radiation experiments, or their next of kin, in cases where:

- efforts were made by the government to keep information secret from these individuals or their families, or the public, for the purpose of avoiding embarrassment or potential legal liability, and where this secrecy had the effect of denying individuals the opportunity to pursue potential grievances.
- there was no prospect of direct medical benefit to the subjects, or interventions considered contro-

versial at the time were presented as standard practice, and physical injury attributable to the experiment resulted.

URANIUM MINERS

- The Interagency Working Group, together with Congress, should give serious consideration to amending the provisions of the Radiation Exposure Compensation Act of 1990 relating to uranium miners in order to provide compensation to *all* miners who develop lung cancer after some minimal duration of employment underground (such as one year), without requiring a specific level of exposure. The act should also be reviewed to determine whether the documentation standards for compensation should be liberalized.

IMPROVED PROTECTION FOR HUMAN SUBJECTS

- The Committee found no differences between human radiation research and other areas of research with respect to human subjects issues, either in the past or the present. In comparison to the practices and policies of the 1940s and 1950s, there have been significant advances in the federal government's system for the protection of the rights and interests of human subjects. But deficiencies remain. Efforts should be undertaken on a national scale to ensure the centrality of ethics in the conduct of scientists whose research involves human subjects.
- One problem in need of immediate attention by the government and the biomedical research community is unrealistic expectations among some patients with serious illnesses about the prospect of direct medical benefit from participating in research. Also, among the consent forms we reviewed, some appear to be overly optimistic in portraying the likely benefits of research, to inadequately explain the impact of research procedures on quality of life and personal finances, and to be incomprehensible to lay people.
- A mechanism should be established to provide for continuing interpretation and application in an open and public forum of ethics rules and principles for the conduct of human subjects research. Three examples of policy issues in need of public resolution that the Advisory Committee confronted in our work are: (1) clarification of the meaning of minimal risk in research with healthy children; (2) regulations to cover the conduct of research

with institutionalized children; and (3) guidelines for research with adults of questionable competence, particularly for research in which subjects are placed at more than minimal risk but are offered no prospect of direct medical benefit.

SECRECY: BALANCING NATIONAL SECURITY AND THE PUBLIC TRUST

Current policies do not adequately safeguard against the recurrence of the kinds of events we studied that fostered distrust. The Advisory Committee concludes that there may be special circumstances in which it may be necessary to conduct human research or intentional releases in secret. However, to the extent that the government conducts such activities with elements of secrecy, special protections of the rights and interests of individuals and the public are needed.

Research Involving Human Subjects. The Advisory Committee recommends the adoption of federal policies requiring:

- the informed consent of all human subjects of classified research. This requirement should not be subject to exemption or waiver.
- that classified research involving human subjects be permitted only after the review and approval of an independent panel of appropriate nongovernmental experts and citizen representatives, with all the necessary security clearances.

Environmental Releases. There must be independent review to assure that the action is needed, that risk is minimized, and that records will be kept to assure a proper accounting to the public at the earliest date consistent with legitimate national security concerns. Specifically, the Committee recommends that:

- Secret environmental releases of hazardous substances should be permitted only after the review and approval of an independent panel. This panel should consist of appropriate, nongovernmental experts and citizen representatives, all with the necessary security clearances.
- An appropriate government agency, such as the Environmental Protection Agency, should maintain a program directed at the oversight of classified programs, with suitably cleared personnel. . . .

TOM REGAN

The Case against Animal Research

THE AUTONOMY OF ANIMALS

Autonomy can be understood in different ways. On one interpretation, which finds its classic statement in Kant's writings, individuals are autonomous only if they are capable of acting on reasons they can will that any other similarly placed individual can act on. For example, if I am trying to decide whether I morally ought to keep a promise, I must, Kant believes, ask whether I could will that everyone else who is similarly placed (i.e., who has made a promise) can act as I do for the same reasons as I have. In asking what I ought to do, in other words, I must determine what others can do, and it is only if I have the ability to think through and reflectively evaluate the merits of acting in one way or another (e.g., to decide to keep the promise or to break it), and, having done this, to make a decision on the basis of my deliberations, that I can be viewed as an autonomous individual.

It is highly unlikely that any animal is autonomous in the Kantian sense. To be so animals would have to be able to reason at a quite sophisticated level indeed, bringing to bear considerations about what other animals (presumably those who belong to their own species) can or ought to do in comparable situations, a process that requires assessing the merits of alternative acts from an impartial point of view. Not only is it doubtful that animals could have the requisite abilities to do this; it is doubtful that we could confirm their possession of these abilities if they had them. . . .

But the Kantian sense of autonomy is not the only one. An alternative view is that individuals are autonomous if they have preferences and have the ability to initiate action with a view to satisfying them. It is not necessary, given this interpretation of autonomy (let us call this *preference autonomy*), that one be able to abstract from one's own desires, goals, and so on, as a preliminary to asking what any other similarly placed individual ought to do; it is enough that one have the ability to initiate action because one has those desires or goals one has and believes, rightly or wrongly, that one's desires or purposes will be satisfied or achieved by acting in a certain way. Where the Kantian sense requires that one be able to think impartially if one is to possess autonomy, the preference sense does not.

Both the Kantian and the preference sense of autonomy obviously exclude some of the same individuals from the class of autonomous beings. Rocks, clouds, rivers, and plants, for example, lack autonomy given either sense. But the preference sense includes some individuals excluded by the Kantian sense, most notably many animals. . . . [M]ammalian animals, at least, are reasonably viewed as creatures meeting the requirements for possession of preference autonomy. These animals are reasonably viewed as possessing the cognitive prerequisites for having desires and goals; they perceive and remember, and have the ability to form and apply general beliefs. From this it is a short step to acknowledging that these animals are reasonably viewed as being capable of making preferential choices.

Two types of cases illustrate the propriety of viewing these animals in this way. The first involves cases where they regularly behave in a given way when given the opportunity to do one thing or another. For example, if, when Fido is both hungry and has not recently had an opportunity to run outdoors, he regularly opts for eating when given the choice between food or the outdoors, we have adequate behavioral grounds for saying that the dog prefers eating to running in such cases and so acts (i.e., chooses) accordingly. A second type of case involves situations where there is not regular behavioral pattern because of the novelty of a given set of circumstances. If Fido is hungry, if we place before him both a bowl of his regular food and a bowl of boiled eggplant, and if, as is predictable, Fido opts for his regular food, then we again have adequate behavioral grounds for saying that the dog prefers his normal food to the eggplant and so acts (i.e., chooses) accordingly. And this we may reasonably contend even if this is the only time Fido is presented with the choice in question.

When autonomy is understood in the preference sense, the case can be made for viewing many animals as autonomous. Which animals it is reasonable to view as autonomous will turn, first, on whether we have reasonable grounds for viewing them as having preferences, understood as desires or goals, and second, on whether we find that how they behave in various situations is intelligibly described and parsimoniously explained by making reference to their preferences and the choices they make because of the preferences they have. Like other comparable issues, where one draws the line is certain to be controversial. But at least in the case of normal mammalian animals, aged one or more — even if not in the case of any others — the conclusions reached [earlier], including the need to view their behavior holistically, underwrite the reasonableness of ascribing preference autonomy to them.

We have, then, two senses of autonomy — the Kantian and the preference sense — each differing significantly from the other. If it could be shown that the Kantian sense is the only true sense of autonomy or that the preference sense is silly, or muddled, or worse, then one could rightfully claim that animals lack autonomy. But none of these options hold any promise. The Kantian interpretation of autonomy does not give us a condition that must be met if one is to be autonomous in any sense. It provides a condition that must be met if one is to be an autonomous *moral agent* — that is, an individual who can be held morally accountable for the acts he performs or fails to perform, one who can rightly be blamed or praised, criticized or condemned. Central to the Kantian sense of autonomy is the idea that autonomous individuals can rise above

thinking about their individual preferences and think about where their moral duty lies by bringing impartial reasons to bear on their deliberations. These two ideas (that of individual preferences, on the one hand, and on the other, one's moral duty) are distinct. Just because I prefer your death or public shame, for example, it does not follow that either I or anyone else has a moral duty to terminate your life or bring about your public disgrace, and there are many things I might be morally obligated to do that I personally do not prefer doing (e.g., keeping a promise). Suppose it is agreed that one must be autonomous in the Kantian sense to have the status of a moral agent. . . . It does not follow that one must be autonomous in *this* sense to be autonomous in *any* sense. So long as one has the ability to act on one's preferences, the ascription of autonomy is intelligible and attributions of it are confirmable. Though normal mammalian animals aged one or more are not reasonably viewed as moral agents because they are not reasonably viewed as autonomous in the Kantian sense, they are reasonably viewed as autonomous in the preference sense.

• • •

MORAL AGENTS AND MORAL PATIENTS

. . . Moral agents are individuals who have a variety of sophisticated abilities, including in particular the ability to bring impartial moral principles to bear on the determination of what, all considered, morally ought to be done and, having made this determination, to freely choose or fail to choose to act as morality, as they conceive it, requires. Because moral agents have these abilities, it is fair to hold them morally accountable for what they do, assuming that the circumstances of their acting as they do in a particular case do not dictate otherwise. If an action is the result of duress, coercion, unavoidable ignorance, or a psychological impairment (e.g., temporary insanity), then the individual may fairly be excused from being held responsible for acting as he or she does in those circumstances. In the absence of such excusing conditions, however, moral agents are justly and fairly held accountable for their deeds. Since it is they who ultimately decide what they do, it is also they who must bear the moral responsibility of doing (or not doing) it. Normal adult human beings are the paradigm individuals believed to be moral agents. To defend this belief would take us far afield from the present inquiry, involving us in debates dealing both with the existence of free will, for example, and with the extent to which we are able to influence how we act by bringing reason to bear on our decision-making. Though it is a large assumption to make, the assumption will be made that normal adult humans are moral agents. To make this assumption in the present case plays no theoretical favorites, since all theories examined in this and the following [discussion] share this assumption.

Now, moral agents not only can do what is right or wrong, they may also be on the receiving end, so to speak, of the right or wrong acts of other moral agents. There is, then, a sort of reciprocity that holds between moral agents. I can do what is right or wrong, and my doing either can affect or involve you; and you can do what is right or wrong, and what you do can affect or involve me. Let us define the notion of *the moral community* as comprising all those individuals who are of direct moral concern or alternatively, as consisting of all those individuals toward whom moral agents have direct duties. Then one possible specification of who belongs to the moral community is that *all and only moral agents belong.* This is the conception of the moral community common to all indirect duty views. Any individual who is not a moral agent stands outside the scope of direct moral concern on these views, and no moral agent can have any direct duty to such individuals. Any duties involving individuals who are not moral agents are indirect duties to those who are.

In contrast to moral agents, *moral patients* lack the prerequisites that would enable them to control their own behavior in ways that would make them morally accountable for what they do. A moral patient lacks the ability to formulate, let alone bring to bear, moral principles in deliberating about which one among a number of possible acts it would be right or proper to perform. Moral patients, in a word, cannot do what is right, nor can they do what is wrong. Granted, what they do may be detrimental to the welfare of others — they may, for example, bring about acute suffering or even death; and granted, it may be necessary, in any given case, for moral agents to use force or violence to prevent such harm being done, either in self-defense or in defense of others. . . . But even when a moral patient causes significant harm to another, the moral patient has not done what is wrong. Only moral agents can do what is wrong. Human infants, young children, and the

mentally deranged or enfeebled of all ages are paradigm cases of human moral patients. More controversial is whether human fetuses and future generations of human beings qualify as moral patients. It is enough for our purposes, however, that some humans are reasonably viewed in this way.

Individuals who are moral patients differ from one another in morally relevant ways. Of particular importance is the distinction between (a) those individuals who are conscious and sentient (i.e., can experience pleasure and pain) but who lack other mental abilities, and (b) those individuals who are conscious, sentient, and possess the other cognitive and volitional abilities . . . (e.g., belief and memory). Some animals, for reasons discussed in previous chapters already advanced, belong in category (b); other animals quite probably belong in category (a). . . . Our primary interest . . . concerns the moral status of animals in category (b). When, therefore, the notion of a *moral patient* is appealed to in the discussions that follow, it should be understood as applying to *animals in category (b) and to those other moral patients like these animals in the relevant respects* — that is, those who have desires and beliefs, who perceive, remember, and can act intentionally, who have a sense of the future, including their own future (i.e., are self-aware or self-conscious), who have an emotional life, who have a psychophysical identity over time, who have a kind of autonomy (namely, preference-autonomy), and who have . . . experiential welfare. . . . Some *human* moral patients satisfy these criteria — for example, young children and those humans who, though they suffer from a variety of mental handicaps and thus fail to qualify as moral agents, possess the abilities just enumerated. Where one draws the line between those humans who have these abilities and those who do not is a difficult question certainly, and it may be that no exact line can be drawn. . . . But how we should approach the question in the case of human beings is the same as how we should approach it in the case of animals. Given any human being, what we shall want to know is whether his/her behavior can be accurately described and parsimoniously explained by making reference to the range of abilities that characterizes animals (desires, beliefs, preferences, etc.). To the extent that the case can be made for describing and explaining the behavior of a human being in these terms, to that extent, assuming that we have further reasons for denying that the human in question has the abilities necessary for moral agency, we have reason to regard that human as a moral patient on all fours, so to speak, with animals. As previously claimed, some human beings *are* moral patients in the relevant sense, and *it is only those individuals who are moral patients in this sense (who have, that is, the abilities previously enumerated), whether these individuals be human or nonhuman, who are being referred to, in this [discussion] and in the sequel, when reference is made to "moral patients."*

Moral patients cannot do what is right or wrong, we have said, and in this respect they differ fundamentally from moral agents. But moral patients can be on the receiving end of the right or wrong acts of moral agents, and so in this respect resemble moral agents. A brutal beating administered to a child, for example, is wrong, even if the child herself can do no wrong, just as attending to the basic biological needs of the senile is arguably right, even if a senile person can no longer do what is right. Unlike the case of the relationship that holds between moral agents, then, the relationship that holds between moral agents, on the one hand, and moral patients, on the other, is not reciprocal. Moral patients can do nothing right or wrong that affects or involves moral agents, but moral agents can do what is right or wrong in ways that affect or involve moral patients.

• • •

INDIVIDUALS AS EQUAL IN VALUE

. . . The inherent value of individual moral agents is to be understood as being conceptually distinct from the intrinsic value that attaches to the experiences they have (e.g., their pleasures or preference satisfactions), as not being reducible to values of this latter kind, and as being incommensurate with these values. To say that inherent value is not reducible to the intrinsic values of an individual's experiences means that we cannot determine the inherent value of individual moral agents by totaling the intrinsic values of their experiences. Those who have a more pleasant or happier life do not therefore have greater inherent value than those whose lives are less pleasant or happy. Nor do those who have more "cultivated" preferences (say, for arts and letters) therefore have greater inherent value. To say that the inherent value of individual moral agents is incommensurate with the intrinsic value of their (or anyone else's) experiences means that the two kinds of value are not comparable and cannot be exchanged one for the other. Like proverbial apples and oranges, the two kinds of value do not fall within the same scale of

comparison. One cannot ask, How much intrinsic value is the inherent value of this individual worth — how much is it equal to? The inherent value of any given moral agent isn't equal to any sum of intrinsic values, neither the intrinsic value of that individual's experiences nor the total of the intrinsic value of the experiences of all other moral agents. To view moral agents as having inherent value is thus to view them as something different from, and something more than, mere receptacles of what has intrinsic value. They have value in their own right, a value that is distinct from, not reducible to, and incommensurate with the values of those experiences which, as receptacles, they have or undergo.

The difference between the utilitarian-receptacle view of value regarding moral agents and the postulate of inherent value might be made clearer by recalling the cup analogy. . . . On the receptacle view of value, it is *what goes into the cup* (the pleasures or preference-satisfactions, for example) that has value; what does not have value is the cup itself (i.e., the individual himself or herself). The postulate of inherent value offers an alternative. The cup (that is, the individual) has value *and* a kind that is not reducible to, and is incommensurate with, what goes into the cup (e.g., pleasure). The cup (the individual) does "contain" (experience) things that are valuable (e.g., pleasures), but the value of the cup (individual) is not the same as any one or any sum of the valuable things the cup contains. *Individual moral agents themselves have a distinctive kind of value,* according to the postulate of inherent value, but not according to the receptacle view to which utilitarians are committed. It's the cup, not just what goes into it, that is valuable.

Two options present themselves concerning the possession by moral agents of inherent value. First, moral agents might be viewed as having this value to varying degrees, so that some may have more of it than others. Second, moral agents might be viewed as having this value equally. The latter view is rationally preferable. If moral agents are viewed as having inherent value to varying degrees, then there would have to be some basis for determining how much inherent value any given moral agent has. Theoretically, the basis could be claimed to be anything — such as wealth or belonging to the "right" race or sex. More likely, the basis might be claimed to be possession of certain virtues or excellences, such as those favored by Aristotle. On this latter (perfectionist) account of inherent value, those who have abundant intellectual or artistic skills would have more inherent value than those who have some, and these latter individuals would have more than those who lack these virtues completely. To accept this view of the inherent value of moral agents is to pave the way for a perfectionist theory of justice: those with less inherent value could *justly* be required to serve the needs and interests of those with more, even if it is not in the interests of those who serve to do so. And the subjugated could have no grounds to complain of the injustice of the treatment they receive. Because they have less inherent value, *they* would get what they deserve. Such an interpretation of justice is unacceptable. Equally unacceptable, therefore, is any view of the inherent value of moral agents that could serve as the basis of such a theory. We must reject the view that moral agents have inherent value in varying degrees. All moral agents are equal in inherent value, if moral agents have inherent value.

. . . [T]he inherent value of moral agents cannot be viewed as something they can earn by dint of their efforts or as something they can lose by what they do or fail to do. A criminal is no less inherently valuable than a saint, if both are moral agents and if moral agents have inherent value. Second, the inherent value of moral agents cannot wax or wane depending upon the degree to which they have utility with respect to the interests of others. The most beneficent philanthropist is neither more nor less inherently valuable than, say, an unscrupulous used-car salesman. Third, the inherent value of moral agents is independent of their being the object of anyone else's interests. When it comes to inherent value, it matters not whether one is liked, admired, respected, or in other ways valued by others. The lonely, forsaken, unwanted, and unloved are no more nor less inherently valuable than those who enjoy a more hospitable relationship with others. To view all moral agents as equal in inherent value is thus decidedly egalitarian and nonperfectionist.

• • •

INHERENT VALUE AND REVERENCE FOR LIFE

Those who, like Kant, restrict inherent value to moral agents limit this value to those individuals who have those abilities essential for moral agency, in particular the ability to bring impartial reasons to bear on one's decision making. The conception of inherent value involved in the postulate of inherent value is more catholic, applying to individuals (e.g., human moral patients), who lack the abilities necessary for moral agency. If moral agents and moral patients, despite their differences, are viewed as having equal inherent value, then it is not unreasonable to demand that we cite some relevant similarity between them that makes attributing inherent value to them intelligible and non-arbitrary. In the nature of the case this similarity cannot be something that varies from individual to individual, since that would allow their inherent value to vary accordingly. Thus, no physical characteristic (e.g., having two eyes or five fingers) can mark the relevant similarity; nor will species membership suffice (e.g., belonging to the species *Canis lupus* or *Homo sapiens*); nor will still more general biological classifications do (e.g., being an animal). One characteristic shared by all moral agents and those moral patients with whom we are concerned is that they are *alive,* and some thinkers evidently believe that it is the possession of this characteristic that marks off the class of individuals who have inherent value from those who do not. Albert Schweitzer is perhaps the most famous thinker whose position invites this interpretation, and his famous ethics of "reverence for life" enjoys wide currency in many public discussions of how we ought to live, not only regarding how we ought to treat one another, in our reciprocal relationships as moral agents, but also regarding how we ought to treat other living things, including moral patients. But there are problems concerning both the scope and precision of Schweitzer's principle, some of which Schweitzer himself, perhaps unwittingly, exposes without resolving in the following passage:

True philosophy must commence with the most immediate and comprehensive facts of consciousness. And this may be formulated as follows: "I am life which wills to live, and I exist in the midst of life which wills to live". . . . Just as in my own will-to-live there is a yearning for more life, and for that mysterious exaltation of the will which is called pleasure, and terror in face of annihilation and that injury to the will-to-live which is called pain; so the same obtains in all the will-to-live around me, equally whether it can express itself to my comprehension or whether it remains unvoiced.

Ethics thus consists in this, that I experience the necessity of practising the same reverence for life toward all will-to-live, as toward my own. Therein I have already the needed fundamental principle of morality. It is *good* to maintain and cherish life; it is *evil* to destroy and to check life. . . . A man is really ethical only when he obeys the constraint laid on him to help all life which he is able to succour, and when he goes out of his way to avoid injuring anything living. He does not ask how far this or that life deserves sympathy as valuable in itself, nor how far it is capable of feeling. To him life as such is sacred. He shatters no ice crystal that sparkles in the sun, tears no leaf from its tree, breaks off no flower, and is careful not to crush any insect as he walks. If he works by lamplight on a summer evening he prefers to keep the window shut and to breathe stifling air, rather than to see insect after insect fall on his table with singed and sinking wings.[1]

Among the many things that are unclear in this passage is why those who are enjoined to have reverence for all *life* should take care not to shatter an ice crystal, since there is no clear sense in which ice crystals are "alive" or exhibit "will to live." That ice crystals may be beautiful, and that conscientious sojourners would not needlessly destroy their beauty or the beauty of nonliving nature generally, is arguable — though not easily! But *if* we are enjoined not to destroy the beauty of the natural order, even when the object of beauty is not alive, then we are in need of a more general principle than that of "reverence for (all) life." More importantly, reliance on a more general principle will imply that *being-alive* is not a necessary condition of something's having inherent value, with the result that "the ethic of reverence for life" will not be the *sole* fundamental principle its champions imply that it is.

In reply to these difficulties it might be suggested that *being-alive* is a *sufficient* condition of an individual's having inherent value. This position would avoid the problems indigenous to the view that being-alive is a necessary condition, but it stands in need of quite considerable analysis and argument if it is to win the day. It is not clear why we have, or how we reasonably could be said to have, direct duties to, say, individual blades of grass, potatoes, or cancer cells. Yet all are alive, and so all should be owed direct duties if all have inherent value. Nor is it clear why we have, or how we reasonably could be said to have, direct duties to collections of such individuals — to lawns, potato fields, or cancerous tumors. If, in reply to these difficulties, we are told that we have direct duties only to some, but not to all, living things, and that it is this subclass of living things whose members have inherent value, then not only will we stand in need of a way to distinguish those living things that have this value from those that do not but more importantly for present purposes, the view that being-alive is a sufficient condition of having such value will have to be abandoned. Because of the difficulties endemic both to the view that being-alive is a necessary condition of having inherent value and to the view that this is a sufficient condition, and granting that moral agents and moral patients share the important characteristic of being alive, it is extremely doubtful that the case could be made for viewing this similarity as the relevant similarity they share, by virtue of which all moral agents and patients have equal inherent value.

INHERENT VALUE AND THE SUBJECT-OF-A LIFE CRITERION

An alternative to viewing being-alive as the relevant similarity is what will be termed *the subject-of-a-life criterion*. To be the subject-of-a-life, in the sense in which this expression will be used, involves more than merely being alive and more than merely being conscious. To be the subject-of-a-life is to be an individual whose life is characterized by those features explored in the [preceding paragraphs]: that is, individuals are subjects-of-a-life if they have beliefs and desires; perception, memory, and a sense of the future, including their own future; an emotional life together with feelings of pleasure and pain; preference- and welfare-interests; the ability to initiate action in pursuit of their desires and goals; a psychophysical identity over time; and an individual welfare in the sense that their experiential life fares well or ill for them, logically independently of their utility for others and logically independently of their being the object of anyone else's interests. Those who satisfy the subject-of-a-life criterion themselves have a distinctive kind of value — inherent value — and are not to be viewed or treated as mere receptacles.

The claim that the value of those individuals who satisfy this criterion is *logically* independent of their utility for, and the interests of, others must be kept distinct from, and not confused with, the obvious fact that the welfare of those who satisfy this criterion is *causally* related to their perceived utility and the interests of others. Actively to harm either a moral agent or patient (e.g., to cause either gratuitous suffering) is to do something that causally detracts from their individual welfare, just as actively to benefit either (e.g., by providing either with the opportunity to pursue their desires, when it is in their interests to do so) is prima facie to contribute to their welfare. Especially in the case of human moral patients, individuals who, because of a variety of conditions, are incapable to varying degrees of taking care of themselves, how they fare in life is to a very considerable degree causally dependent on what we do to them or for them. For example, young children and the mentally enfeebled of all ages lack the requisite knowledge and sometimes even the requisite physical abilities to satisfy even their most basic needs and correlative desires. If we do not act on their behalf, they will fare ill. But even in the case of these individuals, their having a welfare, their being the experiencing subject of a life that fares well or ill *for them,* logically independently of their utility for us or of our taking an interest in them — this fact about them is not causally dependent on what we do to or for them. Indeed, the very possibility of our doing anything that affects their experiential welfare, for good or ill, *presupposes* that they are the experiencing subjects of such a life, on their own, as it were. And the same is true both of those moral patients (e.g., animals in the wild) who can take care of themselves without the need of human intervention and of those humans who are moral agents. Though what we, as moral agents, do to each other causally affects how we fare during the course of our individual lives, that we are the subjects of such a life is not similarly causally dependent on what others do to or for us. We have this status in the world, as do moral patients, whether human or animal, on our own; having this status is *logically* part of what it is for us or them *to be* in the world.

The subject-of-a-life criterion identifies a similarity that holds between moral agents and patients. Is this similarity a relevant similarity, one that makes viewing them as inherently valuable intelligible and nonarbitrary? The grounds for replying affirmatively are as follows: (1) A relevant similarity among all those who are postulated to have equal inherent value must mark a characteristic shared by all those moral agents and patients who are here viewed as having such value. The subject-of-a-life criterion satisfies this requirement. *All* moral agents and *all* those moral patients with whom we are concerned *are* subjects of a life that is better or worse for them, in the sense explained, logically independently of the utility they have for others and logically independently of their being the object of the interests of others. (2) Since inherent value is conceived to be a categorical value, admitting of no degrees, any supposed relevant similarity must itself be categorical. The subject-of-a-life criterion satisfies this requirement. This criterion does not assert or imply that those who

meet it have the status of subject of a life to a greater or lesser degree, depending on the degree to which they have or lack some favored ability or virtue (e.g., the ability for higher mathematics or those virtues associated with artistic excellence). One either *is* a subject of a life, in the sense explained, or one *is* not. All those who are, are so equally. The subject-of-a-life criterion thus demarcates a categorical status shared by all moral agents and those moral patients with whom we are concerned. (3) A relevant similarity between moral agents and patients must go some way toward illuminating why we have direct duties to both and why we have less reason to believe that we have direct duties to individuals who are neither moral agents nor patients, even including those who, like moral agents and those patients we have in mind, are alive. This requirement also is satisfied by the subject-of-a-life criterion. Not all living things are subjects of a life, in the sense explained; thus not all living things are to be viewed as having the same moral status, given this criterion, and the differences concerning our confidence about having direct duties to some (those who are subjects) can be at least partially illuminated because the former meet, while the latter fail to meet, the subject-of-a-life criterion. For these reasons, the subject-of-a-life criterion can be defended as citing a relevant similarity between moral agents and patients, one that makes the attribution of equal inherent value to them both intelligible and nonarbitrary.

•   •   •

THE RIGHTS OF MORAL PATIENTS

. . . The validity of the claim to respectful treatment, and thus the case for recognition of the right to such treatment, cannot be any stronger or weaker in the case of moral patients than it is in the case of moral agents. Both have inherent value, and both have it equally; thus, both are owed respectful treatment, as a matter of justice. Moreover, since the validity of the claim to such treatment in the case of moral agents has been shown, the same is true in the case of the validity of the claim to such treatment in the case of moral patients. It lies within the power of all moral agents to treat all those moral patients with whom they do or might have any dealings with the respect that, as possessors of inherent value, they are due. Similarly in the case of moral patients having valid claims-against moral agents: the individuals against whom the claim holds are all those moral agents who do or might interact with moral patients, and the claims made against

moral agents in this regard are validated by appeal to the respect principle and the postulate of inherent value on which it rests. Because moral patients have inherent value and have neither more nor less inherent value than that possessed by moral agents, they have the same right to respectful treatment possessed by moral agents *and* they possess this right equally—that is, moral agents and moral patients have an equal right to respectful treatment. Moreover, because moral agents have this right independently of the legislative acts (the laws) of this or that nation, the same is true in the case of moral patients. In the case of animals, in particular, therefore, one cannot argue against their having the basic moral right in question on the grounds that it is not recognized as a legal right by any nation.

It would be arbitrary in the extreme, therefore, to accept the postulate of inherent value, the respect principle, the analysis of rights as valid claims, and the argument for the right to respectful treatment in the case of moral agents, and then to deny that moral patients have this right. If the arguments used to validate this right in the case of moral agents are sound, then moral patients, including animals, have this right also. That is the destination toward which this work has been moving from the outset. It is not an act of kindness to treat animals respectfully. It is an act of justice. It is not "the sentimental interests" of moral agents that grounds our duties of justice to children, the retarded, the senile, or other moral patients, including animals. It is respect for their inherent value. The myth of the privileged moral status of moral agents has no clothes.

It is of more than passing interest to note that the argument for recognition of the basic moral rights of moral agents and patients does not depend on appeals to the utility of recognizing these rights. As was observed in the original characterization of the rights view, . . . certain individuals are viewed as having certain rights, according to this view, independently of considerations about the value of the consequences that result from recognizing that they have them. For the rights position, basic moral rights are more basic than utility and independent of it, so that the principal reason why, say, killing a moral agent or patient is wrong, if and when it is, lies in the violation of the individual's moral rights, and not in considerations about all those others who will or who will not receive pleasure or pain or who will or who will not have their preferences satisfied or frustrated. The argument of the present section should make it clear how those who favor the rights view can argue for their position independently of appeals to utility. Certain individuals have the basic right to respectful treatment because of the kind of value they have (inherent value), a kind of value that is itself independent of utility, and the criterion that makes its attribution to certain individuals both intelligible and nonarbitrary (the subject-of-a-life criterion) also makes no reference to, and thus is independent of appeals to, the utility of recognizing it. It is not, then, for utilitarian reasons that we recognize and validate the basic rights of moral agents and patients—not by appeal to "the *general* welfare." Their basic rights are validated by appeals to the respect that, as *individuals* who possess inherent value, they are due as a matter of strict justice.

． ． ．

THE RIGHTS OF ANIMALS

. . . [A]ll moral agents and patients have certain basic moral rights. To say that these individuals possess basic (or unacquired) moral rights means that (1) they possess certain rights independently of anyone's voluntary acts, either their own or those of others, and independently of the position they happen to occupy in any given institutional arrangement; (2) these rights are universal—that is, they are possessed by all relevant similar individuals, independently of those considerations mentioned in (1); and (3) all who possess these rights possess them equally. Basic moral rights thus differ *both* from acquired moral rights (e.g., the right of the promisee against the promisor) because one acquires these rights as a result of someone's voluntary acts or one's place in an institutional arrangement *and* from legal rights (e.g., the right to vote) since legal rights, unlike basic moral rights, are not equal or universal. . . .

The principal basic moral right possessed by all moral agents and patients is the right to respectful treatment. . . . [A]ll moral agents and patients are intelligibly and nonarbitrarily viewed as having a distinctive kind of value (inherent value) and as having this value equally. All moral agents and patients must always be treated in ways that are consistent with the recognition of their equal possession of value of this kind. These individuals have a basic moral right to respectful treatment because the claim made to it is (a) a valid claim-against assignable individuals (namely, all moral agents) and (b) a valid claim-to, the validity of the claim-to resting on appeal to the respect principle. . . . The basic moral right to respectful treatment prohibits treating moral agents or patients as if they were mere receptacles of intrinsic values (e.g., pleasure), lacking any value of their own, since such a view of these individuals would allow harming some (e.g., by making them suffer) on the grounds that the aggregate consequences for all those other "receptacles" affected by the outcome would be "the best." . . . [A]ll moral agents and patients [also] have a prima facie basic moral right not to be harmed. . . .

. . .

SCIENTIFIC RESEARCH

. . . To deny science use of animals in research is, it might be said, to bring scientific and allied medical progress to a halt, and that is reason enough to oppose it. The claim that progress would be "brought to a halt" is an exaggeration certainly. It is not an exaggeration to claim that, given its present dominant tendency, the rights view requires massive redirection of scientific research. The dominant tendency involves routinely harming animals. It should come as no surprise that the rights view has principled objections to its continuation.

A recent statement of the case for unrestricted use of animals in neurobiological research contrasts sharply with the rights view and will serve as an introduction to the critical assessment of using animals in basic research. The situation, as characterized by C. R. Gallistel, a psychologist at the University of Pennsylvania, is as follows:[2] "Behavioral neurobiology tries to establish the manner in which the nervous system mediates behavioral phenomena. It does so by studying the behavioral consequences of one or more of the following procedures: (a) destruction of a part of the nervous system, (b) stimulation of a part, (c) administration of drugs that alter neural functioning. These three techniques are as old as the discipline. A recent addition is (d) the recording of electrical activity. All four cause the animal at least temporary distress. In the past they have frequently caused intense pain, and they occasionally do so now. Also, they often impair an animal's proper functioning, sometimes transiently, sometimes permanently."[3] The animals subjected to these procedures are, in a word, harmed. When it comes to advancing our knowledge in neurobiology, however, "there is no way to establish the relation between the nervous system and behavior without some experimental surgery," where by "experimental surgery" Gallistel evidently means to include the four procedures just outlined. The issue, then, in Gallistel's mind, is not whether to allow such surgery or not; it is whether any restrictions should be placed on the use made of animals. Gallistel thinks not.

In defense of unrestricted use of animals in research, Gallistel claims that "most experiments conducted by neurobiologists, *like scientific experiments generally,* may be seen in retrospect to have been a waste of time, in the sense that they did not prove or yield any new insight." But, claims Gallistel, "there is no way of discriminating in advance the waste-of-time experiments from the illuminating ones with anything approaching certainty."[4] The logical upshot, so Gallistel believes, is that "restricting research on living animals is certain to restrict the progress in our understanding of the nervous system and behavior. Therefore," he concludes, "one should advocate such restrictions only if one believes that the moral value of this scientific knowledge and of the many human and humane benefits that flow from it cannot outweigh the suffering of a rat," something that, writing autobiographically, Gallistel finds "an affront to my ethical sensibility."[5]. . .

[T]he rights view rejects Gallistel's approach at a fundamental level. On the rights view, we cannot justify harming a single rat *merely* by aggregating "the many human and humane benefits" that flow from doing it, since, as stated, this is to assume that the rat has value only as a receptacle, which, on the rights view, is not true. Moreover, . . . [n]ot even a single rat is to be treated as if an animal's value were reducible to his *possible utility* relative to the interests of others, which is what we would be doing if we intentionally harmed the rat on the grounds that this *just might* "prove" something, *just might* "yield" a "new insight," *just might* produce "benefits" for others. . . .

If we are seriously to challenge the use of animals in research, we must challenge the *practice* itself, not only individual instances of it or merely the liabilities in its present methodology. The rights view issues such a challenge. Routine use of animals in research assumes that their value is reducible to their possible utility relative to the interests of others. The rights view rejects this view of animals and their value, as it rejects the justice of institutions that treat them as renewable resources. They, like us, have a value of their own, logically independently of their utility for others and of their being the object of anyone else's interests. To treat them in ways that respect their value, therefore, requires that we *not* sanction practices that institution-alize treating them as if their value was reducible to their possible utility relative to our interests. Scientific research, when it involves routinely harming animals in the name of possible "human and humane benefits," violates this requirement of respectful treatment. Animals are not to be treated as mere receptacles or as renewable resources. Thus does the practice of scientific research on animals violate their rights. Thus ought it to cease, according to the rights view. It is not enough first conscientiously to look for nonanimal alternatives and then, having failed to find any, to resort to using animals.[6] Though that approach is laudable as far as it goes, and though taking it would mark significant progress, it does not go far enough. It assumes that it is all right to allow practices that use animals as if their value were reducible to their possible utility relative to the interests of others, provided that we have done our best not to do so. The rights view's position would have us go further in terms of "doing our best." *The best we can do in terms of not using animals is not to use them.* Their inherent value does not disappear just because we have failed to find a way to avoid harming them in pursuit of our chosen goals. Their value is independent of these goals and their possible utility in achieving them. . . .

The rights view does not oppose using what is learned from conscientious efforts to treat a sick animal (or human) to facilitate and improve the treatment tendered other animals (or humans). In *this* respect, the rights view raises no objection to the "many human and humane benefits" that flow from medical science and the research with which it is allied. What the rights view opposes are practices that cause intentional harm to laboratory animals (for example, by means of burns, shock, amputation, poisoning, surgery, starvation, and sensory deprivation) preparatory to "looking for something that just might yield some human or humane benefit." Whatever benefits happen to accrue from such a practice are irrelevant to assessing its tragic injustice. Lab animals are not our tasters; we are not their kings.

The tired charge of being antiscientific is likely to fill the air once more. It is a moral smokescreen. The rights view is not against research on animals, if this research does not harm these animals or put them at risk of harm. It is apt to remark, however, that this objective will not be accomplished merely by ensuring that test animals are anaesthetized, or given postoperative drugs to ease their suffering, or kept in clean cages with ample food and water, and so forth. For it is

not only the pain and suffering that matters — though they certainly matter — but it is the *harm* done to the animals, including the diminished welfare opportunities they endure as a result of the deprivations caused by the surgery, *and* their untimely death. It is unclear whether a *benign* use of animals in research is possible or, if possible, whether scientists could be persuaded to practice it. That being so, and given the serious risks run by relying on a steady supply of human volunteers, research should take the direction away from the use of any moral agent or patient. If nonanimal alternatives are available, they should be used; if they are not available, they should be sought. That is the moral challenge to research, given the rights view, and it is those scientists who protest that this "can't be done," in advance of the scientific commitment to try — not those who call for the exploration — who exhibit a lack of commitment to, and belief in, the scientific enterprise — who are, that is, antiscientific at the deepest level. Like Galileo's contemporaries, who would not look through the telescope because they had already convinced themselves of what they would see and thus saw no need to look, those scientists who have convinced themselves that there can't be viable scientific alternatives to the use of whole animals in research (or toxicity tests, etc.) are captives of mental habits that true science abhors.

The rights view, then, is far from being antiscientific. On the contrary, as is true in the case of toxicity tests, so also in the case of research: it calls upon scientists *to do science* as they redirect the traditional practice of their several disciplines away from reliance on "animal models" toward the development and use of nonanimal alternatives. All that the rights view prohibits is science that violates individual rights. If that means that there are some things we cannot learn, then so be it. There are also some things we cannot learn by using humans, if we respect their rights. The rights view merely requires moral consistency in this regard.

The rights view's position regarding the use of animals in research cannot be fairly criticized on the grounds that it is antihumanity. The implications of this view in this regard are those that a rational human being should expect, especially when we recall that nature neither respects nor violates our rights. . . . Only moral agents do; indeed, only moral agents *can*. And nature is not a moral agent. We have, then, no basic right against nature not to be harmed by those natural diseases we are heir to. And neither do we have any basic right against humanity in this regard. What we do have, at this point in time at least, is a right to fair treatment on the part of those who have voluntarily decided to offer treatment for these maladies, a right that will not tolerate the preferential treatment of some (e.g., Caucasians) to the detriment of others (e.g., Native Americans). The right to fair treatment of our naturally caused maladies (and the same applies to mental and physical illnesses brought on by human causes, e.g. pollutants) is an *acquired right* we have against those moral agents who acquire the duty to offer fair treatment because they voluntarily assume a role within the medical profession. Both those in this profession, as well as those who do research in the hope that they might improve health care, are not morally authorized to override the *basic rights* of others in the process — rights others have, that is, independently of their place in any institutional arrangement and independently of any voluntary act on the part of anyone. . . . And yet that is what is annually done to literally millions of animals whose services, so to speak, are enlisted in the name of scientific research, including that research allied with medical science. For this research treats these animals as if their value is reducible to their possible utility relative to the interests of others. Thus does it routinely violate their basic right to respectful treatment. Though those of us who today are to be counted among the beneficiaries of the human benefits obtained from this research in the past might stand to lose some future benefits, at least in the short run, if this research is stopped, the rights view will not be satisfied with anything less than its total abolition. Even granting that we face greater prima facie harm than laboratory animals presently endure if future harmful research on these animals is stopped, and even granting that the number of humans and other animals who stand to benefit from allowing this practice to continue exceeds the number of animals used in it, this practice remains wrong because unjust.

· · ·

ANIMALS IN SCIENCE, UTILITARIANISM, AND ANIMAL RIGHTS

The fundamental differences between utilitarianism and the rights view are never more apparent than in the case of the use of animals in science. For the utilitarian, whether the harm done to animals in pursuit of sci-entific ends is justified depends on the balance of the aggregated consequences for all those affected by the outcome. If the consequences that result from harming animals would produce the best aggregate balance of good over evil, then harmful experimentation is obligatory. If the resulting consequences would be at least as good as what are otherwise obtainable, then harmful experimentation is permissible. Only if harmful experimentation would produce less than the best consequences would it be wrong. For a utilitarian to oppose or support harmful experimentation on animals, therefore, requires that he have the relevant facts — who will be benefited or harmed, how much, and so on. *Everyone's* interests, including the interests of those who do the tests or conduct the research, their employers, the dependents of these persons, the retailers and wholesalers of cages, animal breeders, and others, must be taken into account and counted equitably. For utilitarians, such *side effects count.* The animals used in the test have no privileged moral status. Their interests must be taken into account, to be sure, but not any more than anybody else's interests.

As is "almost always" the case, utilitarians simply fail to give us what is needed — the relevant facts, facts that we must have, given their theory, to determine whether use of animals in science is or is not justified. Moreover, for a utilitarian to claim or imply that there must be something wrong with a given experiment, if the experimenter would not be willing to use a less intelligent, less aware human being but would be willing to use a more intelligent, more aware animal, simply lacks a utilitarian basis. For all we know, and for all the utilitarian has thus far told us, the consequences of using such an animal, all considered, might be better than those that would result from using the human being. It is not *who* is used, given utilitarian theory, that matters; it is *the consequences* that do.

The rights view takes a very different stand. No one, whether human or animal, is ever to be treated as if she were a mere receptacle, or as if her value were reducible to her possible utility for others. We are, that is, never to harm the individual merely on the grounds that this will or just might produce "the best" aggregate consequences. To do so is to violate the rights of the individual. That is why the harm done to animals in pursuit of scientific purposes is wrong. The benefits derived are real enough; but some gains are ill-gotten, and all gains are ill-gotten when secured unjustly.

So it is that the rights view issues its challenge to those who do science; advance knowledge, work for the general welfare, but not by allowing practices that violate the rights of the individual. These are, one might say, the terms of the new contract between science and society, a contract that, however belatedly, now contains the signature of those who speak for the rights of animals. *Those who accept the rights view, and who sign for animals, will not be satisfied with anything less than the total abolition of the harmful use of animals in science — in education, in toxicity testing, in basic research.* But the rights view plays no favorites. No scientific practice that violates human rights, whether the humans be moral agents or moral patients, is acceptable. And the same applies to those humans who, for reasons analogous to those advanced in the present [essay] in regard to nonhumans, should be given the benefit of the doubt about having rights because of the weight of our ignorance — the newly born and the soon-to-be born. Those who accept the rights view are committed to denying any and all access to these "resources" on the part of those who do science.

And we do this not because we oppose cruelty (though we do), nor because we favor kindness (though we do), but because justice requires nothing less. . . .

NOTES

1. Albert Schweitzer, *Civilization and Ethics,* Pt. II of *The Philosophy of Civilization,* trans. C. T. Campion (2d ed; London: A. & C. Black, 1929), pp. 246–247.

2. C. R. Gallistel, "Bell, Magendie, and the Proposal to Restrict the Use of Animals in Neurobehavioral Research," *American Psychologist* (April 1981), pp. 357–360.

3. Ibid., p. 357.

4. Ibid., p. 358

5. Ibid., p. 360

6. This is the view recommended in Dale Jamieson and Tom Regan, "On the Ethics of the Use of Animals in Science" [in *And Justice for All,* ed. Tom Regan and VanDeVeer (Totowa, N.J.: Rowman and Littlefield, 1982), 169–196]. In disassociating myself from this earlier view, I speak only for myself. I am in no position to speak for Professor Jamieson.

CARL COHEN

Do Animals Have Rights?

Whether animals have rights is a question of great importance because if they do, those rights must be respected, even at the cost of great burdens for human beings. A right (unlike an interest) is a valid claim, or potential claim, made by a moral agent, under principles that govern both the claimant and the target of the claim. Rights are precious; they are dispositive; they count.

You have a right to the return of money you lent me; we both understand that. It may be very convenient for me to keep the money, and you may have no need of it whatever; but my convenience and your needs are not to the point. You have a *right* to it, and we have courts of law partly to ensure that such rights will be respected.

Reprinted with the permission of the author and the publisher, Lawrence Erlbaum Associates, Inc., from *Ethics & Behavior* 7 (1997), 91–102. Copyright © 1997 Carl Cohen.

If you make me a promise, I have a moral right to its fulfillment — even though there may be no law to enforce my right. It may be very much in your interest to break that promise, but your great interests and the silence of the law cut no mustard when your solemn promise — which we both well understood — had been given. Likewise, those holding power may have a great and benevolent interest in denying my rights to travel or to speak freely — but their interests are overridden by my rights.

A great deal was learned about hypothermia by some Nazi doctors who advanced their learning by soaking Jews in cold water and putting them in refrigerators to learn how hypothermia proceeds. We have no difficulty in seeing that they may not advance medicine in that way; the subjects of those atrocious experiments had rights that demanded respect. For those who ignored their rights we have nothing but moral loathing.

Some persons believe that animals have rights as surely as those Jews had rights, and they therefore look on the uses of animals in medical investigations just as we look at the Nazi use of the Jews, with moral loathing. They are consistent in doing so. If animals have rights they certainly have the right not to be killed, even to advance our important interests.

Some may say, "Well, they have rights, but we have rights too, and our rights override theirs." That may be true in some cases, but it will not solve the problem because, although we may have a weighty *interest* in learning, say, how to vaccinate against polio or other diseases, we do not have a *right* to learn such things. Nor could we honestly claim that we kill research animals in self-defense; they did not attack us. If animals have rights, they certainly have the right not to be killed to advance the interests of others, whatever rights those others may have.

In 1952 there were about 58,000 cases of polio reported in the United States, and 3,000 polio deaths; my parents, parents everywhere, trembled in fear for their children at camp or away from home. Polio vaccination became routine in 1955, and cases dropped to about a dozen a year; today polio has been eradicated completely from the Western Hemisphere. The vaccine that achieved this, partly developed and tested only blocks from where I live in Ann Arbor, could have been developed *only* with the substantial use of animals. Polio vaccines had been tried many times earlier, but from those earlier vaccines children had contracted the disease; investigators had become, understandably, exceedingly cautious.

The killer disease for which a vaccine now is needed most desperately is malaria, which kills about 2 million people each year, most of them children. Many vaccines have been tried—not on children, thank God—and have failed. But very recently, after decades of effort, we learned how to make a vaccine that does, with complete success inoculate mice against malaria. A safe vaccine for humans we do not yet have—but soon we will have it, thanks to the use of those mice, many of whom will have died in the process. To test that vaccine first on children would be an outrage, as it would have been an outrage to do so with the Salk and Sabin polio vaccines years ago. We use mice or monkeys *because there is no other way.* And there never will be an-

other way because untested vaccines are very dangerous; their first use on a living organism is inescapably experimental; there is and will be no way to determine the reliability and safety of new vaccines without repeated tests on live organisms. Therefore, because we certainly may not use human children to test them, we will use mice (or as we develop an AIDS vaccine, primates) *or we will never have such vaccines.*

But if those animals we use in such tests have rights as human children do, what we did and are doing to them is as profoundly wrong as what the Nazis did to those Jews not long ago. Defenders of animal rights need not hold that medical scientists are vicious; they simply believe that what medical investigators are doing with animals is morally wrong. Most biomedical investigations involving animal subjects use rodents: mice and rats. The rat is the animal appropriately considered (and used by the critic) as the exemplar whose moral stature is in dispute here. Tom Regan is a leading defender of the view that rats do have such rights, and may not be used in biomedical investigations. He is an honest man. He sees the consequences of his view and accepts them forthrightly. In *The Case for Animal Rights* (Regan, 1983) he wrote,

> The harms others might face as a result of the dissolution of [some] practice or institution is no defense of allowing it to continue. . . . No one has the right to be protected against being harmed if the protection in question involves violating the rights of others. . . . No one has a right to be protected by the continuation of an unjust practice, one that violates the rights of others. . . . Justice *must* be done, though the . . . heavens fall. (pp. 346–347)

The last line echoes Kant, who borrowed it from an older tradition. Believing that rats have rights as humans do, Regan (1983) was convinced that killing them in medical research was morally intolerable. He wrote,

> On the rights view, [he means, of course, the Regan rights view] we cannot justify harming a single rat *merely* by aggregating "the many human and humane benefits" that flow from doing it. . . . Not even a single rat is to be treated as if that animal's value were reducible to his *possible utility* relative to the interests of others. [see above, p. 492]

If there are some things that we cannot learn because animals have rights, well, as Regan (1983) put it, so be it.

This is the conclusion to which one certainly is driven if one holds that animals have rights. If Regan is correct about the moral standing of rats, we humans can have no right, ever, to kill them—unless perchance a rat attacks a person or a human baby, as rats sometimes do; then our right of self-defense may enter, I suppose. But medical investigations cannot honestly be described as self-defense, and medical investigations commonly require that many mice and rats be killed. Therefore, all medical investigations relying on them, or any other animal subjects—which includes most studies and all the important studies of certain kinds—will have to stop. Bear in mind that the replacement of animal subjects by computer simulations, or tissue samples, and so on, is in most research a phantasm, a fantasy. Biomedical investigations using animal subjects (and of course all uses of animals as food) will have to stop.

This extraordinary consequence has no argumentative force for Regan and his followers; they are not consequentialists. For Regan the *interests* of humans, their desire to be freed of disease or relieved of pain, simply cannot outweigh the *rights* of a single rat. For him the issue is one of justice, and the use of animals in medical experiments (he believes) is simply not just. But the consequences of his view will give most of us, I submit, good reason to weigh very carefully the arguments he offers to support such far-reaching claims. Do you believe that the work of Drs. Salk and Sabin was morally right? Would you support it now, or support work just like it saving tens of thousands of human children from diphtheria, hepatitis, measles, rabies, rubella, and tetanus (all of which relied essentially on animal subjects)—as well as, now, AIDS, Lyme disease, and malaria? I surely do. If you would join me in this support we must conclude that the defense of animal rights is a gigantic mistake. I next aim to explain why animals *cannot* possess rights.

WHY ANIMALS DO NOT HAVE RIGHTS

Many obligations are owed by humans to animals; few will deny that. But it certainly does not follow from this that animals have rights because it is certainly not true that every obligation of ours arises from the rights of another. Not at all. We need to be clear and careful here. Rights entail obligations. If you have a right to the return of the money I borrowed, I have an obligation to repay it. No issue. If we have the right to speak freely on public policy matters, the community has the obligation to respect our right to do so. But the proposition *all rights entail obligations* does not convert simply, as the logicians say. From the true propo-

sition that all trees are plants, it does not follow that all plants are trees. Similarly, not all obligations are entailed by rights. Some obligations, like mine to repay the money I borrowed from you, do arise out of rights. But many obligations are owed to persons or other beings who have no rights whatever in the matter.

Obligations may arise from commitments freely made: As a college professor I accept the obligation to comment at length on the papers my students submit, and I do so; but they have not the right to *demand* that I do so. Civil servants and elected officials surely ought to be courteous to members of the public, but that obligation certainly is not grounded in citizens' rights.

Special relations often give rise to obligations: Hosts have the obligation to be cordial to their guests, but the guest has not the right to demand cordiality. Shepherds have obligations to their dogs, and cowboys to their horses, which do not flow from the rights of those dogs or horses. My son, now 5, may someday wish to study veterinary medicine as my father did; I will then have the obligation to help him as I can, and with pride I shall—but he has not the authority to demand such help as a matter of right. My dog has no right to daily exercise and veterinary care, but I do have the obligation to provide those things for her.

One may be obliged to another for a special act of kindness done; one may be obliged to put an animal out its misery in view of its condition—but neither the beneficiary of that kindness nor that dying animal may have had a claim of right.

Beauchamp and Childress (1994) addressed what they called the "correlativity of rights and obligations" and wrote that they would defend an "untidy" (pp. 73–75) variety of that principle. It would be very untidy indeed. Some of our most important obligations—to members of our family, to the needy, to neighbors, and to sentient creatures of every sort—have no foundation in rights at all. Correlativity appears critical from the perspective of one who holds a right; your right correlates with my obligation to respect it. But the claim that rights and obligations are *reciprocals,* that *every* obligation flows from another's right, is false, plainly inconsistent with our general understanding of the differences between what we think we *ought* to do, and what others can justly *demand* that we do.

I emphasize this because, although animals have no rights, it surely does not follow from this that one is free to treat them with callous disregard. Animals are not stones; they feel. A rat may suffer; surely we have the obligation not to torture it gratuitously, even though it be true that the concept of a right could not possibly apply to it. We humans are obliged to act humanely, that is, being aware of their sentience, to apply to animals the moral principles that govern us regarding the gratuitous imposition of pain and suffering; which is not, of course, to treat animals as the possessors of rights.

Animals cannot be the bearers of rights because the concept of rights is essentially *human;* it is rooted in, and has force within, a human moral world. Humans must deal with rats — all too frequently in some parts of the world — and must be moral in their dealing with them; but a rat can no more be said to have rights than a table can be said to have ambition. To say of a rat that it has rights is to confuse categories, to apply to its world a moral category that has content only in the human moral world.

Try this thought experiment. Imagine, on the Serengeti Plain in East Africa, a lioness hunting for her cubs. A baby zebra, momentarily left unattended by its mother, is the prey; the lioness snatches it, rips open its throat, tears out chunks of its flesh, and departs. The mother zebra is driven nearly out of her wits when she cannot locate her baby; finding its carcass she will not even leave the remains for days. The scene may be thought unpleasant, but it is entirely natural, of course, and extremely common. If the zebra has a right to live, if the prey is just but the predator unjust, we ought to intervene, if we can, on behalf of right. But we do not intervene, of course — as we surely would intervene if we saw the lioness about to attack an unprotected human baby or you. What accounts for the moral difference? We justify different responses to humans and to zebras on the ground (implicit or explicit) that their moral stature is very different. The human has a right not to be eaten alive; it is, after all, a human being. Do you believe the baby zebra has the *right* not to be slaughtered by that lioness? That the lioness has the *right* to kill that baby zebra for her cubs? If you are inclined to say, confronted by such natural rapacity — duplicated with untold variety millions of times each day on planet earth — that neither is right or wrong, that neither has a *right* against the other, I am on your side. Rights are of the highest moral consequence, yes; but zebras and lions and rats are totally amoral; there is

no morality for them; they do no wrong, ever. In their world there are no rights.

A contemporary philosopher who has thought a good deal about animals, referring to them as "moral patients," put it this way:

A moral patient lacks the ability to formulate, let alone bring to bear, moral principles in deliberating about which one among a number of possible acts it would be right or proper to perform. Moral patients, in a word, cannot do what is right, nor can they do what is wrong. . . . Even when a moral patient causes significant harm to another, the moral patient has not done what is wrong. Only moral agents can do what is wrong. (Regan, 1983, [see above, p. 486])

Just so. The concepts of wrong and right are totally foreign to animals, not conceivably within their ken or applicable to them, as the author of that passage clearly understands.

When using animals in our research, therefore, we ought indeed be humane — but we can never violate the rights of those animals because, to be blunt, they have none. Rights do not *apply* to them.

But humans do have rights. Where do our rights come from? Why are we not crudely natural creatures like rats and zebras? This question philosophers have struggled to answer from earliest times. A definitive account of the human moral condition I cannot here present, of course. But reflect for a moment on the kinds of answers that have been widely given:

- Some think our moral understanding, with its attendant duties, to be a divine gift. So St. Thomas said: The moral law is binding, and humans have the power, given by God, to grasp its binding character, and must therefore respect the rights that other humans possess. God makes us (Saint Augustine said before him) in his own image, and therefore with a will that is free, and gives us the power to recognize that, and therefore, unlike other creatures, we must choose between good and evil, between right and wrong.
- Many philosophers, distrusting theological justifications of rights and duties, sought the ground of human morality in the membership by all humans, in a moral community. The English idealist, Bradley, called it an organic moral community; the German idealist, Hegel, called it an objective ethical order. These and like accounts commonly center on human interrelations, on a moral *fabric* within which human agents always

act, and within which animals never act and never can possibly act.

- The highly abstract reasoning from which such views emerge has dissatisfied many; you may find more nearly true the convictions of ethical intuitionists and realists who said, as H.A. Prichard, Sir David Ross, and my friend and teacher C. D. Broad, of happy memory, used to say, that there is a direct, underivative, intuitive cognition of rights as possessed by other humans, but not by animals.
- Or perhaps in the end we will return to Kant, and say with him that critical reason reveals at the core of human action a uniquely moral will, and the unique ability to grasp and to lay down moral laws for oneself and for others — an ability that is not conceivably within the capacity of any nonhuman animal whatever.

To be a moral agent (on this view) is to be able to grasp the generality of moral restrictions on our will. Humans understand that some things, which may be in our interest, *must not be willed;* we lay down moral laws for ourselves, and thus exhibit, as no other animal can exhibit, moral autonomy. My dog knows that there are certain things she must not do — but she knows this only as the outcome of her learning about her interests, the pains she may suffer if she does what had been taught forbidden. She does not know, cannot know (as Regan agrees) that any conduct is wrong. The proposition *It would be highly advantageous to act in such-and-such a way, but I may not because it would be wrong* is one that no dog or mouse or rabbit, however sweet and endearing, however loyal or attentive to its young, can ever entertain, or intend, or begin to grasp. Right is not in their world. But right and wrong are the very stuff of human moral life, the ever-present awareness of human beings who can do wrong, and who by seeking (often) to avoid wrong conduct prove themselves members of a moral community in which rights may be exercised and must be respected.

Some respond by saying, "This can't be correct, for human infants (and the comatose and senile, etc.) surely have rights, but they make no moral claims or judgments and can make none — and any view entailing that children can have no rights must be absurd." Objections of this kind miss the point badly. It is not individual persons who qualify (or are disqualified) for the possession of rights because of the presence or absence in them of some special capacity, thus resulting in the award of rights to some but not to others. Rights

are universally human; they arise in a *human moral world,* in a moral *sphere.* In the human world moral judgments are pervasive; it is the fact that all humans including infants and the senile are members of that moral community — not the fact that as individuals they have or do not have certain special capacities, or merits — that makes humans bearers of rights. Therefore, it is beside the point to insist that animals have remarkable capacities, that they really have a consciousness of self, or of the future, or make plans, and so on. And the tired response that because infants plainly cannot make moral claims they must have no rights at all, or rats must have them too, we ought forever put aside. Responses like these arise out of a misconception of right itself. They mistakenly suppose that rights are tied to some identifiable individual abilities or sensibilities, and they fail to see that rights arise only in a community of moral beings, and that therefore there are spheres in which rights do apply and spheres in which they do not.

Rationality is not an issue; the capacity to communicate is not at issue. My dog can reason, if rather weakly, and she certainly can communicate. Cognitive criteria for the possession of rights, Beauchamp (1997) said, are morally perilous. Indeed they are. Nor is the capacity to suffer here at issue. And, if *autonomy* be understood only as the capacity to choose this course rather than that, autonomy is not to the point either. But *moral autonomy* — that is, *moral self-legislation* — is to the point, because moral autonomy is uniquely human and is for animals out of the question, as we have seen, and as Regan and I agree. In talking about autonomy, therefore, we must be careful and precise.

Because humans do have rights, and these rights can be violated by other humans, we say that some humans commit *crimes.* But whether a crime has been committed depends utterly on the moral state of mind of the actor. If I take your coat, or your book, honestly thinking it was mine, I do not steal it. The *actus reus* (the guilty deed) must be accompanied, in a genuine crime, by a guilty mind, a *mens rea.* That recognition, not just of possible punishment for an act, but of moral duties that govern us, no rat or cow ever can possess. In primitive times humans did sometimes bring cows and horses to the bar of human justice. We chuckle at that practice now, realizing that accusing cows of crimes marks the primitive moral view as inane. Animals never can be criminals because they have no moral state of mind. . . .

WHY ANIMALS ARE MISTAKENLY BELIEVED TO HAVE RIGHTS

From the foregoing discussion it follows that, if some philosophers believe that they have proved that animals have rights, they must have erred in the alleged proof. Regan is a leader among those who claim to *argue* in defense of the rights of rats; he contends that the best arguments are on his side. I aim next to show how he and others with like views go astray.

•   •   •

[Regan's] case is built entirely on the principle that allegedly *carries over* almost everything earlier claimed about human rights to rats and other animals. What principle is that? It is the principle, put in italics but given no name, that equates moral agents with moral patients:

> *The validity of the claim to respectful treatment, and thus the case for the recognition of the right to such treatment, cannot be any stronger or weaker in the case of moral patients than it is in the case of moral agents.* (Regan, [see above, p. 490])

But hold on. Why in the world should anyone think this principle to be true? Back in Section 5.2 [see above, p. 485], where Regan first recounted his view of moral patients, he allowed that some of them are, although capable of experiencing pleasure and pain, lacking in other capacities. But he is interested, he told us there, in those moral patients — those animals — that are like humans in having *inherent value*. This is the key to the argument for animal rights, the possession of inherent value. How that concept functions in the argument becomes absolutely critical. I will say first briefly what will be shown more carefully later: *Inherent value* is an expression used by Regan (and many like him) with two very different senses — in one of which it is reasonable to conclude that those who have inherent value have rights, and in another sense in which that inference is wholly unwarranted. But the phrase, *inherent value* has some plausibility in both contexts, and thus by sliding from one sense of inherent value to the other Regan appears to succeed, in two pages, in making the case for animal rights.

The concept of inherent value first entered the discussion in the seventh chapter of Regan's (1983) book, at which point his principal object is to fault and defeat utilitarian arguments. It is not (he argued there) the pleasures or pains that go "into the cup" of humanity that give value, but the "cups" themselves; humans are equal in value because they are humans, having inherent value. So we are, all of us, equal — equal in being moral agents who have this inherent value. This approach to the moral stature of humans is likely to be found quite plausible. Regan called it the "postulate of inherent value"; all humans, "The lonely, forsaken, unwanted, and unloved are no more nor less inherently valuable than those who enjoy a more hospitable relationship with others" [see above, p. 488]. And Regan went on to argue for the proposition that all moral agents are "equal in inherent value." Holding some such views we are likely to say, with Kant, that all humans are beyond price. Their inherent value gives them moral dignity, a unique role in the moral world, as agents having the capacity to act morally and make moral judgments. This is inherent value in Sense 1.

The expression *inherent value* has another sense, however, also common and also plausible. My dog has inherent value, and so does every wild animal, every lion and zebra, which is why the senseless killing of animals is so repugnant. Each animal is unique, not replaceable in itself by another animal or by any rocks or clay. Animals, like humans, are not just things; they live, and as unique living creatures they have inherent value. This is an important point, and again likely to be thought plausible; but here, in Sense 2, the phrase *inherent value* means something quite distinct from what was meant in its earlier uses.

Inherent value in Sense 1, possessed by all humans but not by all animals, which warrants the claim of human rights, is very different from inherent value in Sense 2, which warrants no such claim. The uniqueness of animals, their intrinsic worthiness as individual living things, does not ground the possession of rights, has nothing to do with the moral condition in which rights arise. Regan's argument reached its critical objective with almost magical speed because, having argued that beings with inherent value (Sense 1) have rights that must be respected, he quickly asserted (putting it in italics lest the reader be inclined to express doubt) that rats and rabbits also have rights because they, too, have inherent value (Sense 2).

This is an egregious example of the fallacy of equivocation: the informal fallacy in which two or more meanings of the same word or phrase have been confused in the several premises of an argument (Cohen & Copi, 1994, pp. 143–144). Why is this slippage not seen at once? Partly because we know the phrase *inherent value* often is used loosely, so the reader is not prone to quibble about its introduction; partly because the two uses of the phrase relied on are both common, so neither signals danger; partly because inherent value in Sense 2 is indeed shared by those who have it in Sense 1; and partly because the phrase *inherent value* is woven into accounts of what Regan (1983) elsewhere called the *subject-of-a-life criterion,* a phrase of his own devising for which he can stipulate any meaning he pleases, of course, and which also slides back and forth between the sphere of genuine moral agency and the sphere of animal experience. But perhaps the chief reason the equivocation between these two uses of the phrase *inherent value* is obscured (from the author, I believe, as well as from the reader) is the fact that the assertion that animals have rights appears only indirectly, as the outcome of the application of the principle that moral patients are entitled to the same respect as moral agents—a principle introduced at a point in the book long after the important moral differences between moral patients and moral agents have been recognized, with a good deal of tangled philosophical argument having been injected in between.

I invite readers to trace out this equivocation in detail; my limited space here precludes more extended quotation. But this assurance I will give: there is no argument or set of arguments in *The Case for Animal Rights* that successfully makes the case for animal rights. Indeed, there *could* not be, any more than any book, however, long and convoluted, could make the case for the emotions of oak trees, or the criminality of snakes.

Animals do not have rights. Right does not apply in their world. We do have many obligations to animals, of course, and I honor Regan's appreciation of their sensitivities. I also honor his seriousness of purpose, and his always civil and always rational spirit. But he is, I submit, profoundly mistaken. I conclude with the observation that, had his mistaken views about the rights of animals long been accepted, most successful medical therapies recently devised—antibiotics, vaccines, prosthetic devices, and other compounds and instruments on which we now rely for saving and improving human lives and for the protection of our children—could not have been developed; and were his views to become general now (an outcome that is unlikely but possible) the consequences for medical science and for human well-being in the years ahead would be nothing less than catastrophic.

Advances in medicine absolutely require experiments, many of which are dangerous. Dangerous experiments absolutely require living organisms as subjects. Those living organisms (we now agree) certainly may not be human beings. Therefore, most advances in medicine will continue to rely on the use of nonhuman animals, or they will stop. Regan is free to say in response, as he does, "so be it." The rest of us must ask if the argument he presents is so compelling as to force us to accept that dreadful result.

REFERENCES

Beauchamp, T. L. (1997). Opposing views on animal experimentation: Do animals have rights? *Ethics & Behavior* 7(1997), 113–121.

Beauchamp, T. L., & Childress, J. F. (1994). *Principles of biomedical ethics* (4th ed.) New York: Oxford University Press.

Cohen, C., & Copi, I. M. (1994). *Introduction to logic* (9th ed.). New York: Macmillan.

Regan, T. (1983). *The case for animal rights.* Berkeley: University of California Press.

ANDREW N. ROWAN

Formulation of Ethical Standards for Use of Animals in Medical Research

· · ·

THE MODERN CONTROVERSY

In the last 20 years, more has been written about the moral status of animals than in the previous 2000, but we seem to be no nearer to resolving some of the central arguments and controversies. For example, what grounds can be used to distinguish humans and animals as different in kind rather than degree? If we choose one [criterion] like reason or language, then what reasons should we give for excluding chimpanzees, while including humans who cannot talk or reason? Whatever criterion is chosen, there are either some animals that appear to meet it or some humans that do not. Moral theories that argue that only those who have duties can have rights[1] would exclude a significant number of humans, who are not deemed capable of having duties, from the category of 'rights-holders.'

If suffering is to be given a critical place in our moral theory, then how do we decide what animals are capable of suffering and is all suffering equivalent? Are humans, with their considerable capacity for abstract thought capable of more intense mental anguish than nonverbal animals? Are insects or other invertebrates capable of suffering given that most theories of suffering require the presence of significant cognitive abilities?

Despite the difficult questions, we may find that it is much easier to come to a broadly supported consensus on the ethics of animal research than the overblown rhetoric and ad hominem attacks in the media would seem to imply. First, however, it is desirable to examine some of the ethical positions[2] that are evident in the modern debate because the various protagonists, most of whom are not trained in the analytical tools of moral philosophy, often have difficulty in articulating their own positions regarding the moral status of animals. As such, it is hardly surprising that they are not aware of all the implications of either their own ethical positions or those of their opponents. The following positions do not represent an exhaustive list but they do provide a broad sweep of the arguments that are evident in the modern debate.

DIVINELY GRANTED DOMINION

People commonly refer to biblical authority to justify the position that we can use and kill animals as we wish provided we are not careless or malevolent. Some go further and suggest that there are no constraints whatever on our use of animals[3] but the prevailing view is that God-granted dominion falls far short of domination and should be interpreted more as stewardship. One is then faced with questions about the extent of the obligations to animals that are required by this position of stewardship.

THE THOMIST/KANTIAN POSITION

Although Aquinas and Kant did not have much to say on the animal issue, they both argued that we should not abuse animals, not because of any inherent value that the animals hold, but because animal abusers are more likely to move on to abuse other humans. There is a strong thread of this philosophy apparent in humane education and in anticruelty laws.

Although research tends to support the link between animal abuse and subsequent aggressive behavior towards other humans,[4] it is also possible that the tendency of some individuals to abuse humans may be reduced by the opportunity to mistreat an animal. In this case, the counter-intuitive nature of the Thomist-Kantian position is evident. Imagine the public reaction if people were encouraged to engage in cruelty to animals as part of their psychotherapy!

UTILITARIANISM

Most of the American public probably rely heavily, albeit unknowingly, on Utilitarian arguments to support their moral behavior. Many laws and regulations are based on Utilitarian ideas of maximizing good and minimizing harm. Early Utilitarians, especially the 18th century British philosopher, Jeremy Bentham, identified suffering as a key harm. Bentham then extended his moral orbit to include animal suffering. Indeed, one of his passages is widely quoted in the animal movement's literature.

It may come one day to be recognized, that the number of legs, the villosity of the skin, or the termination of the os sacrum, are reasons equally insufficient [as blackness of the skin among humans] for abandoning a sensitive being to the same fate. What else is it that should trace insuperable line? Is it the faculty of reason, or perhaps the faculty of discourse? But a full-grown horse or dog is beyond comparison a more rational as well as more conversable animal, than an infant of a day, or a week, or even a month, old. But suppose the case were otherwise, what would it avail? The question is not Can they *reason*? nor Can they *talk*? but, Can they *suffer*?[5], (emphasis [in original]).

The rationality and linguistic skills of the individual being were not important to Bentham. If the creature could suffer and experience pleasure — that is, if it was sentient — then it would be entitled to have its suffering and pleasure compared and weighed against the similar suffering and pleasure of other sentient creatures, including humans. This does not imply that a chicken and a horse should be 'treated' the same, just that their interests in not experiencing the same type of suffering are equal and should be 'considered' equally.

In the area of animal research, Utilitarian arguments are very common. On the scientific side, people argue that animal research is justified because its benefits to humans and animals outweigh the harms to the laboratory animals. On the animal activist side, philosophers such as Singer[6] use Utilitarian arguments to attack the use of animals in research. One could characterize these two opposing positions as Permissive and Restrictive Utilitarianism. Clearly, the two sides are not arguing about the use of Utilitarian theory itself, but rather about the extent of human benefit and animal suffering. Singer holds that animal suffering in the laboratory is considerable and that most of the benefits are either too limited to warrant such suffering or, with sufficient effort, could be achieved without the use of animals. In addition, Singer places an animal's interests in not suffering on a virtually equal footing with a human's interests in not suffering. (Singer's arguments have been an important element in the upsurge of support for the animal movement over the past decade.) By contrast, scientists tend to maximize claims of benefit and argue that animal suffering is minimal or nonexistent.

There are several problems with the Utilitarian approach. For example, it is virtually impossible to develop the necessary calculations that permit a measured and rational balancing of harm against good. Frequently one has to attempt to balance very different outcomes. How, for example, does one compare the suffering of a certain number of rats with the increased understanding of a biological phenomenon? In the United Kingdom, where the law governing animal research requires a balancing of costs and benefits, nobody has yet produced a systematic way to compare them.[7] As in the United States, most of the attention is paid to reducing the costs (i.e., animal suffering).

It has also proved difficult to identify what groups of animals experience suffering and distress (do insects suffer?) and whether the suffering of rats is equivalent to that of dogs, or humans? Suffering is usually not defined but the usual implication is that it requires a minimum level of cognitive ability that may not be present in most invertebrates (the octopus being a possible exception). The concept appears to be like obscenity where everybody thinks they can recognize it but nobody can define it for regulatory purposes.

REVERENCE FOR LIFE

Albert Schweitzer argued that our moral concern should be extended beyond just those life forms capable of feeling or sensation (sentience). He held that all life exhibits a 'will to live' and that it is 'good to maintain and cherish . . . [and] . . . evil to destroy and check.'[8] Nevertheless, his philosophy did not cause him to oppose all animal research, nor was he a vegetarian. His view was that any injury to life must be 'necessary' and 'unavoidable,' but he did not spell out the conditions that make the sacrifice of animals in general, or research animals in particular, 'necessary'.[9] Many people make appeals as to the sanctity of life but such appeals are usually reserved for human life. The taking of animal life is usually considered to be acceptable provided little or no suffering is involved and the animal's death is necessary for some human end. The wanton killing of animals is usually not condoned. However, 'reverence for life' is a common phrase in the lexicon of animal activists and, in its strong form, it usually implies no killing of animals for human benefit.

ANIMAL RIGHTS

Animal rights is not a new concept. People have talked of the rights of animals for centuries. In the 18th and 19th centuries a number of authors discussed the status of animals using the term 'animal rights'. These culminated in the 1892 book by Henry Salt, entitled *Animals' Rights,*[10] which presented a very modern exposition of the issues. Today, the concept of 'animal rights' is a central issue in the clash between opponents and proponents of animal research. Unfortunately, the term animal rights now tends to cloud and confuse rather than clarify the issues because it has come to be used as a convenient hook on which to hang oneself or one's opponents! There are three contexts in which the term is used: (i) the 'common sense', (ii) the political, and (iii) the philosophical—that are rarely distinguished nor identified in the course of debate and argument.

(i) *'Common sense'.* Approximately 80% of the public believes that animals have rights. However, about 85 % of that same public believes that humans have the right to kill and eat animals.[11] Thus, whatever 'rights' the public believes animals have claim to, they do not include the right to life. The concept of animal rights held by the general public probably amounts to no more than a vague and woolly idea that animals have the right to some, rather limited moral considerations.

(ii) *Political views.* In the developed world, there is a growing tendency to couch political claims in 'rights' language. Thus, we talk of civil rights, women's rights, gay rights, and the like. Therefore, in the political arena, a rights claim carries significant political resonance. It is only to be expected that the animal movement would attempt to appropriate the power of rights language for its own cause. In this sense, the public campaign for animal rights also includes the animal welfare movement although there has been some attempt, both inside and outside the animal protection movement, to distinguish between animal welfare and animal rights organizations. Peter Singer who, as a Utilitarian, does not agree with rights language, has ironically accepted his identification with the animal rights movement (although he prefers the term 'animal liberation') because he sees it as primarily a political movement with only loose ties to its philosophical roots.

(iii) *Philosophical arguments.* In philosophical circles, a right can be defined (simply and simplistically) as nothing more than a claim that cannot be over-ridden by claims to human utility. A rights claim can only be over-ridden by another rights claim. Thus, one has to determine just what is being claimed as a right. The fact that most of the philosophical arguments espousing animal rights have been radical challenges to current human use of animals — usually setting forth a claim that animals cannot be used solely as a means to a human end[12] — does not mean that all animal rights positions need be that radical.

The very strong Animal Rights argument — developed by Regan[12] and others — asserts that we cannot use animals merely as a means to our own ends. A weaker, but plausible Animal Rights argument is one where the assertion is made that animals have the right not to be caused to suffer. In both positions, the term 'rights' is used simply to define a claim that cannot be over-ridden merely because it would be useful to do so.

Most rights-based arguments have to identify some characteristic or complex of characteristics that confer moral rights. Regan,[12] for example, suggests that animals that have beliefs and desires are the 'subjects of a life' and this confers inherent worth that gives them the right not to be killed or used to satisfy human ends. He identifies adult mammals as having this capacity and would give the benefit of the doubt to birds and perhaps other vertebrates. Thus, Regan's animal rights philosophy tends to require a vegetarian life style and little or no animal use by humans.

Rights-based moral arguments have difficulties dealing with shades of grey. In Regan's philosophy, an animal either is a 'subject-of-a-life' or it is not. It cannot half fulfill the requirements. This creates certain problems from an evolutionary perspective although it is conceivable that the capacity to have beliefs and desires is an all-or-none property. Nonetheless, Regan runs into difficulties when he argues (as he does in his book) that a human has a richer life than a dog and is therefore to be favored over a dog when faced with a direct conflict of competing rights.[12]

ANOTHER POSSIBLE APPROACH

Nearly every articulated argument on the moral status of animals has presented its arguments on the basis of a single morally relevant characteristic. For example, Schweitzer argues that possession of a life is 'the' important characteristic. For Singer, it is sentience. For Regan, it is the possession of beliefs and desires. However, it is very likely that no single characteristic is sufficient to describe a complete ethical theory on animal treatment. The world is not that simple. One has to consider a tapestry of characteristics,[13] including the possession of life, the possession of sentience, the possession of beliefs and desires, the possession of self-awareness, and the like.[2]

One can develop a two-tiered approach to ethical thinking in which there are proscriptive obligations to animals based on the possession of life, sentience, purposiveness, self-awareness and personhood that establish baseline levels of moral consideration below which one cannot go. On this relatively complex edifice, one can add a layer of prescriptive obligations that are owed to beings with which one has established certain explicit or implicit contracts. Thus, one is required to treat one's family with greater consideration than a stranger but the stranger is owed certain basic obligations that cannot be voided.

This approach has strong Darwinian overtones in that the ranking of obligations tends to follow evolutionary paths. Thus, sentient vertebrates would be accorded more consideration than living, but not sentient coelenterates, and self-aware apes would be accorded more consideration than sentient, but (presumably) not self-aware frogs. The scheme also provides a place for the additional moral obligations incurred by explicit or implicit contracts between humans and animals. Thus, this scheme could explain why we might owe more to the family dog than to a purpose-bred laboratory beagle.

ESTABLISHING A MORAL FRAMEWORK

In actual fact, when one looks at the way that we come to decisions about the ethics of animal research, one finds that a variety of ethical approaches are used. For example, we place a high value on virtue in that we try to identify virtuous people who have high standards of ethical behavior to sit on our animal care and use committees. We also try to identify the values that should guide our decision-making and usually incorporate some mix of the following:

(a) reduce animal suffering as much as possible,
(b) reduce the number of animals required as far as possible,
(c) ensure that the science is properly planned and likely to achieve its goals, and
(d) ensure that those conducting the research are adequately trained so that they will be able to minimize animal suffering.

Finally, we have also established some rules of behavior that should guide our decision-making. Thus, conducting multiple surgeries on a single animal is not permitted unless it is part of the same protocol.

In other words, our every-day approach to moral conduct incorporates such supposedly disparate traditions in ethics as virtue, value, and deontological rules. Whatever the approach used, it is striking to note that nearly every philosopher who has addressed the question of the moral status of animals in the past 20 years has come to the conclusion that not only are the questions difficult but that society should also seriously consider upgrading the moral status of animals. Only a few have taken a contrary view. Fox produced a book justifying the use of animals in research[14] but then recanted his position shortly after the book was published and now argues that animals have rights that prohibit their use as research tools.[15] Cohen argues that not only can animal research be justified but that it is morally mandated.[1] He is one of the few professional philosophers who have come out in unquestioning support of the traditional position.

In conclusion, the issue of the appropriate moral status of animals is neither an easy nor a trivial question. It involves developing theories for the moral weight to be accorded to such qualities as life, sentience and suffering, self-awareness, and the like. It then requires a more sophisticated understanding of the concepts of sentience so that we can identify which animals might satisfy the requirements. In justifying biomedical research, one is faced with difficult questions about the value of basic knowledge and likely therapeutic benefit. Most of the public and many scientists consider the testing of cosmetics and toiletries on animals as an unjustifiable activity. However, people have been severely injured by unsafe personal care products in the past, so what should we do now about testing?

If we agree that animal use in research involves moral costs that need to be taken seriously (a widespread view despite recent tendencies by defenders of science to avoid 'apologizing' for animal use in the media), then how much attention must be paid to the three 'R's of Russell (replacement, reduction, and refinement) and Burch and the idea of alternatives? In toxicology, a broad public consensus on this issue is developing but there is still much suspicion of the concept of alternatives in the halls of the National Institutes of Health, neuroscience, and physiology. Nonetheless, much progress in attending to the moral issues related to animal research and testing is evident although there is still a great deal left to do. We will need wisdom, humor, and a good sense of proportion in the decades to come if we are to continue to make progress on these issues.

NOTES

1. Cohen, C. (1986) The case for the use of animals in biomedical research. N. Engl. J. Med. 315, 865–870.

2. Tannenbaum, J. and Rowan, A.N. (1985) Rethinking the morality of animal research. Hastings Center Rep. 15(5), 32–43.

3. White, R.J. (1990) Animal ethics? Hastings Center Rep. 20(6), 43.

4. Felthouse, A.R. and Kellert, S.R. (1987) Childhood cruelty to animals and later aggression against people: A review. Am J. Psychiatry 144, 710–717.

5. Bentham, J. (1962) The Works of Jeremy Bentham, J. Bowring (Ed.), Vol. 1, Russell and Russell, New York, pp. 142–143.

6. Singer, P. (1975) Animal Liberation. New York Review of Books/Random House, New York.

7. Smith, J.A. and Boyd, K.M. (1992) Lives in the Balance: The Ethics of Using Animals in Biomedical Research. Oxford University Press, Oxford.

8. Schweitzer, A. (1929) Civilization and Ethics, trans. C. Campion, Macmillan, New York, pp. 246–247.

9. Schweitzer, A. (1950) The Philosophy of Civilization, trans. C. Champion. Macmillan, New York, p. 318.

10. Salt, H.S. (1892) Animals' Rights. London. New edition issued by International Society for Animal Rights, Clarks Summit, PA, 1980.

11. Parents Magazine. (1989). Parents Poll on Animal Rights, Attractiveness, Television and Abortion. Kane and Parsons Associates, New York, Sept.–Oct., 1989.

12. Regan, T. (1983) The case for animal rights. University of California Press, Berkeley, CA.

13. Nozick, R. (1983) About mammals and people. New York Times Book Review, November 27, p. 11.

14. Fox, M.A. (1986) The Case for Animal Experimentation: An Evolutionary and Ethical Perspective. University of California Press, Berkeley, CA.

15. Fox, M.A. (1987) Animal experimentation; a philosopher's changing views. Between the Species 3(2), 55–60, 75, 80, 82.

SUGGESTED READINGS

CODES AND GUIDELINES

Bankowski, Z. and Levine, R. J., eds. *Ethics and Research on Human Subjects: International Guidelines.* Geneva: Council for International Organizations of Medical Sciences, 1993.

Brody, Baruch A. *The Ethics of Biomedical Research: An International Perspective.* New York: Oxford University Press, 1998.

Canadian Council on Animal Care. *Guide to the Care and Use of Experimental Animals.* 2d ed. Ottawa: The Council, 1993. Excerpts reprinted in: Brody, Baruch A. *The Ethics of Biomedical Research: An International Perspective.* New York: Oxford University Press, 1998, 338–41.

Council for International Organizations of Medical Sciences. "International Ethical Guidelines for Biomedical Research Involving Human Subjects." In A. Bankowski and R. J. Levin, eds. *Ethics and Research on Human Subjects: International Guidelines.* Geneva: CIOMS, 1993, 231 ff. (1–46). [Excerpts reprinted in this chapter.]

———. *International Guidelines for Ethical Review of Epidemiological Studies.* Geneva: CIOMS, 1991.

———. *International Guiding Principles for Research Involving Animals.* Geneva: CIOMS, 1985. [Excerpts reprinted in this chapter.]

Flanagin, Annette. "Who Wrote the Declaration of Helsinki?" *Journal of the American Medical Association* 277 (1997), 926.

Grodin, Michael A. "Historical Origins of the Nuremberg Code." In George J. Annas, and Michael A. Grodin, eds. *The Nazi Doctors and the Nuremberg Code: Human Rights in Human Experimentation.* New York: Oxford University Press, 1992, 121–144.

ICH [International Conference on Harmonisation] Guidelines for Good Clinical Practice. Media, PA: Barnett International/Parexel Clinical Training Group, 1996. Reprinted in: Brody, Baruch A. *The Ethics of Biomedical Research: An International Perspective.* New York: Oxford University Press, 1998, 219–24.

Institute of Laboratory Animal Resources (U.S.). *Guide for the Care of and Use of Laboratory Animals.* 7th ed. Washington, DC: National Academy Press, 1996.

Katz, Jay. "The Nuremberg Code and the Nuremberg Trial: A Reappraisal." *Journal of the American Medical Association* 276 (1996), 1662–66.

Levine, Robert J. "International Codes and Guidelines for Research Ethics: A Critical Appraisal." In Harold Y. Vanderpool, ed. *The Ethics of Research Involving Human Subjects: Facing the 21st Century.* Frederick, MD: University Publishing Group, 1996, 235–59.

Medical Research Council of Canada; Natural Sciences and Engineering Research Council of Canada; and Social Sciences and Humanities Research Council of Canada. *Tri-Council Policy Statement: Ethical Conduct for Research Involving Human Subjects.* Ottawa: The Three Councils, August 1998.

Moreno, Jonathan D. "'The Only Feasible Means': The Pentagon's Ambivalent Relationship with the Nuremberg Code." *Hastings Center Report* 26 (September–October 1996), 11–19.

———. "Reassessing the Influence of the Nuremberg Code on American Medical Ethics." *Journal of Contemporary Health Law and Policy* 13 (1997), 347–60.

Shevell, Michael I. "Neurology's Witness to History: Part II—Leo Alexander's Contributions to the Nuremberg Code (1946–1947)." *Neurology* 50 (1998), 274–78.

Shuster, Evelyne, "Fifty Years Later: The Significance of the Nuremberg Code." *New England Journal of Medicine* 337 (1997), 1436–40.

Spicer, Carol Mason, ed. "Appendix: IV. Ethical Directives for Human Research." In Warren Thomas Reich, ed. *Encyclopedia of Bioethics*. Revised ed. New York: Simon and Schuster Macmillan, 1995, 2761–2800.

———. "Appendix: V. Ethical Directives Pertaining to the Welfare and Use of Animals." In Warren Thomas Reich, ed. *Encyclopedia of Bioethics*. Revised ed. New York: Simon and Schuster Macmillan, 1995, 2801–17.

United States, National Commission for the Protection of Research Subjects. *The Belmont Report: Ethical Principles and Guidelines for the Protection of Human Subjects of Research and Appendix*. 3 vols. Washington, DC: U.S. Government Printing Office, 1978. [Excerpts published in *Federal Register* 44 (1979), 23192–23197.]

United States, Office of Science and Technology Policy. "Federal Policy for the Protection of Human Subjects: Final Rule." *Federal Register* 56 (1991), 28003–23.

ETHICAL ISSUES IN HUMAN RESEARCH

Annas, George J., *et al., Informed Consent to Human Experimentation: The Subject's Dilemma*. Cambridge, MA: Ballinger, 1977.

Barber, Bernard. *Informed Consent in Medical Therapy and Research*. New Brunswick, NJ: Transaction Books, 1978.

Beauchamp, Tom L., *et al.*, eds. *Ethical Issues in Social Science Research*. Baltimore, MD: Johns Hopkins University Press, 1982.

Beecher, Henry K. *Research and the Individual: Human Studies*. Boston: Little, Brown, 1970.

Brieger, Gert H. "Human Experimentation: History." In Warren T. Reich, ed. *Encyclopedia of Bioethics*. New York: Free Press, 1978, 684–92.

Capron, Alexander M. "Human Experimentation." In Robert M. Veatch, ed. *Medical Ethics*. 2d ed. Sudbury, MA: Jones and Bartlett, 1997, 135–84.

Childress, James F. "Compensating Injured Research Subjects: The Moral Argument." *Hastings Center Report* 6 (December 1976), 21–27.

Coughlan, Steven S., and Beauchamp, Tom L. *Ethics and Epidemiology*. New York: Oxford University Press, 1996.

De Deyn, Peter P., ed. *The Ethics of Animal and Human Experimentation*. London: John Libbey, 1994.

Dickens, Bernard M. "Human Research and the Medical Model: Legal and Ethical Issues." *Medicine and Law* 16 (1997), 687–703.

Freedman, Benjamin; Weijer, Charles; and Glass, Kathleen Cranley. "Placebo Orthodoxy in Clinical Research I: Empirical and Methodological Myths." *Journal of Law, Medicine and Ethics* 24 (1996), 243–51.

———. "Placebo Orthodoxy in Clinical Research II: Ethical, Legal, and Regulatory Myths." *Journal of Law, Medicine and Ethics* 24 (1996), 252–59.

Freund, Paul, ed. *Experimentation with Human Subjects*. New York: George Braziller, 1970.

Fried, Charles. *Medical Experimentation: Personal Integrity and Social Policy*. New York: American Elsevier, 1974.

Gorman, Holly M., and Dane, Francis C. "Balancing Methodological Rigour and Ethical Treatment: The Necessity of Voluntary, Informed Consent." In Peter P. De Deyn, ed. *The Ethics of Animal and Human Experimentation*. London: John Libbey, 1994, 35–41.

Gray, Bradford H. *Human Subjects in Medical Experimentation*. New York: Wiley, 1975.

———, *et al.* "Research Involving Human Subjects," *Science* 201 (September 22, 1978), 1094–1101.

Grodin, Michael A., and Annas, George J. "Legacies of Nuremberg: Medical Ethics and Human Rights." *Journal of the American Medical Association* 276 (1996), 1682–83.

Grodin, Michael A., and Glantz, Leonard H., eds. *Children as Research Subjects: Science, Ethics, and Law*. New York: Oxford University Press, 1994.

Jonas, Hans. "Philosophical Reflections on Experimenting with Human Subjects." *Daedalus* 98 (1969), 219–47.

Karlawish, Jason H. T., and Lantos, John. "Community Equipoise and the Architecture of Clinical Research." *Cambridge Quarterly of Healthcare Ethics* 6 (1997), 385–96.

Kass, Nancy E., and Sugarman, Jeremy. "Are Human Subjects Adequately Protected? A Review and Discussion of Studies Conducted by the Advisory Committee on Human Radiation Experiments." *Kennedy Institute of Ethics Journal* 6 (1996), 271–82.

Katz, Jay. "Human Experimentation and Human Rights." *Saint Louis University Law Journal* 38 (1993), 7–54.

Levine, Robert J. *Ethics and Regulation of Human Research*. 2d ed. Baltimore, MD: Urban & Schwarzenberg, 1986.

Mastroianni, Anna C.; Faden, Ruth; and Federman, Daniel, eds. *Women and Health Research: Ethical and Legal Issues of Including Women in Clinical Studies*. 2 vols. Washington, DC: National Academy Press, 1994.

Marwick, Charles. "Improved Protection for Human Research Subjects." *Journal of the American Medical Association* 279 (1998), 344–45.

Robertson, John A. "Compensating Injured Research Subjects: The Law," *Hastings Center Report* 6 (December 1976), 29–31.

Rothman, David J. "Research, Human: Historical Aspects." In Warren Thomas Reich, ed. *Encyclopedia of Bioethics*. Revised ed. New York: Simon and Schuster Macmillan, 1995, 2248–58.

Schafer, Arthur. "The Ethics of the Randomized Clinical Trial." *New England Journal of Medicine* 307 (1982), 719–24.

Shamoo, Adil E., ed. *Ethics in Neurobiological Research with Human Subjects: The Baltimore Conference on Ethics*. Amsterdam: Gordon and Breach, 1997.

Sidel, Victor W. "The Social Responsibilities of Health Professionals." *Journal of the American Medical Association* 276 (1996), 1679–81.

Sonis, Jeffrey, *et al.* "Teaching of Human Rights in US Medical Schools" *Journal of the American Medical Association* 276 (1996), 1676–78.

United States, Department of Health and Human Services, Office of Inspector General, Office of Evaluation and Inspections, *Institutional Review Boards: A Time for Reform*. Washington, DC: DHHS, June 1998. URL: http://www.dhhs.gov/progorg.oei.

United States, National Commission for the Protection of Research Subjects. *Institutional Review Boards: Report and Recommendations and Appendix.* 2 vols. Washington, DC: U.S. Government Printing Office, 1978.

United States, National Institutes of Health, Office of Extramural Research, *Evaluation of NIH Implementation of Section 491 of the Public Health Service Act, Mandating a Program of Protection for Research Subjects.* Bethesda, MD: NIH, June 15, 1998. URL: http://www.nih.gov/grants/oprr/hsp_rpt/hsp_final_rpt.pdf.

Vanderpool, Harold Y., ed. *The Ethics of Research Involving Human Subjects: Facing the 21st Century.* Frederick, MD: University Publishing Group, 1996.

Veatch, Robert M. *Case Studies in Medical Ethics.* Cambridge, MA: Harvard University Press, 1977. Chapter 11.

———. "Three Theories of Informed Consent." In U.S. National Commission for the Protection of Human Subjects. *The Belmont Report: Appendix:* Vol. II. Washington, DC: U.S. Government Printing Office, 1978, 26-1–26-66.

———. *The Patient as Partner: A Theory of Human Experimentation Ethics.* Bloomington, IN: Indiana University Press, 1987.

Weir, Robert F., and Horton, Jay R. "Genetic Research, Adolescents, and Informed Consent." *Theoretical Medicine* 16 (1995), 347–73.

PAST ABUSES OF HUMAN RESEARCH SUBJECTS

Advisory Committee on Human Radiation Experiments. *Final Report.* Washington, DC: U.S. Government Printing Office, October 1995.

Annas, George J., and Grodin, Michael A., eds. *The Nazi Doctors and the Nuremberg Code: Human Rights in Human Experiments.* New York: Oxford University Press, 1992.

Buchanan, Allen. "Judging the Past: The Case of the Human Radiation Experiments." *Hastings Center Report* 26 (May–June 1996), 25–30.

Faden, Ruth. "The Advisory Committee on Human Radiation Experiments: Reflections on a Presidential Commission." *Hastings Center Report* 26 (September–October 1996), 5–10.

Faden, Ruth R.; Lederer, Susan E.; and Moreno, Jonathan D. "US Medical Researchers, the Nuremberg Doctors Trial, and the Nuremberg Code." *Journal of the American Medical Association* 276 (1996), 1667–71.

Freedman, Benjamin. "Research, Unethical." In Warren Thomas Reich, ed. *Encyclopedia of Bioethics.* Revised ed. New York: Simon and Schuster Macmillan, 1995, 2258–61.

Gillmore, Don. *I Swear by Apollo: Dr. Ewen Cameron and CIA Brainwashing Experiments.* Montreal: Eden Press, 1987.

Grodin, Michael A. "The Japanese Analogue." *Hastings Center Report* 26 (September–October 1996), 37–38.

Hanauske-Abel, Hartmut M. "Not a Slippery Slope or Sudden Subversion: German Medicine and National Socialism in 1933." *British Medical Journal* 313 (1996), 1453–63.

Harkness, Jon M. "Nuremberg and the Issue of Wartime Experiments on US Prisoners: The Green Committee." *Journal of the American Medical Association* 276 (1996), 1672–75.

Harris, Sheldon H. *Factories of Death: Japanese Biological Warfare 1932–45 and the American Cover Up.* New York and London: Routledge, 1994.

Hornblum, Allen M. *Acres of Skin: Human Experiments at Holmesburg Prison: A True Story of Abuse and Exploitation in the Name of Medical Science.* Baltimore: Johns Hopkins University Press, 1998.

———. "They Were Cheap and Available: Prisoners as Research Subjects in Twentieth Century America." *British Medical Journal* 315 (1997), 1437–41.

The Human Radiation Experiments: Final Report of the Advisory Committee. New York: Oxford University Press, 1996.

Jones, James H. *Bad Blood: The Tuskegee Syphilis Experiment.* New and expanded ed. New York: Free Press, 1993.

Katz, Jay, with the assistance of Alexander Morgan Capron and Eleanor Swift Glass. *Experimentation with Human Beings.* New York: Russell Sage Foundation, 1972.

Lederer, Susan E. *Subjected to Science: Human Experimentation in America before the Second World War.* Baltimore: Johns Hopkins University Press, 1995.

Reverby, Susan M. "Everyday Evil." *Hastings Center Report* 26 (September–October 1996), 38–39.

Seidelman, William E. "Nuremberg Lamentation: For the Forgotten Victims of Medical Science." *British Medical Journal* 313 (1996), 1463–67.

Shevell, Michael I. "Neurology's Witness to History: The Combined Intelligence Operative Sub-Committee Reports of Leo Alexander." *Neurology* 47 (1996), 1096–1103.

Thomas, Stephen B., and Quinn, Sandra Crouse. "The Tuskegee Syphilis Study, 1932 to 1972: Implications for HIV Education and AIDS Risk Education Programs in the Black Community." *American Journal of Public Health* 81 (1991). 1498–1505.

United States, Public Health Service. *Final Report of the Tuskegee Syphilis Study Ad Hoc Advisory Panel.* Washington, DC: U.S. Government Printing Office, 1973. Reprinted in part in: Jonsen, Albert R.; Veatch, Robert M.; and Walters, LeRoy, eds. *Source Book in Bioethics: A Documentary History.* Washington, DC: Georgetown University Press, 1998, 76–87.

Weindling, Paul. "Human Guinea Pigs and the Ethics of Experimentation: The *BMJ*'s Correspondent at the Nuremberg Medical Trial." *British Medical Journal* 313 (1996), 1467–70.

ETHICAL ISSUES IN ANIMAL RESEARCH

Barnard, Neal D., Kaufman, Stephen R. "Animal Research Is Wasteful and Misleading." *Scientific American* 276 (February 1997), 80–82.

Bateson, Patrick. "When to Experiment on Animals." *New Scientist* 109 (February 20, 1986), 30–32.

Beauchamp, Tom L. "The Moral Standing of Animals in Medical Research." *Law, Medicine and Health Care* 20 (1992), 7–16.

———. "Opposing Views on Animal Experimentation: Do Animals Have Rights?" *Ethics and Behavior* 7 (1997), 113–21.

———. "Problems in Justifying Research on Animals." In National Institutes of Health, *National Symposium on Imperatives in Research Use: Scientific Needs and Animal Welfare.* Bethesda, MD: NIH, 1985, 79–87.

Botting, Jack H., and Morrison, Adrian R. "Animal Research Is Vital to Medicine." *Scientific American* 276 (February 1997), 83–85.

Brody, Baruch A. *The Ethics of Biomedical Research: An International Perspective.* New York: Oxford University Press, 1998, Chapter 1.

Cavalieri, Paula, and Singer, Peter, eds. *The Great Ape Project: Equality beyond Humanity.* New York: St. Martin's Press, 1994.

Cohen, Carl. "The Case for the Use of Animals in Research." *New England Journal of Medicine* 315 (1986), 865–70.

De Deyn, Peter P., ed. *The Ethics of Animal and Human Experimentation.* London: John Libbey, 1994.

DeGrazia, David, *Taking Animal Seriously: Mental Life and Moral Status.* New York: Cambridge University Press, 1996.

Fox, Michael Allen. *The Case for Animal Experimentation: An Evolutionary and Ethical Perspective.* Berkeley, CA: University of California Press, 1986.

Jamieson, Dale, and Regan, Tom. "On the Ethics of the Use of Animals in Science." In Tom Regan and Donald VanDeVeer, eds. *And Justice for All.* Totowa, NJ: Rowman and Littlefield, 1982, 169–96.

Kahn, Jeffrey, and Dell, Ralph. "Animal Research: III. Law and Policy." In Warren Thomas Reich, ed. *Encyclopedia of Bioethics.* Revised ed. New York: Simon and Schuster Macmillan, 1995, 153–58.

Kuhse, Helga. "Interests." *Journal of Medical Ethics* 11 (1985), 146–49.

Leader, Robert W., and Stark, Dennis. "The Importance of Animals in Biomedical Research." *Perspectives in Biology and Medicine* 30 (1987), 470–85.

McCloskey, H. J. "The Moral Case for Experimentation on Animals." *Monist* 70 (1987), 64–82.

Mukerjee, Madhusree. "Trends in Animal Research." *Scientific American* 276 (February 1997), 86–93.

Orlans, F. Barbara. *In the Name of Science: Issues in Responsible Animal Experimentation.* New York: Oxford University Press, 1993.

————. *et al. The Human Use of Animals: Case Studies in Ethical Choice.* New York: Oxford University Press, 1998.

Parascandola, Mark. "Animal Research." In Ruth Chadwick, ed. *Encyclopedia of Applied Ethics.* San Diego, CA: Academic Press, 1998, 151–60.

Rowan, Andrew N. "The Benefits and Ethics of Animal Research." *Scientific American* 276 (February 1997), 79.

————. *Of Mice, Models, and Men: A Critical Evaluation of Animal Research.* Albany, NY: State University of New York Press, 1984.

Singer, Peter. "Animal Research: II. Philosophical Issues." In Warren Thomas Reich, ed. *Encyclopedia of Bioethics.* Revised ed. New York: Simon and Schuster Macmillan, 1995, 147–53.

Tannenbaum, Jerry and Rowan, Andrew M. "Rethinking the Morality of Animal Research." *Hastings Center Report* 15 (October 1985), 32–43.

United States Congress, Office of Technology Assessment. *Alternatives to the Use of Animals in Research, Education, and Testing.* Washington, DC: OTA, 1984.

United States National Institutes of Health, *National Symposium on Imperatives in Research Animal Use: Scientific Needs and Animal Welfare.* Washington, DC: U.S. Government Printing Office, 1985.

United States National Institutes of Health, Office for Protection from Research Risks. *Public Health Service Policy on Humane Care and Use of Laboratory Animals* Bethesda, MD: Office for Protection from Research Risks, National Institutes of Health, 1986.

Whorton, James C. "Animal Experimentation: I. Historical Aspects." In Warren Thomas Reich, ed. *Encyclopedia of Bioethics.* Revised ed. New York: Simon and Schuster Macmillan, 1995, 143–47.

BIBLIOGRAPHIES

Goldstein, Doris Mueller. *Bioethics: A Guide to Information Sources.* Detroit: Gale Research Company, 1982. See under "Research Involving Human Subjects."

Lineback, Richard H., ed. *Philosopher's Index.* Vols. 1– . Bowling Green OH: Philosophy Documentation Center, Bowling Green State University. Issued quarterly. See under "Animal Experimentation," "Experimentation," and "Research."

Walters, LeRoy, and Kahn, Tamar Joy, eds. *Bibliography of Bioethics.* Vols. 1– . Washington, DC: Kennedy Institute of Ethics, Georgetown University. Issued annually. See under "Animal Experimentation," and "Human Experimentation." (The information contained in the annual *Bibliography* can also be retrieved from BIOETHICSLINE, an online database of the National Library of Medicine.)

WORLD WIDE WEB RESOURCES

National Library of Medicine: PubMed
(http://www.ncbi.nlm.nih.gov/PubMed/)

National Library of Medicine: BIOETHICSLINE
(http://igm.nlm.nih.gov)

University Microfilms: Periodical Abstracts
(http://www.umi.com/proquest)

8.
Eugenics and Human Genetics

INTRODUCTION

This chapter discusses both historical and current issues in human heredity. In the first part of the chapter we examine three attempts to improve society by intervening in the reproductive decisions, or modifying the reproductive capacities, of human beings. The first of these eugenics programs emerged in the United Sates during the first half of the twentieth century; the second was enacted in Germany when that country was governed by Adolf Hitler and the National Socialists. A third program is currently being conducted by the People's Republic of China. The remaining two parts of the chapter explore ethical questions raised by human genetics, a field of science and medicine that began to emerge as a discrete discipline in the late 1940s and early 1950s. Four topics are considered: the human genome project, genetic testing, human gene therapy, and genetic enhancement.

EUGENICS PROGRAMS IN THE TWENTIETH CENTURY

The definition of eugenics is frequently controversial. One simple definition is that eugenics means "the study of human improvement by genetic means."[1] If this definition is accepted, one can discover eugenic proposals in writings as old as Plato's *Republic,* where selective breeding was proposed as a means of improving society.[2] The actual word "eugenics" was coined in 1883 by an English scientist, Francis Galton, who was a cousin of Charles Darwin. In his first major book, *Hereditary Genius,* published in 1869, and in later works, Galton advocated a system of arranged marriages between men and women of distinction, with the aim of producing a group of gifted children and ultimately an improved British population.

In the eugenics programs of the twentieth century, the element of coercion by the state was added to the notion of eugenics as a social goal. The first systematic attempts to develop mandatory eugenics programs occurred in several states of the United States. The central aim of these programs was to prevent reproduction by people who were judged to be feeble-minded. The method by which this aim was to be achieved was involuntary sterilization. Philip Reilly's essay chronicles the history of eugenic sterilization in the United States.

While several state courts struck down mandatory sterilization statutes as unconstitutional, the United States Supreme Court found Virginia's involuntary sterilization law to be compatible with the guarantees of the U.S. Constitution. Oliver Wendell Holmes wrote for the Supreme Court's majority and argued that if Carrie Buck's mother, Carrie herself, and Carrie's daughter were all feeble-minded, the state of Virginia was justified in attempting to prevent any further reproduction by Carrie Buck through involuntary sterilization. In Holmes's chilling words, "Three generations of imbeciles are enough." The full text of the court's 1927 *Buck v. Bell* decision is reprinted in this chapter. In his essay "Carrie Buck's Daughter," paleontologist Stephen Jay Gould critically examines the factual premises on which the Supreme Court based its decision.

The eugenics programs undertaken in several states of the United States were closely monitored by academics and policymakers in other parts of the world, and especially in

Germany. There the method of mandatory sterilization was found to be compatible both with the academic field called racial hygiene and with the political agenda of the National Socialists. Robert Jay Lifton traces the theory and practice of the Nazi sterilization program during the 1930s, when approximately 350,000 persons deemed unfit to reproduce were sterilized. As is well known, this sterilization effort was but an initial step on the road that led eventually to the extermination of "unworthy" individuals and groups in Nazi killing centers and concentration camps.[3]

Veronica Pearson's essay at the conclusion of this part discusses the Maternal and Infant Health Care Law that went into effect in the People's Republic of China in June 1995. The aim of this law is to "prevent new births of inferior quality." It requires physicians to advise a couple to terminate a pregnancy if a hereditary disease makes it likely that their child will be born seriously ill or disabled. According to Pearson, Chinese authorities are particularly concerned about the relatively large numbers of intellectually disabled and mentally ill people within their population. The Chinese eugenics law has been the subject of vigorous debate by psychiatrists and human geneticists in many countries.[4] Pearson suggests that criticizing the statute as unscientific may be a more effective approach to Chinese physicians and policymakers than condemning it on ethical grounds.

THE HUMAN GENOME PROJECT AND GENETIC TESTING

There can be no doubt that we live in the golden age of genetics, especially human genetics. Even before the 1950s, Gregor Mendel's classic work on various modes of inheritance was available as a framework for understanding how specific traits are transmitted from one generation to the next. However, Watson and Crick's discovery of the molecular structure of DNA in 1953 and the rapid advances made feasible by recombinant DNA techniques from the 1970s to the present have opened up entirely new possibilities for genetic diagnosis and therapy.

The genetic structure of human cells is incredibly intricate and complex. Within the nuclei of each human cell there are 46 chromosomes. These chromosomes, in turn, are comprised of 70,000–100,000 genes plus intervening sequences; the function of the intervening sequences is not yet well understood. The simplest units into which the genes and intervening sequences can be analyzed are individual nucleotides or bases, designated by the familiar letters A, C, G, and T; two corresponding nucleotides form a base pair. It is estimated that each human cell contains approximately 3 billion base pairs.

Through the remainder of the twentieth century and into the early years of the twenty-first, we will witness an intensive international effort to map and sequence the human genome. The initial fruits of this labor will undoubtedly be diagnostic: Researchers will be able to locate and analyze the "errors" in genetic sequences that are associated with specific genetic diseases, or even susceptibilities to specific diseases. When tests are developed to identify these errors, new possibilities for prenatal or preimplantation diagnosis, newborn screening, and the counseling of couples considering reproduction will be at hand. Of course, the same tests will also be available for use by insurance companies, employers, or governments seeking to identify individuals who are, or will later be, afflicted with a particular genetic disease or who carry identifiable deleterious genes or combinations of genes.

The first four essays in this part discuss the science and ethics of the human genome project. The Biological Sciences Curriculum Study (BSCS) authors and Lee Rowan *et al.* provide a state-of-the-art review of the international human genome project, as it nears the end of its first decade. The BSCS authors indicate how genetic maps will be followed, in turn, by a physical map of the human genome and finally by a complete sequence of all 3 billion bases in the human genome. The latter project was originally scheduled to be concluded by the year 2005; however, with the aid of new sequencing technologies, the full human sequence may be completed by the end of 2003.[5] Rowan *et al.* note with satisfaction the accelerating pace at which new knowledge about human genes and the location of those genes on particular chromosomes is being accumulated.

In an essay that combines history with ethical and political analysis, James Watson describes the sequence of events that led a reluctant community of U.S. biomedical scientists to accept the importance of mapping and sequencing the human genome. As Watson notes with satisfaction, he insisted that a fixed percentage of the human genome project budget — initially 3 percent, later 5 percent — be set aside to study the ethical, legal, and social implications of the project. The ELSI program, as it came to be known, has allowed philosophers, theologians, lawyers, social scientists, and clinicians to perform normative research on issues like those discussed in the current chapter. At the conclusion of his essay Watson predicts that behavioral genetics and genetic enhancement will become important topics as genetic knowledge continues to accrue. He argues that the main lesson to be drawn from the eugenic excesses of past and present is that governments must be prevented from telling citizens what to do, and what not to do, in the genetic sphere.

That the issues considered by ELSI researchers are not merely speculative becomes clear in the essay by Virginia Lapham *et al.,* "Genetic Discrimination: Perspectives of Consumers." In their survey of families in which one or more members are afflicted with a genetic disorder, Lapham and her colleagues discovered that 40 percent had been asked "questions about genetic diseases of disabilities" on applications for health insurance. Twenty-two percent of respondents were denied health insurance, while 31 percent were denied insurance for a particular service or treatment. Questions about genetic diseases or disabilities were raised less frequently in employment settings; however, 15 percent of respondents said that questions about genetic matters had been raised on job applications filled out by family members, and 13 percent reported that they had been either denied a position or let go by an employer for these health-related reasons.

In anticipation of potential problems like those reported by Lapham *et al.,* an interdisciplinary committee of the Institute of Medicine (IOM) devoted multiple years to studying ethical and legal issues in genetic testing and screening. The fruit of the committee's labor was a 1994 report entitled *Assessing Genetic Risks: Implications for Health and Social Policy.* Substantial excerpts from the executive summary of this report are reprinted in this chapter. In general, the committee advocates that genetic tests be voluntary rather than mandated by government. On the other hand, the committee recommends vigorous government action to prevent discrimination on genetic grounds by employers and health insurance companies. The four ethical principles that underlie the committee's specific recommendations are voluntariness, autonomy, privacy, and confidentiality.

Late in 1997 the United Nations Educational, Scientific and Cultural Organization (UNESCO) issued its "Universal Declaration on the Human Genome and Human Rights." The UNESCO declaration, issued 49 years after the original United Nations Declaration of Human Rights, restates several themes of the human rights tradition and attempts to show their relevance to the global human genome project. The declaration asserts that the human genome underlies the "fundamental unity of all members of the human family." The genome also fosters the recognition of humanity's "inherent dignity and diversity." According to the declaration, the human genome is "the heritage of humanity," at least symbolically.

While the authors of the UNESCO declaration agree with the IOM committee's emphasis on free and informed consent and with its rejection of discrimination on genetic grounds, they also accent themes that are absent from the IOM document. For example, the UNESCO document cautions against reducing human beings to their genetic characteristics, that is, against regarding an individual's genome as his or her "real" identity. The declaration also argues against the reproductive cloning of human beings as an affront to human dignity and urges that the "human genome in its natural state" should not "give rise to financial gain." The latter exhortation and the document's emphasis on the sharing of research information derived from the genome project are at least implicit critiques of attempts to patent human genes and to withhold data from the scientific community for commercial reasons. A final distinctive emphasis of the UNESCO document is its affirmation of "solidarity" toward "individuals, families and population groups who are particularly vulnerable to or affected by disease or disability of a genetic character." Solidarity would seem to be the polar opposite of stereotyping individuals or groups on the basis of their genetic characteristics.

HUMAN GENE THERAPY AND GENETIC ENHANCEMENT

In the history of medicine, diagnosis is often the necessary prelude to a cure. It thus seems likely that the capacity to identify genetic diseases and susceptibilities will provide new impetus for already existing efforts to develop ways to correct, or at least to compensate for, genetic defects. The general name usually given to these therapeutic initiatives is gene therapy, or, more broadly, genetic intervention.

A central distinction in any discussion of genetic intervention is the distinction between reproductive and nonproductive cells, which are often called germ-line and somatic cells, respectively. Somatic cells, like skin or muscle cells, contain the full complement of 46 chromosomes and cannot transmit genetic information to succeeding generations. In other words, the genetic information contained in somatic cells stops with us and is not passed on to our descendants. In contrast, germ-line cells, the egg and sperm cells, contain only 23 chromosomes and are capable of transmitting genetic information to our progeny in the next generation, as well as to their children and grandchildren.

A second important distinction in discussions of human genetic intervention is that between the cure or prevention of disease, on the one hand, and the enhancement of human capabilities, on the other. A genetic approach to the treatment of cystic fibrosis clearly would be regarded as gene therapy. The attempt to increase stature or to improve the efficiency of long-term memory — in a child whose height or memory fall within the normal range — would probably be regarded by most observers as an effort to enhance capabilities rather than to cure disease. Thus, we have four possible categories of genetic intervention, which can be arrayed in the following two-by-two matrix:

	Somatic	Germ-Line
Cure or prevention of disease	1	2
Enhancement of capabilities	3	4

LeRoy Walters and Julie Gage Palmer describe the first approved gene therapy study in the United States. This research is a clear example of a Type-1 genetic intervention. The authors also review the variety of diseases against which the first one hundred U.S. gene therapy studies have been directed. As would be expected, genetic diseases have been among the targets selected by researchers; however, various kinds of cancers have been the principal focus of gene therapists in the early years. One infectious disease, AIDS, has also been approached through this experimental technique. Walters and Gage Palmer then summarize the seven central ethical questions that are asked by the public advisory committee that has reviewed gene therapy proposals for the National Institutes of Health in the 1990s. These specific questions can easily be related to more general ethical principles such as those discussed in the first chapter of this book, including beneficence, justice, and respect for the autonomy of persons.

In the next essay, W. French Anderson, one of the pioneers in developing gene therapy as a treatment for human disease, discusses all four types of genetic intervention. First he reviews the worldwide experience with somatic-cell (Type 1) gene therapy as of early 1998. Anderson notes that in the first seven and one-half years of gene therapy, more than 300 clinical protocols have been reviewed worldwide, and more than 3,000 patients have received gene therapy. Definitive evidence of clinical benefit remains elusive, although the excellent health of two young women who have received both gene therapy and a synthetic enzyme for their severe combined immune deficiency provides a basis for cautious optimism. In the concluding section of his essay, Anderson indicates why he opposes germ-line genetic intervention (Type 2) at present; he also expresses fundamental reservations about the use of genetic means to enhance human functioning (Types 3 and 4).

The last two selections in this chapter consider the more speculative possibility that in the future genetic technology will be employed to enhance human capabilities. In an adventuresome essay Jonathan Glover expresses dissatisfaction with at least some aspects of human nature as we know it. He also attempts to demolish several of the standard ethical objections to genetic enhancement. In the end Glover adopts a "principle of caution" and advocates a mixed system of public oversight for genetic enhancement—one that allows substantial leeway to parents in making decisions about the characteristics of their children while at the same time providing for a social check on possible parental excesses.

Without unconditionally rejecting genetic enhancement, Erik Parens questions whether the goals that proponents of enhancement seek to achieve are, on balance, worthwhile. Parens argues that enhancement seeks to replace change with stability and to substitute control or predictability for chance. In addition, he suggests that proposals for genetic enhancement tend toward utopianism. For Parens change, chance, and struggle are important—perhaps even essential—elements of the good life.

L. W.

NOTES

1. *Encyclopedia Britannica,* Micropaedia, "Eugenics," 1989, p. 593.

2. Plato, *Republic,* III (410), IV (456–61).

3. For the history of Nazi policies on the "unfit" and the "unworthy," see the following works: Lifton's entire book, *The Nazi Doctors* (New York: Basic Books, 1986); Robert N. Proctor, *Racial Hygiene: Medicine under the Nazis* (Cambridge, MA: Harvard University Press, 1988); Michael Burleigh and Wolfgang Wipperman, *The Racial State: Germany 1933–1945* (Cambridge: Cambridge University Press, 1991); and Michael Burleigh, *Death and Deliverance: 'Euthanasia' in Germany 1900–1945* (Cambridge: Cambridge University Press, 1994).

4. See Dennis Normile, "Geneticists Debate Eugenics and China's Infant Health Law," *Science* 281 (August 21, 1998), 1118–19.

5. Francis S. Collins *et al.,* "New Goals for the U.S. Human Genome Project: 1998–2003," *Science* 282 (October 23, 1998), 682–89.

Eugenics Programs in the Twentieth Century

PHILIP R. REILLY

Eugenic Sterilization in the United States

The most important event in the rise of state-supported programs to sterilize the feeble-minded, the insane, and criminals was the rediscovery in about 1900 of Mendel's breeding experiments. The elegant laws of inheritance were seductive, and a few influential scientists, convinced that even conditions such as pauperism were caused by defective germ plasm, rationalized eugenic programs.[1] But by the close of the nineteenth century, the science of eugenics was already well established.

The founding father was Francis Galton, who, in 1864, began to study the heredity of talent. His investigations of the accomplishments of the children of eminent British judges first appeared in the popular press in 1865.[2] Four years later his book *Heredity Genius: An Inquiry into Its Laws and Consequences*[3] provided a cornerstone for eugenics. A man obsessed with measuring, Galton returned to the problem of heredity many times throughout his long life.[4]

In the United States, evolutionary theory was complicated by the race problem. Some scientists argued that human races had degenerated from a common type and that color was a rough index of departure from the original (white) type.[5] Such notions accommodated the Old Testament and reinforced the convictions of Europeans and North Americans that the Negro was inferior. Particularly important was Morton's 1839 study of the cranial volume of 256 skulls from the five major races. He reported that the average Caucasian skull was 7 cubic inches larger than the average Negro skull—a powerful finding to explain "obvious" cultural superiority.[6]

From Aubrey Milunsky and George J. Annas, eds., *Genetics and the Law III* (New York: Plenum Press, 1985), pp. 227–241. Copyright © 1985, Plenum Publishing Corporation. Reprinted by permission of the author and publisher.

Another important progenitor of eugenical theory was Cesar Lombroso, an Italian criminologist. Lombroso argued that the behavior of many criminals was the ineluctable product of their germ plasm. During the postmortem on a famous brigand, Lombroso noted a median occipital fossa, rarely found in human skulls, but commonly seen in rodents. That and similar findings convinced him that the criminal was "an atavistic being who reproduces in his person the ferocious instincts of primitive humanity and the inferior animals."[7] Late-nineteenth-century American criminology felt his influence. For example, a Pennsylvania prison official wrote that "everyone who has visited prisons and observed large numbers of prisoners together has undoubtedly been impressed from the appearance of prisoners alone, that a large portion of them were born to be criminals."[8]

Perhaps the single most important event in the rise of eugenics was a report written by Richard Dugdale, a reform-minded New York prison inspector. At one upstate prison, he was struck by the large number of inmates who were relatives. He eventually amassed a pedigree spanning five generations that included 709 individuals, the collective offspring of an early Dutch settler, all with a propensity for almshouses, taverns, and brothels. His study of "the Jukes" had an immediate success with the general public.[9] The family entered American folklore and came to symbolize a new kind of sociological study, one that eugenicists would repeat and refine in the early years of the twentieth century.

During the 1870s, there was a marked increase in the number of state institutions dedicated to the care of the feebleminded. But by 1880, lawmakers were reassessing their relatively generous funding of these institutions. The U.S. Census of 1880 alarmed those who cared for defective persons; it reported that whereas the general population had grown by 30%, the apparent increase in "idiocy" was 200%.[10] By the 1880s, optimistic views on the educability of the feebleminded were fading, and there was a steady increase in the number of "custodial departments." The "Jukes" stimulated much interest in calculating the cost of providing for the nation's feebleminded, insane, or criminal.

The rediscovery of Mendel's laws was timed perfectly to reinforce the popular suspicion that the defective classes were the products of tainted germ plasm. It prompted a deluge of articles on eugenics in the pages of the popular press. Between 1905 and 1909, there were 27 articles on eugenics listed in *The Reader's Guide to Periodical Literature*. From 1910 to 1914, there were 122 additional entries, making it one of the most referenced subjects in the index. Not a few of them were alarmist in tone.

The popularity of this new subject owed much to Charles B. Davenport, the first director of the Station for Experimental Evolution at Cold Spring Harbor, New York. Trained in mathematics and biology (he took a Ph.D. from Harvard in 1892), young, and ambitious, Davenport was well placed to capture the dramatic implications of Mendelism.[11] After convincing the newly endowed Carnegie Institute to create a research facility, he embarked on genetic studies in domestic animals and plants. But the appeal of human studies was irresistible, and he was soon publishing papers on the inheritance of eye color and skin color.

In 1909, Davenport convinced Mrs. E. H. Harriman, the wealthy matron of a railroad fortune, to underwrite the creation of a Eugenics Record Office (ERO) for five years. His first task was to build a cadre of fieldworkers, young women trained to conduct family studies, to amass the raw data of eugenics. Progress was swift, and the ERO soon was publishing monographs arguing that degeneracy was highly heritable and that affected persons tended also to have large families.[12]

Significant as these works were, the major eugenics document of this century was probably Goddard's 1912 study of "the Kallikaks."[13] In 1907, Goddard, a psychologist doing research at the Vineland Training School, traveled to Europe. In Paris, he visited Simon and Binet and learned their new methods for testing intelligence. When he returned to New Jersey, Goddard, closely assisted by an ERO-trained fieldworker, used the methods to study the families of Vineland patients.

One family fascinated them. It was composed of two branches, both descendants of Martin Kallikak, a soldier in the Revolutionary War. While in the army, Martin had got a girl in the "Piney Woods" pregnant. After the war, he married a respectable Quaker maid and engendered a line of eminent New Jersey citizens. Goddard believed that this natural experiment proved the power of heredity. For generation after generation, the "Piney Woods" line produced paupers and feebleminded persons who, often unaware of their biological ties, sometimes worked as servants to their more eminent cousins.

The Kallikak Family was an immediate success. Written in clear language, embellished with many photographs of the moronic, sinister-looking family, and relatively short, the book hit home with the public. Reprinted in 1913, 1914, 1916, and 1919, it earned Goddard not a little celebrity. Only recently did Stephen Gould discover that the photographs had been altered, thus casting doubt on the integrity of the entire enterprise.[14] But in 1912 or 1919, one could hardly read *The Kallikak Family* without worrying about the consequences of childbearing by the weaker stock in the human family.

The climate of nativism made a large number of Americans particularly receptive to the argument that, if the wrong people had too many children, the nation's racial vigor would decline. No study of eugenic sterilization in the United States can ignore the impact of immigration. The history of the growth of nineteenth-century America is a history of immigration. The first of four great waves rolled across the land in the 1840s. During the 1890s, immigration exceeded the wildest predictions, rising from 225,000 in 1898 to 1,300,000 in 1907. Large-scale assimilation was painful, sometimes agonizing. Perhaps the most dramatic perturbation was competition for jobs. Despite their commitment to internationalism, even the great unions favored restrictive immigration laws. Several states passed laws excluding immigrants from the public works.[15]

Beginning about 1875 proposals to curtail the entry of aliens became a perennial topic before the U.S. Congress. The earliest laws were stimulated by fears in California that the importation of coolie labor had gone too far. Starting with the "Chinese Exclusion Acts," the federal government built the walls even higher. In 1882, a new law expressly excluded lunatics, idiots, and persons likely to become a public charge. During the late 1890s, the most ardent restrictionists sought to condition entry on a literacy test, but success in Congress was damped by President Cleveland's veto.

The early responses to fears of a rapidly growing number of defective persons were proposals that they be incarcerated. The first asylum dedicated to segregating feeble-minded women during their reproductive years was opened in New York in 1878. But by the 1890s, it was obvious that only a tiny fraction of feebleminded women would ever be institutionalized. This harsh reality engendered a successful campaign to enact laws to prohibit marriage by the feebleminded, epileptics, and other "defective" types. Beginning with Connecticut in 1895, many states passed eugenic marriage laws, but this solution was unenforceable. Even the eugenicists dismissed it as ineffective.[16]

Perhaps the most lurid alternative to proposals for lifetime segregation was mass castration. Although never legally implemented, proposals to castrate criminals were seriously debated in a few state legislatures during the 1890s.[17] With the development of the vasectomy, a socially more acceptable operation, procastration arguments (usually aimed at male criminals) faded.

THE SURGICAL SOLUTION

The first American case report of a vasectomy was by Albert Ochsner, a young Chicago surgeon. He argued that the vasectomy could eliminate criminality inherited from the "father's side" and that it "could reasonably be suggested for chronic inebriates, imbeciles, perverts and paupers."[18] Three years later, H. C. Sharp, a surgeon at the Indiana Reformatory, reported the first large study on the effects of vasectomy. He claimed that his 42 patients felt stronger, slept better, performed more satisfactorily in the prison school, and felt less desire to masturbate! Sharp urged physicians to lobby for a law to empower directors of state institutions "to render every male sterile who passes its portals, whether it be almshouse, insane asylum, institute for the feebleminded, reformatory or prison."[19]

In 1907, the governor of Indiana signed the nation's first sterilization law. It initiated the involuntary sterilization of any habitual criminal, rapist, idiot, or imbecile committed to a state institution whom physicians diagnosed as "unimprovable." Having operated on 200 Indiana prisoners, Sharp quickly emerged as the national authority on eugenical sterilization. A tireless advocate, he even underwrote the publication of a pamphlet, *Vasectomy*.[20] In it, he affixed tear-out post cards so that readers could mail a preprinted statement supporting compulsory sterilization laws to their legislative representatives.

Although the simplicity of the vasectomy attracted their attention to defective males, the eugenicists were also concerned with defective women. But the salpingectomy was not yet perfected, and the morbidity from intraabdominal operations was high. Eugenic theoreticians had little choice but to support the long-term segregation of feebleminded women. They were, however, comforted in their belief that most retarded women became prostitutes and were rendered sterile by pelvic inflammatory disease.[21]

Prosterilization arguments peaked in the medical literature in 1910, when roughly one half of the 40 articles published since 1900 appeared. The articles almost unanimously favored involuntary sterilization of the feebleminded. Appeals to colleagues that they lobby for enabling laws were commonly heard at meetings of state medical societies.[22] At the annual meeting of the American Medical Association, Sharp enthralled his listeners with reports on a series of 456 vasectomies performed on defective men in Indiana. After hearing him, a highly placed New Jersey official announced that he would seek a bill for the compulsory sterilization of habitual criminals in his state.[23] New Jersey enacted such a law 18 months later.

The most successful physician lobbyist was F. W. Hatch, Secretary of the State Lunacy Commission in California. In 1909, he drafted a sterilization law and helped convince the legislature (made highly sensitive to eugenic issues by the influx of "racially inferior" Chinese and Mexicans) to adopt it. After the law was enacted, Hatch was appointed General Superintendent of State Hospitals and was authorized to implement the new law. Until his death in 1924, Hatch directed eugenic sterilization programs in 10 state hospitals and approved 3,000 sterilizations, nearly half the nation's total.[24]

THE EARLY STERILIZATION LAWS

In studying the rapid rise of the early sterilization legislation, one is hampered by a paucity of state legislative historical materials.[25] Four small, but influential, groups lobbied hard for these laws: physicians (especially those working at state facilities), scientific eugenicists, lawyers and judges, and a striking number of the nation's richest families. There were, of course, opponents as well. But except for a handful of academic sociologists and social workers, they were less visible and less vocal.

The enthusiastic support that America's wealthiest families provided to the eugenics movement is a most curious feature of its history. First among many was Mrs. E. H. Harriman, who almost single-handedly supported the ERO in its first five years. The second largest financial supporter of the ERO was John D. Rockefeller, who gave it $400 each month. Other famous eugenic philanthropists included Dr. John Harvey Kellogg (brother to the cereal magnate), who organized the First Race Betterment Conference (1914), and Samuel Fels, the Philadelphia soap manufacturer. Theodore Roosevelt was an ardent eugenicist, who favored large families to avoid racial dilution by the weaker immigrant stocks.[26]

Of the few vocal opponents to the eugenics movement, Alexander Johnson and Franz Boas were the most important. Johnson, leader of the National Conference of Charities and Correction, thought that sterilization was less humane than institutional segregation. He dreamed of "orderly celibate communities segregated from the body politic," where the feebleminded and the insane would be safe and could be largely self-supporting.[27] Boas, a Columbia University anthropologist, conducted a special study for Congress to determine whether immigrants were being assimilated into American culture. His findings argued that Hebrews and Sicilians were easily assimiliable — a conclusion that was anathema to eugenicists.[28]

The extraordinary legislative success of proposals to sterilize defective persons suggests that there was substantial support among the general public for such a plan. Between 1905 and 1917, the legislatures of 17 states passed sterilization laws, usually by a large majority vote. Most were modeled after the "Indiana plan," which covered "conformed criminals, idiots, imbeciles, and rapists." In Indiana, if two outside surgeons agreed with the institution's physician that there was no prognosis for "improvement" in such persons, they could be sterilized without their consent. In California, the focus was on sterilizing the insane. The statute permitted authorities to condition a patient's discharge from a state hospital on undergoing sterilization. California law was unique in requiring that the patient or the family consent to the operation, but as the hospitalization was of indeterminate length, people rarely refused sterilization; thus the consent was rendered nugatory.[29]

How vigorously were these laws implemented? From 1907 to 1921, 3,233 sterilizations were performed

under state law. A total of 1,853 men (72 by castration) and 1,380 women (100 by castration) were sterilized. About 2,700 operations were performed on the insane, 400 on the feebleminded, and 130 on criminals. California's program was by far the largest.[30]

Sterilization programs ebbed and flowed according to the views of key state and institutional officials. For example, in 1909, the new governor of Indiana squashed that state's program. In New York, activity varied by institution. In the State Hospital at Buffalo, the superintendent, who believed that pregnancy exacerbated schizophrenia, authorized 12 salpingectomies, but in most other hospitals, no sterilizations were permitted despite the state law. Similar idiosyncratic patterns were documented in other states.[31]

The courts were unfriendly to eugenic policy. Between 1912 and 1921, eight laws were challenged, and seven were held unconstitutional. The first two cases were brought by convicted rapists who argued that sterilization violated the Eighth Amendment's prohibition of cruel and unusual punishment. The Supreme Court of the State of Washington, impressed by Dr. Sharp's reports that vasectomy was simple, quick, and painless, upheld its state law.[32] But a few years later, a federal court in Nevada ruled that the vasectomy was an "unusual" punishment and struck down a criminal sterilization law.[33] Peter Feilen, the appellant in the Washington case, was probably the only man ever forced to undergo a vasectomy pursuant to a law drafted expressly as a punitive rather than an eugenic measure.

In six states (New Jersey, Iowa, Michigan, New York, Indiana, and Oregon), constitutional attacks were leveled at laws that authorized the sterilization of feebleminded or insane persons who resided in state institutions. The plaintiffs argued that laws aimed only at institutionalized persons violated the Equal Protection Clause and that the procedural safeguards were so inadequate that they ran afoul of the Due Process Clause. All six courts invalidated the laws, but they were divided in their reasoning. The three that found a violation of the Equal Protection Clause did not clearly oppose eugenic sterilization; their concern was about uniform treatment of all feebleminded persons. The three that relied on due process arguments to reject the laws were more antagonistic to the underlying policy. An Iowa judge characterized sterilization as a degrading act that could cause "mental torture."[34]

From 1918 to 1921, the years during which these cases were decided, sterilization laws faded as quickly as they had appeared. One reason that the courts were less sympathetic to sterilization laws than the legislatures had been was that sterilization petitions (like commitment orders) touched the judiciary's historic role as protector of the weak. The judges demanded clear proof that the individual would benefit from being sterilized. Another important reason was that scientific challenges to eugenic theories about crime had appeared. For example, two physicians who studied 1,000 recidivists to determine whether inheritance was a factor in criminal behavior found "no proof of the existence of hereditary criminalistic traits."[35] But their voices were soon lost in the storm as another huge wave of immigrants swept across America.

THE RESURGENCE OF THE STERILIZATION MOVEMENT

Despite the judicial rejection of the earlier laws, after World War I arguments that mass eugenic sterilization was critical to the nation's "racial strength" resurfaced. Probably the major impetus was the sudden arrival of hundreds of thousands of southeastern European immigrants.[36] The xenophobia triggered by this massive influx had widespread repercussions. It reinforced concern about the dangers of miscegenation and helped to renew interest in biological theories of crime.

The concurrent concern about miscegenation reflected the weakening of southern white society's control over the lives of blacks. During the eighteenth and nineteenth centuries, the southern states forbade marriage between whites and Negroes. After the Civil War, the burgeoning "colored" population (largely a product of institutionalized rape before then) stimulated amendments that redefined as "negro" persons with ever smaller fractions of black ancestry.[37] This trend culminated when Virginia enacted a marriage law that defined as white "one who has no trace whatsoever of any blood other than Caucasian." It forbade the issuance of marriage licenses until officials had "reasonable assurance" that statements about the color of both the man and the woman were correct, voided all existing interracial marriages (regardless of whether they had been contracted legally elsewhere), and made cohabitation by such couples a felony. Several other states enacted laws modeled on the Virginia plan. It was not until the 1940s that states began to repeal miscegenation laws,

and only recently did the U.S. Supreme Court declare them to be unconstitutional.[38]

The early 1920s were also marked by an interest in biological theories of criminality somewhat akin to those legitimized by Lombroso. Orthodox criminologists were not responsible for this development.[39] The notion of biologically determined criminality was fostered largely by tabloid journalists and a few eugenically minded officials. For example, *World's Work,* a popular monthly, featured five articles on the biological basis of crime. One recounted the innovative efforts of Harry Olson, Chief Justice of the Chicago Municipal Court. Convinced that most criminals were mentally abnormal, Olson started a Psychopathic Laboratory and hired a psychometrician to develop screening tests to identify people with criminal minds.[40]

During the 1920s, many eugenics clubs and societies sprouted, but only two, the American Eugenics Society (AES) and the Human Betterment Foundation (HBF), exerted any significant influence on the course of eugenic sterilization. The AES was conceived at the Second International Congress of Eugenics in 1921. Dr. Henry Fairfield Osborn, President of the American Museum of Natural History, and a small group of patrician New Yorkers initiated the society. By 1923, it was sufficiently well organized to lobby against a bill to support special education for the handicapped, an idea that it considered dysgenic.

In 1925, the AES relocated to New Haven, Connecticut. For the next few years, its major goal was public education. The Great Depression caused a great fall in donations, and when Ellsworth Huntington, a Yale geographer, became president in 1934, the society was moribund. With the aid of a wealthy relative of the founder, Huntington breathed new life into the organization and realized that politically the AES would fare better if it pushed "positive" eugenics policies, such as family planning and personal hygiene. By 1939, the AES had dissociated itself from hard-core sterilization advocates.

The wealthiest eugenics organization was the Human Betterment Foundation (HBF), started by California millionaire Ezra Gosney, who in 1926 convened a group of experts to study the efficacy of California's sterilization program. This group eventually published over 20 articles confirming the safety of being sterilized and concluded that the state had benefitted. Gosney was convinced that a massive sterilization program could reduce the number of mentally defective persons by one half in "three or four generations."[41]

For five years after sterilization statutes were struck down by the courts, there was little legislative activity. Then, in 1923, four states (Oregon, Montana, Delaware, and Ohio) enacted new laws, and by 1925, eight other states had followed suit. The new statutes were drafted with much greater regard for constitutional issues. Besides frequently requiring the assent of parents or guardians, the laws preserved the right to a jury trial of whether the patient was "the potential parent of socially inadequate offspring." Despite concern about the Equal Protection Clause, most laws were still aimed only at institutionalized persons.

Opponents of sterilization quickly attacked the new laws. Battle was joined in Michigan and Virginia. In June 1925, the highest Michigan court ruled that the state's sterilization statute was "justified by the findings of Biological Science."[42] But the crucial case involved a test of the Virginia law. Dr. A. S. Priddy, Superintendent of the State Colony for Epileptics and Feeble-Minded, filed a sterilization petition to test the judicial waters. Carefully amassing a wealth of pro-eugenic testimony, he shepherded the case through the courts. His strategy paid off. In May 1927, Oliver Wendell Holmes, writing for the majority of the U.S. Supreme Court, upheld involuntary sterilization of the feeble-minded, concluding:

It is better for all the world, if instead of waiting to execute degenerative offspring for crime, or to let them starve for their imbecility, society can prevent those who are manifestly unfit from continuing their kind. The principle that sustains compulsory vaccination is broad enough to cover cutting the Fallopian tubes.[43]

YEARS OF TRIUMPH

The Supreme Court's decision to uphold the Virginia law accelerated the pace of legislation: in 1929, nine states adopted similar laws. As was the case before World War I, a small group of activists from influential quarters persuaded scientifically unsophisticated legislators that sterilization was necessary, humane, and just.

The lobbyists succeeded in part because of favorable views expressed in the medical profession. During 1927–1936, about 60 articles, the vast majority in favor of eugenic sterilization, appeared. In the general medical community, support was strong, but not uniform. Only 18 state medical societies officially backed sterilization programs.[44]

The legislative victories of the early 1930s were impressive, but the crucial measure of whether eugenic notions triumphed is to count the number of sterilizations. Data from surveys that were conducted by the Human Betterment Foundation and other groups permit minimal estimates of the extent of mass sterilization and compel some striking conclusions:

1. Between 1907 and 1963, there were eugenic sterilization programs in 30 states. More than 60,000 persons were sterilized pursuant to state laws.
2. Although sterilization reached its zenith during the 1930s, several states vigorously pursued this activity throughout the 1940s and 1950s.
3. At a given time, a few programs were more active than the rest. In the 1920s and 1930s, California and a few midwestern states were most active. After World War II, several southern states accounted for more than half of the involuntary sterilizations performed on institutionalized persons.
4. Beginning in about 1930, there was a dramatic rise in the percentage of women who were sterilized.
5. Revulsion with Nazi sterilization policy did not curtail American sterilization programs. Indeed, more than one half of all eugenic sterilizations occurred after the Nazi program was fully operational.

During 1929–1941, the Human Betterment Foundation conducted annual surveys of state institutions to chart the progress of sterilization. Letters from hospital officials indicate what factors influenced the programs. The most important determinants of the scope of a program's operation seem to have been the complexity of the due process requirements of the relevant laws, the level of funding, and the attitudes of the superintendents themselves. The HBF surveys strongly suggest that the total number of sterilizations performed on institutionalized persons was underreported. Respondents frequently indicated that eugenic operations were conducted outside the confines of state hospitals.[45]

Until 1918, there were only 1,422 eugenic sterilizations reportedly performed pursuant to state law. Ironically, the sterilization rate began to rise during the very period when the courts were rejecting the first round of statutes (1917–1918). From 1918 to 1920, there were 1,811 reported sterilizations, a fourfold increase over the annual rate during the prior decade. During the 1920s, annual sterilization figures were stable. But in 1929, there was a large increase in sterilizations. Throughout the 1930s, more than 2,000 institutionalized persons were sterilized each year, triple the rate of the early 1920s.

This rapid increase reflected changing concerns and changing policy. In the Great Depression years, the superintendents of many hospitals, strapped by tight budgets, decided to sterilize mildly retarded young women. Before 1929, about 53% of all eugenic sterilizations had been performed on men. Between 1929 and 1935, there were 14,651 reported operations, 9,327 on women and 5,324 on men. In several states (e.g., Minnesota, and Wisconsin), virtually all the sterilized persons were women. This fact becomes even more impressive when one recognizes that salpingectomy incurred a relatively high morbidity and a much higher cost than did vasectomy. In California, at least five women died after undergoing eugenic sterilization.[46]

During the 1930s, institutionalized men were also being sterilized in unprecedented numbers, largely because of the great increase in the total number of state programs. Unlike the "menace of the feebleminded" that had haunted policy before World War I, the new concern was to cope with harsh economic realities. As the superintendents saw it, fewer babies born to incompetent parents might mean fewer state wards.

The triumph of eugenic sterilization programs in the United States during the 1930s influenced other nations. Canada, Germany, Sweden, Norway, Finland, France, and Japan enacted sterilization laws. The most important events took place in Germany, where the Nazis sterilized more than 50,000 "unfit" persons within one year of enacting a eugenics law.

The German interest in eugenics had roots that twined with nineteenth-century European racial thought, a topic beyond the scope of this [essay]. In the early years of this century, there was a spate of books that preached the need to protect Nordic germ plasm. A German eugenics society was formed in 1905, and in 1907, the first (unsuccessful) sterilization bill was offered in the Reichstag. The devastation of World War I halted the German eugenic movement, but by 1921, groups were again actively lobbying for eugenics programs. Hitler advocated eugenic sterilization as early as 1923.

When the Nazis swept to power, they quickly implemented a program to encourage larger, healthier families. Tax laws were restructured to favor childbearing. In 1933, a companion law was enacted to prevent reproduction by defective persons. The work of Gosney and Popenoe [see notes 24 and 41] was extremely influential on the Nazi planners.[47]

The law created a system of "hereditary health courts," which judged petitions brought by public health officials that certain citizens burdened with one of a long list of disorders (feeblemindedness, schizophrenia, manic-depressive insanity, epilepsy, Huntington's chorea, hereditary blindness, hereditary deafness, severe physical deformity, and habitual drunkenness) would be subjected to compulsory sterilization. In 1934, the courts heard 64,499 petitions and ordered 56,244 sterilizations, for a "eugenic conviction" rate of 87%.[48] In 1934, the German Supreme Court ruled that the law applied to non-Germans living in Germany, a decision that had special import for Gypsies. From 1935 through 1939, the annual number of eugenic sterilizations grew rapidly. Unfortunately, key records perished during World War II. But in 1951, the "Central Association of Sterilized People in West Germany" charged that, from 1934 to 1945, the Nazis sterilized 3,500,000 people, often on the flimsiest pretext.[49]

The Nazi program was eugenics run amok. In the United States, no program even approached it in scope or daring. But there is no evidence to support the argument, frequently heard, that stories of Nazi horrors halted American sterilization efforts.

THE QUIET YEARS

With the onset of World War II, there was a sharp decline in the number of eugenic sterilizations in the United States. Although manpower shortages (surgeons were unavailable) directly contributed to the decline, other factors were also at work. In 1939, the Eugenics Record Office closed its doors; in 1942, the Human Betterment Foundation also ceased its activities. Later that year, the U.S. Supreme Court, considering its first sterilization case in 15 years, struck down an Oklahoma law that permitted certain thrice-convicted felons to be sterilized.[50] After the war, as the horror of the Nazi eugenics movement became more obvious, the goals of the lingering American programs became more suspect. Yet, despite these changes, many state-mandated sterilization programs continued, albeit at a reduced level of activity.

Between 1942 and 1946, the annual sterilization rate dropped to half that of the 1930s. Reports of institutional officials make it clear that this decline was largely due to a lack of surgeons and nurses.[51] There is little evidence to suggest that the Supreme Court decision had a major impact. Avoiding an opportunity to broadly condemn involuntary sterilization and overrule *Buck v. Bell*,[52] the justices demanded instead that such practices adhere to the precept of the Equal Protection Clause that like persons be treated in a similar fashion. The Oklahoma law was struck down because it spared certain "white-collar" criminals from a punitive measure aimed at other thrice-convicted persons, not simply because it involved sterilization.

During the late 1940s, there was no definite indication that sterilization programs were about to decline. After hitting a low of 1,183 in 1944, there were 1,526 operations in 1950. Slight declines in many states were balanced by rapid increases in North Carolina and Georgia. By 1950, however, there were bellwether signs that sterilization was in disfavor even among institutional officials. For example, during the 1930s and 1940s, 100 persons in San Quentin prison had been sterilized each year. But in 1950, new officials at the California Department of Corrections were "entirely averse" to the program.[53] During that year, sterilization bills were considered in only four states, and all were rejected.[54]

There were major changes in state sterilization programs in 1952. The California program, for years the nation's most active, was moribund, dropping from 275 sterilizations in 1950 to 39 in 1952. By that year, Georgia, North Carolina, and Virginia (having sterilized 673 persons) were responsible for 53% of the national total. General declines in most other states continued throughout the 1950s, and by 1958, these three states were responsible for 76% (574 persons) of the reported operations. The North Carolina program was unique in that it was directed largely at noninstitutionalized rural young women.[55] As recently as 1963, the state paid for the eugenic sterilization of 193 persons, of whom 183 were young women.[56] Despite the persistence, the southern programs must be seen as a local eddy in a tide of decline.

INVOLUNTARY STERILIZATION TODAY

During the 1960s, the practice of sterilizing retarded persons in state institutions virtually ceased. But the laws remained. In 1961, there were eugenic sterilization laws on the books of 28 states, and it was possible to perform involuntary sterilization in 26.[57] Between 1961 and 1976, five laws were repealed, six were amended (to improve procedural safeguards), and one state

(West Virginia in 1975) adopted its first sterilization statute. Currently, eugenic sterilization of institutionalized retarded persons is permissible in 19 states, but the laws are rarely invoked. A few states have enacted laws that expressly forbid the sterilization of any persons in state institutions.

If the mid-1930s saw the zenith of eugenic sterilization, the mid-1960s saw its nadir. But the pendulum of policy continues to swing. The late 1960s saw the first lawsuits brought by the parents of noninstitutionalized retarded females arguing that sterilization was both economically essential and psychologically beneficial to their efforts to maintain their adult daughters at home.[58]

In 1973, the debate over sterilizing institutionalized persons whom officials had decided were unfit to be parents flared in the media. The mother of a young man whom physicians at the Partlow State School in Alabama wished to sterilize challenged the constitutionality of the enabling statute. When Alabama officials cleverly argued that they did not need statutory authority as long as consent was obtained from the retarded person, the federal judge not only overturned the law but decreed strict guidelines to control the process of performing "voluntary" sterilizations at Partlow. The key feature was the creation of an outside committee to review all the sterilization petitions.[59]

Also in 1973, the U.S. Department of Health, Education, and Welfare (HEW) became enmeshed in a highly publicized sterilization scandal. That summer, it was reported that an Alabama physician working at a family-planning clinic funded by HEW had sterilized several young, poor black women without their consent. The National Welfare Rights Organization joined with two of the women and sued to block the use of all federal funds to pay for sterilizations. This move prompted HEW to draft strict regulations governing the use of federal money for such purposes, but a federal judge struck them down and held that HEW could not provide sterilization services to legally incompetent persons.[60] Revamped several times, the HEW guidelines were the subject of continuous litigation for five years. Late in 1978, "final rules" were issued that prohibited the sterilization of some persons (those under 21, and all mentally incompetent persons) and demanded elaborate consent mechanisms when a competent person requested to undergo sterilization to be paid for by public funds.[61]

During the last few years, the debate over sterilizing the mentally retarded, although no longer cast in a eugenic context, reheated. The key issue was to resolve the tensions between the society's duty to protect the incompetent person and the *right* of that person to be sterilized. Of course, exercise of this right presupposes that a family member or guardian is, in fact, properly asserting a right that the subject is incapable of exercising on her own (almost all requests are filed on behalf of retarded young *women*), a matter to which judges devote most of their attention. The court must be convinced that the operation will benefit the patient.

More than 20 appellate courts have been asked to consider sterilization petitions. This spate of litigation has resulted because physicians are now extremely reluctant to run the risk of violating the civil rights of the retarded. The courts have split sharply. In the absence of express statutory authority, six high courts have refused to authorize sterilization orders.[62]

In the more recent decisions, most appellate courts have ruled that (even without statutory authorization) local courts of general jurisdiction do have the power to evaluate petitions to sterilize retarded persons. In a leading case, the highest court in New Jersey held that the parents of an adolescent girl with Down syndrome might obtain surgical sterilization for her if they could provide clear and convincing evidence that it was in "her best interests."[63] Since then, high courts in Colorado, Massachusetts, and Pennsylvania have ruled in a similar manner. These decisions promise that, in the future, the families of some retarded persons will be able to obtain sterilizations for them, regardless of their institutional status.

The great era of sterilization has passed. Yet, grim reminders of unsophisticated programs that once flourished linger. In Virginia, persons sterilized for eugenic reasons decades ago have sued the state, claiming a violation of their civil rights. Although they lost their argument that the operations were performed pursuant to an unconstitutional law, litigation over whether the state failed in its duty to inform them of the consequences of the operations continues. From pretrial discovery, it appears likely that not a few of the persons who were sterilized were not retarded.[64]

What of the future? Is the saga of involuntary sterilization over? Our knowledge of human genetics makes the return of mass eugenic sterilizations unlikely. However, it is more difficult to predict the future of sterilization programs founded on other arguments. During the 1960s, a number of state legislatures considered a bill to tie welfare payments to "voluntary" sterilization.[65] In 1980, a Texas official made a similar suggestion.[66] Unscientific opinion polls conducted by magazines and newspapers in Texas and Massachusetts found significant support for involuntary sterilization of the retarded.[67]

Although it is unlikely to happen in the United States, the pressing demands of population control in India and China have resulted in social policies that create strong incentives to be sterilized. Since launching the "one-child" program in 1979, China has rapidly altered the social fabric of 1 billion people.[68] As our resources continue to shrink and our earthly neighborhood becomes more crowded, compulsory sterilization may someday be as common as compulsory immunizations, but the eugenic vision will no longer provide its intellectual rationale.

REFERENCES AND NOTES

1. Estabrook, A., and Davenport, C. B., *The Nam Family: A Study of Cacogenics,* Eugenics Record Office, Cold Spring Harbor, NY, 1912.

2. Galton, F., Hereditary talent and character, *Macmillan's Magazine* 12:157–66 (1865).

3. Macmillan, London (1869).

4. Two other books by Galton, *English Men of Science: Their Nature and Nurture,* Macmillan, London (1874); and *Inquiries into Human Faculty and Its Development,* Macmillan, London, (1883), did much to legitimize eugenics.

5. Greene, J. C., Some early speculations on the origin of human races, *American Anthropologist* 56:31–41 (1954).

6. Morton, S. G., *Crania Americana,* John Pennington, Philadelphia (1839). After the Civil War, miscegenation took on new importance; the leading opponent of interracial marriages was a South Carolina physician: Nott, J. C., The mulatto a hybrid, *Am. J. Med. Sci.* 6:252–56 (1843).

7. Lombroso-Ferrerr, G., *Lombroso's Criminal Man,* Patterson-Smith, Montclair, NJ (1872).

8. Boies, H. M., *Prisoners and Paupers,* G. P. Putnam's Sons, NY (1893).

9. Dugdale, R. L., A record and study of the relations of crime, pauperism and disease, in *Appendix to the Thirty-first Report of the NY Prison Association,* NY Prison Assoc., Albany, NY (1875).

10. Kerlin, I., Report to the eleventh national conference on charters and reforms, *Proc. A.M.O.* [*Proceedings of the Association of Medical Officers of American Institutions for Idiotic and Feeble-Minded Persons*] (1884), 465.

11. Rosenberg, C. E., Charles Benedict Davenport and the beginning of human genetics, *Bull. Hist. Med.* 35:266–76 (1961).

12. See *supra* note 1; ERO workers also analyzed the inheritance of Huntington's chorea: Davenport, C. B., Huntington's Chorea in relation to heredity and eugenics, *Bull. No. 17,* Cold Spring Har-

bor, NY (1916); and early eugenic work was reported in a climate of scientific respectability.

13. Goddard, H. H., *The Kallikak Family,* Macmillan, New York (1912).

14. Gould, S. J., *The Mismeasure of Man,* Norton, New York (1981).

15. Higham, J., *Strangers in the Land,* Athenaeum, New York (1965).

16. Davenport, C. B., *State Laws Limiting Marriage Selection,* Eugenics Record Office, Cold Spring Harbor, NY (1913).

17. Daniel, F. E., Emasculation for criminal assaults and incest, *Texas Med. J.* 22:347 (1907).

18. Ochsner, A., Surgical treatment of habitual criminals, *JAMA* 53:867–68 (1899).

19. Sharp, H. C. The severing of the vasa deferentia and its relation to the neuropsychiatric constitution, *N.Y. Med. J* (1902), 411–14.

20. Sharp, H. C., *Vasectomy,* privately printed, Indianapolis (1909).

21. Ochsner, supra note 18.

22. Reilly, P. R., The surgical solution: The writings of activist physicians in the early days of eugenical sterilization, *Persp. Biol. Med.* 26:637–56 (1983).

23. Sharp, H. C., Vasectomy as a means of preventing procreation of defectives, *JAMA* 51:1897–1902 (1907).

24. Popenoe, P., The progress of eugenical sterilization, *J. of Heredity* 28:19–25 (1933).

25. But see Rhode Island State Library Legislative Research Bureau, *Sterilization of the Unfit,* Providence (1913); and Laughlin, H. H., *Eugenical Sterilization in the United States,* Chicago Psychopathic Laboratory of the Municipal Court, Chicago (1922).

26. Roosevelt, T., Twisted eugenics, *Outlook* 106:30–34, 1914; Eugene Smith, President of the National Prison Association, was a prominent lawyer pushing for sterilization laws — The cost of crime, *Medico-Legal J.* 27:140–49 (1908) — as was Judge Warren Foster, *Pearson's Magazine* (1909) 565–72.

27. Johnson, A., Race improvement by control of defectives, *Ann. Am. Acad. Penal Soc. Sci.* 34:22–29 (1909).

28. Report by the Immigration Commission, U.S. Government Printing Office, Washington, D.C. (1910).

29. See Laughlin supra, note 25.

30. Id.

31. Id.

32. *State v. Feilen,* 70 Wash. 65 (1912).

33. *Mickle v. Henrichs,* 262 F. 687 (1918).

34. *Davis v. Berry,* 216 F. 413 (1914).

35. Spaulding, E. R., and Healy, W., Inheritance as a factor in criminality, in *Physical Basis of Crime,* American Academy of Med. Press, Easton, PA (1914).

36. Ludmerer, K., *Genetics and American Society,* Johns Hopkins University Press, Baltimore (1972).

37. Mencke, J. G., *Mulattoes and Race Mixture: American Attitudes and Images, 1865–1918,* UMI Research Press, Ann Arbor, MI (1959).

38. *Loving v. Virginia,* 388 U.S. 1 (1967).

39. Parmelee, M., *Criminology,* Macmillan, New York (1918).

40. Strother, F., The cause of crime: Defective brain, *World's Work* 48:275–81 (1924).

41. Gosney, E. S., & Popenoe, P., *Sterilization for Human Betterment,* Macmillan, New York (1929). HBF was the leading source of prosterilization literature during the 1930s, sponsored a "social eugenics" column in the *Los Angeles Times,* aired radio programs, produced pamphlets, and underwrote lectures. It remained vigorous until Gosney's death in 1942.

42. *Smith v. Probate,* 231 Mich. 409 (1925).

43. *Buck v. Bell,* 274 U.S. 200 (1927).

44. Whitten, B. D., Sterilization, *J. Psycho-Asthenics* 40:56–68 (1935). But in some states, like Indiana, support was very strong. Harshman, L. P., Medical and legal aspects of sterilization in Indiana, *J. Psycho-Asthenics* 39:183–206 (1934).

45. See, e.g., Dunham, W. F., Letter to E. S. Gosney, *AVS [Association for Voluntary Sterilization] Archive,* University of Minnesota (1936).

46. Gosney and Popenoe *supra,* note 41.

47. Kopp, M., The German sterilization program, *AVS Archive,* University of Minnesota (1935).

48. Cook, R., A year of German sterilization, *J. Heredity* 26:485–89 (1935).

49. *New York Herald Tribune* (Jan. 14, 1951), 12.

50. *Skinner v. Oklahoma,* 316 U.S. 535 (1942).

51. Taromianz, M. A., Letter to NJ Sterilization League, *AVS Archive,* University of Minnesota (1944).

52. 274 U.S. 200 (1927).

53. Stanley, L. L., Letter to the NJ Sterilization League, *AVS Archive,* University of Minnesota (1950).

54. Butler, F. O., Report, *AVS Archive,* University of Minnesota (1950).

55. Woodside, M., *Sterilization in North Carolina,* University of North Carolina, Chapel Hill (1950).

56. Casebolt, S. L., Letters to Human Betterment Association of America, *AVS Archive,* University of Minnesota (1963).

57. Landman, F. T., and McIntyre, D. M., *The Mentally Disabled and the Law,* University of Chicago Press, Chicago (1961).

58. *Frazier v. Levi,* 440 S.W. 2d 579 (TX 1968).

59. *Wyatt v. Aderholt,* 368 F. Supp. 1382 (Ala. D.C. 1973).

60. *Relf v. Weinberger,* 372 F. Supp. 1196 (1974).

61. *Fed. Reg.* 52146–75 (1978).

62. *In the Matter of S.C.E.,* 378 A. 2d 144 (1977).

63. *In re Grady,* 426 N.W. 2d 467 (NJ 1981).

64. *Poe v. Lynchburg,* 1981.

65. Paul, J., The return of punitive sterilization laws, *Law Soc. Rev.* 4:77–110 (1968).

66. *New York Times* (Feb. 28, 1980), A16.

67. *The Texas Observer* (March 20, 1981), 7; *Boston Globe* (March 31, 1982), 1.

68. *Intercom* 9(8):12–14, 1981.

UNITED STATES SUPREME COURT

Buck v. Bell (1927)

Argued April 22, 1927. Decided May 2, 1927.

On Writ of Error to the Supreme Court of Appeals of the State of Virginia to review a judgment affirming a judgment of the Circuit Court for Amherst County directing the sterilization of an inmate of a Colony for Epileptics and Feeble Minded. Affirmed. . . .*

The facts are stated in the opinion.

Mr. I. P. Whitehead argued the cause and filed a brief for plaintiff in error:

The act of assembly of Virginia does not provide due process of law guaranteed by the 14th Amendment to the Constitution of the United States. . . .

The act of assembly of Virginia denies to the plaintiff and other inmates of the State Colony for Epileptics and Feebleminded the equal protection of the law guaranteed by the 14th Amendment to the Constitution of the United States. . . .

Mr. Aubrey E. Strode argued the cause and filed a brief for defendant in error:

The act affords due process of law. . . .

The act is a valid exercise of the police power.

The statute may be sustained as based upon a reasonable classification. . . .

MR. JUSTICE HOLMES delivered the opinion of the court:

This is a writ of error to review a judgment of the supreme court of appeals of the state of Virginia, affirming a judgment of the circuit court of Amherst county, by which the defendant in error, the superintendent of the State Colony for Epileptics and Feeble Minded, was ordered to perform the operation of sal-

*Editor's note: Some references to other court decisions are omitted or abbreviated.

From *United States [Supreme Court] Reports* 274 (1927), 200–208.

pingectomy upon Carrie Buck, the plaintiff in error, for the purpose of making her sterile. 143 Va. 310, 51 A.L.R. 855, 130 S. E. 516. The case comes here upon the contention that the statute authorizing the judgment is void under the 14th Amendment as denying to the plaintiff in error due process of law and the equal protection of the laws.

Carrie Buck is a feeble minded white woman who was committed to the State Colony above mentioned in due form. She is the daughter of a feeble minded mother in the same institution, and the mother of an illegitimate feeble minded child. She was eighteen years old at the time of the trial of her case in the circuit court, in the latter part of 1924. An Act of Virginia approved March 20, 1924, recites that the health of the patient and the welfare of society may be promoted in certain cases by the sterilization of mental defectives, under careful safeguard, etc.; that the sterilization may be effected in males by vasectomy and in females by salpingectomy, without serious pain or substantial danger to life; that the Commonwealth is supporting in various institutions many defective persons who if now discharged would become a menace but if incapable of procreating might be discharged with safety and become self-supporting with benefit to themselves and to society; and that experience has shown that heredity plays an important part in the transmission of insanity, imbecility, etc. The statute then enacts that whenever the superintendent of certain institutions including the above named State Colony shall be of opinion that it is for the best interests of the patients and of society that an inmate under his care should be sexually sterilized, he may have the operation performed upon any patient afflicted with hereditary forms of insanity, imbecility, etc., on complying with the very careful provisions by which the act protects the patients from possible abuse.

The superintendent first presents a petition to the special board of directors of his hospital or colony, stating the facts and the grounds for his opinion, verified by affidavit. Notice of the petition and of the time and place of the hearing in the institution is to be served upon the inmate, and also upon his guardian, and if there is no guardian the superintendent is to apply to the circuit court of the county to appoint one. If the inmate is a minor notice also is to be given to his parents if any with a copy of the petition. The board is to see to it that the inmate may attend the hearings if desired by him or his guardian. The evidence is all to be reduced to writing, and after the board has made its order for or against the operation, the superintendent, or the inmate, or his guardian, may appeal to the circuit court of the county. The circuit court may consider the record of the board and the evidence before it and such other admissible evidence as may be offered, and may affirm, revise, or reverse the order of the board and enter such order as it deems just. Finally any party may apply to the supreme court of appeals, which, if it grants the appeal, is to hear the case upon the record of the trial in the circuit court and may enter such order as it thinks the circuit court should have entered. There can be no doubt that so far as procedure is concerned the rights of the patient are most carefully considered, and as every step in this case was taken in scrupulous compliance with the statute and after months of observation, there is no doubt that in that respect the plaintiff in error has had due process of law.

The attack is not upon the procedure but upon the substantive law. It seems to be contended that in no circumstances could such an order be justified. It certainly is contended that the order cannot be justified upon the existing grounds. The judgment finds the facts that have been recited and that Carrie Buck "is the probable potential parent of socially inadequate offspring, likewise afflicted, that she may be sexually sterilized without detriment to her general health and that her welfare and that of society will be promoted by her sterilization," and thereupon makes the order. In view of the general declarations of the legislature and the specific findings of the court obviously we cannot say as matter of law that the grounds do not exist, and if they exist they justify the result. We have seen more than once that the public welfare may call upon the best citizens for their lives. It would be strange if it could not call upon those who already sap the strength of the state for these lesser sacrifices, often not felt to be such by those concerned, in order to prevent our being swamped with incompetence. It is better for all the world, if instead of waiting to execute degenerate offspring for crime, or to let them starve for their imbecility, society can prevent those who are manifestly unfit from continuing their kind. The principle that sustains compulsory vaccination is broad enough to cover cutting the Fallopian tubes. Jacobson v. Massachusetts, 197 U.S. 11. Three generations of imbeciles are enough.

But, it is said, however it might be if this reasoning were applied generally, it fails when it is confined to the small number who are in the institutions named and is not applied to the multitudes outside. It is the usual last resort of constitutional arguments to point out shortcomings of this sort. But the answer is that the law does all that is needed when it does all that it can, indicates a policy, applies it to all within the lines, and seeks to bring within the lines all similarly situated so far and so fast as its means allow. Of course so far as the operations enable those who otherwise must be kept confined to be returned to the world, and thus open the asylum to others, the equality aimed at will be more nearly reached.

Judgment affirmed.

MR. JUSTICE BUTLER dissents.

STEPHEN JAY GOULD

Carrie Buck's Daughter

The Lord really put it on the line in his preface to that prototype of all prescriptions, the Ten Commandments:

. . . for I, the Lord thy God, am a jealous God, visiting the iniquity of the fathers upon the children unto the third and fourth generation of them that hate me (Exod. 20:5).

The terror of this statement lies in its patent unfairness—its promise to punish guiltless offspring for the misdeeds of their distant forebears.

A different form of guilt by genealogical association attempts to remove this stigma of injustice by denying a cherished premise of Western thought—human free will. If offspring are tainted not simply by the deeds of their parents but by a material form of evil transferred directly by biological inheritance, then "the iniquity of the fathers" becomes a signal or warning for probable misbehavior of their sons. Thus Plato, while denying that children should suffer directly for the crimes of their parents, nonetheless defended the banishment of a personally guiltless man whose father, grandfather and great-grandfather had all been condemned to death.

It is, perhaps, merely coincidental that both Jehovah and Plato chose three generations as their criterion for establishing different forms of guilt by association. Yet we maintain a strong folk, or vernacular, tradition for viewing triple occurrences as minimal evidence of regularity. Bad things, we are told, come in threes. Two may represent an accidental association; three is a pattern. Perhaps, then, we should not wonder that our

own century's most famous pronouncement of blood guilt employed the same criterion—Oliver Wendell Holmes's defense of compulsory sterilization in Virginia (Supreme Court decision of 1927 in *Buck v. Bell*): "three generations of imbeciles are enough."

Restrictions upon immigration, with national quotas set to discriminate against those deemed mentally unfit by early versions of IQ testing, marked the greatest triumph of the American eugenics movement—the flawed hereditarian doctrine, so popular earlier in our century and by no means extinct today . . . that attempted to "improve" our human stock by preventing the propagation of those deemed biologically unfit and encouraging procreation among the supposedly worthy. But the movement to enact and enforce laws for compulsory "eugenic" sterilization had an impact and success scarcely less pronounced. If we could debar the shiftless and the stupid from our shores, we might also prevent the propagation of those similarly afflicted but already here.

The movement for compulsory sterilization began in earnest during the 1890s, abetted by two major factors—the rise of eugenics as an influential political movement and the perfection of safe and simple operations (vasectomy for men and salpingectomy, the cutting and tying of Fallopian tubes, for women) to replace castration and other socially unacceptable forms of mutilation. Indiana passed the first sterilization act based on eugenic principles in 1907 (a few states had previously mandated castration as a punitive measure for certain sexual crimes, although such laws were rarely enforced and usually overturned by judicial review). Like so many others to follow, it provided for sterilization of afflicted people residing in the state's "care," either as inmates of mental hospitals and homes for the feeble-minded or as inhabitants of prisons. Sterilization could be imposed upon those judged insane, idiotic, imbecilic, or moronic, and upon convicted rapists or criminals when recommended by a board of experts.

By the 1930s, more than thirty states had passed similar laws, often with an expanded list of so-called hereditary defects, including alcoholism and drug addiction in some states, and even blindness and deafness in others. These laws were continually challenged and rarely enforced in most states; only California and Virginia applied them zealously. By January 1935, some 20,000 forced "eugenic" sterilizations had been performed in the United States, nearly half in California.

No organization crusaded more vociferously and successfully for these laws than the Eugenics Record Office, the semiofficial arm and repository of data for the eugenics movement in America. Harry Laughlin, superintendent of the Eugenics Record Office, dedicated most of his career to a tireless campaign of writing and lobbying for eugenic sterilization. He hoped, thereby, to eliminate in two generations the genes of what he called the "submerged tenth" — "the most worthless one-tenth of our present population." He proposed a "model sterilization law" in 1922, designed

to prevent the procreation of persons socially inadequate from defective inheritance, by authorizing and providing for eugenical sterilization of certain potential parents carrying degenerate hereditary qualities.

This model bill became the prototype for most laws passed in America, although few states cast their net as widely as Laughlin advised. (Laughlin's categories encompassed "blind, including those with seriously impaired vision; deaf, including those with seriously impaired hearing; and dependent, including orphans, ne'er-do-wells, the homeless, tramps, and paupers.") Laughlin's suggestions were better heeded in Nazi Germany, where his model act inspired the infamous and stringently enforced *Erbgesundheitsrecht,* leading by the eve of World War II to the sterilization of some 375,000 people, most for "congenital feeblemindedness," but including nearly 4,000 for blindness and deafness.

The campaign for forced eugenic sterilization in America reached its climax and height of respectability in 1927, when the Supreme Court, by an 8–1 vote, upheld the Virginia sterilization bill in *Buck v. Bell.* Oliver Wendell Holmes, then in his mid-eighties and the most celebrated jurist in America, wrote the majority opinion with his customary verve and power of style.

It included the notorious paragraph, with its chilling tag line, cited ever since as the quintessential statement of eugenic principles. Remembering with pride his own distant experiences as an infantryman in the Civil War, Holmes wrote:

We have seen more than once that the public welfare may call upon the best citizens for their lives. It would be strange if it could not call upon those who already sap the strength of the state for these lesser sacrifices. . . . It is better for all the world, if instead of waiting to execute degenerate offspring for crime, or to let them starve for their imbecility, society can prevent those who are manifestly unfit from continuing their kind. The principle that sustains compulsory vaccination is broad enough to cover cutting the Fallopian tubes. Three generations of imbeciles are enough.

Who, then, were the famous "three generations of imbeciles," and why should they still compel our interest?

When the state of Virginia passed its compulsory sterilization law in 1924, Carrie Buck, an eighteen-year-old white woman, lived as an involuntary resident at the State Colony for Epileptics and Feeble-Minded. As the first person selected for sterilization under the new act, Carrie Buck became the focus for a constitutional challenge launched, in part, by conservative Virginia Christians who held, according to eugenical "modernists," antiquated views about individual preferences and "benevolent" state power. (Simplistic political labels do not apply in this case, and rarely in general for that matter. We usually regard eugenics as a conservative movement and its most vocal critics as members of the left. This alignment has generally held in our own decade. But eugenics, touted in its day as the latest in scientific modernism, attracted many liberals and numbered among its most vociferous critics groups often labeled as reactionary and antiscientific. If any political lesson emerges from these shifting allegiances, we might consider the true inalienability of certain human rights.)

But why was Carrie Buck in the State Colony and why was she selected? Oliver Wendell Holmes upheld her choice as judicious in the opening lines of his 1927 opinion:

Carrie Buck is a feeble-minded white woman who was committed to the State Colony. . . . She is the daughter of a feeble-minded mother in the same institution, and the mother of an illegitimate feeble-minded child.

In short, inheritance stood as the crucial issue (indeed as the driving force behind all eugenics). For if measured mental deficiency arose from malnourishment, either of body or mind, and not from tainted genes, then how could sterilization be justified? If decent food, upbringing, medical care, and education might make a worthy citizen of Carrie Buck's daughter, how could the State of Virginia justify the severing of Carrie's Fallopian tubes against her will? (Some forms of mental deficiency are passed by inheritance in family lines, but most are not—a scarcely surprising conclusion when we consider the thousand shocks that beset us all during our lives, from abnormalities in embryonic growth to traumas of birth, malnourishment, rejection, and poverty. In any case, no fair-minded person today would credit Laughlin's social criteria for the identification of hereditary deficiency—ne'er-do-wells, the homeless, tramps, and paupers—although we shall soon see that Carrie Buck was committed on these grounds.)

When Carrie Buck's case emerged as the crucial test of Virginia's law, the chief honchos of eugenics understood that the time had come to put up or shut up on the crucial issue of inheritance. Thus, the Eugenics Record Office sent Arthur H. Estabrook, their crack fieldworker, to Virginia for a "scientific" study of the case. Harry Laughlin himself provided a deposition, and his brief for inheritance was presented at the local trial that affirmed Virginia's law and later worked its way to the Supreme Court as *Buck v. Bell*.

Laughlin made two major points to the court. First, that Carrie Buck and her mother, Emma Buck, were feebleminded by the Stanford-Binet test of IQ then in its own infancy. Carrie scored a mental age of nine years, Emma of seven years and eleven months. (These figures ranked them technically as "imbeciles" by definitions of the day, hence Holmes's later choice of words—though his infamous line is often misquoted as "three generations of idiots." Imbeciles displayed a mental age of six to nine years; idiots performed worse, morons better, to round out the old nomenclature of mental deficiency.) Second, that most feeblemindedness resides ineluctably in the genes, and that Carrie Buck surely belonged with this majority. Laughlin reported:

Generally feeble-mindedness is caused by the inheritance of degenerate qualities; but sometimes it might be caused by environmental factors which are not hereditary. In the case given, the evidence points strongly toward the feeble-mindedness and moral delinquency of Carrie Buck being due, primarily, to inheritance and not to environment.

Carrie Buck's daughter was then, and has always been, the pivotal figure of this painful case. I noted in beginning this essay that we tend (often at our peril) to regard two as potential accident and three as an established pattern. The supposed imbecility of Emma and Carrie might have been an unfortunate coincidence, but the diagnosis of similar deficiency for Vivian Buck (made by a social worker, as we shall see, when Vivian was but six months old) tipped the balance in Laughlin's favor and led Holmes to declare the Buck lineage inherently corrupt by deficient heredity. Vivian sealed the pattern—*three* generations of imbeciles are enough. Besides, had Carrie not given illegitimate birth to Vivian, the issue (in both senses) would never have emerged.

Oliver Wendell Holmes viewed his work with pride. The man so renowned for his principle of judicial restraint, who had proclaimed that freedom must not be curtailed without "clear and present danger"—without the equivalent of falsely yelling "fire" in a crowded theater—wrote of his judgment in *Buck v. Bell:* "I felt that I was getting near the first principle of real reform."

And so *Buck v. Bell* remained for fifty years, a footnote to a moment of American history perhaps best forgotten. Then, in 1980, it reemerged to prick our collective conscience, when Dr. K. Ray Nelson, then director of the Lynchburg Hospital where Carrie Buck had been sterilized, researched the records of his institution and discovered that more than 4,000 sterilizations had been performed, the last as late as 1972. He also found Carrie Buck, alive and well near Charlottesville, and her sister Doris, covertly sterilized under the same law (she was told that her operation was for appendicitis), and now, with fierce dignity, dejected and bitter because she had wanted a child more than anything else in her life and had finally, in her old age, learned why she had never conceived.

As scholars and reporters visited Carrie Buck and her sister, what a few experts had known all along became abundantly clear to everyone. Carrie Buck was a woman of obviously normal intelligence. For example, Paul A. Lombardo of the School of Law at the University of Virginia, and a leading scholar of *Buck v. Bell,* wrote in a letter to me:

As for Carrie, when I met her she was reading newspapers daily and joining a more literate friend to assist at regular bouts with the crossword puzzles. She was not a sophisticated woman, and lacked social graces, but mental health professionals who examined her in later life confirmed my impressions that she was neither mentally ill nor retarded.

On what evidence, then, was Carrie Buck consigned to the State Colony for Epileptics and Feeble-Minded on January 23, 1924? I have seen the text of her commitment hearing; it is, to say the least, cursory and contradictory. Beyond the bald and undocumented say-so of her foster parents, and her own brief appearance before a commission of two doctors and a justice of the peace, no evidence was presented. Even the crude and early Stanford-Binet test, so fatally flawed as a measure of innate worth . . . but at least clothed with the aura of quantitative respectability, had not yet been applied.

When we understand why Carrie Buck was committed in January 1924, we can finally comprehend the hidden meaning of her case and its message for us today. The silent key, again as from the first, is her daughter Vivian, born on March 28, 1924, and then but an evident bump on her belly. Carrie Buck was one of several illegitimate children borne by her mother, Emma. She grew up with foster parents, J. T. and Alice Dobbs, and continued to live with them as an adult, helping out with chores around the house. She was raped by a relative of her foster parents, then blamed for the resulting pregnancy. Almost surely, she was (as they used to say) committed to hide her shame (and her rapist's identity), not because enlightened science had just discovered her true mental status. In short, she was sent away to have her baby. Her case never was about mental deficiency; Carrie Buck was persecuted for supposed sexual immorality and social deviance. The annals of her trial and hearing reek with the contempt of the well-off and well-bred for poor people of "loose morals." Who really cared whether Vivian was a baby of normal intelligence; she was the illegitimate child of an illegitimate woman. Two generations of bastards are enough. Harry Laughlin began his "family history" of the Bucks by writing: "These people belong to the shiftless, ignorant and worthless class of anti-social whites of the South."

We know little of Emma Buck and her life, but we have no more reason to suspect her than her daughter Carrie of true mental deficiency. Their supposed deviance was social and sexual; the charge of imbecility was a cover-up, Mr. Justice Holmes notwithstanding.

We come then to the crux of the case, Carrie's daughter, Vivian. What evidence was ever adduced for her mental deficiency? This and only this: At the original trial in late 1924, when Vivian Buck was seven months old, a Miss Wilhelm, social worker for the Red Cross, appeared before the court. She began by stating honestly the true reason for Carrie Buck's commitment:

> Mr. Dobbs, who had charge of the girl, had taken her when a small child, had reported to Miss Duke [the temporary secretary of Public Welfare for Albemarle County] that the girl was pregnant and that he wanted to have her committed somewhere — to have her sent to some institution.

Miss Wilhelm then rendered her judgment of Vivian Buck by comparing her with the normal granddaughter of Mrs. Dobbs, born just three days earlier:

> It is difficult to judge probabilities of a child as young as that, but it seems to me not quite a normal baby. In its appearance — I should say that perhaps my knowledge of the mother may prejudice me in that regard, but I saw the child at the same time as Mrs. Dobbs' daughter's baby, which is only three days older than this one, and there is a very decided difference in the development of the babies. That was about two weeks ago. There is a look about it that is not quite normal, but just what it is, I can't tell.

This short testimony, and nothing else, formed all the evidence for the crucial third generation of imbeciles. Cross-examination revealed that neither Vivian nor the Dobbs grandchild could walk or talk, and that "Mrs. Dobbs' daughter's baby is a very responsive baby. When you play with it or try to attract its attention — it is a baby that you can play with. The other baby is not. It seems very apathetic and not responsive." Miss Wilhelm then urged Carrie Buck's sterilization: "I think," she said, "it would at least prevent the propagation of her kind." Several years later, Miss Wilhelm denied that she had ever examined Vivian or deemed the child feebleminded.

Unfortunately, Vivian died at age eight of "enteric colitis" (as recorded on her death certificate), an ambiguous diagnosis that could mean many things but may well indicate that she fell victim to one of the preventable childhood diseases of poverty (a grim reminder of the real subject in *Buck v. Bell*). She is therefore mute as a witness in our reassessment of her famous case.

When *Buck v. Bell* resurfaced in 1980, it immediately struck me that Vivian's case was crucial and that evidence for the mental status of a child who died at age eight might best be found in report cards. I have therefore been trying to track down Vivian Buck's school records for the past four years and have finally succeeded. (They were supplied to me by Dr. Paul A. Lombardo, who also sent other documents, including Miss Wilhelm's testimony, and spent several hours answering my questions by mail and Lord knows how much time playing successful detective in re Vivian's school records. I have never met Dr. Lombardo; he did all this work for kindness, collegiality, and love of the game of knowledge, not for expected reward or even requested acknowledgment. In a profession — academics — so often marred by pettiness and silly squabbling over meaningless priorities, this generosity must be recorded and celebrated as a sign of how things can and should be.)

Vivian Buck was adopted by the Dobbs family, who had raised (but later sent away) her mother, Carrie. As Vivian Alice Elaine Dobbs, she attended the Venable Public Elementary School of Charlottesville for four terms, from September 1930 until May 1932, a month before her death. She was a perfectly normal, quite average student, neither particularly outstanding nor much troubled. In those days before grade inflation, when C meant "good, 81–87" (as defined on her report card) rather than barely scraping by, Vivian Dobbs received A's and B's for deportment and C's for all academic subjects but mathematics (which was always difficult for her, and where she scored D) during her first term in Grade 1A, from September 1930 to January 1931. She improved during her second term in 1B, meriting an A in deportment, C in mathematics, and B in all other academic subjects; she was placed on the honor roll in April 1931. Promoted to 2A, she had trouble during the fall term of 1931, failing mathematics and spelling but receiving A in deportment, B in reading, and C in writing and English. She was "retained in 2A" for the next term — or "left back" as we used to say, and scarcely a sign of imbecility as I remember all my buddies who suffered a similar fate. In any case, she again did well in her final term, with B in deportment, reading, and spelling, and C in writing, English, and mathematics during her last month in school. This daughter of "lewd and immoral" women excelled in deportment and performed adequately, although not brilliantly, in her academic subjects.

In short, we can only agree with the conclusion that Dr. Lombardo has reached in his research on *Buck v. Bell* — there were no imbeciles, not a one, among the three generations of Bucks. I don't know that such correction of cruel but forgotten errors of history counts for much, but I find it both symbolic and satisfying to learn that forced eugenic sterilization, a procedure of such dubious morality, earned its official justification (and won its most quoted line of rhetoric) on a patent falsehood.

Carrie Buck died last year. By a quirk of fate, and not by memory or design, she was buried just a few steps from her only daughter's grave. In the umpteenth and ultimate verse of a favorite old ballad, a rose and a brier — the sweet and the bitter — emerge from the tombs of Barbara Allen and her lover, twining about each other in the union of death. May Carrie and Vivian, victims in different ways and in the flower of youth, rest together in peace.

ROBERT JAY LIFTON

Sterilization and the Nazi Biomedical Vision

The Führer holds the cleansing of the medical profession far more important than, for example, that of the bureaucracy, since in his opinion the duty of the physician is or should be one of racial leadership.

— MARTIN BORMANN

The völkisch *state must see to it that only the healthy beget children. . . . Here the state must act as the guardian of a millennial future. . . . It must put the most modern medical means in the service of this knowledge. It must declare unfit for propagation all who are in any way visibly sick or who have inherited a disease and can therefore pass it on.*

— ADOLF HITLER

FIRST STEPS: POLICIES AND THE COURTS

Only in Nazi Germany was sterilization a forerunner of mass murder. Programs of coercive sterilization were not peculiar to Nazi Germany. They have existed in much of the Western world, including the United States, which has a history of coercive and sometimes illegal sterilization applied mostly to the underclass of our society. It was in the United States that a relatively simple form of vasectomy was developed at a penal institution around the turn of the century. This procedure, together with a rising interest in eugenics, led, by 1920, to the enactment of laws in twenty-five states providing for compulsory sterilization of the criminally insane and other people considered genetically inferior.

No wonder that Fritz Lenz, a German physician-geneticist advocate of sterilization (later a leading ideologue in the Nazi program of "racial hygiene"), could, in 1923, berate his countrymen for their backwardness in the domain of sterilization as compared with the United States. Lenz complained that provisions in the Weimar Constitution (prohibiting the infliction of bodily alterations on human beings) prevented widespread use of vasectomy techniques; that Germany had nothing to match the eugenics research institutions in England and the United States (for instance, that at Cold Spring Harbor, New York, led by Charles B. Davenport and funded by the Carnegie Institution in Washington and by Mary Harriman); and that Germany had no equivalent to the American laws prohibiting marriage both for people suffering from such conditions as epilepsy or mental retardation, and between people of different races. Lenz criticized America only for focusing too generally on preserving the "white race" instead of specifically on the "Nordic race" — yet was convinced that "the next round in the thousand year fight for the life of the Nordic race will probably be fought in America."[1]* That single reservation suggests the early German focus on a specific racial entity, the "Nordic" or "Aryan race," however unsupported by existing knowledge.

There had been plenty of racial-eugenic passion in the United States, impulses to sterilize large numbers of criminals and mental patients out of fear of "national degeneration" and of threat to the health of "the civilized

*Lenz did not at this point infer anti-Semitism from his belief in racial differences. Citing him, among others, George L. Mosse has argued that "there is no warrant for the claim to see in the . . . doctrine of 'racial biology and hygiene' an immediate forerunner of the Nazi policy against the Jews."[2] But once the Jews came to be viewed as a race, the connection was readily made.

races," who were seen to be "biologically plunging downward." Associated with the American eugenics movement was a biomedical vision whose extent is suggested by the following quotation from a 1923 book by A. E. Wiggam: "The first warning which biology gives to statesmanship is that the advanced races of mankind are going backward; . . . that civilization, as you have so far administered it, is self-destructive; that civilization always destroys the man that builds it; that your vast efforts to improve man's lot, instead of improving man, are hastening the hour of his destruction."[3]*

(A clear distinction must be made between genetics and eugenics. Genetics was, and is, a legitimate science, though one with limited development at the time [it began as a science with the recognition of Mendel's laws in 1900]; its principles were crudely, often falsely, applied by the Nazis. "Eugenics" is a term coined by Francis Galton in 1883 to denote the principle of strengthening a biological group on the basis of ostensible hereditary worth; despite its evolutionary claims and later reference to genetic laws, eugenics has no scientific standing.)

But the German version of eugenics had a characteristic tone of romantic excess, as in Lenz's earlier (1917) declaration, in a thesis written for his professor, Alfred Ploetz (a social-Darwinist and the founder, in 1904, of the German Society for Racial Hygiene), that "race was the criterion of value" and "the State is not there to see that the individual gets his rights, but to serve the race." Lenz understood his advocacy to be one of "organic socialism" and feared that, without a radical eugenics project, "our [Nordic] race is doomed to extinction."[5]

For Germans like Lenz in the 1920s, establishing widespread compulsory sterilization became a sacred mission — a mission that led them to embrace National Socialism, with its similar commitment. While American and British advocates of eugenics sometimes approached this German romantic excess, the political systems in the two countries allowed for open criticism and for legal redress. In Britain there was continual legal resistance to coercive sterilization; and in the United States, legal questions could be raised concerning individual rights and limited knowledge about heredity, which eventually led to the rescinding or inactivation of sterilization laws in the states where they had been passed.* In Nazi Germany, on the other hand, the genetic romanticism of an extreme biomedical vision combined with a totalistic political structure to enable the nation to carry out relentlessly, and without legal interference, a more extensive program of compulsory sterilization than had ever previously been attempted. Indeed, the entire Nazi regime was built on a biomedical vision that *required* the kind of racial purification that would progress from sterilization to extensive killing.†

As early as his publication of *Mein Kampf* between 1924 and 1926, Hitler had declared the sacred racial mission of the German people to be "assembling and preserving the most valuable stocks of basic racial elements [and] . . . slowly and surely raising them to a dominant position." He was specific about the necessity for sterilization ("*the most modern medical means*") on behalf of an immortalizing vision of the state-mediated race ("*a millennial future*"). And for him the stakes were absolute: "*If the power to fight for one's own health is no longer present, the right to live in this world of struggle ends.*"[9]

Once in power — Hitler took the oath of office as Chancellor of the Third Reich on 30 January 1933 — the Nazi regime made sterilization the first application of the biomedical imagination to this issue of collective life or death. On 22 June, Wilhelm Frick, the minister of the interior, introduced the early sterilization law with a declaration that Germany was in grave danger of *Volkstod* ("death of the people" [or "nation" or "race"]) and that harsh and sweeping measures were therefore imperative. The law was implemented three weeks later, less than six months after Hitler had become chancellor, and was extended by amendation later that year. It became basic sterilization doctrine and set the tone for the regime's medicalized approach to "life unworthy of

---

*In a 1932 study of the sterilization movement in the United States, J. P. Landman spoke of "alarmist eugenics" and of "over zealous and over ardent eugenicists" who "regard the socially inadequate persons, i.e., the feeble-minded, the epileptics, the mentally diseased, the blind, the deformed and the criminals as inimical to the human race . . . [because] these peoples perpetuate their deficiencies and thus threaten the quality of the ensuing generations. It should be our aim to exterminate these undesirables, they contend, since a nation must defend itself against national degeneration as much as against the external foreign enemy."[4]

*In observing Nazi sterilization policies, the *Journal of the American Medical Association* did not so much express outrage as it contrasted America's "more gradual evolution of practice and principles" regarding sterilization.[6] Ardent American sterilizers, such as Dr. Joseph S. De Jarnette of Virginia, could even complain: "The Germans are beating us at our own game."[7]

†Thus Daniel J. Kevles reports: "Within three years, German authorities had sterilized some two hundred and twenty-five thousand people, almost ten times the number so treated in the previous thirty years in America."[8]

life." Included among the "hereditarily sick" who were to be surgically sterilized were the categories of congenital feeblemindedness (now called mental deficiency), an estimated 200,000; schizophrenia, 80,000; manic depressive insanity, 20,000; epilepsy, 60,000; Huntington's chorea (a hereditary brain disorder), 600; hereditary blindness, 4,000; hereditary deafness, 16,000; grave bodily malformation, 20,000; and hereditary alcoholism, 10,000. The projected total of 410,000 was considered only preliminary, drawn mostly from people already in institutions; it was assumed that much greater numbers of people would eventually be identified and sterilized.

Special "Hereditary Health Courts" were set up to make decisions on sterilization, their composition reflecting the desired combination of medicalization and Nazi Party influence. Of the three members, two were physicians — one an administrative health officer likely to have close Party ties and the other ostensibly knowledgeable about issues of hereditary health; the third was a district judge, also likely to be close to the regime, who served as chairman and coordinator. There were also appeals courts, which made final decisions in contested cases and on which some of the regime's most recognized medical leaders served. All physicians were legally required to report to health officers anyone they encountered in their practice or elsewhere who fell into any of the preceding categories for sterilization, and also to give testimony on such matters unrestricted by the principle of patient-doctor confidentiality. Physicians also performed the surgical procedures. The entire process was backed up by law and police power.[10]

On 18 October 1935, a major ordinance regulating sterilization and the issuing of marriage licenses followed directly upon the notorious Nuremberg Laws (15 September), which prohibited marriage or any sexual contact between Jews and non-Jews. The Nuremberg lawmakers described themselves as "permeated with the knowledge that the purity of the German blood is a precondition for the continued existence of the German people, and filled with the inflexible determination to make the German nation secure for all future time."[11]

There were revealing discussions of method. The favored surgical procedures were ligation of the vas deferens in men and of the ovarian tubes in women. Professor G. A. Wagner, director of the University of Berlin's Women's Clinic, advocated that the law provide an option for removing the entire uterus in men-

tally deficient women. His convoluted argument was based on the principle of "hereditary health": mentally deficient women, after being sterilized, were especially likely to attract the opposite sex (who need not worry about impregnating them) and therefore to develop gonorrhea, which is most resistant to treatment when it affects the uterine cervix; the men who would then contract gonorrhea from these women would, in turn, infect other women with desirable hereditary traits and render them sterile. Other medical commentators, making a less genetic and more specifically moralistic argument, favored removal of the uterus in those candidates for sterilization who showed tendencies to promiscuity.* Still more foreboding was an official edict permitting sterilization by irradiation (X rays or radium) in certain specified cases "on the basis of scientific experiments."[13] These experiments, ostensibly in the service of improving medical procedures for specific cases, were a preliminary step toward later X-ray sterilization experiments conducted extensively, harmfully, and sometimes fatally on Jewish men and women in Auschwitz and elsewhere.

Directors of institutions of various kinds had a strong impulse to sterilize in order to eliminate the possible hereditary influence of a wide variety of conditions — blindness, deafness, congenital defects, and such "crippled" states as clubfoot, harelip, and cleft palate.[14] The genetically dominated worldview demanded of physicians led to discussions of the advisability of sterilizing not only the weak and impaired but their relatives, anyone who might be a "carrier" of these defects. Not surprisingly, Fritz Lenz carried the concept farthest in suggesting the advisability of sterilizing people with only slight signs of mental disease, though he recognized that a radical application of this principle would lead to the sterilization of 20 percent of the total German population — something on the order of twenty million people![15]

In that atmosphere, humane efforts were likely to take the form of pleas for restriction and exemption: for example, the recommendation by the distinguished anti-Nazi Berlin psychiatrist Karl Bonhoeffer that people who combined hereditary defects with unusual qualities or talents should not be sterilized; and the Munich psychiatrist Dr. Oswald Bumke's recommendation

---

*There was, indeed, concern that degenerate individuals might seek sterilization to pursue "unrestrained sexual gratification."[12]

against sterilizing people who were schizoid rather than schizophrenic, along with his cautionary statement that schizophrenia itself could not be eliminated by sterilization because of the complexity of hereditary influences.[16] (The eugenics courts sometimes did make exceptions for the artistically gifted.)

But the regime discouraged qualifications and employed a rhetoric of medical emergency: "dangerous patients" and "urgent cases" were people with hereditary taints still in the prime of life. Among "urgent cases" were mentally deficient but physically healthy men and women between the ages of sixteen and forty, schizophrenic and manic-depressive patients in remission, epileptics and alcoholics under the age of fifty, etc.[17] Once a petition was heard before a sterilization court, the die was pretty well cast. More than 90 percent of petitions taken before the special courts in 1934 resulted in sterilization (though a screening process eliminated some before they got to court); and fewer than 5 percent of appeals against sterilization made to higher courts, were upheld.[18] But the principle of legality was nonetheless extremely important, and the strict secrecy surrounding court deliberations lent power and mystery to this expression of medicalized authority.

The legal structure cloaked considerable chaos and arbitrariness in criteria for sterilization (especially concerning mental conditions, which resulted in the greatest number of sterilizations) and concerning alleged hereditary factors. Inevitably, too, political considerations affected diagnoses and decisions—as was made clear by a directive from Martin Bormann, Hitler's private secretary and close associate, instructing that the moral and political behavior of a person be considered in making a diagnosis of feeblemindedness. The clear implication was that one could be quick to label "feebleminded" a person seen as hostile to the Nazis, but that one should be cautious indeed about so labeling an ideologically enthusiastic Party member. Political currents and whims also affected the project in various ways; and, despite its high priority, there were undoubtedly periods of diminished enthusiasm for sterilization. No one really knows how many people were actually sterilized; reliable estimates are generally between 200,000 and 350,000.[19]

In association with the sterilization laws, and as a further expression of racial policy, steps were taken to establish a national card index of people with heredi-

tary taints. Special research institutes for hereditary biology and racial hygiene were set up at universities—for example, the institute established by Otmar von Verschuer, a professor at Frankfurt. These institutes sought genetic information about individuals extending back over several generations, and made use of hospitals, courts, and local and national health institutions. The physician, as genetic counselor and policeman, could be the vigilant "protector of the family that is free from hereditary defects."[20] In other words, sterilization was the medical fulcrum of the Nazi biocracy.

FANATICAL GENETICS: THE ROLE OF ERNST RÜDIN

The predominant medical presence in the Nazi sterilization program was Dr. Ernst Rüdin, a Swiss-born psychiatrist of international renown. Originally a student of Emil Kraepelin, the great classical psychiatrist, Rüdin became a close associate of Alfred Ploetz in establishing the German Society for Racial Hygiene. Rüdin was an indefatigable researcher and saw as his mission the application of Mendelian laws and eugenic principles to psychiatry. A former student and associate of his told me that "the aim of his life" was to establish the genetic basis for psychiatric conditions, and that "he was not so much a fanatical Nazi as a fanatical geneticist."

But a Nazi Rüdin did become, joining the Party in 1937 at the age of sixty. From his prestigious position as director of the Research Institute for Psychiatry of the Kaiser Wilhelm Society in Munich, Rüdin worked closely with a regime whose commitment to genetic principles he applauded, and was one of the principal architects of the sterilization laws. He became a significant source of scientific legitimation for the regime's racial policies (including consultations with Hans F. K. Günther, the leading Nazi anthropologist-publicist on racial matters, whose intellectual repute was generally held to be very low). Rüdin was not involved in the direct medical killing of the "euthanasia" program; but a younger associate to whom I spoke had the impression that his teacher, though not without doubts about the program, could well have favored a version of it with careful medical control.

In a special 1943 issue of his journal, *Archiv für Rassen-und Gesellschaftsbiologie* (Archive of Racial and Social Biology), celebrating ten years of National Socialist rule, Rüdin extolled Hitler and the movement for its "decisive . . . path-breaking step toward making racial hygiene a fact among the German people . . . and inhibiting the propagation of the congenitally ill and inferior." He praised both the Nuremberg Laws for "preventing the further penetration of the German gene pool by Jewish blood," and the SS for "its ultimate goal, the creation of a special group of medically superior and healthy people of the German Nordic type."[21]

A close relative, also a physician, told me that Rüdin felt it "necessary" to write those things and, in response to my question whether he had meant them at the time, answered, "Well, half and half." While Rüdin apparently did eventually become disillusioned with the regime, he could never (according to a former colleague) bring himself to resign his positions but sought always to work from within.*

No one I spoke to thought Rüdin a cruel person; to the contrary, he was seen as decent and dedicated to his work. Yet he not only served the regime but, in his person and scientific reputation, did much to effect the medicalization of racial policies — not quite those of killing but of suppressing in specific groups the continuity of life. He also demonstrates, in extreme form, the attraction of the Nazi biomedical vision for a certain kind of biologically and genetically oriented scientist.

OPPOSITION TO STERILIZATION

There did not seem to be much opposition to sterilization. The Catholic Church disapproved of it, but avoided confronting the issue and did little more than press for the exemption of Catholic judges and doctors from enforcing the law. One judge on a Hereditary Health Appeals Court raised the interesting question of the "burden of unusual responsibility" placed on doctors required to perform operations that "serve no therapeutic purpose." But Gerhard Wagner — then the leading Nazi medical authority and a zealous advocate of sterilization — denied any such moral conflict in doctors; and a Party newspaper ran a column with the significant heading "Life or Death," which made the simple point that the life of the nation took precedence over "dogma and conflicts of conscience," and also that opposition to the government's program would be met with strong retaliation.[23]

The great majority of the doctors I interviewed told me that they approved of the sterilization laws at the time. They believed the laws to be consistent with pre-

vailing medical and genetic knowledge concerning the prevention of hereditary defects, though a few of these doctors had some hesitation about the laws' compulsory features. The doctors all stressed their absolute distinction between those sterilization policies and later "euthanasia."

Decisions about sterilization were affected by bureaucratic struggles both between doctors and lawyers and between extremely ardent and less ardent advocates of the procedure. One doctor I interviewed, Johann S., who had been a leading organizer and high-level participant in Nazi medical programs including sterilization, thought that "the law was totally messed up by the legal people." He and his medical colleagues believed strongly that "it would have been more appropriate to leave this decision [about whom and when to sterilize] to a doctors' team." While psychiatrists later emphasized their restraint, Dr. S. related incidents in which they had to be restrained from sterilizing people with relatively benign psychological difficulties such as treatable depressions. He told how even Gerhard Wagner (whom he tended to glorify) had restrained a physician-health officer with the admonition, "This is not a rabbit hunt." While Dr. S. recognized that excessive zeal was widespread, he tended to excuse it as a product of the idealism of that time: "The great enthusiasm that carried through the developments between 1933 and 1939 cannot be denied. Everybody wanted to contribute. One of the first National Socialist laws to be enacted was the law on [hereditary] health. Thus the [state] health officers demonstrated their ambition to have as many people as possible sterilized."

THE NAZIFICATION OF MEDICINE

Nazification of the medical profession — a key aspect of the transition from sterilization to direct medical killing — was achieved by a combination of ideological enthusiasm and systematic terror. An influential manual by Rudolf Ramm of the medical faculty of the University of Berlin proposed that each doctor was to be no longer merely a caretaker of the sick but was to become a "cultivator of the genes," a "physician to the *Volk*," and a "biological soldier." While Ramm harked back to traditional forms of medical idealism ("inner calling, high ethics, profound knowledge . . . sacrifice and dedication"), he favored abandoning the old "liberal-materialistic spirit" (associated especially with

---

*Rüdin's defenders later claimed that he contested the "euthanasia" program from within. This is unlikely, as efforts in 1940 of two psychiatrists to enlist Rüdin, and through him the German Psychiatric Society, for opposition to the killing met with no success. . . . Rüdin received two high awards from Hitler as the "pathfinder in the field of hereditary hygiene."[22]

the harmful influence of Jews in the profession) and acquiring instead "the idealistic *Weltanschauung* of National Socialism." Thus, the physician could carry out what Gerhard Wagner identified as the task of his Public Health Office: the "promotion and perfection of the health of the German people . . . to ensure that the people realize the full potential of their racial and genetic endowment."[24] Ramm went on to speak of "breakthroughs in biological thinking" under National Socialism that enabled medical leaders to take an important part in projects to reverse racial decay such as the Nuremberg Laws and the sterilization program. To carry these programs out properly, the individual physician must become a "genetics doctor" (*Erbarzt*). He could then become a "caretaker of the race" and a "politician of population." By following "public care" functions of preventing "bastardization through the propagation of unworthy and racially alien elements . . . and maintaining and increasing those of sound heredity," he could attain the national goal of "keeping our blood pure."[25]

Ramm also discussed the virtues of sterilization and labeled "erroneous" the widespread belief that a doctor should under no circumstances take a patient's life, since for the incurably sick and insane, "euthanasia" was the most "merciful treatment" and "an obligation to the *Volk*." That obligation was always central. The physician was to be concerned with the health of the *Volk* even more than with individual disease and was to teach them to overcome the old individualistic principle of "the right to one's own body" and to embrace instead the "duty to be healthy."[26] Thus, Johann S. spoke to me with pride about the principle of being "doctor to the *Volkskörper* ['national body' or 'people's body']" and of "our duty . . . to the collectivity."

Ramm's manual also specified that a doctor was to be a biological militant, "an alert biological soldier" living under "the great idea of the National Socialist biological state structure." . . . For it claimed that "National Socialism, unlike any other political philosophy or Party program, is in accord with the natural history and biology of man."[27]

Physicians could thrill to that message. Dr. S., for instance, described joining the Party immediately after hearing Deputy Party Leader Rudolf Hess say, at a mass meeting in 1934, "National Socialism is nothing but applied biology." And in his work of Nazi medical organizing, this doctor saw himself as primarily

spreading a biological message: "We wanted to put into effect the laws of life, which are biological laws." His medical faction was disdainful of any politics that did not follow that principle: "We understood National Socialism from the biological side — we introduced biological considerations into [Party] policies." He stressed the conviction that physicians alone possess the necessary combination of theoretical knowledge and direct human experience to serve as the authentic biological evangelists: "Every practitioner has much more knowledge about biology than a philosopher or what have you, because he has seen it."

At the same time, it was claimed that the desired identity of the Nazi physician evolved naturally from medical tradition — a tradition that now required "Germanizing" and "eugenicizing." One lavishly illustrated volume by two medical historians was entitled *The Face of the Germanic Doctor over Four Centuries*. It featured Paracelsus, the great sixteenth-century Swiss-German physician-alchemist, and praised him for both his scientific empiricism and his nationalism. He was quoted as saying, "Each country developed its own sickness, medicine, and its own doctor." More recent German scientists, especially Carl Correns who did pioneering work in plant genetics, were hailed as having "created the foundation for the eugenic and racial-biological measures of the National Socialist people's state." The authors' SS ranks are included;* and the introduction by Ernst Robert von Grawitz, chief physician of the SS, puts forward the concept of the physician, past and present, as the "protector of life" who "knows himself to be deeply obligated to the future of our *Volk*."[28]†

Another such introduction to a volume on medical ethics was written by Joachim Mrugowsky, a high-ranking SS doctor who became head of the Hygienic Institute, which was responsible for maintaining and distributing the Zyklon-B gas used at Auschwitz. Mrugowsky was put to death at Nuremberg in 1948 for his extensive involvement in fatal medical experiments. The book he introduced had been written a hundred years earlier by Christoph Wilhelm Hufeland, one of

---

*The SS (*Schutzstaffel,* or defense squadron) began as Hitler's personal guard unit. Particularly after 1929, under the control of Heinrich Himmler, it advertised itself as an élite corps whose members fit the ideal Aryan model. As such, it attracted considerable support from the aristocracy and professional classes, including physicians. . . .

†The concept of "Germanic" physicians included Austrians, Dutch, Belgians, and Scandinavians.

Germany's great modern physician-humanists. In his introduction, Mrugowsky focused upon the doctor's function as "the priest of the holy flame of life" (in Hufeland's words), and on the "art of healing" as the doctor's "divine mission." Partially anticipating his own future, he spoke of the National Socialist breakdown of the distinction between research and healing, since the results of the work of the researcher are for the benefit of the *Volk*.[29]

Inevitably, the Nazi medical ideal went back to Hippocrates and related itself to the Hippocratic oath. The claim was that medicine had been "despiritualized" mainly by what Gerhard Wagner identified as the "mechanically oriented spirit" of Jewish teachers. There was thus a need to "return to the ethics and high moral status of an earlier generation . . . which stood on [the] solid philosophical ground" of the Hippocratic oath.[30] Finally, the *Reichsführer* of the SS and overall head of the Nazi police system, Heinrich Himmler himself embraced Hippocrates as a model for SS physicians. In a brief introduction to a series of short books for SS doctors under the overall title "Eternal Doctors," Himmler spoke of "the great Greek doctor Hippocrates," of the "unity of character and accomplishment" of his life, which "proclaims a morality, the strengths of which are still undiminished today and shall continue to determine medical action and thought in the future." The series was edited by Grawitz and possessed the ultimate imprimatur in being "authorized" by none other than Hitler himself.[31] In testimony at the Nuremberg Medical Trial, a witness referred to the Nazi embrace of Hippocratic principles as "an ironical joke of world history."[32] But this ultimate absurdity had an internal logic: the sense of recasting the medical profession — and the entire German nation — in the service of larger healing.

There was one area in which the Nazis did insist upon a clear break with medical tradition. They mounted a consistent attack upon what they viewed as exaggerated Christian compassion for the weak individual instead of tending to the health of the group, of the *Volk*. This partly Nietzschean position, as articulated by Ramm, included a rejection of the Christian principle of *caritas* or charity, and of the Church's "commandment to attend to the incurably ill person and render him medical aid unto his death."[33] The same position was expressed in the Nazi Party medical outlet *Ziel und Weg* (Aim and Road) from the time of its founding in 1931. The matter was put strongly by Dr. Arthur Guett, a high-ranking health official, who declared that

"the ill-conceived 'love of thy neighbor' has to disappear. . . . It is the supreme duty of the . . . state to grant life and livelihood only to the healthy and hereditarily sound portion of the population in order to secure . . . a hereditarily sound and racially pure folk [*Volk*] for all eternity." He added the visionary-idealistic principle that "the life of the individual has meaning only in the light of that ultimate aim."[34] The doctor, like everyone in Nazi Germany, was expected to become "hardened," to adopt what Hitler himself called the "ice-cold logic" of the necessary.

The keynote of the Nazi policy was transformation, in Ramm's words: "a change in the attitude of each and every doctor, and a spiritual and mental regeneration of the entire medical profession." The true physician, moreover, "must not only be a Party member on the outside, but rather must be convinced in his heart of hearts of the biological laws that form the center of his life." He was also to be a "preacher for these laws."[35] Dr. S. believed that Nazi medicine had achieved some of this transformation: that is, it had overcome the exaggerated stress on "technical things," reversed the prior tendency to "know only cases and not people," and "put in the foreground the questions of the psyche that had been neglected."

But the Nazis sought something more than mere psychosomatic inclusiveness or "holistic" medicine: their quest had the quality of *biological and medical mysticism*. Mrugowsky, for instance, wrote, in the introduction mentioned earlier, that "today the [German] *Volk* is holy to us." Of the physician's relationship to the *Volk*, or "community of fate," Mrugowsky added that "only in the art of healing does he find the myth of life."[36] Other writers had viewed the Third Reich as "immanent in all German history, which strives toward that moment when the *Volk* becomes the vessel of God."[37] But in the vision I am describing, the physician-biologists saw themselves as the core of the mystical body of the *Volk*.

There had to develop, as one Nazi doctor put it, "a totality of the physicians' community, with physicians having total dedication to the *Volk*." This doctor's term for his biological mysticism was "biological socialism." The Nazis, he insisted, had been able to bring together nationalism and socialism because of their "recognition of the natural phenomena of life." Thus, "for the first time, the mind begins to understand that there are powerful forces over it which it must acknowledge"; that "the human being becomes . . . a working member in the kingdom of the living; and that his powers will be fulfilled when working within the balanced interplay of natural forces." We may say that mysticism, especially communal mysticism, was given a biological and medical face.

NOTES

(The numbers in brackets refer to the original, complete citation of a particular reference in each chapter. The dates in brackets denote original publication of a title.)

1. Fritz Lenz, *Menschliche Auslese and Rassenhygiene,* vol. II of Erwin Bauer, Eugen Fischer, and Lenz, *Grundriss der menschlichen Erblichkeitslehre und Rassenhygiene* (Munich: J. F. Lehmanns Verlag, 1923), p. 147. See the expanded version of this joint work's third (1927) edition, especially for American readers: *Human Heredity* (New York: Macmillan, 1931). On Davenport and Cold Spring Harbor, see Daniel J. Kevles, *In the Name of Eugenics: Genetics and the Uses of Human Heredity* (New York: Alfred A. Knopf, 1985), pp. 44–56.

2. George L. Mosse, *Toward the Final Solution: A History of European Racism* (New York: Harper & Row, 1978), p. 81.

3. Albert Edward Wiggam, *New Decalogue of Science* (Indianapolis: Bobbs-Merrill, 1923), pp. 25–26.

4. J[acob] P. Landman, *Human Sterilization: The History of the Sexual Sterilization Movement* (New York: Macmillan, 1932), pp. 4–5.

5. Helmut Krausnick, "The Persecution of the Jews," in Krausnick et al., *Anatomy of the SS State* (New York: Walker, 1968 [1965]), pp. 16–17.

6. "Human Sterilization in Germany and the United States," *JAMA [Journal of the American Medical Association]* 102 (1934): 1501–02; see Kevles, *Eugenics* [1], pp. 113–17.

7. Kevles, *Eugenics* [1], p. 116.

8. Ibid., p. 117.

9. Adolf Hitler, *Mein Kampf* (Boston: Houghton Mifflin, 1943 [1925–26]), pp. 403–04, 257, respectively.

10. *JAMA* 101 (1933):866–67; 102 (1934):630–31, 1501; 103 (1934):849–50. W. W. Peter, "Germany's Sterilization Program," *American Journal of Public Health* 24 (1934):187.

11. *JAMA* 105 (1935):1999.

12. *JAMA* 104 (1935):2109 (Wagner); 101 (1933):867; 106 (1936):1582.

13. *JAMA* 106 (1936):1582.

14. *JAMA* 103 (1934):766–67, 850; 106 (1936):58, 308–09.

15. *JAMA* 104 (1935):2110.

16. *JAMA* 102 (1934):57; 103 (1934):1164; 104 (1935):2110.

17. *JAMA* 104 (1935):1183.

18. *JAMA* 105 (1935):1051.

19. W[alter] von Baeyer, "Die Bestätigung der NS-Ideologie in der Medizin unter besonderer Berücksichtgung der Euthanasie," *Universitätstage* 5 (1966):64; Ernst Klee, *"Euthanasie" im NS-Staat: Die "Vernichtung lebensunwerten Lebens"* (Frankfurt/M.: S. Fischer, 1983), p. 86. Much of my manuscript had been completed when this important book appeared, but I have used it to confirm and supplement information from other sources. Another important recent study is Gisela Bock, "Racism and Sexism in Nazi Germany: Motherhood, Compulsory Sterilization and the State," in *When Biology Became Destiny: Women in Weimar and Nazi Germany,* Renate Bridenthal, Atina Grossmann, and Marion Kaplan, eds. (New York: Monthly Review, 1985), pp. 271–96.

20. *JAMA* 105 (1935):1052–53.

21. Ernst Rüdin, "Zehn Jahre nationalsozialistischer Staat," *Archiv für Rassen- und Gesellschaftsbiologie* 36 (1942):321.

22. Robert Wistrich, *Who's Who in Nazi Germany* (New York: Macmillan, 1982), p. 261. See also B. Schultz, "Ernst Rüdin," *Archiv für Psychiatrie und Zeitschrift für Neurologie* 190 (1953):189–95.

23. Judge Goetz and Wagner quoted in *JAMA* 106 (1936):1582; party paper in *JAMA* 105 (1935):1051.

24. Rudolf Ramm, *Ärztliche Rechts- und Standeskunde: Der Arzt als Gesundheitserzieher,* 2d. rev. ed. (Berlin: W. deGruyter, 1943), pp. iv, 43, 79–80.

25. Ibid., pp. 101, 135.

26. Ibid., pp. 154–56.

27. Ibid. See Kurt Blome, *Arzt im Kampf: Erlebnisse and Gedanken* (Leipzig: J. A. Barth, 1942).

28. Bernward J. Gottlieb and Alexander Berg, *Das Antlitz des Germanischen Arztes in vier Jahrhunderten* (Berlin: Rembrandt-Verlag, 1942), pp. 3, 51–52.

29. Joachim Mrugowsky, "Einleitung," Christoph Wilhelm Hufeland, *Das ärztliche Ethos: Christoph Wilhelm Hufelands Vermächtnis einer fünfzigjährigen Erfahrung* (Munich and Berlin: J. F. Lehmann, 1939), pp. 14–15, 22; see pp. 7–40.

30. Hanns Löhr, *Über die Stellung und Bedeutung der Heilkunde im nationalsozialistischen Staate* (1935), quoted in George L. Mosse, ed., *Nazi Culture: Intellectual, Cultural and Social Life in the Third Reich* (New York: Grosset & Dunlap, 1968), p. 229.

31. Ernst Grawitz, ed., *Hippokrates: Gedanken ärztlicher Ethik aus dem Corpus Hippocraticum,* vol. I: *Ewiges Arzttum* (Prague, Amsterdam, Berlin, and Vienna: Volk und Reich Verlag, 1942), p. 5.

32. Werner Leibbrandt, 27 January 1947, *Nuremberg Medical Case,* vol. II, p. 81.

33. Ramm, *Ärztliche Standeskunde* [24], p. 19. On the Nazis' related elevation of pain, see Michael H. Kater, "Medizinische Fakultäten and Medizinstudenten: Eine Skizze," in Fridolf Kudlien, ed., *Ärzte im Nationalsozialismus* (Cologne: Kiepenheuer & Witsch, 1985), p. 93.

34. *Nuremberg Medical Case* [32], vol. I, p. 58.

35. Ramm, *Ärztliche Standeskunde* [24], pp. 80–83.

36. Mrugowsky, "Einleitung" [29], pp. 9–10, 14.

37. George L. Mosse, *Masses and Man: Nationalist and Fascist Perceptions of Reality* (New York: Fertig, 1980), p. 81.

VERONICA PEARSON

Population Policy and Eugenics in China

Dismay has been expressed by the international psychiatric community at the Chinese government's intention of implementing a eugenicist birth policy through new legislation. Western psychiatrists cannot forget that in 1933, the German government passed the *Law for the Prevention of Offspring with Hereditary Diseases,* which was defined to include those with schizophrenia, manic-depression and learning disability. Between 1934 and 1939 350,000 compulsory sterilisations were carried out. This was followed by a euthanasia programme, resulting in the deaths of at least 70,000 mentally ill people between 1939 and 1941 (Meyer, 1988). These events are seared into the collective consciousness of Western psychiatrists, accompanied by a determination that it will never happen again. Yet from the Chinese perspective, eugenics is simply a matter of quality control, devoid of the moral implications that are so strong for those with a Western professional background.

From the Chinese viewpoint their population is dangerously large (nearly 1.2 billion, around 22% of the world's population with only 7% of the world's arable land) and too many of these people have a handicap. Based on the first ever national survey of people with a disability carried out in 1987 (Li, 1988), the projected figure is 51.64 million (only slightly less than the population of the UK). Of these, 10.17 million were intellectually impaired and 1.94 million were seriously mentally ill (although this may be an underestimate).

Reprinted with the permission of the publisher from *British Journal of Psychiatry* 167 (July 1995), 1–4. Copyright © 1995 by the Royal College of Psychiatrists.

*Editor's note: An English-language paraphrase of this law is available in *International Digest of Health Legislation* 46(1):1995; 39–42.

The Minister of Public Health announced a draft Eugenics Law at the Standing Committee of the fifth meeting of the National People's Congress in December 1993. It caused little stir in China but received a good deal of adverse publicity in the Western press. The aim is to 'prevent new births of inferior quality', particularly in underdeveloped and economically poor areas. Restrictions on marriage and childbirth are to apply to those with hereditary, venereal or reproductive ailments, severe psychoses or contagious diseases. The minister pointed out that as well as 10 million people with a learning disability, China also had another 10 million persons disabled from birth 'who should have been prevented through better controls'. Having become aware of the uproar this announcement caused in the West, the English name of the draft was changed to the Maternal and Infant Health Care Law, but the Chinese name remains unchanged. The law was promulgated in October 1994 and will take effect in June 1995.*

The law requires doctors to advise a couple to terminate a pregnancy if a hereditary disease is liable to result in a birth of a seriously sick or disabled baby, or if continuing the pregnancy would jeopardise the mother's life. The law states that abortions may only be carried out under this legislation with the agreement of the pregnant woman or her guardian (Article 19). With China's record in coercive birth control measures, many people find it hard to accept that assurance.

HISTORICAL CONTINUITIES

This concern with eugenics has been a continuing theme in marriage legislation since the Communists began issuing regulations in the areas of China they controlled in the 1930s and '40s (Meijer, 1971). The National Marriage Law of 1950 prohibited marriage if one of the parties suffered a 'serious illness' such as venereal disease, mental illness, leprosy.

The 1981 Marriage Law, article 6(b) states:

Marriage is not permitted in the following circumstances . . . Where one party is suffering from leprosy, a cure not having been effected, or from any other disease which is regarded by medical science as rendering a person unfit for marriage.

Clearly this leaves a great deal of space for individual interpretation by different provinces and municipalities. An authoritative commentary on the Marriage Law states that the law is not clear and that the relevant judicial and legislative organs have not yet issued any interpretations (Ren, 1988). Based on judicial practice, the two most important illnesses covered by article 6(b) are severe mental illness and mental retardation. The reasons given are that (a) severe mental illness usually develops in youth, that (b) people suffering from it cannot carry out their marital, parental, or civic responsibilities and (c) it is hereditary.

In 1986, the Ministry of Public Health and the Ministry of Civil Affairs issued a *Circular Concerning Pre-marital Medical Check-ups* (Zhi, 1991). This states that the parties concerned can only complete the marriage registration formalities after they have undergone a medical examination, although there is the proviso that "since conditions vary from place to place, no fixed time for implementing the circular has been laid down".

The circular has three categories affecting marriage and childbirth. Marriage is prohibited between close relatives and between people who have very low intelligence. Marriage is to be postponed when one or both parties are suffering from schizophrenia, manic-depression or other psychoses. Marriage is permitted but childbirth forbidden

. . . where either party whose inherited disease, such as schizophrenia, manic-depressive psychosis, or other types of psychosis as well as congenital heart disease is in a stable condition. (Zhi, 1991, p. 18)

The aim of the policy is quite clear:

With the rapid development of eugenics, scientific research work into eugenics and healthier births broke new ground, and health care work in urban and rural areas greatly improved, thereby enabling eugenics to guide marriage and childbirth. (Zhi, 1991, p. 18)

It is often the practice for the Chinese government to have a 'trial run' of proposed legislation by implementing regulations, or trying out legislation in a few areas first. This seems to be the case with this circular. Provisions of the *Gansu People's Congress Concerning Prohibiting Reproduction by Intellectually Impaired Persons* also seem to have been a testing ground for national legislation. Gansu may have been chosen because it is one of the poorest and most backward of China's provinces, and is said to have an unusually large population of people with a learning disability. There are reputed to be some villages where there is virtually no one with a normal intelligence. Iodine deficiency disorder may well be a partial explanation of the problem in this area.

Gansu's rules are tougher than the Ministries of Public Health and Civil Affairs' circular. They categorically state that intellectually impaired persons considering marriage must be sterilised. They also state that an intellectually impaired person who is already married but pregnant must have an abortion (with no provisos concerning the stage of the pregnancy). Officials involved in this process are exhorted "to do a good job". If they do not and intellectually impaired persons are allowed to reproduce, the officials shall be administratively punished (demoted, promotion delayed, severely criticised) and fined; likewise guardians. It has been reported that 1000 women were sterilised during the first year after these regulations were implemented (*Inter Press Service,* February 7, 1994). Contraception does not seem to have been considered.

EUGENICS AND BIRTH CONTROL

For the Chinese, eugenics is intimately bound up with their very rigorous population control programme. The first goal of this programme is fewer but healthier babies with the prevention of birth and genetic defects (Peng, 1994). This policy really began to bite at the beginning of the 1980s.

At present, we advocate one child for every couple. How to ensure that the one and only child born to a couple is healthy and intelligent has become a common concern. Therefore, spreading the knowledge of eugenics and adopting practical measures to improve the hereditary qualities of our children has assumed a more pressing significance. ('Medical Experts', Foreign Broadcast Information Service Daily Report, 1980, quoted in Banister, 1987, p. 222)

In 1983 an exhibition of severely deformed foetuses was held in Beijing. A spokesman for the Family Planning Commission was reported as saying that "our aim is the gradual preparation of public opinion for a law on eugenics" (*South China Morning Post,* 2 November 1983). The same report recalled the *People's Daily* causing a sensation in 1980 when it published an article that gave a list of people who should not be allowed to breed, including imbeciles, haemophiliacs and the colour blind, all of whom, it was claimed, were unproductive and a danger to society.

To the Western observer this policy is misguided on two grounds. First, it is morally unacceptable. Second, it is not effective. At least one of the illnesses mentioned in the 1981 Marriage Law, leprosy, is largely unrelated to heredity. The policy assumes that we know infinitely more than we do about the hereditability of mental retardation, schizophrenia and manic-depressive psychosis. Many instances of learning disability are not hereditable, such as those caused by perinatal trauma or iodine deficiency disorder. Indeed, the government estimates that 80% of intellectual impairment in China is caused by the latter (*Beijing Review,* 11 November 1993). Thus stopping such people from having babies, logically, is not about heredity but about concerns as to who will look after the baby. Child-rearing is generally a family affair in China. Any resulting child would be most unlikely to end up as a charge upon the state. Indeed, from the family's point of view, if the learning disabled or mentally ill adult does not have a child then who will look after parents and grandparents in their old age? The majority of people do not have pensions and especially in the rural areas the issue of children to protect one from a destitute old age is extraordinarily important.

The International Pilot Project on Schizophrenia has established that the course of the illness seems to be more benign and the outcome better in developing countries and in rural areas (Jablensky, 1987; Leff, 1988). One reason for this may be the existence of greater family support. China continues to be a family oriented society where the majority of people with schizophrenia are primarily cared for by family members (Phillips, 1993; Pearson & Phillips, 1994). To the Western observer, this is a wonderful resource and great strength within the Chinese system of care. It should be preserved and strengthened, not undermined by the clumsy attempts at social engineering that eugenics represents.

There is no doubt at all that Chinese psychiatrists are very concerned about the hereditability of schizophrenia (Fang *et al.,* 1982; Liu, 1983; Xun, 1986). Some see it as a justification for restricting marriage and childbirth. Both Fang *et al* (1982) and Xun (1986) are troubled by the higher birth rate among people with schizophrenia among whom, for a variety of reasons, birth control acceptance is not high. One reason is that birth control workers are afraid of them and reluctant to approach them or mobilise them in the face of resistance, in the way that they would other members of the population. The researchers advocate the use of law to restrict marriage and childbirth for people suffering from schizophrenia and frankly advocate a policy of eugenics and compulsory sterilisation. Xun's research involved a population of 250 people with schizophrenia who were sterilised in the Xiang Tan Psychiatric Hospital in Hunan Province, between 1972 and 1983. Likewise, Fang mentions that 22% of his sample of people with schizophrenia were sterilised.

Account has to be taken of the fact that the Chinese do not necessarily share Western priorities. Autonomy, individuality, privacy, the right to have as many children as wanted are selfish values. What is encouraged and valued is concern for the greater good and an ability to fit into the group, rather than to stand out from it. Furthermore, they live in a harsher world. Many people alive in China today remember severe famine, civil war, the horrors of the Japanese occupation and the Cultural Revolution. These are not conditions that encourage a kinder, gentler view of the world. Sterilisations and abortion are already part of their lives through the one-child policy (Banister, 1987; Aird, 1990). They are not inflicted on people with a mental illness or learning disability exclusively. Such a fate is part of many people's lives.

I have never come across even one incidence of a mentally ill person being forbidden to marry and have children despite extensive experience of Chinese psychiatric hospitals. The existing regulations are largely ignored. This is admitted publicly (Liu & Jia, 1994). The reason given is that the health system is already overburdened and the resources are not there to perform the necessary examinations. Privately, Chinese psychiatrists tell me that they do not have the heart for such work. To forbid marriage and children, on a personal level as opposed to on paper, is just too cruel. This situation might change because of the national law, but to implement it the government would have to increase the resources available to the health services (currently 3.2% of GDP

(World Bank, 1992)). Based on current performance (Pearson, 1995) that does not seem very likely.

Chinese psychiatrists are very concerned to be seen as scientific. If a procedure, technique or idea is described as such, it is high praise indeed. Associated with this is their very biological orientation towards psychiatry and the causes and treatments of disease. In my view, at least part of this is self-protection; it is much harder to turn the biological into the political.

For Western psychiatrists to argue that eugenics is morally wrong is unlikely to produce a good effect for it immediately sets up in the minds of the Chinese the spectre of cultural imperialism. They have tried to reassure us that their policies are entirely unlike Hitler's, thus there is no cause for Westerners to be troubled; they do not see the connection between what they are doing and what Hitler did. Any opposition to this law from Western countries is going to be very much more effective if it eschews the moral high ground and focuses on the fact that such a policy cannot produce the desired results; that in short, it is not scientific.

ACKNOWLEDGMENTS

I am grateful to Dr. Linda Johnson of the Faculty of Law, The University of Hong Kong for generously sharing information regarding the law in Gansu with me.

REFERENCES

AIRD, J. (1990) *Slaughter of the Innocents: Coercive Birth Control in China.* Washington, DC: The AEI Press.

BANISTER, J. (1987) *China's Changing Population.* Stanford: Stanford University Press.

FANG, Y. Z., ZHANG, L. J., GUO, B. H. *et al* (1982) A survey of the marital state and family planning behaviour of schizophrenics. *Chinese Journal of Neurology and Psychiatry,* 15, 204–206 (in Chinese).

JABLENSKY, A. (1987) Multicultural studies and the nature of schizophrenia; a review. *Journal of the Royal Society of Medicine,* 80, 162–167.

LEFF, J. (1988) *Psychiatry Around the Globe* (2d ed). London: Gaskell.

LI, R. S. (1988) General discussion on the Chinese 1987 survey of the handicapped. *Population Survey,* 4, 125–27 (in Chinese).

LIU, J. H. & JIA, J. T. (1994) *Medicine and the Law in the People's Republic of China.* Paper presented at a conference *The Taniguchi Foundation, 19th International Symposium, Division of Medical History.* September 4–10, Fuji Institute of Education and Training, Shizuoka, Japan.

LIU, X. E. (1983) A family history study of patients with psychoses, epilepsy and mental retardation. *Chinese Journal of Neurology and Psychiatry,* 16, 99–102.

MEIJER, M. J. (1971) *Marriage Law and Policy in the Chinese People's Republic.* Hong Kong: Hong Kong University Press.

MEYER, J. E. (1988) The fate of the mentally ill in Germany during the Third Reich. *Psychological Medicine,* 18, 575–81.

PEARSON, V. (1995) Health and responsibility; but whose? In *Social Change and Social Policy in Contemporary China* (eds L. Wong & S. MacPherson). Basingstoke: Avebury Press (in press).

——— & PHILLIPS, M. R. (1994) Future opportunities and challenges for the development of psychiatric rehabilitation in China. In *Psychiatric Rehabilitation in China; Models for Change in a Changing Society* (eds M. R. Phillips, V. Pearson & R. W. Wang). *British Journal of Psychiatry,* 65 (suppl. 24), 11–18.

PENG, Y. (1994) China's experience in population matters: an official statement. *Population and Development Review,* 20, 488–91.

PHILLIPS, M. R. (1993) Strategies used by Chinese families coping with schizophrenia. In *Chinese Families in the Post-Mao Era* (eds D. Davis & S. Harrell), pp. 277–306. Berkeley and Los Angeles: University of California Press.

REN, G. (1988) *A General Survey of Marriage Law.* Beijing: Chinese University of Politics and Law Press (in Chinese).

WORLD BANK (1992) *China: Long Term Issues and Options in the Health Transition.* Washington, DC: World Bank.

XUN, M. (1986) The problems of birth control in schizophrenic patients. *Chinese Journal of Neurology and Psychiatry,* 19, 335–38.

ZHI, M. (1991) Pre-marital medical check-ups. *Women of China,* 1, 18–19.

BIOLOGICAL SCIENCES CURRICULUM STUDY

The Human Genome Project

"These are exciting and challenging times for biological researchers. The wealth of information and capabilities now being generated by the various genome projects and other biological endeavors will lead over the next two decades to more insights into living systems than have been amassed in the past two millennia. Biology is truly undergoing a revolution."

—DAVID A. SMITH
(retiring director, Health Effects and Life Sciences Research Division, Office of Health and Environmental Research, DOE [Department of Energy], 19 December 1996)

• • •

WHAT IS THE HUMAN GENOME PROJECT?

The Human Genome Project [HGP] is a large, internationally coordinated effort in biological research directed at creating a series of maps of the DNA of humans and several other species, with each map providing greater detail (resolution). Figure [1] shows the rate of progress of the different aspects of the work on the human genome. The project is large in scope, time line, and funding. The U.S. Department of Energy and the National Institutes of Health (NIH) have jointly defined the project as a 15-year effort that began in 1990, with funding estimated at $3 billion. The ultimate goal is to map and sequence all of the estimated

Reprinted with the permission of the publisher from Biological Sciences Curriculum Study, *The Puzzle of Inheritance: Genetics and the Methods of Science.* (Colorado Springs, CO: BSCS, 1997), pp 8–12. Copyright © 1997 by Biological Sciences Curriculum Study.

80,000 human genes. The genetic map will be at a resolution of 2Mb, and the physical map will be at a resolution of 0.1Mb (Mb is a megabase, or 1 million nucleotides). Additional goals are to collect the human genome as clones of approximately 5kb in length and ultimately to resolve a base-by-base sequence (kb is kilobase, or 1,000 nucleotides). . . .

Detailed maps of the genomes of several other well-studied organisms also are being made. These organisms include several bacterial species (such as . . . *Escherichia coli,* yeast (*Saccharomyces cerevisiae*), nematode (*Caenorhabditis elegans*), fruit fly (*Drosophila melanogaster*), mouse (*Mus musculus*), and a flowering plant (*Arabidopsis thaliana*). By including organisms other than humans, the HGP provides a wealth of data for evolutionary research in addition to the valuable foundation of genetics information for each species studied.

WHO IS DOING THE HUMAN GENOME PROJECT?

The HGP includes a wide variety of professionals in science, education, ethics, medicine, law, engineering, computing, and mathematics. Hundreds of research laboratories contribute, and some large Human Genome Program Centers help focus and coordinate the work. Involvement of different centers changes as the project proceeds. . . . For an update, consult the DOE web site at http://www.ornl.gov/hgmis or the NIH web site at http://[www.nhgri.nih.gov].

In addition to direct efforts to map and sequence particular human chromosomes or those of model organisms, [the genome program] centers improve existing

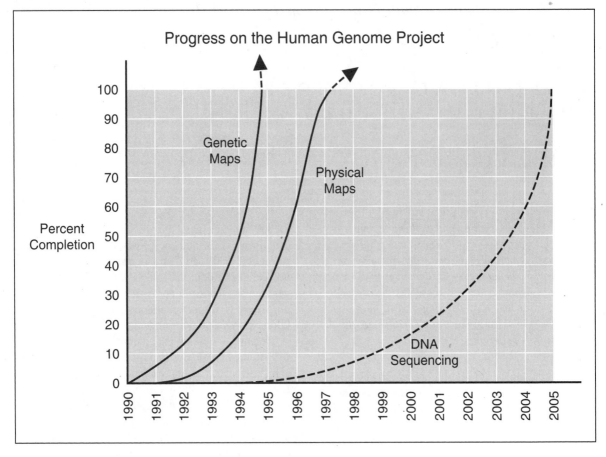

Figure [1]   Progress on the HGP: The rate of each level of inquiry is depicted.

technologies and develop new technologies to increase the speed, accuracy, and cost-effectiveness of the HGP. These centers also act to stimulate and coordinate collaboration among investigators not formally associated with the HGP. The work is not limited to the United States. The Human Genome Organization (HUGO), formed in 1988, coordinates international scientific collaboration between Canada, the United States, Italy, the United Kingdom, France, the Commonwealth of Independent States, the European Community, and Japan. The United Nations Educational, Scientific, and Cultural Organization (UNESCO) promotes the continued involvement of developing nations in genome activities and also supports international conferences and exchanges.

HOW IS THE HUMAN GENOME PROJECT RELATED TO THE NATURE OF SCIENCE?

As David Smith's quote . . . indicates, the Human Genome Project is expanding our collection of genetic data enormously. Simply mapping and sequencing the entire human genome will not, however, provide us with answers to all of our questions about genetics. Knowing the sequence of a stretch of DNA or its location on a given chromosome does *not* reveal the significance of the region. If the region encodes protein, the DNA sequence will predict accurately the corresponding amino acid sequence of the protein, but neither sequence will tell us the *biological function* of the protein in the absence of additional data. Fortunately, much is known about the biological function of various proteins, and data are accumulating rapidly. With the foundation of a detailed and organized bank of genome data, biologists can construct a more complete picture of living systems.

Although the HGP will not answer all questions about genetics, it will provide an invaluable databank. In addition, as they collect data, researchers have made and will continue to make discoveries about specific genes, the organization of genetic information, evolutionary relationships at the molecular level, and new technologies in laboratory and computer applications.

The genome map and sequence data will serve as powerful tools for future research in genetics, evolution, and medicine, in this way fueling the work of scientists in years to come.*

• • •

*Editor's note: See the Genome Issue of *Science,* published annually in October, for more detailed information about the current status of the Human Genome Project.

LEE ROWEN, GREGORY MAHAIRAS, AND LEROY HOOD

Sequencing the Human Genome

At the end of 1997, we are halfway through the time allotted for completing the Human Genome Project. The Human Genome Project aims to sequence the genomes of the human and selected model organisms, identify all of the genes, and develop the technologies required to accomplish these objectives. Significant progress has been made, particularly in identifying and mapping genes, developing a stable DNA-sequencing technology, and in building the computational tools required for the analysis of sequence data. Yet, the large-scale sequencing of the 3 billion base pairs of the human genome has barely begun (Table 1). Approximately 60 million base pairs have been analyzed to date. Of these, the longest contiguous stretch of human DNA sequence in a public database is less than 1.5 million base pairs.[1] Here we discuss today's challenges for sequencing the human genome.

WHAT HAS BEEN DONE SO FAR?

Gene Identification. The expressed genes from hundreds of different human tissues have been partially sequenced after copying the messenger RNAs into

Excerpted with the permission of the authors and the publisher from *Science* 278 (October 24, 1997), 605–07. Copyright © 1997, American Association for the Advancement of Science.

complementary DNA libraries. About 800,000 of these so-called expressed sequence tags (ESTs) are available in public databases and at various Web sites.[2] These represent perhaps 40,000 to 50,000 genes of the estimated total of 70,000 to 100,000 human genes. ESTs from a variety of model organisms are also available.

Mapping. Mapping requires the identification of unique genome markers [for example, ESTs or sequence-tagged sites (STSs)] and their localization to specific chromosomal sites. STSs are unique addresses generated by polymerase chain reaction primers that amplify

Table 1. Current State of Genome Sequence, as of September 1997.

Organism	Size (Mb)	Sequenced	Percent finished
Microbial genomes (~11)	0.6–4.2	0.6–4.2	100
E. coli	4.6	4.6	100
Yeast	13	13	100
Nematode	100	71	71
Drosophila	130	8	6
Mouse	3000	6	0.2
Human	3000	60	2

just a single chromosomal site. Three techniques have been used for marker localization: genetic mapping (generally 1- to 10-Mb resolution), fluorescence in situ hybridization (~1-Mb resolution), and radiation hybrid mapping (down to 50-kb resolution). By means of these techniques, markers have been placed on average every 200 kb across the genome.[3] Using STS landmarks to identify and order clones, researchers have constructed a framework physical map for most of the human genome from large inserts of human DNA cloned into yeast artificial chromosomes (YACs) in 1993.[4] A genetic map with more than 5000 highly polymorphic simple sequence repeats is also available.[5]

Clone Library Construction. Human chromosomes cannot be sequenced directly. Rather, human DNA must be isolated, randomly fragmented, and cloned into vectors capable of stable propagation in a suitable host such as the bacterium *Escherichia coli* or yeast. Before sequencing, clones must be selected from libraries with chromosomal markers as probes, verified for their fidelity to the genome, and ordered in a minimal-overlapping tiling path spanning a portion of a chromosome. Several cloning systems with insert sizes varying from hundreds of base pairs to megabases have been successfully developed. . . .

Large-Scale Sequencing. Beginning with a source clone, most large-scale sequencing centers use the following stops for sequence determination: randomly fragmenting the source clone into small (~1500 base pairs) pieces, subcloning the small pieces into a sequence-ready vector, sequencing 10 to 30 subclones per kilobase of the source clone,[6] and assembling the overlapping sequence reads into a contiguous multiple sequence alignment from which a consensus sequence can be inferred from the highest quality reads.

The development of the automated fluorescent sequencer in the mid-1980s made high throughput genomic sequencing possible.[7] One Perkin-Elmer Applied Biosystems 377 sequencer can produce two runs per day of sequence reads averaging 750 bases in length. Each run produces 64 reads (soon to be 96 reads). Improvements in the sequencing chemistries (better polymerases and higher sensitivity dyes) have resulted in higher quality, more accurate sequence data. Finally, more powerful computers combined with more sophis-

ticated assembly programs have facilitated the determination of a consensus sequence from a given set of sequence reads. Using current sequencing methodologies, several laboratories are now producing contiguous stretches of human sequence in the 300-kb to 1.5-Mb range.[1]

Sequence Analysis. Extensive databases of sequences obtained from expressed genes and genomic clones from hundreds of organisms have been assembled and maintained by the National Center for Biotechnology Information (NCBI), Genome Sequence Data Bank (GSDB), European Molecular Biology Laboratory (EMBL), and the DNA Data Bank of Japan (DDBJ). Powerful search engines, accessible via Web sites, electronic mail, or direct connection to a server and database have enabled biologists to query the sequence data in the context of many different analyses, including gene finding, protein motif identification, regulatory motif analysis, identification of repeated sequences, similarity analyses, nucleotide compositional analyses, and cross-species comparisons. The explosion of data produced by the Human Genome Project has called forth the creation of a new discipline—bioinformatics, whose focus is on the acquisition, storage, analysis, modeling, and distribution of the many types of information embedded in DNA and protein sequence data.

Genomes Sequenced. The genomes of *E. coli,* yeast, and 11 microbes have been completely sequenced.[8] Those of the worm, fruit fly, mouse, and human have been partially sequenced[9] (Table 1). These sequences have dramatically altered the practice of genetics, molecular biology, developmental biology, immunology, and microbiology.

CHALLENGES FOR SEQUENCING THE HUMAN GENOME

Source Material. Over the past decade, numerous clone libraries have been constructed from human sperm and cell lines. With these libraries, physical maps covering significant portions of the genome have been constructed, providing the source material for large-scale sequencing. Virtually all of the existing clone libraries must now be discontinued, however, because the National Institutes of Health (NIH) and the Department of Energy (DOE) have mandated that clone libraries come from donors that have given appropriate consent and are anonymous. This ruling is to prevent possible discrimination against DNA donors or their relatives as information from their genomes becomes available. Sequencing centers must now rebuild physical maps from the new clone libraries that are being constructed with proper [institutional] review board (IRB) approval.

Clone Validation. It has been argued that the genome should be sequenced from multiple libraries so that no individual's chromosomes are dominantly represented in the final sequence. Unfortunately, use of multiple libraries for selecting source clones undermines the ability of sequencing centers to validate the fidelity of their clones. This is so because validation is judged by internal consistency among overlapping clones assayed by restriction enzyme fingerprinting. The rate of polymorphism in the human population is about one variation per 500 base pairs with ~15% of the variations being insertions or deletions.[10] Sequence polymorphisms lead to differences in fingerprints among overlapping clones that cannot be distinguished easily from differences in the fingerprints that arise from deletions or rearrangements of artifactual clones.

Thus, technical considerations argue for using a minimum number of highly redundant clone libraries, and social considerations argue for diversifying the clone libraries.

. . .

Sequence Scale-up. To complete the genome by 2005, starting in 1998, seven large-scale sequencing centers, for example, would each have to complete on the order of 75 Mb/year. Sequencing centers now have a throughput of 2 to 30 Mb/year. If the genome is to be sequenced on time and within budget, sequencing must become significantly faster and cheaper. Technology improvements in mapping, sequencing, and informatics leading to largely automated sequencing production lines will be critical for this scale-up. . . .

Standards. The current standards for sequencing set by the NIH and DOE require that three conditions be met: (i) an error rate of not more than 1 in 10,000; (ii) sequence contiguity, that is, sequence without gaps; and (iii) clone validation, that is, a demonstration that clones faithfully represent the genome. The precision of sequencing and, by inference, the probable error, is estimated by comparing the sequences of overlapping clones. It is also gauged by programs that assign a quality measure to each base in a consensus sequence. Contiguity is gauged by the sequence assembly programs and by the successful overlapping of sequences from adjacent clones. Fingerprint comparison of the clones against other overlapping clones, and in some cases directly against genomic DNA, verifies clone integrity and validity (but see the discussion under "Clone Validation" above). . . .

Dissemination of Data to the Community. Genome centers are currently required to release their data to the community in a timely manner. Currently, finished sequence is available from four large databases (GenBank and GSDB in the United States; EMBL and DDDJ in Europe and Japan, respectively). Unfinished sequence is usually available and searchable from the HTG (high-throughput genomes) division of GenBank (and other databases) or the Web pages of the individual genome centers, or both. Genome centers generally provide a minimum of annotation for finished sequence — identification of repeat sequences, similarity analyses and some indication of the quality of the data. If the data are really to be useful to the biological and medical communities, it is essential that biological information in these sequences be far more completely annotated in the future. Indeed, the complete human genome sequence must be seen as a starting point for new biological investigations, not as an end in itself.

NOTES

1. The longest submitted sequence to date, 1.493 Mb, produced by the Olson laboratory at the University of Washington, derives from the metabotropic glutamate receptor 8 gene on chromosome 7 (GenBank accession number AE000668). Other sequences >1 Mb include the immunoglobulin λ locus (1.025 Mb, accession numbers D86989-D87024 and D88268-D88271); the T cell receptor α locus (1.071 Mb, accession numbers AE000658-AE000662); the DiGeorge critical region (1.25 Mb, http://www.genome.ou.edu/maps/dgcr.gb); and a region of chromosome 19q13 (1.02 Mb, http://www.bio.llnl.gov/sequence-bin/seq_19?band = q13.1). Numerous sequences in the several hundred kilobase range are now being produced by the large sequencing centers in the United States and elsewhere (for example, the Sanger Centre, Cambridge, UK).

2. M. D. Adams *et al., Nature* **377** (suppl.), 3 (1995). EST databases can be accessed via the NCBI BLAST server (http://www.ncbi.nlm.nih.gov/BLAST/).

3. T. J. Hudson *et al., Science* **270,** 1945 (1995).

4. D. Cohen, I. Chumakov, J. Weissenbach, *Nature* **366,** 698 (1993).

5. C. Dib *et al.*, ibid. **380**, 152 (1996).

6. The number of reads per kilobase is a function of the desired redundancy of coverage (typically 5- to 10-fold) and the average read length (typically 400 to 800 bases). A comprehensive review of sequencing technology is found in Adams *et al.* [M. D. Adams, C. Fields, J. C. Venter, Eds. *Automated DNA Sequencing and Analysis* (Academic Press, London, 1994)].

7. L. M. Smith *et al.*, *Nature* **321**, 674 (1986).

8. *Escherichia coli:* F. R. Blattner *et al.*, *Science* **277**, 1453 (1997); yeast: A. Goffeau *et al.*, ibid. **274**, 546 (1996); representative microbial genomes: R. D. Fleischmann *et al.*, ibid. **269**, 496 (1995);

C. M. Fraser *et al.*, ibid. **270**; 397 (1995); C. J. Bult *et al.* ibid. **273**, 1058 (1996); R. Himmelreich *et al.*, *Nucleic Acids Res.* **24**, 4420 (1996); T. Kaneko *et al.*, *DNA Res.* **3**, 109 (1996).

9. The sequencing status of *C. elegans* can be accessed from http://genome/wustl.edu/gsc/gschmpg.html; the *Drosophila melanogaster* sequencing status can be accessed from http://fruitfly.berkeley.edu/. There is no central location for the overall status of human and mouse sequencing progress.

10. Truly reliable estimates of sequence variation rates across the human genome require more data than currently exist. The numbers cited derive from an analysis of 290 kb of the human β T cell receptor locus for which more than one haplotype was sequenced (L. Rowen, unpublished results). These variations are annotated in Gen-Bank accession numbers U66059, U66060, and U66061.

JAMES D. WATSON

Genes and politics

·   ·   ·

GENUINE HUMAN GENETICS EMERGES FROM RECOMBINANT DNA METHODOLOGIES

Long holding back the development of human genetics as a major science was the lack of a genetic map allowing human genes to be located along the chromosomes on which they reside. As long as conventional breeding procedures remained the only route to gene mapping, the precise molecular changes underpinning most human genetic diseases seemed foreordained to remain long mysterious. The key breakthrough opening a path around this seemingly insuperable obstacle came in the late 1970s when it was discovered that the exact sequence (order of the genetic letters A, G, T, and C) of a given gene varies from one person to another. Between any two individuals, roughly 1 in 1000 bases are different, with such variations most frequently occurring within the noncoding DNA regions not involved in specifying specific amino acids. Initially most useful were base differences (polymorphisms) which affected DNA cutting by one of the many just discov-

ered "restriction enzymes" that cut DNA molecules within very specific base sequences.

Soon after the existence of DNA polymorphisms became known, proposals were made that they could provide the genetic markers needed to put together human genetic maps. In a 1980 paper, David Botstein, Ron Davis, Mark Scolnick, and Ray White argued that human maps could be obtained through studying the pattern through which polymorphisms were inherited in the members of large multigenerational families. Those polymorphisms that stay together were likely to be located close to each other on a given chromosome. During the next 5 years, two groups, one led by Helen Donis-Keller in Massachusetts, the other led by Ray White in Utah, rose to this challenge, both using DNA from family blood samples stored at CEPH (Centre d'Étude de Polymorphisme Humain), the mapping center established in Paris by Jean Dausset. By 1985, the mutant genes responsible for Huntington's disease and cystic fibrosis (CF) had been located on chromosomes 4 and 7, respectively.

By using a large number of additional polymorphic markers in the original chromosome 7 region implicated in CF, Francis Collins' group in Ann Arbor and L. C. Tsui's group in Toronto located the DNA segment containing the responsible gene. Its DNA sequence revealed that the CF gene coded for a large

Reprinted with the permission of the author and the publisher from *Journal of Molecular Medicine* 75 (September 1997), 632–36.

membrane protein involved in the transport of chloride ions. The first CF mutant they found contained three fewer bases than its normal equivalent and led to a protein product that was nonfunctional because of its lack of a phenylalanine residue.

THE HUMAN GENOME PROJECT: RESPONDING TO THE NEED FOR EFFICIENT DISEASE GENE MAPPING AND ISOLATION

Although the genes responsible for cystic fibrosis and Huntington's disease were soon accurately mapped using only a small number of DNA polymorphic markers, the genes behind many other important genetic diseases quickly proved to be much harder to map to a specific chromosome, much less assign to a DNA chromosomal segment short enough to generate hopes for its eventual cloning. All too obviously, the genes behind the large set of still very badly understood diseases like Alzheimer's disease, late-onset diabetes, or breast cancer would be mapped much, much sooner if several thousands more newly mapped DNA polymorphisms somehow became available. Likewise, the task of locating the chromosomal DNA segment(s) in which the desired disease genes reside would be greatly shortened if all human DNA were publicly available as sets of overlapping cloned DNA segments (contigs). And the scanning of such DNA segments to look for mutationally altered base sequences would go much faster if the complete sequence of all the human DNA were already known. However, to generate these importantly new resources for human genetics, major new sources of money would be needed. So, by early 1986, serious discussions began as to how to start, soon, the complete sequencing of the 3×10^9 [3 billion] base pairs that collectively make up the human genome (the Human Genome Project or HGP).

Initially, there were more scientific opponents than proponents for what necessarily would be biology's first megaproject. It would require thousands of scientists and the consumption of some $3 billion-like sums. Those disliking its prospects feared that, inevitably, it would be run by governmental bureaucrats not up to the job and would employ scientists too dull for assignment to this intellectually challenging research. Out of many protracted meetings held late in 1986 and through 1987, the argument prevailed that the potential rewards for medicine as well as for biological research itself would more than compensate for the monies the Human Genome Project would consume during the 15 years then thought needed to complete it. Moreover,

completion of each of the two stages — the collection of many more mapped DNA markers and the subsequent ordering of cloned DNA segments into long overlapping sets (contigs) — would by themselves greatly speed up disease gene isolation.

Always equally important to point out, the 15 years projected to complete the Human Genome Project meant that its annual cost of $200 million at most would represent only 1-2% of the money spent yearly for fundamental biomedical research over the world. There was also the realization that some 100,000 human genes believed sited along their chromosomes would be much easier to find and functionally understand if genome sequences were first established for the much smaller, well-studied model organisms such as *Escherichia coli, Saccharomyces cerevisiae, Caenorhabditis elegans,* and *Drosophila melanogaster.* Thus, the biologists who worked with these organisms realized that their own research would be speeded up if the Human Genome Project went ahead.

The American public, as represented by their congressional members, proved initially to be much more enthusiastic about the objectives of the Human Genome Project than most supposedly knowledgeable biologists, with their parochial concerns for how federal monies for biology would be divided up. The first congressionally mandated monies for the Human Genome Project became available late in 1987, when many intelligent molecular geneticists still were sitting on the fence as to whether it made sense. In contrast, Congress, being told that big medical advances would virtually automatically flow out of genome knowledge, saw no reason not to move fast. In doing so, they temporarily set aside the question of what human life would be like when the bad genes behind so many of our major diseases were found. Correctly, to my mind, their overwhelming concern was the current horror of diseases like Alzheimer's, not seeing the need then to, perhaps prematurely, worry about the dilemmas arising when individuals are genetically shown at risk for specific diseases years before they show any symptoms.

GENOME ETHICS: PROGRAMS TO FIND WAYS TO AMELIORATE GENETIC INJUSTICE

The moment I began in October 1988 my almost 4-year period of helping lead the Human Genome Project, I stated that 3% of the NIH-funded component should support research and discussion on the Ethical, Legal, and Social Implications (ELSI) of the new resulting genetic knowledge. A lower percentage might be seen as tokenism, while I then could not see wise use of a larger sum. Under my 3% proposal, some $6 million (3% of $200 million) would eventually be so available, a much larger sum than ever before provided by our government for the ethical implications of biological research.

In putting ethics so soon into the Genome agenda, I was responding to my own personal fear that all too soon critics of the Genome Project would point out that I was a representative of the Cold Spring Harbor Laboratory that once housed the controversial Eugenics Record Office. My not forming a genome ethics program quickly might be falsely used as evidence that I was a closet eugenicist, having as my real long-term purpose the unambiguous identification of genes that lead to social and occupational stratification as well as to genes justifying racial discrimination. So I saw the need to be proactive in making ELSI's major purpose clear from its start — to devise better ways to combat the social injustice that has at its roots bad draws of the genetic dice. Its programs should not be turned into public forums for debating whether genetic inequalities exist. With imperfect gene copying always the evolutionary imperative, there necessarily will always be a constant generation of the new gene disease variants and consequential genetic injustice.

The issues soon considered for ELSI monies were far-ranging. For example, how can we ensure that the results of genetic diagnosis are not misused by prospective employers or insurers? How should we try to see that individuals know what they are committing themselves to when they allow their DNA to be used for genetic analyzing? What concrete steps should be taken to ensure the accuracy of genetic testing? And when a fetus is found to possess genes that will not allow it to develop into a functional human being, who, if anyone, should have the right to terminate the pregnancy?

From their beginnings, our ELSI programs had to reflect primarily the needs of individuals at risk of the oft tragic consequences of genetic disabilities. Only long-term harm would result in the perception of genetics as an honest science if ELSI-type decisions were perceived to be dominated either by the scientists who provided the genetic knowledge or by the government bodies that funded such research. And since women are even in the distant future likely to disproportion-

ately share the burden of caring for the genetically disabled, they should lead the discussion of how more genetic knowledge is to come into our lives.

HUMAN HESITATIONS IN LEARNING THEIR OWN GENETIC FATE

With the initial distribution of American genome monies and the building and equipping the resulting genome centers taking 2 years, the Human Genome Project in its megaphase did not effectively start until the fall of 1990. Decisions to go ahead by funding bodies in the United States helped lead to the subsequent inspired creation of Genethon outside Paris by the French genetic disease charity, Association Française contre les Myopathies (AFM), as well as the building of the now immense Sanger Centre, just south of Cambridge, England, by the British medically oriented charity, the Wellcome Trust. Now effectively 7 years into its projected 15-year life, the Human Genome Project has more than lived up to its role in speeding up genetic disease mapping and subsequent gene cloning. It quickly made successful the search for the gene behind the fragile X syndrome that leads to severe mental retardation in boys preferentially affected by this sex-linked genetic affliction. The molecular defect found was an expansion of preexisting three-base repetitive sequences that most excitingly increase in length from one generation to the next. The long mysterious phenomenon of anticipation, in which the severity of a disease grows through subsequent generations, was thus given a molecular explanation. Then at long last, in 1994, the gene for Huntington's disease was found. Its cause was likewise soon found to be the expansion of a repetitive gene sequence.

While the mapping to a chromosome per se of any disease gene remains an important achievement, the cloning of the disease gene itself is a bigger milestone. Thus, the 1990 finding by Mary Claire King that much hereditary breast cancer is due to a gene on chromosome 17 set off a big gene-cloning race. With that gene in hand, there was a chance that its DNA sequence would reveal the normal function of the protein it codes for. In any case, it gives its possessors the opportunity to examine directly the DNA from individuals known to be at risk for a disease to see whether they had the unwanted gene. Thus, when in 1993 the chromosome 17 breast cancer gene (BRAC1) was isolated by Myriad, the Utah disease gene-finding company, it could inform women so tested for BRAC1 whether or not they had the feared gene.

Initially, concerns were voiced that unbridled commercialization of this capability would all too easily give women knowledge they would not be psychologically prepared to handle. If so, the ethical way to prevent such emotional setbacks might be to regulate both how the tests were given and who should be allowed to be tested. I fear, however, that a major reason behind many such calls for regulation of genetic testing is the hidden agenda of wanting to effectively stop widespread genetic testing by making it so difficult to obtain. Now, however, calls for governmental regulation may fall on increasingly deaf ears. To Myriad's great disappointment, it appears that the great majority of women at 50% risk of being breast cancer gene carriers don't want to be tested. Rather than receive the wrong verdict, they seem to prefer living with uncertainty. Likewise, a very large majority of the individuals at risk for Huntington's disease are also psychologically predisposed against putting themselves at risk of possibly knowing of their genetic damnation.

Although we are certain to learn in the future of many individuals regretting that they subjected themselves to genetic tests and wishing they had been more forewarned of the potential perils of such knowledge, I do not see how the state can effectively enter into such decisons. Committees of well-intentioned outsiders will never have the intimate knowledge to assess a given individual's psychological need, or not, for a particular piece of scientific or medical knowledge. In the last analysis, we should accept the fact that if scientific knowledge exists, individual persons or families should have the right to decide whether it will lead to their betterment.

INARGUABLE EXISTENCE OF GENES PREDISPOSING HUMANS TO BEHAVIORAL DISORDERS

The extraordinarily negative connotation that the term eugenics now conveys is indelibly identified with its past practitioners' unjustified statements that behavioral differences, whether between individuals, families, or the so-called races, largely had their origins in gene differences. Given the primitive power of human genetics, there was no way for such broad-ranging assertions to have been legitimatized by the then methods of science. Even the eugenically minded psychiatrists' claims that defective genes were invariably at the root of their mental patients' symptoms were no more than hunches. Yet, it was by their imputed genetic imperfection that the mentally ill were first sterilized and

then, being of no value to the wartime Third Reich, released from their lives by subsequent "mercy killings."

But past eugenic horrors in no way justify the "Not in Our Genes" politically correct outlook of many left-wing academics. They still spread the unwarranted message that only our bodies, not our minds, have genetic origins. Essentially protecting the ideology that all our troubles have capitalistic exploitative origins, they are particularly uncomfortable with the thought that genes have any influence on intellectual abilities or that unsocial criminal behavior might owe its origins to other than class or racially motivated oppression. Whether these scientists on the left actually believe, say, that the incidence of schizophrenia would seriously lessen if class struggles ended, however, is not worth finding out.

Instead, we should employ, as fast as we can, the powerful new techniques of human genetics to find soon the actual schizophrenia predisposing genes. The much higher concordance of schizophrenia in identical versus nonidentical twins unambiguously tells us that they are there to find. Such twin analysis, however, reveals that genetics cannot be the whole picture. Since the concordance rates for schizophrenia, as well as for manic-depressive disease, are more like 60%, not 100%, environmental predisposing factors must exist and, conceivably, viral infections that affect the brain are sometimes involved.

Unfortunately, still today, the newer statistical tricks for analyzing polymorphic inheritance patterns have not yet led to the unambiguous mapping of even one major schizophrenic gene to a defined chromosomal site. The only convincing data involve only the 1% of schizophrenics whose psychoses seemingly are caused by the small chromosome 22 deletions responsible also for the so-called St. George facial syndrome. Manic-depressive disease also has been more than hard to understand genetically. Only last year did solid evidence emerge for a major predisposing gene on the long arm of chromosome 18. This evidence looks convincing enough for real hopes that the actual gene involved will be isolated over the next several years.

Given that over half the human genes are thought to be involved in human brain development and functioning, we must expect that many other behavioral differences between individuals will also have genetic origins. Recently, there have been claims that both "reckless personalities" and "unipolar depressions" associate with specific polymorphic forms of genes coding for the membrane receptors involved in the transmission of signals between nerve cells. Neither claim now appears to be reproducible, but we should not be surprised to find some subsequent associations to hold water. Now anathematic to left-wing ideologues is the highly convincing report of a Dutch family, many of whose male members display particularly violent behavior. Most excitingly, all of the affected males possess a mutant gene coding for an inactive form of the enzyme monoamine oxidase. Conceivably having too little of this enzyme, which breaks down neurotransmitters, leads to the persistence of destructive thoughts and the consequential aggressive patterns. Subsequent attempts to detect in other violent individuals this same mutant gene have so far failed. We must expect someday, however, to find that other mutant genes that lead to altered brain chemistry also lead to asocial activities. Their existence, however, in no way should be taken to mean that gene variants are the major cause of violence. Nonetheless, continued denials by the scientific left that genes have no role in how people interact with each other will inevitably further diminish their already tainted credibility.

KEEPING GOVERNMENTS OUT OF GENETIC DECISIONS

No rational person should have doubts whether genetic knowledge properly used has the capacity to improve the human condition. Through discovering those genes whose bad variants make us unhealthy or in some other way unable to function effectively, we can fight back in several different ways. For example, knowing what is wrong at the molecular level should let us sometimes develop drugs that will effectively neutralize the harm generated by certain bad genes. Other genetic disabilities should effectively be neutralized by so-called gene therapy procedures restoring normal cell functioning by adding good copies of the missing normal genes. Although gene therapy enthusiasts have promised too much for the near future, it is difficult to imagine that they will not with time cure some genetic conditions.

For the time being, however, we should place most of our hopes for genetics on the use of antenatal diagnostic procedures, which increasingly will let us know whether a fetus is carrying a mutant gene that will seriously proscribe its eventual development into a functional human being. By terminating such pregnancies, the threat of horrific disease genes continuing to blight many families' prospects for future success can be erased. But even among individuals who firmly place themselves on the pro-choice side and do not want to limit women's rights for abortion, opinions frequently are voiced that decisions obviously good for individual persons or families may not be appropriate for the societies in which we live. For example, by not wanting to have a physically or mentally handicapped child or one who would have to fight all its life against possible death from cystic fibrosis, are we not reinforcing the second-rate status of such handicapped individuals? And what would be the consequences of isolating genes that give rise to the various forms of dyslexia, opening up the possibility that women will take antenatal tests to see if their prospective child is likely to have a bad reading disorder? Is it not conceivable that such tests would lead to our devoting less resources to the currently reading-handicapped children whom now we accept as an inevitable feature of human life?

That such conundrums may never be truly answerable, however, should not concern us too much. The truly relevant question for most families is whether an obvious good to them will come from having a child with a major handicap. Is it more likely for such children to fall behind in society or will they through such affliction develop the strengths of character and fortitude that lead, like Jeffrey Tate, the noted British conductor, to the head of their packs? Here I'm afraid that the word handicap cannot escape its true definition — being placed at a disadvantage. From this perspective, seeing the bright side of being handicapped is like praising the virtues of extreme poverty. To be sure, there are many individuals who rise out of its inherently degrading states. But we perhaps most realistically should see it as the major origin of asocial behavior that has among its many bad consequences the breeding of criminal violence.

Only harm, thus, I fear will come from any form of society-based restriction on individual genetic decisions. Decisions from committees of well-intentioned individuals will too often emerge as vehicles for seeming to do good as opposed to doing good. Moreover, we should necessarily worry that once we let governments tell their citizens what they cannot do genetically, we must fear they also have power to tell us what we must do. But for us as individuals to feel comfortable making decisions that affect the genetic makeups of our children, we correspondingly have to become genetically literate. In the future, we must necessarily question any government which does not see this as its responsibility. Will it so not act because it wants to keep such powers for itself?

Those of us who venture forth into the public arena to explain what Genetics can or cannot do for society seemingly inevitably come up against individuals who feel that we are somehow the modern equivalents of Hitler. Here we must not fall into the absurd trap of being against everything Hitler was for. It was in no way evil for Hitler to regard mental disease as a scourge on society. Almost everyone then, as still true today, was made uncomfortable by psychotic individuals. It is how Hitler treated German mental patients that still outrages civilized societies and lets us call him immoral. Genetics per se can never be evil. It is only when we use or misuse it that morality comes in. That we want to find ways to lessen the impact of mental illness is inherently good. The killing by the Nazis of the German mental patients for reasons of supposed genetic inferiority, however, was barbarianism at its worst.

Because of Hitler's use of the term Master Race, we should not feel the need to say that we never want to use genetics to make humans more capable than they are today. The idea that genetics could or should be used to give humans power that they do not now possess, however, strongly upsets many individuals first exposed to the notion. I suspect such fears in some ways are similar to concerns now expressed about the genetically handicapped of today. If more intelligent human beings might someday be created, would we not think less well about ourselves as we exist today? Yet anyone who proclaims that we are now perfect as humans has to be a silly crank. If we could honestly promise young couples that we knew how to give them offspring with superior character, why should we assume they would decline? Those at the top of today's societies might not see the need. But if your life is going nowhere, shouldn't you seize the chance of jump-starting your children's future?

Common sense tells us that if scientists find ways to greatly improve human capabilities, there will be no stopping the public from happily seizing them.

UNITED NATIONS EDUCATIONAL, SCIENTIFIC, AND CULTURAL ORGANIZATION

Universal Declaration on the Human Genome and Human Rights (December 1997)

• • •

Recognizing that research on the human genome and the resulting applications open up vast prospects for progress in improving the health of individuals and of humankind as a whole, but *emphasizing* that such research should fully respect human dignity, freedom and human rights, as well as the prohibition of all forms of discrimination based on genetic characteristics.

Proclaims the principles that follow and *adopts* the present Declaration.

A. HUMAN DIGNITY AND THE HUMAN GENOME

ARTICLE I

The human genome underlies the fundamental unity of all members of the human family, as well as the recognition of their inherent dignity and diversity. In a symbolic sense, it is the heritage of humanity.

ARTICLE 2

a) Everyone has a right to respect for their dignity and for their rights regardless of their genetic characteristics.

b) That dignity makes it imperative not to reduce individuals to their genetic characteristics and to respect their uniqueness and diversity.

ARTICLE 3

The human genome, which by its nature evolves, is subject to mutations. It contains potentialities that are expressed differently according to each individual's natural and social environment including the individual's state of health, living conditions, nutrition and education.

ARTICLE 4

The human genome in its natural state shall not give rise to financial gains.

B. RIGHTS OF THE PERSONS CONCERNED

ARTICLE 5

a) Research, treatment or diagnosis affecting an individual's genome shall be undertaken only after rigorous and prior assessment of the potential risks and benefits pertaining thereto and in accordance with any other requirement of national law.

b) In all cases, the prior, free and informed consent of the person concerned shall be obtained. If the latter is not in a position to consent, consent or authorization shall be obtained in the manner prescribed by law, guided by the person's best interest.

c) The right of each individual to decide whether or not to be informed of the results of genetic examination and the resulting consequences should be respected.

d) In the case of research, protocols shall, in addition, be submitted for prior review in accordance with relevant national and international research standards or guidelines.

e) If according to the law a person does not have the capacity to consent, research affecting his or her genome may only be carried out for his or her direct health benefit, subject to the authorization and the protective conditions prescribed by law. Research which does not have an expected direct health benefit may only be undertaken by way of exception, with the utmost restraint, exposing the person only to a minimal risk and minimal burden and if the research is intended to contribute to the health benefit of other persons in the same age category or with the same genetic condition, subject to the condition prescribed by law, and provided such research is compatible with the protection of the individual's human rights.

ARTICLE 6

No one shall be subjected to discrimination based on genetic characteristics that is intended to infringe or has the effect of infringing human rights, fundamental freedoms and human dignity.

ARTICLE 7

Genetic data associated with an identifiable person and stored or processed for the purposes of research or any other purpose must be held confidential in the conditions set by law.

ARTICLE 8

Every individual shall have the right, according to international and national law, to just reparation for any damage sustained as a direct and determining result of an intervention affecting his or her genome.

ARTICLE 9

In order to protect human rights and fundamental freedoms, limitations to the principles of consent and confidentiality may only be prescribed by law, for compelling reasons within the bounds of public international law and the international law of human rights.

C. RESEARCH ON THE HUMAN GENOME

ARTICLE 10

No research or research applications concerning the human genome, in particular in the fields of biology, genetics and medicine, should prevail over respect for the human rights, fundamental freedoms and human dignity of individuals or, where applicable, of groups of people.

ARTICLE 11

Practices which are contrary to human dignity, such as reproductive cloning of human beings, shall not be permitted. States and competent international organizations are invited to cooperate in identifying such practices and in taking, at [a] national or international level, the measures necessary to ensure that the principles set out in this Declaration are respected.

a) Benefits from advances in biology, genetics and medicine, concerning the human genome, shall be made available to all, with due regard for the dignity and human rights of each individual.

b) Freedom of research, which is necessary for the progress of knowledge, is part of freedom of thought. The applications of research, including applications in biology, genetics and medicine, concerning the human genome, shall seek to offer relief from suffering and improve the health of individuals and humankind as a whole.

D. CONDITIONS FOR THE EXERCISE OF SCIENTIFIC ACTIVITY

ARTICLE 13

The responsibilities inherent in the activities of researchers, including meticulousness, caution, intellectual honesty and integrity in carrying out their research as well as in the presentation and utilization of their findings, should be the subject of particular attention in the framework of research on the human genome, because of its ethical and social implications. Public and private science policymakers also have particular responsibilities in this respect.

ARTICLE 14

States should take appropriate measures to foster the intellectual and material conditions favourable to freedom in the conduct of research on the human genome and to consider the ethical, legal, social and economic implications of such research, on the basis of the principles set out in this Declaration.

ARTICLE 15

States should take appropriate steps to provide the framework for the free exercise of research on the human genome with due regard for the principles set out in this Declaration, in order to safeguard respect for human rights, fundamental freedoms and human dignity and to protect public health. They should seek to ensure that research results are not used for non-peaceful purposes.

ARTICLE 16

States should recognize the value of promoting, at various levels, as appropriate, the establishment of independent, multidisciplinary and pluralist ethics commit-

tees to assess the ethical, legal and social issues raised by research on the human genome and its application.

E. SOLIDARITY AND INTERNATIONAL COOPERATION

ARTICLE 17

States should respect and promote the practice of solidarity towards individuals, families and population groups who are particularly vulnerable to or affected by disease or disability of a genetic character. They should foster, *inter alia,* research on the identification, prevention and treatment of genetically-based and genetically-influenced diseases, in particular rare as well as endemic diseases which affect large numbers of the world's population.

ARTICLE 18

States should make every effort, with due and appropriate regard for the principles set out in this Declaration, to continue fostering the international dissemination of scientific knowledge concerning the human genome, human diversity and genetic research and, in that regard, to foster scientific and cultural cooperation, particularly between industrialized and developing countries.

ARTICLE 19

a) In the framework of international cooperation with developing countries, States should seek to encourage measures enabling:

i) assessment of the risks and benefits pertaining to research on the human genome to be carried out and abuse to be prevented;

ii) the capacity of developing countries to carry out research on human biology and genetics, taking into consideration their specific problems, to be developed and strengthened;

iii) developing countries to benefit from the achievements of scientific and technological research so that their use in favour of economic and social progress can be to the benefit of all;

iv) the free exchange of scientific knowledge and information in the areas of biology, genetics and medicine to be promoted.

b) Relevant international organizations should support and promote the initiatives taken by States for the above-mentioned purposes.

F. PROMOTION OF THE PRINCIPLES
SET OUT IN THE DECLARATION

ARTICLE 20

States should take appropriate measures to promote the principles set out in the Declaration, through education and relevant means, *inter alia* through the conduct of research and training in interdisciplinary fields and through the promotion of education in bioethics, at all levels, in particular for those responsible for science policies.

ARTICLE 21

States should take appropriate measures to encourage other forms of research, training and information dissemination conducive to raising the awareness of society and all of its members of their responsibilities regarding the fundamental issues relating to the defence of human dignity which may be raised by research in biology, in genetics and in medicine, and its applications. They should also undertake to facilitate on this subject an open international discussion, ensuring the free expression of various socio-cultural, religious and philosophical opinions.

G. IMPLEMENTATION OF THE DECLARATION

ARTICLE 22

States should make every effort to promote the principles set out in this Declaration and should, by means of all appropriate measures, promote their implementation.

ARTICLE 23

States should take appropriate measures to promote, through education, training and information dissemination, respect for the above-mentioned principles and to foster their recognition and effective application. States should also encourage exchanges and networks among independent ethics committees, as they are established to foster full collaboration.

ARTICLE 24

The International Bioethics Committee of UNESCO should contribute to the dissemination of the principles set out in this Declaration and to the further examination of issues raised by their applications and by the evolution of the technologies in question. It should organize appropriate consultations with parties concerned, such as vulnerable groups. It should make recommendations, in accordance with UNESCO's statutory procedures, addressed to the General Conference and give advice concerning the follow-up of this Declaration, in particular regarding the identification of practices that could be contrary to human dignity, such as germ-line interventions.

ARTICLE 25

Nothing in this Declaration may be interpreted as implying for any State, group or person any claim to engage in any activity or to perform any act contrary to human rights and fundamental freedoms, including the principles set out in this Declaration.

· · ·

INSTITUTE OF MEDICINE, COMMITTEE ON ASSESSING GENETIC RISKS

Assessing Genetic Risks: Implications for Health and Social Policy

Approximately 3 percent of all children are born with a severe disorder that is presumed to be genetic in origin, and several thousand definite or suspected single-gene diseases have been described. Most of these diseases manifest themselves early in life, although some inherited diseases—and many others that have a genetic component—have their onset much later in life (e.g., diabetes mellitus or mental illness). Then there are many disorders in which both genetic and environmental factors play major roles (e.g., coronary heart disease, hypertension). These "complex" disorders are more common than single-gene diseases and thus, in the aggregate, constitute a greater public health burden. Many disease genes can be detected in individuals before symptoms occur, but for many common diseases with some genetic basis, such as heart disease and cancer, the detection of genetic alterations might only indicate susceptibility, not the certainty of disease.

PROMISE AND PROBLEMS IN GENETIC TESTING

The ability to diagnose genetic disease has developed rapidly over the past 20 years, and the Human Genome Project, with its ambitious goal of mapping and sequencing the entire genome, will bring a further explosion in our knowledge of the structure and function of human genes. The ultimate goals of these scientific advances are the treatment, cure, and eventual prevention of genetic disorders, but effective interventions lag be-

hind the ability to detect disease or increased susceptibility to disease. Thus, many genetic services today consist of diagnosis and counseling; effective treatment is rare. Nevertheless, as more genes are identified, there is growing pressure to broaden existing screening programs, and otherwise increase both the number of available genetic tests and the volume of genetic information they generate.

The rapidly changing science and practice of genetic testing raise a number of scientific, ethical, legal, and social issues. The national investment in the Human Genome Project will greatly increase the capacity to detect genes leading to disease susceptibility. It will also greatly increase the availability of genetic testing over the next 5 to 10 years, identifying the genetic basis for diseases—even some newly discovered to be genetic—and increasing the number of tests for detecting them. The emergence of the biotechnology industry increases the likelihood that these findings will be rapidly translated into widely available test kits and diagnostic products. Entrepreneurial pressure may also lead to the development of commercial and academic "genetic testing services" that would not be regulated under current Food and Drug Administration (FDA) procedures. Problems of laboratory quality control would be heightened by the introduction of "multiplex" tests that detect the presence of numerous genetic markers—for disease, carrier status, and susceptibility alike—at the same time. And the potential for generating all of this genetic information about individuals raises serious questions of informed consent, confidentiality, and discrimination. Over the next five to ten years, there will be an increasing number of personal and public policy decisions related to genetic testing; well-trained health professionals and an interested and informed public will both be key to that decision making.

As genetic screening becomes more widespread, these issues threaten to outrun current ethical and regulatory standards, as well as the training of health professionals. There will be a need for greater numbers of genetics specialists, but genetic testing is no longer just for specialists. Increasingly, primary care providers will be called upon to administer tests, counsel patients, and protect their privacy. Government officials and the broader public will also be called upon to participate in setting public policy for genetic testing and in making difficult decisions, public and private, based on the results of genetic tests. Consequently, there must be a significant increase in genetics education, both in the medical curriculum and for all Americans. Finally, there will be a need for centralized oversight to ensure that new genetic tests are accurate and effective, that they are performed and interpreted with close to "zero-error" tolerance, and that the results of genetic testing are not used to discriminate against individuals in employment or health insurance.

COMMITTEE ON ASSESSING GENETIC RISKS

This study of the scientific, ethical, and social issues implicit in the field of genetic diagnosis, testing, and screening was supported jointly by the National Center for Human Genome Research at the National Institutes of Health and the Department of Energy's Health Effects and Life Sciences Research Office. Supplemental funding was also provided by the Markey Charitable Trust and the Institute of Medicine. The Committee on Assessing Genetic Risks hopes that this report will be widely read, not only by various health professionals interested in genetics and preventive medicine, but by a wide-ranging audience who makes and influences public policy in the United States, including members of genetic support groups and the public.

The establishment of the Ethical, Legal, and Social Implications (ELSI) Program in the Human Genome Project (HGP) and the set-aside of the first 3 to 5 percent of the HGP research budget for the study of ethical, legal, and social issues is unique in the history of science. This support gives us the opportunity to "worry in advance" about the implications and impacts of the mapping and sequencing of the human genome, including several thousand human disease genes, *before* wide-scale genetic diagnosis, testing, and screening come into

practice, rather than *after* the problems have presented themselves in full relief.

The committee took its starting point from the wise advice of the 1975 National Academy of Sciences study *Genetic Screening: Programs, Principles, and Research:*

Screening programs for genetic diseases and characteristics . . . have multiplied rapidly in the past decade, and many have been begun without prior testing and evaluation and not always for reasons of health alone. Changes in disease patterns and a new emphasis on preventive medicine, as well as recent and rapid advances in genetics, indicate that screening for genetic characteristics will become more common in the future. These conditions, together with the mistakes already made, suggested the need for a review of current screening practices that would identify the problems and difficulties and give some procedural guidance, in order to minimize the shortcomings and maximize the effectiveness of future genetic screening programs.

These words, written almost 20 years ago, remain just as valid today for genetic testing and diagnosis. The committee reaffirms the sentiments expressed in the 1975 report and hopes to update and broaden their application for the 1990s and beyond.

As a result, the committee has posed its recommendations in terms of general principles that we hope will be useful today — and for some years into the future — for the evaluation of expanded genetic diagnosis, testing, and screening. Although these recommendations reflect what is known today, and what experts foresee for the next few years, the committee had no crystal ball and, therefore, tried to develop criteria and to suggest processes for assessing when new tests are ready for pilot introduction and for widespread application in the population.

The committee's fundamental ethical principles include *voluntariness, informed consent, and confidentiality,* which in turn derive from respect for autonomy, equity, and privacy. Other committee principles described in the report include the necessity of (1) *high-quality tests (of high specificity and sensitivity) performed with the highest level of proficiency and interpreted correctly; and (2) conveying information to clients — both before and after testing — in an easily understood manner through genetic education and counseling that is relevant to the needs and concerns of the client.* These principles are the absolute foundation of genetic testing.

It is the view of the committee that, *until benefits and risks have been defined, genetic testing and screen-*

Therefore, routine use of tests should be preceded by pilot studies that demonstrate their safety and effectiveness. Standard safeguards should be applied in conducting these pilot studies, and independent review of the pilot studies should be conducted to determine whether the test should be offered clinically. Publicly supported population-based screening programs are justified only for disorders of significant severity, impact, frequency, and distribution, and when there is consensus that the available interventions warrant the expenditure of funds. **Informed consent should be an essential element of all screening. These principles and procedures described above should apply to genetic testing regardless of the setting, whether in primary medical practice, public programs, or any other settings.**

GENETIC TESTING AND ASSESSMENT

Genetic tests include the many different laboratory assays used to diagnose or predict a genetic condition or the susceptibility to genetic disease. *Genetic testing* denotes the use of specific assays to determine the genetic status of individuals already suspected to be at high risk for a particular inherited condition because of family history or clinical symptoms; *genetic screening* involves the use of various genetic tests to evaluate populations or groups of individuals independent of a family history of a disorder. However, these terms are commonly used interchangeably, and the committee has generally used the term *genetic testing* unless a specific aspect of genetic screening alone is being discussed. *Genetic counseling* refers to the communication process by which individuals and their family members are given information about the nature, recurrence risk, burden, risks and benefits of tests, and meaning of test results, including reproductive options of a genetic condition, as well as counseling and support concerning the implications of such genetic information.

NEWBORN SCREENING

At the present time, there are 10 genetic conditions for which some states screen newborns, although the scope of such screening varies by state (see Table 1). It is also possible to extract DNA from the newborn blood "spots" that are used for these tests. There is increasing pressure to test old blood samples for a wide variety of disorders, as well as to do DNA testing on newborns for a wide variety of disorders in the future. **As basic principles to govern newborn screening, the committee**

Table 1. Genetic Disorders for Which Newborns Were Screened in the United States in 1990

Disorder	Number of states that provided screening[a]
Phenylketonuria	52
Congenital hypothyroidism[b]	52
Hemoglobinopathy	42[c]
Glactosemia	38
Maple syrup urine disorder	22
Homocysteinuria	21
Biotinidase deficiency	14
Adrenal hyperplasia	8
Tyrosinemia	5
Cystic fibrosis	3[d]

[a]Includes District of Columbia, Puerto Rico, and U.S. Virgin Islands.
[b]Only a proportion of cases have a genetic etiology.
[c]Utah's hemoglobinopathy pilot study (6-1-90 through 3-31-91) has been discontinued.
[d]Wisconsin's cystic fibrosis screening program is for research purposes only.
SOURCE: Council of Regional Networks for Genetic Services, 1992.

recommends that such screening take place only when (1) there is a clear indication of benefit to the newborn, (2) a system is in place to confirm the diagnosis, and (3) treatment and follow-up are available for affected newborns. In addition, the committee does not believe that newborns should be screened using multiplex testing for many disorders at one time unless all of the disorders meet the principles described by the committee in this report. . . .

To determine clear benefit to the newborn, well-designed and peer-reviewed pilot studies are required to demonstrate the safety and effectiveness of the proposed screening program. In pilot studies for new population-based newborn screening programs, parents should be informed of the investigational nature of the test and have the opportunity to consent to the participation of their infant. **Since some existing programs may not have been subject to careful evaluation, the committee recommends that ongoing programs be reviewed periodically, preferably by an independent body that is authorized to add, eliminate, or modify existing programs.** . . . The need for ongoing review and revision also suggests that detailed statutory requirements for specific tests may be unduly inflexible; state statutes should provide guidance for standards—not prescriptions. **The committee recommends that** states with newborn screening programs for treatable disorders also have programs available to ensure that necessary treatment and follow-up services are provided to affected children identified through newborn screening without regard to ability to pay. Informed consent should also be an integral part of a newborn screening, including disclosure of the benefits and risks of the tests and treatments. **Finally, mandatory screening has not been shown to be essential to achieve maximum public health benefits; however, it is appropriate to mandate the *offering* of established tests (e.g., phenylketonuria, hypothyroidism) where early diagnosis leads to improved treatable outcomes.** . . .

Newborns should not be screened for the purpose of determining the carrier status of the newborn or its parents for autosomal recessive disorders. Instead, couples in high-risk populations who are considering reproduction should be offered carrier screening for themselves (see below). When carrier status may be incidentally determined in newborn screening (e.g., in sickle cell screening), parents should be informed in advance about the benefits and limitations of genetic information, and that this information is not relevant to the health of their child. If they ask for the results of the incidentally determined carrier status for their own reproductive planning, it should be communicated to them in the context of genetic counseling, and they should be informed that misattributed paternity could be revealed. **Newborn screening programs should include provision for counseling of parents who are informed that the child is affected with a genetic disorder.**

The committee recognizes the complexities of identifying information about misattributed paternity. **On balance, the committee recommends that information on misattributed paternity be communicated to the mother, but not be volunteered to the woman's partner.** There may be special circumstances that warrant such disclosure, but these situations present difficult counseling challenges. . . .

Stored newborn blood spots should be made available for additional research only if identifiers have been removed. As with other research involving human subjects, research proposals for the subsequent use of newborn blood spots should be reviewed by an appropriate institutional review board. If identifiable information is to be disclosed, informed consent of the infant's parent or guardian should be obtained prior to use of the specimen. . . . Although DNA typing will provide new tools for newborn screening, in general, the committee recommends that these tools be employed only (1) when genetic heterogeneity of conditions to be detected is small; (2) when the sensitivity of detecting disease-causing mutations is high; (3) when costs are reasonable; and (4) when the benefits to newborns of early detection are clear.

CARRIER IDENTIFICATION

Carrier testing is usually provided for purposes of reproductive planning. **The committee recommends that couples in high-risk populations who are considering reproduction be offered carrier screening before pregnancy if possible. Standard safeguards such as institutional review and demonstrated safety and effectiveness should be applied in initiating any carrier detection program.** First, the test should be accurate, sensitive, and specific. In the future, such screening will be done increasingly as part of routine medical care; the same principles should apply regardless of the setting. Carrier testing and screening should also be voluntary, with high standards of informed consent and attention to telling individuals or couples, in easily understood terms, the medical and social choices available to them should they be found at risk for disease in their offspring, including termination of the pregnancy. Research is needed to develop innovative methods for providing carrier testing in young adults before pregnancy and to evaluate these methods through pilot studies. The committee had reservations about carrier screening programs in the high school setting in the United States and about carrier screening of persons younger than age 18.

With improving technology, carrier status for many different rare autosomal and X-linked recessive disorders will be detectable by multiplex technology. . . . Obtaining appropriate informed consent before testing for each of these disorders will be a challenge. . . . **Multiplexed tests should, therefore, be grouped into categories of tests (and disorders) that raise similar issues and implications for informed consent and for genetic education and counseling.** . . . If carrier status is detected, individuals should be informed of their carrier status to allow testing and counseling to be offered to their partners. Usually, the partner will be found not to be a carrier; however, if both partners are carriers, they should be referred for genetic counseling to help them understand available reproductive options, in-

PRENATAL DIAGNOSIS

Anyone considering prenatal diagnosis must be fully informed about the risks and benefits of both the testing procedure and the possible outcomes, as well as alternative options that might be available. Disclosure should include full information concerning the spectrum of severity of the genetic disorders for which prenatal diagnosis is being offered (e.g. cystic fibrosis or fragile X). Furthermore, invasive prenatal diagnosis is only justified if the diagnostic procedures are accurate, sensitive, and specific for the disorder(s) for which prenatal diagnosis is being offered. **Standards of care for prenatal screening and diagnosis should also include education and counseling before and after the test, either directly or by referral, and ongoing counseling should also be available following termination of pregnancies.**

The committee believes that *offering* prenatal diagnosis is an appropriate standard of care in circumstances associated with increased risk of carrying a fetus with a diagnosable genetic disorder, including the increased risks associated with advanced maternal age. However, the committee was concerned about the use of prenatal diagnosis for identification of trivial characteristics or conditions. **It was the consensus of this committee that prenatal diagnosis should only be offered for the diagnosis of genetic disorders and birth defects.** A family history of a diagnosable genetic disorder warrants the offering of prenatal diagnosis, regardless of maternal age, as does determination of carrier status in both parents of an autosomal recessive disorder for which prenatal diagnosis is available. Prenatal diagnostic services for detection of genetic disease for which there is a family history should be reimbursed by insurers. . . . Ability to pay should not restrict appropriate access to prenatal diagnosis or termination of pregnancy of an affected fetus.

The committee felt strongly that the use of fetal diagnosis for determination of fetal sex and the subsequent use of abortion for the purpose of preferential selection of the sex of the fetus represents a misuse of genetic services that is inappropriate and should be discouraged by health professionals. More broadly, reproductive genetic services should not be used to pursue eugenic goals, but should be aimed at increasing individual control over reproductive options. As a consequence, additional research is needed on the impact of prenatal diagnosis, particularly its immediate and long-term impact on women, and on the design and evaluation of genetic counseling techniques for prenatal diagnosis for the future.

TESTING FOR LATE-ONSET DISORDERS

Science is moving closer to defining the genetics of such adult disorders as Alzheimer disease, a variety of cancers, heart disease, and arthritis, to name a few. . . . A combination of genetic and environmental factors plays a predominant role in most people afflicted with these disorders, but we do not yet understand why some people with a certain gene(s) develop a disease and others do not. Although further work may eventually elucidate the gene(s) involved, there may be long delays until the time when effective interventions are available for many disorders. Furthermore, not all affected individuals will have an identifiable genetic basis to their disorder. Thus, the complexities involved in determining and establishing susceptibility, sorting out potential environmental influences, and devising a strategy for counseling and treatment will pose tremendous challenges in the future.

Many of these diseases do not manifest clinically until adulthood and may become apparent only in middle age or later. *Predictive* or *presymptomatic* testing and screening can provide clues about genetic susceptibility or predisposition to genetic disorders. For monogenic disorders of late onset, such as Huntington disease, tests will usually be highly predictive. Many common diseases usually have multifactorial — or complex — causation, including both multiple genetic factors and environmental effects; for these disorders, prediction will be less certain. Many common diseases of adulthood, including coronary artery disease, some cancers, diabetes, high blood pressure, rheumatoid arthritis, and some psychiatric diseases, fall into this category. However, in rare forms of these common diseases, single genes may play the decisive role; screening for disease-causing alleles of these genes will be of much greater predictive value.

The committee therefore recommends caution in the use and interpretation of presymptomatic or predictive tests. The nature of these predictions will usually be probabilistic (i.e., with a certain degree of likelihood of occurrence) and not deterministic (i.e., not definite, settled, or without doubt). The dangers of stigmatization and discrimination are areas of concern, as is the potential for harm due to inappropriate preventive or therapeutic measures. Since environmental factors are often essential for the manifestation of complex diseases, the detection of those at high risk will identify certain individuals who will most benefit from certain interventions (e.g., dietary measures in coronary heart disease). Identification of some persons at high risk for certain cancers suggests that more frequent monitoring may identify the earliest manifestations of cancer when treatability is greatest (e.g., colon cancer); research is needed on the psychosocial implications of such testing in both adults and children.

Further research and the unfolding of the Human Genome Project are likely to reveal the underlying genes mediating predisposition to numerous common diseases, and genetic susceptibility testing will be increasingly possible. Certain environmental factors may interact with only one set of genes and not with another. There may also be interaction between the various genes involved, so that the effects of multiple gene action cannot be predicted by separate analyses of each of the single genes. In such cases, definitive prediction will rarely, if ever, be possible. When dealing with genetic testing for some non-Mendelian diseases, it will be impossible to group individuals into two distinct categories—those at no (or very low) risk and those at high risk. Extensive counseling and education will be essential in any testing for genetic susceptibility. The benefits of the various presymptomatic interventions must be weighed against the potential anxiety, stigmatization, and other possible harms to individuals who are informed that they are at increased risk of developing future disease.

Population screening for predisposition to late-onset monogenic diseases should only be considered for treatable or preventable conditions of relatively high frequency. Under such guidelines, population screening should only be offered after appropriate, reliable, sensitive, and specific tests become available. Such tests do not yet exist. The committee recommends that the predictive value of genetic tests be thoroughly validated in prospective studies of sufficient size and statistical power before their widespread application. Since there will be a considerable time lag before the appearance of confirmatory symptoms, these studies will require support for long periods of time. . . .

In the case of predictive tests for mental disorders, results must be handled with stringent atten-tion to confidentiality to protect an already vulnerable population. If no effective treatment is available, testing may not be appropriate since more harm than good could result from improper use of test results. On the other hand, future research might result in psychological or drug treatments that could prevent the onset of these diseases. Carefully designed pilot studies should be conducted to determine the effectiveness of such interventions and to measure the desirability and psychosocial impact of such testing. Interpretation and communication of predictive test results in psychiatry will be particularly difficult. To prepare for the issues associated with genetic testing for psychiatric diseases in the future, psychiatrists and other mental health professionals will need more training in genetics and genetic counseling; such training should include the ethical, legal, and social issues in genetic testing.

Because of their wide applicability, it is likely there will be strong commercial interests in the introduction of genetic tests for common, high-profile complex disorders. **Strict guidelines for efficacy therefore will be necessary to prevent premature introduction of this technology.**

TESTING OF CHILDREN OR MINORS

Children should generally be tested only for genetic disorders for which there exists an effective curative or preventive treatment that must be instituted early in life to achieve maximum benefit. Childhood testing is not appropriate for carrier status, untreatable childhood diseases, and late-onset diseases that cannot be prevented or forestalled by early treatment. In general, the committee believes that testing of minors should be discouraged unless delaying such testing would reduce benefits of available treatment or monitoring. It is essential that the individual seeking testing understand the potential abuse of such information in society, including in employment or insurance practice, and that the provider should ensure that confidentiality is respected. . . .

Because only certain types of genetic testing are appropriate for children, multiplex testing that includes tests specifically directed to obtaining information about carrier status, untreatable childhood diseases, or late-onset diseases should not be included in the multiplex tests offered to children. **Research should be undertaken to determine the appropriate age for testing and screening for genetic disorders, both to maximize the benefits of therapeutic intervention and to avoid the possibility of generating**

genetic information about a child when there is no likely benefit and there is possibility of harm to the child.

. . .

FINANCING OF GENETIC TESTING SERVICES

The cost and financing of genetic testing and counseling have had a profound effect on access to these services in the United States. No matter what aspect of genetics is discussed, it is almost impossible to keep the discussion from turning to issues related to financing, in particular the role of health insurance in genetic testing and counseling. . . . The United States is the only developed country in the world without a social insurance or statutory system to cover basic expenses for medical services for most of its population. This creates problems of access and equity, especially for those low-income or high-risk individuals who are self-employed, work part-time, or are employed by small businesses and who may not be able to afford or obtain health insurance. Over 37 million people are without health insurance coverage in the United States.

Even for those who have health insurance, coverage for most preventive, screening, and counseling services may be excluded. These limitations of health care coverage in the United States particularly affect genetic services, which have an important counseling component. Insurance reimbursement or other financing of genetic testing is not generally available now in the United States. The committee also heard testimony that individuals whose insurance does cover some or all genetic services may be reluctant or unwilling to file claims for such services. They may fear that the genetic information they sought might be used to evaluate and deny their future applications for health or life insurance coverage, or lead to higher premiums or limited coverage. And, because so much coverage in the United States is employment based, people may also worry that their employer will have access to the information and use it (overtly or covertly) to discriminate against them. . . .

In order to develop appropriate financing for genetic testing and counseling services, private and public health plans, and geneticists and consumers, should work together to develop guidelines for the reimbursement of genetic services. Such guidelines should address the issue of how each new genetic test should be assessed for its sensitivity and specificity in light of the availability of effective treatment, the con-

sequences of the test, the evaluation of pilot study results, and when new tests are appropriate for use in routine clinical practice. . . .

In addition, the insurance concept of what is considered *medically necessary* (and therefore reimbursable) should be expanded to include the *offering* of *appropriate genetic testing* and related education and counseling, making these genetic services reimbursable under health insurance plans. Medical appropriateness can often be established by a family history of the disorder. In pregnancy, medical necessity should be considered established for cytogenetic testing in pregnancies in women of advanced maternal age or considered at high risk based on other methods of assessing risk. The committee also recommends that newborn screening and MSAFP [maternal serum alpha-fetoprotein] screening in pregnant women of any age be considered within the insurance definition of medically appropriate and be reimbursable under health insurance plans. . . .

SOCIAL, LEGAL, AND ETHICAL ISSUES IN GENETIC TESTING

The committee recommends that vigorous protection be given to *autonomy, privacy, confidentiality, and equity.* These principles should be breached only in rare instances and only when the following conditions are met: (1) the action must be aimed at an important goal — such as the protection of others from serious harm — that outweighs the value of autonomy, privacy, confidentiality, or equity in the particular instance; (2) it must have a high probability of realizing that goal; (3) there must be no acceptable alternatives that can also realize the goal without breaching those principles; and (4) the degree of infringement of the principle must be the minimum necessary to realize the goal.

VOLUNTARINESS

Voluntariness should be the cornerstone of any genetic testing program. The committee found no justification for a state-sponsored *mandatory* public health program involving genetic testing of adults or for unconsented-to genetic testing of patients in the clinical setting. There is evidence that voluntary screening programs achieve a higher level of efficacy in screening, and there is no evidence that mandating newborn screening is necessary or sufficient to ensure that the vast majority of newborns are screened. Mandatory *offering* of newborn screening is appropriate for disorders with treatments of demonstrated efficacy where very early intervention is essential to improve health outcomes (e.g., phenylketonuria and congenital hypothyroidism). One benefit of voluntariness and informing parents about newborn screening is that of quality assurance: parents can check to see if the sample was actually drawn. In addition, since people will be facing the possibility of undergoing many more genetic tests in their lifetimes, the disclosure of information to parents about newborn screening prior to the event can be an important tool for education about genetics.

INFORMED CONSENT

Obtaining informed consent should be the method of ensuring that genetic testing is voluntary. By *informed consent* the committee means a *process* of education and the opportunity to have questions answered—not merely the signing of a form. The patient or client should be given information about the risks, benefits, efficacy, and alternatives to the testing; information about the severity, potential variability, and treatability of the disorder being tested for; information about the subsequent decisions that will be likely if the test is positive (such as a decision about abortion); and information about any potential conflicts of interest of the person or institution offering the test. . . . **Research should therefore also be undertaken to determine what patients *want* to know in order to make a decision about whether or not to undergo a genetic test.** People often have less interest in the label for the disorder and its mechanisms of action than in how certainly the test predicts the disorder, what effects the disorder has on physical and mental functioning, and how intrusive, difficult, or effective any existing treatment protocol would be. Research is also necessary to determine the advantages and disadvantages of various means of conveying that information (e.g., through specialized genetic counselors, primary care providers, single disorder counselors, brochures, videos, audiotapes, computer programs).

CONFIDENTIALITY

All forms of genetic information should be considered confidential and should not be disclosed without the individual's consent (except as required by state law, or in rare instances discussed in [other parts of the committee's report]. This includes genetic information that is obtained through specific genetic testing of a person, as well as genetic information about that person that is obtained in other ways (e.g., physical examination, past treatment, or a relative's genetic status). The confidentiality of genetic information should be protected no matter who obtains or maintains that information. This includes genetic information collected or maintained by health care professionals, health care institutions, researchers, employers, insurance companies, laboratory personnel, and law enforcement officials. To the extent that current statues do not ensure such confidentiality, they should be amended.

Codes of ethics for professionals providing genetic services should contain specific provisions to protect autonomy, privacy, and confidentiality. The committee endorses the 1991 National Society of Genetic Counselors (NSGC) statement of guiding principles on confidentiality of test results:

The NSGC support individual confidentiality regarding results of genetic testing. It is the right and responsibility of the individual to determine who shall have access to medical information, particularly results of testing for genetic conditions.

Confidentiality should be breached and relatives informed about genetic risks *only* when (1) attempts to elicit voluntary disclosure fail, (2) there is a high probability of irreversible harm that the disclosure will prevent, and (3) there is no other reasonable way to avert the harm. When disclosure is to be attempted over the patient's refusal, the burden should be on the person who wishes to disclose to justify to the patient, to an ethics committee, and perhaps in court that the disclosure was necessary and met the committee's test. Thus, the committee has determined that the disadvantages of informing relatives over the patient's refusal generally outweigh the advantages, except in the rare instances described above. . . . **The committee recommends that health care providers not reveal genetic information about a patient's carrier status to the patient's spouse without the patient's permission, and that information on misattributed paternity should be given to the mother, but not be volunteered to her partner.**

As a matter of general principle, the committee believes strongly that patients should disclose to relatives genetic information relevant to ensuring the

health of those relatives. Patients should be encouraged and aided in sharing appropriate genetic information with spouses and relatives. To facilitate the disclosure of relevant genetic information to family members, accurate and balanced materials should be developed to assist individuals in informing their families, and in providing access to further information, as well as access to testing if relatives should choose to be tested. Under those rare circumstances where unauthorized disclosure of genetic information is deemed warranted, the genetic counselor should first try to obtain the permission of the person to release the information.

The committee also endorses the principles on the protection of DNA data and DNA data banking developed in 1990 by the ASHG [American Society of Human Genetics] Ad Hoc Committee on Identification by DNA Analysis. In short, patients' consent should be obtained before their names are provided to a genetic disease registry, and their consent should also be obtained before information is redisclosed. **Each entity that receives or maintains genetic information or samples should have procedures in place to protect confidentiality.** Information or samples should be kept free of identifiers and instead use encoding to link the information or sample to the individual's name. Finally, any entity that releases genetic information about an individual to someone other than that individual should ensure that the recipient of the genetic information has procedures in place to protect the confidentiality of the information.

GENETIC DISCRIMINATION IN HEALTH INSURANCE

Legislation should be adopted to prevent medical risks, including genetic risks, from being taken into account in decisions on whether to issue or how to price health care insurance. Because health insurance differs significantly from other types of insurance in that it regulates access to health care — an important social good — risk-based health insurance should be eliminated. Access to health care should be available to every American without regard to the individual's present health status or condition; in particular, the committee recommends that insurability decisions not be based on genetic status. . . .

Some of the committee's concerns about genetic discrimination in health insurance would be obviated by current proposals for national health insurance reform that would eliminate most, if not all, aspects of medical underwriting. **The committee recommends that insurance reform preclude the use of genetic information in establishing eligibility for health insurance.** As health insurance reform proposals are developed, those concerned with genetic disorders will need to assess whether they adequately protect genetic information and persons with genetic disorders from health insurance discrimination and discrimination in the provision of medical services. . . .

GENETIC DISCRIMINATION IN EMPLOYMENT

Legislation should be adopted that forbids employers to collect genetic information on prospective or current employees unless it is clearly job related. Sometimes employers will have employees submit to medical exams to see if they are capable of performing particular job tasks. If an individual consents to the release of genetic information to an employer or potential employer, the releasing entity should not release specific information, but instead answer only yes or no regarding whether the individual was fit to perform the job at issue.

The committee urges the Equal Employment Opportunity Commission to recognize that the language of the Americans with Disabilities Act (ADA) provides protection for presymptomatic people with genetic risks for late-onset disorders, unaffected carriers of disorders that might affect their children, and individuals with genetic profiles indicating the possibility of increased risk of a multifactorial disorder. State legislatures should adopt laws to protect people from genetic discrimination in employment. In addition, ADA should be amended (and similar state statues adopted) to limit the type of medical testing employers can request and to ensure that the medical information they can collect is job related.

•   •   •

E. VIRGINIA LAPHAM, CHAHIRA KOZMA, AND JOAN O. WEISS

Genetic Discrimination: Perspectives of Consumers

The rapid advances in human genetics, largely fueled by the Human Genome Project (HGP), have resulted in the expansion of the number and range of genetic tests.[1] These tests are capable of providing carrier and presymptomatic information including risk of future disease, disability, and early death. In addition, these tests may reveal genetic information not only about the health of the individual, but also about his or her family members.[2]

Concern about access to genetic information by health insurers has historical support.[3, 4] In the early 1970s, several insurance companies discriminated against individuals who were carriers of sickle cell anemia, even though they were quite healthy.[5] The use of genetic information to deny life insurance to individuals leaves their dependents more vulnerable to economic consequences than is the case with the 70% of adults who are covered.[6] The use of genetic screening to identify workers who may be particularly sensitive to noxious environments has been the principal focus of concern about workplace genetic testing even when done for benevolent reasons.[7] Issues of genetic discrimination in employment and insurance have become more urgent as a result of the genome project.[8]

Overall concerns about privacy and confidentiality have led the Ethical, Legal, and Social Issues (ELSI) Branch of the National Center for Human Genome Research to identify this issue as a top priority with the goal of proposing legislation specifically designed to protect people against genetic discrimination.[9] Additionally, several working groups and scholars are focusing on this issue and have developed background

papers and policy recommendations about the use of genetic information in health insurance as well as other areas such as life insurance and employment.[10, 11] Despite these concerns about potential genetic discrimination and documentation of individual cases, there is little information about the incidence and range of the problem.[12]

This report provides information on the experiences of 332 individuals with one or more family members with a genetic disorder who are affiliated with genetic support groups. The study was part of the Human Genome Education Model (HuGEM) Project of the Georgetown University Child Development Center and the Alliance of Genetic Support Groups. It was the first phase of the HuGEM Project with the aim of getting input from 300 consumers in order to develop, implement, and evaluate a collaborative education model for consumers and health care providers.

Participants were recruited primarily through the national, regional, and local genetic support groups affiliated with the Alliance of Genetic Support Groups. Notices were put in two issues of the monthly *Alliance Alert* and letters were sent to the directors of 101 genetic support groups (representing an estimated 585,800 members). The notices contained information about the study and requested volunteers that were at least 18 years old and with one or more persons in the family with a genetic disorder who would be willing to participate in a 30-min telephone interview to provide opinions on the ethical, legal, and social issues of the HGP as well as priority topics for education. Volunteers were assured confidentiality of their responses. Random sampling was considered and ruled out because of time, cost, and the primarily educational focus of the project. Thus, the findings are applicable only to

Reprinted with the permission of the publisher from *Science* 274 (October 25, 1996), 621–24. Copyright © 1996 American Association for the Advancement of Science.

this group. Support group leaders were requested to distribute the letter requesting volunteers at meetings and in newsletters. Persons interested in participating were to complete a form at the bottom of the letter or call a 1-800 number for more information.

As a result of information provided by the support groups to the members or through the *Alliance Alert,* a group of 483 persons (from 73 different groups) contacted the Alliance of Genetic Support Groups about the study. They were sent information about the study and about the Human Genome Project. Of these, 336 (70%) returned consent forms.[13] From this group, four persons decided not to participate after the interviews started, 306 persons completed telephone interviews, and 26 requested and completed the questionnaire by mail, for a total return of 332 respondents from 44 states and the District of Columbia.[14]

Respondents were primarily female, highly educated, married, and Caucasian[15] — characteristics believed to be typical of genetic support groups.[16] Age categories ranged from the twenties through seventies with a median age in the forties. A range of religious preferences was reported.[17] There was an average of 2.1 affected family members per respondent with a range of 1 to 12 affected members reported.

The study questionnaire was composed primarily of questions with multiple choice responses. Telephone interviews were conducted by four social workers, a genetic counselor, and a consumer administrator[18] and lasted an average of 40 min with a range of 29 to 90 min. The content covered five areas: demographic information; knowledge of the Human Genome Project (61% had heard about the HGP before volunteering to participate in the study, 74% considered the HGP very important to their families, and 81% considered it very important to society); personal and family experience in areas related to genetic testing and research; opinions on a range of ethical, legal, and social issues; and priority topics for education. The education priorities were used to develop and implement educational forums in the mid-Atlantic and Pacific Northwest regions and will be described elsewhere.

Respondents were asked whether they or other family members had encountered problems with health insurance, life insurance, and employment.[19] The term "genetic discrimination" was not used in the survey. It is used in this report to describe prejudicial actions as perceived by the respondents that resulted from insurers' or employers' knowledge of an individual's genetic condition, carrier status, or presumed carrier sta-

tus, based on observation, family history, genetic testing, or other means of gathering genetic information.[20]

Respondents reported 101 different primary genetic disorders. The 18% of families with two or more disorders were asked to select one for purposes of the study. Of the primary disorders 68% were single-gene disorders, 10% were chromosome disorders, 11% were multifactorial disorders, 11% were major malformation syndromes, and less than 1% were mitochondrial and endocrine diseases.

Data analysis included frequency responses and comparison of responses to the questions on genetic discrimination by education, religious preference, and health of respondent and they showed no statistically significant differences (Pearson value of $P < 0.05$ was considered significant). Gender and ethnicity showed no significant differences when controlled for sample size.

Consumer experiences with health insurers were deemed important because the availability of affordable health insurance often determines who does and who does not have access to health care.[4] For many people with genetic disorders, health insurance may mean the difference between life and death.[21]

Although considerable genetic information may already be available to insurers in medical records, 40% of the respondents recalled being specifically asked about genetic diseases or disabilities on their applications for health insurance (Table 1). It cannot be assumed that the remaining 60% had not been asked questions about genetic diseases and disabilities. Many of them volunteered the information that they had never applied for health insurance. Some were able to maintain the coverage they had prior to diagnosis of a genetic disorder. Others had not applied because they assumed the genetic condition in the family would result in being turned down. Whether or not this information was then used to deny insurance to these people based on their genetic condition is not known.

Twenty-two percent of the respondents (Table 1) said that they or a family member were refused health insurance as a result of the genetic condition in the family. Since insurers do not need to provide reasons for turning down applications, it might be argued that respondents may have subjectively assumed that the denials were made because of the genetic condition. In this study, however, 83% of those who were refused health insurance had also been asked about genetic diseases or disabilities on their applications. Looked at in another way,

Table 1. Questions and Responses about Experiences of Consumers in Areas of Health Insurance, Life Insurance, and Employment. The Total Number of Respondents Is 332.

Question	Responses (%)		
	Yes	No	Don't know
As a result of the genetic condition in your family, have you or a member of your family been—			
Asked questions about genetic diseases or disabilities on an application for health insurance?	40	55	5
Refused health insurance?	22	76	2
Refused insurance coverage of some service or treatment?	31	67	2
Refused life insurance?	25	70	6
Asked questions about genetic diseases or disabilities on a job application?	15	83	2
Denied a job or let go from a job?	13	85	2

Table 2. Questions and Responses to Opinions about Genetic Information in Insurance and Employment.

Question	Responses (%)		
	Strongly agree or agree	Disagree or strongly disagree	Not sure or don't know
Genetic testing should be part of pre-employment physical exams.	4	94	2
Health insurers should be able to get genetic information if they pay for the tests.	16	78	6
	Yes	No	Not sure
If you were tested and found to be at high risk for a genetic disorder with serious complications, which of the following would you want to know the results of the test?			
a. Your employers?	6	87	7
b. Your insurance company?	11	83	6

nearly half (47%) of those who were asked about genetic diseases or disabilities on an application for health insurance were subsequently turned down. As health and life insurers are primarily regulated by states and most states are just beginning to address genetic issues in legislation,[22] it is not known how many insurers actually ask genetic questions on applications.

The 31% of respondents with health insurance coverage who were denied reimbursement for some service or treatment indicated reasons such as the treatments were considered experimental, and services such as physical or occupational therapy were not considered a medical necessity. Time limits for submitting claims were also an issue, with insurers not paying claims that were more than a year old even when they had been submitted within the year and returned for more information. In several instances, payment was

denied even though preapproval for a treatment or service had been given.

The large majority (83%) of respondents (Table 2) said they would not want their insurers to know if they were tested and found to be at high risk for a genetic disorder. The rate decreased to 78% when a similar question was asked that added the condition, "if the insurer pays for the tests." Some of the respondents noted that they would pay for genetic tests themselves or not be tested if they wanted to keep their genetic information confidential. The fear of genetic discrimination, as shown in Table 3, resulted in 9% of the respondents or a family member refusing to be tested for a genetic condition. This fear eliminates the opportunities of individuals to learn that they are not at increased risk for the genetic disorder in the family or to make life-style changes to reduce the risks or seriousness of the con-

Table 3. Percentage of Respondents Withholding Information or Refusing to Be Tested for a Genetic Condition as a Result of Fear.

Question	Responses (%)		
	Yes	No	Don't know
As a result of a genetic condition, have you or a member of your family—			
Refused to be tested for a genetic condition for fear of your insurance coverage being dropped.	9	89	2
Not revealed genetic information to an insurance company.	18	79	3
Not revealed genetic information to an employer.	17	81	2

dition. It may also affect the number of people willing to participate in scientific research.[10] Fear also prevented 18% of the respondents from revealing genetic information to an insurance company.

Approximately 70% of adults in the United States have some form of life insurance.[23] It is widely available, and only 3% of those who apply for coverage are declined. Of the 97% accepted, 5% are required to pay higher than standard premiums.[24] This may be compared to the respondents in this study in which 25% (Table 1) of the respondents or affected family member have been refused life insurance.[25]

Two questions were asked about the employment experiences of the study population. As noted in Table 1, 15% of the respondents said that they or affected family members had been asked questions about genetic diseases or disabilities on job applications. This increased to 29% of affected respondents ($P = 0.006$). It is not clear how often this information was used to subsequently deny the job to the applicants but the possibility exists and was of concern to respondents. In this study, 87% of respondents (Table 2) would not want their employers to know if they were tested and found to be at high risk for a genetic disorder with serious complications.

Thirteen percent of all respondents (Table 1) reported that they or another family member had been denied a job or let go from a job because of the genetic condition in the family. This was true for 21% of affected respondents and 4% of unaffected respondents ($P = 0.00001$). The percent was reduced to 9% ($P = 0.006$) for those with an affected child, even though a higher proportion of these respondents were in the workforce than the total population.

During the course of the analysis, a question was raised as to whether the perceived problems encoun-

tered in job application or denial or dismissal emanated from an employer's perception of a visible disability. To approach this question, analysis was done for the 77 unaffected respondents whose only affected family member was a child of less than 16 years of age. It was found that 7% of this population was asked about genetic diseases or disabilities on a job application and 3% were denied or let go from a job. These numbers should only be used as a starting point for future analyses.

For the affected respondents, some specific examples highlight the kinds of problems experienced. A man with a sex chromosome disorder reported that he had been denied a job following a pre-employment physical exam after the doctor wrote the name of the possible disorder on his medical report. The employer, in this case, knew it was illegal to use the diagnosis in the hiring decision and told the applicant that he would deny the conversation in the future if asked. A woman with a skeletal disorder reported that she was given termination notice the day after she informed her employer of a genetic diagnosis. The notice was withdrawn after she sought legal counsel. Examples provided by other respondents focused on effects of the genetic condition that could come under the protection of the 1995 interpretations of the Americans with Disabilities Act.[26] The dilemma for persons with genetic disorders is that they must show not only that they have a genetic defect but also that they were regarded as "disabled" by an employer and discriminated against because of that perception. This raises concerns about the privacy and confidentiality of genetic information in the workplace.

A total of 17% have not revealed genetic information to their employers (Table 3) for fear of losing their jobs or insurance coverage. This increased to 25% of affected respondents ($P = 0.00001$). Overall, 43% of the respondents reported that they or members of their family have experienced genetic discrimination in one or more of the three areas. This included health insurance only (9%), life insurance only (11%), employment only (6%), and more than one category (17%).

Additional studies of persons with genetic disorders are indicated to confirm or deny the perceptions of the consumers in this study. It is possible that members of genetic support groups who have experienced genetic discrimination may have been more motivated to volunteer for this study. On the other hand, persons with these resources of higher education and membership in support groups traditionally have the skills and means to work with and influence social systems and may have experienced less discrimination than other groups. With adequate funding, a random sampling of respondents from support group or clinic populations could be selected with probability methods and objective as well as subjective information could be gathered.

Another goal would be to design more detailed questions to elicit information on genetic discrimination from respondents. Distinctions between the implications of overt genetic disease and conditions on each person and the effects on unaffected family members, or persons who are carriers or do not overtly express the consequences of the genetic condition will require further study. Consumers may be willing to participate if confidentiality is assured and trust is established. In this study, it was also found important for the interviewers to have clinical as well as technical skills in interviewing to facilitate the comfort level of discussing sensitive issues. This would also be recommended for future studies.

Although the goal of the HGP (and other genetic testing and research) is to help people, it could also cause harm if the level of perceived discrimination is in fact true. Neither the authors nor the respondents (as indicated in earlier responses) are suggesting that the HGP should not continue. On the contrary, there is strong support to continue research and to find ways to deal with genetic discrimination including federal or state legislation, guidelines, and standards among insurers, employers, researchers, and health professionals, and citizen advocacy to establish protections.[27]

NOTES

1. National Center for Human Genome Research, National Institutes of Health, *The Human Genome Project: From Maps to Medicine* (NIH Publication No. 95-3897, Bethesda, MD, 1995).

2. G. Geller *et al. J. Law Med. Ethics* **21,** 238 (1993).

3. N. E. Kass, *Hastings Cent. Rep.* **22,** S6 (1992); T. H. Murray, ibid., p. S12.

4. E. Draper, ibid., p. S15.

5. L. B. Andrews, J. E. Fullarton, N. A. Holtzman, A. G. Mutulsky, Eds. *Assessing Genetic Risks: Implications for Health and Social Policy* (National Academy Press, Washington, DC, 1994).

6. The Ad Hoc Committee on Genetic Testing/Insurance Issues, *Am. J. Hum. Genet.* **56,** 327 (1995).

7. T. H. Murray, "The Human Genome Project and Genetic Testing: Ethical Implications," Report of a Conference on the Ethical and Legal Implications of Genetic Testing: The Genome, Ethics and the Law," American Association for the Advancement of Science, 14 to 16 June 1991.

8. R. M. Cook-Deegan, in *Biomedical Politics,* K. E. Hanna, Ed. (National Academy Press, Washington, DC, 1991). p. 148.

9. F. S. Collins, *J. Clin. Ethics* **2,** 4 (1991).

10. H. Ostrer, *Am. J. Hum. Genet.* **52,** 565 (1993); U.S. Congress, Office of Technology Assessment, *Genetic Monitoring and Screening in the Workplace,* OTA-BA-455 (U.S. Government Printing Office, Washington, DC, 1990).

11. *Genetic Information and Health Insurance: Report of the Task Force on Genetic Information and Insurance* (National Institutes of Health–Department of Energy Working Group on the Ethical, Legal, and Social Implications of Human Genome Research, 10 May 1993).

12. See, for example, P. R. Billings *et al., Am. J. Hum. Genet.* **50,** 476 (1992).

13. As the interviews progressed and it was apparent that few members of ethnic or racial minorities were volunteering, additional telephone outreach was made to support groups to increase awareness of the project and opportunities for volunteering. This was only partially successful as seen in the demographic data.

14. There were no statistically significant differences in the responses on the telephone and written interviews so they are reported here together.

15. Of the 332 respondents, 80% were female, 57% have at least a bachelors degree, and 90% were Caucasian. Other characteristics were: 75% were married and living with their spouses, 76% have children, and 63% work outside the home. Family relationship, whether or not the respondent or family members were affected, age of diagnosis, and current age were also recorded.

16. Precise data on the demographics of genetic support groups are not available. Impressions are from staff of the Alliance of Genetic Support Groups based on their conversations and communications with the member organizations and attendance at national, regional, and local meetings.

17. Religious preferences were Roman Catholic, 26%; Protestant, 41%; Christian-other, 9%; Jewish, 11%; other, 2%; and none, 12%.

18. The interviewers were trained in interview techniques by the principal investigator and participated in pretesting the questionnaire.

19. The questions on possible genetic discrimination were taken from a questionnaire developed by Dr. Dorothy C. Wertz, The Shriver Center, Waltham, MA, entitled, *Ethical Issues in Genetics, Part 1,* p. 33, No. 34, and used with permission of Dr. Wertz (letter of 16 December 1993).

20. This definition of genetic discrimination differs from the one used by Billings *et al.* (*12*) as they did not include actions against persons who were symptomatic or visibly affected by their genetic disorders. The design of our questionnaire does not permit analysis according to the definition of Billings *et al.* (1993). Because the questions on discrimination ask about all family members at once,

the questions do not distinguish among: (i) the direct consequences of ongoing genetic disease or conditions, (ii) the effect of genetic disease on other family members, and (iii) the consequences of genetic information gained through testing.

21. M. J. Ellis Kahn, in a video by the HuGEM Project, *An Overview of the Human Genome Project and Its Ethical, Legal, and Social Issues* (Georgetown University Medical Center, Washington, DC, 1995).

22. K. H. Rothenberg, *J. Law Med. Ethics* **23**, 313 (1995).

23. The Ad Hoc Committee on Genetic Testing/Insurance Issues, *Am. J. Hum. Genet.* **56**, 328 (1995).

24. "Report of the ACLI-HIAA Task Force on Genetic Testing," The American Council of Life Insurance and The Health Insurance Association of America (1991).

25. Many respondents said they had never applied for life insurance because they assumed they would be turned down.

26. Since 1990, the Americans with Disabilities Act (ADA) has provided protection for persons with disabilities in the workplace. The ADA prevents employers from openly denying employment or firing an individual solely on the basis of a "disability" if there are "reasonable accommodations" that can be made in the work setting to allow the person to perform his or her job. In April 1995, the ADA was interpreted by the U.S. Equal Employment Opportunity Commission to include healthy people who are carriers of genetic disorders. Implementation in general relies on employers and employees knowing and similarly interpreting the law as well as having good faith efforts to comply.

27. We wish to thank the HuGEM Advisory Committee; N. A. Holtzman, F. Neal-Smith, E. O. Nightingale, K. H. Rothenberg, and L. Walters, for assistance in planning and carrying out the study. We also wish to thank L. Palincsar, M. A. Wilson, S. Rennert, and M. Volner, for their assistance with the telephone interviews and M. J. Verdieck and M. O'Reilly for research assistance. Most of all, we wish to thank the consumers who provided the data. Funded by the National Institutes of Health at the National Center of Human Genome Research in the branch of Ethical, Legal and Social Issues, grant number RO1-HG00786-03. This support does not constitute an endorsement of the views expressed in this article.

Human Gene Therapy and Genetic Enhancement

LEROY WALTERS AND JULIE GAGE PALMER

The Ethics of Human Gene Therapy

SCIENTIFIC ISSUES

GENE THERAPY FOR ADA DEFICIENCY

On September 14, 1990, the first officially sanctioned human somatic-cell gene therapy experiment began. A 4-year-old girl was the first of two children to receive a dose of her own cells in which a functioning counterpart of her malfunctioning gene had been previously inserted. As early as December of the same year, and continuing through the end of the first phase of the experiment in July 1991, newspaper headlines dramatically cheered news of the experiment's success.[1]

The subjects of this successful gene therapy experiment were children suffering from a rare genetic disease called *adenosine deaminase (ADA) deficiency.* ADA deficiency arises from the malfunction of a gene expressed in bone marrow *stem cells,* long-lived cells that differentiate into multiple types of blood cells, including infection-fighting T and B cells (varieties of white blood cells). The malfunctioning ADA genes in these cells fail to produce functional versions of adenosine deaminase, an enzyme that normally metabolizes a compound called *deoxyadenosine.* Absent ADA, toxic levels of deoxyadenosine accumulate. T cells suffer the most from this buildup. These important infection-fighting cells are devastated, leaving the patient prey to infections which healthy individuals could easily withstand. Ultimately, most patients suffering from this rare disease die from infection unless a matched bone marrow donor can be found.[2] Unfortunately, matched donors are available for only about 30% of patients.[3] ADA-deficiency patients usually die before they reach the age of 2.[4]

ADA deficiency was an appropriate initial candidate for gene therapy for several reasons. First, researchers had long been convinced that even a small level of ADA production would be sufficient to operate as a cure for an ADA-deficient patient. They therefore did not have to achieve high expression levels in order to test the therapy. Additionally, the ADA gene is subject to relatively simple regulation, which made the achievement of appropriate ADA gene expression less complex than for other genes. Most significant was the hope that T cells armed with properly functioning ADA genes might have a selective advantage in the human body, allowing them to persist and multiply while noncorrected, ADA-deficient T cells expired.[5] Indeed, research had shown that human T cells, to which the ADA gene was added, survived in the bloodstreams of laboratory mice for months, while the cells with defective ADA genes died rapidly. The mouse experiments were evidence that T cells containing an inserted, functioning ADA gene were likely to thrive in patients suffering from ADA deficiency.[6]

In addition, numerous other animal experiments, in mice and in monkeys, had demonstrated that T cells could be successfully grown in vitro (literally, "in glass," meaning in a test tube), genetically altered, and reintroduced into animals where they would function appropriately as immune cells.[7] Although researchers had initially hoped to insert the functioning ADA gene into bone marrow stem cells, where the gene could be expected to persist indefinitely, they were, until recently, unable to purify the stem cells in the laboratory. Nevertheless, the T-cell results in animals were good enough to warrant a human experiment of the therapy.[8]

A team of investigators, led by National Institutes of Health doctors W. French Anderson, R. Michael Blaese, Kenneth W. Culver, and Steven Rosenberg, designed the first human gene therapy experiments in accordance with these extensive, preliminary animal experiments. During the human gene therapy experiment, doctors obtained blood from each ADA-deficient patient. The research team isolated T cells from these blood samples in the laboratory and grew the T cells in vitro. Then they inserted properly functioning ADA genes into the T cell using a process known as *transduction* in which an engineered RNA virus called a *retrovirus* carried the genes into the T cells. . . . Finally, doctors reinfused into each patient her (both are female) own altered T cells. The patients each received approximately six doses of transduced cells during the several-month first phase of the experiment.[9]

In conjunction with the gene therapy, the patients received a drug called *polyethyleneglycol (PEG)-ADA,* a version of the ADA enzyme itself. PEG-ADA had previously proven somewhat effective, but not effective enough to allow patients to fully regain immune function. Although able to decrease extracellular levels of deoxyadenosine, PEG-ADA cannot gain entrance to the T cells. Hence, PEG-ADA treatment by itself left the patients' T cells disabled. The investigators hoped that gene therapy would correct the T cells themselves and decrease intracellular levels of deoxyadenosine.[10]

The first scientific report on this initial gene therapy study was published in *Science* in October 1995.[11] Both young patients continue to receive PEG-ADA, although the dose has been reduced by more than half.[12] In laboratory measures of immune system function, both patients have shown improvement since the initiation of gene therapy in late 1990 and early 1991. In fact, the T-cell count for the younger of the two patients rose from below normal (about 500) to the normal range (1,200–1,800), and her blood levels for the enzyme ADA rose to about 50% of the levels in heterozygotes who carry one normal and one nonfunctioning ADA gene. The researchers estimate that about half of the T cells in the circulation of this younger patient carry the ADA gene.[13] In contrast, the older patient has much lower levels of ADA, and only 0.1–1.0% of her circulating T cells carry the ADA gene.[14]

More important than the laboratory values of these two patients is the effect of gene therapy plus PEG-ADA on their daily lives. Here is the researchers' summary of their clinical progress.

The effects of this treatment on the clinical well-being of these patients is more difficult to quantitate. Patient 1 [the younger patient], who had been kept in relative isolation in her home for her first 4 years, was enrolled in public kindergarten after 1 year on the protocol and has missed no more school because of infectious disease than her classmates or siblings. She has grown normally in height and weight and is considered to be normal by her parents. Patient 2 was regularly attending public school while receiving PEG-ADA treatment alone and has continued to do well clinically. Chronic sinusitis and headaches, which had been a recurring problem for several years, cleared completely a few months after initiation of the protocol.[15]

The same issue of *Science* in which the U.S. ADA study was reported also included a report by Italian researchers on their study of gene therapy in two young children with ADA deficiency. The Italian research team was led by Claudio Bordingnon of the Scientific Research Institute H. S. Raffaele in Milan. Both Italian patients had been started on enzyme therapy with PEG-ADA at the age of 2 years, and both had "failed" — that is, their immune systems were not adequately protecting them against infection — after treatment with PEG-ADA alone.[16] In the Italian study the two patients received both genetically modified T cells and genetically modified bone marrow cells plus ongoing support with PEG-ADA. Three years after the start of gene therapy in patient 1 (at age 5) and 2½ years after the start of treatment in patient 2 (at age 4), both patients are doing well clinically. The Italian researchers report that the genetically modified T cells have gradually died off after remaining in the children's circulation for 6–12 months but that the percentage of new T cells produced by genetically modified bone marrow progenitor cells is gradually increasing.[17]

The news media have greeted these two gene therapy studies with cautious optimism. For example, the headline of the story announcing the *Science* article on the U.S. study read, "Gene Therapy's First Success Is Claimed, But Doubts Remain."[18] These doubts have to do mainly with two features of the studies performed to date. First, for understandable reasons the researchers have been reluctant to withdraw PEG-ADA from children who are doing well on a combination of PEG-ADA and (past) gene therapy. Second, the experimental step of removing, selecting, and expanding the number of T cells may have a beneficial effect for patients, in addition to the beneficial effects of the genetic modification itself. Further research will help to resolve these remaining questions.[19]

• • •

DEVELOPMENTS IN GENE THERAPY SINCE 1990

Five years after the treatment of the first gene therapy patient in an approved protocol there [were] 100 protocols that [had] either been approved by the NIH Recombinant DNA Advisory Committee or that [were]

under review at the U.S. Food and Drug Administration. The target diseases in these 100 studies [were] the following (numbers refer to number of studies):

Cancers of various types: 63 (63%)

HIV infection/AIDS: 12 (12%)

Genetic diseases: 22 (22%)

Other diseases: 3 (3%)

   Rheumatoid arthritis: 1

   Peripheral artery disease: 1

   Arterial restenosis: 1

The category "Genetic Diseases" can be further subdivided among the following disorders (numbers refer to number of studies):

Cystic fibrosis: 12

Gaucher disease (Type I): 3

SCID due to adenosine deaminase (ADA) deficiency: 1

Familial hypercholesterolemia: 1

Alpha 1-antitrypsin deficiency: 1

Fanconi anemia: 1

Hunter syndrome (mild form): 1

Chronic granulomatous disease: 1

Purine nucleoside phosphorylase (PNP) deficiency: 1

• • •

ETHICAL ISSUES

AN INITIAL QUESTION: IS THIS KIND OF TREATMENT DIFFERENT?

In the ethical discussions that began in the late 1960s, commentators on human gene therapy sometimes seemed to assume that this technique was qualitatively different from other types of therapeutic interventions. However, as the ethical discussion of gene therapy has progressed, somatic cell gene therapy has increasingly been viewed as a natural and logical *extension* of current techniques for treating disease. Which of these views is correct?

On balance, the gene-therapy-as-extension view seems to be the more appropriate one. There are several reasons for adopting this view. First, because somatic cell gene therapy affects only nonreproductive cells, none of the genetic changes produced by somatic cell gene therapy will be passed on to the patient's children. Second, in some cases the products of the genetically modified somatic cells are similar to medications that patients can take as an alternative treatment. For example, there are enzyme therapies currently available for both ADA deficiency and Gaucher disease, but both enzyme therapies are very expensive and must be administered frequently. Third, some of the techniques currently used in somatic cell gene therapy closely resemble other widely used medical interventions — especially the transplantation of organs or tissues.

Several examples . . . illustrate how similar at least some somatic cell approaches are to transplantation. In the protocol for treating ADA deficiency, some of the patients' T cells were removed from their bodies and had the missing ADA gene added to them. The genetically modified cells were then returned to the patients' bodies, where they began to produce the missing enzyme, ADA. If the patients involved in this early gene therapy study had had healthy siblings whose cells closely matched their own, the alternative to gene therapy would have been a bone marrow transplant. In effect, the T cells of the healthy sibling (or more technically the stem cells that produce the T cells) would have replaced the patients' own ADA-deficient T cells.

The case is similar with cystic fibrosis (CF). Increasingly, lung transplants are being employed in the treatment of this disease. The cells in the transplanted lung will not have the genetic defect that causes CF and will therefore be able to function normally in the recipient. However, such transplants are expensive and highly invasive procedures, and there is a perpetual shortage of healthy organs for transplantation. Further, because transplanted organs never match the recipient's genotype exactly, except in the case of identical twins, the recipients will likely have to take drugs indefinitely to prevent his or her immune system from rejecting the transplant as foreign tissue. Somatic cell gene therapy seems to many observers to be a less invasive approach than the transplantation of a major organ. In addition, because it is the patient's own cells that are being genetically modified, there is a much lower probability that the cells will be rejected as foreign.

MAJOR ETHICAL QUESTIONS CONCERNING GENE-THERAPY RESEARCH

In the review of proposals to perform gene therapy research with human beings, seven questions are central:

1. What is the disease to be treated?
2. What alternative interventions are available for the treatment of this disease?
3. What is the anticipated or potential harm of the experimental gene therapy procedure?
4. What is the anticipated or potential benefit of the experimental gene therapy procedure?
5. What procedure will be followed to ensure fairness in the selection of patient-subjects?
6. What steps will be taken to ensure that patients, or their parents or guardians, give informed and voluntary consent to participating in the research?
7. How will the privacy of patients and the confidentiality of their medical information be protected?

Taken together, questions 1–4 constitute a kind of first hurdle, or initial threshold, that gene therapy research proposals must clear. If these questions are not satisfactorily answered, questions 5–7 will not even need to be asked. However, if the first four questions are satisfactorily answered, and the risk-benefit ratio for the proposed research seems appropriate, questions 5–7 remain as a second hurdle — a set of important procedural safeguards for prospective subjects in the research. [These seven questions are elaborated in more detail in a set of guidelines called the "Points to Consider." For the full text of these guidelines see http://www.nih.gov/od/ordanot.]

What is the Disease to Be Treated? Question 1 asks both a simple and a more profound question. It asks simply for the name of a condition or a disorder that is regarded by reasonable people to be a malfunction in the human body. Thus, "cystic fibrosis" would be an acceptable answer to the first question, while "average height" would not. At a more profound level, question 1 asks whether the disease or condition put forward as an early candidate for somatic cell gene therapy is sufficiently serious or life-threatening to merit being treated with a highly experimental technique. As the list of disorders treated in the first 100 gene therapy studies indicates, the conditions proposed for possible treatment by means of gene therapy do gravely compromise the quality and duration of human life.

It must be acknowledged that two of the disorders included in the above list do not qualify as life-threatening: rheumatoid arthritis and peripheral artery disease. Rheumatoid arthritis is a chronic condition that often causes severe pain to the person who is suffering from it, but this disease alone generally does not cause a patient's death. Similarly, peripheral artery disease in, for example, the lower leg and ankle of a person with diabetes will not cause the patient's death. However, this condition can be limb-threatening. That is, a limb that does not receive a sufficient flow of oxygen may need to be amputated in order to prevent gangrene from developing in the limb. In the future, gene therapy protocols may also be submitted that seek to preserve sight by taking new approaches to the treatment of currently untreatable eye diseases.

Philosophers have argued at considerable length about the precise definitions of health and disease.[20] For our analysis we have adopted a rather standard definition of health, "species-typical functioning."[21] It seems clear that all of the conditions to be treated by the first 100 gene therapy protocols represent significant deviations from the physiological norm of species-typical functioning and therefore qualify as bona fide diseases. But are there reasonable limits to the notion of disease? How far would we will be willing to extend the concept? At the far extremes exemplified in discriminatory social programs both past and present, we would never want to see human characteristics like gender, ethnicity, or skin color regarded as diseases. However, serious mental illness would be included within the scope of our definition. We would not consider mild obesity or a crooked nose or larger-than-average ears to be significant deviations from species-typical functioning. However, serious obesity that threatened to shorten life might well qualify as a disease. In each case a condition will need to be evaluated in the light of species-typical functioning and a judgment will have to be made about the extent to which the condition compromises such functioning.[22]

What Alternative Interventions Are Available for the Treatment of This Disease? Question 2 asks about alternative therapies. If available modes of treatment provide relief from the most serious consequences of a disease without major side effects and at reasonable cost, the disease may not be a good candidate for early clinical trials of gene therapy in humans. For example, phenylketonuria (PKU) is a hereditary disorder that can be detected in newborns through a simple blood test. Dietary therapy suffices to prevent the brain damage that would otherwise occur in children afflicted with the disorder. Therefore, PKU is probably not a good early candidate for gene therapy. Similarly, the harmful effects of diabetes can be controlled quite well in most patients through the use of insulin produced by recombinant

DNA techniques. Thus, diabetes may be a later rather than a earlier candidate for gene therapy research.

The determination that an alternative therapy is sufficiently effective is always a judgment call. In the review process for the first ADA deficiency study, it was noted that bone marrow transplantation was an effective treatment for children who had genetically matched siblings and that a synthetic form of ADA was available for use in ADA-deficient patients. The synthetic form of ADA was derived from the ADA produced by cattle and was linked, or conjugated, with the chemical PEG. The proponents of gene therapy for ADA deficiency pointed out that PEG-ADA could stimulate a hostile response by the human immune system because the synthetic compound was derived from cattle and thus might be perceived as foreign. The proponents also noted that, while most ADA-deficient patients benefited somewhat from treatment with PEG-ADA, they were still susceptible to many infections. Further, the high cost of PEG-ADA, about $250,000 per year, put this synthetic treatment out of the reach of most families. Thus, the reviewers of the initial ADA gene therapy protocol ultimately concluded that in families where children had no matched sibling donors, the alternative therapy of PEG-ADA was not wholly satisfactory. There was therefore space or justification for the development of gene therapy as a possibly superior approach to the treatment of this life-threatening pediatric disease.

As the field of gene therapy matures, the requirement that there be no effective alternative therapy may need to be relaxed. At some point there will need to be well-controlled studies that compare the gene therapy approach with alternative approaches to treatment of the same disease. However, given the novelty of gene therapy in 1990 and the uncertainty about its potential benefits and harms, it seems to us to have been appropriate to limit the earliest gene therapy trials to diseases and groups of patients for whom no alternative therapies were available.

What Is the Anticipated or Potential Harm of the Experimental Gene-Therapy Procedure? Question 3 concerns the anticipated or possible harm of somatic cell gene therapy. In responding to this question, researchers are asked to base their statements on the best available *data* from preclinical studies in vitro or in laboratory animal models like mice or monkeys. The use of domesticated (technically, replication-deficient) viruses as vectors in many somatic-cell gene-therapy studies raises one important safety question: How certain can researchers be that the domesticated viruses will not regain the genes that have been removed from them and thus regain the capacity to reproduce and cause an infection in the patient? A second kind of safety question arises from the "unguided-missile" quality of retroviral vectors. . . . [R]esearchers cannot predict where a retroviral vector with its attached gene and marker will "land" within the nucleus of a target cell. It is possible that the vector will integrate into the middle of a gene that is essential to the functioning of the cell and will therefore kill the cell. A further concern is the theoretical possibility that a retroviral vector might integrate beside a quiescent oncogene (cancer-causing gene) and stimulate it into becoming active. If so, a previously healthy cell might begin to divide uncontrollably and even start a cancer in a particular site. Because of these concerns about risk and safety, researchers are asked to provide data about preclinical studies in animals that, insofar as possible, exactly duplicate the gene therapy studies that they propose to do in human subjects.

What Is the Anticipated or Potential Benefit of the Experimental Gene Therapy Procedure? The fourth question is in many ways the mirror image of the third. It asks researchers once again to provide data from preclinical studies, but in this case the data should indicate that there is a reasonable expectation of benefit to human patients from their participation in the gene therapy study. One step in the review process for the first approved human gene therapy study in 1990 illustrates the importance of this point. Drs. Blaese and Anderson had provided impressive safety data to the RAC (the Recombinant DNA Advisory Committee — established in 1974 by NIH) . . . based on their long-term studies in mice and monkeys. However, RAC members were not convinced that the genetic modification of ADA-deficient T cells would be beneficial to human patients. What if the T cells died off quickly, or what if they were overwhelmed by the patients' own ADA-deficient T cells? Fortunately there was a researcher in Milan, Italy, Dr. Claudio Bordignon, who was willing to speak to the RAC about his own research in mice that had an immune deficiency similar to the one that afflicts ADA-deficient human patients. In these animals Dr. Bordignon was able to show that *human* T cells that carry a functioning ADA gene survive longer than ADA-deficient T cells. This was the information that the RAC was seeking, and Dr. Bordignon's report helped to ensure the approval of the Blaese-Anderson proposal.

There has been considerable debate about the appropriate relationship between question 3 and question 4 — or between anticipated harm and anticipated benefit of a gene therapy study. Some researchers have argued that if a gene therapy study is not likely to make patients worse off, it should be approved even if the probability of benefit is very low. This rationale may have been the basis for the controversial approval of a gene therapy protocol by former NIH director Bernadine Healy in December 1992. The proposal to treat a single cancer patient had not gone through regular view by the NIH RAC, and there was, in the opinion of most experts, little probability that it would benefit the terminally ill patient. Nonetheless, Dr. Healy approved the protocol on a "compassionate use" basis.[23] Since late 1992 the RAC has further discussed the requisite harm-benefit ratio in gene therapy studies. A majority of the committee members seem to have adopted the following view: Even if a gene therapy protocol provides a satisfactory answer to question 3 (about harm), it must also offer at least a low probability of benefit to the patients who are invited to enter the protocol, *and* it must have an excellent scientific design, so that the information gathered from studying the early patients will be useful to later patients and to the entire field of gene therapy research. That is, there must also be a satisfactory answer to question 4.

If these first four questions are satisfactorily answered, researchers have cleared a first hurdle or crossed an important threshold. They have demonstrated that the ratio of probable benefit to probable harm in a proposed study is sufficiently positive to justify proceeding to research in human beings. The remaining three questions ask how the research will be done, or, in other words, outline procedural safeguards for the patients who will be invited to take part in the gene therapy studies.

What Procedure Will Be Followed to Ensure Fairness in the Selection of Patient-Subjects? The first of the procedural questions, and the fifth question overall, asks how patients will be selected in a fair manner. With very rare disorders, like familial hypercholesterol-emia and ADA deficiency, fairness in the selection process was relatively unproblematic. Virtually every patient with the condition who was not too ill to participate was considered a candidate for gene therapy and invited to enroll in the studies. However, when somatic cell gene therapy began to be used for more prevalent conditions like brain tumors, the selection process became much more difficult. For example, the first study of gene therapy for brain tumors was led by Edward Oldfield and Kenneth Culver at the National Institutes of Health. Their proposal was initially approved for the study of 20 patients. Within the first year of their study the offices of Drs. Oldfield and Culver received more than 1,000 inquiries by patients, their family members and friends, and even governors and legislators. It was therefore quite important that a fair procedure, like first-come first-served, be in place to use in selecting among the many candidates for treatment.

In the review of the first 100 gene therapy protocols two other questions of fairness in selecting subjects have also arisen. The first question is whether children should be included in the initial studies, assuming that some children do survive to adulthood with the disease. The first gene therapy study, for severe combined immune deficiency (SCID), involved children precisely because, until now, almost no children with this disorder live to complete their teenage years. However, some patients with familial hypercholesterolemia do live to be 30, as do an increasing number of cystic fibrosis (CF) patients. There are two opposing ethical perspectives on the involvement of children in the early stages of clinical trials. The classical position, formulated in the early 1970s in the United States, was that clinical trials should be completed in adults first, before children are exposed to the potential harms of such trials.[24] The revisionist position of the late 1980s and 1990s is that participants in clinical trials are carefully monitored and that they often are the first people in a society to have access to new and possibly effective treatments. Therefore no class of individuals, whether women or members of ethnic minorities or children, should be excluded from the potential benefits of timely participation in clinical trials.[25]

A second question is closely related to the alternative-therapy question discussed above. It concerns the stage of disease at which people with serious disease should receive gene therapy. Already in 1987, during the review of the "Preclinical Data Document," there had been vigorous debate about whether gene therapy should be regarded as last-ditch therapy. In the early studies of gene therapy, patients had generally not been helped by alternative therapies, or no alternative therapies were available. As the field has matured, and as researchers have gained more confidence in the safety of gene therapy (if not in its effectiveness), the question has increasingly been raised, "Why not employ gene therapy at earlier stages in the disease process where it might have a better chance to prevent the deterioration of the patient's condition?"

What Steps Will Be Taken to Ensure that Patients, or Their Parents or Guardians, Give Informed and Voluntary Consent to Participating in the Research? The next procedural question, and the sixth question overall, concerns the voluntary and informed consent of patients or, in the case of minors, of their parents or guardians. It is always a challenge for researchers to convey to potential patient-subjects the important facts about their disease or condition, the major alternative treatments, and the precise procedures to be followed in the research. With a cutting-edge technology like human gene therapy this generic problem becomes even more difficult. For gene therapy studies, patients or their parents or guardians will frequently need a short course on how recombinant DNA research is conducted, how vectors are constructed, what cell types are targeted, how genes are inserted into cells, and how genes function in cells. In the case of specific gene therapy studies, additional modules may have to be added to the short course. For example, in the case of gene therapy for SCID, patients or their parents or guardians will need additional information on the human immune system and how specific kinds of cells, like T cells, function. While this educational responsibility may initially seem daunting, the question about voluntary, informed consent simply points to the importance of an extensive and ongoing dialogue between researchers and subjects, rather than the momentary act of signing a multiple-page consent form.

The response of researchers to question 6 has varied considerably. Some gene therapy proposals have included detailed information, including charts that outline the sequence and timing of proposed procedures, for patients. Other written consent forms have been woefully incomplete or have included ambiguous wording about who pays for procedures required by the research or about how the sponsoring institution deals with patients who are accidentally injured while they participate in research. Further, no external observers are present to monitor the quality of the consent *process* as patients are invited to take part in gene therapy studies. All that can be said with certainty is that the RAC has provided detailed guidance to researchers about the major points that RAC members think should be included in consent forms and that the consent forms themselves are reviewed in a public forum by peers who are not employees of the sponsoring institutions.

How Will the Privacy of Patients and the Confidentiality of Their Medical Information Be Protected? The third procedural question, and the seventh question overall, concerns privacy and confidentiality. There is no single "correct" answer to this question. It merely asks researchers to think through in advance how they and the subjects participating in gene therapy studies will deal with inquiries from the press and the general public. A particular concern was that patients have sufficient privacy and rest following their treatment to allow them "space" to benefit from this experimental approach to treatment. Different researchers and families have adopted varying policies regarding privacy and confidentiality. In the case of the ADA-deficiency protocol, the first two young women treated remained relatively anonymous until the second anniversary (in September 1992) of the first child's initial treatment. Less than a year later, the two children were featured, named, and pictured in a *Time* magazine story.[26] In contrast, the parents of two newborns treated at birth (in a modification of the same protocol) by a different technique using stem cells from umbilical cord blood allowed their names and pictures, and the names and pictures of their infants, to be disclosed almost immediately.[27] Similarly, the first patient in the study that aims to treat peripheral artery disease was interviewed by a reporter for the *New York Times* before he received his first gene transfer.[28]

This final question was included in the "Points to Consider" not to prescribe or proscribe any particular actions by patients or researchers but simply to encourage all parties involved in gene therapy studies to think through, in advance, a strategy for dealing with the press and the media. There had, in fact, been veritable media circuses when several earlier biomedical technologies had first been introduced. One thinks, for example, of the earliest heart transplant recipients, of Barney Clark and his artificial heart, of Baby Fae and

her baboon heart, and of Louise Brown, the first "test tube baby." In general, the introduction of gene therapy has been, in our view, more respectful of patients and their families.

. . .

NOTES

1. Larry Thompson, "Human Gene Therapy Test Working," *Washington Post,* December 16, 1990, p. A6; Natalie Angier, "Doctors Have Success Treating a Blood Disease by Altering Genes," *New York Times,* July 28, 1991, Section I, p. 20.

2. Experimental protocol submitted to the Human Gene Therapy Subcommittee of the Recombinant DNA Advisory Committee, entitled "Treatment of Severe Combined Immunodeficiency Disease (SCID) due to Adenosine Deaminase (ADA) Deficiency with Autologous Lymphocytes Transduced with a Human ADA Gene," pp. 2–3.

3. Ibid., p. 3.

4. Eve K. Nichols, *Human Gene Therapy* (Cambridge, MA: Harvard University Press, 1988), p. 217.

5. Response to Points to Consider for ADA Deficiency protocol, p. 15.

6. Thomas D. Gelehrter and Francis S. Collins, *Principles of Medical Genetics* (Baltimore: Williams & Wilkins, 1990), p. 295; Natalie Angier, "New Genetic Treatment Given Vote of Confidence," *New York Times,* June 3, 1990, Section I, p. 25.

7. Response to Points to Consider, p. 13 (22).

8. W. French Anderson, "Prospects for Human Gene Therapy," *Science* 226(4673): 402; 26 October 1984; John E. Dick, "Retrovirus-Mediated Gene Transfer into Hematopoietic Stem Cells," *Annals of the New York Academy of Sciences* 507: 242–51; 1987. Shortly after the human ADA gene therapy experiment achieved success, the U.S. Patent and Trademark Office granted a patent to Stanford University molecular biologist Irving Weissman and colleagues at SyStemix, a biotechnology company, for their process for isolating stem cells and for the isolated stem cells themselves. See Beverly Merz, "Researchers Find Stem Cell; Clinical Possibilities Touted," *American Medical News,* November 25, 1991, p. 2.

9. Angier, "Doctors Have Success," (note 1); experimental protocol (note 2), p. 24 (59).

10. Response to Points to Consider (note 5), p. 12 (21).

11. R. Michael Blaese, et al., "T Lymphocyte-Directed Gene Therapy for ADA-SCID: Initial Trial Results after 4 Years," *Science* 270(5235): 475–80; 20 October 1995.

12. Ibid., p. 479.

13. Ibid., pp. 475–76.

14. Ibid., p. 477.

15. Ibid., p. 478. For more detailed accounts of this initial gene therapy study in the United States, see Larry Thompson, *Correcting the Code: Inventing the Genetic Cure for the Human Body* (New York: Simon and Schuster, 1994), and Jeff Lyon and Peter Gorner, *Altered Fates: Gene Therapy and the Retooling of Human Life* (New York: W. W. Norton & Company, 1995). For an excellent survey of the status of somatic cell gene therapy in 1995 see Ronald G. Crystal, "Transfer of Genes to Humans: Early Lessons and Obstacles to Success," *Science* 270(5235): 404–10; 20 October 1995.

16. Claudio Bordignon, et al., "Gene Therapy in Peripheral Blood Lymphocytes and Bone Marrow for ADA-Immunodeficient Patients," *Science* 270(5235): 470–75; 20 October 1995.

17. Ibid., pp. 473–74.

18. Gina Kolata, *New York Times,* October 20, 1995, p. A22.

19. A few weeks before the two *Science* articles on gene therapy were published, a newborn substudy of the Blaese–Anderson protocol reported initial results in the treatment of three newborn infants. According to the authors, the genetic modification of CD34+ cells in the umbilical cord blood of three ADA-deficient newborns had resulted in the persistence of the introduced gene in leukocytes (white blood cells) from bone marrow and peripheral blood for 18 months after the initial treatment. All three patients are also receiving PEG-ADA, although the dosages have been reduced. No clinical effects of the genetic modification were expected or observed at the time the article was published. See Donald B. Kohn, et al., "Engraftment of Gene-Modified Umbilical Cord Blood Cells in Neonates with Adenosine Deaminase Deficiency," *Nature Medicine* 1(10): 1017–1023; October 1995.

20. See, for example, Arthur L. Caplan, H. Tristram Engelhardt, Jr., and James J. McCartney, eds. *Concepts of Health and Disease: Interdisciplinary Perspectives* (Reading, MA: Addison-Wesley, 1981); and H. Tristram Engelhardt, Jr., and Kevin Wm. Wildes, "Health and Disease. IV. Philosophical Perspectives," in Warren T. Reich, ed.-in-chief, *Encyclopedia of Bioethics* (revised ed.; New York: Simon and Schuster Macmillan, 1995), Vol. II, pp. 1101–06.

21. Norman Daniels, *Just Health Care* (Cambridge: Cambridge University Press, 1985), esp. pp. 26–32; Christopher Boorse, "Health as a Theoretical Concept," *Philosophy of Science* 44(4): 542–73; December 1977; and Christopher Boorse, "On the Distinction Between Disease and Illness," *Philosophy and Public Affairs* 5(1): 49–68; Fall 1975.

22. Two helpful discussions of the just allocation of human gene therapy are Norman Daniels, "The Genome Project, Individuals, and Just Health Care," in Timothy F. Murphy and Marc A. Lappé, eds., *Justice and the Human Genome Project* (Berkeley: University of California Press, 1994), pp. 110–32; and Leonard M. Fleck, "Just Genetics: A Problem Agenda," ibid., pp. 133–52.

23. For discussion of this case, see Larry Thompson, "Healy Approves an Unproven Treatment," *Science* 259(5092): 172; 8 January 1993; and Larry Thompson, "Should Dying Patients Receive Untested Genetic Methods?" *Science* 259(5094): 452; 22 January 1993.

24. See, for example, Jay Katz, with Alexander Morgan Capron and Eleanor Swift Glass, *Experimentation with Human Beings: The Authority of the Investigator, Subject, Professions, and State in the Human Experimentation Process* (New York: Russell Sage Foundation, 1972).

25. See, for example, Anna C. Mastroianni, Ruth Faden, and Daniel Federman, eds., *Women and Health Research: Ethical and Legal Issues of Including Women in Clinical Studies* (2 vols.; Washington, DC: National Academy Press, 1994).

26. Larry Thompson, "The First Kids with New Genes," *Time,* June 7, 1993, pp. 50–53.

27. Leon Jaroff, "Brave New Babies," *Time* May 31, 1993, pp. 56–57.

28. Gina Kolata, "Novel Bypass Method: A Dose of New Genes," *New York Times,* December 13, 1994, p. C1.

W. FRENCH ANDERSON

Human Gene Therapy

The first approved clinical protocol for somatic gene therapy started trials in September 1990.[1] Since then, in just 7½ years, more than 300 clinical protocols have been approved worldwide and over 3,000 patients have carried genetically engineered cells in their body. The conclusions from these trials are that gene therapy has the potential for treating a broad array of human diseases and that the procedure appears to carry a very low risk of adverse reactions; the efficiency of gene transfer and expression in human patients is, however, still disappointingly low. Except for anecdotal reports of individual patients being helped, there is still no conclusive evidence that a gene-therapy protocol has been successful in the treatment of a human disease. Why not?

In this review I will examine the 'why not?' by evaluating the promise and the problems of gene therapy. There are various categories of somatic cell gene therapy, distinguished by the mode of delivery of the gene to the affected tissue (see Box 1). The challenge is to develop gene therapy as an efficient and safe drug-delivery system. This goal is more difficult to achieve than many investigators had predicted 5 years ago. The human body has spent many thousands of years learning to protect itself from the onslaught of environmental hazards, including the incorporation of foreign DNA

Reprinted with the permission of the author and the publisher from *Nature* 392 (Supplement, April 30, 1998), pp. 25–30. Copyright © 1998 Macmillan Magazines Ltd.

into its genome. Viruses, however, have been partially successful in overcoming these barriers and being able to insert their genetic material into human cells. Hence the initial efforts at gene therapy have been directed towards engineering viruses so that they could be used as vectors to carry therapeutic genes into patients. A number of reviews on aspects of gene therapy have been published recently[2-10]; this review will consider the categories of the various virus vectors in turn.

VECTORS BASED ON RNA VIRUSES

Retroviruses were initially chosen as the most promising gene-transfer vehicles.[11] Currently, about 60% of all approved clinical protocols utilize retroviral vectors. These RNA viruses can carry out efficient gene transfer into many cell types and can stably integrate into the host cell genome, thereby providing the possibility of long-term expression. They have minimal risk because retroviruses have evolved into relatively non-pathogenic parasites (although there are exceptions, such as the human immunodeficiency viruses (HIV) and human T-cell lymphotropic viruses (HTLV)). In particular, murine leukaemia virus (MuLV) has traditionally been used as the vector of choice for clinical gene-therapy protocols, and a variety of packaging systems to enclose the vector genome within viral particles have been developed. The vectors themselves have all of

the viral genes removed, are fully replication-defective and can accept up to about 8 kilobases (kb) of exogenous DNA.

The problems that investigators face in developing retroviral vectors that are effective in treating disease are of four main types: obtaining efficient delivery, transducing non-dividing cells, sustaining long-term gene expression, and developing a cost-effective way to manufacture the vector.

• • •

VECTORS BASED ON DNA VIRUSES

Adenoviral Vectors. The DNA virus used most widely for *in situ* gene transfer vectors is the adenovirus (specifically serotypes 2 and 5). Adenoviral vectors have several positive attributes: they are large and can therefore potentially hold large DNA inserts (up to 35 kb . . .); they are human viruses and are able to transduce a large number of different human cell types at a very high efficiency (often reaching nearly 100% *in vitro*); they can transduce non-dividing cells; and they can be produced at very high titres in culture. They have been the vector of choice for several laboratories trying to treat the pulmonary complications of cystic fibrosis, as well as for a variety of protocols attempting to treat cancer.

• • •

Adeno-associated Viral Vectors. Another DNA virus used in clinical trials is the adeno-associated virus (AAV). This is a non-pathogenic virus that is widespread in the human population (about 80% of humans have antibodies directed against AAV). Initial interest in this virus arose because it is the only known mammalian virus that shows preferential integration into a specific region in the genome (into the short arm of human chromosome 19). As the virus does not produce disease, its insertion site appears to be a 'safe' region in the genome. It would be useful, therefore, to engineer the sequences that dictate this site-specific insertion into gene-therapy vectors. Unfortunately, the present AAV vectors appear to integrate in a nonspecific manner, although it has been suggested that vectors could be designed that retain some specificity.[12] . . .

OTHER DNA VIRUS-BASED VECTORS

Other DNA viruses are being studied as possible gene-therapy vectors for specific situations. For example, herpes simplex virus (HSV) vectors have a propensity for transducing cells of the nervous system,[13, 14] as well as several other cell types. A stripped-down version of the HSV, called an amplicon, may have certain advantages, particularly when combined with components from other viral systems.[15] A number of other DNA virus vectors are under study including poxviruses.

Several investigators are examining replication-competent, or attenuated, viral vectors (both DNA and RNA). In addition, hybrid systems have been reported where an adenoviral vector is used to carry a retoviral vector into a cell that is normally inaccessible to retroviral transduction.[16]

NON-VIRAL VECTORS

Although viral systems are potentially very efficient, two factors suggest that non-viral gene delivery systems will be the preferred choice in the future: safety, and ease of manufacturing. A totally synthetic gene-delivery system could be engineered to avoid the danger of producing recombinant virus or other toxic effects engendered by biologically active viral particles. Also, manufacturing a synthetic product should be less complex than using tissue culture cells as bioreactors, and QA/QC [Quality Assurance/Quality Control] procedures should be simplified. . . .

CLINICAL STUDIES

At present over 300 clinical protocols have been approved. Detailed information is available on the 232 protocols that had been approved in the USA as of 3 February 1998[17] (Table 1).

Only one phase III and several phase II clinical trials are now underway; all the rest of the approved gene therapy clinical protocols are for smaller phase I/II trials. Genetic Therapy Inc./Novartis is carrying out the phase III clinical trial. The target disease is glioblastoma multiforma, a malignant brain tumour.[18] The rationale is to insert a gene capable of directing cell killing into the tumour while protecting the normal brain cells.

. . .

Several phase II trials are underway testing gene-therapy vectors as 'vaccines,' either against cancer[19] or against AIDS.[20] . . .

Finally, a comment on the original adenosine deaminase (ADA) deficiency gene-therapy trial.[1, 21] ADA deficiency is a rare genetic disorder that produces severe immunodeficiency in children. Starting in 1990, gene-corrected autologous T lymphocytes were given to two

Table 1. Disease Targets and Gene Therapy Protocols

(a) Types of gene therapy clinical protocols*

Type	Number	Percentage of total
Therapy	200	(86%)
Marker	30	(13%)
Non-therapeutic†	2	(1%)
Total	232	(100%)

(b) Disease targets for therapeutic gene therapy clinical protocols

Target	Number	Percentage of total
Cancer	138	(69%)
Genetic Diseases	33	(16.5%)
CF	16	
Other‡	17	
AIDS	23	(11.5%)
Others§	6	(3%)
Total	200	(100%)

*Roughly 60% of all protocols use retroviral vectors, 20% use non-viral delivery systems, 10% use adenoviral vectors and the remainder use other viral vectors.

†A 'non-therapeutic' protocol means a non-therapeutic portion of a non-gene-therapy clinical protocol.

‡These 17 include 12 other monogenic diseases.

§The five 'other' are: peripheral artery disease, rheumatoid arthritis, arterial restenosis, cubital tunnel syndrome and coronary artery disease (2).

girls suffering from this disease. Both girls are doing well and continue to lead essentially normal lives. Patient 1 (A.D.) received a total of 11 infusions, the last being in the summer of 1992. Her total T-cell level and her level of transduced T cells have remained essentially constant for the past 5½ years. She contracted chickenpox in late 1996 and experienced the same clinical course as would have been expected for any normal 10-year-old. Both she and patient 2 (C.C.) continue to receive polyethylene glycol (PEG)-ADA. Although both girls have gene-engineered T lymphocytes in their circulation after more than 7 years, no definitive conclusion can be drawn as to the relative roles of PEG-ADA and gene therapy in their excellent clinical course.

ETHICAL ISSUES

Somatic cell gene therapy for the treatment of serious disease is now accepted as ethically appropriate. Indeed, it is so well accepted, and the side effects from gene-therapy protocols have been so minimal, that the danger now exists that genetic engineering may be used for non-disease conditions, that is for functional enhancement or 'cosmetic' purposes. The first Gene Therapy Policy Conference organized by the NIH RAC focused on this issue in September 1997. The conclusion was that enhancement engineering is about to take place, and could slip through the regulatory process if RAC and the FDA (and similar organizations in other countries) are not vigilant. As an example, a US biotechnology company has developed the technology for transferring genes (specifically the tyrosinase gene) into hair follicle cells.[22] They are now looking for genes that promote hair growth with the clinical objective of reversing the hair loss that occurs after chemotherapy in cancer patients. The application to the FDA for product licensing would list chemotherapy-induced alopecia as the product indication. The risk-benefit analysis here would be very favourable. However, once a product is licensed for any indication, it can be prescribed by physicians for any 'off-label' use that is felt by the physician to be clinically justified. The result could be millions of balding men receiving gene therapy to treat their hair loss. The conference concluded that the FDA should use a risk-benefit analysis that takes into account the extensive off-label usage for cosmetic reasons that could take place.

Using genetic engineering to treat baldness is not a major issue in itself, of course. But this is just one example of how our society is moving towards a slippery slope where genetic engineering might very well be used for a broad range of enhancement purposes, including larger size from a growth hormone gene, increased muscle mass from a dystrophin gene and so on. If we knew that there would be no long-term negative effects of genetic engineering, then widespread, or even frivolous, use of genetic engineering technology might not be detrimental. But just as with nuclear energy, pesticides and fluorocarbons, we as a society tend to see the benefits but are caught off guard by the bad effects of our powerful new technologies. What society wants to do 100 years from now with regard to genetic engineering is their business, but it is our duty to begin the era of genetic engineering in as responsible a manner as possible. Until we have learned about the long-term effects of somatic cell gene therapy in the treatment of disease, we should not use this technology for any other purpose than where it is medically indicated.[23]

In utero somatic gene therapy of the fetus will be undertaken in the foreseeable future. The same care should be exercised here as with somatic cell gene-therapy protocols for adults, children and newborns. So long as only serious disease is targeted and the risk-benefit ratios for both mother and the fetus are acceptable, *in utero* gene therapy should be ethically appropriate.[24] Germline gene therapy should not be attempted at this time for the reasons outlined elsewhere.[25]

A situation with the potential for real abuse of the new technologies would be the combination of cloning and genetic engineering. This combination has already been achieved in sheep where single cells have been obtained from fetal fibroblasts, transduced with a gene (human factor IX), and the gene-engineered cells grown into living sheep producing human factor IX.[26] Attempts to use such techniques to produce genetically engineered humans would provoke an even greater ethical storm than the present suggestion by a Chicago scientist to clone humans.*

THE FUTURE

The ultimate goal of gene-therapy research is the development of vectors that can be injected, will target specific cells, will result in safe and efficient gene transfer into a high percentage of those cells, will insert themselves into appropriate regions of the genome (or will persist as stable episomes), will be regulated either by administered agents or by the body's own physiological signals, will be cost-effective to manufacture and will cure disease. As the number of target cells may be in the billions, very high efficiency of gene transfer and the injection of a large number of gene-therapy vectors may be necessary. How soon can we expect significant progress in each of these areas?

The next 5 years should bring the first successes for gene therapy, that means statistically significant data that a gene-therapy protocol results in significant improvement in the clinical condition of patients. Within this time frame the first vectors that can target specific tissues should begin clinical trials and tissue-specific gene expression should have made its way into clinical trials.

---

*Editor's note: See Gina Kolata, "Proposal for Human Cloning Draws Dismay and Disbelief," *New York Times,* January 8, 1998, p. A1.

In a time frame of 5–15 years from now, I expect that the number of gene-therapy products will begin to increase exponentially, coinciding with the enormous increase in characterized genes as a result of the Human Genome Project. The first injectable vectors will reach clinical trials and efficient tissue-specific gene transfer will be available in a few cases. It will probably take longer to develop site-specific integration, efficiently regulated genes and the correction of genes *in situ* by means of homologous recombination. Beyond this, our imagination is the limit.

For many gene-therapy applications in the future, it is probable that a synthetic hybrid system will be used that incorporates engineered viral components for target-specific binding and core entry, immunosuppressive genes from various viruses and some mechanism that allows site-specific integration, perhaps utilizing AAV sequences or an engineered retroviral integrase protein. In addition, regulatory sequences from the target cell itself will be utilized to allow physiological control of expression of the inserted genes. All these components would be assembled *in vitro* in a liposome-like formulation with additional measures taken to reduce immunogenicity . . . .

CONCLUSIONS

Gene therapy is a powerful new technology that still requires several years before it will make a noticeable impact on the treatment of disease. Several major deficiencies still exist including poor delivery systems, both viral and non-viral, and poor gene expression after genes are delivered. The reason for the low efficiency of gene transfer and expression in human patients is that we still lack a basic understanding of how vectors should be constructed, what regulatory sequences are appropriate for which cell types, how *in vivo* immune defences can be overcome, and how to manufacture efficiently the vectors that we do make. It is not surprising that we have not yet had notable clinical successes. Nonetheless, the lessons we are learning in the clinic are invaluable in illuminating the problems that future research must solve.

Despite our present lack of knowledge, gene therapy will almost certainly revolutionize the practice of medicine over the next 25 years. In every field of medicine, the ability to give the patient therapeutic genes offers extraordinary opportunities to treat, cure and ultimately prevent a vast range of diseases that now plague mankind.

ACKNOWLEDGEMENTS

I want to thank the many individuals who offered valuable comments on early drafts of this review. I am a consultant to GTI/Novartis.

NOTES

1. Blaese, R. M., *et al.* T lymphocyte-directed gene therapy for ADA-SCID: initial trial results after 4 years. *Science* 270, 475–80 (1995).

2. Kay, N. A., Liu, D. & Hoogerbrugge, P. M. Gene therapy. *Proc. Natl Acad. Sci. USA* **94,** 12744–746 (1997).

3. Verma, I. M. & Somia, N. Gene therapy: promises, problems and prospects. *Nature* **389,** 239–42 (1997).

4. Havenga, M., Hoogerbrugge, P., Valerio, D. & van Es, H. H. G. Retroviral stem cell gene therapy. *Stem Cells* **15,** 162–79 (1997).

5. Dass, C. R. *et al.* Cationic liposomes and gene therapy for solid tumors. *Drug Delivery* **4,** 151–65 (1997).

6. Miller, N. & Whelan, J. Progress in transcriptionally targeted and regulatable vectors for genetic therapy. *Hum. Gene Ther.* **8,** 803–15 (1997).

7. Cosset, F.-L. & Russell, S. J. Targeting retrovirus entry. *Gene Ther.* **3,** 946–56 (1996).

8. Cristiano, R. J. & Curiel, D. T. Strategies to accomplish gene delivery via the receptor-mediated endocytosis pathway. *Cancer Gene Ther.* **3,** 49–57 (1996).

9. Brenner, M. Gene marking. *Hum. Gene Ther.* **7,** 1927–36 (1996).

10. Schnierle, B. S. & Groner, B. Retroviral targeted delivery. *Gene Ther.* **3,** 1069–73 (1996).

11. Anderson, W. F. Prospects for human gene therapy. *Science* **226,** 401–09 (1984).

12. Linden, R. M. & Berns, K. I. Site-specific integration by adeno-associated virus: a basis for a potential gene therapy vector. *Gene Ther.* **4,** 4–5 (1997).

13. Breakefield, X. O. & DeLuca, N. A. Herpes simplex virus for gene delivery to neurons. *New Biol.* **3,** 203–18 (1991).

14. Fink, D. J. & Glorioso, J. C. Engineering herpes simplex virus vectors for gene transfer to neurons. *Nature Med.* **3,** 357–59 (1997).

15. Jacoby, D. R., Fraefel, C. & Breakefield, X. O. Hybrid vectors: a new generation of virus-based vectors designed to control the cellular fate of delivered genes. *Gene Ther.* **4,** 1281–83 (1997).

16. Bilbao, G. *et al.* Adenoviral/retroviral vector chimeras: a novel strategy to achieve high-efficiency stable transduction in vivo. *FASEB J.* **11,** 624–34 (1997).

17. ORDA Report: Human Gene Therapy Protocols (2/3/98) (Office of Recombinant DNA Activities, NIH, Bethesda, MD, 1998).

18. Ram, Z. *et al.* Therapy of malignant brain tumors by intratumoral implantation of retroviral vector-producing cells. *Nature Med.* **3,** 1354–61 (1997).

19. Stopeck, A. T. *et al.* Phase I study of direct gene transfer of an allogeneic histocompatibility antigen, HLA-B7, in patients with metastatic melanoma. *J. Clin. Oncol.* **15,** 341–49 (1997).

20. Haubrich, [*et al.*] An open label, phase I/II clinical trial to evaluate the safety and biological activity of HIV-IT (V) (HIV-1$_{\text{IIIB}}^{\text{env/rev}}$ retroviral vector) in HIV-I-infected subjects. *Hum. Gene Ther.* **6**, 941–55 (1995).

21. Anderson, W. F. Human gene therapy. *Science* **256**, 808–13 (1992).

22. Hoffman, R. M. *et al.* The feasibility of targeted selective gene therapy of the hair follicle. *Nature Med* **1,** 705–06 (1995).

23. Anderson, W. F. Human gene therapy: why draw a line? *J. Med. Philos.* **14**, 681–93 (1989).

24. Fletcher, J. C. & Richter, G. Human fetal gene therapy: moral and ethical questions. *Hum. Gene Ther.* **7**, 1605–14 (1996).

25. Fletcher, J. C. & Anderson, W. F. Germ-line gene therapy: a new stage of debate. *Law Med. Health Care* **20**, 26–39 (1992).

26. Schnieke, A. E. *et al.* Human factor IX transgenic sheep produced by transfer of nuclei from transfected fetal fibroblasts. *Science* **278**, 2130–33 (1997).

JONATHAN GLOVER

Questions about Some Uses of Genetic Engineering

There is a widespread view that any project for the genetic improvement of the human race ought to be ruled out: that there are fundamental objections of principle. The aim of this discussion is to sort out some of the main objections. It will be argued that our resistance is based on a complex of different values and reasons, none of which is, when examined, adequate to rule out in principle this use of genetic engineering. The debate on human genetic engineering should become like the debate on nuclear power: one in which large possible benefits have to be weighed against big problems and the risk of great disasters. The discussion has not reached this point, partly because the techniques have not yet been developed. But it is also partly because of the blurred vision which fuses together many separate risks and doubts into a fuzzy-outlined opposition in principle.

1. AVOIDING THE DEBATE ABOUT GENES AND THE ENVIRONMENT

In discussing the question of genetic engineering, there is everything to be said for not muddling the issue up with the debate over the relative importance of genes and environment in the development of such characteristics as intelligence. One reason for avoiding that debate is that it arouses even stronger passions than genetic engineering, and so is filled with as much acrimony as

argument. But, apart from this fastidiousness, there are other reasons.

The nature-nurture dispute is generally seen as an argument about the relative weight the two factors have in causing differences within the human species: 'IQ is 80 per cent hereditary and 20 per cent environmental' versus 'IQ is 80 per cent environmental and 20 per cent hereditary.' No doubt there is some approximate truth of this type to be found if we consider variations within a given population at a particular time. But it is highly unlikely that there is any such statement which is simply true of human nature regardless of context. To take the extreme case, if we could iron out all environmental differences, any residual variations would be 100 per cent genetic. It is only if we make the highly artificial assumption that different groups at different times all have an identical spread of relevant environmental differences that we can expect to find statements of this kind applying to human nature in general. To say this is not to argue that studies on the question should not be conducted, or are bound to fail. It may well be possible, and useful, to find out the relative weights of the two kinds of factor for a given characteristic among a certain group at a particular time. The point is that any such conclusions lose relevance, not only when environmental differences are stretched out or compressed, but also when genetic differences are. And this last case is what we are considering.

We can avoid this dispute because of its irrelevance. Suppose the genetic engineering proposal were to try to make people less aggressive. On a superficial view, the proposal might be shown to be unrealistic if there were evidence to show that variation in aggressiveness is hardly genetic at all: that it is 95 per cent environmental. (Let us grant, most implausibly, that such a figure turned out to be true for the whole of humanity, regardless of social context.) But all this would show is that, within our species, the distribution of genes relevant to aggression is very uniform. It would show nothing about the likely effects on aggression if we use genetic engineering to give people a different set of genes from those they now have.

In other words, to take genetic engineering seriously, we need take no stand on the relative importance or unimportance of genetic factors in the explanation of the present range of individual differences found in people. We need only the minimal assumption that different genes could give us different characteristics. To deny *that* assumption you need to be the sort of person who thinks it is only living in kennels which make dogs different from cats.

2. METHODS OF CHANGING THE GENETIC COMPOSITION OF FUTURE GENERATIONS

There are essentially three ways of altering the genetic composition of future generations. The first is by environmental changes. Discoveries in medicine, the institution of a National Health Service, schemes for poverty relief, agricultural changes, or alterations in the tax position of large families, all alter the selective pressure on genes.[1] It is hard to think of any social change which does not make some difference to who survives or who is born.

The second method is to use eugenic policies aimed at altering breeding patterns or patterns of survival of people with different genes. Eugenic methods are 'environmental' too: the difference is only that the genetic impact is intended. Possible strategies range from various kinds of compulsion (to have more children, fewer children, or no children, or even compulsion over the choice of sexual partner) to the completely voluntary (our present genetic counselling practice of giving prospective parents information about probabilities of their children having various abnormalities).

The third method is genetic engineering: using enzymes to add to or subtract from a stretch of DNA.

Most people are unworried by the fact that a side-effect of an environmental change is to alter the gene pool, at least where the alteration is not for the worse. And even in cases where environmental factors increase the proportion of undesirable genes in the pool, we often accept this. Few people oppose the National Health Service, although setting it up meant that some people with genetic defects, who would have died, have had treatment enabling them to survive and reproduce. On the whole, we accept without qualms that much of what we do has genetic impact. Controversy starts when we think of aiming deliberately at genetic changes, by eugenics or genetic engineering. I want to make some brief remarks about eugenic policies, before suggesting that policies of deliberate intervention are best considered in the context of genetic engineering.

Scepticism has been expressed about whether eugenic policies have any practical chance of success. Medawar has pointed out the importance of genetic polymorphism: the persistence of genetically different types in a population.[2] (Our different blood groups are a familiar example.) For many characteristics, people get a different gene from each parent. So children do not simply repeat parental characteristics. Any simple picture of producing an improved type of person, and then letting the improvement be passed on unchanged, collapses.

But, although polymorphism is a problem for this crudely utopian form of eugenics, it does not show that more modest schemes of improvement must fail. Suppose the best individuals for some quality (say, colour vision) are heterozygous, so that they inherit a gene A from one parent, and a gene B from the other. These ABs will have AAs and BBs among their children, who will be less good than they are. But AAs and BBs may still be better than ACs or ADs, and perhaps much better than CCs or CDs. If this were so, overall improvement could still be brought about by encouraging people whose genes included an A or a B to have more children than those who had only Cs or Ds. The point of taking a quality like colour vision is that it may be genetically fairly simple. Qualities like kindness or intelligence are more likely to depend on the interaction of many genes, but a similar point can be made at a higher level of complexity.

Polymorphism raises a doubt about whether the offspring of the three 'exceptionally intelligent women' fertilized by Dr. Shockley or other Nobel prize-winners will have the same IQ as the parents, even apart from environmental variation. But it does not show the inevitable failure of any large-scale attempts to alter human characteristics by varying the relative numbers of children different kinds of people have. Yet any attempt, say, to raise the level of intelligence, would be a very slow affair, taking many generations to make much of an impact. This is no reason for preferring to discuss genetic engineering. For the genetic engineering of human improvements, if it becomes possible, will have an immediate effect, so we will not be guessing which qualities will be desirable dozens of generations later.

There is the view that the genetic-engineering techniques required will not become a practical possibility. Sir MacFarlane Burnet, writing in 1971 about using genetic engineering to cure disorders in people already born, dismissed the possibility of using a virus to carry a new gene to replace a faulty one in cells throughout the body: 'I should be willing to state in any company that the chance of doing this will remain infinitely small to the last syllable of recorded time.'[3] Unless engineering at the stage of sperm cell and egg is easier, this seems a confident dismissal of the topic to be discussed here. More recent work casts doubt on this confidence.[4] So, having mentioned this skepticism, I shall disregard it. We will assume that genetic engineering of people may become possible, and that it is worth discussing. (Sir MacFarlane Burnet's view has not yet been falsified as totally as Rutherford's view about atomic energy. But I hope that the last syllable of recorded time is still some way off.)

The main reason for casting the discussion in terms of genetic engineering rather than eugenics is not a practical one. Many eugenic policies are open to fairly straightforward moral objections, which hide the deeper theoretical issues. Such policies as compulsory sterilization, compulsory abortion, compelling people to pair off in certain ways, or compelling people to have more or fewer children than they would otherwise have, are all open to objection on grounds of overriding people's autonomy. Some are open to objection on grounds of damage to the institution of the family. And the use of discriminatory tax- and child-benefit policies is an intolerable step towards a society of different genetic castes.

Genetic engineering need not involve overriding anyone's autonomy. It need not be forced on parents against their wishes, and the future person being engineered has no views to be overridden. (The view that despite this, it is still objectionable to have one's genetic characteristics decided by others, will be considered later.) Genetic engineering will not damage the family in the obvious ways that compulsory eugenic policies would. Nor need it be encouraged by incentives which create inequalities. Because it avoids these highly visible moral objections, genetic engineering allows us to focus more clearly on other values that are involved.

(To avoid a possible misunderstanding, one point should be added before leaving the topic of eugenics. Saying that some eugenic policies are open to obvious moral objections does not commit me to disapproval of all eugenic policies. In particular, I do not want to be taken to be opposing two kinds of policy. One is genetic counselling: warning people of risks in having children, and perhaps advising them against having them. The other is the introduction of screening-programmes to detect foetal abnormalities, followed by giving the mother the option of abortion where serious defects emerge.)

Let us now turn to the question of what, if anything, we should do in the field of human genetic engineering.

3. THE POSITIVE-NEGATIVE DISTINCTION

We are not yet able to cure disorders by genetic engineering. But we do sometimes respond to disorders by adopting eugenic policies, at least in voluntary form. Genetic counselling is one instance, as applied to those thought likely to have such disorders as Huntington's chorea. This is a particularly appalling inherited disorder, involving brain degeneration, leading to mental decline and lack of control over movement. It does not normally come on until middle age, by which time many of its victims would in the normal course of things have had children. Huntington's chorea is caused by a dominant gene, so those who find that one of the parents has it have themselves a 50 per cent chance of developing it. If they do have it, each of their children will in turn have a 50 per cent chance of the disease. The risks are so high and the disorder so bad that the potential parents often decide not to have children, and are often given advice to this effect by doctors and others.

Another eugenic response to disorders is involved in screening-programmes for pregnant women. When tests pick up such defects as Down's syndrome (mongolism) or spina bifida, the mother is given the possibility of an abortion. The screening-programmes are eugenic because part of their point is to reduce the incidence of severe genetic abnormality in the population.

These two eugenic policies come in at different stages: before conception and during pregnancy. For this reason the screening-programme is more controversial, because it raises the issue of abortion. Those who are sympathetic to abortion, and who think it would be good to eliminate these disorders will be sympathetic to the programme. Those who think abortion is no different from killing a fully developed human are obviously likely to oppose the programme. But they are likely to feel that elimination of the disorders would be a good thing, even if not an adequate justification for killing. Unless they also disapprove of contraception, they are likely to support the genetic-counselling policy in the case of Huntington's chorea.

Few people object to the use of eugenic policies to eliminate disorders, unless those policies have additional features which are objectionable. Most of us are resistant to the use of compulsion, and those who oppose abortion will object to screening-programmes. But apart from these other moral objections, we do not object to the use of eugenic policies against disease. We do not object to advising those likely to have Huntington's chorea not to have children, as neither compulsion nor killing is involved. Those of us who take this view have no objection to altering the genetic composition of the next generation, where this alteration consists in reducing the incidence of defects.

If it were possible to use genetic engineering to correct defects, say at the foetal stage, it is hard to see how those of us who are prepared to use the eugenic measure just mentioned could object. In both cases, it would be pure gain. The couple, one of whom may develop Huntington's chorea, can have a child if they want, knowing that any abnormality will be eliminated. Those sympathetic to abortion will agree that cure is preferable. And those opposed to abortion prefer babies to be born without handicap. It is hard to think of any objection to using genetic engineering to eliminate defects, and there is a clear and strong case for its use.

But accepting the case for eliminating genetic mistakes does not entail accepting other uses of genetic engineering. The elimination of defects is often called 'negative' genetic engineering. Going beyond this, to bring about improvements in normal people, is by contrast 'positive' engineering. (The same distinction can be made for eugenics.)

The positive-negative distinction is not in all cases completely sharp. Some conditions are genetic disorders whose identification raises little problem. Huntington's chorea or spina bifida are genetic 'mistakes' in a way that cannot seriously be disputed. But with other conditions, the boundary between a defective state and normality may be more blurred. If there is a genetic disposition towards depressive illness, this seems a defect, whose elimination would be part of negative genetic engineering. Suppose the genetic disposition to depression involves the production of lower levels of an enzyme than are produced in normal people. The negative programme is to correct the genetic fault so that the enzyme level is within the range found in normal people. But suppose that within 'normal' people also, there are variations in the enzyme level, which correlate with ordinary differences in [the] tendency to be cheerful or depressed. Is there a sharp boundary between 'clinical' depression and the depression sometimes felt by those diagnosed as 'normal'? Is it clear that a sharp distinction can be drawn between raising someone's enzyme level so that it falls within the normal range and raising someone else's level from the bottom of the normal range to the top?

The positive-negative distinction is sometimes a blurred one, but often we can at least roughly see where it should be drawn. If there is a rough and ready distinction, the question is: how important is it? Should we go on from accepting negative engineering to accepting positive programmes, or should we say that the line between the two is the limit of what is morally acceptable?

There is no doubt that positive programmes arouse the strongest feelings on both sides. On the one hand, many respond to positive genetic engineering or positive eugenics with Professor Tinbergen's thought: 'I find it morally reprehensible and presumptuous for anybody to put himself forward as a judge of the qualities for which we should breed' [*Guardian*, 5 March, 1980].

But other people have held just as strongly that positive policies are the way to make the future of mankind better than the past. Many years ago H. J. Muller expressed this hope:

And so we foresee the history of life divided into three main phases. In the long preparatory phase it was the helpless creature of its environment, and natural selection gradually ground it into human shape. In the second—our own short transitional phase—it reaches out at the immediate environment, shaking, shaping and grinding to suit the form, the requirements, the wishes, and the whims of man. And in the long third phase, it will reach down into the secret places of the great universe of its own nature, and by aid of its ever growing intelligence and cooperation, shape itself into an increasingly sublime creation—a being beside which the mythical divinities of the past will seem more and more ridiculous, and which setting its own marvellous inner powers against the brute Goliath of the suns and the planets, challenges them to contest.[5]

The case for positive engineering is not helped by adopting the tones of the mad scientist in a horror film. But behind the rhetoric is a serious point. If we decide on a positive programme to change our nature, this will be a central moment in our history, and the transformation might be beneficial to a degree we can now scarcely imagine. The question is: how are we to weigh this possibility against Tinbergen's objection, and against other objections and doubts?

For the rest of this discussion, I shall assume that, subject to adequate safeguards against things going wrong, negative genetic engineering is acceptable. The issue is positive engineering. I shall also assume that we can ignore problems about whether positive engineering will be technically possible. Suppose we have the power to choose people's genetic characteristics. Once we have eliminated genetic defects, what, if anything, should we do with this power? . . .

4. THE VIEW THAT OVERALL IMPROVEMENT IS UNLIKELY OR IMPOSSIBLE

There is one doubt about the workability of schemes of genetic improvement which is so widespread that it would be perverse to ignore it. This is the view that, in any genetic alteration, there are no gains without compensating losses. On this view, if we bring about a genetically based improvement, such as higher intelligence, we are bound to pay a price somewhere else: perhaps the more intelligent people will have less resistance to disease, or will be less physically agile. If correct, this might so undermine the practicability of applying eugenics or genetic engineering that it would be hardly worth discussing the values involved in such programmes.

This view perhaps depends on some idea that natural selection is so efficient that, in terms of gene survival, we must already be as efficient as it is possible to be. If it were possible to push up intelligence without weakening some other part of the system, natural selection would already have done so. But this is a naive version of evolutionary theory. In real evolutionary theory, far from the genetic status quo always being the best possible for a given environment, some mutations turn out to be advantageous, and this is the origin of evolutionary progress. If natural mutations can be

beneficial without a compensating loss, why should artificially induced ones not be so too?

It should also be noticed that there are two different ideas of what counts as a gain or a loss. From the point of view of evolutionary progress, gains and losses are simply advantages and disadvantages from the point of view of gene survival. But we are not compelled to take this view. If we could engineer a genetic change in some people which would have the effect of making them musical prodigies but also sterile, this would be a hopeless gene in terms of survival, but this need not force us, or the musical prodigies themselves, to think of the changes as for the worse. It depends on how we rate musical ability as against having children, and evolutionary survival does not dictate priorities here.

The view that gains and losses are tied up with each other need not depend on the dogma that natural selection *must* have created the best of all possible sets of genes. A more cautiously empirical version of the claim says there is a tendency for gains to be accompanied by losses. John Maynard Smith, in his paper on 'Eugenics and Utopia',[6] takes this kind of 'broad balance' view and runs it the other way, suggesting, as an argument in defence of medicine, that any loss of genetic resistance to disease is likely to be a good thing: 'The reason for this is that in evolution, as in other fields, one seldom gets something for nothing. Genes which confer disease-resistance are likely to have harmful effects in other ways: this is certainly true of the gene for sickle-cell anaemia and may be a general rule. If so, absence of selection in favour of disease-resistance may be eugenic.'

It is important that different characteristics may turn out to be genetically linked in ways we do not yet realize. In our present state of knowledge, engineering for some improvement might easily bring some unpredicted but genetically linked disadvantage. But we do not have to accept that there will in general be a broad balance, so that there is a presumption that any gain will be accompanied by a compensating loss (or Maynard Smith's version that we can expect a compensating gain for any loss). The reason is that what counts as a gain or loss varies in different contexts. Take Maynard Smith's example of sickle-cell anaemia. The reason why sickle-cell anaemia is widespread in Africa is that it is genetically linked with resistance to malaria. Those who are heterozygous (who inherit one sickle-cell gene and one normal gene) are resistant to malaria, while those who are homozygous (whose genes are both sickle-cell) get sickle-cell anaemia. If we use genetic engineering to knock out sickle-cell anaemia where malaria is common, we will pay the price of having more malaria. But when we eradicate malaria, the gain will not involve this loss. Because losses are relative to context, any generalization about the impossibility of overall improvements is dubious.

5. THE FAMILY AND OUR DESCENDANTS

Unlike various compulsory eugenic policies, genetic engineering need not involve any interference with decision by couples to have children together, or with their decisions about how many children to have. And let us suppose that genetically engineered babies grow in the mother's womb in the normal way, so that her relationship to the child is not threatened in the way it might be if the laboratory or the hospital were substituted for the womb. The cruder threats to family relationships are eliminated.

It may be suggested that there is a more subtle threat. Parents like to identify with their children. We are often pleased to see some of our own characteristics in our children. Perhaps this is partly a kind of vanity, and no doubt sometimes we project on to our children similarities that are not really there. But, when the similarities do exist, they help the parents and children to understand and sympathize with each other. If genetic engineering resulted in children fairly different from their parents, this might make their relationship have problems.

There is something to this objection, but it is easy to exaggerate. Obviously, children who were like Midwich cuckoos, or comic-book Martians, would not be easy to identify with. But genetic engineering need not move in such sudden jerks. The changes would have to be detectable to be worth bringing about, but there seems no reason why large changes in appearance, or an unbridgeable psychological gulf, should be created in any one generation. We bring about environmental changes which make children different from their parents, as when the first generation of children in a remote place are given schooling and made literate. This may cause some problems in families, but it is not usually thought a decisive objection. It is not clear that genetically induced changes of similar magnitude are any more objectionable.

A related objection concerns our attitude to our remoter descendants. We like to think of our descendants stretching on for many generations. Perhaps this is in part an immortality substitute. We hope they will to some extent be like us, and that, if they think of us, they

will do so with sympathy and approval. Perhaps these hopes about the future of mankind are relatively unimportant to us. But, even if we mind about them a lot, they are unrealistic in the very long term. Genetic engineering would make our descendants less like us, but this would only speed up the natural rate of change. Natural mutations and selective pressures make it unlikely that in a few million years our descendants will be physically or mentally much like us. So what genetic engineering threatens here is probably doomed anyway. . . .

[6.] RISKS AND MISTAKES

Although mixing different species and cloning are often prominent in people's thoughts about genetic engineering, they are relatively marginal issues. This is partly because there may be no strong reasons in favour of either. Our purposes might be realized more readily by improvements to a single species, whether another or our own, or by the creation of quite new types of organism, than by mixing different species. And it is not clear what advantage cloning batches of people might have, to outweigh the drawbacks. This is not to be dogmatic that species mixing and cloning could never be useful, but to say that the likelihood of other techniques being much more prominent makes it a pity to become fixated on the issues raised by these ones. And some of the most serious objections to positive genetic engineering have wider application than to these rather special cases. One of these wider objections is that serious risks may be involved.

Some of the risks are already part of the public debate because of current work on recombinant DNA. The danger is of producing harmful organisms that would escape from our control. The work obviously should take place, if at all, only with adequate safeguards against such a disaster. The problem is deciding what we should count as adequate safeguards. I have nothing to contribute to this problem here. If it can be dealt with satisfactorily, we will perhaps move on to genetic engineering of people. And this introduces another dimension of risk. We may produce unintended results, either because our techniques turn out to be less finely tuned than we thought, or because different characteristics are found to be genetically linked in unexpected ways.

If we produce a group of people who turn out worse than expected, we will have to live with them. Perhaps we would aim for producing people who were especially imaginative and creative, and only too late find we had produced people who were also very violent and aggressive. This kind of mistake might not only be disastrous, but also very hard to 'correct' in subsequent generations. For when we suggested sterilization to the people we had produced, or else corrective genetic engineering for *their* offspring, we might find them hard to persuade. They might like the way they were, and reject, in characteristically violent fashion, our explanation that they were a mistake.

The possibility of an irreversible disaster is a strong deterrent. It is enough to make some people think we should rule out genetic engineering altogether, and to make others think that, while negative engineering is perhaps acceptable, we should rule out positive engineering. The thought behind this second position is that the benefits from negative engineering are clearer, and that, because its aims are more modest, disastrous mistakes are less likely.

The risk of disasters provides at least a reason for saying that, if we do adopt a policy of human genetic engineering, we ought to do so with extreme caution. We should alter genes only where we have strong reasons for thinking the risk of disaster is very small, and where the benefit is great enough to justify the risk. (The problems of deciding when this is so are familiar from the nuclear power debate.) This 'principle of caution' is less strong than one ruling out all positive engineering, and allows room for the possibility that the dangers may turn out to be very remote, or that greater risks of a different kind are involved in *not* using positive engineering. These possibilities correspond to one view of the facts in the nuclear power debate. Unless with genetic engineering we think we can already rule out such possibilities, the argument from risk provides more justification for the principle of caution than for the stronger ban on all positive engineering. . . .

DECISIONS

Some of the strongest objections to positive engineering are not about specialized applications or about risks. They are about the decisions involved. The central line of thought is that we should not start playing God by redesigning the human race. The suggestion is that there is no group (such as scientists, doctors, public officials, or politicians) who can be entrusted with decisions about what sort of people there should be. And it is also doubted whether we could have any adequate

grounds for basing such decisions on one set of values rather than another. . . .

1. NOT PLAYING GOD

Suppose we could use genetic engineering to raise the average IQ by fifteen points. (I mention, only to ignore, the boring objection that the average IQ is always by definition 100.) Should we do this? Objectors to positive engineering say we should not. This is not because the present average is preferable to a higher one. We do not think that, if it were naturally fifteen points higher, we ought to bring it down to the present level. The objection is to our playing God by deciding what the level should be.

On one view of the world, the objection is relatively straightforward. On this view, there really is a God, who has a plan for the world which will be disrupted if we stray outside the boundaries assigned to us. (It is *relatively* straightforward: there would still be the problem of knowing where the boundaries came. If genetic engineering disrupts the programme, how do we know that medicine and education do not?)

The objection to playing God has a much wider appeal than to those who literally believe in a divine plan. But, outside such a context, it is unclear what the objection comes to. If we have a Darwinian view, according to which features of our nature have been selected for their contribution to gene survival, it is not blasphemous, or obviously disastrous, to start to control the process in the light of our own values. We may value other qualities in people, in preference to those which have been most conducive to gene survival.

The prohibition on playing God is obscure. If it tells us not to interfere with natural selection at all, this rules out medicine, and most other environmental and social changes. If it only forbids interference with natural selection by the direct alteration of genes, this rules out negative as well as positive genetic engineering. If these interpretations are too restrictive, the ban on positive engineering seems to need some explanation. If we can make positive changes at the environmental level, and negative changes at the genetic level, why should we not make positive changes at the genetic level? What makes this policy, but not the others, objectionably God-like?

Perhaps the most plausible reply to these questions rests on a general objection to any group of people trying to plan too closely what human life should be like. Even if it is hard to distinguish in principle between the use of genetic and environmental means, genetic changes are likely to differ in degree from most environmental ones. Genetic alterations may be more drastic or less reversible, and so they can be seen as the extreme case of an objectionably God-like policy by which some people set out to plan the lives of others.

This objection can be reinforced by imagining the possible results of a programme of positive engineering, where the decisions about the desired improvements were taken by scientists. Judging by the literature written by scientists on this topic, great prominence would be given to intelligence. But can we be sure that enough weight would be given to other desirable qualities? And do things seem better if for scientists we substitute doctors, politicians or civil servants? Or some committee containing businessmen, trade unionists, academics, lawyers and a clergyman?

What seems worrying here is the circumscribing of potential human development. The present genetic lottery throws up a vast range of characteristics, good and bad, in all sorts of combinations. The group of people controlling a positive engineering policy would inevitably have limited horizons, and we are right to worry that the limitations of their outlook might become the boundaries of human variety. The drawbacks would be like those of town-planning or dog-breeding, but with more important consequences.

When the objection to playing God is separated from the idea that intervening in this aspect of the natural world is a kind of blasphemy, it is a protest against a particular group of people, necessarily fallible and limited, taking decisions so important to our future. This protest may be on grounds of the bad consequences, such as loss of variety of people, that would come from the imaginative limits of those taking the decisions. Or it may be an expression of opposition to such concentration of power, perhaps with the thought: 'What right have *they* to decide what kinds of people there should be?' Can these problems be side-stepped?

2. THE GENETIC SUPERMARKET

Robert Nozick is critical of the assumption that positive engineering has to involve any centralized decision about desirable qualities: 'Many biologists tend to think the problem is one of *design,* of specifying the best types of persons so that biologists can proceed to produce them. Thus they worry over what sort(s) of person there is to be and who will control this process. They do not tend to think, perhaps because it diminishes the importance of their role, of a system in which they run a "genetic supermarket," meeting the individual specifications (within certain moral limits) of prospective parents. Nor do they think of seeing what limited number of types of persons people's choices would converge upon, if indeed there would be any such convergence. This supermarket system has the great virtue that it involves no centralized decision fixing the future human type(s).'[7]

This idea of letting parents choose their children's characteristics is in many ways an improvement on decisions being taken by some centralized body. It seems less likely to reduce human variety, and could even increase it, if genetic engineering makes new combinations of characteristics available. (But we should be cautious here. Parental choice is not a guarantee of genetic variety, as the influence of fashion or of shared values might make for a small number of types on which choices would converge.)

To those sympathetic to one kind of liberalism, Nozick's proposal will seem more attractive than centralized decisions. On this approach to politics, it is wrong for the authorities to institutionalize any religious or other outlook as the official one of the society. To a liberal of this kind, a good society is one which tolerates and encourages a wide diversity of ideals of the good life. Anyone with these sympathies will be suspicious of centralized decisions about what sort of people should form the next generation. But some parental decisions would be disturbing. If parents chose characteristics likely to make their children unhappy, or likely to reduce their abilities, we might feel that the children should be protected against this. (Imagine parents belonging to some extreme religious sect, who wanted their children to have a religious symbol as a physical mark on their face, and who wanted them to be unable to read, as a protection against their faith being corrupted.) Those of us who support restrictions protecting children from parental harm after birth (laws against cruelty, and compulsion on parents to allow their children to be educated and to have necessary medical treatment) are likely to support protecting children from being harmed by their parents' genetic choices.

No doubt the boundaries here will be difficult to draw. We already find it difficult to strike a satisfactory balance between protection of children and parental freedom to choose the kind of upbringing their children should have. But it is hard to accept that society should set no limits to the genetic choices parents can make for their children. Nozick recognizes this when he says the genetic supermarket should meet the specifications of parents 'within certain moral limits'. So, if the supermarket came into existence, some centralized policy, even if only the restrictive one of ruling out certain choices harmful to the children, should exist. It would be a political decision where the limits should be set.

There may also be a case for other centralized restrictions on parental choice, as well as those aimed at preventing harm to the individual people being designed. The genetic supermarket might have more oblique bad effects. An imbalance in the ratio between the sexes could result. Or parents might think their children would be more successful if they were more thrusting, competitive and selfish. If enough parents acted on this thought, other parents with different values might feel forced into making similar choices to prevent their own children being too greatly disadvantaged. Unregulated individual decisions could lead to shifts of this kind, with outcomes unwanted by most of those who contribute to them. If a majority favour a roughly equal ratio between the sexes, or a population of relatively uncompetitive people, they may feel justified in supporting restrictions on what parents can choose. (This is an application to the case of genetic engineering of a point familiar in other contexts, that unrestricted individual choices can add up to a total outcome which most people think worse than what would result from some regulation.)

Nozick recognizes that there may be cases of this sort. He considers the case of avoiding a sexual imbalance and says that 'a government could require that genetic manipulation be carried on so as to fit a certain ratio.'[8] He clearly prefers to avoid governmental intervention of this kind, and, while admitting that the desired result would be harder to obtain in a purely libertarian system, suggests possible strategies for doing so. He says: 'Either parents would subscribe to an information service monitoring the recent births and so know which sex was in shorter supply (and hence would be more in demand in later life), thus adjusting their activities, or interested individuals would contribute to a charity that offers bonuses to maintain the ratios, or the ratio would leave 1:1, with new family and social patterns developing.' The proposals for avoiding the sexual imbalance without central regulation are not reassuring. Information about likely prospects for marriage or sexual partnership might not be decisive for parents' choices. And, since those most likely to be 'interested individuals' would be in the age group being genetically engineered, it is not clear that the charity would be given donations adequate for its job.[9]

If the libertarian methods failed, we would have the choice between allowing a sexual imbalance or imposing some system of social regulation. Those who dislike central decisions favouring one sort of person over others might accept regulation here, on the grounds that neither sex is being given preference: the aim is rough equality of numbers.

But what about the other sort of case, where the working of the genetic supermarket leads to a general change unwelcome to those who contribute to it? Can we defend regulation to prevent a shift towards a more selfish and competitive population as merely being the preservation of a certain ratio between characteristics? Or have we crossed the boundary, and allowed a centralized decision favouring some characteristics over others? The location of the boundary is obscure. One view would be that the sex-ratio case is acceptable because the desired ratio is equality of numbers. On another view, the acceptability derives from the fact that the present ratio is to be preserved. (In this second view, preserving altruism would be acceptable, so long as no attempt was made to raise the proportion of altruistic people in the population. But is *this* boundary an easy one to defend?)

If positive genetic engineering does become a reality, we may be unable to avoid some of the decisions being taken at a social level. Or rather, we could avoid this, but only at what seems an unacceptable cost, either to the particular people being designed, or to their generation as a whole. And, even if the social decisions are only restrictive, it is implausible to claim that they are all quite free of any taint of preference for some characteristics over others. But, although this suggests that we should not be doctrinaire in our support of the liberal view, it does not show that the view has to be abandoned altogether. We may still think that social decisions in favour of one type of person rather than another should be few, even if the consequences of excluding them altogether are unacceptable. A genetic supermarket, modified by some central regulation, may still be better than a system of purely central decisions. The liberal value is not obliterated because it may sometimes be compromised for the sake of other things we care about.

3. A MIXED SYSTEM

The genetic supermarket provides a partial answer to the objection about the limited outlook of those who would take the decisions. The choices need not be concentrated in the hands of a small number of people. The genetic supermarket should not operate in a completely unregulated way, and so some centralized decisions would have to be taken about the restrictions that should be imposed. One system that would answer many of the anxieties about centralized decision-making would be to limit the power of the decision-makers to one of veto. They would then only check departures from the natural genetic lottery, and so the power to bring about changes would not be given to them, but spread through the whole population of potential parents. Let us call this combination of parental initiative and central veto a 'mixed system.' If positive genetic engineering does come about, we can imagine the argument between supporters of a mixed system and supporters of other decision-making systems being central to the political theory of the twenty-first century, parallel to the place occupied in the nineteenth and twentieth centuries by the debate over control of the economy.[10]

My own sympathies are with the view that, if positive genetic engineering is introduced, this mixed system is in general likely to be the best one for making decisions. I do not want to argue for an absolutely inviolable commitment to this, as it could be that some centralized decision for genetic change was the only way of securing a huge benefit or avoiding a great catastrophe. But, subject to this reservation, the dangers of concentrating the decision-making create a strong presumption in favour of a mixed system rather than one in which initiatives come from the centre. And, if a mixed system was introduced, there would have to be a great deal of political argument over what kinds of restrictions on the supermarket should be imposed. Twenty-first-century elections may be about issues rather deeper than economics.

If this mixed system eliminates the anxiety about genetic changes being introduced by a few powerful people with limited horizons, there is a more general unease which it does not remove. May not the limitations of one generation of parents also prove disastrous? And, underlying this, is the problem of what values parents should appeal to in making their choices. How can we be confident that it is better for one sort of person to be born than another?

4. VALUES

The dangers of such decisions, even spread through all prospective parents, seem to me very real. We are swayed by fashion. We do not know the limitations of

our own outlook. There are human qualities whose value we may not appreciate. A generation of parents might opt heavily for their children having physical or intellectual abilities and skills. We might leave out a sense of humour. Or we might not notice how important to us is some other quality, such as emotional warmth. So we might not be disturbed in advance by the possible impact of the genetic changes on such a quality. And, without really wanting to do so, we might stumble into producing people with a deep coldness. This possibility seems one of the worst imaginable. It is just one of the many horrors that could be blundered into by our lack of foresight in operating the mixed system. Because such disasters are a real danger, there is a case against positive genetic engineering, even when the changes do not result from centralized decisions. But this case, resting as it does on the risk of disaster, supports a principle of caution rather than a total ban. We have to ask the question whether there are benefits sufficiently great and sufficiently probable to outweigh the risks.

But perhaps the deepest resistance, even to a mixed system, is not based on risks, but on a more general problem about values. Could the parents ever be justified in choosing, according to some set of values, to create one sort of person rather than another?

Is it sometimes better for us to create one sort of person rather than another? We say 'yes' when it is a question of eliminating genetic defects. And we say 'yes' if we think that encouraging some qualities rather than others should be an aim of the upbringing and education we give our children. Any inclination to say 'no' in the context of positive genetic engineering must lay great stress on the two relevant boundaries. The positive-negative boundary is needed to mark off the supposedly unacceptable positive policies from the acceptable elimination of defects. And the genes-environment boundary is needed to mark off positive engineering from acceptable positive aims of educational policies. But it is not clear that confidence in the importance of these boundaries is justified. . . .

NOTES

1. Chris Graham has suggested to me that it is misleading to say this without emphasizing the painful slowness of this way of changing gene frequencies.

2. *The Future of Man* (The Reith Lectures, 1959), London, 1960, chapter 3; and in 'The Genetic Improvement of Man', in *The Hope of Progress,* London, 1972.

3. *Genes, Dreams and Realities,* London, 1971, p . 81.

4. 'Already they have pushed Cline's results further, obtaining transfer between rabbit and mouse, for example, and good expression of the foreign gene in its new host. Some, by transferring the genes into the developing eggs, have managed to get the new genes into every cell in the mouse, including the sex cells; those mice have fathered offspring who also contain the foreign gene.' Jeremy Cherfas: *Man Made Life,* Oxford, 1982, pp. 229–30.

5. *Out of the Night,* New York, 1935. To find a distinguished geneticist talking like this after the Nazi period is not easy.

6. John Maynard Smith: *On Evolution,* Edinburgh, 1972; the article is reprinted from the issue on 'Utopia' of *Daedalus, Journal of the American Academy of Arts and Sciences,* 1965.

7. *Anarchy, State and Utopia,* New York, 1974, p. 315.

8. Op. cit., p. 315.

9. This kind of unworldly innocence is part of the engaging charm of Nozick's dotty and brilliant book.

10. Decision-taking by a central committee (perhaps of a dozen elderly men) can be thought of as a 'Russian' model. The genetic supermarket (perhaps with genotypes being sold by TV commercials) can be thought of as an 'American' model. The mixed system may appeal to Western European social democrats.

ERIK PARENS

The Goodness of Fragility: On the Prospect of Genetic Technologies Aimed at the Enhancement of Human Capacities

Currently, genetic technology cannot be used to significantly enhance human capacities. Although, for instance, genetically engineered bovine somatotropin (BST) is now used to enhance the milk production of cows, no one suggests an analogous enhancement of humans. And while human growth hormone (hGH) has been administered to enhance the stature of children who are not hGH deficient, it is not clear whether the procedure has worked (White 1993).

Yet if it is true that humans cannot now significantly enhance their capacities with genetic technology, it is also true that they always have sought to enhance their capacities with whatever means have been available. For example, we enhance our intellectual capacities with education, our bodily capacities with exercise, and our capacity to attract sexual partners with a variety of cosmetic techniques. From this I infer two things: (1) that it would make no sense to argue that the enhancement of human capacities is, in itself, a bad thing; and (2) that when genetic technology gets to the point where enhancement is possible, there will be a powerful drive to employ it.

Indeed, there seems to be no reason why, in principle, the gene-therapy techniques used to replace defec-

tive genes with "healthy" ones could not be used to replace healthy genes with "enhanced" or "better" ones.[1] Nor is there any reason why, in principle, the genetic-engineering techniques used to make products that the body cannot make could not be used to make more of a product that the body already makes.

If today, a drug like fluoxetine (Prozac) can enhance the capacity of a significant minority of users to compete in a consumer society by raising the level of the neurotransmitter serotonin (Kramer 1993; Sherman 1994), then there is reason to think that genetic technology will be able to enhance human capacities in similarly significant ways.[2] Indeed, a recent issue of *Science* reports on researchers who generated mice that lacked the gene for one of the serotonin receptors (5-HT$_{1B}$) (Saudou et al. 1994). As one might predict from fluoxetine's ability to increase serotonin levels in humans by inhibiting the reuptake of serotonin, the researchers found that the aggressiveness of the mice was increased. While these researchers clearly did not have in mind the significant minority of fluoxetine users whose competitiveness is enhanced by increased levels of serotonin, they apparently did have in mind the possibility of using genetic technology to achieve the same therapeutic effect that drugs like fluoxetine have. Furthermore, although enhancing the aggressiveness of mice is a long way from enhancing the competitiveness of humans with genetic

Reprinted by permission from *Kennedy Institute of Ethics Journal* 5 (June 1995), 141–53. Copyright © 1995 by the Johns Hopkins University Press.

technology, such enhancements no longer seem the stuff of science fiction.

Given the apparently enduring desire of humans to enhance their capacities, and given the likelihood that new genetic technologies will at some point enable us to enhance our capacities in significant and perhaps unprecedented ways, now is the time for society to begin thinking about how far it ought to go in this regard.[3] While there are good and self-evident reasons to go in the direction of such enhancements, a chief aim of this essay is to reflect on some good and less-evident reasons why our society ought to exercise extreme caution as it contemplates such a move.

Urging caution with respect to genetic enhancement is nothing new (see, e.g., President's Commission 1982; Davis and Engelhardt 1984; Anderson 1989; Walters 1991). But the problem does not admit of a neat solution. It is, rather, the sort of problem that requires ongoing engagement. My attempt to engage it will take the form of the following question: Will we, in some of our attempts to enhance humans, inadvertently impoverish them by reducing what I will call their fragility.[4] Before beginning to answer this question, I want to make three preliminary points.

First, my use of the term "fragility" might seem strange. When I say that we are fragile creatures, I mean that we are creatures subject to change and to chance. In this essay I attempt to reflect upon what life would be like if we could significantly reduce the change and chance to which we — creatures whose forms are largely determined by the genetic hand dealt us by nature — have hitherto been subject.

Second, I am not trying to argue that genetic technology aimed at enhancement could rid life of fragility. Even if human beings were to become uniformly beautiful, marvelously tempered, hugely healthy, and massively smart, there still would be plenty of change and chance for everyone to be subject to. I am merely exploring what might be lost if, to an unprecedented extent, we could reduce our vulnerability to change and chance.

Finally, I am not making the unconditional or absolute claim that we ought never to use genetic technology to enhance human beings. Nor am I attempting to provide an algorithm that we could simply apply when faced with the prospect of a given technology. Rather, I am attempting to articulate a series of considerations that ought to be factored into any decision about whether to go ahead with a given technology aimed at enhancement. I undertake to articulate these considerations because, given the potential for prodigious benefits, we might overlook them. In the end, I will speculate about what besides benevolence inclines us to overlook such considerations as we contemplate the use of technologies aimed at the enhancement of human capacities.

THE DESIRE TO REDUCE CHANGE

One of the easiest ways to begin appreciating what is valuable about fragility is to think about the pleasure we take in our experience of some forms of the beautiful. Consider the ordinary experience of beholding other organisms — such as flowers. The intensity of one sort of pleasure we receive from beholding flowers depends decisively on their transience, on the fact that they undergo change. Crucial ingredients in our pleasure are our anticipation of the blossoming and our anxiety about, and memory of, its passing.

That the blossom comes into being and passes away may be a source of anxiety — but it is an anxiety that heightens our pleasure: this flower, in this form, is here but for a few, beautiful days. It may even be that this "little" anxiety in the face of the flower's coming into being and passing away is an occasion for our reflection upon the "great" anxiety we experience in the face of our own mortality. Though we often turn away from anxiety, both little and great, doing so is to turn away from an important part of being human and thus is to impoverish our experience.

The goodness of this sort of fragility receives one of its most beautiful expressions in the poetry of Wallace Stevens:

Is there no change of death in paradise?
Does ripe fruit never fall? Or do the boughs
Hang always heavy in that perfect sky,
Unchanging, yet so like our perishing earth,
With rivers like our own that seek for seas
They never find, the same receding shores
That never touch with inarticulate pang? . . .
Death is the mother of beauty. . . .[5]

If there is no change in paradise, then, according to Stevens, neither is there beauty of a fundamental sort.

If the attempt to reduce our subjection to change could affect for the worse our experience of some forms of the beautiful, it could do the same for our experience of caring and being cared for.[6] Suppose enhancement technology were aimed at removing the difficulties of aging, thereby altering our conception and experience of, for example, relationships between the generations. Given that figuring out how to care for a burgeoning elderly population is one of our most pressing social problems, it might, at first glance, seem quite wonderful if we could, say, enhance the capacities of ninety-five-year-olds so that they could act and feel like twenty-five-year-olds.

Furthermore, while we're thinking about trying to reduce the time spent on the elderly members of our society, we could also think about trying to reduce the time spent on the young. We could, I suppose, strive to discover an "acceleration hormone"—a hormone aimed at making children grow faster. Much money and energy would be saved if we could compress not only old age, but childhood too. I can well imagine the complaint that I have created a straw man. After all, children are sweet; no one would make such a proposal. But what about accelerating adolescence? No one ever claimed that adolescents are sweet; moreover, adolescence is a time of pain and danger to the people undergoing it, as well as to the rest of us. Compressing this difficult period could significantly reduce pain and the expenditure of valuable social resources.

I assume that one reason no one would assent to my modest proposal is that we think that we ought to caringly respond to the pain of adolescence rather than engineer a way around it. There is a point beyond which the reduction of our subjection to some sorts of change costs too much. Though it would be naive to forget just how burdensome the need for care can be to both the giver of care and the receiver, it would be equally naive to forget that the shared recognition and acceptance of human neediness can be profoundly valuable. That is, I take it to be valuable for us to recognize and accept our nature, and neediness is a constituent of that nature.

Further, as I will discuss more fully below, when we consider whether to proceed with a given technology aimed at enhancement, we ought to consider whether that technology threatens to reduce the great diversity of human forms. Given what appears to be a deep human tendency to fear and hate the different, we ought to be especially vigilant about promoting technologies that could—by engineering sameness—collude with that tendency. At the point where a given enhancement technology diminishes difference across the life span, where it promises to make us all look and act more alike, the good that is diversity across the life span is threatened.

In a word, before we attempt to enhance human beings by reducing their subjection to change—before attempting to reduce their fragility—we ought to consider how such attempts would affect the good that is our experience of some forms of the beautiful, the good that is relationships of care, and the good that is diversity across the life span.

THE DESIRE TO REDUCE CHANCE

Let me invite you now to think about the pleasure we take in our experience of some human excellences. Why is it, for example, that our knowledge of a runner's use of steroids diminishes our pleasure in his or her performance? Why is it that watching Ben Johnson run does not give track fans the same sort of pleasure as watching, say, Carl Lewis? Part of the reason is no doubt simply a sense of fairness: Johnson has an unfair, steroid-induced advantage. I want to suggest, however, that something subtler is at work as well. Part of our experience of the particular excellence of a winning runner resides in our intuition that this performance is the result of an extraordinary combination of human effort and chance. It could have been otherwise, and it almost always is, but this time a human being ran 100 meters in well under 10 seconds. To reduce the role of chance—to alter with steroids the hand that nature dealt the runner—is to diminish, if not ruin, our experience of this form of excellence.

Sport is neither the only, nor the most significant, area of human endeavor where chance plays a crucial role. When we speak of equal opportunity, for example, we mean that within the constraints of those gifts that come to people from the natural lottery, we give each an equal opportunity to compete. When there no longer is a natural lottery such as we have understood it heretofore, when what we are depends not upon the hand nature dealt us, but—even more than now—upon the hand our parents bought us, then concepts such as equal opportunity will have to undergo fundamental transformations.[7]

It is predictable, for example, that an even larger chasm will open between the rich who can afford enhancement treatment and the poor who cannot. This prediction rests on the assumption that enhancement treatment will be distributed unevenly, according to peoples' ability to pay. But let us change the assumption. What would happen if resources were not limited and enhancement treatment were available to all? At first glance, it might seem that nothing could be lost; it might seem that, finally, we had discovered how to make humankind happier. Reducing the chance to which humans are subject in the natural lottery might seem like a brilliant way to end the competitiveness and resentment that are the root of clashes in the kindergarten and on the battlefield. Imagine: Everyone could be porcelain-skinned, blond, blue-eyed, straight, tall, small-waisted, big-chested, smart, and nice. Nobody would have to have skin too dark anymore. Nobody would have to have hair too kinky anymore. Nobody would have to be gay. Nobody would be too short. Nobody would have too big a nose or too small a chest. Nobody would be too mean or too nice. Everybody would be just right (see Fielder 1985).

If society could in fact enhance away the "imperfections" resulting from chance, it could, once again, reduce one of its most pressing burdens: the burden of responding to the needs of those who are marginalized because they do not possess the specifications deemed valuable. And once again the questions arise: Would it be a good thing to reduce the diversity — to diminish the difference — that results from our subjection to chance? Would it be a good thing to reduce the need to respond to the vulnerability of others that results from our subjection to chance? For the reasons offered above in the context of attempting to reduce our subjection to change, my tentative answers to those questions are clear.

Just as I suggested that it is in exuberant moments — of imagining how much better life might be if we could rid it of change — that we forget about the goodness of change, so in exuberant moments we forget about the goodness of chance.[8] When we are carried away by our benevolent desires to reduce the suffering of vulnerable people and, less benevolently, their cost to society, we forget that the vulnerability of others not only burdens us (though it surely does so), but also elicits from us the awesome capacity to care for others. Although — and I cannot be too emphatic about this — it would be a profound mistake to romanticize the need to care for vulnerable others and the need of vulnerable others to be cared for, it would be equally mistaken to ignore the goodness that those relationships can possess.[9]

THE DESIRE FOR PARADISE

In my attempt to articulate the considerations that ought to be factored into any decision to implement a given technology aimed at enhancement, there operates an as-yet unarticulated premise involving a particular conception of the proper relationship between humans and the rest of the natural world. Indeed it seems that significantly different conceptions of the value and the meaning of human life — profoundly different conceptions of our proper relationship to ourselves and to the rest of the natural world — are at work in the argument between those who tend to favor enhancement technologies and those who tend to be critical of them. I would like now to suggest one way to begin thinking about that difference.

Those who tend to favor genetic enhancement proceed from a conception of the relationship between humans and the rest of the world much like that of Francis Bacon. Bacon's project to conquer and control nature is relentlessly commented upon, yet one element of the project is often forgotten. Bacon thinks that his project has a divine sanction; in *The New Organon* (I, cxxix), for instance, he writes that the human race has a "right over nature which belongs to it by divine bequest." Consistent with his Calvinism, Bacon believes, as one scholar succinctly puts it, that "the mission of science [is] to repair the damage done by the Fall of Man and to restore man to his original glory" (Finch 1963, p. xiii).[10]

It goes without saying that Bacon's project has benefited humankind enormously. It does not, however, go without saying that Bacon's project is embedded in a very particular conception of the proper relationship between humans and the rest of nature. In fact, we are so embedded in Bacon's conception that it does not seem particular to us at all. Medicine, for example, has been one of the greatest beneficiaries of that project's success. When Ronald Munson and Lawrence Davis (1992) argue in this journal that medicine ought to employ germ-line therapy for the treatment of disease, they speak as if the aim of medicine were self-evident. Like Bacon, they proceed as if the Western biomedical conception were ordained by God. Because the aim of medicine is self-evident for Munson and Davis, the only remaining problem is to find the means to achieve it. As they write, "The basic standard of evaluation [for medicine] must be practical or instrumental success with respect to its specific aim." What, in their view is the aim of medicine? It is to achieve "control over the factors affecting health. . . . [Knowledge] is important to medicine because it leads to control" (Munson and Davis 1992, p. 155). Given that control is the aim, and given that germ-line therapy "is the most effective form of control," they conclude that medicine has a prima facie duty to employ germ-line therapy.

Although the view that the proper relationship between humans and the rest of the world is one of control is so entrenched as to seem self-evident, there are alternative perspectives: certainly many feminists, environmentalists, and peoples from different cultures have articulated such views. But people in the bioethical conversation also have attempted to articulate an alternative vision; Hans Jonas is one such person.

Whereas Bacon proceeds from the assumption that the mission of science is to repair the damage done by the Fall of Man and to restore Man to his original glory, Jonas — to translate his thought into theological terms — proceeds from the assumption that leaving Paradise did not constitute a Fall at all, but rather marked the beginning of peculiarly difficult and good human life. Whereas Bacon thinks that creation needs restoration to a former state of perfection, Jonas thinks that creation is owed preservation in its altogether "imperfect" state. Whereas Bacon thinks that nature is ours to use in whatever ways conduce to our desires, Jonas thinks that because nature is in an important sense not ours — "being [is] strictly on loan" (1992, p. 36) — we ought not so to use it.[11]

The archenemy of the Baconian project — death — is of course the ultimate form of fragility. Whereas, according to Bacon, death is the enemy and life extension is medicine's "noblest goal" (Amundsen 1978, p. 27), according to Jonas, death is both a "bitter burden" and a "blessing." Following Heidegger, Jonas (1992, p. 36) writes of death: "only in confrontation with ever-possible not-being could being come to feel itself, affirm itself, make itself its own purpose." For Jonas, death is not an accidental part of life that we ought to try to overcome, but rather is an essential part of life, the goodness of which we need to try to understand.

Those who seek to understand the goodness of death — that ultimate form of fragility — hope that we are the sort of animals who can decide that, although technologies aimed at enhancement might gratify both pedestrian and noble desires, we won't go ahead with some of those technologies because to do so would be to lose too much that makes life good. As valuable as the human capacity for self-transformation and control of the world is, the human capacity to relinquish control and to resist the desire for transformation is equally valuable. We are the animals that can ask: When does that marvelous capacity to manipulate and control the world, when does that marvelous and peculiarly human capacity to change ourselves, go too far?

With respect to genetic technology, we can begin by saying that it goes too far when — in an attempt to establish paradise on earth — it threatens the good that is the pleasure we take in some forms of the beautiful and excellent, or when it threatens the good that is some relationships of care, or when it threatens the good that is the diversity of human forms. When we ask whether it makes a difference if we figure out when our capacity to manipulate and control the world and ourselves has gone too far, we might think about what that capacity has wrought, in the last forty years, on the diversity of life forms on this planet.

Since Watson and Crick discovered the double helix in 1953, the world's population has more than doubled and its economic activity has more than quadrupled (Kennedy 1993, p. 97). According to an appeal sent to Latin American presidents by Gabriel Garcia Marquez and others, "By the year 2000 three-quarters of America's tropical forests may have been felled and 50 percent of their species lost forever" (Kennedy 1993, p. 100). Thus, it is possible that in approximately the same time it will have taken us to garner the knowledge necessary to diminish the diversity of human forms by making ourselves more alike, we also will have reduced by one-half the diversity of other animal forms in some places.[12]

It seems to me that it would be profoundly tragic if the virtue that is our capacity for self-transformation became a vice. It would be profoundly tragic and paradoxical if what Nietzsche calls "the unfixed animal" — due to its capacity for change and its desire for perfection — were to "fix itself" (see Jonas 1974, p. 153).

Let me emphasize: It would be cruel, if not stupid, to suggest that we ought never to use genetic technology to heal the sick. It probably would be foolish to suggest that technology ought never to be used for the enhancement of human beings. So too would it be foolish to forget that without the desire to control and master the world there would be no desire to control and master ourselves.[13] My suggestion has not been that we should figure out a way to extirpate our desire to control and alter ourselves and the world; rather, it has been simply that we should think more deeply about how attempts at control and alteration that truly enhance life are different from those that impoverish it.

It may be that thinking more deeply about that difference will entail rethinking some basic beliefs about our proper relationship to ourselves and the rest of nature.

To paraphrase the Czech novelist, Milan Kundera, whose native country has been subjected to relentless political violence in the name of establishing Paradise on earth, "Humankind's longing for Paradise is humankind's longing not to be human." No less than the nobility, we should remember the peril of that longing.

This essay was prepared for The Hastings Center Project on Priorities in the Clinical Application of Human Genome Research, funded by the National Center for Human Genome Research of the National Institutes of Health grant R01HG00418-0. I am deeply grateful to Hilde Lindemann Nelson, James Lindemann Nelson, and Andrea Kott Parens for their critical and generous readings of earlier versions of this essay.

NOTES

1. I am keenly aware that, given the extent to which concepts such as health and enhancement are socially constructed, the distinction between treatment aimed at health and treatment aimed at enhancement is highly contestable. For an account of the reasonableness of the distinction, see Normal Daniels (1992).

2. Although Prozac's effectiveness is correlated with altered serotonin levels, research suggests that increased serotonin is a necessary, but not sufficient, cause for the effects now associated with Prozac. Nonetheless, my point remains: if we can enhance behavior with a drug like Prozac, it stands to reason that we can do the same with genetic technology.

3. It seems to me that we should respond to the prospect of genetic enhancement (somatic and germ-line) as Nelson Wivel and LeRoy Walters respond to the prospect of germ-line treatment aimed at the prevention of disease: "Because the readily identifiable technical problems necessarily consign germ-line gene modification to the relatively distant future, a discussion of the ethical issues might be viewed as an exercise in the abstract. . . . It [nonetheless] would, in our view, be a useful investment of time and energy to continue and in fact to intensify the public discussion . . . *even though the application of this new technology to humans is not likely to be proposed in the near future*" (Wivel and Walters 1993, p. 537, emphasis added).

4. Always in the background for me will be the words of Martha Nussbaum (1986, p. 2), "Human excellence is seen . . . in the Greek poetic tradition . . . as something whose very nature it is to be in need, a growing thing in the world that could not be made invulnerable and keep its own peculiar fineness."

5. My attention was first called to Stevens's "Sunday Morning" by Leon Kass's essay "Mortality and Morality: The Virtues of Finitude" (1985).

6. For the dangers of such "care talk," see Adrienne Asch (1993).

7. Concerning the implications of the genetic technologies for (1) our concept of equality of opportunity, (2) our conception of humans as responsible agents, and (3) our conception of normality, see Dan Brock (1992).

8. See Hans Jonas (1985, p. 500): "The random nature of the sexual process is both the irreplaceable blessing and the inescapable burden of our lot. . . . "

9. See Bruce Jennings, Daniel Callahan and Arthur Caplan (1988, p. 15): "The provision of care and social support for persons with chronic illness by temporarily well and able-bodied citizens reflects an acknowledgment of the links that join the sick and the well, the young and the old in a community of common humanness and vulnerability."

10. See also Charles Taylor's discussion of the Calvinist desire to "clean up the human mess" (Taylor, 1989, pp. 227–28).

11. Though here I am contrasting Jonas's world view with the Calvinist one, the respect in which Jonas's view is commensurate with much of Christian thought is clear.

12. This desire to McDonaldize the world — to reduce the diversity of animate and inanimate forms — is as deep as it is demanding of our attention. Benjamin R. Barber's (1992) "Jihad vs. McWorld" is pertinent. For a closely related argument, see James V. Neel (1993, p. 127): "The elucidation of the precise nature of our genetic material, four billion years in evolving, occurred only 40 years ago. Despite the incredible advances in molecular genetics, we still have a very limited knowledge of the anatomy of our DNA, but even less understanding of how it transacts its excruciatingly complex business. Right now the ecosystem is reeling under the impact of an intellectual arrogance which assumed unbridled license to perturb that system. We are a part of that ecosystem, the last frontier, so to speak. Is there any informed person who, surveying the current evidence of the profound consequences of precipitous human action, believes we are now ready for a serious consideration of how to mold ourselves genetically?"

13. Similarly, it would be foolish to suggest that Bacon and his contemporary followers are without awe or reverence for nature; there are, however, "reverences" or "awes" with different emphases. See Renée Fox's discussion of the difference between the awe Barbara McClintock brings to the study of molecular biology and the awe Albert Claude brings to it (Fox 1989, pp. 190–94).

REFERENCES

Amundsen, Darrel W. 1978. The Physician's Obligation to Prolong Life: A Medical Duty without Classical Roots. *Hastings Center Report* 8 (4): 23–30.

Anderson, W. French, 1989. Human Gene Therapy: Why Draw a Line? *Journal of Medicine and Philosophy* 14: 681–93.

Asch, Adrienne. 1993. Abused or Neglected Clients — Abusive or Neglectful Service Systems? In *Ethical Conflicts in the Management of Home Care,* ed. Rosalie A. Kane and Arthur L. Caplan, pp. 113–21. New York: Springer Publishing Co.

Barber, Benjamin R. 1992. Jihad vs. McWorld. *Atlantic Monthly* (March): 53–65.

Brock, Dan. 1992. The Human Genome Project and Human Identity. *Houston Law Review* 29 (1): 7–22.

Daniels, Norman. 1992. Growth Hormone Therapy for Short Stature: Can We Support the Treatment/Enhancement Distinction? *Growth: Genetics & Hormones* 8 (Supplement 1): 46–48.

Davis, Bernard D., and Engelhardt, H. Tristram, Jr. 1984. Genetic Engineering: Prospects and Recommendations. *Zygon* 19: 277–80.

Fielder, Leslie A. 1985. The Tyranny of the Normal. In *Which Babies Shall Live?,* ed. Thomas H. Murray and Arthur L. Caplan, pp. 151–60. Clifton, NJ: Humana Press.

Finch, Henry LeRoy, ed. 1963. *The Complete Essays of Francis Bacon.* New York: Washington Square Press.

Fox, Renée. 1989. *The Sociology of Medicine: A Participant Observer's View.* Englewood Cliffs, NJ: Prentice-Hall.

Jennings, Bruce; Callahan, Daniel; and Caplan, Arthur. 1988. Ethical Challenges of Chronic Illness. *Hastings Center Report* 18 (1, Special Supplement): 1–16.

Jonas, Hans. 1974. Biological Engineering—A Preview. In *Philosophical Essays: From Ancient Creed to Technological Man,* ed. Hans Jonas, pp. 141–67. Englewood Cliffs, NJ: Prentice-Hall.

———. 1985. Ethics and Biogenic Art. *Social Research* 52: 491–504.

———. 1992. The Burden and Blessing of Mortality. *Hastings Center Report* 22 (1): 34–40.

Kass, Leon. 1985. Mortality and Morality: The Virtues of Finitude. In *Toward a More Natural Science,* ed. Leon Kass, pp. 299–317. New York: The Free Press.

Kennedy, Paul. 1993. *Preparing for the Twenty-First Century.* New York: Random House.

Kramer, Peter D. 1993. *Listening to Prozac.* New York: Viking.

Munson, Ronald, and Davis, Lawrence H. 1992. Germ-Line Therapy and the Medical Imperative. *Kennedy Institute of Ethics Journal* 2: 137–58.

Neel, James V. 1993. Germ-Line Gene Therapy: Another View. *Human Gene Therapy* 4: 127–28.

Nussbaum, Martha. 1986. *The Fragility of Goodness.* New York: Cambridge University Press.

President's Commission for the Study of Ethical Problems in Medicine and Biomedical and Behavioral Research. 1982. *Splicing Life: The Social and Ethical Issues of Genetic Engineering with Human Beings.* Washington, DC: U.S. Government Printing Office.

Saudou, Frédéric; Amara, Djamel Aït; Dierich, Andrée; et al. 1994. Enhanced Aggressive Behavior in Mice Lacking 5-HT$_{1B}$ Receptor. *Science* 265: 1875–78.

Sherman, Carl. 1994. Depression's Complex, Tangled Biologic Roots. *Clinical Psychiatry News* 22 (2): 3, 15.

Taylor, Charles. 1989. *Sources of the Self: The Making of the Modern Identity.* Cambridge: Harvard University Press.

Walters, LeRoy. 1991. Human Gene Therapy: Ethics and Public Policy. *Human Gene Therapy* 2: 115–22.

White, Gladys. 1993. Human Growth Hormone: The Dilemma of Expanded Use in Children. *Kennedy Institute of Ethics Journal* 3: 401–9.

Wivel, Nelson A., and Walters, LeRoy. 1993. Germ-line Gene Modification and Disease Prevention: Some Medical and Ethical Perspectives. *Science* 262: 533–38.

SUGGESTED READINGS

GENERAL ISSUES

Andrews, Lori B., *et al.* "Genetics and the Law." *Emory Law Journal* 39 (1990), 619–853. Symposium.

Asch, Anrienne, and Geller, Gail. "Feminism, Bioethics, and Genetics." In Susan M. Wolf, ed. *Feminism and Bioethics: Beyond Reproduction.* New York: Oxford University Press, 1996, 318–50.

Annas, George J., and Elias, Sherman, eds. *Gene Mapping: Using Law and Ethics as Guides.* New York: Oxford University Press, 1992.

Bankowski, Zbigniew, and Capron, Alexander Morgan, eds. Council for International Organizations of Medical Sciences. *Genetics, Ethics, and Human Values: Human Genome Mapping, Genetic Screening and Gene Therapy.* Geneva: CIOMS, 1990.

Davis, Bernard D., ed. *The Genetic Revolution: Scientific Prospects and Public Perceptions.* Baltimore: Johns Hopkins University Press, 1991.

Fletcher, Joseph. *The Ethics of Genetic Control: Ending Reproductive Roulette.* Garden City, NY: Anchor Books, 1974.

Frankel, Mark S., and Teich, Albert, eds. *The Genetic Frontier: Ethics Law, and Policy.* Washington, DC: American Association for the Advancement of Science, 1994.

Gert, Bernard, *et al. Morality and the New Genetics: A Guide for Students and Health Care Providers.* Boston: Jones and Bartlett, 1996.

Harris, John. *Clones, Genes, and Immortality: Ethics and the Genetic Revolution.* New York: Oxford University Press, 1998. (Earlier edition entitled *Wonderwoman and Superman.*)

House of Commons, Select Committee on Science and Technology. *Human Genetics: The Science and Its Consequences* (Third Report). 4 vols. London: Her Majesty's Stationery Office, 1995. (HC41.)

Hubbard, Ruth, and Wald, Elijah. *Exploding the Gene Myth.* Boston: Beacon Press, 1993.

Kitcher, Philip. *The Lives to Come: The Genetic Revolution and Human Possibilities.* New York: Simon and Schuster, 1996.

Krimsky, Sheldon. *Biotechnics and Society: The Rise of Industrial Genetics.* Westport, CT: Praeger, 1991.

Mahowald, Mary B., *et al.* "The New Genetics and Women." *Milbank Quarterly* 74 (1996), 239–83.

McGee, Glenn. *The Perfect Baby: A Pragmatic Approach to Genetics.* Lanham, MD: Rowman and Littlefield, 1997.

———. "Parenting in an Era of Genetics." *Hastings Center Report* 27 (March–April 1997), 16–22.

Nelkin, Dorothy, and Lindee, M. Susan. *The DNA Mystique: The Gene as a Cultural Icon.* New York: Freeman, 1995.

Nuffield Council on Bioethics. *Mental Disorders and Genetics: The Ethical Context.* London: The Council, September 1998.

Ramsey, Paul. *Fabricated Man: The Ethics of Genetic Control* New Haven: Yale University Press, 1970.

Rifkin, Jeremy. *The Biotech Century: Harnessing the Gene and Remaking the World.* New York: Penguin Putnam, 1998.

Suzuki, David, and Knudtson, Peter. *Genethics: The Clash between the New Genetics and Human Values.* Revised and updated edition. Cambridge, MA: Harvard University Press, 1990.

Tong, Rosemarie. "Feminist and Nonfeminist Perspectives on Genetic Screening, Diagnosis, Counseling, and Therapy." In her *Feminist Approaches to Bioethics: Theoretical Reflections and Practical Applications.* Boulder, CO: Westview Press: 213–42, 268–71.

United States Congress, Office of Technology Assessment. *New Developments in Biotechnology—Background Paper: Public Perceptions of Biotechnology.* Washington, DC: U.S. Government Printing Office, May 1987.

Walters, LeRoy. "Human Genetic Intervention and the Theologians: Cosmic Theology and Casuistic Analysis." In Lisa Sowle Cahill and James F. Childress, eds. *Christian Ethics: Problems and Prospects.* Cleveland: Pilgrim Press, 1996: 235–49.

Weir, Robert F.; Lawrence, Susan C.; and Fales, Evan, eds. *Genes and Human Self-Knowledge: Historical and Philosophical Re-*

flections on Modern Genetics. Iowa City, IA: Iowa University Press, 1994.

Wolf, Susan M. "Beyond 'Genetic Discrimination'; Toward the Broader Harm of Geneticism." *Journal of Law, Medicine and Ethics* 23 (1995), 345–53.

Wolpe, Paul. "If I Am Only My Genes, What Am I? Genetic Essentialism and a Jewish Response." *Kennedy Institute of Ethics Journal* 7 (1997), 213–30.

EUGENICS PROGRAMS IN THE TWENTIETH CENTURY

Adams, Mark B., ed. *The Wellborn Science: Eugenics in Germany, France, Brazil, and Russia.* New York: Oxford University Press, 1990.

Allen, Garland E. "The Social and Economic Origins of Genetic Determinism: A Case History of the American Eugenics Movement, 1900–1940, and Its Lessons for Today." *Genetica* 99 (1997), 77–88.

Barondess, Jeremiah A. "Medicine Against Society: Lessons from the Third Reich." *Journal of the American Medical Association* 276 (1996), 1657–61.

Burleigh, Michael, and Wippermann, Wolfgang. *The Racial State: Germany 1933–1945.* Cambridge: Cambridge University Press, 1991.

China. "Presidential Decree No. 33 of 27 October 1994 Promulgating the Law of the People's Republic of China on the Protection of Maternal and Child Health." *International Digest of Health Legislation* 46:1(1995), 39–42.

Dikötter, Frank. *Imperfect Conceptions: Medical Knowledge, Birth Defects, and Eugenics in China.* New York: Columbia University Press, 1998.

———. "Race Culture: Recent Perspectives on the History of Eugenics." *American Historical Review* 103 (1998), 467–78.

Duster, Troy. *Backdoor to Eugenics.* New York: Routledge, Chapman and Hall, 1990.

Haller, Mark H. *Eugenics: Hereditarian Attitudes in American Thought.* New Brunswick, NJ: Rutgers University Press, 1963.

Hesketh, Therese, and Zhu, Wei Xiang. "Maternal and Child Health in China." *British Medical Journal* 314 (1997), 1898–1900.

Kevles, Daniel J. "Eugenics: I. Historical Aspects." in Warren Thomas Reich, ed. *Encyclopedia of Bioethics.* Revised ed. New York: Simon and Schuster Macmillan, 1995, 765–70.

———. *In the Name of Eugenics: Genetics and the Uses of Human Heredity.* New York: Knopf, 1985.

Lappé, Marc. "Eugenics: II. Ethical Issues." In Warren Thomas Reich, ed. *Encyclopedia of Bioethics.* Revised ed. New York: Simon and Schuster Macmillan, 1995, 770–77.

Ludmerer, Kenneth M. *Genetics and American Society: A Historical Appraisal.* Baltimore: Johns Hopkins University Press, 1972.

Pernick, Martin S. "Eugenics and Public Health in American History." *American Journal of Public Health* 87 (1997), 1767–72.

Proctor, Robert N. *Racial Hygiene: Medicine under the Nazis.* Cambridge, MA: Harvard University Press, 1988.

Reilly, Philip R. *The Surgical Solution: A History of Involuntary Sterilization in the United States.* Baltimore: Johns Hopkins University Press, 1991.

Smith, J. David, and Nelson, K. Ray. *The Sterilization of Carrie Buck.* Far Hills, NJ: New Horizon Press, 1989.

Wachbroit, Robert. "What Is Wrong with Eugenics?" In Edward Erwin, Sidney Gendin, and Lowell Kleiman, eds. *Ethical Issues in Scientific Research.* New York: Garland Publishing, 1994, 329–36.

Watson, James D. "Genes and Politics." *Journal of Molecular Medicine* 75 (1997), 624–36.

Weindling, Paul. *Health, Race, and German Politics between National Unification and Nazism, 1870–1945.* Cambridge: Cambridge University Press, 1989.

THE HUMAN GENOME PROJECT

Boyle, Philip J., *et al.* "Genetic Grammar: 'Health,' 'Illness,' and the Human Genome Project." *Hastings Center Report* 22 (July–August 1992; Supplement), S1–S10.

Brock, Dan W. "The Human Genome Project and Human Identity." in Robert F. Weir, Susan C. Lawrence, and Evan Fales, eds. *Genes and Human Self-Knowledge: Historical and Philosophical Reflections on Modern Genetics.* Iowa City: Iowa University Press, 1994: 18–33.

Brower, Vicki, "Mining the Genetics Riches of Human Populations." *Nature Biotechnology* 16 (1998), 337–40.

Campbell, Paulette Walker. "Private Company's Plan Creates Doubt about U.S. Project on Human Genome." *Chronicle of Higher Education* 44 (May 22, 1998), A38–39.

Cantor, Charles R. "How Will the Human Genome Project Improve Our Quality of Life?" *Nature Biotechnology* 16 (1998), 212–13.

Capron, Morgan Alexander. "Which Ills to Bear?: Reevaluating the 'Threat' of Modern Genetics." *Emory Law Journal* 39 (1990), 665–96.

Collins, Francis S. "Medical and Ethical Consequences of the Human Genome Project." *Journal of Clinical Ethics* 2 (1991), 260–67.

———. "Ahead of Schedule and under Budget: The Genome Project Passes Its Fifth Birthday." *Proceedings of the National Academy of Sciences* 92 (1995), 10821–23.

Collins, Francis S.; Guyer, Mark S.; and Chakravarti, Aravinda. "Variations on a Theme: Cataloging Human DNA Sequence Variation." *Science* (1997), 1580–81.

Francis S. Collins, *et al.* "New Goals for the Human Genome Project: 1998–2003." *Science* 282 (1998), 682–89.

Cook-Deegan, Robert M. *The Gene Wars: Science, Politics, and the Human Genome* New York: W. W. Norton, 1993.

———. "Genome Mapping and Sequencing." in Warren Thomas Reich, ed. *Encyclopedia of Bioethics.* Revised ed. New York: Simon and Schuster Macmillan, 1995: 1011–20.

Doll, John J. "The Patenting of DNA." *Science* (1998), 689–90.

Ganten, Detlev. "James D. Watson at the Congress of Molecular Medicine." *Journal of Molecular Medicine* 75 (1997), 615–17.

Hanna, Kathi E. "The Ethical, Legal, and Social Implications Program of the National Center for Human Genome Research: A Missed Opportunity?" In Ruth Ellen Bulger, Elizabeth Meyer Bobby, and Harvey F. Fineberg, eds. Institute of Medicine, Committee on the Social and Ethical Impacts of Developments in Biomedicine. *Society's Choices: Social and Ethical Decision Making in Biomedicine.* Washington, DC: National Academy Press, 1995, 432–57.

Hedgecoe, Adam M. "Genome Analysis." In Ruth Chadwick, ed. *Encyclopedia of Applied Ethics.* San Diego, CA: Academic Press, 1998, 463–70.

Heller, Michael A., and Eisenberg, Rebecca S. "Can Patents Deter Innovation? The Anticommons in Biomedical Research." *Science* 280 (1998), 698–701.

Juengst, Eric T. "Respecting Human Subjects in Genome Research: A Preliminary Policy Agenda." In Harold Y. Vanderpool, ed. *The Ethics of Research Involving Human Subjects: Facing the 21st Century.* Frederick, MD: University Publishing Group, 1996, 401–29.

———. "Self-Critical Federal Science? The Ethics Experiment within the U.S. Human Genome Project." *Social Philosophy and Policy* 13 (1996), 63–95.

Karjala, Dennis S. "A Legal Research Agenda for the Human Genome Initiative." *Jurimetrics Journal* 32 (1992), 121–222.

Kevles, Daniel J., and Hood, Leroy, eds. *The Code of Codes: Scientific and Social Issues in the Human Genome Project.* Cambridge, MA: Harvard University Press, 1992.

Koonin, Steven E. "An Independent Perspective on the Human Genome Project." *Science* (1998), 36–37.

Lenoir, Noelle. "UNESCO, Genetics, and Human Rights." *Kennedy Institute of Ethics Journal* 7 (1997), 31–42.

McKusick, Victor A. "The Human Genome Project: Plans, Status, and Applications in Biology and Medicine." In George J. Annas, and Sherman Elias, eds. *Genome Mapping: Using Law and Ethics as Guides.* New York: Oxford University Press, 1992: 18–42.

Meslin, Eric M.; Thomson, Elizabeth J.; and Boyer, Joy T. "The Ethical, Legal, and Social Implications Research Program at the National Human Genome Research Institute." *Kennedy Institute of Ethics Journal* 7 (1997), 291–98.

Murray, Thomas H.; Rothstein, Mark A.; and Murray, Robert F. Jr., eds. *The Human Genome Project and the Future of Health Care.* Bloomington and Indianapolis, IN: Indiana University Press, 1996.

National Research Council. *Mapping and Sequencing the Human Genome.* Washington, DC: National Academy Press, 1988.

Olson, Maynard V. "The Human Genome Project." *Proceedings of the National Academy of Sciences* 90 (1993), 4338–44.

Poste, George. "The Case for Genomic Patenting." *Nature* 378 (1995), 534–36.

Proctor, Robert N. "Genomics and Eugenics: How Fair Is the Comparison?" In George J. Annas, and Sherman Elias, eds. *Gene Mapping: Using Law and Ethics as Guides.* New York: Oxford University Press, 1992, 75–93.

Rosenberg, Alexander. "The Human Genome Project: Research Tactics and Economic Strategies." *Social Philosophy and Policy* 13 (1996), 1–17.

Rothman, Barbara Katz. "Of Maps and Imaginations: Sociology Confronts the Genome." *Social Problems* 42 (1995), 1–10.

Rothstein, Mark A., ed. *Legal and Ethical Issues Raised by the Human Genome Project.* Houston, TX: University of Houston, Health Law and Policy Institute, 1991.

United States Congress, Office of Technology Assessment. *Mapping Our Genes—The Genome Projects: How Big, How Fast?* Washington, DC: U.S. Government Printing Office, April 1988.

Venter, J. Craig, et al. "Shotgun Sequencing of the Human Genome." *Science* 280 (1998), 1540–42.

Wade, Nicholas. "The Struggle to Decipher Human Genes." *New York Times,* March 10, 1998, p. F1.

———. "Impresario of the Genome Looks Back with Candor." *New York Times,* April 7, 1998, p. F1.

———. "Beyond Sequencing of Human DNA" *New York Times,* May 12, 1998, p. F3.

Weiss, Kenneth M. "In Search of Human Variation." *Genome Research* 8 (1998), 691–97.

GENETIC TESTING AND SCREENING

AAAS-ABA National Conference of Lawyers and Scientists and AAAS Committee on Scientific Freedom and Responsibility. *The Genome, Ethics, and the Law: Issues in Genetic Testing.* Washington, DC: American Association for the Advancement of Science, 1992.

Advisory Committee on Genetic Testing. *Code of Practice and Guidance on Human Genetic Testing Services Supplied to the Public.* London: Her Majesty's Stationery Office, 1997.

American Medical Association, Council on Ethical and Judicial Affairs, "Use of Genetic Testing by Employers." *Journal of the American Medical Association* 266 (1991), 1827–30.

Andrews, Lori B., et al. Institute of Medicine, Committee on Assessing Genetic Risks. *Assessing Genetic Risks: Implications for Health and Social Policy.* Washington, DC: National Academy Press, 1994.

Association of British Insurers. *Genetic Testing: ABI Code of Practice.* London: ABI, 1997.

Bartels, Dianne M.; LeRoy, Bonnie S.; and Caplan, Arthur L., eds. *Prescribing Our Future: Ethical Challenges in Genetic Counseling.* New York: Aldine De Gruyter, 1993.

Billings, Paul R., ed. *DNA on Trial: Genetic Identification and Criminal Justice.* Plainview, NY: Cold Spring Harbor Laboratory Press, 1992.

Billings, Paul R., et al. "Discrimination as a Consequence of Genetic Testing." *American Journal of Human Genetics* 50 (1992), 476–82.

Burke, Wylie, et al. "Recommendations for Follow-Up Care for Individuals with an Inherited Predisposition to Cancer. I. Hereditary Nonpolyposis Colon Cancer. Cancer Genetics Studies Consortium." *Journal of the American Medical Association* 277 (1997), 915–19.

Clayton, Ellen Wright. "Genetic Testing in Children." *Journal of Medicine and Philosophy* 22 (1997), 233–51.

Cohen, Cynthia B., and McCloskey, Elizabeth Leibold, eds. "Special Issue: Genetic Testing." *Kennedy Institute of Ethics Journal* 8 (1998), vii–200.

DeGrazia, David. "The Ethical Justification for Minimal Paternalism in the Use of the Predictive Test for Huntington's Disease." *Journal of Clinical Ethics* 2 (1991), 219–28.

Gostin, Larry. Genetic Discrimination: The Use of Genetically Based Diagnostic and Prognostic Tests by Employers and Insurers." *American Journal of Law and Medicine* 17 (1991), 109–44.

Hoedemaekers, Rogeer; ten Have, Henk; and Chadwick, Ruth. "Genetic Screening: A Comparative Analysis of Three Recent Reports." *Journal of Medical Ethics* 23 (1997), 135–41.

Holtzman, Neil A. *Proceed with Caution: Predicting Genetic Risks in the Recombinant DNA Era.* Baltimore: Johns Hopkins University Press, 1989.

Holtzman, Neil A., and Shapiro, David. "Genetic Testing and Public Policy." *British Medical Journal* 316 (1998), 852–56.

Holtzman, Neil A., et al. "Predictive Genetic Testing: From Basic Research to Clinical Practice." *Science* 278 (1997), 602–05.

Hudson, Kathy L., et al. "Genetics Discrimination and Health Insurance: An Urgent Need for Reform." *Science* 270 (1995), 391–93.

Lerman, Caryn, et al. "BRCA1 Testing in Families with Hereditary Breast-Ovarian Cancer: A Prospective Study of Patient Decision

Making and Outcomes." *Journal of the American Medical Association* 275 (1996), 1885–92.

Lippman, Abby. "Prenatal Genetic Testing and Screening: Constructing Needs and Reinforcing Inequities." *American Journal of Law and Medicine* 17 (1991), 15–50.

Koenig, Barbara A., *et al.* "Genetics Testing for BRCA1 and BRCA2: Recommendations of the Stanford Program in Genomics, Ethics, and Society." *Journal of Women's Health* 7 (1998), 531–45.

Marteau, Theresa M., and Crooyle, Robert T. "Psychological Responses to Genetic Testing." *British Medical Journal* 316 (1998), 693–96.

National Academy of Sciences, Committee on DNA Technology in Forensic Science. *DNA Technology in Forensic Science.* Washington, DC: National Academy Press, 1992.

National Research Council, Committee for the Study of Inborn Errors of Metabolism. *Genetic Screening: Programs, Principles and Research.* Washington, DC: National Academy of Science, 1975.

Natowicz, Marvin R.; Alper, Jane K.; and Alper, Joseph S. "Genetic Discrimination and the Law." *American Journal of Human Genetics* 50 (1992), 465–75.

Nelkin, Dorothy, and Tancredi, Laurence. *Dangerous Diagnostics: The Social Power of Biological Information.* New York: Basic Books, 1989.

Nuffield Council on Bioethics. *Genetic Screening: Ethical Issues.* London: The Council, 1993.

Powers, Madison. "Privacy and the Control of Genetic Information." In Mark S. Frankel, and Albert Teich, eds. *The Genetic Frontier: Ethics, Law, and Policy.* Washington, DC: American Association for the Advancement of Science, 1994, 77–100.

Robertson, John A. "Ethical and Legal Issues in Preimplantation Genetic Screening." *Fertility and Sterility* 57 (1992), 1–11.

———. "Genetic Selection of Offspring Characteristics." *Boston University Law Review* 76 (1996), 421–82.

Rothenberg, Karen H. "Genetic Information and Health Insurance: State Legislative Approaches." *Journal of Law, Medicine, and Ethics* 23 (1995), 312–19.

Rothenberg, Karen H., and Thomson, Elizabeth J., eds. *Women and Prenatal Testing. Facing the Challenges of Genetic Technology.* Columbus, OH: Ohio State University Press, 1994.

Rothenberg, Karen H., *et al.* "Genetic Information and the Workplace: Legislative Approaches and Policy Challenges." *Science* 275 (1997), 1755–57.

Rothman, Barbara Katz. *The Tentative Pregnancy: Prenatal Diagnosis and the Future of Motherhood.* New York: Viking Penguin, 1986.

Task Force on Genetic Testing. *Promoting Safe and Effective Testing in the United States. Final Report.* Baltimore: Johns Hopkins University Press, 1998.

Testart, Jacques. "The New Eugenics and Medicalized Reproduction." *Cambridge Quarterly of Healthcare Ethics* 4 (1995), 304–12.

United States, Congress, Office of Technology Assessment. *Cystic Fibrosis and DNA Tests: Implications of Carrier Screening.* Washington, DC: U.S. Government Printing Office, August 1992.

United States, Congress, Office of Technology Assessment. *Genetic Monitoring and Screening in the Workplace.* Washington, DC: U.S. Government Printing Office, October 1990.

United States, Congress, Office of Technology Assessment. *Genetic Witness: Forensic Uses of DNA Tests.* Washington, DC: U.S. Government Printing Office, July 1990.

United States, President's Commission for the Study of Ethical Problems in Medicine and Biomedical and Behavioral Research.

Screening and Counseling for Genetic Conditions. Washington, DC: U.S. Government Printing Office, February 1983.

Wertz, Dorothy C., and Fletcher, John C., eds. *Ethics and Human Genetics: A Cross-Cultural Perspective.* Berlin and New York: Springer-Verlag, 1989.

Wolf, Susan M. "Beyond 'Genetic Discrimination': Toward the Broader Harm of Geneticism." *Journal of Law, Medicine and Ethics* 23 (1995), 345–53.

Xin, Mao, and Wertz, Dorothy C. "China's Genetics Services Providers' Attitudes towards Several Ethical Issues: A Cross-Cultural Survey." *Clinical Genetics* 52 (1997), 100–109.

HUMAN GENE THERAPY

Anderson, W. French. "Human Gene Therapy: Why Draw a Line?" *Journal of Medicine and Philosophy* 14 (1989), 681–93.

———. "Human Gene Therapy." *Science* 256 (1992), 808–13.

Fletcher, John C., and Anderson, W. French. "Germ-Line Gene Therapy: A New Stage of Debate." *Law, Medicine and Health Care* 20 (1992), 26–39.

Fletcher, John C., and Richter, Gerd. "Human Fetal Gene Therapy: Moral and Ethical Questions." *Human Gene Therapy* 7 (1996), 1605–14.

Fowler, Gregory; Juengst, Eric T.; and Zimmerman, Burke K. "Germ-Line Gene Therapy and the Clinical Ethos of Medical Genetics." *Theoretical Medicine* 10 (1989), 151–65.

Hedgecoe, Adam M. "Gene Therapy." In Ruth Chadwick, ed. *Encyclopedia of Applied Ethics.* San Diego, CA: Academic Press, 1998, 383–90.

Juengst, Eric T., ed. "Human Germ-Line Engineering." *Journal of Medicine and Philosophy* 16 (1991), 587–694. Thematic issue.

Nichols, Eve K., and Institute of Medicine, National Academy of Sciences. *Human Gene Therapy.* Cambridge, MA: Harvard University Press, 1988.

Pollack, Andrew. "Gene Therapy's Focus Shifts from Rare Illness." *New York Times,* August 4, 1998, p. F1.

Ross, Gail, *et al.* "Gene Therapy in the United States: A Five-Year Status Report." *Human Gene Therapy* 7 (1996), 1781–90.

United States, National Institutes of Health, Recombinant DNA Advisory Committee. "Appendix M: The Points to Consider in the Design and Submission of Protocols for the Transfer of Recombinant DNA Molecules into the Genome of One or More Human Subjects (Points to Consider), National Institutes of Health Guidelines for Research Involving Recombinant DNA Molecules (NIH Guidelines)." *Federal Register* 62 (1997), 59032–46. [For the most recent version of the "Points to Consider," please consult the following URL: http://www.nih.gov/od/orda]

United States, President's Commission for the Study of Ethical Problems in Medicine and Biomedical and Behavioral Research. *Splicing Life: A Report on the Social and Ethical Issues of Genetic Engineering with Human Beings.* Washington, DC: U.S. Government Printing Office, November 1982.

Verma, Inder M., and Somia, Nikunj. "Gene Therapy—Promises, Problems, and Projects." *Nature* 389 (1998), 239–42.

Walters, LeRoy. "Ethical Issues in Human Gene Therapy." *Journal of Clinical Ethics* 2 (1991), 267–74.

———. "Human Gene Therapy: Ethics and Public Policy." *Human Gene Therapy* 2 (1991), 115–22.

Walters, LeRoy, and Palmer, Julie Gage. *The Ethics of Human Gene Therapy.* New York: Oxford University Press, 1997.

Wivel, Nelson A., and Walters, LeRoy. "Germ-Line Gene Modification and Disease Prevention: Some Medical and Ethical Perspectives." *Science* 262 (1993), 533–38.

GENETIC ENHANCEMENT

Engelhardt, Tristram H. "Germ-Line Genetics Engineering and Moral Diversity: Moral Controversies in a Post-Christian World." *Social Philosophy and Policy* 13 (1996), 47–62.

Gardner, William. "Can Human Genetic Enhancement Be Prohibited?" *Journal of Medicine and Philosophy* 20 (1995), 65–84.

Glover, Jonathan. *What Sort of People Should There Be?* New York: Penguin Books, 1984.

Juengst, Eric T. "Can Enhancement Be Distinguished from Prevention in Genetic Medicine?" *Journal of Medicine and Philosophy* 22 (1997), 125–42.

Muller, Hermann J. "The Guidance of Human Evolution." *Perspectives in Biology and Medicine* 3, (1959), 1–43.

Parens, Erik, ed. *Enhancing Human Traits: Ethical and Social Implications.* Washington, DC: Georgetown University Press, 1998.

Walters, LeRoy, and Palmer, Julie Gage. *The Ethics of Human Gene Therapy.* New York: Oxford University Press, 1997. Chapter 4.

BIBLIOGRAPHIES

Darragh, Martina, and McCarrick, Pat Milmoe. "Genetics and Ethics: Selections from Updated *Scope Notes.*" *Kennedy Institute of Ethics Journal* 7 (1997), 299–318.

Goldstein, Doris Mueller. *Bioethics: A Guide to Information Sources.* Detroit: Gale Research Company, 1982. See under "Genetic Intervention."

Lineback, Richard H., ed. *Philosopher's Index.* Vols. 1– . Bowling Green, OH: Philosophy Documentation Center, Bowling Green State University. Issued quarterly. See under "Eugenics," "Genes," "Genetic Engineering", "Genetic Enhancement," "Genetic Screening," "Genetic Therapy," and "Genetics."

Walters, LeRoy, and Kahn, Tamar Joy, eds. *Bibliography of Bioethics.* Vols. 1– . Washington, DC: Kennedy Institute of Ethics, Georgetown University. Issued annually. See under "Eugenics," "Gene Therapy," "Genetic Counseling," "Genetic Intervention," "Genetic Screening," and "Genome Mapping." (The information contained in the annual *Bibliography* can also be retrieved from BIOETHICSLINE.)

WORLD WIDE WEB RESOURCES

National Library of Medicine: PubMed
(http://www.ncbi.nlm.nih.gov/PubMed/)

National Library of Medicine: BIOETHICSLINE
(http://igm.nlm.nih.gov)

University Microfilms: Periodical Abstracts
(http://www.umi.com/proquest)

9.
Reproductive Technologies and
Surrogate Parenting Arrangements

INTRODUCTION

This chapter considers the moral quandaries faced by individuals or couples contemplating the conception, gestation, birth, and rearing of a child or multiple children. In the idealized traditional model, the members of a heterosexual couple make a rational decision about whether to have a child, or another child. If their decision is positive, they proceed to conceive a child by means of sexual intercourse. It is always understood, of course, that the process of rational decision making may occur after the unintended initiation of a pregnancy.

The idealized traditional model is not always realized in practice. In the latter part of the twentieth century, health professionals and couples alike have made the general public increasingly aware of the problem of involuntary infertility. As a response to this problem, both older and newer technologies of assisted reproduction have been developed and increasingly employed. At the same time, novel social arrangements for the bearing, begetting, and rearing of children are becoming more prevalent. In turn, these new arrangements and technologies have called into question the previously settled notions of "family," "parent," "mother," and "father."

PARENTING AND THE FAMILY

In the first part of this chapter, Ruth Macklin and Barbara Katz Rothman explore the implications of assisted reproductive techniques for the notions of family and motherhood. Macklin notes that there are four major determinants of what is meant by the term "family": biological connection, law, custom, and subjective intentions. On this view, a homosexual couple, a single woman and child, or a commissioning couple and surrogate mother could each be viewed as a family from a certain perspective. Macklin cautions against seeking a "single, univocal concept of the family." In contrast, Katz Rothman proposes a revisionary and univocal definition of motherhood. She argues that men have imposed a seed-based notion of parenthood on women, in part because men are biologically incapable of gestation, giving birth, and breast-feeding a child. These unique and intimate relationships of nurturance are, in her view, much more important than the genetic contribution of a sperm or egg cell could ever be. Katz Rothman's thesis has clear implications for the question of who the real mother is in cases where a surrogate carries and delivers a child to whom she has not made a genetic contribution.

THE PROBLEM OF INFERTILITY

The most comprehensive recent survey suggests that approximately 2.1 million (or 7.1%) U.S. married couples were infertile in the mid-1990s.[1] (For this survey infertility was defined as not conceiving after at least twelve months of unprotected intercourse.) Similar surveys of cohabiting couples in Canada found that between 7 percent and 8.5 percent were infertile; the variation in rates depended on whether a one-year or two-year criterion was used for establishing infertility.[2] The causes of infertility vary from couple to couple, but seem to include lower fertility rates among couples who defer having children until the spouses are in their thirties, and the deleterious effects on fertility of sexually transmitted diseases such as chlamydia. The excerpt from a 1998 report of the New York State Task Force on Life and the Law discusses both the definition and the prevalence of infertility.

But how should the problem of infertility be viewed, philosophically and ethically? Some critics of the new reproductive technologies have argued that infertility is not a disease and that medical intervention to alleviate infertility amounts to nothing more than doctoring the desires of patients.[3] The three remaining selections in this part adopt a different approach. The first, an excerpt from the Warnock Committee report in the United Kingdom, argues that even if infertility is not a disease in the strict sense, it is a bodily "malfunction" that health professionals can and should help to remedy. In her essay, Barbara Katz Rothman employs a different metaphor, suggesting that involuntary infertility should be regarded as a disability. While accepting the view that women should be totally free to choose whether or not to become parents, the author presents a nuanced approach to the problems faced by couples, and especially women, who are surprised to discover that they cannot easily bear children. With the aid of the disability metaphor, Katz Rothman notes that infertility can sometimes be prevented, sometimes cured. In other cases, the disabled person must simply find ways to compensate for the disability. Whatever path is chosen, the author argues, it is the person herself and not a successful reproductive outcome that should remain the central focus of attention.

A 1998 decision of the U.S. Supreme Court parallels Katz Rothman's analysis in the legal sphere. The question before the court was whether a woman's HIV infection placed a substantial limitation on her ability "to reproduce and to bear children" and, if so, whether reproduction is one of the "major life activities" covered by the Americans with Disabilities Act (ADA) of 1990. By a 5–4 margin, the Supreme Court agreed that limitations on a woman's ability to reproduce *do* constitute a disability under the terms of the ADA. Excerpts from the majority opinion written by Justice Kennedy and a vigorous dissent by Chief Justice Rehnquist are reprinted in this chapter.

IN VITRO FERTILIZATION

The birth of Louise Brown in Lancashire, England, in 1978 inaugurated a new era in the history of reproductive technologies. Louise had not been conceived inside her mother's body, but in a petri dish, where eggs removed from her mother had been mixed with sperm from her father and fertilization had taken place.

In vitro fertilization (literally, "fertilization in glass") is most often proposed as a technique for overcoming infertility in married couples. The simplest case involves the use of semen from the husband and eggs from the wife. No reproductive cells are donated to the couple, and no "surplus" embryos are produced. All embryos that result from in vitro fertilizations (IVF) contain the parents' genes, and all are transferred to the uterus of the wife in the hope that at least one pregnancy will be achieved. In addition, the simplest case involves no freezing and storage of early human embryos.

There are, of course, variations on this simplest case. Either the sperm cells or the egg cells or the early embryo may be derived from sources other than the husband and the wife (donors or vendors). Even if the sperm and egg cells are provided by the husband and wife, there are numerous options. The developing embryos may be tested for genetic or chromosomal abnormalities, frozen and stored, donated to other couples, provided for research, or allowed to die. Thus, multiple procedures that previously had been possible only with semen or prenatally (that is, after implantation) are now able to be performed after fertilization and before implantation.

IVF is no longer a radically "new" reproductive technology. In fact, one expert group has estimated that 300,000 infants have been born worldwide with the assistance of IVF.[4] Nonetheless, as the essays in this chapter indicate, IVF raises a series of interesting metaphysical and ethical problems. John Robertson's essay provides an overview of ethical and public policy issues surrounding the practice of IVF, with special emphasis on the biological, moral, and legal status of preimplantation embryos. In the concluding sections of his essay Robertson also addresses what he calls "consumer protection issues" and the question of patient access to a relatively expensive reproductive technology. Susan Sherwin notes several issues treated by moral philosophers and theologians in their discussions of IVF, then proceeds to identify a series of feminist themes that have been neglected in traditional analyses. Among these themes are discriminatory criteria for selecting among candidates for IVF, unexamined assumptions about women's natural roles as mothers, and an undue emphasis on the importance of a genetic connection between parents and the children they rear.

SURROGATE PARENTING ARRANGEMENTS

In contrast to the new technology of IVF, surrogate parenting involves the combination of a relatively old technology, assisted insemination (formerly called "artificial insemination"), with a new social arrangement. The first documented attempt to establish a fee-for-service surrogate motherhood arrangement in the United States occurred in 1976 under the direction of Michigan attorney Noel Keane.[5] According to the terms of such arrangements, usually spelled out in written contracts, a woman agrees to become pregnant on behalf of a couple and to deliver the resulting infant to the couple, in exchange for the couple's payment of a fee to the surrogate. In the early years of this new social practice, the technique of assisted insemination donor (AID) was generally employed, using sperm provided by the husband of the future social mother. Thus, the child in the usual or "full" surrogate motherhood arrangement contains genes from the egg of the surrogate mother and the sperm of the would-be social father. However, in 1985 the first instance of surrogate motherhood assisted by IVF occurred. The future social mother was able to produce fertilizable eggs but was medically unable to carry a pregnancy. Her eggs were therefore fertilized in vitro with sperm from her husband, and the resulting embryos were transferred to the uterus of a surrogate mother. In this arrangement, which is sometimes called "partial" surrogacy, the surrogate mother can also be designated a "surrogate carrier" because she makes no genetic contribution to the embryo or infant. (Note that genetic, gestational, and social motherhood can be distinguished in surrogate motherhood arrangements.)

The most celebrated early case of surrogate motherhood involved Noel Keane as attorney and arranger, Mary Beth Whitehead as surrogate mother, William Stern as semen donor and intended social father, and an infant, "Baby M," who became the object of an intense and protracted custody dispute. This case eventually came before the New Jersey Supreme Court, which announced its decision in early 1988. First, the court noted, surrogate motherhood contracts are unenforceable in New Jersey, both because they contradict existing statutes and because they are against "the public policies of this state."[6] Second, the court awarded custody of the child to Stern and his wife because, in the court's judgment, the stable environment of the Sterns' home would be a better setting for the child's rearing than the rather turbulent household of the Whiteheads. Finally, the court directed that the trial court award visitation rights to Whitehead, the genetic and gestational mother of Baby M.

Paid, or commercial, surrogacy is not a prevalent method of reproduction in the United States or any other country. The best estimates are that approximately 1,000 infants are born each year in all types of surrogacy arrangements.[7] However, the ethical and legal issues raised by this reproductive alternative are so sweeping and so profound that surrogate parenting has spawned a substantial bioethics literature.

The two essays reprinted in the fourth part of this chapter present diametrically opposed perspectives on the ethical acceptability of surrogacy. According to Elizabeth Anderson, paid surrogate parenting arrangements transform the work of "bringing forth children into the world" into a commodity. In Anderson's view, commercial norms are inherently manipulative when applied to "the sphere of parental love." In contrast, Laura Purdy argues that, if reasonably regulated, the practice of surrogacy can "empower women and increase their status in society." In many cases, this option will be less risky to women's health than alternative occupations. Purdy does acknowledge, however, that oppressive stipulations in surrogate parenting contracts can render this otherwise permissible practice wrong in certain cases.

CLONING

In the February 27th, 1997, issue of *Nature* Scottish researcher Ian Wilmut and his colleagues published an article modestly titled "Viable Offspring Derived from Fetal and Adult Mammalian Cells." The one viable offspring deprived from an adult mammalian cell was a sheep named "Dolly," who became an overnight celebrity. The research of Wilmut and his colleagues and subsequent success in the cloning of other mammals have stimulated a global debate on the question: "Now or in the future, would it be morally justifiable to clone a human being?"

Once again in this instance, conceptual clarification is necessary. Cloning can be defined quite technically as the transfer of the nucleus from one (nonreproductive) cell into an egg cell from which the nucleus has been removed. This broad definition would cover the transfer of a nucleus from an early embryonic cell as well as from a nonreproductive cell of an adult. Robert Winston's brief essay includes a discussion of this kind of cloning. In contrast, the type of cloning that has provoked the most vigorous ethical discussion would transfer the nucleus of a cell taken from an already-born individual into an enucleated egg cell. Someone who cloned a human being in this sense would be attempting to produce a genetically identical twin to a visible and recognizable individual — whether that individual were an infant, a college student, or a person nearing retirement age. This narrower (and more popular) conception of cloning is the one presupposed in the analyses by Daniel Callahan, Lee Silver, and the U.S. National Bioethics Advisory Commission (NBAC).

In response to a request by President Clinton, NBAC completed an ethical evaluation of human cloning in just over three months. The commission's conclusion was that the cloning of a human being in 1997 or in the next few years would be unethical, both because many questions about the safety of the technique for offspring remain unresolved and because broader social concerns about the technique will require further deliberation. NBAC went on to recommend a legislative ban on human cloning in the United States — both in the public and private sectors — for a period of three to five years.

Winston expresses concern that any call for the banning of human cloning may inadvertently prohibit kinds of nuclear transfer in embryos that could assist couples in preventing disease. Specifically, he cites a clinical situation in which DNA from the cytoplasm of a woman's eggs (the mitochondrial DNA) could transmit a serious genetic disease to her offspring. He therefore suggests a transfer of the nucleus from the at-risk woman's egg to the cytoplasm of an enucleated donor egg.[8]

In their commentaries on the ethics of cloning in the more popular sense, Callahan and Silver adopt positions that are almost polar opposites. Callahan, a philosopher, notes pessimistically that American society in the late 1990s is much more receptive to human cloning than it had been in the late 1960s and early 1970s. During the earlier period, thinkers like Hans Jonas, Leon Kass, and Paul Ramsey eloquently described the dangers of cloning and other new reproductive techniques. As we approach the 21st century and a new millennium, Callahan notes, most bioethicists have jumped onto the technological bandwagon. Silver, on the other hand, adduces several standard ethical objections to cloning and attempts to show that these objections do not withstand critical scrutiny. In his view, there are no convincing secular or philosophical arguments against the cloning of a human being. According to Silver, only religious objections to cloning will remain when the defeat of philosophical arguments is more widely recognized.

REGULATING ASSISTED REPRODUCTION

The final two selections in this chapter contrast two modes of public oversight for the assisted reproductive technologies. In the United Kingdom, the Human Fertilisation and Embryology Authority (HFEA) is a statutory body that regulates donor insemination, IVF, and research involving early human embryos. An excerpt from HFEA's sixth annual report describes the role of the Authority and several of the public policy questions that the Authority was confronting in 1997.

Within the United States, the reproductive technologies have developed within an environment that can only be described as laissez faire. A working group from the Institute for Science, Law, and Technology (ISLAT) in Chicago has now proposed federal legislation that would set minimum standards for U.S. clinics that offer assistance in reproduction. According to the working group, these standards should cover such issues as approval of new techniques by a research review committee, more systematic data collection and reporting, and fuller disclosure to those who seek reproductive assistance. The group stops short of recommending a regulatory body like HFEA for the United States.

L. W.

NOTES

1. Joyce C. Abma, *et al.,* "Fertility, Family Planning, and Women's Health: New Data from the 1995 National Survey of Family Growth," *Vital and Health Statistics,* Series 23: Data from the National Survey of Family Growth, No. 19, May 1997, pp. 7 and 61.

2. New York State Task Force on Life and the Law, *Assisted Reproductive Technologies: Analysis and Recommendations for Public Policy* (New York: The Task Force, April 1998), pp. 12–13 [reprinted in this chapter].

3. See, for example, Leon R. Kass, "Making Babies: The New Biology and the 'Old' Morality," *Public Interest,* No. 26 (1972), pp. 18–56.

4. ISLAT Working Group, "ART into Science: Regulation of Fertility Techniques," *Science* 281 (July 31, 1998), p. 651 [reprinted in this chapter].

5. Noel P. Keane and Dennis L. Breo, *The Surrogate Mother* (New York: Dodd, Mead, 1981).

6. New Jersey Supreme Court, *In the Matter of Baby M,* Atlantic Reporter, 537 A.2d 1227 (1988), Pt. II.

7. ISLAT Working Group, *op. cit.,* p. 651.

8. For more detailed discussion of this clinical scenario, see Donald S. Rubinstein, *et al.,* "Germ-Line Therapy to Cure Mitochondrial Disease: Protocol and Ethics of *in vitro* Ovum Nuclear Transplantation," *Cambridge Quarterly of Healthcare Ethics* 4 (Summer 1995), 316–39.

RUTH MACKLIN

Artificial Means of Reproduction and Our Understanding of the Family

It is an obvious truth that scientific and technologic innovations produce changes in our traditional way of perceiving the world around us. We have only to think of the telescope, the microscope, and space travel to recall that heretofore unimagined perceptions of the macrocosm and the microcosm have become commonplace. Yet it is not only perceptions, but also conceptions of the familiar that become altered by advances in science and technology. As a beginning student of philosophy, I first encountered problems in epistemology generated by scientific knowledge: If physical objects are really composed of molecules in motion, how is it that we perceive them as solid? Why is it that objects placed on a table don't slip through the empty spaces between the molecules? If the mind is nothing but electrical processes occurring in the brain, how can we explain Einstein's ability to create the special theory of relativity or Bach's ability to compose the Brandenburg Concertos?

Now questions are being raised about how a variety of modes of artificial means of reproduction might alter our conception of the family. George Annas has observed:

Dependable birth control made sex without reproduction possible. . . . Now medicine is closing the circle . . . by offering methods of reproduction without sex, including artificial insemination by donor (AID), in vitro fertilization (IVF), and surrogate embryo transfer (SET). As with birth control, artificial reproduction is defended as life-affirming and loving by its proponents, and denounced as unnatural by its detractors.[1]

From *Hastings Center Report* 21 (January–February 1991), 5–11. Reprinted by permission of The Hastings Center.

Opponents of artificial reproduction have expressed concerns about its effects on the family. This concern has centered largely but not entirely on surrogacy arrangements. Among the objections to surrogacy made by the Roman Catholic Church is the charge that "the practice of surrogate motherhood is a threat to the stability of the family."[2] But before the consequences for the family of surrogacy arrangements or other new reproductive practices can be assessed, we need to inquire into our understanding of the family. Is there a single, incontrovertible conception of the family? And who are the "we" presupposed in the phrase, "our understanding"? . . .

THE BIOLOGICAL CONCEPT OF FAMILY

It is possible, of course, to settle these conceptual matters simply and objectively by adopting a biological criterion for determining what counts as a family. According to this criterion, people who are genetically related to one another would constitute a family, with the type and degree of relatedness described in the manner of a family tree. This sense of *family* is important and interesting for many purposes, but it does not and cannot encompass everything that is actually meant by *family,* nor does it reflect the broader cultural customs and kinship systems that also define family ties. . . .

Newly developed artificial means of reproduction have rendered the term *biological* inadequate for making some critical conceptual distinctions, along with consequent moral decisions. The capability of separating the process of producing eggs from the act of gestation renders obsolete the use of the word *biological* to modify the word *mother.* The techniques of egg retrieval, in vitro fertilization (IVF), and gamete intrafallopian transfer (GIFT) now make it possible for two different women to make a biological contribution to the creation of a new life. It would be a prescriptive rather than a descriptive definition to maintain that the egg donor should properly be called the biological mother. The woman who contributes her womb during gestation—whether she is acting as a surrogate or is the intended rearing mother—is also a biological mother. We have only to reflect on the many ways that the intrauterine environment and maternal behavior during pregnancy can influence fetal and later child development to acknowledge that a gestating woman is also a biological mother. I will return to this issue later in considering how much genetic contributions should count in disputed surrogacy arrangements.

ADDITIONAL DETERMINANTS OF THE MEANING OF *FAMILY*

In addition to the biological meaning, there appear to be three chief determinants of what is meant by *family*. These are law, custom, and what I shall call subjective intentions. All three contribute to our understanding of the family. The effect of artificial means of reproduction on our understanding of the family will vary, depending on which of these three determinants is chosen to have priority. There is no way to assign a priori precedence to any one of the three. Let me illustrate each briefly.

LAW AS A DETERMINANT OF FAMILY

Legal scholars can elaborate with precision and detail the categories and provisions of family law. This area of law encompasses legal rules governing adoption, artificial insemination by donor, foster placement, custody arrangements, and removal of children from a home in which they have been abused or neglected. For present purposes, it will suffice to summarize the relevant areas in which legal definitions or decisions have determined what is to count as a family.

Laws governing adoption and donor insemination stipulate what counts as a family. In the case of adoption, a person or couple genetically unrelated to a child is deemed that child's legal parent or parents. By this legal rule, a new family is created. The biological parent or parents of the child never cease to be genetically related, of course. But by virtue of law, custom, and usually emotional ties, the adoptive parents become the child's family.

The Uniform Parentage Act holds that a husband who consents to artificial insemination by donor (AID) of his wife by a physician is the legal father of the child. Many states have enacted laws in conformity with this legal rule. I am not aware of any laws that have been enacted making an analogous stipulation in the case of egg donation, but it is reasonable to assume that there will be symmetry of reasoning and legislation.

Commenting on the bearing of family law on the practice of surrogacy, Alexander M. Capron and Margaret J. Radin contend that the "legal rules of greatest immediate relevance" to surrogacy are those on adoption. These authors identify a number of provisions of state laws on adoption that should apply in the case of surrogacy. The provisions include allowing time for a "change of heart" period after the agreement to release a child, and prohibition of agreements to relinquish parental rights prior to the child's birth.[3]

Capron and Radin observe that in the context of adoption, "permitting the birth mother to reclaim a child manifests society's traditional respect for biological ties."[4] But how does this observation bear on artificial reproduction where the biological tie can be either genetic or gestational?

Consider first the case of the gestational surrogate who is genetically unrelated to the child. Does society's traditional respect for biological ties give her or the genetic mother the right to "reclaim" (or claim in the first place) the child? Society's traditional respect is more likely a concern for genetic inheritance than a recognition of the depth of the bond a woman may feel toward a child she has given birth to.

Secondly, consider the case of egg donation and embryo transfer to the wife of the man whose sperm was used in IVF. If the sperm donor and egg recipient were known to the egg donor, could the donor base her claim to the child on "society's traditional respect for biological ties"? As I surmised earlier, it seems reasonable to assume that any laws enacted for egg donation will be similar to those now in place for donor insemination. In the latter context, society's traditional respect for biological ties gave way to other considerations arising out of the desire of couples to have a child who is genetically related to at least one of the parents.

CUSTOM AS A DETERMINANT OF FAMILY

The most telling examples of custom as a determinant of family are drawn from cultural anthropology. Kinship systems and incest taboos dictated by folkways and mores differ so radically that few generalizations are possible.

Ruth Benedict writes: "No known people regard all women as possible mates. This is not in an effort, as is so often supposed, to prevent inbreeding in our sense, for over great parts of the world it is an own cousin, often the daughter of one's mother's brother, who is the predestined spouse."[5] In contrast, Benedict notes, some incest taboos are

extended by a social fiction to include vast numbers of individuals who have no traceable ancestors in common.... This social fiction receives unequivocal expression in the terms of relationship which are used. Instead of distinguishing lineal from collateral kin as we do in the distinction between father and uncle, brother and cousin, one term means literally "man of my father's group (relationship, locality, etc.) or his generation." ... Certain tribes of eastern Australia use an extreme form of this so-called classificatory kinship system. Those whom they call brothers and sisters are all those of their generation with whom they recognize any relationship.[6]

One anthropologist notes that "the family in all societies is distinguished by a stability that arises out of the fact that it is based on marriage, that is to say, on socially sanctioned mating entered into with the assumption of permanency."[7] If we extend the notion of socially sanctioned mating to embrace socially sanctioned procreation, it is evident that the new artificial means of reproduction call for careful thought about what should be socially sanctioned before policy decisions are made.

SUBJECTIVE INTENTION AS A DETERMINANT OF FAMILY

This category is most heterogeneous and amorphous. It includes a variety of ways in which individuals — singly, in pairs, or as a group — consider themselves a family even if their arrangement is not recognized by law or custom. Without an accompanying analysis, I list here an array of examples, based on real people and their situations.

- A homosexual couple decides to solidify their relationship by taking matrimonial vows. Despite the fact that their marriage is not recognized by civil law, they find an ordained minister who is willing to perform the marriage ceremony. Later they apply to be foster parents of children with AIDS whose biological parents have died or aban-

doned them. The foster agency accepts the couple. Two children are placed in foster care with them. They are now a family.
- A variation on this case: A lesbian couple has a long-term monogamous relationship. They decide they want to rear a child. Using "turkey-baster" technology, one of the women is inseminated, conceives, and gives birth to a baby. The three are now a family, with one parent genetically related to the child.
- Pat Anthony, a forty-seven-year-old grandmother in South Africa, agreed to serve as gestational surrogate for her own daughter. The daughter had had her uterus removed, but could still produce eggs and wanted more children. The daughter's eggs were inseminated with her husband's sperm, and the resulting embryos implanted in her own mother. Mrs. Anthony gave birth to triplets when she was forty-eight. She was the gestational mother and the genetic grandmother of the triplets.
- Linda Kirkman was the gestational mother of a baby conceived with a sister's egg and destined to live with the infertile sister and her husband. Linda Kirkman said, "I always considered myself her aunt." Carol Chan donated eggs so that her sister Susie could bear and raise a child. Carol Chan said: "I could never regard the twins as anything but my nephews." The two births occurred in Melbourne within weeks of each other.[8]

My point in elucidating this category of heterogeneous examples is to suggest that there may be entirely subjective yet valid elements that contribute to our understanding of the family, family membership, or family relationships. I believe it would be arbitrary and narrow to rule out all such examples by fiat. The open texture of our language leaves room for conceptions of family not recognized by law or preexisting custom.

Posing the question, Who counts as family? Carol Levine replies: "The answer to this apparently simple question is by no means easy. It depends on why the question is being asked and who is giving the answer."[9] Levine's observation, made in the context of AIDS, applies equally well to the context of artificial means of reproduction.

THE GESTATIONAL VERSUS THE GENETIC MOTHER

One critical notion rendered problematic by the new technological capabilities of artificial reproduction is the once-simple concept of a mother. The traditional concept is complicated by the possibility that a woman can gestate a fetus genetically unrelated to her. This prospect has implications both for public policy and our understanding of the family. The central policy question is, How much should genetic relatedness count in disputed surrogacy arrangements?

A MATTER OF DISCOVERY OR DECISION?

Which criterion — genetic or gestational — should be used to determine who is the "real" mother? I contend that this question is poorly formulated. Referring to the "real" mother implies that it is a matter of discovery, rather than one calling for a decision. To speak of "the real x" is to assume that there is an underlying metaphysical structure to be probed by philosophical inquiry. But now that medical technology has separated the two biological contributions to motherhood, in place of the single conjoint role provided by nature, some decisions will have to be made.

One decision is conceptual, and a second is moral. The conceptual question is: Should a woman whose contribution is solely gestational be termed a mother of the baby? We may assume, by analogy with our concept of paternity, that the woman who makes the genetic contribution in a surrogacy arrangement can properly be termed a mother of the baby. So it must be decided whether there can be only one mother, conceptually speaking, or whether this technological advance calls for new terminology.

Conceptual decisions often have implications beyond mere terminology. A decision not to use the term *mother* (even when modified by the adjective *gestational*) to refer to a woman who acts in this capacity can have important consequences for ethics and public policy. As a case in point, the Wayne County Circuit Court in Michigan issued an interim order declaring a gamete donor couple to be the biological parents of a fetus being carried to term by a woman hired to be the gestational mother. Upon birth, the court entered an order that the names of the ovum and sperm donors be listed on the birth certificate, rather than that of the woman who gave birth, who was termed by the court a "human incubator."[10]

The ethical question posed by the separation of biological motherhood into genetic and gestational components is, Which role should entitle a woman to a greater claim on the baby, in case of dispute? Since the answer to this question cannot be reached by discovery, but is, like the prior conceptual question, a matter

for decision, we need to determine which factors are morally relevant and which have the greatest moral weight. To avoid begging any ethical questions by a choice of terminology, I use the terms *genetic mother* and *gestational mother* to refer to the women who make those respective contributions. And instead of speaking of the "real" mother, I'll use the phrase *primary mother* when referring to the woman presumed to have a greater claim on the child.

MORALLY RELEVANT FACTORS

The possibilities outlined below are premised on the notion that surrogacy contracts are voidable. I take this to mean that no legal presumption is set up by the fact that there has been a prior contract between the surrogate and the intended rearing parents. From an ethical perspective, that premise must be argued for independently, and convincing arguments have been advanced by a number of authors.[11] If we accept the premise that a contractual provision to relinquish a child born of a surrogacy agreement has no legal force, the question then becomes, Is there a morally relevant distinction between the two forms of surrogacy with respect to a claim on the child? Who has the weightiest moral claim when a surrogate is unwilling to give the baby up after its birth? Where should the moral presumption lie? The question may be answered in one of three ways.

1. Gestation. According to this position, whether a woman is merely the gestational surrogate, or also contributes her genetic material, makes no difference in determining moral priorities. In either case, the surrogate is the primary mother because the criterion is gestation.

The gestational position is adopted by George Annas and others who have argued that the gestational mother should be legally presumed to have the right and responsibility to rear the child. One reason given in support of this presumption is "the greater biological and psychological investment of the gestational mother in the child."[12] This is referred to as "sweat equity." A related yet distinct reason is "the biological reality that the mother at this point has contributed more to the child's development, and that she will of necessity be present at birth and immediately thereafter to care for the child.[13]

The first reason focuses on what the gestational mother deserves, based on her investment in the child, while the second reason, though mentioning her contribution, also focuses on the interests of the child during and immediately after birth. Annas adds that "to designate the gestational mother, rather than the genetic mother, the legal or 'natural mother' would be protective of children."[14]

2. Genetics. In surrogacy arrangements, it is the inseminating male who is seen as the father, not the husband of the woman who acts as a surrogate. This is because the genetic contribution is viewed as determinative for fatherhood. By analogy, the woman who makes the genetic contribution is the primary mother. This position sharply distinguishes between the claim to the child made by the two different types of surrogate. It makes the surrogate who contributes her egg as well as her womb the primary (or sole) mother. But now recall the fact that in AID, the law recognizes the husband of the inseminated woman as the father—proof that laws can be made to go either way.

This position was supported by the court in *Smith & Smith v. Jones & Jones,* on grounds of the analogy with paternity. The court said: "The donor of the ovum, the biological mother, is to be deemed, in fact, the natural mother of this infant, as is the biological father to be deemed the natural father of this child."[15]

Legal precedents aside, is there a moral reason that could be invoked in support of this position? One possibility is "ownership" of one's genetic products. Since each individual has a unique set of genes, people might be said to have a claim on what develops from their own genes, unless they have explicitly relinquished any such claims. This may be a metaphorical sense of ownership, but it reflects the felt desire to have genetically related children—the primary motivation behind all forms of assisted reproduction.

Another possible reason for assigning greater weight to the genetic contribution is the child-centered position. Here it is argued that it is in children's best interest to be reared by parents to whom they are genetically related. Something like this position is taken by Sidney Callahan. She writes:

The most serious ethical problems in using third-party donors in alternative reproduction concern the well-being of the potential child. . . . A child who has donor(s) intruded into its parentage will be cut off from its genetic heritage and part of its kinship relations in new ways. Even if there is no danger of transmitting unknown genetic disease or causing physiological harm to the child, the psychological relationship of the child to its parents is endangered—with or without the practice of deception and secrecy about its origins.[16]

Additional considerations lending plausibility to this view derive from data concerning adopted children who have conducted searches for their biological parents, and similar experiences of children whose birth was a result of donor insemination and who have sought out their biological fathers. In the case of gestational surrogacy, the child is genetically related to both of the intended rearing parents. However, there [are] no data to suggest whether children born of gestational mothers might someday begin to seek out those women in a quest for their "natural" or "real" mothers.

3. Gestation and genetics. According to this position, the surrogate who contributes both egg and womb has more of a claim to being the primary mother than does the surrogate who contributes only her womb. Since the first type of surrogate makes both a genetic and a gestational contribution, in case of a dispute she gets to keep the baby instead of the biological father, who has made only one contribution. But this does not yet settle the question of who has a greater moral claim to the infant in cases where the merely gestational surrogate does not wish to give up the baby to the genetic parents. To determine that, greater weight must be given either to the gestational component or the genetic component.

SUBSIDIARY VIEWS

One may reject the notion that the only morally relevant considerations are the respective contributions of each type of surrogate. Another possible criterion draws on the biological conception of family, and thus takes into account the contribution of the genetic father. According to this position, two genetic contributions count more than none. This leads to three subsidiary views, in addition to the three main positions outlined above.

4. Gestational surrogates have less of a moral claim to the infant than the intended parents, both of whom have made a genetic contribution. This is because two (genetic) contributions count more than one (gestational) contribution. This view, derived from "society's traditional respect for biological ties," gives greatest weight to the concept of family based on genetic inheritance.

5. A woman who contributes both egg and womb has a claim equal to that of the biological father, since

both have made genetic contributions. If genetic contribution is what determines both "true" motherhood and fatherhood, the policy implications of this view are that each case in which a surrogate who is both genetic and gestational mother wishes to keep the baby would have to go to court and be settled in the manner of custody disputes.

As a practical suggestion, this model is of little value. It throws every case of this type of surrogacy — the more common variety — open to this possibility, which is to move backwards in public policy regarding surrogacy.

6. However, if genetic and gestational contributions are given equal weight, but it is simply the number of contributions that counts, the artificially inseminated surrogate has the greater moral claim since she has made two contributions — genetic and gestational — while the father has made only one, the genetic contribution.

What can we conclude from all this about the effects of artificial means of reproduction on the family and on our conception of the family? Several conclusions emerge, although each requires a more extended elaboration and defense than will be given here.

A broad definition of *family* is preferable to a narrow one. A good candidate is the working definition proposed by Carol Levine: "Family members are individuals who by birth, adoption, marriage, or declared commitment share deep personal connections and are mutually entitled to receive and obligated to provide support of various kinds to the extent possible, especially in times of need."[17]

Some of the effects of the new reproductive technologies on the family call for the development of public policy, while others remain private, personal matters to be decided within a given family. An example of the former is the determination of where the presumptions should lie in disputed surrogacy arrangements, whose rights and interests are paramount, and what procedures should be followed to safeguard those rights and interests. An example of the latter is disclosure to a child of the facts surrounding genetic paternity or maternity in cases of donor insemination or egg donation, including the identity of the donor when that is known. These are profound moral decisions, about which many people have strong feelings, but they are not issues to be addressed by public policy.

It is not at all clear that artificial modes of reproduction threaten to produce greater emotional difficulties for family members affected, or pose more serious ethical problems, than those already arising out of long-standing practices such as adoption and artificial insemination. The analogy is often made between the impact on women who serve as surrogates and those who have lost their biological offspring in other ways.

Warning of the dangers of surrogacy, defenders of birth mothers have related the profound emotional trauma and lasting consequences for women who have given their babies up for adoption. One such defender is Phyllis Chesler, a psychologist who has written about the mother-infant bond and about custody battles in which mothers have lost their children to fathers. Dr. Chesler reports that many women never get over having given up their child for adoption. Their decision "leads to thirty to forty years of being haunted."[18] Chesler contends that the trauma to women who have given up their babies for adoption is far greater than that of incest, and greater than that felt by mothers who have lost custody battles for their children.

Additional evidence of the undesirable consequences for birth mothers of adoption is provided by Alison Ward, a woman who serves as an adoption reform advocate. Having given up her own daughter for adoption in 1967, she found and was reunited with her in 1980. Ms. Ward said to an audience assembled to hear testimony on surrogacy:

I think that you lack the personal experience I have: that of knowing what it is like to terminate your parental rights and go for years not knowing if your child is dead or alive. All the intellectual and philosophical knowledge in the world cannot begin to touch having to live your life as a birthparent. Last Sunday was Mother's Day. It seems ironic, as our country gives such lip service to the values of motherhood and the sanctity of the bond between mother and child, that we even consider legalizing a process [surrogacy] which would destroy all that.[19]

The effects of these practices on children are alleged to be equally profound and damaging. Scholarly studies conducted in recent years have sought to evaluate the adjustment of children to adoption. One expert notes that "the pattern emerging from the more recent clinical and nonclinical studies that have sampled widely and used appropriate controls, generally supports the view that, on the average, adopted children are more likely to manifest psychological problems than nonadopted children."[20] The additional fact that numerous adopted children have sought to find their biological parents, despite their being in a loving family setting, suggests that psychological forces can intrude on the dictates of law or custom regarding what counts as a family. Although it is easier to keep secret from a child the circumstances surrounding artificial insemination and egg donation, such secrets have sometimes been revealed with terrible emotional consequences for everyone involved.

Alison Ward compares the impact of surrogacy on children to both situations:

There will always be pain for these children. Just as adoptive parents have learned that they cannot love the pain of their adopted children away, couples who raise children obtained through surrogacy will have to deal with a special set of problems. Donor offspring . . . rarely find out the truth of their origins. But, some of them do, and we must listen to them when they speak of their anguish, of not knowing who fathered them; we must listen when they tell us how destructive it is to their self-esteem to find out their father sold the essence of his lineage for $40 or so, without ever intending to love or take responsibility for them. For children born of surrogacy contracts, it will be even worse: their own mothers did this to them.[21]

Phyllis Chesler paints a similarly bleak picture of the effect on children of being adopted away from their birth mothers. She contends that this has "dramatic, extreme psychological consequences." She cites evidence indicating that adopted children seem more prone to mental and emotional disorders than other children, and concludes that "children need to know their natural origins."[22]

These accounts present only one side, and there is surely another, more positive picture of parents and children flourishing in happy, healthy families that would not have existed but for adoption or artificial insemination. Yet the question remains, What follows in any case from such evidence? Is it reasonable to conclude that the negative consequences of these practices, which have altered traditional conceptions of the family, are reasons for abolishing them? Or for judging that it was wrong to institute them in the first place, since for all practical purposes they cannot be reversed? A great deal more evidence, on a much larger scale, would be needed before a sound conclusion could be reached that adoption and artificial insemination have had such negative consequences for the family that they ought never to have been socially sanctioned practices.

Similarly, there is no simple answer to the question of how artificial means of reproduction affect our understanding of the family. We need to reflect on the variety of answers, paying special attention to what follows from answering the question one way rather than another. Since there is no single, univocal concept of the family, it is a matter for moral and social decision just which determinants of "family" should be given priority.

REFERENCES

1. George J. Annas, "Redefining Parenthood and Protecting Embryos," in *Judging Medicine* (Clifton, NJ: Humana Press, 1988), p. 59. Reprinted from the *Hastings Center Report* 14, no. 5 (1984).

2. William F. Bolan, Jr., Executive Director, New Jersey Catholic Conference, "Statement of New Jersey Catholic Conference in Connection with Public Hearing on Surrogate Mothering," Commission on Legal and Ethical Problems in the Delivery of Health Care, Newark, NJ:, 11 May 1988.

3. Alexander M. Capron and Margaret J. Radin, "Choosing Family Law over Contract Law as a Paradigm for Surrogate Motherhood," *Law, Medicine & Health Care* 16 (Spring–Summer 1988): 35.

4. Capron and Radin, "Choosing Family Law over Contract Law," p. 35.

5. Ruth Benedict, *Patterns of Culture* (New York: Mentor Books, 1934), p. 29.

6. Benedict, *Patterns of Culture,* p. 30.

7. Melville J. Herskovits, *Cultural Anthropology* (New York: Alfred A. Knopf, 1955), p. 171.

8. R. Alta Charo, "Legislative Approaches to Surrogate Motherhood," *Law, Medicine & Health Care* 16 (Spring–Summer 1988): 104

9. Levine, "AIDS and Changing Concepts of Family," *Milbank Quarterly* 68, supp. 1 (1990): 35.

10. O.T.A. [Office of Technology Assessment] report, "Infertility: Medical and Social Choices," [Washington, DC: OTA, 1988], p. 284; case cited *Smith & Smith v. Jones & Jones,* 85-532014 DZ, Detroit, MI, 3rd Dist. (15 March 1986), as reported in *BioLaw,* ed. James F. Childress, . . . et al. (Frederick, MD: University Publishers of America, 1986). See also George J. Annas, "The Baby Broker Boom," *Hastings Center Report* 16, no. 3 (1986): 30–31.

11. See, e.g., George J. Annas, "Death without Dignity for Commercial Surrogacy: The Case of Baby M," *Hastings Center Report,* 18, no. 2 (1988): 21–24; and Bonnie Steinbock, "Surrogate Motherhood as Prenatal Adoption," in *Surrogate Motherhood: Politics and Privacy,* ed. Larry Gostin (Bloomington: Indiana University Press, 1990), pp. 123–35.

12. Sherman Elias and George J. Annas, "Noncoital Reproduction," *JAMA* 255 (3 January 1986): 67.

13. Annas, "Death without Dignity," p. 23.

14. Annas, "Death without Dignity," p. 24.

15. Annas, "The Baby Broker Boom," p. 31.

16. "The Ethical Challenge of the New Reproductive Technology," presentation before the Task Force on New Reproductive Practices; published in John F. Monagle and David C. Thomasma, eds., *Medical Ethics: A Guide for Health Care Professionals* (Frederick, MD: Aspen Publishers, 1987).

17. Levine, "AIDS and Changing Concepts of Family," p. 36.

18. This statement and subsequent ones attributed to Phyllis Chesler are taken from her unpublished remarks made at a public hearing on surrogacy conducted by the New Jersey Bioethics Commission, Newark, NJ, 11 May 1988, in which the author was a participant.

19. Written testimony, presented orally at the New Jersey Bioethics Commission's public hearing on surrogacy, 11 May 1988.

20. David M. Brodzinsky, "Adjustment to Adoption: A Psychosocial Perspective," *Clinical Psychology Review* 7 (1987): 29.

21. Ward, written testimony from New Jersey public hearing.

22. Chesler, oral testimony at New Jersey public hearing.

BARBARA KATZ ROTHMAN

Motherhood: Beyond Patriarchy*

INTRODUCTION

Law works by precedent and by analogy. While that has shown extraordinary advantages in maintaining an orderly system and avoiding capriciousness, it has its limitations. The law has a hard time confronting something new. New things can be incorporated only by stressing their points of similarity to old things, to concepts already embedded in the law.

The "something new" to which I refer here is not so much surrogacy arrangements and new reproductive technology per se, as it is the issues and concerns, the *interests,* of women where those are not the same as, or analogous to, those of men.

American law has, since the time of the constitution, continually if haltingly expanded the definition of citizen, of individual entitled to full legal rights. The rights and privileges of the white men framers of the constitution have thus been extended to men of color, to native American men, and eventually to women. In the areas of employment, housing, education — all of the areas of what we think of as the "public sphere" — this has been an effective technique to achieve a more just society.

As new concerns arise around family and procreation — the areas we think of in America as "private life" — the limitations of the workings of the law become apparent. It is these limitations which I address here.

PATRIARCHY, PATERNITY AND MATERNITY

Legal definitions of the family are reflections not of biological relationships, but rather of cultural values and ideology. The law reifies the values and beliefs of the law-makers. American family law has its roots in patriarchy, and in men's view of family relationships.

The term "patriarchy" is often used loosely as a synonym for "sexism," or to refer to any social system where men rule. The term has a more specific, technical meaning, however: the rule of fathers. It is in that specific sense that I am using it here.

Patriarchal kinship is the core of what is meant by patriarchy: the idea that paternity is the definitive social relationship. A very clear statement of patriarchal kinship is found in the book of Genesis, in the "begats." Each man, from Adam onward, is described as having begot a son in his likeness, after his image. After the birth of this firstborn son, the men are described as having lived so many years, and having begot sons and daughters. The text then turns to that firstborn son, and in turn his firstborn son after him. Women appear as "the daughters of men who bore them offspring." In a patriarchal kinship system, children are reckoned as being born to men, out of women. Women, in this system of patriarchy, bear the children of men.

The central concept here is the "seed," that part of men that grows into children of their likeness within

From *Nova Law Review* 13 (Spring 1989), 481–86. Copyright © 1989 by *Nova Law Review.* Reprinted by permission of the publisher.

*Parts of this article are drawn from the author's book, *Recreating Motherhood: Ideology and Technology in a Patriarchal Society* (W. W. Norton & Co. 1989).

the bodies of women. Such a system is inevitably male dominated, but it is a particular kind of male domination. Men control women as daughters, much as they control their sons, but they also control women as the mothers of men's children. It is women's motherhood that men must control to maintain patriarchy. In a patriarchy, because what is valued is the relationship of a man to his sons, women are a vulnerability that men have: to beget these sons, men must pass their seed through the body of a woman.

While all societies appear to be male dominated to some degree, not all societies are patriarchal. In some, the line of descent is not from father to son, but along the lines of the women. These are called "matrilineal" societies: it is a shared woman that makes for shared lineage of the family group. Men still rule in these groups, but they do not rule as fathers. They rule the women and children who are related to them through their mother's line. In such a system, people are not men's children coming through the bodies of women, but the children of women.

Our society developed out of a patriarchal system, in which paternity was the fundamentally important relationship. Some of our social customs and traditions, as well as such laws as those defining "illegitimacy," reflected men's concern for maintaining paternity. But the modern American society's kinship system is not classically patriarchal. It is what anthropologists call a bilateral system, in that individuals are considered to be equally related to both their mother's and their father's "sides" of the family.

We carry our history with us, though. Out of the patriarchal focus on the seed as the source of being, on the male production of children from men's seed, has grown our current thinking about procreation.

Modern procreative technology has been forced to go beyond the sperm as seed, to recognize the egg as seed also. But the central concept of patriarchy, the importance of the seed, was retained by extending the concept to women. Women too have seed, and women too can be said to have their "own" children, just as men do. In this modified system based on the older ideology of patriarchy, women's "rights" to their children are not based on the unique relationship of pregnancy, the long months of gestation and nurturance, the intimate connections of birth and suckling, but on women's status as producers of seed. Women gain their control over their children not as mothers, but as father-equivalents. Thus the rights and privileges of men are extended to women. But there are costs, as we are increasingly coming to see.

REDEFINING MOTHERHOOD AND FATHERHOOD

When biological paternity could only be assumed and never proved, the legal relationship between men and women in marriage gave men control over the children of women: any child of a man's wife was legally a child of the man. Motherhood was obvious; and fatherhood was reckoned by the relationship of the man to the mother.

Now that biological paternity can be brought under the control of science, with doctors both controlling paternity by moving insemination from the bed to the operating table or petri dish, and by proving paternity with newly definitive paternity testing, the legal relationship between men, women and their children has begun to shift.

A man's paternity need no longer be reckoned through his legal relationship with the mother of the child, but can now be ascertained directly. In consequence, we occasionally find ourselves reckoning maternity through a woman's legal relationship with the father. Consider here the newly available technology which permits a woman to carry to term a fetus not conceived of her ovum. There is nothing in *in vitro* technology that requires the fertilized ovum to be placed in the uterus of the same woman from whom the ovum was originally retrieved. We have, to put it simply, a technology that takes Susan's egg and puts it in Mary's body. And so who, we ask, is the mother? Is Mary substituting for Susan's body, growing Susan's baby for Susan? Or is Susan's egg substituting for Mary's, growing into Mary's baby in Mary's body?

The way American society has been answering that question depends on which woman is married to the baby's father. If Mary's husband is the father, then Mary is the mother, and Susan considered an "ovum donor," comparable to a sperm donor, with no recognized claim to the child. But if Susan's husband is the father, then Susan is the mother, and Mary the surrogate, the hired uterus, the incubator. There exist now in the U.S., birth certificates that list as the mother the ovum donor, and the name of the woman who carried the pregnancy and birthed the baby is nowhere on the birth certificate. Just as there exist birth certificates that list as the mother the woman who carried the baby, and not the name of the woman who donated the egg. Legal motherhood is being determined by the relationship of the woman to the father.

Thus, while we have moved beyond traditional patriarchal definitions, we have not moved beyond the focus on seeds and genetics, and sperm and paternity specifically. This focus on the genetic connection between parents and their children is not a simple reflection of biological reality. The parent-child relationship is invested with social and legal rights and claims that are not recognized, in this society, in any other genetic relationship. And that is not because it is a uniquely close relationship. If an individual carries a certain gene, the chances that a sibling will carry the same gene are fifty-fifty, the same as the parent-child relationship. Genetically, "there is nothing special about the parent-offspring relationship except its close degree and a certain fundamental asymmetry. The full-sib relationship is just as close."[1]

The significance we claim for the parent-child relationship is rooted in our social heritage of patriarchy: that genetic connection was the basis for men's control over the children of women. The contemporary modification of traditional patriarchy has been to recognize the genetic parenthood of women as being equivalent to the genetic parenthood of men. Genetic parenthood is the only parenthood men could have biologically, and thus in our legal system, the only parenthood that is recognized for women. The significance of gestation, having no analogy to the experience of men's parenthood, is dismissed.

SURROGACY: BEYOND BABY M

It is in this context, in which genetic parenthood is acknowledged and pregnancy ignored, that the marketing of mothering services, commercial surrogacy, has developed.

Surrogacy, some people tell us, is not new; it is as old as the bible, as old as the story of Abraham, Sarah and Hagar. But Hagar was not a surrogate mother for Ishmael. She was unquestionably the mother of that child. Sarah was not Ishmael's adoptive, foster, rearing, or social mother. She was Abraham's wife, and Hagar was the mother of the child, *his* child, the child of Abraham. If Hagar served as a surrogate, it was as a surrogate wife, bearing a child for Abraham, the child of his seed, in her body.

Abraham and Hagar were living in a true patriarchy; William Stern and Mary Beth Whitehead do not. Our society, recognizing the genetic tie between mother and child, understood Baby M to be "half his, half hers."

But the child might just as well have grown in the backyard. The unique relationship of pregnancy, the motherhood experience, received no recognition. Even without a legal contract for a surrogacy arrangement, Stern had as much right to the child, in our modified patriarchy, as did Whitehead. Abraham claimed his child but acknowledged the mother. Stern claimed his child but recognized no mother, only a rented uterus, a human incubator. The court ultimately rejected his argument, but only to the extent of recognizing Whitehead's *genetic* tie to the child, not the significance of her mothering of that child through pregnancy and birth.

The "Baby M" case simply highlighted what is true for all mothers in this system: we are only recognized as half owners of the children of our bodies. Women have gained recognition of our genetic ties to our children, but we have lost recognition of our nurturance, our motherhood. In a sense, we have gained paternity rights at the cost of maternity rights.

And now that women's genetic parenthood can be split off from gestational parenthood, the costs of equating our parenthood with that of men comes clear. If parenthood is understood as a genetic relationship, divided equally between sperm and ovum donors, then where is the place for pregnancy?

The new reproductive technology permits the development of surrogacy arrangements quite different from that of the Baby M situation. What will happen as the new technology allows brokers to hire women who are not related genetically to the babies that are to be sold? Like the poor and non-white women who are hired to do other kinds of nurturing and caretaking tasks, these mothers can be paid very little, with few benefits, and no long-term commitment. The same women who are pushing white babies in strollers, [or] white old folks in wheelchairs, can be carrying white babies in their bellies. Poor, uneducated, third world women and women of color from the United States and elsewhere, with fewer economic alternatives, can be hired more cheaply. They can also be controlled more tightly. With a legally supported surrogate motherhood contract, and with new technology, the marketing possibilities are enormous — and terrifying. Just as Perdue and Holly Farms advertise their chickens based on superior breeding and feeding, the baby brokers could begin to advertise their babies: brand-name, state-of-the-art babies, produced from the "finest" of genetic materials and an all-natural, vitamin-enriched diet.

IN SUM: BEYOND PATERNITY

We cannot allow the law to inch along, extending to women some of the privileges of patriarchy, but understanding the experiences of women only as they are analogous to those of men. What is needed is to move beyond the principles of patriarchy and beyond its modifications, to an explicit recognition of *motherhood*. Women are not, and must not be thought of as, incubators, bearing the children of others—not the children of men, and not the children of other women. Every woman is the mother of the child she bears, regardless of the source of the sperm, and regardless of the source of the egg. The law must come to such an explicit recognition of the maternity relationship.

NOTE

1. Hamilton, "The Genetic Evolution of Social Behavior," in *The Sociobiology Debate: Readings on Ethical and Scientific Issues* 191 (A. Caplan, ed. 1978).

The Problem of Infertility

NEW YORK STATE TASK FORCE ON LIFE AND THE LAW

The Prevalence of Infertility

. . .

Estimates of how many people are affected by infertility vary widely depending on the way infertility is defined. Clinicians, demographic researchers, and the public tend to define infertility differently, and experts disagree as to the appropriate definition to use.[1] This section presents the results of available survey data and comments on the benefits and limitations of the measures used, trends over time, and implications for the use of ARTs [Assisted Reproductive Technologies].

The National Survey of Family Growth (NSFG), conducted by the National Center for Health Statistics, provides the only comprehensive national data on infertility and impaired fecundity in the United States. The most recent information, collected in 1995, is based on interviews with 10,847 women between the ages of 15 and 44. The interviews encompassed a range of topics related to reproduction, including the physical ability to have children, contraceptive use, pregnancies and their outcome, marriage and cohabitation, use of family planning and infertility services, certain risk factors for infertility, and various [types of] demographic information.[2]

Based on data obtained from these surveys, researchers have used a variety of measures to estimate the prevalence of infertility, impaired fecundity, and unwanted childlessness, including the following:

INFERTILITY IN MARRIED COUPLES

The 1995 NSFG survey found that an estimated 2.1 million married couples were currently infertile, meaning that they had not conceived after at least twelve months of unprotected intercourse.[3] This figure represents 7.1 percent of the 29.7 million married couples with wives of childbearing age.[4] The incidence of infertility is 10.5 percent among married couples with non-Hispanic black women, roughly 1.5 times greater than

Reprinted from The New York State Task Force on Life and the Law, *Assisted Reproductive Technologies: Analysis and Recommendations for Public Policy* (New York: The Task Force, April 1998), pp. 10–16. Notes have been renumbered.

Definitions Commonly Used in Studies of Fertility

Fertility. The ability to conceive a pregnancy.

Fecundity. The ability to conceive a pregnancy and carry it to term.

Infertility. Difficulty achieving conception. In most studies, infertility is defined as the failure of a couple to conceive, despite unprotected intercourse, after a certain amount of time.

Impaired fecundity. Difficulty conceiving or carrying a pregnancy to term, including situations in which pregnancy has been deemed medically risky for the woman and/or her offspring.

Primary infertility. Infertility in persons who have never had children.

Secondary infertility. Infertility in persons who have already had children.

Sterility. Permanent infertility.

Surgical sterility. Inability to conceive or carry a pregnancy to term as a result of surgery. This category includes both the "contraceptively sterile," people who have had sterilizing operations such as tubal ligation or vasectomy, and the "noncontraceptively sterile," people who are sterile as a result of surgery for other medical conditions (such as endometriosis, fibroid tumors, or cancer).

---

among Hispanic or non-Hispanic white women.[5] The percentage of infertile couples has declined since 1965, when the first national survey revealed that 11.2 percent of married couples were infertile.[6] However, even with the decreasing rate, the total number of infertile couples is approximately the same as it was in 1982 because of an increase in the total number of married couples in the relevant age group.[7]

Although no increase has been detected in the overall prevalence of infertility, more couples today experience infertility before they have had any children. The number of women with primary infertility increased from about half a million in 1965 to one million in 1995, a change attributed to large numbers of women in the post-World War II baby boom generation entering the reproductive years and delaying marriage and attempts to conceive a first pregnancy. While primary infertility increased, secondary infertility decreased from 2.5 million in 1965 to 1.1 million in 1995, a change attributed to a smaller desired family size and more frequent surgical sterilization.[8]

The twelve-month definition of infertility used in the NSFG survey has the potential to both over- and underestimate reproductive difficulty. First, the calculation is inherently inexact because it relies on detailed behavioral information about couples' sexual and contraceptive practices.[9] For example, if regular contraceptive use is reported but not practiced, cases of infertility may be missed. If regular intercourse is assumed because a couple is married, and the interviewee fails to report months in which intercourse did not occur, a couple may be classified as infertile when they are not.

In addition, twelve-month estimates may overstate the problem of infertility because the measure is time limited and does not indicate a specific diagnosis or permanent condition. In fact, the measure seems to be a poor predictor of future fertility; one study found that less than 15 percent of couples meeting this definition actually remained infertile for the following ten years.[10] Therefore, some commentators argue that the one-year timespan produces an inflated number; they suggest that inability to conceive within two years is a more appropriate measure to use, for both recommending how soon couples should seek treatment and estimating the extent of the problem in the population.[11] In three surveys conducted among Canadian couples, using the two-year criterion as compared to a one-year criterion reduced the percentage of cohabiting couples deemed infertile from 8.5 percent to 7 percent.[12]

IMPAIRED FECUNDITY IN WOMEN

Infertility estimates may understate the total number of couples who want to have children but cannot, because the definition of infertility does not include couples who are capable of conceiving but cannot carry a pregnancy to term.[13] The broader concept of fecundity, rather than fertility, yields a more accurate picture of the number of couples experiencing difficulty having a child.

Based on women's interview responses, the NSFG classified women as having impaired fecundity if they said that (1) it was impossible to have a baby for some reason other than a sterilization operation—such as accident, illness, or unexplained inability to conceive; (2) it was physically difficult for them to conceive or deliver a baby, or a doctor had told them never to become pregnant again because a pregnancy would pose a danger to the woman, the baby, or both; or (3) they were continuously married, did not use contraception, and did not become pregnant for three years or longer.[14]

In 1995, 10.2 percent of women age[d] 15 to 44, or 6.1 million women, had impaired fecundity, an increase of 1.2 million women since 1988.[15] Among married couples, 12.9 percent reported some form of impaired fecundity in 1995.[16]

Most women reporting impaired fecundity had already had one child or more.[17] Among childless women, the percentage with impaired fecundity increased with age from 5.5 percent at ages 15 to 24 to 25.7 percent at ages 35 to 44.[18] Between 1982 and 1995, trends in delayed childbearing created a large increase in the number of women in their later reproductive years (between 35 and 44) who had impaired fecundity and had never had children. In 1982, an estimated 454,000 women were in that category, compared with more than a million in 1995.[19]

In classifying women as infertile or having impaired fecundity, the NSFG does not take into account whether a woman of a couple is interested in having a child. In the 1995 NSFG survey, 71 percent of women with impaired fecundity—or about 4.4 million women—stated that they currently wanted to have a baby (or another baby).[20]

USE OF MEDICAL INFERTILITY SERVICES

In 1995, 1.2 million women (about 2 percent of all women of reproductive age) reported having used infertility services within the last twelve months.[21] Of the 60.2 million women of reproductive age in 1995, 9.3 million (15 percent) had used some kind of infertility service—whether tests, medical advice, medications, surgery, ARTs, or specialized prenatal care designed to prevent miscarriage—at some point in life.[22] One in every five women between the ages of 34 and 44 reported that she had received infertility services.[23]

The use of infertility services, particularly assisted reproductive procedures such as in vitro fertilization (IVF),[24] differs by age, race, and whether a woman has previously had children. For example, non-Hispanic white women are twice as likely as Hispanic women, and four times as likely as black women, to have utilized ARTs.[25] In general, women receiving assisted reproductive services tend to be white, older, wealthier, better educated, married, and childless.[26] Discrepancies in education, income, and race are not striking when the use of all infertility services [is] considered.[27]

In earlier studies, younger couples sought infertility consultation more frequently than older couples. That pattern has shifted, and recent studies show that couples in which the woman is older are now more likely to use infertility services.[28]

In New York State, a 1989 survey revealed that 71 percent of women with a history of infertility had sought medical services for their problem. Age, education, and income were positively correlated with the use of infertility services.[29] In a more recent small survey in New York State, two out of three women who reported difficulty becoming pregnant had sought advice from a physician.[30]

USE OF ADOPTION SERVICES

In 1995, about 0.9 percent of women of childbearing age reported that they were currently seeking to adopt a child; 0.2 percent had applied to an agency or engaged a lawyer in the adoption process.[31] The percentages seeking to adopt were twice as high among women who had used infertility services.[32]

More specific analysis, based on data from the NSFG's 1988 survey, reveals that less than one-third of childless women with impaired fecundity (ages 30 to 44) had ever taken initial steps toward adoption—contacting a lawyer or adoption agency or formally applying to adopt. Even among those who had sought infertility services and were presumably highly motivated toward family building, less than half had taken any steps toward adoption.[33]

IMPLICATIONS FOR INFERTILITY SERVICES

Although surveys detect no overall rise in the prevalence of infertility, there are several reasons why the demand for infertility services is increasing.

First, medical services for infertile couples are more widely available, offer increasing options for treatment, and are well publicized.[34] As the technologies expand, increasing the number of indications deemed appropriate for intervention, the number of infertile couples considered potentially treatable also rises. Recent examples include developments in the micromanipulation of sperm,[35] which makes IVF possible for couples in which the man produces very few sperm; and the use of donor eggs,[36] which makes it possible to treat postmenopausal women and others without functioning ovaries. As a greater number of services or more complicated or time-intensive sources are offered to each couple, the number of patient visits will also increase.

Second, there are more women of reproductive age than in the past, so that even if the rate of infertility continues to decline or remains stable, the number of women with fertility problems may increase. The last of the baby boom generation will not reach the end of the reproductive years (approximately 44) until 2010.

Third, there is an ongoing trend toward delayed childbearing, particularly among professional and highly educated women. Between 1976 and 1986, the rate of the first births among women 40 years of age or older doubled.[37] One in five women who reached 35 years of age by 1989 had not had children; in contrast, only 9 percent of women who turned 35 in 1970 were childless.[38] According to a national survey, half of the women who are married and childless at 30 to 34 years of age expect to have at least one child.[39] With increasing rates of divorce and remarriage, women who have already borne children are also increasingly likely to attempt future childbearing in their later reproductive years. Since infertility increases with a woman's age,[40] a higher proportion of these women will seek infertility services.

Fourth, important risk factors for infertility are increasing among younger women. In particular, increasing rates of chlamydia in the young may result in an increased prevalence of tubal infertility.[41]

Finally, adoption is no longer an easy method of family building, which may increase the demand for medical intervention. Although the public impression may overstate the shortage of adoptable infants, adoption can be a slow and complicated process. According to one estimate, in a given year there are approximately 3.3 couples seeking adoption for every one who succeeds.[42]

• • •

NOTES

1. Population Information Program, "Infertility and Sexually Transmitted Disease: A Public Health Challenge," *Population Reports* 11 (1983): 113; W. Mosher, "Infertility: Why Business Is Booming," *American Demographics* 9 (1987): 42; G. S. Berkowitz, "Epidemiology of Infertility and Early Pregnancy Wastage", in *Reproductive Failure*, ed. A. DeCherney (New York: Churchill Livingstone, 1986), 17–18.

2. J. C. Abma et al., "Fertility, Family Planning, and Women's Health: New Data from the 1995 National Survey of Family Growth," *Vital and Health Statistics* 23, no. 19 (1997): 1. The most comprehensive data specific to New York State is found in a reproductive health survey conducted by the New York State Department of Health in 1989. The New York Reproductive Health Survey (NYRHS) included interviews with 1,910 women living in New York State, excluding New York City, between the ages of 15 and 44. Centers for Disease Control and Prevention and New York State Department of Health, *New York Reproductive Health Survey, 1989* (Atlanta: Department of Health and Human Services, 1991), 37–40.

3. Abma et al., 108. According to NSFG researchers, the survey measures infertility only for married couples because "the concept assumes continuous exposure to intercourse and no underreporting of pregnancies, which can be assumed only of currently married women." W. D. Mosher and W. F. Pratt, "Fecundity and Infertility in the United States, 1965-88," *Advance Data* 192 (1990): 1, 5.

4. Abma et al., 7, 61. These percentages are less than widely publicized estimates that approximately one in seven couples is infertile. The discrepancy reflects a difference in the way the NSFG data from 1982 was sometimes reported. Although the definition of infertility was the same, the denominator (total number of couples) excluded those who had been surgically sterilized. This reduction had the impact of substantially underestimating the number of couples without fertility problems since many fertile people choose sterilization as a form of contraception.

5. Abma et al, 61. The highest incidence of infertility, 13.6 percent, is reported among women categorized by race as "non-Hispanic other," a grouping that includes Asian, Pacific Islander, Alaskan native, and American Indian women. Ibid., 112. Commentators emphasize that more accurate, comprehensive data on race and infertility is essential to guide planning and decision making by policymakers. E. Heitman and M. Schlachtenhaufen, "The Differential Effects of Race, Ethnicity, and Socioeconomic Status on Infertility and Its Treatment: Ethical and Policy Issues for Oocyte Donation," in *New Ways of Making Babies: The Case of Egg Donation*, ed. C. B. Cohen (Bloomington: Indiana University Press, 1996), 188, 194.

6. Mosher and Pratt, 5.

7. Abma et al., "Fertility, Family Planning, and Women's Health," 7.

8. R. H. Gray and A. Fuentes, "Infertility Epidemiology: Current Scene," *Contemporary OB/GYN* 39, no. 5 (1994): 70, 73–74; Abma et al., 7.

9. E. Greenhall and M. Vessey, "The Prevalence of Subfertility: A Review of the Current Confusion and a Report of Two New Studies," *Fertility and Sterility* 54 (1990): 978.

10. P. Marchbanks et al., "Research on Infertility: Definition Makes a Difference," *American Journal of Epidemiology* 130 (1989): 259. In the NYRHS, researchers measured a history of infertility (having ever tried to get pregnant for twelve consecutive months or more without success) rather than current infertility. Fourteen percent of the women surveyed indicated a history of infertility; 65 percent of these women had experienced a live birth after recognizing the problem. Centers for Disease Control and Prevention and New York State Department of Health, *Reproductive Health Survey,* 38.

11. Population Information Program, "Infertility and Sexually Transmitted Disease," 116; Berkowitz, "Epidemiology of Infertility," 18; J. Menken, J. Trussell, and U. Larsen, "Age and Infertility," *Science* 233 (1986): 1389.

12. Royal Commission on New Reproductive Technologies, *Proceed with Care: Final Report of the Royal Commission on New Reproductive Technologies,* vol. 1 (Ottawa, Canada: Minister of Government Services, 1993), 195–96.

13. Mosher and Pratt, "Fecundity and Infertility," 5.

14. Abma et al., "Fertility, Family Planning, and Women's Health," 107.

15. Ibid., 59; Mosher and Pratt, 3. The researchers noted that this increase "may be an artifact of the baby boom generation" or the result of a reduction in the number of people surgically sterile for noncontraceptive reasons. Abma et al., 7.

16. Abma et al., 60

17. Ibid., 59.

18. Ibid.

19. Mosher and Pratt, 3; Abma et al., 59.

20. Telephone interview with Anjani Chandra, Ph.D., Statistician, National Center for Health Statistics, July 10, 1997.

21. Abma et al., "Fertility, Family Planning, and Women's Health," 7. NSFG calculations of the recent use of infertility services do not indicate whether the reported visits were for an initial consultation or follow-up treatment. Therefore, techniques that involve many visits, over extended periods of time, could raise the number of times that infertility services are used even if the proportion of infertile couples who seek treatment remains constant.

22. Ibid.

23. Ibid.

24. For a description of IVF, see Chapter 2, pages 51–60 [not reprinted].

25. Abma et al., 65.

26. Ibid.

27. Ibid.

28. S. O. Aral and W. Cates, Jr., "The Increasing Concern with Infertility: Why Now?" *Journal of the American Medical Association* 250 (1983): 2327.

29. Centers for Disease Control and Prevention and New York State Department of Health, *Reproductive Health Survey,* 39.

30. G. Buck et al., "A Population-Based Study of Infertile Couples Who Do and Do Not Seek Services from Physicians," *Assisted Reproduction Reviews* 7 (1997): 82, 84.

31. Abma et al., "Fertility, Family Planning, and Women's Health," 76, 113.

32. Ibid., 76.

33. C. A. Bachrach, K. A. London, and P. L. Maza, "On the Path to Adoption: Adoption Seeking in the United States, 1988," *Journal of Marriage and the Family* 53 (1991): 705, 713.

34. Mosher and Pratt, "Fecundity and Infertility," 6.

35. See Chapter 2, pages 63–66 [not reprinted].

36. See ibid., pages 76–80 [not reprinted].

37. R. C. Fretts et al., "Increased Maternal Age and the Risk of Fetal Death," *New England Journal of Medicine* 333 (1995): 953.

38. F. G. Cunningham and K. J. Leveno, "Childbearing among Older Women — The Message Is Cautiously Optimistic," *New England Journal of Medicine* 333 (1995): 1002.

39. Ibid.

40. See pages 16–18 [not reprinted].

41. Division of STD Prevention, "Sexually Transmitted Disease Surveillance 1995: National Profile Chlamydia," Centers for Disease Control and Prevention website: *http://wonder.cdc.gov/rchtml/Convert/STD/CSTD3808.PCW.html,* visited August 28, 1997.

42. Bachrach, London, and Maza, "Path to Adoption," 715.

WARNOCK COMMITTEE

Infertility

In the past, there was considerable public ignorance of the causes and extent of infertility, as well as ignorance of possible remedies. At one time, if a couple were childless, there was very little they could do about it. Generally the cause of infertility was thought to be something in the woman which made her childless; only occasionally was it thought that there might be something wrong with the man. Even today, there is very little factual information about the prevalence of infertility. A commonly quoted figure is that one couple in ten is childless, but accurate statistics are not available, nor is it known what proportion of this figure

relates to couples who choose not to have children. In certain religious and cultural traditions, infertility was, and still is, considered sufficient grounds for divorce. In our own society childless couples used to be advised to adopt a child. Now, as a result of improved contraception, the wider availability of legal abortion and changed attitudes toward the single mother, far fewer babies are placed for adoption.

Childlessness can be a source of stress even to those who have deliberately chosen it. Family and friends often expect a couple to start a family, and express their expectations, either openly or by implication. The family is a valued institution within our present society: within it the human infant receives nurture and protection during its prolonged period of dependence. It is also the place where social behaviour is learnt and where the child develops its own identity and feeling of

From United Kingdom, Department of Health and Social Security, *Report on the Committee of Inquiry into Human Fertilisation and Embryology* (London: Her Majesty's Stationery Office, July 1984), pp. 8–10. Crown copyright is reproduced with the permission of the Controller of Her Majesty's Stationery Office.

self-value. Parents likewise feel their identity in society enhanced and confirmed by their role in the family unit. For those who long for children, the realisation that they are unable to found a family can be shattering. It can disrupt their picture of the whole of their future lives. They may feel that they will be unable to fulfil their own and other people's expectations. They may feel themselves excluded from a whole range of human activity and particularly the activities of their child-rearing contemporaries. In addition to social pressures to have children there is, for many, a powerful urge to perpetuate their genes through a new generation. This desire cannot be assuaged by adoption.

Arguments have been put to us both for and against the treatment of infertility. First, we have encountered the view that in an over-populated world it is wrong to take active steps to create more human beings who will consume finite resources. However strongly a couple may wish to have children, such a wish is ultimately selfish. It has been said that if they cannot have children without intervention, they should not be helped to do so. Secondly, there is a body of opinion which holds that it is wrong to interfere with nature, or with what is perceived to be the will of God. Thirdly, it has been argued that the desire to have children is no more than a wish; it cannot be said to constitute a need. Other people have genuine needs which must be satisfied if they are to survive. Thus services designed to meet these needs must have priority for scarce resources.

In answer to the first point, it is never easy to counter an argument based on the situation of the world as a whole with an argument relying on the desires of individuals. We saw it as our function to concentrate on individuals rather than on the world at large. Questions about the distribution of resources within the world as a whole lie far outside our terms of reference. In any event, the number of children born as a result of techniques to assist in the treatment of infertility will always be insignificant in comparison with the naturally increasing world population. On the second point, the argument that to offer treatment to the infertile is contrary to nature fails to convince in view of the ambiguity of the concepts "natural" and "unnatural." We took the view that actions taken with the intention of overcoming infertility can, as a rule, be regarded as acceptable substitutes for natural fertilisation. Thirdly, the argument that the desire to have children is only a wish, not a need, and therefore should not be satisfied at the expense of other more urgent demands on resources can be answered in several ways. There are many other treatments not designed to satisfy absolute needs (in the sense that the patient would die without them) which are readily available within the NHS [National Health Service]. Medicine is no longer exclusively concerned with the preservation of life, but with remedying the malfunctions of the human body. On this analysis, an inability to have children is a malfunction and should be considered in exactly the same way as any other. Furthermore infertility may be the result of some disorder which in itself needs treatment for the benefit of the patient's health. Infertility is not something mysterious, nor a cause of shame, nor necessarily something that has to be endured without attempted cure. In addition, the psychological distress that may be caused by infertility in those who want children may precipitate a mental disorder warranting treatment. It is, in our view, better to treat the primary cause of such distress than to alleviate the symptoms. In summary, we conclude that infertility is a condition meriting treatment.

BARBARA KATZ ROTHMAN

Infertility as Disability

The treatment of infertility needs to be recognized as an issue of self-determination. It is as important an issue for women as access to contraception and abortion, and freedom from forced sterilization. There is no contradiction in assuring access to both infertility services and abortion services for all women who would choose them. Not only do different women have different needs, but the same women have different needs at different points in their lives. A woman who had an unwanted pregnancy and abortion at eighteen may very well need, for unrelated reasons, treatment for infertility at twenty-eight. Being infertile at twenty-eight, or thirty-eight, does not necessarily make a woman regret abortions she may have had at eighteen — what the woman wants is to have a child now, not to have spent the past decade of her life raising a child she didn't want then.[1] And a woman who needed to have medical treatment for infertility at one point in her life may very well have an accidental, unwanted pregnancy at some later point, and want an abortion. The issue is not getting more women pregnant or fewer: the concern is women having as much control as they can over entry into motherhood.

Of course the issue of individual control is inherently complicated. It raises the basic questions of free will, individual choice in any social structure, and our limitations as embodied beings whose bodies do not always accede to our will.

Feminists have been struggling with all of these questions in one area or another. In regard to motherhood, we have become particularly sensitive to the loss of individual choice in a pro-natalist system. There is

no question but that women have been forced into motherhood, and into repeated motherhood, when that is not what they themselves wanted. And it is also true that social systems create our wants as surely as they create the ways in which we meet them. Women have been carefully trained to want motherhood, to experience themselves and their womanhood, their very purpose in life, through motherhood. And that is wrong.

And yet. Wanting children, and wanting our children to want children, is not such an awful thing. I am frankly at a loss as to how I could possibly raise my own children in a way that was not pro-natalist. I love them, I love having them in my life, my children bring me joy — and I share that with them. I love friendships, and long talks — and I share that with them, too. And it delights me when I see them developing their own friendships, learning the pleasures of conversations with friends. How can it delight me less to see them develop their own interest in children? I love it when someone brings a baby around, and my son is eager for his turn to hold and play with it. I love to watch him teaching his sister and her friend how mirrors work, or helping them work a problem through. I look at him and I think, He's going to be a great father. It's not that I insist on this for them, or insist that they experience children in the same way I do, as a parent, but I want them to have the pleasures life can bring, and to me children are one such pleasure.

Certainly a world in which nobody much cared whether or not they had children would be a sad place. So pro-natalism, in a general, joyous, but not coercive way, is a good thing.

Like all the things we teach our children, some lessons are learned more powerfully by some children than by others. Some of our children will learn from us the joys of having children to raise, and will want that for themselves very much, and some won't. How much a person wants to have children, how well they learned that lesson, is not connected to the condition of their tubes, their exposure to infection, or to any other cause of infertility.

In this sense, infertility is just like any other adult-onset disability. I have a good friend who ultimately had to have a leg amputated. He fought it as hard as it could be fought, for years. He endured great pain, repeated prolonged hospitalizations, the loss of a business he had developed, risks to his health from drugs, and repeated surgery. I thought he was crazy. It's only a leg—use crutches. Other people thought *I* was crazy to suggest such a thing. It's his *leg,* they'd say, how can he not fight to save his leg?

I watch women go through painful, dangerous, expensive, life-encompassing infertility treatments, and hear the same kinds of discussions among their friends and family. Some say, "So she won't have children, what's the big deal. She can join 'Big Sister,' take her nephews to the circus. It's nice to have children in your life, but it's not worth risking all this." And others say, "If there's a chance, the slightest chance that she could get pregnant, how can she not take it?"

If we are to recognize and respect choice, we have to respect these choices as well: the choice to accept infertility and the choice to fight it.

Thinking about infertility as a disability does gives us a particularly useful model for developing social policy.

We begin with the "simple idea that society defines, implicitly, a population of 'normal' people; that is, people tend to think of the 'standard human model' as able-bodied, having what are considered typical functional abilities."[2] Disability then can be understood only in the context of normal abilities, and is inherently a *social* and not a *medical* concept. The relevant medical concept is impairment, defined as "the expression of a physiological, anatomical or mental loss or abnormality. . . . an impairment can be the result of accident, disease or congenital condition."[3] Examples of impairment which result in infertility include scarred fallopian tubes, congenital malformations of the uterus, testicular damage done by mumps, and so on.

Disability is most often based on an impairment, and is a "'dis' (lack of) 'ability' to perform certain functions. . . . Disabilities apply to generic or basic human functions: walking, speaking, grasping, hearing, excreting and so on."[4] Procreation—sperm production and ejaculation in the male, the ability to ovulate, conceive, and gestate in the female—can certainly be considered a basic human function, and the loss of ability to perform such functions a disability.

The third level of analysis, beyond impairment and disability, is handicap, defined as a "socially, environmentally and personally specified limitation. Aspirations or life goals must be taken into account when defining or identifying a handicap."[5] In the case of infertility, a person who does not want (any or any more) children is not handicapped by an impairment in procreative capacity—surgical sterilization is in fact the purposeful creation of such an impairment. But for a person who does want a child, the same impairment constitutes the basis for a handicap.

Even under these circumstances, the handicapping effects of any given impairment vary, depending on the social environment. For me, a very sedentary person, a below-the-knee amputation of one leg would not be particularly handicapping—I don't think it would change my life dramatically, provided I had an adequate prosthesis, good banisters to hand when I needed them, cars with hand controls, etc. For my friend, the loss of a leg was experienced as handicapping. For a professional athlete or dancer, it would be even more profoundly handicapping.

Similarly, an infertile person who can adopt a baby, and so enter into the social role of parent, may not be handicapped by infertility. The handicap depends on how goals are defined (having a baby rather than having a pregnancy) and the societal resources (babies available for adoption) to which the person has access. For a man who is infertile, the availability of a sperm donation, enabling his mate to become pregnant, can offset the handicapping effects of his impairment and resulting disability.

An advantage of thinking about infertility as a disability is that we can see the proper place for medical treatment. Some treatments can cure the cause of the impairment: blocked tubes can be unblocked, ending an impairment, whether it's a fallopian tube and the impairment caused infertility, or the eustachian tube and the impairment caused hearing loss. Other treatments can bypass the impairment and prevent the disability: in vitro fertilization offsets the disabling effects of tubal impairment. But there are equally important, non-medical ways of managing disability, ways that address the handicapping effects of the disability—like learning sign language, having wheelchair ramps, adopting babies.

This analysis leaves two unresolved issues, however. One is deciding which ways of overcoming the handicap are socially acceptable. Kidnapping newborns would also ameliorate the handicap of disability—and was the story in the film *Raising Arizona.* That is quite obviously not an acceptable solution, any more than buying a human slave to carry around a person without a leg or purchasing corneas from starving people to cure blindness would be acceptable. So while the principle of providing services to overcome a handicap is not unique to infertility, there remains with all handicaps the problem of deciding which services, medical or other, are socially acceptable.

Second, we have to remember that not all ways of solving the handicap are equally acceptable to the *individual.* Returning to the example of the leg amputation, a wheelchair, crutches, and various levels of sophistication in prosthetic devices will all help overcome the handicap. But some (technologically sophisticated replacement leg) may be better than others (crutches). With infertility, as with other disabilities, ways of overcoming the handicap that most closely approximate normal functioning are usually the most acceptable: donor insemination or in vitro fertilization rather than adoption, for example. But these are individual decisions: some people with an amputated leg might find adjustment to a prosthetic too difficult, painful, or aesthetically unappealing, and prefer crutches. And some infertile couples might prefer adoption to the risks and discomforts of infertility treatments, especially those of in vitro fertilization.

For now, while there are babies needing homes, adoption is the preferred solution of many infertile couples. But adoption is problematic. . . . As a long-range feminist social policy, we cannot rely on adoption, but are going to have to address directly the prevention and treatment of the impairments that cause infertility.

As a rule, prevention generally makes more sense than treatment when designing social policy. On an individual, clinical level, we certainly have to respond to a crisis with appropriate treatment, but as a plan, we can put our efforts into avoiding crises.

Much infertility is avoidable, though no one knows quite how much. We need more basic research on the causes of infertility, with particular attention paid to the neglected areas of environmental and iatrogenic causes. Infertility is approximately one and a half times as common among women of color as among white women[6]—access to good nutrition, a generally higher standard of living, and better medical care, high priorities in any feminist agenda, would prevent some infertility.

But a focus on prevention has its negative side as well, in that it may lead to a "victim-blaming" stance, individuals being held accountable for their own infertility. Consider the attention paid in recent years to the infertility problems of the so-called delayed-childbearing women, the women who "put off" motherhood until their thirties, or sometimes even forties. One reason their infertility gets so much attention is that precisely because they are older, and put off childbearing to develop careers, they are the ones who can now afford the high-tech, high-cost treatments. But their infertility is often blamed on their own choice, as if they're now paying the piper for their carefree years in graduate school or the years establishing jobs, businesses, and careers rather than making babies.

Besides its unkindness, there are at least two problems with holding women accountable for their own infertility. In the first place, the data are not all that clear on just how much fertility is actually lost as originally fertile women enter their mid to late thirties. While common sense tells us that infertility must increase with age, simply because each year of life presents that many more opportunities for damage to fertility, it is very difficult to get an accurate measure of the extent of this loss.

Until recently, fertility data were collected on married women only. Particularly prior to the legalization of abortion, a period which covers the early reproductive years of today's "delayed-childbearing" women, many of the most fertile women became wives and mothers. Many highly fertile young women were the pregnant brides of twenty years ago, pushed into marriage and motherhood by fertility. On the other hand, among those who avoided early motherhood and early marriage were those women who were markedly less fertile. Simply put, young married women have been likely to be fertile—it's one of the reasons they've married young. Older women who have never had children are likely to have higher rates of infertility—it's one of the reasons they were able to avoid having had children. It is not altogether clear what percentage of women discovering infertility at say, thirty-seven were any more fertile at twenty-two.

Second, and I think even more important, this blaming of the women themselves ignores the context in which women have "chosen" to delay childbearing: a lack of maternity leave, of child care, of shared parenting by men, and so on. Shall we blame the woman for putting off childbearing while she became a lawyer, art historian, physician, set designer, or engineer? Or shall we blame the system that makes it so very difficult for young lawyers, art historians, physicians, set designers, and engineers to have children without having wives to care for them? Men did not have to delay entry into parenthood for nearly as many years in the pursuit of their careers as women now do.

It is easier to blame the individual woman than to understand the political and economic context in which she must act, but it does not make for good social policy. If we want to decrease infertility in part by having women concentrate childbearing in their twenties and early thirties, we have to make that possible for them.

Unfortunately, we have no reason to think that we can prevent all infertility: even if everyone had excellent health care, a safe working environment, good nutrition, and tried to get pregnant at twenty-four, we'd still have some people experiencing infertility. If prevention won't solve it, and adoption should not be relied on as a long-range solution, then we're left with medical management.

One school of thought among feminists has been to do away with high-technology infertility treatments. For all of the reasons I have outlined, I don't think that is acceptable policy.

But neither is business as usual. Infertility treatment embodies all that is bad in our medical care: it is available only to the well-to-do, it is male dominated, and it is offered in a way that is totally divorced from the context of one's life. And worse, it doesn't work. In vitro fertilization (IVF) fails 90 percent of the women who try it.

Much has been written about the skewed reporting of IVF clinics. Some of it is like the psychological self-protection in which many medical workers engage. Calling a "chemical pregnancy" (a positive pregnancy test even if the woman "miscarries" in time for a normal period) a success is a way of shifting blame for the failure to achieve a baby from the clinic staff (*we* got you pregnant) to the woman (*you* lost it). Blaming the patient for failing when the treatment was "successful" is a fairly common medical practice.

Some of the reporting, I think, is deliberately misleading. Some clinics cite the best success rates available for IVF even if they themselves have never achieved a baby. Half of the IVF clinics in the United States have not, in fact, ever gotten a baby born. There are more subtle misleading reports, too: dividing the number of babies by the number of women; for example, as if two sets of twins and one set of triplets among twenty women was the same as seven out of twenty women having babies. I've only seen one IVF clinic, but I'd be willing to bet that its wall of baby photos near the intake area is a near-universal feature. A few minutes of study and I realized that the same babies were pictured repeatedly — here at birth, there dressed for "First Christmas," over in the top corner showing off a new tooth. Innocent enough — grateful parents send photos, pleased staff puts them up — but the image is one of lots and lots of babies, a misleading image of lots and lots of "successes."

IVF clinics are having more success these days, getting more women pregnant and more babies born. But I fear it has as much to do with a change in admissions as anything else. Where the original candidates had no other chance of a pregnancy — no tubes at all, for example — today IVF and the related procedure GIFT (gamete intra-fallopian transfer) are being used with less and less indication, earlier and earlier in the infertility workup. That is, IVF and GIFT are now being used with women of greater fertility, women who might very well have conceived on their own in another few months. There are now women who do get pregnant while on the waiting list for IVF treatment.

The most significant shift in IVF use, however, is that it is now being used to treat male infertility. A man with a very low sperm count, or with other fertility problems, can use IVF to have his sperm fertilize an ovum. This means that fertile women, women who could get pregnant readily with another man, or with insemination with donor sperm, are being subjected to IVF treatment, including hormonal stimulation, sonograms, and surgery, to maintain their husband's genetic paternity.

The medical community likes to talk about infertility as a problem "of the couple." Since fertility level is a continuum (some of us get pregnant very readily, some less so; some men have higher sperm counts, some lower) this often makes sense. Two people of lower fertility will have more trouble conceiving with each other than either would with a highly fertile partner.

But if a man has a high sperm count the infertility problem is treated entirely as the woman's, whereas if the man has a low sperm count, the problem is *still* treated largely as the woman's. Further, Judith Lorber reports that most women who are undergoing IVF or GIFT for male infertility are told about "some little thing wrong" in themselves as well.[7] Which of course is probably quite true. Even very fertile people aren't perfectly fertile, and nobody seems to get pregnant at every possible opportunity.

This inclusion of "some little problem" of the woman's in the treatment makes the treatment of the woman as the patient for male infertility "more acceptable medically to the couple and to the staff."[8] All of this is particularly problematic when "sexual dysfunction" seems to be a common reason why couples present themselves for infertility treatment, and why there are so many 'waiting list pregnancies.' It may also be the reason why the husband's inability to masturbate to ejaculation on demand is a perennial problem in IVF clinics the world over."[9]

A couple may be a social unit, but it is not a physiological unit. If a man cares deeply enough about an impairment which prevents him from producing adequate sperm, that impairment should be treated. We do therefore need more research on *male* treatment of *male* infertility, an area now neglected in favor of female treatment of male infertility. But if a man is more concerned about simply overcoming the handicapping effects of his impairment, insemination with donor sperm should be encouraged.

Many men do care less about the infertility per se than they care about what it is doing to their lives and to their wives.[10] Women have been very protective of men, and ultimately of themselves and their potential children, concerned that the man may not feel he is the social father to a child if he is not the genetic father. Doctors have colluded with women to protect genetic paternity, at the cost of women's safety and health. I think that a focus on men's nurturing capacities is more than appropriate, and that many more men would in fact accept the use of insemination with donor sperm (that is, accept the loss of their own genetic paternity) if it were recommended by infertility specialists as a

relatively inexpensive, quick, and safe way to achieve a pregnancy and, as so many infertile men and women have expressed with longing, "get on with their lives." The more we learn to think of fathering as a social, emotional, nurturing, loving relationship, the less important genetic paternity will be.

In sum, I think we as a society need to think about infertility as we need to think about any other disability. We need to see it as a multifaceted problem. Some of it can be prevented, some can be cured, and some needs to be lived with. Part of the solution to any disability problem is a change in societal attitudes; part is a change in societal services. Disability is not doom, life is not over, and one does learn to cope. But recognizing that blind people can live wonderful and full lives neither excuses us from preventing and treating that blindness which is preventable and treatable nor gives us cause to deny the sadness in loss of sight.

We can recognize and acknowledge and fully appreciate the depth of grief that may accompany infertility, just as such grief may accompany the loss of a leg or of sight. To say that women are more than just mothers, that we are persons in our own right, does not mean that we have to deny the sadness of loss of motherhood.

NOTES

1. Joan Leibmann-Smith, 1988, "Delayed Childbearing and Infertility: Social Antecedents and Consequences," dissertation in progress, City University of New York.

2. Office of Technology Assessment (OTA) of the U.S. Congress, 1982, *Technology and Handicapped People,* p. 19.

3. Ibid.

4. Ibid., p. 20.

5. Ibid.

6. OTA, 1988, *Infertility: Medical and Social Choices,* p. 51.

7. Judith Lorber, 1988, "Whose Problem, Whose Decision: The Use of In Vitro Fertilization in Male Infertility," unpublished paper presented to the Eastern Sociological Society, Philadelphia.

8. Ibid.

9. Ibid.

10. Arthur L. Greil, Thomas A. Leitko, and Karen L. Porter, 1988, "Infertility: His and Hers," *Gender & Society,* Vol. 2; No. 2, in press.

UNITED STATES SUPREME COURT

Reproduction as a 'Major Life Activity' (Bragdon v. Abbott, 1998)

[Editor's summary of the case. Sidney Abbott, the respondent, has been infected with HIV since 1986. In September of 1994 Ms. Abbott went to the dental office of Randon Bragdon, the petitioner, in Bangor, Maine, for a checkup. Ms. Abbott disclosed her HIV infection on the patient registration form. Dr. Bragdon then performed a dental examination, discovered a cavity, and informed Ms. Abbott of his policy against filling the cavities of HIV-infected patients in his office. He offered to fill the cavity at a hospital, with no added fee for his services, although Ms. Abbott would have had to pay the cost of using the hospital's facilities. Ms. Abbott declined the dentist's offer.

Shortly thereafter, Ms. Abbott sued Dr. Bragdon for discrimination. Part of her complaint was that a federal law, the Americans with Disabilities Act (ADA) of 1990, prohibits anyone who operates a "place of public accommodation" from refusing services to a person on the basis of that person's disability.

In 1994 Ms. Abbott's HIV infection had not yet manifested the most serious symptoms of late-stage HIV disease, including AIDS. However, Ms. Abbott argued that her HIV infection was already a disabling condition because it "placed a substantial limitation on her ability to reproduce and have children." Ms. Abbot's claim gave the U.S. Supreme Court the opportunity to consider whether reproduction is one of the "major life activities" covered by the ADA and whether impairment of the capacity to reproduce constitutes a disability under the terms of the statute. The Court's discussion of this issue follows.]

JUSTICE KENNEDY delivered the opinion of the Court.

Reprinted from 118 *S. Ct.* 2196 (1998). References omitted.

• • •

The statute [the Americans with Disabilities Act of 1990] defines disability as:

. . . a physical or mental impairment that substantially limits one or more of the major life activities of [an] individual.

• • •

The statute is not operative, and the definition not satisfied, unless [an] impairment affects a major life activity. Respondent's claim throughout this case has been that the HIV infection placed a substantial limitation on her ability to reproduce and to bear children. Given the pervasive, and invariably fatal, course of the disease [HIV infection], its effect on major life activities of many sorts might have been relevant to our inquiry. Respondent and a number of *amici* make arguments about HIV's profound impact on almost every phase of the infected person's life. In light of these submissions, it may seem legalistic to circumscribe our discussion to the activity of reproduction. We have little doubt that had different parties brought the suit they would have maintained that an HIV infection imposes substantial limitations on other major life activities.

From the outset, however, the case has been treated as one in which reproduction was the major life activity limited by the impairment. It is our practice to decide cases on the grounds raised and considered in the Court of Appeals and included in the question on which we granted certiorari. We ask, then, whether reproduction is a major life activity.

We have little difficulty concluding that it is. As the Court of Appeals held, "[t]he plain meaning of the word 'major' denotes comparative importance" and "suggest[s] that the touchstone for determining an activity's inclusion under the statutory rubric is its significance."

Reproduction falls well within the phrase "major life activity." Reproduction and the sexual dynamics surrounding it are central to the life process itself.

While petitioner [Dr. Bragdon] concedes the importance of reproduction, he claims that Congress intended the ADA [Americans with Disabilities Act] only to cover those aspects of a person's life which have a public, economic, or daily character. The argument founders on the statutory language. Nothing in the definition suggests that activities without a public, economic, or daily dimension may somehow be regarded as so unimportant or insignificant as to fall outside the meaning of the word "major." The breadth of the term confounds the attempt to limit its construction in this manner.

. . . [T]he ADA must be construed to be consistent with regulations issued to implement the Rehabilitation Act. Rather than enunciating a general principle for determining what is and is not a major life activity, the Rehabilitation Act regulations instead provide a representative list, defining [the] term to include "functions such as caring for one's self, performing manual tasks, walking, seeing, hearing, speaking, breathing, learning, and working." As the use of the term "such as" confirms, the list is illustrative, not exhaustive.

These regulations are contrary to petitioner's attempt to limit the meaning of the term "major" to public activities. The inclusion of activities such as caring for one's self and performing manual tasks belies the suggestion that a task must have a public or economic character in order to be a major life activity for purposes of the ADA. On the contrary, the Rehabilitation Act regulations support the inclusion of reproduction as a major life activity, since reproduction could not be regarded as any less important than working and learning. Petitioner advances no credible basis for confining major life activities to those with a public, economic, or daily aspect. In the absence of any reason to reach a contrary conclusion, we agree with the Court of Appeals' determination that reproduction is a major life activity for the purposes of the ADA.

. . .

CHIEF JUSTICE REHNQUIST, with whom JUSTICE SCALIA and JUSTICE THOMAS join, and with whom JUSTICE O'CONNOR joins as to Part II, concurring in the judgment in part and dissenting in part.

. . . [T]he Court is simply wrong in concluding as a general matter that reproduction is a "major life activity." Unfortunately, the ADA does not define the phrase "major life activities." But the Act does incorporate by reference a list of such activities contained in regulations issued under the Rehabilitation Act. The Court correctly recognizes that this list of major life activities "is illustrative, not exhaustive," but then makes no attempt to demonstrate that reproduction is a major life activity in the same sense that "caring for one's self, performing manual tasks, walking, seeing, hearing, speaking, breathing, learning, and working" are.

Instead, the Court argues that reproduction is a "major" life activity in that it is "central to the life process itself." In support of this reading, the Court focuses on the fact that "'major'" indicates "'comparative importance,'"; see . . . Webster's Collegiate Dictionary 702 (10th ed. 1994) ("greater in dignity, rank, importance, or interest"), ignoring the alternative definition of "major" as "greater in quantity, number, or extent," *ibid.* It is the latter definition that is most consistent with the ADA's illustrative list of major life activities.

No one can deny that reproductive decisions are important in a person's life. But so are decisions as to who to marry, where to live, and how to earn one's living. Fundamental importance of this sort is not the common thread linking the statute's listed activities. The common thread is rather that the activities are repetitively performed and essential in the day-to-day existence of a normally functioning individual. They are thus quite different from the series of activities leading to the birth of a child.

Both respondent and the United States as *amicus curiae,* argue that reproduction must be a major life activity because regulations issued under the ADA define the term "physical impairment" to include physiological disorders affecting the reproductive system. If reproduction were not a major life activity, they argue, then it would have made little sense to include the reproductive disorders in the roster of physical impairments. This argument is simply wrong. There are numerous disorders of the reproductive system, such as dysmenorrhea [painful menstrual periods] and endometriosis [the presence of lining from the uterus in other pelvic organs, for example, the ovaries], which are so painful that they limit a woman's ability to engage in major life activities such as walking and working. And, obviously, cancer of the various reproductive organs limits one's ability to engage in numerous activities other than reproduction.

• • •

Justice O'Connor, concurring in the judgment in part and dissenting in part.

I agree with The Chief Justice that [the respondent] . . . has not proven that her asymptomatic HIV status substantially limited one or more of her major life activities. In my view, the act of giving birth to a child, while a very important part of the lives of many women, is not generally the same as the representative major life activities of all persons — "caring for one's self, performing manual tasks, walking, seeing, hearing, speaking, breathing, learning, and working" — listed in regulations relevant to the Americans with Disabilities Act of 1990. Based on that conclusion, there is no need to address whether other aspects of intimate or family relationships not raised in the case could constitute major life activities; nor is there reason to consider whether HIV status would impose a substantial limitation on one's ability to reproduce if reproduction were a major life activity.

• • •

In Vitro Fertilization

JOHN A. ROBERTSON

IVF, Infertility, and the Status of Embryos

In vitro fertilization (IVF) emerged as a major treatment for infertility in the 1980s. Its reliance on extracorporeal fertilization of human eggs raises questions about the status, control, and disposition of embryos. As a high-tech reproductive procedure, it also presents issues of access, efficacy, and truthful disclosure that test the limits of procreative freedom. To explore these issues, this [essay] addresses the conflicts and controversies that arise when husband and wife provide egg and sperm for IVF.[1]

• • •

Robertson, John A., *Children of Choice: Freedom and the New Reproductive Technologies,* pp. 97–105, 107–11, 113–18. Copyright © 1994 by Princeton University Press. Reprinted by permission of Princeton University Press.

IN VITRO FERTILIZATION

IVF treats infertility problems by bypassing the natural place of fertilization in the fallopian tube. It operates by collecting eggs surgically after ovarian stimulation, fertilizing them in vitro in the laboratory, and, after 48–72 hours, placing the cleaving embryos into the uterus.

Originally developed to overcome tube blockage by bypassing the fallopian tubes altogether, IVF is increasingly used to treat infertility due to other conditions, such as endometriosis, cervical mucus problems, and the great number of cases of unexplained infertility. In addition, IVF can be used to treat oligospermia or low sperm count by putting sperm directly in contact with the egg in a dish, where there is a shorter distance to travel to conception. In severe cases, it would enable conception to occur by drilling of the egg's zona pellucida or by microinjection of [a] single sperm into the egg.

The first birth of a child from IVF occurred in 1978 in Great Britain, capping off a long period of research by Steptoe, Edwards, and others. Since then more than 30,000 children conceived in this way have been born worldwide. The United States has more than 180 programs offering IVF. Over 8,230 children have been born as a result of the procedure in the last four years alone.[2] However, IVF will not provide all patients with a baby. While the best programs have a success rate of 20 to 25 percent per egg retrieval cycle, many programs cannot approach this record.[3] At present women have to undergo on the average two IVF cycles to start a pregnancy, at a cost of $5,000 to $7,000 per cycle. Improvements in success rates will occur as research and experience with the technique grow.

To increase the chances of pregnancy, most IVF programs stimulate the ovaries to obtain multiple eggs, and place several fertilized eggs or embryos in the uterus in each IVF cycle (American programs place on average 3.5 embryos in the uterus per cycle). If too many fertilized eggs are placed in the uterus, there is a great risk of multiple pregnancy, and may create the need for selective reduction (abortion) of the pregnancy. Embryo freezing, now practiced in most clinics, permits extra embryos to be preserved and then thawed for use in later cycles. This will increase the overall efficacy of an egg retrieval cycle and reduce the costs or burdens of later cycles.

Increasingly, eggs are collected by means of ultrasound-guided transvaginal aspiration, which eliminates the need for laparoscopy and general anesthesia.[4] When tubes are patent, the embryos may also be placed directly into the fallopian tube, in a procedure known as ZIFT (zygote intrafallopian transfer). Egg and sperm may also be inserted directly into a patent tube before fertilization occurs (known as GIFT, or gamete intrafallopian transfer). Since the fallopian tube is the natural site of fertilization and early embryo development, these procedures may offer a better chance of success in certain cases.

SHOULD IVF BE DONE AT ALL?

Basic IVF raises many issues that force us to consider the scope and meaning of procreative liberty. At the most fundamental level, the question is whether IVF should occur at all. Engineering conception in the bright glare of the laboratory rather than the dark recesses of the fallopian tube strikes some people as wrong or undesirable. They would deny or severely limit access to this procedure.

Their objection has several strands. One is an antitechnology bias against medical interventions, especially reproductive interventions. A second strand is theological, exemplified by the Catholic position that any separation of the unitive (sexual) and procreative is improper. A third feminist strand sees any reproductive technology as exploiting the socially engrained view that infertile women are inadequate — that women must produce children for their husbands. IVF, which bombards a woman's body with powerful hormones and then invades the body to harvest eggs, is in their view a prime example of such an exploitive technology. It holds out the false promise of success when the chance of taking home a baby is actually quite low.[5] Finally, right-to-life groups would ban IVF because they think that it harms embryos.

Whatever the merits of these objections, they have not dampened demand or had a significant impact on public policy. Although a 1987 Vatican directive urged that civil law be enacted to ban procedures such as IVF, no state has done so and no groups appear to be lobbying for such a measure.[6] Indeed, the incidence of IVF in the United States (and throughout the world) continues to grow. In 1990, 19,079 stimulation cycles for IVF were reported, 16,405 of which went to egg retrieval, with an additional 3,750 retrieval cycles done for gamete intrafallopian transfer (GIFT), in which the egg and sperm are placed directly into the fallopian tube.[7]

If a law banning IVF or GIFT were passed, it would no doubt be found unconstitutional because it directly impeded the efforts of infertile married couples to have offspring, thus interfering with their fundamental right to procreate.[8] The moral objections to IVF made by the Catholic Church, feminists, and others do not constitute the compelling evidence of tangible harm necessary to justify interference with procreative liberty. Ancillary rules for the conduct of IVF, which are discussed below, should also have to satisfy the compelling-interest test when they substantially interfere with access to IVF.

EMBRYO STATUS ISSUES

IVF is unique because it externalizes the earliest stages of human life, and subjects it to observation and manipulation. Moral and legal controversies over basic IVF concern the control and disposition of embryos created in the process. What is the status of preimplantation embryos?[9] Who has dispositional control over them? What actions may be done with them?

These questions pit deeply felt views about respect for the earliest stages of human life against the needs of infertile couples to create embryos to serve their reproductive goals. Their resolution will have a great impact on the scope of procreative freedom and the use of IVF to treat infertility. The biological, moral, and legal status of the embryo is first discussed before issues of ownership and limitations on what may be done with embryos is addressed.

THE BIOLOGICAL STATUS OF EMBRYOS

Conception occurs when a single spermatozoa enters the egg and the chromosomes of each fuse into a single cell of forty-six chromosomes. Fertilization is not instantaneous, but occurs gradually over several hours after penetration of the egg by a single sperm.[10] At this stage a new and unique genome beginning a new generation exists within a single cell.[11]

During the next three days the one-celled zygote divides several times to become an undifferentiated aggregate of two, four, six, or eight cells. In IVF programs the embryo will be transferred to a uterus when it reaches the four-, six-, or eight-cell stage, some 48 to 72 hours after conception. In ZIFT, transfer directly into the fallopian tube occurs via laparoscopy at the one-cell or zygote stage. It is also at this stage that the embryo would be cryopreserved for later use.

Further growth produces the cell clusters of the morula and then blastocyst stage of development. At the blastocyst stage the simple cellular aggregate of the fertilized egg starts to show a central cavity surrounded by a peripheral cellular layer with some distinguishable inner cells.[12] The outer cells develop into a trophoblastic or feeding layer that becomes the placenta rather than the embryo proper. At this time only cells of the inner mass can give rise to an embryo.

The blastocyst stage marks the developing capability to interact with maternal cells of the uterine lining, which is essential for implantation and later development to occur. At six to nine days the developing cellular mass acquires the ability to implant or embed in the uterine wall as the placenta, jointly derived from embryonic and maternal cells, begins to form.[13] Implantation marks the beginning of pregnancy as a maternal state. At this stage the embryonic mass has a clearly distinguishable outer cellular layer which plays the major role in the implantation process. It is the as yet undeveloped inner cell mass, however, that is the source of the embryo proper. It is for this reason that preimplantation stages are more accurately called the "preembryo."

When the blastocyst is well established in the uterine wall (early in the second postfertilization week), the inner cell mass reorganizes into two layers that make up the embryonic disk. This first true rudiment of the embryo is the site of the formation of the embryonic axis, along which the major organs and structures of the body will be differentiated.[14] By the end of the fourth postconception week, the major organs are more fully formed and cardiovascular circulation has begun.[15] By the eighth week an anatomically recognizable human miniature exists, displaying very primitive neuromuscular function but still extremely immature by all structural and functional criteria.[16] The higher parts of the brain do not show any electrical activity or nerve cell connections until twelve weeks after conception.[17] If abortion does not occur, the birth of a newborn infant will complete the gestational process.

THE MORAL STATUS OF EMBRYOS

While scientists largely agree about these facts of zygote, preembryo, and embryo development, there is also a growing consensus about their moral significance. Three major ethical positions have been articulated in the debate of embryo status. At one extreme is the view of the embryo as a human subject after fertilization, which requires that it be accorded the rights of a person. This position entails an obligation to provide an opportunity for implantation to occur and tends to ban any action before transfer that might harm the embryo or that is not immediately therapeutic, such as freezing and embryo research. Its weakness is that it ignores the reality of biological development just described.

At the opposite extreme is the view that the embryo has a status no different from that of any other human tissue, and can be treated accordingly. Other than requiring the consent of those who have ownership or decision-making authority over embryos, no limits should be imposed on actions taken with them. The problem with this view is that it ignores the fact that a new genome has been formed and that actions with this tissue could affect whether a new child will be born.

The most widely held view of embryo status takes an intermediate position between the other two. It holds that the embryo deserves respect greater than that accorded to other human tissue, because of its potential to become a person and the symbolic meaning it carries for many people. Yet it should not be treated as a person, because it has not yet developed the features of personhood, is not yet established as developmentally individual, and may never realize its biologic potential.[18]

It is noteworthy that law, ethical commentary, and the reports of most official or professional advisory bodies share the view that the embryo has a special moral status less than that of a person. For example, the United States' Ethics Advisory Board unanimously agreed in 1979 that "the human preembryo is entitled to profound respect, but this respect does not necessarily encompass the full legal and moral rights attributed to persons."[19]

In 1984, the Warnock Committee in Great Britain took a similar position when it stated: "The human preembryo . . . is not under the present law of the United Kingdom accorded the same status as a living child or an adult, nor do we necessarily wish it to be accorded the same status. Nevertheless, we were agreed that the preembryo of the human species ought to have a special status."[20]

The Ontario Law Reform Commission (Canada), which completed an extensive review of the issue in 1985, also took this view, as have nearly all other professional and official advisory bodies that have reviewed the question of embryo status.[21] The most recent pronouncement to this effect came from the Tennessee Supreme Court in 1992 when it overturned a trial court finding that embryos were "children" but held that because of their special status they deserved "special respect."[22]

For the most part, only groups holding the view that "personhood" begins at conception have rejected this middle position. However, Father Richard McCormick, a noted Catholic bioethicist who believes that abortion is immoral, has looked carefully at the biologic facts about the embryo and concluded that because the embryo is not developmentally individual until implantation, it has not clearly been determined to be a person in Catholic theology.[23]

Legal status—position or standing in law—will define what rights, if any, embryos have and what duties are owed to them, thus determining what might be done with these entities, and by whom.

Do Embryos Have Legal Rights? The advisory body conclusions parallel the traditional Anglo-American legal view of prenatal life. In that tradition, legal personhood does not exist until live birth and separation from the mother. Common law prohibitions on abortion protected fetuses only after quickening (roughly sixteen weeks of gestation). While many American states did pass restrictive abortion laws in the nineteenth and twentieth centuries, those laws applied only to termination of pregnancy, and thus did not address the status of preimplantation embryos outside the body. Wrongful death statutes did not compensate for the wrongful death of a fetus until the late 1940s, and then only if the fetus was viable at the time of the injury.

At the present time, then, the law does not regard embryos as rights-bearing entities, although it has recognized that prenatal actions could affect the postnatal well-being of persons. In most states the embryo is not a legal subject in its own right and is not protected by laws against homicide or wrongful death, nor is embryo discard prohibited. However, three states (Minnesota, Louisiana, and Illinois) have altered their homicide laws in such a way that they arguably ban the intentional destruction of extracorporeal embryos.[24] Aside from those states, the embryo generally has legal cognizance only if the interests of an actual person are at stake, such as when transfer occurs and offspring may be affected or when someone wrongfully interferes with another person's right to determine disposition of the embryo.

The biology of early human embryo development supports this legal status. Since the embryo does not have differentiated organs, much less the developed brain, nervous system, and capacity for sentience that legal subjects ordinarily have, it cannot easily be regarded as a legal subject. Indeed, the embryo is not yet individual, because twinning or mosaicism can still occur. It is not surprising that the law does not recognize the embryo itself as a legal subject.

This legal status of embryos is not dependent on the continued survival of *Roe v. Wade* and the right to abortion. Because abortion laws penalized termination of pregnancy, they never applied to the destruction of embryos before pregnancy occurred. Thus *Roe* has not been a direct barrier to states wishing to protect embryos in situations other than abortion. A reversal of *Roe v. Wade* is not necessary to have states protect extracorporeal embryos more extensively than they previously have. IVF programs are also free to set their own standards concerning the extent to which embryos will be protected.

Dispositional Control over Embryos. An important question of legal status concerns the locus and scope of decisional authority over embryos. "Who" has the right or authority to choose among available options for disposition of embryos is a question separate from "what" those dispositional options are.

The question of decisional authority is really the question of who "owns"—has a "property" interest in—the embryo. However, using terms such as "ownership" or "property" risks misunderstanding. Ownership does not signify that embryos may be treated in all respects like other property. Rather, the term merely designates who decides which legally available options will occur, such as creation, freezing, discard, donation, use in research, and placement in a uterus. Although the bundle of property rights attached to one's ownership of an embryo may be more circumscribed than for other things, it is an ownership or property interest nonetheless.

While the individuals who provided the gametes, the couple jointly, their transferees, the physicians or embryologists who directly create the embryos, or the IVF program or embryo storage bank that has actual possession are all possible candidates for decisional authority over embryos, the persons who provide the egg and sperm have the strongest claim to ownership of the embryo. The more interesting questions concern whether and how they have exercised that authority, and whether advance instructions for disposition will be binding if their preferences or circumstances change.

While legislation has not yet explicitly recognized the gamete providers' joint ownership of extracorporeal embryos, it is reasonable to assume that the courts would so hold when confronted with disputes raising this issue.[25] It is also likely that a right of survivorship in embryos would be recognized as well. The Uniform Anatomical Gift Act and other precedents concerning disposition of body parts support that view, even though they do not address it specifically.

Since most IVF programs and storage banks are likely to honor the couple's ownership, the issue would be directly joined only if a program or bank refused to follow the couple's dispositional instructions. The question would also arise if the program intentionally or negligently destroyed embryos.

• • •

Limits on the Scope of Authority over Embryos. Having seen that the gamete providers and their transferees have decisional authority over embryos, we now consider the limits that the state and IVF programs may impose on exercise of the authority. Is the couple's "ownership" of embryos absolute, or may the state qualify or limit it in certain ways? As noted previously, the answer to this question will depend on the reproductive interests implicated and the state's reasons for limiting the couple's ownership. While resolution of some issues will turn on views of embryo moral status, most will turn on the reproductive interests at stake and the degree to which procreative liberty is recognized. The main questions that arise here are limits on discard and freezing of embryos.

Discard or Nontransfer of Embryos. Because most IVF programs hyperstimulate the ovaries and retrieve multiple eggs, couples and programs must decide whether all fertilized eggs will be placed in the uterus, or whether surplus or unwanted embryos may be discarded or donated to others. If all fertilized eggs are to placed in the uterus, the number fertilized may have to be limited, because of the very serious risks of multiple gestation.[26] Yet limiting the number fertilized might yield too few embryos to initiate a viable pregnancy. Freezing extra embryos may solve the problem in some cases, but not all frozen embryos will be placed in the woman producing them.

The procedure most likely to produce pregnancy is to fertilize all viable eggs, transfer only the three or four embryos that can safely be placed in the uterus at one time, and either freeze the remaining embryos, discard them, or donate them to others. A problem arises when people object to discard of embryos because they believe that embryos are persons with rights, or because they find the symbolic effects of such a practice distasteful and take action to implement their view.

Legally, IVF programs are free to determine their own policy about embryo discard, but must inform couples of their policies before embryos are created. Except in Minnesota, Louisiana, and possibly Illinois, destruction or discard of an embryo is not covered by homicide or other criminal laws.[27] While many programs will allow couples the option of discard, some will apply restrictive policies, either because of their own moral qualms or because of institutional constraints.[28]

An important public policy question is whether couples and programs should be free to decide these matters as they wish, or whether government should intervene to limit their choice. A limitation on embryo discard (by limiting the number of eggs that may be inseminated, banning discard, or requiring donation of unwanted embryos) would interfere with the procreative liberty of a couple that wished to employ this alternative.[29] Would such laws be constitutional? Are they desirable?

The constitutionality of laws that prevent the discard or destruction of IVF embryos is independent of the right to abortion established in *Roe v. Wade* and upheld in *Planned Parenthood v. Casey.*[30] *Roe* and *Casey* protect a woman's interest in not having embryos placed in her body and in terminating implantation (pregnancy) that has occurred. Under *Roe-Casey* the state would be free to treat external embryos as persons or give as much protection to their potential life as it chooses, as long as it did not trench on a woman's bodily integrity or other procreative rights.

Embryo protection laws, however, even if they do not infringe bodily integrity, do interfere with decisions about having biologic offspring and thus limit procreative choice. For example, laws that require donation of unwanted embryos in lieu of discard force people to have biologic offspring against their will, thus infringing the right not to procreate. Even if no child-rearing obligations follow, as would ordinarily be the case if the embryos are donated anonymously to others, the couple would still face the possibility that they had produced genetic offspring. One could argue that genetic reproduction *tout court* is such a significant personal event that it should be included in the fundamental right not to procreate. If this argument were accepted, a state's desire to signify the importance of human life by requiring donation of unwanted embryos would not constitute the compelling interest necessary to justify infringement of a fundamental right to avoid reproduction.

A counterargument to this position is that the Supreme Court is unlikely to recognize the right to avoid biologic offspring *tout court* as a fundamental right, and therefore the state's interest in protecting prenatal life provides a rational basis for embryo protection laws. *Griswold, Roe,* and *Casey* establish a right to avoid reproduction when reproduction is necessarily coupled with gestation or rearing burdens. Laws that mandate embryo donation impose only the psychological burden of having unknown biologic offspring. Such a purely psychosocial interest is not likely to be granted fundamental right status as part of the right to avoid reproduction. In that case a state concerned with protecting prenatal life would easily satisfy the rational basis test by which such a statute would be judged. The reaffirmation of *Roe v. Wade* in *Casey* does not lessen the state's power to protect extracorporeal embryos, because the right of women to end pregnancy is not at issue.

One could also argue that bans on embryo discard interfere with the right to procreate. By limiting the number of eggs that can be fertilized or requiring that extra embryos be donated, such policies will deter couples from using IVF to treat infertility, thus infringing their right to use noncoital means of procreation. The validity of this argument rests on the degree of deterrence that such policies entail. It is possible that this policy would not "unduly burden" efforts to treat infertility. After all, the couple may still undergo IVF. They just are limited in the number of eggs they can inseminate, or must accept anonymous donation of extras to others. If deemed unlikely to deter resort to IVF, embryo protection policies would not violate the freedom to procreate.

Resolving the question of embryo discard requires coming to terms with two very different value questions. One is the importance of the genetic tie *tout court*—an issue never previously faced in this way. The other is the detriment to values of respect for human life that flow from embryo discard. While the view of many people would be that embryos are too rudimentary to make embryo discard very costly in symbolic terms, some persons—and IVF programs—will hold different views. The values that people hold about these two aspects of reproduction will determine what policies ultimately control embryo discard.

Embryo Freezing. Cryopreservation or embryo freezing is a rapidly growing aspect of IVF practice. In 1990 there were 23,865 embryos frozen as a result of the

IVF process, an increase of 14,657 over the number reported in 1988.[31] In addition, 3,290 frozen embryos were thawed and placed in a uterus, a 70 percent increase over 1988, resulting in 382 pregnancies and 291 live births. The frozen embryo cycles involved more than 129 clinics, with 19 clinics performing fifty or more transfer cycles.

Embryo freezing is growing in popularity for several reasons. It could increase the efficacy of IVF by making use of all retrieved eggs. By eliminating the need for additional stimulation and egg retrieval cycles, it reduces the physical and financial costs of later IVF cycles. It also reduces the chance that surplus embryos (those that cannot be safely implanted in the uterus) will be destroyed. Yet many aspects of embryo freezing are controversial and are likely to generate proposals to limit the practice.

Harm to Embryos. Persons opposed to embryo discard also object to embryo freezing on the ground that the freeze-thaw process harms or destroys embryos by damaging particular blastomeres or cells that render the embryo unable to divide further. It is true that frozen-thawed embryos divide and start pregnancies at a lesser rate than do fresh embryos, and that freezing does damage some blastomeres. It is not clear, however, whether the damaged embryos are viable, and thus would have successfully implanted if freezing had not occurred.

A ban on embryo freezing would actually reduce the number of embryos in existence. Rather than risk the possibility of multiple gestation (and the chance of selective reduction of the pregnancy), fewer embryos would be created, since all embryos would have to be placed in the uterus. This reduction might also lead to fewer IVF pregnancies, because one cannot always guarantee that fertilizing three or four eggs will yield three or four viable embryos (the optimal number of embryos to transfer).

Reasonable people, however, could find that embryo freezing is sufficiently respectful of prenatal human life that it should be permitted as an option for infertile couples trying to become pregnant through IVF. Fewer embryos are destroyed than by outright discard. Moreover, it leads to the creation of embryos that would never have existed if freezing were not available. Even if some embryos are harmed by the freezing process, the total number of embryos available for implantation has increased. Even if discard were prohibited, freezing seems more protective than destructive of

embryos and should be permitted as part of procreative choice in the IVF process.

Length of Storage. For most infertile couples embryo storage will be temporary, with most frozen embryos thawed within six to eighteen months in efforts to start pregnancy. Technically, however, there may be no outer limit on the length of time that embryos could be frozen before they are thawed and implanted in a uterus. Inevitably, some embryos will end up being frozen for years, as plans change or other factors intervene. An important question for IVF programs and public policy is whether the length of storage should be limited.

Proposals for such limits vary, from set terms such as five to ten years to the reproductive life of the woman providing the egg. Time limits are thought to be easier to administer and more desirable, because it will prevent children from being born to women who are much older.[32] It will also prevent simultaneously conceived siblings from being born years apart.

As a matter of public policy, such considerations are not sufficient to justify time limits on embryo freezing. None of them pose such dangers to offspring — who might not otherwise be born — that the wishes of couples to freeze for longer periods should be infringed. IVF programs should assess more carefully the purposes of time limits on storage, and not impose them unless clearly necessary. If programs adopt such policies, they should clearly inform couples in advance and permit them to remove frozen embryos to other facilities when the period elapses.

Posthumous Implantation. Embryo freezing also makes possible the posthumous implantation and birth of children conceived before death occurs. While such cases will not be frequent, situations will arise in which the husband or wife dies before previously frozen embryos are thawed and implanted. A surviving wife may request that "her" embryos be implanted in her, so that she may reproduce the "child" that she and her now dead husband created. A surviving husband might wish [that] the thawed embryos be placed in a new partner or in a host uterus engaged for that purpose.

Respect for the procreative liberty of the surviving spouse should permit posthumous thawing and implantation to occur. The survivor has a real interest in procreating, which the frozen embryo serves well. The fear that the child will have only one parent is not sufficient to override the spouse's procreative liberty. Many children thrive with single parents, especially if they have the resources and support to parent, and births to women pregnant at the time of their husband's death occasionally occur. A law that prohibited posthumous implantation would infringe the survivor's procreative liberty, and is unnecessary. IVF programs should not set such a restriction.

The question is somewhat different if both husband and wife die while the embryos are frozen. If the couple has directed that any frozen embryos be donated for implantation, their wishes should be respected. On the other hand, if they directed or accepted the program's condition that remaining embryos would be discarded, that too may be honored. However, a state law that required all frozen embryos remaining at time of death of both to be implanted would probably not violate the procreative rights of the couple, since the prospect of posthumous donation is unlikely to influence their reproductive decision making.[33]

• • •

Resolving Disputes over Frozen Embryos. The practice of freezing embryos will also raise questions about embryo disposition when the couple divorces, dies, is unavailable, is unable to agree, or is in arrears in paying storage charges. As noted earlier, the best way to handle these questions is by dispositional agreements made at the time of creation or cryopreservation of embryos. Such agreements should be binding on the parties, and enforced even if their circumstances or desires change. IVF programs that have reasonable grounds for thinking that the agreements were freely and knowingly made should be free to rely on them, without more. This is the best policy to give all parties some control of the process, as well as reliable advance certainty about future outcomes. It also will reduce the administrative costs and difficulty of resolving any disputes that arise.

The advantage of relying on prior dispositional agreements to resolve disputes over frozen embryos is illustrated by the widely publicized 1989 Tennessee divorce case of *Davis v. Davis* concerning disposition of seven frozen embryos. The couple had made no prior agreement for embryo disposition in case of divorce or disagreement. At the time of divorce, the wife insisted that the embryos be available to her for thawing and placement in her uterus or donation to another couple. The husband objected to the idea of children from a marriage that had failed. The trial judge awarded "custody" of the embryos to the wife, on the ground that the embryos were "children" whose best interests required the chance to implant and come to term.

A Tennessee intermediate appellate court reversed the trial court decision, requiring that any disposition of the embryos be jointly agreed to by the husband and wife. The Tennessee Supreme Court affirmed this decision on somewhat different grounds.[34] It upheld advance agreements for disposition in the case of divorce or disagreement, but rejected the notion that the freezing of embryos alone constituted an agreement to later implantation. It also recognized that a right to "procreational autonomy" existed under both the United States and Tennessee constitutions that outweighed the state's "at best slight" interest in "the potential life embodied by these four- to eight-cell preembryos."[35]

In this case, however, the choice of the husband not to procreate conflicted with the wife's desire to use the embryos to procreate. To resolve that conflict, the Court compared the relative burdens and concluded that the burdens of unwanted reproduction to the husband, even if genetic only, outweighed the burden to the wife of not having the embryos donated to another couple, as she now desired. Even if she had wanted them for herself, her claim to have them would be strong only if she had no way to achieve parenthood by other reasonable means. If she could go through another IVF cycle without excessive burdens to her, her interest in procreating with the disputed embryos should not take precedence over the husband's wishes to avoid unwanted reproduction.

The Tennessee Supreme Court's decision is eminently sound and will be a major precedent for the conduct of IVF and the resolution of disputes about frozen embryos for years to come. It nicely illustrates the advantages of relying on a prior agreement in these cases, rather than having to balance the procreative interests anew in lengthy and expensive litigation.[36]

• • •

CONSUMER PROTECTION ISSUES

Questions about the control and disposition of embryos have attracted much attention, but questions of safety, efficacy, and access raise equally important policy issues. For most couples, the most important question concerning IVF is whether it will work. The ethical niceties of control over embryos may be much less important.

Unfortunately, IVF does not work nearly as often as people would like. In the very best programs, pregnancy and take-home baby rates are around 20 percent of IVF egg retrieval cycles, which means that fewer than one in ten IVF-created embryos implant and come to term. Only ten to twenty programs achieve this level of success. Many other programs have much weaker records, and many have very few pregnancies at all. One survey in 1987 found that over half of the then existing American IVF programs had never produced a live birth. Other programs have misstated their success rates to consumers and been the subject of Federal Trade Commission charges of misleading advertising.[37]

The reasons for this relatively poor track record are several. The whole process of IVF is extremely complicated with many unknowns. What eggs best fertilize, what culture medium to use for embryos, when to transfer, what instruments to use, and many other questions will determine the outcome of IVF. Also crucial is the skill and experience of the physicians involved, the reliability of their laboratories, and the age and condition of patients. It is no accident that the biggest and most experienced programs consistently have the highest success rates.

The efficacy situation raises three important policy issues for protecting consumers. One concerns the need to support and fund research to improve success rates. Because of pro-life opposition, the federal government funded no IVF research during the twelve years of the Reagan-Bush administrations. Under the Clinton administration, federal funding of IVF research will now occur, though the amount of funding will have to compete with the many other demands for the federal health research dollar.

A second policy issue is the need to make infertile couples more aware of the varying success rates of IVF programs, so that they can make informed choices about whether and where to seek IVF. Complaints from unhappy consumers about misleading claims by IVF clinics led Congressman Ron Wyden (D-Oregon) to conduct hearings and seek legislation that requires that IVF success rates be uniformly kept and accurately disclosed. Uniform reporting and disclosure will prevent infertile couples from being misled by claims of success rates overall vs. success of the particular clinic, or claims that successful fertilization and even clinical pregnancy is the equivalent of a live-born child, the bottom line issue of interest to patients. Prodded by Congressman Wyden's interest, the American Fertility Society and the Society for Assisted Reproductive Technology began to collect and publish overall and clinic specific data about IVF, GIFT, and ZIFT success rates. The Fertility Clinic Success Rate and Certification Act of 1992 now requires that each IVF program report annually to the Centers for Disease Control their pregnancy success rates as defined in the act.[38]

A third policy issue is the need for oversight of the laboratory settings in which IVF programs handle human oocytes, sperm, and embryos. Laboratories vary widely in the quality and replicability of their procedures, and are thought to be an important factor in the wide variance in IVF success rates. The Fertility Clinic Success Rate and Certification Act of 1992 directs the Secretary of Health and Human Services to develop a model program for the certification of embryo laboratories. This program will be made available to states that wish to adopt it. The act also provides for states to have private accrediting bodies such as the College of American Pathology and the American Fertility Society, which have adopted a joint inspection program, conduct the certification. Greater attention to laboratory conditions and practices should improve the efficacy of IVF.

Questions of IVF efficacy and consumer awareness show that IVF, while a novel reproductive procedure, also presents policy problems typical of most new medical technologies. Medical zeal and interest in self-promotion may mislead patients about its efficacy, and induce women to undergo expensive, invasive procedures that may have less chance of helping them than they thought. A 1992 proposed public offering of stock in IVF America, a chain of IVF clinics that planned to expand across the country, revealed the importance of the profit motive in providing IVF services and the need for ongoing monitoring of the industry.[39] Laboratory certification and accurate disclosure of success rates relative to other clinics is an appropriate policy response to protect the procreative freedom of infertile couples. However, it is they who will have to decide whether the risks and benefits of the procedure are worth it.

FUNDING AND ACCESS ISSUES

Another important policy issue with IVF and other reproductive technologies is cost and access. IVF costs

$5,000 to $7,000 per cycle and is often ineffective, with two or three cycles necessary to achieve pregnancy when it is successful. Insurance may pay none or only some of the costs, making IVF a procedure that only wealthier couples can afford. Indeed, the cost may be prohibitive for many middle-class couples.

The high cost of IVF raises questions of access and justice in allocation of health care resources. Given the high rate of infertility, its impact on couples, and insurance coverage of many kinds of infertility treatment, there is a reasonable case for including IVF in private or public health insurance plans. Ten states have laws that require insurance coverage of infertility services. Five of these states (Arkansas, Hawaii, Massachusetts, Maryland, and Texas) currently require health insurers to include IVF as an option.[40] Courts have also ruled that insurance plans that cover surgical repair of blocked fallopian tubes as treatment for an "existing physical or mental illness" must also cover IVF, though other courts have found that IVF is not a medically necessary treatment for illness.[41]

While insurance coverage will increase access to IVF, it also increases the cost of insurance for all policyholders. Depending on the size of the pool, however, this subsidy may not be unfair. Infertility may reasonably be viewed, because of its frequency, expense, and personal importance, as one of the health risks for which people should be insured. Spread over a large group, the cost of IVF coverage is relatively small. It should not be singled out for exclusion if other infertility services are covered.

On the other hand, a policy that covered no infertility services or which excluded IVF and other high-tech procedures might not be unreasonable. At a time of great strain in the health care system, limiting coverage for procedures based on judgments about their cost, efficacy, and benefits to patients is also reasonable. If choices have to be made, people might well prefer coverage for catastrophic or life-threatening illness and preventive services rather than for infertility.

Such a judgment would support exclusion of IVF (and other fertility treatments) from public insurance programs such as Medicaid as well. Despite stereotypes of unrestrained reproduction, the poor actually have higher rates of infertility due to poverty, nutrition, and more infectious disease than does the middle class. If infertility is considered an "illness" for which "med-

ical treatment" is available, existing law would require that Medicaid cover IVF and other infertility treatments.

Yet many people would object to spending increasingly scarce Medicaid funds on IVF when life-threatening illnesses are not adequately covered. It is not surprising that the Oregon health care plan for rationing medical resources for Medicaid patients ranked infertility treatment near the bottom.[42] Such a ranking does deny the poor infertility services available to those who have the means to pay directly. Yet if differences between public and private funding of health care are to exist, one may reasonably conclude that infertility is one place to draw the line. Such a judgment illustrates the limitations of procreative liberty as a negative right that does not entitle people to government resources to fulfill their reproductive goals.

A final issue of access is the control that IVF programs exercise over who receives their services. Many IVF programs will not treat unmarried persons. Nearly all will test couples for HIV, and may refuse the procedure if one or both of the partners test positive.[43] Some may exclude couples whom they think are unstable or unfit parents. The exclusion is usually justified on the "ethical" ground of protecting offspring who would be born in disadvantageous circumstances. However, providing IVF services to these groups would not harm children who have no other way to be born, and thus may ethically be provided if a program is so inclined.[44] Because private IVF clinics have wide discretion in selecting patients for treatment, they may in most circumstances be legally free to set the criteria for selecting patients.

CONCLUSION

This account of IVF shows how different strands of procreative liberty and different views about the status of preimplantation embryos are entwined in the use of this technology. Restriction of IVF to protect embryos will, in most cases, interfere with an infertile couple's interest in procreating and may affect other reproductive interests.

Resolution of the ethical, legal, and policy conflicts that arise in IVF depends, for the most part, on determining the relative importance of these reproductive interests vs. the perceived threat to embryos and respect for prenatal life. The widely held view that the preimplantation embryo is not a person but deserves special respect would resolve most of these conflicts in favor of the infertile couple. However, a more protective view of embryo status would not necessarily exclude central aspects of IVF practice, including embryo freezing, even though it prevents embryo discard from occurring.[45]

A final point to note is how issues of efficacy and access turn out to be as important to IVF as issues of embryo status. The legal right to use IVF is embedded in a set of socioeconomic and structural circumstances that affect exercise of the right. Socially constructed attitudes about the need to overcome infertility will be a main determinant of use. Money also counts when one is seeking access to IVF. IVF shows that procreative liberty is not a fully meaningful concept unless one has the knowledge and means to obtain IVF from the best programs, or the will to resist its allure when its use seems excessive.

NOTES

1. The focus is on married couples because most women seeking IVF are married, and most IVF programs treat only married couples. Whether the state could prohibit single persons access to IVF is discussed later in the chapter.

2. Medical Research International, Society for Assisted Reproduction, the American Fertility Society, "In Vitro Fertilization-Embryo Transfer (IVF-ET) in the United States: 1990 Results from the IVF-ET Registry," *Fertility and Sterility* 57(1992):15. This study reports 2,345 deliveries from IVF in 1990. By extrapolation the number of births for the last four years is over eight thousand.

3. Success here is measured by take-home baby rate per stimulation or egg retrieval cycle, and not clinical pregnancy rate, which many programs use to improve their statistics.

4. Eventually egg retrieval will occur in the physician's office, which will reduce the costs of the procedure. Retrieving eggs during a natural cycle without stimulation will also reduce costs, though it may also reduce efficacy.

5. Elizabeth Bartholet vividly expresses concerns about infertile women feeling compelled by their own sense of inadequacy to try IVF and to keep trying because there "is often no logical stopping point." *Family Bonds: Adoption and the Politics of Parenting* (Boston: Houghton Mifflin, 1993), 202.

6. Catholic Church, Congregation for the Doctrine of the Faith, "Instruction on Respect for Human Life in Its Origin and on the Dignity of Procreation," *Origins* 16(1987):698–711.

7. 1990 Results from the IVF-ET Registry, note [2] supra at pp. 16–19.

8. See chapter 2 [not reprinted], where the argument for infertile married couples having the same right to reproduce that fertile married couples have is developed.

9. For the sake of convenience, the term "embryo" is used throughout this [essay] rather than the technically more accurate "preembryo." Embryo thus refers to all postfertilization, preimplantation stages of development.

10. Grobstein, "The Early Development of Human Embryos," *Journal of Medicine and Philosophy* 10(1985):213, 214. Much of the ensuing description is based on Grobstein's excellent survey of early human and mammalian development.

11. However, the fertilized egg is not yet individual, as only at implantation can a single new individual be identified. Also, recent studies suggest that a new genome is not expressed until the four- to eight-cell stage of development. See Braude, Bolton, and Moore, "Human Gene Expression First Occurs between the Four- and Eight-Cell Stages of Preimplantation Development," *Nature* 332(1988): 459, 460.

12. Grobstein, "Early Development," 216–17.

13. Ibid., 219, 232.

14. Ibid., 219–20

15. Ibid., 223.

16. Ibid.

17. Ibid., 223–25.

18. This view parallels the view described in chapter 3 [not reprinted] of respecting fetuses because of their symbolic value. Although not persons or entities which themselves have rights, embryos are potent symbols of human life and deserve some degree of respect on that basis alone.

19. Department of Health and Human Services, the Ethical Advisory Board in the United States, U.S. Department of Health, Education and Welfare, Ethics Advisory Board, HEW Support of Research Involving Human In Vitro Fertilization and Embryo Transfer, 44 Fed.Reg. 35033 (1979).

20. The Warnock Committee Report in Great Britain, United Kingdom, Department of Health and Social Security, Report of the Committee of Inquiring into Human Fertilisation and Embryology (1984).

21. Ontario Law Reform Commission, Report on Human Artificial Reproduction and Related Matters (1985).

22. *Davis v. Davis,* 842 S.W.2d 588 (Tenn. 1992). In reaching that conclusion, the Court relied heavily on the American Fertility Society's report "Ethical Considerations of the New Reproductive Technologies," which articulated a view similar to that set forth in the text. *Fertility and Sterility* 46, (supp. 1) (1986):295–305.

23. "Who or What is a Preembryo?" *Kennedy Institute of Ethics Journal* 1(1991):1–15.

24. John A. Robertson, "In the Beginning: The Legal Status of Early Embryos," *Virginia Law Review* 76(1990):437, 452.

25. It follows then that an IVF program must have the consent of both partners before thawing, transferring, implanting, discarding, or donating embryos.

26. Elizabeth Rosenthal, "Cost of High-Tech Fertility: Too Many Tiny Babies," *New York Times,* 26 May 1992, discusses some of the problems of the higher rate of multigestational pregnancies that occurs when more than two embryos are placed in a woman's uterus. See also chapter 9 [not reprinted], where selective reduction of multifetal pregnancies is discussed.

27. See note 22.

28. Some programs will not permit discard of fresh embryos, but will allow embryos that have been frozen for a period of time to be discarded.

29. Although the issue raises questions of the couple's right to avoid genetic reproduction, the embryo discard policy might also influence their willingness to use IVF in the first place, thus implicating their right to reproduce as well.

30. *Roe v. Wade,* 410 U.S. 113 (1973); *Planned Parenthood v. Casey,* 112 S.Ct. 2791 (1992).

31. Medical Research International, 15, 21. [See note 2.]

32. Of course, it would not harm children to be born to older mothers, even if younger mothers are more desirable rearers of offspring,

if the children in question had no alternative way of being born. See chapters 4 and 8 [not reprinted].

33. For further discussion of this issue, see J. Robertson, "Posthumous Reproduction," *Indiana Law Journal* (forthcoming, 1994).

34. 842 S.W.2d 588 (Tenn. 1992).

35. "When weighed against the interests of the individuals and the burdens inherent in parenthood, the state's interest in the potential life of these preembryos is not sufficient to justify any infringement upon the freedom of these individuals to make their own decisions as to whether to allow a process to continue that may result in such a dramatic change in their lives as becoming parents." *Davis v. Davis,* 842 S.W.2d 588, 602–03 (Tenn. 1992).

36. In cases where there is no prior agreement on disposition, the courts should, as the Tennessee court recommended, resolve such disputes according to whether the party wishing to preserve the embryos has a realistic possibility of achieving his or her reproductive goals by other means. If there are no alternative opportunities to reproduce, or if going through IVF again would be unduly burdensome, it may be fairer to award the embryos to the party for whom they represent the last chance to have offspring, as might occur if the wife has lost ovarian function since the embryos were preserved. In that case, the unconsenting party should also be relieved of child support obligations. In most cases, however, the party wishing the embryos to be destroyed should prevail. See Robertson, "Resolving Disputes over Frozen Embryos," *Hastings Center Report,* November/December 1989; Robertson, "In the Beginning," 473–83.

37. Robert Pear, "Fertility Clinics Face Crackdown, *New York Times,* 26 October 1992.

38. Public Law 102-493 (H.R.4773), 24 October 1992. The act calls for reporting of the live birth rate for IVF and other assisted reproductive techniques, defined as the ratio of live births divided (1) by the number of ovarian stimulation procedures attempted at each program, and (2) by the number of successful oocyte retrieval procedures performed by each program. Section 2(b)(2)(A) and (B). Virginia now also requires clinic-specific disclosure of success rates to patients before IVF treatments occur. Va. Code Ann. Sec. 54.1-2971.1 (Michie 1991).

39. Alison Leigh Cowan, "Can a Baby-Making Venture Deliver?" *New York Times,* 1 June 1992. However, the public offering was never made.

40. Ark. Code Ann. Sec. 23-85-137 (Michie 1992); Haw. Rev. Stat. Ann. Sec. 431:10A-116.5 (1992); Md. Ann. Code art. 48A, Sec. 354DD (1992); Tex. Ins. Code Ann. art. 3.51-6, Sec. 3A (West 1993).

41. *Egert v. Connecticut General Life Ins. Co.,* 900 F.2d 1032 (7th Cir.)(infertility an illness and IVF necessary to treat it); *Kinzie v. Physician's Liability Insur. Co.,* 750 P. 2d 1140 (Okl. App. 1987) (IVF not a medically necessary procedure under the insurance contract).

42. David C. Hadorn, "Setting Health Care Priorities in Oregon: Cost Effectiveness Meets the Rule of Rescue," *Journal of the American Medical Association* 265(1991):2218.

43. Such discrimination against persons with HIV may be a violation of the Americans with Disabilities Act, because HIV status qualifies as a disability within the meaning of that law and an infertility clinic may be considered a place of public accommodation. 42 U.S.C. 12182 (1990).

44. The patient groups in question may have a right against a state that denies them access to IVF or other reproductive services, but they would not have the same right to services from private actors unless civil rights or antidiscrimination laws apply. See chapters 2 and 4 [not reprinted].

45. Persons who view the fertilized egg and embryo as persons from the time of fertilization may differ over the extent to which IVF should be permitted at all. Some may permit it with no freezing, or with freezing but no embryo discard.

S U S A N   S H E R W I N

Feminist Ethics and In Vitro Fertilization[1]

New technology in human reproduction has provoked wide ranging arguments about the desirability and moral justifiability of many of these efforts. Authors of biomedical ethics have ventured into the field to offer the insight of moral theory to these complex moral problems of contemporary life. I believe, however, that the moral theories most widely endorsed today are problematic and that a new approach to ethics is necessary if we are to address the concerns and perspectives identified by feminist theorists in our considerations of such topics. Hence, I propose to look at one particular technique in the growing repertoire of new reproductive technologies, in vitro fertilization (IVF), in order to consider the insight which the mainstream approaches to moral theory have offered to this debate, and to see the difference made by a feminist approach to ethics.

From Marsha Hanen and Kai Nielsen, eds., *Science, Morality and Feminist Theory* (Calgary, Alberta: University of Calgary Press, 1987), pp. 265–84. Reprinted by permission of the author and the University of Calgary Press.

I have argued elsewhere that the most widely accepted moral theories of our time are inadequate for addressing many of the moral issues we encounter in our lives, since they focus entirely on such abstract qualities of moral agents as autonomy or quantities of happiness, and they are addressed to agents who are conceived of as independent, non-tuistic individuals. In contrast, I claimed, we need a theory which places the locus of ethical concerns in a complex social network of interrelated persons who are involved in special sorts of relations with one another. Such a theory, as I envision it, would be influenced by the insights and concerns of feminist theory, and hence, I have called it feminist ethics.[2]

In this [essay], I propose to explore the differences between a feminist approach to ethics and other, more traditional approaches in examining the propriety of developing and implementing in vitro fertilization and related technologies. This is a complicated task, since each sort of ethical theory admits of a variety of interpretations and hence of a variety of conclusions on concrete ethical issues. Nonetheless, certain themes and trends can be seen to emerge. Feminist thinking is also ambivalent in application, for feminists are quite torn about their response to this sort of technology. It is my hope that a systematic theoretic evaluation of IVF from the point of view of a feminist ethical theory will help feminists like myself sort through our uncertainty on these matters.

Let me begin with a quick description of IVF for the uninitiated. In vitro fertilization is the technology responsible for what the media likes to call 'test tube babies.' It circumvents, rather than cures, a variety of barriers to conception, primarily those of blocked fallopian tubes and low sperm counts. In vitro fertilization involves removing ova from the woman's body, collecting sperm from the man's, combining them to achieve conception in the laboratory, and, a few days later, implanting some number of the newly fertilized eggs directly into the woman's womb with the hope that pregnancy will continue normally from this point on. This process requires that a variety of hormones be administered to the woman — which involve profound emotional and physical changes — that her blood and urine be monitored daily, and then at 3 hour intervals, [and] that ultrasound be used to determine when ovulation occurs. In some clinics, implantation requires that she remain immobile for 48 hours (including 24 hours in the head down position). IVF is successful in about 10–15% of the cases selected as suitable, and commonly involves multiple efforts at implantation.

Let us turn now to the responses that philosophers working within the traditional approaches to ethics have offered on this subject. A review of the literature in bioethics identifies a variety of concerns with this technology. Philosophers who adopt a theological perspective tend to object that such technology is wrong because it is not 'natural' and undermines God's plan for the family. Paul Ramsey, for instance, is concerned about the artificiality of IVF and other sorts of reproductive technology with which it is potentially associated, e.g. embryo transfer, ova as well as sperm donation or sale, increased eugenic control, etc.:

> But there is as yet no discernible evidence that we are recovering a sense for man [sic] as a natural object . . . toward whom a . . . form of "natural piety" is appropriate . . . parenthood is certainly one of those "courses of action" natural to man, which cannot without violation be disassembled and put together again.[3]

Leon Kass argues a similar line in '"Making Babies" Revisited.'[4] He worries that our conception of humanness will not survive the technological permutations before us, and that we will treat these new artificially conceived embryos more as objects than as subjects; he also fears that we will be unable to track traditional human categories of parenthood and lineage, and that this loss would cause us to lose track of important aspects of our identity. The recent position paper of the Catholic Church on reproductive technology reflects related concerns:

> It is through the secure and recognized relationship to his [sic] own parents that the child can discover his own identity and achieve his own proper human development . . .
> Heterologous artificial fertilization violates the rights of the child; it deprives him of his filial relationship with his parental origins and can hinder the maturing of his personal identity.[5]

Philosophers partial to utilitarianism prefer a more scientific approach; they treat these sorts of concerns as sheer superstition. They carefully explain to their theological colleagues that there is no clear sense of 'natural' and certainly no sense that demands special moral status. All medical activity, and perhaps all human activity, can be seen in some sense as being 'interference with nature,' but that is hardly grounds for avoiding such action. 'Humanness,' too, is a concept that admits of many interpretations; generally, it does not provide satisfactory grounds for moral distinctions. Further, it is no longer thought appropriate to focus too strictly on questions of lineage and strict biological parentage, and, they note, most theories of personal identity do not rely on such matters.

Where some theologians object that 'fertilization achieved outside the bodies of the couple remains by this very fact deprived of the meanings of the values which are expressed in the language of the body and the union of human persons,'[6] utilitarians quickly dismiss the objection against reproduction without sexuality in a properly sanctified marriage. See, for instance, Michael Bayles in *Reproductive Ethics:* '. . . even if reproduction should occur only within a context of marital love, the point of that requirement is the nurturance of offspring. Such nurturance does not depend on the sexual act itself. The argument confuses the biological act with the familial context.'[7]

Another area of disagreement between theological ethicists and their philosophical critics is the significance of the wedge argument to the debate about IVF. IVF is already a complex technology involving research on superovulation, 'harvesting' of ova, fertilization, and embryo implants. It is readily adaptable to technology involving the transfer of ova and embryos, and hence their donation or sale, as well as to the 'rental of womb space'; it also contributes to an increasing ability to foster fetal growth outside of the womb and, potentially, to the development of artificial wombs covering the whole period of gestation. It is already sometimes combined with artificial insemination and is frequently used to produce surplus fertilized eggs to be frozen for later use. Theological ethicists worry that such activity, and further reproductive developments we can anticipate (such as human cloning), violate God's plan for human reproduction. They worry about the cultural shift involved in viewing reproduction as a scientific enterprise, rather than the 'miracle of love' which religious proponents prefer: '[He] cannot be desired or conceived as the product of an intervention of medical or biological techniques; that would be equivalent to reducing him to an object of scientific technology.'[8] And, worse, they note, we cannot anticipate the ultimate outcome of this rapidly expanding technology.

The where-will-it-all-end hand-wringing that comes with this sort of religious futurology is rejected by most analytical philosophers; they urge us to realize that few slopes are as slippery as the pessimists would have us believe, that scientists are moral people and quite capable of evaluating each new form of technology on its own merits, and that IVF must be judged by its own consequences and not the possible result of some future technology with which it may be linked. Samuel Gorovitz is typical:

It is not enough to show that disaster awaits if the process is not controlled. A man walking East in Omaha will drown in the Atlantic — if he does not stop. The argument must also rest on the evidence about the likelihood that judgment and control will be exercised responsibly . . . Collectively we have significant capacity to exercise judgment and control . . . our record has been rather good in regard to medical treatment and research.[9]

The question of the moral status of the fertilized eggs is more controversial. Since the superovulation involved in producing eggs for collection tends to produce several at once, and the process of collecting eggs is so difficult, and since the odds against conception on any given attempt are so slim, several eggs are usually collected and fertilized at once. A number of these fertilized eggs will be introduced to the womb with the hope that at least one will implant and gestation will begin, but there are frequently some 'extras.' Moral problems arise as to what should be done with these surplus eggs. They can be frozen for future use (since odds are against the first attempt 'taking'), or they can be used as research material, or simply discarded. Canadian clinics get around the awkwardness of their ambivalence on the moral status of these cells by putting them all into the woman's womb. This poses the devastating threat of six or eight 'successfully' implanting, and a woman being put into the position of carrying a litter; something, we might note, her body is not constructed to do.

Those who take a hard line against abortion and argue that the embryo is a person from the moment of conception object to all these procedures, and, hence, they argue, there is no morally acceptable means of conducting IVF. To this line, utilitarians offer the standard responses. Personhood involves moral, not biological categories. A being neither sentient nor conscious is not a person in any meaningful sense. For example, Gorovitz argues, 'Surely the concept of person involves in some fundamental way the capacity for sentience, or an awareness of sensations at the very least.'[10] Bayles says, 'For fetuses to have moral status they must be capable of good or bad in their lives . . . What happens to them must make a difference to them. Consequently some form of awareness is necessary for moral status.'[11] (Apparently, clinicians in the field have been trying to avoid this whole issue by coining a new term in the hopes of identifying a new ontological category, that of the 'pre-embryo.')[12]

Many bioethicists have agreed here, as they have in the abortion debate, that the principal moral question of IVF is the moral status and rights of the embryo. Once they resolve that question, they can, like Engelhardt, conclude that since fetuses are not persons, and since reproductive processes occurring outside a human body pose no special moral problems, 'there will be no sustainable moral arguments in principle . . . against in vitro fertilization.'[13] He argues,

in vitro fertilization and techniques that will allow us to study and control human reproduction are morally neutral instruments for the realization of profoundly important human goals, which are bound up with the realization of the good of others: children for infertile parents and greater health for the children that will be born.[14]

Moral theorists also express worries about the safety of the process, and by that they tend to mean the safety to fetuses that may result from this technique. Those fears have largely been put to rest in the years since the first IVF baby was born in 1978, for the couple of thousand infants reportedly produced by this technique to date seem no more prone to apparent birth defects than the population at large, and, in fact, there seems to be evidence that birth defects may be less common in this group — presumably because of better monitoring and pre and post natal care. (There is concern expressed, however, in some circles outside of the bioethical literature about the longterm effect of some of the hormones involved, in light of our belated discoveries of the effect of DES usage on offspring. This concern is aggravated by the chemical similarity of clomid, one of the hormones used in IVF, to DES.)[15]

Most of the literature tends to omit comment on the uncertainties associated with the effect of drugs inducing superovulation in the woman concerned, or with the dangers posed by the general anaesthetic required for the laparoscopy procedure; the emotional costs associated with this therapy are also overlooked, even though there is evidence that it is extremely stressful in the 85–90% of the attempts that fail, and that those

who succeed have difficulty in dealing with common parental feelings of anger and frustration with a child they tried so hard to get. Nonetheless, utilitarian theory could readily accommodate such concerns, should the philosophers involved think to look for them. In principle, no new moral theory is yet called for, although a widening of perspective (to include the effects on the women involved) would certainly be appropriate.

The easiest solution to the IVF question seems to be available to ethicists of a deontological orientation who are keen on autonomy and rights and free of religious prejudice. For them, IVF is simply a private matter, to be decided by the couple concerned together with a medical specialist. The desire to have and raise children is a very common one and generally thought to be a paradigm case of a purely private matter. Couples seeking this technology face medical complications that require the assistance of a third party, and it is thought, 'it would be unfair to make infertile couples pass up the joys of rearing infants or suffer the burdens of rearing handicapped children.'[16] Certainly, meeting individuals' desires/needs is the most widely accepted argument in favour of the use of this technology.

What is left, then, in the more traditional ethical discussions, is usually some hand waving about costs. This is an extremely expensive procedure; estimates range from $1500 to $6000 per attempt. Gorovitz says, for instance, 'there is the question of the distribution of costs, a question that has heightened impact if we consider the use of public funds to pay for medical treatment.'[17] Debate tends to end here in the mystery of how to balance soaring medical costs of various sorts and a comment that no new ethical problems are posed.

Feminists share many of these concerns, but they find many other moral issues involved in the development and use of such technology and note the silence of the standard moral approaches in addressing these matters. Further, feminism does not identify the issues just cited as the primary areas of moral concern. Nonetheless, IVF is a difficult issue for feminists.

On the one hand, most feminists share the concern for autonomy held by most moral theorists, and they are interested in allowing women freedom of choice in reproductive matters. This freedom is most widely discussed in connection with access to safe and effective contraception and, when necessary, to abortion services. For women who are unable to conceive because of blocked fallopian tubes, or certain fertility problems of their partners, IVF provides the technology to permit pregnancy which is otherwise impossible. Certainly most of the women seeking IVF perceive it to be technology that increases their reproductive freedom of choice. So, it would seem that feminists should support this sort of technology as part of our general concern to foster the degree of reproductive control women may have over their own bodies. Some feminists have chosen this route. But feminists must also note that IVF as practiced does not altogether satisfy the motivation of fostering individual autonomy.

It is, after all, the sort of technology that requires medical intervention, and hence it is not really controlled by the women seeking it, but rather by the medical staff providing this 'service.' IVF is not available to every woman who is medically suitable, but only to those who are judged to be worthy by the medical specialists concerned. To be a candidate for this procedure, a woman must have a husband and an apparently stable marriage. She must satisfy those specialists that she and her husband have appropriate resources to support any children produced by this arrangement (in addition, of course, to the funds required to purchase the treatment in the first place), and that they generally 'deserve' this support. IVF is not available to single women, lesbian women, or women not securely placed in the middle class or beyond. Nor is it available to women whom the controlling medical practitioners judge to be deviant with respect to their norms of who makes a good mother. The supposed freedom of choice, then, is provided only to selected women who have been screened by the personal values of those administering the technology.

Further, even for these women, the record on their degree of choice is unclear. Consider, for instance, that this treatment has always been very experimental: it was introduced without the prior primate studies which are required for most new forms of medical technology, and it continues to be carried out under constantly shifting protocols, with little empirical testing, as clinics try to raise their very poor success rates. Moreover, consent forms are perceived by patients to be quite restrictive procedures and women seeking this technology are not in a particularly strong position to bargain to revise the terms; there is no alternate clinic down the street to choose if a women dislikes her treatment at some clinic, but there are usually many other women waiting for access to her place in the clinic should she choose to withdraw.

Some recent studies indicate that few of the women participating in current programs really know how low the success rates are.[18] And it is not apparent that participants are encouraged to ponder the medical unknowns associated with various aspects of the technique, such as the long term consequences of superovulation and the use of hormones chemically similar to DES. Nor is it the case that the consent procedure involves consultation on how to handle the disposal of 'surplus' zygotes. It is doubtful that the women concerned have much real choice about which procedure is followed with the eggs they will not need. These policy decisions are usually made at the level of the clinic. It should be noted here that at least one feminist argues that neither the woman, nor the doctors have the right to choose to destroy these embryos: '. . . because no one, not even its parents, owns the embryo/fetus, no one has the *right* to destroy it, even at a very early development stage . . . to destroy an embryo is not an automatic entitlement held by anyone, including its genetic parents.'[19]

Moreover, some participants reflect deep seated ambivalence on the part of many women about the procedure—they indicate that their marriage and status depends on a determination to do 'whatever is possible' in pursuit of their 'natural' childbearing function—and they are not helped to work through the seeming imponderables associated with their long term well-being. Thus, IVF as practiced involves significant limits on the degree of autonomy deontologists insist on in other medical contexts, though the non-feminist literature is insensitive to this anomaly.

From the perspective of consequentialism, feminists take a long view and try to see IVF in the context of the burgeoning range of techniques in the area of human reproductive technology. While some of this technology seems to hold the potential of benefitting women generally—by leading to better understanding of conception and contraception, for instance—there is a wary suspicion that this research will help foster new techniques and products such as human cloning and the development of artificial wombs which can, in principle, make the majority of women superfluous. (This is not a wholly paranoid fear in a woman-hating culture: we can anticipate that there will be great pressure for such techniques in subsequent generations, since one of the 'successes' of reproductive technology to date has been to allow parents to control the sex of their offspring; the 'choice' now made possible clearly threatens to result in significant imbalances in the ratio of boy to girl infants. Thus, it appears, there will likely be significant shortages of women to bear children in the future, and we can anticipate pressures for further technological solutions to the 'new' problem of reproduction that will follow.)

Many authors from all traditions consider it necessary to ask why it is that some couples seek this technology so desperately. Why is it so important to so many people to produce their 'own' child? On this question, theorists in the analytic tradition seem to shift to previously rejected ground and suggest that this is a natural, or at least a proper, desire. Engelhardt, for example, says 'The use of technology in the fashioning of children is integral to the goal of rendering the world congenial to persons.'[20] Bayles more cautiously observes that 'A desire to beget for its own sake . . . is probably irrational'; nonetheless, he immediately concludes, 'these techniques for fulfilling that desire have been found ethically permissible.'[21] R. G. Edwards and David Sharpe state the case most strongly: 'the desire to have children must be among the most basic of human instincts, and denying it can lead to considerable psychological and social difficulties.'[22] Interestingly, although the recent pronouncement of the Catholic Church assumes that 'the desire for a child is natural,'[23] it denies that a couple has a right to a child: 'The child is not an object to which one has a right.'[24]

Here, I believe, it becomes clear why we need a deeper sort of feminist analysis. We must look at the sort of social arrangements and cultural values that underlie the drive to assume such risks for the sake of biological parenthood. We find that the capitalism, racism, sexism, and elitism of our culture have combined to create a set of attitudes which views children as commodities whose value is derived from their possession of parental chromosomes. Children are valued as privatized commodities, reflecting the virility and heredity of their parents. They are also viewed as the responsibility of their parents and are not seen as the social treasure and burden that they are. Parents must tend their needs on pain of prosecution, and, in return, they get to keep complete control over them. Other adults are inhibited from having warm, stable interactions with the children of others — it is as suspect to try to hug and talk regularly with a child who is not one's own as it is to fondle and hang longingly about a car or a bicycle which belongs to someone else — so those who wish to know children well often find they must have their own.

Women are persuaded that their most important purpose in life is to bear and raise children; they are told repeatedly that their life is incomplete, that they are lacking in fulfillment if they do not have children. And, in fact, many women do face a barren existence without children. Few women have access to meaningful, satisfying jobs. Most do not find themselves in the centre of the romantic personal relationships which the culture pretends is the norm for heterosexual couples. And they have been socialized to be fearful of close friendships with others — they are taught to distrust other women, and to avoid the danger of friendship with men other than their husbands. Children remain the one hope for real intimacy and for the sense of accomplishment which comes from doing work one judges to be valuable.

To be sure, children can provide that sense of self worth, although for many women (and probably for all mothers at some times) motherhood is not the romanticized satisfaction they are led to expect. But there is something very wrong with a culture where childrearing is the only outlet available to most women in which to pursue fulfillment. Moreover, there is something wrong with the ownership theory of children that keeps other adults at a distance from children. There ought to be a variety of close relationships possible between children and adults so that we all recognize that we have a stake in the well-being of the young, and we all benefit from contact with their view of the world.

In such a world, it would not be necessary to spend the huge sums on designer children which IVF requires while millions of other children starve to death each year. Adults who enjoyed children could be involved in caring for them whether or not they produced them biologically. And, if the institution of marriage survives, women and men would marry because they wished to share their lives together, not because the men needed someone to produce heirs for them and women needed financial support for their children. That would be a world in which we might have reproductive freedom of choice. The world we now live in has so limited women's options and self-esteem, it is legitimate to question the freedom behind women's demand for this technology, for it may well be largely a reflection of constraining social perspectives.

Nonetheless, I must acknowledge that some couples today genuinely mourn their incapacity to produce children without IVF, and there are very significant and unique joys which can be found in producing and raising one's own children which are not accessible to persons in infertile relationships. We must sympathize with these people. None of us shall live to see the implementation of the ideal cultural values outlined above which would make the demand for IVF less severe. It is with real concern that some feminists suggest that the personal wishes of couples with fertility difficulties may not be compatible with the overall interests of women and children.

Feminist thought, then, helps us to focus on different dimensions of the problem than do other sorts of approaches. But, with this perspective, we still have difficulty in reaching a final conclusion on whether to encourage, tolerate, modify, or restrict this sort of reproductive technology. I suggest that we turn to the developing theories of feminist ethics for guidance in resolving this question.[25]

In my view, a feminist ethics is a moral theory that focuses on relations among persons as well as on individuals. It has as a model an inter-connected social fabric, rather than the familiar one of isolated, independent atoms; and it gives primacy to bonds among people rather than to rights to independence. It is a theory that focuses on concrete situations and persons and not on free-floating abstract actions.[26] Although many details have yet to be worked out, we can see some of its implications in particular problem areas such as this.

It is a theory that is explicitly conscious of the social, political, and economic relations that exist among persons; in particular, as a feminist theory, it attends to the implications of actions or policies on the status of women. Hence, it is necessary to ask questions from the perspective of feminist ethics in addition to those which are normally asked from the perspective of mainstream ethical theories. We must view issues such as this one in the context of the social and political realities in which they arise, and resist the attempt to evaluate actions or practices in isolation (as traditional responses in biomedical ethics often do). Thus, we cannot just address the question of IVF per se without asking how IVF contributes to general patterns of women's oppression. As Kathryn Payne Addleson has argued about abortion,[27] a feminist perspective raises questions that are inadmissible within the traditional ethical frameworks, and yet, for women in a patriarchal society, they are value questions of greater urgency. In particular, a feminist ethics, in contrast to other approaches in biomedical ethics, would take seriously the concerns just reviewed which are part of the debate in the feminist literature.

A feminist ethics would also include components of theories that have been developed as 'feminine ethics,' as sketched out by the empirical work of Carol Gilligan.[28] (The best example of such a theory is the work of Nel Noddings in her influential book *Caring*.[29]) In other words, it would be a theory that gives primacy to interpersonal relationships and woman-centered values such as nurturing, empathy, and cooperation. Hence, in the case of IVF, we must care for the women and men who are so despairing about their infertility as to want to spend the vast sums and risk the associated physical and emotional costs of the treatment, in pursuit of 'their own children.' That is, we should, in Noddings' terms, see their reality as our own and address their very real sense of loss. In so doing, however, we must also consider the implications of this sort of solution to their difficulty. While meeting the perceived desires of some women—desires which are problematic in themselves, since they are so compatible with the values of a culture deeply oppressive to women—this technology threatens to further entrench those values which are responsible for that oppression. A larger vision suggests that the technology offered may, in reality, reduce women's freedom and, if so, it should be avoided.

A feminist ethics will not support a wholly negative response, however, for that would not address our obligation to care for those suffering from infertility; it is the responsibility of those who oppose further implementation of this technology to work towards the changes in the social arrangements that will lead to a reduction of the sense of need for this sort of solution. On the medical front, research and treatment ought to be stepped up to reduce the rates of [puerperal] sepsis and gonorrhea which often result in tubal blockage, more attention should be directed at the causes and possible cures for male infertility, and we should pursue techniques that will permit safe reversible sterilization providing women with better alternatives to tubal ligation as a means of fertility control; these sorts of technology would increase the control of many women over their own fertility and would be compatible with feminist objectives. On the social front, we must continue the social pressure to change the status of women and children in our society from that of breeder and possession respectively; hence, we must develop a vision of society as community where all participants are valued members, regardless of age or gender. And we must challenge the notion that having one's wife produce a child with his own genes is sufficient cause for the wives of men with low sperm counts to be expected to undergo the physical and emotional assault such technology involves.

Further, a feminist ethics will attend to the nature of the relationships among those concerned. Annette Baier has eloquently argued for the importance of developing an ethics of trust,[30] and I believe a feminist ethics must address the question of the degree of trust appropriate to the relationships involved. Feminists have noted that women have little reason to trust the medical specialists who offer to respond to their reproductive desires, for commonly women's interests have not come first from the medical point of view.[31] In fact, it is accurate to perceive feminist attacks on reproductive technology as expressions of the lack of trust feminists have in those who control the technology. Few feminists object to reproductive technology per se; rather they express concern about who controls it and how it can be used to further exploit women. The problem with reproductive technology is that it concentrates power in reproductive matters in the hands of those who are not directly involved in the actual bearing and rearing of the child; i.e., in men who relate to their clients in a technical, professional, authoritarian manner. It is a further step in the medicalization of pregnancy and birth which, in North America, is marked by relationships between pregnant women and their doctors which are very different from the traditional relationships between pregnant women and midwives. The latter relationships fostered an atmosphere of mutual trust which is impossible to replicate in hospital deliveries today. In fact, current approaches to pregnancy, labour, and birth tend to view the mother as a threat to the fetus who must be coerced to comply with medical procedures designed to ensure delivery of healthy babies at whatever cost necessary to the mother. Frequently, the fetus-mother relationship is medically characterized as adversarial and the physicians choose to foster a sense of alienation and passivity in the role they permit the mother. However well IVF may serve the interests of the few women with access to it, it more clearly serves the interests (be they commercial, professional, scholarly, or purely patriarchal) of those who control it.

Questions such as these are a puzzle to those engaged in the traditional approaches to ethics, for they always urge us to separate the question of evaluating the morality of various forms of reproductive technology in themselves, from questions about particular uses of that technology. From the perspective of a feminist ethics, however, no such distinction can be meaningfully made. Reproductive technology is not an abstract activity; it is an activity done in particular contexts and it is those contexts which must be addressed.

Feminist concerns cited earlier made clear the difficulties we have with some of our traditional ethical concepts; hence, feminist ethics directs us to rethink our basic ethical notions. Autonomy, or freedom of choice, is not a matter to be determined in isolated instances, as is commonly assumed in many approaches to applied ethics. Rather it is a matter that involves reflection on one's whole life situation. The freedom of choice feminists appeal to in the abortion situation is freedom to define one's status as a childbearer, given the social, economic, and political significance of reproduction for women. A feminist perspective permits us to understand that reproductive freedom includes control of one's sexuality, protection against coerced sterilization (or iatrogenic sterilization, e.g. as caused by the Dalkon shield), and the existence of a social and economic network of support for the children we may choose to bear. It is the freedom to redefine our roles in society according to our concerns and needs as women.

In contrast, the consumer freedom to purchase technology, allowed only to a few couples of the privileged classes (in traditionally approved relationships), seems to entrench further the patriarchal notions of woman's role as childbearer and of heterosexual monogamy as the only acceptable intimate relationship. In other words, this sort of choice does not seem to foster autonomy for women on the broad scale. IVF is a practice which seems to reinforce sexist, classist, and often racist assumptions of our culture; therefore, on our revised understanding of freedom, the contribution of this technology to the general autonomy of women is largely negative.

We can now see the advantage of a feminist ethics over mainstream ethical theories, for a feminist analysis explicitly accepts the need for a political component to our understanding of ethical issues. In this, it differs from traditional ethical theories and it also differs from a simply feminine ethics approach, such as the one Noddings offers, for Noddings seems to rely on individual relations exclusively and is deeply suspicious of political alliances as potential threats to the pure relation of caring. Yet, a full understanding of both the threat of IVF, and the alternative action necessary should we decide to reject IVF, is possible only if it includes a political dimension reflecting on the role of women in society.

From the point of view of feminist ethics, the primary question to consider is whether this and other forms of reproductive technology threaten to reinforce the lack of autonomy which women now experience in our culture — even as they appear, in the short run, to be increasing freedom. We must recognize that the interconnections among the social forces oppressive to women underlie feminists' mistrust of this technology which advertises itself as increasing women's autonomy.[32] The political perspective which directs us to look at how this technology fits in with general patterns of treatment for women is not readily accessible to traditional moral theories, for it involves categories of concern not accounted for in those theories — e.g., the complexity of issues which makes it inappropriate to study them in isolation from one another, the role of oppression in shaping individual desires, and potential differences in moral status which are connected with differences in treatment.

It is the set of connections constituting women's continued oppression in our society which inspires feminists to resurrect the old slippery slope arguments to warn against IVF. We must recognize that women's existing lack of control in reproductive matters begins the debate on a pretty steep incline. Technology with the potential to further remove control of reproduction from women makes the slope very slippery indeed. This new technology, though offered under the guise of increasing reproductive freedom, threatens to result, in fact, in a significant decrease in freedom, especially since it is a technology that will always include the active involvement of designated specialists and will not ever be a private matter for the couple or women concerned.

Ethics ought not to direct us to evaluate individual cases without also looking at the implications of our decisions from a wide perspective. My argument is that a theory of feminist ethics provides that wider perspective, for its different sort of methodology is sensitive to both the personal and the social dimensions of issues. For that reason, I believe it is the only ethical perspective suitable for evaluating issues of this sort.

NOTES

1. I appreciate the helpful criticism I have received from colleagues in the Dalhousie Department of Philosophy, the Canadian Society for Women in Philosophy, and the Women's Studies program of the University of Alberta where earlier versions of this paper were read. I am particularly grateful for the careful criticism it has received from Linda Williams and Christine Overall.

2. Susan Sherwin, 'A Feminist Approach to Ethics,' *Dalhousie Review* 64, 4 (Winter 1984–85) 704–13.

3. Paul Ramsey, 'Shall We Reproduce?' *Journal of the American Medical Association* 220 (June 12, 1972), 1484.

4. Leon Kass, '"Making Babies" Revisited,' *The Public Interest* 54 (Winter 1979), 32–60.

5. Joseph Cardinal Ratzinger and Alberto Bovone, 'Instruction on Respect for Human Life in its Origin and on the Dignity of Procreation: Replies to Certain Questions of the Day' (Vatican City: Vatican Polyglot Press 1987), 23–24.

6. Ibid., 28.

7. Michael Bayles, *Reproductive Ethics* (Englewood Cliffs, NJ: Prentice-Hall 1984), 15.

8. Ratzinger and Bovone, 28.

9. Samuel Gorovitz, *Doctors' Dilemmas: Moral Conflict and Medical Care* (New York: Oxford University Press 1982), 168.

10. Ibid., 173.

11. Bayles, 66.

12. I owe this observation to Linda Williams.

13. H. Tristram Engelhardt, *The Foundations of Bioethics* (Oxford: Oxford University Press 1986), 237.

14. Ibid., 241.

15. Anita Direcks, 'Has the Lesson Been Learned?' *DES Action Voice* 28 (Spring 1986), 1–4; and Nikita A. Crook, 'Clomid,' DES Action/Toronto Factsheet #442 (available from 60 Grosvenor St., Toronto, M5S 1B6).

16. Bayles, 32. Though Bayles is not a deontologist, he does concisely express a deontological concern here.

17. Gorovitz, 177.

18. Michael Soules, 'The In Vitro Fertilization Pregnancy Rate: Let's Be Honest with One Another,' *Fertility and Sterility* 43, 4 (1985) 511–13.

19. Christine Overall, *Ethics and Human Reproduction: A Feminist Analysis* (Allen and Unwin, forthcoming), 104 ms.

20. Engelhardt, 239.

21. Bayles, 31.

22. Robert G. Edwards and David J. Sharpe, 'Social Values and Research in Human Embryology,' *Nature* 231 (May 14, 1971), 87.

23. Ratzinger and Bovone, 33.

24. Ibid., 34.

25. Many authors are now working on an understanding of what feminist ethics entail. Among the Canadian papers I am familiar with are Kathryn Morgan's 'Women and Moral Madness,' Sheila Mullet's 'Only Connect: The Place of Self-Knowledge in Ethics,' [in Marsha Hanen and Kai Nielsen, eds., *Science, Monthly, and Feminist Theory* (Calgary, Alberta: University of Calgary Press, 1987)], and Leslie Wilson's 'Is a Feminine Ethics Enough?' *Atlantis* (forthcoming).

26. Sherwin, 'A Feminist Approach to Ethics.'

27. Kathryn Payne Addelson, 'Moral Revolution,' in Marilyn Pearsall, ed., *Women and Values* (Belmont, CA: Wadsworth 1986), 291–309.

28. Carol Gilligan, *In a Different Voice* (Cambridge, MA: Harvard University Press 1982).

29. Nel Noddings, *Caring* (Berkeley: University of California Press 1984).

30. Annette Baier, 'What Do Women Want in a Moral Theory?' *Nous* 19 (March 1985), 53–64, and 'Trust and Antitrust,' *Ethics* 96 (January 1986), 231–60.

31. Linda Williams presents this position particularly clearly in her invaluable work 'But What Will They Mean for Women? Feminist Concerns About the New Reproductive Technologies,' No. 6 in the *Feminist Perspectives* Series, CRIAW.

32. Marilyn Frye vividly describes the phenomenon of interrelatedness which supports sexist oppression by appeal to the metaphor of a bird cage composed of thin wires, each relatively harmless in itself, but, collectively, the wires constitute an overwhelming barrier to the inhabitant of the cage. Marilyn Frye, *The Politics of Reality: Essays in Feminist Theory* (Trumansburg, NY: The Crossing Press 1983), 4–7.

Surrogate Parenting Arrangements

ELIZABETH S. ANDERSON

Is Women's Labor a Commodity?

In the past few years the practice of commercial surrogate motherhood has gained notoriety as a method for acquiring children. A commercial surrogate mother is anyone who is paid money to bear a child for other people and terminate her parental rights, so that the others may raise the child as exclusively their own. The growth of commercial surrogacy has raised with new urgency a class of concerns regarding the proper scope of the market. Some critics have objected to commercial surrogacy on the ground that it improperly treats children and women's reproductive capacities as commodities.[1] The prospect of reducing children to consumer durables and women to baby factories surely inspires revulsion. But are there good reasons behind the revulsion? And is this an accurate description of what commercial surrogacy implies? This article offers a

The author thanks David Anderson, Steven Darwell, Ezekiel Emanuel, Daniel Hausman, Don Herzog, Robert Nozick, Richard Pildes, John Rawls, Michael Sandel, Thomas Scanlon, and Howard Wial for helpful comments and criticisms.

Elizabeth S. Anderson, "Is Women's Labor a Commodity?" *Philosophy and Public Affairs* 19 (Winter 1990), 71–92. Copyright © 1990 by Princeton University Press. Reprinted by permission of Princeton University Press.

theory about what things are properly regarded as commodities which supports the claim that commercial surrogacy constitutes an unconscionable commodification of children and of women's reproductive capacities.

WHAT IS A COMMODITY?

The modern market can be characterized in terms of the legal and social norms by which it governs the production, exchange, and enjoyment of commodities. To say that something is properly regarded as a commodity is to claim that the norms of the market are appropriate for regulating its production, exchange, and enjoyment. To the extent that moral principles or ethical ideals preclude the application of market norms to a good, we may say that the good is not a (proper) commodity.

Why should we object to the application of a market norm to the production or distribution of a good? One reason may be that to produce or distribute the good in accordance with the norm is to *fail to value it in an appropriate way.* Consider, for example, a standard Kantian argument against slavery, or the commodification of persons. Slaves are treated in accordance with the market norm that owners may use commodities to satisfy their own interests without regard for the interests of the commodities themselves. To treat a person without regard for her interests is to fail to respect her. But slaves are persons who may not be merely used in this fashion, since as rational beings they possess a dignity which commands respect. In Kantian theory, the problem with slavery is that it treats beings worthy of *respect* as if they were worthy merely of *use*. "Respect" and "use" in this context denote what we may call different *modes of valuation*. We value things and persons in other ways than by respecting and using them. For example, love, admiration, honor, and appreciation constitute distinct modes of valuation. To value a thing or person in a distinctive way involves treating it in accordance with a particular set of norms. For example, courtesy expresses a mode of valuation we may call "civil respect," which differs from Kantian respect in that it calls for obedience to the rules of etiquette rather than to the categorical imperative.

Any ideal of human life includes a conception of how different things and persons should be valued. Let us reserve the term "use" to refer to the mode of valuation proper to commodities, which follows the market norm of treating things solely in accordance with the owner's nonmoral preferences. Then the Kantian argument against commodifying persons can be generalized to apply to many other cases. It can be argued that many objects which are worthy of a higher mode of valuation than use are not properly regarded as mere commodities.[2] Some current arguments against the colorization of classic black-and-white films take this form. Such films have been colorized by their owners in an attempt to enhance their market value by attracting audiences unused to black-and-white cinematography. But some opponents of the practice object that such treatment of the film classics fails to appreciate their aesthetic and historical value. True appreciation of these films would preclude this kind of crass commercial exploitation, which debases their aesthetic qualities in the name of profits. Here the argument rests on the claim that the goods in question are worthy of appreciation, not merely of use.

The ideals which specify how one should value certain things are supported by a conception of human flourishing. Our lives are enriched and elevated by cultivating and exercising the capacity to appreciate art. To fail to do so reflects poorly on ourselves. To fail to value things appropriately is to embody in one's life an inferior conception of human flourishing.[3]

These considerations support a general account of the sorts of things which are appropriately regarded as commodities. Commodities are those things which are properly treated in accordance with the norms of the modern market. We can question the application of market norms to the production, distribution, and enjoyment of a good by appealing to ethical ideals which support arguments that the good should be valued in some other way than use. Arguments of the latter sort claim that to allow certain market norms to govern our treatment of a thing expresses a mode of valuation not worthy of it. If the thing is to be valued appropriately, its production, exchange, and enjoyment must be removed from market norms and embedded in a different set of social relationships.

THE CASE OF COMMERCIAL SURROGACY

Let us now consider the practice of commercial surrogate motherhood in the light of this theory of commodities. Surrogate motherhood as a commercial enterprise is based upon contracts involving three parties: the intended father, the broker, and the surrogate mother. The intended father agrees to pay a lawyer to find a suitable surrogate mother and make the requisite medical and legal arrangements for the conception and birth of the child, and for the transfer of legal custody to himself.[4] The surrogate mother agrees to become impregnated with the intended father's sperm, to carry the resulting child to term, and to relinquish her parental rights to it, transferring custody to the father in return for a fee and medical expenses. Both she and her husband (if she has one) agree not to form a parent-child bond with her child and to do everything necessary to effect the transfer of the child to the intended father. At current market prices, the lawyer arranging the contract can expect to gross $15,000 from the contract, while the surrogate mother can expect a $10,000 fee.[5]

The practice of commercial surrogacy has been defended on four main grounds. First, given the shortage of children available for adoption and the difficulty of qualifying as adoptive parents, it may represent the only hope for some people to be able to raise a family. Commercial surrogacy should be accepted as an effective means for realizing this highly significant good. Second, two fundamental human rights support commercial surrogacy: the right to procreate and freedom of contract. Fully informed autonomous adults should have the right to make whatever arrangements they wish for the use of their bodies and the reproduction of children, so long as the children themselves are not harmed. Third, the labor of the surrogate mother is said to be a labor of love. Her altruistic acts should be permitted and encouraged.[6] Finally, it is argued that commercial surrogacy is no different in its ethical implications from many already accepted practices which separate genetic, gestational, and social parenting, such as artificial insemination by donor, adoption, wet-nursing, and day care. Consistency demands that society accept this new practice as well.[7]

In opposition to these claims, I shall argue that commercial surrogacy does raise new ethical issues, since it represents an invasion of the market into a new sphere of conduct, that of specifically women's labor — that is, the labor of carrying children to term in pregnancy. When women's labor is treated as a commodity, the women who perform it are degraded. Furthermore, commercial surrogacy degrades children by reducing their status to that of commodities. Let us consider each of the goods of concern in surrogate motherhood — the child, and women's reproductive labor — to see how the commercialization of parenthood affects people's regard for them.

CHILDREN AS COMMODITIES

The most fundamental calling of parents to their children is to love them. Children are to be loved and cherished by their parents, not to be used or manipulated by them for merely personal advantage. Parental love can be understood as a passionate, unconditional commitment to nurture one's child, providing it with the care, affection, and guidance it needs to develop its capacities to maturity. This understanding of the way parents should value their children informs our interpretation of parental rights over their children. Parents' rights over their children are trusts, which they must always exercise for the sake of the child. This is not to deny that parents have their own aspirations in raising children. But the child's interests beyond subsistence are not definable independently of the flourishing of the family, which is the object of specifically parental aspirations. The proper exercise of parental rights includes those acts which promote their shared life as a family, which realize the shared interests of the parents and the child.

The norms of parental love carry implications for the ways other people should treat the relationship between parents and their children. If children are to be loved by their parents, then others should not attempt to compromise the integrity of parental love or work to suppress the emotions supporting the bond between parents and their children. If the rights to children should be understood as trusts, then if those rights are lost or relinquished, the duty of those in charge of transferring custody to others is to consult the best interests of the child.

Commercial surrogacy substitutes market norms for some of the norms of parental love. Most importantly, it requires us to understand parental rights no longer as trusts but as things more like property rights — that is, rights of use and disposal over the things owned. For in this practice the natural mother deliberately conceives a child with the intention of giving it up for material advantage. Her renunciation of parental responsibilities is not done for the child's sake, nor for the sake of fulfilling an interest she shares with the child, but typically for her own sake (and possibly, if "altruism" is a motive, for the intended parents' sakes). She and the couple who pay her to give up her parental rights over her child thus treat her rights as a kind of property right. They thereby treat the child itself as a kind of commodity, which may be properly bought and sold.

Commercial surrogacy insinuates the norms of commerce into the parental relationship in other ways. Whereas parental love is not supposed to be conditioned upon the child having particular characteristics, consumer demand is properly responsive to the characteristics of commodities. So the surrogate industry provides opportunities to adoptive couples to specify the height, I.Q., race, and other attributes of the surrogate mother, in the expectation that these traits will be passed on to the child.[8] Since no industry assigns agents to look after the "interests" of its commodities, no one represents the child's interests in the surrogate industry. The surrogate agency promotes the adoptive parents' interests and not the child's interests where matters of custody are concerned. Finally, as the agent of the adoptive parents, the broker has the task of policing the surrogate (natural) mother's relationship to her child, using persuasion, money, and the threat of a lawsuit to weaken and destroy whatever parental love she may develop for her child.[9]

All of these substitutions of market norms for parental norms represent ways of treating children as commodities which are degrading to them. Degradation occurs when something is treated in accordance with a lower mode of valuation than is proper to it. We value things not just "more" or "less," but in qualitatively higher and lower ways. To love or respect someone is to value her in a higher way than one would if one merely used her. Children are properly loved by their parents and respected by others. Since children are valued as mere use-objects by the mother and the surrogate agency when they are sold to others, and by the adoptive parents when they seek to conform the child's genetic makeup to their own wishes, commercial surrogacy degrades children insofar as it treats them as commodities.[10]

One might argue that since the child is most likely to enter a loving home, no harm comes to it from permitting the natural mother to treat it as property. So the purchase and sale of infants is unobjectionable, at least from the point of view of children's interests.[11] But the sale of an infant has an expressive significance which this argument fails to recognize. By engaging in the transfer of children by sale, all of the parties to the surrogate contract express a set of attitudes toward children which undermine the norms of parental love. They all agree in treating the ties between a natural mother and her children as properly loosened by a monetary incentive. Would it be any wonder if a child born of a surrogacy agreement feared resale by parents who have such an attitude? And a child who knew how anxious her parents were that she have the "right" genetic makeup might fear that her parent's love was contingent upon her expression of these characteristics.[12]

The unsold children of surrogate mothers are also harmed by commercial surrogacy. The children of some surrogate mothers have reported their fears that they may be sold like their half-brother or half-sister, and express a sense of loss at being deprived of a sibling.[13] Furthermore, the widespread acceptance of commercial surrogacy would psychologically threaten all children. For it would change the way children are valued by people (parents and surrogate brokers) — from being loved by their parents and respected by others, to being sometimes used as objects of commercial profit-making.[14]

Proponents of commercial surrogacy have denied that the surrogate industry engages in the sale of children. For it is impossible to sell to someone what is already his own, and the child is already the father's own natural offspring. The payment to the surrogate mother is not for her child, but for her services in carrying it to term.[15] The claim that the parties to the surrogate contract treat children as commodities, however, is based on the way they treat the *mother's* rights over her child. It is irrelevant that the natural father also has some rights over the child; what he pays for is exclusive rights to it. He would not pay her for the "service" of carrying the child to term if she refused to relinquish her parental rights to it. That the mother regards only her labor and not her child as requiring compensation is also irrelevant. No one would argue that the baker does not treat his bread as property just because he sees the income from its sale as compensation for his labor and expenses and not for the bread itself, which he doesn't care to keep.[16]

Defenders of commercial surrogacy have also claimed that it does not differ substantially from other already accepted parental practices. In the institutions of adoption and artificial insemination by donor (AID), it is claimed, we already grant parents the right to dispose of their children.[17] But these practices differ in significant respects from commercial surrogacy. The purpose of adoption is to provide a means for placing children in families when their parents cannot or will not discharge their parental responsibilities. It is not a sphere for the existence of a supposed parental right to dispose of one's children for profit. Even AID does not sanction the sale of fully formed human beings. The semen donor sells only a product of his body, not his child, and does not initiate the act of conception.

Two developments might seem to undermine the claim that commercial surrogacy constitutes a degrading commerce in children. The first is technological: the prospect of transplanting a human embryo into the womb of a genetically unrelated woman. If commercial surrogacy used women only as gestational mothers and not as genetic mothers, and if it was thought that only genetic and not gestational parents could properly claim that a child was "theirs," then the child born of a surrogate mother would not be hers to sell in the first place. The second is a legal development: the establishment of the proposed "consent-intent" definition of parenthood.[18] This would declare the legal parents of a child to be whoever consented to a procedure which leads to its birth, with the intent of assuming parental responsibilities for it. This rule would define away the problem of commerce in children by depriving the surrogate mother of any legal claim to her child at all, even if it were hers both genetically and gestationally.[19]

There are good reasons, however, not to undermine the place of genetic and gestational ties in these ways. Consider first the place of genetic ties. By upholding a system of involuntary (genetic) ties of obligation among people, even when the adults among them prefer to divide their rights and obligations in other ways, we help to secure children's interests in having an assured place in the world, which is more firm than the wills of their parents. Unlike the consent-intent rule, the principle of respecting genetic ties does not make the obligation to care for those whom one has created (intentionally or not) contingent upon an arbitrary desire to do so. It thus provides children with a set of preexisting social sanctions which give them a more secure place in the world. The genetic principle also places children in a far wider network of associations and obligations than the consent-intent rule sanctions. It supports the roles of grandparents and other relatives in the nurturing of children, and provides children with a possible focus of stability and an additional source of claims to care if their parents cannot sustain a well-functioning household.

In the next section I will defend the claims of gestational ties to children. To deny these claims, as commercial surrogacy does, is to deny the significance of reproductive labor to the mother who undergoes it and thereby to dehumanize and degrade the mother herself. Commercial surrogacy would be a corrupt practice even if it did not involve commerce in children.

WOMEN'S LABOR AS A COMMODITY

Commercial surrogacy attempts to transform what is specifically women's labor — the work of bringing forth children into the world — into a commodity. It does so by replacing the parental norms which usually govern the practice of gestating children with the economic norms which govern ordinary production processes. The application of commercial norms to women's labor reduces the surrogate mothers from persons worthy of respect and consideration to objects of mere use.

Respect and consideration are two distinct modes of valuation whose norms are violated by the practices of the surrogate industry. To respect a person is to treat her in accordance with principles she rationally accepts — principles consistent with the protection of her autonomy and her rational interests. To treat a person with consideration is to respond with sensitivity to her and to her emotional relations with others, refraining from manipulating or denigrating these for one's own purposes. Given the understanding of respect as a dispassionate, impersonal regard for people's interests, a different ethical concept — consideration — is needed to capture the engaged and sensitive regard we should have for people's emotional relationships. The failure

of consideration on the part of the other parties to the surrogacy contract explains the judgment that the contract is not simply disrespectful of the surrogate mother, but callous as well.[20]

The application of economic norms to the sphere of women's labor violates women's claims to respect and consideration in three ways. First, by requiring the surrogate mother to repress whatever parental love she feels for the child, these norms convert women's labor into a form of alienated labor. Second, by manipulating and denying legitimacy to the surrogate mother's evolving perspective on her own pregnancy, the norms of the market degrade her. Third, by taking advantage of the surrogate mother's noncommercial motivations without offering anything but what the norms of commerce demand in return, these norms leave her open to exploitation. The fact that these problems arise in the attempt to commercialize the labor of bearing children shows that women's labor is not properly regarded as a commodity.

The key to understanding these problems is the normal role of the emotions in noncommercialized pregnancies. Pregnancy is not simply a biological process but also a social practice. Many social expectations and considerations surround women's gestational labor, marking it off as an occasion for the parents to prepare themselves to welcome a new life into their family. For example, obstetricians use ultrasound not simply for diagnostic purposes but also to encourage material bonding with the fetus.[21] We can all recognize that it is good, although by no means inevitable, for loving bonds to be established between the mother and her child during this period.

In contrast with these practices, the surrogate industry follows the putting-out system of manufacturing. It provides some of the raw materials of production (the father's sperm) to the surrogate mother, who then engages in production of the child. Although her labor is subject to periodic supervision by her doctors and by the surrogate agency, the agency does not have physical control over the product of her labor as firms using the factory system do. Hence, as in all putting-out systems, the surrogate industry faces the problem of extracting the final product from the mother. This problem is exacerbated by the fact that the social norms surrounding pregnancy are designed to encourage parental love for the child. The surrogate industry addresses this problem by requiring the mother to engage in a form of emotional labor.[22] In the surrogate contract, she agrees not to form or attempt to form a parent-child relationship with her offspring.[23] Her labor is alienated, because she must divert it from the end which the social practices of pregnancy rightly promote—an emotional bond with her child. The surrogate contract thus replaces a norm of parenthood, that during pregnancy one create a loving attachment to one's child, with a norm of commercial production, that the producer shall not form any special emotional ties to her product.

The demand to deliberately alienate oneself from one's love for one's own child is a demand which can reasonably and decently be made of no one. Unless we were to remake pregnancy into a form of drudgery which is only performed for a wage, there is every reason to expect that many women who do sign a surrogate contract will, despite this fact, form a loving attachment to the child they bear. For this is what the social practices surrounding pregnancy encourage. Treating women's labor as just another kind of commercial production process violates the precious emotional ties which the mother might rightly and properly establish with her "product," the child, and thereby violates her claims to consideration.[24]

Commercial surrogacy is also a degrading practice. The surrogate mother, like all persons, has an independent evaluative perspective on her activities and relationships. The realization of her dignity demands that the other parties to the contract acknowledge rather than evade the claims which her independent perspective makes upon them. But the surrogate industry has an interest in suppressing, manipulating, and trivializing her perspective, for there is an ever-present danger that she will see her involvement in her pregnancy from the perspective of a parent rather than from the perspective of a contract laborer.

How does this suppression and trivialization take place? The commercial promoters of surrogacy commonly describe the surrogate mothers as inanimate objects: mere "hatcheries," "plumbing," or "rented property"—things without emotions which could make claims on others.[25] They also refuse to acknowledge any responsibility for the consequences of the mother's emotional labor. Should she suffer psychologically from being forced to give up her child, the father is not liable to pay for therapy after her pregnancy, although he is liable for all other medical expenses following her pregnancy.[26]

The treatment and interpretation of surrogate mothers' grief raises the deepest problems of degradation. Most surrogate mothers experience grief upon giving up their children—in 10 percent of cases, seriously enough to require therapy.[27] Their grief is not compensated by the $10,000 fee they receive. Grief is not an intelligible response to a successful deal, but rather reflects the subject's judgment that she has suffered a grave and personal loss. Since not all cases of grief resolve themselves into cases of regret, it may be that some surrogate mothers do not regard their grief, in retrospect, as reflecting an authentic judgment on their part. But in the circumstances of emotional manipulation which pervade the surrogate industry, it is difficult to determine which interpretation of her grief more truly reflects the perspective of the surrogate mother. By insinuating a trivializing interpretation of her emotional responses to the prospect of losing her child, the surrogate agency may be able to manipulate her into accepting her fate without too much fuss, and may even succeed in substituting its interpretation of her emotions for her own. Since she has already signed a contract to perform emotional labor—to express or repress emotions which are dictated by the interests of the surrogate industry—this might not be a difficult task.[28] A considerate treatment of the mothers' grief, on the other hand, would take the evaluative basis of their grief seriously.

Some defenders of commercial surrogacy demand that the provision for terminating the surrogate mother's parental rights in her child be legally enforceable, so that peace of mind for the adoptive parents can be secured.[29] But the surrogate industry makes no corresponding provision for securing the peace of mind of the surrogate. She is expected to assume the risk of a transformation of her ethical and emotional perspective on herself and her child with the same impersonal detachment with which a futures trader assumes the risk of a fluctuation in the price of pork bellies. By applying the market norms of enforcing contracts to the surrogate mother's case, commercial surrogacy treats a moral transformation as if it were merely an economic change.[30]

The manipulation of the surrogate mother's emotions which is inherent in the surrogate parenting contract also leaves women open to grave forms of exploitation. A kind of exploitation occurs when one party to a transaction is oriented toward the exchange of "gift" values, while the other party operates in accordance with the norms of the market exchange of commodities. Gift values, which include love, gratitude, and appreciation of others, cannot be bought or obtained through piecemeal calculations of individual advantage. Their exchange requires a repudiation of a self-interested attitude, a willingness to give gifts to others without demanding some specific equivalent good in return each time one gives. The surrogate mother often operates according to the norms of gift relationships. The surrogate agency, on the other hand, follows market norms. Its job is to get the best deal for its clients and itself, while leaving the surrogate mother to look after her own interests as best as she can. This situation puts the surrogate agencies in a position to manipulate the surrogate mothers' emotions to gain favorable terms for themselves. For example, agencies screen prospective surrogate mothers for submissiveness, and emphasize to them the importance of the motives of generosity and love. When applicants question some of the terms of the contract, the broker sometimes intimidates them by questioning their character and morality: if they were really generous and loving they would not be so solicitous about their own interests.[31]

Some evidence supports the claim that most surrogate mothers are motivated by emotional needs and vulnerabilities which lead them to view their labor as a form of gift and not a purely commercial exchange. Only 1 percent of applicants to surrogate agencies would become surrogate mothers for money alone; the others have emotional as well as financial reasons for applying. One psychiatrist believes that most, if not all, of the 35 percent of applicants who had had a previous abortion or given up a child for adoption wanted to become surrogate mothers in order to resolve their guilty feelings or deal with their unresolved loss by going through a process of losing a child again.[32] Women who feel that giving up another child is an effective way to punish themselves for past abortions, or a form of therapy for their emotional problems, are not likely to resist manipulation by surrogate brokers.

Many surrogate mothers see pregnancy as a way to feel "adequate," "appreciated," or "special." In other words, these women feel inadequate, unappreciated, or unadmired when they are not pregnant.[33] Lacking the power to achieve some worthwhile status in their own right, they must subordinate themselves to others' definitions of their proper place (as baby factories) in order to get from them the appreciation they need to attain a sense of self-worth. But the sense of self-worth one can attain under such circumstances is precarious and ultimately self-defeating. For example, those who seek gratitude on the part of the adoptive parents and

some opportunity to share the joys of seeing their children grow discover all too often that the adoptive parents want nothing to do with them.[34] For while the surrogate mother sees in the arrangement some basis for establishing the personal ties she needs to sustain her emotionally, the adoptive couple sees it as an impersonal commercial contract, one of whose main advantages to them is that all ties between them and the surrogate are ended once the terms of the contract are fulfilled.[35] To them, her presence is a threat to marital unity and a competing object for the child's affections.

These considerations should lead us to question the model of altruism which is held up to women by the surrogacy industry. It is a strange form of altruism which demands such radical self-effacement, alienation from those whom one benefits, and the subordination of one's body, health, and emotional life to the independently defined interests of others.[36] Why should this model of "altruism" be held up to *women*? True altruism does not involve such subordination, but rather the autonomous and self-confident exercise of skill, talent, and judgment. (Consider the dedicated doctor.) The kind of altruism we see admired in surrogate mothers involves a lack of self-confidence, a feeling that one can be truly worthy only through self-effacement. This model of altruism, far from affirming the freedom and dignity of women, seems all too conveniently designed to keep their sense of self-worth hostage to the interests of a more privileged class.[37]

The primary distortions which arise from treating women's labor as a commodity — the surrogate mother's alienation from loved ones, her degradation, and her exploitation — stem from a common source. This is the failure to acknowledge and treat appropriately the surrogate mother's emotional engagement with her labor. Her labor is alienated, because she must suppress her emotional ties with her own child, and may be manipulated into reinterpreting these ties in a trivializing way. She is degraded, because her independent ethical perspective is denied, or demoted to the status of a cash sum. She is exploited, because her emotional needs and vulnerabilities are not treated as characteristics which call for consideration, but as factors which may be manipulated to encourage her to make a grave self-sacrifice to the broker's and adoptive couple's advantage. These considerations provide strong grounds for sustaining the claims of women's labor to its "product," the child. The attempt to redefine parenthood so as to strip women of parental claims to the children they bear does violence to their emotional engagement with the project of bringing children into the world.

COMMERCIAL SURROGACY, FREEDOM, AND THE LAW

In the light of these ethical objections to commercial surrogacy, what position should the law take on the practice? At the very least, surrogate contracts should not be enforceable. Surrogate mothers should not be forced to relinquish their children if they have formed emotional bonds with them. Any other treatment of women's ties to the children they bear is degrading.

But I think these arguments support the stronger conclusion that commercial surrogate contracts should be illegal, and that surrogate agencies who arrange such contracts should be subject to criminal penalties.[38] Commercial surrogacy constitutes a degrading and harmful traffic in children, violates the dignity of women, and subjects both children and women to a serious risk of exploitation. But are these problems inherent in the practice of commercial surrogacy? Defenders of the practice have suggested three reforms intended to eliminate these problems: (1) give the surrogate mother the option of keeping her child after birth; (2) impose stringent regulations on private surrogate agencies; (3) replace private surrogate agencies with a state-run monopoly on surrogate arrangements. Let us consider each of these options in turn.

Some defenders of commercial surrogacy suggest that the problem of respecting the surrogate mother's potential attachment to her child can be solved by granting the surrogate mother the option to reserve her parental rights after birth.[39] But such an option would not significantly change the conditions of the surrogate mother's labor. Indeed, such a provision would pressure the agency to demean the mother's self-regard more than ever. Since it could not rely on the law to enforce the adoptive parents' wishes regardless of the surrogate's feelings, it would have to make sure that she assumed the perspective which it and its clients have of her: as "rented plumbing."

Could such dangers be avoided by careful regulation of the surrogate industry? Some have suggested that exploitation of women could be avoided by such measures as properly screening surrogates, setting low fixed fees (to avoid tempting women in financial duress), and requiring independent counsel for the surrogate mother.[40] But no one knows how to predict who will suffer grave psychological damage from surrogacy, and the main forms of duress encountered in the industry are emotional rather than financial. Furthermore, there is little hope that regulation would check the exploitation of surrogate mothers. The most significant encounters between the mothers and the surrogate agencies take place behind closed doors. It is impossible to regulate the multifarious ways in which brokers can subtly manipulate the emotions of the vulnerable to their own advantage. Advocates of commercial surrogacy claim that their failure rate is extremely low, since only five out of the first five hundred cases were legally contested by surrogate mothers. But we do not know how many surrogate mothers were browbeaten into relinquishing their children, feel violated by their treatment, or would feel violated had their perspectives not been manipulated by the other parties to the contract. The dangers of exploiting women through commercial surrogacy are too great to ignore, and too deep to effectively regulate.

Could a state-run monopoly on surrogate arrangements eliminate the risk of degrading and exploiting surrogate mothers?[41] A nonprofit state agency would arguably have no incentive to exploit surrogates, and it would screen the adoptive parents for the sake of the best interests of the child. Nevertheless, as long as the surrogate mother is paid money to bear a child and terminate her parental rights, the commercial norms leading to her degradation still apply. For these norms are constitutive of our understanding of what the surrogate contract is for. Once such an arrangement becomes socially legitimized, these norms will govern the understandings of participants in the practice and of society at large, or at least compete powerfully with the rival parental norms. And what judgment do these norms make of a mother who, out of love for her child, decides that she cannot relinquish it? They blame her for commercial irresponsibility and flighty emotions. Her transformation of moral and emotional perspective, which she experiences as real but painful growth, looks like a capricious and selfish exercise of will from the standpoint of the market, which does not distinguish the deep commitments of love from arbitrary matters of taste.[42]

The fundamental problem with commercial surrogacy is that commercial norms are inherently manipulative when they are applied to the sphere of parental love. Manipulation occurs whenever norms are deployed to psychologically coerce others into a position where they cannot defend their own interests or articulate their own perspective without being charged with irresponsibility or immorality for doing so. A surrogate contract is inherently manipulative, since the very form of the contract invokes commercial norms which, whether upheld by the law or by social custom only, imply that the mother should feel guilty and irresponsible for loving her own child.

But hasn't the surrogate mother decided in advance that she is not interested in viewing her relationship to her child in this way? Regardless of her initial state of mind, once she enters the contract, she is not free to develop an autonomous perspective on her relationship with her child. She is contractually bound to manipulate her emotions to agree with the interests of the adoptive parents. Few things reach deeper into the self than a parent's evolving relationship with her own child. To lay claim to the course of this relationship in virtue of a cash payment constitutes a severe violation of the mother's personhood and a denial of the mother's autonomy.

Two final objections stand in the way of criminalizing commercial surrogacy. Prohibiting the practice might be thought to infringe two rights: the right of procreation, and the right to freedom of contract. Judge Harvey Sorkow, in upholding the legality and enforceability of commercial surrogate parenting contracts, based much of his argument on an interpretation of the freedom to procreate. He argued that the protection of the right to procreate requires the protection of non-coital means of procreation, including commercial surrogacy. The interests upheld by the creation of the family are the same, regardless of the means used to bring the family into existence.[43]

Sorkow asserts a blanket right to procreate, without carefully examining the specific human interests protected by such a right. The interest protected by the right to procreate is that of being able to create and sustain a family life with some integrity. But the enforcement of surrogate contracts against the will of the mother destroys one family just as surely as it creates another. And the same interest which generates the right to procreate also generates an obligation to uphold the integrity of family life which constrains the exercise of this right.[44] To recognize the legality of commercial surrogate contracts would undermine the integrity of families by giving public sanction to a practice which expresses contempt for the moral and emotional ties which bind a mother to her children, legitimates the view that these ties are merely the product of arbitrary

will, properly loosened by the offering of a monetary incentive, and fails to respect the claims of genetic and gestational ties to children which provide children with a more secure place in the world than commerce can supply.

The freedom of contract provides weaker grounds for supporting commercial surrogacy. This freedom is already constrained, notably in preventing the purchase and sale of human beings. Yet one might object that prohibiting surrogate contracts could undermine the status of women by implying that they do not have the competence to enter into and rationally discharge the obligations of commercial contracts. Insofar as the justification for prohibiting commercial surrogacy depends upon giving special regard to women's emotional ties to their children, it might be thought to suggest that women as a group are too emotional to subject themselves to the dispassionate discipline of the market. Then prohibiting surrogate contracts would be seen as an offensive, paternalistic interference with the autonomy of the surrogate mothers.

We have seen, however, that the content of the surrogate contract itself compromises the autonomy of surrogate mothers. It uses the norms of commerce in a manipulative way and commands the surrogate mothers to conform their emotions to the interests of the other parties to the contract. The surrogate industry fails to acknowledge the surrogate mothers as possessing an independent perspective worthy of consideration. And it takes advantage of motivations — such as self-effacing "altruism" — which women have formed under social conditions inconsistent with genuine autonomy. Hence the surrogate industry itself, far from expanding the realm of autonomy for women, actually undermines the external and internal conditions required for fully autonomous choice by women.

If commercial surrogate contracts were prohibited, this would be no cause for infertile couples to lose hope for raising a family. The option of adoption is still available, and every attempt should be made to open up opportunities for adoption to couples who do not meet standard requirements — for example, because of age. While there is a shortage of healthy white infants available for adoption, there is no shortage of children of other races, mixed-race children, and older and handicapped children who desperately need to be adopted. Leaders of the surrogate industry have proclaimed that commercial surrogacy may replace adoption as the method of choice for infertile couples who wish to raise families. But we should be wary of the racist and eugenic motivations which make some people rally to the surrogate industry at the expense of children who already exist and need homes.

The case of commercial surrogacy raises deep questions about the proper scope of the market in modern industrial societies. I have argued that there are principled grounds for rejecting the substitution of market norms for parental norms to govern the ways women bring children into the world. Such substitutions express ways of valuing mothers and children which reflect an inferior conception of human flourishing. When market norms are applied to the ways we allocate and understand parental rights and responsibilities, children are reduced from subjects of love to objects of use. When market norms are applied to the ways we treat and understand women's reproductive labor, women are reduced from subjects of respect and consideration to objects of use. If we are to retain the capacity to value children and women in ways consistent with a rich conception of human flourishing, we must resist the encroachment of the market upon the sphere of reproductive labor. Women's labor is *not* a commodity.

NOTES

1. See, for example, Gena Corea, *The Mother Machine* (New York: Harper and Row, 1985), pp. 216, 219; Angela Holder, "Surrogate Motherhood: Babies for Fun and Profit," *Case and Comment* 90 (1985): 3–11; and Margaret Jane Radin, "Market Inalienability," *Harvard Law Review* 100 (June 1987): 1849–1937.

2. The notion of valuing something more highly than another can be understood as follows. Some preferences are neither obligatory nor admirable. To value a thing as a mere use-object is to treat it solely in accordance with such nonethical preferences. To value a thing or person more highly than as a mere use-object is to recognize it as having some special intrinsic worth, in virtue of which we form preferences about how to treat the thing which we regard as obligatory or admirable. The person who truly appreciates art does not conceive of art merely as a thing which she can use as she pleases, but as something which commands appreciation. It would be contemptible to willfully destroy the aesthetic qualities of a work of art simply to satisfy some of one's nonethical preferences, and it is a mark of a cultivated and hence admirable person that she has preferences for appreciating art. This account of higher and lower modes of valuation is indebted to Charles Taylor's account of higher and lower values. See Charles Taylor, "The Diversity of Goods," in *Utilitarianism and Beyond*, ed. Amartya Sen and Bernard Williams (Cambridge: Cambridge University Press, 1982), pp. 129–44.

3. This kind of argument shows why treating something as a commodity may be deplorable. Of course, more has to be said to justify prohibiting the commodification of a thing. I shall argue below that the considerations against the commodification of children and

of women's labor are strong enough to justify prohibiting the practice of commercial surrogacy.

4. State laws against selling babies prevent the intended father's wife (if he has one) from being a party to the contract.

5. See Katie Marie Brophy, "A Surrogate Mother Contract to Bear a Child," *Journal of Family Law* 20 (1981–82): 263–91, and Noel Keane, "The Surrogate Parenting Contract," *Adelphia Law Journal* 2 (1983): 45–53, for examples and explanations of surrogate parenting contracts.

6. Mary Warnock, *A Question of Life* (Oxford: Blackwell, 1985), p. 45. This book reprints the Warnock Report on Human Fertilization and Embryology, which was commissioned by the British government for the purpose of recommending legislation concerning surrogacy and other issues. Although the Warnock Report mentions the promotion of altruism as one defense of surrogacy, it strongly condemns the practice overall.

7. John Robertson, "Surrogate Mothers: Not So Novel after All," *Hastings Center Report,* October 1983, pp. 28–34; John Harris, *The Value of Life* (Boston: Routledge and Kegan Paul, 1985).

8. See "No Other Hope for Having a Child," *Time,* 19 January 1987, pp. 50–51. Radin argues that women's traits are also commodified in this practice. See "Market Inalienability," pp. 1932–35.

9. Here I discuss the surrogate industry as it actually exists today. I will consider possible modifications of commercial surrogacy in the final section below.

10. Robert Nozick has objected that my claims about parental love appear to be culture-bound. Do not parents in the Third World, who rely on children to provide for the family subsistence, regard their children as economic goods? In promoting the livelihood of their families, however, such children need not be treated in accordance with market norms—that is, as commodities. In particular, such children usually remain a part of their families, and hence can still be loved by their parents. But insofar as children are treated according to the norms of modern capitalist markets, this treatment is deplorable wherever it takes place.

11. See Elizabeth Landes and Richard Posner, "The Economics of the Baby Shortage," *Journal of Legal Studies* 7 (1978): 323–48, and Richard Posner, "The Regulation of the Market in Adoptions," *Boston University Law Review* 67 (1987): 59–72.

12. Of course, where children are concerned, it is irrelevant whether these fears are reasonable. One of the greatest fears of children is separation from their parents. Adopted children are already known to suffer from separation anxiety more acutely than children who remain with their natural mothers, for they feel that their original mothers did not love them. In adoption, the fact that the child would be even worse off if the mother did not give it up justifies her severing of ties and can help to rationalize this event to the child. But in the case of commercial surrogacy, the severing of ties is done not for the child's sake, but for the parents' sakes. In the adoption case there are explanations for the mother's action which may quell the child's doubts about being loved which are unavailable in the case of surrogacy.

13. Kay Longcope, "Surrogacy: Two Professionals on Each Side of Issue Give Their Arguments for Prohibition and Regulation," *Boston Globe,* 23 March 1987, pp. 18–19; and Iver Peterson, "Baby M Case: Surrogate Mothers Vent Feelings," *New York Times,* 2 March 1987, pp. B1, B4.

14. Herbert Krimmel, "The Case against Surrogate Parenting," *Hastings Center Report,* October 1983, pp. 35–37.

15. Judge Sorkow made this argument in ruling on the famous case of Baby M. See *In Re Baby M,* 217 N.J. Super 313. Reprinted in *Family Law Reporter* 13 (1987): 2001–30. Chief Justice Wilentz of the New Jersey Supreme Court overruled Sorkow's judgment. See *In the Matter of Baby M,* 109 N.J. 396, 537 A:2d 1227 (1988).

16. Sallyann Payton has observed that the law does not permit the sale of parental rights, only their relinquishment or forced termination by the state, and these acts are subject to court review for the sake of the child's best interests. But this legal technicality does not change the moral implications of the analogy with baby-selling. The mother is still paid to do what she can to relinquish her parental rights and to transfer custody of the child to the father. Whether or not the courts occasionally prevent this from happening, the actions of the parties express a commercial orientation to children which is degrading and harmful to them. The New Jersey Supreme Court ruled that surrogacy contracts are void precisely because they assign custody without regard to the child's best interests. See *In the Matter of Baby M*, p. 1246.

17. Robertson, "Surrogate Mothers: Not So Novel after All," p. 32; Harris, *The Value of Life*, p. 144–45.

18. See Philip Parker, "Surrogate Motherhood: The Interaction of Litigation, Legislation and Psychiatry," *International Journal of Law and Psychiatry* 5 (1982): 341–54.

19. The consent-intent rule would not, however, change the fact that commercial surrogacy replaces parental norms with market norms. For the rule itself embodies the market norm which acknowledges only voluntary, contractual relations among people as having moral force. Whereas familial love invites children into a network of unwilled relationships broader than those they have with their parents, the willed contract creates an exclusive relationship between the parents and the child only.

20. I thank Steven Darwall and David Anderson for clarifying my thoughts on this point.

21. I am indebted to Dr. Ezekiel Emanuel for this point.

22. One engages in emotional labor when one is paid to express or repress certain emotions. On the concept of emotional labor and its consequences for workers, see Arlie Hochschild, *The Managed Heart* (Berkeley and Los Angeles: University of California Press, 1983).

23. Noel Keane and Dennis Breo, *The Surrogate Mother* (New York: Everest House, 1981), p. 291; Brophy, "A Surrogate Mother Contract," p. 267. The surrogate's husband is also required to agree to this clause of the contract.

24. One might ask why this argument does not extend to all cases in which one might form an emotional attachment to an object one has contracted to sell. If I sign a contract with you to sell my car to you, can I back out if I decide I am too emotionally attached to it? My argument is based upon the distinctive characteristics of parental love — a mode of valuation which should not be confused with less profound modes of valuation which generate sentimental attachments to things. The degree to which other modes of valuation generate claims to consideration which tell against market norms remains an open question.

25. Corea, *The Mother Machine*, p. 222.

26. Keane and Breo, *The Surrogate Mother*, p. 292.

27. Kay Longcope, "Standing Up for Mary Beth," *Boston Globe*, 5 March 1987, p. 83; Daniel Goleman, "Motivations of Surrogate Mothers," *New York Times*, 20 January 1987, p. C1; Robertson, "Surrogate Mothers: Not So Novel after All," pp. 30, 34 n. 8. Neither the surrogate mothers themselves nor psychiatrists have been able to predict which women will experience such grief.

28. See Hochschild, *The Managed Heart*, for an important empirical study of the dynamics of commercialized emotional labor.

29. Keane and Breo, *The Surrogate Mother*, pp. 236–37.

30. For one account of how a surrogate mother who came to regret her decision viewed her own moral transformation, see Elizabeth Kane, *Birth Mother: The Story of America's First Legal Surrogate Mother* (San Diego: Harcourt Brace Jovanovich, 1988). I argue below that the implications of commodifying women's labor are not significantly changed even if the contract is unenforceable.

31. Susan Ince, "Inside the Surrogate Industry," in *Test-Tube Women*, ed. Rita Arditti, Renate Duelli Klein, and Shelley Minden (Boston: Pandora Press, 1984), p. 110.

32. Philip Parker, "Motivation of Surrogate Mothers: Initial Findings," *American Journal of Psychiatry* 140 (1983): 117–18.

33. The surrogate broker Noel Keane is remarkably open about reporting the desperate emotional insecurities which shape the lives of so many surrogate mothers, while displaying little sensitivity to the implications of his taking advantage of these motivations to make his business a financial success. See especially Keane and Breo, *The Surrogate Mother*, pp. 247ff.

34. See, for example, the story of the surrogate mother Nancy Barrass in Anne Fleming, "Our Fascination with Baby M," *New York Times Magazine*, 29 March 1987, p. 38.

35. For evidence of these disparate perspectives, see Peterson, "Baby M Case: Surrogate Mothers Vent Feelings," p. B4.

36. The surrogate mother is required to obey all doctor's orders made in the interests of the child's health. (See Brophy, "A Surrogate Mother Contract"; Keane, "The Surrogate Parenting Contract"; and Ince, "Inside the Surrogate Industry.") These orders could include forcing her to give up her job, travel plans, and recreational activities. The doctor could confine her to bed, and order her to submit to surgery and take drugs. One can hardly exercise an autonomous choice over one's health if one could be held in breach of contract and liable for $35,000 damages for making a decision contrary to the wishes of one's doctor.

37. See Corea, *The Mother Machine*, pp. 227–33, and Christine Overall, *Ethics and Human Reproduction* (Boston: Allen and Unwin, 1987), pp. 122–28. Both emphasize the social conditions which undermine the claim that women choose to be surrogate mothers under conditions of autonomy.

38. Both of these conclusions follow the Warnock commission's recommendations. See Warnock, *A Question of Life*, pp. 43–44, 46–47. Since the surrogate mother is a victim of commercial surrogacy arrangements, she should not be prosecuted for entering into them. And my arguments are directed only against surrogacy as a commercial enterprise.

39. Barbara Cohen, "Surrogate Mothers: Whose Baby Is It?" *American Journal of Law and Medicine* 10 (1984): 282; Peter Singer and Deane Wells, *Making Babies* (New York: Scribner, 1985), pp. 106–7, 111.

40. Harris, *The Value of Life*, pp. 143–44, 156.

41. Singer and Wells support this recommendation in *Making Babies*, pp. 110–11. See also the dissenting opinion of the Warnock commission, *A Question of Life*, pp. 87–89.

42. See Fleming, "Our Fascination with Baby M," for a sensitive discussion of Americans' conflicting attitudes toward surrogate mothers who find they cannot give up their children.

43. *In Re Baby M*, p. 2022. See also Robertson, "Surrogate Mothers: Not So Novel after All," p. 32.

44. The Catholic Church makes this principle the fundamental basis for its own criticism of surrogate motherhood. See Congregation for the Doctrine of the Faith, "Instruction on Respect for Human Life In Its Origin and on the Dignity of Procreation: Replies to Certain Questions of the Day," reproduced in *New York Times*, 11 March 1987, pp. A14–A17.

LAURA M. PURDY

Surrogate Mothering: Exploitation or Empowerment?

INTRODUCTION

'Pregnancy is barbaric'[1] proclaimed Shulamith Firestone in the first heady days of the new women's movement; she looked forward to the time when technology would free women from the oppression of biological reproduction. Yet as reproductive options multiply, some feminists are making common cause with conservatives for a ban on innovations. What is going on?

Firestone argued that nature oppresses women by leaving them holding the reproductive bag, while men are free of such burden; so long as this biological inequality holds, women will never be free. (Firestone, 198–200) It is now commonplace to point out the naivety of her claim: it is not the biological difference, per se, that oppresses women, but its social significance. So we need not change biology, only attitudes and institutions.

This insight has helped us to see how to achieve a better life for women, but I wonder if it is the whole story. Has Firestone's brave claim no lesson at all for us?

Her point was that being with child is uncomfortable and dangerous, and it can limit women's lives. We have become more sensitive to the ways in which social arrangements can determine how much these difficulties affect us. However, even in feminist utopias, where sex or gender are considered morally irrelevant except where they may entail special needs, a few difficulties would remain. Infertility, for instance, would exist, as would the desire for a child in circumstances where pregnancy is impossible or undesirable.

At present, the problem of infertility is generating a whole series of responses and solutions. Among them are high-tech procedures like IVF, and social arrangements like surrogate motherhood. Both these techniques are also provoking a storm of concern and protest. As each raises a distinctive set of issues, they need to be dealt with separately, and I shall here consider only surrogate motherhood.

One might argue that no feminist paradise would need any practice such as this. As Susan Sherwin argues, it could not countenance 'the capitalism, racism, sexism, and elitism of our culture [that] have combined to create a set of attitudes which views children as commodities whose value is derived from their possession of parental chromosomes.'[2] Nor will society define women's fulfilment as only in terms of their relationship to genetically related children. No longer will children be needed as men's heirs or women's livelihood.

We will, on the contrary, desire relationships with children for the right reasons: the urge to nurture, teach and be close to them. No longer will we be driven by narcissistic wishes for clones or immortality to seek genetic offspring no matter what the cost. Indeed, we will have recognized that children are the promise and responsibility of the whole human community. And childrearing practices will reflect these facts, including at least a more diffuse family life that allows children to have significant relationships with others. Perhaps childbearing will be communal.

This radically different world is hard to picture realistically, even by those like myself who—I think—most ardently wish for it. The doubts I feel are fanned by the visions of so-called 'cultural feminists' who glorify traditionally feminine values. Family life can be suffocating, distorting, even deadly.[3] Yet there is a special closeness that arises from being a child's primary caretaker, just as there can be a special thrill in witnessing the unfolding of biologically driven traits in that child. These pleasures justify risking neither the health of the child[4] nor that of the mother; nobody's general well-being should be sacrificed to them, nor do they warrant huge social investments. However, they are things that, other things being equal, it would be desirable to preserve so long as people continue to have anything like their current values. If this is so, then evaluating the morality of practices that open up new ways of creating children is worthwhile.[5]

MORAL OR IMMORAL?

What is surrogate mothering exactly? Physically, its essential features are as follows: a woman is inseminated with the sperm of a man to whom she is not married. When the baby is born she relinquishes her claim to it in favour of another, usually the man from whom the sperm was obtained. As currently practiced, she provides the egg, so her biological input is at least equal to that of the man. 'Surrogate' mothering may not therefore be the best term for what she is doing.[6]

By doing these things she also acts socially—to take on the burden and risk of pregnancy for another, and to separate sex and reproduction, reproduction and childrearing, and reproduction and marriage. If she takes money for the transaction (apart from payment of medical bills), she may even be considered to be selling a baby.

The bare physical facts would not warrant the welter of accusation and counter-accusation that surrounds the practice.[7] It is the social aspects that have engendered the acrimony about exploitation, destruction of the family, and baby-selling. So far we have reached no consensus about the practice's effect on women or its overall morality.

I believe that the appropriate moral framework for addressing questions about the social aspects of contracted pregnancy is consequentialist.[8] This framework requires us to attempt to separate those consequences that invariably accompany a given act from those that accompany it only in particular circumstances. Doing this compels us to consider whether a practice's necessary features lead to unavoidable overridingly bad consequences. It also demands that we look at how different circumstances are likely to affect the outcome. Thus a practice which is moral in a feminist society may well be immoral in a sexist one. This distinction allows us to tailor morality to different conditions for optimum results without thereby incurring the charge of malignant relativism.

Before examining arguments against the practice of contracted pregnancy, let us take note of why people might favour it. First, as noted before, alleviating infertility can create much happiness. Secondly, there are often good reasons to consider transferring burden and risk from one individual to another. Pregnancy may be a serious burden or risk for one woman, whereas it is much less so for another. Some women love being pregnant, others hate it; pregnancy interferes with work for some, not for others; pregnancy also poses much higher levels of risk to health (or even life) for some than for others. Reducing burden and risk is a benefit not only for the woman involved, but also for the resulting child. High-risk pregnancies create, among other things, serious risk of prematurity, one of the major sources of handicap in babies. Furthermore, we could prevent serious genetic diseases by allowing carriers to avoid pregnancy. A third benefit of 'surrogate mothering' is that it makes possible the creation of non-traditional families. This can be a significant source of happiness to single women and gay couples.

All of the above presuppose that there is some advantage in making possible at least partially genetically based relationships between parents and offspring. Although, as I have argued above, we might be better off without this desire, I doubt that we will soon be free of it. Therefore, if we can satisfy it at little cost, we should try to do so.

IS SURROGATE MOTHERING ALWAYS WRONG?

Despite the foregoing advantages, some feminists argue that the practice is *necessarily* wrong: it is wrong because it must betray women's and society's basic interests.[9]

What, if anything is wrong with the practice? Let us consider the first three acts I described earlier: transferring burden and risk, separating sex and reproduction, and separating reproduction and childrearing. Separation of reproduction and marriage will not be dealt with here.

Is it wrong to take on the burden of pregnancy for another? Doing this is certainly supererogatory, for pregnancy can threaten comfort, health, even life. One might argue that women should not be allowed to take these risks, but that would be paternalistic. We do not forbid mountain-climbing or riding a motorcycle on these grounds. How could we then forbid a woman to undertake this particular risk?

Perhaps the central issue is the transfer of burden from one woman to another. However, we frequently do just that—much more often than we recognize. Anyone who has her house cleaned, her hair done, or her clothes dry-cleaned is engaging in this procedure;[10] so is anyone who depends on agriculture or public works such as bridges.[11] To the objection that in this case the bargain includes the risk to life and limb, as well as use of time and skills, the answer is that the other activities just cited entail surprisingly elevated risk rates from exposure to toxic chemicals or dangerous machinery.[12]

Furthermore, it is not even true that contracted pregnancy merely shifts the health burden and risks associated with pregnancy from one woman to another. In some cases (infertility, for example) it makes the impossible possible; in others (for women with potentially high-risk pregnancies) the net risk is lowered.[13] As we saw, babies benefit, too, from better health and fewer handicaps. Better health and fewer handicaps in both babies and women also means that scarce resources can be made available for other needs, thus benefiting society in general.

I do think that there is, in addition, something suspect about all this new emphasis on risk. Awareness of risks inherent in even normal pregnancy constitutes progress: women have always been expected to forge ahead with childbearing oblivious to risk. Furthermore, childbearing has been thought to be something women owed to men or to society at large, regardless of their own feelings about a given—or any—pregnancy. When women had little say about these matters, we never heard about risk.[14] Why are we hearing about risk only now, now that women finally have some choices, some prospect of remuneration?[15] For that matter, why is our attention not drawn to the fact that surrogacy is one of the least risky approaches to non-traditional reproduction?[16]

Perhaps what is wrong about this kind of transfer is that it necessarily involves exploitation. Such exploitation may take the form of exploitation of women by men and exploitation of the rich by the poor. This possibility deserves serious consideration, and will be dealt with shortly.

Is there anything wrong with the proposed separation of sex and reproduction? Historically, this separation—in the form of contraception—has been beneficial to women and to society as a whole. Although there are those who judge the practice immoral, I do not think we need belabour the issue here.

It may be argued that not all types of separation are morally on a par. Contraception is permissible, because it spares women's health, promotes autonomy, strengthens family life, and helps make population growth manageable. But separation of sex and reproduction apart from contraception is quite another kettle of fish: it exploits women, weakens family life, and may increase population. Are these claims true and relevant?

Starting with the last first, if we face a population problem, it would make sense to rethink overall population policy, not exploit the problems of the infertile.[17] If family strengthening is a major justification for contraception, we might point out that contracted pregnancy will in some cases do the same. Whether or not having children can save a failing marriage, it will certainly prevent a man who wants children from leaving a woman incapable of providing them. We may bewail his priorities, but if his wife is sufficiently eager for the relationship to continue it would again be paternalistic for us to forbid 'surrogacy' in such circumstances. That 'surrogacy' reduces rather than promotes women's autonomy may be true under some circumstances, but there are good grounds for thinking that it can also enhance autonomy. It also remains to be shown that the practice systematically burdens women, or one class of women. In principle, the availability of new choices can be expected to nourish rather than stunt women's lives, so long as they retain control over their bodies and lives. The claim that contracted pregnancy destroys women's individuality and constitutes alienated labour, as Christine Overall argues, depends not only on a problematic Marxist analysis, but on the assumption that other jobs available to women are seriously less alienating.[18]

Perhaps what is wrong here is that contracted pregnancy seems to be the other side of the coin of prostitution. Prostitution is sex without reproduction; 'surrogacy' is reproduction without sex. But it is difficult to form a persuasive argument that goes beyond mere guilt by association. Strictly speaking, contracted pregnancy is not prostitution; a broad-based Marxist definition would include it, but also traditional marriage. I think that in the absence of further argument, the force of this accusation is primarily emotional.

Perhaps the dread feature contracted pregnancy shares with prostitution is that it is a lazy person's way of exploiting their own 'natural resources'. But I suspect that this idea reveals a touchingly naive view of what it takes to be a successful prostitute, not to mention the effort involved in running an optimum pregnancy. Overall takes up this point by asserting that it

is not and cannot be merely one career choice among others. It is not a real alternative. It is implausible to suppose that fond parents would want it for their daughters. We are unlikely to set up training courses for surrogate mothers. Schools holding 'career days' for their future graduates will surely not invite surrogate mothers to address the class on advantages of 'vocation'. And surrogate motherhood does not seem to be the kind of thing one would put on one's curriculum vitae. (p. 126)

But this seems to me to be a blatant *ad populum* argument.

Such an objection ought, in any case, to entail general condemnation of apparently effortless ways of life that involved any utilization of our distinctive characteristics.

We surely exploit our personal 'natural resources' whenever we work. Ditchdiggers use their bodies, professors use their minds. Overall seems particularly to object to some types of 'work': contracted pregnancy 'is no more a real job option than selling one's blood or one's gametes or one's bodily organs can be real job options' (p. 126). But her discussion makes clear that her denial that such enterprises are 'real' jobs is not based on any social arrangements that preclude earning a living wage doing these things, but rather on the moral judgement that they are wrong. They are wrong because they constitute serious 'personal and bodily alienation.' Yet her arguments for such alienation are weak. She contends that women who work as 'surrogates' are deprived of any expression of individuality (p. 126), are interchangeable (p. 127), and they have no choice about whose sperm to harbor (p. 128). It is true that, given a reasonable environment (partly provided by the woman herself), bodies create babies without conscious effort. This fact, it seems to me, has no particular moral significance: many tasks can be accomplished in similar ways yet are not thought valueless.[19]

It is also usually true that women involved in contracted pregnancy are, in some sense, interchangeable. But the same is true, quite possibly necessarily so, of most jobs. No one who has graded mounds of logic exams or introductory ethics essays could reasonably withhold their assent to this claim, even though college teaching is one of the most autonomous careers available. Even those of us lucky enough to teach upper level courses that involve more expression of individual expertise and choice can be slotted into standardized job descriptions. Finally, it is just false that a woman can have no say about whose sperm she accepts: this could be guaranteed by proper regulation.

I wonder whether there is not some subtle devaluing of the physical by Overall. If so, then we are falling into the trap set by years of elitist equations of women, nature and inferiority.

What I think is really at issue here is the disposition of the fruit of contracted pregnancy: babies. However, it seems to be generally permissible to dispose of or barter what we produce with both our minds and our bodies — except for that which is created by our reproductive organs. So the position we are considering may just be a version of the claim that it is wrong to separate reproduction and childrearing.

Why? It is true that women normally expect to become especially attached to the product of this particular kind of labour, and we generally regard such attachment as desirable. It seems to be essential for successfully rearing babies the usual way. But if they are to be reared by others who are able to form the appropriate attachment, then what is wrong if a surrogate mother fails to form it? It seems to me that the central question here is whether this 'maternal instinct' really exists, and, if it does, whether suppressing it is always harmful.

Underlying these questions is the assumption that bonding with babies is 'natural' and therefore 'good'. Perhaps so: the evolutionary advantage of such a tendency would be clear. It would be simpleminded, however, to assume that our habits are biologically determined: our culture is permeated with pronatalist bias.[20] 'Natural' or not, whether a tendency to such attachment is desirable could reasonably be judged to depend on circumstance. When infant mortality is high[21] or responsibility for childrearing is shared by the community, it could do more harm than good. Beware the naturalistic fallacy![22]

But surely there is something special about gestating a baby. That is, after all, the assumption behind the judgement that Mary Beth Whitehead, not William Stern, had a stronger claim to Baby M. The moral scoreboard seems clear: they both had the same genetic input, but she gestated the baby, and therefore has a better case for social parenthood.[23]

We need to be very careful here. Special rights have a way of being accompanied by special responsibilities:

women's unique gestational relationship with babies may be taken as reason to confine them once more to the nursery. Furthermore, positing special rights entailed directly by biology flirts again with the naturalistic fallacy and undermines our capacity to adapt to changing situations and forge our destiny.[24]

Furthermore, we already except many varieties of such separation. We routinely engage in sending children to boarding school, foster parenting, daycare, and so forth; in the appropriate circumstances, these practices are clearly beneficial. Hence, any blanket condemnation of separating reproduction and childrearing will not wash; additional argument is needed for particular classes of cases.

John Robertson points out that the arguments against separating reproduction and childrearing used against contracted pregnancy are equally valid—but unused—with respect to adoption.[25] Others, such as Herbert Krimmel, reject this view by arguing that there is a big moral difference between giving away an already existing baby and deliberately creating one to give away. This remains to be shown, I think. It is also argued that as adoption outcomes are rather negative, we should be wary of extending any practice that shares its essential features. In fact, there seems to be amazingly little hard information about adoption outcomes. I wonder if the idea that they are bad results from media reports of offspring seeking their biological forbears. There is, in any case, reason to think that there are differences between the two practices such that the latter is likely to be more successful than the former.[26]

None of the social descriptions of surrogacy thus seem to clearly justify the outcry against the practice. I suspect that the remaining central issue is the crucial one: surrogacy is baby-selling and participating in this practice exploits and taints women.

IS SURROGACY BABY-SELLING?

In the foregoing, I deliberately left vague the question of payment in contracted pregnancy. It is clear that there is a recognizable form of the practice that does not include payment; however, it also seems clear that controversy is focusing on the commercial form. The charge is that it is baby-selling and that this is wrong.

Is paid 'surrogacy' baby-selling? Proponents deny that it is, arguing that women are merely making available their biological services. Opponents retort that as women are paid little or nothing if they fail to hand over a live, healthy child, they are indeed selling a baby. If they are merely selling their services they would get full pay, even if the child were born dead.

It is true [that] women who agree to contracts relieving clients of responsibility in this case are being exploited. They, after all, have done their part, risked their risks, and should be paid—just like the physicians involved. Normal childbearing provides no guarantee of a live, healthy child—why should contracted pregnancy?

There are further reasons for believing that women are selling their services, not babies. Firstly, we do not consider children property. Therefore, as we cannot sell what we do not own, we cannot be selling babies. What creates confusion here is that we do think we own sperm and ova. (Otherwise, how could men sell their sperm?) Yet we do not own what they become, persons. At what point, then, does the relationship cease to be describable as 'ownership'?

Resolution of this question is not necessary to the current discussion. If we can own babies, there seems to be nothing problematic about selling them. If ownership ceases at some time before birth (and could thus be argued to be unconnected with personhood), then it is not selling of babies that is going on.

Although this response deals with the letter of the objection about babyselling, it fails to heed its spirit, which is that we are trafficking in persons, and that such trafficking is wrong. Even if we are not 'selling', something nasty is happening.

The most common analogy, with slavery, is weak. Slavery is wrong according to any decent moral theory: the institution allows people to be treated badly. Their desires and interests, whose satisfaction is held to be essential for a good life, are held in contempt. Particularly egregious is the callous disregard of emotional ties to family and self-determination generally. But the institution of surrogate mothering deprives babies of neither.[27] In short, as Robertson contends, 'the purchasers do not buy the right to treat the child . . . as a commodity or property. Child abuse and neglect laws still apply' (p. 655).

If 'selling babies' is not the right description of what is occurring, then how are we to explain what happens when the birth mother hands the child over to others? One plausible suggestion is that she is giving up her parental right to have a relationship with the child.[28] That it is wrong to do this for pay remains to be shown. Although it would be egoistic and immoral to 'sell' an ongoing, friendly relationship (doing so would raise questions about whether it was friendship at all), the immorality of selling a relationship with an organism your body has created but with which you do not yet have a unique social bond, is a great deal less clear.[29]

People seem to feel much less strongly about the wrongness of such acts when motivated by altruism; refusing compensation is the only acceptable proof of such altruism. The act is, in any case, socially valuable. Why then must it be motivated by altruistic considerations? We do not frown upon those who provide other socially valuable services even when they do not have the 'right' motive. Nor do we require them to be unpaid. For instance, no one expects physicians, no matter what their motivation, to work for beans. They provide an important service; their motivation is important only to the extent that it affects quality.

In general, workers are required to have appropriate skills, not particular motivations.[30] Once again, it seems that there is a different standard for women and for men.

One worry is that women cannot be involved in contracted pregnancy without harming themselves, as it is difficult to let go of a child without lingering concern. So far, despite the heavily publicized Baby M case, this appears not to be necessarily true.[31]

Another worry is that the practice will harm children. Children's welfare is, of course, important. Children deserve the same consideration as other persons, and no society that fails to meet their basic needs is morally satisfactory. Yet I am suspicious of the objections raised on their behalf in these discussions: recourse to children's alleged well-being is once again being used as a trump card against women's autonomy.

First, we hear only about possible risks, never possible benefits, which, as I have been arguing, could be substantial.[32] Second, the main objection raised is the worry about how children will take the knowledge that their genetic mother conceived on behalf of another. We do not know how children will feel about having had such 'surrogate' mothers. But as it is not a completely new phenomenon we might start our inquiry about this topic with historical evidence, not pessimistic speculation. In any case, if the practice is dealt with in an honest and commonsense way, particularly if it becomes quite common (and therefore 'normal'), there is likely to be no problem. We are also hearing about the worries of existing children of women who are involved in the practice: there are reports that they fear their mother will give them away, too. But surely we can make clear to children the kinds of distinctions that distinguish the practice from slavery or baby-selling in the first place.

Although we must try to foresee what might harm children, I cannot help but wonder about the double standards implied by this speculation. The first double standard occurs when those who oppose surrogacy (and reproductive technologies generally) also oppose attempts to reduce the number of handicapped babies born.[33] In the latter context, it is argued that despite their problems handicapped persons are often glad to be alive. Hence it would be paternalistic to attempt to prevent their birth.

Why then do we not hear the same argument here? Instead, the possible disturbance of children born of surrogacy is taken as a reason to prevent their birth. Yet this potential problem is both more remote and most likely involves less suffering than such ailments as spina bifida, Huntington's disease or cystic fibrosis, which some do not take to be reasons to refrain from childbearing.[34]

Considering the sorts of reasons why parents have children, it is hard to see why the idea that one was conceived in order to provide a desperately wanted child to another is thought to be problematic. One might well prefer that to the idea that one was an 'accident', adopted, born because contraception or abortion were not available, conceived to cement a failing marriage, to continue a family line, to qualify for welfare aid, to sex-balance a family, or as an experiment in childrearing. Surely what matters for a child's well-being in the end is whether it is being raised in a loving, intelligent environment.

The second double standard involves a disparity between the interests of women and children. Arguing that surrogacy is wrong because it may upset children suggests a disturbing conception of the moral order. Women should receive consideration at least equal to that accorded children. Conflicts of interest between the two should be resolved according to the same rules we use for any other moral subjects. Those rules should never prescribe sacrificing one individual's basic interest at the mere hint of harm to another.

In sum, there seems to be no reason to think that there is anything necessarily wrong with 'surrogate mothering', even the paid variety. Furthermore, some objections to it depend on values and assumptions that have been the chief building blocks of women's inequality. Why are some feminists asserting them? Is it because 'surrogacy' as currently practiced often exploits women?

IS 'SURROGATE MOTHERING' WRONG IN CERTAIN SITUATIONS?

Even if 'surrogate mothering' is not necessarily immoral, circumstances can render it so. For instance, it is obviously wrong to coerce women to engage in the practice. Also, certain conditions are unacceptable. Among them are clauses in a contract that subordinate a woman's reasonable desires and judgements to the will of another contracting party,[35] clauses legitimating inadequate pay for the risks and discomforts involved, and clauses that penalize her for the birth of a handicapped or dead baby through no fault of her own. Such contracts are now common.[36]

One popular solution to the problem of such immoral contracts is a law forbidding all surrogacy agreements; their terms would then be unenforceable. But I believe that women will continue to engage in surrogate mothering, even if it is unregulated, and this approach leaves them vulnerable to those who change their mind, or will not pay. Fair and reasonable regulations are essential to prevent exploitation of women. Although surrogate mothering may seem risky and uncomfortable to middle-class persons safely ensconced in healthy, interesting, relatively well-paid jobs, with adequate regulation it becomes an attractive option for some women. That these women are more likely than not to be poor is no reason to prohibit the activity.

As I suggested earlier, poor women now face substantial risks in the workplace. Even a superficial survey of hazards in occupations available to poor women would give pause to those who would prohibit surrogacy on the grounds of risk.[37]

Particularly shocking is the list of harmful substances and conditions to which working women are routinely exposed. For instance, cosmeticians and hairdressers, dry cleaners and dental technicians are all exposed to carcinogens in their daily work. (Stellman, Appendixes 1 and 2) Most low-level jobs also have high rates of exposure to toxic chemicals and dangerous machinery, and women take such jobs in disproportionate numbers. It is therefore unsurprising that poor women sicken and die more often than other members of society.[38]

This is not an argument in favour of adding yet another dangerous option to those already facing such women. Nor does it follow that the burdens they already bear justify the new ones. On the contrary, it is imperative to clean up dangerous workplaces. However, it would be utopian to think that this will occur in the near future. We must therefore attempt to improve women's lot under existing conditions. Under these circumstances it would be irrational to prohibit surrogacy on the grounds of risk when women would instead have to engage in still riskier pursuits.

Overall's emphatic assertion that contracted pregnancy is not a 'real choice' for women is unconvincing. Her major argument, as I suggested earlier, is that it is an immoral, alienating option. But she also believes that such apparently expanded choices simply mask an underlying contraction of choice (p. 124). She also fears that by 'endorsing an uncritical freedom of reproductive choice, we may also be implicitly endorsing all conceivable alternatives that an individual might adopt; we thereby abandon the responsibility for evaluating substantive actions in favour of advocating merely formal freedom of choice' (p. 125). Both worries are, as they stand, unpersuasive.

As I argued before, there is something troubling here about the new and one-sided emphasis on risk. If nothing else, we need to remember that contracted pregnancy constitutes a low-tech approach to a social problem, one which would slow the impetus toward expensive and dangerous high-tech solutions.[39]

A desire for children on the part of those who normally could not have them is not likely to disappear anytime soon. We could discount it, as many participants in debate about new reproductive technologies do. After all, nobody promised a rose garden to infertile couples, much less to homosexuals or to single women. Nor is it desirable to propagate the idea that having children is essential for human fulfilment.

But appealing to the sacrosancity of traditional marriage or of blood ties to prohibit otherwise acceptable practices that would satisfy people's desires hardly makes sense, especially when those practices may provide other benefits. Not only might contracted pregnancy be less risky and more enjoyable than other jobs women are forced to take, but there are other advantages as well. Since being pregnant is not usually a full-time occupation, 'surrogate mothering' could buy time for women to significantly improve their lot; students, aspiring writers, and social activists could make real progress toward their goals.

Women have until now done this reproductive labour for free.[40] Paying women to bear children should force us all to recognize this process as the socially useful enterprise that it is, and children as socially valuable creatures whose upbringing and welfare are critically important.

In short, 'surrogate mothering' has the potential to empower women and increase their status in society. The darker side of the story is that it also has frightening potential for deepening their exploitation. The outcome of the current warfare over control of new reproductive possibilities will determine which of these alternatives comes to pass.

NOTES

1. Shulamith Firestone, *The Dialectic of Sex* (New York: Bantam Books, 1970), p. 198. A version of this paper was given at the Eastern SWIP meeting, 26 March 1988. I would like especially to thank Helen B. Holmes and Sara Ann Ketchum for their useful comments on this paper; they are, of course, in no way responsible for its perverse position! Thanks also to the editors and referees of *Bioethics* for their helpful criticisms.

2. Susan Sherwin, 'Feminist Ethics and In Vitro Fertilization,' *Science, Morality and Feminist Theory,* ed. Marsha Hanen and Kai Nielsen, *The Canadian Journal of Philosophy* supplementary volume 13, 1987, p. 277.

3. Consider the many accounts of the devastating things parents have done to children, in particular.

4. See L. M. Purdy 'Genetic Diseases: Can Having Children be Immoral?' *Moral Problems in Medicine,* ed. Samuel Gorovitz, (NJ: Prentice-Hall, 1983), 377–84.

5. Another critical issue is that no feminist utopia will have a supply of 'problem' children whom no one wants. Thus the proposal often heard nowadays that people should just adopt all those handicapped, non-white kids will not do. (Nor does it 'do' now.)

6. I share with Sara Ann Ketchum the sense that this term is not adequate, although I am not altogether happy with her suggestions that we call it 'contracted motherhood' ('New Reproductive Technologies and the Definition of Parenthood: A Feminist Perspective', paper given at the 1987 *Feminism and Legal Theory Conference,* at the University of Wisconsin at Madison, summer 1987, p. 44ff.) It would be better, I think, to reserve terms like 'mother' for the social act of nurturing. I shall therefore substitute the terms 'contracted pregnancy' and 'surrogacy' (in scare quotes).

7. This is not to say that no one would take the same view as I: the Catholic Church, for instance, objects to the masturbatory act required for surrogacy to proceed.

8. The difficulty in choosing the 'right' moral theory to back up judgments in applied ethics, given that none are fully satisfactory continues to be vexing. I would like to reassure those who lose interest at the mere sight of consequentialist — let alone utilitarian — judgment, that there are good reasons for considering justice an integral part of moral reasoning, as it quite obviously has utility.
A different issue is raised by the burgeoning literature on feminist ethics. I strongly suspect that utilitarianism could serve feminists well, if properly applied. (For a defence of this position, see my paper 'Do Feminists Need a New Moral Theory', to be given at the University of Minnesota, Duluth, at the conference *Explorations in Feminist Ethics: Theory and Practice,* 8–9 October 1988.)

9. See for example Gena Corea, *The Mother Machine,* and Christine Overall, *Ethics and Human Reproduction* (Winchester, MA: Allen and Unwin, 1987).

10. These are just a couple of examples in the sort of risky service that we tend to take for granted.

11. Modern agricultural products are brought to us at some risk by farm workers. Any large construction project will also result in some morbidity and mortality.

12. Even something so mundane as postal service involves serious risk on the part of workers.

13. The benefit to both high-risk women and to society is clear. Women need not risk serious deterioration of health or abnormally high death rates.

14. See Laura Purdy, 'The Morality of New Reproductive Technologies,' *The Journal of Social Philosophy* (Winter 1987), pp. 38–48.

15. For elaboration of this view, consider Jane Ollenburger and John Hamlin, '"All Birthing Should Be Paid Labor"—A Marxist Analysis of the Commodification of Motherhood,' *On the Problem of Surrogate Parenthood: Analyzing the Baby M Case,* ed. Herbert Richardson (Lewistong, NY: The Edwin Mellen Press, 1987).

16. Compare the physical risk with that of certain contraceptive technologies, and high-tech fertility treatments like IVF.

17. Infertility is often a result of social arrangements. This process would therefore be especially unfair to those who already have been exposed to more than their share of toxic chemicals or other harmful conditions.

18. Christine Overall, *Ethics and Human Reproduction* (Winchester, MA: Allen & Unwin, 1987), ch. 6. Particularly problematic are her comments about women's loss of individuality, as I will be arguing shortly.

19. Men have been getting handsome pay for sperm donation for years; by comparison with childbearing, such donation is a lark. Yet there has been no outcry about its immorality. Another double standard?

20. See Ellen Peck and Judith Senderowitz, *Pronatalism: The Myth of Mom and Apple Pie* (New York: Thomas Y. Crowell Co., 1974).

21. As it has been at some periods in the past: see for example information about family relationships in Philippe Ariès, *Centuries of Childhood: A Social History of Family Life,* trans. Robert Baldick (New York, 1982), and Lloyd DeMause's work.

22. Consider the arguments in chapter 8 of *Women's Work,* by Ann Oakley (New York: Vintage Books, 1974).

23. One of the interesting things about the practice of contracted pregnancy is that it can be argued to both strengthen and weaken the social recognition of biological relationships. On the one hand, the pregnant woman's biological relationship is judged irrelevant beyond a certain point; on the other, the reason for not valuing it is to enhance that of the sperm donor. This might be interpreted as yet another case where men's interests are allowed to overrule women's. But it might also be interpreted as a salutary step toward awareness that biological ties can and sometimes should be subordinated to social ones. Deciding which interpretation is correct will depend on the facts of particular cases, and the arguments taken to justify the practice in the first place.

24. Science fiction, most notably John Wyndham's *The Midwich Cuckoos,* provides us with thought-provoking material.

25. John Robertson, 'Surrogate Mothers: Not So Novel After All', *Hastings Center Report,* vol. 13, no. 5 (October 1983). This article is reprinted in *Bioethics,* ed. Rem B. Edwards and Glen C. Graber, San Diego, CA: Harcourt, Brace Jovanovich, 1988). Krimmel's article ('The Case Against Surrogate Parenting') was also originally published in the *Hastings Center Report* and is reprinted in *Bioethics.* References here are to the latter.

26. One major difference between adoption and contracted pregnancy is that the baby is handed over virtually at birth, thus ensuring that the trauma sometimes experienced by older adoptees is not experienced. Although children of contracted pregnancy might well be

curious to know about their biological mother, I do not see this as a serious obstacle to the practice, since we could change our policy about this. There is also reason to believe that carefully screened women undertaking a properly regulated contracted pregnancy are less likely to experience lingering pain of separation. First, they have deliberately chosen to go through pregnancy, knowing that they will give the baby up. The resulting sense of control is probably critical to both their short- and long-term well-being. Second, their pregnancy is not the result of trauma. See also Monica B. Morris, 'Reproductive Technology and Restraints,' *Transaction/SOCIETY,* March/April 1988, pp. 16–22, especially p. 18.

27. There may be a problem for the woman who gives birth, as the Baby M case has demonstrated. There is probably a case for a waiting period after the birth during which the woman can change her mind.

28. Heidi Malm suggested this position in her comment on Sara Ann Ketchum's paper 'Selling Babies and Selling Bodies: Surrogate Motherhood and the Problem of Commodification,' at the Eastern Division *APA* meetings, 30 December 1987.

29. Mary Anne Warren suggests, alternatively, that this objection could be obviated by women and children retaining some rights and responsibilities toward each other in contracted pregnancy. Maintaining a relationship of sorts might also, she suggests, help forestall and alleviate whatever negative feelings children might have about such transfers. I agree that such openness is probably a good idea in any case. (Referee's comment.)

30. Perhaps lurking behind the objections of surrogacy is some feeling that it is wrong to earn money by letting your body work, without active effort on your part. But this would rule out sperm selling, as well as using women's beauty to sell products and services.

31. See, for example, James Rachels 'A Report from America: The Baby M Case,' *Bioethics,* vol. 1, n. 4 (October 1987), p. 365. He reports that there have been over six hundred successful cases; see also the above note on adoption.

32. Among them the above mentioned one of being born healthier.

33. To avoid the difficulties about abortion added by the assumption that we are talking about existing foetuses, let us consider here only the issue of whether certain couples should risk pregnancy.

34. There is an interesting link here between these two aspects of reproduction, as the promise of healthier children is, I think, one of the strongest arguments for contracted pregnancy.

35. What this may consist of naturally requires much additional elucidation.

36. See Susan Ince, 'Inside the Surrogate Industry,' *Test-Tube Women,* ed. Rita Arditti, Renate Duelli Klein, and Shelley Minden (London: Pandora Press, 1984).

37. See, for example, Jeanne Mager Stellman, *Women's Work, Women's Health* (New York: Pantheon 1977).

38. See George L. Waldbott, *Health Effects of Environmental Pollutants* (St. Louis: The C.V. Mosby Co., 1973); Nicholas Ashford, *Crisis in the Workplace: Occupational Disease and Injury* (Cambridge: MIT Press, 1976); *Cancer and the Worker* (The New York Academy of Science, 1977); *Environmental Problems in Medicine,* ed. William D. McKee (Springfield, IL: Charles C. Thomas, 1977).

39. These are the ones most likely to put women in the clutches of the paternalistic medical establishment. Exploitation by commercial operations such as that of Noel Keane could be avoided by tight regulation or prohibition altogether of for-profit enterprises.

40. The implications of this fact remain to be fully understood; I suspect that they are detrimental to women and children, but that this is a topic for another paper.

Cloning

R O B E R T   W I N S T O N

The Promise of Cloning for Human Medicine

The production of a sheep clone, Dolly, from an adult somatic cell[1] is a stunning achievement of British science. It also holds great promise for human medicine.

This article was first published in the BMJ [*British Medical Journal*] 1997; 314: 913–14, and is reproduced by permission of the BMJ. Copyright © 1997 by the British Medical Association.

Sadly, the media have sensationalised the implications, ignoring the huge potential of this experiment. Accusations that scientists have been working secretively and without the chance for public debate are invalid. Successful cloning was publicised in 1975,[2] and it is over eight years since Prather *et al.* published details of the first piglet clone after nuclear transfer.[3]

Missing from much of the debate about Dolly is recognition that she is not an identical clone. Part of our genetic material comes from the mitochondria [small "organs" in the cytoplasm that contain DNA] in the cytoplasm of the egg. In Dolly's case only the nuclear DNA was transferred. Moreover, we are a product of our nurture as much as our genetic nature. Monovular twins are genetically closer than are artificially produced clones, and no one could deny that such twins have quite separate identities.

Dolly's birth provokes fascinating questions. How old is she? Her nuclear DNA gives her potentially adult status, but her mitochondria are those of a newborn. Mitochondria are important in the aging process because aging is related to acquired mutations in mitochondrial DNA, possibly caused by oxygen damage during an individual's life.[4] Experimental nuclear transfer in animals and in human cell lines could help elucidate mechanisms for many of these processes.

Equally extraordinary is the question concerning the role of the egg's cytoplasm in mammalian development. Once the quiescent nucleus had been transferred to the recipient egg cell, developmental genes expressed only in very early life were switched on. There are likely to be powerful factors in the cytoplasm of the egg that make this happen. Egg cytoplasm is perhaps the new royal jelly. Studying why and how these genes switch on would give important information about both human development and genetic disease.

Research on nuclear transfer into human eggs has immense clinical value. Here is a model for learning more about somatic cell differentiation. If, in due course, we could influence differentiation to give rise to targeted cell types we might generate many tissues of great value in transplantation. These could include skin and blood cells, and possibly neuronal tissue, for the treatment of injury, for bone marrow transplants for leukaemia, and for degenerative diseases such as Parkinson's disease. One problem to be overcome is the existence of histocompatibility antigens encoded by mitochondrial DNA,[5] but there may be various ways of altering their expression. Cloning techniques might also be useful in developing transgenic animals — for example, for human xenotransplantation [transplantation of organs from non-human animals].

There are also environmental advantages in pursuing this technology. Mention has been made of the use of these methods to produce dairy herds and other livestock. This would be of limited value because animals with genetic diversity derived by sexual reproduction will always be preferable to those produced asexually. The risk of a line of farm animals prone to a particular disease would be ever present. However, cloning offers real prospects for preservation of endangered or rare species.

In human reproduction, cloning techniques could offer prospects to sufferers from intractable infertility. At present there is no treatment, for example, for those men who exhibit total germ cell failure. Clearly it is far fetched to believe that we are now able to reproduce the process of meiosis, but it may be possible in future to produce a haploid cell from the male which could be used for fertilisation of female gametes. Even if straight cloning techniques were used, the mother would contribute important constituents — her mitochondrial genes, intrauterine influences, and subsequent nurture.

Regulation of cloning is needed, but British law already covers this. Talk of "legal loopholes"[6] is wrong. The Human Fertilisation and Embryology Act may need modification, but there is no particular urgency. A precipitate ban on human nuclear transfer would, for example, prevent the use of in vitro fertilisation and preimplantation diagnosis for those couples at risk of having children who have appalling mitochondrial diseases.[7] Self regulation and legislation already work well. Apart from any other consideration, it seems highly unlikely that doctors would transfer human clones to the uterus out of simple self interest. Many of the animal clones that have been produced show serious developmental abnormalities,[8] and, apart from ethical considerations, doctors would not run the medicolegal risks involved. Transgenic technology has been with us for 20 years, but no clinician has been foolish enough to experiment with human germ cell therapy. The production of Dolly should not be seen as a moral threat, but rather as an exciting challenge. To answer this good science with a knee jerk political reaction, as did President Clinton recently,[9] shows poor judgment. In a society which is still scientifically illiterate, the onus is on researchers to explain the potential good that can be gained in the laboratory.

REFERENCES

1. Wilmut T, Schnieke AK, McWhir J, Kind AJ, Campbell KHS. Viable offspring derived from fetal and adult mammalian cells. *Nature* 1997;385:810–13.

2. Gurdon JB, Laskey RA, Reeves OR. The developmental capacity of nuclei transplanted from keratinised skin cells of adult frogs. *J Embryol Exp Morph* 1975;34:93–112.

3. Prather RS, Simms MM, First NL. Nuclear transplantation in early pig embryos. *Biol Reprod* 1989;41:414–18.

4. Ozawa T. Mitochondrial DNA mutations associated with aging and degenerative diseases. *Exp Gerontol* 1995;30:269–90.

5. Dabhi VM, Lindahl KF. MtDNA-encoded histocompatibility antigens. *Methods Enzymol* 1995;260;466–85.

6. Masood E. Cloning technique "reveals legal loophole." *Nature* 1997;385:757.

7. Winston RM, Handyside AH. New challenges in human in vitro fertilization. *Science* 1993;260:932–36.

8. Campbell KHS, McWhir J, Ritchie WA, Wilmut I. Sheep cloned by nuclear transfer from a cultured cell line. *Nature* 1996; 380:64–66.

9. Wise J. Sheep cloned from mammary gland cells. *BMJ* 1997; 314:623.

NATIONAL BIOETHICS ADVISORY COMMISSION

Cloning Human Beings: Executive Summary (1997)

The idea that humans might someday be cloned — created from a single somatic cell without sexual reproduction — moved further away from science fiction and closer to a genuine scientific possibility on February 23, 1997. On that date, *The Observer* broke the news that Ian Wilmut, a Scottish scientist, and his colleagues at the Roslin Institute were about to announce the successful cloning of a sheep by a new technique which had never before been fully successful in mammals. The technique involved transplanting the genetic material of an adult sheep, apparently obtained from a differentiated somatic cell, into an egg from which the nucleus had been removed. The resulting birth of the sheep, named Dolly, on July 5, 1996, was different from prior attempts to create identical offspring since Dolly contained the genetic material of only one parent, and was, therefore, a "delayed" genetic twin of a single adult sheep.

This cloning technique is an extension of research that had been ongoing for over 40 years using nuclei derived from non-human embryonic and fetal cells. The demonstration that nuclei from cells derived from an adult animal could be "reprogrammed," or that the

full genetic complement of such a cell could be reactivated well into the chronological life of the cell, is what sets the results of this experiment apart from prior work. In this report we refer to the technique, first described by Wilmut, of nuclear transplantation using nuclei derived from somatic cells other than those of an embryo or fetus as "somatic cell nuclear transfer."

Within days of the published report of Dolly, President Clinton instituted a ban on federal funding related to attempts to clone human beings in this manner. In addition, the President asked the recently appointed National Bioethics Advisory Commission (NBAC) to address within ninety days the ethical and legal issues that surround the subject of cloning human beings. This provided a welcome opportunity for initiating a thoughtful analysis of the many dimensions of the issue, including a careful consideration of the potential risks and benefits. It also presented an occasion to review the current legal status of cloning and the potential constitutional challenges that might be raised if new legislation were enacted to restrict the creation of a child through somatic cell nuclear transfer cloning.

The Commission began its discussions fully recognizing that any effort in humans to transfer a somatic cell nucleus into an enucleated egg involves the creation of an embryo, with the apparent potential to be implanted in utero and developed to term. Ethical con-

Reprinted from *Cloning Human Beings: Report and Recommendations of the National Bioethics Advisory Committee* (Rockville, MD: The Commission, June 1997), pp. i–v.

cerns surrounding issues of embryo research have recently received extensive analysis and deliberation in our country. Indeed, federal funding for human embryo research is severely restricted, although there are few restrictions on human embryo research carried out in the private sector. Thus, under current law, the use of somatic cell nuclear transfer to create an embryo solely for research purposes is already restricted in cases involving federal funds. There are, however, no current federal regulations on the use of private funds for this purpose.

The unique prospect, vividly raised by Dolly, is the creation of a new individual genetically identical to an existing (or previously existing) person—a "delayed" genetic twin. This prospect has been the source of the overwhelming public concern about such cloning. While the creation of embryos for research purposes alone always raises serious ethical questions, the use of somatic cell nuclear transfer to create embryos raises no new issues in this respect. The unique and distinctive ethical issues raised by the use of somatic cell nuclear transfer to create children relate to, for example, serious safety concerns, individuality, family integrity, and treating children as objects. Consequently, the Commission focused its attention on the use of such techniques for the purpose of creating an embryo which would then be implanted in a woman's uterus and brought to term. It also expanded its analysis of this particular issue to encompass activities in both the public and private sector.

In its deliberations, NBAC reviewed the scientific developments which preceded the Roslin announcement, as well as those likely to follow in its path. It also considered the many moral concerns raised by the possibility that this technique could be used to clone human beings. Much of the initial reaction to this possibility was negative. Careful assessment of that response revealed fears about harms to the children who may be created in this manner, particularly psychological harms associated with a possibly diminished sense of individuality and personal autonomy. Others expressed concern about a degradation in the quality of parenting and family life.

In addition to concerns about specific harms to children, people have frequently expressed fears that the widespread practice of somatic cell nuclear transfer cloning would undermine important social values by opening the door to a form of eugenics or by tempting some to manipulate others as if they were objects instead of persons. Arrayed against these concerns are

other important social values, such as protecting the widest possible sphere of personal choice, particularly in matters pertaining to procreation and child rearing, maintaining privacy and the freedom of scientific inquiry, and encouraging the possible development of new biomedical breakthroughs.

To arrive at its recommendations concerning the use of somatic cell nuclear transfer techniques to create children, NBAC also examined long-standing religious traditions that guide many citizens' responses to new technologies and found that religious positions on human cloning are pluralistic in their premises, modes of argument, and conclusions. Some religious thinkers argue that the use of somatic cell nuclear transfer cloning to create a child would be intrinsically immoral and thus could never be morally justified. Other religious thinkers contend that human cloning to create a child could be morally justified under some circumstances, but hold that it should be strictly regulated in order to prevent abuses.

The public policies recommended with respect to the creation of a child using somatic cell nuclear transfer reflect the Commission's best judgments about both the ethics of attempting such an experiment and our view of traditions regarding limitations on individual actions in the name of the common good. At present, the use of this technique to create a child would be a premature experiment that would expose the fetus and the developing child to unacceptable risks. This in itself might be sufficient to justify a prohibition on cloning human beings at this time, even if such efforts were to be characterized as the exercise of a fundamental right to attempt to procreate.

Beyond the issue of the safety of the procedure, however, NBAC found that concerns relating to the potential psychological harms to children and effects on the moral, religious, and cultural values of society merited further reflection and deliberation. Whether upon such further deliberation our nation will conclude that the use of cloning techniques to create children should be allowed or permanently banned is, for the moment, an open question. Time is an ally in this regard, allowing for the accrual of further data from animal experimentation, enabling an assessment of the prospective safety and efficacy of the procedure in humans, as well as granting a period of fuller national debate on ethical and social concerns. The Commission therefore concluded that there should be imposed a period of time in which no attempt is made to create a child using somatic cell nuclear transfer.[1]

Within this overall framework the Commission came to the following conclusions and recommendations:

I. The Commission concludes that at this time it is morally unacceptable for anyone in the public or private sector, whether in a research or clinical setting, to attempt to create a child using somatic cell nuclear transfer cloning. We have reached a consensus on this point because current scientific information indicates that this technique is not safe to use in humans at this time. Indeed, we believe it would violate important ethical obligations were clinicians or researchers to attempt to create a child using these particular technologies, which are likely to involve unacceptable risks to the fetus and/or potential child. Moreover, in addition to safety concerns, many other serious ethical concerns have been identified, which require much more widespread and careful public deliberation before this technology may be used.

The Commission, therefore, recommends the following for immediate action:

- A continuation of the current moratorium on the use of federal funding in support of any attempt to create a child by somatic cell nuclear transfer.
- An immediate request to all firms, clinicians, investigators, and professional societies in the private and non-federally funded sectors to comply voluntarily with the intent of the federal moratorium. Professional and scientific societies should make clear that any attempt to create a child by somatic cell nuclear transfer and implantation into a woman's body would at this time be an irresponsible, unethical, and unprofessional act.

II. The Commission further recommends that:

- Federal legislation should be enacted to prohibit anyone from attempting, whether in a research or clinical setting, to create a child through somatic cell nuclear transfer cloning. It is critical, however, that such legislation include a sunset clause to ensure that Congress will review the issue after a specified time period (three to five years) in order to decide whether the prohibition continues to be

needed. If state legislation is enacted, it should also contain such a sunset provision. Any such legislation or associated regulation also ought to require that at some point prior to the expiration of the sunset period, an appropriate oversight body will evaluate and report on the current status of somatic cell nuclear transfer technology and on the ethical and social issues that its potential use to create human beings would raise in light of public understandings at that time.

III. The Commission also concludes that:

- Any regulatory or legislative actions undertaken to effect the foregoing prohibition on creating a child by somatic cell nuclear transfer should be carefully written so as not to interfere with other important areas of scientific research. In particular, no new regulations are required regarding the cloning of human DNA sequences and cell lines, since neither activity raises the scientific and ethical issues that arise from the attempt to create children through somatic cell nuclear transfer, and these fields of research have already provided important scientific and biomedical advances. Likewise, research on cloning animals by somatic cell nuclear transfer does not raise the issues implicated in attempting to use this technique for human cloning, and its continuation should only be subject to existing regulations regarding the humane use of animals and review by institution-based animal protection committees.
- If a legislative ban is not enacted, or if a legislative ban is ever lifted, clinical use of somatic cell nuclear transfer techniques to create a child should be preceded by research trials that are governed by the twin protections of independent review and informed consent, consistent with existing norms of human subjects protection.
- The United States Government should cooperate with other nations and international organizations to enforce any common aspects of their respective policies on the cloning of human beings.

IV. The Commission also concludes that different ethical and religious perspectives and traditions are divided on many of the important moral issues that surround any attempt to create a child using somatic cell nuclear transfer techniques. Therefore, we recommend that:

- The federal government, and all interested and concerned parties, encourage widespread and continuing deliberation on these issues in order to further our understanding of the ethical and social implications of this technology and to enable society to produce appropriate long-term policies regarding this technology should the time come when present concerns about safety have been addressed.

V. Finally, because scientific knowledge is essential for all citizens to participate in a full and informed fashion in the governance of our complex society, the Commission recommends that:

- Federal departments and agencies concerned with science should cooperate in seeking out and supporting opportunities to provide information and education to the public in the area of genetics, and on other developments in the biomedical sciences, especially where these affect important cultural practices, values, and beliefs.

NOTE

1. The Commission also observes that the use of any other technique to create a child genetically identical to an existing (or previously existing) individual would raise many, if not all, of the same non-safety-related ethical concerns raised by the creation of a child by somatic cell nuclear transfer.

DANIEL CALLAHAN

Cloning: Then and Now

The possibility of human cloning first surfaced in the 1960s, stimulated by the report that a salamander had been cloned. James D. Watson and Joshua Lederberg, distinguished Nobel laureates, speculated that the cloning of human beings might one day be within reach; it was only a matter of time. Bioethics was still at that point in its infancy — indeed, the term "bioethics" was not even widely used then — and cloning immediately caught the eye of a number of those beginning to write in the field. They included Paul Ramsey, Hans Jonas, and Leon Kass. Cloning became one of the symbolic issues of what was, at that time, called "the new biology," a biology that would be dominated by molecular genetics. Over a period of five years or so in the early 1970s a number of articles and book chapters on the ethical issues appeared, discussing cloning in its own right and cloning as a token of the radical genetic possibilities.

While here and there a supportive voice could be found for the prospect of human cloning, the overwhelming reaction, professional and lay, was negative. Although there was comparatively little public discussion, my guess is that there would have been as great a sense of repugnance then as there has been recently. And if there had been some kind of government commission to study the subject, it would almost certainly have recommended a ban on any efforts to clone a human being.

Now if my speculation about the situation 20 to 25 years ago is correct, one might easily conclude that nothing much has changed. Is not the present debate simply a rerun of the earlier debate, with nothing very new added? In essence that is true. No arguments have been advanced this time that were not anticipated and discussed in the 1970s. As had happened with other problems in bioethics (and with genetic engineering most notably), the speculative discussions prior to important scientific breakthroughs were remarkably prescient. The actuality of biological progress often adds little to what can be imagined in advance.

Yet if it is true that no substantially new arguments have appeared over the past two decades, there are I believe some subtle differences this time. Three of them are worth some comment. In bioethics, there is by far a more favorable response to scientific and technological developments than was then the case. Permissive, quasi-libertarian attitudes toward reproductive rights

From *Cambridge Quarterly for Healthcare Ethics* 7 (Spring 1998), 141–44. Copyright © 1998 Cambridge University Press. Reprinted with the permission of Cambridge University Press.

that were barely noticeable earlier now have far more substance and support. And imagined or projected research benefits have a stronger prima facie claim now, particularly for the relief of infertility.

1. THE RESPONSE TO SCIENTIFIC AND TECHNOLOGICAL DEVELOPMENTS

Bioethics came to life in the mid- to late-1960s, at a time not only of great technological advances in medicine but also of great social upheaval in many areas of American cultural life. Almost forgotten now as part of the "sixties" phenomenon was a strong anti-technology strain. A common phrase, "the greening of America," caught well some of that spirit, and there were a number of writers as prepared to indict technology for America's failing as they were to indict sexism, racism, and militarism.

While it would be a mistake to see Ramsey, Jonas, and Kass as characteristic sixties thinkers—they would have been appalled at such a label—their thinking about biological and genetic technology was surely compatible with the general suspicion of technology that was then current. In strongly opposing the idea of human cloning, they were not regarded as Luddites, or radicals, nor were they swimming against the tide. In mainline intellectual circles it was acceptable enough to be wary of technology, even to assault it. It is probably no accident that Hans Jonas, who wrote so compellingly on technology and its potentially deleterious effects, was lauded in Germany well into the 1990s, that same contemporary Germany that has seen the most radical "green" movement and the most open, enduring hostility to genetic technology.

There has been considerable change since the 1960s and 1970s. Biomedical research and technological innovation now encounter little intellectual resistance. Enthusiasm and support are more likely. There is no serious "green" movement in biotechnology here as in Germany. Save possibly for Jeremy Rifkin, there are no regular, much less celebrated, critics of biotechnology. Technology-bashing has gone out of style. The National Institutes of Health, and *particularly* its Human Genome Project, receive constant budget increases, and that at a time of budget cutting more broadly of government programs. The genome project, moreover, has no notable opponents in bioethics—and it would probably have support *even* if it did not lavish so much money on bioethics.

Cloning, in a word, now has behind it a culture far more supportive of biotechnological innovation than was the case in the 1960s and 1970s. Even if human cloning itself has been, for the moment, rejected, animal cloning will go forward. If some *clear* potential benefits can be envisioned for human cloning, the research will find a background culture likely to be welcoming rather than hostile. And if money can be made off of such a development, its chances will be greatly enhanced.

2. REPRODUCTIVE RIGHTS

The right to procreate, as a claimed human right, is primarily of post-World War II vintage. It took hold first in the United States with the acceptance of artificial insemination (AID) and was strengthened by a series of court decisions upholding contraception and abortion. The emergence of in vitro fertilization in 1978, widespread surrogate motherhood in the 1980s, and a continuous stream of other technological developments over the past three decades have provided a wide range of techniques to pursue reproductive choice. It is not clear what, if any, limits remain any longer to an exercise of those rights. Consider the progression of a claimed right: from a right to have or not have children as one chooses, to a right to have them any way one can, and then to a right to have the kind of child one wants.

While some have contended that there is no natural right to knowingly procreate a defective or severely handicapped child, there have been no serious moves to legally or otherwise limit such procreation. The right to procreation has, then, slowly become almost a moral absolute. But that was not the case in the early 1970s, when the reproductive rights movement was just getting off the ground. It was the 1973 *Roe v. Wade* abortion decision that greatly accelerated it.

While the National Bioethics Advisory Commission ultimately rejected a reproductive rights claim for human cloning, it is important to note that it felt the need to give that viewpoint ample exposure. Moreover, when the commission called for a five-year ban followed by a sunset provision—to allow time for more scientific information to develop and for public discussion to go forward—it surely left the door open for another round of reproductive rights advocacy. For that matter, if the proposed five-year ban is eventually to be lifted because of a change in public attitudes, then it is likely that putative reproductive rights will be a principal reason for that happening. Together with the possibility of more effective relief from infertility (to which I will next turn) it is the most powerful viewpoint waiting in the wings to be successfully deployed. If procreation is, as claimed, purely a private matter, and if it is thought wrong to morally judge the means people choose to have children, or their reasons for having them, then it is hard to see how cloning can long be resisted.

3. INFERTILITY RELIEF AND RESEARCH POSSIBILITIES

The potential benefits of scientific research have long been recognized in the United States, going back to the enthusiasm of Thomas Jefferson in the early years of American history. Biomedical research has in recent years had a particularly privileged status, commanding constant increases in government support even in the face of budget restrictions and cuts. Meanwhile, lay groups supportive of research on one undesirable medical condition or another have proliferated. Together they constitute a powerful advocacy force. The fact that the private sector profits enormously from the fruits of research adds still another potent factor supportive of research.

A practical outcome of all these factors working together is that in the face of ethical objections to some biotechnological aspirations there is no more powerful antidote than the claim of potential scientific and clinical benefits. Whether it be the basic biological knowledge that research can bring, or the direct improvements to health, it is a claim difficult to resist. What seems notably different now from two decades ago is the extent of the imaginative projections of research and clinical benefits from cloning. This is most striking in the area of infertility relief. It is estimated that one in seven people desiring to procreate are infertile for one reason or another. Among the important social causes of infertility are late procreation and the effects of sexually transmitted diseases. The relief of infertility has thus emerged as a major growth area in medicine. And, save for the now-traditional claims that some new line of research may lead to a cure for cancer, no claim seems so powerful as the possibility of curing infertility or otherwise dealing with complex procreation issues.

In its report, the bioethics commission envisioned, through three hypothetical cases, some reasons why people would turn to cloning: to help a couple both of whom are carriers of a lethal recessive gene; to procreate a child with the cells of a deceased husband; and to save the life of a child who needs a bone marrow transplant. What is striking about the offering of them, however, is that it now seems to be considered plausible to take seriously rare cases, as if — because they show how human cloning could benefit some few individuals — that creates reasons to accept it. The commission did not give in to such claims, but it treated them with a seriousness that I doubt would have been present in the 1970s.

Hardly anyone, so far as I can recall, came forward earlier with comparable idiosyncratic scenarios and offered them as serious reasons to support human cloning. But it was also the case in those days that the relief of infertility, and complex procreative problems, simply did not command the kind of attention or have the kind of political and advocacy support now present. It is as if infertility, once accepted as a fact of life, even if a sad one, is now thought to be some enormous menace to personal happiness, to be eradicated by every means possible. It is an odd turn in a world not suffering from underpopulation and in a society where a large number of couples deliberately choose not to have children.

WHAT OF THE FUTURE?

In citing what I take to be three subtle but important shifts in the cultural and medical climate since the 1960s and 1970s, I believe the way has now been opened just enough to increase the likelihood that human cloning will be hard to resist in the future. It is that change also, I suggest, that is responsible for the sunset clause proposed by the bioethics commission. That clause makes no particular sense unless there was on the part of the commission some intuition that both the scientific community and the general public could change their minds in the relatively near future — and that the idea of such a change would not be preposterous, much less unthinkable.

In pointing to the changes in the cultural climate since the 1970s, I do not want to imply any approval. The new romance with technology, the seemingly unlimited aims of the reproductive rights movement, and the obsession with scientific progress generally, and the relief of infertility particularly, are nothing to be proud of. I would like to say it is time to turn back the clock. But since it is the very nature of a progress-driven culture to find such a desire reprehensible, I will suggest instead that we turn the clock forward, skipping the present era, and moving on to one that is more sensible and balanced. It may not be too late to do that.

LEE M. SILVER

Cloning, Ethics, and Religion*

On Sunday morning, 23 February 1997, the world awoke to a technological advance that shook the foundations of biology and philosophy. On that day, we were introduced to Dolly, a 6-month-old lamb that had been cloned directly from a single cell taken from the breast tissue of an adult donor. Perhaps more astonished by this accomplishment than any of their neighbors were the scientists who actually worked in the field of mammalian genetics and embryology. Outside the lab where the cloning had actually taken place, most of us thought it could never happen. Oh, we would say that perhaps at some point in the distant future, cloning might become feasible through the use of sophisticated biotechnologies far beyond those available to us now. But what many of us really believed, deep in our hearts, was that this was one biological feat we could never master. New life—in the special sense of a conscious being—must have its origins in a embryo formed through the merger of gametes from a mother and father. It was impossible, we thought, for a cell from an adult mammal to become reprogrammed, to start all over again, to generate another entire animal or person in the image of the one born earlier.

How wrong we were.

Of course, it wasn't the cloning of a sheep that stirred the imaginations of hundreds of millions of people. It was the idea that humans could now be cloned as well, and many people were terrified by the prospect. Ninety percent of Americans polled within the first week after the story broke felt that human cloning should be banned.[1] And while not unanimous, the opinions of many

media pundits, ethicists, and policymakers seemed to follow that of the public at large. The idea that humans might be cloned was called "morally despicable," "repugnant," "totally inappropriate," as well as "ethically wrong, socially misguided and biologically mistaken."[2]

Scientists who work directly in the field of animal genetics and embryology were dismayed by all the attention that now bore down on their research. Most unhappy of all were those associated with the biotechnology industry, which has the most to gain in the short-term from animal applications of the cloning technology.[3] Their fears were not unfounded. In the aftermath of Dolly, polls found that two out of three Americans considered the cloning of *animals* to be morally unacceptable, while 56% said they would not eat meat from cloned animals.[4]

It should not be surprising, then, that scientists tried to play down the feasibility of human cloning. First they said that it might not be possible *at all* to transfer the technology to human cells.[5] And even if human cloning is possible in theory, they said, "it would take years of trial and error before it could be applied successfully," so that "cloning in humans is unlikely any time soon."[6] And even if it becomes possible to apply the technology successfully, they said, "there is no clinical reason why you would do this."[7] And even if a person wanted to clone him- or herself or someone else, he or she wouldn't be able to find trained medical professionals who would be willing to do it.

Really? That's not what science, history, or human nature suggest to me. The cloning of Dolly broke the technological barrier. There is no reason to expect that the technology couldn't be transferred to human cells. On the contrary, there is every reason to expect that it *can* be transferred. If nuclear transplantation works in every mammalian species in which it has been seriously tried, then nuclear transplantation *will* work with

*This article is based on material extracted from Silver, L. M., *Remaking Eden: Cloning and Beyond in a Brave New World.* Avon Books, 1997.

From *Cambridge Quarterly of Heathcare Ethics* 7 (Spring 1998), 168–72. Copyright © 1998 Cambridge University Press. Reprinted with the permission of Cambridge University Press.

human cells as well. It requires only equipment and facilities that are already standard, or easy to obtain by biomedical laboratories and freestanding in vitro fertilization clinics across the world. Although the protocol itself demands the services of highly trained and skilled personnel, there are thousands of people with such skills in dozens of countries.

The initial horror elicited by the announcement of Dolly's birth was due in large part to a misunderstanding by the lay public and the media of what biological cloning is and is not. The science critic Jeremy Rifkin exclaimed: "It's a horrendous crime to make a Xerox (copy) of someone,"[8] and the Irvine, California, rabbi Bernard King was seriously frightened when he asked, "Can the cloning create a soul? Can scientists create the soul that would make a being ethical, moral, caring, loving, all the things we attribute humanity to?"[9] The Catholic priest Father Saunders suggested that "cloning would only produce humanoids or androids — soulless replicas of human beings that could be used as slaves."[10] And *New York Times* writer Brent Staples warned us that "synthetic humans would be easy prey for humanity's worst instincts."[11]

Anyone reading this volume already knows that real human clones will simply be later-born identical twins — nothing more and nothing less. Cloned children will be full-fledged human beings, indistinguishable in biological terms from all other members of the species. But even with this understanding, many ethicists, scholars, and scientists are still vehemently opposed to the use of cloning as means of human reproduction under any circumstances whatsoever. Why do they feel this way? Why does this new reproductive technology upset them so?

First, they say, it's a question of "safety." The cloning procedure has not been proven safe and, as a result, its application toward the generation of newborn children could produce deformities and other types of birth defects. Second, they say that even if physical defects can be avoided, there is the psychological well-being of the cloned child to consider. And third, above and beyond each individual child, they are worried about the horrible effect that cloning will have on society as a whole.

What I will argue here is that people who voice any one or more of these concerns are — either consciously or subconsciously — hiding the real reason they oppose cloning. They have latched on to arguments about safety, psychology, and society because they are simply unable to come up with an ethical argument that is not based on the religious notion that by cloning human beings man will be playing God, and it is wrong to play God.

Let us take a look at the safety argument first. Throughout the 20th century, medical scientists have sought to develop new protocols and drugs for treating disease and alleviating human suffering. The safety of all these new medical protocols was initially unknown. But through experimental testing on animals first, and then volunteer human subjects, safety could be ascertained and governmental agencies — such as the Food and Drug Administration in the United States — could make a decision as to whether the new protocol or drug should be approved for use in standard medical practice.

It would be ludicrous to suggest that legislatures should pass laws banning the application of each newly imagined medical protocol before its safety has been determined. Professional ethics committees, institutional review boards, and the individual ethics of each medical practitioner are relied upon to make sure that hundreds of new experimental protocols are tested and used in an appropriate manner each year. And yet the question of unknown safety alone was the single rationale used by the National Bioethics Advisory Board (NBAC) to propose a ban on human cloning in the United States.

Opposition to cloning on the basis of safety alone is almost surely a losing proposition. Although the media have concocted fantasies of dozens of malformed monster lambs paving the way for the birth of Dolly, fantasy is all it was. Of the 277 fused cells created by Wilmut and his colleagues, only 29 developed into embryos. These 29 embryos were placed into 13 ewes, of which 1 became pregnant and gave birth to Dolly.[12] If safety is measured by the percentage of lambs born in good health, then the record, so far, is 100% for nuclear transplantation from an adult cell (albeit with a sample size of 1).

In fact, there is no scientific basis for the belief that cloned children will be any more prone to genetic problems than naturally conceived children. The commonest type of birth defect results from the presence of an abnormal number of chromosomes in the fertilized egg. This birth defect arises during gamete production and, as such, its frequency should be greatly reduced in embryos formed by cloning. The second most common class of birth defects results from the inheritance of two mutant copies of a gene from two parents who are silent carriers. With cloning, any silent mutation in a donor will be silent in the newly formed embryo and child as well. Finally, much less frequently, birth defects can be caused by new mutations; these will occur with the same frequency in embryos derived through conception or cloning. (Although some scientists have suggested that chromosome shortening in the donor cell will cause cloned children to have a shorter lifespan, there is every reason to expect that chromosome repair in the embryo will eliminate this problem.) Surprisingly, what our current scientific understanding suggests is that birth defects in cloned children could occur less frequently than birth defects in naturally conceived ones.

Once safety has been eliminated as an objection to cloning, the next concern voiced is the psychological well-being of the child. Daniel Callahan, the former director of the Hastings Center, argues that "engineering someone's entire genetic makeup would compromise his or her right to a unique identity."[13] But no such 'right' has been granted by nature — identical twins are born every day as natural clones of each other. Dr. Callahan would have to concede this fact, but he might still argue that just because twins occur naturally does not mean we should create them on purpose.

Dr. Callahan might argue that a cloned child is harmed by knowledge of her future condition. He might say that it's unfair to go through childhood knowing what you will look like as an adult, or being forced to consider future medical ailments that might befall you. But even in the absence of cloning, many children have some sense of the future possibilities encoded in the genes they got from their parents. Furthermore, genetic screening already provides people with the ability to learn about hundreds of disease predispositions. And as genetic knowledge and technology become more and more sophisticated, it will become possible for any human being to learn even more about his or her genetic future than a cloned child could learn from his or her progenitor's past.

It might also be argued that a cloned child will be harmed by having to live up to unrealistic expectations placed on her by her parents. But there is no reason to believe that her parents will be any more unreasonable than many other parents who expect their children to accomplish in their lives what they were unable to accomplish in their own. No one would argue that parents with such tendencies should be prohibited from having children.

But let's grant that among the many cloned children brought into this world, some *will* feel badly about the fact that their genetic constitution is not unique. Is this alone a strong enough reason to ban the practice of cloning? Before answering this question, ask yourself another: Is a child having knowledge of an older twin worse off than a child born into poverty? If we ban the former, shouldn't we ban the latter? Why is it that so many politicians seem to care so much about cloning but so little about the welfare of children in general?

Finally, there are those who argue against cloning based on the perception that it will harm society at large in some way. The *New York Times* columnist William Safire expresses the opinion of many others when he says that "cloning's identicality would restrict evolution."[14] This is bad, he argues, because "the continued interplay of genes . . . is central to humankind's progress." But Mr. Safire is wrong on both practical and theoretical grounds. On practical grounds, even if human cloning became efficient, legal, and popular among those in the moneyed classes (which is itself highly unlikely), it would still only account for a fraction of a percent of all the children born onto this earth. Furthermore, each of the children born by cloning to different families would be different from each other, so where does the identicality come from?

On theoretical grounds, Safire is wrong because humankind's progress has nothing to do with unfettered evolution, which is always unpredictable and not necessarily upward bound. H. G. Wells recognized this principle in his 1895 novel *The Time Machine,* which portrays the evolution of humankind into weak and dimwitted but cuddly little creatures. And Kurt Vonnegut follows this same theme in *Galápagos,* where he suggests that our "big brains" will be the cause of our downfall, and future humans with smaller brains and powerful flippers will be the only remnants of a once great species, a million years hence.

As is so often the case with new reproductive technologies, the real reason that people condemn cloning has nothing to do with technical feasibility, child psychology, societal well-being, or the preservation of the human species. The real reason derives from religious beliefs. It is the sense that cloning leaves God out of the process of human creation, and that man is venturing into places he does not belong. Of course, the 'playing God' objection only makes sense in the context of one definition of God, as a supernatural being who plays a role in the birth of each new member of our species. And even if one holds this particular view of God, it does not necessarily follow that cloning is equivalent to playing God. Some who consider themselves to be religious have argued that if God didn't want man to clone, "he" wouldn't have made it possible.

Should public policy in a pluralist society be based on a narrow religious point of view? Most people would say no, which is why those who hold this point of view are grasping for secular reasons to support their call for an unconditional ban on the cloning of human beings. When the dust clears from the cloning debate, however, the secular reasons will almost certainly have disappeared. And then, only religious objections will remain.

NOTES

1. Data extracted from a *Time/CNN* poll taken over the 26th and 27th of February 1997 and reported in *Time* on 10 March 1997; and an ABC Nightline poll taken over the same period, with results reported in the *Chicago Tribune* on 2 March 1997.

2. Quotes from the bioethicist Arthur Caplan in *Denver Post* 1997; Feb 24; the bioethicist Thomas Murray in *New York Times* 1997;Mar 6; Congressman Vernon [Ehlers] in *New York Times* 1997;Mar 6; and evolutionary biologist Francisco Ayala in *Orange County Register* 1997;Feb 25.

3. James A. Geraghty, president of Genzyme Transgenics Corporation (a Massachusetts biotech company), testified before a Senate committee that "everyone in the biotechnology industry shares the unequivocal conviction that there is no place for the cloning of human beings in our society." *Washington Post* 1997;Mar 13.

4. Data obtained from a Yankelovich poll of 1,005 adults reported in *St. Louis Post-Dispatch* 1997;Mar 9 and a *Time/CNN* poll reported in *New York Times* 1997;Mar 5.

5. Leonard Bell, president and chief executive of Alexion Pharmaceuticals, is quoted as saying, "There is a healthy skepticism whether you can accomplish this efficiently in another species." *New York Times* 1997;Mar 3.

6. Interpretation of the judgments of scientists, reported by Specter M, Kolata G. *New York Times* 1997;Mar 3, and by Herbert W, Sheler JL, Watson T. *U.S. News & World Report* 1997;Mar 10.

7. Quote from Ian Wilmut, the scientist who brought forth Dolly, in Friend T. *USA Today* 1997;Feb 24.

8. Quoted in Kluger J. *Time* 1997;Mar 10.

9. Quoted in McGraw C, Kelleher S. *Orange County Register* 1997;Feb 25.

10. Quoted in the on line version of the *Arlington Catholic Herald* (http://www.catholicherald.com/bissues.htm) 1997;May 16.

11. Staples B. [Editorial]. *New York Times* 1997;Feb 28.

12. Wilmut I, Schnieke AE, McWhir J, Kind AJ, Campbell KHS. Viable offspring derived from fetal and adult mammalian cells. *Nature* 1997;385:810–13.

13. Callahan D. [op-ed]. *New York Times* 1997;Feb 26.

14. Safire W. [op-ed]. *New York Times* 1997;Feb 27.

Regulating Assisted Reproduction

HUMAN FERTILISATION AND EMBRYOLOGY AUTHORITY (UNITED KINGDOM)

Annual Report (1997)

THE HUMAN FERTILISATION AND EMBRYOLOGY AUTHORITY

The Human Fertilisation and Embryology Authority was the first statutory body in the world established to regulate and monitor certain fertility treatments

Reprinted from Human Fertilisation and Embryology Authority, *Sixth Annual Report* (London: HFEA, 1997), pp. 3–4, 10–12.

and human embryo research. A product of the 1984 Warnock Committee's report,[1] the Authority was created by the Human Fertilisation and Embryology Act 1990 and assumed its full powers on 1 August 1991.

THE AUTHORITY'S ROLE

The HFEA's principal tasks are to license and monitor those clinics that carry out *in vitro* fertilisation (IVF), donor insemination (DI) and embryo research. The HFEA also regulates the storage of gametes (sperm and eggs) and embryos.

Underlying all its activities is the Authority's primary aim—to safeguard all relevant interests: patients; children; the wider public; and future generations. Its objectives are to ensure that both treatment and research are undertaken with the utmost respect and responsibility.

The HFEA's other main functions under the 1990 Act are:

- to keep a formal register of information about donors, treatments and children born from those treatments. This is so that children born as a result of donated eggs or sperm can find out, if they wish, something about their genetic history;
- to produce a Code of Practice which gives guidelines to clinics about the proper conduct of licensed activities;
- to publicise its role and provide relevant advice and information to patients and donors and clinics;
- to keep under review information about embryos and any subsequent development of embryos and about the provision of treatment services and activities governed by the 1990 Act and advise the Secretary of State if he asks about those matters.

THE AUTHORITY'S MEMBERSHIP

The Authority's 21 Members are appointed by UK Health Ministers. The 1996 appointments were made for the first time after national advertising and in accordance with Nolan guidelines.

Authority Members determine the Authority's policies and scrutinise treatment and research license applications. They are not appointed as representatives of different groups, but bring to the Authority a broad range of medical, scientific, social, legal, religious and philosophical knowledge and experience. In order that an independent perspective can be maintained, the 1990 Act requires that the Chairman, Deputy Chairman and at least half of the Authority's Membership are neither doctors nor scientists involved in research or practice relevant to infertility.

THE AUTHORITY'S EXECUTIVE

The Authority has an Executive composed of 29 staff who are responsible for implementing the Authority's

policies and licensing decisions and conducting the Authority's day-to-day activities.

• • •

ETHICAL ISSUES

Ethical issues are always being considered by the HFEA. Current concerns include pre-implantation genetic diagnosis, payment to gamete donors, . . . and cloning.

PRE-IMPLANTATION GENETIC DIAGNOSIS (PGD)

PGD is a technique used to detect whether an embryo created *in vitro* is carrying a genetic defect which will give rise to a serious inherited disorder. It can also be used to determine the sex of an embryo where a family is at risk of passing on a serious sex-linked disorder, such as Duchenne's muscular dystrophy, to a male child. Four centres are licensed to carry out this technique clinically while four others hold Authority research licenses.

While PGD is now practised on a small scale, it is expected that, as knowledge about the genes responsible for different conditions increases and people become more aware of genetics, demand will grow. The Authority, and its Ethics Committee in particular, have been considering the issues surrounding PGD in order to determine what guidance should be produced and what criteria should be used in deciding when PGD is, and is not, acceptable. As part of this exercise a joint working group has been established with the Advisory Committee on Genetic Testing.

PAYMENTS TO GAMETE DONORS

Under the 1990 Act, payments to donors may only be made if authorised by the Authority. The Authority's first working group on this subject developed two broad principles which have guided the Authority on this issue:

- fully informed consent, free from any inducement and pressure, is fundamental to gamete donation; and,
- the potential for human life inherent in a donation made with the specific intent of producing children should be respected.

The authority is still considering the implications surrounding the withdrawal of payments for donors and intends to consult before taking any final decisions. If changes are made to the present system, these will not be introduced until after responses to the consultation have been discussed in depth by the Authority, and clinics will be given sufficient time to prepare for such changes.

• • •

CLONING

The 1990 Act prohibits cloning by nuclear replacement and bringing about the creation, keeping or using of an embryo except in accordance with a license from the Authority.[2] The Authority decided in 1994 that it would not license embryo splitting for treatment purposes or for research where the intention is to increase the number of embryos for replacement (transfer).

In February 1997 the Roslin Institute (Edinburgh) reported the cloning of Dolly the sheep.[3] Their research provoked a public response which focused almost entirely on the possibility of using the Roslin technique for human cloning.

This experiment prompted the House of Commons' Science and Technology Committee to conduct an inquiry into the Roslin experiment. In particular, the Committee wished to explore, "the adequacy of the law relating to cloning and related issues in both animals and humans."

In giving evidence to the Committee, the Authority's Chairman said that much depended on the definition of "embryo" as contained in the 1990 Act. The Authority informed the Committee that it was taking legal advice with the Department of Health on this point.[4]

REVIEW OF WRITTEN CONSENT PROVISIONS

a) The Diane Blood Case. Sperm were taken from the late Mr. Blood while he was in a coma. He died shortly afterwards without regaining consciousness and thus had no opportunity to give the informed, written consent required by the 1990 Act for storage or use of sperm. The Authority was asked to exercise its discretion to allow the export of the sperm, but refused this request. An application was made to the High Court. The President of the Family Division rejected the application and an appeal against that decision was made to the Court of Appeal.

The Court of Appeal in its ruling confirmed that a person's gametes must not be stored or used in the UK (whether or not for export) without that person's informed written consent. In light of the judgement, the Authority decided to exercise its discretion and allowed the export of Mr. Blood's sperm for Mrs. Blood's treatment abroad.

b) The Review of Written Consent Provisions. As a consequence of the issues raised in the case, the Government in February 1997 announced that Professor Sheila McLean, Professor of Law and Ethics in Medicine at the University of Glasgow, had agreed to undertake a review for the UK Health Ministers of the written consent requirements for the storage and use of gametes (sperm or eggs) contained in the Human Fertilisation and Embryology Act 1990.[5] The Authority welcomes this review. A working group of Authority Members chaired by the Authority Chairman has been set up to prepare the Authority's response.

NOTES

1. Committee of Inquiry into Human Fertilisation and Embryology.

2. Section 3 HFE Act 1990.

3. *Nature,* volume 385, 27 February, 1997.

4. Science and Technology Committee, Fifth Report, *The Cloning of Animals from Adult Cells,* HC 373-I, 18 March 1997.

5. The Review's Terms of Reference are: to review whether—and in which circumstances—explicit consent under the common law to the removal of gametes might be waived; to consider in the light of the above whether changes are required to the Human Fertilisation and Embryology Act 1990 whereby effective consent to storage and use of gametes must always be given in writing; to consider the implications of any changes to the present consent regime in the Human Fertilisation and Embryology Act 1990 for the remainder of the Act including for the operation of the Human Fertilisation and Embryology Authority; and to consider the implications for the above of the judgement given by the Court of Appeal in the case of *R v. Human Fertilisation and Embryology Authority ex parte Diane Blood.*

ISLAT WORKING GROUP*

ART into Science: Regulation of Fertility Techniques

On 25 July 1998, Louise Brown, the first child born through in vitro fertilization, was 20 years old. Since her birth, 300,000 other children have been created worldwide by in vitro fertilization (IVF). Variations of the technology abound, including the use of donor gametes, transfer of the embryo into a surrogate, and preimplantation genetic screening of in vitro embryos. Potential parents now seemingly have greater control over how they bring children into the world. They can even, as did a California couple, choose an egg donor, sperm donor, and surrogate gestational mother, thus creating a child with five or more potential legal parents.[1]

The assisted reproductive technology (ART) industry, with an annual revenue of $2 billion,[2] is growing to serve an estimated one of six American couples who are infertile.[3] Annually, in the United States alone, approximately 60,000 births result from donor insemination,[4] 15,000 from IVF,[5] and at least 1000[6] from surrogacy arrangements. In contrast, only about 30,000 healthy infants are available for adoption.[7] What is striking about this comparison is that every state has an elaborate regulatory mechanism for adoption whereas only two states, Virginia and New Hampshire, have enacted legislation to comprehensively address ARTs.

Despite the fact that many families have been created with ART, the field has not been without problems. These include experimentation without appropriate review, use of embryos without consent, inadequate informed consent, conflicts regarding control over stored gametes and embryos, and failure to routinely screen donors for disease. Currently, the United States has taken a laissez faire approach toward ART. In contrast, other countries combine outright prohibitions of certain procedures, such as sex selection for nonmedical purposes [for example, in Canada],[8] and licensing requirements to limit who may perform reproductive technologies [for example, in the United Kingdom].[9] Despite the existence of voluntary guidelines by the American Society [for] Reproductive Medicine abuses continue to occur. Medical researchers in other fields risk losing federal funds or academic positions if they do not comply with human subjects' protections. Reproductive technologists, many of whom practice in private clinics, do not have such constraints.

REGULATION OF ART

In the United Kingdom a licensing authority was established under the Human Fertilization and Embryology Authority. When such an oversight group was suggested in the United States, reproductive technologists argued that they should not be singled out for regulations that do not apply to other areas of medicine. Yet enhanced regulation is justified in this area because the constraints usually in place in other fields of medicine are lacking here.

For several reasons, reproductive technology has been insulated from regulations that apply to other medical fields. For example, the political undertow from the abortion debate has led every administration from the late 1970s to the present to reject federal funding of embryo and fetal research. As a result, IVF clinics, which do not receive federal research funding, are not required to set up institutional review boards (IRBs) or to review

*Working Group members: Lori Andrews and Nanette Elster, co-chairs; Robert Gatter, Terri Finesmith Horwich, Ami Jaeger, Susan Klock, Eugene Pergament, Francis Pizzulli, Robyn Shapiro, Mark Siegler, Peggie Smith, and Shirley Zager. The Group is located at The Institute for Science, Law, and Technology (ISLAT), Illinois Institute of Technology, Chicago, IL 60661-3691, USA.

Reprinted with permission from *Science* 281 (July 31, 1998), 651–52. Copyright © 1998 by the American Association for the Advancement of Science.

innovative therapies under the human research subject regulations of the Department of Health and Human Services. In fact, IRB review is so rare in this field that it has been viewed as "remarkable."[10]

Unlike new drugs and new medical equipment, which are regulated by the Food and Drug Administration, no similar review of innovative ART medical procedures is required.[11] Consequently, if ART practitioners wanted to undertake an innovative and unproven technique like human cloning, there would be nothing to stop them (other than the legislative bans on human cloning in California and Michigan). In fact, one ART provider has suggested that even though the success rate of cloning is low (1 in 277 in the Dolly experiment), this may not be a barrier because all new reproductive technologies have high failure rates.[12]

ART also differs from other medical procedures because it is rarely covered by health insurance. For other types of health services, insurers, through managed care outcome studies and evaluation of services, have required proof of efficacy before medical services are reimbursed.

Additionally, medical malpractice litigation, which serves as a quality control mechanism in other areas of health care, does not work as well in the ART field because of the high failure rate (which means that patients do not know whether their lack of success was due to negligence or not). Risks to the children may not be discernible for many years, which may be past the period of time a statute of limitations on a legal suit has run. In "wrongful life" cases, courts have been reluctant to impose liability on medical providers and laboratories for children born with birth defects where the child would not have been born if the negligent act had been avoided.[13]

In 1992 a federal law was passed to require ART clinics to report success rates to the Centers for Disease Control.[14] Implementation was slow — the first report was published in December of 1997. In 1992 there was concern that the federal government did not have the constitutional authority to regulate ART clinics, because medicine is traditionally regulated at the state level. Since then, however, federal court cases have established Congress' ability to regulate medical clinics, whether or not they receive federal funds, if patients travel across state lines to use them, if supplies come from out of state, and if the doctors attend conferences in other states.[15] All of these factors are present in ARTs.

The consequences of the laissez-faire approach have been documented by the report of the New York State Task Force on Life and the Law.[16] They identified various major problems, such as clinics' lack of oversight, variability in success rates, failure to assess risks associated with ovarian hyperstimulation, failure to disclose multiple gestation risks, insufficient follow-up data collection efforts, and inconsistent reporting of risk data for egg donation.[16] Despite their criticisms, the New York Task Force would impose few new responsibilities on physicians to change practices or curb abuses. In contrast, we recommend a federal law to set a minimum standard requiring IRB approval of new ARTs, data collection, reporting, record keeping, and informed consent. Noncompliance would result in criminal or civil liability.

DATA COLLECTION, REPORTING, RECORDS

ART should be treated as a science. Currently, ART practitioners experiment on patients in the clinical setting without required peer review of research methods or protocol oversight. With ARTs, experimental techniques have been introduced rapidly in many of the more than 280 ART clinics in the United States without sufficient prior animal experimentation, randomized clinical trials, or the rigorous data collection that would occur in federally funded studies.[17, 18]

Intracytoplasmic sperm injection (ICSI) has been used since 1993 as a therapy for male factor infertility. Only recently has it been observed that children born after this procedure are twice as likely to have major congenital abnormalities as children conceived naturally.[19] The newly discovered risks include an unbalanced chromosome complement and male infertility.[20] Children conceived through ICSI may experience mild or significant developmental delays during their first year more often than children conceived by natural conception or IVF.[21]

ART procedures may present risks to women as well. ARTs increase pregnancy-related risks to women — higher rates of preeclampsia, diabetes mellitus, bleeding, and anemia.[22] There is some indication that hormonal stimulation during ART may increase the risk of ovarian cancer.[23] Yet new techniques are used on women before being adequately researched in animals. IVF itself was applied to women years before it was applied to baboons, chimpanzees, or rhesus monkeys, leading some embryologists to observe that it seemed as if women have served as the model for the nonhuman primates.[24]

Our analysis of public health implications of ART indicates the need for more consistent record keeping and review. Sperm and egg donation account for more than 60,000 births annually, yet there is no uniform procedure for storing information regarding the donor, the resulting birth, and medical history information. The recent discovery that a California semen donor transmitted polycystic kidney disease to at least one child and possibly many other children,[25] and the case of Dr. Cecil Jacobson[26] who secretly inseminated over 70 of his patients with his own sperm, are striking examples.

Data should also be collected on long-term health risks of treating women with fertility drugs. Studies should be undertaken on ART children to assess the long-term medical and psychological effects of ART procedures, especially cryopreservation. All ART clinics should be required to obtain and maintain updated medical and family information about both donors and ART children, including any reported change in medical status of donors.

NUMBER OF EMBRYOS TRANSFERRED

Unlike England, where doctors are prohibited from implanting more than three or four embryos, the laws in the United States set no limits on how many embryos a physician may implant. The New York State Task Force deferred to the American Society for Reproductive Medicine's voluntary recommendation that generally only four embryos be transferred, but it is clear that the guidelines are not being followed. In fact, the recently published report by the Centers for Disease Control,[5] examining data collected from 281 ART programs in 1995, shows that in some programs seven or more embryos are being transferred during an IVF cycle. Out of ART births, 37% are multiples as compared with 2% in the general population. Multiple pregnancies present significant risks to the resulting children in terms of increased frequency of death within the first year and long-term disability.[27] We recommend that a federal law be adopted limiting the number of embryos transferred per cycle to women to four.

INFORMED CONSENT AND DISCLOSURE

Basic informed consent requires that the patient or patients be told the risks, benefits, and alternatives of a treatment. Clinics should, at minimum, be required by federal law to disclose pregnancy rates; how pregnancy is confirmed; the live birth rate for the clinic; and the risks, benefits, and specific procedures for the technique being considered. Clinics should also disclose the risks associated with fertility drugs. They should disclose the risks of multiple births, including potential medical and psychological problems for the offspring.

The clinic should be required to disclose all embryo disposition options: storage, donation for use by another couple (known or unknown), donation for research, or destruction. Moreover, the clinic should disclose which services it actually offers, including the costs, duration, and location of gamete and embryo storage, and which services it does not offer that other clinics do.

CONCLUSION

ART involves creating children and building families, a fundamental social value. These minimum scientific standards for the practice of ART were designed to protect the interests of all participants — couples, children, donors, and health care providers.

REFERENCES AND NOTES

1. *Buzzanca v. Buzzanca,* 72 Cal. Rptr. 280 (10 March 1998).

2. M. Beck *et al., Newsweek,* 17 January 1994, p. 54.

3. D. Kong, *The Boston Globe,* 4 August 1996, p. A35.

4. Personal communication with American Society [for] Reproductive Medicine, 2 April 1998. Information is based on anecdotal reports from 1994.

5. *1995 Assisted Reproductive Technology Success Rates, National Summary and Fertility Clinic Reports* [Centers for Disease Control (CDC), Atlanta, GA, 1997].

6. Personal communication with the Organization of Parents Through Surrogacy, 25 March 1997.

7. *Hotline Information Packet 1* (National Council for Adoption, Washington, DC, 1997).

8. *Government of Canada, New Reproductive and Genetic Technologies: Setting Boundaries, Enhancing Health* (Minister of Supply and Services Canada, Canada, 1996).

9. Human Fertilization and Embryology Act 1990, Ministry of Health, United Kingdom.

10. B. Harrison, *The Atlanta Journal and Constitution,* 21 December 1997, p. D06, quoting Dr. Mark Sauer.

11. M. Siegler and L. Bergman, *Transplant. Proc.,* in press.

12. P. Kendall and W. Neikirk, *Chicago Tribune,* 25 February 1997, p. 1.

13. L. B. Andrews, *Hous. L. Rev.* 23, 149 (1992); M. Hibbert, proceedings from *Changing Conceptions: A Symposium on Reproductive Technologies,* Institute for Science, Law, and Technology, Chicago, IL, 1 to 26 December 1997 (Chicago: Chicago-Kent College of Law, 1997).

14. 42 U.S.C. 263a-1 through 263a-7 (Suppl. 1998).

15. *Abbott v. Bragdon,* 912 F. Supp. 580 (D. Me 1995) aff'd; 66 USLW 460 (U.S., 25 June 1998); *United States v. Wilson,* 73 F. 3d 675 (7th Circuit, 1995).

16. The New York State Task Force on Life and the Law, Assisted Reproductive Technologies: Analysis and Recommendations for Public Policy (1998).

17. K. Saunders, J. Spensley, J. Munro, G. Halasz, *Pediatrics* **97,** 688 (1996).

18. E. R. te Veld, A. L. van Baar, R. J. van Kooij, *Lancet* **351,** 1524 (1998).

19. J. Kurinczuk and C. Bower, *Br. Med. J.* **315,** 1260 (1997).

20. See, for example, P. A. In't Veld *et al., Lancet* **350,** 490 (1997).

21. J. R. Bowen, F. L. Gibson, G. I. Leslie, D. M. Saunders, *ibid.* **351,** 1529 (1998).

22. J. G. Schenken, *Fertil. Steril.* **61,** 411 (1994).

23. A. Venn *et al., Lancet* **346,** 995 (1995).

24. D. P. Wolf and M. M. Quigley, Eds., *Human in Vitro Fertilization and Embryo Transfer* (Plenum, New York, 1984), pp. 3–4.

25. See J. Marquis, *Los Angeles Times,* 9 August 1997, p. A1.

26. *U.S. v. Jacobson,* 785 F. Suppl. 563 (E. D. Va. 1992).

27. B. Guyer *et al., Pediatrics* **100,** 905 (1997).

SUGGESTED READINGS

GENERAL ISSUES

Alpern, Kenneth D. *The Ethics of Reproductive Technology.* New York: Oxford University Press, 1992.

American Fertility Society, Ethics Committee. "Ethical Considerations of the New Reproductive Technologies." *Fertility and Sterility* 62 (Supplement 1; 1994), 1S-125S.

American Society for Reproductive Medicine. "Ethical Considerations of Assisted Reproductive Technologies." *Fertility and Sterility* 67 (Supplement 1; 1997), I-III.

Andrews, Lori B. "Control and Compensation: Laws Governing Extracorporeal Generative Materials." *Journal of Medicine and Philosophy* 14 (1989), 541–60.

Australia, National Health and Medical Research Council. *Long-Term Effects on Women from Assisted Conception.* Canberra: NH&MRC, 1996.

Bartels, Diane M., *et al.,* eds. *Beyond Baby M: Ethical Issues in New Reproductive Techniques.* Clifton, NJ: Humana Press, 1990.

Blank, Robert H. *Regulating Reproduction.* New York: Columbia University Press, 1990.

Cahill, Lisa Sowle. "Moral Traditions, Ethical Language, and Reproductive Technologies." *Journal of Medicine and Philosophy* 14 (1989), 497–522.

Canada, Law Reform Commission. *Medically Assisted Procreation.* Working Paper 65. Ottawa: Minister of Supply and Services, 1992.

Canada, Royal Commission on New Reproductive Technologies. *Proceed with Care: Final Report.* 2 vols. Ottawa: The Commission, November 15, 1993.

Caplan, Arthur L. "And Baby Makes—Moral Muddles." In his *Am I My Brother's Keeper: The Ethical Frontiers of Biomedicine.* Bloomington and Indianapolis, IN: Indiana University Press, 1997, 3–21.

Cohen, Cynthia. "Reproductive Technologies: VII. Ethical Issues." In Warren Thomas Reich, ed. *Encyclopedia of Bioethics.* Revised ed. New York: Simon and Schuster Macmillan, 1995, 2233–41.

Corea, Gena. *Man-Made Women: How New Reproductive Technologies Affect Women.* Bloomington, IN: Indiana University Press, 1987.

———. *The Mother Machine: Reproductive Technologies from Artificial Insemination to Artificial Wombs.* New York: Harper & Row, 1985.

Glover, Jonathan, *et al. Ethics of New Reproductive Technologies: The Glover Report to the European Commission.* DeKalb: Northern Illinois University Press, 1989.

Harris, John. *Clones, Genes, and Immortality: Ethics and the Genetic Revolution.* Oxford: Oxford University Press, 1998. (Earlier edition entitled *Wonderwoman and Superman.*)

———, and Holm, Søren, eds. *The Future of Human Reproduction: Ethics, Choice and Regulation.* New York: Oxford University Press, 1998.

Holmes, Helen Bequaert. "Reproductive Technologies." In Lawrence C. Becker, and Charlotte B. Becker, eds. *Encyclopedia of Ethics.* New York: Garland, 1992, 1083–89.

Hull, Richard T., ed. *Ethical Issues in the New Reproductive Technologies.* Belmont, CA: Wadsworth, 1990.

Humber, James M., and Almeder, Robert F., eds. *Biomedical Ethics Reviews, 1995: Reproduction, Technology, and Rights.* Totowa, NJ: Humana Press, 1996.

Institute of Medicine and National Research Council, Committee on the Basic Science Foundations of Medically Assisted Conception. *Medically Assisted Conception: An Agenda for Research.* Washington, DC: National Academy Press, 1989.

Knoppers, Bartha M., and LeBris, Sonia. "Recent Advances in Medically Assisted Conception: Legal, Ethical and Social Issues." *American Journal of Law and Medicine* 17 (1991), 329–61.

Kondratowicz, Diane M. "Approaches Responsive to Reproductive Technologies: A Need for Critical Assessment and Directions for Further Study." *Cambridge Quarterly of Healthcare Ethics* 6 (1997), 148–56.

Lauritzen, Paul. *Pursuing Parenthood: Ethical Issues in Assisted Reproduction.* Bloomington, IN: Indiana University Press, 1993.

McCullough, Laurence B., and Chervenak, Frank A. *Ethics in Obstetrics and Gynecology.* New York: Oxford University Press, 1994.

Melo-Martin, Immaculada de. *Making Babies: Biomedical Technologies, Reproductive Ethics, and Public Policy.* Dordrecht and Boston: Kluwer Academic, 1998.

New York State Task Force on Life and the Law. *Assisted Reproductive Technologies: Analysis and Recommendations for Public Policy.* New York: The Task Force, April 1998.

Overall, Christine. *Ethics and Human Reproduction: A Feminist Analysis.* Boston: Allen & Unwin, 1987.

———, ed. *The Future of Human Reproduction.* Toronto: The Women's Press, 1989.

Pellegrino, Edmund D.; Harvey, John Collins; and Langan, John P., eds. *Gift of Life: Catholic Scholars Respond to the Vatican Instruction.* Washington, DC: Georgetown University Press, 1990.

Robertson, John A. "Assisted Reproductive Technology and the Family." *Hastings Law Journal* 47 (1996), 911–33.

———. *Children of Choice: Freedom and the New Reproductive Technologies.* Princeton, NJ: Princeton University Press, 1994.

Rothman, Barbara Katz. *Recreating Motherhood: Ideology and Technology in a Patriarchal Society.* New York: W.W. Norton, 1989.

Rowland, Robyn. *Living Laboratories: Women and Reproductive Technology.* Bloomington, IN: Indiana University Press, 1992.

Ryan, Maura A. "The Argument for Unlimited Procreative Liberty: A Feminist Critique." *Hastings Center Report* 20 (July–August 1990), 6–12.

Sherwin, Susan. "The Ethics of Babymaking" [Book Review Essay]. *Hastings Center Report* 25 (March–April 1995), 34–37.

Singer, Peter, and Wells, Deane. *Making Babies: The New Science and Ethics of Conception.* New York: Scribner's Sons, 1985.

Steinberg, Deborah Lynn. *Bodies in Glass: Genetics, Eugenics, Embryo Ethics.* Manchester: Manchester University Press (distributed in the United States by St. Martin's Press), 1997.

Steinbock, Bonnie. *Life Before Birth: The Moral and Legal Status of Embryos and Fetuses.* New York: Oxford University Press, 1992.

United Kingdom, Human Fertilisation and Embryology Authority. *Sixth Annual Report.* London: HFEA, 1997.

———. *The Patients' Guide to DI [Donor Insemination] and IVF [In Vitro Fertilization] Clinics.* 3d ed. London: HFEA, 1997.

United States, Centers for Disease Control and Prevention; American Society for Reproductive Medicine and Society for Assisted Reproductive Technology; and RESOLVE. *1995 Assisted Reproductive Technology Success Rates.* 3 vols. Atlanta: CDC, December 1997.

United States, Congress, Office of Technology Assessment. *Artificial Insemination: Practice in the United States—Summary of a 1987 Survey.* Background Paper. Washington, DC: U.S. Government Printing Office, August 1988.

———. *Infertility: Medical and Social Choices.* Washington, DC: U.S. Government Printing Office, May 1988.

Walters, LeRoy. "Ethics and New Reproductive Technologies: An International Review of Committee Statements." *Hastings Center Report* 17 (June 1987; Supplement), 3–9.

———. "Reproductive Technologies and Genetics." In Robert M. Veatch, ed. *Medical Ethics.* 2d ed. Boston: Jones and Bartlett Publishers, 1997, 209–38.

Warnock, Mary, and United Kingdom, Department of Health and Social Security, Committee of Inquiry into Human Fertilisation and Embryology. *A Question of Life: The Warnock Report on Human Fertilisation and Embryology.* New York: Basil Blackwell, 1985.

INFERTILITY

Abma, Joyce C., *et al.* "Fertility, Family Planning, and Women's Health: New Data from the 1995 National Survey of Family Growth." *Vital and Health Statistics,* Series 23: Data from the National Survey of Family Growth, No. 19, May 1997.

Chandra, Anjani, and Stephen, Elizabeth Hervey. "Impaired Fecundity in the United States: 1982–1995." *Family Planning Perspectives* 30 (January/February 1998), 34–42.

Fein, Esther B. "Calling Infertility a Disease, Couples Battle with Insurers." *New York Times,* February 22, 1998, p. 1.

Shanner, Laura. "Bioethics through the Back Door: Phenomenology, Narratives, and Insights into Infertility." In L. Wayne Sumner and Joseph Boyle, eds. *Philosophical Perspectives on Bioethics.* Buffalo, NY: University of Toronto Press, 1996, 115–42.

United States, Congress, Office of Technology Assessment. *Infertility: Medical and Social Choices.* Washington, DC: U.S. Government Printing Office, May 1988.

Bonnicksen, Andrea L. *In Vitro Fertilization: Building Policy from Laboratories to Legislatures.* New York: Columbia University Press, 1989.

———. "Reproductive Technologies: IV. In Vitro Fertilization and Embryo Transfer." In Warren Thomas Reich, ed. *Encyclopedia of Bioethics.* Revised ed. New York: Simon and Schuster Macmillan, 1995, 2221–25.

Caplan, Arthur L. "The Ethics of In Vitro Fertilization." *Primary Care* 13 (1986), 241–53.

Capron, Alexander M. "Parenthood and Frozen Embryos: More Than Property and Privacy." *Hastings Center Report* 22 (September–October 1992), 32–33.

Cohen, Cynthia B., ed. *New Ways of Making Babies: The Case of Egg Donation.* Bloomington and Indianapolis, IN: Indiana University Press, 1996.

Dawson, Karen, and Singer, Peter. "Should Fertile People Have Access to In Vitro Fertilization?" *British Medical Journal* 300 (1990), 167–70.

Fleischer, Eva. "Ready for Any Sacrifice? Women in IVF Programmes." *Issues in Reproductive and Genetic Engineering* 3 (1990), 1–11.

Klein, Renate D. "IVF Research: A Question of Feminist Ethics." *Issues in Reproductive and Genetic Engineering* 3 (1990), 243–51.

Rothman, Barbara Katz. "Not All That Glitters Is Gold." *Hastings Center Report* 22 (July–August 1992; Supplement), S11–S15.

Singer, Peter, *et al. Embryo Experimentation.* New York: Cambridge University Press, 1990.

Tennessee, Supreme Court. *Davis v. Davis. Southwestern Reporter,* SW.2d 842, 588–604 (1992).

Tong, Rosemarie. "Nonfeminist and Feminist Perspectives on Artificial Insemination and In-Vitro Fertilization." In her *Feminist Approaches to Bioethics: Theoretical Reflections and Practical Applications.* Boulder, CO: Westview Press, 1997, 156–86, 261–65.

Van der Wilt, Gert Jan. "Health Care and the Principle of Fair Equality of Opportunity: A Report from the Netherlands." *Bioethics* 8 (1994), 329–49.

SURROGATE PARENTING ARRANGEMENTS

Allen, Anita L. "Surrogacy, Slavery, and the Ownership of Life." *Harvard Journal of Law and Public Policy* 13 (1990), 139–49.

American College of Obstetricians and Gynecologists, Committee on Ethics. "Ethical Issues in Surrogate Motherhood." *Women's Health Issues* 1 (1991), 129–34. See also pp. 135–60.

Annas, George J. "Crazy Making: Embryos and Gestational Mothers." *Hastings Center Report* 21 (January–February 1991), 35–38.

Arneson, Richard J. "Commodification and Commercial Surrogacy." *Philosophy and Public Affairs* 21 (1992), 132–64.

Capron, Alexander M. "Surrogate Motherhood: Legal Issues Raised by the New Reproductive Alternatives." In Mark I. Evans, *et al.,* eds. *Fetal Diagnosis and Therapy: Science, Ethics, and the Law.* Philadelphia: J. B. Lippincott, 1989, 372–86.

———. "Whose Child Is This?" *Hastings Center Report* 21 (November–December 1991), 37–38.

———, and Radin, Margaret Jane. "Choosing Family Law over Contract Law as a Paradigm for Surrogate Motherhood." *Law Medicine, and Health Care* 16 (1988), 34–43.

Field, Martha A. *Surrogate Motherhood.* Cambridge, MA: Harvard University Press, 1988.

Gostin, Larry, ed. *Surrogate Motherhood: Politics and Privacy.* Bloomington: Indiana University Press, 1990.

Macklin, Ruth. *Surrogates and Other Mothers: The Debates over Assisted Reproduction.* Philadelphia: Temple University Press, 1994.

New Jersey, Commission on Legal and Ethical Problems in the Delivery of Health Care. *After Baby M: The Legal, Ethical and Social Dimensions of Surrogacy.* Trenton, NJ: The Commission, September 1992.

New Jersey, Supreme Court. *In the Matter of Baby M. Atlantic Reporter* 537 A.2d 1227 (1988).

Posner, Richard A. "The Ethics and Economics of Enforcing Contracts of Surrogate Motherhood." *Journal of Contemporary Health Law and Policy* 5 (1989), 21–29.

Rae, Scott B. *The Ethics of Commercial Surrogate Motherhood: Brave New Families?* Westport, CT: Praeger, 1994.

Rothenberg, Karen H. "Gestational Surrogacy and the Health Care Provider: Put Part of the 'IVF Genie' Back in the Bottle." *Law, Medicine and Health Care* 18 (1990), 345–52.

Satz, Debra. "Markets in Women's Reproductive Labor." *Philosophy and Public Affairs* 21 (1992), 107–31.

Shapiro, Michael H. "How (Not) to Think about Surrogacy and Other Reproductive Innovations." *University of San Francisco Law Review* 28 (1994), 647–80.

Tong, Rosemarie. "Feminist and Nonfeminist Perspectives on Surrogacy." In her *Feminist Approaches to Bioethics: Theoretical Reflections and Practical Applications.* Boulder, CO: Westview Press, 1997, 187–212, 266–68.

———. "Reproductive Technologies: V. Surrogacy." In Warren Thomas Reich, ed. *Encyclopedia of Bioethics.* Revised ed. New York: Simon and Schuster Macmillan, 1995, 2225–29.

Wadlington, Walter J. "Baby M: Catalyst for Family Law Reform?" *Journal of Contemporary Health Law and Policy* 5 (1989), 1–20.

Wertheimer, Alan. "Commercial Surrogacy." In his *Exploitation.* Princeton: Princeton University Press, 1996, 96–122.

CLONING

Andrews, Lori B. "Mom, Dad, Clone: Implications for Reproductive Privacy." *Cambridge Quarterly for Healthcare Ethics* 7 (1998), 176–86.

Fitzgerald, Kevin T. "Human Cloning: Analysis and Evaluation." *Cambridge Quarterly for Healthcare Ethics* 7 (1998), 218–22.

Group of Adviser on the Ethical Implications of Biotechnology. "Ethical Aspects of Cloning Techniques: Opinion of the Group of Advisers on the Ethical Implications of Biotechnology of the European Commission. *Cambridge Quarterly of Healthcare Ethics* 7 (1998), 187–93.

Harris, John. "Cloning and Human Dignity." *Cambridge Quarterly for Healthcare Ethics* 7 (1998), 163–67.

Humber, James M., and Almeder, Robert F., eds. *Biomedical Ethics Reviews: Human Cloning.* Totowa, NJ: Humana Press, 1998.

Kass, Leon R. "The Wisdom of Repugnance." *New Republic* 216 (June 2, 1997), 17–26.

———, and Wilson, James Q. *The Ethics of Cloning.* Washington, DC: AEI [American Enterprise Institute] Press, 1998.

Kolata, Gina. *Clone: The Road to Dolly, and the Path Ahead.* New York: William Morrow and Company, 1998.

Newman, Stephen A. "Human Cloning and the Family: Reflections on Cloning Existing Children." *New York Law School Journal on Human Rights* 13 (1997), 523–30.

Pence, Gregory E. *Who's Afraid of Human Cloning?* Lanham, MD: Rowman and Littlefield, 1998.

———, ed. *Flesh of My Flesh: The Ethics of Cloning Humans: A Reader.* Lanham, MD: Rowman and Littlefield, 1998.

Silver, Lee M. *Remaking Eden: Cloning and Beyond in a Brave New World.* New York: Avon Books, 1997.

Sunstein, Cass R., and Nussbaum, Martha, eds. *Clones and Clones: Facts and Fantasies about Human Cloning.* New York: W.W. Norton, 1998.

United States, National Bioethics Advisory Commission. *Cloning Human Beings: Report and Recommendations of the National Bioethics Advisory Commission.* Rockville, MD: The Commission, June 1997.

Wakayama, T., *et al.* "Full-Term Development of Mice from Enucleated Oocytes Injected with Cumulus Cell Nuclei." *Nature* 394 (1998), 369–74.

Wilmut, I., *et al.* "Viable Offspring Derived from Fetal and Adult Mammalian Cells." *Nature* 385 (1997), 810–13.

REGULATING ASSISTED REPRODUCTION

Baird, Patricia A. "New Reproductive Technologies: The Canadian Perspective" *Women's Health Issues* 6 (1996), 156–66.

Charo, R. Alta. "Reproductive Technologies: VIII. Legal and Regulatory Issues." In Warren Thomas Reich, ed. *Encyclopedia of Bioethics.* Revised ed. New York: Simon and Schuster Macmillan, 1995, 2241–48.

Cohen, Cynthia B. "Unmanaged Care: The Need to Regulate New Reproductive Technologies in the United States." *Bioethics* 11 (1997), 348–65.

Jones, Howard W., Jr. "The Time Has Come." *Fertility and Sterility* 65 (1996), 1090–92.

———, *et al.* "Accountability in the Advertising and Marketing of Assisted Reproduction." *Women's Health Issues* 7 (1997), 167–71.

Jonsen, Albert R.; Macklin, Ruth; and White, Gladys B. "Assisted Reproduction: A Process Ripe for Regulation: A Conference of the National Advisory Board on Ethics in Reproduction." *Women's Health Issues* 6 (1996), 117–21

Steinbock, Bonnie. "Regulating Assisted Reproductive Technologies: An Ethical Framework." *Women's Health Issues* 6 (1996), 167–74.

Warnock, Mary. "The Regulation of Technology." *Cambridge Quarterly for Healthcare Ethics* 7 (1998), 173–75.

Wilcox, Lynne S., and Marks, James S. "Regulating Assisted Reproductive Technologies: Public Health, Consumer Protection, and Public Resources." *Women's Health Issues* 6 (1996), 175–80.

BIBLIOGRAPHIES

Goldstein, Doris Mueller. *Bioethics: A Guide to Information Sources.* Detroit: Gale Research Company, 1982. See under "Reproductive Technologies."

Lineback, Richard H., ed. *Philosopher's Index.* Vols. 1– . Bowling Green, OH: Philosophy Documentation Center, Bowling Green State University. Issued quarterly. See under "Artificial Insemination," "Cloning," "In Vitro Fertilization," and "Surrogates."

Walters, LeRoy, and Kahn, Tamar Joy, eds. *Bibliography of Bioethics.* Vols. 1– . Washington, DC: Kennedy Institute of Ethics,

Georgetown University. Issued annually. See under "Artificial Insemination," "Cloning," "In Vitro Fertilization," "Reproduction," "Reproductive Technologies," and "Surrogate Mothers." (The information contained in the annual *Bibliography* can also be retrieved from BIOETHICSLINE, an online database of the National Library of Medicine.)

National Library of Medicine: PubMed
(http://www.ncbi.nlm.nih.gov/PubMed/)

National Library of Medicine: BIOETHICSLINE
(http://igm.nlm.nih.gov)

University Microfilms: Periodical Abstracts
(http://www.umi.com/proquest)

10.
The Global AIDS Epidemic

INTRODUCTION

No public health problem of the twentieth century is as threatening to human welfare as the global epidemic of AIDS. From small beginnings in a few sites about 1980, this epidemic has spread to every continent on earth. By early 1992 almost 13 million people worldwide were infected with the human immunodeficiency virus (HIV), the virus that causes AIDS. Of these 13 million people, almost 3 million were estimated to have advanced to the end-stage of HIV infection, the life-threatening clinical diagnosis of AIDS.[1] At the end of 1997 updated and more precise figures on the extent of the epidemic were collected by the Joint United Nations Programme on HIV/AIDS (UNAIDS) and the World Health Organization (WHO). These two public health agencies reported that 30.6 million people were living with HIV infection or AIDS in 1997. Of these, an estimated 21 million resided in sub-Saharan Africa.[2]

How is this virus transmitted, and why has the epidemic been so difficult to control? The simplest answer is that HIV infection is predominantly a sexually transmitted disease. Thus, it is associated with one of the strongest drives in human beings and with a sphere of behavior that is both intimate and private in most people's lives. There are, of course, other sexually transmitted diseases, but the ingenuity of twentieth-century medicine has provided effective treatments for bacterial diseases such as syphilis and gonorrhea, if they are diagnosed early, and has helped people who contract genital herpes to cope with the discomfort of that chronic viral infection. Unlike these sexually transmitted diseases, however, HIV infection is at present incurable and uncontrollable. Its long-term effect, over the course of 10–20 years, is to weaken the infected person's immune system until he or she becomes susceptible to some life-threatening secondary infection.

There are, to be sure, non-sexual modes of transmission for this potent virus. For example, in the early years of the epidemic, many hemophiliacs were infected through their use of clotting factor unknowingly made from the blood products of HIV-infected people. Similarly, several thousand patients were infected through receiving HIV-infected blood transfusions. These modes of transmission have virtually ceased in industrialized countries because of reliable tests for antibody to the virus in blood and new methods of treating clotting factor that kill the virus. Still important as a mode of infection in some countries is the sharing of needles among injecting drug users. Because injecting drug use occurs despite being illegal in most of these countries, and because some injecting drug users are addicted to the drugs they inject, this mode of transmission is also quite difficult to control. A final important mode of transmission is from pregnant women to the fetuses they are carrying. In the United States the rate of maternal-fetal transmission, without prenatal drug therapy, is approximately 25 percent.

The following essays represent the effort of people in numerous academic fields to respond to this major epidemic. Among the fields of training represented by the authors are philosophy, theology, medicine, law, political science, and public health. All of the authors whose works are reprinted here share the goal of fighting and eventually defeating the global epidemic of AIDS, in a manner that is compatible with our other moral obligations and with human rights.

GENERAL ISSUES

In June of 1998 the UNAIDS Programme and the World Health Organization issued a comprehensive report on the global HIV/AIDS epidemic. While there are glimmers of hope in the report, the overall impression it conveys is one of sadness and pessimism. Since the beginning of the epidemic, 11.7 million people have died of AIDS. That figure equals the total population of the state of Illinois. In 1997 alone, 2.3 million people—the number of residents in the cities of Philadelphia and Houston combined—succumbed to the ravages of the epidemic. The number of orphans left behind by these deaths was a staggering 8.2 million. There were 5.8 million new HIV infections acquired in 1997, or 16,000 new infections per day. In terms of overall mortality, AIDS has now become one of the top ten diseases worldwide; in the next few years it could become one of the top five. New modes of therapy have helped to slow the course of the epidemic in industrialized countries, but even that welcome news highlights the fact that the best modes of current treatment are too expensive for most third-world countries. The first selection in this chapter presents extended excerpts from the June 1998 UNAIDS-WHO report.

The three remaining essays in this part explore the ethical dimensions and the social implications of the HIV/AIDS epidemic. LeRoy Walters surveys major issues in the prevention and treatment of HIV infection and AIDS in three distinct spheres: public health, the delivery of health care, and biomedical research. In the public health sphere, Walters advocates a voluntary rather than a mandatory approach, with major emphasis on educating people at risk of infection about ways to reduce the probability of their infecting others and, simultaneously, their risk of being infected. In the author's view, only the screening of blood, semen, and tissues or organs should be required by law. In the health care sphere, Walters argues that health providers have a moral obligation to care for people with HIV infection but that policies should be implemented to ensure that the health risks to such providers remain at a reasonable level. Further, at the level of the health care system, better access to timely health care should be provided to all HIV-infected people. Biomedical research will also raise important ethical questions, especially when researchers initiate large-scale clinical trials of vaccines for the prevention of HIV infection. The author notes the relevance of three major ethical principles—beneficence, justice, and respect for autonomy—to the AIDS epidemic but suggests that these principles may need to be supplemented by at least one additional principle.

The excerpt from a National Research Council (NRC) panel report on *The Social Impact of AIDS in the United States* responds in part to an earlier study of the AIDS epidemic by an interdisciplinary group of scholars. The prior study, entitled *A Disease of Society: Cultural Responses to AIDS,* had opened with the following words:

> AIDS is no "ordinary" epidemic. More than a devastating disease, it is freighted with profound social and cultural meaning. More than a passing tragedy, it will have long-term, broad-ranging effects on personal relationships, social institutions, and cultural configurations.[3]

The NRC panel questions whether the consequences of AIDS will be either as pervasive or as long-lasting as this quotation suggests. Quite provocatively, the panel compares the current AIDS epidemic with the "forgotten" influenza epidemic of 1918, which killed perhaps

30 million people worldwide but arguably had no major impact on the social institutions and practices of the time. In a similar fashion, the panel asserts, AIDS is increasingly affecting the most marginalized groups in the United States, especially the urban poor, many of whom belong to ethnic minorities. Thus, if the current pattern of the epidemic holds, the threat of AIDS may seem to disappear in the United States not because the virus has been controlled or eliminated but "because those who continue to be affected by [the epidemic] are socially invisible, beyond the sight and attention of the majority population."

The essay by Ronald Bayer and Jeff Stryker reports both medical progress and new ethical dilemmas. The good news is that triple combination chemotherapy, including a protease inhibitor, can reduce the viral loads of people with AIDS and can delay the progression of disease, at least for a time. The less good news is that combination chemotherapy costs $10,000 to $15,000 per year in the United States. A patchwork of private health insurance, Medicaid plans, and the AIDS Drug Assistance Program provides access to chemotherapy to most people who need it, but not without complexity and compromise. Bayer and Stryker adopt a relatively rigorous approach to people with AIDS who are, at present, unable or unwilling to take all of their prescribed medications on a regular basis. Their concern is that a haphazard approach to chemotherapy will not only be ineffective for the patient, but that partial compliance will also allow HIV to mutate and to develop resistance to even the newest generation of AIDS-fighting drugs. In their conclusion, Bayer and Stryker return to one of the major themes in the UNAIDS/WHO report, the utter unavailability of expensive chemotherapy in most third-world countries.

THE DUTY TO WARN AND THE DUTY NOT TO HARM

The duty to warn and the duty not to harm apply not just to health professionals, but to everyone. The authors of the three essays in the second part of this chapter examine the moral obligations of actual or potential sexual partners to each other, as well as the obligations of health professionals to at-risk third parties.

In their letter to the *New England Journal of Medicine* entitled "Sex, Lies, and HIV," Susan Cochran and Vickie Mays report on a survey of 665 college students from southern California. The students reported on their past practice in withholding information from, or lying to, sexual partners, and on their willingness to deceive in the future. Of particular importance for the topic of this chapter was the prospective willingness of 20 percent of the men and 4 percent of the women surveyed to lie about their HIV-antibody status. Also worthy of note was the willingness of almost half of the men and more than 40 percent of the women to understate the number of previous sexual partners.

Ronald Bayer describes a subtle shift in sexual ethics that has occurred in the midst of the AIDS epidemic. According to Bayer, in the early years of the epidemic commentators were reluctant to discuss the moral responsibility of people with HIV infection or AIDS to warn or otherwise protect their sexual partners. Instead, the accent was on the more egoistic goal of self-protection. Part of the rationale for this approach was a concern that HIV-infected people, already subject to stigmatization, would have unique duties imposed on them by an intolerant society. Bayer applauds the development of a more balanced, mature, and altruistic ethic that includes attention to the welfare of others. However, he notes that ambiguities remain, especially regarding the role of trust in sexual ethics.

Philosopher Ferdinand Schoeman discusses the "standard of care" that should be employed in intimate sexual relationships by a person who knows that he or she is, or might be, HIV-infected. While acknowledging the difficulty of fulfilling such a moral obligation in practice, the author asserts that an HIV-infected person has a clear moral obligation to disclose his or her HIV status to the potential partner. At least two arguments are advanced to justify this position. The first argument concerns the seriousness of the potential harm to the partner: HIV infection is a life-threatening disease. The second relies on Annette Baier's notion of trust; according to Schoeman, conditions of trust and intimacy that are worth respecting should be characterized by openness and honesty between the parties to the relationship. Schoeman notes that there are questions of legal accountability in intimate relationships, as well. Thus, a male who, contrary to fact, asserted to a female that he was free of sexually transmitted disease and who subsequently transmitted his herpes infection to her was not allowed by a California court to hide behind an asserted constitutional right of privacy. Whatever the right of privacy may mean, the court found, it does not include misrepresenting the facts about one's health status in a way that leads to serious harm to another person.

Schoeman goes on to raise a second, quite different question: Do health professionals have a moral or legal obligation to warn at-risk third parties in this life-and-death context? Schoeman argues that a therapeutic relationship aims to promote a patient's welfare "within the context of social responsibility." Therefore, in his view, the professional has a clear moral obligation to warn in cases where a patient adamantly refuses to fulfill his or her own moral duty.

TESTING AND SCREENING PROGRAMS

The essays in this section ask the questions: Under what circumstances should individuals be tested for HIV infection (through an antibody test), and should such testing be mandatory or voluntary? Debate about these questions has been a central feature of the AIDS policy discussion since a reasonably accurate antibody test became available in mid-1985. Note that the answers to the questions depend in part on the facts about how HIV infection is transmitted. That is, if HIV infection were transmitted through the air like the common cold or influenza, the risk of transmission to bystanders and casual acquaintances would be considerably higher and the argument for widespread testing and screening correspondingly stronger. In addition, the facts about whether an effective treatment for an infection exists may also influence one's judgments about the moral justification for testing and screening programs.

In his overview, James Childress accents the ethical principle of respect for persons and cites three types of rules that can be derived from this principle: rules of liberty, rules of privacy, and rules of confidentiality. The author then asks what set of conditions could justify overriding this principle and these prima facie rules. He suggests five conditions that, in his view, would be individually necessary and jointly sufficient to justify infringements of the rules. Childress's formal analysis is then applied to an interesting variety of potential screenees: hospital patients, couples applying for marriage licenses, pregnant women and newborns, prisoners, and immigrants. In general, Childress concludes that mandatory testing and screening of these groups is not justified, given the current fact-situation.

The last two essays in this part focus on proposals to screen either pregnant women or newborn infants for HIV infection. As Childress noted and Howard Minkoff and Anne Willoughby discuss in greater detail, the shape of the ethical questions surrounding prenatal HIV testing was radically changed by the decisive results of a randomized, placebo-controlled clinical trial. In November 1994, AIDS researchers reported that treatment of pregnant women and newborn infants with AZT (also called zidovudine) reduced the rate of HIV infection in the infants by two-thirds—from 25.5 percent to 8.3 percent. This clinical result was the most dramatic success story in the AIDS epidemic to that time. The question therefore arose: Should all pregnant women be required to be tested for HIV infection? Minkoff and Willoughby argue that pregnant women should not be *required* to be tested because such a requirement would violate the civil liberties of adults and would affect only one gender. The authors also note that mandatory testing of pregnant women would be ineffective unless one were prepared to forcibly administer AZT to HIV-infected women who refused to initiate therapy themselves. On the other hand, Minkoff and Willoughby contend, the prenatal test for HIV infection should not be singled out as one that requires special justification or an inquiry by the clinician into each patient's risk factors. Rather, it should be assumed that virtually all pregnant women will want to take reasonable steps to protect the fetuses they are carrying and that most will welcome the offer of a test that can assist them in the achievement of that goal.

A second question discussed by Minkoff and Willoughby is whether there should be mandatory testing of newborn infants. This type of mandatory program, modeled on the testing of newborns for certain genetic conditions (see Chapter 8), avoids the difficulty of forcing a pregnant woman to accept a test on behalf of another — the fetus that she is carrying. However, the neonatal test, if positive, will disclose both the HIV status of the infant and of the infant's mother. Minkoff and Willoughby argue that a neonatal test occurs too late to be helpful to the newborn because no effective treatment currently exists. Despite this kind of expert opinion, the United States Congress has enacted legislation requiring states to reduce the level of perinatal transmission or face a federal requirement that they institute mandatory neonatal testing. In the meantime, New York state has established such a program. Deborah Sontag's *New York Times* article reports on the initial experience in that program.

CLINICAL RESEARCH ON HIV/AIDS

The six selections in the final part of this chapter discuss one of the most controversial topics in contemporary bioethics. As noted above, the AIDS epidemic is most devastating in third-world settings. After a U.S. clinical trial had demonstrated a two-thirds reduction in the transmission of HIV infection from pregnant women to the fetuses they were carrying, the question quite naturally arose, Can the drug regimen that was successfully employed for pregnant women and fetuses in this clinical trial be provided to pregnant women and infants in developing countries? Because of the high cost of AZT, it was immediately clear that the administration of the drug to pregnant women during the second and third trimesters of pregnancy would not be feasible in less affluent countries. In addition, most countries in the third world could not afford to provide intravenous AZT to pregnant women during labor and delivery. Accordingly, a less expensive alternative was sought. International experts in public health agreed with the health officers in several countries — including Thailand and Côte d'Ivoire — that a short course of oral AZT treatment for pregnant women would be an affordable alternative to the U.S. regimen. Thus, plans were laid to study how effective oral AZT would be in preventing transmission of HIV infection to fetuses if the oral AZT were administered only during the last two to four weeks of pregnancy.

All participants in the debate about the study of AZT during pregnancy in third-world settings would, I think, agree with the preceding description of the factual situation as clinical trials were planned. Here, however, the agreement ends. Several commentators, including Peter Lurie, Sidney Wolf, and Marcia Angell, argue that the optimal design for the third-world study would have been an *equivalency* trial comparing the expensive U.S. regimen from the earlier study against a shorter course of oral AZT during the final weeks of pregnancy. (This design was, in fact, employed in one study led by a researcher from the Harvard School of Public Health.) In sharp contrast, other commentators — including Harold Varmus, David Satcher, Danstan Bagenda, and Philippa Musoke-Mudido — assert that the most efficient and reliable study design was one that aimed to demonstrate the *superiority* of short-term oral AZT to a placebo (an inactive pill). Praphan Phanuphak adopts a mediating position in this complex, often emotional debate. He argues that placebo-controlled trials were morally justifiable in Thailand in 1994, when AZT was not readily available to Thai pregnant women, but that the continuation of the placebo-controlled studies was no longer justifiable in January 1997, when AZT was made accessible to all Thai pregnant women through the Thai Red Cross Society.

When the moral debate about the placebo-controlled trials in Thailand and other third-world countries was at its peak in 1997, the studies were still in progress and study results had not been made public. Early in 1998, the results of the U.S.-sponsored placebo-controlled trial in Thailand were released. The final selection in this chapter reports those results. Researchers found that HIV infection had been transmitted to 35 of 198 infa (18.6 percent) in the placebo arm of the study, and to 17 of 193 infants (9.2 percent) in the AZT arm.

L. W.

NOTES

1. For further details on these estimates, see Jonathan Mann, Daniel J. M. Tarantola, and Thomas W. Netter, eds. *AIDS in the World* (Cambridge, MA: Harvard University Press, 1992), pp. 2–4.

2. United Nations Joint Programme on HIV/AIDS and World Health Organization, *Report on the Global HIV/AIDS Epidemic, June 1998* (Geneva: UNAIDS/WHO, 1998), p. 6.

3. Dorothy Nelkin, David P. Willis, and Scott V. Parris, "Introduction," in Dorothy Nelkin, David P. Willis, and Scott V. Parris, eds., *A Disease of Society: Cultural and Institutional Responses to AIDS* (New York: Cambridge University Press, 1991), p. 1.

General Issues

JOINT UNITED NATIONS PROGRAMME ON HIV/AIDS AND WORLD HEALTH ORGANIZATION

Report on the Global HIV/AIDS Epidemic: June 1998

HIV AND AIDS: THE GLOBAL SITUATION

The human immunodeficiency virus (HIV) continues to spread around the world, insinuating itself into communities previously little troubled by the epidemic and strengthening its grip on areas where AIDS is already the leading cause of death in adults (defined here as those aged 15–49).

Estimates by the Joint United Nations Programme on HIV/AIDS (UNAIDS) and the World Health Organization (WHO), a cosponsor of the Joint Programme, indicate that by the beginning of 1998 over 30 million people were infected with HIV, the virus that causes AIDS, and that 11.7 million people around the world had already lost their lives to the disease. [See Table 1.]

Unless a cure is found or life-prolonging therapy can be made more widely available, the majority of those now living with HIV will die within a decade.

These deaths will not be the last; there is worse to come. The virus continues to spread, causing nearly 16,000 new infections a day. During 1997 alone, that meant 5.8 million new HIV infections, despite the fact that more is known now than ever before about what works to prevent the spread of the epidemic.

It is possible that momentum for prevention will build up as the epidemic becomes more visible. Today, although one in every 100 adults in the most sexually active age bracket (15–49) is living with HIV, only a

tiny fraction know about their infection. Because people can live for many years with HIV before showing any sign of illness, the virus can spread unobserved for a long time. In the face of other pressing concerns, it has been relatively easy in many parts of the world for political, religious and community leaders to overlook the significance of the epidemic. But AIDS cases, and AIDS deaths, are growing the world over, and there are few countries where it is still possible to be ignorant of the scale of the disease. Some 2.3 million people died of AIDS during the course of 1997. In roughly the same number again HIV infection developed into symptomatic AIDS. HIV has more than doubled the adult death rate in some places, and is the single biggest cause of adult death in many others. . . . Indeed HIV/AIDS is among the top ten killers worldwide, and given current levels of HIV infection, it may soon move into the top five, overtaking such well-established causes of death as diarrhoeal diseases.

Nearly 600,000 children were infected with HIV in 1997, mostly through their mothers before or during birth or through breastfeeding. The number of children under 15 who have lived or are living with HIV since the start of the epidemic in the late 1970s has reached around 3.8 million — 2.7 million of them have already died. However, recent developments in the understanding of mother-to-child transmission and in drug research hold out a promise of reducing the number of child infections, at least in populations where pregnant women can choose to be tested for HIV.

. . . HIV infections are concentrated in the developing world, mostly in countries least able to afford to care

Table 1. Global Estimates of the HIV/AIDS Epidemic as of End of 1997

	Adults	Women	Children	Total
People newly infected with HIV in 1997	5,200,000	2,100,000	590,000	5,800,000
Number of people living with HIV/AIDS	29,400,000	12,200,000	1,100,000	30,600,000
AIDS deaths in 1997	1,800,000	800,000	460,000	2,300,000
Total number of AIDS deaths since the beginning of the epidemic	9,000,000	3,900,000	2,700,000	11,700,000
Total number of AIDS orphans* since the beginning of the epidemic				8,200,000

*Defined as children who lost their mothers or both parents to AIDS when they were under the age of 15.

for infected people. In fact, 89% of people with HIV live in sub-Saharan Africa and the developing countries of Asia, which between them account for less than 10% of global Gross National Product. [See Table 2.]

... While in some countries HIV has remained at roughly the same low levels for a number of years, others, currently at similar absolute levels of prevalence, are experiencing a rapid spread of the virus. It is these countries that have the greatest potential to avert epidemic spread by acting quickly. ...

It is clear that infection rates are rising rapidly in much of Asia, Eastern Europe and southern Africa. The picture in Latin America is mixed, with prevalence in some countries rising rapidly. In other parts of Latin America and many industrialized countries, infection is falling or close to stable. This is also the case in Uganda, one of the earliest countries to record epidemic growth in HIV infection; in Thailand, where the rapid spread of HIV has been checked by active prevention programmes; and in some West African countries. Nevertheless, although the situation is improving among many groups, large numbers of new infections still occur every year in these countries.

Table 2. Adults and Children Living with HIV/AIDS — Total 30,600,000

North America	860,000
Caribbean	310,000
Latin America	1,300,000
Western Europe	480,000
North Africa & Middle East	210,000
Sub-Saharan Africa	21,000,000
Eastern Europe & Central Asia	190,000
East Asia & Pacific	420,000
South & South-East Asia	5,800,000
Australia & New Zealand	12,000

ORPHANS

HIV has often caused huge increases in death rates among younger adults — just the age when people are forming families and having children. ... This inevitably leads to an increase in orphans. In rural areas of East Africa, 4 of every 10 children who have lost one of their parents by age 15 have been orphaned by HIV/AIDS.

... [F]rom the beginning of the epidemic until the start of 1998, some 8.2 million children around the world had lost their mothers to AIDS. Many of those had lost their fathers as well. In 1997 alone, around 1.6 million children were orphaned by HIV. Over 90% of those orphans live in sub-Saharan Africa.

Extended family structures have in many countries been able to absorb some of the stress of increasing orphanhood. However, urbanization and the migration of labour, often across borders, is eating away at those structures. As the number of orphans grows and the number of potential caregivers shrinks, traditional coping mechanisms stretch to breaking point. That point may be reached much more rapidly in countries such as Thailand, where the nuclear family is increasingly the norm, and in Cambodia, where decades of war and civil strife have already taken a heavy toll on family structures and social coping mechanisms. These two countries already have the highest proportion of AIDS orphans in Asia.

THE EVOLVING PICTURE REGION BY REGION

SUB-SAHARAN AFRICA

Over two-thirds of all the people now living with HIV in the world — nearly 21 million men, women and children — live in Africa south of the Sahara desert, and fully 83% of the world's AIDS deaths have been in this region. Since the very start of the epidemic, HIV in sub-Saharan Africa has mostly spread through sex between men and women. . . . [T]his means that women are more heavily affected in Africa than in other regions, where the virus initially spread most quickly among men by male-to-male sex or drug injecting. Four out of five HIV-positive women in the world live in Africa.

An even higher proportion of the children living with HIV in the world are in Africa—an estimated 87%. There are a number of reasons for this. First, more women of childbearing age are HIV-infected in Africa than elsewhere. Secondly, African women have more children on average than those in other continents, so one infected woman may pass the virus on to a higher than average number of children. Thirdly, nearly all children in Africa are breastfed. Breastfeeding is thought to account for between a third and half of all HIV transmission from mother to child. Finally, new drugs which help reduce transmission from mother to child before and around childbirth are less readily available in developing countries, including those in Africa, than in the industrialized world.

. . .

ASIA: LOW INFECTION RATES BUT RAPID SPREAD

HIV was a latecomer to Asia, but its spread has been swift. Until the late 1980s, no country in Asia experienced a major epidemic—the continent appeared practically immune. By 1992, however, a number of countries, led by Thailand, were facing increasing numbers of infections. These were generally concentrated in groups such as drug injectors and sex workers whose behaviour was known to put them at risk. Although no Asian country has reached anything like the prevalence levels common in sub-Saharan Africa, HIV was by 1997 well established across the continent. The countries of South-East Asia, with the exception of Indonesia, the Philippines and Laos, are comparatively hard hit, as is India. While prevalence remains low in China, that country too has been recording an increasing number of cases.

Only a few countries in the region have developed sophisticated systems for monitoring the spread of the virus, so HIV estimates in Asia often have to be made on the basis of less information than in other regions. Because over half of the world's population lives in the region, small differences in rates can make a huge difference in the absolute numbers of people infected.

. . .

[A]bout 6.4 million people are currently believed to be living with HIV in Asia and the Pacific—just over 1 in 5 of the world's total. By the end of the year 2000, that proportion is expected to grow to 1 in 4. Around 94,000 children in Asia now live with HIV.

LATIN AMERICA AND THE CARIBBEAN: MOST INFECTIONS ARE IN MARGINALIZED GROUPS

In Latin America the picture is fragmented, although nearly every country in the continent now reports HIV infections. The pattern of HIV spread in Latin America is much the same as that in industrialized countries. Men who have unprotected sex with other men and drug injectors who share needles are the focal points of HIV infection in many countries in the region. Studies in Mexico suggest that up to 30% of men who have sex with men may be living with HIV. Between 3% and 11% of drug injectors in Mexico are HIV-infected, and in Argentina and Brazil the proportion may be close to half of all injectors.

Rising rates in women nevertheless show that heterosexual transmission is becoming more prominent. In Brazil in 1986, 1 AIDS case in 17 was a woman. Now the figure for AIDS is one in four, and a quarter of the 555,000 adults currently living with HIV in Brazil are women. In the region as a whole the proportion is around one-fifth.

In some places there is clear evidence of increasing infection among poorer and less educated members of the population. For example, in Brazil most of the early AIDS cases were in people with secondary or university education; today 60% of people living with AIDS never studied beyond primary school.

Some [1.6] million people are believed to be living with HIV in Latin America and the Caribbean. HIV prevalence is estimated at under 1 adult in 100 in all but a handful of the region's 44 countries and territories. . . .

EASTERN EUROPE: DRUG INJECTION DRIVES HIV

Until the mid-1990s, most of the countries of Eastern Europe appeared to have been spared the worst of the HIV epidemic. Mass screening of blood samples from people whose behaviour put them at risk of HIV showed extremely low levels of infection, right up to 1994. The whole of Eastern Europe put together had around 30,000 infections among its 450 million people at the start of 1995. At that time, Western Europe had over 15 times as many cases, while in sub-Saharan

Africa over 400 times as many people were living with the virus. But in the last few years, the former socialist economies of Eastern Europe and Central Asia have seen infections increase around six-fold. By the end of 1997, some 190,000 adults in the region were living with HIV infection.

The pattern of consistently low prevalence began to change in 1995 in several of the countries of the former Soviet Union. Belarus, Moldova, the Russian Federation and Ukraine have all registered astronomical growth in HIV infection rates over the last three years, most related to unsafe drug injecting. Now there may be nearly four times as many infections in Ukraine alone as there were in the whole Eastern European region just three years ago.

•   •   •

THE INDUSTRIALIZED WORLD: AIDS IS FALLING

In general, HIV infection rates appear to be dropping in Western Europe, with new infections concentrated among drug injectors in the southern countries of the continent, particularly Greece and Portugal. It is estimated that 30,000 Western Europeans were newly infected with HIV in 1997. Antiretroviral drugs given to women during pregnancy and the availability of safe alternatives to breastfeeding . . . kept mother-to-child transmission low; it is estimated that fewer than 500 children under the age of 15 were infected with HIV in 1997.

North America estimated it had around 44,000 new HIV infections in 1997, close to half of them among injecting drug users. As in Western Europe, transmission from mother to child was rare, with fewer than 500 new cases.

Generally, industrialized countries concentrate on following AIDS cases rather than tracking HIV. And as HIV infections continue to rise in the developing world, AIDS cases in many industrialized countries are falling. . . .

In Western Europe, new AIDS cases (corrected for delays in reporting) fell from 23,954 in 1995 to 14,874 in 1997 — a 38% drop. The fall in AIDS cases is due in part to prevention measures taken since the late 1980s by gay communities, and to a sustained rise in the proportion of young people using condoms, which led to a drop in the number of people infected with HIV. Because of the long lag time between HIV infection and symptomatic AIDS, the behaviour change of the late 1980s is only now being reflected in fewer new cases

of AIDS. But the downturn is probably due most of all to new antiretroviral drug therapies which postpone the development of AIDS and prolong the life of people living with HIV. . . .

In the United States, AIDS case reports indicate that the first-ever annual decrease in new cases — 6% — occurred in 1996, and an even larger reduction was expected in 1997. The biggest improvement — a drop of 11% — was in homosexual men. In some disadvantaged sections of society, however, AIDS continues to rise. Among African-Americans, new AIDS cases rose by 19% among heterosexual men and 12% among heterosexual women in 1996. In the Hispanic community, there were 13% more cases among men and 5% more among women than a year earlier. This is partly because these communities may find it hard to access the expensive new drugs that could stave off the onset of AIDS. It is partly, too, because prevention efforts in minority communities, where transmission is often through heterosexual intercourse and drug injecting, have been less successful than in the predominantly well-educated and well-organized gay community.

NORTH AFRICA AND THE MIDDLE EAST: THE GREAT UNKNOWN

Less is known about HIV infection rates in North Africa or the Middle East than in other parts of the world. Some countries, particularly those with large populations of immigrant workers, carry out mass screening for the virus, but none estimates infections at more than 1 adult in 100. Just over 200,000 people are estimated to be living with HIV in these countries, under 1% of the world total.

Risk behaviour does, however, exist. At least one country in the region has started a programme to reduce risky drug-injecting practices. The generally conservative social and political attitudes in the Middle East and North Africa often make it difficult for governments to address risk behaviour directly. However, in some countries in the region, governments have created elbow room for community and nongovernmental organizations to help sex workers and others whose behaviour puts them at risk to protect themselves from HIV.

UNDERSTANDING THE EPIDEMIC

NO SIMPLE EXPLANATIONS

Since HIV first began its march across the globe, people have been trying to explain why some countries are more affected than others. Because most of the worst-hit countries are among the world's poorest, for instance, there has been a temptation to say "AIDS is a disease of poverty." Because many of the populations most affected are also among the world's least educated, there has been a temptation to say "AIDS is a disease of ignorance."

Globally, it is certainly the poorer and less educated who are feeling the brunt of the HIV epidemic. But the epidemic has spread in different ways and through different groups of people in different parts of the world. Neighbouring countries often have very different epidemics. And even within a single nation, HIV can strike different populations or different geographic areas in dissimilar ways, ways that may change over the course of time.

An analysis of the relationship between education and HIV illustrates the pitfalls of drawing deceptively simple conclusions about the determinants of the epidemic. Relationships that seem clear at a global level can look very different at a regional level, and even more complex over time in a single setting.

It is reasonable to assume that better-educated people have better access to information about HIV, how it is transmitted, and how it can be avoided. On top of that, better-educated people are more likely to have better-paid jobs, and can afford the sorts of goods and services that allow them to act on their AIDS knowledge. If we take overall levels of literacy as an indication of educational levels in a country, we might, then, expect to find that countries with high levels of literacy have low levels of HIV. And indeed, if we compare literacy and HIV for the 161 countries in the world for which there are data on both HIV and literacy, a statistically significant pattern of just this kind emerges. . . .

But if we look just at the region of the world worst affected by HIV, sub-Saharan Africa, a very different picture emerges. In the 44 countries of the region for which figures exist, the analysis also reveals a relationship between HIV and literacy. But the direction of the relationship is now reversed. In this region, . . . the countries with the highest levels of HIV infection are also those whose men and women are most literate.

In this region as in all others, more-educated people are likely to be better informed about the dangers of HIV and have more disposable income than the illiterate. So why do the figures suggest they are also more likely to be HIV-infected? There are several possible explanations. It may be that social changes that accompany more schooling are also associated with behaviour that increases the risk of HIV infection. This may be especially the case for women, who without education may have very much less social mobility and be exposed to a much narrower spectrum of social and sexual relationships, for instance.

Another plausible explanation may be that educated people with higher earning power use their disposable income to support behaviours that put them at risk of infection. While a rich man is more able to afford a condom than a poor man, he is also more able to afford to invite a potential partner to a night-club, to support a number of wives or to visit sex workers. And where men tend to have at least some partners of a similar social and educational standing as themselves, higher HIV rates among educated men will translate into higher HIV prevalence among educated women.

. . .

UNDERSTANDING BEHAVIOUR

Clearly, the HIV epidemic progresses differently in different situations. It is driven by individual behaviour which put people at risk of infection. These behaviours may in turn be driven by poverty, by unequal relationships between men and women or between old and young people, or by cultural and religious norms that leave people little control over their exposure to the virus. The social, economic and cultural situations that create this kind of vulnerability to HIV infection have not been adequately studied or explained. Perhaps more surprisingly, there is still virtually no information in many countries on the basic sexual and drug-taking behaviours and patterns of sexual networking that determine how the virus spreads through a population.

Many countries have set up surveillance systems to track the spread of HIV through their populations — systems that have largely been pioneered by the countries of sub-Saharan Africa. But far fewer have collected any information on the sexual and drug-taking behaviours that are central to the spread of HIV. Since these behaviours precede infection, information about them can act as an early warning system. Such behavioural data can indicate how exposed a community may be to HIV. The information can identify groups who are especially vulnerable, and can pinpoint particular risk behaviours which threaten to drive the spread of the virus. When collected over time, it can also indicate trends in risk behaviour and vulnerability, validating existing prevention approaches or suggesting what changes need to be made for greater impact.

. . .

PREVENTION WORKS

For many years, HIV was a silent epidemic. Even when millions of people were infected with the virus, very few showed outward signs of illness. But now, as the epidemic matures in many parts of the world, its effects have become more visible. People are developing the illnesses associated with AIDS in ever-greater numbers. Because of this, communities are becoming increasingly concerned about caring for people who are affected by illness. But as the horrifying consequences of the epidemic become more visible, there is also increased momentum for preventing its further spread.

Even in places where the epidemic is less visible, well-designed and carefully-focused prevention campaigns have managed to arrest or reverse HIV trends. The best prevention campaigns work simultaneously on many levels—increasing knowledge of HIV and how to avoid it; creating an environment where safer sexual or drug-taking behaviours can be discussed and acted upon; providing services such as HIV testing, treatment for other sexually transmitted diseases (which if left untreated greatly magnify the risk of HIV transmission) and access to cheap condoms and clean injection equipment; and helping people to acquire the skills they need to protect themselves and their partners. Structural changes can help, too, by empowering people and reducing their vulnerability. Changes in laws, employment practices and even economic policy can create an environment in which people can more easily reduce or control their exposure to HIV, although it is hard to demonstrate a direct link between such changes and HIV infection levels.

Programmes to prevent the spread of HIV work best as a package, with each initiative reinforcing the others. It is almost impossible, therefore, to attribute changing behaviour or low or falling rates of infection with HIV and other STDs to a single element of a prevention campaign. Careful monitoring of both HIV prevalence and the behaviours that lead to its spread can, however, indicate whether such campaigns are having a collective impact.

. . .

FINDING OUT ONE'S HIV STATUS

In industrialized countries, counselling services and voluntary testing for HIV are widely available. Testing seems to be sought out more and more by people with high-risk behaviour now that therapies are available to those who know they are HIV-positive. In a study of new AIDS cases in Germany, the proportion of people who did not know they were HIV-infected until they were diagnosed with AIDS remained constant until 1996. Then, once widespread availability of effective antiretroviral therapy increased the incentive to get tested, the proportion of people who learned they were seropositive only when they were diagnosed with AIDS dropped by half in 1997.

There are valuable reasons to increase access to testing and counselling even in countries where expensive antiretroviral therapy is not widely available. People who know they are infected may be able to maintain their health better by eating appropriately and by seeking affordable prophylaxis and treatment for common opportunistic infections and other illnesses. They can choose to use condoms to protect their sex partners and children from infection. They can make informed choices about childbearing, and can seek advice on alternatives to breastfeeding to protect their infants. They can plan for their future needs and those of the families. They may choose to join together with others to increase support in the community for HIV-affected people, so as to gradually reduce the stigma which can eat away at prevention and care efforts. And they may increase pressure on local or national authorities to improve standards of care and services for affected individuals, families and communities.

It is difficult to attribute behaviour change directly to the provision of testing and counselling versus counselling alone. Even without testing, counselling helps people assess their risk of infection and provides information so that people can reduce the risk of acquiring HIV or passing it on. Counselling is also essential to reinforce safe behaviour among those who test negative. And it helps people cope with the results of a positive test. However, counselling along with testing probably offers the greatest benefits. There is a growing body of evidence to suggest that people who have received counselling and know their serostatus are more likely to adopt or maintain safe behaviours, either to protect themselves from future infection if they are uninfected, or, if HIV-positive, to protect their partners from infection. A study of HIV-infected homosexual men in Norway recorded a drop in the number of sex partners after testing. Men in the study averaged 4.3 partners a year before they learned of their HIV infection. After testing and counselling, that average fell to 1.6.

Preliminary results from a study in developing countries — Botswana, Côte d'Ivoire, Kenya, Rwanda, Tanzania, Thailand, Trinidad, Uganda and Zambia — show that voluntary testing and counselling does not always reduce the number of casual partners a person chooses. But it may contribute to increased condom use with those partners. Most groups reported a reduction of between 40% and 46% in unprotected casual sex after testing and counselling.

. . .

TREATMENT REDUCES AIDS DEATHS IN COUNTRIES THAT CAN AFFORD IT

In industrialized nations, a few countries in Latin America, and Thailand, many people who test positive for HIV have access to combination antiretroviral therapy which reduces the amount of HIV in the body and delays the onset of AIDS. In other countries combination antiretroviral therapy is also used, but by a very small proportion of HIV-infected people. Such therapies are expensive, hard to administer, and require regular medical monitoring.

Combination therapy with at least three antiretroviral drugs was introduced in 1995 and became widespread in 1996. While it is not yet known how long these therapies will prolong life, and while it is clear that they do not work for everyone, their use is already having a visible impact on AIDS incidence and AIDS mortality.

. . .

MOTHER-TO-CHILD TRANSMISSION

Altogether, 2.7 million children have died of AIDS since the beginning of the epidemic. Another million were estimated to be living with the disease at the end of 1997, half of them infected last year alone.

The overwhelming majority of these children acquired the infection from their mothers before or around the time of birth, or through breast milk. An equally great majority live in the developing world.

The gap between rich and poor countries in terms of transmission of HIV from mother to child has been growing. In France and the USA, for instance, fewer than 5% of children born to HIV-positive women in 1997 were infected with the virus. In developing countries, the average was between 25% and 35%. There are two major reasons for the difference — breastfeed-

ing practices and access to drugs for reducing mother-to-child transmission.

Since it first became clear that HIV could be transmitted through breast milk, very few infected women in industrialized countries have chosen to breastfeed their children, so transmission of infection at the nipple is negligible. In developing countries, however, between one-third and half of all HIV infections in young children are acquired through breastmilk.

There are several reasons for this. First, more than 9 out of 10 HIV-positive women in developing countries have no idea they are infected. They therefore cannot make informed choices about how to feed their children. Secondly, a woman may choose to breastfeed even if she knows about her infection, and knows she might pass it on through breast milk. Breastfeeding protects the infant against a range of other infections. It is convenient, approved by most cultures, and free. By choosing artificial feeding a woman may avoid passing on HIV. But where the water-supply is unsafe she may expose her child to other deadly diseases. Since prolonged breastfeeding has a naturally contraceptive effect, she may also expose herself to pregnancy again, repeating the dilemma. In most developing countries she will stretch the family budget. A year's supply of artificial milk for infants will cost a Vietnamese family more than the country's per capita GDP, and the same is true elsewhere in the developing world. And if bottle-feeding becomes a badge of HIV status, a woman may expose herself to stigma and social rejection.

Increasingly, developing countries are providing information about safe infant feeding to HIV-infected women who are pregnant. Some governments such as Thailand's distribute free or subsidized artificial milk to such women. But in many countries, the critical first step remains to provide counselling, voluntary HIV testing and information about safe feeding to all women considering pregnancy or already pregnant.

In 1994, it was shown that giving an antiretroviral drug to women during pregnancy and delivery and to the infant after birth could cut HIV transmission from mother to child by as much as two-thirds. This quickly became common practice in industrialized countries, but is hard to imagine as a standard in countries where many women do not get even basic antenatal care. The regimen is difficult to administer, involving regular drug-taking over several months and an intravenous drip during delivery. And it is expensive — currently, around US$ 1000 per pregnancy. A country such as Côte d'Ivoire, where both fertility and HIV prevalence are high, would have to spend 70% of its total current drug budget to provide this regimen for all women who risk passing HIV on to their children. This does not include the cost of counselling or testing.

Because the regimen used in the industrialized world is clearly out of reach for most people in the countries where it is most needed, new trials were initiated to identify more practical and affordable alternatives. A trial recently concluded in Thailand shows that a short course of antiretroviral pills given to pregnant women during the last weeks prior to and during labour successfully cuts the rate of vertical transmission during pregnancy and delivery by half. Because the Thai women were also given safe alternatives to breast milk and did not breastfeed, the short course of treatment was able to cut overall mother-to-child transmission in the study population to 9%, compared with a norm in developing countries of up to 35%.

The cost of treating HIV-positive women with a short course of antiretrovirals in late pregnancy and around the time of delivery compares well with that of many other health interventions. The cost-effectiveness varies according to the level of infection in a country. One study suggests that in Tanzania, counselling, testing and short-course antiretrovirals for pregnant women would cost under US$ 600 per HIV infection that is averted. This translates into around US$ 30 per healthy year of life gained — less than half the cost of providing food supplementation to avoid malnutrition in preschool children and around the same price per healthy year of life saved through immunization for polio and DPT (diphtheria, pertussis and tetanus). In high-prevalence areas of Thailand the cost per infection averted is around US$ 2800, just over twice the cost of caring for a child with AIDS.

• • •

LEROY WALTERS

Ethical Issues in the Prevention and Treatment of HIV Infection and AIDS

An adequate ethical framework for evaluating public policies regarding infection with the human immunodeficiency virus (HIV) will include the following considerations: (i) the outcomes, often categorized as benefits and harms, of the policies; (ii) the distribution of these outcomes within the population; and (iii) the liberty-rights, or freedoms, of those who are affected by the policies. A recent presidential commission on bioethics called these three considerations well-being, equity, and respect (*1*). In their *Principles of Biomedical Ethics,* Beauchamp and Childress designate these

Reprinted with permission from *Science* 239 (February 5, 1988), 597–603. Copyright © 1988 by the American Association for the Advancement of Science.

considerations beneficence and nonmaleficence, justice, and respect for autonomy (*2*).

As we and other societies attempt to confront the AIDS epidemic, the central problem we face is the following: How can we control the epidemic and the harm that it causes without unjustly discriminating against particular social groups and without unnecessarily infringing on the freedom of individuals? This formulation accepts the importance of halting the transmission of HIV infection but recognizes that the achievement of that goal may at times be in tension with other moral constraints, namely, constraints based on justice or respect for autonomy. At the same time, however, these three considerations, or moral vectors, may all point in the same direction, for example, if a particular policy is simultaneously counterproductive, discriminatory, and intrusive.

In this [essay] I will indicate how the ethical principles of beneficence, justice, and respect for autonomy relate to the epidemic of HIV infection in the United States (3). I will argue that, because these three principles are all of importance, none of them should be ignored in the formulation of public policy. While one principle may predominate in a given situation or sphere, it should not be allowed to overwhelm or displace the other two.

Three types of policies will be considered: public health policies, policies for the delivery of health care to people with HIV infection, and research policies.

PUBLIC HEALTH POLICIES

PUBLIC EDUCATION

Until more effective medical therapies and preventive measures are developed, public education is likely to be one of the most important means for controlling the epidemic. If the education appeals to the rational capacities of the hearer, it respects his or her autonomy. If public education simultaneously leads to risk-reducing behavioral change, it also promotes the health of the hearer and his or her associates.

Imaginative public education will be moral education in the sense that it helps the hearer to see clearly the possible effects of his or her behavior on others. One possible approach to such education involves the use of ethical if-then statements such as the following. "We have discussed the pros and cons of engaging in behavior X. If you choose to do X, then, in order to avoid harming others, you should adopt measures A, B, and C." Fortunately, many of the measures that protect others are also self-protective. Thus, public educators can simultaneously appeal to both the self-interested and altruistic sentiments of their audiences.

While everyone who is at risk of contracting or transmitting HIV infection should be educated, there are strong moral arguments for targeting educational efforts especially toward people who are most likely to engage in risky behaviors — for example, behaviors like receptive anal intercourse, intravenous (IV) drug use with shared needles, or vaginal intercourse with IV drug users. Such targeted programs can be justified on either or both of two grounds. Intensive coverage of the groups most at risk for infection is likely to be more efficient in controlling the epidemic than general educational programs alone will be. It can also be argued that

groups at higher than average risk need, or even deserve, stronger than average warnings of the risks to which they may be exposed (4).

MODIFIED APPROACHES TO IV DRUG USE

Twenty-five percent of clinical AIDS cases involve the illegal use of IV drugs (5). The sharing of needles and syringes, sometimes a ritual in settings where multiple drug users self-inject together, seems to be the principal mode of transmission among IV drug users. People who become infected through sharing contaminated needles and syringes may, in turn, infect nondrug-using people through sexual intercourse.

Members of ethnic and racial minority groups are represented in disproportionate numbers among U.S. IV drug users who have AIDS. In AIDS cases involving IV drug use as the sole risk, 51% of patients are black and 28% are Hispanic (5). Among minority group women, the correlation between IV drugs and AIDS is particularly strong: 70% of black women with AIDS and 83% of Hispanic women with AIDS are either IV drug users or the sexual partners of IV drug users. Two-thirds of black children and three-fourths of Hispanic children with AIDS contracted their infections from mothers who were members of the same two risk groups (6,7).

It is clear that current programs for IV drug users in the United States are failing in many respects and that new and bold measures are needed. These measures may not be politically popular, given the misunderstanding and fear that frequently surround drug use and given our society's traditional neglect of IV drug users. But the initiatives will be essential for controlling the epidemic, for meeting the needs of people who are often stigmatized, and for enabling IV drug users to make autonomous choices about their lives.

The first initiative that should be undertaken is the expansion of drug-treatment programs to accommodate, on a timely basis, all IV drug users who desire treatment. Reports of 3-month waiting lists in U.S. drug-treatment programs are commonplace (8, pp. 108–109; 9). Our failure to provide treatment to people who indicate an interest in discontinuing drug use is both short-sighted and counterproductive. It is encouraging to note that the Presidential Commission on Human Immunodeficiency Virus Epidemic is making the lack of programs to treat IV drug users one of four major areas for initial study (10, pp. 22–23).

A second initiative that will probably be necessary to control the epidemic among IV drug users is the establishment of public programs for the exchange of sterile needles and syringes for used and possibly contaminated equipment. Three countries—the Netherlands, the United Kingdom, and Australia—have experimented with free needle-exchange programs and have reported initially encouraging results—although it is too early to know for certain that the exchange programs actually reduce the rate of infection transmission (9, 11, 12). Proposals to initiate needle-exchange programs in the United States have not yet been implemented, in part because they appear to condone or even to encourage IV drug use. Perhaps for this reason U.S. law-enforcement officials have generally opposed such programs (8, pp. 109–110; 9). However, the ethical if-then statements discussed above may also pertain here. Moral and legal prohibitions of IV drug use have not achieved universal acceptance in our society. Given that fact, one seeks to formulate rules of morally responsible drug use: "If you choose to use IV drugs, then you should take steps, including the use of sterile needles and syringes, to minimize the chance of your becoming infected and infecting others with HIV."

If the foregoing measures, coupled with targeted education for IV drug users, are insufficient, more radical initiatives will need to be contemplated. One of the most controversial initiatives, at least among law-enforcement officials, would be the provision of controlled access to injectable drugs by IV drug users in an effort to bring addiction and its social context above ground. Such a policy was endorsed editorially in May 1987 by the British journal The Lancet (13). Pilot programs of controlled access to injectable drugs, with simultaneous decriminalization of IV drug use, could provide valuable data on the potential effectiveness of this initiative.

MODIFIED APPROACHES TO PROSTITUTION

Male or female prostitutes who have unprotected intercourse with multiple sexual partners expose themselves to considerable risk of HIV infection in areas of moderate to high seroprevalence. This theoretical risk has been actualized among female prostitutes who have been studied epidemiologically in both the United States and equatorial Africa. For example, a recent cross-sectional survey of female prostitutes in the Newark, New Jersey, area indicated that 51.7% tested positive

for antibody to HIV in 1987; in Miami the seroprevalence rate among incarcerated female prostitutes was 18.7% (14). A high infection rate among prostitutes imperils not only their own health but also the health of their clients and their clients' other sexual partners.

Official policies on prostitution in this country are set by states and localities. In most U.S. jurisdictions the general approach has been to criminalize the practice of prostitution; in some jurisdictions, the patronizing of a prostitute is also a crime. In contrast, many European countries and several counties in Nevada have adopted a licensing or regulatory approach that includes periodic screening of prostitutes for infectious disease (14; 15, pp. 2–20).

An ethically appropriate response to prostitution will be based not simply on our evaluation of prostitution as a practice but also on careful assessment of the extent to which alternative public policies on prostitution are compatible with the principles of beneficence, respect for autonomy, and justice. Although the intervening variables are numerous, the available evidence from Nevada and Europe suggests that, compared with the outlaw and arrest approach, the licensing and regulatory approach to prostitution is at least correlated with lower rates of infection with several other sexually transmitted diseases among prostitutes (14, 16, 17). At the same time, a licensing and regulatory approach displays greater respect for the autonomy of adult persons to perform acts that affect chiefly the persons themselves, especially if the transmission of disease is prevented through the use of condoms and through regular health examinations.

Again in this case we should be willing to become pragmatic and experimental in our approach to controlling the epidemic. The legal prohibition of prostitution has not been notably successful in preventing a rapid rise in seropositivity among prostitutes, at least in some cities. Pilot studies of less restrictive approaches in selected localities, taken together with evidence from Nevada and Western Europe, might reveal that alternative policies are, on balance, ethically preferable (18).

MODIFIED APPROACHES TO HOMOSEXUAL AND BISEXUAL SEXUAL ACTIVITY

As of December 1987, 65% of AIDS cases in the United States involve homosexual or bisexual males; an additional 8% of cases involve homosexual or bisexual males who also admit to IV drug use (5). Thus, in a substantial fraction of U.S. AIDS cases to date, HIV seems to have been transmitted through sexual intercourse between males. Receptive anal intercourse is one of the principal modes of viral transmission (*19, 20*).

Many homosexual and bisexual males with AIDS or HIV infection became infected before AIDS was described as a clinical syndrome and before the primary modes of transmission were identified. Thus, while they may have known that they were at increased risk for a series of treatable sexually transmitted diseases, for example, gonorrhea or hepatitis B, they could not have known that they were at risk for contracting an infection that might lead to AIDS. Since the facts about HIV transmission have become well known, homosexual and bisexual men have been heavily involved in targeted public education programs and in humane health care programs for people with AIDS. There is also substantial evidence to indicate that considerable numbers of homosexual and bisexual males have altered their sexual practices to reduce their probability of becoming infected and infecting others with HIV (*21–23*).

It might seem that, short of traditional public health measures such as increased testing and screening, little more can be done to encourage the cooperation of homosexual and bisexual males in controlling the epidemic. However, two public policy initiatives might conceivably have a salutary effect: (i) in jurisdictions that currently outlaw such acts, the decriminalization of private homosexual acts between consenting adults; and (ii) in jurisdictions that currently lack such antidiscrimination statutes, the legal prohibition of discrimination against people who engage in private consensual homosexual acts.

There would be strong moral arguments for these legal changes even in the absence of a major epidemic (*24–27*). However, in the midst of an epidemic that has already affected large numbers of homosexual and bisexual men, the following additional arguments can be advanced. First, decriminalization and antidiscrimination initiatives would encourage homosexual and bisexual males to disclose their patterns of sexual activity to health providers and hospitals without fear that a breach of confidentiality could lead to criminal prosecution. Such open disclosure could, in turn, lead to the discussion of risk-reducing practices such as the use of condoms or the avoidance of anal intercourse. Second, the legal changes could facilitate the gathering of more accurate data on current patterns of sexual activity in the United States — patterns that have not been studied in depth since the research of Alfred Kinsey and associates in the 1940s (*28*). By reducing respondents' fears about being stigmatized, the proposed legal changes could enhance the accuracy of data that would then be used for educational and epidemiological purposes. Third, the proposed legal changes would send a clear signal to homosexuals and bisexuals that heterosexuals intend to treat them with what Ronald Dworkin has termed "equal concern and respect" (*29*). More specifically, these policies would help all of us, regardless of sexual orientation or pattern of sexual practice, jointly to reassess whether the magnitude of our national effort to control the current epidemic has been proportionate to the gravity of the threat posed by the epidemic.

TESTING AND SCREENING PROGRAMS

The moral and legal justification for testing individuals or screening populations for antibody to HIV has been extensively debated (*8*, pp. 112–130; *15*, chap. 2; *30–35*). James Childress has proposed a helpful taxonomy of screening programs (*31*):

	Degree of Voluntariness	
Extent of screening	Voluntary	Compulsory
Universal	1	2
Selective	3	4

A recent amendment to the voluntary category in this matrix is "routine" counseling and testing, which is defined in Public Health Service guidelines as "a policy to provide these services to all clients after informing them that testing will be done." The Public Health Service guidelines add that "Except where testing is required by law, individuals have the right to decline to be tested without being denied health care or other services" (*34*).

There is scant justification and little public support for universal HIV antibody screening programs, whether voluntary or compulsory. The principal arguments against such programs are consequential. The usual screening test has poor predictive value in populations where the prevalence of seropositivity is low; thus, large numbers of people who are in fact antibody-negative would be falsely identified as positive during initial screening (*36*). Further, the cost of universal screening would be high, especially given the fact that screening would need to be repeated at regular intervals to track changes in antibody status. In short, universal screening is incompatible with the principle of beneficence. Mandatory universal screening would involve a massive violation of the respect for autonomy principle, as well.

The crux of the current debate is whether selective screening for HIV antibody should be undertaken and, if so, whether the screening should be compulsory or voluntary. To date, most commentators on the ethics of HIV antibody screening have argued that only carefully targeted, voluntary screening programs are morally justifiable and that such programs are morally justified only if they fulfill three conditions: (i) the programs include adequate counseling of screenees; (ii) they protect the confidentiality of information about individuals, except in carefully specified exceptional circumstances; and (iii) they are conducted in a context that provides guarantees of nondiscrimination to seropositive individuals (30–34). Categories of persons often nominated for selective, voluntary screening programs include hemophiliacs, IV drug users, homosexual and bisexual men, prostitutes, patients at clinics for sexually transmitted diseases, heterosexual sexual partners of infected persons, prisoners, military recruits and personnel, applicants for marriage licenses, and hospital patients, especially patients undergoing surgery or hemodialysis.

It is not possible here to discuss each of these population groups (37). I will, however, comment on the three conditions for ethically acceptable voluntary screening programs. The provision of face-to-face counseling to all persons participating in a large-scale, voluntary screening program may be infeasible on financial grounds. Thus, it might at first glance seem reasonable to reserve counseling for screenees who are confirmed to be HIV antibody positive. However, if voluntary screening programs are targeted to selected groups with much higher than average prevalence, then the screening context would seem an ideal setting for carefully tailored education regarding risk reduction. Such counseling demonstrates a program's respect for the autonomy of screenees and should help to slow the progress of the epidemic, as well.

The protection of patient confidentiality in all but carefully delineated circumstances also demonstrates respect for the autonomy of screenees (15, chap. 4; 38). Guarantees of confidentiality can be strengthened by statutes that impose criminal sanctions for unauthorized, medically nonindicated disclosure of antibody status. At the same time, however, guarantees of confidentiality should not be absolute. Several commentators have argued, for example, that health care providers have a moral duty to warn known intimate associates of an antibody-positive person who refuses to inform the associates of his or her antibody status and who continues to place those associates at risk (31, 32, 34, 39). In this case, the health provider cannot simultaneously respect the autonomy of both the screenee and the associates.

The level of participation in voluntary screening programs is likely to be higher if legal guarantees against discrimination are provided to antibody-positive persons (15, chap. 5; 40, pp. 347–350; 41). These guarantees would complement the general guarantees of nondiscrimination discussed above. One formulation of such a guarantee in a major federal bill reads as follows:

A person may not discriminate against an otherwise qualified individual in employment, housing, public accommodations, or governmental services solely by reason of the fact that such individual is, or is regarded as being, infected with the etiologic agent for acquired immune deficiency syndrome (42).

In a democratic society, the presumption should be in favor of voluntary rather than mandatory public health programs. This presumption should be overridden only as a last resort, after voluntary alternatives have been vigorously employed and have failed, and only if there is a reasonable hope that a mandatory program would succeed (43). In my judgment, voluntary screening programs that include adequate counseling and appropriate guarantees of confidentiality and nondiscrimination have not yet received a sufficient trial in the United States. Such screening programs, coupled with anonymous testing for those who desire it and with the other public health strategies outlined above offer us a reasonable hope of bringing the AIDS epidemic under control. Thus, I conclude that mandatory screening programs — other than those involving persons who voluntarily donate blood, semen, or organs — are not morally justifiable at this time (44).

POLICIES FOR THE DELIVERY OF HEALTH CARE

Even as public health efforts to prevent the further spread of HIV infection proceed, some of the approximately 1.5 million already infected people in the United States will experience initial symptoms, become ill, develop full-blown AIDS, or die. As of 7 December 1987, 47,436 infected adults and 703 infected children had been diagnosed as having clinical AIDS; 26,816 (60.3%) of the adults and 419 (59.6%) of the children had died (5). HIV infection produces a broad clinical spectrum that includes, at its extremes, asymptomatic status and terminal illness. The health care delivery issue is currently focused on people who are symptomatic as a result of HIV infection and who know that they are infected with HIV. Increasingly, however, people at risk for HIV infection are likely to call on the health care system for help in clarifying their antibody status. Further, the health care system may be able to offer medical interventions to asymptomatic infected people that will prevent, or at least delay, some of the possible sequelae of HIV infection (45).

THE DUTY TO PROVIDE CARE

This issue can be considered at two levels: the level of the individual health care worker and the level of health-related institutions and the health care system.

Surveys of attitudes toward caring for AIDS patients in one high-prevalence area have revealed considerable anxiety among physicians and nurses. A study conducted at four New York residency programs in 1986 noted that 36% of medical house officers and 17% of pediatric house officers reported needlestick exposure to the blood of AIDS patients. Twenty-five percent of respondents indicated that they "would not continue to care for AIDS patients if given a choice" (46). A 1984 survey of nurses at the Westchester (New York) County Hospital found that 39% would ask for a transfer if they had to care for AIDS patients on a regular basis (47).

Studies suggest that the probability of infection transmission from patient to health care worker is very low. Yet ten reasonably well-documented cases of seroconversion in health care workers have been reported, with six of these workers having been exposed by accidental needlesticks and the remainder by exposure of the eyes, mouth, or hands and arms to infectious body fluids (48, 49). HIV seems to be much less infectious than the hepatitis B virus. Yet this comparison is not entirely pertinent; hepatitis B is not usually a lethal disease, and an effective vaccine against the disease is available. Thus, there remains a very small but nonetheless real probability that health care workers will acquire HIV infection from the blood or other body fluids of people with HIV infection. In an unknown proportion of these workers, the infection will have lethal consequences.

Despite these attitudes and risks, it might seem at first blush that the ethical obligation of health care workers to care for people with HIV infection is clear. The words "profession" and "professional" leap readily to mind, as do images of real or fictional heroines and heroes such as Florence Nightingale, Benjamin Rush, or Bernard Rieux (50). Yet the scope of the term health care worker is broad and includes the medical technologist, the phlebotomist, and the person who transports infective waste to the incinerator. Further, the basis for and the extent of the health care worker's obligation to provide care for patients are matters of dispute — despite several vigorous reassertions of the physician's moral duty to treat people with HIV infection (51).

A reasonable ethic for health care workers will not require of them heroic self-sacrifice or works of supererogation. Such a requirement would violate both the principles of autonomy and beneficence. On the other hand, a reasonable ethic will not allow people who are in need of care to be refused treatment or abandoned solely because they are infectious. Such refusal and abandonment would violate the principle of beneficence. Universal infection-control precautions such as those suggested by the Centers for Disease Control (CDC) (49) are likely to reduce substantially the risks to health care workers; thus, heroic self-sacrifice will not be required. If these measures are insufficient in certain high-risk settings, or if the universal precautions seriously impede patient care, testing of selected categories of patients — for example, surgical patients — may be justifiable. This testing should be carried out only with the prior knowledge and consent of patients and should include counseling for seropositive persons. Patients who decline testing will be presumed to be antibody-positive. Testing measures will seem less threatening to patients when carried out in a social context that respects confidentiality and opposes discrimination.

At the level of health care institutions and the health care system, the AIDS epidemic has exacerbated already existing problems regarding access to health care. The access problems faced by people with AIDS or HIV infection do not differ qualitatively from those faced by many other U.S. citizens with chronic or terminal illness. However, because people with HIV infection are almost always under 65 years of age, their health care needs graphically illustrate major deficiencies in the current U.S. system for providing health care to the nonelderly.

Even before the AIDS epidemic became a major factor in health care financing, it was almost commonplace to assert that 15 to 17.5% of U.S. residents under age 65 lack both public and private health insurance. These percentages translate into 30 to 35 million Americans (52). An additional 10 to 15% of these under age 65 who are insured are not adequately protected against chronic or catastrophic illness (53). Of the 150 million Americans under 65 who are privately insured, at least 80% have their health insurance tied to group plans at their place of employment (54).

People with HIV infection who are currently employed and who have group health insurance coverage through their employers are in the best position to cope with the medical costs that may result from their infection. However, even for these most well-off people a double threat looms. If they become so ill that they can no longer continue employment, they face the prospect of losing both their source of income and their group health insurance coverage. Although federal legislation enacted in 1985 provides for continuing individual health insurance coverage for 18 months after the termination of employment, the cost of such coverage may be prohibitive for an unemployed person. Other people with HIV infection who become symptomatic — the underinsured, the uninsured, and the unemployed — are likely to rely on Medicaid for assistance, if they can meet complex eligibility requirements. Actuaries from the Health Care Financing Administration estimate that 40% of patients with clinical AIDS are assisted by Medicaid with their direct medical care expenses and that an average of 23% of such expenses are born by Medicaid. In fiscal year 1987 federal and state Medicaid expenditures for AIDS patients were estimated at $400 million (15, p. 6–5).

The future looks bleak, both in terms of costs and in terms of shortages of needed services for chronically and terminally ill patients. In the cost projections made to date, the estimates of personal medical costs for AIDS patients alone in 1991 range from a low of $3.5 billion to a high of $9.4 billion (in 1984 dollars) (55). Already in 1988, there are shortages of nursing home facilities, home care programs, hospice facilities, and counseling

services for clinically ill people with HIV infection (8, chap. 5; 10, pp. 19–21; 15, chaps. 6 and 8).

Divergent views exist about the appropriate role of the private sector in the provision of health care to people infected with HIV, as well as to other people with health care needs (8, 162–173; 56). What is clear, however, is that we as a society cannot expect private hospitals and nursing homes to operate at a loss. Nor can we expect private health insurers or self-insuring employers to ignore the financial impact of an unanticipated epidemic.

The central ethical question confronting the U.S. health care system was evident long before HIV was discovered or named. That question is: Does our society have a moral obligation to provide a basic level of health care to every one of its members? Several commentators on the ethics of health care allocation have argued that our society does have such an obligation (57). They have based their argument on the principles of beneficence (the unpredictability of health care needs and the harms caused by lack of access) and justice (the inequities that result from current differentials in access). They assert that the principle of respect for autonomy must take second place, as those of us who are financially well off are called upon to share in meeting the needs of the less well off, presumably through the payment of increased premiums and taxes.

This judgment seems to me to be correct. If so, the major policy question is no longer whether we should attempt to meet the needs of the medically less well off. Rather, we should address the questions "What constitutes a basic level of care?" and "How can this level best be provided to everyone, including people infected with HIV?"

NEUROLOGICAL INVOLVEMENT
AND CONSENT TO CARE

An unknown proportion of people with HIV infection experience involvement of the central nervous system, including the brain (58). Indeed, the CDC has recently expanded the clinical definition of AIDS to include such neurological complications (59). The extent of neurological involvement may range from minor symptoms of cognitive impairment to totally disabling dementia.

Brain involvement resulting from HIV infection, like brain involvement due to other causes, inevitably complicates the relation between patient and health provider. Two methods of extending patient autonomy forward in time have proved helpful in other health care settings and may also be beneficial in the treatment of HIV-infected patients with early symptoms of neurological deterioration. Advance directives about preferred modes of care of nontreatment are now expressly recognized by the statutes of 38 states and the District of Columbia (60). In addition, 18 states make legal provision for a patient's appointment of a spokesperson with durable power of attorney, who can express the patient's wishes if the patient should become incapacitated or be adjudged legally incompetent (61). The patient's spokesperson is usually a trusted friend or family member. Both modes of anticipatory decision-making were strongly endorsed by the President's Commission on Bioethics in 1983 (62) and both seem well adapted to the needs of HIV-infected patients with neurological symptoms (63).

THE CARE OF DYING AIDS PATIENTS

When treatment fails and death within a few months becomes inevitable, people with AIDS deserve compassion and support. Individual patient preferences vary, but many terminally ill patients have expressed a desire to die at home in the company of friends or in a hospice-like institutional setting. These alternatives should be provided by an upgraded system of care for all terminally ill patients.

A central role in patient management should be played by the patient's own directives and, if the patient becomes mentally incapacitated, by the patient-designated proxy. If at all possible, future decisions about resuscitation and the use of artificial nutrition and hydration measures should be explicitly discussed with the competent AIDS patient (64). Like other terminally ill patients who face the probability of severe physical deterioration and the possibility of a painful death, some AIDS patients will also want to discuss the options of suicide or voluntary active euthanasia. Both of these topics have received intensive study, especially in the Netherlands, the United Kingdom, and the United States (65). Respect for the autonomy of terminally ill patients would seem to require us to place these difficult issues on the agenda for sustained local and national discussion.

RESEARCH POLICIES

In the long term, the best hope for controlling the AIDS epidemic lies in biomedical research. A vaccine against HIV would seem to be the ideal solution but if immunization strategies prove to be infeasible, chemoprophylactic measures may succeed. For people already infected with HIV, new interventions are under development, but progress has been slow. Epidemiological, social-scientific, educational, and social-intervention studies will also be key elements in an overall research strategy.

A general question that has been raised about the U.S. research effort is whether it has been proportionate to the gravity of the threat posed by the current epidemic. A 1986 report from the Institute of Medicine and the National Academy of Sciences concluded that at that time the response was inadequate (8, pp. 28 and 238–249). A less than adequate response to the epidemic violates both the principle of beneficence and the principle of justice. It fails to prevent avoidable harm to thousands if not millions of people, and it conveys the impression that policy-makers do not care about the welfare of the groups most at risk. Even in the best of times, members of several groups at increased risk for HIV infection experience neglect or even stigmatization by many of their fellow-citizens. These are not the best of times.

Clinical trials of various treatments are being conducted in asymptomatic and symptomatic people with HIV infection as well as in patients with clinical AIDS. The usual practice in early trials is to use a placebo-controlled design with each subgroup of people until an effective therapy for that group is discovered. When the efficacy of an agent has been demonstrated, placebos are no longer given; rather, various dosages of the effective agent are compared, or a new candidate therapy is compared against the older, effective therapy.

Some critics have questioned whether it is ethical to conduct placebo-controlled trials with HIV-infected patients. They have suggested that all symptomatic people with HIV infection should be given immediate access to potentially promising therapies that have not been validated in randomized controlled trials (66). Here one can, in my view, make a justice-based argument for subjecting potential treatments for HIV infection to the same kind of rigorous study that other new treatments must undergo. Further, from the perspective of beneficence, unnecessary suffering would be visited on people with HIV infection if they were provided immediate access to ineffective "therapies" or treatments with toxic effects that far outweigh their therapeutic benefits.

The testing of vaccines for the prevention of HIV infection will also raise important ethical questions. For example, it will be necessary for uninfected volunteers to be exposed to inoculations that will make them antibody-positive by ELISA and Western blot tests. Further, research subjects who participate in unsuccessful vaccine trials may thereby be made more susceptible to HIV or other infections than they would have been had they not taken part in the trials. Equally disturbing is the possibility that some subjects, having received an ineffective vaccine, may be rendered incapable of being immunized by subsequently developed effective vaccines. Because the numbers of participants in early trials may reach into the thousands or tens of thousands, they could constitute a serious additional public health problem for society.

The risks associated with vaccine trials have prompted some researchers to consider testing vaccines against HIV in countries of equatorial Africa, where the prevalence of infection is known to be higher than in the United States and where the number of trial participants could therefore be lower. In addition, the risk of litigation for research-related injury might be reduced in a non-U.S. setting. However, the proposal to export research risks raises questions of fairness in its own right.

Partial solutions to the ethical quandaries presented by vaccine trials can be found in policies that exemplify the principles of respect for autonomy, beneficence, and justice. The autonomy of participants in vaccine trials will be respected if they are warned clearly and in advance of the potential physical and social harms to which they will be exposed. The careful planning and foresight of researchers can also reduce the harms associated with vaccine-induced seropositivity. For example, in a vaccine trial sponsored by the National Institutes of Health, volunteers will be provided with official documentation certifying that their antibody status had been negative before they participated in a vaccine trial (67). Nonetheless, if participants in vaccine trials are injured as a result of their participation, they may have a legitimate claim to compensation for disabilities incurred in a publicly declared war on a major disease. Indeed, the principle of justice may require the establishment of a compensation program for research-related injuries (8, pp. 228–229; 68).

Epidemiologic research will provide a scientific basis for policies in public health and health care delivery. Longitudinal studies among members of at-risk groups will help to clarify the natural history of HIV infection and the role of cofactors in the development of clinical symptoms. Homosexual and bisexual men, in particular, have been active participants in published longitudinal studies (23, 69). Cross-sectional studies of demographic groups—newborn infants, patients in "sentinel" hospitals, and residents in selected metropolitan areas—will facilitate more refined estimates of the number of people infected with HIV (70). One of the major ethical questions in cross-sectional studies has been whether to retain the identifying links between blood samples and the individuals from whom the samples were taken. Anonymous, unlinked testing without consent seems to be emerging as the method of choice, in part because a recent interview survey indicated a likely refusal rate of about 30% among adult Americans if they were invited to be tested in a national seroprevalence study (71). The advantages of anonymous epidemiologic studies are that no identifiable subjects are placed at risk and that the research results are not skewed by refusals. The disadvantage is that seropositive individuals cannot be identified, notified, and counseled.

Other types of research can also play important roles in understanding and coping with the current epidemic. Social science and behavioral research will help to elucidate such questions as the extent of homosexual sexual activity among U.S. adults—a topic that has not been studied in large, rigorously selected samples since the 1940s. Educational research will assist public health officials and counselors in communicating more effectively about lifesaving alternatives in the most intimate realms of human behavior (8, pp. 230–238; 72). Finally, social-intervention research can provide public policymakers with essential information about the effects of innovative approaches to social practices such as IV drug use and prostitution (73).

CONCLUSION

At the beginning of this [essay] I mentioned three ethical principles that are thought to be of central importance in contemporary biomedical ethics: beneficence, justice, and respect for autonomy. These principles have informed the preceding analysis. However, as I have reflected on the complexities of the current epidemic, it has occurred to me that a fourth ethical principle may be required to guide our actions and policies in response to this major threat to the public health. I do not have a precise name for this additional principle, but I will venture to suggest some first approximations: mutuality, solidarity, or community (74).

REFERENCES AND NOTES

1. President's Commission for the Study of Ethical Problems in Medicine and Biomedical and Behavioral Research, *Summing Up* (Government Printing Office, Washington, DC, March 1983), pp. 66–71.

2. T. L. Beauchamp and J. F. Childress, *Principles of Biomedical Ethics* (Oxford Univ. Press, New York, 2d ed., 1983), chaps. 3–6.

3. Although the focus of this article is limited to the situation in the United States, I think that the same general ethical principles are also applicable elsewhere. However, the discussion of alternative public policy options would not necessarily fit other social and cultural settings. Other essays on ethics and HIV infection or AIDS include: A. R. Jonsen, M. Cooke, B. A. Koening, *Issues Sci. Technol.* **2,** 56 (1986); R. Bayer, *Milbank Mem. Fund Q.* **64** (Suppl. 1), 168 (1986). See also two special supplements to the *Hastings Center Report,* one published in August 1985, the other in December 1986; and C. Pierce and D. VanDeVeer, Eds., *AIDS: Ethics and Public Policy* (Wadsworth, Belmont, CA, 1988). On legal aspects of the epidemic and its control, see (*15*) and (*40*) below; H. E. Lewis, *J. Am. Med. Assoc.* **258,** 2410 (1987); and two special issues of *Law Med. Health Care* published in December 1986 and summer 1987.

4. For discussions of general and targeted public education in the context of the current epidemic, see (*8,* pp. 96–112 and 130–133) and (*15,* chap. 9). The illustrated version of the *Surgeon General's Report on Acquired Immune Deficiency Syndrome* (Department of Health and Human Services, Public Health Service, Washington, DC, 1986) is a model of factual, explicit general education about HIV infection and AIDS.

5. Centers for Disease Control (CDC), *AIDS Weekly Surveillance Report United States,* 7 December 1987.

6. L. Thompson, *Washington Post,* 11 August 1987, Health, p. 7.

7. D. S. Weinberg and H. W. Murray, *N. Engl. J. Med.* **317,** 1469 (1987).

8. Institute of Medicine, National Academy of Sciences, *Confronting AIDS: Directions for Public Health, Health Care, and Research* (National Academy Press, Washington, DC, 1986).

9. D. C. Des Jarlais and S. R. Friedman, *AIDS* **1,** 67 (1987).

10. Presidential Commission on the Human Immunodeficiency Virus Epidemic, *Preliminary Report* (The Commission, Washington, DC, 2 December 1987).

11. A. R. Moss, *Br. Med. J.* **294,** 389 (1987).

12. A. Wodak *et al., Med. J. Australia* **147,** 275 (1987).

13. Anonymous, "Management of drug addicts: Hostility, humanity, and pragmatism," *Lancet* **1987-I,** 1068 (1987). See also J. B. Bakalar and L. Grinspoon, *Drug Control in a Free Society* (Cambridge Univ. Press, Cambridge, 1984) and A. S. Trebach, *The Heroin Solution* (Yale Univ. Press, New Haven, CT, 1982).

14. CDC, *J. Am. Med. Assoc.* **257,** 2011 (1987).

15. U.S. Department of Health and Human Services, Public Health Service, *AIDS: A Public Health Challenge* (Intergovernmental Health Policy Project, George Washington University, Washington, DC, October 1987), vols. 1–3.

16. G. L. Smith and K. F. Smith, *Lancet* **1987-II,** 1392 (1987).

17. G. Papaevangelou, A. Roumeliotou-Karayannis, G. Kallinkos, G. Papoutsakis, *ibid.* **1985-II,** 1018 (1985).

18. For a general discussion of regulatory policy on prostitution, see F. M. Shaver, *Can. Public Policy* **11,** 493 (1985).

19. L. A. Kingsley *et al., Lancet* **1987-I,** 345 (1987).

20. J. S. Chmiel *et al., Am. J. Epidemiol.* **126,** 568 (1987).

21. CDC, *Morbid. Mortal. Weekly Rep.* **34,** 613 (1985).

22. L. W. McKusick, W. Horstman, T. J. Coates, *Am. J. Public Health* **75,** 493 (1985).

23. W. Winkelstein, Jr., *et al.,* ibid. **76,** 685 (1987).

24. J. Feinberg, *The Moral Limits of the Criminal Law,* vol. 2, *Offense to Others* (Oxford Univ. Press, New York, 1985).

25. D. A. J. Richards, *Sex, Drugs, Death, and the Law: An Essay on Human Rights and Overcriminalization* (Rowman and Littlefield, Totowa, NJ, 1982), pp. 29–83.

26. U.S. Supreme Court, *"Bowers v. Hardwick,"* S. Ct. **106,** 2841 (1986), dissents by Justices Blackmun and Stevens.

27. R. Mohr, *Bioethics* **1,** 35 (1987).

28. A. C. Kinsey, W. B. Pomeroy, C. E. Martin, *Sexual Behavior in the Human Male* (Saunders, Philadelphia, 1948.)

29. R. Dworkin, *Taking Rights Seriously* (Harvard Univ. Press, Cambridge, MA, 1977), chaps. 6 and 7.

30. R. Bayer, C. Levine, S. M. Wolf, *J. Am. Med. Assoc.* **256,** 1768 (1986).

31. J. F. Childress, *AIDS Public Policy J.* 28 (1987).

32. L. Gostin and W. J. Curran, *Am. J. Public Health* **77,** 361 (1987).

33. D. P. Francis and J. Chin, *J. Am. Med. Assoc.* **257,** 1357 (1987); L. O. Gostin, W. J. Curran, M. E. Clark, *Am. J. Law Med.* **12,** 7 (1987); CDC, *Recommended Additional Guidelines for HIV Antibody Counseling and Testing in the Prevention of HIV Infection and AIDS* (CDC, Atlanta, 30 April 1987).

34. CDC, *Morbid. Mortal. Weekly Rep.* **36,** 509 (1987).

35. P. D. Cleary *et al., J. Am. Med. Assoc.* **258,** 1757 (1987).

36. K. B. Meyer and S. G. Pauker, *N. Engl. J. Med.* **317,** 238 (1987).

37. For an original approach to casuistic analysis in situations like these, see A. R. Jonsen and S. Toulmin, *The Abuse of Casuistry* (Univ. of California Press, Berkeley, 1988).

38. R. Gillon, *Br. Med. J.* **294,** 1675 (1987).

39. American Medical Association, Board of Trustees, *J. Am. Med. Assoc.* **258,** 2103 (1987).

40. G. W. Matthews and V. S. Neslund, *ibid.* **257,** 344 (1987).

41. The decision of the U.S. Supreme Court in *"School Board of Nassau County, Florida v. Arline,"* seems clearly to extend the antidiscrimination protections contained in Section 504 of the Rehabilitation Act of 1973 to *symptomatic* people with HIV infection. The Court explicitly reserved judgment on the status of asymptomatic carriers of contagious disease (fn. 7 in the decision). The Rehabilitation Act applies only to programs receiving federal financial assistance. See *S. Ct.* **107**; 1123 (1987).

42. U.S. Congress, House, 100th Congr. 1st Sess., H.R. 3071; see Appendix 10, p. 437.

43. These formal conditions closely resemble the criteria of the just-war tradition. See L. B. Walters, Jr., *Five Classic Just-War Theories: A Study in the Thought of Thomas Aquinas, Vitoria, Súarez, Gentili, and Grotius* (unpublished dissertation, Yale University, 1971).

44. If substantial neurological compromise were conclusively demonstrated to be present in, say, 25% of asymptomatic people with HIV infection, then a strong case could be made for mandatory

screening of people who are responsible for the lives of large numbers of other people, for example, airline pilots or public officials with decision-making authority over the use of nuclear weapons. However, strictly speaking, this would be a public safety rather than a public health justification. For recent data on HIV infection and neurological status, see I. Grant *et al., Ann. Intern. Med.* **107**, 828 (1987); and D. Price, *Science* **239**, 586 (1988). . . .

45. Clinical trials of zidovudine (AZT) among asymptomatic people with HIV infection are currently in progress.

46. R. N. Link, A. R. Feingold, M. H. Charap, K. Freeman, S. Shelov, *Third Int. Conf. on AIDS, Washington, DC, Abstr.* (U.S. Dept. Health and Human Services and WHO, Washington, DC 1987).

47. M. Blumfield *et al, Gen. Hosp. Psychiatry* **9**, 58 (1987).

48. CDC, *J. Am. Med. Assoc.* **257**, 3032 (1987).

49. *Ibid.* **258**, 1293 (1987); ibid., p. 1441.

50. L. H. Butterfield, Ed., *Letters of Benjamin Rush* (Princeton Univ. Press, Princeton, NJ, 1951), vol. 2, p. 664; F. Nightingale, *Notes on Nursing* (Dover, New York, 1969 repr. of 1860 ed.), pp. 33–34; A. Camus, *The Plague*, S. Gilbert, translator (Knopf, New York, 1948).

51. R. Gillon, *Br. Med. J.* **294**, 1332 (1987); A. Zuger and S. H. Miles, *J. Am. Med. Assoc.* **258**, 1924 (1987); E. D. Pellegrino, *ibid.*, p. 939; American Medical Association, Council on Ethical and Judicial Affairs, *Report: A (I-87): Ethical Issues Involved in the Growing AIDS Crisis* (American Medical Association, Chicago, November 1987).

52. U.S. Bureau of the Census, Current Population Reports, Series P-60 (no. 155), *Receipt of Selected Noncash Benefits: 1985* (Government Printing Office, Washington, DC, 1987), pp. 15 and 19; D. Chollet, "A profile of the nonelderly population without health insurance," *Employee Benefit Research Institute Issue Brief*, no. 66, May 1987.

53. K. Davis and D. Rowland, *Milbank Mem. Fund Q./Health and Society* **61**, 149 (1983).

54. U.S. Bureau of the Census, Current Population Reports, Series P-70 (no. 8), *Disability, Functional Limitation, and Health Insurance Coverage: 1984/85* (Government Printing Office, Washington, DC, 1986), pp. 36–37.

55. A. A. Scitovsky and D. P. Rice, *Public Health Rep.* **102**, 5 (1987).

56. American Council of Life Insurance and Health Insurance Association of America, *AIDS Public Policy J.* **2**, 32 (1987); J. E. Harris, *Technol. Rev.* **90**, 59 (1987); J. K. Iglehart, *N. Engl. J. Med.* **317**, 180 (1987); D. P. Andrulis, V. S. Beers, J. D. Bentley, L. S. Gage, *J. Am. Med. Assoc.* **258**, 1343 (1987).

57. President's Commission for the Study of Ethical Problems in Medicine and Biomedical and Behavioral Research, *Securing Access to Health Care* (Government Printing Office, Washington, DC,

March 1983), vols. 1–3; N. Daniels, *Just Health Care* (Cambridge Univ. Press, New York, 1985); A Buchanan, *Phil. Public Aff.* **13**, 55 (1984).

58. B. A. Navia, B. D. Jordan, R. W. Price, *Ann. Neurol.* **19**, 517 (1986); S. W. Burton, *Br. Med. J.* **295**, 228 (1987).

59. CDC, *J. Am. Med. Assoc.* **258**, 1143 (1987). . . .

60. *Handbook of Living Will Laws: 1987 Edition* (Society for the Right to Die, New York, 1987).

61. E. N. Cohen, *Appointing a Proxy for Health-Care Decisions: Analysis and Chart of State Laws* (Society for the Right to Die, New York, October 1987).

62. President's Commission for the Study of Ethical Problems in Medicine and Biomedical and Behavioral Research, *Deciding to Forego Life-Sustaining Treatment* (Government Printing Office, Washington, DC, March 1983), pp. 136–153.

63. In cases involving the use of experimental therapeutic procedures, the patient's proxy may also be called upon to give consent to research. On this issue, see J. C. Fletcher, F. W. Dommel, Jr., D. D. Cowell, *IRB: A Review of Human Subjects Research* **7**, 1 (November/December 1985).

64. R. Steinbrook et al., *N. Engl. J. Med.* **314**, 457 (1986).

65. J. Rachels, *The End of Life: Euthanasia and Morality* (Oxford Univ. Press, New York, 1986); A. B. Downing and B. Smoker, Eds., *Voluntary Euthanasia* (Humanities Press, Atlantic Heights, NJ, rev. ed., 1986); J. K. M. Gevers, *Bioethics* **1**, 156 (1987).

66. E. Eckholm, *New York Times*, 13 July 1986, p. E30; R. Macklin and G. Friedland, *Law Med. Health Care* **14**, 273 (1986).

67. B. Merz, *J. Am. Med. Assoc.* **258**, 1433 (1987).

68. President's Commission for the Study of Ethical Problems in Medicine and Biomedical and Behavioral Research, *Compensating for Research Injuries* (Government Printing Office, Washington, DC, June 1982), vols. 1 and 2.

69. J. J. Goedert *et al., Science* **231**, 992 (1986).

70. E. Eckholm, *New York Times*, 10 January 1987, p. 6; P. M. Boffey, *ibid.*, 3 December 1987, p. A20.

71. W. Booth, *Science* **238**, 747 (1987).

72. M. Barinaga, *Nature (London)* **330**, 99 (1987).

73. A. Rivlin and M. P. Timpane, Eds., *Ethical and Legal Issues of Social Experimentation* (Brookings Institution, Washington, DC, 1975).

74. I thank M. Stanley and C. Williams for assistance in manuscript preparation and E. Meslin, S. Meinke, P. M. McCarrick for bibliographic assistance. I also thank the following people for helpful comments: L. B. Andrews, T. L. Beauchamp, J. F. Childress, R. M. Cook-Deegan, M. A. G. Cutter, B. M. Dickens, R. R. Faden, E. Locke, A. R. Jonsen, C. R. McCarthy, E. Meslin, J. Porter, E. E. Shelp, R. M. Veatch, and three anonymous reviewers for *Science*. This article is dedicated with gratitude to Jane M. Walters, my wife, who died on 15 January 1988 after open heart surgery.

NATIONAL RESEARCH COUNCIL, PANEL ON MONITORING THE SOCIAL IMPACT OF THE AIDS EPIDEMIC

The Social Impact of AIDS in the United States

An epidemic is both a medical and social occurrence. Medically, it is the appearance of a serious, often fatal, disease in numbers far greater than normal. Socially, it is an event that disrupts the life of a community and causes uncertainty, fear, blame, and flight. The etymology of the word itself suggests the broader, social meaning: *epi demos,* in ancient Greek, means "upon the people or the community."

The epidemic of acquired immune deficiency syndrome (AIDS)—which was recognized in the United States in 1981, continues today, and will continue into the foreseeable future—mirrors epidemics of the past. The medical meaning of the epidemic has been revealed in the sobering numbers reported in epidemiologic studies. During 1991, 45,506 new AIDS cases were reported to the Centers for Disease Control (CDC), which brought the cumulative total of cases in the United States to 206,392; 133,233 (65 percent) deaths have been tallied (Centers for Disease Control, 1992). It is estimated that 1 million people are currently infected with the human immunodeficiency virus (HIV), which causes AIDS (Centers for Disease Control, 1990), but this number is very uncertain. . . .

These numbers identify the first and most obvious impact of the HIV/AIDS epidemic on American society: the large population of infected, sick, and dying persons attacked by a previously unknown disease. Behind the epidemiologic reports and the statistical estimates lies the social disruption of the epidemic: the destroyed life for which each of the numbers stands and

the changed lives of many others touched by the disease. And behind the individual lives are the manifold ways in which a variety of institutions and practices have been affected by the epidemic.

• • •

EPIDEMICS, IMPACTS, AND RESPONSES

. . . It is common to find references to the impact of AIDS and HIV. It is also rather common to find such references expressed in quite strong terms. For example, *Milbank Quarterly's* two-volume study, *A Disease of Society: Cultural Responses to AIDS,* opens with these words (Nelkin et al., 1991:1):

> AIDS is no "ordinary" epidemic. More than a devastating disease, it is freighted with profound social and cultural meaning. More than a passing tragedy, it will have long-term, broad-ranging effects on personal relationships, social institutions, and cultural configurations. AIDS is clearly affecting mortality—though in some communities more than others. It is also costly in terms of the resources—both people and money—required for research and medical care. But the effects of the epidemic extend far beyond their medical and economic costs to shape the very ways we organize our individual and collective lives.

It is not clear what an "ordinary" epidemic would be. No epidemic seems ordinary to those who experience it. The AIDS epidemic has invoked comparison with many epidemics of the past. Most commonly, the bubonic plague (the Black Death) that devastated Europe in the fourteenth century is recalled: between 1348 and 1350, some 20 million people, one-third of the population of Europe, died. (Additional tens of millions had died in

Asia during the preceding decade [McNeil, 1976].) This epidemic had unquestionable impacts. Historians attribute to it, at least in part, the emergence of nation states, the rise of mercantile economies, and the religious movements that led to the Reformation (Campbell, 1931; McNeil, 1976; Tuchman, 1978). As Anna Campbell (1931) noted, the Black Death "changed the minds of men" bringing new ways of understanding God, the meaning of death, the place of tradition, and the role of authority in religious and social life. Changes in the collective mind of a society might be the most profound of all impacts, for the new ideas generated by a major social tragedy can propel institutional change and outlast immediate changes to affect lives far in the future. Difficult though it might be to predict the future import of the present impact of the HIV/AIDS epidemic, one should not shrink from the task, especially when one must plan for that future.

AIDS has been compared with other epidemics, too: the resurgence of bubonic plague in England in the mid-seventeenth century, the cholera epidemics of the nineteenth century, the venereal disease epidemics of the sixteenth century and the early twentieth century, and the polio epidemics of the twentieth century (Brandt, 1988; Risse, 1988; Slack, 1988). AIDS has its analogies to each of these epidemics—number of deaths, methods of prevention, stigmatization of sufferers and presumed carriers, and responses of authorities—all can be compared in general or in detail. The comparisons are often illuminating, but sometimes misleading (Fee and Fox, 1988). It can be said with some assurance, however, that none of the historical epidemics was "ordinary." Each had impacts that struck its sufferers and subsequent commentators as "extraordinary."

The comparison with epidemics of the past invokes the features that are remembered about those plagues. They have, in this respect, had an impact on history or, as Campbell wrote (1931), "on the minds of men." They also left social institutions that sometimes affect present-day thinking about the AIDS epidemic: cholera, for example, left a public health approach to epidemic disease that stressed quarantine; venereal diseases gave rise to the public health approach of contact tracing. These established public health practices have had to be reconsidered in the current epidemic. Many of the prominent, even dramatic impacts of past epidemics, however, have so melded into the social fabric that people are often astonished to hear of them today, and

some, interesting though they be, seem of little relevance to the current problem. For example, to attribute the existence of Protestant Christianity to the effects of the Black Death on religious ideas and sentiments has little influence on the ways in which people today think about religion or about epidemics. Similarly, to attribute the existence of Canada as an independent nation to the fact that British troops had been vaccinated against smallpox before the Battle of Quebec, but American troops were decimated by the disease, is certainly to point to an effect of epidemic and, indeed, an impact. Yet that impact has been of little relevance to subsequent citizens and governments, except that "some Canadians to this day worship smallpox as the deliverer from United States citizenship" (Foege, 1988:332).

Many features of epidemics are no longer remembered and have left little imprint on the societies that they ravished for a time. Indeed, one of the greatest of epidemics, the influenza [outbreak] of 1918–1920, has been called by its historian "the forgotten epidemic" (Crosby, 1989). Worldwide, perhaps 30 million people died; in the United States, 675,000 people died, most of whom were not the usual victims of influenza (the very old, infants, and children), but men and women in their 20s and 30s. This terrible scourge might have had a great impact, but it passed and left almost no mark on the social institutions and practices of the time. Many people were mourned, but life quickly returned to normal. Even the absence of impact has a lesson for this study: it is possible that many of the effects currently taken as important and lasting will pass or be absorbed into the course of American life and culture. It is not entirely clear how confidently one should accept the words of *Milbank* editors Nelkin, Willis, and Parris (1991:1,2):

> More than a passing tragedy, it [AIDS] will have long-term, broad-ranging effects on personal relationships, social institutions, and cultural configurations . . . AIDS will reshape many aspects of society, its norms and values, its interpersonal relationships and its cultural representations . . . [T]he future will be [unlike] both the present and the past.

Our report *[The Social Impact of AIDS in the United States]* suggests that, in some respects, the AIDS epidemic may be more like the influenza [outbreak] of 1918 than the bubonic plague of 1348: many of its most striking features will be absorbed in the flow of American life, but, hidden beneath the surface, its worst effects will continue to devastate the lives and cultures of certain communities.

Historically, certain epidemics have done great damage to social institutions: the Black Death in a 3-year sweep through Europe wiped out enough laborers to cause a major restructuring of the economy of the continent. The HIV/AIDS epidemic, although often compared to the Black Death, has not affected U.S. social institutions to any such extent. Although it had by the end of 1991 infected perhaps 1 million people, brought devastating sickness to 206,392, and death to 133,233, it had not significantly altered the structures or directions of the social institutions that we studied. Many of the responses have been ad hoc and may be reversed when pressures subside. Others may be more lasting, but only because they reinforced or accelerated changes already latent or budding within the institutions.

It is the panel's opinion that the limited responsiveness of institutions can in part be explained because the absolute numbers of the epidemic, relative to the U.S. population, are not overwhelming, and because U.S. social institutions are strong, complex, and resilient. However, we believe that another major reason for this limited response is the concentration of the epidemic in socially marginalized groups. The convergence of evidence shows that the HIV/AIDS epidemic is settling into spatially and socially isolated groups and possibly becoming endemic within them. Many observers have recently commented that, instead of spreading out to the broad American population, as was once feared, HIV is concentrating in pools of persons who are also caught in the "synergism of plagues" (see Wallace, 1988): poverty, poor health and lack of health care, inadequate education, joblessness, hopelessness, and social disintegration converge to ravage personal and social life. These coexisting conditions foster and aggravate HIV infection and AIDS. Our study of New York City . . . illustrates this dramatically for one epicenter of the epidemic. We believe that the patterns shown there are repeated throughout the country: many geographical areas and strata of the population are virtually untouched by the epidemic and probably never will be; certain confined areas and populations have been devastated and are likely to continue to be.

This epidemiological direction reveals the disconcerting implications of our major conclusion. The institutions that we studied are particularly weak at those points at which the epidemic is likely to be most destructive. For example, the health care system, which responded to the appearance of a new disease with some alacrity, is weakest organizationally and economically in those places where the affected populations are concentrated. The problems of caring for those who are infected are magnified by the particular configuration of the U.S. health care system, which emphasizes to a greater extent than other developed countries private insurance and ability-to-pay criteria. Providers, hospitals, and public health mechanisms can [respond] and have responded to a flood of patients with AIDS, but those responses were most successful where health care was better organized and financed and where the populations to be served had sufficient knowledge to understand the disease and its modes of transmission and were capable of organizing themselves in ways that supported and supplemented the health care system.

Thus, our most general conclusion about the epidemic is that its impact has hit institutions hardest where they are weakest: serving the most disadvantaged people in U.S. society. Predictions of the imminent collapse of the health care system due to the epidemic, for example, now look shrill, but, conversely, hopes that the epidemic would force the country toward more rational and equitable reform of the system now also seem unrealistic. In the panel's judgment, the HIV/AIDS epidemic has effected many transient changes in the institutions that we studied and relatively few changes that we expect to be permanent. Among the more permanent, however, two are particularly noteworthy.

First, the institutions of public health, of health care delivery, and of scientific research have become more responsive to cooperation and collaboration with "outsiders." Policies and practices have been modified in these three institutions under pressure from and in collaboration with those who are affected by the epidemic and their advocates. Many of these changes are positive and will contribute to the efficiency and efficacy of the institutions. Similarly, volunteer organizations stimulated by the challenge of the epidemic not only have discovered ways of supplying help where extant institutions were lacking, they have also influenced the policies and practices of those institutions.

Second, even in institutions with very defined purposes and strong constraints—institutions as different as religious groups and correctional agencies—the response to the epidemic has reflected awareness of the scientific realities, as well as the social implications, of HIV/AIDS. Traditionally based doctrinal constraints in the case of religious groups and the stringent requirements of civil punishment in the case of correctional agencies are powerful forces that could and did dictate rigid and narrow response. Yet, powerful as those forces were, they did not negate more reflective responses that contributed to containment of the epidemic and respected the rights of individuals. We are concerned, however, that as the epidemic strikes with greater force in socially and economically deprived communities, the directions toward more communal involvement and respect for civil and personal liberties might be constricted and diverted.

The panel believes that a failure by scientists and policy makers to appreciate the interaction between social, economic, and cultural conditions and the propagation of HIV/AIDS disease has often led to public misunderstanding and policy mistakes about the epidemic. Although in the beginning of the epidemic, gay life and behavior were certainly at the center of attention, even then they were noted primarily as "modes of transmission" and not as social contexts in which the disease had particular meanings around which strong forces for care, prevention, and political action could rally. Similarly, intravenous drug use was understood as a social behavior that could transmit infection, but its place in a matrix of social, cultural, and economic conditions was ignored.

A constant theme of this report and of the AIDS literature is the stigma, discrimination, and inequalities of the AIDS epidemic. At its outset, HIV disease settled among socially disvalued groups, and as the epidemic has progressed, AIDS has increasingly been an affliction of people who have little economic, political, and social power. In this sense, AIDS is an undemocratic affliction. In "democratic epidemics" (Arras, 1988), communicable illnesses cut across class, racial, and ethnic lines and threaten the community at large. In traditional societies with limited medical knowledge and technology, epidemics fall on most, if not all, of the people. In the modern world, particularly in industrial societies, inequalities in morbidity and mortality are often more social than biological phenomena. With HIV/AIDS, the concentration of the epidemic from its beginnings was among those who were, for a variety of reasons, members of marginalized social groups. In this case, the biology of viral transmission matched existing social inequalities and resulted in an unequal concentration of HIV/AIDS in certain regions and among certain populations (see Grmek, 1990). This pattern has created tension between the social and ge-

ographical localization of the epidemic and the need to mobilize resources to deal with the epidemic from among individuals, groups, and institutions that are removed from the social groups that are at the epicenter of the epidemic. As the epidemic becomes endemic in already deprived and segregated populations, this tension will be intensified.

If the current pattern of the epidemic holds, U.S. society at large will have been able to wait out the primary impact of the epidemic even though the crisis period will have stretched out over 15 years. HIV/AIDS will "disappear," not because, like smallpox, it has been eliminated, but because those who continue to be affected by it are socially invisible, beyond the sight and attention of the majority population. . . .

REFERENCES

Arras, J.D. (1988) The fragile web of responsibility: AIDS and the duty to treat. *Hastings Center Report* 18(Suppl.):10–20.

Brandt, A.M. (1988) AIDS and metaphor: toward the social meaning of epidemic disease. *Social Research* 55:413–432.

Brookmeyer, R. (1991) Reconstruction and future trends of the AIDS epidemic in the United States. *Science* 253:37–42.

Campbell, A.M. (1931) *The Black Death and Men of Learning.* New York: Columbia University Press.

Centers for Disease Control (CDC) (1990) HIV prevalence and AIDS case projections for the United States: report based on a workshop. *Morbidity and Mortality Weekly Report* 39:(RR-16):1–31.

Centers for Disease Control (CDC) (1991) Mortality attributable to HIV infection/AIDS—United States, 1981–1990. *Morbidity and Mortality Weekly Report* 40:41–46.

Centers for Disease Control (CDC) (1992) *HIV/AIDS Surveillance Report.* Atlanta, Ga.: Centers for Disease Control.

Crosby, A.W. (1989) *Epidemic and Peace, 1918: America's Forgotten Pandemic.* New York: Cambridge University Press.

Fee, E., and D. Fox (1988) *AIDS: The Burdens of History.* Berkeley, Calif.: University of California Press.

Foege, W.H. (1988) Plagues: perceptions of risk and social responses. *Social Research* 55:331–342.

Grmek, M.D. (1990) *The History of AIDS: Emergence and Origin of a Modern Pandemic.* Princeton, N.J.: Princeton University Press.

Harris, J. (1990) Reporting delays and the incidence of AIDS. *Journal of the American Statistical Association* 85:915–924.

McNeil, W.H. (1976) *Plagues and Peoples.* New York: Doubleday.

Miller, H.G., C.F. Turner, and L.E. Moses, eds. (1990) *AIDS: The Second Decade.* Committee on AIDS Research and the Behavioral, Social, and Statistical Sciences, Commission on Behavior and Social Sciences and Education, National Research Council. Washington, D.C.: National Academy Press.

Nelkin, D., D.P. Willis, and S.V. Parris (1991) Introduction. In D. Nelkin, D.P. Willis, and S.V. Parris, eds., *A Disease of Society: Cultural Responses to AIDS.* New York: Cambridge University Press.

Risse, G.B. (1988) Epidemics and history: ecological perspectives and social responses. In E. Fee and D.M. Fox, eds., *AIDS: The Burdens of History.* Berkeley, Calif.: University of California Press.

Slack, P. (1988) Responses to plague in early modern Europe: the implications of public health. *Social Research* 55:433–453.

Tuchman, B. (1978) *A Distant Mirror: The Calamitous 14th Century.* New York: Knopf.

Turner, C.F., H.G. Miller, and L.E. Moses, eds. (1989) *AIDS: Sexual Behavior and Intravenous Drug Use.* Committee on AIDS Research and the Behavioral, Social, and Statistical Sciences, Commission on Behavioral and Social Sciences and Education, National Research Council. Washington, D.C.: National Academy Press.

Wallace, R. (1988) A synergism of plagues: "planned shrinkage," contagious housing destruction and AIDS in the Bronx. *Environmental Research* 47:1–33.

RONALD BAYER AND JEFF STRYKER

Ethical Challenges Posed by Clinical Progress in AIDS

INTRODUCTION

The past year has witnessed an extraordinary transformation in the climate surrounding the treatment of human immunodeficiency virus (HIV) infection. The clinical despair expressed by many in the wake of the Ninth International AIDS Conference in Berlin, where the results of the Concorde zidovudine trial were presented, has now given way to a posture of therapeutic enthusiasm. Combination therapies relying on two nucleoside analogs and a protease inhibitor have emerged as the standard of care.[1]

At the 11th International AIDS Conference in Vancouver in July 1996, researchers presented evidence suggesting the possibility of dramatically reducing the viral load of HIV-infected individuals.[2] Such an achievement, it was presumed, could extend periods of symptom-free life and possibly improve survival. There was even speculation about eradicating HIV from those already infected.[3] In the press, these reversals of fortune have been described as the "Lazarus syndrome"[4] or "the death of a death sentence."[5]

Some have remained skeptical, recalling the ultimately unfounded enthusiasm for monotherapy with zidovudine and the mistaken assumption that CD4 counts could provide a reliable surrogate marker for disease progression.[6] Nevertheless, for many clinicians and thousands of their patients, a new era of AIDS treatment has begun.

Reprinted with permission of the publisher from *American Journal of Public Health* 87 (October 1997), 1599–1602. Copyright © 1997 by the American Public Health Association.

However today's hopes will be viewed from the vantage point of the coming years, this new sense of therapeutic efficacy has produced ethical challenges demanding immediate attention.

The new therapeutic advances will test the vitality of our conception of equity of access to medical care; pose questions about the limits of patient autonomy, the legitimacy of medical paternalism, and the claims of the public health when poor adherence to medical regimens may foster the emergence of drug resistance; and confront the industrialized world with questions about what is owed to the developing world, where upwards of 90% of new HIV infections are now occurring.[7]

ACCESS TO CARE

The new combination therapies are costly. Adding protease inhibitors to the therapeutic armamentarium has tripled the retail prescription cost of drugs used in treating HIV disease, bringing the average to $10,000 to 15,000 per year per patient.[8,9] The viral load assays necessary to monitor the drugs' effectiveness add a further expense.[10] These costs impede access for many. Richman's review of dramatically improved therapeutic prospects added the disheartening caveat "at least for those socioeconomically privileged."[11]

Approximately 40% to 50% of persons with AIDS are covered by Medicaid.[12] States with fee-for-service Medicaid plans cover all three protease inhibitors licensed by the Food and Drug Administration. The coverage is less straightforward in Medicaid managed care, where formularies operating pursuant to Medicaid contracts are not necessarily required to include each of the protease inhibitors. States operating under Health Care Financing Administration (HCFA) Medicaid waivers with managed care contracts often have global budgets. The cost of the protease inhibitors may impinge upon the delivery of other services. In the wake of the approval of protease inhibitors by the Food and Drug Administration, HCFA instructed state Medicaid directors to "examine their existing contracts to determine if prescription drugs are covered through managed care plans, what (if any) benefit restrictions may apply, and whether the capitation rates should be adjusted to account for the introduction of new drugs such as protease inhibitors" (S. Richardson, HCFA Medicaid Bureau, written communication, June 1996).

More than 20% of people with AIDS lack private insurance coverage, yet are not covered by Medicaid or Medicare. The AIDS Drug Assistance Program was created to address this gap. Administered by the states as part of the Ryan White CARE Act's Title II, the program served 70,030 people in 1995, an increase of 20% from the previous year,[13] and about 80,000 in 1996. Nearly three quarters (74%) of the program's funding comes from federal resources. Despite the addition of specifically earmarked federal funds (bringing the fiscal year 1997 total to approximately $249.6 million), burgeoning needs have continually outpaced the ability of the program to keep up.[14]

Persistent shortfalls in AIDS Drug Assistance Program (ADAP) funding have prompted various rationing strategies and invited considerable media attention to the plight of individuals seeking access to the new therapies. Nearly half of the states' ADAP programs limit access to protease inhibitors.[15] Some have established waiting lists or dollar ceilings; others limit the number of prescriptions per patient per month. Missouri both limited the number of patients eligible to receive protease inhibitors to 132 and established a limit of $10,000 for any patient's combination therapy.[16] To cover a single protease inhibitor, Illinois removed 84 other drugs from its AIDS Drug Assistance Program formulary, including all antibiotics. In four states — Arkansas, Nevada, South Dakota, and Oregon — the program does not cover any protease inhibitors. The coordinator of Oregon's program explained that such coverage "would blow our budget out of the water."[17]

Despite the expense of the new drugs, they may produce a cost saving in the short run. A model developed by Moore and Bartlett showed that pharmaceutical costs could, in part, be offset by reduced expenditures in hospitalization and ambulatory care.[18] But even the additional cost per year of life saved would be, according to this model, well within the range of costs for other widely accepted life-extending therapies. Given the nature of the American health care system, it is unlikely that such savings will be viewed as sufficiently compelling to warrant rapid expansion in budgets for outpatient drug prescriptions.

From the perspective of medical ethics, the inequalities in access to the new therapies are unacceptable. Whether due to economic barriers or accidents of geography, the current situation represents a profoundly troubling affront to conceptions of equity. Even applying the anemic formulation proffered by the President's Commission for the Study of Ethical Issues in Medicine more than a decade ago — that society has an ethical obligation to ensure that individuals have access to an adequate level of care without undue burden — such barriers would be a violation of the principle of justice.[19] In a nation where 40 million people lack health insurance, and millions more do not have adequate coverage, the issue posed here is not unique. It does, however, take on special significance in a disease as dire as AIDS.

It is in this context that the sometimes unseemly battle by disease lobbyists takes place. Yet the struggle on the part of AIDS activists for coverage of the new therapies is morally compelling. The plight of individuals with other critical medical conditions will not necessarily be advanced if those with a special concern for AIDS adopt a less demanding posture.

Finally, an issue too often neglected by bioethicists, the fairness of drug pricing, must be addressed. It is clear that the market price for a new drug that may prolong the lives of the desperate is not necessarily the fair price for such a drug. Failure to address this issue places public funders, private insurers, and patients in a vulnerable position. Therefore, as Baruch Brody has noted, "We need to develop a system of drug pricing that provides adequate economic incentives for drug research and development, taking into account the uncertainties and length of time involved while limiting excessive promotional costs and profits."[20]

COMPLIANCE AND RESISTANCE

The new combination regimens are demanding and involve taking 15 to 20 pills a day. If simply remembering to take the various drugs at the proper time were the only problem, compliance would be difficult enough. Some of the drugs must be taken on an empty stomach; others are best tolerated following a high-fat meal. Ritonavir must be refrigerated. Even relatively healthy patients may have difficulties tolerating side effects, which may include nausea, diarrhea, vomiting, and anorexia.

A rapid rate of replication of viral particles combined with a high rate of mutation can lead to the development of resistance, "particularly in the presence of a selective pressure by anti-retroviral therapies."[9(p150)] Hence, resistance can develop if drug dosages are inadequate or doses are missed.[21] In early trials of protease inhibitors, patients received sub-optimal dosages and HIV readily developed resistance, which persisted even in the face of higher dosages. Incomplete treatment may also yield cross resistance to other HIV treatment agents not yet prescribed.

Given the difficulties of securing complete adherence to any drug regimen, the challenges involved in combination therapy for HIV are daunting. The prospect of resistance not only makes individual patients more vulnerable, it also raises the specter of a public health threat that could well neutralize recent therapeutic advances.[22] Clinicians have been concerned about how to communicate the extraordinary urgency of strict compliance to their patients. Patient-oriented newsletters and magazines have warned against taking "drug holidays."[23]

The threat of drug resistance emerging as a result of noncompliance raises profound ethical questions. Should some therapies not be offered to patients who might have difficulty in adhering to the demanding regimens? Should such concerns ever be cause for denying drug therapies to patients who request them? Should decisions to withhold combination therapies be based on demonstrated noncompliance with previous treatment demands or on predictions about future behavior based on defined patient characteristics? Are there entire classes of individuals (i.e., the homeless, those suffering from certain types of mental illness, and injection drug users) to whom the drugs ought not be offered?

Such questions have been broached by clinicians with a steadfast dedication to working with disenfranchised and vulnerable populations. According to one physician:

We have many patients who can and will benefit right now. But we have many others whose lives are in too much turmoil to prescribe them the therapy. We have patients using illicit drugs, some are homeless, some don't even have enough to eat. It won't be helpful to start them on the medication until their lives are more stable. From a pubic health point of view, for the larger community, that would be disastrous.[8]

A New York City health official went so far as to say that the lack of access to the drugs by the homeless and injection drug users was a "perverse blessing."[24] Indeed, so striking is the specter of physicians denying access to life-extending treatments that it has become the subject of newspaper accounts.[25,26]

Compliance and resistance has been at the center of discussions of tuberculosis treatment for more than 4 decades. It is within that context that the ubiquity of noncompliance with therapeutic regimes became a central concern. Class, socioeconomic status, and gender could not predict adherence. With the upsurge in tuberculosis in the late 1980s and the increasing incidence of multidrug-resistant tuberculosis, directly observed therapy emerged as the standard of care.[27] Given the difficulty of predicting who would be adherent, many called for universal directly observed therapy.[28] But supervised therapy regimens for tuberculosis involve taking drugs at most once a day and often only two or three times per week. The sheer logistics of combination therapies, which require medication several times a day, preclude directly observed therapy as a useful approach. Other strategies will thus be necessary to enhance patient adherence.

Were the problem exclusively one of individual patient welfare, the question would be whether predictions regarding adherence could justify denying access to a life-enhancing and life-extending therapy. Could a refusal to prescribe protease inhibitors in the short term be justified by hopes that an improved prospect for adherence in the future could make treatment efficacious in the long run? This is an exquisite dilemma of medical paternalism. We believe it would be very difficult to justify denial of access to protease inhibitors in the face of expressed patient preference for treatment except in the presence of clear and compelling evidence that a patient could not or would not be adherent. But there may indeed be such instances. And, when they arise, a failure to act paternalistically may represent an abrogation of professional responsibility.

But the issue is clearly not one of individual patient welfare alone. Failure to adhere to therapy may have profound public health consequences, most notably the development of resistant strains of HIV that could be transmitted to sexual and needle-sharing partners as well as to the infants born to infected women. In the face of these risks, we believe that only an individualized determination that a given patient will not be adherent and that he or she is likely to engage in behavior that could transmit resistant strains of HIV could justify the withholding of protease inhibitors on public health grounds.

Patient autonomy should, as a matter of principle, be the guiding norm in clinical determinations. But autonomy is not absolute, and it may be overridden when the well-being of the community is at stake. Typically, this occurs in the context of infectious diseases such as tuberculosis, for which patients may be compelled to undergo testing and treatment. The interests of the public health and the patient are thus served. What makes the current situation so difficult and troubling is that the interest of the public may be in conflict with the preference of the patient for therapy. Indeed, it may require that a patient be denied therapy.

Denials of access to therapy should never be based on broad social characteristics such as mental illness, homelessness, or drug use, although such conditions might well increase the index of suspicion and trigger a careful, individualized assessment of the individual's prospects for compliance.[28] Given the common problem of nonadherence, however, such assessments are crucial even with those who are not typically expected to pose a risk. When denials of treatment occur, patients must be apprised of the rationale for withholding therapy, and such decisions must be reviewed periodically because changed patient behavior could affect the determination. Decisions to limit access to therapies because of concerns about adherence must not become a pretext for rationing, cloaking denials based on economic considerations. To the extent that deprivations such as homelessness or inadequate access to mental health services or drug abuse treatment create the context of nonadherence, justice demands addressing those underlying conditions. It would be a cruel irony to deny the most vulnerable individuals access to life-extending therapies when remediable social condition undermine their capacity for adherence.

The threat of viral resistance must also be understood in the context of physician practices. Failure to provide appropriate combinations at appropriate dosage levels could produce viral resistance even in patients who were completely adherent. There is, thus, a strong professional obligation for physicians to understand how these drugs should be prescribed. This moral imperative takes place within a context of considerable uncertainty. But such uncertainty does not provide a warrant for poorly informed decision making. The problem of appropriate physician practice must also be considered in the light of the movement toward managed care for the poor and the trend toward emphasizing the role of general practitioners without special training in the treatment of HIV disease. The imperatives of cost containment may thus conflict with the demands of appropriate patient care.

Finally, we address the challenge of the expensive new therapies for HIV infection in the developing world. Because of cost, the new drugs are out of reach in areas where AIDS poses the greatest burden. This situation is unique only because, within recent memory, the United States shared with the most impoverished nations a common fate of therapeutic impotence.

Given the current cost of the new drug therapies, there is little likelihood that they will become available in the areas where they are so desperately needed. Even if the costs declined and prices reflected some concept of fairness rather than the play of market forces, the medical infrastructure and expertise necessary for monitoring the clinical course of those on combination therapies would not be available in many nations. This state of affairs underscores the consequence of disease in a world characterized by deep and widening gulfs in wealth, a profound inequality that should fuel our moral concern. It also underscores the necessity of a continued commitment to vaccine development that could provide those who are poor and desperately in need of effective AIDS prevention with affordable and manageable prophylaxis. Whether the mobilization of resources for such an endeavor will be sustained in the face of the therapeutic transformation now occurring in the wealthiest nations remains to be seen.

The new therapeutic approaches heralded at Vancouver may signal the beginning of the end of the era of relative therapeutic impotence in HIV disease. But these advances, as with all such medical progress, pose ethical challenges demanding wisdom and a commitment to justice that may be in shorter supply than the resources needed to fund the path of medical progress.

ACKNOWLEDGMENT

This work was supported by National Institute of Mental Health grant K05 MH01376-01.

REFERENCES

1. Corey L, Holmes KK. Therapy for human immunodeficiency virus infection—what have we learned? *N Engl J Med.* 1996;335: 1142–1143.

2. Sharp D. Vancouver meeting highlights combination attack on HIV. *Lancet.* 1996;348:115.

3. Pennisi E, Cohen J. Eradicating HIV from a patient: not just a dream? *Science* 1996;272:1884.

4. Goodman E. Living with AIDS: the Lazarus syndrome. *Baltimore Sun.* March 18, 1997:9A.

5. Hopper L. The death of a death sentence: HIV patients plot career courses. *Austin American Statesman.* November 15, 1996:A1.

6. Levy JA. Surrogate markers in AIDS research. Is there truth in numbers? *JAMA.* 1997;276:61–62.

7. Mann J, Tarantola D. eds. *AIDS in the World: Global Dimensions, Social Roots, and Responses.* New York, NY: Oxford University Press Inc; 1996.

8. Waldholz M. Precious pills: new AIDS treatment raises tough questions of who will get it. *Wall Street Journal.* July 3, 1996:A1.

9. Deeks SG, Smith M, Holodniy, M, et al. HIV-1 protease inhibitors: a review for clinicians. *JAMA.* 1997;277:145–153.

10. Saag MS, Holodniy M, Kuritzkes DR, et al. Viral load markers in clinical practice. *Nature Med.* 1996;1:625–629.

11. Richman DD. HIV therapeutics. *Science.* 1996;272:1886–1887.

12. Diaz T, Chu SY, Conti L, et al. Health insurance coverage among persons with AIDS: results from a multistate surveillance project. *Am J Public Health.* 1994;84:1015–1018.

13. Kolata G. AIDS patients slipping through safety net. *New York Times.* September 15, 1996:A1.

14. *State AIDS Drug Assistance Programs: A National Status Report on Access (1997).* Washington, DC: National Alliance of State and Territorial AIDS Directors; 1997.

15. Carton B. New AIDS drug brings hope to Provincetown, but unexpected woes. *Wall Street Journal.* October 3, 1996:A1.

16. Pear R. Expense means many can't get drugs for AIDS. *New York Times.* February 15, 1997:A1.

17. Goldstein A. New treatments put AIDS program in a dilemma. *Washington Post.* August 15, 1996:A1.

18. Moore RD, Bartlett JG. Combination antiretroviral therapy in HIV infection. *PharmacoEconomics.* 1996;10:109–113.

19. *Securing Access to Health Care: The Ethical Implications of Differences in the Availability of Health Services.* Washington, DC: President's Commission for the Study of Ethical Problems in Medicine and Biomedical and Behavioral Research; 1993.

20. Brody B. Public goods and fair prices: balancing technological innovation with social well-being. *Hastings Cent Rep.* 1996;26:5–11.

21. Schapiro JM, Winters MA, Vierra M, et al. *Causes of Long-Term Efficacy and/or Drug Failure in Protease (PR) Inhibitor Monotherapy.* Vancouver, British Columbia, Canada: 11th International Conference on AIDS; 1996.

22. Gold HS, Moellering RC. Antimicrobial-drug resistance. *N Engl J Med.* 1996;335:1445–1446.

23. White EC. Pill-stopping: drug holidays are routine for double-digit-dosing PWAs. So is drug resistance. *POZ.* September–October 1996.

24. Schoofs M. Drug resistance: the next AIDS crisis. *Village Voice.* July 9, 1996:15.

25. Sontag D, Richardson L. Doctors withhold HIV pill regimen from some. *New York Times.* March 2, 1997:A1.

26. Baxter D. Casting off the "unreliable" AIDS patient. *New York Times.* March 6, 1997:A23.

27. Bayer R, Wilkinson D. Directly observed therapy for tuberculosis: a history of an idea. *Lancet.* 1995;345:1545–1548.

28. Sbarbaro JA. All patients should receive directly observed therapy in tuberculosis. *Am Rev Respir Dis.* 1980;212:611–614.

The Duty to Warn and the Duty Not to Harm

S U S A N   D .   C O C H R A N   A N D   V I C K I E   M .   M A Y S

Sex, Lies, and HIV

To the Editor: Reducing the risk of human immunodeficiency virus (HIV) transmission among sexually active teenagers and young adults is a major public health concern.[1] Young people are advised to select potential sexual partners from groups at lower risk for HIV,[2] in part by asking about partners' risk histories.[3] Unfortunately, this advice overlooks the possibility that people may lie about their risk history.[4]

Reprinted with the permission of the publisher from the *New England Journal of Medicine* 322 (March 15, 1990), 774–775. Copyright © 1990 by the Massachusetts Medical Society.

Table 1. Dishonesty in Dating.

Variable	Men (N = 196)	Women (N = 226)
	percent	
History of disclosure		
Has told a lie in order to have sex	34	10*
Lied about ejaculatory control	38	
or likelihood of pregnancy		14
Sexually involved with more than one person	32	23†
Partner did not know	68	59
Experience of being lied to		
Has been lied to for purposes of sex	47	60‡
Partner lied about ejaculatory control		46
or likelihood of pregnancy	34	
Willingness to deceive§		
Would lie about having negative HIV-antibody test	20	4*
Would lie about ejaculatory control	29	
or likelihood of pregnancy		2*
Would understate number of previous partners	47	42
Would disclose existence of other partner to new partner		
Never	22	10 ⎤
After a while, when safe to do so	34	28 ⎬ *
Only if asked	31	33 ⎟
Yes	13	29 ⎦
Would disclose a single episode of sexual infidelity		
Never	43	34 ⎤
After a while, when safe to do so	21	20 ⎬ †
Only if asked	14	11 ⎟
Yes	22	35 ⎦

*P < 0.001 by chi-square test.

†P < 0.05 by chi-square test.

‡P < 0.01 by chi-square test.

§Hypothetical scenarios were described in which honesty would threaten either the opportunity to have sex or the maintenance of a sexually active relationship.

In a sample of 18-to-25-year-old students attending colleges in southern California (n = 665), we found strong evidence that undermines faith in questioning partners as an effective primary strategy of risk reduction. The young adults, of whom 422 were sexually active, completed anonymous 18-page questionnaires assessing sexual behavior, HIV-related risk reduction, and their experiences with deception when dating.

We found that sizable percentages of the 196 men and 226 women who were sexually experienced reported having told a lie in order to have sex. Men reported telling lies significantly more frequently than women (Table 1). Women more often reported that they had been lied to by a dating partner. When asked what they would do in hypothetical situations, both men and women frequently reported that they would actively or passively deceive a dating partner, although again, men were significantly more likely than women to indicate a willingness to do so.

Although we cannot be certain that our subjects were fully forthcoming in their responses (e.g., they reported more frequent dishonesty from others than they admitted to themselves), one can probably assume that their reports of their own dishonesty underestimate rather than overestimate the problem. The implications of our findings are clear. In counseling patients, particularly young adults, physicians need to consider realistically the patients' capacity for assessing the risk of

HIV in sexual partners through questioning them.[5] Patients should be cautioned that safe-sex strategies are always advisable,[5-7] despite arguments to the contrary from partners. This is particularly important for heterosexuals in urban centers where distinctions between people at low risk and those at high risk may be less obvious because of higher rates of experimentation with sex and the use of intravenous drugs and undisclosed histories of high-risk behavior.

NOTES

1. Koop CE. Surgeon General's report on acquired immune deficiency syndrome. Washington, D.C.: Public Health Service, 1986.

2. Hearst N, Hulley SB. Preventing the heterosexual spread of AIDS: Are we giving our patients the best advice? *JAMA* 1988; 259:2428-32.

3. Fox M. Asking the right questions. *Health* 1988; February:38-9, 98-100.

4. Potterat JJ, Phillips L., Muth JB. Lying to military physicians about risk factors for HIV infections. *JAMA* 1987; 257:1727.

5. Schulman K. Preventing the heterosexual spread of AIDS. *JAMA* 1988; 260:1879-80.

6. Padian NS, Francis DP. Preventing the heterosexual spread of AIDS. *JAMA* 1988; 260:1879.

7. Goedert JJ. Preventing the heterosexual spread of AIDS. *JAMA* 1988; 260:1880.

RONALD BAYER

AIDS Prevention — Sexual Ethics and Responsibility

Do people infected with the human immunodeficiency virus (HIV) have special responsibilities to their sexual partners? If so, what do these responsibilities involve? Merely raising these questions directly has tended, until recently, to disquiet many people involved in AIDS-prevention efforts.

From the onset of the AIDS epidemic in 1981, it became increasingly clear that questions of sexual ethics could not be avoided. Here was a new fatal disease, spread in the context of sexual relations that are typically consensual. The questions posed by AIDS were not fundamentally different from those raised by other sexually transmitted diseases. But the lethality of HIV infection added an urgency that made refusing to consider such matters more problematic.

The following questions had to be answered: Is there a moral obligation on the part of someone infected with HIV to use condoms when engaging in penetrative sex? If condoms are used, is there an additional obligation to inform one's partner that one is in-

Reprinted with the permission of the publisher from the *New England Journal of Medicine* 334, (June 6, 1996), pp. 1540–42. Copyright © 1996 by the Massachusetts Medical Society.

fected? Does this obligation change if the sexual acts in question are thought to involve a relatively low risk, or risks that are a matter of dispute? Does it matter whether the sexual contact occurs in the context of an ongoing relationship, one that is thought to be monogamous, a casual relationship, or an anonymous encounter? Does it matter if the infected person is man or a woman or the sexual encounter gay or heterosexual? Is there an obligation to inform past sexual partners about one's HIV infection, and if so, partners from how long ago? Is the obligation to use condoms or to disclose infection obviated if there is a real or assumed threat of violence? Does the anticipation of rejection justify a failure to use condoms or to disclose one's HIV status? Does concern about possible secondary disclosure justify keeping silent about one's infection? What obligations do health departments and AIDS service organizations have to foster an ethic of personal responsibility? Should concern about stigmatizing people affect that obligation?

In the early years of the epidemic, the very idea of responsibility raised by these questions was viewed as alien and threatening. It was a concept more common to the moral and religious right, which had shown a profound indifference to the plight of those with AIDS. The emphasis on personal responsibility was often associated with condemnation of those whose sexual or drug-using behavior had exposed them to HIV, as well as with calls for invasions of privacy and deprivations of liberty. It seemed, finally, to echo the moralistic disapproval of sexual pleasure in general and of homosexuality more specifically.

Pragmatic, philosophical, and political objections to the concept of responsibility were raised. On a pragmatic level, it was claimed that a public health policy focusing on the responsibility of people with HIV to behave in ways that protected the uninfected — either by using condoms or by disclosing the fact of their infection — would, paradoxically, increase the risk of HIV transmission. Misled by false expectations, people would fail to protect themselves. Some did not know they were infected. Others knew they were at high risk but sought to avoid HIV testing. Finally, it was believed that some would lie about whether they were infected. Given these prospects, it made sense to stress self-protection rather than self-disclosure. Each person had to be responsible for condom use,[1] and this obligation was shared equally by the infected and the uninfected. Because each sexual partner was responsible for his or her own health, neither was ultimately responsible for the health of the other.

Even some health departments sought to promote condom use because it was the only way of ensuring self-protection. In an AIDS-prevention advertisement produced by the New York City Health Department, in the style of pop art, a man and woman are shown embracing and thinking, "I hope he [she] doesn't have AIDS!" To this, the voice of the Health Department responds, "You can't live on hope." The text of the advertisement continues:

You hope this guy is finally the right guy.
You hope this time she just might be the right one.
And you both hope the other one is not infected with the AIDS virus.
Of course, you could ask. But your partner might not know.
That's because it's possible to carry the AIDS virus for many years without showing any symptoms.
The only way to prevent getting infected is to protect yourself. Start using condoms.
Every time. Ask him to use them. If he says no, so can you.

When the question of disclosure was considered in the first decade of the epidemic, it was commonly discussed in terms of the psychological burdens associated with secrecy rather than the sexual partner's right to be informed.

From a philosophical perspective, it was asserted that since HIV was primarily transmitted in the context of consensual sex, each person bore the responsibility of self-protection. Mohr wrote, "The disease's mode of contagion argues that those at risk are those whose actions contribute to their own risk of infection."[2] Relying on the legal maxim "to one who consents, no harm is done,"[3] Illingworth concluded that people who did not protect themselves had no claim against those who infected them.

Haunting the philosophical perspective on the dangerous concept of sexual responsibility was the specter of criminalization. If the protection of others was a moral duty and the consequence of disregarding that duty was a lethal infection, would it not be logical to impose criminal sanctions for unsafe sex? Many state legislatures enacted statues imposing criminal penalties on those whose actions could result in HIV transmission, and they sometimes refused to distinguish between those who did use condoms and those who did not.[4]

A final, political objection was made to the claim that those with HIV infection had a special responsibility not to transmit the virus. In the face of indifference, hostility, and stigma, it was considered crucial to articulate an ideology of solidarity, one that rejected as divisive all efforts to distinguish the infected from the uninfected. Such distinctions, it was feared, would lead to "viral apartheid." Solidarity was endangered to the extent that the infected were held to have special duties — protecting the uninfected, even recognizing their right to choose not to have penetrative sex with them — and to the extent that the uninfected had a special need to remain uninfected. Cohesiveness could best be grounded in the concepts of universal vulnerability to HIV and the universal importance of safe sexual practices.

It is important not to overstate the extent to which the principle of self-protection rendered impossible any discussion of the responsibility of people with HIV infection. Some philosophers underscored the obligation to notify sexual partners about one's HIV status by drawing on the doctrine of informed consent.[5] And while virtually always rejecting the idea that there was a duty to disclose one's HIV status, many AIDS service organizations urged universal condom use.[6] Public health departments and the Centers for Disease Control and Prevention paid considerable attention to issues of partner notification and explicitly sought to define strategies to protect the unsuspecting sexual contacts of persons with HIV. "Privilege to disclose" legislation in many states made it possible for physicians to breach confidentiality to warn unsuspecting sexual partners.[7]

Nevertheless, self-protection was accorded a central conceptual role in AIDS-prevention efforts, especially by community-based organizations and health departments sensitive to the fears of those most at risk. In a 1995 review of preventive efforts among drug users, Des Jarlais noted that "most programs that have urged intravenous drug users to use condoms thus far have focused on the self-protective efforts of condom use. Appealing to altruistic feelings of protecting others from HIV infection may be an untapped source of motivation for increasing condom use." (Des Jarlais D: personal communication).

How deeply rooted the ideology of self-protection had become and how difficult developing programs that appealed to "altruistic feelings" might be was starkly revealed in New York City in 1993. To mark the occasion of the city's 50,000th AIDS case, efforts were made to launch a prevention campaign that would focus on protecting others as well as oneself. Those efforts were aborted when AIDS specialists inside the health department denounced the proposal as "victim blaming."

The emerging recognition of the limitations of self-protection reflects a growing awareness that new epidemiologic trends demand a new approach to prevention. Self-protection has little to offer the increasing number of women infected through heterosexual contact, who often cannot protect themselves. Patterns of new infections among young gay men suggest that, at least in part, they are vulnerable to infection from an older generation in which the prevalence of HIV infection is high.

Although a growing literature in the late 1980s and early 1990s detailed the patterns of self-disclosure of HIV status to sexual partners,[8-13] the debate about responsibility was largely inaudible. In 1995, however, the *New York Times* published a piece in which the gay journalist Michelangelo Signorile wrote, "If I am positive, I have a responsibility: not to put others at risk and to understand that not all HIV-negative people are

equipped to deal with the responsibility of safer sex."[14] AIDS service organizations, he charged, had failed to address this matter. Signorile's challenge was echoed by Gabriel Rotello, a gay columnist for *New York Newsday:* "The focus on self-protection allows some who are HIV-positive to reason that if an infected partner is willing to take risks, that's the partner's choice. And if that choice results in infection, it's the partner's fault."[15]

Even more striking were the observations in 1995 by Dr. Lawrence Mass, a cofounder of Gay Men's Health Crisis (GMHC), New York's largest community-based organization devoted to AIDS prevention:

When I wrote the earliest version of GMHC's Medical Answers about AIDS . . . I was maximally concerned about civil liberties. Today, I remain so, but with behavior modification looking as if it will remain the sole form of prevention for years to come, I am even more aware of and concerned about personal and moral responsibility.[16]

The endorsement of personal responsibility by prominent and vocal people should not be taken to mean that the world of AIDS prevention has done an about-face. Nevertheless, it represents a profoundly important challenge, one that would require fundamentally reformulating the messages conveyed in counseling and public efforts at education about AIDS.

Acknowledging that personal responsibility has a central role in AIDS prevention raises a number of complex questions. Some proponents of this concept view it primarily as an alternative strategy of motivating people to use condoms. Others underscore the concomitant obligation to disclose one's HIV infection. After all, condoms sometimes fail. Even AIDS-prevention groups refer to sexual intercourse with the use of condoms as being "safer" rather than "safe." Should not uninfected persons be given the opportunity to decide whether to take the risk, however small, entailed by engaging in protected sex with an infected partner?

What are the implications, if people infected with HIV are obligated both to wear condoms during penetrative sex and to disclose their status to their partners? Should those who have been told that a partner is not infected agree to intercourse without a condom? Should such arrangements between partners be thought of as "negotiated safety" or "negotiated danger"?[17] Most important, should AIDS-prevention programs link the concept of candor with that of trust by suggesting that condoms may not be needed by monogamous, uninfected couples?

Alarmed at the extent to which infected people may not know that they are infected or may not be willing to share the fact, some have recommended that intercourse always be protected, even in ongoing relationships. For them, the very concept of trust — even between husband and wife — "disempowers"[18] partners by making the routine use of condoms unacceptable to those who deem their relationship completely monogamous. Sobo notes, "Unsafe sex within a so-called faithful union helps a woman maintain her state of denial and her belief that her partnership is one of love, trust and fidelity. . . ." AIDS risk denial is tied to monogamy ideals. . . ."[19] From that perspective, some, not surprisingly, have argued that romantic feelings are an impediment to effective AIDS prevention.[20] And so, in view of the risks faced by those who follow the romantic maxim "Love conquers all," it has been suggested that safety can be found only in the warning, "Let the buyer beware" — a warning appropriate to commercial exchanges.

Is such a perspective compatible with lasting relationships, heterosexual or gay. Can efforts to prevent AIDS subvert the expectation of trust within intimate relationships and still remain socially and psychologically credible? It may be appealing to assert that AIDS-prevention efforts should have it both ways, encouraging an ethic of responsibility as well as a posture of self-defense. But can candor be fostered when the continued need for vigilance and self-protection is underscored?

There are no simple answers that address the needs both for trust and candor in intimate relationships and for security in the era of AIDS. Systematic behavioral research is essential, as is searching inquiry into the ethical and psychological underpinnings of intimate relationships. Nonetheless, these questions make it clear that matters of sexual ethics are not moralistic diversions. They are at the heart of AIDS prevention.

This week is the 15th anniversary of the first report of AIDS by the Centers for Disease Control. All public and community-based programs of HIV prevention should mark this occasion by confronting openly the challenge of sexual responsibility, a challenge that too many have addressed for too long in at best an oblique and morally cramped fashion.

Supported by a grant (K05 MH01376-01) from the National Institute of Mental Health.

REFERENCES

1. Cochran SD, Mays VM. Sex, lies, and HIV. N Engl J Med 1990;322:774–5.

2. Mohr RD. Gay life, state coercion. Raritan 1986;6:38–62.

3. Illingworth P. AIDS and the good society. London Routledge, 1990.

4. Bayer R. Fairchild-Carrino A. AIDS and the limits of control: public health orders, quarantine, and recalcitrant behavior. Am J Public Health 1993;83:1471–6.

5. Yeo M. Sexual ethics and AIDS: a liberal view. In: Overall C, Zion WP, eds. Perspectives on AIDS: ethical and social issues. Toronto: Oxford University Press, 1991:75–90.

6. Chambers DL. Gay men, AIDS, and the code of the condom. Harvard Civil Rights/Civil Liberties Law Rev 1994;29:353–85.

7. Bayer R, Toomey KE. HIV prevention and the two faces of partner notification. Am J Public Health 1992;82:1158–62.

8. Kegeles SM, Catania JA, Coates TJ. Intentions to communicate positive HIV-antibody status to sex partners. JAMA 1988;259:216–7.

9. Marks G, Richardson JL, Maldonado N. Self-disclosure of HIV infection to sexual partners. Am J Public Health 1991;81:1321–2.

10. Marks G, Richardson JL, Ruiz MS, Maldonado N. HIV-infected men's practices in notifying past sexual partners of infection risk. Public Health Rep 1992;107:100–5.

11. Perry SW, Card CA, Moffatt M Jr, Ashman T, Fishman B, Jacobsberg LB. Self-disclosure of HIV infection to sexual partners after repeated counseling. AIDS Educ Prev 1994;6:403–11.

12. Simoni JM, Mason HR, Marks G, Ruiz MS, Reed D, Richardson JL. Women's self-disclosure of HIV infection: rates, reasons, and reactions. J Consult Clin Psychol 1995;63:474–8.

13. Mason HR, Marks G, Simoni JN, Ruiz MS, Richardson JL. Culturally sanctioned secrets? Latino men's nondisclosure of HIV infection to family, friends, and lovers. Health Psychol 1995;14:6–12.

14. Signorile M. HIV-positive and careless. New York Times. February 26, 1995;4:15.

15. Rotello G. [Letter to the editor]. The Nation. April 17, 1995:510.

16. Mass L. [Letter to the editor]. The Nation. April 17, 1995;540.

17. Ekstrand M, Stall R, Kegeles S, Hays R, DeMayo M. Coates T. Safer sex among gay men: what is the ultimate goal? AIDS 1993;7:281–2.

18. Willig C. I wouldn't have married the guy if I'd have to do that: heterosexual adults' constructions of condom use and their implications for sexual practice. J Community Appl Psychol 1995;4:74–87.

19. Sobo EJ. Choosing unsafe sex: AIDS-risk denial among disadvantaged women. Philadelphia: University of Pennsylvania Press, 1995.

20. Pinkington CJ, Kern W, Indest D. Is safer sex necessary with a "safe" partner? Condom use and romantic feelings. J Sex Res 1994; 31:203–10.

FERDINAND SCHOEMAN

AIDS and Privacy

Issues of privacy surface in nearly every dimension of AIDS, from diagnosis, to treatment, to epidemiology, to prevention. A sampling of issues includes topics like reporting human immunodeficiency virus (HIV) infection to public health agencies, confidentiality of the therapist-patient relationship, and the duty, on the part of the individual or public health authorities, to disclose one's condition to a sexual partner, surgeon, employer, or insurance provider. No group in society is more vulnerable to both biological and social repercussions of a disease than those infected with HIV. Tragically, some aspects of protecting the privacy of those who are HIV infected have frightening potential for others who understandably wish to avoid contagion, as well as for those who recognize the social costs of the increasing numbers and changing profile of AIDS victims. AIDS, as we will see, is destined to have as much impact on the contours of our notion of privacy as computerization of records and the legalization of abortion did.

Conflict and the inevitability of unmet and haunting needs is nowhere more manifest than in the case of AIDS. AIDS is a lethal disease that is communicable in controllable ways. To think of it as a fatal disease invokes one pattern of normative responses: sympathetic and protecting attitudes. To think of it as a condition that is communicable in a controllable way invokes another set of normative responses: those attributing accountability for harming others. Being sick diminishes one's accountability for some things — things over which one has impaired capacity. The negligence or recklessness involved in infecting another with HIV is *not,* however

typically the result of impaired capacity (*United States v. Sergeant Nathaniel Johnson, Jr.*).[1] A person who deserves compassion for having a disease *may* also deserve admonition for acquiring or condemnation for transmitting it. Spouses or partners of those HIV infected may have cause for complaint on either ground.

People infected with HIV have much to fear besides the disease. Because of the association of AIDS with promiscuity, primarily homosexual but also heterosexual, or the self-abandonment connected with intravenous (IV) drug usage, any adult with AIDS is suspected of degeneracy. One in five Americans regard those with AIDS as deserving their suffering because of their immorality (Blendon and Donelan 1988). Homophobia is widespread in the United States, and the intrusion of AIDS as a public health problem has in many people's minds lent legitimacy to hostility toward gay individuals (Goleman 1990). The level of public ignorance about the disease, the deficiency of scientific understanding surrounding aspects of its transmission, and the general hysteria about AIDS mean that people diagnosed as HIV positive must face social, economic, and medical hurdles no one with such dire medical prospects should have to confront. These prejudices extend to those who care for AIDS victims and even to the dwellings of those with AIDS. A diagnosis of HIV infection, or even a suspicion of this, is sufficient in some cases to deprive people of housing, employment, life and health insurance, social tolerance, routine and even emergency medical treatment like mouth-to-mouth resuscitation, schooling, social contacts, friendships, the right to travel in and out of countries — a social identity.

Studies of public attitudes toward those with AIDS make crystal clear the social consequences AIDS sufferers will confront (Blendon and Donelan 1988). One in four questioned in a survey indicated that he or she would refuse to work with someone with AIDS; the same percentage believe that employers should be able to fire employees with AIDS; 39 percent of people surveyed agreed that public school employees should be dismissed if found to have AIDS. In 1988, 18 percent felt that children with AIDS should be barred from school. Nearly one-third indicated that out of concern for their own children's health they would keep their children from attending schools that admitted children with AIDS. In surveys conducted in 1987, a substantial minority (between 21 and 40 percent, depending on the wording) favored isolating people with AIDS from the general community, from public places, and from their own neighborhoods. Panic over the prospect of becoming contaminated is even widespread among health professionals (see Zuger's essay in [Frederic G. Reamer, ed., *AIDS and Ethics* (New York: Columbia University Press, 1991), chapter 9]). Also widespread is skepticism about the accuracy of risk assessments promulgated in the best medical journals. Tragically, fear of discrimination is itself an important obstacle to both greater epidemiological understanding of HIV transmission and implementation of public health measures aimed at minimizing HIV infection.

Further complicating the terrifying social and medical dimensions of HIV infection is the awareness of having been infected by and/or potentially infecting those with whom one is most intimate. This is a moral burden few could find anything but crushing. And yet, discovering and revealing one's own HIV status threatens this source of meaning and support perhaps more than any other.

CONCEPTUAL FOUNDATIONS OF PRIVACY

Because of the way AIDS is transmitted and because of the social, financial, and medical consequences of being identified as HIV positive, it is no wonder that AIDS and privacy intersect at every dimension of the disease. Let us turn our attention to some of the foundational issues related to privacy, beginning with the meaning of privacy.[2] There are broader and narrower conceptions of privacy. On the narrower range of conceptions, privacy relates exclusively to information of a personal sort about an individual and describes the extent to which others have access to this information.[3] A broader conception extends beyond the informational domain and encompasses anonymity and restricted physical

access. Thus far the characterizations allow a sharp contrast between privacy and autonomy. Embracing some aspects of autonomy within the definition of privacy, it has been defined as control over the intimacies of personal identity. At the broadest end of the spectrum, privacy is thought to be the measure of the extent an individual is afforded the social and legal space to develop the emotional, cognitive, spiritual, and moral powers of an autonomous agent. An advocate of one of the narrower conceptions can agree about the value of autonomous development but think that privacy as properly defined makes an important but limited contribution to its achievement.

Privacy is important as a means of respecting or even socially constructing moral personality, comprising qualities like independent judgment, creativity, self-knowledge, and self-respect. It is important because of the way control over one's thoughts and body enables one to develop trust for, or love and friendships with, one another and more generally modulate relationships with others (Fried 1960). It is important too for the political dimensions of a society that respects individual privacy, finding privacy instrumental in protecting rights of association, individual freedom, and limitations on governmental control over thoughts and actions (Benn 1971). Finally, it has been argued that privacy is important as a means of protecting people from overreaching social (as opposed to legal) pressures and sanctions and is thus critical if people are to enjoy a measure of social freedom. This is a dimension of privacy I return to below.

Respecting privacy does not commit us to elevating it above all other concerns. We respect privacy even when we abridge it provided we do so for good reason. What I shall be arguing as we proceed is that HIV status is to be regarded as private information about a person, deserving protection, unless there is "a need to know" on someone's part that in the circumstances makes withholding information unreasonable. In assessing the need to know, we have a responsibility to use the best available information about risk factors. What is protected in one informational context may be unprotected in another. Assessing whether a risk is reasonable is not just a function of the probability of harm. Relevant too are the consequences of abstaining from that behavior and the alternatives available for achieving similar objectives.

In assessing the need to know, many factors depend for their strength on social perceptions, ones that can vary over cultures and within a culture over time and circumstance. They can also vary over class and gender within a culture. By offering some examples of the variability of these standards, we can recognize that many acts we would regard as intrusive, others would not so regard. For instance, in some cultures that place a high premium on the virginity of brides and consummation of marriage as initiating the married state, the first act of intercourse between the man and woman is publicly monitored (Stone 1979). In colonial New England, people were required to live within a household, thinking it improper that a person not be supervised in his private affairs. There was a village officer, the tithingsman, whose role was to pry into the private lives of people to ensure compliance with local social standards (Flaherty 1972). In some communities within the contemporary United States, having a child out of wedlock would be something important to conceal. In other communities, it is the norm. We can and should be sensitive to the class, cultural, and even gender differences in attitudes toward the importance of treating something as private. Inevitably, policies in a pluralistic society will grate against some sensibilities, however judicious the policies are.

PRIVACY AND SEXUALLY TRANSMITTED DISEASES

As the discussion of AIDS and privacy proceeds, some additional theoretical categories will be introduced. AIDS is not the first disease to raise privacy issues. Most states require that a test for venereal diseases be made prior to marriage (Krause 1986:43–44) and that a doctor certify that the partners either are free of disease or have it in noncommunicable stages. All states have public health laws that require reporting sexually transmitted diseases (STDs). Most states do not deal with AIDS or the presence of the HIV antibody as falling under public health regulations pertaining to STDs proper, though they usually have equivalent regulations for AIDS.

As of July 1989, a total of 28 states required health care providers to report cases of persons infected with HIV to their state public health departments. The clear trend is toward reporting of HIV infection, with many states having such proposals before their legislatures (Gostin 1990a:1962).

Although it is certain that one major route of infection is through sexual contact, there is concern that if AIDS or HIV infection is treated as an STD, requiring reporting, those who are infected with HIV will face additional social, medical, and economic isolation in addition to the ravages of the disease (Gostin 1990a). Ironically, treating AIDS as an STD would automatically engage those confidentiality requirements associated with the relevant public health laws.

PRIVACY AND AIDS

The range of privacy issues that arise in the AIDS environment is bewildering (Gostin 1990a). These include confidentiality in relationships with health professionals and disclosure of HIV status to insurers and employers, to state health agencies, to family members or sexual or other partners where transmission is a possibility, to schools, and to residential settings of almost any kind, including correctional facilities. Privacy arises as an issue in considering proposals for HIV screening and in partner notification.

AIDS also has an impact on consideration of public norms that govern private relationships. AIDS and privacy intersect not only for the health care provider, the state, and the HIV-infected person but also for people in their ordinary and informal contact with others. The law both reflects and influences the moral and social rules governing these ordinary and informal contacts. Because AIDS is typically transmitted under circumstances that lie somewhere between the intimate and the private, we tend to think that enforceable public standards are not quite the appropriate levers for directing conduct. This attitude about public standards in private relationships is something I will reconsider. Especially I will want to consider how privacy norms operate vis-à-vis moral norms in general. Clarifying this relationship will help us discern which norms are applicable and what they impose or permit.

The standards I employ are those associated with our responsibility not to harm people, the state's responsibility to maintain public health, and our responsibility as members of society for maintaining practices of social trust and caring. At times the consequences of being guided by one of these standards frustrate the influence of the others.

• • •

PRIVACY AND THE THERAPEUTIC CONTEXT

In discussing limitations on the confidentiality privileges thought appropriate in the therapist-patient relationship, various forms of disclosure could be at issue. There could be disclosure to governmental health agencies, local, state, or federal. There could be disclosure to those who might help the patient, like physician or parent. There could be disclosure to those who might be or might have been endangered by the patient, like a sexual partner. Finally, there could be disclosure to courts, various criminal justice agencies, or those who might threaten the patient's welfare in other respects, like a health insurance provider or people seeking civil damages in court. In the discussion that follows, I am primarily concerned with disclosures to those medically endangered by contact with a patient. Here a case can be made for abridging the patient's privacy on the basis of someone else's need to know of her own risks.

Therapists counseling patients at various stages of HIV infection are aware of dangers their patients at times have posed for others. While some would maintain that the confidentiality of the therapist-patient relationship insulates the therapist from responsibility for those endangered, others would argue that such a restriction would violate the therapist's social responsibility. In this section I discuss the responsibility of the therapist in the context of a relationship with an HIV-infected patient who poses a danger for others. This issue brings us right to the heart of the conflict discussed in the beginning of this paper between seeing a person as ill and seeing a person as a threat to others.

Apparently, a person who confesses to his priest that he has contracted a contagious disease that he might infect his fiancée with is not entitled to confidentiality vis-à-vis his priest's communications with his fiancée.

> Catholic teaching holds that a man forfeits any vow of professional secrecy about an incurable and contagious venereal disease through his intent to act in a way that might gravely injure his bride (Regan 1943).

Analogously, the *Tarasoff* cases (*Tarasoff v. Regents of the University of California* 1974, and *Tarasoff v. Regents of the University of California* 1976) and subsequent others that have raised similar issues establish a duty to warn and protect potential victims of patients undergoing therapy (Lewis 1986, Fulero 1988). Is this a reasonable basis for uprooting a profoundly significant confidential relationship? To address this question and apply it in the therapeutic relationship, we will consider some additional material on the foundations of respect for privacy. I will draw some distinctions

whose relevance for the scope and limit of therapist-patient confidentiality will become clear.

There is no one answer to why privacy is important; in different settings, privacy is important for different reasons. Some of our activities, particularly those connected with bodily or biological functioning or malfunctioning, are associated with privacy norms: elimination, sexual reproduction, illness. Such norms, though widespread and diverse, are not universal. Still, for us they are associated with respect for people, perhaps connected with practices that obscure some of what we share with lower animals.

Privacy norms governing such activities or areas of life are not typically directed to providing those carrying out these functions discretion about how to manage. Instead, these functions, though carried out in private, are traditionally strictly governed by norms that were internalized when young and vigorously sustained on pain of shame. Let us call the privacy norms that are so regulated *discretionless privacy norms.* In the case of discretionless privacy norms one has a duty *not* to present certain faces of oneself in public. The point of this restriction is decidedly not liberation from social control.

Next comes an area of life that is highly regulated but one in which the discretion of how to carry out the objectives is left to the agents. Parent-child relationships characteristically fall into this category. The authoritative discretion parents are accorded in raising their children is rationalized on the grounds that it is to be exercised solely for the purpose of promoting the child's best interest. People will disagree about what does promote the child's interest, and it is in this area of interpretation that a parent is afforded her discretion. Let us call the privacy norms that permit discretion in the achievement of a given objective *narrow privacy.*

Finally, norms that restrict access of others to a person or to a sphere of life may be in place to enable wide discretion in behavior and interpretation of roles. This discretion encompasses discretion both in the ends to be achieved, something lacking in the narrow privacy domain, and in the means by which the ends are to be reached, something shared with the narrow privacy domain. Today we think of the privacy associated with intimate adult relationships as entitled to this full measure of discretion. It is not merely that gratuitous surveillance by others is regarded as out of bounds, as is the case in the discretionless and narrow discretion domains. It is that the couple is thought to be at liberty to develop the relationship as they see fit and to explore possibilities that suit the contours of their individual personalities. Let us call such privacy norms *wide privacy norms*.[4]

Now we can locate the therapist-patient relationship on this spectrum of privacy norms. I argue that therapeutic relationships fall into the middle region, the region of narrow privacy norms. The privacy and discretion afforded the therapist-patient relationship must be exercised to serve specific goals, and it is not up to the therapist and patient to develop other goals or interpret the goals already embraced in eccentric ways. Or at least, it is only within these confines that the relationship becomes socially and legally privileged. Lest one think this is too confining a restriction, recall that this is no narrower discretion than that regulating the parent-child relationship, one that offers considerable latitude in interpreting where the child's good lies and that allows the development of considerable personal and interpersonal meaning within its confines (Schoeman 1989).

In the therapist-patient relationship, anything that does not serve the patient's interest within the general bounds recognized as socially responsible is out of line, a misuse of the discretion, a violation of the relevant norms. Though privacy norms protect many violations from public exposure, this does not redeem their character as violations.

Another consideration that the parent-child relationship shares with therapist-patient relationship has to do with the notion of social responsibility. Parents are entrusted to use their discretion to promote their children's welfare. But parents are also responsible for raising their children to be decent and law-abiding citizens. Just as a person's own welfare can conflict with what is right for her to do, so a parent's regard of her child's welfare can conflict with her attitude about what it is right for the child to do or to become. It could be, for instance, in a child's long-term best interest to be coached on how to cheat in certain endeavors. Nevertheless, we think it wrong for parents to promote the child's interest through such advice. This illustrates that there is a complex goal or a complex set of side constraints that govern parents in the discharge of their responsibilities to promote their children's welfare.

A therapist operates also to promote the welfare of the patient in the context of standards of social decency. Central to our understanding what it is to help someone is a compatibility with a measure of social responsibility. The way the notion of helping works, we are helping only when we do so in a way that is so-

cially responsible. We do not "help" a child molester by teaching him how to get away with abusing children, even if that is the advice he seeks. People for whom helping them is actually inconsistent with respect for others are people we are willing to change but not willing to serve. We tell them, and sincerely believe, that changing them will help them, but that claim is beside the point. For whether it helps them or not, changing them is the first priority.

This distinction between the patient's welfare and social welfare applies very directly to AIDS counseling. The therapist-patient relationship may take on a value in its own right, independent of the relationship serving the patient's narrowly therapeutic interests. But the privacy and confidentiality privileges associated with the relationship are not warranted because of this additional meaning. Confidentiality privileges are afforded because it is presumed that in this way the patient's welfare is promoted in a socially responsible manner.

In claiming that therapists are bound by principles of social responsibility, am I also saying that therapists are best thought as of agents of the state?[5] The question suggests a conflation between the political and the moral. Principles of social responsibility may require therapists to circumvent political requirements, as when a therapist illegally informs a patient about birth control or abortion. Nevertheless, ideally we would hope that the standards that the state expects therapists to adhere to are morally appropriate. If there is no discrepancy, then acting in a way that is socially responsible is coincidentally acting in a way that the state endorses or requires. Furthermore, the therapist is there to assist the patient. To discuss constraints on this does not undermine the point of the relationship, though the constraints do reveal something about it. What they reveal is that a therapeutic relationship requires a sense of distance from the patient. This distance is required for professional judgment and presupposed in our practices of according professional privileges.

So now we recognize some structure in the account of privacy that pertains to patient-therapist relationships. Unlike spousal intimacy, the patient-therapist relationship is not primarily an end in itself but a vehicle to enable the patient to respond to problems with professional help in the context of limitations on the costs to others that providing such help can exact.

One might object on the grounds that parent-child privacy is not just there for the purpose of promoting the child's interests but has an independent dignity founded on the intimacy of the parent-child bond (Schoeman 1980). So similarly, one might extrapolate, the therapist-patient relationship can also involve intimate sharing, and insofar as it does so, it deserves the respect with which norms of privacy can grace a relationship.

There is something to be said for this objection, but it goes only so far as there is consensus between therapist and patient, just as it extends in the parent-child relationship only so far as there is consensus between parent and child. For if there is discord between parental and child will, then the parent is accorded authority only insofar as the parent acts in (her interpretation of) the child's best interest. That is why in many contexts children can obviate the requirement of parental consent by establishing to another objective evaluator that the child's interest is served by not involving the parent.

So in the therapist-patient relationship, it is assumed that there is a convergence of interest *and* that this convergence has already passed whatever moral thresholds responsible social agents will recognize. Therapists are not entitled to help patients shirk fundamental social responsibilities.

Someone might object to this bald claim, suggesting that lawyers are entitled to benefit their clients and work with unconditional confidentiality rules that seem blind to standards of social responsibility. To the extent that lawyers are at liberty to act as "hired guns," their practice has been subjected to intense criticism (Luban 1988). But independent of that, the comparison is more complex than suggested.[6] The therapist, we are presuming, is required to breach confidentiality, to prevent a serious harm that threatens. Rule 1.6 of The American Bar Association Model Rules of Professional Conduct allows (though does not require) lawyers to breach confidentiality "to prevent the client from committing a criminal act the lawyer believes is likely to result in imminent death or substantial bodily harm." Rule 3.3 of this same code makes lawyers responsible for assuring that false evidence is not presented to a court. If the lawyer is not effective at persuading the client to withdraw false testimony, the lawyer is then duty bound to disclose the fraud to the court.

Still, unlike psychotherapists, it is *not* clear that attorneys are required to act to protect potential victims of their client's violent intentions. In *Hawkins v. King*

County an attorney was held not liable for failure to notify officials at his client's bail hearing of his client's dangerousness and was held not liable for failure to notify his client's mother, a victim of his client's dangerousness. Nevertheless, *Hawkins* is different from *Tarasoff v. Regents* in three important respects. The defendant in *Hawkins* did not have specific indications of the direction of his client's dangerousness. He only knew that he was dangerous to himself and others. The defendant in *Hawkins* was not in a position to make a specific evaluation of his client's dangerousness; it is something he learned from others. Third, the victim of the client's aggression was as much aware of the client's dangerousness as the attorney was. If the fact situation had been different in *Hawkins,* the outcome might also have been different.

A difference between the lawyer-client relationship and the therapist-patient relationship is that the right to representation at a criminal trial is a constitutional right. No similar constitutional right is recognized for medical or psychological services. Furthermore, a lawyer's client faces criminal prosecution wherein the full power of the state is aimed at convicting and then punishing him. The therapist in reporting an endangering of others is not acting in response to a threat to her patient posed by the state. Though there may be consequences of the disclosure for her patient, the point of the disclosure is not to hurt the patient. Reporting statutes and judicial decisions require that health agencies and endangered persons be notified, not that the police or prosecutors be notified.

Above, we established that the privacy accorded a therapeutic relationship is aimed at an outcome: promoting the patient's welfare within the context of social responsibility. Realizing this aim helps us situate the confidentiality privileges associated with therapy. The confidentiality of the patient's condition does not preclude the therapist from taking steps to ensure notification of those endangered by the patient. Therapists should notify public health officials who in turn would notify those put at risk. Those endangered have a need to know of their vulnerability, and this need warrants breach of confidentiality.

Which behaviors constitute a risk that therapists must take responsibility for notifying others of their risks? Here we can use as a standard the following: if it is unreasonable for a patient to fail to inform others of a life-threatening risk, then the therapist owes it to these other persons to notify them of the risk. In [the next section of this essay] I discuss when it is unreasonable for people not to inform others of risks they pose to them.

FERDINAND SCHOEMAN   739

* * *

THE INDIVIDUAL'S DUTY TO WARN

In the last [section], I addressed the question of what responsibilities therapists have to breach confidentiality and protect those endangered by patients with AIDS. . . . In this section, I discuss what responsibilities a person has to warn others whom he may be endangering because of his HIV infection. Since this often arises in the context of a sexual relationship, I focus here on standards of care that are enforceable despite arising in a private setting. . . .

Conditions of trust and intimacy that are worth respecting should be transparent, in that if partners were to be more fully informed of the other, the basis of the trust and intimacy would not be undermined (Baier 1986). Should this ideal be imposed by those not party to the relationship? Could not the information be misleading, or might not it be aberrational, or does it presuppose too much rationality in the agents? How does it affect matters when the behavior in question is life threatening?

What responsibilities does a person who knows he is or might be HIV infected have toward those he might transmit the virus to? Let us restrict our attention here to those who would not willingly be part of an interchange in which HIV might be transmitted. As this relates to privacy, we might ask more specifically whether the intimacy or privacy of the relationship might bar public or legal accountability on the part of someone who transmits the virus.

A further refinement of the question is in order. What we are here concerned with is what standard the state will impose if it is addressed to resolve a dispute between parties disagreeing over the proper standard of care. This involves, not surveillance on the part of the state into relationships where it is not invited, but a response to a complaint brought by people who were sexually intimate, even within the context of marriage.

Although not dispositive of the moral, the legal framework for assessing liability between sexual partners for transmission of disease is relevant. The leading relevant case here is *Kathleen K. v. Robert B.* (1984). The California Court of Appeals held that the constitutional right of privacy does not "insulate one sexual partner who by intentionally tortious conduct causes physical injury to another."

Kathleen K. alleged that she contracted genital herpes, a contagious and debilitating condition for which there is at present no cure, as a result of sexual intercourse with Robert B. at a time when he knew or should have known that he was a carrier. She also alleged that Robert B. misrepresented to her that he was free from venereal disease and that she relied on his assertion. Robert B. alleged that his right to privacy precluded a court's intrusion into the case, its jurisdiction in this domain.

The court found that Robert B.'s right to privacy was not absolute and was subordinate to the state's fundamental right to enact laws that promote public health, welfare, and safety. The court cited penal statutes covering consensual sexual acts, registration of convicted sex offenders, laws relating to paternity, even to marital rape legislation, to illustrate its jurisdiction in the private domain.

Recent Minnesota and New Jersey cases, *R.A.P. v. B.J.P.,* and *G.L. v. M.L.,* respectively, would allow a person to claim damages against a former spouse for transmitting genital herpes *during the tenure of the marriage.* Recovery is permitted on the basis of a duty to refrain from acts that might transmit a disease or minimally warn the spouse of her contagious condition. The New Jersey court endorsed the position that courts were instrumental in defining the level of care spouses owe one another.

The Supreme Court of Ohio (*Mussivand v. David*) held that if person A has a venereal disease and is having an affair with a married person B but has not informed B of his condition, A owes *B's spouse* notification of his, B's spouse's, vulnerability to the disease. (The duty A owes *B* was not an issue in this case.) Anything less subjects B's spouse to an unreasonable risk of contracting the disease, making A liable for damages.

These cases illustrate that sexual intimacy brings with it an enforceable standard of care despite being located within the private precincts of life. Most of the cases mentioned involved a risk of contracting genital herpes. Because the risks associated with AIDS are so much more threatening than those associated with herpes, there is every reason to think that the standard of care expected of those who might transmit AIDS will be more vigorously applied than that expected of those who might transmit herpes (Gostin 1990a; Lambert 1990).[7]

The standard of care required by law is implicit in public attitudes toward what people in intimate relationships owe one another. In one study of people who presented themselves at an STD clinic, when offered confidential HIV testing, 79 percent accepted; 71 percent of those accepting the test offered as a reason concern for transmitting HIV to their sexual partner(s).[8]

The intimate or delicate nature of many aspects of AIDS transmission is a real barrier to frank discussion of risk factors. Not surprisingly many people about to embark on a sexual relationship would not regard it as fitting to discuss prospects for transmission of venereal disease in general or HIV in particular. The more such issues are discussed in public contexts, the more people will in fact feel comfortable in raising them in private contexts without feeling as if they are doing something offensive and unreasonable. Very clearly people need more incentives or fewer inhibitions in taking safety precautions related to sexual behavior and frank sexual conversations. Much about our social upbringing disposes us to feel skittish about broaching such topics even with people we know well. More open discussion of such issues in schools, homes, churches, and other settings of exemplary social norms will go some way toward facilitating open expressions of concern when it is important to do so in sexual settings. The less prevalent the ravages of AIDS are within a community, the less awareness there will be that such privacy barriers are dangerous.

• • •

I mentioned at the outset that in cases of real moral conflict we are haunted by needs and concerns that cannot be addressed because of the pressing nature of the other values involved. Tragically, this is what we confront commonly when we consider the needs of those infected with HIV in cases where people legitimately raise privacy concerns.

The fact that people infected with HIV may be thought to be living under a death sentence, both physically and socially, argues in favor of respecting the privacy interests of these people to the extent possible. Being so fated, however, does not release these people from standards of decency and care they owe others. After all, if AIDS is horrible to endure, it is horrible to transmit. A person's right to privacy concerning his HIV-positive status is properly abridged when doing so represents the least invasive and most efficient means of protecting others from contracting or spreading the disease.

We cannot afford to be anything but compassionate in our policies toward those infected with HIV. But because of the physical and social ruin this infection occasions, we cannot afford to be ambivalent toward those who unreasonably risk infecting others or who will not share information that can literally save lives. . . .

ACKNOWLEDGMENTS

I express appreciation to Robert Ball, Nora Bell, Nathan Crystal, Patricia Conway, Linda Kettinger, Susan Lake, Robert Post, Bosko Postic, Frederic Reamer, Laurence Thomas, and Deborah Valentine for valuable discussions and resource materials that helped me develop an understanding of issues related to AIDS. Frederic Reamer has been an ideal editor, offering wise comments and constructively prodding me on numerous issues that arose in the myriad versions of this paper. The paper owes much to his care and commitment to making it the most valuable contribution it can be. . . .

NOTES

1. *United States v. Sergeant Nathaniel Johnson, Jr.* upholds Sergeant Johnson's conviction for aggravated assault for attempting to engage in anal sex while knowing his condition to be HIV positive — making his semen deadly.

2. For a collection of much of the best writing on privacy along with a philosophical overview of this literature, see Schoeman (1984a). For a review of the philosophical dimension of central privacy issues, see Schoeman (1984c).

3. There is an even narrower conception, one that limits the range of privacy to personal information that is "undocumented."

4. One criterion of the difference between the narrow and the wide privacy norms can be phrased in terms of the distinction between a role and a relationship. While a role is relatively limited in the range of responses thought appropriate and the ends to be achieved, a relationship is treated as more flexible on both counts. Our standing as a parent is role governed insofar as we owe our children certain attitudes almost independently of how they behave; our standing as a spouse is much more responsive to the actual behavior of the partner (Greenhouse 1986).

5. I am indebted to Robert Post for suggesting that I address this question.

6. I am indebted to Nathan Crystal and Robert Post for coaching me on the intricacies of the lawyer-client confidentiality privilege.

7. Marc Christian, Rock Hudson's long-term companion, "won a multimillion-dollar award from Rock Hudson's estate in a suit alleging that the movie star lied about his illness and continued having unsafe sex" (Lambert 1990:15A). Because Mr. Christian was not HIV infected, the basis of the award must have been infliction of emotional distress and violation of a duty to inform (*Christian v. Sheft*).

8. Personal communication, Dr. Jeffrey Jones, Disease Control Division, South Carolina Department of Health and Environmental Control.

Baier, A. 1986. Trust and Antitrust. *Ethics* 96:231–260.

Benn, S. 1971. Privacy, Freedom, and Respect for Persons. In F. Schoeman, ed., *Philosophical Dimensions of Privacy: An Anthology,* pp. 223–244. New York: Cambridge University Press, 1984.

Blendon, R. and K. Donelan. 1988. Discrimination against People with AIDS. *New England Journal of Medicine* 319:1022–1026.

Christian v. Sheft. 1988. Super Ct. LA City: *AIDS Literature Reporter* (June 24).

Flaherty, D. 1972. *Privacy in Colonial New England.* Charlottesville: University Press of Virginia.

Fried, C. 1960. Privacy. In F. Schoeman, ed., *Philosophical Dimensions of Privacy,* pp. 203–222.

Fulero, S. 1988. *Tarasoff:* 10 Years Later. *Professional Psychology: Research and Practice* 19: 184–190.

G.L. v. M.L. 1988. 550 A.2d 525 (N.J. Super. Ct.).

Goleman, D. 1990. Studies Discover Clues to the Roots of Homophobia. *New York Times* (July 10), p. B1.

Gostin, L. 1990a. The AIDS Litigation Project: A National Review of Court and Human Rights Commission Decisions. Part I: The Social Impact of AIDS. *JAMA* 263:1961–1970.

Greenhouse, C. 1986. *Praying for Justice: Faith, Order, and Community in an American Town.* Ithaca, N.Y.: Cornell University Press.

Hawkins v. King County. 1979. 602 P.2d 361.

Kathleen K. v. Robert B. 1984. 198 *California Reporter* 273.

Krause, H. 1986. *Family Law.* St. Paul: West Publishing.

Lambert, B. 1990. AIDS: Keeping Track of the Infected. *New York Times* (May 13), p. 15A.

Lewis, M. 1986. Duty to Warn Versus Duty to Maintain Confidentiality: Conflicting Demands on Mental Health Professionals. *Suffolk Law Review* 20:579–615.

Luban, D. 1988. *Lawyers and Justice: An Ethical Study.* Princeton, N.J.: Princeton University Press.

Mussivand v. David. 544 N.E. 2d 265.

R.A.P. v. B.J.P. 1988. 428 N.W.2b 103 (Minn. Ct. App.).

Regan, R. 1943. *Professional Secrecy in Light of Moral Principles.* Washington, D.C.: Augustinian Press. Cited in S. Eth. 1988. The Sexually Active, HIV Infected Patient: Confidentiality Versus the Duty to Protect. *Psychiatric Annals* 18:571–576.

Schoeman, F. 1980. Rights of Children, Rights of Parents, and the Moral Basis of the Family. *Ethics* 91:6–19.

Schoeman, F., ed. 1984a. *Philosophical Dimensions of Privacy.* New York: Cambridge University Press.

Schoeman, F. 1984c. Introduction. In F. Schoeman, ed., *Philosophical Dimensions of Privacy,* pp. 1–33.

Schoeman, F. 1989. Adolescent Confidentiality and Family Privacy. In G. Graham and H. LaFollette, eds., *Person to Person,* pp. 213–234. Philadelphia: Temple University Press.

Stone, L. 1979. *The Family, Sex, and Marriage in England, 1500–1800.* New York: Harper & Row.

Tarasoff v. Regents of the University of California. 1974. 118 *California Reporter* 129.

Tarasoff v. Regents of the University of California. 1976. 17 Cal.3d 425.

United States v. Sergeant Nathaniel Johnson, Jr. 27 M.J. 798.

Testing and Screening Programs

JAMES F. CHILDRESS

Mandatory HIV Screening and Testing

Faced with epidemics societies frequently curtail individual rights and liberties, often in ways later considered to be excessive and unnecessary. Even liberal societies

From Frederic G. Reamer, ed., *AIDS and Ethics,* copyright © 1991 Columbia University Press. This updated version of the essay is reprinted from James F. Childress, *Practical Reasoning in Bioethics* (Bloomington and Indianapolis, IN: Indiana University Press, 1997), pp. 95–118, 339–343.

have protected the public health by such measures as compulsory screening and testing, quarantine, and isolation, and contact tracing. For a liberal society — that is, a society that recognizes and protects individual rights and liberties — the difficult question is when the public health justifies overriding these rights and liberties.[1] For several years — roughly from the late 1950s to the early 1980s — the United States considered itself immune to major public health crises. Even though debates lingered about policies to control sexually transmitted diseases, these diseases were not viewed as major threats to individual or communal survival. During the same period, laws, public policies and social practices, including health care, increasingly protected various individual rights and liberties. Then came AIDS with its major threat to the public health and, upon the development in mid-1985 of tests for antibodies to the human immunodeficiency virus (HIV), calls to use these diagnostic tools to identify seropositive individuals through consensual and/or mandatory screening and testing.[2] Numerous bills were introduced in state legislatures to require testing in various context, such as application for marriage licenses, and the federal government instituted mandatory screening of selected groups, including immigrants, inmates in federal prisons, and military personnel.

Advocates of mandatory screening and testing, who often invoke the metaphor of war against AIDS, frequently fail to indicate what actions would, or should, follow the identification of HIV antibody positive individuals. Yet it is not possible to isolate mandatory (or even consensual) screening and testing from other possible interventions because, quite in contrast to a vaccine, screening and testing by themselves have no direct impact on an epidemic. What is done with the information, and with the people who test positive, will determine its effect on the AIDS epidemic. Hence, a first question for all proposed HIV antibody tests is why the information is wanted and what will be done with that information (as well as with the people who test positive). Debates have raged about whether sexual contacts should be traced, whether current sexual partners should be warned, whether certain employers should be notified, whether seropositive individuals should be quarantined, and the like. Such questions provide the backdrop for much of the debate about mandatory screening and testing.

In this essay I will assume the social and political principles and rules embedded in a liberal society, then try to determine when such a society, under the public health threat from AIDS, may justifiably resort to mandatory screening and testing for HIV antibodies, thereby overriding some of its important principles and rules. After sketching the major presumptive or prima facie principles and rules that may constrain public health efforts in a liberal society, I will identify

some conditions that need to be met to justify infringing those principles and rules in the pursuit of public health. Then I will develop a typology of screening/testing policies, stressing the distinction between consensual and man-datory screening/testing, and examine the issues raised by different policies. Throughout this discussion I will note the central role of analogical reasoning, and I will conclude with an analysis of the impact of the metaphor "war against AIDS" on our society's continuing debates about mandatory screening and testing.

A SOCIAL-ETHICAL FRAMEWORK FOR ASSESSING POLICIES OF SCREENING AND TESTING

It is not necessary to belabor why control of HIV infection and AIDS is a public health concern rather than merely a private, individual matter. AIDS is an infectious disease; people may be infected—and infectious—for many years before they become aware of their condition; there is no known cure for AIDS, which has an extremely high death rate (apparently 100 percent, given enough time); the suffering of AIDS patients and others is tremendous; the cost of caring for AIDS patients is very high; and so on. Protecting the public health, including the health of individuals, is a legitimate moral concern—even a moral imperative—based on fundamental moral principles affirmed by a liberal society, including beneficence, nonmaleficence, and justice, as well as respect for persons and their autonomy.[3] "Public health is what we, as a society, do collectively to assure the conditions in which people can be healthy. This requires that continuing and emerging threats to the health of the public be successfully countered."[4] AIDS is a paradigmatic instance of the public health threats that must be effectively countered by the society.

If the goal of controlling AIDS is a strong moral imperative for the society as well as for individuals, we have to determine which measures may and should be adopted to achieve this goal. "The AIDS virus has no civil rights"—that rhetoric often suggests that the moral imperative to control AIDS cancels all other moral imperatives. Of course, few who use this rhetoric attempt to justify compulsory universal screening accompanied by mass quarantine or even mass slaughter. Even so, their position rarely takes seriously enough other significant moral principles and rules, also embedded in a liberal society's laws, policies, and practices. I want to examine some of those principles and rules and sketch what they imply for public policies to control this infectious disease. This argument hinges on the best available scientific and medical information, including evidence that the spread of AIDS usually involves consensual, intimate contact, in the form of sexual activity or sharing intravenous drug needles and syringes, and that casual contact is not a mode of transmission. A different set of facts could justify different screening and testing policies. (Below I will indicate where my judgments about particular policies have been revised since the publication of the original version of this essay because of changes in scientific and medical evidence; the main example appears in maternal-fetal screening and testing because of the evidence that AZT substantially reduces the risk of maternal-fetal HIV transmission.) Indeed, different policies may be justified for HIV infection and tuberculosis because of differences in modes and ease of transmission, in risks to more casual contacts, and in treatments.[5]

The principle of respect for persons is a primary principle in the ethical framework of a liberal society.[6] It implies that we should not treat people merely as means to ends. From this principle (and others) we can derive more specific rules that also direct and limit policies. Three such roles are especially important for this analysis: rules of liberty, including freedom of association; rules of privacy, including bodily integrity and decisional space; and rules of confidentiality. The principle of respect for persons and its derivative rules can be stated as individual rights or as societal obligations and duties—for example, the individual's right to privacy or the society's obligation not to violate an individual's privacy. Even if some of these rules are independent rather than derived, they are closely related to personal autonomy—for instance, the individual can autonomously waive the rights expressed in the rules or, perhaps more accurately, can exercise those rights by yielding liberty or privacy or by granting access to previously confidential information. Furthermore, in a liberal society, overriding the principle of respect for autonomy and these rules can be justified more easily to protect others than to protect the agent himself or herself. Thus, there is a strong suspicion of paternalism, which infringes these principles and rules to protect the agent rather than others.[7] (Of course, the goals of intervention are often mixed.) Rather than offering a theoretical foundation for the principle of respect for autonomy and various derivative rules, I will assume that they can be discerned in our constitution, laws, policies, and practices—in short, in the social ethics or political morality operative in a liberal society.

CONDITIONS FOR OVERRIDING PRIMA FACIE PRINCIPLES AND RULES

Which, if any, policies of mandatory screening and testing for HIV antibodies can be ethically justified in a liberal society in view of its moral obligation to control AIDS and its other moral principles and rules? In order to answer this question we have to determine both what these principles and rules mean and how much weight they have relative to other principles and rules. (For brevity I will sometimes use "principles" or "rules" to cover both principles and rules.) Some apparent violations of rules may not really be violations; upon closer inspection they may turn out to be consistent with the rules properly interpreted. And none of these rules is absolute—each one can be justifiably overridden in order to protect the public health under some conditions. However, in a liberal society these principles and rules are more than mere maxims or rule of thumb that yield to any and every utilitarian objection. If these principles and rules are not absolute or mere maxims, is there an alternative conception of their weight or stringency? They may be construed as prima facie binding, that is, they have heavy moral weight or strong binding power in and of themselves. Because they are morally weighty and binding, other things being equal, it is necessary to justify any departures from them, and the process of justification involves meeting a significant burden of proof.[8]

At least five conditions must be met to justify infringements of these rules.[9] These conditions, which will be called *justificatory conditions,* are effectiveness, proportionality, necessity, least infringement, and explanation and justification to the parties protected by the rules. They express the logic of prima facie duties or rights, that is, how principles and rules with such weight or strength are to be approached, as well as the substance of liberal principles and rules. A presupposition of these justificatory conditions is that the goal—both expressed and latent—is to protect public health, that is, the health of the community and the individuals within it, rather than to express moralistic judgments about individuals and their conduct or to exclude seropositive individuals from the community by subjecting them to discrimination or denying them access to needed services.[10]

First, it is necessary to show that infringing these rules will probably realize the goal of protecting public health. This first condition is one of effectiveness. A policy that cannot realize its public-health goal and also infringes these moral rules simply has no justification—it is arbitrary and capricious. An ineffective policy to control HIV infection that does not infringe these (or other) moral rules may be wasteful, unwise, and even stupid, but if it infringes moral rules, there is, in addition, a decisive moral argument against it.

Second, it is necessary to show that the probable benefits of a policy infringing these moral rules outweigh both the rules infringed and any negative consequences. This condition, which may be called proportionality, is complex, for it involves considering not only the weight of the infringed moral rule but also other harms, costs, and burdens that may flow from the infringement. For example, it is necessary to consider not only the weight or strength of the rule of privacy but also other probable negative effects, such as discrimination, that may befall the one whose privacy is infringed. (As I will argue later, in order to justify policies that *impose* community, it may also be essential to *express* community through measures to avoid or reduce such negative consequences. Indeed, if community is expressed through such measures, it may be unnecessary to impose community.)

Third, it is not sufficient to meet the first two conditions of effectiveness and proportionality and thus to show that infringement of these rules will produce better consequences for more people. As prima facie binding, these rules direct us to seek alternative ways to realize the end of public health before infringing the rules. For example, if it is possible to protect the public health without infringing liberty and privacy (and other moral rules), then the society should do so. This condition is one of necessity, last resort, or lack of a feasible alternative. Priority belongs to policies that do not infringe the rules of liberty, privacy, and confidentiality. Thus, policies that seek to *educate* people about acting in certain ways have moral priority over policies that *force* people to act in certain ways. However, under some circumstances, where coercive policies would be effective and proportionate, they can be justified if they are also necessary means to protect the public health. Many of the proposed policies of mandatory screening fail this third test.

Fourth, even when a liberal society is justified in infringing its own moral rules to protect the public health, it is obligated to seek policies that least infringe its rules. Only the degree or extent of infringement that is necessary to realize the important end can be justified. For example, when liberty is at stake, the liberal society should seek the least restrictive alternative; when privacy is at stake, it should seek the least intrusive and invasive alternative; and when confidentiality is at stake, it should disclose only the amount and kind of information needed for effective action. This fourth condition may be called that of "least infringement."

Finally, even when a public policy that infringes one or more moral rules satisfies all four prior conditions, the underlying principle of respect for persons may generate additional requirements. This principle may, for instance, require informing those whose liberty, privacy, and confidential relations are infringed. In many cases, such as coercive screening for HIV antibody, where blood has not already been drawn for other purposes, the infringements will be evident to the parties affected. However, this may not be true in all cases, especially if secrecy or deception is involved. In some contexts, as Sissela Bok notes, secret or deceptive actions may be more disrespectful and insulting to the parties affected than coercive actions.[11] Hence, the society may have a duty to disclose, and even to justify, the actions to the person and perhaps even sometimes to undertake compensatory measures. Even if it is essential to infringe a person's rights to protect the public health, that person should not be reduced to a mere means to the goal of public health. This crucial point can also be stated through an image drawn from Robert Nozick: Overridden moral principles and rules leave "moral traces."[12] They do not evaporate or simply disappear when they are justifiably overridden—they are outweighed, not canceled. And they may require subsequent corrective or compensatory actions.

As is true of much moral, political, and legal reasoning, this process of reasoning about the justification of mandatory HIV antibody tests is to a great extent analogical. The principle of universalizability or formal justice requires treating similar cases in a similar way. Hence it is necessary to consider the relevant similarities and differences among candidate targets for screening, not only for HIV antibodies but also for other conditions, such as genetic ones. Reasoning in a liberal society certainly considers precedent cases—for example, the relevant similarities and differences between HIV antibody screening and other mandatory screening policies that have been held to be justifiable—but also the precedents mandatory HIV antibody screening would create. "HIV and AIDS must not be treated in isolation," Margaret Somerville argues; "comparison with analogous situations is mandatory."[13]

In addition to formal justice, material criteria of justice, also embedded in a liberal society, are relevant to assessments of public policies of screening and testing that override the prima facie rules of liberty, privacy, and confidentiality. Standards of justice, in both broad and narrow senses, serve as the backdrop for debates about such policies and provide specific challenges to some actual and proposed policies, particularly because of discrimination, procedural deficiencies, the maldistribution of benefits and burdens, and the like. One of the major negative social effects of breaches of confidentiality about HIV infection is discrimination in various settings, such as housing.

MAJOR TYPES OF SCREENING/TESTING POLICIES

In order to apply the principle of respect for personal autonomy and its derivative rules—all conceived as prima facie binding—along with the conditions for justifying their infringement, it is necessary to identify the main types of proposed policies of mandatory screening and testing for HIV antibodies. The following chart indicates some of the most important options: Policies of screening/testing may be consensual or compulsory, and universal or selective.

Screening/Testing Policies

| | | Degree of Voluntariness | |
		Consensual	Compulsory
Extent of Screening	Universal	1	2
	Selective	3	4

The term "screening" usually refers to testing groups, while the term "testing" usually refers to testing individuals. However, even in mass screening, the individual is tested as part of the targeted group. Thus, I will continue to use both terms as appropriate without drawing a sharp distinction between them. A more important distinction concerns the *scope* of the screening or testing: Is it universal or selective?

UNIVERSAL SCREENING

There is simply no adequate justification for *universal screening,* whether voluntary or compulsory. Even serious proposals for widespread screening usually fall short of universal screening. For example, Rhame and Maki have recommended "HIV testing vigorously to all U.S. adults under the age of sixty regardless of their reported risk history."[14] The arguments against universal screening are compelling: Universal screening is not necessary to protect the public health; HIV infection is not widespread outside groups engaging in high risk activities; screening in groups or areas with low seroprevalence produces a high rate of false positives; universal screening would be very costly and would not be cost effective—the funds could be spent more effectively on education; and its potential negative effects, including discrimination, would outweigh any potential benefits. It is not even justifiable to encourage everyone to be tested.

If universal consensual screening is not justifiable, there is, a fortiori, no justification for universal compulsory screening since it would infringe the principle of respect for autonomy and the rules of liberty and privacy (and probably confidentiality) without compensating benefit. The main rationale for compulsory universal screening is that seropositive individuals could then reduce risks to others. While there is evidence of some individual behavior change following disclosure of seropositivity, especially with counseling,[15] there is no evidence that mandatory testing would produce equivalent voluntary change in taking risks and in subjecting others to risk.[16]

Identification of and disclosure to the individuals who are seropositive do not necessarily translate into benefits for others, without additional interventions. And appropriate education and counseling, apart from mandatory testing, could be effective ways to realize the same end, especially because universal precautions are recommended in risky situations whether a person is seropositive or seronegative.[17] In light of the current scientific and medical evidence, compulsory universal screening thus fails to meet the five conditions identified earlier for justified breaches of relevant moral principles and rules. Universal precautions, pursued through education, are morally preferable to mandatory universal screening, and the latter is not demonstrably more effective and would, in addition, produce some serious negative consequences.

SELECTIVE SCREENING

Consensual or voluntary selective screening may appear to pose no moral problems. However, it does raise some important questions—for example, who should be encouraged to be tested, who should bear the costs, what sort of pretest and posttest counseling should be provided, and what conditions make the decision to have the test a rational one. Individuals making rational choices will consent to testing only when they perceive a favorable risk-benefit ratio. And "more than most medical tests, HIV screening has major benefits and harms that must be weighed."[18] In all risk-benefit analyses, the comparison is between the probability of harm of some magnitude and the probability of benefit of some magnitude. Perhaps because "risk" is a probabilistic term, while "benefit" is not, risk-benefit analyses sometimes neglect to determine both the probability and the magnitude of both benefits and harms of proposed policies, which any adequate analysis must include.

If we assume the accuracy of the test results, the possible *benefits* of testing to *seronegative* individuals include reassurance, the possibility of making future plans, and the motivation to make behavioral changes to prevent infection, while the possible *benefits* to *seropositive* individuals include closer medical follow-up, including prognoses at various stages, earlier use of AZT (and any other treatments), prophylaxis or other care for associated diseases, protection of loved ones, and clearer plans for the future. There appear to be no *harms* to *seronegative* individuals, if we assume the accuracy of the test results, while there are major *risks* to *seropositive* individuals.[19] These risks may be identified as both psychological and social (with considerable overlap and interaction). The psychological risks include anxiety and depression—followed by a higher rate of suicide than for the population at large[20]—while the social risks include stigma, discrimination, and breaches of confidentiality.

Clearly the society can have a major impact on the risk-benefit analyses of potential candidates for voluntary testing. On the one hand, the medical benefits of early diagnosis are possible only if seropositive individuals have adequate access to health care. Hence, even on the benefit side, the problem is not merely medical, because of the social problem of access to health care. On the other hand, the risks can be greatly reduced by societal decisions to allocate funds and to establish strong rules to protect individual rights and liberties. The society should provide resources for pretest and posttest counseling both to help the indi-

vidual and also to reduce risks to others, and it should protect discrimination in such areas as housing, employment, and insurance. Without such societal support and protection, the risks of the test may outweigh its benefits, including any medical benefits, for rational individuals.

If voluntary or consensual testing of selected groups can be effective, in some contexts, then there is no justification for compulsory screening of those groups. The liberal justificatory framework imposes this necessary condition: Moral principles and rules are not to be infringed if the same important ends—in this case, the public health—can be realized without their infringement. Furthermore, the society may even have to bear additional costs to protect its important principles and rules.

The requirement, expressed by the terms "mandatory" and "compulsory," may be imposed on the one to be tested or on the tester or on both. For example, in the context of screening blood donated for transfusions, the term "mandatory" refers in the first instance to the obligation imposed on organizations collecting blood. And such "mandatory" screening may be imposed or only permitted by the state. The one area of mandatory selective screening that is morally settled and uncontroversial is screening all donated (or sold) blood, organs, sperm, and ova, in part because recipients cannot take other measures to protect themselves. In this area universal precautions cannot work without screening and testing.

Many policies of screening are actually mixes of voluntary actions and compulsory actions, as is evident in programs of screening donated blood. While individuals can choose to donate blood or not, their blood will be tested if they do donate. Another good example is the policy of screening recruits into the military. The U.S. armed forces now consist of volunteers, who are tested for HIV antibodies upon entry (and then again at least once a year). It could be argued that volunteers for the armed forces consent to HIV testing, because they voluntarily enter an institution where screening is compulsory, and that the mandatory screening thus does not violate any of the volunteers' rights. This argument has merit, but it does not adequately address the question whether the society can justify its policy by the conditions identified earlier. The major express justification is that each member of the armed forces is a potential donor of blood for transfusions on the battlefield hence the rationale is comparable to the one that governs screening donated blood. Even if this rationale is solid, along with the rationale of protecting HIV-infected people from live virus vaccines used in the armed forces, there is also reason to suspect that the military's homophobia was a factor in the decision. Furthermore, there is concern about the precedent this mandatory screening creates, especially when, as sometimes happens, proponents also appeal to the cost of future health care for HIV-infected former members of the armed forces.[21]

Voluntariness may be compromised in various ways. We tend to think of coercion as the major compromise of voluntariness — for example, forcing someone to undergo a test for HIV antibodies. However, conditional requirements — if you want X, then you have to do Y — may also be morally problematic. For example, requiring HIV antibody testing as a condition for some strongly desired benefit, such as a marriage license, may constitute an undue incentive, even if it is not, strictly speaking, coercive because the person can choose to decline the benefit.[22] One important question then is whether it is fair to impose the condition, even if the person is free to take it or leave it. This question expresses the important general point that selection of targets for mandatory screening — or even for voluntary screening — is in part a matter of justice in the distribution of benefits and burdens[23] and that not all important moral issues are reducible to a determination of the voluntariness of choices. The justificatory conditions identified earlier serve as important selection criteria.

Nevertheless, because of the centrality of the principle of respect for personal autonomy in a liberal framework, it is not surprising that consent plays such an important role in the analysis and assessment of screening policies. When an individual gives valid consent to testing, there is no violation of his or her personal autonomy and liberty of action. Nor does consensual testing violate the rule of privacy, for the individual voluntarily surrenders some of his or her privacy. And, finally, if a person grants others access to the information about his or her HIV antibody status, the rule of confidentiality is not violated. In a liberal framework, valid consent creates rights that did not previously exist. (I will use the terms "voluntary" testing and "consensual" testing interchangeably to refer to testing with the individual's voluntary, informed consent — it is irrelevant, for our purposes, whether he or she requested the test or only accepted a recommended test.)

What counts as consent? This question becomes important because people have been held to consent in various ways, not simply by express oral or written statements. And some varieties of consent have even been invoked to override a person's express wishes and choices. I shall discuss this topic in the context of screening hospital patients for HIV antibodies. One difficult question is whether the institutional rules of consent should be structured to authorize HIV antibody testing without express, specific consent.

VARIETIES OF CONSENT IN THE CONTEXT OF SCREENING HOSPITAL PATIENTS

The term "routine" often covers several types of screening and testing. However, this term is seriously misleading without further qualification, for its ethical significance is unclear until we can determine whether the screening will be done routinely, without notice or the possibility of refusal, or whether it will be offered routinely with the possibility of refusal.[24]

When a hospital patient consents to HIV antibody testing after being informed about the risks and benefits of the test — including whether the intended benefits are primarily for the patient or for care givers — there is no breach of moral principles. But are there forms of consent in addition to express and specific oral or written consent that can create rights on the part of hospitals to test patients who have not provided specific, express consent?

Consider, first, *tacit consent,* a favorite tool of political theorists in the contract tradition. Tacit consent is expressed silently or passively by omissions or by failure to indicate or signify dissent.[25] If a newly admitted hospital patient is silent when told that the HIV antibody test will be performed, along with other tests, unless he objects, his silence may constitute valid (though tacit) consent, as long as there is understanding and voluntariness — the same conditions that are important for express oral or written consent. According to some interpreters, even if a patient is not notified of or given any information about the test, his or her failure to dissent from the test may be *presumed* to be consent on the basis of a presumed general understanding of hospital testing policy. However, its moral validity as consent is suspect, despite the patient's right to dissent or opt out.

Whereas tacit consent or presumed consent is expressed through failures to dissent, *implied* or implicit consent is, in part, inferred from actions. Consent to a specific action may be implied by general consent to professional authority or by consent to a set of actions. Does a person's voluntary admission to the hospital imply consent to the HIV antibody test without express consent? Again much will depend on the patient's understanding. However, rather than relying on a general consent or consent to several tests, hospitals should be obligated to seek specific, express consent for HIV antibody tests because of the psychological and social risks of the tests and their results.

There are two major reasons for explicit, specific disclosure and explicit, specific consent. On the one hand, the diagnostic or therapeutic procedure may be invasive — for example, drawing blood. However, if a patient has consented to blood drawing for various tests to determine his or her medical condition, there is no additional invasion of his or her body to test that blood for HIV antibodies. Then the second major reason for specific disclosure and consent enters — the risk to the patient. Even where the blood has already been drawn, the test has the psychological and social risks noted above, and explicit, specific consent should be sought.[26] (This argument does not exclude the possibility and justifiability of unlinked testing of blood samples in the hospital in order to determine seroprevalence as part of epidemiological studies, since such studies do not involve psychological and social risks.)

A Virginia law (Virginia Code 32.1–45.21) invokes "deemed consent" in permitting a health care provider to test a patient's blood, without specific consent, following the provider's exposure to the patient's body fluids under circumstances where HIV infection might be spread. In such a case, "the patient whose body fluids were involved in the exposures shall be deemed to have consented to testing for infection with human immunodeficiency virus (and) to have consented to the release of such test results to the person who was exposed." The law assigns health care providers the responsibility, in other than emergency circumstances, to inform patients of this provision of deemed consent prior to the provision of health care services. Presumably, the patient's acceptance of health care following disclosure of this statutory provision counts as, or is deemed to be, consent. Even if such consent is valid, the fairness of imposing this condition remains an important question.

Because consent is so important an implication of the principle of respect for personal autonomy, we often resort to fictions such as deemed consent or an-

other variety of consent even when they do not appear to constitute valid consent. We tend to extend the meaning of rules of consent and of the principle of respect for personal autonomy in order to avoid conflicts with our other moral principles. Such fictions may, however, obscure important moral conflicts. It may be more defensible, for instance, for the society to indicate that it believes it can justifiably *override* a patient's autonomy, liberty, privacy, and confidentiality in order to obtain and provide information about an individual's HIV antibody status to a health care provider who has been exposed to the risk of infection in the provision of care. A fiction such as deemed consent may appear defensible in part because it incorporates the patient into a larger moral community of shared concern, but this does not negate the cost of the fiction.

There is evidence that hospitals sometimes test patients for HIV antibodies without their consent (and without providing information about actions to reduce risks).[27] In general, hospitals are not justified in testing patients for HIV antibodies without specific consent, either to benefit the patients themselves or to enable caregivers to take extra precautions. Information that a patient is seronegative may create false security on the part of the professionals in view of the long period that may elapse between exposure to HIV and the development of antibodies. Thus, the best protection, though not an inexpensive or perfect one, is offered by universal precautions. According to one study, there is no evidence "that preoperative testing for HIV infection would reduce the frequency of accidental exposures to blood."[28]

Where exposure has already occurred, and the blood is not available for testing, it is very difficult to justify forcible extraction of the patient's blood to test for HIV antibodies to reduce the caregiver's anxieties. Where the blood is already available, it is easier to justify testing after exposure, even against the patient's wishes. However, the analogy with the hepatitis B virus argues against mandatory testing, whether before or after exposure.[29] One ethically acceptable possibility would be to obtain patients' advance express consent — not merely deemed consent — to testing if accidental exposure occurs. (I will discuss testing health care professionals below.)

PREMARITAL SCREENING

State-mandated premarital screening for HIV antibodies also mixes voluntary choices with compulsory screening: While individuals choose to apply for marriage licenses, the test is required as a condition of application. Debates about such a policy often invoke historical analogies. For example, Gary Bauer, former assistant to President Reagan for Policy Development, uses mandatory premarital screening as an example of the "routine testing" that is similar to measures taken in the past to deal with threatening epidemics. And he argues that mandatory premarital screening for syphilis contributed to a "sharp reduction in the infant mortality rate from syphilis."[30] By contrast, Larry O. Gostin contends that "statutes for syphilis screening were largely regarded as a failed experiment" and notes they have been repealed by most states.[31]

The analogy with screening for syphilis is interesting in part because, in contrast to HIV infection, syphilis is treatable and infected individuals can be rendered noninfectious. Many argue that it is even more imperative to require premarital HIV tests as a condition for marriage licenses because there is no cure for AIDS, a fatal disease. By contrast, opponents contend that the absence of effective treatment is a good reason not to require the tests. Because antibiotics can cure syphilis, it is justifiable to withhold a marriage license until there is proof of a cure, but "it would be contrary to public policy to bar marriage to seropositive individuals," who cannot now be cured.[32]

Legislatures (Illinois and Louisiana) that passed statues mandating premarital screening subsequently rescinded those statutes, largely on grounds that they were not cost effective. A report on the first six months of experience in Illinois indicated that only eight of 70,846 applicants for marriage licenses were found to be seropositive, while the cost of the testing program for that period was estimated at $2.5 million, or $312,000 for each seropositive individual identified.[33] Furthermore, half of those identified as seropositive admitted having engaged in risky behavior and could probably have been identified more efficiently through voluntary programs aimed at populations with a higher seroprevalence rate. Illinois also experienced a 22.5 percent decrease (a total of approximately 10,300) in the number of marriage licenses, while neighboring states granted licenses to a significantly larger number of Illinois residents than usual. Since the applicants had to cover the costs of the tests, the state of Illinois did not have to determine the most cost-effective ways to spend public money and make trade-offs.[34] However, Illinois did lose the revenue from marriage licenses, estimated at $77,250 for six months. The authors conclude what policy analysts had predicted prior

to the experiment: "The Illinois experience with premarital testing provides a strong argument against widespread or publicly supported HIV antibody screening of low prevalence populations."[35]

While many of the proposed policies of compulsory selective screening fail the test of necessity because there are viable alternatives, the policy of mandatory premarital screening also fails to meet the conditions of effectiveness and proportionality. There is no evidence that the screening program prevented any additional illnesses or that it was a "rational or effective public health policy."[36] It mistakenly assumed that sexual relations only begin after the marriage, and it may even have been counterproductive in driving some couples away from the institution of marriage. Furthermore, the costs may have kept some low-income people from applying for marriage licenses. Finally, the important public health objective of protecting spouses (and future offspring) can be pursued in other ways that will not compromise respect for personal autonomy and yet will probably be more effective and cost effective—for instance, providing information about HIV risks and providing of voluntary testing with counseling, perhaps free of charge, to all applicants for marriage licenses. The context of applying for a marriage license appears to be an appropriate one "for promoting individual HIV risk assessment with educational materials."[37]

SCREENING PREGNANT WOMEN AND NEWBORNS

One major goal of premarital screening is to prevent infected offspring of the marriage. In the United States approximately four million women give birth each year. Of those, an estimated 7,000 are infected with HIV, and perhaps 2,000 of their children will be HIV infected. Studies investigating the mechanisms of maternal-fetal HIV transmission identify two major factors: the level of virus in the pregnant woman's blood, and birth events that expose infants to maternal blood.[38]

Because mandatory premarital screening programs are failures, because voluntary premarital screening is limited, and because HIV infections may occur after marriage, many have proposed screening pregnant women and newborns at least in selected settings. Since all fifty states and the District of Columbia mandate neonatal screening for several diseases, the question arises: Why not treat HIV "just like any other disease"? Even if HIV infection were strictly analogous to these other medical conditions, such as phenylketonuria (PKU), Kathleen Nolan notes that it would be difficult to determine what it would mean to treat HIV infection "just like any other disease," because states have a wide variety of laws — for example, there is no condition for which all states mandate screening, and many states allow parental refusal.[39] Furthermore, HIV infection differs from most other diseases because of its social risks. For example, so-called "boarder babies" cannot leave the hospital because no one will take these HIV-infected babies. Hence, HIV infection, Nolan argues, is best viewed as a "separate case."

Still within the context of analogical reasoning, Nolan identifies three criteria for justifying neonatal *genetic* screening: (1) the seriousness of the genetic condition; (2) availability of presymptomatic interventions that effectively prevent serious injury; and (3) an acceptable benefit-cost ratio. While HIV infection clearly satisfies the first criterion, it did not clearly satisfy the other two in neonatal cases, at least until the mid-1990s, except where there were specific reasons for testing — and parents usually consent under those circumstances. (Furthermore, neonatal and infant screening, for over a year, will reflect maternal antibodies without specifically indicating neonatal or infant infection.) In summary, Nolan argued, "calls for mandatory neonatal screening emerge primarily from beneficent clinical attitudes towards newborns, and they are rejected primarily on the grounds that not enough benefit accrues at present to justify overriding parental autonomy and family values."[40] The situation changed significantly with convincing evidence about ways to reduce the risk of maternal-fetal HIV transmission, but there is still considerable debate about whether it changed enough to warrant mandatory neonatal screening or prenatal testing.

Up to 1994, the following argument against mandatory prenatal testing, here presented in summary form, was quite persuasive: Mandatory prenatal testing to protect offspring appears relatively ineffective because nothing can be done to prevent the infection of the fetus; it is morally controversial because abortion is the only way to prevent another HIV-infected infant and yet only 25–40 percent of the offspring of HIV-infected pregnant women are also infected; and it is potentially counterproductive because it drives pregnant women away from settings where HIV screening is compulsory. The most defensible policy — because the most respectful of pregnant women's autonomy and also the most productive of desirable consequences — was to offer pregnant women, in high seroprevalence areas or with risk factors, prenatal testing for HIV with adequate information so that they could make their own decisions, with appropriate pretest and posttest counseling and support services.[41]

Then in 1994 a clinical trial established a way to reduce the risk of maternal-fetal HIV transmission. In a major multicenter, randomized, double-blind, placebo-controlled trial, HIV-infected women with CD4 counts greater than 200, who were symptom-free and who had not received zidovudine (AZT) earlier, received AZT (or a placebo) during pregnancy and during labor, and their infants received AZT for the first six weeks of life. This trial was terminated early (at the first interim analysis) on ethical grounds because of the great disparity between HIV transmission in the placebo and AZT groups: Thirteen babies (9.3 percent) in the AZT group and forty (25.5 percent) in the placebo group were HIV infected, as determined by at least one viral culture. Hence, AZT reduced the risk of maternal-fetal transmission by 67.5 percent.[42]

These scientific data presented challenges to the dominant approaches to both neonatal and prenatal screening and testing. Much of the subsequent controversy centered on anonymous newborn screening. For several years the Centers for Disease Control and Prevention (CDC) had supported state health departments around the country — forty-five states in all participated — in the epidemiological surveillance of HIV infection by testing, anonymously, blood samples from patients in hospitals, clinics, and emergency rooms. This program did not require specific informed consent because the blood samples were taken for other purposes (and thus involved no additional bodily invasions) and because they were stripped of identifiers (and thus did not subject patients to additional social risks). Furthermore, efforts to secure specific consent would have precluded universal testing in the relevant institutions, and mandatory testing could not be ethically justified because of the conditions identified earlier. Many concurred that such blinded surveillance satisfied both ethical and legal standards.

Furthermore, this blinded surveillance program produced important data about the incidence of HIV infection, including the rate of maternal-fetal HIV transmission, which could then be used to shape more effective policies and practices. Neonates' blood samples are available because of various state-mandated neonatal tests. However, because these samples are tested anonymously, the women whose babies are HIV infected (and who are themselves infected) cannot be notified, in contrast to the approach taken to most other diseases. (Of course, these women may already know — or may subsequently learn — that they are HIV positive from other sources, including voluntary testing.) One rationale for CDC's approach is that testing infants is a surrogate test for their mothers because all babies born to HIV-infected women test positive at birth because of the presence of their mother's antibodies, even though many of the babies are not actually HIV infected.

Critics charged that this information could and should be used to help infants and their mothers and thus needed to be unblinded. As a consequence, a bill ("The Newborn Infant Notification Act") was introduced into Congress to prohibit anonymous tests of blood samples drawn from newborns and to authorize screening only when it would be possible to notify mothers of HIV-positive babies. In response, the CDC announced that it would suspend its tests.

The congressional bill generated wide support as a way to protect mothers and children, and CDC's recent practice, according to many critics, appeared to be similar to the notorious Tuskegee syphilis experiment, in which African-American men were left untreated, even after the availability of penicillin, a safe and effective treatment, in order to determine the natural history of untreated syphilis. Although the Nazi analogy is more widely used to oppose various research projects, the Tuskegee syphilis experiment analogy is also powerful where information is generated that either cannot be or is not shared with patients or other subjects.

Pediatrician Arthur Amman, for instance, insists that the "maintenance of anonymous test results at a time when treatment and prevention are readily available will be recorded in history as analogous to the Tuskegee 'experiment.'"[43] However, Ronald Bayer disputes the analogy: "In the case of Tuskegee, individuals who were known to be afflicted with syphilis were willfully deprived of that knowledge," and public health officials conspired to "prevent those impoverished African American men from knowing about their situation or about the availability of therapy." Such a situation differs greatly from blinded surveillance of HIV infection. "To compare blinded surveillance for HIV infection to Tuskegee," Bayer continues, "is to threaten the interest of the mothers and babies who could benefit from carefully targeted efforts to identify those in need of care. Clever political slogans about the right of mothers to

know about their babies' lethal infections should not serve to justify an attack on studies that have proved so invaluable in the past and that remain crucial today."[44] We should, Bayer argues, vigorously encourage voluntary HIV testing and yet also retain the anonymous surveillance studies to guide effective public health efforts. Furthermore, since AZT can reduce the risk of transmission of HIV from pregnant women to their offspring, it is important to use resources to encourage testing prior to birth. And women and babies who are identified as seropositive through voluntary testing need to have access to various clinical and social services.

Even with the new data about the value of AZT to reduce maternal-fetal HIV transmission, the most defensible approach to protect offspring remains voluntary prenatal (and neonatal) testing, with all the necessary support, for all pregnant women. In contrast to its earlier recommendation of voluntary testing for pregnant women at high risk of infection, such as intravenous drug users and prostitutes, the CDC in mid-1995 issued guidelines to set a new standard of prenatal care: All pregnant women should be offered a test, following counseling, to determine whether they are HIV infected. And women who do not receive prenatal care should be offered HIV testing for themselves or their infants after delivery.

Such efforts to reduce maternal-fetal HIV transmission are not unproblematic, particularly in relation to other possible priorities, such as preventing HIV infection in women and detecting HIV infection in women early and facilitating pregnancy prevention. One major concern involves the unknown long-term effects [of AZT] on children, especially since 60 to 75 percent of the children of HIV-infected mothers would not be infected even without AZT. In addition, from a public health standpoint, concerns emerge about producing AZT-resistant strains of HIV through its increased use. And, finally, the cost of AZT is beyond the reach of many women who are HIV infected.[45]

Such concerns, along with persistent social risks, further support a pregnant woman's voluntary decision to undergo or decline testing and to accept or refuse AZT therapy. In addition, her decision to accept AZT therapy will obviously depend, in many cases, on the availability of insurance or other financial resources to cover its costs. Voluntary prenatal testing followed by a recommendation of AZT therapy will be ineffective without the necessary funds. Here again it is crucial for public policies to *express* community. Even efforts to *impose* community through mandatory prenatal and neonatal testing will be ineffective without the expression of community through policies to fund AZT and other needed care.

Much of the debate about mandatory and voluntary testing hinges on claims that some women, perhaps especially black and Hispanic women, who account for 75 percent of all AIDS cases among women in the United States, will avoid care if they know that they will be subjected to mandatory testing for HIV infection. Whatever the outcome of this debate, which often follows ideological lines, it is difficult to justify mandatory testing without asking about the availability of resources for AZT and other care, and it is difficult to justify mandatory testing when there is evidence that pregnant women will accept prenatal testing when it is offered in certain contexts and certain ways. Variations in the rate of acceptance appear to be correlated with such factors as perceived risk of infection, the risk of social discrimination, and whether testing is universally and routinely offered to all or only to a targeted high-risk population. According to one study of poor pregnant women in Baltimore, 91 percent consented to be tested when they could view it as part of routine treatment, which they could accept or decline.[46]

In conclusion, it is also important — as this analysis suggests and as Nolan reminds us — to consider whether we are following defensible precedents (historical analogies) for genetic diseases and what precedents our policies regarding HIV testing may set for other genetic diseases that in the future can be detected in utero. Indeed, she notes, our different responses to cystic fibrosis and HIV infection suggest that morally extraneous factors such as race and geography play significant parts in our societal and professional judgments, particularly in the movement from nondirective to directive counseling (for example, at least prior to 1994, counselors appeared to be more directive in urging HIV-infected women to abort).

PRISONERS AND OTHERS IN STATE CUSTODY

Mandatory screening might appear to be justified in several institutional settings, mainly custodial settings, such as prisons and institutions for the mentally infirm or mentally ill. I will concentrate on prisoners, with brief attention to arrested prostitutes and patients in public psychiatric facilities.

Many prisoners have been subjected to mandatory screening because of the risk of rape and the frequency of consensual sexual intercourse in prisons where there is also high seroprevalence. Evidence indicates that HIV transmission is not uncommon in prisons. According to the authors of one study of hundreds of prisoners incarcerated in the Florida state prison system since the late 1970s, "the discovery of HIV-positive individuals in a long-term, continuously incarcerated population is strong, though presumptive, evidence for intraprison transmission of HIV infection."[47] Even if mandatory screening of prisoners, followed by quarantine or isolation, could reduce the spread of HIV infection, it is not clearly cost-effective and it imposes risks of injustice on seropositive prisoners, "ranging from unequal facilities for inmates to violations of a number of hard-won rights of prisoners."[48] Furthermore, it is not the least intrusive or restrictive alternative. Indeed, on grounds of respect for persons, as well as other moral principles, it is crucial for the society to reduce nonconsensual sexual intercourse in prisons.[49] It is also important to educate prisoners — and perhaps even to provide condoms — to reduce the risk of transmission of HIV through consensual sexual activities. Even providing voluntary testing may be useful. According to one study in Oregon, "two-thirds of all inmates, including those at highest risk for HIV, sought HIV counseling and testing when given the opportunity."[50] Nevertheless, as Ruth Macklin rightly argues, "it would not be unethical to subject to a blood test any prisoner who has sexually assaulted another inmate, and if he is found seropositive, to isolate him permanently from the general prison population."[51]

Similarly, it would not be unethical, in terms of the principles of a liberal society, to confine a recalcitrant prostitute who puts others at serious risk, for example, by continuing to practice unsafe sex. A more difficult question is whether it is justifiable to require prostitutes to undergo HIV testing. Although prostitution is widely viewed as a major route for the spread of HIV infection among heterosexuals, Martha Field argues that the overall HIV infection rate among prostitutes does not justify targeting them for mandatory testing, that prostitutes tend to be well informed about safe sex practices, and that over 99 percent of all prostitutes are never arrested. Thus, mandatory testing of prostitutes does not appear to satisfy the conditions identified earlier. However, if states pass laws to require prostitutes to be tested when in state custody, Field views two conditions as essential. First, testing should be required only of those who are convicted, because of the legal presumption of innocence. Second, patrons should be tested if prostitutes are tested—"although patrons are seldom arrested or convicted, both parties are guilty of criminal behavior that is capable of transmission."[52]

Patients in state psychiatric institutions may also be at risk of transmitting HIV infection through sexual intercourse. As in the case of prisoners, the state should attempt to prevent rape in psychiatric institutions—and not only because of the risk of HIV infection. Since many psychiatric patients are unable to benefit from education about HIV infection and safe sex, there may be a stronger argument than in some other contexts for identifying and isolating HIV-infected patients. Even so, it is necessary to make sure that there are no other effective alternatives and to choose the least restrictive alternative.

IMMIGRATION AND INTERNATIONAL TRAVEL

"Seeking to secure our national borders against an 'invasion' of AIDS," Carol Wolchok writes, "the United States now requires HIV antibody testing of 500,000 immigrants, nonimmigrants, and refugees annually. In addition, in what may be the most massive use of HIV testing in this country, more than 2.5 million aliens living in the United States must be tested in order to qualify for legal residence."[53] Historically, societies have responded to epidemics by closing their borders, but the current U.S. policy is ironic because the United States is probably a net exporter of HIV infection. Nevertheless, HIV infection was added to the list of designated diseases (now eight, including infectious leprosy, active tuberculosis, gonorrhea, and infectious syphilis) for which aliens can be excluded from the United States. In view of the precedent set by listing the other exclusionary diseases, it did not seem to many to be unreasonable to add HIV infection. Now temporary visitors to the United States have to indicate their HIV antibody status when they apply for a visa, and the immigration officer may require a test. Applicants for permanent residence must undergo a serologic test for HIV infection (and syphilis) and if positive cannot receive permanent residence. Because the costs of the program fall on the applicants, the society does not have to face the question of trade-offs in the use of public funds.

Analogical reasoning is also significant here, not only in considering historical precedents but also in considering the implications of the mandatory screening of aliens for the other groups in the society. As Margaret Somerville notes, viewing prospective immigrants who are HIV infected as "a danger to public health and safety would necessarily set a precedent that all HIV-infected people [already in the country] could be similarly characterized."[54] In addition, it sets precedents for genetic screening as more and more genetic tests become available.

"A just and efficacious travel and immigration policy," according to Gostin and his colleagues, "would not exclude people because of their serologic status unless they posed a danger to the community through casual transmission."[55] Indeed, the list of excludable conditions should be revised because only active tuberculosis poses a threat of casual transmission. Immigrants are thus not a major threat to the public health, and screening them will have only a modest impact on the course of the epidemic in the United States, which already has over one million HIV-infected persons. In addition, the screening program discourages travelers from being treated and "drives further underground undocumented aliens who live in the United States and reduces their incentive to seek counseling and preventative care."[56] Finally, current U.S. policy does not contribute to efforts to control HIV infection in the international community.[57]

Since the current screening program does not contribute significantly to public health objectives, the major argument for excluding seropositive immigrants appears to be the cost to the society of providing health care. It may not be intrinsically unjust for a society to exclude immigrants on grounds of the costs of providing health care, but several commentators cogently argue that "it is inequitable . . . to use cost as a reason to exclude people infected with HIV, for there are no similar exclusionary policies for those with other costly chronic diseases, such as heart disease or cancer."[58] This argument rests on the requirement of justice to treat similar cases in a similar way. And, as is the case for each proposed screening target, screening immigrants raises larger philosophical and ethical questions about the boundaries of the moral communities.

OTHER AREAS OF SELECTIVE SCREENING

I have concentrated on a few areas to indicate how the liberal framework of principles, rules, and justificatory conditions applies to proposed policies of mandatory

HIV antibody screening and testing. The arguments extend, mutatis mutandis, to other proposed policies. What we know about the transmission of HIV renders mandatory screening in the workplace, for example, utterly inappropriate, unless there is exposure to bodily fluids under circumstances that would transmit the virus.

Concern has been expressed about the possibility that health care professionals, particularly dentists and surgeons, might transmit the virus to their patients during invasive procedures. In July, 1990, the Centers for Disease Control (CDC) reported a case of "possible transmission" of HIV to a patient during the removal of two of her teeth by a dentist who had AIDS. Although the "possibility of another source of infection cannot be entirely excluded," the CDC noted the absence of any other reported risk factors and a close relation between the viral DNA sequences from the patient and the dentist.[59] Subsequent investigations concluded that this dentist infected at least six of his patients, including Kimberly Bergalis, who made a powerful appeal for mandatory HIV testing of health care professionals in poignant testimony before Congress — what George Annas called "the most dangerous two minutes in the history of the AIDS epidemic." Controversy has persisted about these cases, in part because of the absence of a cogent explanation of the mode of transmission, in part because the CDC's investigation did not pursue other acknowledged risk factors in these patients, and in part because of the absence of evidence of transmission in many other interactions between HIV-infected dentists and surgeons and their patients in the context of health care.

During the same week as the first report of dental-patient transmission, researchers reported that there was no evidence that a Tennessee surgeon with HIV infection had infected any of his surgical patients, many of whom consented to HIV tests.[60] Other studies have reached similar conclusions. According to the researchers involved in a study of the patients of an HIV-infected general dentist in Florida, "the risk for transmission of HIV from a general dentist to his patients is minimal in a setting in which universal precautions are strictly observed. Programs to ensure compliance with universal precautions would appear preferable to programs for widespread testing of adults."[61]

Nevertheless, in view of the mode of transmission of HIV "it would be unexpected if HIV transmission" did not sometimes occur in some surgical procedures.[62] It is important, however, to keep the risk of such transmission in perspective. The probability is very low, perhaps between one in 100,000 [and] one in one million operations.[63] While the risk is "exceedingly remote" of infection for any single patient, "the cumulative risk over a surgical career is real."[64] The main risk appears to be in seriously invasive procedures, particularly vaginal hysterectomies or pelvic surgery, where there is "blind" (i.e., not directly visualized) use of sharp surgical tools.[65]

If there are grounds for restricting the activities of any surgeon — or dentist — who is known to be HIV infected, then there are probably grounds for mandatory testing to determine which ones are HIV infected. This area continues to require careful attention, as well as appropriate monitoring, and the conclusions — at least for some forms of surgery — are likely to be applicable to both health care professionals and patients, since each party may put the other at risk of HIV infection.

Sometimes the goal of screening or testing is to reduce economic costs rather than to prevent transmission of HIV infection. Both goals appear in some screening policies — for example, both immigration and military screening. The goal of saving funds is often primary in workplace screening, and it is clearly the only concern in insurance screening. It is not unreasonable or even unjust for insurance companies to screen and for states to allow them to screen applicants for life and health insurance for HIV antibodies, just as they screen for other conditions. However, it is a failure of justice as well as of compassion and care, for the society, through the federal and state governments, not to provide funds so that HIV-infected individuals and other sick people can obtain needed health care. In short, the fundamental problem is not the actions of insurance companies but the larger societal failure to respond effectively and justly to the health care needs of its citizens, including those with HIV infection.

CONCLUSION: THE WAR AGAINST AIDS

Not only do societies often react — and, at least in retrospect, overreact — through coercive measures to epidemics of communicable diseases, they frequently do so in the name of *war* against the diseases. The metaphor of "the war against AIDS" has been very prominent in justifications of mandatory screening and testing. "Under the guise of a war against AIDS," one commentator notes, "American politics have recently become enamored of an argument over testing citizens" for HIV antibody.[66] Further reflecting the prominence of military metaphors, Gostin observes that it often appears that "the first line of defense in combating AIDS is to identify carriers of the virus by systematic screening."[67] And, in a sensitive discussion of major vocabularies of concern about AIDS, Monroe Price notes that "the crisis of epidemic is a natural substitute for the crisis of war," and that "the question is whether the AIDS epidemic will become such a serious threat that, in the public's mind, it takes on the stature of war."[68]

The metaphor of war is natural in our sociocultural context when a serious threat to a large number of human lives requires the mobilization of societal resources, especially when that threat comes from biological organisms, such as viruses, which attack the human body. For example, the military metaphor is one way to galvanize the society and to marshal its resources for an effective counterattack, and AIDS activists may even exploit it for this purpose.[69] However, the metaphor has other entailments that need to be questioned and perhaps even opposed, especially in our sociocultural context.[70]

From the beginning of the war against AIDS, identification of the enemy has been a major goal. Once the virus was identified as the primary enemy, it became possible to develop technologies to identify human beings who carry or harbor the virus. This led to what Ronald Bayer calls the "politics of identification."[71] How are antibody-positive individuals viewed? As carriers of HIV, are they enemies to be fought? Should the society try to identify them? And how should it act on the information that a particular individual carries or harbors the virus? The line between the virus and the carrier becomes very tenuous, and the carrier tends to become an enemy just as the virus he or she carries. However much Surgeon General C. Everett Koop could argue that this war is against the virus, not against people, the distinction is too subtle for many in the community. Furthermore, it is not surprising that this metaphor of war often coexists with metaphors of AIDS as punishment or as otherness, because many deny that several actions that lead to exposure to HIV are "innocent" and, furthermore, view the associated lifestyles as threats to dominant social values.[72]

The military metaphor tends to justify coercive measures, such as quarantine and isolation of internal threats. In World War II the United States sent Japanese-Americans to internment camps, without due process, and with the approval of the U.S. Supreme Court in *Korematsu v. United States* in 1944. These coercive policies were later discredited, and Congress even approved reparation to those who were interned. However, the coercive polity of identification and internment "demonstrates how, in times of war, like times of public health crisis, the actions of government become clothed with an unusual inviolability."[73] And it becomes even worse when the public health crisis is itself construed as warfare, because of the perceived disjunction between "peacetime procedures" and "wartime needs."[74]

The metaphor of war against AIDS would not be so dangerous if our society had a better appreciation of the moral constraints on resort to and conduct of warfare, represented in particular in the just-war or limited-war tradition.[75] The justification and limitation of war, including the means employed, follow the pattern of the prima facie principles and conditions for justified infringements identified earlier. In general, like a dinosaur, the United States has been slow to engage in war but then hard to control once it starts to act. After AIDS appeared, the early societal response was limited in part because the disease was viewed as a threat mainly to those on the margins of society, especially gays, but then when AIDS was viewed as threat to the larger society, the response was conceived in terms of war. In general, the United States tends to engage in total war, with unlimited objectives and unlimited means, as expressed in our willingness to destroy cities in Vietnam in order to save them. In the war against AIDS it is important to recognize both limited objectives and limited means. I do not believe, in contrast to Susan Sontag,[76] that we must retire the metaphor of war, but we should explore its logic carefully, limit its application by just-war criteria, and supplement and correct it with other metaphors.

Caring has often been viewed as an alternative metaphor.[77] If the military metaphor tends to conflate the virus and the carriers of the virus, the caring metaphor tends to focus concern on the individuals who carry the virus. Even a liberal society need not be a society of mere strangers—it can at least be a society of "friendly strangers." This friendliness can be expressed in care, compassion, and empathy. Insofar as the metaphor of war against AIDS tends to divide the community by casting HIV-infected individuals in the role of enemies, it thereby undermines some of the conditions that sustain voluntaristic policies. After all, trust is indispensable for voluntaristic policies—otherwise the social risks are significant—and it presupposes communal commitments to provide funds for health care and to enforce rules against discrimination, breaches of confidentiality, and the like.

These communal efforts are critically important, because the groups most affected by AIDS — gay men and intravenous drug users — exist on the "margins" of the community.[78] They thus tend to view coercive policies to identify antibody-positive individuals as analogous to the Nazi efforts to identify Jews and others for nefarious purposes.[79] When the "politics of identification" reflects the socio-cultural metaphor of war, it is easy to understand the fears of HIV-infected individuals, especially those in marginalized sub-communities. The war metaphor tends to exclude HIV-infected individuals, as enemies, from the larger community, while the metaphor of care tends to include them in the community. Compulsory measures, such as mandatory screening, appear to *impose* community, but, unless the society also *expresses* community — for example, through the allocation of funds for health care and protection of individual rights and liberties — it largely excludes coerced individuals from the community.

If the society expresses solidarity with HIV-infected individuals, it is less likely to need coercive policies in place of voluntaristic ones, which can be made more effective through the reduction of social risks and the provision of essential means. And if the society fails to extend solidarity to all, coercive policies are likely to be ineffective and even counterproductive, because they too presuppose voluntary cooperation at many points, often for individuals to enter situations where testing is encouraged or required and usually to implement measures to protect others (e.g., disclosure of sexual contacts).

Mandatory HIV screening, in most settings, would set a precedent of overriding rights in a crisis — in a war against disease — even when it produces no benefits, when the burdens outweigh the benefits, or when alternative ways exist to protect the public health. We need to respond out of metaphors other than — or at least in addition to — war, with careful attention to the moral commitments of a liberal society and the justificatory conditions for overriding, under some circumstances, our prima facie principles and rules. How we respond to HIV's threat to public health will shape and express our "identity and community in a democracy under siege."[80]

REFERENCES

1. I will define a liberal society as one that recognizes various individual rights and liberties, including free speech, freedom of association, liberty of action, freedom of conscience, etc. These are identified, with varying emphases, by many interpreters, including John Rawls, *A Theory of Justice* (Cambridge: Harvard University Press, 1971), and *Political Liberalism* (New York: Columbia University Press, 1993).

2. For the history of developments in the United States, see Randy Shilts, *And the Band Played On: Politics, People, and the AIDS Epidemic* (New York: Penguin Books, 1987), and Ronald Bayer, *Private Acts, Social Consequences: AIDS and the Politics of Public Health* (New York: Free Press, 1989).

3. For these principles, see Tom L. Beauchamp and James F. Childress, *Principles of Biomedical Ethics,* 4th ed. (New York: Oxford University Press, 1994).

4. Committee for the Study of the Future of Public Health, Division of Health Care Services, Institute of Medicine, *The Future of Public Health* (Washington, D.C.: National Academy Press, 1988), p. 1.

5. For a fuller discussion of the impact on justifiable policies of the relevant differences between HIV infection and tuberculosis, see Beauchamp and Childress, *Principles of Biomedical Ethics,* chap 7.

6. See James F. Childress, *Who Should Decide? Paternalism in Health Care* (New York: Oxford University Press, 1982); Childress, "An Ethical Framework for Assessing Policies to Screen for Antibodies to HIV," *AIDS & Public Policy Journal* 2 (Winter 1987): 28–31; and Childress, "The Place of Autonomy in Bioethics," *Hastings Center Report* 20 (January/February 1990): 12–17.

7. Childress, *Who Should Decide?*

8. See Beauchamp and Childress, *Principles of Biomedical Ethics,* esp. chaps. 1 and 2.

9. See Childress, "An Ethical Framework for Assessing Policies to Screen for Antibodies to HIV," from which parts of this essay have been drawn with permission. For other justificatory frameworks, with important similarities to the current one, see Ronald Bayer, Carol Levine, and Susan M. Wolf, "HIV Antibody Screening: An Ethical Framework for Evaluating Proposed Programs," *Journal of the American Medical Association* 256 (October 3, 1986): 1768–74; Carol Levine and Ronald Bayer, "The Ethics of Screening for Early Intervention in HIV Disease," *American Journal of Public Health* 79 (December 1989): 1661–67; Maura O'Brien, "Mandatory HIV Antibody Testing Policies: An Ethical Analysis," *Bioethics* 3 (October 1989): 273–300; and Martha A. Field "Testing for AIDS: Uses and Abuses," *American Journal of Law and Medicine* 16 (1990): 33–106.

10. Field, "Testing for AIDS," p. 54.

11. Sissela Bok, *Lying: Moral Choice in Public and Private Life* (New York: Pantheon Books, 1978).

12. Robert Nozick, "Moral Complications and Moral Structures," *Natural Law Forum* 13 (1968):1–50.

13. Margaret Sommerville, "The Case Against HIV Antibody Testing of Refugees and Immigrants," *Canadian Medical Association Journal* 141 (November 1, 1989): 869–94.

14. Frank S. Rhame and Dennis G. Maki, "The Case for Wider Use of Testing for HIV Infection," *New England Journal of Medicine* 320 (May 11, 1989): 1253.

15. Willard Cates, Jr., and H. Hunter Handsfield, "HIV Counseling and Testing: Does It Work?" *American Journal of Public Health* 78 (December 1988): 1533–34; Jane McCusker et al., "Effects of HIV Antibody Test Knowledge on Subsequent Sexual Be-

haviors in a Cohort of Homosexually Active Men," *American Journal of Pubic Health* 78 (April 1988): 462–67.

16. Larry O. Gostin, "A Decade of a Maturing Epidemic: An Assessment and Directions for Future Public Policy," *American Journal of Law & Medicine* 16 (1990): 9–10; Field, "Testing for AIDS," pp. 58–59.

17. For a survey of published reports, see Marshall H. Becker and Jill G. Joseph, "AIDS and Behavioral Change to Reduce Risk: A Review," *American Journal of Public Health* 78 (April 1988): 394–410.

18. Bernard L., Robert L. Steinbrook, Molly Cooke et al., "Voluntary Screening for Human Immunodeficiency Virus (HIV) Infection: Weighing the Benefits and Harms," *Annals of Internal Medicine* 110 (May 1989): 730.

19. For these risks and possible benefits, see ibid, pp. 727–33.

20. Peter Marzuk et al., "Increased Risk of Suicide in Persons with AIDS," *Journal of the American Medical Association* 259 (1988): 1333–37.

21. Bayer, *Private Acts, Social Consequences,* pp. 158–61.

22. For an important discussion of coercion, see Alan Wertheimer, *Coercion* (Princeton: Princeton University Press, 1987).

23. See John C. Fletcher, "AIDS Screening: A Response to Gary Bauer," *AIDS & Public Policy Journal* 2 (Fall/Winter 1987): 5–7.

24. See LeRoy Walters, "Ethical Issues in HIV Testing during Pregnancy" (publication information in n. 41, below).

25. See A. John Simmons, "Tacit Consent and Political Obligation," *Philosophy and Public Affairs* 5 (Spring 1976): 274–91. For an analysis of varieties of consent, with special reference to medicine and health care, see Childress, *Who Should Decide?* chap. 4.

26. Martha S. Swartz, "AIDS Testing and Informed Consent," *Journal of Health Politics, Policy and Law* 13 (Winter 1988): 607–721.

27. See Keith Henry and Kent Crossley, "Analysis of the Use of HIV Antibody Testing in a Minnesota Hospital," *Journal of the American Medical Association* 259 (January 8, 1988): 264–65.

28. Julie Louise Gerberding, Gary Littell, Ada Tarkington et al., "Risk of Exposure of Surgical Personnel to Patient's Blood during Surgery at San Francisco General Hospital," *New England Journal of Medicine* 322 (June 21, 1990): 1788.

29. Field, "Testing for AIDS," p. 104.

30. Gary Bauer, "AIDS Testing," *AIDS & Public Policy Journal* 2 (Fall/Winter 1987): 1.

31. Larry O. Gostin, "Screening for AIDS: Efficacy, Cost, and Consequences," *AIDS & Public Health Journal* 2 (Fall/Winter 1987): 16.

32. Ibid., p. 17.

33. Bernard J. Turnock and Chester J. Kelly, "Mandatory Premarital Testing for Human Immunodeficiency Virus: The Illinois Experience," *Journal of the American Medical Association* 261 (June 16, 1989): 3415–18.

34. Field, "Testing for AIDS."

35. Turnock and Kelly, "Mandatory Premarital Testing." See also the earlier predictions by Paul D. Cleary et al., "Compulsory Premarital Screening for the Human Immunodeficiency Virus: Technical and Public Health Considerations," *Journal of the American Medical Association* 258 (October 1987): 1757–62.

36. Edward A. Belongia, James M. Vergeront, and Jeffrey P. Davis, "Premarital HIV Screening" (Letter to the Editor), *Journal of the American Medical Association* 261 (April 21, 1989): 2198.

37. Stephen C. Joseph, "Premarital AIDS Testing: Public Policy Abandoned at the Altar," *Journal of the American Medical Association* 261 (June 16, 1989): 3456.

38. See, for example, Pamela Boyer et al., "Factors Predictive of Maternal-Fetal Transmission of HIV-1," *Journal of the American Medical Association* 271 (June 22/29, 1994): 1925–30; Srisakul C. Kliks et al., "Features of HIV-1 That Could Influence Maternal-Child Transmission," *Journal of the American Medical Association* 272 (August 10, 1994): 467–73; Louise Kuhn et al., "Maternal-Infant HIV Transmission and Circumstances of Delivery," *American Journal of Public Health* 84 (July 1994): 1110–15.

39. Kathleen Nolan, "Ethical Issues in Caring for Pregnant Women and Newborns at Risk for Human Immunodeficiency Virus Infection," *Seminars in Perinatology* 13 (February 1989): 55–65.

40. Ibid. p. 59. See also Levine and Bayer, "Ethics of Screening for Early Intervention in HIV Disease."

41. See LeRoy Walters, "Ethical Issues in HIV Testing during Pregnancy," in *AIDS, Women and the Next Generation,* ed. Ruth Faden, Gail Geller, and Madison Powers (New York: Oxford University Press, 1991), chap. 11. Various essays in this important volume, which appeared after I had prepared earlier versions of this chapter, sketch legal, ethical, social, psychological, and medical factors in prenatal and neonatal HIV screening and testing. A consensus statement at the end holds that there is no clinical or public health justification for mandatory prenatal or neonatal screening (p. 341).

42. See "Zidovudine for the Prevention of HIV Transmission from Mother to Infant," *Journal of the American Medical Association* 271 (May 25, 1994): 1567–68; "Birth Outcomes Following Zidovudine Therapy in Pregnant Women," *Journal of the American Medical Association* 272 (July 6, 1994): 17.

43. See Nat Hentoff, "Another 'Tuskegee,'" *Washington Post,* May 20, 1995, p. A23. Hentoff also accepts this analogy.

44. Ron Bayer, "It's Not 'Tuskegee' Revisited," *Washington Post,* May 26, 1995, p. A27.

45. These and other concerns appear in James J. Goedert and Timothy R. Cote, "Public Health Interventions to Reduce Pediatric AIDS" (Editorial), *American Journal of Public Health* 84 (July 1994): 1065–66.

46. See Ruth R. Faden et al., "Prenatal HIV-Antibody Testing and the Meaning of Consent," *AIDS and Public Policy Journal* 9 (Fall 1994): 151–59.

47. Randal C. Mutter, Richard M. Grimes, and Darwin Labarthe, "Evidence of Intraprison Spread of HIV Infection," *Archives of Internal Medicine* 154 (April 11, 1994): 793–95.

48. Ruth Macklin, "Predicting Dangerousness and the Public Health Response to AIDS," *Hastings Center Report* 16 (December 1986): 22.

49. Gostin, "Screening for AIDS," p. 21; Field, "Testing for AIDS," pp. 81–91.

50. Jon K. Andrus et al., "HIV Testing in Prisoners: Is Mandatory Testing Mandatory?" *American Journal of Public Health* 79 (July 1989): 842.

51. Macklin, "Predicting Dangerousness and the Public Health Response to AIDS," p. 22.

52. Field, "Testing for AIDS," p. 94.

53. Carol Leslie Wolchok, "AIDS at the Frontier: United States Immigration Policy," *Journal of Legal Medicine* 10 (1989): 128.

54. Somerville, "The Case Against HIV Antibody Testing of Refugees and Immigrants," p. 891.

1995), 1165–68. Copyright © 1995 by the American Medical Association.

Pediatric HIV Disease, Zidovudine in Pregnancy, and Unblinding Heelstick Surveys: Reframing the Debate on Prenatal HIV Testing

Federal and state legislatures have recently taken up the issue of identification of newborns exposed to the human immunodeficiency virus (HIV). Proposed legislation (eg, the Coburn/Waxman HIV testing amendment to the Ryan White CARE Act, the Ackerman Newborn HIV Notification Act [HR 1289], and NY A4413 and NY 52704) would include consideration of "unblinding" newborn heelstick surveys, which, until quite recently, were performed anonymously for surveillance purposes. These surveys, which relied on the detection of passively acquired maternal antibody to HIV, allowed health departments to track the course of the HIV epidemic among women of reproductive age. By unblinding these surveys, ie, ending the anonymity built into current protocols, health departments would identify exposed newborns, who could then be provided with appropriate therapeutic and prophylactic interventions. Since identification of exposed newborns relies on serological testing for passively acquired maternal antibody, such unblinding identifies infected women, and this discussion becomes, in essence, only the most recent iteration of a decade-long debate on the appropriate standards for HIV testing of women. Although some of the ethical principles that underpin this debate are inured to change (eg, maternal autonomy and fetal beneficence), the backdrop against which these discussions are held has recently undergone dramatic clinical changes.

On November 3, 1994, the results of AIDS [acquired immunodeficiency syndrome] Clinical Trials Group (ACTG) Protocol 076, a double-blind, placebo-controlled study of zidovudine use in pregnancy, were published.[1] Zidovudine prevented two thirds of expected perinatal HIV infections (25.5% transmission in the placebo group vs 8.3% in the zidovudine-treated group). By the time of that publication, the consequences of the 076 trial results had already been felt. On February 17 of that year, an independent Data Safety Monitoring Board overseeing the results of the study had recommended its discontinuation, citing the demonstrated advantage of therapy over placebo,[2] and in August 1994 the Public Health Service had published recommendations for an altered standard of care in light of the results.[3] It was a defining moment in the history of the AIDS epidemic, marking what was in a sense one of the first major successes in the "war" on AIDS. Although zidovudine was obviously not a vaccine or cure as traditionally defined, the consequence of its perinatal use was essentially to protect the child during the journey through pregnancy and parturition by mechanisms still to be described. While much needs to be learned regarding which component of therapy (antepartum, intrapartum, or postpartum) is most essential, and while efforts must continue to find ways to protect those children still being infected, the work to date should be recognized as a substantial triumph.

The public policy consequences of these findings are also substantial, fueling the current debate on peri-

natal HIV testing. Clearly, the ratio of benefits to burdens associated with prenatal testing has been altered. The question now is, what is the testing policy that most appropriately derives from these new data?

PRENATAL HIV TESTING: HISTORICAL OVERVIEW

The history of prenatal HIV testing has been marked by an evolution in policy. When testing first became a practical possibility, clinicians were chastened by the discriminatory consequences of known positive HIV status, which were being widely reported at a time when little medical advantage accrued to those whose status was known. Hence, enthusiasm for testing was tepid, and prenatal testing, if offered at all, was done in a selective manner focused on individuals who acknowledged "risk" behaviors. Given the stigmatizing nature of those behaviors, it was not surprising that only a small percentage of HIV-infected women were identified by those programs in which testing was targeted to individuals acknowledging risk behaviors.[4,5] Subsequent to the recognition of the failure of that approach, the routine offering of tests was adopted by many programs,[6] and testing rates moved incrementally upward. When antiretroviral therapy and *Pneumocystis carinii* pneumonia (PCP) prophylaxis became available for HIV-infected adults and various therapies were shown to ameliorate the course of pediatric disease, many clinicians chose to invoke the authority of the white coat and to recommend, rather than merely offer, prenatal HIV testing.[7] Although voices were heard arguing for a more aggressive approach,[5] the equivocal nature of the maternal-fetal benefits was such that no clear consensus for anything other than recommended and consensual testing emerged. Now the ACTG 076 results compel a revisit to this issue.

The results of ACTG 076 do not substantively change our understanding of the risks of prenatal exposure to zidovudine. Previously published data, though minimal and short term, revealed no serious harm,[8] and no significant morbidity was seen among ACTG 076 participants. Greater degrees of reassurance must await experience with substantially increased numbers of prenatal exposures and much longer durations of follow-up (ACTG protocol 219 mandates long-term follow-up of children exposed to zidovudine as a consequence of maternal-child participation in ACTG 076.) It is also unclear whether a mother's prenatal use of zidovudine will compromise the drug's efficacy if it is subsequently required as part of the woman's medical management. Beyond those concerns, the burden side of the ledger remains essentially unchanged. The benefit side, however, has undergone a quantum change. For the first time, the benefits of an HIV therapeutic are not being discussed in terms of palliation or marginally prolonged survival, but rather as the difference between life and death for the neonate who would otherwise be infected. Admittedly and critically, however, this agent is not perfect.

In 8% of treated pregnancies, maternal-fetal HIV transmission still occurred (compared with 25.5% in the placebo group). Outside the somewhat narrow inclusion criteria of ACTG 076 and in a clinical world not as rigorously controlled as the research setting, failure rates could be much higher. Women excluded from ACTG 076, such as those with low CD4+ counts and those who have already had prolonged exposure to zidovudine, with the concomitant increased likelihood of resistant organisms, may not witness as high a success rate when given perinatal doses of zidovudine. Women who register for prenatal care after 34 weeks' gestation may be similarly disadvantaged. Thus, what has been reported so far may overstate the advantage that will accrue in the real world of clinical obstetrics, given the heterogeneous status and variable time of presentation of the approximately 7000 HIV-infected women who bear live children annually.[9]

What then is the testing policy that most appropriately follows from these realities? The standard that existed before this evidence of fetal protection was reported was routinely recommended testing and informed written consent.[7] In areas of the country with very low seroprevalence and scant resources to commit to counseling and testing, the policy has sometimes been routine offering instead of recommending. If the remarkable benefits of this agent are confirmed and the agent is accessible, there is a need for consideration of a more aggressive policy.

Under the rubric of a more aggressive policy, several possible approaches exist. The current approach of routine consensual testing could be bolstered with enhanced resources to ensure that every prenatal patient receives counseling. In many geographic areas today, particularly those that are medically disadvantaged, access to counseling can be haphazard. There is compelling evidence that when consensual testing programs are rigorously applied and supported, extremely high percentages of women will agree to be tested.[10] However, a policy of recommended consensual testing would still make the HIV test unique among antenatal tests, a distinction now perhaps less justified given the apparent advantage that accrues to the treated fetus. The consent for almost all other tests is included within the global "patient care" consent, and from a practical point of view these tests are either subject to "right of refusal" or mandatory (eg, syphilis testing in New York State).

INFORMED RIGHT OF REFUSAL AND MANDATORY TESTING

Giving patients the right to informed refusal without requiring written consent would result in a de facto deemphasis on both the HIV test and the unique stigma attached to a positive result. Changing the "exceptional" nature of the consenting process for HIV tests[11] would be significant, because it is not only the fear of social consequences that results in testing rates much lower than those seen with other prenatal tests such as gonorrhea cultures. The low rates also stem from the requirement that the patient give specific attention to the HIV test and take an affirmative action (written consent) to have that test performed, while for other tests it is deferring the test that requires an action (refusal). It is specifically worth noting that a woman is asked to consent to HIV testing after being counseled about modes of transmission — in essence, being told that only unsafe sex or needle use would put her at risk. Thus, a patient who might be interested in taking the test, but not in sharing her risk-taking background, might feel compelled to eschew the test to ensure her privacy. For a reasonable analogy, consider what the impact on universal Papanicolaou test screening would be if, prior to a Papanicolaou test, women were first informed that cervical cancer was caused by human papillomavirus, a sexually transmitted disease that could not be acquired if one [were] in a lifelong mutually monogamous relationship. Signing a consent at that point would allow for the test but would simultaneously provide a de facto confession of unsafe sex.

When an informed right of refusal approach is used instead of written informed consent, a psychological burden is shifted from those who would choose the test to those who would refuse — in essence, requiring a special effort to say no. The confessional nature of testing (implicitly acknowledging risk behavior through the act of signing consent) would be removed. Although some patients would choose to opt out of testing even if they had to assert their rights to do so, the percentage of individuals tested would undoubtedly rise dramatically.

A right of refusal policy, however, could not guarantee universal testing. Testing would have to be mandatory to ensure that every exposed fetus would be identified, though even that step would not be sufficient to ensure therapy. If the purpose of mandatory testing is universal perinatal therapy, then treatment as well would have to be mandated. Taking away maternal rights without ensuring benefits would be illogical and indefensible. Therefore, a woman's right to balance her own and her child's risks from prenatal zidovudine (eg, theoretical reduction in duration of drug efficacy when it becomes medically indicated plus as yet unknown long-term consequences for the child) against fetal benefits (rigorously and scientifically demonstrated reduction in vertical transmission) would be abrogated.

In an editorial accompanying the ACTG 076 results, Bayer[12] dismissed mandatory screening, stating, "[M]andatory screening of pregnant women is objectionable because mandatory treatment of competent adults is virtually never acceptable." However, if the balance between maternal risk and fetal benefit is overwhelmingly tilted in one direction, then negating the mother's right to refuse either testing or therapy would not be unprecedented. For example, despite the risk of anaphylaxis from penicillin, prenatal testing and treatment for syphilis are mandated in some states. However, two substantive differences between penicillin and zidovudine must be pointed out. First, penicillin's cure rate is close to 100%, while fetal protection from zidovudine would appear to be much less; and second, treatment with penicillin involves, at most, three injections. In the absence of maternal cooperation, ensuring zidovudine therapy following the ACTG 076 regimen could, as pointed out by Bayer,[12] involve incarceration of the pregnant woman and forcibly coerced oral therapy for 6 months, forced intravenous infusion of medications during labor and delivery, and 6 weeks of forcible oral therapy for the child—all of this done with the knowledge that 75% of the offspring of infected mothers are not and have never been at risk of infection. That degree of encumbrance on civil liberties in pursuit of possible fetal benefit would be unprecedented.

In practical terms, the barrier that civil liberties place[s] on the implementation of mandatory HIV testing should not be seen as a lethal, or even a serious, blow to fetal beneficence. The need to override a patient refusal and to mandate testing for, and treatment of, syphilis in the prenatal setting is an extremely rare event because women do not refuse. Allowing an individual to assert her right to refuse HIV testing and zidovudine therapy in the face of counseling about the life-saving potential of the regimen is the price we pay to avoid subjecting civil liberties to gender and child-bearing status distinctions.

The failure to achieve high rates of testing in many settings is not solely related to failed policies or patient recalcitrance. Despite published recommendations for widespread implementation of counseling and testing,[7] there has been, in many instances, a failure or clinicians to effect those guidelines. Clinician attitudes, beliefs, HIV-related knowledge, involvement with HIV-infected patients, and training in counseling skills, as well as institutional and patient characteristics, influence whether clinicians encourage their patients to take the HIV test. For example, one survey found that time and shared language were the best predictors of physician-conducted HIV risk assessment and counseling.[13] Simplifying the process by uncoupling detailed counseling from the consenting process might also have a salutary influence on physicians' willingness to engage in HIV testing programs. Thus, although the focus of this discussion is on policies and statutes designed to remedy a perceived inability to identify large numbers of HIV-infected women, the role of the clinician in the success of failure of any program must be recognized.

UNBLINDING HEELSTICK SURVEYS

The most recently proposed statutes would bypass all of the approaches discussed above and, as previously noted, require unblinding of newborn heelstick surveys. Although the focus of this approach would apparently shift testing from the prenatal to the newborn period, it would still involve detection of maternal antibody and, as was the case with prenatal testing, identify mothers who are HIV infected and newborns who have been exposed to HIV. This approach would seem to have some logistic advantage, with an extant infrastructure and no requirement whatsoever for any consenting. However, in a benefit-burden calculus that factors in the well-being and rights of children, mothers, and society, it is hard to conjure a rational justification for this approach. Given current knowledge, few if any children will be spared an AIDS-related death by the initiation of either primary treatment or prophylaxis for opportunistic infections during the first days, weeks, or months of life. No scientist has presented data suggesting that current therapies can cure any HIV-infected child, regardless of the age at which the child was identified. The palliation that will be gained through institution of PCP prophylaxis will be a prolonged life expectancy of uncertain duration and uncertain quality for that very small minority of children currently unidentified who would otherwise have succumbed to PCP as their initial clinical presentation of HIV disease. Clearly, scientific advances that invalidate any of these suppositions will compel a revisit to the issue of HIV testing policy.

It has been suggested that an additional advantage of unblinding the heelstick survey would be to provide an opportunity to counsel recent parturients against breast-feeding, thereby reducing HIV transmission to neonates. However, breast-feeding, particularly prolonged breast-feeding, is not known to be common in US populations at high risk for HIV infection. Additionally, by the time HIV results are available and women can be traced and informed of their results, exposure to potentially infected breast milk will already have occurred. Most importantly, those women who had refused persuasive efforts to be tested during their pregnancy and now discover that, contrary to their stated request, they have been HIV tested and are infected, must be enlisted in efforts either to avoid transmission through cessation of breast-feeding or to initiate palliative therapies recommended by a medical establishment that has disregarded their refusal of HIV testing.

Some advocates of unblinding newborn heelstick results justify its compulsory nature, in part, by suggesting that some HIV-infected mothers may be drug addicted and will not assume responsibility for getting their newborns tested, let alone ensuring that their children receive treatment. However, current law already allows testing under circumstances in which a mother has abandoned her child, and no further legislative redress is required. If a physician believes that the child's medical condition warrants an HIV test and that the mother is being negligent in refusing to permit one, the physician can, as in other circumstances of medical negligence, pursue a court order. Finally, the ethical foundations for blinded screening have been widely accepted by public health organizations and ethicists alike.[14]

The burdens associated with unblinding the newborn heelstick survey are substantial. It will introduce a gender-specific exclusion to the concept of informed consent. Even those tested in the military know they will be tested and could have chosen not to enlist if they did not wish their status known. The documented social and psychological difficulties of people identified after they consented to HIV testing have been sufficiently daunting to give pause to any who would assume responsibility for those learning their status without first agreeing to the process.

The literature describing the hypothesized benefits of mandatory unblinding of HIV seroprevalence surveys in newborns has not explored the significant difficulties and expense of a system of notification, posttest counseling, and the drawing into accessible and effective care of 7000 women and children annually. The burden would fall on dozens of state departments of health, which would need to design new systems to address these new needs and issues in a population some of whom will not welcome the information that they have been administered a test they did not want or know about.

CONCLUSION

Instituting a routine *informed* right of refusal policy might be the most appropriate compromise, allowing testing policies to keep pace with evolving clinical realities without abrogating in toto women's rights. In ideal circumstances, such a policy would permit the overwhelming majority of children to be the beneficiaries of a significant scientific advance, and mothers would be assured that they would remain the ultimate arbiters of their own fate. In the real world, however, the danger exists that a right of refusal policy could evolve into a routine testing program with little attention paid to ensuring that the process be informed. Here the distinction between Papanicolaou test screening and HIV testing is most germane. Women diagnosed with cervical dysplasia do not have their homes, jobs, or insurance status imperiled. Given that reality, in addition to educational and power inequities between providers and patients as well as barriers of language and literacy, it is incumbent on all physicians to make efforts to vouchsafe the pregnant woman's right to make a choice based on a full and frank discussion of risks and benefits.

In sum, a policy that destigmatizes and facilitates the voluntary testing of women for HIV *before* the birth of a child would have the greatest chance to save the lives of infants and would best represent women as autonomous and rational. Preserving consent will best preserve the woman's role as fetal champion and the clinician's role as patient advocate.

REFERENCES

1. Connor EM, Sperling RS, Gelber R, et al. Reduction of maternal-infant transmission of human immunodeficiency virus with zidovudine treatment. *N Engl J Med.* 1994;331:1173–80.

2. Cotton P. Trial halted after drug cuts maternal HIV transmission rate by two thirds. *JAMA.* 1994;271:807.

3. Centers for Disease Control and Prevention. Recommendations of the U.S. Public Health Service Task Force on the use of zidovudine to reduce perinatal transmission of human immunodeficiency virus. *MMWR Morb Mortal Wkly Rep.* 1994;43:115.

4. Landesman S, Minkoff HL, Holman S, McCalla S, Sijin O. Serosurvey of human immunodeficiency virus infection in parturients: implications for human immunodeficiency virus testing programs of pregnant women. *JAMA.* 1987;258:2701–03.

5. Krasinsky K, Borkowsky W, Bebenroth D, Moore T. Failure of voluntary testing for human immunodeficiency virus to identify infected parturient women in a high-risk population. *N Engl J Med.* 1988;318:185.

6. Minkoff HL, Landesman SH, Delke I, et al. Routinely offered prenatal HIV testing. *N Engl J Med.* 1988;319:1018.

7. *Human Immunodeficiency Virus Infection.* Washington, DC: American College of Obstetricians and Gynecologists; 1992;162: 1–11.

8. Sperling RS, Stratton P, O'Sullivan MJ, et al. A survey of zidovudine use in pregnant women with human immunodeficiency virus infection. *N Engl J Med.* 1992;326:857–61.

9. Centers for Disease Control and Prevention. *National HIV Serosurveillance Summary: Results Through 1992.* Atlanta, GA: US Dept of Health and Human Services, Public Health Service; 1994:3.

10. Lindsay MK, Peterson HB, Feng TI, Slade BA, Willis S, Klein L. Routine antepartum human immunodeficiency virus infection screening in an inner-city population. *Obstet Gynecol.* 1989;74: 289–94.

11. Bayer R. Public health policy and the AIDS epidemic: an end to HIV exceptionalism? *N Engl J Med.* 1991;324:1500–04.

12. Bayer R. Ethical challenges posted by zidovudine treatment to reduce vertical transmission of HIV. *N Engl J Med.* 1994;318: 1223–25.

13. Wheat ME, Hyman RB, Devons C, Solomon S. Preventing HIV transmission: behaviors and attitudes of medical house staff in a high-prevalence area. *Am J Prev Med.* 1993;9:307–16.

14. Bayer R. It's not Tuskegee revisited. *Washington Post.* May 26, 1995:A27.

DEBORAH SONTAG

H.I.V. Testing for Newborns Debated Anew

New York hospitals quietly began the open mandatory testing of newborns for H.I.V. this month in the first such program in the nation. And, in maternity wards and nurseries across the state, as they drew blood from babies and counseled new mothers, doctors, nurses and social workers continued to wrangle over the value of such testing with the undiluted passion that has inflamed the political debate for years.

Technically, the state, which for several years has conducted anonymous — blind — H.I.V. testing of newborns for statistical purposes, will now simply "unblind"

the results. Ten months ago, New York hospitals began asking mothers for their consent to be notified of the test results. On Feb. 1, hospitals eliminated the consent forms and agreed often begrudgingly, to the mandatory disclosure of tests results — which means tracking down and counseling the mothers weeks after they leave the hospital.

The issue of consent has been a thorny one, since the test on the baby reveals not the newborn's but the mother's H.I.V. status, through the presence or absence of her antibodies in the baby's blood. Only a quarter of the babies exposed to H.I.V. in the womb become infected, and the virus, which causes AIDS, cannot yet be detected at birth.

But consent has not been the only issue. Most health care professionals believe in prenatal testing since treatment of the mother can prevent transmission of the virus.

So, although the test is a simple prick of a baby's heel, it has provoked a furious controversy in New York and across the country, often posing unnatural antagonisms between advocates for mothers and those for children, between obstetricians and pediatricians.

"Certainly, this is a very charged issue and an extraordinary undertaking, politically and as a public health program," Dr. Barbara DeBuono, the State Health Commissioner said. "It is being watched very closely by other states and by the C.D.C. to see if it has any significant impact."

TO SOME PARENTS, TEST COMES AS A BIG SURPRISE

So far, the reality of carrying out the new law has been far more mundane than the debate swirling around it. After working frantically to devise elaborate plans to cope with the new law, hospitals were forced to slow down and wait. It will be several weeks until the first test results are in, so the principal new task has been informing mothers the test is being conducted. While public health law requires informed consent for all medical tests, the Legislature, in passing the new law last summer, has specifically exempted women immediately after childbirth.

Of 10 hospitals queried, so far none have had patients who balked at the testing.

At New York Hospital-Cornell Medical Center, counselors have tried to make it clear that it is the woman who is being tested when the baby's heel is pricked, said Dr. Margaret Polaneczky, who directs the hospital's maternal-pediatric H.I.V. counseling and testing program and oversees the law's implementation there. "It gets very touchy because there are issues between couples," she said. "We have to kick dad out of the room so we can have a frank conversation with mom about her sexual behavior."

But many hospitals have chosen simply to alert mothers to the new test through a form letter or a quick comment.

Some new parents, particularly patients of private obstetricians, have been confused and taken aback. When Steven Cohen, a Federal prosecutor, learned that his 2-day-old son Ethan was to be tested for H.I.V. before being discharged from Beth Israel Hospital, he was puzzled.

"It's not like he has had time to do drugs or have sex yet," he said.

No one at the hospital had explained the concept of the perinatal transmission of infection, or that the test would reflect his wife's H.I.V. status. Mr. Cohen said their obstetrician had not mentioned H.I.V., which is not uncommon for doctors in private practices since their patients, whose risk of infection is low, are nonetheless often more resistant than poorer women to being tested.

On Bellevue Hospital Center's maternity ward, the new mothers were far more savvy. Five of five new mothers interviewed Friday evening had taken prenatal H.I.V. tests at clinics; all five said they tested negative, and so were unconcerned about the babies' tests. Still, they said they believed in mandatory testing.

"I think the testing is very, very important because the baby's health is more important than the mother's feelings," said Mabel Buritica, 25, as she cradled day-old Jennifer, inhaling her sweet smell. "Maybe the mother thinks she has no need to worry, but even if she knows about herself, she can never know exactly what her man has been up to."

Statewide, some 1,100 women who were H.I.V. positive gave birth in New York State during the first 10 months of last year. That number has steadily declined since 1990, which health officials attribute to public education campaigns.

MONEY AND EXTRA WORK ARE ISSUES IN HOSPITALS

Judging by State Health Department statistics, most hospitals will deal with very small numbers of H.I.V.-positive mothers, probably no more than four a month at the largest public hospitals in New York City. And most will know they are H.I.V.-positive by the time they give birth. This law then intends to enhance the quality of healthy life for those few babies, probably not more than 25 statewide in a year, whose infections may not have been discovered without mandatory testing.

"If we identify these kids early, then we can offer them treatment that might dramatically alter the course of their life," said Dr. William Borkowski, the director of pediatric infectious diseases at N.Y.U. Medical Center/Bellevue Hospital Center.

No one in the health care community argues that children with the virus should not be found and treated, or that their mothers should remain ignorant of their own conditions. But many believe that the law is misguided.

"All of us in the medical profession would like to see women tested, but think it should be done in the prenatal setting," said Dr. Polaneczky of New York Hospital. "If you're going to mandate that all women be tested without their permission, then at least do it when you can make a difference. Postpartum is too late."

H.I.V.-infected women treated with AZT prenatally and during delivery drastically reduce the likelihood that their babies will be infected—from 23 percent without AZT to about 8 percent with it. A baby treated after birth has a longer, healthier life but a life defined by the virus.

Dr. DeBuono said she hoped that the new law would "motivate the health care community to improve their rate of prenatal counseling and testing." And many doctors said it probably would.

. . .

Since hospitals receive test results from two to six weeks after the baby's birth, tracking down mothers and children after they leave the hospital is a greater concern. Time is of the essence; breastfeeding greatly increases the chance that H.I.V.-positive mothers will pass the virus to their babies. Last summer, after the state began disclosing H.I.V. results to women who requested them, hospitals began developing systems for tracking them down.

"It just takes time, because we often have an incorrect address or phone number, or the child is in foster care, or the mother doesn't really have a home," said Dr. Ian R. Holzman, the chief of newborn medicine at Mount Sinai Medical Center in Manhattan. "But we use birth certificate information, or Medicaid information, or look in shelters and so on. Still, it's not like Kansas where we can send out the sheriff, so we don't always find someone."

FOR MANY WOMEN, A DEEPLY PERSONAL ISSUE

At the Einstein-Weiler Hospital in the Bronx, a division of Montefiore Medical Center, one-third of the H.I.V.-positive mothers are never found, said Dr. Carlos Vega-Rich, the director of newborn services.

And once a woman is located, she must be persuaded to return to the hospital to get the results. "After they've spent three weeks with their babies at home, they don't want to hear that there's a problem," Dr. Vega-Rich said. "And we have to be vague: We can't mention H.I.V. over the phone, because you need to give the news in a confidential setting."

The new law poses peculiar predicaments for hospitals and doctors. Many hospitals, for instance, com-

puterize all test results for newborns, but given the stringent confidentiality rules, H.I.V. information is not supposed to be available at the click of a mouse. Also, it requires results to be sent to the newborns' pediatricians, yet many new mothers have yet to select their pediatricians.

Before the mandatory disclosure began this month, the state had already required hospitals to ask women whether they wanted to know the test results. The overwhelming majority of mothers—about 93 percent, according to the Health Department—did agree to notification. Some doctors wonder, then, whether it was necessary to mandate disclosure.

"I want voluntary programs that strongly encourage women, because in them there are very high acceptance rates for testing," said Laurie Solomon, director of ambulatory obstetrics and gynecology for Bronx Lebanon Hospital Center. "Then women can decide when they are ready to deal with their fears and come forward."

A state analysis of the newborn testing program during a three-month period last year found that only 13 of 269 H.I.V.-positive mothers declined notifications of their results.

And 32 more H.I.V.-positive mothers were not offered a chance to learn their test results. . . .

To many women, the law does not present a daunting public health issue but a deeply personal one. Waiting for a friend to be discharged from the maternity ward at The Long Island College Hospital in Brooklyn, Alma Velez sat rubbing her belly on Friday morning.

She is a week away from delivery, with two young children in school. She has never submitted to an H.I.V. test, although it was advised by a doctor at her health clinic. And, at first, she was quite upset when she learned that new baby would be tested, and that the test would reveal if she had the virus.

"They have no right at all, and I'll sue them if they try it," she said belligerently. Within minutes, though, her face crumpled.

"I've always been too scared to do the test, but I always wondered," she said. "I had this boyfriend who was into the drugs, and his habits [weren't] too cleanly. I was healthy, and my kids [were] healthy, but I always still wondered. It would be a relief to know, actually. And if I have to face the music, I guess I will. The thought of an innocent baby getting it—ay, Dios mio."

PETER LURIE AND SIDNEY M. WOLFE

Unethical Trials of Interventions to Reduce Perinatal Transmission of the Human Immunodeficiency Virus in Developing Countries

It has been almost three years since the *Journal*[1] published the results of AIDS Clinical Trials Group (ACTG) Study 076, the first randomized, controlled trial in which an intervention was proved to reduce the incidence of human immunodeficiency virus (HIV) infection. The antiretroviral drug zidovudine [AZT], administered orally to HIV-positive pregnant women in the United States and France, administered intravenously during labor, and subsequently administered to the newborn infants, reduced the incidence of HIV infection by two thirds.[2] The regimen can save the life of one of every seven infants born to HIV-infected women.

Because of these findings, the study was terminated at the first interim analysis and within two months after the results had been announced, the Public Health Service had convened a meeting and concluded that the ACTG 076 regimen should be recommended for all HIV-positive pregnant women without substantial prior exposure to zidovudine and should be considered for other HIV-positive pregnant women on a case-by-case basis.[3] The standard of care for HIV-positive pregnant women thus became the ACTG 076 regimen.

In the United States, three recent studies of clinical practice report that the use of the ACTG 076 regimen is associated with decreases of 50 percent or more in perinatal HIV transmission.[4-6] But in developing countries, especially in Asia and sub-Saharan Africa, where it is projected that by the year 2000, 6 million pregnant women will be infected with HIV,[7] the potential of the ACTG 076 regimen remains unrealized primarily because of the drug's exorbitant cost in most countries.

Reprinted with permission from the *New England Journal of Medicine* 337 (September 18, 1997), pp. 835–56. Copyright © 1997 by the Massachusetts Medical Society.

Clearly, a regimen that is less expensive than ACTG 076 but effective is desirable, in both developing and industrialized countries. But there has been uncertainty about what research design to use in the search for a less expensive regimen. In June 1994, the World Health Organization (WHO) convened a group in Geneva to assess the agenda for research on perinatal HIV transmission in the wake of ACTG 076. The group, which included no ethicists, concluded, "Placebo-controlled trials offer the best option for a rapid and scientifically valid assessment of alternative antiretroviral drug regimens to prevent [perinatal] transmission of HIV."[8] This unpublished document has been widely cited as justification for subsequent trials in developing countries. In our view, most of these trials are unethical and will lead to hundreds of preventable HIV infections in infants.

Primarily on the basis of documents obtained from the Centers for Disease Control and Prevention (CDC), we have identified 18 randomized, controlled trials of interventions to prevent perinatal HIV transmission that either began to enroll patients after the ACTG 076 study was completed or have not yet begun to enroll patients. The studies are designed to evaluate a variety of interventions: antiretroviral drugs such as zidovudine (usually in regimens that are less expensive or complex than the ACTG 076 regimen), vitamin A and its derivatives, intrapartum vaginal washing, and HIV immune globulin, a form of immunotherapy. These trials involve a total of more than 17,000 women.

In the two studies being performed in the United States, the patients in all the study groups have unrestricted access to zidovudine or other antiretroviral drugs. In 15 of the 16 trials in developing countries, however, some or all of the patients are not provided with antiretroviral drugs. Nine of the 15 studies being conducted outside the United States are funded by the U.S. government through the CDC or the National Institutes of Health (NIH), 5 are funded by other governments, and 1 is funded by the United Nations AIDS Program. The studies are being conducted in Côte d'Ivoire, Uganda, Tanzania, South Africa, Malawi, Thailand, Ethiopia, Burkina Faso, Zimbabwe, Kenya, and the Dominican Republic. These 15 studies clearly violate recent guidelines designed specifically to address ethical issues pertaining to studies in developing countries. According to these guidelines, "The ethical standards applied should be no less exacting than they would be in the case of research carried out in [the sponsoring] country."[9] In addition, U.S. regulations governing studies performed with federal funds domestically or abroad specify that research procedures must "not unnecessarily expose subjects to risk."[10]

The 16th study is noteworthy both as a model of an ethically conducted study attempting to identify less expensive antiretroviral regimens and as an indication of how strong the placebo-controlled trial orthodoxy is. In 1994, Marc Lallemant, a researcher at the Harvard School of Public Health, applied for NIH funding for an equivalency study in Thailand in which three shorter zidovudine regimens were to be compared with a regimen similar to that used in the ACTG 076 study. An equivalency study is typically conducted when a particular regimen has already been proved effective and one is interested in determining whether a second regimen is about as effective but less toxic or expensive.[11] The NIH study section repeatedly put pressure on Lallemant and the Harvard School of Public Health to conduct a placebo-controlled trial instead, prompting the director of Harvard's human subjects committee to reply, "The conduct of a placebo-controlled trial for [zidovudine] in pregnant women in Thailand would be unethical and unacceptable, since an active-controlled trial is feasible."[12] The NIH eventually relented, and the study is now under way. Since the nine studies of antiretroviral drugs have attracted the most attention, we focus on them in this article.

ASKING THE WRONG RESEARCH QUESTION

There are numerous areas of agreement between those conducting or defending these placebo-controlled studies in developing countries and those opposing such trials. The two sides agree that perinatal HIV transmission is a grave problem meriting concerted international attention; that the ACTG 076 trial was a major breakthrough in perinatal HIV prevention; that there is

a role for research on this topic in developing countries; that identifying less expensive, similarly effective interventions would be of enormous benefit given the limited resources for medical care in most developing countries; and that randomized studies can help identify such interventions.

The sole point of disagreement is the best comparison group to use in assessing the effectiveness of less-expensive interventions once an effective intervention has been identified. The researchers conducting the placebo-controlled trials assert that such trials represent the only appropriate research design, implying that they answer the question, "Is the shorter regimen better than nothing?" We take the more optimistic view that, given the findings of ACTG 076 and other clinical information, researchers are quite capable of designing a shorter antiretroviral regimen that is approximately as effective as the ACTG 076 regimen. The proposal for the Harvard study in Thailand states the research question clearly: "Can we reduce the duration of prophylactic [zidovudine] treatment without increasing the risk of perinatal transmission of HIV, that is, without compromising the demonstrated efficacy of the standard ACTG 076 [zidovudine] regimen?"[13] We believe that such equivalency studies of alternative antiretroviral regimens will provide even more useful results than placebo-controlled trials, without the deaths of hundreds of newborns that are inevitable if placebo groups are used.

At a recent congressional hearing on research ethics, NIH director Harold Varmus was asked how the Department of Health and Human Services could be funding both a placebo-controlled trial (through the CDC) and a non-placebo-controlled equivalency study (through the NIH) in Thailand. Dr. Varmus conceded that placebo-controlled studies are "not the only way to achieve results."[14] If the research can be satisfactorily conducted in more than one way, why not select the approach that minimizes loss of life?

INADEQUATE ANALYSIS OF DATA FROM ACTG 076 AND OTHER SOURCES

The NIH, CDC, WHO, and the researchers conducting the studies we consider unethical argue that differences in the duration and route of administration of antiretroviral agents in the shorter regimens, as compared with the ACTG 076 regimen, justify the use of a placebo group.[15-18] Given that ACTG 076 was a well-conducted, randomized, controlled trial, it is disturbing that the rich data available from the study were not adequately used by the group assembled by WHO in June 1994, which recommended placebo-controlled trials after ACTG 076, or by the investigators of the 15 studies we consider unethical.

In fact, the ACTG 076 investigators conducted a subgroup analysis to identify an appropriate period for prepartum administration of zidovudine. The approximate median duration of prepartum treatment was 12 weeks. In a comparison of treatment for 12 weeks or less (average, 7) with treatment for more than 12 weeks (average, 17), there was no univariate association between the duration of treatment and its effect in reducing perinatal HIV transmission ($P=0.99$) (Gelber R: personal communication). This analysis is somewhat limited by the number of infected infants and its post hoc nature. However, when combined with information such as the fact that in non-breast-feeding populations an estimated 65 percent of cases of perinatal HIV infection are transmitted during delivery and 95 percent of the remaining cases are transmitted within two months of delivery,[19] the analysis *suggests* that the shorter regimens may be equally effective. This finding should have been explored in later studies by randomly assigning women to longer or shorter treatment regimens.

What about the argument that the use of the oral route for intrapartum administration of zidovudine in the present trials (as opposed to the intravenous route in ACTG 076) justifies the use of a placebo? In its protocols for its two studies in Thailand and Côte d'Ivoire, the CDC acknowledged that previous "pharmacokinetic modelling data suggest that [zidovudine] serum levels obtained with this [oral] dose will be similar to levels obtained with an intravenous infusion."[20]

Thus, on the basis of the ACTG 076 data, knowledge about the timing of perinatal transmission, and pharmacokinetic data, the researchers should have had every reason to believe that well-designed shorter regimens would be more effective than placebo. These findings seriously disturb the equipoise (uncertainty over the likely study result) necessary to justify a placebo-controlled trial on ethical grounds.[21]

DEFINING PLACEBO AS THE STANDARD OF CARE IN DEVELOPING COUNTRIES

Some officials and researchers have defended the use of placebo-controlled studies in developing countries

by arguing that the subjects are treated at least according to the standard of care in these countries, which consists of unproven regimens or no treatment at all. This assertion reveals a fundamental misunderstanding of the concept of the standard of care. In developing countries, the standard of care (in this case, not providing zidovudine to HIV-positive pregnant women) is not based on a consideration of alternative treatments or previous clinical data, but is instead an economically determined policy of governments that cannot afford the prices set by drug companies. We agree with the Council for International Organizations of Medical Sciences that researchers working in developing countries have an ethical responsibility to provide treatment that conforms to the standard of care in the sponsoring country, when possible.[9] An exception would be a standard of care that required an exorbitant expenditure, such as the cost of building a coronary care unit. Since zidovudine is usually made available free of charge by the manufacturer for use in clinical trials, excessive cost is not a factor in this case. Acceptance of a standard of care that does not conform to the standard in the sponsoring country results in a double standard in research. Such a double standard, which permits research designs that are unacceptable in the sponsoring country, creates an incentive to use as research subjects those with the least access to health care.

What are the potential implications of accepting such a double standard? Researchers might inject live malaria parasites into HIV-positive subjects in China in order to study the effect on the progression of HIV infection, even though the study protocol had been rejected in the United States and Mexico. Or researchers might randomly assign malnourished San (bushmen) to receive vitamin-fortified or standard bread. One might also justify trials of HIV vaccines in which the subjects were not provided with condoms or state-of-the-art counseling about safe sex by arguing that they are not customarily provided in the developing countries in question. These are not simply hypothetical worst-case scenarios; the first two studies have already been performed,[22,23] and the third has been proposed and criticized.[24]

Annas and Grodin recently commented on the characterization and justification of placebos as a standard of care: " 'Nothing' is a description of what happens; 'standard of care' is a normative standard of effective medical treatment, whether or not it is provided to a particular community."[25]

Researchers have also sought to justify placebo-controlled trials by arguing that they require fewer subjects than equivalency studies and can therefore be completed more rapidly. Because equivalency studies are simply concerned with excluding alternative interventions that fall below some preestablished level of efficacy (as opposed to establishing which intervention is superior), it is customary to use one-sided statistical testing in such studies.[11] The numbers of women needed for a placebo-controlled trial and an equivalency study are similar.[26] In a placebo-controlled trial of a short course of zidovudine, with rates of perinatal HIV transmission of 25 percent in the placebo group and 15 percent in the zidovudine group, an alpha level of 0.05 (two-sided), and a beta level of 0.2, 500 subjects would be needed. An equivalency study with a transmission rate of 10 percent in the group receiving the ACTG 076 regimen, a difference in efficacy of 6 percent (above the 10 percent), an alpha level of 0.05 (one-sided), and a beta level of 0.2 would require 620 subjects (McCarthy W: personal communication).

TOWARD A SINGLE INTERNATIONAL STANDARD OF ETHICAL RESEARCH

Researchers assume greater ethical responsibilities when they enroll subjects in clinical studies, a precept acknowledged by Varmus recently when he insisted that all subjects in an NIH-sponsored needle-exchange trial be offered hepatitis B vaccine.[27] Residents of impoverished, postcolonial countries, the majority of whom are people of color, must be protected from potential exploitation in research. Otherwise, the abominable state of health care in these countries can be used to justify studies that could never pass ethical muster in the sponsoring country.

With the increasing globalization of trade, government research dollars becoming scarce, and more attention being paid to the hazards posed by "emerging infections" to the residents of industrialized countries, it is likely that studies in developing countries will increase. It is time to develop standards of research that preclude the kinds of double standards evident in these trials. In an editorial published nine years ago in the *Journal,* Marcia Angell stated, "Human subjects in any part of the world should be protected by a irreducible set of ethical standards."[28] Tragically, for the hundreds of infants who have needlessly contracted HIV infection in the perinatal-transmission studies that have al-

ready been completed, any such protection will have come too late.

REFERENCES

1. Connor EM, Sperling RS, Gelber R, et al. Reduction of maternal-infant transmission of human immunodeficiency virus type 1 with zidovudine treatment. N Engl J Med 1994;331:1173–80.

2. Sperling RS, Shapiro DE, Coombs RW, et al. Maternal viral load, zidovudine treatment, and the risk of transmission of human immunodeficiency virus type 1 from mother to infant. N Engl J Med 1996;335:1621–29.

3. Recommendations of the U.S. Public Health Service Task Force on the use of zidovudine to reduce perinatal transmission of human immunodeficiency virus. MMWR Morb Mortal Wkly Rep 1994;43(RR-11):1–20.

4. Fiscus SA, Adimora AA, Schoenbach VJ, et al. Perinatal HIV infection and the effect of zidovudine therapy on transmission in rural and urban countries. JAMA 1996;275:1483–88.

5. Cooper E, Diaz D, Pitt J, et al. Impact of ACTG 076: use of zidovudine during pregnancy and changes in the rate of HIV vertical transmission. In: Program and abstracts of the Third Conference on Retroviruses and Opportunistic Infections, Washington, D.C., January 28–February 1, 1996. Washington, D.C.: Infectious Diseases Society of America, 1996:57.

6. Simonds RJ, Nesheim S, Matheson P, et al. Declining mother to child HIV transmission following perinatal ZDV recommendations. Presented at the 11th International Conference on AIDS, Vancouver, Canada, July 7–12, 1996. abstract.

7. Scarlatti G. Paediatric HIV infection. Lancet 1996;348:863–68.

8. Recommendations from the meeting on mother-to-infant transmission of HIV by use of antiretrovirals, Geneva, World Health Organization, June 23–25, 1994.

9. World Health Organization. International ethical guidelines for biomedical research involving human subjects. Geneva: Council for International Organizations of Medical Sciences, 1993.

10. 45 CFR 46.111(a)(1).

11. Testing equivalence of two binomial proportions. In: Machin D, Campbell MJ. Statistical tables for the design of clinical trials. Oxford, England: Blackwell Scientific, 1987:35–53.

12. Brennan TA. Letter to Gilbert Meier, NIH Division of Research Ethics, December 28, 1994.

13. Lallemant M, Vithayasai V. A short ZDV course to prevent perinatal HIV in Thailand. Boston: Harvard School of Public Health, April 28, 1995.

14. Varmus H. Testimony before the Subcommittee on Human Resources, Committee on Government Reform and Oversight, U.S. House of Representatives, May 8, 1997.

15. Draft talking points: responding to Public Citizen press conference. Press release of the National Institutes of Health, April 22, 1997.

16. Questions and answers: CDC studies of AZT to prevent mother-to-child HIV transmission in developing countries. Press release of the Centers for Disease Control and Prevention, Atlanta. (undated document.)

17. Questions and answers on the UNAIDS sponsored trials for the prevention of mother-to-child transmission: background brief to assist in responding to issues raised by the public and the media. Press release of the United Nations AIDS Program. (undated document.)

18. Halsey NA, Meinert CK, Ruff AJ, et al. Letter to Harold Varmus, Director of National Institutes of Health. Baltimore: Johns Hopkins University, May 6, 1997.

19. Wiktor SZ, Ehounou E. A randomized placebo-controlled intervention study to evaluate the safety and effectiveness of oral zidovudine administered in late pregnancy to reduce the incidence of mother-to-child transmission of HIV-1 in Abidjan, Côte D'Ivoire. Atlanta: Centers for Disease Control and Prevention. (undated document.)

20. Rouzioux C, Costagliola D. Burgard M. et al. Timing of mother-to-child HIV-1 transmission depends on maternal status. AIDS 1993;7:Suppl 2:S49–S52.

21. Freedman B. Equipoise and the ethics of clinical research. N Engl J Med 1987;317:141–45.

22. Heimlich HJ, Chen XP, Xiao BQ, et al. CD4 response in HIV-positive patients treated with malaria therapy. Presented at the 11th International Conference on AIDS, Vancouver, B.C., July 7–12, 1996. abstract.

23. Bishop WB, Laubscher I, Labadarios D, Rehder P, Louw ME, Fellingham SA. Effect of vitamin-enriched bread on the vitamin status of an isolated rural community — a controlled clinical trial. S Afr Med J 1996;86:Suppl:458–62.

24. Lurie P, Bishaw M, Chesney MA, et al. Ethical, behavioral, and social aspects of HIV vaccine trials in developing countries. JAMA 1994;271:295–301.

25. Annas G, Grodin M. An apology is not enough. Boston Globe. May 18, 1997:C1–C2.

26. Freedman B, Weijer C, Glass KC. Placebo orthodoxy in clinical research. I. Empirical and methodological myths. J Law Med Ethics 1996;24:243–51.

27. Varmus H. Comments at the meeting of the Advisory Committee to the Director of the National Institutes of Health, December 12, 1996.

28. Angell M. Ethical imperialism? Ethics in international collaborative clinical research. N Engl J Med 1988;319:1081–83.

MARCIA ANGELL

The Ethics of Clinical Research in the Third World

An essential ethical condition for a randomized clinical trial comparing two treatments for a disease is that there be no good reason for thinking one is better than the other.[1,2] Usually, investigators hope and even expect that the new treatment will be better, but there should not be solid evidence one way or the other. If there is, not only would the trial be scientifically redundant, but the investigators would be guilty of knowingly giving inferior treatment to some participants in the trial. The necessity for investigators to be in this state of equipoise[2] applies to placebo-controlled trials, as well. Only when there is no known effective treatment is it ethical to compare a potential new treatment with a placebo. When effective treatment exists, a placebo may not be used. Instead, subjects in the control group of the study must receive the best known treatment. Investigators are responsible for all subjects enrolled in a trial, not just some of them, and the goals of the research are always secondary to the well-being of the participants. Those requirements are made clear in the Declaration of Helsinki of the World Health Organization (WHO), which is widely regarded as providing the fundamental guiding principles of research involving human subjects.[3] It states, "In research on man [sic] , the interest of science and society should never take precedence over considerations related to the wellbeing of the subject," and "In any medical study, every patient — including those of a control group, if any — should be assured of the best proven diagnostic and therapeutic method."

One reason ethical codes are unequivocal about investigators' primary obligation to care for the human subjects of their research is the strong temptation to subordinate the subjects' welfare to the objectives of the study. That is particularly likely when the research question is extremely important and the answer would probably improve the care of future patients substantially. In those circumstances, it is sometimes argued explicitly that obtaining a rapid, unambiguous answer to the re-

Reprinted with permission from the *New England Journal of Medicine,* 337 (September 18, 1997), pp. 847–49. Copyright © 1997 by the Massachusetts Medical Society.

search question is the primary ethical obligation. With the most altruistic of motives, then, researchers may find themselves slipping across a line that prohibits treating human subjects as means to an end. When that line is crossed, there is very little left to protect patients from a callous disregard of their welfare for the sake of research goals. Even informed consent, important though it is, is not protection enough, because of the asymmetry in knowledge and authority between researchers and their subjects. And approval by an institutional review board, though also important, is highly variable in its responsiveness to patients' interests when they conflict with the interests of researchers.

A textbook example of unethical research is the Tuskegee Study of Untreated Syphilis.[4] In that study, which was sponsored by the U.S. Public Health Service and lasted from 1932 to 1972, 412 poor African-American men with untreated syphilis were followed and compared with 204 men free of the disease to determine the natural history of syphilis. Although there was no very good treatment available at the time the study began (heavy metals were the standard treatment), the research continued even after penicillin became widely available and was known to be highly effective against syphilis. The study was not terminated until it came to the attention of a reporter and the outrage provoked by front-page stories in the *Washington Star* and *New York Times* embarrassed the Nixon administration into calling a halt to it.[5] The ethical violations were multiple: Subjects did not provide informed consent (indeed, they were deliberately deceived); they were denied the best known treatment; and the study was continued even after highly effective treatment became available. And what were the arguments in favor of the Tuskegee study? That these poor African-American men probably would not have been treated anyway, so the investigators were merely observing what would have happened if there were no study; and that the study was important (a "never-to-be-repeated opportunity," said one physician after penicillin became available).[6] Ethical concern was even stood on its head when it was suggested that not only was the information valuable, but it was especially so for people like the subjects—an impoverished rural population with a very high rate of untreated syphilis. The only lament seemed to be that many of the subjects inadvertently received treatment by other doctors.

Some of these issues are raised by Lurie and Wolfe elsewhere in this issue of the *Journal*. They discuss the ethics of ongoing trials in the Third World of regimens to prevent the vertical transmission of human immunodeficiency virus (HIV) infection.[7] All except one of the trials employ placebo-treated control groups, despite the fact that zidovudine has already been clearly shown to cut the rate of vertical transmission greatly and is now recommended in the United States for all HIV-infected pregnant women. The justifications are reminiscent of those for the Tuskegee study: Women in the Third World would not receive antiretroviral treatment anyway, so the investigators are simply observing what would happen to the subjects' infants if there were no study. And a placebo-controlled study is the fastest, most efficient way to obtain unambiguous information that will be of greatest value in the Third World. Thus, in response to protests from Wolfe and others to the secretary of Health and Human Services, the directors of the National Institutes of Health (NIH) and the Centers for Disease Control and Prevention (CDC)—the organizations sponsoring the studies—argued, "It is an unfortunate fact that the current standard of perinatal care for the HIV-infected pregnant women in the sites of the studies does not include any HIV prophylactic intervention at all," and the inclusion of placebo controls "will result in the most rapid, accurate, and reliable answer to the question of the value of the intervention being studied compared to the local standard of care."[8]

. . . As mentioned earlier, the Declaration of Helsinki requires control groups to receive the "best" current treatment, not the local one. The shift in wording between "best" and "local" may be slight, but the implications are profound. Acceptance of this ethical relativism could result in widespread exploitation of vulnerable Third World populations for research programs that could not be carried out in the sponsoring country.[9] Furthermore, it directly contradicts the Department of Health and Human Services' own regulations governing U.S.-sponsored research in foreign countries,[10] as well as joint guidelines for research in the Third World issued by WHO and the Council for International Organizations of Medical Sciences,[11] which require that human subjects receive protection at least equivalent to that in the sponsoring country. . . .

. . . There appears to be a general retreat from the clear principles enunciated in the Nuremberg Code and the Declaration of Helsinki as applied to research in the Third World. Why is that? Is it because the "local standard of care" is different? I don't think so. In my view, that is merely a self-serving justification after the fact. Is it because diseases and their treatments are very different in the Third World, so that information gained in the industrialized world has no relevance and we have to start from scratch? That, too, seems an unlikely explanation, although here again it is often offered as a justification. Sometimes there may be relevant differences between populations, but that cannot be assumed. Unless there are specific indications to the contrary, the safest and most reasonable position is that people everywhere are likely to respond similarly to the same treatment.

I think we have to look elsewhere for the real reasons. One of them may be a slavish adherence to the tenets of clinical trials. According to these, all trials should be randomized, double-blind, and placebo-controlled, if at all possible. That rigidity may explain the NIH's pressure on Marc Lallemant to include a placebo group in his study, as described by Lurie and Wolfe.[7] Sometimes journals are blamed for the problem because they are thought to demand strict conformity to the standard methods. That is not true, at least not at this journal. We do not want a scientifically neat study if it is ethically flawed, but like Lurie and Wolfe we believe that in many cases it is possible, with a little ingenuity, to have both scientific and ethical rigor.

The retreat from ethical principles may also be explained by some of the exigencies of doing clinical research in an increasingly regulated and competitive environment. Research in the Third World looks relatively attractive as it becomes better funded and regulations at home become more restrictive. Despite the existence of codes requiring that human subjects receive at least the same protection abroad as at home,

they are still honored partly in the breach. The fact remains that many studies are done in the Third World that simply could not be done in the countries sponsoring the work. Clinical trials have become a big business, with many of the same imperatives. To survive, it is necessary to get the work done as quickly as possible, with a minimum of obstacles. When these considerations prevail, it seems as if we have not come very far from Tuskegee after all. Those of us in the research community need to redouble our commitment to the highest ethical standards, no matter where the research is conducted, and sponsoring agencies need to enforce those standards, not undercut them.

REFERENCES

1. Angell M. Patients' preferences in randomized clinical trials. N Engl J Med 1984;310:1385–87.

2. Freedman B. Equipoise and the ethics of clinical research. N Engl J Med 1987;317:141–45.

3. Declaration of Helsinki IV, 41st World Medical Assembly, Hong Kong, September 1989. In: Annas GJ, Grodin MA, eds. The Nazi doctors and the Nuremberg Code: human rights in human experimentation. New York: Oxford University Press, 1992:339–42.

4. Twenty years after: the legacy of the Tuskegee syphilis study. Hastings Cent Rep 1992;22(6):29–40.

5. Caplan AL. When evil intrudes. Hastings Cent Rep 1992; 22(6):29–32.

6. The development of consent requirements in research ethics. In: Faden RR, Beauchamp TL. A history and theory of informed consent. New York: Oxford University Press, 1986:151–99.

7. Lurie P, Wolfe SM. Unethical trials of interventions to reduce perinatal transmission of the human immunodeficiency virus in developing countries. N Engl J Med 1997;337:853–86.

8. The conduct of clinical trials of maternal-infant transmission of HIV supported by the United States Department of Health and Human Services in developing countries. Washington, D.C.: Department of Health and Human Services, July 1997.

9. Angell M. Ethical imperialism? Ethics in international collaborative clinical research. N Engl J Med 1988;319:1081–83.

10. Protection of human subjects, 45 CFR § 46 (1996).

11. International ethical guidelines for biomedical research involving human subjects. Geneva: Council for International Organizations of Medical Sciences, 1993.

HAROLD VARMUS AND DAVID SATCHER

Ethical Complexities of Conducting Research in Developing Countries

One of the great challenges in medical research is to conduct clinical trials in developing countries that will lead to therapies that benefit the citizens of these countries. Features of many developing countries — poverty, endemic diseases, and a low level of investment in health care systems — affect both the ease of performing trials and the selection of trials that can benefit the populations of the countries. Trials that make use of impoverished populations to test drugs for use solely in developed countries violate our most basic understanding of ethical behavior. Trials that apply scientific knowledge to interventions that can be used to benefit such populations are appropriate but present their own ethical challenges. How do we balance the ethical premises on which our work is based with the calls for public health partnerships from our colleagues in developing countries?

Some commentators have been critical of research performed in developing countries that might not be found ethically acceptable in developed countries. Specifically, questions have been raised about trials of interventions to prevent maternal-infant transmission of the human immunodeficiency virus (HIV) that have been sponsored by the National Institutes of Health (NIH) and the Centers for Disease Control and Prevention (CDC).[1,2] Although these commentators raise important issues, they have not adequately considered the purpose and complexity of such trials and the needs of the countries involved. They also allude inappropriately to the infamous Tuskegee study, which did not test an intervention. The Tuskegee study ultimately deprived people of a known, effective, affordable intervention. To claim that countries seeking help in stemming the tide of maternal-infant HIV transmission by seeking usable interventions have followed that path trivializes the suffering of the men in the Tuskegee study and shows a serious lack of understanding of today's trials.

After the Tuskegee study was made public, in the 1970s, a national commission was established to develop principles and guidelines for the protection of research subjects. The new system of protection was described in the Belmont report.[3] Although largely compatible with the World Medical Association's Declaration of Helsinki,[4] the Belmont report articulated three principles: respect for persons (the recognition of the right of persons to exercise autonomy), beneficence (the minimization of risk incurred by research subjects and the maximization of benefits to them and to others), and justice (the principle that therapeutic investigations should not unduly involve persons from groups unlikely to benefit from subsequent applications of the research).

There is an inherent tension among these three principles. Over the years, we have seen the focus of debate shift from concern about the burdens of participation in research (beneficence) to equitable access to clinical trials (justice). Furthermore, the right to exercise autonomy was not always fully available to women, who were excluded from participating in clinical trials perceived as jeopardizing their safety; their exclusion clearly limited their ability to benefit from the research. Similarly, persons in developing countries deserve research that addresses their needs.

How should these principles be applied to research conducted in developing countries? How can we — and they — weigh the benefits and risks? Such research must be developed in concert with the developing countries in which it will be conducted. In the case of the NIH and CDC trials, there has been strong and consistent support and involvement of the scientific and

Reprinted with permission from the *New England Journal of Medicine* 337 (October 2, 1997), pp. 1003–05. Copyright © 1997 by the Massachusetts Medical Society.

public health communities in the host countries, with local as well as United States–based scientific and ethical reviews and the same requirements for informed consent that would exist if the work were performed in the United States. But there is more to this partnership. Interventions that could be expected to be made available in the United States might be well beyond the financial resources of a developing country or exceed the capacity of its health care infrastructure. Might we support a trial in another country that would not be offered in the United States? Yes, because the burden of disease might make such a study more compelling in that country. Even if there were some risks associated with intervention, such a trial might pass the test of beneficence. Might we elect not to support a trial of an intervention that was beyond the reach of the citizens of the other country? Yes, because that trial would not pass the test of justice.

Trials supported by the NIH and the CDC, which are designed to reduce the transmission of HIV from mothers to infants in developing countries, have been held up by some observers as examples of trials that do not meet ethical standards. We disagree. The debate does not hinge on informed consent, which all the trials have obtained. It hinges instead of whether it is ethical to test interventions against a placebo control when an effective intervention is in use elsewhere in the world. A background paper sets forth our views on this matter more fully.[5] The paper is also available on the World Wide Web (at http://www.nih.gov/news/mathiv/mathiv.htm).

One such effective intervention — known as AIDS Clinical Trials Group protocol 076 — was a major breakthrough in the search for a way to interrupt the transmission of HIV from mother to infant. The regimen tested in the original study, however, was quite intensive for pregnant women and the health care system. Although this regimen has been proved effective, it requires that women undergo HIV testing and receive counseling about their HIV status early in pregnancy, comply with a lengthy oral regimen and with intravenous administration of the relatively expensive antiretroviral drug zidovudine, and refrain from breast-feeding. In addition, the newborn infants must receive six weeks of oral zidovudine, and both mothers and infants must be carefully monitored for adverse effects of the drug. Unfortunately, the burden of maternal-infant transmission of HIV is greatest in countries where women present late

for prenatal care, have limited access to HIV testing and counseling, typically deliver their infants in settings not conducive to intravenous drug administration, and depend on breast-feeding to protect their babies from many diseases, only one of which is HIV infection. Furthermore, zidovudine is a powerful drug, and its safety in the populations of developing countries, where the incidences of other diseases, anemia, and malnutrition are higher than in developed countries, is unknown. Therefore, even though the 076 protocol has been shown to be effective in some countries, it is unlikely that it can be successfully exported to many others.

In addition to these hurdles, the wholesale cost of zidovudine in the 076 protocol is estimated to be in excess of $800 per mother and infant, an amount far greater than most developing countries can afford to pay for standard care. For example, in Malawi, the cost of zidovudine alone for the 076 regimen for one HIV-infected woman and her child is more than 600 times the annual per capita allocation for health care.

Various representatives of the ministries of health, communities, and scientists in developing countries have joined with other scientists to call for less complex and less expensive interventions to counteract the staggering impact of maternal-infant transmission of HIV in the developing world. The World Health Organization moved promptly after the release of the results of the 076 protocol, convening a panel of researchers and public health practitioners from around the world. This panel recommended the use of the 076 regimen throughout the industrialized world, where it is feasible, but also called for studies of alternative regimens that could be used in developing countries, observing that the logistical issues and costs precluded the widespread application of the 076 regimen.[6] To this end, the World Health Organization asked UNAIDS, the Joint United Nations Programme on HIV/AIDS, to coordinate international research efforts to develop simpler, less costly interventions.

The scientific community is responding by carrying out trials of several promising regimens that developing countries recognize as candidates for widespread delivery. However, these trials are being criticized by some people because of the use of placebo controls. Why not test these new interventions against the 076 regimen? Why not test them against other interventions that might offer some benefit? These questions were carefully considered in the development of these research projects and in their scientific and ethical review.

An obvious response to the ethical objection to placebo-controlled trials in countries where there is no current intervention is that the assignment to a placebo group does not carry a risk beyond that associated with standard practice, but this response is too simple. An additional response is that a placebo-controlled study usually provides a faster answer with fewer subjects, but the same result might be achieved with more sites or more aggressive enrollment. The most compelling reason to use a placebo-controlled study is that it provides definitive answers to questions about the safety and value of an intervention in the setting in which the study is performed, and these answers are the point of the research. Without clear and firm answers to whether and, if so, how well an intervention works, it is impossible for a country to make a sound judgment about the appropriateness and financial feasibility of providing the intervention.

For example, testing two or more interventions of unknown benefit (as some people have suggested) will not necessarily reveal whether either is better than nothing. Even if one surpasses the other, it may be difficult to judge the extent of the benefit conferred, since the interventions may differ markedly in other ways — for example, cost or toxicity. A placebo-controlled study would supply that answer. Similarly, comparing an intervention of unknown benefit — especially one that is affordable in a developing country — with the only intervention with a known benefit (the 076 regimen) may provide information that is not useful for patients. If the affordable intervention is less effective than the 076 regimen — not an unlikely outcome — this information will be of little use in a country where the more effective regimen is unavailable. Equally important, it will still be unclear whether the affordable intervention is better than nothing and worth the investment of scarce health care dollars. Such studies would fail to meet the goal of determining whether a treatment that could be implemented is worth implementing.

A placebo-controlled trial is not the only way to study a new intervention, but as compared with other approaches, it offers more definitive answers and a clearer view of side effects. This is not a case of treating research subjects as a means to an end, nor does it reflect "a callous disregard of their welfare."[2] Instead, a placebo-controlled trial may be the only way to obtain an answer that is ultimately useful to people in similar circumstances. If we enroll subjects in a study that exposes them to unknown risks and is designed in a way this is unlikely to provide results that are useful to the subjects or others in the population, we have failed the test of beneficence.

Finally, the NIH- and CDC-supported trials have undergone a rigorous process of ethical review, including not only the participation of the public health and scientific communities in the developing countries where the trials are being performed but also the application of the U.S. rules for the protection of human research subjects by relevant institutional review boards in the United States and in the developing countries. Support from local governments has been obtained, and each active study has been and will continue to be reviewed by an independent data and safety monitoring board.

To restate our main points: these studies address an urgent need in the countries in which they are being conducted and have been developed with extensive in-country participation. The studies are being conducted according to widely accepted principles and guidelines in bioethics. And our decisions to support these trials rest heavily on local support and approval. In a letter to the NIH dated May 8, 1997, Edward K. Mbidde, chairman of the AIDS Research Committee of the Uganda Cancer Institute, wrote:

These are Ugandan studies conducted by Ugandan investigators on Ugandans. Due to lack of resources we have been sponsored by organizations like yours. We are grateful that you have been able to do so. . . . There is a mix up of issues here which needs to be clarified. It is not NIH conducting the studies in Uganda but Ugandans conducting their study on their people for the good of their people.

The scientific and ethical issues concerning studies in developing countries are complex. It is a healthy sign that we are debating these issues so that we can continue to advance our knowledge and our practice. However, it is essential that the debate take place with a full understanding of the nature of the science, the interventions in question, and the local factors that impede or support research and its benefits.

REFERENCES

1. Lurie P, Wolfe SM. Unethical trials of interventions to reduce perinatal transmission of the human immunodeficiency virus in developing countries. N Engl J Med 1997;337:853–56.

2. Angell M. The ethics of clinical research in the third world. N Engl J Med 1997;337:847–49.

3. National Commission for the Protection of Human Subjects of Biomedical and Behavioral Research. Belmont report: ethical

principles and guidelines for the protection of human subjects of research. Washington, D.C.: Government Printing Office, 1988. (GPO 887-809.)

4. World Medical Association Declaration of Helsinki. Adopted by the 18th World Medical Assembly, Helsinki, 1964, as revised by the 48th World Medical Assembly, Republic of South Africa, 1996.

5. The conduct of clinical trials of maternal-infant transmission of HIV supported by the United States Department of Health and Human Services in developing countries. Washington, D.C.: Department of Health and Human Services, July 1997.

6. Recommendations from the meeting on mother-to-infant transmission of HIV by use of antiretrovirals, Geneva, World Health Organization, June 23–25, 1994.

DANSTAN BAGENDA AND PHILIPPA MUSOKE-MUDIDO

We're Trying to Help Our Sickest People, Not Exploit Them

Every day, like the beat of a drum heard throughout Africa, 1,000 more infants here are infected with HIV, the virus that causes AIDS. At Old Mulago Hospital, we are trying to educate people about AIDS, as well as study new therapies to prevent the disease's rampant spread. Recently, some of these studies have been attacked, with comparisons made to the notorious Tuskegee experiment in which black men in the United States were denied treatment for syphilis. Tuskegee? Is this really what is happening here in our mother-child clinic?

Our country lies in the heart of Africa, along the Great Rift Valley and Lake Victoria. It is one of those hardest hit by the AIDS epidemic. A few years ago, visitors here in the capital were greeted by the macabre sight of empty coffins for sale — piled in pyramids from adult to baby size — along the main road. These grim reminders have since been removed by city authorities, but the AIDS epidemic is omnipresent. In this city of 1 million, about one out of every six adults is infected with HIV. Hospitals and clinics like ours, which provide free medical care and therefore serve the poorest communities, are stretched beyond their resources.

At the Mulago Hospital, where more than 20,000 women deliver each year, we are trying to find effective therapies to stop transmission of HIV from pregnant women to their babies. About one in five babies becomes infected with HIV during pregnancy and delivery. If the mother breast-feeds her baby, there is an additional 15- to 25-percent chance that the baby will later become infected. There is no available treatment for the disease in Uganda. After careful consideration among researchers from developing and developed countries, the World Health Organization (WHO) recommended in 1994 that the best way to find safe and effective treatment for sufferers in countries in the developing world is to conduct studies in which new treatments, better tailored to the local population, are compared with placebos (inactive pills).

Women who enroll in our studies undergo intensive education and individual counseling. They are given a comprehensive consent form, written in the local language, which they are encouraged to take home and discuss with their families. It describes the potential risks of participating in the study and their chances of receiving a placebo. Only when they and their counselors are satisfied that all questions have been answered are they asked to sign the form. Our careful attention to these measures has consistently met the standards of national and international ethical review committees.

Results from a clinical trial in the United States and France, known as the ACTG 076 protocol, showed as long ago as 1994 that if a mother takes zidovudine

(AZT) daily from the middle of her pregnancy until delivery, receives intravenous AZT during delivery, gives her infant oral AZT for the first six weeks of life and does not breast-feed, the transmission of HIV from mother to child can be reduced by two-thirds. The ACTG 076 protocol immediately became the recommended therapy in the United States. But it is not possible to simply transplant this protocol to Uganda for three main reasons: At a cost of between $800 and $1,000 per person, it is far too expensive; it requires treatment to begin in the middle of a pregnancy; and it means mothers must abstain from breast-feeding.

Some critics in the United States have asserted that we should compare new therapies with the ACTG 076 protocol rather than with a placebo. But in Uganda, the government health expenditure is $3 per person per year, and the average citizen makes less than $1 per day. We think it is unethical to impose expensive treatment protocols that could never be used here. The situations are not parallel. In America, for instance, antibiotics are often over-prescribed; but here in Uganda we have difficulty even obtaining many needed antibiotics — to treat common complaints like ear infections. It is also naive to assume that what works for Americans will work for the rest of the world. Differences in nutrition, economics, societal norms and culture, and the frequency of tropical diseases make such extrapolations dangerously ethnocentric and wrong.

Many pregnant women here never show up for prenatal care and, of those who do, 70 percent make their first visit after the 30th week of pregnancy — too late for the U.S. treatment protocol. Should we make a study available only to the minority of women who come early for care and tell the others, sorry, you came too late? We need to find treatments that will reach the most women possible — ones that can be given late in pregnancy or during labor.

There is also a huge gap between the United States and Uganda in breast-feeding practices. Should we apply the ACTG 076 protocol and tell women in the clinic not to breast-feed and instead give their babies infant formula? Access to clean water is a formidable challenge here, and we still remember the shocking epidemics of infant diarrhea and mortality in the early 1970s, when multinational companies shamelessly marketed formula in Africa. Despite the known risks of transmitting HIV through breast milk, the Ugandan Ministry of Health, UNICEF and WHO still encourage African women to breast-feed as the nutritional benefits outweigh the risks of HIV transmission.

There are other factors we need to take into account. Every day, we treat both mothers and infants for malaria and iron deficiency. Both diseases contribute to anemia, which is also a major side effect of AZT. We are worried that AZT will exacerbate anemia in women and infants here. If we are to find out whether the new treatments are safe, the best way is to compare them with a placebo. How could we evaluate the safety of a new treatment if we compared it with the treatment used in America — one that has its own side effects? Could we really tell Ugandans that we had evaluated a new therapy for side effects using the best possible methods?

The AIDS epidemic has touched all our lives. Each of the 90 staff members in the mother-child health clinic has lost a family member, a loved one or a close friend. There is no dividing line between patients with HIV and those of us who care for them. A few years ago, we all chipped in money when a staff member needed to pay for the burial of a loved one, but recently we realized that we were all giving and receiving the same.

The ethical issues in our studies are complicated, but they have been given careful thought by the local community, ethicists, physicians and activists. Those who can speak with credibility for AIDS patients in Africa are those who live among and know the people here or have some basic cross-cultural sensitivity. We are suspicious of those who claim to speak for our people, yet have never worked with them. Callous accusations may help sell newspapers and journals, but they demean the people here and the horrible tragedy that we live daily.

In the next several months, we expect to see results from our study and others like it in Ivory Coast, South Africa, Tanzania and Thailand. We hope they will help bring appropriate and safe therapies to the people of the developing world. That hope is the driving force that brings us back to our work in the clinic after each of the all-too frequent burials.

PRAPHAN PHANUPHAK

Ethical Issues in Studies in Thailand of the Vertical Transmission of HIV

In response to the controversy over placebo-controlled trials in developing countries of treatments to prevent mother-to-child transmission of the human immunodeficiency virus (HIV),[1] I would like to offer the perspective of someone who lives and works in Thailand, a developing country with limited resources that is the site of several such trials.

PLACEBO-CONTROLLED TRIALS IN DEVELOPING COUNTRIES

I believe that placebo-controlled trials are sometimes justified in countries where treatment is otherwise totally unavailable, because at least half the patients (those receiving active treatment) will probably benefit. This is particularly true if the trial will generate results that will directly benefit the patient population under study. But the availability of resources is usually relative. It depends on the judgment and commitment of policy makers, who can always reshuffle budget priorities. There are different levels of constraints in developing countries. Some countries, such as those in Central Africa, may have virtually no resources. Some may have limited resources; examples are Thailand, the Philippines, Brazil, and South Africa. Therefore, recommendations by international agencies such as the World Health Organization[2] should not be too general. If they are, policy makers from countries with some, albeit limited, resources may too readily claim poverty as an excuse to do less than they are able to do.

Scientifically sound alternatives to placebo-controlled trials exist. Equivalency studies are one of the examples mentioned by Lurie and Wolfe.[1] The investigators or the sponsors may have to enroll more patients, spend more money, or take more time to perform an equivalency study than a placebo-controlled trial. In my view, they ought to do so rather than to risk the lives of the patients (or their offspring) receiving placebo. This is particularly true of trials involving zidovudine, which has been proved effective in preventing mother-to-child transmission of HIV and which has been accepted as the standard of care in all developed countries.[3]

APPROVAL OF PLACEBO-CONTROLLED TRIALS IN THAILAND

Placebo-controlled studies of short-course zidovudine (given for two to four weeks) in the prevention of vertical transmission of HIV started in Thailand as early as 1994. At that time, only a small portion of Thai obstetricians thought zidovudine would benefit their HIV-infected pregnant patients. There was also no clear-cut recommendation from the Ministry of Public Health for the routine use of zidovudine. Although financial constraints were a reason, the chief concern was uncertainty about whether the infrastructure needed to implement any such recommendations was ready. In particular, there was no system for ensuring HIV testing and counseling, follow-up of mothers and infants, or formula feeding. It was in this context that the protocols for the placebo-controlled trials were approved by both the institutional review boards and the Ethical Committee for Human Experimentation of the Ministry of Public Health.

CHANGING CIRCUMSTANCES

It takes time before a trial can actually get started. It also takes a few years to finish it. As the studies in Thailand

Reprinted with permission from the *New England Journal of Medicine* 338 (March 19, 1998), 834–35. Copyright © 1998 by the Massachusetts Medical Society.

proceeded, and as knowledge and experience accumulated, more obstetricians came to believe zidovudine was beneficial, and at the same time the drug became more readily available. Thus, a trial that might have seemed ethical in 1994 could come to be seen as unethical in 1997. Such an evolution is underscored by the zidovudine-donation campaign of the Thai Red Cross Society. This campaign, under the patronage of Princess Soamsawali, started in February 1996 with the aim of collecting donations from the general public to procure zidovudine for poor, HIV-infected pregnant women throughout Thailand. Contributions continue to grow and are supplemented by funds from the Ministry of Public Health. By the end of August 1997, 1040 pregnant women at 57 government hospitals throughout Thailand had received zidovudine through this program, and about half had already delivered their babies.

The increased availability of zidovudine through the Thai Red Cross donation program and the Ministry of Public Health led to the early termination, in January 1997, of the placebo-controlled trial of two weeks of zidovudine therapy, conducted at Chulalongkorn University Hospital in Bangkok. However, the other placebo-controlled study in Bangkok, led by the U.S. Centers for Disease Control and Prevention (CDC),[4] is at this writing slated to continue until its completion early this year. This decision has created considerable controversy both locally and globally. The ethical concerns are heightened by the fact that some pregnant women who sought antenatal care early in pregnancy were not offered complete information or told about the full benefits of the AIDS Clinical Trials Group Protocol 076 regimen but, rather, were left untreated until the 36th week of gestation, when they were randomly assigned to the zidovudine or placebo group.

UNETHICAL STUDIES IN DEVELOPING COUNTRIES

In addition to the CDC-sponsored study, there is another study being undertaken in Thailand, sponsored by the U.S. government, that I believe is unjustified and unethical. This is a study conducted by the Walter Reed Army Institute of Research in Lampang, a city in the north of Thailand. The purpose of the study is to determine the natural history of perinatal HIV infection among the infants born to pregnant women attending a hospital-based antenatal clinic in Lampang.[5]

Measurements of CD4 levels and of viral loads in the blood, cervicovaginal secretions, and colostrum are among the expensive and sophisticated laboratory tests in this two-to-three-year prospective study. None of the women have received zidovudine, even though its cost would constitute only a small fraction of the study budget. As of October 31, 1997, all but 10 to 15 of the 125 women enrolled had delivered their babies. Local U.S. investigators have since been asked to consider giving zidovudine to the remaining pregnant women and their newborns, and the response has been positive.

Although placebo-controlled studies may be scientifically acceptable, they may not always be ethically acceptable. Ethical standards may vary according to culture, the availability of resources, and evolving scientific knowledge. Therefore, scientists may have to reconsider or change their approaches as circumstances change. That is the only way that clinical trials can survive — both for the good of science and for the good of the research subjects.

Editor's note: Dr. Phanuphak's article was referred to Dr. Merlin L. Robb, chief of vaccine research at the Division of Retrovirology, Walter Reed Army Institute of Research, who responds in the Correspondence section of this issue. Also in the Correspondence section is a response from Dr. Suchint Wongchoosri, director of Lampang Hospital, and colleagues.

REFERENCES

1. Lurie P, Wolfe SM. Unethical trials of interventions to reduce perinatal transmission of the human immunodeficiency virus in developing countries. N Engl J Med 1997;337:853–56.

2. Recommendations from the meeting on mother-to-infant transmission of HIV by use of antiretrovirals, Geneva, World Health Organization, June 23–25, 1994.

3. Conor EM, Sperling RS, Gelber R, et al. Reduction of maternal–infant transmission of human immunodeficiency virus type 1 with zidovudine treatment. N Engl J Med 1994;331:1173–80.

4. Chaisilwattana P, Shaffer N, Chearskul S, et al. Randomized placebo-controlled trial of short-course zidovudine (ZDV) to reduce perinatal HIV transmission in Thailand. Presented at the Conference on Global Strategies for the Prevention of HIV Transmission from Mothers to Infants, Washington, D.C., September 3–6, 1997, abstract.

5. Sriplienchan S, Vancott T, Wera-arpachai M, et al. Evaluation of the epidemiology and biology of perinatal transmission in a provincial hospital in northern Thailand. Presented at the Conference on Global Strategies for the Prevention of HIV Transmission from Mothers to Infants, Washington, D.C., September 3–6, 1997, abstract.

P .   V U T H I P O N G S E ,   E T   A L .

Administration of Zidovudine During Late Pregnancy and Delivery to Prevent Perinatal HIV Transmission — Thailand, 1996–1998

Worldwide, approximately 500,000 infants are perinatally infected with human immunodeficiency virus (HIV) each year, most of whom are born in developing countries (1). In 1994, a clinical trial in the United States and France demonstrated that zidovudine (ZDV) administered orally five times a day to HIV-infected pregnant women starting at 14–34 weeks' gestation, intravenously during labor, and orally to their newborns for 6 weeks reduced the risk for perinatal HIV transmission by two-thirds (2). In 1994, this regimen was recommended as standard care in the United States (3); however, because of its complexity and cost, this regimen has not been implemented in most developing countries, and no other intervention had been efficacious in reducing perinatal HIV transmission. In 1996, the Ministry of Public Health of Thailand and Mahidol University, in collaboration with CDC, initiated a randomized, placebo-controlled trial of a simpler and less expensive regimen of ZDV to prevent perinatal HIV transmission. This report describes preliminary trial results, which indicate that a short-term antenatal regimen of ZDV reduced the risk for perinatal HIV transmission by approximately half.

HIV-infected pregnant women gave written informed consent for participation and were randomly selected at each of two study hospitals in Bangkok to receive either ZDV or a placebo. The ZDV regimen consisted of 300 mg orally twice a day from 36 weeks' gestation until onset of labor and 300 mg every 3 hours from onset of labor until delivery. All women were provided infant formula and counseled not to breast-feed, consistent with national guidelines for HIV-infected women in

Reprinted from *MMWR (Morbidity and Mortality Weekly Report)* 47 (March 6, 1998), 151–54.

Thailand. The planned sample size was 392 women, selected to provide 80% power to detect a 50% lower transmission rate in the ZDV group compared with a transmission rate of 24% in the placebo group. The study endpoint was the HIV-infection status of the infant at age 6 months, determined by results of polymerase chain reaction (PCR) testing for HIV DNA performed on blood specimens obtained at birth, 2 months, and 6 months. The proportion of children found to be infected by age 6 months in each treatment group was estimated by using the Kaplan-Meier method. The null hypothesis of no treatment effect was tested by using a normally distributed Z statistic computed from these estimates. As a result of two interim evaluations of treatment efficacy for data and safety monitoring in July 1997 and January 1998, the critical value of the Z statistic for rejecting the null hypothesis of no treatment effect at the end of the study was 2.05. The trial protocol was approved by human subjects committees in Thailand and at CDC, and the conduct of the trials was monitored by a data and safety monitoring board at the U.S. National Institutes of Health, which included a senior health official from Thailand.

From May 23, 1996, through December 31, 1997, a total of 397 women were enrolled; four women were lost to follow-up before delivery, and 393 women delivered 395 live-born infants (Table 1). At enrollment, the median age was 24 years, and the median CD4+ cell count was 424 cells/μL. Fourteen percent of women had cesarean deliveries. The median duration of antenatal treatment was 25 days, and the median number of doses during labor was three. Of these enrollees, 99% took at least 90% of the prescribed doses of ZDV during the antepartum period, and 99% took at least one dose during labor; 96% of study visits were kept. Base-

Table 1. Study Outcome of Perinatal Zidovudine (ZDV) Trial, by Treatment Group — Bangkok, Thailand, 1998

	Treatment group	
Category	ZDV (n = 198)	Placebo (n = 199)
Median CD4+ count (cells/µL) at enrollment	428	410
Number of women lost to follow-up before delivery	3	1
Number of women who delivered infants	195	198
Number of live-born children*	196	199
Number of children with at least one polymerase chain reaction (PCR) result[†]	193	198
Number of children with positive PCR	17	35
Risk for perinatal transmission	9.2%	18.6%
(95% confidence interval)[§]	(5.0%–13.5%)	(13.0%–24.0%)
Number of children that died	3	4

*Included one set of twins in each treatment group.

[†]Excludes one child from each set of twins. In addition, one child died without a PCR result, and one child's first result is pending.

[§]Estimated using the Kaplan-Meier method.

line and delivery characteristics, protocol adherence, and adverse event rates were similar in the two trial groups. No women breastfed their infants.

As of February 13, 1998, PCR data were available for 391 children (Table 1). Of these, 52 children have tested PCR positive (17 in the ZDV group and 35 in the placebo group), all by their 2-month visit. Of the remaining 339 children, 310 tested PCR negative at age ≥ 2 months, and 29 children tested PCR negative at birth but have not yet been evaluated further. The estimated HIV transmission risk for the ZDV and placebo groups were 9.2% (95% confidence interval [CI]=5.0%–13.5%) and 18.6% (95% CI=13.0%–24.0%), respectively, representing a 51% (95% CI=15%–71%) decrease in transmission risk. On the basis of these data, the Z statistic for testing for a difference between the groups was 2.67 (p=0.008). Assuming that all infected children will be detected by their 2-month visit and that the transmission risk among the children whose infection status is pending is as high as 24%, the probability is >98% that the null hypothesis of no treatment effect will be rejected when all results are available.

Reported by: P Vuthipongse, MD, Ministry of Public Health; C Bhadrakom, MD, P Chaisilwattana, MD, A Roongpisuthipong, MD, A Chalermchokcharoenkit, MD, Dept of OB/GYN; S Chearskul, MD, N Wanprapa, MD, K Chokephaibulkit, MD, M Tuchinda, MD, Dept of Pediatrics; C Wasi, MD, R Chuachoowong, MD, Dept of Microbiology, Siriraj Hospital, Mahidol Univ; W Siriwasin, MD, P Chinayon, MD, S Asavapiriyanont, MD, Dept of OB/GYN, Rajavithi Hospital; T Chotpitayasunondh, MD, N Waranawat, MD, V Sangtaweesin, MD, S Horpaopan, MD, Queen Sirikit National Institute for Child Health, Bangkok; The HIV/AIDS Collaboration, Nonthaburi, Thailand. Div of HIV/AIDS Prevention-Surveillance and Epidemiology, National Center for HIV, STD and TB Prevention, CDC.

EDITORIAL NOTE

This report is the first to describe the efficacy of a short-term regimen of an antiretroviral drug for preventing perinatal HIV transmission. The regimen studied in this trial is more feasible for implementation in Thailand and other developing countries than the regimen now used in the United States (3) because it is less expensive (i.e., $50 versus $800) and logistically simpler (i.e., later start in pregnancy, shorter duration, less frequent dosing, oral labor dosing, and no infant treatment). If implemented, thousands of perinatal HIV infections annually could be prevented in Thailand, where an estimated 20,000 HIV-infected women deliver infants each year.

Although this trial was not designed to compare the short-term ZDV regimen to the longer regimen (2), the decrease in transmission rate (51%) using the shorter regimen is less than the 66% decrease with the longer regimen. The smaller treatment effect could result from the shorter duration of treatment, oral rather than intravenous administration during labor, lack of treatment for the infant, different study populations, random variation, or a combination of these factors.

However, this clinical trial demonstrates that a shorter regimen of ZDV given only during pregnancy can substantially reduce perinatal transmission.

Reasons are unknown for the lower transmission rate in the placebo group (18.6%) than in untreated women (24.2%) studied in the same hospitals during 1993–1994 (4). The lower than expected background transmission rate highlights the importance of having included a randomized, concurrently enrolled, untreated control group. Had the test regimen been inactive, a transmission rate of 18.6% may have suggested some efficacy when compared with historical data.

CDC has sponsored another placebo-controlled trial of the same regimen of ZDV in collaboration with the Ministry of Public Health in Côte d'Ivoire in west Africa, where most HIV-infected women breastfeed their infants. Because the trial in Thailand demonstrated that the short-term regimen is efficacious in reducing transmission around the time of birth, and because preliminary data from the trial in Côte d'Ivoire have shown the regimen to be safe in this population, enrollment in the placebo group of the Côte d'Ivoire trial has been stopped. All women enrolled in the study are being offered the short-term ZDV regimen. Because breastfeeding is associated with postnatal HIV transmission from mothers to infants (5), follow-up of enrolled infants will continue to determine whether the short-term ZDV regimen results in an overall lower risk for mother-infant HIV transmission in populations where HIV-infected women routinely breastfeed.

To implement these findings, ministries of health, donor agencies, and other international agencies should develop policies and practices to strengthen access to prenatal care, testing and counseling for HIV infection, and provision of ZDV for HIV-infected pregnant women. Operational research is needed to optimize provision of this intervention to HIV-infected women in resource-poor settings. Further evaluation is needed of the effect of breastfeeding on the efficacy of this regimen.

REFERENCES

1. World Health Organization, Global AIDS surveillance — part 1. Wkly Epidemiol Rec 1997;72:357–60.

2. Sperling RS, Shapiro DE, Coombs RW, et al. Maternal viral load, zidovudine treatment, and the risk of transmission of human immunodeficiency virus type 1 from mother to infant. N Engl J Med 1996;335:1621–29.

3. CDC. Recommendations of the U.S. Public Health Service Task Force on the Use of Zidovudine to Reduce Perinatal Transmission of Human Immunodeficiency Virus. MMWR 1994;43 (no. RR-11).

4. Shaffer N, Bhiraleus P, Chinayon P, et al. High viral load predicts perinatal HIV-1 subtype E transmission, Bangkok, Thailand [Abstract]. Vancouver, Canada: XIth International Conference on AIDS, July 1996.

5. Bertolli J, St. Louis ME, Simonds RJ, et al. Estimating the timing of mother-to-child transmission of human immunodeficiency virus in a breast-feeding population in Kinshasa, Zaire. J Infec Dis 1996;174:722–26.

SUGGESTED READINGS

GENERAL ISSUES

Allen, James R., *et al.* "AIDS: The Responsibilities of Health Professionals" [Special Supplement]. *Hastings Center Report* 18 (April–May 1988), S1–S32.

Almond, Brenda, ed. *AIDS: A Moral Issue—the Ethical, Legal and Social Aspects.* New York: St. Martin's Press, 1990.

Battin, Margaret P. "Going Early, Going Late: The Rationality of Decisions about Suicide in AIDS." *Journal of Medicine and Philosophy* 19 (1994), 571–94

Bayer, Ronald. "AIDS: I. Public-Health Issues." In Warren Thomas Reich, ed. *Encyclopedia of Bioethics.* Revised ed. New York: Simon and Schuster Macmillan, 1995, 108–13.

————. "AIDS and Ethics." In Robert M. Veatch, ed. *Medical Ethics.* 2d ed. Sudbury, MA: Jones and Bartlett, 1997, 395–413.

————. *Private Acts, Social Consequences: AIDS and the Politics of Public Health.* New York: Free Press, 1989.

————. "Science, Politics, and AIDS Prevention Policy." *Journal of Acquired Immune Deficiency Syndromes and Human Retrovirology* 14 (Suppl. 2; 1997), S22–S29.

Berridge, Virginia. *AIDS in the UK: The Making of a Policy, 1981–1994.* New York: Oxford University Press, 1996.

Blendon, Robert J.; Donelan, Karen; and Knox, Richard A. "Public Opinion and AIDS: Lessons for the Second Decade." *Journal of the American Medical Association* 267 (1992), 981–86.

Brandt, Allan M. "The Syphilis Epidemic and Its Relationship to AIDS." *Science* 239 (1988), 375–80.

Brennan, Troyen A. "The Challenge of AIDS." In his *Just Doctoring: Medical Ethics in the Liberal State.* Berkeley, CA: University of California Press, 1991, 147–74, 264–68.

Cameron, Miriam E. *Living with AIDS: Experiencing Ethical Problems.* Newbury Park, CA: Sage Publications, 1993.

Cook, Molly, *et al.* "Informal Caregivers and the Intention to Hasten AIDS-Related Death." *Archives of Internal Medicine* 158 (1998), 69–75.

Daniels, Norman. "Insurability and the HIV Epidemic: Ethical Issues in Underwriting." *Milbank Quarterly* 68 (1990), 497–525.

Dickens, Bernard M. "Legal Rights and Duties in the AIDS Epidemic." *Science* 239 (188), 580–87.

Epstein, Steven. *Impure Science: AIDS, Activism, and the Politics of Knowledge.* Berkeley, CA: University of California Press, 1996.

Faden, Ruth R., and Kass, Nancy E., eds. *HIV, AIDS, and Childbearing: Public Policy, Private Lives.* New York: Oxford University Press, 1996.

————. "Women as Vessels and Vectors: Lessons from the HIV Epidemic." In Susan M. Wolf, ed. *Feminism and Bioethics: Beyond Reproduction.* New York: Oxford University Press, 1996: 252–81.

Foley, Kathleen M. "Competent Care for the Dying Instead of Physician-Assisted Suicide" [Editorial]. *New England Journal of Medicine* 336 (1997), 54–58.

Gostin, Lawrence O. "The AIDS Litigation Project: A National Review of Court and Human Rights Commission Decisions" [Two Parts]. *Journal of the American Medical Association* 263 (1990), 1961–70, 2086–93.

Gostin, Lawrence O., ed. *AIDS and the Health Care System.* New Haven: Yale University Press, 1990.

———, *et al.* "Prevention of HIV/AIDS and Other Blood-Borne Diseases among Injection Drug Users: A National Survey on the Regulation of Syringes and Needles." *Journal of the American Medical Association* 277 (1997), 53–62.

———, and Lazzarini, Zita. *Human Rights and Public Health in the AIDS Pandemic.* New York: Oxford University Press, 1997.

———, and Webber, David W. "HIV Infection and AIDS in the Public Health and Health Care Systems: The Role of Law and Litigation." *Journal of the American Medical Association* 279 (1998), 1108–13.

Graubard, Stephen R., ed. *Living with AIDS.* Cambridge, MA: MIT Press, 1990.

Hastings Center. *AIDS: An Epidemic of Ethical Puzzles.* Brookfield, VT: Dartmouth, 1991.

Humber, James M., and Almeder, Robert F. *Biomedical Ethics Reviews, 1988: AIDS and Ethics.* Clifton, NJ: Humana Press, 1989.

Institute of Medicine, Committee for the Oversight of AIDS Activities. *Confronting AIDS: Update 1988.* Washington, DC: National Academy Press, 1988.

Joint United Nations Programme on HIV/AIDS (UNAIDS) and World Health Organization (WHO). *Report on the Global HIV/AIDS Epidemic: June 1998.* Geneva: UNAIDS/WHO, 1998.

Juengst, Eric T., and Koenig, Barbara A., eds. *The Meaning of AIDS: Implications for Medical Science, Clinical Practice, and Public Health Policy.* New York: Praeger, 1989.

Kahn, James. "Success and Sadness." *Journal of the American Medical Association* 280 (1998), 89.

Kass, Nancy E., *et al.* "Homosexual and Bisexual Men's Perceptions of Discrimination in Health Services." *American Journal of Public Health* 82 (1992), 1277–79.

Kondro, Wayne. "Canadian AIDS Doctor Convicted of Physician-Assisted Suicide." *Lancet* 351 (1998), 121.

Lo, Bernard. "AIDS: II. Health-Care and Research Issues." In Warren Thomas Reich, ed. *Encyclopedia of Bioethics.* Revised ed. New York: Simon and Schuster Macmillan, 1995, 113–20.

———. "Ethical Dilemmas in HIV Infection: What Have We Learned?" *Law, Medicine and Health Care* 20 (1992), 92–103.

Loewy, Erich H., ed. "Ethical and Communal Issues in AIDS." *Theoretical Medicine* 11 (1990), 173–226. Thematic Issue.

Mann, Jonathan, and Tarantola, Daniel, eds. *AIDS in the World II: Global Dimensions, Social Roots, and Responses.* New York: Oxford University Press, 1996.

Mann, Jonathan; Tarantola, Daniel J. M.; and Netter, Thomas W., eds. *AIDS in the World: A Global Report.* Cambridge, MA: Harvard University Press, 1992.

McKenzie, Nancy F., ed. *The AIDS Reader: Social, Political, Ethical Issues.* New York: Meridian, 1991.

Miller, Heather G.; Turner, Charles F.; and Moses, Lincoln E., eds. *AIDS: The Second Decade.* Washington, DC: National Academy Press, 1990.

Mohr, Richard D. *Gays/Justice: A Study of Ethics, Society, and Law.* New York: Columbia University Press, 1988.

Murphy, Timothy F. "AIDS." In Ruth Chadwick, ed. *Encyclopedia of Applied Ethics.* San Diego, CA: Academic Press, 1998, 111–22.

———. "No Time for an AIDS Backlash." *Hastings Center Report* 21 (March–April 1991), 7–11.

National Research Council, Commission on Behavioral and Social Sciences and Education, Committee on AIDS Research and the Behavioral, Social, and Statistical Sciences. *AIDS: Sexual Behavior and Intravenous Drug Use.* Edited by Charles F. Turner, Heather G. Miller, and Lincoln E. Moses. Washington, DC: National Academy Press, 1989.

National Research Council, Panel on Monitoring the Social Impact of the AIDS Epidemic. *The Social Impact of AIDS in the United States.* Washington, DC: National Academy Press, 1993.

Nelkin, Dorothy; Willis, David P.; and Parris, Scott V., eds. *A Disease of Society: Cultural and Institutional Responses to AIDS.* New York: Cambridge University Press, 1991.

Nichols, Eve K., Institute of Medicine, National Academy of Sciences. *Mobilizing Against AIDS.* Newly revised and enlarged ed. Cambridge: Harvard University Press, 1989.

Onwuteaka-Philipsen, Bregje D., and van der Wal, Gerrit. "Cases of Euthanasia and Physician Assisted Suicide among AIDS Patients Reported to the Public Prosecutor in North Holland." *Public Health* 112 (1998), 53–56.

Parmet, Wendy E., and Jackson, Daniel J. "No Longer Disabled: The Legal Impact of the New Social Construction of HIV." *American Journal of Law and Medicine* 23 (1997), 7–43.

Pierce, Christine, and VanDeVeer, Donald, eds. *AIDS: Ethics and Public Policy.* Belmont, CA: Wadsworth, 1988.

Reamer, Frederic G., ed. *AIDS and Ethics.* New York: Columbia University Press, 1991.

Rubenstein, William B.; Eisenberg, Ruth; and Gostin, Lawrence O. *The Rights of People Who Are HIV Positive: The Authoritative ACLU Guide to the Rights of People Living with HIV Disease and AIDS.* Carbondale, IL: Southern Illinois University Press, 1996.

Schüklenk, Udo, *et al.* "AIDS in the Developing World." In Ruth Chadwick, ed. *Encyclopedia of Applied Ethics.* San Diego, CA: Academic Press, 1998: 123–27.

Shilts, Randy. *And the Band Played On.* New York: Penguin, 1988.

Slome, Lee R., *et al.* "Physician-Assisted Suicide and Patients with Human Immunodeficiency Virus Disease." *New England Journal of Medicine* 336 (1997), 417–21.

United States. "Americans with Disabilities Act of 1990" (Public Law No. 101-336). *[United States] Statutes at Large* 104, 327 ff.

United States, National Commission on AIDS. *AIDS: An Expanding Tragedy—The Final Report of the National Commission on AIDS.* Washington, DC: U.S. Government Printing Office, 1993.

Wang, Yan Guang. "AIDS and Bioethics: Ethical Dilemmas Facing China in HIV Prevention: A Report from China." *Bioethics* 11 (1997), 323–27.

Zhu, T. "An African HIV-1 Sequence from 1959 and Implications for the Origin of the Epidemic." *Nature* 391 (February 5, 1998), 594–97.

THE DUTY TO WARN AND THE DUTY NOT TO HARM

Altman, Lawrence L. "Sex, Privacy and Tracking H.I.V. Infections." *New York Times,* November 4, 1997, A1.

Bayer, Ronald. "Discrimination, Informed Consent, and the HIV Infected Clinician." *British Medical Journal* 314 (1997), 915–16.

Brennan, Troyen A. "Transmission of the Human Immunodeficiency Virus in the Health Care Setting—Time for Action." *New England Journal of Medicine* 324 (1991), 1504–09.

Daniels, Norman. "HIV-Infected Professionals, Patient Rights, and the 'Switching Dilemma.'" *Journal of the American Medical Association* 267 (1992), 1368–71.

Dickens, Bernard M. "Confidentiality and the Duty to Warn." In Lawrence O. Gostin, ed. *AIDS and the Health Care System.* New Haven: Yale University Press, 1990, 98–112, 259–61.

Erridge, Peter. "The Rights of HIV Infected Healthcare Workers: Ignoring Them May Put the Public at Risk" [Editorial]. *British Medical Journal* 312 (1996), 1625–26.

Fein, Esther B. "Medical Professionals with H.I.V. Keep Silent, Fearing Reprisals." *New York Times,* December 21, 1997, 41, 45.

Fleck, Leonard, and Angell, Marcia. "Please Don't Tell!" [Case Study]. *Hastings Center Report* 21 (November–December 1991), 39–40.

Freedman, Benjamin. "Violating Confidentiality to Warn of a Risk of HIV Infection: Ethical Work in Progress." *Theoretical Medicine* 12 (1991), 309–23.

Gostin, Larry. "The HIV-Infected Health Professional: Public Policy, Discrimination, and Patient Safety. *Law, Medicine and Health Care* 18 (1990), 303–10.

Harris, John, and Holm, Søren. "Is There a Moral Obligation Not to Infect Others?" *British Medical Journal* 311 (1995), 1215–17.

Lo, Bernard, and Steinbrook, Robert. "Health Care Workers Infected with the Human Immunodeficiency Virus: The Next Steps." *Journal of the American Medical Association* 267 (1992), 1100–05.

Macklin, Ruth. "HIV-Infected Psychiatric Patients: Beyond Confidentiality." *Ethics and Behavior* 1 (1991), 3–20.

Murphy, Timothy F. "Health Care Workers with HIV and a Patient's Right to Know." *Journal of Medicine and Philosophy* 19 (1994), 553–69.

Rothenberg, Karen H., and North, Richard L. "Partner Notification and the Threat of Domestic Violence against Women with HIV Infection." *New England Journal of Medicine* 329 (1993), 1194–96.

Rothenberg, Karen H., and Paskey, Stephen J. "The Risk of Domestic Violence and Women with HIV Infection: Implications for Partner Notification, Public Policy, and the Law." *American Journal of Public Health* 85 (1995), 1569–76.

Rothenberg, Karen H., *et al.* "Domestic Violence and Partner Notification: Implications for Treatment and Counseling of Women with HIV." *Journal of the American Medical Women's Association* 50 (1995), 87–93.

Schorr, Andrew F. "Health Care Workers, Patients, and HIV: An Analysis of the Policy and Ethical Debate." *Pharos* 58 (1995), 7–13.

Simon, Stephanie; Hartz, Jay N.; and Micco, Guy. "A Family's Right to Know?" [Case Study and Commentaries]. *Cambridge Quarterly of Healthcare Ethics* 6 (1997), 93–99.

Simons, Marlise. "French Doctor with AIDS Reportedly Infected Patient in Surgery." *New York Times,* January 17, 1997, p. A5.

———. "French Group Appeals to H.I.V.-Positive Doctors to Halt Surgery." *New York Times,* January 22, 1997, p. A5.

Smolkin, Doran. "HIV Infection, Risk Taking, and the Duty to Treat." *Journal of Medicine and Philosophy* 22 (1997), 55–74.

Stein, Michael D. "Sexual Ethics: Disclosure of HIV-Positive Status to Partners." *Archives of Internal Medicine* 158 (1998), 253–57.

United States, Supreme Court. *Bragdon v. Abbott.* June 25, 1998 (date of decision). 118 *S. Ct.* 2196 (1998).

TESTING, SCREENING, AND REPORTING PROGRAMS

Ammann, Arthur J. "Unrestricted Routine Prenatal HIV Testing: The Standard of Care." *Journal of the American Medical Women's Association* 50 (1995), 83–84.

Angell, Marcia. "A Dual Approach to the AIDS Epidemic." *New England Journal of Medicine* 324 (1991), 1498–1500.

Asch, David A., and Patton, James P. "Conflicts over Post-Exposure Testing for Human Immunodeficiency Virus: Can Negotiated Settlements Help?" *Journal of Medicine and Philosophy* 19 (1994), 41–59.

Bayer, Ronald. "Rethinking the Testing of Babies and Pregnant Women for HIV Infection." *Journal of Clinical Ethics* (1996), 85–89.

———. "Women's Rights, Babies' Interests: Politics, and Science in the Debate of Newborn HIV Screening." In Howard L. Minkoff; Jack A. DeHovitz; and Ann Duerr, eds. *HIV Infection in Women.* New York: Raven Press, 1995, 293–307.

Berger, Jeffrey T.; Rosner, Fred; and Farnsworth, Peter. "The Ethics of Mandatory HIV Testing in Newborns." *Journal of Clinical Ethics* 7 (1997), 77–84.

Brandt, Allan M.; Cleary, Paul D.; and Gostin, Lawrence O. "Routine Hospital Testing for HIV: Health Policy Considerations." In Lawrence O. Gostin, ed. *AIDS and the Health Care System.* New Haven: Yale University Press, 1990, 125–39, 264–67.

Britton, Carolyn Barley. "An Argument for Universal HIV Counseling and Voluntary Testing of Women." *Journal of the American Medical Women's Association* 50 (1995), 85–86.

Cooper, Elizabeth B. "HIV Disease in Pregnancy: Ethics, Law, and Policy." *Obstetrics and Gynecology Clinics of North America* 24 (1997), 899–910.

Crawford, Colin. "Protecting the Weakest Link: A Proposal for Universal, Unblinded Pediatric HIV Testing, Counseling and Treatment." *Journal of Community Health* 20 (1995), 125–41.

Danziger, Renée, and Gil, Noel. "HIV Testing and HIV Prevention in Sweden" [Article and Commentary]. *British Medical Journal* 316 (1998), 293–96.

David, Dena S. "Mandatory HIV Testing in Newborns: Not Yet, Maybe." *Journal of Clinical Ethics* 7 (1996), 191–92.

De Cock, Kevin M., and Johnson, Anne M. "From Exceptionalism to Normalisation: A Reappraisal of Attitudes and Practices around HIV Testing." *British Medical Journal* 316 (1998), 290–93.

Dumois, Ana O. "The Case Against Mandatory Newborn Screening for HIV Antibodies." *Journal of Community Health* 20 (1995), 143–59.

Faden, Ruth; Geller, Gail; and Powers, Madison, eds. *AIDS, Women and the Next Generation.* New York: Oxford University Press, 1991.

Fisher, Ian. "Bill Would Order AID-Virus Testing to Protect Babies." *New York Times,* May 1, 1996, p. A1.

Gorsky, Robin D., *et al.* "Preventing Perinatal Transmission of HIV—Costs and Effectiveness of a Recommended Intervention." *Public Health Reports* 111 (1996), 335–41.

Gostin, Lawrence O.; Ward, John W.; and Baker, A. Cornelius. "National HIV Case Reporting for the United States: A Defining Moment in the History of the Epidemic." *New England Journal of Medicine* 337 (1997), 1162–67.

Gunderson, Martin; Mayo, David J.; and Rhame, Frank S. *AIDS: Testing and Privacy.* Salt Lake City: University of Utah Press, 1989.

———. "Routine HIV Testing of Hospital Patients and Pregnant Women: Informed Consent in the Real World." *Kennedy Institute of Ethics Journal* 6 (1996), 161–82.

Hardy, Leslie M., ed. Institute of Medicine, Committee on Prenatal and Newborn Screening for HIV Infection. *HIV Screening of Pregnant Women and Newborns.* Washington, DC: National Academy Press, 1991.

Hernandez, Raymond. "Law Requires Giving Results of H.I.V. Tests of Newborns." *New York Times,* June 27, 1996, p. B4.

Institute of Medicine and National Research Council, Committee on Perinatal Transmission of HIV. *Reducing the Odds: Preventing Perinatal Transmission of HIV in the United States.* Washington, DC: National Academy Press, 1998.

Kopelman, Loretta M. "Informed Consent and Anonymous Tissue Samples: The Case of HIV Seroprevalence Studies." *Journal of Medicine and Philosophy* 19 (1994), 525–52.

Landers Daniel, V., and Sweet, Richard L. "Reducing Mother-Infant Transmission of HIV—the Door Remains Open" [Editorial]. *New England Journal of Medicine* 334 (1996), 1664–65.

Leary, Warren E. "Medical Panel Urges H.I.V. Tests for All Pregnant Women." *New York Times,* October 15, 1998, p. A24.

Lovvorn, Amy E.; Quinn, Sandra Crouse; and Jolly, David H. "HIV Testing of Pregnant Women: A Policy Analysis." *Journal of Public Health Policy* 18 (1997), 401–32.

Madison, Mellinda. "Tragic Life or Tragic Death: Mandatory Testing of Newborns for HIV—Mothers' Rights versus Children's Health." *Journal of Legal Medicine* 18 (1997), 361–86.

Minkoff, Howard, and Willoughby, Anne. "The Future of Prenatal HIV Testing." *Acta Paediatrica, Supplement* 421 (1997), 72–77.

Minkoff, Howard, and O'Sullivan, Mary Jo. "The Case for Rapid HIV Testing During Labor." *Journal of the American Medical Association* 279 (1998), 1743–44.

O'Brien, Maura. "Mandatory HIV Antibody Testing Policies: An Ethical Analysis." *Bioethics* 3 (1989) 273–300.

Ploughman, Penelope. "Public Policy versus Private Rights: The Medical, Social, Ethical, and Legal Implications of the Testing of Newborns for HIV." *AIDS and Public Policy Journal* 10 (1995/1996), 182–204.

Rogers, David E., and Osborn, June E. "Another Approach to the AIDS Epidemic." *New England Journal of Medicine* 325 (1991), 806–08.

Samson, Lindy, and King, Susan. "Evidence-Based Guidelines for Universal Counseling and Offering of HIV Testing in Pregnancy in Canada." *Canadian Medical Association Journal* 158 (1998), 1149–57.

Schneider, Carl E. "Testing Testing." *Hastings Center Report* 27 (July–August 1997), 22–23.

Sternlight, Jean R. "Mandatory Non-Anonymous Testing of Newborns for HIV: Should It Ever Be Allowed?" *John Marshall Law Review* 29 (1994), 373–91.

Touchette, Nancy. "CDC and Congress at Odds over Mandatory HIV Testing." *Nature Medicine* 1 (1995), 723–24.

United States, Centers for Disease Control and Prevention. "U.S. Public Health Service Recommendations for Human Immunodeficiency Virus Counseling and Voluntary Testing for Pregnant Women." *Morbidity and Mortality Weekly Report* 44 (1995; RR-7), 1–15.

United States, Congress, House, Committee on Commerce, Subcommittee on Health and the Environment. *HIV Testing of Women and Infants.* 104th Congress, 1st Session, May 11, 1995. Washington, DC: U.S. Government Printing Office, 1995.

Wilfert, Catherine M. "Mandatory Screening of Pregnant Women for the Human Immunodeficiency Virus." *Clinical Infectious Diseases* 19 (1996), 664–66.

Working Group on HIV Testing of Pregnant Women and Newborns. "HIV Infection, Pregnant Women and Newborns: A Policy for Information and Testing." *Journal of the American Medical Association* 264 (1990), 2416–20.

CLINICAL RESEARCH ON HIV/AIDS

Altman, Lawrence K. "F.D.A. Authorizes First Full Testing for H.I.V. Vaccine." *New York Times,* June 4, 1998, p. A1.

Angell, Marcia. "Tuskegee Revisited." *Wall Street Journal,* October 28, 1997, p. A22.

Annas, George J. and Grodin, Michael A. "Human Rights and Maternal-Fetal HIV Transmission Prevention Trials in Africa." *American Journal of Public Health* 88 (1998), 560–63.

Baker, Robert. "A Theory of International Bioethics: The Negotiable and the Non-Negotiable." *Kennedy Institute of Ethics Journal* 8 (1998), 233–73, esp. 260–66.

Bayer, Ronald. "The Debate over Maternal-Fetal HIV Transmission Prevention Trials in Africa, Asia, and the Caribbean: Racist Exploitation or Exploitation of Racism?" *American Journal of Public Health* 88 (1998), 567–70.

———. "Ethical Challenges Posed by Zidovudine Treatment to Reduce Vertical Transmission of HIV." *New England Journal of Medicine* 331 (1994), 1123–25.

Bloom, Barry R. "The Highest Attainable Standard: Ethical Issues in AIDS Vaccines." *Science* 279 (1998), 186–88.

Cohen, Jon. "Ethics of AZT Studies in Poorer Countries Attacked." *Science* 276 (1997), 1022.

Connor, Edward M., *et al.* "Reduction of Maternal-Infant Transmission of Human Immunodeficiency Virus Type 1 with Zidovudine Treatment." *New England Journal of Medicine* 331 (1994), 1173–80.

de Zoysa, Isabelle; Elias, Christopher J.; and Bentley, Margaret E. "Ethical Challenges in Efficacy Trials of Vaginal Microbicides for HIV Prevention." *American Journal of Public Health* 88 (1998), 571–75.

Grady, Christine. "HIV Preventive Vaccine Research: Selected Ethical Issues." *Journal of Medicine and Philosophy* (1994), 595–612.

———. *The Search for an AIDS Vaccine: Ethical Issues in the Development and Testing of a Preventive HIV Vaccine.* Bloomington, IN: Indiana University Press, 1995.

Gray, Joni N.; Lyons, Phillip M.; and Melton, Gary B. *Ethical and Legal Issues in AIDS Research.* Baltimore: Johns Hopkins University Press, 1995.

Halsey, Neal A., *et al.* "Ethics and International Research." *British Medical Journal* 315 (1997), 965–66.

Karim, Salim S. A. "Placebo Controls in HIV Perinatal Transmission Trials: A South African's Viewpoint." *American Journal of Public Health* 88 (1998), 564–66.

Karlawish, Jason H. T., and Lantos, John. "Community Equipoise and the Architecture of Clinical Research." *Cambridge Quarterly of Healthcare Ethics* 6 (1997), 385–96.

Kerns, Thomas A. *Ethical Issues in HIV Vaccine Trials.* New York: St. Martin's Press, 1997.

Kuhn, Louise, and Stein, Zena. "Infant Survival, HIV Infection, and Feeding Alternatives." *American Journal of Public Health* 87 (1997), 926–31.

Marshall, Eliot. "Controversial Trial Offers Hopeful Result." *Science* 279 (1998), 1299.

Marwick, Charles. "Bioethics Group Considers Transnational Research." *Journal of the American Medical Association* 279 (1998), 1425.

Mbidde, Edward. "Bioethics and Local Circumstances." *Science* 279 (1998), 155.

Merson, Michael H., *et al.* "Ethics of Placebo-Controlled Trials of Zidovudine to Prevent the Perinatal Transmission of HIV in the Third World." *New England Journal of Medicine* 338 (1998), 836–41.

Robb, Merlin L.; Khambaroong, Chirasak; and Nelson, Kenrad E. "Studies in Thailand of the Vertical Transmission of HIV." *New England Journal of Medicine* 338 (1998), 843–44.

Schüklenk, Udo, and Hogan, Carlton. "Patient Access to Experimental Drugs and AIDS Clinical Trial Designs: Ethical Issues." *Cambridge Quarterly of Healthcare Ethics* 5 (1996), 400–09.

Stolberg, Sheryl Gay. "Placebo Use Is Suspended in Overseas AIDS Trials." *New York Times* February 19, 1998, p. A16.

United States Centers for Disease Control and Prevention. "Recommendations of the U.S. Public Health Service Task Force on the Use of Zidovudine to Reduce Perinatal Transmission of Human Immunodeficiency Virus." *Morbidity and Mortality Weekly Report* 43 (1994; RR-11), 1–20.

Wadman, Meredith. "Controversy Flares over AIDS Prevention Trials in Third World." *Nature* 389 (1997), 894.

Zion, Deborah, "Ethical Considerations of Clinical Trials to Prevent Vertical Transmission of HIV in Developing Countries." *Nature Medicine* 4 (1998), 11–12.

BIBLIOGRAPHIES

Darragh, Martina, and McCarrick, Pat Milmoe. "Public Health by the Numbers." *Kennedy Institute of Ethics Journal* 8 (1998), 339–58.

Lineback, Richard H., ed. *Philosopher's Index.* Vols. 1– . Bowling Green OH: Philosophy Documentation Center, Bowling Green State University. Issued quarterly. See under "AIDS" and "HIV."

Walters, LeRoy, and Kahn, Tamar Joy, eds. *Bibliography of Bioethics.* Vols. 1– . Washington, DC: Kennedy Institute of Ethics, Georgetown University. Issued annually. See under "AIDS." (The information contained in the annual *Bibliography* can also be retrieved from BIOETHICSLINE, an online database of the National Library of Medicine.)

WORLD WIDE WEB RESOURCES

National Library of Medicine: PubMed
(http://www.ncbi.nlm.nih.gov/PubMed/)

National Library of Medicine: BIOETHICSLINE
(http://igm.nlm.nih.gov)

National Library of Medicine: AIDSLINE
(http://igm.nlm.nih.gov)

University Microfilms: Periodical Abstracts
(http://www.umi.com/proquest)